The
C++
Programming
Language

Fourth Edition

Bjarne Stroustrup

Addison-Wesley

Upper Saddle River, NJ • Boston • Indianapolis • San Francisco
New York • Totonto • Montreal • London • Munich • Paris • Madrid
Capetown • Sydney • Tokyo • Singapore • Mexico City

The publisher offers excellent discounts on this book when ordered in quantity for bulk purchases or special sales, which may include electronic versions and/or custom covers and content particular to your business, training goals, marketing focus, and branding interests. For more information, please contact:

U.S. Corporate and Government Sales
(800) 382-3419
corpsales@pearsontechgroup.com
For sales outside the United States, please contact:
International Sales
international@pearsoned.com

Visit us on the Web: informit.com/aw

Library of Congress Cataloging-in-Publication Data

Stroustrup, Bjarne.
   The C++ programming language / Bjarne Stroustrup.—Fourth edition.
      pages cm
   Includes bibliographical references and index.
   ISBN 978-0-321-56384-2 (pbk. : alk. paper)—ISBN 0-321-56384-0 (pbk. : alk. paper)
   1. C++ (Computer programming language) I. Title.

QA76.73.C153 S77 2013
005.13'3—dc23   2013002159

This book was typeset in Times and Helvetica by the author.

ISBN-13: 978-0-321-56384-2
ISBN-10:   0-321-56384-0
Text printed in the United States on recycled paper at Edwards Brothers Malloy in Ann Arbor, Michigan.
First printing, May 2013

Contents

Part III: Abstraction Mechanisms   447

Part IV: The Standard Library   857

Index   1281

Preface

All problems in computer science
can be solved by another level of indirection,
except for the problem of too many layers of indirection.
– David J. Wheeler

C++ feels like a new language. That is, I can express my ideas more clearly, more simply, and more directly in C++11 than I could in C++98. Furthermore, the resulting programs are better checked by the compiler and run faster.

In this book, I aim for *completeness*. I describe every language feature and standard-library component that a professional programmer is likely to need. For each, I provide:

- *Rationale*: What kinds of problems is it designed to help solve? What principles underlie the design? What are the fundamental limitations?
- *Specification*: What is its definition? The level of detail is chosen for the expert programmer; the aspiring language lawyer can follow the many references to the ISO standard.
- *Examples*: How can it be used well by itself and in combination with other features? What are the key techniques and idioms? What are the implications for maintainability and performance?

The use of C++ has changed dramatically over the years and so has the language itself. From the point of view of a programmer, most of the changes have been improvements. The current ISO standard C++ (ISO/IEC 14882-2011, usually called C++11) is simply a far better tool for writing quality software than were previous versions. How is it a better tool? What kinds of programming styles and techniques does modern C++ support? What language and standard-library features support those techniques? What are the basic building blocks of elegant, correct, maintainable, and efficient C++ code? Those are the key questions answered by this book. Many answers are not the same as you would find with 1985, 1995, or 2005 vintage C++: progress happens.

C++ is a general-purpose programming language emphasizing the design and use of type-rich, lightweight abstractions. It is particularly suited for resource-constrained applications, such as those found in software infrastructures. C++ rewards the programmer who takes the time to master techniques for writing quality code. C++ is a language for someone who takes the task of programming seriously. Our civilization depends critically on software; it had better be quality software.

There are billions of lines of C++ deployed. This puts a premium on stability, so 1985 and 1995 C++ code still works and will continue to work for decades. However, for all applications, you can do better with modern C++; if you stick to older styles, you will be writing lower-quality and worse-performing code. The emphasis on stability also implies that standards-conforming code you write today will still work a couple of decades from now. All code in this book conforms to the 2011 ISO C++ standard.

This book is aimed at three audiences:

- C++ programmers who want to know what the latest ISO C++ standard has to offer,
- C programmers who wonder what C++ provides beyond C, and
- People with a background in application languages, such as Java, C#, Python, and Ruby, looking for something "closer to the machine" – something more flexible, something offering better compile-time checking, or something offering better performance.

Naturally, these three groups are not disjoint – a professional software developer masters more than just one programming language.

This book assumes that its readers are programmers. If you ask, "What's a for-loop?" or "What's a compiler?" then this book is not (yet) for you; instead, I recommend my *Programming: Principles and Practice Using C++* to get started with programming and C++. Furthermore, I assume that readers have some maturity as software developers. If you ask "Why bother testing?" or say, "All languages are basically the same; just show me the syntax" or are confident that there is a single language that is ideal for every task, this is not the book for you.

What features does C++11 offer over and above C++98? A machine model suitable for modern computers with lots of concurrency. Language and standard-library facilities for doing systems-level concurrent programming (e.g., using multicores). Regular expression handling, resource management pointers, random numbers, improved containers (including, hash tables), and more. General and uniform initialization, a simpler for-statement, move semantics, basic Unicode support, lambdas, general constant expressions, control over class defaults, variadic templates, user-defined literals, and more. Please remember that those libraries and language features exist to support programming techniques for developing quality software. They are meant to be used in combination – as bricks in a building set – rather than to be used individually in relative isolation to solve a specific problem. A computer is a universal machine, and C++ serves it in that capacity. In particular, C++'s design aims to be sufficiently flexible and general to cope with future problems undreamed of by its designers.

Acknowledgments

In addition to the people mentioned in the acknowledgment sections of the previous editions, I would like to thank Pete Becker, Hans-J. Boehm, Marshall Clow, Jonathan Coe, Lawrence Crowl, Walter Daugherty, J. Daniel Garcia, Robert Harle, Greg Hickman, Howard Hinnant, Brian Kernighan, Daniel Krügler, Nevin Liber, Michel Michaud, Gary Powell, Jan Christiaan van Winkel, and Leor Zolman. Without their help this book would have been much poorer.

Thanks to Howard Hinnant for answering many questions about the standard library.

Andrew Sutton is the author of the Origin library, which was the testbed for much of the discussion of emulating concepts in the template chapters, and of the matrix library that is the topic of Chapter 29. The Origin library is open source and can be found by searching the Web for "Origin" and "Andrew Sutton."

Thanks to my graduate design class for finding more problems with the "tour chapters" than anyone else.

Had I been able to follow every piece of advice of my reviewers, the book would undoubtedly have been much improved, but it would also have been hundreds of pages longer. Every expert reviewer suggested adding technical details, advanced examples, and many useful development conventions; every novice reviewer (or educator) suggested adding examples; and most reviewers observed (correctly) that the book may be too long.

Thanks to Princeton University's Computer Science Department, and especially Prof. Brian Kernighan, for hosting me for part of the sabbatical that gave me time to write this book.

Thanks to Cambridge University's Computer Lab, and especially Prof. Andy Hopper, for hosting me for part of the sabbatical that gave me time to write this book.

Thanks to my editor, Peter Gordon, and his production team at Addison-Wesley for their help and patience.

College Station, Texas

Bjarne Stroustrup

Preface to the Third Edition

Programming is understanding.
– Kristen Nygaard

I find using C++ more enjoyable than ever. C++'s support for design and programming has improved dramatically over the years, and lots of new helpful techniques have been developed for its use. However, C++ is not *just* fun. Ordinary practical programmers have achieved significant improvements in productivity, maintainability, flexibility, and quality in projects of just about any kind and scale. By now, C++ has fulfilled most of the hopes I originally had for it, and also succeeded at tasks I hadn't even dreamt of.

This book introduces standard C++† and the key programming and design techniques supported by C++. Standard C++ is a far more powerful and polished language than the version of C++ introduced by the first edition of this book. New language features such as namespaces, exceptions, templates, and run-time type identification allow many techniques to be applied more directly than was possible before, and the standard library allows the programmer to start from a much higher level than the bare language.

About a third of the information in the second edition of this book came from the first. This third edition is the result of a rewrite of even larger magnitude. It offers something to even the most experienced C++ programmer; at the same time, this book is easier for the novice to approach than its predecessors were. The explosion of C++ use and the massive amount of experience accumulated as a result makes this possible.

The definition of an extensive standard library makes a difference to the way C++ concepts can be presented. As before, this book presents C++ independently of any particular implementation, and as before, the tutorial chapters present language constructs and concepts in a "bottom up" order so that a construct is used only after it has been defined. However, it is much easier to use a well-designed library than it is to understand the details of its implementation. Therefore, the standard library can be used to provide realistic and interesting examples well before a reader can be assumed to understand its inner workings. The standard library itself is also a fertile source of programming examples and design techniques.

This book presents every major C++ language feature and the standard library. It is organized around language and library facilities. However, features are presented in the context of their use.

---

† ISO/IEC 14882, Standard for the C++ Programming Language.

That is, the focus is on the language as the tool for design and programming rather than on the language in itself. This book demonstrates key techniques that make C++ effective and teaches the fundamental concepts necessary for mastery. Except where illustrating technicalities, examples are taken from the domain of systems software. A companion, *The Annotated C++ Language Standard*, presents the complete language definition together with annotations to make it more comprehensible.

The primary aim of this book is to help the reader understand how the facilities offered by C++ support key programming techniques. The aim is to take the reader far beyond the point where he or she gets code running primarily by copying examples and emulating programming styles from other languages. Only a good understanding of the ideas behind the language facilities leads to mastery. Supplemented by implementation documentation, the information provided is sufficient for completing significant real-world projects. The hope is that this book will help the reader gain new insights and become a better programmer and designer.

Acknowledgments

In addition to the people mentioned in the acknowledgement sections of the first and second editions, I would like to thank Matt Austern, Hans Boehm, Don Caldwell, Lawrence Crowl, Alan Feuer, Andrew Forrest, David Gay, Tim Griffin, Peter Juhl, Brian Kernighan, Andrew Koenig, Mike Mowbray, Rob Murray, Lee Nackman, Joseph Newcomer, Alex Stepanov, David Vandevoorde, Peter Weinberger, and Chris Van Wyk for commenting on draft chapters of this third edition. Without their help and suggestions, this book would have been harder to understand, contained more errors, been slightly less complete, and probably been a little bit shorter.

I would also like to thank the volunteers on the C++ standards committees who did an immense amount of constructive work to make C++ what it is today. It is slightly unfair to single out individuals, but it would be even more unfair not to mention anyone, so I'd like to especially mention Mike Ball, Dag Brück, Sean Corfield, Ted Goldstein, Kim Knuttila, Andrew Koenig, Dmitry Lenkov, Nathan Myers, Martin O'Riordan, Tom Plum, Jonathan Shopiro, John Spicer, Jerry Schwarz, Alex Stepanov, and Mike Vilot, as people who each directly cooperated with me over some part of C++ and its standard library.

After the initial printing of this book, many dozens of people have mailed me corrections and suggestions for improvements. I have been able to accommodate many of their suggestions within the framework of the book so that later printings benefitted significantly. Translators of this book into many languages have also provided many clarifications. In response to requests from readers, I have added appendices D and E. Let me take this opportunity to thank a few of those who helped: Dave Abrahams, Matt Austern, Jan Bielawski, Janina Mincer Daszkiewicz, Andrew Koenig, Dietmar Kühl, Nicolai Josuttis, Nathan Myers, Paul E. Sevinç, Andy Tenne-Sens, Shoichi Uchida, Ping-Fai (Mike) Yang, and Dennis Yelle.

Murray Hill, New Jersey   *Bjarne Stroustrup*

Preface to the Second Edition

As promised in the first edition of this book, C++ has been evolving to meet the needs of its users. This evolution has been guided by the experience of users of widely varying backgrounds working in a great range of application areas. The C++ user-community has grown a hundredfold during the six years since the first edition of this book; many lessons have been learned, and many techniques have been discovered and/or validated by experience. Some of these experiences are reflected here.

The primary aim of the language extensions made in the last six years has been to enhance C++ as a language for data abstraction and object-oriented programming in general and to enhance it as a tool for writing high-quality libraries of user-defined types in particular. A "high-quality library," is a library that provides a concept to a user in the form of one or more classes that are convenient, safe, and efficient to use. In this context, *safe* means that a class provides a specific type-safe interface between the users of the library and its providers; *efficient* means that use of the class does not impose significant overheads in run-time or space on the user compared with hand-written C code.

This book presents the complete C++ language. Chapters 1 through 10 give a tutorial introduction; Chapters 11 through 13 provide a discussion of design and software development issues; and, finally, the complete C++ reference manual is included. Naturally, the features added and resolutions made since the original edition are integral parts of the presentation. They include refined overloading resolution, memory management facilities, and access control mechanisms, type-safe linkage, `const` and `static` member functions, abstract classes, multiple inheritance, templates, and exception handling.

C++ is a general-purpose programming language; its core application domain is systems programming in the broadest sense. In addition, C++ is successfully used in many application areas that are not covered by this label. Implementations of C++ exist from some of the most modest microcomputers to the largest supercomputers and for almost all operating systems. Consequently, this book describes the C++ language itself without trying to explain a particular implementation, programming environment, or library.

This book presents many examples of classes that, though useful, should be classified as "toys." This style of exposition allows general principles and useful techniques to stand out more clearly than they would in a fully elaborated program, where they would be buried in details. Most of the useful classes presented here, such as linked lists, arrays, character strings, matrices, graphics classes, associative arrays, etc., are available in "bulletproof" and/or "goldplated" versions from a wide variety of commercial and non-commercial sources. Many of these "industrial strength" classes and libraries are actually direct and indirect descendants of the toy versions found here.

This edition provides a greater emphasis on tutorial aspects than did the first edition of this book. However, the presentation is still aimed squarely at experienced programmers and endeavors not to insult their intelligence or experience. The discussion of design issues has been greatly expanded to reflect the demand for information beyond the description of language features and their immediate use. Technical detail and precision have also been increased. The reference manual, in particular, represents many years of work in this direction. The intent has been to provide a book with a depth sufficient to make more than one reading rewarding to most programmers. In other words, this book presents the C++ language, its fundamental principles, and the key techniques needed to apply it. Enjoy!

Acknowledgments
In addition to the people mentioned in the acknowledgements section in the preface to the first edition, I would like to thank Al Aho, Steve Buroff, Jim Coplien, Ted Goldstein, Tony Hansen, Lorraine Juhl, Peter Juhl, Brian Kernighan, Andrew Koenig, Bill Leggett, Warren Montgomery, Mike Mowbray, Rob Murray, Jonathan Shopiro, Mike Vilot, and Peter Weinberger for commenting on draft chapters of this second edition. Many people influenced the development of C++ from 1985 to 1991. I can mention only a few: Andrew Koenig, Brian Kernighan, Doug McIlroy, and Jonathan Shopiro. Also thanks to the many participants of the "external reviews" of the reference manual drafts and to the people who suffered through the first year of X3J16.

Murray Hill, New Jersey   *Bjarne Stroustrup*

Preface to the First Edition

Language shapes the way we think,
and determines what we can think about.
— B.L. Whorf

C++ is a general purpose programming language designed to make programming more enjoyable for the serious programmer. Except for minor details, C++ is a superset of the C programming language. In addition to the facilities provided by C, C++ provides flexible and efficient facilities for defining new types. A programmer can partition an application into manageable pieces by defining new types that closely match the concepts of the application. This technique for program construction is often called *data abstraction.* Objects of some user-defined types contain type information. Such objects can be used conveniently and safely in contexts in which their type cannot be determined at compile time. Programs using objects of such types are often called *object based.* When used well, these techniques result in shorter, easier to understand, and easier to maintain programs.

The key concept in C++ is *class.* A class is a user-defined type. Classes provide data hiding, guaranteed initialization of data, implicit type conversion for user-defined types, dynamic typing, user-controlled memory management, and mechanisms for overloading operators. C++ provides much better facilities for type checking and for expressing modularity than C does. It also contains improvements that are not directly related to classes, including symbolic constants, inline substitution of functions, default function arguments, overloaded function names, free store management operators, and a reference type. C++ retains C's ability to deal efficiently with the fundamental objects of the hardware (bits, bytes, words, addresses, etc.). This allows the user-defined types to be implemented with a pleasing degree of efficiency.

C++ and its standard libraries are designed for portability. The current implementation will run on most systems that support C. C libraries can be used from a C++ program, and most tools that support programming in C can be used with C++.

This book is primarily intended to help serious programmers learn the language and use it for nontrivial projects. It provides a complete description of C++, many complete examples, and many more program fragments.

Acknowledgments

C++ could never have matured without the constant use, suggestions, and constructive criticism of many friends and colleagues. In particular, Tom Cargill, Jim Coplien, Stu Feldman, Sandy Fraser, Steve Johnson, Brian Kernighan, Bart Locanthi, Doug McIlroy, Dennis Ritchie, Larry Rosler, Jerry Schwarz, and Jon Shopiro provided important ideas for development of the language. Dave Presotto wrote the current implementation of the stream I/O library.

In addition, hundreds of people contributed to the development of C++ and its compiler by sending me suggestions for improvements, descriptions of problems they had encountered, and compiler errors. I can mention only a few: Gary Bishop, Andrew Hume, Tom Karzes, Victor Milenkovic, Rob Murray, Leonie Rose, Brian Schmult, and Gary Walker.

Many people have also helped with the production of this book, in particular, Jon Bentley, Laura Eaves, Brian Kernighan, Ted Kowalski, Steve Mahaney, Jon Shopiro, and the participants in the C++ course held at Bell Labs, Columbus, Ohio, June 26-27, 1985.

Murray Hill, New Jersey   *Bjarne Stroustrup*

Part I

Introduction

This introduction gives an overview of the major concepts and features of the C++ programming language and its standard library. It also provides an overview of this book and explains the approach taken to the description of the language facilities and their use. In addition, the introductory chapters present some background information about C++, the design of C++, and the use of C++.

Chapters

"... and you, Marcus, you have given me many things; now I shall give you this good advice. Be many people. Give up the game of being always Marcus Cocoza. You have worried too much about Marcus Cocoza, so that you have been really his slave and prisoner. You have not done anything without first considering how it would affect Marcus Cocoza's happiness and prestige. You were always much afraid that Marcus might do a stupid thing, or be bored. What would it really have mattered? All over the world people are doing stupid things ... I should like you to be easy, your little heart to be light again. You must from now, be more than one, many people, as many as you can think of ..."

     – Karen Blixen,
          The Dreamers from *Seven Gothic Tales* (1934)

1

Notes to the Reader

Hurry Slowly
(festina lente).
– Octavius, Caesar Augustus

- The Structure of This Book
    Introduction; Basic Facilities; Abstraction Mechanisms; The Standard Library; Examples and References
- The Design of C++
    Programming Styles; Type Checking; C Compatibility; Language, Libraries, and Systems
- Learning C++
    Programming in C++; Suggestions for C++ Programmers; Suggestions for C Programmers; Suggestions for Java Programmers
- History
    Timeline; The Early Years; The 1998 Standard; The 2011 Standard; What is C++ Used for?
- Advice
- References

1.1 The Structure of This Book

A pure tutorial sorts its topics so that no concept is used before it has been introduced; it must be read linearly starting with page one. Conversely, a pure reference manual can be accessed starting at any point; it describes each topic succinctly with references (forward and backward) to related topics. A pure tutorial can in principle be read without prerequisites – it carefully describes all. A pure reference can be used only by someone familiar with all fundamental concepts and techniques. This book combines aspects of both. If you know most concepts and techniques, you can access it on a per-chapter or even on a per-section basis. If not, you can start at the beginning, but try not to get bogged down in details. Use the index and the cross-references.

Making parts of the book relatively self-contained implies some repetition, but repetition also serves as review for people reading the book linearly. The book is heavily cross-referenced both to itself and to the ISO C++ standard. Experienced programmers can read the (relatively) quick "tour" of C++ to gain the overview needed to use the book as a reference. This book consists of four parts:

Part I	*Introduction*: Chapter 1 (this chapter) is a guide to this book and provides a bit of C++ background. Chapters 2-5 give a quick introduction to the C++ language and its standard library.
Part II	*Basic Facilities*: Chapters 6-15 describe C++'s built-in types and the basic facilities for constructing programs out of them.
Part III	*Abstraction Mechanisms*: Chapters 16-29 describe C++'s abstraction mechanisms and their use for object-oriented and generic programming.
Part IV	Chapters 30-44 provide an overview of the standard library and a discussion of compatibility issues.

1.1.1 Introduction

This chapter, Chapter 1, provides an overview of this book, some hints about how to use it, and some background information about C++ and its use. You are encouraged to skim through it, read what appears interesting, and return to it after reading other parts of the book. Please do not feel obliged to read it all carefully before proceeding.

The following chapters provide an overview of the major concepts and features of the C++ programming language and its standard library:

Chapter 2	*A Tour of C++: The Basics* describes C++'s model of memory, computation, and error handling.
Chapter 3	*A Tour of C++: Abstraction Mechanisms* presents the language features supporting data abstraction, object-oriented programming, and generic programming.
Chapter 4	*A Tour of C++: Containers and Algorithms* introduces strings, simple I/O, containers, and algorithms as provided by the standard library.
Chapter 5	*A Tour of C++: Concurrency and Utilities* outlines the standard-library utilities related to resource management, concurrency, mathematical computation, regular expressions, and more.

This whirlwind tour of C++'s facilities aims to give the reader a taste of what C++ offers. In particular, it should convince readers that C++ has come a long way since the first, second, and third editions of this book.

1.1.2 Basic Facilities

Part II focuses on the subset of C++ that supports the styles of programming traditionally done in C and similar languages. It introduces the notions of type, object, scope, and storage. It presents the fundamentals of computation: expressions, statements, and functions. Modularity – as supported by namespaces, source files, and exception handling – is also discussed:

Chapter 6	*Types and Declarations*: Fundamental types, naming, scopes, initialization, simple type deduction, object lifetimes, and type aliases

I assume that you are familiar with most of the programming concepts used in Part I. For example, I explain the C++ facilities for expressing recursion and iteration, but I do not go into technical details or spend much time explaining how these concepts are useful.

The exception to this rule is exceptions. Many programmers lack experience with exceptions or got their experience from languages (such as Java) where resource management and exception handling are not integrated. Consequently, the chapter on exception handling (Chapter 13) presents the basic philosophy of C++ exception handling and resource management. It goes into some detail about strategy with a focus on the "Resource Acquisition Is Initialization" technique (RAII).

1.1.3 Abstraction Mechanisms

Part III describes the C++ facilities supporting various forms of abstraction, including object-oriented and generic programming. The chapters fall into three rough categories: classes, class hierarchies, and templates.

The first four chapters concentrate of the classes themselves:

Classes can be organized into hierarchies:

Chapter 20   *Derived Classes* presents the basic language facilities for building hierarchies out of classes and the fundamental ways of using them. We can provide complete separation between an interface (an abstract class) and its implementations (derived classes); the connection between them is provided by virtual functions. The C++ model for access control (**public**, **protected**, and **private**) is presented.

Chapter 21   *Class Hierarchies* discusses ways of using class hierarchies effectively. It also presents the notion of multiple inheritance, that is, a class having more than one direct base class.

Chapter 22   *Run-Time Type Information* presents ways to navigate class hierarchies using data stored in objects. We can use **dynamic_cast** to inquire whether an object of a base class was defined as an object of a derived class and use the **typeid** to gain minimal information from an object (such as the name of its class).

Many of the most flexible, efficient, and useful abstractions involve the parameterization of types (classes) and algorithms (functions) with other types and algorithms:

Chapter 23   *Templates* presents the basic principles behind templates and their use. Class templates, function templates, and template aliases are presented.

Chapter 24   *Generic Programming* introduces the basic techniques for designing generic programs. The technique of *lifting* an abstract algorithm from a number of concrete code examples is central, as is the notion of *concepts* specifying a generic algorithm's requirements on its arguments.

Chapter 25   *Specialization* describes how templates are used to generate classes and functions, *specializations*, given a set of template arguments.

Chapter 26   *Instantiation* focuses on the rules for name binding.

Chapter 27   *Templates and Hierarchies* explains how templates and class hierarchies can be used in combination.

Chapter 28   *Metaprogramming* explores how templates can be used to generate programs. Templates provide a Turing-complete mechanism for generating code.

Chapter 29   *A Matrix Design* gives a longish example to show how language features can be used in combination to solve a complex design problem: the design of an N-dimensional matrix with near-arbitrary element types.

The language features supporting abstraction techniques are described in the context of those techniques. The presentation technique in Part III differs from that of Part II in that I don't assume that the reader knows the techniques described.

1.1.4 The Standard Library

The library chapters are less tutorial than the language chapters. In particular, they are meant to be read in any order and can be used as a user-level manual for the library components:

Chapter 30   *Standard-Library Overview* gives an overview of the standard library, lists the standard-library headers, and presents language support and diagnostics support, such as **exception** and **system_error**.

Chapter 31   *STL Containers* presents the containers from the iterators, containers, and algorithms framework (called *the STL*), including **vector**, **map**, and **unordered_set**.

1.1.5 Examples and References

This book emphasizes program organization rather than the design of algorithms. Consequently, I avoid clever or harder-to-understand algorithms. A trivial algorithm is typically better suited to illustrate an aspect of the language definition or a point about program structure. For example, I use a Shell sort where, in real code, a quicksort would be better. Often, reimplementation with a more suitable algorithm is an exercise. In real code, a call of a library function is typically more appropriate than the code used here to illustrate language features.

Textbook examples necessarily give a warped view of software development. By clarifying and simplifying the examples, the complexities that arise from scale disappear. I see no substitute for writing realistically sized programs in order to get an impression of what programming and a programming language are really like. This book concentrates on the language features and the standard-library facilities. These are the basic techniques from which every program is composed. The rules and techniques for such composition are emphasized.

The selection of examples reflects my background in compilers, foundation libraries, and simulations. The emphasis reflects my interest in systems programming. Examples are simplified versions of what is found in real code. The simplification is necessary to keep programming language and design points from getting lost in details. My ideal is the shortest and clearest example that illustrates a design principle, a programming technique, a language construct, or a library feature. There are no "cute" examples without counterparts in real code. For purely language-technical examples, I use variables named x and y, types called A and B, and functions called f() and g().

Where possible, the C++ language and library features are presented in the context of their use rather than in the dry manner of a manual. The language features presented and the detail in which they are described roughly reflect my view of what is needed for effective use of C++. The purpose is to give you an idea of how a feature can be used, often in combination with other features. An understanding of every language-technical detail of a language feature or library component is neither necessary nor sufficient for writing good programs. In fact, an obsession with understanding every little detail is a prescription for awful – overelaborate and overly clever – code. What is needed is an understanding of design and programming techniques together with an appreciation of application domains.

I assume that you have access to online information sources. The final arbiter of language and standard-library rules is the ISO C++ standard [C++,2011].

References to parts of this book are of the form §2.3.4 (Chapter 2, section 3, subsection 4) and §iso.5.3.1 (ISO C++ standard, §5.3.1). Italics are used sparingly for emphasis (e.g., "a string literal is *not* acceptable"), for first occurrences of important concepts (e.g., *polymorphism*), and for comments in code examples.

To save a few trees and to simplify additions, the hundreds of exercises for this book have been moved to the Web. Look for them at www.stroustrup.com.

The language and library used in this book are "pure C++" as defined by the C++ standard [C++,2011]. Therefore, the examples should run on every up-to-date C++ implementation. The major program fragments in this book were tried using several C++ implementations. Examples using features only recently adopted into C++ didn't compile on every implementation. However, I see no point in mentioning which implementations failed to compile which examples. Such information would soon be out of date because implementers are working hard to ensure that their implementations correctly accept every C++ feature. See Chapter 44 for suggestions on how to cope with older C++ compilers and with code written for C compilers.

I use C++11 features freely wherever I find them most appropriate. For example, I prefer {}-style initializers and using for type aliases. In places, that usage may startle "old timers." However, being startled is often a good way to start reviewing material. On the other hand, I don't use new features just because they are new; my ideal is the most elegant expression of the fundamental ideas – and that may very well be using something that has been in C++ or even in C for ages.

Obviously, if you have to use a pre-C++11 compiler (say, because some of your customers have not yet upgraded to the current standard), you have to refrain from using novel features. However, please don't assume that "the old ways" are better or simpler just because they are old and familiar. §44.2 summarizes the differences between C++98 and C++11.

1.2   The Design of C++

The purpose of a programming language is to help express ideas in code. In that, a programming language performs two related tasks: it provides a vehicle for the programmer to specify actions to be executed by the machine, and it provides a set of concepts for the programmer to use when thinking about what can be done. The first purpose ideally requires a language that is "close to the machine" so that all important aspects of a machine are handled simply and efficiently in a way that is reasonably obvious to the programmer. The C language was primarily designed with this in mind. The second purpose ideally requires a language that is "close to the problem to be solved" so that the concepts of a solution can be expressed directly and concisely. The facilities added to C to create C++, such as function argument checking, const, classes, constructors and destructors, exceptions, and templates, were primarily designed with this in mind. Thus, C++ is based on the idea of providing both

- *direct mappings of built-in operations and types to hardware* to provide efficient memory use and efficient low-level operations, and
- *affordable and flexible abstraction mechanisms* to provide user-defined types with the same notational support, range of uses, and performance as built-in types.

This was initially achieved by applying ideas from Simula to C. Over the years, further application of these simple ideals resulted in a far more general, efficient, and flexible set of facilities. The result supports a synthesis of programming styles that can be simultaneously *efficient* and *elegant*.

The design of C++ has focused on programming techniques dealing with fundamental notions such as memory, mutability, abstraction, resource management, expression of algorithms, error handling, and modularity. Those are the most important concerns of a systems programmer and more generally of programmers of resource-constrained and high-performance systems.

By defining libraries of classes, class hierarchies, and templates, you can write C++ programs at a much higher level than the one presented in this book. For example, C++ is widely used in financial systems, for game development, and for scientific computation (§1.4.5). For high-level applications programming to be effective and convenient, we need libraries. Using just the bare language features makes almost all programming quite painful. That's true for every general-purpose language. Conversely, given suitable libraries just about any programming task can be pleasant.

My standard introduction of C++ used to start:

- *C++ is a general-purpose programming language with a bias toward systems programming.*

This is still true. What has changed over the years is an increase in the importance, power, and flexibility of C++'s abstraction mechanisms:

- *C++ is a general-purpose programming language providing a direct and efficient model of hardware combined with facilities for defining lightweight abstractions.*

Or terser:

- *C++ is a language for developing and using elegant and efficient abstractions.*

By *general-purpose programming language* I mean a language designed to support a wide variety of uses. C++ has indeed been used for an incredible variety of uses (from microcontrollers to huge distributed commercial applications), but the key point is that C++ is not deliberately specialized for any given application area. No language is ideal for every application and every programmer, but the ideal for C++ is to support the widest possible range of application areas well.

By *systems programming* I mean writing code that directly uses hardware resources, has serious resource constraints, or closely interacts with code that does. In particular, the implementation of software infrastructure (e.g., device drivers, communications stacks, virtual machines, operating systems, operations systems, programming environments, and foundation libraries) is mostly systems programming. The importance of the "bias toward systems programming" qualification in my long-standing characterization of C++ is that C++ has not been simplified (compromised) by ejecting the facilities aimed at the expert-level use of hardware and systems resources in the hope of making it more suitable for other application areas.

Of course, you can also program in ways that completely hide hardware, use expensive abstractions (e.g., every object on the free store and every operation a virtual function), use inelegant styles (e.g., overabstraction), or use essentially no abstractions ("glorified assembly code"). However, many languages can do that, so those are not distinguishing characteristics of C++.

The *Design and Evolution of C++* book [Stroustrup,1994] (known as *D&E*) outlines the ideas and design aims of C++ in greater detail, but two principles should be noted:

- *Leave no room for a lower-level language below C++* (except for assembly code in rare cases). If you can write more efficient code in a lower-level language then that language will most likely become the systems programming language of choice.
- *What you don't use you don't pay for.* If programmers can hand-write reasonable code to simulate a language feature or a fundamental abstraction and provide even slightly better performance, someone will do so, and many will imitate. Therefore, a language feature and a fundamental abstraction must be designed not to waste a single byte or a single processor cycle compared to equivalent alternatives. This is known as *the zero-overhead principle*.

These are Draconian principles, but essential in some (but obviously not all) contexts. In particular, the zero-overhead principle repeatedly led C++ to simpler, more elegant, and more powerful facilities than were first envisioned. The STL is an example (§4.1.1, §4.4, §4.5, Chapter 31, Chapter 32, Chapter 33). These principles have been essential in the effort to raise the level of programming.

1.2.1 Programming Style

Languages features exist to provide support for programming styles. Please don't look at an individual language feature as a solution, but as one building brick from a varied set which can be combined to express solutions.

The general ideals for design and programming can be expressed simply:

- Express ideas directly in code.
- Express independent ideas independently in code.
- Represent relationships among ideas directly in code.
- Combine ideas expressed in code freely – where and only where combinations make sense.
- Express simple ideas simply.

These are ideals shared by many people, but languages designed to support them can differ dramatically. A fundamental reason for that is that a language embodies a set of engineering tradeoffs reflecting differing needs, tastes, and histories of various individuals and communities. C++'s answers to the general design challenges were shaped by its origins in systems programming (going back to C and BCPL [Richards,1980]), its aim to address issues of program complexity through abstraction (going back to Simula), and its history.

The C++ language features most directly support four programming styles:

- Procedural programming
- Data abstraction
- Object-oriented programming
- Generic programming

However, the emphasis is on the support of effective combinations of those. The best (most maintainable, most readable, smallest, fastest, etc.) solution to most nontrivial problems tends to be one that combines aspects of these styles.

As is usual with important terms in the computing world, a wide variety of definitions of these terms are popular in various parts of the computing industry and academia. For example, what I refer to as a "programming style," others call a "programming technique" or a "paradigm." I prefer to use "programming technique" for something more limited and language-specific. I feel uncomfortable with the word "paradigm" as pretentious and (from Kuhn's original definition) having implied claims of exclusivity.

My ideal is language facilities that can be used elegantly in combination to support a continuum of programming styles and a wide variety of programming techniques.

- *Procedural programming*: This is programming focused on processing and the design of suitable data structures. It is what C was designed to support (and Algol, and Fortran, as well as many other languages). C++'s support comes in the form of the built-in types, operators, statements, functions, **structs**, **unions**, etc. With minor exceptions, C is a subset of C++. Compared to C, C++ provides further support for procedural programming in the form of many additional language constructs and a stricter, more flexible, and more supportive type system.

- *Data abstraction*: This is programming focused on the design of interfaces, hiding implementation details in general and representations in particular. C++ supports concrete and abstract classes. The facilities for defining classes with private implementation details, constructors and destructors, and associated operations directly support this. The notion of an abstract class provides direct support for complete data hiding.

- *Object-oriented programming*: This is programming focused on the design, implementation, and use of class hierarchies. In addition to allowing the definition lattices of classes, C++ provides a variety of features for navigating class lattices and for simplifying the definition of a class out of existing ones. Class hierarchies provide run-time polymorphism (§20.3.2, §21.2) and encapsulation (§20.4, §20.5).

- *Generic programming*: This is programming focused on the design, implementation, and use of general algorithms. Here, "general" means that an algorithm can be designed to accept a wide variety of types as long as they meet the algorithm's requirements on its arguments. The template is C++'s main support for generic programming. Templates provide (compile-time) parametric polymorphism.

Just about anything that increases the flexibility or efficiency of classes improves the support of all of those styles. Thus, C++ could be (and has been) called *class oriented*.

Each of these styles of design and programming has contributed to the synthesis that is C++. Focusing exclusively on one of these styles is a mistake: except for toy examples, doing so leads to wasted development effort and suboptimal (inflexible, verbose, poorly performing, unmaintainable, etc.) code.

I wince when someone characterizes C++ exclusively through one of these styles (e.g., "C++ is an object-oriented language") or uses a term (e.g., "hybrid" or "mixed paradigm") to imply that a more restrictive language would be preferable. The former misses the fact that all the styles mentioned have contributed something significant to the synthesis; the latter denies the validity of the synthesis. The styles mentioned are not distinct alternatives: each contributes techniques to a more expressive and effective style of programming, and C++ provides direct language support for their use in combination.

From its inception, the design of C++ aimed at a synthesis of programming and design styles. Even the earliest published account of C++ [Stroustrup,1982] presents examples that use these different styles in combination and presents language features aimed at supporting such combinations:

- *Classes* support all of the mentioned styles; all rely on the user representing ideas as user-defined types or objects of user-defined types.
- *Public/private access control* supports data abstraction and object-oriented programming by making a clear distinction between interface and implementation.
- *Member functions, constructors, destructors, and user-defined assignment* provide a clean functional interface to objects as needed by data abstraction and object-oriented programming. They also provide a uniform notation as needed for generic programming. More general overloading had to wait until 1984 and uniform initialization until 2010.
- *Function declarations* provide specific statically checked interfaces to member functions as well as freestanding functions, so they support all of the mentioned styles. They are necessary for overloading. At the time, C lacked "function prototypes" but Simula had function declarations as well as member functions.
- *Generic functions and parameterized types* (generated from functions and classes using macros) support generic programming. Templates had to wait until 1988.
- *Base and derived classes* provide the foundation for object-oriented programming and some forms of data abstraction. Virtual functions had to wait until 1983.
- *Inlining* made the use of these facilities affordable in systems programming and for building run-time and space efficient libraries.

These early features are general abstraction mechanisms, rather than support for disjoint programming styles. Today's C++ provides much better support for design and programming based on lightweight abstraction, but the aim of elegant and efficient code was there from the very beginning. The developments since 1981 provide much better support for the synthesis of the programming styles ("paradigms") originally considered and significantly improve their integration.

The fundamental object in C++ has identity; that is, it is located in a specific location in memory and can be distinguished from other objects with (potentially) the same value by comparing addresses. Expressions denoting such objects are called *lvalues* (§6.4). However, even from the earliest days of C++'s ancestors [Barron,1963] there have also been objects without identity (objects for which an address cannot be safely stored for later use). In C++11, this notion of *rvalue* has been developed into a notion of a value that can be moved around cheaply (§3.3.2, §6.4.1, §7.7.2). Such objects are the basis of techniques that resemble what is found in functional programming (where the notion of objects with identity is viewed with horror). This nicely complements the techniques and language features (e.g., lambda expressions) developed primarily for generic programming. It also solves classical problems related to "simple abstract data types," such as how to elegantly and efficiently return a large matrix from an operation (e.g., a matrix +).

From the very earliest days, C++ programs and the design of C++ itself have been concerned about resource management. The ideal was (and is) for resource management to be
- simple (for implementers and especially for users),
- general (a resource is anything that has to be acquired from somewhere and later released),
- efficient (obey the zero-overhead principle; §1.2),
- perfect (no leaks are acceptable), and
- statically type-safe.

Many important C++ classes, such as the standard library's vector, string, thread, mutex, unique_ptr, fstream, and regex, are resource handles. Foundation and application libraries beyond the standard provided many more examples, such as Matrix and Widget. The initial step in supporting the notion of resource handles was taken with the provision of constructors and destructors in the very first "C with Classes" draft. This was soon backed with the ability to control copy by defining assignment as well as copy constructors. The introduction of move constructors and move assignments (§3.3) in C++11 completes this line of thinking by allowing cheap movement of potentially large objects from scope to scope (§3.3.2) and to simply control the lifetime of polymorphic or shared objects (§5.2.1).

The facilities supporting resource management also benefit abstractions that are not resource handles. Any class that establishes and maintains an invariant relies on a subset of those features.

1.2.2 Type Checking

The connection between the language in which we think/program and the problems and solutions we can imagine is very close. For this reason, restricting language features with the intent of eliminating programmer errors is, at best, dangerous. A language provides a programmer with a set of conceptual tools; if these are inadequate for a task, they will be ignored. Good design and the absence of errors cannot be guaranteed merely by the presence or absence of specific language features. However, the language features and the type system are provided for the programmer to precisely and concisely represent a design in code.

The notion of static types and compile-time type checking is central to effective use of C++. The use of static types is key to expressiveness, maintainability, and performance. Following Simula, the design of user-defined types with interfaces that are checked at compile time is key to the expressiveness of C++. The C++ type system is extensible in nontrivial ways (Chapter 3, Chapter 16, Chapter 18, Chapter 19, Chapter 21, Chapter 23, Chapter 28, Chapter 29), aiming for equal support for built-in types and user-defined types.

C++ type-checking and data-hiding features rely on compile-time analysis of programs to prevent accidental corruption of data. They do not provide secrecy or protection against someone who is deliberately breaking the rules: C++ protects against accident, not against fraud. They can, however, be used freely without incurring run-time or space overheads. The idea is that to be useful, a language feature must not only be elegant, it must also be affordable in the context of a real-world program.

C++'s static type system is flexible, and the use of simple user-defined types implies little, if any overhead. The aim is to support a style of programming that represents distinct ideas as distinct types, rather than just using generalizations, such as integer, floating-point number, string, "raw memory," and "object," everywhere. A type-rich style of programming makes code more readable, maintainable, and analyzable. A trivial type system allows only trivial analysis, whereas a type-rich style of programming opens opportunities for nontrivial error detection and optimization. C++ compilers and development tools support such type-based analysis [Stroustrup,2012].

Maintaining most of C as a subset and preserving the direct mapping to hardware needed for the most demanding low-level systems programming tasks implies the ability to break the static type system. However, my ideal is (and always was) complete type safety. In this, I agree with Dennis Ritchie, who said, "C is a strongly typed, weakly checked language." Note that Simula was both type-safe and flexible. In fact, my ideal when I started on C++ was "Algol68 with Classes" rather than "C with Classes." However, the list of solid reasons against basing my work on type-safe Algol68 [Woodward,1974] was long and painful. So, perfect type safety is an ideal that C++ as a language can only approximate. But it is an ideal that C++ programmers (especially library builders) can strive for. Over the years, the set of language features, standard-library components, and techniques supporting that ideal has grown. Outside of low-level sections of code (hopefully isolated by type-safe interfaces), code that interfaces to code obeying different language conventions (e.g., an operating system call interface), and the implementations of fundamental abstractions (e.g., **string** and **vector**), there is now little need for type-unsafe code.

1.2.3 C Compatibility

C++ was developed from the C programming language and, with few exceptions, retains C as a subset. The main reasons for relying on C were to build on a proven set of low-level language facilities and to be part of a technical community. Great importance was attached to retaining a high degree of compatibility with C [Koenig,1989] [Stroustrup,1994] (Chapter 44); this (unfortunately) precluded cleaning up the C syntax. The continuing, more or less parallel evolution of C and C++ has been a constant source of concern and requires constant attention [Stroustrup,2002]. Having two committees devoted to keeping two widely used languages "as compatible as possible" is not a particularly good way of organizing work. In particular, there are differences in opinion as to the value of compatibility, differences in opinion on what constitutes good programming, and differences in opinion on what support is needed for good programming. Just keeping up communication between the committees is a large amount of work.

One hundred percent C/C++ compatibility was never a goal for C++ because that would compromise type safety and the smooth integration of user-defined and built-in types. However, the definition of C++ has been repeatedly reviewed to remove gratuitous incompatibilities; C++ is now more compatible with C than it was originally. C++98 adopted many details from C89 (§44.3.1). When C then evolved from C89 [C,1990] to C99 [C,1999], C++ adopted almost all of the new features, leaving out VLAs (variable-length arrays) as a misfeature and designated initializers as redundant. C's facilities for low-level systems programming tasks are retained and enhanced; for example, see inlining (§3.2.1.1, §12.1.5, §16.2.8) and **constexpr** (§2.2.3, §10.4, §12.1.6).

Conversely, modern C has adopted (with varying degrees of faithfulness and effectiveness) many features from C++ (e.g., **const**, function prototypes, and inlining; see [Stroustrup,2002]).

The definition of C++ has been revised to ensure that a construct that is both legal C and legal C++ has the same meaning in both languages (§44.3).

One of the original aims for C was to replace assembly coding for the most demanding systems programming tasks. When C++ was designed, care was taken not to compromise the gains in this area. The difference between C and C++ is primarily in the degree of emphasis on types and structure. C is expressive and permissive. Through extensive use of the type system, C++ is even more expressive without loss of performance.

Knowing C is not a prerequisite for learning C++. Programming in C encourages many techniques and tricks that are rendered unnecessary by C++ language features. For example, explicit type conversion (casting) is less frequently needed in C++ than it is in C (§1.3.3). However, *good* C programs tend to be C++ programs. For example, every program in Kernighan and Ritchie, *The C Programming Language, Second Edition* [Kernighan,1988], is a C++ program. Experience with any statically typed language will be a help when learning C++.

1.2.4 Language, Libraries, and Systems

The C++ fundamental (built-in) types, operators, and statements are those that computer hardware deals with directly: numbers, characters, and addresses. C++ has no built-in high-level data types and no high-level primitive operations. For example, the C++ language does not provide a matrix type with an inversion operator or a string type with a concatenation operator. If a user wants such a type, it can be defined in the language itself. In fact, defining a new general-purpose or application-specific type is the most fundamental programming activity in C++. A well-designed user-defined type differs from a built-in type only in the way it is defined, not in the way it is used. The C++ standard library (Chapter 4, Chapter 5, Chapter 30, Chapter 31, etc.) provides many examples of such types and their uses. From a user's point of view, there is little difference between a built-in type and a type provided by the standard library. Except for a few unfortunate and unimportant historical accidents, the C++ standard library is written in C++. Writing the C++ standard library in C++ is a crucial test of the C++ type system and abstraction mechanisms: they must be (and are) sufficiently powerful (expressive) and efficient (affordable) for the most demanding systems programming tasks. This ensures that they can be used in large systems that typically consist of layer upon layer of abstraction.

Features that would incur run-time or memory overhead even when not used were avoided. For example, constructs that would make it necessary to store "housekeeping information" in every object were rejected, so if a user declares a structure consisting of two 16-bit quantities, that structure will fit into a 32-bit register. Except for the `new`, `delete`, `typeid`, `dynamic_cast`, and `throw` operators, and the `try`-block, individual C++ expressions and statements need no run-time support. This can be essential for embedded and high-performance applications. In particular, this implies that the C++ abstraction mechanisms are usable for embedded, high-performance, high-reliability, and real-time applications. So, programmers of such applications don't have to work with a low-level (error-prone, impoverished, and unproductive) set of language features.

C++ was designed to be used in a traditional compilation and run-time environment: the C programming environment on the UNIX system [UNIX,1985]. Fortunately, C++ was never restricted to UNIX; it simply used UNIX and C as a model for the relationships among language, libraries, compilers, linkers, execution environments, etc. That minimal model helped C++ to be successful on essentially every computing platform. There are, however, good reasons for using C++ in environments that provide significantly more run-time support. Facilities such as dynamic loading, incremental compilation, and a database of type definitions can be put to good use without affecting the language.

Not every piece of code can be well structured, hardware-independent, easy to read, etc. C++ possesses features that are intended for manipulating hardware facilities in a direct and efficient way without concerns for safety or ease of comprehension. It also possesses facilities for hiding such code behind elegant and safe interfaces.

Naturally, the use of C++ for larger programs leads to the use of C++ by groups of programmers. C++'s emphasis on modularity, strongly typed interfaces, and flexibility pays off here. However, as programs get larger, the problems associated with their development and maintenance shift from being language problems to being more global problems of tools and management.

This book emphasizes techniques for providing general-purpose facilities, generally useful types, libraries, etc. These techniques will serve programmers of small programs as well as programmers of large ones. Furthermore, because all nontrivial programs consist of many semi-independent parts, the techniques for writing such parts serve programmers of all applications.

I use the implementation and use of standard-library components, such as vector, as examples. This introduces library components and their underlying design concepts and implementation techniques. Such examples show how programmers might design and implement their own libraries. However, if the standard library provides a component that addresses a problem, it is almost always better to use that component than to build your own. Even if the standard component is arguably slightly inferior to a home-built component for a particular problem, the standard component is likely to be more widely applicable, more widely available, and more widely known. Over the longer term, the standard component (possibly accessed through a convenient custom interface) is likely to lower long-term maintenance, porting, tuning, and education costs.

You might suspect that specifying a program by using a more detailed type structure would increase the size of the program source text (or even the size of the generated code). With C++, this is not so. A C++ program declaring function argument types, using classes, etc., is typically a bit shorter than the equivalent C program not using these facilities. Where libraries are used, a C++ program will appear much shorter than its C equivalent, assuming, of course, that a functioning C equivalent could have been built.

C++ supports systems programming. This implies that C++ code is able to effectively interoperate with software written in other languages on a system. The idea of writing all software in a single language is a fantasy. From the beginning, C++ was designed to interoperate simply and efficiently with C, assembler, and Fortran. By that, I meant that a C++, C, assembler, or Fortran function could call functions in the other languages without extra overhead or conversion of data structures passed among them.

C++ was designed to operate within a single address space. The use of multiple processes and multiple address spaces relied on (extralinguistic) operating system support. In particular, I assumed that a C++ programmer would have the operating systems command language available for composing processes into a system. Initially, I relied on the UNIX Shell for that, but just about any "scripting language" will do. Thus, C++ provided no support for multiple address spaces and no support for multiple processes, but it was used for systems relying on those features from the earliest days. C++ was designed to be part of large, concurrent, multilanguage systems.

1.3 Learning C++

No programming language is perfect. Fortunately, a programming language does not have to be perfect to be a good tool for building great systems. In fact, a general-purpose programming language cannot be perfect for all of the many tasks to which it is put. What is perfect for one task is often seriously flawed for another because perfection in one area implies specialization. Thus, C++ was designed to be a good tool for building a wide variety of systems and to allow a wide variety of ideas to be expressed directly.

Not everything can be expressed directly using the built-in features of a language. In fact, that isn't even the ideal. Language features exist to support a variety of programming styles and techniques. Consequently, the task of learning a language should focus on mastering the native and natural styles for that language – not on understanding of every little detail of every language feature. Writing programs is essential; understanding a programming language is not just an intellectual exercise. Practical application of ideas is necessary.

In practical programming, there is little advantage in knowing the most obscure language features or using the largest number of features. A single language feature in isolation is of little interest. Only in the context provided by techniques and by other features does the feature acquire meaning and interest. Thus, when reading the following chapters, please remember that the real purpose of examining the details of C++ is to be able to use language features and library facilities in concert to support good programming styles in the context of sound designs.

No significant system is built exclusively in terms of the language features themselves. We build and use libraries to simplify the task of programming and to increase the quality of our systems. We use libraries to improve maintainability, portability, and performance. Fundamental application concepts are represented as abstractions (e.g., classes, templates, and class hierarchies) in libraries. Many of the most fundamental programming concepts are represented in the standard library. Thus, learning the standard library is an integral part of learning C++. The standard library is the repository of much hard-earned knowledge of how to use C++ well.

C++ is widely used for teaching and research. This has surprised some who – correctly – point out that C++ isn't the smallest or cleanest language ever designed. It is, however:

- Sufficiently clean for successfully teaching basic design and programming concepts
- Sufficiently comprehensive to be a vehicle for teaching advanced concepts and techniques
- Sufficiently realistic, efficient, and flexible for demanding projects
- Sufficiently commercial to be a vehicle for putting what is learned into nonacademic use
- Sufficiently available for organizations and collaborations relying on diverse development and execution environments

C++ is a language that you can grow with.

The most important thing to do when learning C++ is to focus on fundamental concepts (such as type safety, resource management, and invariants) and programming techniques (such as resource management using scoped objects and the use of iterators in algorithms) and not get lost in language-technical details. The purpose of learning a programming language is to become a better programmer, that is, to become more effective at designing and implementing new systems and at maintaining old ones. For this, an appreciation of programming and design techniques is far more important than understanding all the details. The understanding of technical details comes with time and practice.

C++ programming is based on strong static type checking, and most techniques aim at achieving a high level of abstraction and a direct representation of the programmer's ideas. This can usually be done without compromising run-time and space efficiency compared to lower-level techniques. To gain the benefits of C++, programmers coming to it from a different language must learn and internalize idiomatic C++ programming style and technique. The same applies to programmers used to earlier and less expressive versions of C++.

Thoughtlessly applying techniques effective in one language to another typically leads to awkward, poorly performing, and hard-to-maintain code. Such code is also most frustrating to write because every line of code and every compiler error message reminds the programmer that the language used differs from "the old language." You can write in the style of Fortran, C, Lisp, Java, etc., in any language, but doing so is neither pleasant nor economical in a language with a different philosophy. Every language can be a fertile source of ideas about how to write C++ programs. However, ideas must be transformed into something that fits with the general structure and type system of C++ in order to be effective in C++. Over the basic type system of a language, only Pyrrhic victories are possible.

In the continuing debate on whether one needs to learn C before C++, I am firmly convinced that it is best to go directly to C++. C++ is safer and more expressive, and it reduces the need to focus on low-level techniques. It is easier for you to learn the trickier parts of C that are needed to compensate for its lack of higher-level facilities after you have been exposed to the common subset of C and C++ and to some of the higher-level techniques supported directly in C++. Chapter 44 is a guide for programmers going from C++ to C, say, to deal with legacy code. My opinion on how to teach C++ to novices is represented by [Stroustrup,2008].

There are several independently developed implementations of C++. They are supported by a wealth of tools, libraries, and software development environments. To help master all of this you can find textbooks, manuals, and a bewildering variety of online resources. If you plan to use C++ seriously, I strongly suggest that you obtain access to several such sources. Each has its own emphasis and bias, so use at least two.

1.3.1 Programming in C++

The question "How does one write good programs in C++?" is very similar to the question "How does one write good English prose?" There are two answers: "Know what you want to say" and "Practice. Imitate good writing." Both appear to be as appropriate for C++ as they are for English – and as hard to follow.

The main ideal for C++ programming – as for programming in most higher-level languages – is to express concepts (ideas, notions, etc.) from a design directly in code. We try to ensure that the concepts we talk about, represent with boxes and arrows on our whiteboard, and find in our (non-programming) textbooks have direct and obvious counterparts in our programs:

[1]   Represent ideas directly in code.
[2]   Represent relationships among ideas directly in code (e.g., hierarchical, parametric, and ownership relationships).
[3]   Represent independent ideas independently in code.
[4]   Keep simple things simple (without making complex things impossible).

More specifically:

- [5] Prefer statically type-checked solutions (when applicable).
- [6] Keep information local (e.g., avoid global variables, minimize the use of pointers).
- [7] Don't overabstract (i.e., don't generalize, introduce class hierarchies, or parameterize beyond obvious needs and experience).

More specific suggestions are listed in §1.3.2.

1.3.2 Suggestions for C++ Programmers

By now, many people have been using C++ for a decade or two. Many more are using C++ in a single environment and have learned to live with the restrictions imposed by early compilers and first-generation libraries. Often, what an experienced C++ programmer has failed to notice over the years is not the introduction of new features as such, but rather the changes in relationships between features that make fundamental new programming techniques feasible. In other words, what you didn't think of when first learning C++ or found impractical just might be a superior approach today. You find out only by reexamining the basics.

Read through the chapters in order. If you already know the contents of a chapter, you can be done in minutes. If you don't already know the contents, you'll have learned something unexpected. I learned a fair bit writing this book, and I suspect that hardly any C++ programmer knows every feature and technique presented. Furthermore, to use the language well, you need a perspective that brings order to the set of features and techniques. Through its organization and examples, this book offers such a perspective.

Take the opportunity offered by the new C++11 facilities to modernize your design and programming techniques:

- [1] Use constructors to establish invariants (§2.4.3.2, §13.4, §17.2.1).
- [2] Use constructor/destructor pairs to simplify resource management (RAII; §5.2, §13.3).
- [3] Avoid "naked" `new` and `delete` (§3.2.1.2, §11.2.1).
- [4] Use containers and algorithms rather than built-in arrays and ad hoc code (§4.4, §4.5, §7.4, Chapter 32).
- [5] Prefer standard-library facilities to locally developed code (§1.2.4).
- [6] Use exceptions, rather than error codes, to report errors that cannot be handled locally (§2.4.3, §13.1).
- [7] Use move semantics to avoid copying large objects (§3.3.2, §17.5.2).
- [8] Use `unique_ptr` to reference objects of polymorphic type (§5.2.1).
- [9] Use `shared_ptr` to reference shared objects, that is, objects without a single owner that is responsible for their destruction (§5.2.1).
- [10] Use templates to maintain static type safety (eliminate casts) and avoid unnecessary use of class hierarchies (§27.2).

It might also be a good idea to review the advice for C and Java programmers (§1.3.3, §1.3.4).

1.3.3 Suggestions for C Programmers

The better one knows C, the harder it seems to be to avoid writing C++ in C style, thereby losing many of the potential benefits of C++. Please take a look at Chapter 44, which describes the differences between C and C++.

[1]   Don't think of C++ as C with a few features added. C++ can be used that way, but only suboptimally. To get really major advantages from C++ as compared to C, you need to apply different design and implementation styles.

[2]   Don't write C in C++; that is often seriously suboptimal for both maintenance and performance.

[3]   Use the C++ standard library as a teacher of new techniques and programming styles. Note the difference from the C standard library (e.g., = rather than strcpy() for copying and == rather than strcmp() for comparing).

[4]   Macro substitution is almost never necessary in C++. Use const (§7.5), constexpr (§2.2.3, §10.4), enum or enum class (§8.4) to define manifest constants, inline (§12.1.5) to avoid function-calling overhead, templates (§3.4, Chapter 23) to specify families of functions and types, and namespaces (§2.4.2, §14.3.1) to avoid name clashes.

[5]   Don't declare a variable before you need it, and initialize it immediately. A declaration can occur anywhere a statement can (§9.3), in for-statement initializers (§9.5), and in conditions (§9.4.3).

[6]   Don't use malloc(). The new operator (§11.2) does the same job better, and instead of realloc(), try a vector (§3.4.2). Don't just replace malloc() and free() with "naked" new and delete (§3.2.1.2, §11.2.1).

[7]   Avoid void∗, unions, and casts, except deep within the implementation of some function or class. Their use limits the support you can get from the type system and can harm performance. In most cases, a cast is an indication of a design error. If you must use an explicit type conversion, try using one of the named casts (e.g., static_cast; §11.5.2) for a more precise statement of what you are trying to do.

[8]   Minimize the use of arrays and C-style strings. C++ standard-library strings (§4.2), arrays (§8.2.4), and vectors (§4.4.1) can often be used to write simpler and more maintainable code compared to the traditional C style. In general, try not to build yourself what has already been provided by the standard library.

[9]   Avoid pointer arithmetic except in very specialized code (such as a memory manager) and for simple array traversal (e.g., ++p).

[10]   Do not assume that something laboriously written in C style (avoiding C++ features such as classes, templates, and exceptions) is more efficient than a shorter alternative (e.g., using standard-library facilities). Often (but of course not always), the opposite is true.

To obey C linkage conventions, a C++ function must be declared to have C linkage (§15.2.5).

1.3.4 Suggestions for Java Programmers

C++ and Java are rather different languages with similar syntaxes. Their aims are significantly different and so are many of their application domains. Java is *not* a direct successor to C++ in the sense of a language that can do the same as its predecessor, but better and also more. To use C++ well, you need to adopt programming and design techniques appropriate to C++, rather than trying to write Java in C++. It is not just an issue of remembering to delete objects that you create with new because you can't rely on the presence of a garbage collector:

[1]   Don't simply mimic Java style in C++; that is often seriously suboptimal for both maintainability and performance.

[2]   Use the C++ abstraction mechanisms (e.g., classes and templates): don't fall back to a C style of programming out of a false feeling of familiarity.

[3]   Use the C++ standard library as a teacher of new techniques and programming styles.

[4]   Don't immediately invent a unique base for all of your classes (an Object class). Typically, you can do better without it for many/most classes.

[5]   Minimize the use of reference and pointer variables: use local and member variables (§3.2.1.2, §5.2, §16.3.4, §17.1).

[6]   Remember: a variable is never implicitly a reference.

[7]   Think of pointers as C++'s equivalent to Java references (C++ references are more limited; there is no reseating of C++ references).

[8]   A function is not virtual by default. Not every class is meant for inheritance.

[9]   Use abstract classes as interfaces to class hierarchies; avoid "brittle base classes," that is, base classes with data members.

[10] Use scoped resource management ("Resource Acquisition Is Initialization"; RAII) whenever possible.

[11] Use a constructor to establish a class invariant (and throw an exception if it can't).

[12] If a cleanup action is needed when an object is deleted (e.g., goes out of scope), use a destructor for that. Don't imitate finally (doing so is more ad hoc and in the longer run far more work than relying on destructors).

[13] Avoid "naked" new and delete; instead, use containers (e.g., vector, string, and map) and handle classes (e.g., lock and unique_ptr).

[14] Use freestanding functions (nonmember functions) to minimize coupling (e.g., see the standard algorithms), and use namespaces (§2.4.2, Chapter 14) to limit the scope of freestanding functions.

[15] Don't use exception specifications (except noexcept; §13.5.1.1).

[16] A C++ nested class does not have access to an object of the enclosing class.

[17] C++ offers only the most minimal run-time reflection: dynamic_cast and typeid (Chapter 22). Rely more on compile-time facilities (e.g., compile-time polymorphism; Chapter 27, Chapter 28).

Most of this advice applies equally to C# programmers.

1.4 History

I invented C++, wrote its early definitions, and produced its first implementation. I chose and formulated the design criteria for C++, designed its major language features, developed or helped to develop many of the early libraries, and was responsible for the processing of extension proposals in the C++ standards committee.

C++ was designed to provide Simula's facilities for program organization [Dahl,1970] [Dahl,1972] together with C's efficiency and flexibility for systems programming [Kernighan,1978] [Kernighan,1988]. Simula is the initial source of C++'s abstraction mechanisms. The class concept (with derived classes and virtual functions) was borrowed from it. However, templates and exceptions came to C++ later with different sources of inspiration.

The evolution of C++ was always in the context of its use. I spent a lot of time listening to users and seeking out the opinions of experienced programmers. In particular, my colleagues at AT&T Bell Laboratories were essential for the growth of C++ during its first decade.

This section is a brief overview; it does not try to mention every language feature and library component. Furthermore, it does not go into details. For more information, and in particular for more names of people who contributed, see [Stroustrup,1993], [Stroustrup,2007], and [Stroustrup,1994]. My two papers from the ACM History of Programming Languages conference and my *Design and Evolution of C++* book (known as "D&E") describe the design and evolution of C++ in detail and document influences from other programming languages.

Most of the documents produced as part of the ISO C++ standards effort are available online [WG21]. In my FAQ, I try to maintain a connection between the standard facilities and the people who proposed and refined those facilities [Stroustrup,2010]. C++ is not the work of a faceless, anonymous committee or of a supposedly omnipotent "dictator for life"; it is the work of many dedicated, experienced, hard-working individuals.

1.4.1 Timeline

The work that led to C++ started in the fall of 1979 under the name "C with Classes." Here is a simplified timeline:

1979 Work on "C with Classes" started. The initial feature set included classes and derived classes, public/private access control, constructors and destructors, and function declarations with argument checking. The first library supported non-preemptive concurrent tasks and random number generators.

1984 "C with Classes" was renamed to C++. By then, C++ had acquired virtual functions, function and operator overloading, references, and the I/O stream and complex number libraries.

1985 First commercial release of C++ (October 14). The library included I/O streams, complex numbers, and tasks (nonpreemptive scheduling).

1985 *The C++ Programming Language* ("TC++PL," October 14) [Stroustrup,1986].

1989 *The Annotated C++ Reference Manual* ("the ARM").

1991 *The C++ Programming Language, Second Edition* [Stroustrup,1991], presenting generic programming using templates and error handling based on exceptions (including the "Resource Acquisition Is Initialization" general resource management idiom).

1997 *The C++ Programming Language, Third Edition* [Stroustrup,1997] introduced ISO C++, including namespaces, `dynamic_cast`, and many refinements of templates. The standard library added the STL framework of generic containers and algorithms.

1998 ISO C++ standard.

2002 Work on a revised standard, colloquially named C++0x, started.

2003 A "bug fix" revision of the ISO C++ standard was issued. A C++ Technical Report introduced new standard-library components, such as regular expressions, unordered containers (hash tables), and resource management pointers, which later became part of C++0x.

2006 An ISO C++ Technical Report on Performance was issued to answer questions of cost, predictability, and techniques, mostly related to embedded systems programming.

2009 C++0x was feature complete. It provided uniform initialization, move semantics, variadic template arguments, lambda expressions, type aliases, a memory model suitable for concurrency, and much more. The standard library added several components, including threads, locks, and most of the components from the 2003 Technical Report.

2011 ISO C++11 standard was formally approved.

2012 The first complete C++11 implementations emerged.

2012 Work on future ISO C++ standards (referred to as C++14 and C++17) started.

2013 *The C++ Programming Language, Fourth Edition* introduced C++11.

During development, C++11 was known as C++0x. As is not uncommon in large projects, we were overly optimistic about the completion date.

1.4.2 The Early Years

I originally designed and implemented the language because I wanted to distribute the services of a UNIX kernel across multiprocessors and local-area networks (what are now known as multicores and clusters). For that, I needed some event-driven simulations for which Simula would have been ideal, except for performance considerations. I also needed to deal directly with hardware and provide high-performance concurrent programming mechanisms for which C would have been ideal, except for its weak support for modularity and type checking. The result of adding Simula-style classes to C, "C with Classes," was used for major projects in which its facilities for writing programs that use minimal time and space were severely tested. It lacked operator overloading, references, virtual functions, templates, exceptions, and many, many details [Stroustrup,1982]. The first use of C++ outside a research organization started in July 1983.

The name C++ (pronounced "see plus plus") was coined by Rick Mascitti in the summer of 1983 and chosen as the replacement for "C with Classes" by me. The name signifies the evolutionary nature of the changes from C; "++" is the C increment operator. The slightly shorter name "C+" is a syntax error; it had also been used as the name of an unrelated language. Connoisseurs of C semantics find C++ inferior to ++C. The language was not called D, because it was an extension of C, because it did not attempt to remedy problems by removing features, and because there already existed several would-be C successors named D. For yet another interpretation of the name C++, see the appendix of [Orwell,1949].

C++ was designed primarily so that my friends and I would not have to program in assembler, C, or various then-fashionable high-level languages. Its main purpose was to make writing good programs easier and more pleasant for the individual programmer. In the early years, there was no C++ paper design; design, documentation, and implementation went on simultaneously. There was no "C++ project" either, or a "C++ design committee." Throughout, C++ evolved to cope with problems encountered by users and as a result of discussions among my friends, my colleagues, and me.

1.4.2.1 Language Features and Library Facilities

The very first design of C++ (then called "C with Classes") included function declarations with argument type checking and implicit conversions, classes with the **public/private** distinction between the interface and the implementation, derived classes, and constructors and destructors. I used macros to provide primitive parameterization. This was in use by mid-1980. Late that year, I was able to present a set of language facilities supporting a coherent set of programming styles; see §1.2.1. In retrospect, I consider the introduction of constructors and destructors most significant. In the terminology of the time, "a constructor creates the execution environment for the member functions and the destructor reverses that." Here is the root of C++'s strategies for resource management (causing a demand for exceptions) and the key to many techniques for making user code short and clear. If there were other languages at the time that supported multiple constructors capable of executing general code, I didn't (and don't) know of them. Destructors were new in C++.

C++ was released commercially in October 1985. By then, I had added inlining (§12.1.5, §16.2.8), consts (§2.2.3, §7.5, §16.2.9), function overloading (§12.3), references (§7.7), operator overloading (§3.2.1.1, Chapter 18, Chapter 19), and virtual functions (§3.2.3, §20.3.2). Of these features, support for run-time polymorphism in the form of virtual functions was by far the most controversial. I knew its worth from Simula but found it impossible to convince most people in the systems programming world of its value. Systems programmers tended to view indirect function calls with suspicion, and people acquainted with other languages supporting object-oriented programming had a hard time believing that virtual functions could be fast enough to be useful in systems code. Conversely, many programmers with an object-oriented background had (and many still have) a hard time getting used to the idea that you use virtual function calls only to express a choice that must be made at run time. The resistance to virtual functions may be related to a resistance to the idea that you can get better systems through more regular structure of code supported by a programming language. Many C programmers seem convinced that what really matters is complete flexibility and careful individual crafting of every detail of a program. My view was (and is) that we need every bit of help we can get from languages and tools: the inherent complexity of the systems we are trying to build is always at the edge of what we can express.

Much of the design of C++ was done on the blackboards of my colleagues. In the early years, the feedback from Stu Feldman, Alexander Fraser, Steve Johnson, Brian Kernighan, Doug McIlroy, and Dennis Ritchie was invaluable.

In the second half of the 1980s, I continued to add language features in response to user comments. The most important of those were templates [Stroustrup,1988] and exception handling [Koenig,1990], which were considered experimental at the time the standards effort started. In the design of templates, I was forced to decide among flexibility, efficiency, and early type checking. At the time, nobody knew how to simultaneously get all three, and to compete with C-style code for demanding systems applications, I felt that I had to choose the first two properties. In retrospect, I think the choice was the correct one, and the search for better type checking of templates continues [Gregor,2006] [Sutton,2011] [Stroustrup,2012a]. The design of exceptions focused on multilevel propagation of exceptions, the passing of arbitrary information to an error handler, and the integrations between exceptions and resource management by using local objects with destructors to represent and release resources (what I clumsily called "Resource Acquisition Is Initialization"; §13.3).

I generalized C++'s inheritance mechanisms to support multiple base classes [Stroustrup,1987a]. This was called *multiple inheritance* and was considered difficult and controversial. I considered it far less important than templates or exceptions. Multiple inheritance of abstract classes (often called *interfaces*) is now universal in languages supporting static type checking and object-oriented programming.

The C++ language evolved hand in hand with some of the key library facilities presented in this book. For example, I designed the complex [Stroustrup,1984], vector, stack, and (I/O) stream [Stroustrup,1985] classes together with the operator overloading mechanisms. The first string and list classes were developed by Jonathan Shopiro and me as part of the same effort. Jonathan's string and list classes were the first to see extensive use as part of a library. The string class from the standard C++ library has its roots in these early efforts. The task library described in [Stroustrup,1987b] was part of the first "C with Classes" program ever written in 1980. I wrote it and its associated classes to support Simula-style simulations. Unfortunately, we had to wait until 2011 (30 years!) to get concurrency support standardized and universally available (§1.4.4.2, §5.3, Chapter 41). The development of the template facility was influenced by a variety of vector, map, list, and sort templates devised by Andrew Koenig, Alex Stepanov, me, and others.

C++ grew up in an environment with a multitude of established and experimental programming languages (e.g., Ada [Ichbiah,1979], Algol 68 [Woodward,1974], and ML [Paulson,1996]). At the time, I was comfortable in about 25 languages, and their influences on C++ are documented in [Stroustrup,1994] and [Stroustrup,2007]. However, the determining influences always came from the applications I encountered. That was a deliberate policy to have the development of C++ "problem driven" rather than imitative.

1.4.3 The 1998 Standard

The explosive growth of C++ use caused some changes. Sometime during 1987, it became clear that formal standardization of C++ was inevitable and that we needed to start preparing the ground for a standardization effort [Stroustrup,1994]. The result was a conscious effort to maintain contact between implementers of C++ compilers and major users. This was done through paper and electronic mail and through face-to-face meetings at C++ conferences and elsewhere.

AT&T Bell Labs made a major contribution to C++ and its wider community by allowing me to share drafts of revised versions of the C++ reference manual with implementers and users. Because many of those people worked for companies that could be seen as competing with AT&T, the significance of this contribution should not be underestimated. A less enlightened company could have caused major problems of language fragmentation simply by doing nothing. As it happened, about a hundred individuals from dozens of organizations read and commented on what became the generally accepted reference manual and the base document for the ANSI C++ standardization effort. Their names can be found in *The Annotated C++ Reference Manual* ("the ARM") [Ellis,1989]. The X3J16 committee of ANSI was convened in December 1989 at the initiative of Hewlett-Packard. In June 1991, this ANSI (American national) standardization of C++ became part of an ISO (international) standardization effort for C++ and named WG21. From 1990, these joint C++ standards committees have been the main forum for the evolution of C++ and the refinement of its definition. I served on these committees throughout. In particular, as the chairman of the working group for extensions (later called the evolution group), I was directly responsible for handling proposals for major changes to C++ and the addition of new language features. An initial draft standard for public review was produced in April 1995. The first ISO C++ standard (ISO/IEC 14882-1998) [C++,1998] was ratified by a 22-0 national vote in 1998. A "bug fix release" of this standard was issued in 2003, so you sometimes hear people refer to C++03, but that is essentially the same language as C++98.

1.4.3.1 Language Features

By the time the ANSI and ISO standards efforts started, most major language features were in place and documented in the ARM [Ellis,1989]. Consequently, most of the work involved refinement of features and their specification. The template mechanisms, in particular, benefited from much detailed work. Namespaces were introduced to cope with the increased size of C++ programs and the increased number of libraries. At the initiative of Dmitry Lenkov from Hewett-Packard, minimal facilities to use run-time type information (RTTI; Chapter 22) were introduced. I had left such facilities out of C++ because I had found them seriously overused in Simula. I tried to get a facility for optional conservative garbage collection accepted, but failed. We had to wait until the 2011 standard for that.

Clearly, the 1998 language was far superior in features and in particular in the detail of specification to the 1989 language. However, not all changes were improvements. In addition to the inevitable minor mistakes, two major features were added that in retrospect should not have been:

- Exception specifications provide run-time enforcement of which exceptions a function is allowed to throw. They were added at the energetic initiative of people from Sun Microsystems. Exception specifications turned out to be worse than useless for improving readability, reliability, and performance. They are deprecated (scheduled for future removal) in the 2011 standard. The 2011 standard introduced **noexcept** (§13.5.1.1) as a simpler solution to many of the problems that exception specifications were supposed to address.
- It was always obvious that separate compilation of templates and their uses would be ideal [Stroustrup,1994]. How to achieve that under the constraints from real-world uses of templates was not at all obvious. After a long debate in the committee, a compromise was reached and something called **export** templates were specified as part of the 1998 standard. It was not an elegant solution to the problem, only one vendor implemented **export** (the Edison Design Group), and the feature was removed from the 2011 standard. We are still looking for a solution. My opinion is that the fundamental problem is not separate compilation in itself, but that the distinction between interface and implementation of a template is not well specified. Thus, **export** solved the wrong problem. In the future, language support for "concepts" (§24.3) may help by providing precise specification of template requirements. This is an area of active research and design [Sutton,2011] [Stroustrup,2012a].

1.4.3.2 The Standard Library

The greatest and most important innovation in the 1998 standard was the inclusion of the STL, a framework of algorithms and containers, in the standard library (§4.4, §4.5, Chapter 31, Chapter 32, Chapter 33). It was the work of Alex Stepanov (with Dave Musser, Meng Le, and others) based on more than a decade's work on generic programming. Andrew Koenig, Beman Dawes, and I did much to help get the STL accepted [Stroustrup,2007]. The STL has been massively influential within the C++ community and beyond.

Except for the STL, the standard library was a bit of a hodgepodge of components, rather than a unified design. I had failed to ship a sufficiently large foundation library with Release 1.0 of C++ [Stroustrup,1993], and an unhelpful (non-research) AT&T manager had prevented my colleagues and me from rectifying that mistake for Release 2.0. That meant that every major organization (such as Borland, IBM, Microsoft, and Texas Instruments) had its own foundation library by the time the standards work started. Thus, the committee was limited to a patchwork of components based on what had always been available (e.g., the complex library), what could be added without interfering with the major vendor's libraries, and what was needed to ensure cooperation among different nonstandard libraries.

The standard-library string (§4.2, Chapter 36) had its origins in early work by Jonathan Shopiro and me at Bell Labs but was revised and extended by several different individuals and groups during standardization. The valarray library for numerical computation (§40.5) is primarily the work of Kent Budge. Jerry Schwarz transformed my streams library (§1.4.2.1) into the iostreams library (§4.3, Chapter 38) using Andrew Koenig's manipulator technique (§38.4.5.2) and other ideas. The iostreams library was further refined during standardization, where the bulk of the work was done by Jerry Schwarz, Nathan Myers, and Norihiro Kumagai.

By commercial standards the C++98 standard library is tiny. For example, there is no standard GUI, database access library, or Web application library. Such libraries are widely available but are not part of the ISO standard. The reasons for that are practical and commercial, rather than technical. However, the C standard library was (and is) many influential people's measure of a standard library, and compared to that, the C++ standard library is huge.

1.4.4 The 2011 Standard

The current C++, C++11, known for years as C++0x, is the work of the members of WG21. The committee worked under increasingly onerous self-imposed processes and procedures. These processes probably led to a better (and more rigorous) specification, but they also limited innovation [Stroustrup,2007]. An initial draft standard for public review was produced in 2009. The second ISO C++ standard (ISO/IEC 14882-2011) [C++,2011] was ratified by a 21-0 national vote in August 2011.

One reason for the long gap between the two standards is that most members of the committee (including me) were under the mistaken impression that the ISO rules required a "waiting period" after a standard was issued before starting work on new features. Consequently, serious work on new language features did not start until 2002. Other reasons included the increased size of modern languages and their foundation libraries. In terms of pages of standards text, the language grew by about 30% and the standard library by about 100%. Much of the increase was due to more detailed specification, rather than new functionality. Also, the work on a new C++ standard obviously had to take great care not to compromise older code through incompatible changes. There are billions of lines of C++ code in use that the committee must not break.

The overall aims for the C++11 effort were:
- Make C++ a better language for systems programming and library building.
- Make C++ easier to teach and learn.

The aims are documented and detailed in [Stroustrup,2007].

A major effort was made to make concurrent systems programming type-safe and portable. This involved a memory model (§41.2) and a set of facilities for lock-free programming (§41.3), which is primarily the work of Hans Boehm, Brian McKnight, and others. On top of that, we added the threads library. Pete Becker, Peter Dimov, Howard Hinnant, William Kempf, Anthony Williams, and others did massive amounts of work on that. To provide an example of what can be achieved on top of the basic concurrency facilities, I proposed work on "a way to exchange information between tasks without explicit use of a lock," which became futures and async() (§5.3.5); Lawrence Crowl and Detlef Vollmann did most of the work on that. Concurrency is an area where a complete and detailed listing of who did what and why would require a very long paper. Here, I can't even try.

1.4.4.1 Language Features

The list of language features and standard-library facilities added to C++98 to get C++11 is presented in §44.2. With the exception of concurrency support, every addition to the language could be deemed "minor," but doing so would miss the point: language features are meant to be used in combination to write better programs. By "better" I mean easier to read, easier to write, more elegant, less error-prone, more maintainable, faster-running, consuming fewer resources, etc.

Here are what I consider the most widely useful new "building bricks" affecting the style of C++11 code with references to the text and their primary authors:

- Control of defaults: =delete and =default: §3.3.4, §17.6.1, §17.6.4; Lawrence Crowl and Bjarne Stroustrup.
- Deducing the type of an object from its initializer, auto: §2.2.2, §6.3.6.1; Bjarne Stroustrup. I first designed and implemented auto in 1983 but had to remove it because of C compatibility problems.
- Generalized constant expression evaluation (including literal types), constexpr: §2.2.3, §10.4, §12.1.6; Gabriel Dos Reis and Bjarne Stroustrup [DosReis,2010].
- In-class member initializers: §17.4.4; Michael Spertus and Bill Seymour.
- Inheriting constructors: §20.3.5.1; Bjarne Stroustrup, Michael Wong, and Michel Michaud.
- Lambda expressions, a way of implicitly defining function objects at the point of their use in an expression: §3.4.3, §11.4; Jaakko Jarvi.
- Move semantics, a way of transmitting information without copying: §3.3.2, §17.5.2; Howard Hinnant.
- A way of stating that a function may not throw exceptions noexcept: §13.5.1.1; David Abrahams, Rani Sharoni, and Doug Gregor.
- A proper name for the null pointer, §7.2.2; Herb Sutter and Bjarne Stroustrup.
- The range-for statement: §2.2.5, §9.5.1; Thorsten Ottosen and Bjarne Stroustrup.
- Override controls: final and override: §20.3.4. Alisdair Meredith, Chris Uzdavinis, and Ville Voutilainen.
- Type aliases, a mechanism for providing an alias for a type or a template. In particular, a way of defining a template by binding some arguments of another template: §3.4.5, §23.6; Bjarne Stroustrup and Gabriel Dos Reis.
- Typed and scoped enumerations: enum class: §8.4.1; David E. Miller, Herb Sutter, and Bjarne Stroustrup.
- Universal and uniform initialization (including arbitrary-length initializer lists and protection against narrowing): §2.2.2, §3.2.1.3, §6.3.5, §17.3.1, §17.3.4; Bjarne Stroustrup and Gabriel Dos Reis.
- Variadic templates, a mechanism for passing an arbitrary number of arguments of arbitrary types to a template: §3.4.4, §28.6; Doug Gregor and Jaakko Jarvi.

Many more people than can be listed here deserve to be mentioned. The technical reports to the committee [WG21] and my C++11 FAQ [Stroustrup,2010a] give many of the names. The minutes of the committee's working groups mention more still. The reason my name appears so often is (I hope) not vanity, but simply that I chose to work on what I consider important. These are features that will be pervasive in good code. Their major role is to flesh out the C++ feature set to better support programming styles (§1.2.1). They are the foundation of the synthesis that is C++11.

Much work went into a proposal that did not make it into the standard. "Concepts" was a facility for specifying and checking requirements for template arguments [Gregor,2006] based on previous research (e.g., [Stroustrup,1994] [Siek,2000] [DosReis,2006]) and extensive work in the committee. It was designed, specified, implemented, and tested, but by a large majority the committee decided that the proposal was not yet ready. Had we been able to refine "concepts," it would have been the most important single feature in C++11 (its only competitor for that title is concurrency support). However, the committee decided against "concepts" on the grounds of complexity, difficulty of use, and compile-time performance [Stroustrup,2010b]. I think we (the committee) did the right thing with "concepts" for C++11, but this feature really was "the one that got away." This is currently a field of active research and design [Sutton,2011] [Stroustrup,2012a].

1.4.4.2 Standard Library

The work on what became the C++11 standard library started with a standards committee technical report ("TR1"). Initially, Matt Austern was the head of the Library Working Group, and later Howard Hinnant took over until we shipped the final draft standard in 2011.

As for language features, I'll only list a few standard-library components with references to the text and the names of the individuals most closely associated with them. For a more detailed list, see §44.2.2. Some components, such as unordered_map (hash tables), were ones we simply didn't manage to finish in time for the C++98 standard. Many others, such as unique_ptr and function were part of a technical report (TR1) based on Boost libraries. Boost is a volunteer organization created to provide useful library components based on the STL [Boost].

- Hashed containers, such as unordered_map: §31.4.3; Matt Austern.
- The basic concurrency library components, such as thread, mutex, and lock: §5.3, §42.2; Pete Becker, Peter Dimov, Howard Hinnant, William Kempf, Anthony Williams, and more.
- Launching asynchronous computation and returning results, future, promise, and async(): §5.3.5, §42.4.6; Detlef Vollmann, Lawrence Crowl, Bjarne Stroustrup, and Herb Sutter.
- The garbage collection interface: §34.5; Michael Spertus and Hans Boehm.
- A regular expression library, regexp: §5.5, Chapter 37; John Maddock.
- A random number library: §5.6.3, §40.7; Jens Maurer and Walter Brown. It was about time. I shipped the first random number library with "C with Classes" in 1980.

Several utility components were tried out in Boost:

- A pointer for simply and efficiently passing resources, unique_ptr: §5.2.1, §34.3.1; Howard E. Hinnant. This was originally called move_ptr and is what auto_ptr should have been had we known how to do so for C++98.
- A pointer for representing shared ownership, shared_ptr: §5.2.1, §34.3.2; Peter Dimov. A successor to the C++98 counted_ptr proposal from Greg Colvin.

- The tuple library: §5.4.3, §28.5, §34.2.4.2; Jaakko Jarvi and Gary Powell. They credit a long list of contributors, including Doug Gregor, David Abrahams, and Jeremy Siek.
- The general bind(): §33.5.1; Peter Dimov. His acknowledgments list a veritable who's who of Boost (including Doug Gregor, John Maddock, Dave Abrahams, and Jaakko Jarvi).
- The function type for holding callable objects: §33.5.3; Doug Gregor. He credits William Kempf and others with contributions.

1.4.5 What is C++ used for?

By now (2013), C++ is used just about everywhere: it is in your computer, your phone, your car, probably even in your camera. You don't usually see it. C++ is a systems programming language, and its most pervasive uses are deep in the infrastructure where we, as users, never look.

C++ is used by millions of programmers in essentially every application domain. Billions (thousands of millions) of lines of C++ are currently deployed. This massive use is supported by half a dozen independent implementations, many thousands of libraries, hundreds of textbooks, and dozens of websites. Training and education at a variety of levels are widely available.

Early applications tended to have a strong systems programming flavor. For example, several early operating systems have been written in C++: [Campbell,1987] (academic), [Rozier,1988] (real time), [Berg,1995] (high-throughput I/O). Many current ones (e.g., Windows, Apple's OS, Linux, and most portable-device OSs) have key parts done in C++. Your cellphone and Internet routers are most likely written in C++. I consider uncompromising low-level efficiency essential for C++. This allows us to use C++ to write device drivers and other software that rely on direct manipulation of hardware under real-time constraints. In such code, predictability of performance is at least as important as raw speed. Often, so is the compactness of the resulting system. C++ was designed so that every language feature is usable in code under severe time and space constraints (§1.2.4) [Stroustrup,1994,§4.5].

Some of today's most visible and widely used systems have their critical parts written in C++. Examples are Amadeus (airline ticketing), Amazon (Web commerce), Bloomberg (financial information), Google (Web search), and Facebook (social media). Many other programming languages and technologies depend critically on C++'s performance and reliability in their implementation. Examples include the most widely used Java Virtual Machines (e.g., Oracle's HotSpot), JavaScript interpreters (e.g., Google's V8), browsers (e.g., Microsoft's Internet Explorer, Mozilla's Firefox, Apple's Safari, and Google's Chrome), and application frameworks (e.g., Microsoft's .NET Web services framework). I consider C++ to have unique strengths in the area of infrastructure software [Stroustrup,2012a].

Most applications have sections of code that are critical for acceptable performance. However, the largest amount of code is not in such sections. For most code, maintainability, ease of extension, and ease of testing are key. C++'s support for these concerns has led to its widespread use in areas where reliability is a must and where requirements change significantly over time. Examples are financial systems, telecommunications, device control, and military applications. For decades, the central control of the U.S. long-distance telephone system has relied on C++, and every 800 call (i.e., a call paid for by the called party) has been routed by a C++ program [Kamath,1993]. Many such applications are large and long-lived. As a result, stability, compatibility, and scalability have been constant concerns in the development of C++. Multimillion-line C++ programs are common.

Games is another area where a multiplicity of languages and tools need to coexist with a language providing uncompromising efficiency (often on "unusual" hardware). Thus, games has been another major applications area for C++.

What used to be called systems programming is widely found in embedded systems, so it is not surprising to find massive use of C++ in demanding embedded systems projects, including computer tomography (CAT scanners), flight control software (e.g., Lockheed-Martin), rocket control, ship's engines (e.g., the control of the world's largest marine diesel engines from MAN), automobile software (e.g., BMW), and wind turbine control (e.g., Vesta).

C++ wasn't specifically designed with numerical computation in mind. However, much numerical, scientific, and engineering computation is done in C++. A major reason for this is that traditional numerical work must often be combined with graphics and with computations relying on data structures that don't fit into the traditional Fortran mold (e.g., [Root,1995]). I am particularly pleased to see C++ used in major scientific endeavors, such as the Human Genome Project, NASA's Mars Rovers, CERN's search for the fundamentals of the universe, and many others.

C++'s ability to be used effectively for applications that require work in a variety of application areas is an important strength. Applications that involve local- and wide-area networking, numerics, graphics, user interaction, and database access are common. Traditionally, such application areas were considered distinct and were served by distinct technical communities using a variety of programming languages. However, C++ is widely used in all of those areas, and more. It is designed so that C++ code can coexist with code written in other languages. Here, again, C++'s stability over decades is important. Furthermore, no really major system is written 100% in a single language. Thus, C++'s original design aim of interoperability becomes significant.

Major applications are not written in just the raw language. C++ is supported by a variety of libraries (beyond the ISO C++ standard library) and tool sets, such as Boost [Boost] (portable foundation libraries), POCO (Web development), QT (cross-platform application development), wxWidgets (a cross-platform GUI library), WebKit (a layout engine library for Web browsers), CGAL (computational geometry), QuickFix (Financial Information eXchange), OpenCV (real-time image processing), and Root [Root,1995] (High-Energy Physics). There are many thousands of C++ libraries, so keeping up with them all is impossible.

1.5 Advice

Each chapter contains an "Advice" section with a set of concrete recommendations related to its contents. Such advice consists of rough rules of thumb, not immutable laws. A piece of advice should be applied only where reasonable. There is no substitute for intelligence, experience, common sense, and good taste.

I find rules of the form "never do this" unhelpful. Consequently, most advice is phrased as suggestions for what to do. Negative suggestions tend not to be phrased as absolute prohibitions and I try to suggest alternatives. I know of no major feature of C++ that I have not seen put to good use. The "Advice" sections do not contain explanations. Instead, each piece of advice is accompanied by a reference to an appropriate section of the book.

For starters, here are a few high-level recommendations derived from the sections on design, learning, and history of C++:

[1]   Represent ideas (concepts) directly in code, for example, as a function, a class, or an enumeration; §1.2.

[2]   Aim for your code to be both elegant and efficient; §1.2.

[3]   Don't overabstract; §1.2.

[4]   Focus design on the provision of elegant and efficient abstractions, possibly presented as libraries; §1.2.

[5]   Represent relationships among ideas directly in code, for example, through parameterization or a class hierarchy; §1.2.1.

[6]   Represent independent ideas separately in code, for example, avoid mutual dependencies among classes; §1.2.1.

[7]   C++ is not just object-oriented; §1.2.1.

[8]   C++ is not just for generic programming; §1.2.1.

[9]   Prefer solutions that can be statically checked; §1.2.1.

[10] Make resources explicit (represent them as class objects); §1.2.1, §1.4.2.1.

[11] Express simple ideas simply; §1.2.1.

[12] Use libraries, especially the standard library, rather than trying to build everything from scratch; §1.2.1.

[13] Use a type-rich style of programming; §1.2.2.

[14] Low-level code is not necessarily efficient; don't avoid classes, templates, and standard-library components out of fear of performance problems; §1.2.4, §1.3.3.

[15] If data has an invariant, encapsulate it; §1.3.2.

[16] C++ is not just C with a few extensions; §1.3.3.

In general: To write a good program takes intelligence, taste, and patience. You are not going to get it right the first time. Experiment!

1.6 References

[Austern,2003]   Matt Austern et al.: *Untangling the Balancing and Searching of Balanced Binary Search Trees.* Software – Practice & Experience. Vol 33, Issue 13. November 2003.

[Barron,1963]   D. W. Barron et al.: *The main features of CPL.* The Computer Journal. 6 (2): 134. (1963). comjnl.oxfordjournals.org/content/6/2/134.full.pdf+html.

[Barton,1994]   J. J. Barton and L. R. Nackman: *Scientific and Engineering C++: An Introduction with Advanced Techniques and Examples.* Addison-Wesley. Reading, Massachusetts. 1994. ISBN 0-201-53393-6.

[Berg,1995]   William Berg, Marshall Cline, and Mike Girou: *Lessons Learned from the OS/400 OO Project.* CACM. Vol. 38, No. 10. October 1995.

[Boehm,2008]   Hans-J. Boehm and Sarita V. Adve: *Foundations of the C++ concurrency memory model.* ACM PLDI'08.

[Boost]   The Boost library collection. www.boost.org.

[Budge,1992]   Kent Budge, J. S. Perry, and A. C. Robinson: *High-Performance Scientific Computation Using C++.* Proc. USENIX C++ Conference. Portland, Oregon. August 1992.

[C,1990]	X3 Secretariat: *Standard – The C Language*. X3J11/90-013. ISO Standard ISO/IEC 9899-1990. Computer and Business Equipment Manufacturers Association. Washington, DC.
[C,1999]	ISO/IEC 9899. *Standard – The C Language*. X3J11/90-013-1999.
[C,2011]	ISO/IEC 9899. *Standard – The C Language*. X3J11/90-013-2011.
[C++,1998]	ISO/IEC JTC1/SC22/WG21: *International Standard – The C++ Language*. ISO/IEC 14882:1998.
[C++Math,2010]	*International Standard – Extensions to the C++ Library to Support Mathematical Special Functions*. ISO/IEC 29124:2010.
[C++,2011]	ISO/IEC JTC1/SC22/WG21: *International Standard – The C++ Language*. ISO/IEC 14882:2011.
[Campbell,1987]	Roy Campbell et al.: *The Design of a Multiprocessor Operating System*. Proc. USENIX C++ Conference. Santa Fe, New Mexico. November 1987.
[Coplien,1995]	James O. Coplien: *Curiously Recurring Template Patterns*. The C++ Report. February 1995.
[Cox,2007]	Russ Cox: *Regular Expression Matching Can Be Simple And Fast*. January 2007. swtch.com/~rsc/regexp/regexp1.html.
[Czarnecki,2000]	K. Czarnecki and U. Eisenecker: *Generative Programming: Methods, Tools, and Applications*. Addison-Wesley. Reading, Massachusetts. 2000. ISBN 0-201-30977-7.
[Dahl,1970]	O-J. Dahl, B. Myrhaug, and K. Nygaard: *SIMULA Common Base Language*. Norwegian Computing Center S-22. Oslo, Norway. 1970.
[Dahl,1972]	O-J. Dahl and C. A. R. Hoare: *Hierarchical Program Construction* in *Structured Programming*. Academic Press. New York. 1972.
[Dean,2004]	J. Dean and S. Ghemawat: *MapReduce: Simplified Data Processing on Large Clusters*. OSDI'04: Sixth Symposium on Operating System Design and Implementation. 2004.
[Dechev,2010]	D. Dechev, P. Pirkelbauer, and B. Stroustrup: *Understanding and Effectively Preventing the ABA Problem in Descriptor-based Lock-free Designs*. 13th IEEE Computer Society ISORC 2010 Symposium. May 2010.
[DosReis,2006]	Gabriel Dos Reis and Bjarne Stroustrup: *Specifying C++ Concepts*. POPL06. January 2006.
[DosReis,2010]	Gabriel Dos Reis and Bjarne Stroustrup: *General Constant Expressions for System Programming Languages*. SAC-2010. The 25th ACM Symposium On Applied Computing. March 2010.
[DosReis,2011]	Gabriel Dos Reis and Bjarne Stroustrup: *A Principled, Complete, and Efficient Representation of C++*. Journal of Mathematics in Computer Science. Vol. 5, Issue 3. 2011.
[Ellis,1989]	Margaret A. Ellis and Bjarne Stroustrup: *The Annotated C++ Reference Manual*. Addison-Wesley. Reading, Mass. 1990. ISBN 0-201-51459-1.
[Freeman,1992]	Len Freeman and Chris Phillips: *Parallel Numerical Algorithms*. Prentice Hall. Englewood Cliffs, New Jersey. 1992. ISBN 0-13-651597-5.
[Friedl,1997]:	Jeffrey E. F. Friedl: *Mastering Regular Expressions*. O'Reilly Media. Sebastopol, California. 1997. ISBN 978-1565922570.

[Gamma,1995]   Erich Gamma et al.: *Design Patterns: Elements of Reusable Object-Oriented Software*. Addison-Wesley. Reading, Massachusetts. 1994. ISBN 0-201-63361-2.

[Gregor,2006]   Douglas Gregor et al.: *Concepts: Linguistic Support for Generic Programming in C++*. OOPSLA'06.

[Hennessy,2011]   John L. Hennessy and David A. Patterson: *Computer Architecture, Fifth Edition: A Quantitative Approach*. Morgan Kaufmann. San Francisco, California. 2011. ISBN 978-0123838728.

[Ichbiah,1979]   Jean D. Ichbiah et al.: *Rationale for the Design of the ADA Programming Language*. SIGPLAN Notices. Vol. 14, No. 6. June 1979.

[Kamath,1993]   Yogeesh H. Kamath, Ruth E. Smilan, and Jean G. Smith: *Reaping Benefits with Object-Oriented Technology*. AT&T Technical Journal. Vol. 72, No. 5. September/October 1993.

[Kernighan,1978]   Brian W. Kernighan and Dennis M. Ritchie: *The C Programming Language*. Prentice Hall. Englewood Cliffs, New Jersey. 1978.

[Kernighan,1988]   Brian W. Kernighan and Dennis M. Ritchie: *The C Programming Language, Second Edition*. Prentice-Hall. Englewood Cliffs, New Jersey. 1988. ISBN 0-13-110362-8.

[Knuth,1968]   Donald E. Knuth: *The Art of Computer Programming*. Addison-Wesley. Reading, Massachusetts. 1968.

[Koenig,1989]   Andrew Koenig and Bjarne Stroustrup: *C++: As close to C as possible – but no closer*. The C++ Report. Vol. 1, No. 7. July 1989.

[Koenig,1990]   A. R. Koenig and B. Stroustrup: *Exception Handling for C++ (revised)*. Proc USENIX C++ Conference. April 1990.

[Kolecki,2002]   Joseph C. Kolecki: *An Introduction to Tensors for Students of Physics and Engineering*. NASA/TM-2002-211716.

[Langer,2000]   Angelika Langer and Klaus Kreft: *Standard C++ IOStreams and Locales: Advanced Programmer's Guide and Reference*. Addison-Wesley. 2000. ISBN 978-0201183955.

[McKenney]   Paul E. McKenney: *Is Parallel Programming Hard, And, If So, What Can You Do About It?* kernel.org. Corvallis, Oregon. 2012. http://kernel.org/pub/linux/kernel/people/paulmck/perfbook/perfbook.html.

[Maddock,2009]   John Maddock: *Boost.Regex*. www.boost.org. 2009.

[Orwell,1949]   George Orwell: *1984*. Secker and Warburg. London. 1949.

[Paulson,1996]   Larry C. Paulson: *ML for the Working Programmer*. Cambridge University Press. Cambridge. 1996. ISBN 0-521-56543-X.

[Pirkelbauer,2009]   P. Pirkelbauer, Y. Solodkyy, and B. Stroustrup: *Design and Evaluation of C++ Open Multi-Methods*. Science of Computer Programming. Elsevier Journal. June 2009. doi:10.1016/j.scico.2009.06.002.

[Richards,1980]   Martin Richards and Colin Whitby-Strevens: *BCPL – The Language and Its Compiler*. Cambridge University Press. Cambridge. 1980. ISBN 0-521-21965-5.

[Root,1995]   *ROOT: A Data Analysis Framework*. root.cern.ch. It seems appropriate to represent a tool from CERN, the birthplace of the World Wide Web, by a

Web address.

[Rozier,1988]   M. Rozier et al.: *CHORUS Distributed Operating Systems*. Computing Systems. Vol. 1, No. 4. Fall 1988.

[Siek,2000]   Jeremy G. Siek and Andrew Lumsdaine: *Concept checking: Binding parametric polymorphism in C++*. Proc. First Workshop on C++ Template Programming. Erfurt, Germany. 2000.

[Solodkyy,2012]   Y. Solodkyy, G. Dos Reis, and B. Stroustrup: *Open and Efficient Type Switch for C++*. Proc. OOPSLA'12.

[Stepanov,1994]   Alexander Stepanov and Meng Lee: *The Standard Template Library*. HP Labs Technical Report HPL-94-34 (R. 1). 1994.

[Stewart,1998]   G. W. Stewart: *Matrix Algorithms, Volume I. Basic Decompositions*. SIAM. Philadelphia, Pennsylvania. 1998.

[Stroustrup,1982]   B. Stroustrup: *Classes: An Abstract Data Type Facility for the C Language*. Sigplan Notices. January 1982. The first public description of "C with Classes."

[Stroustrup,1984]   B. Stroustrup: *Operator Overloading in C++*. Proc. IFIP WG2.4 Conference on System Implementation Languages: Experience & Assessment. September 1984.

[Stroustrup,1985]   B. Stroustrup: *An Extensible I/O Facility for C++*. Proc. Summer 1985 USENIX Conference.

[Stroustrup,1986]   B. Stroustrup: *The C++ Programming Language*. Addison-Wesley. Reading, Massachusetts. 1986. ISBN 0-201-12078-X.

[Stroustrup,1987]   B. Stroustrup: *Multiple Inheritance for C++*. Proc. EUUG Spring Conference. May 1987.

[Stroustrup,1987b]   B. Stroustrup and J. Shopiro: *A Set of C Classes for Co-Routine Style Programming*. Proc. USENIX C++ Conference. Santa Fe, New Mexico. November 1987.

[Stroustrup,1988]   B. Stroustrup: *Parameterized Types for C++*. Proc. USENIX C++ Conference, Denver. 1988.

[Stroustrup,1991]   B. Stroustrup: *The C++ Programming Language (Second Edition)*. Addison-Wesley. Reading, Massachusetts. 1991. ISBN 0-201-53992-6.

[Stroustrup,1993]   B. Stroustrup: *A History of C++: 1979-1991*. Proc. ACM History of Programming Languages conference (HOPL-2). ACM Sigplan Notices. Vol 28, No 3. 1993.

[Stroustrup,1994]   B. Stroustrup: *The Design and Evolution of C++*. Addison-Wesley. Reading, Mass. 1994. ISBN 0-201-54330-3.

[Stroustrup,1997]   B. Stroustrup: *The C++ Programming Language, Third Edition*. Addison-Wesley. Reading, Massachusetts. 1997. ISBN 0-201-88954-4. Hardcover ("Special") Edition. 2000. ISBN 0-201-70073-5.

[Stroustrup,2002]   B. Stroustrup: *C and C++: Siblings, C and C++: A Case for Compatibility*, and *C and C++: Case Studies in Compatibility*. The C/C++ Users Journal. July-September 2002. www.stroustrup.com/papers.html.

[Stroustrup,2007]   B. Stroustrup: *Evolving a language in and for the real world: C++ 1991-2006*. ACM HOPL-III. June 2007.

[Stroustrup,2008]	B. Stroustrup: *Programming – Principles and Practice Using C++*. Addison-Wesley. 2009. ISBN 0-321-54372-6.
[Stroustrup,2010a]	B. Stroustrup: *The C++11 FAQ*. www.stroustrup.com/C++11FAQ.html.
[Stroustrup,2010b]	B. Stroustrup: *The C++0x "Remove Concepts" Decision*. Dr. Dobb's Journal. July 2009.
[Stroustrup,2012a]	B. Stroustrup and A. Sutton: *A Concept Design for the STL*. WG21 Technical Report N3351==12-0041. January 2012.
[Stroustrup,2012b]	B. Stroustrup: *Software Development for Infrastructure*. Computer. January 2012. doi:10.1109/MC.2011.353.
[Sutton,2011]	A. Sutton and B. Stroustrup: *Design of Concept Libraries for C++*. Proc. SLE 2011 (International Conference on Software Language Engineering). July 2011.
[Tanenbaum,2007]	Andrew S. Tanenbaum: *Modern Operating Systems, Third Edition*. Prentice Hall. Upper Saddle River, New Jersey. 2007. ISBN 0-13-600663-9.
[Tsafrir,2009]	Dan Tsafrir et al.: *Minimizing Dependencies within Generic Classes for Faster and Smaller Programs*. ACM OOPSLA'09. October 2009.
[Unicode,1996]	The Unicode Consortium: *The Unicode Standard, Version 2.0*. Addison-Wesley. Reading, Massachusetts. 1996. ISBN 0-201-48345-9.
[UNIX,1985]	*UNIX Time-Sharing System: Programmer's Manual. Research Version, Tenth Edition*. AT&T Bell Laboratories, Murray Hill, New Jersey. February 1985.
[Vandevoorde,2002]	David Vandevoorde and Nicolai M. Josuttis: *C++ Templates: The Complete Guide*. Addison-Wesley. 2002. ISBN 0-201-73484-2.
[Veldhuizen,1995]	Todd Veldhuizen: *Expression Templates*. The C++ Report. June 1995.
[Veldhuizen,2003]	Todd L. Veldhuizen: *C++ Templates are Turing Complete*. Indiana University Computer Science Technical Report. 2003.
[Vitter,1985]	Jefferey Scott Vitter: *Random Sampling with a Reservoir*. ACM Transactions on Mathematical Software, Vol. 11, No. 1. 1985.
[WG21]	ISO SC22/WG21 The C++ Programming Language Standards Committee: *Document Archive*. www.open-std.org/jtc1/sc22/wg21.
[Williams,2012]	Anthony Williams: *C++ Concurrency in Action – Practical Multithreading*. Manning Publications Co. ISBN 978-1933988771.
[Wilson,1996]	Gregory V. Wilson and Paul Lu (editors): *Parallel Programming Using C++*. The MIT Press. Cambridge, Mass. 1996. ISBN 0-262-73118-5.
[Wood,1999]	Alistair Wood: *Introduction to Numerical Analysis*. Addison-Wesley. Reading, Massachusetts. 1999. ISBN 0-201-34291-X.
[Woodward,1974]	P. M. Woodward and S. G. Bond: *Algol 68-R Users Guide*. Her Majesty's Stationery Office. London. 1974.

2

A Tour of C++: The Basics

> *The first thing we do, let's*
> *kill all the language lawyers.*
> *– Henry VI, Part II*

- Introduction
- The Basics
    Hello, World!; Types, Variables, and Arithmetic; Constants; Tests and Loops; Pointers, Arrays, and Loops
- User-Defined Types
    Structures; Classes; Enumerations
- Modularity
    Separate Compilation; Namespaces; Error Handling
- Postscript
- Advice

2.1 Introduction

The aim of this chapter and the next three is to give you an idea of what C++ is, without going into a lot of details. This chapter informally presents the notation of C++, C++'s model of memory and computation, and the basic mechanisms for organizing code into a program. These are the language facilities supporting the styles most often seen in C and sometimes called *procedural programming*. Chapter 3 follows up by presenting C++'s abstraction mechanisms. Chapter 4 and Chapter 5 give examples of standard-library facilities.

The assumption is that you have programmed before. If not, please consider reading a textbook, such as *Programming: Principles and Practice Using C++* [Stroustrup,2009], before continuing here. Even if you have programmed before, the language you used or the applications you wrote may be very different from the style of C++ presented here. If you find this "lightning tour" confusing, skip to the more systematic presentation starting in Chapter 6.

This tour of C++ saves us from a strictly bottom-up presentation of language and library facilities by enabling the use of a rich set of facilities even in early chapters. For example, loops are not discussed in detail until Chapter 10, but they will be used in obvious ways long before that. Similarly, the detailed description of classes, templates, free-store use, and the standard library are spread over many chapters, but standard-library types, such as **vector**, **string**, **complex**, **map**, **unique_ptr**, and **ostream**, are used freely where needed to improve code examples.

As an analogy, think of a short sightseeing tour of a city, such as Copenhagen or New York. In just a few hours, you are given a quick peek at the major attractions, told a few background stories, and usually given some suggestions about what to see next. You do *not* know the city after such a tour. You do *not* understand all you have seen and heard. To really know a city, you have to live in it, often for years. However, with a bit of luck, you will have gained a bit of an overview, a notion of what is special about the city, and ideas of what might be of interest to you. After the tour, the real exploration can begin.

This tour presents C++ as an integrated whole, rather than as a layer cake. Consequently, it does not identify language features as present in C, part of C++98, or new in C++11. Such historical information can be found in §1.4 and Chapter 44.

2.2 The Basics

C++ is a compiled language. For a program to run, its source text has to be processed by a compiler, producing object files, which are combined by a linker yielding an executable program. A C++ program typically consists of many source code files (usually simply called *source files*).

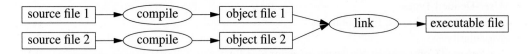

An executable program is created for a specific hardware/system combination; it is not portable, say, from a Mac to a Windows PC. When we talk about portability of C++ programs, we usually mean portability of source code; that is, the source code can be successfully compiled and run on a variety of systems.

The ISO C++ standard defines two kinds of entities:
- *Core language features*, such as built-in types (e.g., **char** and **int**) and loops (e.g., **for**-statements and **while**-statements)
- *Standard-library components*, such as containers (e.g., **vector** and **map**) and I/O operations (e.g., **<<** and **getline()**)

The standard-library components are perfectly ordinary C++ code provided by every C++ implementation. That is, the C++ standard library can be implemented in C++ itself (and is with very minor uses of machine code for things such as thread context switching). This implies that C++ is sufficiently expressive and efficient for the most demanding systems programming tasks.

C++ is a statically typed language. That is, the type of every entity (e.g., object, value, name, and expression) must be known to the compiler at its point of use. The type of an object determines the set of operations applicable to it.

2.2.1 Hello, World!

The minimal C++ program is

```
int main() { }        // the minimal C++ program
```

This defines a function called **main**, which takes no arguments and does nothing (§15.4).

Curly braces, { }, express grouping in C++. Here, they indicate the start and end of the function body. The double slash, //, begins a comment that extends to the end of the line. A comment is for the human reader; the compiler ignores comments.

Every C++ program must have exactly one global function named **main()**. The program starts by executing that function. The **int** value returned by **main()**, if any, is the program's return value to "the system." If no value is returned, the system will receive a value indicating successful completion. A nonzero value from **main()** indicates failure. Not every operating system and execution environment make use of that return value: Linux/Unix-based environments often do, but Windows-based environments rarely do.

Typically, a program produces some output. Here is a program that writes **Hello, World!**:

```
#include <iostream>

int main()
{
    std::cout << "Hello, World!\n";
}
```

The line **#include <iostream>** instructs the compiler to *include* the declarations of the standard stream I/O facilities as found in **iostream**. Without these declarations, the expression

```
std::cout << "Hello, World!\n"
```

would make no sense. The operator << ("put to") writes its second argument onto its first. In this case, the string literal **"Hello, World!\n"** is written onto the standard output stream **std::cout**. A string literal is a sequence of characters surrounded by double quotes. In a string literal, the backslash character \ followed by another character denotes a single "special character." In this case, \n is the newline character, so that the characters written are **Hello, World!** followed by a newline.

The **std::** specifies that the name **cout** is to be found in the standard-library namespace (§2.4.2, Chapter 14). I usually leave out the **std::** when discussing standard features; §2.4.2 shows how to make names from a namespace visible without explicit qualification.

Essentially all executable code is placed in functions and called directly or indirectly from **main()**. For example:

```
#include <iostream>
using namespace std;        // make names from std visible without std:: (§2.4.2)

double square(double x)     // square a double precision floating-point number
{
    return x*x;
}
```

```
void print_square(double x)
{
    cout << "the square of " << x << " is " << square(x) << "\n";
}

int main()
{
    print_square(1.234);      // print: the square of 1.234 is 1.52276
}
```

A "return type" **void** indicates that a function does not return a value.

2.2.2 Types, Variables, and Arithmetic

Every name and every expression has a type that determines the operations that may be performed on it. For example, the declaration

```
int inch;
```

specifies that **inch** is of type **int**; that is, **inch** is an integer variable.

A *declaration* is a statement that introduces a name into the program. It specifies a type for the named entity:

- A *type* defines a set of possible values and a set of operations (for an object).
- An *object* is some memory that holds a value of some type.
- A *value* is a set of bits interpreted according to a type.
- A *variable* is a named object.

C++ offers a variety of fundamental types. For example:

```
bool      // Boolean, possible values are true and false
char      // character, for example, 'a', 'z', and '9'
int       // integer, for example, 1, 42, and 1066
double    // double-precision floating-point number, for example, 3.14 and 299793.0
```

Each fundamental type corresponds directly to hardware facilities and has a fixed size that determines the range of values that can be stored in it:

A **char** variable is of the natural size to hold a character on a given machine (typically an 8-bit byte), and the sizes of other types are quoted in multiples of the size of a **char**. The size of a type is implementation-defined (i.e., it can vary among different machines) and can be obtained by the **sizeof** operator; for example, **sizeof(char)** equals **1** and **sizeof(int)** is often **4**.

The arithmetic operators can be used for appropriate combinations of these types:

```
x+y        // plus
+x         // unary plus
x−y        // minus
−x         // unary minus
x∗y        // multiply
x/y        // divide
x%y        // remainder (modulus) for integers
```

So can the comparison operators:

```
x==y       // equal
x!=y       // not equal
x<y        // less than
x>y        // greater than
x<=y       // less than or equal
x>=y       // greater than or equal
```

In assignments and in arithmetic operations, C++ performs all meaningful conversions (§10.5.3) between the basic types so that they can be mixed freely:

```
void some_function()      // function that doesn't return a value
{
    double d = 2.2;       // initialize floating-point number
    int i = 7;            // initialize integer
    d = d+i;              // assign sum to d
    i = d∗i;              // assign product to i (truncating the double d*i to an int)
}
```

Note that = is the assignment operator and == tests equality.

C++ offers a variety of notations for expressing initialization, such as the = used above, and a universal form based on curly-brace-delimited initializer lists:

```
double d1 = 2.3;
double d2 {2.3};

complex<double> z = 1;          // a complex number with double-precision floating-point scalars
complex<double> z2 {d1,d2};
complex<double> z3 = {1,2};      // the = is optional with { ... }

vector<int> v {1,2,3,4,5,6};     // a vector of ints
```

The = form is traditional and dates back to C, but if in doubt, use the general {}-list form (§6.3.5.2). If nothing else, it saves you from conversions that lose information (narrowing conversions; §10.5):

```
int i1 = 7.2;       // i1 becomes 7
int i2 {7.2};       // error: floating-point to integer conversion
int i3 = {7.2};     // error: floating-point to integer conversion (the = is redundant)
```

A constant (§2.2.3) cannot be left uninitialized and a variable should only be left uninitialized in extremely rare circumstances. Don't introduce a name until you have a suitable value for it. User-defined types (such as **string**, **vector**, **Matrix**, **Motor_controller**, and **Orc_warrior**) can be defined to be implicitly initialized (§3.2.1.1).

When defining a variable, you don't actually need to state its type explicitly when it can be deduced from the initializer:

```
auto b = true;        // a bool
auto ch = 'x';        // a char
auto i = 123;         // an int
auto d = 1.2;         // a double
auto z = sqrt(y);     // z has the type of whatever sqrt(y) returns
```

With **auto**, we use the = syntax because there is no type conversion involved that might cause problems (§6.3.6.2).

We use **auto** where we don't have a specific reason to mention the type explicitly. "Specific reasons" include:

- The definition is in a large scope where we want to make the type clearly visible to readers of our code.
- We want to be explicit about a variable's range or precision (e.g., **double** rather than **float**).

Using **auto**, we avoid redundancy and writing long type names. This is especially important in generic programming where the exact type of an object can be hard for the programmer to know and the type names can be quite long (§4.5.1).

In addition to the conventional arithmetic and logical operators (§10.3), C++ offers more specific operations for modifying a variable:

```
x+=y      // x = x+y
++x       // increment: x = x+1
x-=y      // x = x-y
--x       // decrement: x = x-1
x*=y      // scaling: x = x*y
x/=y      // scaling: x = x/y
x%=y      // x = x%y
```

These operators are concise, convenient, and very frequently used.

2.2.3 Constants

C++ supports two notions of immutability (§7.5):

- **const**: meaning roughly "I promise not to change this value" (§7.5). This is used primarily to specify interfaces, so that data can be passed to functions without fear of it being modified. The compiler enforces the promise made by **const**.
- **constexpr**: meaning roughly "to be evaluated at compile time" (§10.4). This is used primarily to specify constants, to allow placement of data in memory where it is unlikely to be corrupted, and for performance.

For example:

```
const int dmv = 17;                      // dmv is a named constant
int var = 17;                            // var is not a constant
constexpr double max1 = 1.4*square(dmv); // OK if square(17) is a constant expression
constexpr double max2 = 1.4*square(var); // error: var is not a constant expression
const double max3 = 1.4*square(var);     // OK, may be evaluated at run time
```

```
double sum(const vector<double>&);        // sum will not modify its argument (§2.2.5)
vector<double> v {1.2, 3.4, 4.5};         // v is not a constant
const double s1 = sum(v);                 // OK: evaluated at run time
constexpr double s2 = sum(v);             // error: sum(v) not constant expression
```

For a function to be usable in a *constant expression*, that is, in an expression that will be evaluated by the compiler, it must be defined **constexpr**. For example:

```
constexpr double square(double x) { return x∗x; }
```

To be **constexpr**, a function must be rather simple: just a **return**-statement computing a value. A **constexpr** function can be used for non-constant arguments, but when that is done the result is not a constant expression. We allow a **constexpr** function to be called with non-constant-expression arguments in contexts that do not require constant expressions, so that we don't have to define essentially the same function twice: once for constant expressions and once for variables.

In a few places, constant expressions are required by language rules (e.g., array bounds (§2.2.5, §7.3), case labels (§2.2.4, §9.4.2), some template arguments (§25.2), and constants declared using **constexpr**). In other cases, compile-time evaluation is important for performance. Independently of performance issues, the notion of immutability (of an object with an unchangeable state) is an important design concern (§10.4).

2.2.4 Tests and Loops

C++ provides a conventional set of statements for expressing selection and looping. For example, here is a simple function that prompts the user and returns a Boolean indicating the response:

```
bool accept()
{
        cout << "Do you want to proceed (y or n)?\n";     // write question

        char answer = 0;
        cin >> answer;                                     // read answer

        if (answer == 'y') return true;
        return false;
}
```

To match the << output operator ("put to"), the >> operator ("get from") is used for input; **cin** is the standard input stream. The type of the right-hand operand of >> determines what input is accepted, and its right-hand operand is the target of the input operation. The \n character at the end of the output string represents a newline (§2.2.1).

The example could be improved by taking an **n** (for "no") answer into account:

```
bool accept2()
{
        cout << "Do you want to proceed (y or n)?\n";     // write question

        char answer = 0;
        cin >> answer;                                     // read answer
```

```
        switch (answer) {
        case 'y':
            return true;
        case 'n':
            return false;
        default:
            cout << "I'll take that for a no.\n";
            return false;
        }
}
```

A **switch**-statement tests a value against a set of constants. The case constants must be distinct, and if the value tested does not match any of them, the **default** is chosen. If no **default** is provided, no action is taken if the value doesn't match any case constant.

Few programs are written without loops. For example, we might like to give the user a few tries to produce acceptable input:

```
bool accept3()
{
    int tries = 1;
    while (tries<4) {
        cout << "Do you want to proceed (y or n)?\n";     // write question
        char answer = 0;
        cin >> answer;                                     // read answer

        switch (answer) {
        case 'y':
            return true;
        case 'n':
            return false;
        default:
            cout << "Sorry, I don't understand that.\n";
            ++tries;   // increment
        }
    }
    cout << "I'll take that for a no.\n";
    return false;
}
```

The **while**-statement executes until its condition becomes **false**.

2.2.5 Pointers, Arrays, and Loops

An array of elements of type **char** can be declared like this:

```
    char v[6];              // array of 6 characters
```

Similarly, a pointer can be declared like this:

```
    char* p;                // pointer to character
```

In declarations, [] means "array of" and * means "pointer to." All arrays have **0** as their lower bound, so **v** has six elements, **v[0]** to **v[5]**. The size of an array must be a constant expression (§2.2.3). A pointer variable can hold the address of an object of the appropriate type:

```
char* p = &v[3];        // p points to v's fourth element
char x = *p;            // *p is the object that p points to
```

In an expression, prefix unary * means "contents of" and prefix unary & means "address of." We can represent the result of that initialized definition graphically:

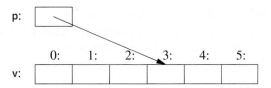

Consider copying ten elements from one array to another:

```
void copy_fct()
{
    int v1[10] = {0,1,2,3,4,5,6,7,8,9};
    int v2[10];                 // to become a copy of v1

    for (auto i=0; i!=10; ++i)  // copy elements
        v2[i]=v1[i];
    // ...
}
```

This **for**-statement can be read as "set **i** to zero; while **i** is not **10**, copy the ith element and increment **i**." When applied to an integer variable, the increment operator, **++**, simply adds **1**. C++ also offers a simpler **for**-statement, called a range-**for**-statement, for loops that traverse a sequence in the simplest way:

```
void print()
{
    int v[] = {0,1,2,3,4,5,6,7,8,9};

    for (auto x : v)            // for each x in v
        cout << x << '\n';

    for (auto x : {10,21,32,43,54,65})
        cout << x << '\n';
    // ...
}
```

The first range-**for**-statement can be read as "for every element of **v**, from the first to the last, place a copy in **x** and print it." Note that we don't have to specify an array bound when we initialize it with a list. The range-**for**-statement can be used for any sequence of elements (§3.4.1).

If we didn't want to copy the values from **v** into the variable **x**, but rather just have **x** refer to an element, we could write:

```
void increment()
{
    int v[] = {0,1,2,3,4,5,6,7,8,9};

    for (auto& x : v)
        ++x;
    // ...
}
```

In a declaration, the unary suffix **&** means "reference to." A reference is similar to a pointer, except that you don't need to use a prefix * to access the value referred to by the reference. Also, a reference cannot be made to refer to a different object after its initialization. When used in declarations, operators (such as **&**, *, and []) are called *declarator operators*:

```
T a[n];     // T[n]: array of n Ts (§7.3)
T* p;       // T*: pointer to T (§7.2)
T& r;       // T&: reference to T  (§7.7)
T f(A);     // T(A): function taking an argument of type A returning a result of type T (§2.2.1)
```

We try to ensure that a pointer always points to an object, so that dereferencing it is valid. When we don't have an object to point to or if we need to represent the notion of "no object available" (e.g.,for an end of a list), we give the pointer the value **nullptr** ("the null pointer"). There is only one **nullptr** shared by all pointer types:

```
double* pd = nullptr;
Link<Record>* lst = nullptr;    // pointer to a Link to a Record
int x = nullptr;                // error: nullptr is a pointer not an integer
```

It is often wise to check that a pointer argument that is supposed to point to something, actually points to something:

```
int count_x(char* p, char x)
    // count the number of occurrences of x in p[]
    // p is assumed to point to a zero-terminated array of char (or to nothing)
{
    if (p==nullptr) return 0;
    int count = 0;
    for (; *p!=0; ++p)
        if (*p==x)
            ++count;
    return count;
}
```

Note how we can move a pointer to point to the next element of an array using **++** and that we can leave out the initializer in a **for**-statement if we don't need it.

The definition of **count_x()** assumes that the **char** * is a *C-style string*, that is, that the pointer points to a zero-terminated array of **char**.

In older code, **0** or **NULL** is typically used instead of **nullptr** (§7.2.2). However, using **nullptr** eliminates potential confusion between integers (such as **0** or **NULL**) and pointers (such as **nullptr**).

2.3 User-Defined Types

We call the types that can be built from the fundamental types (§2.2.2), the **const** modifier (§2.2.3), and the declarator operators (§2.2.5) *built-in types*. C++'s set of built-in types and operations is rich, but deliberately low-level. They directly and efficiently reflect the capabilities of conventional computer hardware. However, they don't provide the programmer with high-level facilities to conveniently write advanced applications. Instead, C++ augments the built-in types and operations with a sophisticated set of *abstraction mechanisms* out of which programmers can build such high-level facilities. The C++ abstraction mechanisms are primarily designed to let programmers design and implement their own types, with suitable representations and operations, and for programmers to simply and elegantly use such types. Types built out of the built-in types using C++'s abstraction mechanisms are called *user-defined types*. They are referred to as classes and enumerations. Most of this book is devoted to the design, implementation, and use of user-defined types. The rest of this chapter presents the simplest and most fundamental facilities for that. Chapter 3 is a more complete description of the abstraction mechanisms and the programming styles they support. Chapter 4 and Chapter 5 present an overview of the standard library, and since the standard library mainly consists of user-defined types, they provide examples of what can be built using the language facilities and programming techniques presented in Chapter 2 and Chapter 3.

2.3.1 Structures

The first step in building a new type is often to organize the elements it needs into a data structure, a **struct**:

```
struct Vector {
    int sz;          // number of elements
    double* elem;   // pointer to elements
};
```

This first version of **Vector** consists of an **int** and a **double***.

A variable of type **Vector** can be defined like this:

```
Vector v;
```

However, by itself that is not of much use because **v**'s **elem** pointer doesn't point to anything. To be useful, we must give **v** some elements to point to. For example, we can construct a **Vector** like this:

```
void vector_init(Vector& v, int s)
{
    v.elem = new double[s];   // allocate an array of s doubles
    v.sz = s;
}
```

That is, **v**'s **elem** member gets a pointer produced by the **new** operator and **v**'s **size** member gets the number of elements. The **&** in **Vector&** indicates that we pass **v** by non-**const** reference (§2.2.5, §7.7); that way, **vector_init()** can modify the vector passed to it.

The **new** operator allocates memory from an area called *the free store* (also known as *dynamic memory* and *heap*; §11.2).

A simple use of **Vector** looks like this:

```
double read_and_sum(int s)
     // read s integers from cin and return their sum; s is assumed to be positive
{
     Vector v;
     vector_init(v,s);            // allocate s elements for v
     for (int i=0; i!=s; ++i)
          cin>>v.elem[i];         // read into elements

     double sum = 0;
     for (int i=0; i!=s; ++i)
          sum+=v.elem[i];         // take the sum of the elements
     return sum;
}
```

There is a long way to go before our **Vector** is as elegant and flexible as the standard-library **vector**. In particular, a user of **Vector** has to know every detail of **Vector**'s representation. The rest of this chapter and the next gradually improve **Vector** as an example of language features and techniques. Chapter 4 presents the standard-library **vector**, which contains many nice improvements, and Chapter 31 presents the complete **vector** in the context of other standard-library facilities.

I use **vector** and other standard-library components as examples
* to illustrate language features and design techniques, and
* to help you learn and use the standard-library components.

Don't reinvent standard-library components, such as **vector** and **string**; use them.

We use . (dot) to access **struct** members through a name (and through a reference) and –> to access **struct** members through a pointer. For example:

```
void f(Vector v, Vector& rv, Vector* pv)
{
     int i1 = v.sz;          // access through name
     int i2 = rv.sz;         // access through reference
     int i4 = pv–>sz;        // access through pointer
}
```

2.3.2 Classes

Having the data specified separately from the operations on it has advantages, such as the ability to use the data in arbitrary ways. However, a tighter connection between the representation and the operations is needed for a user-defined type to have all the properties expected of a "real type." In particular, we often want to keep the representation inaccessible to users, so as to ease use, guarantee consistent use of the data, and allow us to later improve the representation. To do that we have to distinguish between the interface to a type (to be used by all) and its implementation (which has access to the otherwise inaccessible data). The language mechanism for that is called a *class*. A class is defined to have a set of *members*, which can be data, function, or type members. The interface is defined by the **public** members of a class, and **private** members are accessible only through that interface. For example:

```
class Vector {
public:
    Vector(int s) :elem{new double[s]}, sz{s} { }    // construct a Vector
    double& operator[](int i) { return elem[i]; }     // element access: subscripting
    int size() { return sz; }
private:
    double* elem;  // pointer to the elements
    int sz;        // the number of elements
};
```

Given that, we can define a variable of our new type **Vector**:

```
Vector v(6);    // a Vector with 6 elements
```

We can illustrate a **Vector** object graphically:

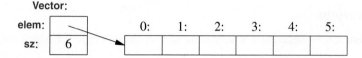

Basically, the **Vector** object is a "handle" containing a pointer to the elements (**elem**) plus the number of elements (**sz**). The number of elements (6 in the example) can vary from **Vector** object to **Vector** object, and a **Vector** object can have a different number of elements at different times (§3.2.1.3). However, the **Vector** object itself is always the same size. This is the basic technique for handling varying amounts of information in C++: a fixed-size handle referring to a variable amount of data "elsewhere" (e.g., on the free store allocated by **new**; §11.2). How to design and use such objects is the main topic of Chapter 3.

Here, the representation of a **Vector** (the members **elem** and **sz**) is accessible only through the interface provided by the **public** members: **Vector()**, **operator[]()**, and **size()**. The **read_and_sum()** example from §2.3.1 simplifies to:

```
double read_and_sum(int s)
{
    Vector v(s);                         // make a vector of s elements
    for (int i=0; i!=v.size(); ++i)
        cin>>v[i];                       // read into elements

    double sum = 0;
    for (int i=0; i!=v.size(); ++i)
        sum+=v[i];                       // take the sum of the elements
    return sum;
}
```

A "function" with the same name as its class is called a *constructor*, that is, a function used to construct objects of a class. So, the constructor, **Vector()**, replaces **vector_init()** from §2.3.1. Unlike an ordinary function, a constructor is guaranteed to be used to initialize objects of its class. Thus, defining a constructor eliminates the problem of uninitialized variables for a class.

Vector(int) defines how objects of type **Vector** are constructed. In particular, it states that it needs an integer to do that. That integer is used as the number of elements. The constructor initializes the **Vector** members using a member initializer list:

```
:elem{new double[s]}, sz{s}
```

That is, we first initialize **elem** with a pointer to **s** elements of type **double** obtained from the free store. Then, we initialize **sz** to **s**.

Access to elements is provided by a subscript function, called **operator[]**. It returns a reference to the appropriate element (a **double&**).

The **size()** function is supplied to give users the number of elements.

Obviously, error handling is completely missing, but we'll return to that in §2.4.3. Similarly, we did not provide a mechanism to "give back" the array of **double**s acquired by **new**; §3.2.1.2 shows how to use a destructor to elegantly do that.

2.3.3 Enumerations

In addition to classes, C++ supports a simple form of user-defined type for which we can enumerate the values:

```
enum class Color { red, blue, green };
enum class Traffic_light { green, yellow, red };


Color col = Color::red;
Traffic_light light = Traffic_light::red;
```

Note that enumerators (e.g., **red**) are in the scope of their **enum class**, so that they can be used repeatedly in different **enum class**es without confusion. For example, **Color::red** is **Color**'s **red** which is different from **Traffic_light::red**.

Enumerations are used to represent small sets of integer values. They are used to make code more readable and less error-prone than it would have been had the symbolic (and mnemonic) enumerator names not been used.

The **class** after the **enum** specifies that an enumeration is strongly typed and that its enumerators are scoped. Being separate types, **enum class**es help prevent accidental misuses of constants. In particular, we cannot mix **Traffic_light** and **Color** values:

```
Color x = red;                  // error: which red?
Color y = Traffic_light::red;   // error: that red is not a Color
Color z = Color::red;           // OK
```

Similarly, we cannot implicitly mix **Color** and integer values:

```
int i = Color::red;             // error: Color::red is not an int
Color c = 2;                    // error: 2 is not a Color
```

If you don't want to explicitly qualify enumerator names and want enumerator values to be **int**s (without the need for an explicit conversion), you can remove the **class** from **enum class** to get a "plain **enum**" (§8.4.2).

By default, an **enum class** has only assignment, initialization, and comparisons (e.g., **==** and **<**; §2.2.2) defined. However, an enumeration is a user-defined type so we can define operators for it:

```
Traffic_light& operator++(Traffic_light& t)
      // prefix increment: ++
{
      switch (t) {
      case Traffic_light::green:        return t=Traffic_light::yellow;
      case Traffic_light::yellow:       return t=Traffic_light::red;
      case Traffic_light::red:          return t=Traffic_light::green;
      }
}

Traffic_light next = ++light;          // next becomes Traffic_light::green
```

C++ also offers a less strongly typed "plain" **enum** (§8.4.2).

2.4 Modularity

A C++ program consists of many separately developed parts, such as functions (§2.2.1, Chapter 12), user-defined types (§2.3, §3.2, Chapter 16), class hierarchies (§3.2.4, Chapter 20), and templates (§3.4, Chapter 23). The key to managing this is to clearly define the interactions among those parts. The first and most important step is to distinguish between the interface to a part and its implementation. At the language level, C++ represents interfaces by declarations. A *declaration* specifies all that's needed to use a function or a type. For example:

```
double sqrt(double);      // the square root function takes a double and returns a double

class Vector {
public:
      Vector(int s);
      double& operator[](int i);
      int size();
private:
      double* elem;  // elem points to an array of sz doubles
      int sz;
};
```

The key point here is that the function bodies, the function *definitions*, are "elsewhere." For this example, we might like for the representation of **Vector** to be "elsewhere" also, but we will deal with that later (abstract types; §3.2.2). The definition of **sqrt()** will look like this:

```
double sqrt(double d)      // definition of sqrt()
{
      // ... algorithm as found in math textbook ...
}
```

For **Vector**, we need to define all three member functions:

```
Vector::Vector(int s)                  // definition of the constructor
      :elem{new double[s]}, sz{s}       // initialize members
{
}
```

```
double& Vector::operator[](int i)        // definition of subscripting
{
    return elem[i];
}

int Vector::size()                       // definition of size()
{
    return sz;
}
```

We must define **Vector**'s functions, but not **sqrt()** because it is part of the standard library. However, that makes no real difference: a library is simply some "other code we happen to use" written with the same language facilities as we use.

2.4.1 Separate Compilation

C++ supports a notion of separate compilation where user code sees only declarations of types and functions used. The definitions of those types and functions are in separate source files and compiled separately. This can be used to organize a program into a set of semi-independent code fragments. Such separation can be used to minimize compilation times and to strictly enforce separation of logically distinct parts of a program (thus minimizing the chance of errors). A library is often a separately compiled code fragments (e.g., functions).

Typically, we place the declarations that specify the interface to a module in a file with a name indicating its intended use. For example:

```
// Vector.h:

class Vector {
public:
    Vector(int s);
    double& operator[](int i);
    int size();
private:
    double* elem;        // elem points to an array of sz doubles
    int sz;
};
```

This declaration would be placed in a file **Vector.h**, and users will *include* that file, called a *header file*, to access that interface. For example:

```
// user.cpp:

#include "Vector.h"      // get Vector's interface
#include <cmath>         // get the the standard-library math function interface including sqrt()
using namespace std;     // make std members visible (§2.4.2)
```

```
double sqrt_sum(Vector& v)
{
    double sum = 0;
    for (int i=0; i!=v.size(); ++i)
        sum+=sqrt(v[i]);                    // sum of square roots
    return sum;
}
```

To help the compiler ensure consistency, the **.cpp** file providing the implementation of **Vector** will also include the **.h** file providing its interface:

```
// Vector.cpp:

#include "Vector.h" // get the interface

Vector::Vector(int s)
    :elem{new double[s]}, sz{s}
{
}

double& Vector::operator[](int i)
{
    return elem[i];
}

int Vector::size()
{
    return sz;
}
```

The code in **user.cpp** and **Vector.cpp** shares the **Vector** interface information presented in **Vector.h**, but the two files are otherwise independent and can be separately compiled. Graphically, the program fragments can be represented like this:

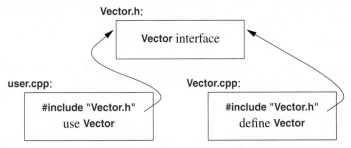

Strictly speaking, using separate compilation isn't a language issue; it is an issue of how best to take advantage of a particular language implementation. However, it is of great practical importance. The best approach is to maximize modularity, represent that modularity logically through language features, and then exploit the modularity physically through files for effective separate compilation (Chapter 14, Chapter 15).

2.4.2 Namespaces

In addition to functions (§2.2.1, Chapter 12), classes (Chapter 16), and enumerations (§2.3.3, §8.4), C++ offers *namespaces* (Chapter 14) as a mechanism for expressing that some declarations belong together and that their names shouldn't clash with other names. For example, I might want to experiment with my own complex number type (§3.2.1.1, §18.3, §40.4):

```
namespace My_code {
    class complex { /* ... */ };
    complex sqrt(complex);
    // ...
    int main();
}

int My_code::main()
{
    complex z {1,2};
    auto z2 = sqrt(z);
    std::cout << '{' << z2.real() << ',' << z2.imag() << "}\n";
    // ...
};

int main()
{
    return My_code::main();
}
```

By putting my code into the namespace **My_code**, I make sure that my names do not conflict with the standard-library names in namespace **std** (§4.1.2). The precaution is wise, because the standard library does provide support for **complex** arithmetic (§3.2.1.1, §40.4).

The simplest way to access a name in another namespace is to qualify it with the namespace name (e.g., **std::cout** and **My_code::main**). The "real **main()**" is defined in the global namespace, that is, not local to a defined namespace, class, or function. To gain access to names in the standard-library namespace, we can use a **using**-directive (§14.2.3):

```
using namespace std;
```

Namespaces are primarily used to organize larger program components, such as libraries. They simplify the composition of a program out of separately developed parts.

2.4.3 Error Handling

Error handling is a large and complex topic with concerns and ramifications that go far beyond language facilities into programming techniques and tools. However, C++ provides a few features to help. The major tool is the type system itself. Instead of painstakingly building up our applications from the built-in types (e.g., **char**, **int**, and **double**) and statements (e.g., **if**, **while**, and **for**), we build more types that are appropriate for our applications (e.g., **string**, **map**, and **regex**) and algorithms (e.g., **sort()**, **find_if()**, and **draw_all()**). Such higher level constructs simplify our programming, limit our opportunities for mistakes (e.g., you are unlikely to try to apply a tree traversal to a dialog box), and increase the compiler's chances of catching such errors. The majority of C++ constructs are dedicated to the design and implementation of elegant and efficient abstractions (e.g., user-defined types and algorithms using them). One effect of this modularity and abstraction (in particular, the use of libraries) is that the point where a run-time error can be detected is separated from the point where it can be handled. As programs grow, and especially when libraries are used extensively, standards for handling errors become important.

2.4.3.1 Exceptions

Consider again the **Vector** example. What *ought* to be done when we try to access an element that is out of range for the vector from §2.3.2?

- The writer of **Vector** doesn't know what the user would like to have done in this case (the writer of **Vector** typically doesn't even know in which program the vector will be running).
- The user of **Vector** cannot consistently detect the problem (if the user could, the out-of-range access wouldn't happen in the first place).

The solution is for the **Vector** implementer to detect the attempted out-of-range access and then tell the user about it. The user can then take appropriate action. For example, **Vector::operator[]()** can detect an attempted out-of-range access and throw an **out_of_range** exception:

```
double& Vector::operator[](int i)
{
    if (i<0 || size()<=i) throw out_of_range{"Vector::operator[]"};
    return elem[i];
}
```

The **throw** transfers control to a handler for exceptions of type **out_of_range** in some function that directly or indirectly called **Vector::operator[]()**. To do that, the implementation will unwind the function call stack as needed to get back to the context of that caller (§13.5.1). For example:

```
void f(Vector& v)
{
    // ...
    try { // exceptions here are handled by the handler defined below

        v[v.size()] = 7;  // try to access beyond the end of v
    }
    catch (out_of_range) {    // oops: out_of_range error
        // ... handle range error ...
    }
    // ...
}
```

We put code for which we are interested in handling exceptions into a **try**-block. That attempted assignment to v[v.size()] will fail. Therefore, the **catch**-clause providing a handler for **out_of_range** will be entered. The **out_of_range** type is defined in the standard library and is in fact used by some standard-library container access functions.

Use of the exception-handling mechanisms can make error handling simpler, more systematic, and more readable. See Chapter 13 for further discussion, details, and examples.

2.4.3.2 Invariants

The use of exceptions to signal out-of-range access is an example of a function checking its argument and refusing to act because a basic assumption, a *precondition*, didn't hold. Had we formally specified **Vector**'s subscript operator, we would have said something like "the index must be in the [**0:size**()) range," and that was in fact what we tested in our **operator[]()**. Whenever we define a function, we should consider what its preconditions are and if feasible test them (see §12.4, §13.4).

However, **operator[]()** operates on objects of type **Vector** and nothing it does makes any sense unless the members of **Vector** have "reasonable" values. In particular, we did say "**elem** points to an array of **sz** doubles" but we only said that in a comment. Such a statement of what is assumed to be true for a class is called a *class invariant*, or simply an *invariant*. It is the job of a constructor to establish the invariant for its class (so that the member functions can rely on it) and for the member functions to make sure that the invariant holds when they exit. Unfortunately, our **Vector** constructor only partially did its job. It properly initialized the **Vector** members, but it failed to check that the arguments passed to it made sense. Consider:

```
Vector v(-27);
```

This is likely to cause chaos.

Here is a more appropriate definition:

```
Vector::Vector(int s)
{
    if (s<0) throw length_error{};
    elem = new double[s];
    sz = s;
}
```

I use the standard-library exception **length_error** to report a non-positive number of elements because some standard-library operations use that exception to report problems of this kind. If operator **new** can't find memory to allocate, it throws a **std::bad_alloc**. We can now write:

```
void test()
{
    try {
        Vector v(-27);
    }
    catch (std::length_error) {
        // handle negative size
    }
    catch (std::bad_alloc) {
        // handle memory exhaustion
    }
}
```

You can define your own classes to be used as exceptions and have them carry arbitrary information from a point where an error is detected to a point where it can be handled (§13.5).

Often, a function has no way of completing its assigned task after an exception is thrown. Then, "handling" an exception simply means doing some minimal local cleanup and rethrowing the exception (§13.5.2.1).

The notion of invariants is central to the design of classes, and preconditions serve a similar role in the design of functions. Invariants

- helps us to understand precisely what we want
- forces us to be specific; that gives us a better chance of getting our code correct (after debugging and testing).

The notion of invariants underlies C++'s notions of resource management supported by constructors (§2.3.2) and destructors (§3.2.1.2, §5.2). See also §13.4, §16.3.1, and §17.2.

2.4.3.3 Static Assertions

Exceptions report errors found at run time. If an error can be found at compile time, it is usually preferable to do so. That's what much of the type system and the facilities for specifying the interfaces to user-defined types are for. However, we can also perform simple checks on other properties that are known at compile time and report failures as compiler error messages. For example:

```
static_assert(4<=sizeof(int), "integers are too small");   // check integer size
```

This will write **integers are too small** if **4<=sizeof(int)** does not hold, that is, if an **int** on this system does not have at least 4 bytes. We call such statements of expectations *assertions*.

The **static_assert** mechanism can be used for anything that can be expressed in terms of constant expressions (§2.2.3, §10.4). For example:

```
constexpr double C = 299792.458;             // km/s

void f(double speed)
{
     const double local_max = 160.0/(60*60);      // 160 km/h == 160.0/(60*60) km/s

     static_assert(speed<C,"can't go that fast");    // error: speed must be a constant
     static_assert(local_max<C,"can't go that fast");  // OK

     // ...
}
```

In general, **static_assert(A,S)** prints **S** as a compiler error message if **A** is not **true**.

The most important uses of **static_assert** come when we make assertions about types used as parameters in generic programming (§5.4.2, §24.3).

For runtime-checked assertions, see §13.4.

2.5 Postscript

The topics covered in this chapter roughly correspond to the contents of Part II (Chapters 6–15). Those are the parts of C++ that underlie all programming techniques and styles supported by C++. Experienced C and C++ programmers, please note that this foundation does not closely correspond to the C or C++98 subsets of C++ (that is, C++11).

2.6 Advice

[1]   Don't panic! All will become clear in time; §2.1.
[2]   You don't have to know every detail of C++ to write good programs; §1.3.1.
[3]   Focus on programming techniques, not on language features; §2.1.

3

A Tour of C++: Abstraction Mechanisms

Don't Panic!
– Douglas Adams

- Introduction
- Classes
    Concrete Types; Abstract Types; Virtual Functions; Class Hierarchies
- Copy and Move
    Copying Containers; Moving Containers; Resource Management; Suppressing Operations
- Templates
    Parameterized Types; Function Templates; Function Objects; Variadic Templates; Aliases
- Advice

3.1 Introduction

This chapter aims to give you an idea of C++'s support for abstraction and resource management without going into a lot of detail. It informally presents ways of defining and using new types (*user-defined types*). In particular, it presents the basic properties, implementation techniques, and language facilities used for *concrete classes*, *abstract classes*, and *class hierarchies*. Templates are introduced as a mechanism for parameterizing types and algorithms with (other) types and algorithms. Computations on user-defined and built-in types are represented as functions, sometimes generalized to *template functions* and *function objects*. These are the language facilities supporting the programming styles known as *object-oriented programming* and *generic programming*. The next two chapters follow up by presenting examples of standard-library facilities and their use.

The assumption is that you have programmed before. If not, please consider reading a textbook, such as *Programming: Principles and Practice Using C++* [Stroustrup,2009], before continuing here. Even if you have programmed before, the language you used or the applications you wrote may be very different from the style of C++ presented here. If you find this "lightning tour" confusing, skip to the more systematic presentation starting in Chapter 6.

As in Chapter 2, this tour presents C++ as an integrated whole, rather than as a layer cake. Consequently, it does not identify language features as present in C, part of C++98, or new in C++11. Such historical information can be found in §1.4 and Chapter 44.

3.2 Classes

The central language feature of C++ is the *class*. A class is a user-defined type provided to represent a concept in the code of a program. Whenever our design for a program has a useful concept, idea, entity, etc., we try to represent it as a class in the program so that the idea is there in the code, rather than just in our head, in a design document, or in some comments. A program built out of a well chosen set of classes is far easier to understand and get right than one that builds everything directly in terms of the built-in types. In particular, classes are often what libraries offer.

Essentially all language facilities beyond the fundamental types, operators, and statements exist to help define better classes or to use them more conveniently. By "better," I mean more correct, easier to maintain, more efficient, more elegant, easier to use, easier to read, and easier to reason about. Most programming techniques rely on the design and implementation of specific kinds of classes. The needs and tastes of programmers vary immensely. Consequently, the support for classes is extensive. Here, we will just consider the basic support for three important kinds of classes:

- Concrete classes (§3.2.1)
- Abstract classes (§3.2.2)
- Classes in class hierarchies (§3.2.4)

An astounding number of useful classes turn out to be of these three kinds. Even more classes can be seen as simple variants of these kinds or are implemented using combinations of the techniques used for these.

3.2.1 Concrete Types

The basic idea of *concrete classes* is that they behave "just like built-in types." For example, a complex number type and an infinite-precision integer are much like built-in **int**, except of course that they have their own semantics and sets of operations. Similarly, a **vector** and a **string** are much like built-in arrays, except that they are better behaved (§4.2, §4.3.2, §4.4.1).

The defining characteristic of a concrete type is that its representation is part of its definition. In many important cases, such as a **vector**, that representation is only one or more pointers to more data stored elsewhere, but it is present in each object of a concrete class. That allows implementations to be optimally efficient in time and space. In particular, it allows us to

- place objects of concrete types on the stack, in statically allocated memory, and in other objects (§6.4.2);
- refer to objects directly (and not just through pointers or references);
- initialize objects immediately and completely (e.g., using constructors; §2.3.2); and
- copy objects (§3.3).

The representation can be private (as it is for **Vector**; §2.3.2) and accessible only through the member functions, but it is present. Therefore, if the representation changes in any significant way, a user must recompile. This is the price to pay for having concrete types behave exactly like built-in types. For types that don't change often, and where local variables provide much-needed clarity and efficiency, this is acceptable and often ideal. To increase flexibility, a concrete type can keep major parts of its representation on the free store (dynamic memory, heap) and access them through the part stored in the class object itself. That's the way **vector** and **string** are implemented; they can be considered resource handles with carefully crafted interfaces.

3.2.1.1 An Arithmetic Type

The "classical user-defined arithmetic type" is **complex**:

```
class complex {
      double re, im;  // representation: two doubles
public:
      complex(double r, double i) :re{r}, im{i} {}    // construct complex from two scalars
      complex(double r) :re{r}, im{0} {}              // construct complex from one scalar
      complex() :re{0}, im{0} {}                      // default complex: {0,0}

      double real() const { return re; }
      void real(double d) { re=d; }
      double imag() const { return im; }
      void imag(double d) { im=d; }

      complex& operator+=(complex z) { re+=z.re, im+=z.im; return *this; }   // add to re and im
                                                                             // and return the result
      complex& operator-=(complex z) { re-=z.re, im-=z.im; return *this; }

      complex& operator*=(complex);      // defined out-of-class somewhere
      complex& operator/=(complex);      // defined out-of-class somewhere
};
```

This is a slightly simplified version of the standard-library **complex** (§40.4). The class definition itself contains only the operations requiring access to the representation. The representation is simple and conventional. For practical reasons, it has to be compatible with what Fortran provided 50 years ago, and we need a conventional set of operators. In addition to the logical demands, **complex** must be efficient or it will remain unused. This implies that simple operations must be inlined. That is, simple operations (such as constructors, **+=**, and **imag()**) must be implemented without function calls in the generated machine code. Functions defined in a class are inlined by default. An industrial-strength **complex** (like the standard-library one) is carefully implemented to do appropriate inlining.

A constructor that can be invoked without an argument is called a *default constructor*. Thus, **complex()** is **complex**'s default constructor. By defining a default constructor you eliminate the possibility of uninitialized variables of that type.

The **const** specifiers on the functions returning the real and imaginary parts indicate that these functions do not modify the object for which they are called.

Many useful operations do not require direct access to the representation of **complex**, so they can be defined separately from the class definition:

```
complex operator+(complex a, complex b) { return a+=b; }
complex operator–(complex a, complex b) { return a–=b; }
complex operator–(complex a) { return {–a.real(), –a.imag()}; }      // unary minus
complex operator*(complex a, complex b) { return a*=b; }
complex operator/(complex a, complex b) { return a/=b; }
```

Here, I use the fact that an argument passed by value is copied, so that I can modify an argument without affecting the caller's copy, and use the result as the return value.

The definitions of == and != are straightforward:

```
bool operator==(complex a, complex b)        // equal
{
      return a.real()==b.real() && a.imag()==b.imag();
}

bool operator!=(complex a, complex b)        // not equal
{
      return !(a==b);
}

complex sqrt(complex);

// ...
```

Class **complex** can be used like this:

```
void f(complex z)
{
      complex a {2.3};           // construct {2.3,0.0} from 2.3
      complex b {1/a};
      complex c {a+z*complex{1,2.3}};
      // ...
      if (c != b)
            c = –(b/a)+2*b;
}
```

The compiler converts operators involving **complex** numbers into appropriate function calls. For example, **c!=b** means **operator!=(c,b)** and **1/a** means **operator/(complex{1},a)**.

User-defined operators ("overloaded operators") should be used cautiously and conventionally. The syntax is fixed by the language, so you can't define a unary /. Also, it is not possible to change the meaning of an operator for built-in types, so you can't redefine + to subtract **ints**.

3.2.1.2 A Container

A *container* is an object holding a collection of elements, so we call **Vector** a container because it is the type of objects that are containers. As defined in §2.3.2, **Vector** isn't an unreasonable container of **doubles**: it is simple to understand, establishes a useful invariant (§2.4.3.2), provides range-checked access (§2.4.3.1), and provides **size()** to allow us to iterate over its elements. However, it does have a fatal flaw: it allocates elements using **new** but never deallocates them. That's not a good idea because although C++ defines an interface for a garbage collector (§34.5), it is not guaranteed that one is available to make unused memory available for new objects. In some environments you can't use a collector, and sometimes you prefer more precise control of destruction (§13.6.4) for logical or performance reasons. We need a mechanism to ensure that the memory allocated by the constructor is deallocated; that mechanism is a *destructor*:

```
class Vector {
private:
        double* elem;          // elem points to an array of sz doubles
        int sz;
public:
        Vector(int s) :elem{new double[s]}, sz{s}        // constructor: acquire resources
        {
                for (int i=0; i!=s; ++i) elem[i]=0;        // initialize elements
        }

        ~Vector() { delete[] elem; }                       // destructor: release resources

        double& operator[](int i);
        int size() const;
};
```

The name of a destructor is the complement operator, ˜, followed by the name of the class; it is the complement of a constructor. **Vector**'s constructor allocates some memory on the free store (also called the *heap* or *dynamic store*) using the **new** operator. The destructor cleans up by freeing that memory using the **delete** operator. This is all done without intervention by users of **Vector**. The users simply create and use **Vectors** much as they would variables of built-in types. For example:

```
void fct(int n)
{
        Vector v(n);

        // ... use v ...

        {
                Vector v2(2*n);
                // ... use v and v2 ...
        } // v2 is destroyed here

        // ... use v ..

} // v is destroyed here
```

Vector obeys the same rules for naming, scope, allocation, lifetime, etc., as does a built-in type, such as **int** and **char**. For details on how to control the lifetime of an object, see §6.4. This **Vector** has been simplified by leaving out error handling; see §2.4.3.

The constructor/destructor combination is the basis of many elegant techniques. In particular, it is the basis for most C++ general resource management techniques (§5.2, §13.3). Consider a graphical illustration of a **Vector**:

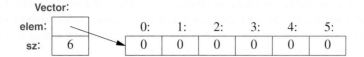

The constructor allocates the elements and initializes the **Vector** members appropriately. The de-structor deallocates the elements. This *handle-to-data model* is very commonly used to manage data that can vary in size during the lifetime of an object. The technique of acquiring resources in a constructor and releasing them in a destructor, known as *Resource Acquisition Is Initialization* or *RAII*, allows us to eliminate "naked **new** operations," that is, to avoid allocations in general code and keep them buried inside the implementation of well-behaved abstractions. Similarly, "naked **delete** operations" should be avoided. Avoiding naked **new** and naked **delete** makes code far less error-prone and far easier to keep free of resource leaks (§5.2).

3.2.1.3 Initializing Containers

A container exists to hold elements, so obviously we need convenient ways of getting elements into a container. We can handle that by creating a **Vector** with an appropriate number of elements and then assigning to them, but typically other ways are more elegant. Here, I just mention two favorites:

- *Initializer-list constructor*: Initialize with a list of elements.
- **push_back()**: Add a new element at the end (at the back of) the sequence.

These can be declared like this:

```
class Vector {
public:
    Vector(std::initializer_list<double>);      // initialize with a list
    // ...
    void push_back(double);                     // add element at end increasing the size by one
    // ...
};
```

The **push_back()** is useful for input of arbitrary numbers of elements. For example:

```
Vector read(istream& is)
{
    Vector v;
    for (double d; is>>d;)        // read floating-point values into d
        v.push_back(d);           // add d to v
    return v;
}
```

The input loop is terminated by an end-of-file or a formatting error. Until that happens, each num-ber read is added to the **Vector** so that at the end, **v**'s size is the number of elements read. I used a **for**-statement rather than the more conventional **while**-statement to keep the scope of **d** limited to the loop. The implementation of **push_back()** is discussed in §13.6.4.3. The way to provide **Vector** with a move constructor, so that returning a potentially huge amount of data from **read()** is cheap, is explained in §3.3.2.

The std::initializer_list used to define the initializer-list constructor is a standard-library type known to the compiler: when we use a {}-list, such as {1,2,3,4}, the compiler will create an object of type initializer_list to give to the program. So, we can write:

```
Vector v1 = {1,2,3,4,5};           // v1 has 5 elements
Vector v2 = {1.23, 3.45, 6.7, 8};  // v2 has 4 elements
```

Vector's initializer-list constructor might be defined like this:

```
Vector::Vector(std::initializer_list<double> lst)    // initialize with a list
    :elem{new double[lst.size()]}, sz{lst.size()}
{
    copy(lst.begin(),lst.end(),elem);           // copy from lst into elem
}
```

3.2.2 Abstract Types

Types such as complex and Vector are called *concrete types* because their representation is part of their definition. In that, they resemble built-in types. In contrast, an *abstract type* is a type that completely insulates a user from implementation details. To do that, we decouple the interface from the representation and give up genuine local variables. Since we don't know anything about the representation of an abstract type (not even its size), we must allocate objects on the free store (§3.2.1.2, §11.2) and access them through references or pointers (§2.2.5, §7.2, §7.7).

First, we define the interface of a class Container which we will design as a more abstract version of our Vector:

```
class Container {
public:
    virtual double& operator[](int) = 0;    // pure virtual function
    virtual int size() const = 0;           // const member function (§3.2.1.1)
    virtual ~Container() {}                  // destructor (§3.2.1.2)
};
```

This class is a pure interface to specific containers defined later. The word virtual means "may be redefined later in a class derived from this one." Unsurprisingly, a function declared virtual is called a *virtual function*. A class derived from Container provides an implementation for the Container interface. The curious =0 syntax says the function is *pure virtual*; that is, some class derived from Container *must* define the function. Thus, it is not possible to define an object that is just a Container; a Container can only serve as the interface to a class that implements its operator[]() and size() functions. A class with a pure virtual function is called an *abstract class*.

This Container can be used like this:

```
void use(Container& c)
{
    const int sz = c.size();

    for (int i=0; i!=sz; ++i)
        cout << c[i] << '\n';
}
```

Note how **use()** uses the **Container** interface in complete ignorance of implementation details. It uses **size()** and **[]** without any idea of exactly which type provides their implementation. A class that provides the interface to a variety of other classes is often called a *polymorphic type* (§20.3.2).

As is common for abstract classes, **Container** does not have a constructor. After all, it does not have any data to initialize. On the other hand, **Container** does have a destructor and that destructor is **virtual**. Again, that is common for abstract classes because they tend to be manipulated through references or pointers, and someone destroying a **Container** through a pointer has no idea what resources are owned by its implementation; see also §3.2.4.

A container that implements the functions required by the interface defined by the abstract class **Container** could use the concrete class **Vector**:

```
class Vector_container : public Container {    // Vector_container implements Container
    Vector v;
public:
    Vector_container(int s) : v(s) { }    // Vector of s elements
    ~Vector_container() {}

    double& operator[](int i) { return v[i]; }
    int size() const { return v.size(); }
};
```

The :**public** can be read as "is derived from" or "is a subtype of." Class **Vector_container** is said to be *derived* from class **Container**, and class **Container** is said to be a *base* of class **Vector_container**. An alternative terminology calls **Vector_container** and **Container** *subclass* and *superclass*, respectively. The derived class is said to inherit members from its base class, so the use of base and derived classes is commonly referred to as *inheritance*.

The members **operator[]()** and **size()** are said to *override* the corresponding members in the base class **Container** (§20.3.2). The destructor (~**Vector_container()**) overrides the base class destructor (~**Container()**). Note that the member destructor (~**Vector()**) is implicitly invoked by its class's destructor (~**Vector_container()**).

For a function like **use(Container&)** to use a **Container** in complete ignorance of implementation details, some other function will have to make an object on which it can operate. For example:

```
void g()
{
    Vector_container vc {10, 9, 8, 7, 6, 5, 4, 3, 2, 1, 0};
    use(vc);
}
```

Since **use()** doesn't know about **Vector_container**s but only knows the **Container** interface, it will work just as well for a different implementation of a **Container**. For example:

```
class List_container : public Container {// List_container implements Container
    std::list<double> ld;    // (standard-library) list of doubles (§4.4.2)
public:
    List_container() { }    // empty List
    List_container(initializer_list<double> il) : ld{il} { }
    ~List_container() {}
```

```
        double& operator[](int i);
        int size() const { return ld.size(); }

};

double& List_container::operator[](int i)
{
    for (auto& x : ld) {
        if (i==0) return x;
        --i;
    }
    throw out_of_range("List container");
}
```

Here, the representation is a standard-library **list<double>**. Usually, I would not implement a container with a subscript operation using a **list**, because performance of **list** subscripting is atrocious compared to **vector** subscripting. However, here I just wanted to show an implementation that is radically different from the usual one.

A function can create a **List_container** and have **use()** use it:

```
void h()
{
    List_container lc = { 1, 2, 3, 4, 5, 6, 7, 8, 9 };
    use(lc);
}
```

The point is that **use(Container&)** has no idea if its argument is a **Vector_container**, a **List_container**, or some other kind of container; it doesn't need to know. It can use any kind of **Container**. It knows only the interface defined by **Container**. Consequently, **use(Container&)** needn't be recompiled if the implementation of **List_container** changes or a brand-new class derived from **Container** is used.

The flip side of this flexibility is that objects must be manipulated through pointers or references (§3.3, §20.4).

3.2.3 Virtual Functions

Consider again the use of **Container**:

```
void use(Container& c)
{
    const int sz = c.size();

    for (int i=0; i!=sz; ++i)
        cout << c[i] << '\n';
}
```

How is the call **c[i]** in **use()** resolved to the right **operator[]()**? When **h()** calls **use()**, **List_container**'s **operator[]()** must be called. When **g()** calls **use()**, **Vector_container**'s **operator[]()** must be called. To achieve this resolution, a **Container** object must contain information to allow it to select the right function to call at run time. The usual implementation technique is for the compiler to convert the name of a virtual function into an index into a table of pointers to functions. That table is usually called the *virtual function table* or simply the **vtbl**. Each class with virtual functions has its own **vtbl** identifying its virtual functions. This can be represented graphically like this:

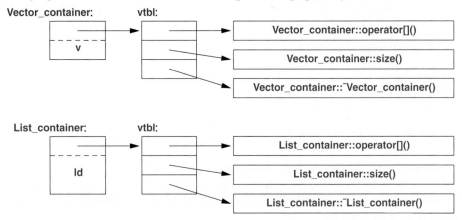

The functions in the **vtbl** allow the object to be used correctly even when the size of the object and the layout of its data are unknown to the caller. The implementation of the caller needs only to know the location of the pointer to the **vtbl** in a **Container** and the index used for each virtual function. This virtual call mechanism can be made almost as efficient as the "normal function call" mechanism (within 25%). Its space overhead is one pointer in each object of a class with virtual functions plus one **vtbl** for each such class.

3.2.4 Class Hierarchies

The **Container** example is a very simple example of a class hierarchy. A *class hierarchy* is a set of classes ordered in a lattice created by derivation (e.g., : **public**). We use class hierarchies to represent concepts that have hierarchical relationships, such as "A fire engine is a kind of a truck which is a kind of a vehicle" and "A smiley face is a kind of a circle which is a kind of a shape." Huge hierarchies, with hundreds of classes, that are both deep and wide are common. As a semi-realistic classic example, let's consider shapes on a screen:

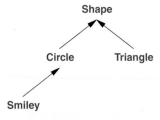

The arrows represent inheritance relationships. For example, class **Circle** is derived from class **Shape**. To represent that simple diagram in code, we must first specify a class that defines the general properties of all shapes:

```
class Shape {
public:
    virtual Point center() const =0;        // pure virtual
    virtual void move(Point to) =0;

    virtual void draw() const = 0;          // draw on current "Canvas"
    virtual void rotate(int angle) = 0;

    virtual ˜Shape() {}                      // destructor
    // ...
};
```

Naturally, this interface is an abstract class: as far as representation is concerned, *nothing* (except the location of the pointer to the **vtbl**) is common for every **Shape**. Given this definition, we can write general functions manipulating vectors of pointers to shapes:

```
void rotate_all(vector<Shape∗>& v, int angle) // rotate v's elements by angle degrees
{
    for (auto p : v)
        p–>rotate(angle);
}
```

To define a particular shape, we must say that it is a **Shape** and specify its particular properties (including its virtual functions):

```
class Circle : public Shape {
public:
    Circle(Point p, int rr);                // constructor

    Point center() const { return x; }
    void move(Point to) { x=to; }

    void draw() const;
    void rotate(int) {}                     // nice simple algorithm
private:
    Point x;    // center
    int r;      // radius
};
```

So far, the **Shape** and **Circle** example provides nothing new compared to the **Container** and **Vector_container** example, but we can build further:

```
class Smiley : public Circle {  // use the circle as the base for a face
public:
    Smiley(Point p, int r) : Circle{p,r}, mouth{nullptr} { }

    ˜Smiley()
    {
        delete mouth;
        for (auto p : eyes) delete p;
    }
```

```
        void move(Point to);

        void draw() const;
        void rotate(int);

        void add_eye(Shape* s) { eyes.push_back(s); }
        void set_mouth(Shape* s);
        virtual void wink(int i);          // wink eye number i

        // ...

private:
        vector<Shape*> eyes;               // usually two eyes
        Shape* mouth;
};
```

The push_back() member function adds its argument to the vector (here, eyes), increasing that vector's size by one.

We can now define Smiley::draw() using calls to Smiley's base and member draw()s:

```
void Smiley::draw()
{
        Circle::draw();
        for (auto p : eyes)
                p->draw();
        mouth->draw();
}
```

Note the way that Smiley keeps its eyes in a standard-library vector and deletes them in its destructor. Shape's destructor is virtual and Smiley's destructor overrides it. A virtual destructor is essential for an abstract class because an object of a derived class is usually manipulated through the interface provided by its abstract base class. In particular, it may be deleted through a pointer to a base class. Then, the virtual function call mechanism ensures that the proper destructor is called. That destructor then implicitly invokes the destructors of its bases and members.

In this simplified example, it is the programmer's task to place the eyes and mouth appropriately within the circle representing the face.

We can add data members, operations, or both as we define a new class by derivation. This gives great flexibility with corresponding opportunities for confusion and poor design. See Chapter 21. A class hierarchy offers two kinds of benefits:

- *Interface inheritance*: An object of a derived class can be used wherever an object of a base class is required. That is, the base class acts as an interface for the derived class. The Container and Shape classes are examples. Such classes are often abstract classes.
- *Implementation inheritance*: A base class provides functions or data that simplifies the implementation of derived classes. Smiley's uses of Circle's constructor and of Circle::draw() are examples. Such base classes often have data members and constructors.

Concrete classes – especially classes with small representations – are much like built-in types: we define them as local variables, access them using their names, copy them around, etc. Classes in class hierarchies are different: we tend to allocate them on the free store using new, and we access them through pointers or references. For example, consider a function that reads data describing shapes from an input stream and constructs the appropriate **Shape** objects:

```
enum class Kind { circle, triangle, smiley };

Shape* read_shape(istream& is)     // read shape descriptions from input stream is
{
    // ... read shape header from is and find its Kind k ...

    switch (k) {
    case Kind::circle:
        // read circle data {Point,int} into p and r
        return new Circle{p,r};
    case Kind::triangle:
        // read triangle data {Point,Point,Point} into p1, p2, and p3
        return new Triangle{p1,p2,p3};
    case Kind::smiley:
        // read smiley data {Point,int,Shape,Shape,Shape} into p, r, e1 ,e2, and m
        Smiley* ps = new Smiley{p,r};
        ps->add_eye(e1);
        ps->add_eye(e2);
        ps->set_mouth(m);
        return ps;
    }
}
```

A program may use that shape reader like this:

```
void user()
{
    std::vector<Shape*> v;
    while (cin)
        v.push_back(read_shape(cin));
    draw_all(v);                    // call draw() for each element
    rotate_all(v,45);               // call rotate(45) for each element
    for (auto p : v) delete p;      // remember to delete elements
}
```

Obviously, the example is simplified – especially with respect to error handling – but it vividly illustrates that **user()** has absolutely no idea of which kinds of shapes it manipulates. The **user()** code can be compiled once and later used for new **Shapes** added to the program. Note that there are no pointers to the shapes outside **user()**, so **user()** is responsible for deallocating them. This is done with the **delete** operator and relies critically on **Shape**'s virtual destructor. Because that destructor is virtual, **delete** invokes the destructor for the most derived class. This is crucial because a derived class may have acquired all kinds of resources (such as file handles, locks, and output streams) that need to be released. In this case, a **Smiley** deletes its **eyes** and **mouth** objects.

Experienced programmers will notice that I left open two obvious opportunities for mistakes:

- A user might fail to **delete** the pointer returned by **read_shape()**.
- The owner of a container of **Shape** pointers might not **delete** the objects pointed to.

In that sense, functions returning a pointer to an object allocated on the free store are dangerous.

One solution to both problems is to return a standard-library **unique_ptr** (§5.2.1) rather than a "naked pointer" and store **unique_ptr**s in the container:

```
unique_ptr<Shape> read_shape(istream& is) // read shape descriptions from input stream is
{
    // read shape header from is and find its Kind k

    switch (k) {
    case Kind::circle:
        // read circle data {Point,int} into p and r
        return unique_ptr<Shape>{new Circle{p,r}};        // §5.2.1
    // ...
    }
}

void user()
{
    vector<unique_ptr<Shape>> v;
    while (cin)
        v.push_back(read_shape(cin));
    draw_all(v);              // call draw() for each element
    rotate_all(v,45);              // call rotate(45) for each element
} // all Shapes implicitly destroyed
```

Now the object is owned by the **unique_ptr** which will **delete** the object when it is no longer needed, that is, when its **unique_ptr** goes out of scope.

For the **unique_ptr** version of **user()** to work, we need versions of **draw_all()** and **rotate_all()** that accept **vector<unique_ptr<Shape>>**s. Writing many such _all() functions could become tedious, so §3.4.3 shows an alternative.

3.3   Copy and Move

By default, objects can be copied. This is true for objects of user-defined types as well as for built-in types. The default meaning of copy is memberwise copy: copy each member. For example, using **complex** from §3.2.1.1:

```
void test(complex z1)
{
    complex z2 {z1};        // copy initialization
    complex z3;
    z3 = z2;              // copy assignment
    // ...
}
```

Now **z1**, **z2**, and **z3** have the same value because both the assignment and the initialization copied both members.

When we design a class, we must always consider if and how an object might be copied. For simple concrete types, memberwise copy is often exactly the right semantics for copy. For some sophisticated concrete types, such as **Vector**, memberwise copy is not the right semantics for copy, and for abstract types it almost never is.

3.3.1 Copying Containers

When a class is a *resource handle*, that is, it is responsible for an object accessed through a pointer, the default memberwise copy is typically a disaster. Memberwise copy would violate the resource handle's invariant (§2.4.3.2). For example, the default copy would leave a copy of a **Vector** referring to the same elements as the original:

```
void bad_copy(Vector v1)
{
    Vector v2 = v1;     // copy v1's representation into v2
    v1[0] = 2;          // v2[0] is now also 2!
    v2[1] = 3;          // v1[1] is now also 3!
}
```

Assuming that **v1** has four elements, the result can be represented graphically like this:

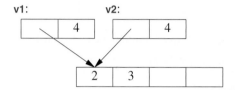

Fortunately, the fact that **Vector** has a destructor is a strong hint that the default (memberwise) copy semantics is wrong and the compiler should at least warn against this example (§17.6). We need to define better copy semantics.

Copying of an object of a class is defined by two members: a *copy constructor* and a *copy assignment*:

```
class Vector {
private:
    double* elem;   // elem points to an array of sz doubles
    int sz;
public:
    Vector(int s);                          // constructor: establish invariant, acquire resources
    ~Vector() { delete[] elem; }            // destructor: release resources

    Vector(const Vector& a);                // copy constructor
    Vector& operator=(const Vector& a);     // copy assignment

    double& operator[](int i);
    const double& operator[](int i) const;

    int size() const;
};
```

A suitable definition of a copy constructor for **Vector** allocates the space for the required number of elements and then copies the elements into it, so that after a copy each **Vector** has its own copy of the elements:

```
Vector::Vector(const Vector& a)     // copy constructor
    :elem{new double[sz]},          // allocate space for elements
     sz{a.sz}
{
    for (int i=0; i!=sz; ++i)       // copy elements
        elem[i] = a.elem[i];
}
```

The result of the v2=v1 example can now be presented as:

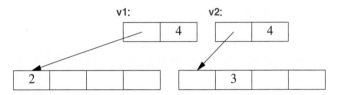

Of course, we need a copy assignment in addition to the copy constructor:

```
Vector& Vector::operator=(const Vector& a)          // copy assignment
{
    double* p = new double[a.sz];
    for (int i=0; i!=a.sz; ++i)
        p[i] = a.elem[i];
    delete[] elem;        // delete old elements
    elem = p;
    sz = a.sz;
    return *this;
}
```

The name this is predefined in a member function and points to the object for which the member function is called.

A copy constructor and a copy assignment for a class X are typically declared to take an argument of type const X&.

3.3.2 Moving Containers

We can control copying by defining a copy constructor and a copy assignment, but copying can be costly for large containers. Consider:

```
Vector operator+(const Vector& a, const Vector& b)
{
    if (a.size()!=b.size())
        throw Vector_size_mismatch{};

    Vector res(a.size());
    for (int i=0; i!=a.size(); ++i)
        res[i]=a[i]+b[i];
    return res;
}
```

Returning from a + involves copying the result out of the local variable **res** and into some place where the caller can access it. We might use this + like this:

```
void f(const Vector& x, const Vector& y, const Vector& z)
{
      Vector r;
      // ...
      r = x+y+z;
      // ...
}
```

That would be copying a **Vector** at least twice (one for each use of the + operator). If a **Vector** is large, say, 10,000 **doubles**, that could be embarrassing. The most embarrassing part is that **res** in **operator+()** is never used again after the copy. We didn't really want a copy; we just wanted to get the result out of a function: we wanted to *move* a **Vector** rather than to *copy* it. Fortunately, we can state that intent:

```
class Vector {
      // ...

      Vector(const Vector& a);            // copy constructor
      Vector& operator=(const Vector& a);     // copy assignment

      Vector(Vector&& a);                 // move constructor
      Vector& operator=(Vector&& a);          // move assignment
};
```

Given that definition, the compiler will choose the *move constructor* to implement the transfer of the return value out of the function. This means that **r=x+y+z** will involve no copying of **Vector**s. Instead, **Vector**s are just moved.

As is typical, **Vector**'s move constructor is trivial to define:

```
Vector::Vector(Vector&& a)
      :elem{a.elem},         // "grab the elements" from a
       sz{a.sz}
{
      a.elem = nullptr;       // now a has no elements
      a.sz = 0;
}
```

The && means "rvalue reference" and is a reference to which we can bind an rvalue (§6.4.1). The word "rvalue" is intended to complement "lvalue," which roughly means "something that can appear on the left-hand side of an assignment." So an rvalue is – to a first approximation – a value that you can't assign to, such as an integer returned by a function call, and an rvalue reference is a reference to something that nobody else can assign to. The **res** local variable in **operator+()** for **Vec**tors is an example.

A move constructor does *not* take a **const** argument: after all, a move constructor is supposed to remove the value from its argument. A *move assignment* is defined similarly.

A move operation is applied when an rvalue reference is used as an initializer or as the right-hand side of an assignment.

After a move, a moved-from object should be in a state that allows a destructor to be run. Typically, we should also allow assignment to a moved-from object (§17.5, §17.6.2).

Where the programmer knows that a value will not be used again, but the compiler can't be expected to be smart enough to figure that out, the programmer can be specific:

```
Vector f()
{
    Vector x(1000);
    Vector y(1000);
    Vector z(1000);
    // ...
    z = x;                // we get a copy
    y = std::move(x);     // we get a move
    // ...
    return z;             // we get a move
};
```

The standard-library function **move()** returns an rvalue reference to its argument.

Just before the **return** we have:

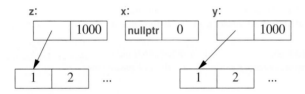

When **z** is destroyed, it too has been moved from (by the **return**) so that, like **x**, it is empty (it holds no elements).

3.3.3 Resource Management

By defining constructors, copy operations, move operations, and a destructor, a programmer can provide complete control of the lifetime of a contained resource (such as the elements of a container). Furthermore, a move constructor allows an object to move simply and cheaply from one scope to another. That way, objects that we cannot or would not want to copy out of a scope can be simply and cheaply moved out instead. Consider a standard-library **thread** representing a concurrent activity (§5.3.1) and a **Vector** of a million **doubles**. We can't copy the former and don't want to copy the latter.

```
std::vector<thread> my_threads;

Vector init(int n)
{
    thread t {heartbeat};              // run heartbeat concurrently (on its own thread)
    my_threads.push_back(move(t));     // move t into my_threads
    // ... more initialization ...
```

```
            Vector vec(n);
            for (int i=0; i<vec.size(); ++i) vec[i] = 777;
            return vec;                              // move res out of init()
    }

    auto v = init();  // start heartbeat and initialize v
```

This makes resource handles, such as Vector and thread, an alternative to using pointers in many cases. In fact, the standard-library "smart pointers," such as unique_ptr, are themselves resource handles (§5.2.1).

I used the standard-library vector to hold the threads because we don't get to parameterize Vector with an element type until §3.4.1.

In very much the same way as new and delete disappear from application code, we can make pointers disappear into resource handles. In both cases, the result is simpler and more maintainable code, without added overhead. In particular, we can achieve *strong resource safety*; that is, we can eliminate resource leaks for a general notion of a resource. Examples are vectors holding memory, threads holding system threads, and fstreams holding file handles.

3.3.4 Suppressing Operations

Using the default copy or move for a class in a hierarchy is typically a disaster: given only a pointer to a base, we simply don't know what members the derived class has (§3.2.2), so we can't know how to copy them. So, the best thing to do is usually to *delete* the default copy and move operations, that is, to eliminate the default definitions of those two operations:

```
    class Shape {
    public:
            Shape(const Shape&) =delete;            // no copy operations
            Shape& operator=(const Shape&) =delete;

            Shape(Shape&&) =delete;                 // no move operations
            Shape& operator=(Shape&&) =delete;

            ˜Shape();
            // ...
    };
```

Now an attempt to copy a Shape will be caught by the compiler. If you need to copy an object in a class hierarchy, write some kind of clone function (§22.2.4).

In this particular case, if you forgot to delete a copy or move operation, no harm is done. A move operation is *not* implicitly generated for a class where the user has explicitly declared a destructor. Furthermore, the generation of copy operations is deprecated in this case (§44.2.3). This can be a good reason to explicitly define a destructor even where the compiler would have implicitly provided one (§17.2.3).

A base class in a class hierarchy is just one example of an object we wouldn't want to copy. A resource handle generally cannot be copied just by copying its members (§5.2, §17.2.2).

The =delete mechanism is general, that is, it can be used to suppress any operation (§17.6.4).

3.4 Templates

Someone who wants a vector is unlikely always to want a vector of **double**s. A vector is a general concept, independent of the notion of a floating-point number. Consequently, the element type of a vector ought to be represented independently. A *template* is a class or a function that we parameterize with a set of types or values. We use templates to represent concepts that are best understood as something very general from which we can generate specific types and functions by specifying arguments, such as the element type **double**.

3.4.1 Parameterized Types

We can generalize our vector-of-doubles type to a vector-of-anything type by making it a **template** and replacing the specific type **double** with a parameter. For example:

```
template<typename T>
class Vector {
private:
        T* elem;   // elem points to an array of sz elements of type T
        int sz;
public:
        Vector(int s);                  // constructor: establish invariant, acquire resources
        ~Vector() { delete[] elem; }    // destructor: release resources

        // ... copy and move operations ...

        T& operator[](int i);
        const T& operator[](int i) const;
        int size() const { return sz; }
};
```

The **template<typename T>** prefix makes **T** a parameter of the declaration it prefixes. It is C++'s version of the mathematical "for all T" or more precisely "for all types T."
     The member functions might be defined similarly:

```
template<typename T>
Vector<T>::Vector(int s)
{
        if (s<0) throw Negative_size{};
        elem = new T[s];
        sz = s;
}

template<typename T>
const T& Vector<T>::operator[](int i) const
{
        if (i<0 || size()<=i)
                throw out_of_range{"Vector::operator[]"};
        return elem[i];
}
```

Given these definitions, we can define Vectors like this:

```
Vector<char> vc(200);          // vector of 200 characters
Vector<string> vs(17);         // vector of 17 strings
Vector<list<int>> vli(45);     // vector of 45 lists of integers
```

The >> in Vector<list<int>> terminates the nested template arguments; it is not a misplaced input operator. It is not (as in C++98) necessary to place a space between the two >s.

We can use Vectors like this:

```
void write(const Vector<string>& vs)          // Vector of some strings
{
    for (int i = 0; i!=vs.size(); ++i)
        cout << vs[i] << '\n';
}
```

To support the range-for loop for our Vector, we must define suitable begin() and end() functions:

```
template<typename T>
T* begin(Vector<T>& x)
{
    return &x[0];          // pointer to first element
}

template<typename T>
T* end(Vector<T>& x)
{
    return x.begin()+x.size(); // pointer to one-past-last element
}
```

Given those, we can write:

```
void f2(const Vector<string>& vs)  // Vector of some strings
{
    for (auto& s : vs)
        cout << s << '\n';
}
```

Similarly, we can define lists, vectors, maps (that is, associative arrays), etc., as templates (§4.4, §23.2, Chapter 31).

Templates are a compile-time mechanism, so their use incurs no run-time overhead compared to "handwritten code" (§23.2.2).

3.4.2 Function Templates

Templates have many more uses than simply parameterizing a container with an element type. In particular, they are extensively used for parameterization of both types and algorithms in the standard library (§4.4.5, §4.5.5). For example, we can write a function that calculates the sum of the element values of any container like this:

```
template<typename Container, typename Value>
Value sum(const Container& c, Value v)
{
    for (auto x : c)
        v+=x;
    return v;
}
```

The Value template argument and the function argument v are there to allow the caller to specify the type and initial value of the accumulator (the variable in which to accumulate the sum):

```
void user(Vector<int>& vi, std::list<double>& ld, std::vector<complex<double>>& vc)
{
    int x = sum(vi,0);                    // the sum of a vector of ints (add ints)
    double d = sum(vi,0.0);               // the sum of a vector of ints (add doubles)
    double dd = sum(ld,0.0);              // the sum of a list of doubles
    auto z = sum(vc,complex<double>{});   // the sum of a vector of complex<double>
                                          // the initial value is {0.0,0.0}
}
```

The point of adding ints in a double would be to gracefully handle a number larger than the largest int. Note how the types of the template arguments for sum<T,V> are deduced from the function arguments. Fortunately, we do not need to explicitly specify those types.

This sum() is a simplified version of the standard-library accumulate() (§40.6).

3.4.3 Function Objects

One particularly useful kind of template is the *function object* (sometimes called a *functor*), which is used to define objects that can be called like functions. For example:

```
template<typename T>
class Less_than {
    const T val;     // value to compare against
public:
    Less_than(const T& v) :val(v) { }
    bool operator()(const T& x) const { return x<val; } // call operator
};
```

The function called operator() implements the "function call," "call," or "application" operator ().

We can define named variables of type Less_than for some argument type:

```
Less_than<int> lti {42};         // lti(i) will compare i to 42 using < (i<42)
Less_than<string> lts {"Backus"}; // lts(s) will compare s to "Backus" using < (s<"Backus")
```

We can call such an object, just as we call a function:

```
void fct(int n, const string & s)
{
    bool b1 = lti(n);     // true if n<42
    bool b2 = lts(s);     // true if s<"Backus"
    // ...
}
```

Such function objects are widely used as arguments to algorithms. For example, we can count the occurrences of values for which a predicate returns true:

```
template<typename C, typename P>
int count(const C& c, P pred)
{
    int cnt = 0;
    for (const auto& x : c)
        if (pred(x))
            ++cnt;
    return cnt;
}
```

A *predicate* is something that we can invoke to return true or false. For example:

```
void f(const Vector<int>& vec, const list<string>& lst, int x, const string& s)
{
    cout << "number of values less than " << x
        << ": " << count(vec,Less_than<int>{x})
        << '\n';
    cout << "number of values less than " << s
        << ": " << count(lst,Less_than<string>{s})
        << '\n';
}
```

Here, Less_than<int>{x} constructs an object for which the call operator compares to the int called x; Less_than<string>{s} constructs an object that compares to the string called s. The beauty of these function objects is that they carry the value to be compared against with them. We don't have to write a separate function for each value (and each type), and we don't have to introduce nasty global variables to hold values. Also, for a simple function object like Less_than inlining is simple, so that a call of Less_than is far more efficient than an indirect function call. The ability to carry data plus their efficiency make function objects particularly useful as arguments to algorithms.

Function objects used to specify the meaning of key operations of a general algorithm (such as Less_than for count()) are often referred to as *policy objects*.

We have to define Less_than separately from its use. That could be seen as inconvenient. Consequently, there is a notation for implicitly generating function objects:

```
void f(const Vector<int>& vec, const list<string>& lst, int x, const string& s)
{
    cout << "number of values less than " << x
        << ": " << count(vec,[&](int a){ return a<x; })
        << '\n';
    cout << "number of values less than " << s
        << ": " << count(lst,[&](const string& a){ return a<s; })
        << '\n';
}
```

The notation [&](int a){ return a<x; } is called a *lambda expression* (§11.4). It generates a function object exactly like Less_than<int>{x}. The [&] is a *capture list* specifying that local names used (such as x) will be passed by reference. Had we wanted to "capture" only x, we could have said so: [&x]. Had we wanted to give the generated object a copy of x, we could have said so: [=x]. Capture nothing is [], capture all local names used by reference is [&], and capture all local names used by value is [=].

Using lambdas can be convenient and terse, but also obscure. For nontrivial actions (say, more than a simple expression), I prefer to name the operation so as to more clearly state its purpose and to make it available for use in several places in a program.

In §3.2.4, we noticed the annoyance of having to write many functions to perform operations on elements of vectors of pointers and unique_ptrs, such as draw_all() and rotate_all(). Function objects (in particular, lambdas) can help by allowing us to separate the traversal of the container from the specification of what is to be done with each element.

First, we need a function that applies an operation to each object pointed to by the elements of a container of pointers:

```cpp
template<class C, class Oper>
void for_all(C& c, Oper op)          // assume that C is a container of pointers
{
    for (auto& x : c)
        op(*x);          // pass op() a reference to each element pointed to
}
```

Now, we can write a version of user() from §3.2.4 without writing a set of _all functions:

```cpp
void user()
{
    vector<unique_ptr<Shape>> v;
    while (cin)
        v.push_back(read_shape(cin));
    for_all(v,[](Shape& s){ s.draw(); });          // draw_all()
    for_all(v,[](Shape& s){ s.rotate(45); });          // rotate_all(45)
}
```

I pass a reference to Shape to a lambda so that the lambda doesn't have to care exactly how the objects are stored in the container. In particular, those for_all() calls would still work if I changed v to a vector<Shape*>.

3.4.4 Variadic Templates

A template can be defined to accept an arbitrary number of arguments of arbitrary types. Such a template is called a *variadic template*. For example:

```cpp
template<typename T, typename... Tail>
void f(T head, Tail... tail)
{
    g(head);    // do something to head
    f(tail...);    // try again with tail
}

void f() { }       // do nothing
```

The key to implementing a variadic template is to note that when you pass a list of arguments to it, you can separate the first argument from the rest. Here, we do something to the first argument (the head) and then recursively call f() with the rest of the arguments (the tail). The ellipsis, ..., is used to indicate "the rest" of a list. Eventually, of course, tail will become empty and we need a separate function to deal with that.

We can call this f() like this:

```
int main()
{
    cout << "first: ";
    f(1,2.2,"hello");

    cout << "\nsecond: "
    f(0.2,'c',"yuck!",0,1,2);
    cout << "\n";
}
```

This would call f(1,2.2,"hello"), which will call f(2.2,"hello"), which will call f("hello"), which will call f(). What might the call g(head) do? Obviously, in a real program it will do whatever we wanted done to each argument. For example, we could make it write its argument (here, head) to output:

```
template<typename T>
void g(T x)
{
    cout << x << " ";
}
```

Given that, the output will be:

```
first: 1 2.2 hello
second: 0.2 c yuck! 0 1 2
```

It seems that f() is a simple variant of printf() printing arbitrary lists or values – implemented in three lines of code plus their surrounding declarations.

The strength of variadic templates (sometimes just called *variadics*) is that they can accept any arguments you care to give them. The weakness is that the type checking of the interface is a possibly elaborate template program. For details, see §28.6. For examples, see §34.2.4.2 (N-tuples) and Chapter 29 (N-dimensional matrices).

3.4.5 Aliases

Surprisingly often, it is useful to introduce a synonym for a type or a template (§6.5). For example, the standard header <cstddef> contains a definition of the alias size_t, maybe:

```
using size_t = unsigned int;
```

The actual type named size_t is implementation-dependent, so in another implementation size_t may be an unsigned long. Having the alias size_t allows the programmer to write portable code.

It is very common for a parameterized type to provide an alias for types related to their template arguments. For example:

```
template<typename T>
class Vector {
public:
    using value_type = T;
    // ...
};
```

In fact, every standard-library container provides value_type as the name of its value type (§31.3.1). This allows us to write code that will work for every container that follows this convention. For example:

```
template<typename C>
using Element_type = typename C::value_type;

template<typename Container>
void algo(Container& c)
{
    Vector<Element_type<Container>> vec; // keep results here
    // ...
}
```

The aliasing mechanism can be used to define a new template by binding some or all template arguments. For example:

```
template<typename Key, typename Value>
class Map {
    // ...
};

template<typename Value>
using String_map = Map<string,Value>;

String_map<int> m; // m is a Map<string,int>
```

See §23.6.

3.5 Advice

[1]   Express ideas directly in code; §3.2.
[2]   Define classes to represent application concepts directly in code; §3.2.
[3]   Use concrete classes to represent simple concepts and performance-critical components; §3.2.1.
[4]   Avoid "naked" new and delete operations; §3.2.1.2.
[5]   Use resource handles and RAII to manage resources; §3.2.1.2.
[6]   Use abstract classes as interfaces when complete separation of interface and implementation is needed; §3.2.2.
[7]   Use class hierarchies to represent concepts with inherent hierarchical structure; §3.2.4.

[8]   When designing a class hierarchy, distinguish between implementation inheritance and interface inheritance; §3.2.4.

[9]   Control construction, copy, move, and destruction of objects; §3.3.

[10] Return containers by value (relying on move for efficiency); §3.3.2.

[11] Provide strong resource safety; that is, never leak anything that you think of as a resource; §3.3.3.

[12] Use containers, defined as resource handle templates, to hold collections of values of the same type; §3.4.1.

[13] Use function templates to represent general algorithms; §3.4.2.

[14] Use function objects, including lambdas, to represent policies and actions; §3.4.3.

[15] Use type and template aliases to provide a uniform notation for types that may vary among similar types or among implementations; §3.4.5.

A Tour of C++: Containers and Algorithms

*Why waste time learning
when ignorance is instantaneous?*
– Hobbes

4.1 Libraries

No significant program is written in just a bare programming language. First, a set of libraries is developed. These then form the basis for further work. Most programs are tedious to write in the bare language, whereas just about any task can be rendered simple by the use of good libraries.

Continuing from Chapters 2 and 3, this chapter and the next give a quick tour of key standard-library facilities. I assume that you have programmed before. If not, please consider reading a textbook, such as *Programming: Principles and Practice Using C++* [Stroustrup,2009], before continuing. Even if you have programmed before, the libraries you used or the applications you wrote may be very different from the style of C++ presented here. If you find this "lightning tour" confusing, you might skip to the more systematic and bottom-up language presentation starting in Chapter 6. Similarly, a more systematic description of the standard library starts in Chapter 30.

I very briefly present useful standard-library types, such as **string**, **ostream**, **vector**, **map** (this chapter), **unique_ptr**, **thread**, **regex**, and **complex** (Chapter 5), as well as the most common ways of using them. Doing this allows me to give better examples in the following chapters. As in Chapter 2 and Chapter 3, you are strongly encouraged not to be distracted or discouraged by an incomplete understanding of details. The purpose of this chapter is to give you a taste of what is to come and to convey a basic understanding of the most useful library facilities.

The specification of the standard library is almost two thirds of the ISO C++ standard. Explore it, and prefer it to home-made alternatives. Much though have gone into its design, more still into its implementations, and much effort will go into its maintenance and extension.

The standard-library facilities described in this book are part of every complete C++ implementation. In addition to the standard-library components, most implementations offer "graphical user interface" systems (GUIs), Web interfaces, database interfaces, etc. Similarly, most application development environments provide "foundation libraries" for corporate or industrial "standard" development and/or execution environments. Here, I do not describe such systems and libraries. The intent is to provide a self-contained description of C++ as defined by the standard and to keep the examples portable, except where specifically noted. Naturally, a programmer is encouraged to explore the more extensive facilities available on most systems.

4.1.1 Standard-Library Overview

The facilities provided by the standard library can be classified like this:

- Run-time language support (e.g., for allocation and run-time type information); see §30.3.
- The C standard library (with very minor modifications to minimize violations of the type system); see Chapter 43.
- Strings and I/O streams (with support for international character sets and localization); see Chapter 36, Chapter 38, and Chapter 39. I/O streams is an extensible framework to which users can add their own streams, buffering strategies, and character sets.
- A framework of containers (such as **vector** and **map**) and algorithms (such as **find()**, **sort()**, and **merge()**); see §4.4, §4.5, Chapters 31-33. This framework, conventionally called the STL [Stepanov,1994], is extensible so users can add their own containers and algorithms.
- Support for numerical computation (such as standard mathematical functions, complex numbers, vectors with arithmetic operations, and random number generators); see §3.2.1.1 and Chapter 40.
- Support for regular expression matching; see §5.5 and Chapter 37.
- Support for concurrent programming, including **threads** and **locks**; see §5.3 and Chapter 41. The concurrency support is foundational so that users can add support for new models of concurrency as libraries.
- Utilities to support template metaprogramming (e.g., type traits; §5.4.2, §28.2.4, §35.4), STL-style generic programming (e.g., **pair**; §5.4.3, §34.2.4.1), and general programming (e.g., **clock**; §5.4.1, §35.2).
- "Smart pointers" for resource management (e.g., **unique_ptr** and **shared_ptr**; §5.2.1, §34.3) and an interface to garbage collectors (§34.5).
- Special-purpose containers, such as **array** (§34.2.1), **bitset** (§34.2.2), and **tuple** (§34.2.4.2).

The main criteria for including a class in the library were that:
- it could be helpful to almost every C++ programmer (both novices and experts),
- it could be provided in a general form that did not add significant overhead compared to a simpler version of the same facility, and
- that simple uses should be easy to learn (relative to the inherent complexity of their task).

Essentially, the C++ standard library provides the most common fundamental data structures together with the fundamental algorithms used on them.

4.1.2 The Standard-library Headers and Namespace

Every standard-library facility is provided through some standard header. For example:

```
#include<string>
#include<list>
```

This makes the standard `string` and `list` available.

The standard library is defined in a namespace (§2.4.2, §14.3.1) called `std`. To use standard library facilities, the `std::` prefix can be used:

```
std::string s {"Four legs Good; two legs Baaad!"};
std::list<std::string> slogans {"War is peace", "Freedom is Slavery", "Ignorance is Strength"};
```

For simplicity, I will rarely use the `std::` prefix explicitly in examples. Neither will I always `#include` the necessary headers explicitly. To compile and run the program fragments here, you must `#include` the appropriate headers (as listed in §4.4.5, §4.5.5, and §30.2) and make the names they declare accessible. For example:

```
#include<string>        // make the standard string facilities accessible
using namespace std;     // make std names available without std:: prefix

string s {"C++ is a general–purpose programming language"};    // OK: string is std::string
```

It is generally in poor taste to dump every name from a namespace into the global namespace. However, in this book, I use the standard library almost exclusively and it is good to know what it offers. So, I don't prefix every use of a standard library name with `std::`. Nor do I `#include` the appropriate headers in every example. Assume that done.

Here is a selection of standard-library headers, all supplying declarations in namespace `std`:

Selected Standard Library Headers (continues)			
`<algorithm>`	copy(), find(), sort()	§32.2	§iso.25
`<array>`	array	§34.2.1	§iso.23.3.2
`<chrono>`	duration, time_point	§35.2	§iso.20.11.2
`<cmath>`	sqrt(), pow()	§40.3	§iso.26.8
`<complex>`	complex, sqrt(), pow()	§40.4	§iso.26.8
`<fstream>`	fstream, ifstream, ofstream	§38.2.1	§iso.27.9.1
`<future>`	future, promise	§5.3.5	§iso.30.6
`<iostream>`	istream, ostream, cin, cout	§38.1	§iso.27.4

Selected Standard Library Headers (continued)			
<map>	map, multimap	§31.4.3	§iso.23.4.4
<memory>	unique_ptr, shared_ptr, allocator	§5.2.1	§iso.20.6
<random>	default_random_engine, normal_distribution	§40.7	§iso.26.5
<regex>	regex, smatch	Chapter 37	§iso.28.8
<string>	string, basic_string	Chapter 36	§iso.21.3
<set>	set, multiset	§31.4.3	§iso.23.4.6
<sstream>	istrstream, ostrstream	§38.2.2	§iso.27.8
<thread>	thread	§5.3.1	§iso.30.3
<unordered_map>	unordered_map, unordered_multimap	§31.4.3.2	§iso.23.5.4
<utility>	move(), swap(), pair	§35.5	§iso.20.1
<vector>	vector	§31.4	§iso.23.3.6

This listing is far from complete; see §30.2 for more information.

4.2 Strings

The standard library provides a **string** type to complement the string literals. The **string** type provides a variety of useful string operations, such as concatenation. For example:

```
string compose(const string& name, const string& domain)
{
    return name + '@' + domain;
}

auto addr = compose("dmr","bell-labs.com");
```

Here, **addr** is initialized to the character sequence **dmr@bell-labs.com**. "Addition" of strings means concatenation. You can concatenate a **string**, a string literal, a C-style string, or a character to a **string**. The standard **string** has a move constructor so returning even long **strings** by value is efficient (§3.3.2).

In many applications, the most common form of concatenation is adding something to the end of a **string**. This is directly supported by the += operation. For example:

```
void m2(string& s1, string& s2)
{
    s1 = s1 + '\n';    // append newline
    s2 += '\n';        // append newline
}
```

The two ways of adding to the end of a **string** are semantically equivalent, but I prefer the latter because it is more explicit about what it does, more concise, and possibly more efficient.

A **string** is mutable. In addition to = and +=, subscripting (using []) and substring operations are supported. The standard-library **string** is described in Chapter 36. Among other useful features, it provides the ability to manipulate substrings. For example:

```
string name = "Niels Stroustrup";

void m3()
{
    string s = name.substr(6,10);        // s = "Stroustrup"
    name.replace(0,5,"nicholas");        // name becomes "nicholas Stroustrup"
    name[0] = toupper(name[0]);          // name becomes "Nicholas Stroustrup"
}
```

The **substr()** operation returns a **string** that is a copy of the substring indicated by its arguments. The first argument is an index into the **string** (a position), and the second is the length of the desired substring. Since indexing starts from 0, s gets the value **Stroustrup**.

The **replace()** operation replaces a substring with a value. In this case, the substring starting at 0 with length 5 is **Niels**; it is replaced by **nicholas**. Finally, I replace the initial character with its uppercase equivalent. Thus, the final value of **name** is **Nicholas Stroustrup**. Note that the replacement string need not be the same size as the substring that it is replacing.

Naturally, **strings** can be compared against each other and against string literals. For example:

```
string incantation;

void respond(const string& answer)
{
    if (answer == incantation) {
        // perform magic
    }
    else if (answer == "yes") {
        // ...
    }
    // ...
}
```

The **string** library is described in Chapter 36. The most common techniques for implementing **string** are presented in the **String** example (§19.3).

4.3 Stream I/O

The standard library provides formatted character input and output through the **iostream** library. The input operations are typed and extensible to handle user-defined types. This section is a very brief introduction to the use of **iostreams**; Chapter 38 is a reasonably complete description of the **iostream** library facilities.

Other forms of user interaction, such as graphical I/O, are handled through libraries that are not part of the ISO standard and therefore not described here.

4.3.1 Output

The I/O stream library defines output for every built-in type. Further, it is easy to define output of a user-defined type (§4.3.3). The operator << ("put to") is used as an output operator on objects of type **ostream**; **cout** is the standard output stream and **cerr** is the standard stream for reporting errors. By default, values written to **cout** are converted to a sequence of characters. For example, to output the decimal number **10**, we can write:

```
void f()
{
    cout << 10;
}
```

This places the character **1** followed by the character **0** on the standard output stream.

Equivalently, we could write:

```
void g()
{
    int i {10};
    cout << i;
}
```

Output of different types can be combined in the obvious way:

```
void h(int i)
{
    cout << "the value of i is ";
    cout << i;
    cout << '\n';
}
```

For **h(10)**, the output will be:

the value of i is 10

People soon tire of repeating the name of the output stream when outputting several related items. Fortunately, the result of an output expression can itself be used for further output. For example:

```
void h2(int i)
{
    cout << "the value of i is " << i << '\n';
}
```

This **h2()** produces the same output as **h()**.

A character constant is a character enclosed in single quotes. Note that a character is output as a character rather than as a numerical value. For example:

```
void k()
{
    int b = 'b';        // note: char implicitly converted to int
    char c = 'c';
    cout << 'a' << b << c;
}
```

The integer value of the character **'b'** is **98** (in the ASCII encoding used on the C++ implementation that I used), so this will output **a98c**.

4.3.2 Input

The standard library offers **istreams** for input. Like **ostreams**, **istreams** deal with character string representations of built-in types and can easily be extended to cope with user-defined types.

The operator **>>** ("get from") is used as an input operator; **cin** is the standard input stream. The type of the right-hand operand of **>>** determines what input is accepted and what is the target of the input operation. For example:

```
void f()
{
    int i;
    cin >> i;        // read an integer into i

    double d;
    cin >> d;        // read a double-precision floating-point number into d
}
```

This reads a number, such as **1234**, from the standard input into the integer variable **i** and a floating-point number, such as **12.34e5**, into the double-precision floating-point variable **d**.

Often, we want to read a sequence of characters. A convenient way of doing that is to read into a **string**. For example:

```
void hello()
{
    cout << "Please enter your name\n";
    string str;
    cin >> str;
    cout << "Hello, " << str << "!\n";
}
```

If you type in **Eric** the response is:

    Hello, Eric!

By default, a whitespace character (§7.3.2), such as a space, terminates the read, so if you enter **Eric Bloodaxe** pretending to be the ill-fated king of York, the response is still:

    Hello, Eric!

You can read a whole line (including the terminating newline character) using the **getline()** function. For example:

```
void hello_line()
{
    cout << "Please enter your name\n";
    string str;
    getline(cin,str);
    cout << "Hello, " << str << "!\n";
}
```

With this program, the input **Eric Bloodaxe** yields the desired output:

    Hello, Eric Bloodaxe!

The newline that terminated the line is discarded, so cin is ready for the next input line.

The standard strings have the nice property of expanding to hold what you put in them; you don't have to precalculate a maximum size. So, if you enter a couple of megabytes of semicolons, the program will echo pages of semicolons back at you.

4.3.3 I/O of User-Defined Types

In addition to the I/O of built-in types and standard strings, the iostream library allows programmers to define I/O for their own types. For example, consider a simple type Entry that we might use to represent entries in a telephone book:

```
struct Entry {
    string name;
    int number;
};
```

We can define a simple output operator to write an Entry using a {"name",number} format similar to the one we use for initialization in code:

```
ostream& operator<<(ostream& os, const Entry& e)
{
    return os << "{\"" << e.name << "\", " << e.number << "}";
}
```

A user-defined output operator takes its output stream (by reference) as its first argument and returns it as its result. See §38.4.2 for details.

The corresponding input operator is more complicated because it has to check for correct formatting and deal with errors:

```
istream& operator>>(istream& is, Entry& e)
    // read { "name" , number } pair. Note: formatted with { " " , and }
{
    char c, c2;
    if (is>>c && c=='{' && is>>c2 && c2=='"') { // start with a { "
        string name;                    // the default value of a string is the empty string: ""
        while (is.get(c) && c!='"')     // anything before a " is part of the name
            name+=c;

        if (is>>c && c==',') {
            int number = 0;
            if (is>>number>>c && c=='}') { // read the number and a }
                e = {name,number};      // assign to the entry
                return is;
            }
        }
    }
    is.setf(ios_base::failbit);          // register the failure in the stream
    return is;
}
```

An input operation returns a reference to its istream which can be used to test if the operation succeeded. For example, when used as a condition, is>>c means "Did we succeed at reading from is into c?"

The is>>c skips whitespace by default, but is.get(c) does not, so that this Entry-input operator ignores (skips) whitespace outside the name string, but not within it. For example:

```
{ "John Marwood Cleese" , 123456        }
{"Michael Edward Palin",987654}
```

We can read such a pair of values from input into an Entry like this:

```
for (Entry ee; cin>>ee; )   // read from cin into ee
      cout << ee << '\n';    // write ee to cout
```

The output is:

```
{"John Marwood Cleese", 123456}
{"Michael Edward Palin", 987654}
```

See §38.4.1 for more technical details and techniques for writing input operators for user-defined types. See §5.5 and Chapter 37 for a more systematic technique for recognizing patterns in streams of characters (regular expression matching).

4.4 Containers

Most computing involves creating collections of values and then manipulating such collections. Reading characters into a string and printing out the string is a simple example. A class with the main purpose of holding objects is commonly called a *container*. Providing suitable containers for a given task and supporting them with useful fundamental operations are important steps in the construction of any program.

To illustrate the standard-library containers, consider a simple program for keeping names and telephone numbers. This is the kind of program for which different approaches appear "simple and obvious" to people of different backgrounds. The Entry class from §4.3.3 can be used to hold a simple phone book entry. Here, we deliberately ignore many real-world complexities, such as the fact that many phone numbers do not have a simple representation as a 32-bit int.

4.4.1 vector

The most useful standard-library container is vector. A vector is a sequence of elements of a given type. The elements are stored contiguously in memory:

The Vector examples in §3.2.2 and §3.4 give an idea of the implementation of vector and §13.6 and §31.4 provide an exhaustive discussion.

We can initialize a vector with a set of values of its element type:

```
vector<Entry> phone_book = {
    {"David Hume",123456},
    {"Karl Popper",234567},
    {"Bertrand Arthur William Russell",345678}
};
```

Elements can be accessed through subscripting:

```
void print_book(const vector<Entry>& book)
{
    for (int i = 0; i!=book.size(); ++i)
        cout << book[i] << '\n';
}
```

As usual, indexing starts at 0 so that book[0] holds the entry for David Hume. The vector member function size() gives the number of elements.

The elements of a vector constitute a range, so we can use a range-for loop (§2.2.5):

```
void print_book(const vector<Entry>& book)
{
    for (const auto& x : book)        // for "auto" see §2.2.2
        cout << x << '\n';
}
```

When we define a vector, we give it an initial size (initial number of elements):

```
vector<int> v1 = {1, 2, 3, 4};       // size is 4
vector<string> v2;                   // size is 0
vector<Shape*> v3(23);               // size is 23; initial element value: nullptr
vector<double> v4(32,9.9);           // size is 32; initial element value: 9.9
```

An explicit size is enclosed in ordinary parentheses, for example, (23), and by default the elements are initialized to the element type's default value (e.g., nullptr for pointers and 0 for numbers). If you don't want the default value, you can specify one as a second argument (e.g., 9.9 for the 32 elements of v4).

The initial size can be changed. One of the most useful operations on a vector is push_back(), which adds a new element at the end of a vector, increasing its size by one. For example:

```
void input()
{
    for (Entry e; cin>>e;)
        phone_book.push_back(e);
}
```

This reads Entrys from the standard input into phone_book until either the end-of-input (e.g., the end of a file) is reached or the input operation encounters a format error. The standard-library vector is implemented so that growing a vector by repeated push_back()s is efficient.

A vector can be copied in assignments and initializations. For example:

```
vector<Entry> book2 = phone_book;
```

Copying and moving of **vector**s are implemented by constructors and assignment operators as described in §3.3. Assigning a **vector** involves copying its elements. Thus, after the initialization of **book2**, **book2** and **phone_book** hold separate copies of every **Entry** in the phone book. When a **vector** holds many elements, such innocent-looking assignments and initializations can be expensive. Where copying is undesirable, references or pointers (§7.2, §7.7) or move operations (§3.3.2, §17.5.2) should be used.

4.4.1.1 Elements

Like all standard-library containers, **vector** is a container of elements of some type **T**, that is, a **vector<T>**. Just about any type qualifies as an element type: built-in numeric types (such as **char**, **int**, and **double**), user-defined types (such as **string**, **Entry**, **list<int>**, and **Matrix<double,2>**), and pointers (such as **const char∗**, **Shape∗**, and **double∗**). When you insert a new element, its value is copied into the container. For example, when you put an integer with the value **7** into a container, the resulting element really has the value **7**. The element is not a reference or a pointer to some object containing **7**. This makes for nice compact containers with fast access. For people who care about memory sizes and run-time performance this is critical.

4.4.1.2 Range Checking

The standard-library **vector** does not guarantee range checking (§31.2.2). For example:

```
void silly(vector<Entry>& book)
{
    int i = book[ph.size()].number;        // book.size() is out of range
    // ...
}
```

That initialization is likely to place some random value in **i** rather than giving an error. This is undesirable, and out-of-range errors are a common problem. Consequently, I often use a simple range-checking adaptation of **vector**:

```
template<typename T>
class Vec : public std::vector<T> {
public:
    using vector<T>::vector;  // use the constructors from vector (under the name Vec); see §20.3.5.1

    T& operator[](int i)                   // range check
        { return vector<T>::at(i); }

    const T& operator[](int i) const       // range check const objects; §3.2.1.1
        { return vector<T>::at(i); }
};
```

Vec inherits everything from **vector** except for the subscript operations that it redefines to do range checking. The **at()** operation is a **vector** subscript operation that throws an exception of type **out_of_range** if its argument is out of the **vector**'s range (§2.4.3.1, §31.2.2).

For **Vec**, an out-of-range access will throw an exception that the user can catch. For example:

```
void checked(Vec<Entry>& book)
{
    try {
        book[book.size()] = {"Joe",999999};        // will throw an exception
        // ...
    }
    catch (out_of_range) {
        cout << "range error\n";
    }
}
```

The exception will be thrown, and then caught (§2.4.3.1, Chapter 13). If the user doesn't catch an exception, the program will terminate in a well-defined manner rather than proceeding or failing in an undefined manner. One way to minimize surprises from uncaught exceptions is to use a **main()** with a **try**-block as its body. For example:

```
int main()
try {
    // your code
}
catch (out_of_range) {
    cerr << "range error\n";
}
catch (...) {
    cerr << "unknown exception thrown\n";
}
```

This provides default exception handlers so that if we fail to catch some exception, an error message is printed on the standard error-diagnostic output stream **cerr** (§38.1).

Some implementations save you the bother of defining **Vec** (or equivalent) by providing a range-checked version of **vector** (e.g., as a compiler option).

4.4.2 list

The standard library offers a doubly-linked list called **list**:

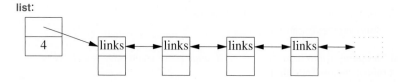

We use a **list** for sequences where we want to insert and delete elements without moving other elements. Insertion and deletion of phone book entries could be common, so a **list** could be appropriate for representing a simple phone book. For example:

```
list<Entry> phone_book = {
    {"David Hume",123456},
```

        {"Karl Popper",234567},
        {"Bertrand Arthur William Russell",345678}
    };

When we use a linked list, we tend not to access elements using subscripting the way we commonly do for vectors. Instead, we might search the list looking for an element with a given value. To do this, we take advantage of the fact that a **list** is a sequence as described in §4.5:

```
int get_number(const string& s)
{
    for (const auto& x : phone_book)
        if (x.name==s)
            return x.number;
    return 0;  // use 0 to represent "number not found"
}
```

The search for **s** starts at the beginning of the list and proceeds until **s** is found or the end of **phone_book** is reached.

Sometimes, we need to identify an element in a **list**. For example, we may want to delete it or insert a new entry before it. To do that we use an *iterator*: a **list** iterator identifies an element of a **list** and can be used to iterate through a **list** (hence its name). Every standard-library container provides the functions **begin()** and **end()**, which return an iterator to the first and to one-past-the-last element, respectively (§4.5, §33.1.1). Using iterators explicitly, we can – less elegantly – write the **get_number()** function like this:

```
int get_number(const string& s)
{
    for (auto p = phone_book.begin(); p!=phone_book.end(); ++p)
        if (p–>name==s)
            return p–>number;
    return 0;  // use 0 to represent "number not found"
}
```

In fact, this is roughly the way the terser and less error-prone range-**for** loop is implemented by the compiler. Given an iterator **p**, ∗**p** is the element to which it refers, ++**p** advances **p** to refer to the next element, and when **p** refers to a class with a member **m**, then **p–>m** is equivalent to (∗**p**).m.

Adding elements to a **list** and removing elements from a **list** is easy:

```
void f(const Entry& ee, list<Entry>::iterator p, list<Entry>::iterator q)
{
    phone_book.insert(p,ee);   // add ee before the element referred to by p
    phone_book.erase(q);       // remove the element referred to by q
}
```

For a more complete description of **insert()** and **erase()**, see §31.3.7.

These **list** examples could be written identically using **vector** and (surprisingly, unless you understand machine architecture) perform better with a small **vector** than with a small **list**. When all we want is a sequence of elements, we have a choice between using a **vector** and a **list**. Unless you have a reason not to, use a **vector**. A **vector** performs better for traversal (e.g., **find()** and **count()**) and for sorting and searching (e.g., **sort()** and **binary_search()**).

4.4.3 map

Writing code to look up a name in a list of *(name,number)* pairs is quite tedious. In addition, a linear search is inefficient for all but the shortest lists. The standard library offers a search tree (a red-black tree) called map:

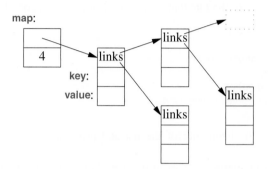

In other contexts, a map is known as an associative array or a dictionary. It is implemented as a balanced binary tree.

The standard-library map (§31.4.3) is a container of pairs of values optimized for lookup. We can use the same initializer as for vector and list (§4.4.1, §4.4.2):

```
map<string,int> phone_book {
    {"David Hume",123456},
    {"Karl Popper",234567},
    {"Bertrand Arthur William Russell",345678}
};
```

When indexed by a value of its first type (called the *key*), a map returns the corresponding value of the second type (called the *value* or the *mapped type*). For example:

```
int get_number(const string& s)
{
    return phone_book[s];
}
```

In other words, subscripting a map is essentially the lookup we called get_number(). If a key isn't found, it is entered into the map with a default value for its value. The default value for an integer type is 0; the value I just happened to choose represents an invalid telephone number.

If we wanted to avoid entering invalid numbers into our phone book, we could use find() and insert() instead of [] (§31.4.3.1).

4.4.4 unordered_map

The cost of a map lookup is O(log(n)) where n is the number of elements in the map. That's pretty good. For example, for a map with 1,000,000 elements, we perform only about 20 comparisons and indirections to find an element. However, in many cases, we can do better by using a hashed lookup rather than comparison using an ordering function, such as <. The standard-library hashed containers are referred to as "unordered" because they don't require an ordering function:

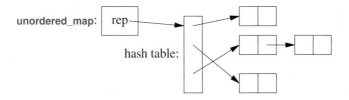

For example, we can use an unordered_map from <unordered_map> for our phone book:

```
unordered_map<string,int> phone_book {
    {"David Hume",123456},
    {"Karl Popper",234567},
    {"Bertrand Arthur William Russell",345678}
};
```

As for a map, we can subscript an unordered_map:

```
int get_number(const string& s)
{
    return phone_book[s];
}
```

The standard-library unordered_map provides a default hash function for strings. If necessary, you can provide your own (§31.4.3.4).

4.4.5 Container Overview

The standard library provides some of the most general and useful container types to allow the programmer to select a container that best serves the needs of an application:

Standard Container Summary	
vector<T>	A variable-size vector (§31.4)
list<T>	A doubly-linked list (§31.4.2)
forward_list<T>	A singly-linked list (§31.4.2)
deque<T>	A double-ended queue (§31.2)
set<T>	A set (§31.4.3)
multiset<T>	A set in which a value can occur many times (§31.4.3)
map<K,V>	An associative array (§31.4.3)
multimap<K,V>	A map in which a key can occur many times (§31.4.3)
unordered_map<K,V>	A map using a hashed lookup (§31.4.3.2)
unordered_multimap<K,V>	A multimap using a hashed lookup (§31.4.3.2)
unordered_set<T>	A set using a hashed lookup (§31.4.3.2)
unordered_multiset<T>	A multiset using a hashed lookup (§31.4.3.2)

The unordered containers are optimized for lookup with a key (often a string); in other words, they are implemented using hash tables.

The standard containers are described in §31.4. The containers are defined in namespace std and presented in headers <vector>, <list>, <map>, etc. (§4.1.2, §30.2). In addition, the standard library provides container adaptors queue<T> (§31.5.2), stack<T> (§31.5.1), deque<T> (§31.4), and priority_queue<T> (§31.5.3). The standard library also provides more specialized container-like types, such as a fixed-size array array<T,N> (§34.2.1) and bitset<N> (§34.2.2).

The standard containers and their basic operations are designed to be similar from a notational point of view. Furthermore, the meanings of the operations are equivalent for the various containers. Basic operations apply to every kind of container for which they make sense and can be efficiently implemented. For example:

- begin() and end() give iterators to the first and one-beyond-the-last elements, respectively.
- push_back() can be used (efficiently) to add elements to the end of a vector, forward_list, list, and other containers.
- size() returns the number of elements.

This notational and semantic uniformity enables programmers to provide new container types that can be used in a very similar manner to the standard ones. The range-checked vector, Vector (§2.3.2, §2.4.3.1), is an example of that. The uniformity of container interfaces also allows us to specify algorithms independently of individual container types. However, each has strengths and weaknesses. For example, subscripting and traversing a vector is cheap and easy. On the other hand, vector elements are moved when we insert or remove elements; list has exactly the opposite properties. Please note that a vector is usually more efficient than a list for short sequences of small elements (even for insert() and erase()). I recommend the standard-library vector as the default type for sequences of elements: you need a reason to choose another.

4.5 Algorithms

A data structure, such as a list or a vector, is not very useful on its own. To use one, we need operations for basic access such as adding and removing elements (as is provided for list and vector). Furthermore, we rarely just store objects in a container. We sort them, print them, extract subsets, remove elements, search for objects, etc. Consequently, the standard library provides the most common algorithms for containers in addition to providing the most common container types. For example, the following sorts a vector and places a copy of each unique vector element on a list:

```
bool operator<(const Entry& x, const Entry& y)    // less than
{
    return x.name<y.name;        // order Entrys by their names
}

void f(vector<Entry>& vec, list<Entry>& lst)
{
    sort(vec.begin(),vec.end());                        // use < for order
    unique_copy(vec.begin(),vec.end(),lst.begin());     // don't copy adjacent equal elements
}
```

The standard algorithms are described in Chapter 32. They are expressed in terms of sequences of elements. A *sequence* is represented by a pair of iterators specifying the first element and the one-beyond-the-last element:

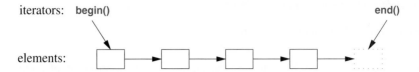

In the example, **sort()** sorts the sequence defined by the pair of iterators **vec.begin()** and **vec.end()** – which just happens to be all the elements of a **vector**. For writing (output), you need only to specify the first element to be written. If more than one element is written, the elements following that initial element will be overwritten. Thus, to avoid errors, **lst** must have at least as many elements as there are unique values in **vec**.

If we wanted to place the unique elements in a new container, we could have written:

```
list<Entry> f(vector<Entry>& vec)
{
    list<Entry> res;
    sort(vec.begin(),vec.end());
    unique_copy(vec.begin(),vec.end(),back_inserter(res)); // append to res
    return res;
}
```

A **back_inserter()** adds elements at the end of a container, extending the container to make room for them (§33.2.2). Thus, the standard containers plus **back_inserter()**s eliminate the need to use error-prone, explicit C-style memory management using **realloc()** (§31.5.1). The standard-library **list** has a move constructor (§3.3.2, §17.5.2) that makes returning **res** by value efficient (even for **list**s of thousands of elements).

If you find the pair-of-iterators style of code, such as **sort(vec.begin(),vec.end())**, tedious, you can define container versions of the algorithms and write **sort(vec)** (§4.5.6).

4.5.1 Use of Iterators

When you first encounter a container, a few iterators referring to useful elements can be obtained; **begin()** and **end()** are the best examples of this. In addition, many algorithms return iterators. For example, the standard algorithm **find** looks for a value in a sequence and returns an iterator to the element found:

```
bool has_c(const string& s, char c)      // does s contain the character c?
{
    auto p = find(s.begin(),s.end(),c);
    if (p!=s.end())
        return true;
    else
        return false;
}
```

Like many standard-library search algorithms, **find** returns **end()** to indicate "not found." An equivalent, shorter, definition of **has_c()** is:

```
bool has_c(const string& s, char c)        // does s contain the character c?
{
      return find(s.begin(),s.end(),c)!=s.end();
}
```

A more interesting exercise would be to find the location of all occurrences of a character in a string. We can return the set of occurrences as a **vector** of **string** iterators. Returning a **vector** is efficient because of **vector** provides move semantics (§3.3.1). Assuming that we would like to modify the locations found, we pass a non-**const** string:

```
vector<string::iterator> find_all(string& s, char c)        // find all occurrences of c in s
{
      vector<string::iterator> res;
      for (auto p = s.begin(); p!=s.end(); ++p)
            if (*p==c)
                  res.push_back(p);
      return res;
}
```

We iterate through the string using a conventional loop, moving the iterator **p** forward one element at a time using **++** and looking at the elements using the dereference operator *∗*. We could test find_all() like this:

```
void test()
{
      string m {"Mary had a little lamb"};
      for (auto p : find_all(m,'a'))
            if (*p!='a')
                  cerr << "a bug!\n";
}
```

That call of find_all() could be graphically represented like this:

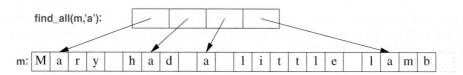

Iterators and standard algorithms work equivalently on every standard container for which their use makes sense. Consequently, we could generalize find_all():

```
template<typename C, typename V>
vector<typename C::iterator> find_all(C& c, V v)        // find all occurrences of v in c
{
      vector<typename C::iterator> res;
      for (auto p = c.begin(); p!=c.end(); ++p)
            if (*p==v)
                  res.push_back(p);
      return res;
}
```

The **typename** is needed to inform the compiler that **C**'s **iterator** is supposed to be a type and not a value of some type, say, the integer **7**. We can hide this implementation detail by introducing a type alias (§3.4.5) for **Iterator**:

```
template<typename T>
using Iterator<T> = typename T::iterator;

template<typename C, typename V>
vector<Iterator<C>> find_all(C& c, V v)          // find all occurrences of v in c
{
     vector<Iterator<C>> res;
     for (auto p = c.begin(); p!=c.end(); ++p)
          if (*p==v)
               res.push_back(p);
     return res;
}
```

We can now write:

```
void test()
{
     string m {"Mary had a little lamb"};
     for (auto p : find_all(m,'a'))          // p is a string::iterator
          if (*p!='a')
               cerr << "string bug!\n";

     list<double> ld {1.1, 2.2, 3.3, 1.1};
     for (auto p : find_all(ld,1.1))
          if (*p!=1.1)
               cerr << "list bug!\n";

     vector<string> vs { "red", "blue", "green", "green", "orange", "green" };
     for (auto p : find_all(vs,"green"))
          if (*p!="green")
               cerr << "vector bug!\n";

     for (auto p : find_all(vs,"green"))
          *p = "vert";
}
```

Iterators are used to separate algorithms and containers. An algorithm operates on its data through iterators and knows nothing about the container in which the elements are stored. Conversely, a container knows nothing about the algorithms operating on its elements; all it does is to supply iterators upon request (e.g., **begin()** and **end()**). This model of separation between data storage and algorithm delivers very general and flexible software.

4.5.2 Iterator Types

What are iterators really? Any particular iterator is an object of some type. There are, however, many different iterator types, because an iterator needs to hold the information necessary for doing its job for a particular container type. These iterator types can be as different as the containers and the specialized needs they serve. For example, a **vector**'s iterator could be an ordinary pointer, because a pointer is quite a reasonable way of referring to an element of a **vector**:

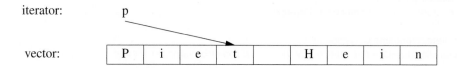

Alternatively, a **vector** iterator could be implemented as a pointer to the **vector** plus an index:

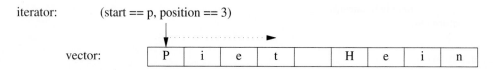

Using such an iterator would allow range checking.

A **list** iterator must be something more complicated than a simple pointer to an element because an element of a **list** in general does not know where the next element of that **list** is. Thus, a **list** iterator might be a pointer to a link:

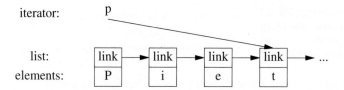

What is common for all iterators is their semantics and the naming of their operations. For example, applying ++ to any iterator yields an iterator that refers to the next element. Similarly, * yields the element to which the iterator refers. In fact, any object that obeys a few simple rules like these is an iterator (§33.1.4). Furthermore, users rarely need to know the type of a specific iterator; each container "knows" its iterator types and makes them available under the conventional names **iterator** and **const_iterator**. For example, **list<Entry>::iterator** is the general iterator type for **list<Entry>**. We rarely have to worry about the details of how that type is defined.

4.5.3 Stream Iterators

Iterators are a general and useful concept for dealing with sequences of elements in containers. However, containers are not the only place where we find sequences of elements. For example, an input stream produces a sequence of values, and we write a sequence of values to an output stream. Consequently, the notion of iterators can be usefully applied to input and output.

To make an **ostream_iterator**, we need to specify which stream will be used and the type of objects written to it. For example:

```
ostream_iterator<string> oo {cout};      // write strings to cout
```

The effect of assigning to *oo is to write the assigned value to **cout**. For example:

```
int main()
{
    *oo = "Hello, ";      // meaning cout<<"Hello, "
    ++oo;
    *oo = "world!\n";     // meaning cout<<"world!\n"
}
```

This is yet another way of writing the canonical message to standard output. The **++oo** is done to mimic writing into an array through a pointer.

Similarly, an **istream_iterator** is something that allows us to treat an input stream as a read-only container. Again, we must specify the stream to be used and the type of values expected:

```
istream_iterator<string> ii {cin};
```

Input iterators are used in pairs representing a sequence, so we must provide an **istream_iterator** to indicate the end of input. This is the default **istream_iterator**:

```
istream_iterator<string> eos {};
```

Typically, **istream_iterator**s and **ostream_iterator**s are not used directly. Instead, they are provided as arguments to algorithms. For example, we can write a simple program to read a file, sort the words read, eliminate duplicates, and write the result to another file:

```
int main()
{
    string from, to;
    cin >> from >> to;                          // get source and target file names

    ifstream is {from};                         // input stream for file "from"
    istream_iterator<string> ii {is};           // input iterator for stream
    istream_iterator<string> eos {};            // input sentinel

    ofstream os{to};                            // output stream for file "to"
    ostream_iterator<string> oo {os,"\n"};      // output iterator for stream

    vector<string> b {ii,eos};                  // b is a vector initialized from input [ii:eos)
    sort(b.begin(),b.end());                    // sort the buffer

    unique_copy(b.begin(),b.end(),oo);          // copy buffer to output, discard replicated values

    return !is.eof() || !os;                    // return error state (§2.2.1, §38.3)
}
```

An **ifstream** is an **istream** that can be attached to a file, and an **ofstream** is an **ostream** that can be attached to a file. The **ostream_iterator**'s second argument is used to delimit output values.

Actually, this program is longer than it needs to be. We read the strings into a **vector**, then we **sort()** them, and then we write them out, eliminating duplicates. A more elegant solution is not to store duplicates at all. This can be done by keeping the **string**s in a **set**, which does not keep duplicates and keeps its elements in order (§31.4.3). That way, we could replace the two lines using a **vector** with one using a **set** and replace **unique_copy()** with the simpler **copy()**:

```
set<string> b {ii,eos};              // collect strings from input
copy(b.begin(),b.end(),oo);          // copy buffer to output
```

We used the names **ii**, **eos**, and **oo** only once, so we could further reduce the size of the program:

```
int main()
{
    string from, to;
    cin >> from >> to;               // get source and target file names

    ifstream is {from};              // input stream for file "from"
    ofstream os {to};                // output stream for file "to"

    set<string> b {istream_iterator<string>{is},istream_iterator<string>{}}; // read input
    copy(b.begin(),b.end(),ostream_iterator<string>{os,"\n"});           // copy to output

    return !is.eof() || !os;         // return error state (§2.2.1, §38.3)
}
```

It is a matter of taste and experience whether or not this last simplification improves readability.

4.5.4 Predicates

In the examples above, the algorithms have simply "built in" the action to be done for each element of a sequence. However, we often want to make that action a parameter to the algorithm. For example, the **find** algorithm (§32.4) provides a convenient way of looking for a specific value. A more general variant looks for an element that fulfills a specified requirement, a *predicate* (§3.4.2). For example, we might want to search a **map** for the first value larger than **42**. A **map** allows us to access its elements as a sequence of *(key,value)* pairs, so we can search a **map<string,int>**'s sequence for a **pair<const string,int>** where the **int** is greater than **42**:

```
void f(map<string,int>& m)
{
    auto p = find_if(m.begin(),m.end(),Greater_than{42});
    // ...
}
```

Here, **Greater_than** is a function object (§3.4.3) holding the value (**42**) to be compared against:

```
struct Greater_than {
    int val;
    Greater_than(int v) : val{v} { }
    bool operator()(const pair<string,int>& r) { return r.second>val; }
};
```

Alternatively, we could use a lambda expression (§3.4.3):

```
int cxx = count_if(m.begin(), m.end(), [](const pair<string,int>& r) { return r.second>42; });
```

4.5.5 Algorithm Overview

A general definition of an algorithm is "a finite set of rules which gives a sequence of operations for solving a specific set of problems [and] has five important features: Finiteness ... Definiteness ... Input ... Output ... Effectiveness" [Knuth,1968,§1.1]. In the context of the C++ standard library, an algorithm is a function template operating on sequences of elements.

The standard library provides dozens of algorithms. The algorithms are defined in namespace **std** and presented in the **<algorithm>** header. These standard-library algorithms all take sequences as inputs (§4.5). A half-open sequence from **b** to **e** is referred to as [**b:e**). Here are a few I have found particularly useful:

Selected Standard Algorithms	
p=find(b,e,x)	p is the first p in [b:e) so that *p==x
p=find_if(b,e,f)	p is the first p in [b:e) so that f(*p)==true
n=count(b,e,x)	n is the number of elements *q in [b:e) so that *q==x
n=count_if(b,e,f)	n is the number of elements *q in [b:e) so that f(*q,x)
replace(b,e,v,v2)	Replace elements *q in [b:e) so that *q==v by v2
replace_if(b,e,f,v2)	Replace elements *q in [b:e) so that f(*q) by v2
p=copy(b,e,out)	Copy [b:e) to [out:p)
p=copy_if(b,e,out,f)	Copy elements *q from [b:e) so that f(*q) to [out:p)
p=unique_copy(b,e,out)	Copy [b:e) to [out:p); don't copy adjacent duplicates
sort(b,e)	Sort elements of [b:e) using < as the sorting criterion
sort(b,e,f)	Sort elements of [b:e) using f as the sorting criterion
(p1,p2)=equal_range(b,e,v)	[p1:p2) is the subsequence of the sorted sequence [b:e) with the value v; basically a binary search for v
p=merge(b,e,b2,e2,out)	Merge two sorted sequences [b:e) and [b2:e2) into [out:p)

These algorithms, and many more (see Chapter 32), can be applied to elements of containers, **strings**, and built-in arrays.

4.5.6 Container Algorithms

A sequence is defined by a pair of iterators [**begin:end**). This is general and flexible, but most often, we apply an algorithm to a sequence that is the contents of a container. For example:

```
sort(v.begin(),v.end());
```

Why don't we just say **sort(v)**? We can easily provide that shorthand:

```
namespace Estd {
    using namespace std;

    template<class C>
    void sort(C& c)
    {
        sort(c.begin(),c.end());
    }
```

```
template<class C, class Pred>
void sort(C& c, Pred p)
{
    sort(c.begin(),c.end(),p);
}

// ...
}
```

I put the container versions of **sort()** (and other algorithms) into their own namespace **Estd** ("extended **std**") to avoid interfering with other programmers' uses of namespace **std**.

4.6 Advice

[1]   Don't reinvent the wheel; use libraries; §4.1.
[2]   When you have a choice, prefer the standard library over other libraries; §4.1.
[3]   Do not think that the standard library is ideal for everything; §4.1.
[4]   Remember to #include the headers for the facilities you use; §4.1.2.
[5]   Remember that standard-library facilities are defined in namespace **std**; §4.1.2.
[6]   Prefer **string**s over C-style strings (a **char**∗; §2.2.5); §4.2, §4.3.2.
[7]   **iostream**s are type sensitive, type-safe, and extensible; §4.3.
[8]   Prefer **vector<T>**, **map<K,T>**, and **unordered_map<K,T>** over **T[]**; §4.4.
[9]   Know your standard containers and their tradeoffs; §4.4.
[10]   Use **vector** as your default container; §4.4.1.
[11]   Prefer compact data structures; §4.4.1.1.
[12]   If in doubt, use a range-checked vector (such as **Vec**); §4.4.1.2.
[13]   Use **push_back()** or **back_inserter()** to add elements to a container; §4.4.1, §4.5.
[14]   Use **push_back()** on a **vector** rather than **realloc()** on an array; §4.5.
[15]   Catch common exceptions in **main()**; §4.4.1.2.
[16]   Know your standard algorithms and prefer them over handwritten loops; §4.5.5.
[17]   If iterator use gets tedious, define container algorithms; §4.5.6.

5

A Tour of C++: Concurrency and Utilities

> *When you wish to instruct,*
> *be brief.*
> *– Cicero*

- Introduction
- Resource Management
    unique_ptr and shared_ptr
- Concurrency
    Tasks and threads; Passing Arguments; Returning Results; Sharing Data; Communicating Tasks
- Small Utility Components
    Time; Type Functions; pair and tuple
- Regular Expressions
- Math
    Mathematical Functions and Algorithms; Complex Numbers; Random Numbers; Vector Arithmetic; Numeric Limits
- Advice

5.1 Introduction

From an end-user's perspective, the ideal standard library would provide components directly supporting essentially every need. For a given application domain, a huge commercial library can come close to that ideal. However, that is not what the C++ standard library is trying to do. A manageable, universally available, library cannot be everything to everybody. Instead, the C++ standard library aims to provide components that are useful to most people in most application areas. That is, it aims to serve the intersection of all needs rather than their union. In addition, support for a few widely important application areas, such as mathematical computation and text manipulation, have crept in.

5.2 Resource Management

One of the key tasks of any nontrivial program is to manage resources. A resource is something
that must be acquired and later (explicitly or implicitly) released. Examples are memory, locks,
sockets, thread handles, and file handles. For a long-running program, failing to release a resource
in a timely manner ("a leak") can cause serious performance degradation and possibly even a miserable crash. Even for short programs, a leak can become an embarrassment, say by a resource
shortage increasing the run time by orders of magnitude.

The standard library components are designed not to leak resources. To do this, they rely on the
basic language support for resource management using constructor/destructor pairs to ensure that a
resource doesn't outlive an object responsible for it. The use of a constructor/destructor pair in
Vector to manage the lifetime of its elements is an example (§3.2.1.2) and all standard-library containers are implemented in similar ways. Importantly, this approach interacts correctly with error
handling using exceptions. For example, the technique is used for the standard-library lock classes:

```
mutex m;  // used to protect access to shared data
// ...
void f()
{
       unique_lock<mutex> lck {m};  // acquire the mutex m
       // ... manipulate shared data ...
}
```

A **thread** will not proceed until **lck**'s constructor has acquired its **mutex, m** (§5.3.4). The corresponding destructor releases the resource. So, in this example, **unique_lock**'s destructor releases the
mutex when the thread of control leaves **f()** (through a return, by "falling off the end of the function," or through an exception throw).

This is an application of the "Resource Acquisition Is Initialization" technique (RAII; §3.2.1.2,
§13.3). This technique is fundamental to the idiomatic handling of resources in C++. Containers
(such as **vector** and **map**), **string**, and **iostream** manage their resources (such as file handles and buffers) similarly.

5.2.1 unique_ptr and shared_ptr

The examples so far take care of objects defined in a scope, releasing the resources they acquire at
the exit from the scope, but what about objects allocated on the free store? In **<memory>**, the standard library provides two "smart pointers" to help manage objects on the free store:

[1]   **unique_ptr** to represent unique ownership (§34.3.1)

[2]   **shared_ptr** to represent shared ownership (§34.3.2)

The most basic use of these "smart pointers" is to prevent memory leaks caused by careless programming. For example:

```
void f(int i, int j)     // X* vs. unique_ptr<X>
{
       X* p = new X;                   // allocate a new X
       unique_ptr<X> sp {new X};       // allocate a new X and give its pointer to unique_ptr
       // ...
```

```
        if (i<99) throw Z{};          // may throw an exception
        if (j<77) return;             // may return "early"
        p->do_something();            // may throw an exception
        sp->do_something();           // may throw an exception
        // ...
        delete p;                     // destroy *p
}
```

Here, we "forgot" to delete **p** if **i<99** or if **j<77**. On the other hand, **unique_ptr** ensures that its object is properly destroyed whichever way we exit **f()** (by throwing an exception, by executing **return**, or by "falling off the end"). Ironically, we could have solved the problem simply by *not* using a pointer and *not* using **new**:

```
void f(int i, int j)       // use a local variable
{
        X x;
        // ...
}
```

Unfortunately, overuse of **new** (and of pointers and references) seems to be an increasing problem.

However, when you really need the semantics of pointers, **unique_ptr** is a very lightweight mechanism with no space or time overhead compared to correct use of a built-in pointer. Its further uses include passing free-store allocated objects in and out of functions:

```
unique_ptr<X> make_X(int i)
        // make an X and immediately give it to a unique_ptr
{
        // ... check i, etc. ...
        return unique_ptr<X>{new X{i}};
}
```

A **unique_ptr** is a handle to an individual object (or an array) in much the same way that a **vector** is a handle to a sequence of objects. Both control the lifetime of other objects (using RAII) and both rely on move semantics to make **return** simple and efficient.

The **shared_ptr** is similar to **unique_ptr** except that **shared_ptr**s are copied rather than moved. The **shared_ptr**s for an object share ownership of an object and that object is destroyed when the last of its **shared_ptr**s is destroyed. For example:

```
void f(shared_ptr<fstream>);
void g(shared_ptr<fstream>);

void user(const string& name, ios_base::openmode mode)
{
        shared_ptr<fstream> fp {new fstream(name,mode)};
        if (!*fp) throw No_file{};   // make sure the file was properly opened

        f(fp);
        g(fp);
        // ...
}
```

Now, the file opened by **fp**'s constructor will be closed by the last function to (explicitly or implicitly) destroy a copy of **fp**. Note that **f()** or **g()** may spawn a task holding a copy of **fp** or in some other way store a copy that outlives **user()**. Thus, **shared_ptr** provides a form of garbage collection that respects the destructor-based resource management of the memory-managed objects. This is neither cost free nor exorbitantly expensive, but does make the lifetime of the shared object hard to predict. Use **shared_ptr** only if you actually need shared ownership.

Given **unique_ptr** and **shared_ptr**, we can implement a complete "no naked **new**" policy (§3.2.1.2) for many programs. However, these "smart pointers" are still conceptually pointers and therefore only my second choice for resource management – after containers and other types that manage their resources at a higher conceptual level. In particular, **shared_ptr**s do not in themselves provide any rules for which of their owners can read and/or write the shared object. Data races (§41.2.4) and other forms of confusion are not addressed simply by eliminating the resource management issues.

Where do we use "smart pointers" (such as **unique_ptr**) rather than resource handles with operations designed specifically for the resource (such as **vector** or **thread**)? Unsurprisingly, the answer is "when we need pointer semantics."

- When we share an object, we need pointers (or references) to refer to the shared object, so a **shared_ptr** becomes the obvious choice (unless there is an obvious single owner).
- When we refer to a polymorphic object, we need a pointer (or a reference) because we don't know the exact type of the object referred to or even its size), so a **unique_ptr** becomes the obvious choice.
- A shared polymorphic object typically requires **shared_ptr**s.

We do *not* need to use a pointer to return a collection of objects from a function; a container that is a resource handle will do that simply and efficiently (§3.3.2).

5.3 Concurrency

Concurrency – the execution of several tasks simultaneously – is widely used to improve throughput (by using several processors for a single computation) or to improve responsiveness (by allowing one part of a program to progress while another is waiting for a response). All modern programming languages provide support for this. The support provided by the C++ standard library is a portable and type-safe variant of what has been used in C++ for more than 20 years and is almost universally supported by modern hardware. The standard-library support is primarily aimed at supporting systems-level concurrency rather than directly providing sophisticated higher-level concurrency models; those can be supplied as libraries built using the standard-library facilities.

The standard library directly supports concurrent execution of multiple threads in a single address space. To allow that, C++ provides a suitable memory model (§41.2) and a set of atomic operations (§41.3). However, most users will see concurrency only in terms of the standard library and libraries built on top of that. This section briefly gives examples of the main standard-library concurrency support facilities: **thread**s, **mutex**es, **lock()** operations, **packaged_task**s, and **future**s. These features are built directly upon what operating systems offer and do not incur performance penalties compared with those.

5.3.1 Tasks and threads

We call a computation that can potentially be executed concurrently with other computations a *task*.
A *thread* is the system-level representation of a task in a program. A task to be executed concurrently with other tasks is launched by constructing a **std::thread** (found in **<thread>**) with the task as
its argument. A task is a function or a function object:

```
void f();                 // function

struct F {                // function object
    void operator()();    // F's call operator (§3.4.3)
};

void user()
{
    thread t1 {f};        // f() executes in separate thread
    thread t2 {F()};      // F()() executes in separate thread

    t1.join();            // wait for t1
    t2.join();            // wait for t2
}
```

The **join()**s ensure that we don't exit **user()** until the threads have completed. To "join" means to
"wait for the thread to terminate."

Threads of a program share a single address space. In this, threads differ from processes, which
generally do not directly share data. Since threads share an address space, they can communicate
through shared objects (§5.3.4). Such communication is typically controlled by locks or other
mechanisms to prevent data races (uncontrolled concurrent access to a variable).

Programming concurrent tasks can be *very* tricky. Consider possible implementations of the
tasks **f** (a function) and **F** (a function object):

```
void f() { cout << "Hello "; }

struct F {
    void operator()() { cout << "Parallel World!\n"; }
};
```

This is an example of a bad error: Here, **f** and **F()** each use the object **cout** without any form of synchronization. The resulting output would be unpredictable and could vary between different executions of the program because the order of execution of the individual operations in the two tasks is
not defined. The program may produce "odd" output, such as

PaHerallllel o World!

When defining tasks of a concurrent program, our aim is to keep tasks completely separate except
where they communicate in simple and obvious ways. The simplest way of thinking of a concurrent task is as a function that happens to run concurrently with its caller. For that to work, we just
have to pass arguments, get a result back, and make sure that there is no use of shared data in
between (no data races).

5.3.2 Passing Arguments

Typically, a task needs data to work upon. We can easily pass data (or pointers or references to the data) as arguments. Consider:

```
void f(vector<double>& v);        // function do something with v

struct F {                        // function object: do something with v
    vector<double>& v;
    F(vector<double>& vv) :v{vv} { }
    void operator()();            // application operator; §3.4.3
};

int main()
{
    vector<double> some_vec {1,2,3,4,5,6,7,8,9};
    vector<double> vec2 {10,11,12,13,14};

    thread t1 {f,some_vec};  // f(some_vec) executes in a separate thread
    thread t2 {F{vec2}};     // F(vec2)() executes in a separate thread

    t1.join();
    t2.join();
}
```

Obviously, F{vec2} saves a reference to the argument vector in F. F can now use that array and hopefully no other task accesses vec2 while F is executing. Passing vec2 by value would eliminate that risk.

The initialization with {f,some_vec} uses a thread variadic template constructor that can accept an arbitrary sequence of arguments (§28.6). The compiler checks that the first argument can be invoked given the following arguments and builds the necessary function object to pass to the thread. Thus, if F::operator()() and f() perform the same algorithm, the handling of the two tasks are roughly equivalent: in both cases, a function object is constructed for the thread to execute.

5.3.3 Returning Results

In the example in §5.3.2, I pass the arguments by non-const reference. I only do that if I expect the task to modify the value of the data referred to (§7.7). That's a somewhat sneaky, but not uncommon, way of returning a result. A less obscure technique is to pass the input data by const reference and to pass the location of a place to deposit the result as a separate argument:

```
void f(const vector<double>& v, double* res);// take input from v; place result in *res

class F {
public:
    F(const vector<double>& vv, double* p) :v{vv}, res{p} { }
    void operator()();                // place result in *res
```

```cpp
private:
    const vector<double>& v;    // source of input
    double* res;                // target for output
};

int main()
{
    vector<double> some_vec;
    vector<double> vec2;
    // ...

    double res1;
    double res2;

    thread t1 {f,some_vec,&res1}; // f(some_vec,&res1) executes in a separate thread
    thread t2 {F{vec2,&res2}};    // F{vec2,&res2}() executes in a separate thread

    t1.join();
    t2.join();

    cout << res1 << ' ' << res2 << '\n';
}
```

I don't consider returning results through arguments particularly elegant, so I return to this topic in §5.3.5.1.

5.3.4 Sharing Data

Sometimes tasks need to share data. In that case, the access has to be synchronized so that at most one task at a time has access. Experienced programmers will recognize this as a simplification (e.g., there is no problem with many tasks simultaneously reading immutable data), but consider how to ensure that at most one task at a time has access to a given set of objects.

The fundamental element of the solution is a **mutex**, a "mutual exclusion object." A **thread** acquires a mutex using a **lock()** operation:

```cpp
mutex m; // controlling mutex
int sh;  // shared data

void f()
{
    unique_lock<mutex> lck {m}; // acquire mutex
    sh += 7;                    // manipulate shared data
}   // release mutex implicitly
```

The **unique_lock**'s constructor acquires the mutex (through a call **m.lock()**). If another thread has already acquired the mutex, the thread waits ("blocks") until the other thread completes its access. Once a thread has completed its access to the shared data, the **unique_lock** releases the **mutex** (with a call **m.unlock()**). The mutual exclusion and locking facilities are found in **<mutex>**.

The correspondence between the shared data and a **mutex** is conventional: the programmer simply has to know which **mutex** is supposed to correspond to which data. Obviously, this is error-prone, and equally obviously we try to make the correspondence clear through various language means. For example:

```
class Record {
public:
    mutex rm;
    // ...
};
```

It doesn't take a genius to guess that for a **Record** called **rec**, **rec.rm** is a **mutex** that you are supposed to acquire before accessing the other data of **rec**, though a comment or a better name might have helped a reader.

It is not uncommon to need to simultaneously access several resources to perform some action. This can lead to deadlock. For example, if **thread1** acquires **mutex1** and then tries to acquire **mutex2** while **thread2** acquires **mutex2** and then tries to acquire **mutex1**, then neither task will ever proceed further. The standard library offers help in the form of an operation for acquiring several locks simultaneously:

```
void f()
{
    // ...
    unique_lock<mutex> lck1 {m1,defer_lock};    // defer_lock: don't yet try to acquire the mutex
    unique_lock<mutex> lck2 {m2,defer_lock};
    unique_lock<mutex> lck3 {m3,defer_lock};
    // ...
    lock(lck1,lck2,lck3);                        // acquire all three locks
    // ... manipulate shared data ...
} // implicitly release all mutexes
```

This **lock()** will only proceed after acquiring all its **mutex** arguments and will never block ("go to sleep") while holding a **mutex**. The destructors for the individual **unique_lock**s ensure that the **mutex**es are released when a **thread** leaves the scope.

Communicating through shared data is pretty low level. In particular, the programmer has to devise ways of knowing what work has and has not been done by various tasks. In that regard, use of shared data is inferior to the notion of call and return. On the other hand, some people are convinced that sharing must be more efficient than copying arguments and returns. That can indeed be so when large amounts of data are involved, but locking and unlocking are relatively expensive operations. On the other hand, modern machines are very good at copying data, especially compact data, such as **vector** elements. So don't choose shared data for communication because of "efficiency" without thought and preferably not without measurement.

5.3.4.1 Waiting for Events

Sometimes, a **thread** needs to wait for some kind of external event, such as another **thread** completing a task or a certain amount of time having passed. The simplest "event" is simply time passing. Consider:

```
using namespace std::chrono;        // see §35.2

auto t0 = high_resolution_clock::now();
this_thread::sleep_for(milliseconds{20});
auto t1 = high_resolution_clock::now();
cout << duration_cast<nanoseconds>(t1−t0).count() << " nanoseconds passed\n";
```

Note that I didn't even have to launch a **thread**; by default, **this_thread** refers to the one and only thread (§42.2.6).

I used **duration_cast** to adjust the clock's units to the nanoseconds I wanted. See §5.4.1 and §35.2 before trying anything more complicated than this with time. The time facilities are found in <chrono>.

The basic support for communicating using external events is provided by **condition_variables** found in <condition_variable> (§42.3.4). A **condition_variable** is a mechanism allowing one **thread** to wait for another. In particular, it allows a **thread** to wait for some *condition* (often called an *event*) to occur as the result of work done by other **threads**.

Consider the classical example of two **threads** communicating by passing messages through a queue. For simplicity, I declare the **queue** and the mechanism for avoiding race conditions on that **queue** global to the producer and consumer:

```
class Message {      // object to be communicated
    // ...
};
```

```
queue<Message> mqueue;        // the queue of messages
condition_variable mcond;     // the variable communicating events
mutex mmutex;                 // the locking mechanism
```

The types **queue**, **condition_variable**, and **mutex** are provided by the standard library.

The **consumer()** reads and processes **Message**s:

```
void consumer()
{
    while(true) {
        unique_lock<mutex> lck{mmutex};        // acquire mmutex
        while (mcond.wait(lck)) /* do nothing */;  // release lck and wait;
                                                   // re-acquire lck upon wakeup

        auto m = mqueue.front();                // get the message
        mqueue.pop();
        lck.unlock();                           // release lck
        // ... process m ...
    }
}
```

Here, I explicitly protect the operations on the **queue** and on the **condition_variable** with a **unique_lock** on the **mutex**. Waiting on **condition_variable** releases its lock argument until the wait is over (so that the queue is non-empty) and then reacquires it.

The corresponding **producer** looks like this:

```
void producer()
{
    while(true) {
        Message m;
        // ... fill the message ...
        unique_lock<mutex> lck {mmutex};       // protect operations
        mqueue.push(m);
        mcond.notify_one();                    // notify
    }                                          // release lock (at end of scope)
}
```

Using **condition_variable**s supports many forms of elegant and efficient sharing, but can be rather tricky (§42.3.4).

5.3.5 Communicating Tasks

The standard library provides a few facilities to allow programmers to operate at the conceptual level of tasks (work to potentially be done concurrently) rather than directly at the lower level of threads and locks:

[1]   **future** and **promise** for returning a value from a task spawned on a separate thread
[2]   **packaged_task** to help launch tasks and connect up the mechanisms for returning a result
[3]   **async()** for launching of a task in a manner very similar to calling a function.
These facilities are found in **<future>**.

5.3.5.1 future and promise

The important point about **future** and **promise** is that they enable a transfer of a value between two tasks without explicit use of a lock; "the system" implements the transfer efficiently. The basic idea is simple: When a task wants to pass a value to another, it puts the value into a **promise**. Somehow, the implementation makes that value appear in the corresponding **future**, from which it can be read (typically by the launcher of the task). We can represent this graphically:

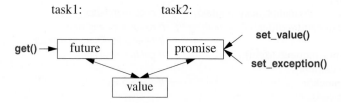

If we have a **future<X>** called **fx**, we can **get()** a value of type **X** from it:

   X v = fx.get();   // if necessary, wait for the value to get computed

If the value isn't there yet, our thread is blocked until it arrives. If the value couldn't be computed, **get()** might throw an exception (from the system or transmitted from the task from which we were trying to **get()** the value).

The main purpose of a **promise** is to provide simple "put" operations (called **set_value()** and **set_exception()**) to match **future**'s **get()**. The names "future" and "promise" are historical; please don't blame me. They are yet another fertile source of puns.

If you have a **promise** and need to send a result of type **X** to a **future**, you can do one of two things: pass a value or pass an exception. For example:

```
void f(promise<X>& px)   // a task: place the result in px
{
     // ...
     try {
          X res;
          // ... compute a value for res ...
          px.set_value(res);
     }
     catch (...) {          // oops: couldn't compute res
          // pass the exception to the future's thread:
          px.set_exception(current_exception());
     }
}
```

The **current_exception()** refers to the caught exception (§30.4.1.2).

To deal with an exception transmitted through a **future**, the caller of **get()** must be prepared to catch it somewhere. For example:

```
void g(future<X>& fx)          // a task: get the result from fx
{
     // ...
     try {
          X v = fx.get();   // if necessary, wait for the value to get computed
          // ... use v ...
     }
     catch (...) {          // oops: someone couldn't compute v
          // ... handle error ...
     }
}
```

5.3.5.2 packaged_task

How do we get a **future** into the task that needs a result and the corresponding **promise** into the thread that should produce that result? The **packaged_task** type is provided to simplify setting up tasks connected with **futures** and **promises** to be run on **threads**. A **packaged_task** provides wrapper code to put the return value or exception from the task into a **promise** (like the code shown in §5.3.5.1). If you ask it by calling **get_future**, a **packaged_task** will give you the **future** corresponding to its **promise**. For example, we can set up two tasks to each add half of the elements of a **vector<double>** using the standard-library **accumulate()** (§3.4.2, §40.6):

```
double accum(double* beg, double * end, double init)
     // compute the sum of [beg:end) starting with the initial value init
{
     return accumulate(beg,end,init);
}

double comp2(vector<double>& v)
{
     using Task_type = double(double*,double*,double);          // type of task

     packaged_task<Task_type> pt0 {accum};                      // package the task (i.e., accum)
     packaged_task<Task_type> pt1 {accum};

     future<double> f0 {pt0.get_future()};                      // get hold of pt0's future
     future<double> f1 {pt1.get_future()};                      // get hold of pt1's future

     double* first = &v[0];
     thread t1 {move(pt0),first,first+v.size()/2,0};            // start a thread for pt0
     thread t2 {move(pt1),first+v.size()/2,first+v.size(),0};   // start a thread for pt1

     // ...

     return f0.get()+f1.get();                                  // get the results
}
```

The **packaged_task** template takes the type of the task as its template argument (here **Task_type**, an alias for **double(double*,double*,double)**) and the task as its constructor argument (here, **accum**). The **move()** operations are needed because a **packaged_task** cannot be copied.

Please note the absence of explicit mention of locks in this code: we are able to concentrate on tasks to be done, rather than on the mechanisms used to manage their communication. The two tasks will be run on separate threads and thus potentially in parallel.

5.3.5.3 async()

The line of thinking I have pursued in this chapter is the one I believe to be the simplest yet still among the most powerful: Treat a task as a function that may happen to run concurrently with other tasks. It is far from the only model supported by the C++ standard library, but it serves well for a wide range of needs. More subtle and tricky models, e.g., styles of programming relying on shared memory, can be used as needed.

To launch tasks to potentially run asynchronously, we can use **async()**:

```
double comp4(vector<double>& v)
     // spawn many tasks if v is large enough
{
     if (v.size()<10000) return accum(v.begin(),v.end(),0.0);

     auto v0 = &v[0];
     auto sz = v.size();
```

```
auto f0 = async(accum,v0,v0+sz/4,0.0);              // first quarter
auto f1 = async(accum,v0+sz/4,v0+sz/2,0.0);         // second quarter
auto f2 = async(accum,v0+sz/2,v0+sz*3/4,0.0);       // third quarter
auto f3 = async(accum,v0+sz*3/4,v0+sz,0.0);         // fourth quarter

return f0.get()+f1.get()+f2.get()+f3.get();  // collect and combine the results
}
```

Basically, async() separates the "call part" of a function call from the "get the result part," and separates both from the actual execution of the task. Using async(), you don't have to think about threads and locks. Instead, you think just in terms of tasks that potentially compute their results asynchronously. There is an obvious limitation: Don't even think of using async() for tasks that share resources needing locking – with async() you don't even know how many threads will be used because that's up to async() to decide based on what it knows about the system resources available at the time of a call. For example, async() may check whether any idle cores (processors) are available before deciding how many threads to use.

Please note that async() is not just a mechanism specialized for parallel computation for increased performance. For example, it can also be used to spawn a task for getting information from a user, leaving the "main program" active with something else (§42.4.6).

5.4 Small Utility Components

Not all standard-library components come as part of obviously labeled facilities, such as "containers" or "I/O." This section gives a few examples of small, widely useful components:

- clock and duration for measuring time.
- Type functions, such as iterator_traits and is_arithmetic, for gaining information about types.
- pair and tuple for representing small potentially heterogeneous sets of values.

The point here is that a function or a type need not be complicated or closely tied to a mass of other functions and types to be useful. Such library components mostly act as building blocks for more powerful library facilities, including other components of the standard library.

5.4.1 Time

The standard library provides facilities for dealing with time. For example, here is the basic way of timing something:

```
using namespace std::chrono;        // see §35.2

auto t0 = high_resolution_clock::now();
do_work();
auto t1 = high_resolution_clock::now();
cout << duration_cast<milliseconds>(t1−t0).count() << "msec\n";
```

The clock returns a time_point (a point in time). Subtracting two time_points gives a duration (a period of time). Various clocks give their results in various units of time (the clock I used measures nanoseconds), so it is usually a good idea to convert a duration into a known unit. That's what duration_cast does.

The standard-library facilities for dealing with time are found in the subnamespace **std::chrono** in **<chrono>** (§35.2).

Don't make statements about "efficiency" of code without first doing time measurements. Guesses about performance are most unreliable.

5.4.2 Type Functions

A *type function* is a function that is evaluated at compile-time given a type as its argument or returning a type. The standard library provides a variety of type functions to help library implementers and programmers in general to write code that take advantage of aspects of the language, the standard library, and code in general.

For numerical types, **numeric_limits** from **<limits>** presents a variety of useful information (§5.6.5). For example:

```
constexpr float min = numeric_limits<float>::min();     // smallest positive float (§40.2)
```

Similarly, object sizes can be found by the built-in **sizeof** operator (§2.2.2). For example:

```
constexpr int szi = sizeof(int); // the number of bytes in an int
```

Such type functions are part of C++'s mechanisms for compile-time computation that allow tighter type checking and better performance than would otherwise have been possible. Use of such features is often called *metaprogramming* or (when templates are involved) *template metaprogramming* (Chapter 28). Here, I just present two facilities provided by the standard library: **iterator_traits** (§5.4.2.1) and type predicates (§5.4.2.2).

5.4.2.1 iterator_traits

The standard-library **sort()** takes a pair of iterators supposed to define a sequence (§4.5). Furthermore, those iterators must offer random access to that sequence, that is, they must be *random-access iterators*. Some containers, such as **forward_list**, do not offer that. In particular, a **forward_list** is a singly-linked list so subscripting would be expensive and there is no reasonable way to refer back to a previous element. However, like most containers, **forward_list** offers *forward iterators* that can be used to traverse the sequence by algorithms and for-statements (§33.1.1).

The standard library provides a mechanism, **iterator_traits** that allows us to check which kind of iterator is supported. Given that, we can improve the range **sort()** from §4.5.6 to accept either a **vector** or a **forward_list**. For example:

```
void test(vector<string>& v, forward_list<int>& lst)
{
    sort(v);    // sort the vector
    sort(lst);  // sort the singly-linked list
}
```

The techniques needed to make that work are generally useful.

First, I write two helper functions that take an extra argument indicating whether they are to be used for random-access iterators or forward iterators. The version taking random-access iterator arguments is trivial:

```
template<typename Ran>                                          // for random-access iterators
void sort_helper(Ran beg, Ran end, random_access_iterator_tag)  // we can subscript into [beg:end)
{
    sort(beg,end);         // just sort it

}
```

The version for forward iterators is almost as simple; just copy the list into a **vector**, sort, and copy back again:

```
template<typename For>                                    // for forward iterators
void sort_helper(For beg, For end, forward_iterator_tag)  // we can traverse [beg:end)
{
    vector<decltype(*beg)> v {beg,end};     // initialize a vector from [beg:end)
    sort(v.begin(),v.end());
    copy(v.begin(),v.end(),beg);            // copy the elements back
}
```

The **decltype()** is a built-in type function that returns the declared type of its argument (§6.3.6.3). Thus, **v** is a **vector<X>** where **X** is the element type of the input sequence.

The real "type magic" is in the selection of helper functions:

```
template<typname C>
void sort(C& c)
{
    using Iter = Iterator_type<C>;
    sort_helper(c.begin(),c.end(),Iterator_category<Iter>{});
}
```

Here, I use two type functions: **Iterator_type<C>** returns the iterator type of **C** (that is, **C::iterator**) and then **Iterator_category<Iter>{}** constructs a "tag" value indicating the kind of iterator provided:

- **std::random_access_iterator_tag** if **C**'s iterator supports random access.
- **std::forward_iterator_tag** if **C**'s iterator supports forward iteration.

Given that, we can select between the two sorting algorithms at compile time. This technique, called *tag dispatch* is one of several used in the standard library and elsewhere to improve flexibility and performance.

The standard-library support for techniques for using iterators, such as tag dispatch, comes in the form of a simple class template **iterator_traits** from **<iterator>** (§33.1.3). This allows simple definitions of the type functions used in **sort()**:

```
template<typename C>
    using Iterator_type = typename C::iterator;    // C's iterator type

template<typename Iter>
    using Iterator_category = typename std::iterator_traits<Iter>::iterator_category;  // Iter's category
```

If you don't want to know what kind of "compile-time type magic" is used to provide the standard-library features, you are free to ignore facilities such as **iterator_traits**. But then you can't use the techniques they support to improve your own code.

5.4.2.2 Type Predicates

A standard-library type predicate is a simple type function that answers a fundamental question about types. For example:

```
bool b1 = Is_arithmetic<int>();      // yes, int is an arithmetic type
bool b2 = Is_arithmetic<string>();   // no, std::string is not an arithmetic type
```

These predicates are found in **<type_traits>** and described in §35.4.1. Other examples are **is_class**, **is_pod**, **is_literal_type**, **has_virtual_destructor**, and **is_base_of**. They are most useful when we write templates. For example:

```
template<typename Scalar>
class complex {
    Scalar re, im;
public:
    static_assert(Is_arithmetic<Scalar>(), "Sorry, I only support complex of arithmetic types");
    // ...
};
```

To improve readability compared to using the standard library directly, I defined a type function:

```
template<typename T>
constexpr bool Is_arithmetic()
{
    return std::is_arithmetic<T>::value ;
}
```

Older programs use **::value** directly instead of **()**, but I consider that quite ugly and it exposes implementation details.

5.4.3 pair and tuple

Often, we need some data that is just data; that is, a collection of values, rather than an object of a class with a well-defined semantics and an invariant for its value (§2.4.3.2, §13.4). In such cases, we could define a simple **struct** with an appropriate set of appropriately named members. Alternatively, we could let the standard library write the definition for us. For example, the standard-library algorithm **equal_range** (§32.6.1) returns a **pair** of iterators specifying a sub-sequence meeting a predicate:

```
template<typename Forward_iterator, typename T, typename Compare>
    pair<Forward_iterator,Forward_iterator>
    equal_range(Forward_iterator first, Forward_iterator last, const T& val, Compare cmp);
```

Given a sorted sequence [first:last), equal_range() will return the **pair** representing the subsequence that matches the predicate **cmp**. We can use that to search in a sorted sequence of **Record**s:

```
auto rec_eq = [](const Record& r1, const Record& r2) { return r1.name<r2.name;};// compare names

void f(const vector<Record>& v)      // assume that v is sorted on its "name" field
{
    auto er = equal_range(v.begin(),v.end(),Record{"Reg"},rec_eq);
```

```
                 for (auto p = er.first; p!=er.second; ++p)      // print all equal records
                      cout << *p;                                // assume that << is defined for Record
         }
```

The first member of a **pair** is called **first** and the second member is called **second**. This naming is not particularly creative and may look a bit odd at first, but such consistent naming is a boon when we want to write generic code.

The standard-library **pair** (from **<utility>**) is quite frequently used in the standard library and elsewhere. A **pair** provides operators, such as =, ==, and <, if its elements do. The **make_pair()** function makes it easy to create a **pair** without explicitly mentioning its type (§34.2.4.1). For example:

```
     void f(vector<string>& v)
     {
          auto pp = make_pair(v.begin(),2);   // pp is a pair<vector<string>::iterator,int>
          // ...
     }
```

If you need more than two elements (or less), you can use **tuple** (from **<utility>**; §34.2.4.2). A **tuple** is a heterogeneous sequence of elements; for example:

```
     tuple<string,int,double> t2("Sild",123, 3.14);   // the type is explicitly specified

     auto t = make_tuple(string("Herring"),10, 1.23);   // the type is deduced
                                                         // t is a tuple<string,int,double>

     string s = get<0>(t); // get first element of tuple
     int x = get<1>(t);
     double d = get<2>(t);
```

The elements of a **tuple** are numbered (starting with zero), rather than named the way elements of **pair**s are (**first** and **second**). To get compile-time selection of elements, I must unfortunately use the ugly **get<1>(t)**, rather than **get(t,1)** or **t[1]** (§28.5.2).

Like **pair**s, **tuple**s can be assigned and compared if their elements can be.

A **pair** is common in interfaces because often we want to return more than one value, such as a result and an indicator of the quality of that result. It is less common to need three or more parts to a result, so **tuple**s are more often found in the implementations of generic algorithms.

5.5 Regular Expressions

Regular expressions are a powerful tool for text processing. They provide a way to simply and tersely describe patterns in text (e.g., a U.S. ZIP code such as **TX 77845**, or an ISO-style date, such as **2009–06–07**) and to efficiently find such patterns in text. In **<regex>**, the standard library provides support for regular expressions in the form of the **std::regex** class and its supporting functions. To give a taste of the style of the **regex** library, let us define and print a pattern:

```
     regex pat (R"(\w{2}\s*\d{5}(-\d{4})?)");   // ZIP code pattern: XXddddd-dddd and variants
     cout << "pattern: " << pat << '\n';
```

People who have used regular expressions in just about any language will find \w{2}\s*\d{5}(–\d{4})? familiar. It specifies a pattern starting with two letters \w{2} optionally followed by some space \s* followed by five digits \d{5} and optionally followed by a dash and four digits –\d{4}. If you are not familiar with regular expressions, this may be a good time to learn about them ([Stroustrup,2009], [Maddock,2009], [Friedl,1997]). Regular expressions are summarized in §37.1.1.

To express the pattern, I use a *raw string literal* (§7.3.2.1) starting with R"(and terminated by)". This allows backslashes and quotes to be used directly in the string.

The simplest way of using a pattern is to search for it in a stream:

```
int lineno = 0;
for (string line; getline(cin,line);) {          // read into line buffer
    ++lineno;
    smatch matches;                              // matched strings go here
    if (regex_search(line,matches,pat))          // search for pat in line
        cout << lineno << ": " << matches[0] << '\n';
}
```

The regex_search(line,matches,pat) searches the line for anything that matches the regular expression stored in pat and if it finds any matches, it stores them in matches. If no match was found, regex_search(line,matches,pat) returns false. The matches variable is of type smatch. The "s" stands for "sub" and an smatch is a vector of sub-matches. The first element, here matches[0], is the complete match.

For a more complete description see Chapter 37.

5.6 Math

C++ wasn't designed primarily with numerical computation in mind. However, C++ is heavily used for numerical computation and the standard library reflects that.

5.6.1 Mathematical Functions and Algorithms

In <cmath>, we find the "usual mathematical functions," such as sqrt(), log(), and sin() for arguments of type float, double, and long double (§40.3). Complex number versions of these functions are found in <complex> (§40.4).

In <numeric>, we find a small set of generalized numerical algorithms, such as accumulate(). For example:

```
void f()
{
    list<double> lst {1, 2, 3, 4, 5, 9999.99999};
    auto s = accumulate(lst.begin(),lst.end(),0.0); // calculate the sum
    cout << s << '\n';                               // print 10014.9999
}
```

These algorithms work for every standard-library sequence and can have operations supplied as arguments (§40.6).

5.6.2 Complex Numbers

The standard library supports a family of complex number types along the lines of the **complex** class described in §2.3. To support complex numbers where the scalars are single-precision floating-point numbers (**floats**), double-precision floating-point numbers (**doubles**), etc., the standard library **complex** is a template:

```
template<typename Scalar>
class complex {
public:
    complex(const Scalar& re ={}, const Scalar& im ={});
    // ...
};
```

The usual arithmetic operations and the most common mathematical functions are supported for complex numbers. For example:

```
void f(complex<float> fl, complex<double> db)
{
    complex<long double> ld {fl+sqrt(db)};
    db += fl*3;
    fl = pow(1/fl,2);
    // ...
}
```

The **sqrt()** and **pow()** (exponentiation) functions are among the usual mathematical functions defined in **<complex>**. For more details, see §40.4.

5.6.3 Random Numbers

Random numbers are useful in many contexts, such as testing, games, simulation, and security. The diversity of application areas is reflected in the wide selection of random number generators provided by the standard library in **<random>**. A random number generator consists of two parts:

[1]   an *engine* that produces a sequence of random or pseudo-random values.

[2]   a *distribution* that maps those values into a mathematical distribution in a range.

Examples of distributions are **uniform_int_distribution** (where all integers produced are equally likely), **normal_distribution** ("the bell curve"), and **exponential_distribution** (exponential growth); each for some specified range. For example:

```
using my_engine = default_random_engine;              // type of engine
using my_distribution = uniform_int_distribution<>;   // type of distribution

my_engine re {};                                      // the default engine
my_distribution one_to_six {1,6};                     // distribution that maps to the ints 1..6
auto die = bind(one_to_six,re);                       // make a generator

int x = die();                                        // roll the die: x becomes a value in [1:6]
```

The standard-library function **bind()** makes a function object that will invoke its first argument (here, **one_to_six**) given its second argument (here, **re**) as its argument (§33.5.1). Thus a call **die()** is equivalent to a call **one_to_six(re)**.

Thanks to its uncompromising attention to generality and performance one expert has deemed the standard-library random number component "what every random number library wants to be when it grows up." However, it can hardly be deemed "novice friendly." The **using** statements makes what is being done a bit more obvious. Instead, I could just have written:

```
auto die = bind(uniform_int_distribution<>{1,6}, default_random_engine{});
```

Which version is the more readable depends entirely on the context and the reader.

For novices (of any background) the fully general interface to the random number library can be a serious obstacle. A simple uniform random number generator is often sufficient to get started. For example:

```
Rand_int rnd {1,10};            // make a random number generator for [1:10]
int x = rnd();                  // x is a number in [1:10]
```

So, how could we get that? We have to get something like **die()** inside a class **Rand_int**:

```
class Rand_int {
public:
    Rand_int(int low, int high) :dist{low,high} { }
    int operator()() { return dist(re); }       // draw an int
private:
    default_random_engine re;
    uniform_int_distribution<> dist;
};
```

That definition is still "expert level," but the *use* of **Rand_int()** is manageable in the first week of a C++ course for novices. For example:

```
int main()
{
    Rand_int rnd {0,4};         // make a uniform random number generator

    vector<int> histogram(5);           // make a vector of size 5
    for (int i=0; i!=200; ++i)
        ++histogram[rnd()];             // fill histogram with the frequencies of numbers [0:4]

    for (int i = 0; i!=mn.size(); ++i) {    // write out a bar graph
        cout << i << '\t';
        for (int j=0; j!=mn[i]; ++j) cout << '*';
        cout << endl;
    }
}
```

The output is a (reassuringly boring) uniform distribution (with reasonable statistical variation):

```
0    *********************************************
1    *******************************************
2    *****************************
3    **********************************************
4    *********************************************
```

There is no standard graphics library for C++, so I use "ASCII graphics." Obviously, there are lots of open source and commercial graphics and GUI libraries for C++, but in this book I'll restrict myself to ISO standard facilities.

For more information about random numbers, see §40.7.

5.6.4 Vector Arithmetic

The **vector** described in §4.4.1 was designed to be a general mechanism for holding values, to be flexible, and to fit into the architecture of containers, iterators, and algorithms. However, it does not support mathematical vector operations. Adding such operations to **vector** would be easy, but its generality and flexibility precludes optimizations that are often considered essential for serious numerical work. Consequently, the standard library provides (in **<valarray>**) a **vector**-like template, called **valarray**, that is less general and more amenable to optimization for numerical computation:

```
template<typename T>
class valarray {
    // ...
};
```

The usual arithmetic operations and the most common mathematical functions are supported for valarrays. For example:

```
void f(valarray<double>& a1, valarray<double>& a2)
{
    valarray<double> a = a1*3.14+a2/a1;        // numeric array operators *, +, /, and =
    a2 += a1*3.14;
    a = abs(a);
    double d = a2[7];
    // ...
}
```

For more details, see §40.5. In particular, **valarray** offers stride access to help implement multidimensional computations.

5.6.5 Numeric Limits

In **<limits>**, the standard library provides classes that describe the properties of built-in types – such as the maximum exponent of a **float** or the number of bytes in an **int**; see §40.2. For example, we can assert that a **char** is signed:

```
static_assert(numeric_limits<char>::is_signed,"unsigned characters!");
static_assert(100000<numeric_limits<int>::max(),"small ints!");
```

Note that the second assert (only) works because **numeric_limits<int>::max()** is a **constexpr** function (§2.2.3, §10.4).

5.7 Advice

[1]   Use resource handles to manage resources (RAII); §5.2.
[2]   Use unique_ptr to refer to objects of polymorphic type; §5.2.1.
[3]   Use shared_ptr to refer to shared objects; §5.2.1.
[4]   Use type-safe mechanisms for concurrency; §5.3.
[5]   Minimize the use of shared data; §5.3.4.
[6]   Don't choose shared data for communication because of "efficiency" without thought and preferably not without measurement; §5.3.4.
[7]   Think in terms of concurrent tasks, rather than threads; §5.3.5.
[8]   A library doesn't have to be large or complicated to be useful; §5.4.
[9]   Time your programs before making claims about efficiency; §5.4.1.
[10] You can write code to explicitly depend on properties of types; §5.4.2.
[11] Use regular expressions for simple pattern matching; §5.5.
[12] Don't try to do serious numeric computation using only the language; use libraries; §5.6.
[13] Properties of numeric types are accessible through numeric_limits; §5.6.5.

Part II

Basic Facilities

This part describes C++'s built-in types and the basic facilities for constructing programs out of them. The C subset of C++ is presented together with C++'s additional support for traditional styles of programming. It also discusses the basic facilities for composing a C++ program out of logical and physical parts.

Chapters

"... I have long entertained a suspicion, with regard to the decisions of philosophers upon all subjects, and found in myself a greater inclination to dispute, than assent to their conclusions. There is one mistake, to which they seem liable, almost without exception; they confine too much their principles, and make no account of that vast variety, which nature has so much affected in all her operations. When a philosopher has once laid hold of a favourite principle, which perhaps accounts for many natural effects, he extends the same principle over the whole creation, and reduces to it every phænomenon, though by the most violent and absurd reasoning. ..."

– David Hume,
Essays, Moral, Political, and Literary. PART I. (1752)

6

Types and Declarations

Perfection is achieved
only on the point of collapse.
– C. N. Parkinson

- The ISO C++ Standard
    Implementations; The Basic Source Character Set
- Types
    Fundamental Types; Booleans; Character Types; Integer Types; Floating-Point Types; Prefixes and Suffixes; **void**; Sizes; Alignment
- Declarations
    The Structure of Declarations; Declaring Multiple Names; Names; Scope; Initialization; Deducing a Type: **auto** and **decltype()**
- Objects and Values
    Lvalues and Rvalues; Lifetimes of Objects
- Type Aliases
- Advice

6.1 The ISO C++ Standard

The C++ language and standard library are defined by their ISO standard: ISO/IEC 14882:2011. In this book, references to the standard are of the form §iso.23.3.6.1. In cases where the text of this book is considered imprecise, incomplete, or possibly wrong, consult the standard. But don't expect the standard to be a tutorial or to be easily accessible by non-experts.

Strictly adhering to the C++ language and library standard doesn't by itself guarantee good code or even portable code. The standard doesn't say whether a piece of code is good or bad; it simply says what a programmer can and cannot rely on from an implementation. It is easy to write perfectly awful standard-conforming programs, and most real-world programs rely on features that the standard does not guarantee to be portable. They do so to access system interfaces and hardware features that cannot be expressed directly in C++ or require reliance on specific implementation details.

Many important things are deemed *implementation-defined* by the standard. This means that each implementation must provide a specific, well-defined behavior for a construct and that behavior must be documented. For example:

```
unsigned char c1 = 64;      // well defined: a char has at least 8 bits and can always hold 64
unsigned char c2 = 1256;    // implementation-defined: truncation if a char has only 8 bits
```

The initialization of `c1` is well defined because a `char` must be at least 8 bits. However, the behavior of the initialization of `c2` is implementation-defined because the number of bits in a `char` is implementation-defined. If the `char` has only 8 bits, the value `1256` will be truncated to `232` (§10.5.2.1). Most implementation-defined features relate to differences in the hardware used to run a program.

Other behaviors are *unspecified*; that is, a range of possible behaviors are acceptable, but the implementer is not obliged to specify which actually occur. Usually, the reason for deeming something unspecified is that the exact behavior is unpredictable for fundamental reasons. For example, the exact value returned by `new` is unspecified. So is the value of a variable assigned to from two threads unless some synchronization mechanism has been employed to prevent a data race (§41.2).

When writing real-world programs, it is usually necessary to rely on implementation-defined behavior. Such behavior is the price we pay for the ability to operate effectively on a large range of systems. For example, C++ would have been much simpler if all characters had been 8 bits and all pointers 32 bits. However, 16-bit and 32-bit character sets are not uncommon, and machines with 16-bit and 64-bit pointers are in wide use.

To maximize portability, it is wise to be explicit about what implementation-defined features we rely on and to isolate the more subtle examples in clearly marked sections of a program. A typical example of this practice is to present all dependencies on hardware sizes in the form of constants and type definitions in some header file. To support such techniques, the standard library provides `numeric_limits` (§40.2). Many assumptions about implementation-defined features can be checked by stating them as static assertions (§2.4.3.3). For example:

```
static_assert(4<=sizeof(int),"sizeof(int) too small");
```

Undefined behavior is nastier. A construct is deemed *undefined* by the standard if no reasonable behavior is required by an implementation. Typically, some obvious implementation technique will cause a program using an undefined feature to behave very badly. For example:

```
const int size = 4*1024;
char page[size];

void f()
{
    page[size+size] = 7; // undefined
}
```

Plausible outcomes of this code fragment include overwriting unrelated data and triggering a hardware error/exception. An implementation is not required to choose among plausible outcomes. Where powerful optimizers are used, the actual effects of undefined behavior can become quite unpredictable. If a set of plausible and easily implementable alternatives exist, a feature is deemed unspecified or implementation-defined rather than undefined.

It is worth spending considerable time and effort to ensure that a program does not use something deemed unspecified or undefined by the standard. In many cases, tools exist to help do this.

6.1.1 Implementations

A C++ implementation can be either *hosted* or *freestanding* (§iso.17.6.1.3). A hosted implementation includes all the standard-library facilities as described in the standard (§30.2) and in this book. A freestanding implementation may provide fewer standard-library facilities, as long as the following are provided:

Freestanding Implementation Headers		
Types	<cstddef>	§10.3.1
Implementation properties	<cfloat> <limits> <climits>	§40.2
Integer types	<cstdint>	§43.7
Start and termination	<cstdlib>	§43.7
Dynamic memory management	<new>	§11.2.3
Type identification	<typeinfo>	§22.5
Exception handling	<exception>	§30.4.1.1
Initializer lists	<initializer_list>	§30.3.1
Other run-time support	<cstdalign> <cstdarg> <cstdbool>	§12.2.4, §44.3.4
Type traits	<type_traits>	§35.4.1
Atomics	<atomic>	§41.3

Freestanding implementations are meant for code running with only the most minimal operating system support. Many implementations also provide a (non-standard) option for not using exceptions for really minimal, close-to-the-hardware, programs.

6.1.2 The Basic Source Character Set

The C++ standard and the examples in this book are written using the *basic source character set* consisting of the letters, digits, graphical characters, and whitespace characters from the U.S. variant of the international 7-bit character set ISO 646-1983 called ASCII (ANSI3.4-1968). This can cause problems for people who use C++ in an environment with a different character set:

- ASCII contains punctuation characters and operator symbols (such as], {, and !) that are not available in some character sets.
- We need a notation for characters that do not have a convenient character representation (such as newline and "the character with value 17").
- ASCII doesn't contain characters (such as ñ, Þ, and Æ) that are used for writing languages other than English.

To use an extended character set for source code, a programming environment can map the extended character set into the basic source character set in one of several ways, for example, by using universal character names (§6.2.3.2).

6.2 Types

Consider:

```
x = y+f(2);
```

For this to make sense in a C++ program, the names x, y, and f must be suitably declared. That is, the programmer must specify that entities named x, y, and f exist and that they are of types for which = (assignment), + (addition), and () (function call), respectively, are meaningful.

Every name (identifier) in a C++ program has a type associated with it. This type determines what operations can be applied to the name (that is, to the entity referred to by the name) and how such operations are interpreted. For example:

```
float x;        // x is a floating-point variable
int y = 7;      // y is an integer variable with the initial value 7
float f(int);   // f is a function taking an argument of type int and returning a floating-point number
```

These declarations would make the example meaningful. Because y is declared to be an int, it can be assigned to, used as an operand for +, etc. On the other hand, f is declared to be a function that takes an int as its argument, so it can be called given the interger 2.

This chapter presents fundamental types (§6.2.1) and declarations (§6.3). Its examples just demonstrate language features; they are not intended to do anything useful. More extensive and realistic examples are saved for later chapters. This chapter simply provides the most basic elements from which C++ programs are constructed. You must know these elements, plus the terminology and simple syntax that go with them, in order to complete a real project in C++ and especially to read code written by others. However, a thorough understanding of every detail mentioned in this chapter is not a requirement for understanding the following chapters. Consequently, you may prefer to skim through this chapter, observing the major concepts, and return later as the need for understanding more details arises.

6.2.1 Fundamental Types

C++ has a set of *fundamental types* corresponding to the most common basic storage units of a computer and the most common ways of using them to hold data:

   §6.2.2 A Boolean type (bool)
   §6.2.3 Character types (such as char and wchar_t)
   §6.2.4 Integer types (such as int and long long)
   §6.2.5 Floating-point types (such as double and long double)
   §6.2.7 A type, void, used to signify the absence of information

From these types, we can construct other types using declarator operators:

   §7.2   Pointer types (such as int∗)
   §7.3   Array types (such as char[])
   §7.7   Reference types (such as double& and vector<int>&&)

In addition, a user can define additional types:

   §8.2   Data structures and classes (Chapter 16)
   §8.4   Enumeration types for representing specific sets of values (enum and enum class)

The Boolean, character, and integer types are collectively called *integral types*. The integral and floating-point types are collectively called *arithmetic types*. Enumerations and classes (Chapter 16) are called *user-defined types* because they must be defined by users rather than being available for use without previous declaration, the way fundamental types are. In contrast, fundamental types, pointers, and references are collectively referred to as *built-in types*. The standard library provides many user-defined types (Chapter 4, Chapter 5).

The integral and floating-point types are provided in a variety of sizes to give the programmer a choice of the amount of storage consumed, the precision, and the range available for computations (§6.2.8). The assumption is that a computer provides bytes for holding characters, words for holding and computing integer values, some entity most suitable for floating-point computation, and addresses for referring to those entities. The C++ fundamental types together with pointers and arrays present these machine-level notions to the programmer in a reasonably implementation-independent manner.

For most applications, we could use **bool** for logical values, **char** for characters, **int** for integer values, and **double** for floating-point values. The remaining fundamental types are variations for optimizations, special needs, and compatibility that are best ignored until such needs arise.

6.2.2 Booleans

A Boolean, **bool**, can have one of the two values **true** or **false**. A Boolean is used to express the results of logical operations. For example:

```
void f(int a, int b)
{
    bool b1 {a==b};
    // ...
}
```

If **a** and **b** have the same value, **b1** becomes **true**; otherwise, **b1** becomes **false**.

A common use of **bool** is as the type of the result of a function that tests some condition (a predicate). For example:

```
bool is_open(File*);
```

```
bool greater(int a, int b) { return a>b; }
```

By definition, **true** has the value **1** when converted to an integer and **false** has the value **0**. Conversely, integers can be implicitly converted to **bool** values: nonzero integers convert to **true** and **0** converts to **false**. For example:

```
bool b1 = 7;     // 7!=0, so b becomes true
bool b2 {7};     // error: narrowing (§2.2.2, §10.5)

int i1 = true;   // i1 becomes 1
int i2 {true};   // i2 becomes 1
```

If you prefer to use the {}-initializer syntax to prevent narrowing, yet still want to convert an **int** to a **bool**, you can be explicit:

```
void f(int i)
{
    bool b {i!=0};
    // ...
};
```

In arithmetic and logical expressions, **bool**s are converted to **int**s; integer arithmetic and logical operations are performed on the converted values. If the result needs to be converted back to **bool**, a **0** is converted to **false** and a nonzero value is converted to **true**. For example:

```
bool a = true;
bool b = true;

bool x = a+b;   // a+b is 2, so x becomes true
bool y = a||b;  // a||b is 1, so y becomes true ("||" means "or")
bool z = a–b;   // a-b is 0, so z becomes false
```

A pointer can be implicitly converted to a **bool** (§10.5.2.5). A non-null pointer converts to **true**; pointers with the value **nullptr** convert to **false**. For example:

```
void g(int* p)
{
    bool b = p;           // narrows to true or false
    bool b2 {p!=nullptr}; // explicit test against nullptr

    if (p) {       // equivalent to p!=nullptr
        // ...
    }
}
```

I prefer **if (p)** over **if (p!=nullptr)** because it more directly expresses the notion "if **p** is valid" and also because it is shorter. The shorter form leaves fewer opportunities for mistakes.

6.2.3 Character Types

There are many character sets and character set encodings in use. C++ provides a variety of character types that reflect that – often bewildering – variety:

- **char**: The default character type, used for program text. A **char** is used for the implementation's character set and is usually 8 bits.
- **signed char**: Like **char**, but guaranteed to be signed, that is, capable of holding both positive and negative values.
- **unsigned char**: Like **char**, but guaranteed to be unsigned.
- **wchar_t**: Provided to hold characters of a larger character set such as Unicode (see §7.3.2.2). The size of **wchar_t** is implementation-defined and large enough to hold the largest character set supported by the implementation's locale (Chapter 39).
- **char16_t**: A type for holding 16-bit character sets, such as UTF-16.
- **char32_t**: A type for holding 32-bit character sets, such as UTF-32.

These are six distinct types (despite the fact that the _t suffix is often used to denote aliases; §6.5). On each implementation, the **char** type will be identical to that of either **signed char** or **unsigned**

char, but these three names are still considered separate types.

A **char** variable can hold a character of the implementation's character set. For example:

```
char ch = 'a';
```

Almost universally, a **char** has 8 bits so that it can hold one of 256 different values. Typically, the character set is a variant of ISO-646, for example ASCII, thus providing the characters appearing on your keyboard. Many problems arise from the fact that this set of characters is only partially standardized.

Serious variations occur between character sets supporting different natural languages and between character sets supporting the same natural language in different ways. Here, we are interested only in how such differences affect the rules of C++. The larger and more interesting issue of how to program in a multilingual, multi-character-set environment is beyond the scope of this book, although it is alluded to in several places (§6.2.3, §36.2.1, Chapter 39).

It is safe to assume that the implementation character set includes the decimal digits, the 26 alphabetic characters of English, and some of the basic punctuation characters. It is *not* safe to assume that:

- There are no more than 127 characters in an 8-bit character set (e.g., some sets provide 255 characters).
- There are no more alphabetic characters than English provides (most European languages provide more, e.g., æ, þ, and ß).
- The alphabetic characters are contiguous (EBCDIC leaves a gap between 'i' and 'j').
- Every character used to write C++ is available (e.g., some national character sets do not provide {, }, [,], |, and \).
- A **char** fits in 1 byte. There are embedded processors without byte accessing hardware for which a **char** is 4 bytes. Also, one could reasonably use a 16-bit Unicode encoding for the basic **char**s.

Whenever possible, we should avoid making assumptions about the representation of objects. This general rule applies even to characters.

Each character has an integer value in the character set used by the implementation. For example, the value of 'b' is **98** in the ASCII character set. Here is a loop that outputs the the integer value of any character you care to input:

```
void intval()
{
    for (char c; cin >> c; )
        cout << "the value of '" << c << "' is " << int{c} << '\n';
}
```

The notation **int{c}** gives the integer value for a character **c** ("the **int** we can construct from **c**"). The possibility of converting a **char** to an integer raises the question: is a **char** signed or unsigned? The 256 values represented by an 8-bit byte can be interpreted as the values **0** to **255** or as the values **–127** to **127**. No, not **–128** to **127** as one might expect: the C++ standard leaves open the possibility of one's-complement hardware and that eliminates one value; thus, a use of **–128** is nonportable. Unfortunately, the choice of signed or unsigned for a plain **char** is implementation-defined. C++ provides two types for which the answer is definite: **signed char**, which can hold at least the values **–127** to **127**, and **unsigned char**, which can hold at least the values **0** to **255**.

Fortunately, the difference matters only for values outside the **0** to **127** range, and the most common characters are within that range.

Values outside that range stored in a plain **char** can lead to subtle portability problems. See §6.2.3.1 if you need to use more than one type of **char** or if you store integers in **char** variables.

Note that the character types are integral types (§6.2.1) so that arithmetic and bitwise logical operations (§10.3) apply. For example:

```
void digits()
{
    for (int i=0; i!=10; ++i)
        cout << static_cast<char>('0'+i);
}
```

This is a way of writing the ten digits to **cout**. The character literal **'0'** is converted to its integer value and **i** is added. The resulting **int** is then converted to a **char** and written to **cout**. Plain **'0'+i** is an **int**, so if I had left out the **static_cast<char>**, the output would have been something like **48**, **49**, and so on, rather than **0**, **1**, and so on.

6.2.3.1 Signed and Unsigned Characters

It is implementation-defined whether a plain **char** is considered signed or unsigned. This opens the possibility for some nasty surprises and implementation dependencies. For example:

```
char c = 255;   // 255 is "all ones," hexadecimal 0xFF
int i = c;
```

What will be the value of **i**? Unfortunately, the answer is undefined. On an implementation with 8-bit bytes, the answer depends on the meaning of the "all ones" **char** bit pattern when extended into an **int**. On a machine where a **char** is unsigned, the answer is **255**. On a machine where a **char** is signed, the answer is –1. In this case, the compiler might warn about the conversion of the literal **255** to the **char** value –1. However, C++ does not offer a general mechanism for detecting this kind of problem. One solution is to avoid plain **char** and use the specific **char** types only. Unfortunately, some standard-library functions, such as **strcmp()**, take plain **chars** only (§43.4).

A **char** must behave identically to either a **signed char** or an **unsigned char**. However, the three **char** types are distinct, so you can't mix pointers to different **char** types. For example:

```
void f(char c, signed char sc, unsigned char uc)
{
    char* pc = &uc;            // error: no pointer conversion
    signed char* psc = pc;     // error: no pointer conversion
    unsigned char* puc = pc;   // error: no pointer conversion
    psc = puc;                 // error: no pointer conversion
}
```

Variables of the three **char** types can be freely assigned to each other. However, assigning a too-large value to a signed **char** (§10.5.2.1) is still undefined. For example:

```
void g(char c, signed char sc, unsigned char uc)
{
    c = 255;   // implementation-defined if plain chars are signed and have 8 bits
```

```
c = sc;     // OK
c = uc;     // implementation-defined if plain chars are signed and if uc's value is too large
sc = uc;    // implementation defined if uc's value is too large
uc = sc;    // OK: conversion to unsigned
sc = c;     // implementation-defined if plain chars are unsigned and if c's value is too large
uc = c;     // OK: conversion to unsigned
}
```

To be concrete, assume that a **char** is 8 bits:

```
signed char sc = –160;
unsigned char uc = sc;    // uc == 116 (because 256-160==116)
cout << uc;               // print 't'

char count[256];          // assume 8-bit chars
++count[sc];              // likely disaster: out-of-range access
++count[uc];              // OK
```

None of these potential problems and confusions occur if you use plain **char** throughout and avoid negative character values.

6.2.3.2 Character Literals

A *character literal* is a single character enclosed in single quotes, for example, 'a' and '0'. The type of a character literal is **char**. A character literal can be implicitly converted to its integer value in the character set of the machine on which the C++ program is to run. For example, if you are running on a machine using the ASCII character set, the value of '0' is **48**. The use of character literals rather than decimal notation makes programs more portable.

A few characters have standard names that use the backslash, \, as an escape character:

Name	ASCII Name	C++ Name
Newline	NL (LF)	\n
Horizontal tab	HT	\t
Vertical tab	VT	\v
Backspace	BS	\b
Carriage return	CR	\r
Form feed	FF	\f
Alert	BEL	\a
Backslash	\	\\
Question mark	?	\?
Single quote	'	\'
Double quote	"	\"
Octal number	*ooo*	*ooo*
Hexadecimal number	*hhh*	\x*hhh* ...

Despite their appearance, these are single characters.

We can represent a character from the implementation character set as a one-, two-, or three-digit octal number (\ followed by octal digits) or as a hexadecimal number (\x followed by hexadecimal digits). There is no limit to the number of hexadecimal digits in the sequence. A sequence of octal or hexadecimal digits is terminated by the first character that is not an octal digit or a hexadecimal digit, respectively. For example:

Octal	Hexadecimal	Decimal	ASCII
'\6'	'\x6'	6	ACK
'\60'	'\x30'	48	'0'
'\137'	'\x05f'	95	'_'

This makes it possible to represent every character in the machine's character set and, in particular, to embed such characters in character strings (see §7.3.2). Using any numeric notation for characters makes a program nonportable across machines with different character sets.

It is possible to enclose more than one character in a character literal, for example, 'ab'. Such uses are archaic, implementation-dependent, and best avoided. The type of such a multicharacter literal is int.

When embedding a numeric constant in a string using the octal notation, it is wise always to use three digits for the number. The notation is hard enough to read without having to worry about whether or not the character after a constant is a digit. For hexadecimal constants, use two digits. Consider these examples:

```
char v1[] = "a\xah\129";        // 6 chars: 'a' '\xa' 'h' '\12' '9' '\0'
char v2[] = "a\xah\127";        // 5 chars: 'a' '\xa' 'h' '\127' '\0'
char v3[] = "a\xad\127";        // 4 chars: 'a' '\xad' '\127' '\0'
char v4[] = "a\xad\0127";       // 5 chars: 'a' '\xad' '\012' '7' '\0'
```

Wide character literals are of the form L'ab' and are of type wchar_t. The number of characters between the quotes and their meanings are implementation-defined.

A C++ program can manipulate character sets that are much richer than the 127-character ASCII set, such as Unicode. Literals of such larger character sets are presented as sequences of four or eight hexadecimal digits preceded by a U or a u. For example:

```
U'\UFADEBEEF'
u'\uDEAD'
u'\xDEAD'
```

The shorter notation u'\uXXXX' is equivalent to U'\U0000XXXX' for any hexadecimal digit X. A number of hexadecimal digits different from four or eight is a lexical error. The meaning of the hexadecimal number is defined by the ISO/IEC 10646 standard and such values are called *universal character names*. In the C++ standard, universal character names are described in §iso.2.2, §iso.2.3, §iso.2.14.3, §iso.2.14.5, and §iso.E.

6.2.4 Integer Types

Like char, each integer type comes in three forms: "plain" int, signed int, and unsigned int. In addition, integers come in four sizes: short int, "plain" int, long int, and long long int. A long int can be referred to as plain long, and a long long int can be referred to as plain long long. Similarly, short is a synonym for short int, unsigned for unsigned int, and signed for signed int. No, there is no long short int equivalent to int.

The **unsigned** integer types are ideal for uses that treat storage as a bit array. Using an **unsigned** instead of an **int** to gain one more bit to represent positive integers is almost never a good idea. Attempts to ensure that some values are positive by declaring variables **unsigned** will typically be defeated by the implicit conversion rules (§10.5.1, §10.5.2.1).

Unlike plain **chars**, plain **ints** are always signed. The signed **int** types are simply more explicit synonyms for their plain **int** counterparts, rather than different types.

If you need more detailed control over integer sizes, you can use aliases from **<cstdint>** (§43.7), such as **int64_t** (a signed integer with exactly 64 bits), **uint_fast16_t** (an unsigned integer with exactly 8 bits, supposedly the fastest such integer), and **int_least32_t** (a signed integer with at least 32 bits, just like plain int). The plain integer types have well-defined minimal sizes (§6.2.8), so the **<cstdint>** are sometimes redundant and can be overused.

In addition to the standard integer types, an implementation may provide *extended integer types* (signed and unsigned). These types must behave like integers and are considered integer types when considering conversions and integer literal values, but they usually have greater range (occupy more space).

6.2.4.1 Integer Literals

Integer literals come in three guises: decimal, octal, and hexadecimal. Decimal literals are the most commonly used and look as you would expect them to:

```
7   1234   976   12345678901234567890
```

The compiler ought to warn about literals that are too long to represent, but an error is only guaranteed for {} initializers (§6.3.5).

A literal starting with zero followed by **x** or **X** (**0x** or **0X**) is a hexadecimal (base 16) number. A literal starting with zero but not followed by **x** or **X** is an octal (base 8) number. For example:

Decimal	Octal	Hexadecimal
	0	0x0
2	02	0x2
63	077	0x3f
83	0123	0x63

The letters **a**, **b**, **c**, **d**, **e**, and **f**, or their uppercase equivalents, are used to represent **10**, **11**, **12**, **13**, **14**, and **15**, respectively. Octal and hexadecimal notations are most useful for expressing bit patterns. Using these notations to express genuine numbers can lead to surprises. For example, on a machine on which an **int** is represented as a two's complement 16-bit integer, **0xffff** is the negative decimal number **–1**. Had more bits been used to represent an integer, it would have been the positive decimal number **65535**.

The suffix **U** can be used to write explicitly **unsigned** literals. Similarly, the suffix **L** can be used to write explicitly **long** literals. For example, **3** is an **int**, **3U** is an **unsigned int**, and **3L** is a **long int**.

Combinations of suffixes are allowed. For example:

```
cout << 0xF0UL << ' ' << 0LU << '\n';
```

If no suffix is provided, the compiler gives an integer literal a suitable type based on its value and the implementation's integer sizes (§6.2.4.2).

It is a good idea to limit the use of nonobvious constants to a few well-commented **const** (§7.5), **constexpr** (§10.4), and enumerator (§8.4) initializers.

6.2.4.2 Types of Integer Literals

In general, the type of an integer literal depends on its form, value, and suffix:

- If it is decimal and has no suffix, it has the first of these types in which its value can be represented: **int, long int, long long int**.
- If it is octal or hexadecimal and has no suffix, it has the first of these types in which its value can be represented: **int, unsigned int, long int, unsigned long int, long long int, unsigned long long int**.
- If it is suffixed by **u** or **U**, its type is the first of these types in which its value can be represented: **unsigned int, unsigned long int, unsigned long long int**.
- If it is decimal and suffixed by **l** or **L**, its type is the first of these types in which its value can be represented: **long int, long long int**.
- If it is octal or hexadecimal and suffixed by **l** or **L**, its type is the first of these types in which its value can be represented: **long int, unsigned long int, long long int, unsigned long long int**.
- If it is suffixed by **ul, lu, uL, Lu, Ul, lU, UL,** or **LU**, its type is the first of these types in which its value can be represented: **unsigned long int, unsigned long long int**.
- If it is decimal and is suffixed by **ll** or **LL**, its type is **long long int**.
- If it is octal or hexadecimal and is suffixed by **ll** or **LL**, its type is the first of these types in which its value can be represented: **long long int, unsigned long long int**.
- If it is suffixed by **llu, llU, ull, Ull, LLu, LLU, uLL,** or **ULL**, its type is **unsigned long long int**.

For example, **100000** is of type **int** on a machine with 32-bit **int**s but of type **long int** on a machine with 16-bit **int**s and 32-bit **long**s. Similarly, **0XA000** is of type **int** on a machine with 32-bit **int**s but of type **unsigned int** on a machine with 16-bit **int**s. These implementation dependencies can be avoided by using suffixes: **100000L** is of type **long int** on all machines and **0XA000U** is of type **unsigned int** on all machines.

6.2.5 Floating-Point Types

The floating-point types represent floating-point numbers. A floating-point number is an approximation of a real number represented in a fixed amount of memory. There are three floating-point types: **float** (single-precision), **double** (double-precision), and **long double** (extended-precision).

The exact meaning of single-, double-, and extended-precision is implementation-defined. Choosing the right precision for a problem where the choice matters requires significant understanding of floating-point computation. If you don't have that understanding, get advice, take the time to learn, or use **double** and hope for the best.

6.2.5.1 Floating-Point Literals

By default, a floating-point literal is of type **double**. Again, a compiler ought to warn about floating-point literals that are too large to be represented. Here are some floating-point literals:

    1.23   .23   0.23   1.   1.0   1.2e10   1.23e–15

Note that a space cannot occur in the middle of a floating-point literal. For example, **65.43 e–21** is not a floating-point literal but rather four separate lexical tokens (causing a syntax error):

    65.43   e   –   21

If you want a floating-point literal of type **float**, you can define one using the suffix **f** or **F**:

    3.14159265f   2.0f   2.997925F   2.9e–3f

If you want a floating-point literal of type **long double**, you can define one using the suffix **l** or **L**:

    3.14159265L   2.0L   2.997925L   2.9e–3L

6.2.6 Prefixes and Suffixes

There is a minor zoo of suffixes indicating types of literals and also a few prefixes:

Arithmetic Literal Prefixes and Suffixes					
Notation		*fix	**Meaning**	**Example**	**Reference**	**ISO**
0		prefix	octal	0776	§6.2.4.1	§iso.2.14.2
0x	0X	prefix	hexadecimal	0xff	§6.2.4.1	§iso.2.14.2
u	U	suffix	unsigned	10U	§6.2.4.1	§iso.2.14.2
l	L	suffix	long	20000L	§6.2.4.1	§iso.2.14.2
ll	LL	suffix	long long	20000LL	§6.2.4.1	§iso.2.14.2
f	F	suffix	float	10f	§6.2.5.1	§iso.2.14.4
e	E	infix	floating-point	10e–4	§6.2.5.1	§iso.2.14.4
.		infix	floating-point	12.3	§6.2.5.1	§iso.2.14.4
'		prefix	char	'c'	§6.2.3.2	§iso.2.14.3
u'		prefix	char16_t	u'c'	§6.2.3.2	§iso.2.14.3
U'		prefix	char32_t	U'c'	§6.2.3.2	§iso.2.14.3
L'		prefix	wchar_t	L'c'	§6.2.3.2	§iso.2.14.3
"		prefix	string	"mess"	§7.3.2	§iso.2.14.5
R"		prefix	raw string	R"(\b)"	§7.3.2.1	§iso.2.14.5
u8"	u8R"	prefix	UTF-8 string	u8"foo"	§7.3.2.2	§iso.2.14.5
u"	uR"	prefix	UTF-16 string	u"foo"	§7.3.2.2	§iso.2.14.5
U"	UR"	prefix	UTF-32 string	U"foo"	§7.3.2.2	§iso.2.14.5
L"	LR"	prefix	wchar_t string	L"foo"	§7.3.2.2	§iso.2.14.5

Note that "string" here means "string literal" (§7.3.2) rather than "of type **std::string**."

Obviously, we could also consider **.** and **e** as infix and **R"** and **u8"** as the first part of a set of delimiters. However, I consider the nomenclature less important than giving an overview of the bewildering variety of literals.

The suffixes **l** and **L** can be combined with the suffixes **u** and **U** to express **unsigned long** types. For example:

```
1LU          // unsigned long
2UL          // unsigned long
3ULL         // unsigned long long
4LLU         // unsigned long long
5LUL         // error
```

The suffixes l and L can be used for floating-point literals to express **long double**. For example:

```
1L           // long int
1.0L         // long double
```

Combinations of R, L, and u prefixes are allowed, for example, uR"**(foo\(bar))**". Note the dramatic difference in the meaning of a U prefix for a character (**unsigned**) and for a string UTF-32 encoding (§7.3.2.2).

In addition, a user can define new suffixes for user-defined types. For example, by defining a user-defined literal operator (§19.2.6), we can get

```
"foo bar"s   // a literal of type std::string
123_km       // a literal of type Distance
```

Suffixes not starting with _ are reserved for the standard library.

6.2.7 void

The type **void** is syntactically a fundamental type. It can, however, be used only as part of a more complicated type; there are no objects of type **void**. It is used either to specify that a function does not return a value or as the base type for pointers to objects of unknown type. For example:

```
void x;      // error: there are no void objects
void& r;     // error: there are no references to void
void f();    // function f does not return a value (§12.1.4)
void* pv;    // pointer to object of unknown type (§7.2.1)
```

When declaring a function, you must specify the type of the value returned. Logically, you would expect to be able to indicate that a function didn't return a value by omitting the return type. However, that would make a mess of the grammar (§iso.A). Consequently, **void** is used as a "pseudo return type" to indicate that a function doesn't return a value.

6.2.8 Sizes

Some of the aspects of C++'s fundamental types, such as the size of an **int**, are implementation-defined (§6.1). I point out these dependencies and often recommend avoiding them or taking steps to minimize their impact. Why should you bother? People who program on a variety of systems or use a variety of compilers care a lot because if they don't, they are forced to waste time finding and fixing obscure bugs. People who claim they don't care about portability usually do so because they use only a single system and feel they can afford the attitude that "the language is what my compiler implements." This is a narrow and shortsighted view. If your program is a success, it will be ported, so someone will have to find and fix problems related to implementation-dependent features. In addition, programs often need to be compiled with other compilers for the same system, and even a future release of your favorite compiler may do some things differently from the current one. It is far easier to know and limit the impact of implementation dependencies when a program is written than to try to untangle the mess afterward.

It is relatively easy to limit the impact of implementation-dependent language features. Limiting the impact of system-dependent library facilities is far harder. Using standard-library facilities wherever feasible is one approach.

The reason for providing more than one integer type, more than one unsigned type, and more than one floating-point type is to allow the programmer to take advantage of hardware characteristics. On many machines, there are significant differences in memory requirements, memory access times, and computation speed among the different varieties of fundamental types. If you know a machine, it is usually easy to choose, for example, the appropriate integer type for a particular variable. Writing truly portable low-level code is harder.

Here is a graphical representation of a plausible set of fundamental types and a sample string literal (§7.3.2):

char	'a'
bool	1
short	756
int	100000000
long	1234567890
long long	1234567890
int*	&c1
double	1234567e34
long double	1234567e34
char[14]	Hello, world!\0

On the same scale (.2 inch to a byte), a megabyte of memory would stretch about 3 miles (5 km) to the right.

Sizes of C++ objects are expressed in terms of multiples of the size of a **char**, so by definition the size of a **char** is **1**. The size of an object or type can be obtained using the **sizeof** operator (§10.3). This is what is guaranteed about sizes of fundamental types:

- $1 \equiv$ **sizeof(char)** $\leq$ **sizeof(short)** $\leq$ **sizeof(int)** $\leq$ **sizeof(long)** $\leq$ **sizeof(long long)**
- $1 \leq$ **sizeof(bool)** $\leq$ **sizeof(long)**
- **sizeof(char)** $\leq$ **sizeof(wchar_t)** $\leq$ **sizeof(long)**
- **sizeof(float)** $\leq$ **sizeof(double)** $\leq$ **sizeof(long double)**
- **sizeof(N)** $\equiv$ **sizeof(signed N)** $\equiv$ **sizeof(unsigned N)**

In that last line, N can be char, short, int, long, or long long. In addition, it is guaranteed that a char has at least 8 bits, a short at least 16 bits, and a long at least 32 bits. A char can hold a character of the machine's character set. The char type is supposed to be chosen by the implementation to be the most suitable type for holding and manipulating characters on a given computer; it is typically an 8-bit byte. Similarly, the int type is supposed to be chosen to be the most suitable for holding and manipulating integers on a given computer; it is typically a 4-byte (32-bit) word. It is unwise to assume more. For example, there are machines with 32-bit chars. It is extremely unwise to assume that the size of an int is the same as the size of a pointer; many machines ("64-bit architectures") have pointers that are larger than integers. Note that it is not guaranteed that sizeof(long)<sizeof(long long) or that sizeof(double)<sizeof(long double).

Some implementation-defined aspects of fundamental types can be found by a simple use of sizeof, and more can be found in <limits>. For example:

```
#include <limits>    // §40.2
#include <iostream>

int main()
{
    cout << "size of long " << sizeof(1L) << '\n';
    cout << "size of long long " << sizeof(1LL) << '\n';

    cout << "largest float == " << std::numeric_limits<float>::max() << '\n';
    cout << "char is signed == " << std::numeric_limits<char>::is_signed << '\n';
}
```

The functions in <limits> (§40.2) are constexpr (§10.4) so that they can be used without run-time overhead and in contexts that require a constant expression.

The fundamental types can be mixed freely in assignments and expressions. Wherever possible, values are converted so as not to lose information (§10.5).

If a value v can be represented exactly in a variable of type T, a conversion of v to T is value-preserving. Conversions that are not value-preserving are best avoided (§2.2.2, §10.5.2.6).

If you need a specific size of integer, say, a 16-bit integer, you can #include the standard header <cstdint> that defines a variety of types (or rather type aliases; §6.5). For example:

```
int16_t x {0xaabb};                    // 2 bytes
int64_t xxxx {0xaaaabbbbccccdddd};     // 8 bytes
int_least16_t y;                       // at least 2 bytes (just like int)
int_least32_t yy                       // at least 4 bytes (just like long)
int_fast32_t z;                        // the fastest int type with at least 4 bytes
```

The standard header <cstddef> defines an alias that is very widely used in both standard-library declarations and user code: size_t is an implementation-defined unsigned integer type that can hold the size in bytes of every object. Consequently, it is used where we need to hold an object size. For example:

```
void* allocate(size_t n);    // get n bytes
```

Similarly, <cstddef> defines the signed integer type ptrdiff_t for holding the result of subtracting two pointers to get a number of elements.

6.2.9 Alignment

An object doesn't just need enough storage to hold its representation. In addition, on some machine architectures, the bytes used to hold it must have proper *alignment* for the hardware to access it efficiently (or in extreme cases to access it at all). For example, a 4-byte int often has to be aligned on a word (4-byte) boundary, and sometimes an 8-byte **double** has to be aligned on a word (8-byte) boundary. Of course, this is all very implementation specific, and for most programmers completely implicit. You can write good C++ code for decades without needing to be explicit about alignment. Where alignment most often becomes visible is in object layouts: sometimes **struct**s contain "holes" to improve alignment (§8.2.1).

The **alignof()** operator returns the alignment of its argument expression. For example:

```
auto ac = alignof('c');      // the alignment of a char
auto ai = alignof(1);        // the alignment of an int
auto ad = alignof(2.0);      // the alignment of a double

int a[20];
auto aa = alignof(a);        // the alignment of an int
```

Sometimes, we have to use alignment in a declaration, where an expression, such as **alignof(x+y)** is not allowed. Instead, we can use the type specifier **alignas**: **alignas(T)** means "align just like a **T**." For example, we can set aside uninitialized storage for some type **X** like this:

```
void user(const vector<X>& vx)
{
    constexpr int bufmax = 1024;
    alignas(X) buffer[bufmax];        // uninitialized

    const int max = min(vx.size(),bufmax/sizeof(X));
    uninitialized_copy(vx.begin(),vx.begin()+max,buffer);
    // ...
}
```

6.3 Declarations

Before a name (identifier) can be used in a C++ program, it must be declared. That is, its type must be specified to inform the compiler what kind of entity the name refers to. For example:

```
char ch;
string s;
auto count = 1;
const double pi {3.1415926535897};
extern int error_number;

const char* name = "Njal";
const char* season[] = { "spring", "summer", "fall", "winter" };
vector<string> people { name, "Skarphedin", "Gunnar" };
```

```
struct Date { int d, m, y; };
int day(Date* p) { return p->d; }
double sqrt(double);
template<class T> T abs(T a) { return a<0 ? -a : a; }

constexpr int fac(int n) { return (n<2)?1:n*fac(n-1); }    // possible compile-time evaluation (§2.2.3)
constexpr double zz { ii*fac(7) };                         // compile-time initialization

using Cmplx = std::complex<double>;                        // type alias (§3.4.5, §6.5)
struct User;                                               // type name
enum class Beer { Carlsberg, Tuborg, Thor };
namespace NS { int a; }
```

As can be seen from these examples, a declaration can do more than simply associate a type with a name. Most of these *declarations* are also *definitions*. A definition is a declaration that supplies all that is needed in a program for the use of an entity. In particular, if it takes memory to represent something, that memory is set aside by its definition. A different terminology deems declarations parts of an interface and definitions parts of an implementation. When taking that view, we try to compose interfaces out of declarations that can be replicated in separate files (§15.2.2); definitions that set aside memory do not belong in interfaces.

Assuming that these declarations are in the global scope (§6.3.4), we have:

```
char ch;                          // set aside memory for a char and initialize it to 0
auto count = 1;                   // set aside memory for an int initialized to 1
const char* name = "Njal";        // set aside memory for a pointer to char
                                  // set aside memory for a string literal "Njal"
                                  // initialize the pointer with the address of that string literal

struct Date { int d, m, y; };     // Date is a struct with three members
int day(Date* p) { return p->d; } // day is a function that executes the specified code

using Point = std::complex<short>;// Point is a name for std::complex<short>
```

Of the declarations above, only three are not also definitions:

```
double sqrt(double);              // function declaration
extern int error_number;          // variable declaration
struct User;                      // type name declaration
```

That is, if used, the entity they refer to must be defined elsewhere. For example:

```
double sqrt(double d) { /* ... */ }
int error_number = 1;
struct User { /* ... */ };
```

There must always be exactly one definition for each name in a C++ program (for the effects of #include, see §15.2.3). However, there can be many declarations.

All declarations of an entity must agree on its type. So, this fragment has two errors:

```
int count;
int count;          // error: redefinition
```

```
extern int error_number;
extern short error_number;        // error: type mismatch
```

This has no errors (for the use of **extern**, see §15.2):

```
extern int error_number;
extern int error_number; // OK: redeclaration
```

Some definitions explicitly specify a "value" for the entities they define. For example:

```
struct Date { int d, m, y; };
using Point = std::complex<short>;        // Point is a name for std::complex<short>
int day(Date* p) { return p->d; }
const double pi {3.1415926535897};
```

For types, aliases, templates, functions, and constants, the "value" is permanent. For non-**const** data types, the initial value may be changed later. For example:

```
void f()
{
    int count {1};                     // initialize count to 1
    const char* name {"Bjarne"}; // name is a variable that points to a constant (§7.5)
    count = 2;                         // assign 2 to count
    name = "Marian";
}
```

Of the definitions, only two do not specify values:

```
char ch;
string s;
```

See §6.3.5 and §17.3.3 for explanations of how and when a variable is assigned a default value. Any declaration that specifies a value is a definition.

6.3.1 The Structure of Declarations

The structure of a declaration is defined by the C++ grammar (§iso.A). This grammar evolved over four decades, starting with the early C grammars, and is quite complicated. However, without too many radical simplifications, we can consider a declaration as having five parts (in order):

- Optional prefix specifiers (e.g., **static** or **virtual**)
- A base type (e.g., **vector<double>** or **const int**)
- A declarator optionally including a name (e.g., **p[7]**, **n**, or *(*)[])
- Optional suffix function specifiers (e.g., **const** or **noexcept**)
- An optional initializer or function body (e.g., **={7,5,3}** or **{return x;}**)

Except for function and namespace definitions, a declaration is terminated by a semicolon. Consider a definition of an array of C-style strings:

```
const char* kings[] = { "Antigonus", "Seleucus", "Ptolemy" };
```

Here, the base type is **const char**, the declarator is *kings[]*, and the initializer is the = followed by the {}-list.

A specifier is an initial keyword, such as **virtual** (§3.2.3, §20.3.2), **extern** (§15.2), or **constexpr** (§2.2.3), that specifies some non-type attribute of what is being declared.

A declarator is composed of a name and optionally some declarator operators. The most common declarator operators are:

<table>
<tr><th colspan="3" align="center">Declarator Operators</th></tr>
<tr><td>prefix</td><td>*</td><td>pointer</td></tr>
<tr><td>prefix</td><td>*const</td><td>constant pointer</td></tr>
<tr><td>prefix</td><td>*volatile</td><td>volatile pointer</td></tr>
<tr><td>prefix</td><td>&</td><td>lvalue reference (§7.7.1)</td></tr>
<tr><td>prefix</td><td>&&</td><td>rvalue reference (§7.7.2)</td></tr>
<tr><td>prefix</td><td>auto</td><td>function (using suffix return type)</td></tr>
<tr><td>postfix</td><td>[]</td><td>array</td></tr>
<tr><td>postfix</td><td>()</td><td>function</td></tr>
<tr><td>postfix</td><td>-></td><td>returns from function</td></tr>
</table>

Their use would be simple if they were all either prefix or postfix. However, *, [], and () were designed to mirror their use in expressions (§10.3). Thus, * is prefix and [] and () are postfix. The postfix declarator operators bind tighter than the prefix ones. Consequently, char*kings[] is an array of pointers to char, whereas char(*kings)[] is a pointer to an array of char. We have to use parentheses to express types such as "pointer to array" and "pointer to function"; see the examples in §7.2.

Note that the type cannot be left out of a declaration. For example:

```
const c = 7;    // error: no type

gt(int a, int b)    // error: no return type
{
     return (a>b) ? a : b;
}

unsigned ui;    // OK: "unsigned" means "unsigned int"
long li;        // OK: "long" means "long int"
```

In this, standard C++ differs from early versions of C and C++ that allowed the first two examples by considering int to be the type when none was specified (§44.3). This "implicit int" rule was a source of subtle errors and much confusion.

Some types have names composed out of multiple keywords, such as long long and volatile int. Some type names don't even look much like names, such as decltype(f(x)) (the return type of a call f(x); §6.3.6.3).

The volatile specifier is described in §41.4.

The alignas() specifier is described in §6.2.9.

6.3.2 Declaring Multiple Names

It is possible to declare several names in a single declaration. The declaration simply contains a list of comma-separated declarators. For example, we can declare two integers like this:

```
int x, y;       // int x; int y;
```

Operators apply to individual names only – and not to any subsequent names in the same declaration. For example:

```
int* p, y;    // int* p; int y;    NOT int* y;
int x, *q;    // int x; int* q;
int v[10], *pv; // int v[10]; int* pv;
```

Such declarations with multiple names and nontrivial declarators make a program harder to read and should be avoided.

6.3.3 Names

A name (identifier) consists of a sequence of letters and digits. The first character must be a letter. The underscore character, _, is considered a letter. C++ imposes no limit on the number of characters in a name. However, some parts of an implementation are not under the control of the compiler writer (in particular, the linker), and those parts, unfortunately, sometimes do impose limits. Some run-time environments also make it necessary to extend or restrict the set of characters accepted in an identifier. Extensions (e.g., allowing the character $ in a name) yield nonportable programs. A C++ keyword (§6.3.3.1), such as **new** or **int**, cannot be used as a name of a user-defined entity. Examples of names are:

hello	this_is_a_most_unusually_long_identifier_that_is_better_avoided			
DEFINED	foO	bAr	u_name	HorseSense
var0	var1	CLASS	_class	___

Examples of character sequences that cannot be used as identifiers are:

012	a fool	$sys	class	3var
pay.due	foo˜bar	.name	if	

Nonlocal names starting with an underscore are reserved for special facilities in the implementation and the run-time environment, so such names should not be used in application programs. Similarly, names starting with a double underscore (__) or an underscore followed by an uppercase letter (e.g., _Foo) are reserved (§iso.17.6.4.3).

When reading a program, the compiler always looks for the longest string of characters that could make up a name. Hence, **var10** is a single name, not the name **var** followed by the number **10**. Also, **elseif** is a single name, not the keyword **else** followed by the keyword **if**.

Uppercase and lowercase letters are distinct, so **Count** and **count** are different names, but it is often unwise to choose names that differ only by capitalization. In general, it is best to avoid names that differ only in subtle ways. For example, in some fonts, the uppercase "o" (**O**) and zero (**0**) can be hard to tell apart, as can the lowercase "L" (**l**), uppercase "i" (**I**), and one (**1**). Consequently, **l0**, **lO**, **l1**, **ll**, and **l1l** are poor choices for identifier names. Not all fonts have the same problems, but most have some.

Names from a large scope ought to have relatively long and reasonably obvious names, such as **vector**, **Window_with_border**, and **Department_number**. However, code is clearer if names used only in a small scope have short, conventional names such as **x**, **i**, and **p**. Functions (Chapter 12), classes (Chapter 16), and namespaces (§14.3.1) can be used to keep scopes small. It is often useful to keep frequently used names relatively short and reserve really long names for infrequently used entities.

Choose names to reflect the meaning of an entity rather than its implementation. For example, **phone_book** is better than **number_vector** even if the phone numbers happen to be stored in a **vector** (§4.4). Do not encode type information in a name (e.g., **pcname** for a name that's a **char∗** or **icount** for a count that's an **int**) as is sometimes done in languages with dynamic or weak type systems:

- Encoding types in names lowers the abstraction level of the program; in particular, it prevents generic programming (which relies on a name being able to refer to entities of different types).
- The compiler is better at keeping track of types than you are.
- If you want to change the type of a name (e.g., use a **std::string** to hold the name), you'll have to change every use of the name (or the type encoding becomes a lie).
- Any system of type abbreviations you can come up with will become overelaborate and cryptic as the variety of types you use increases.

Choosing good names is an art.

Try to maintain a consistent naming style. For example, capitalize names of user-defined types and start names of non-type entities with a lowercase letter (for example, **Shape** and **current_token**). Also, use all capitals for macros (if you must use macros (§12.6); for example, **HACK**) and never for non-macros (not even for non-macro constants). Use underscores to separate words in an identifier; **number_of_elements** is more readable than **numberOfElements**. However, consistency is hard to achieve because programs are typically composed of fragments from different sources and several different reasonable styles are in use. Be consistent in your use of abbreviations and acronyms. Note that the language and the standard library use lowercase for types; this can be seen as a hint that they are part of the standard.

6.3.3.1 Keywords

The C++ keywords are:

C++ Keywords					
alignas	alignof	and	and_eq	asm	auto
bitand	bitor	bool	break	case	catch
char	char16_t	char32_t	class	compl	const
constexpr	const_cast	continue	decltype	default	delete
do	double	dynamic_cast	else	enum	explicit
extern	false	float	for	friend	goto
if	inline	int	long	mutable	namespace
new	noexcept	not	not_eq	nullptr	operator
or	or_eq	private	protected	public	register
reinterpret_cast	return	short	signed	sizeof	static
static_assert	static_cast	struct	switch	template	this
thread_local	throw	true	try	typedef	typeid
typename	union	unsigned	using	virtual	void
volatile	wchar_t	while	xor	xor_eq	

In addition, the word **export** is reserved for future use.

6.3.4 Scope

A declaration introduces a name into a scope; that is, a name can be used only in a specific part of the program text.

- *Local scope*: A name declared in a function (Chapter 12) or lambda (§11.4) is called a *local name*. Its scope extends from its point of declaration to the end of the block in which its declaration occurs. A *block* is a section of code delimited by a {} pair. Function and lambda parameter names are considered local names in the outermost block of their function or lambda.
- *Class scope*: A name is called a *member name* (or a *class member name*) if it is defined in a class outside any function, class (Chapter 16), enum class (§8.4.1), or other namespace. Its scope extends from the opening { of the class declaration to the end of the class declaration.
- *Namespace scope*: A name is called a *namespace member name* if it is defined in a namespace (§14.3.1) outside any function, lambda (§11.4), class (Chapter 16), enum class (§8.4.1), or other namespace. Its scope extends from the point of declaration to the end of its namespace. A namespace name may also be accessible from other translation units (§15.2).
- *Global scope*: A name is called a *global name* if it is defined outside any function, class (Chapter 16), enum class (§8.4.1), or namespace (§14.3.1). The scope of a global name extends from the point of declaration to the end of the file in which its declaration occurs. A global name may also be accessible from other translation units (§15.2). Technically, the global namespace is considered a namespace, so a global name is an example of a namespace member name.
- *Statement scope*: A name is in a statement scope if it is defined within the () part of a **for**-, **while**-, **if**-, or **switch**-statement. Its scope extends from its point of declaration to the end of its statement. All names in statement scope are local names.
- *Function scope*: A label (§9.6) is in scope from its point of declaration until the end of the function.

A declaration of a name in a block can hide a declaration in an enclosing block or a global name. That is, a name can be redefined to refer to a different entity within a block. After exit from the block, the name resumes its previous meaning. For example:

```
int x;              // global x

void f()
{
    int x;          // local x hides global x
    x = 1;          // assign to local x
    {
        int x;      // hides first local x
        x = 2;      // assign to second local x
    }
    x = 3;          // assign to first local x
}

int* p = &x;        // take address of global x
```

Hiding names is unavoidable when writing large programs. However, a human reader can easily fail to notice that a name has been hidden (also known as *shadowed*). Because such errors are relatively rare, they can be very difficult to find. Consequently, name hiding should be minimized. Using names such as i and x for global variables or for local variables in a large function is asking for trouble.

A hidden global name can be referred to using the scope resolution operator, ::. For example:

```
int x;

void f2()
{
    int x = 1;   // hide global x
    ::x = 2;     // assign to global x
    x = 2;       // assign to local x
    // ...
}
```

There is no way to use a hidden local name.

The scope of a name that is not a class member starts at its point of declaration, that is, after the complete declarator and before the initializer. This implies that a name can be used even to specify its own initial value. For example:

```
int x = 97;

void f3()
{
    int x = x;     // perverse: initialize x with its own (uninitialized) value
}
```

A good compiler warns if a variable is used before it has been initialized.

It is possible to use a single name to refer to two different objects in a block without using the :: operator. For example:

```
int x = 11;

void f4()          // perverse: use of two different objects both called x in a single scope
{
    int y = x;     // use global x: y = 11
    int x = 22;
    y = x;         // use local x: y = 22
}
```

Again, such subtleties are best avoided.

The names of function arguments are considered declared in the outermost block of a function. For example:

```
void f5(int x)
{
    int x;     // error
}
```

This is an error because x is defined twice in the same scope.

Names introduced in a for-statement are local to that statement (in statement scope). This allows us to use conventional names for loop variables repeatedly in a function. For example:

```
void f(vector<string>& v, list<int>& lst)
{
    for (const auto& x : v) cout << x << '\n';
    for (auto x : lst) cout << x << '\n';
    for (int i = 0, i!=v.size(), ++i) cout << v[i] << '\n';
    for (auto i : {1, 2, 3, 4, 5, 6, 7}) cout << i << '\n';
}
```

This contains no name clashes.

A declaration is not allowed as the only statement on the branch of an if-statement (§9.4.1).

6.3.5 Initialization

If an initializer is specified for an object, that initializer determines the initial value of an object. An initializer can use one of four syntactic styles:

```
X a1 {v};
X a2 = {v};
X a3 = v;
X a4(v);
```

Of these, only the first can be used in every context, and I strongly recommend its use. It is clearer and less error-prone than the alternatives. However, the first form (used for a1) is new in C++11, so the other three forms are what you find in older code. The two forms using = are what you use in C. Old habits die hard, so I sometimes (inconsistently) use = when initializing a simple variable with a simple value. For example:

```
int x1 = 0;
char c1 = 'z';
```

However, anything much more complicated than that is better done using {}. Initialization using {}, *list initialization*, does not allow narrowing (§iso.8.5.4). That is:

- An integer cannot be converted to another integer that cannot hold its value. For example, char to int is allowed, but not int to char.
- A floating-point value cannot be converted to another floating-point type that cannot hold its value. For example, float to double is allowed, but not double to float.
- A floating-point value cannot be converted to an integer type.
- An integer value cannot be converted to a floating-point type.

For example:

```
void f(double val, int val2)
{
    int x2 = val;        // if val==7.9, x2 becomes 7
    char c2 = val2;      // if val2==1025, c2 becomes 1
```

```
    int x3 {val};        // error: possible truncation
    char c3 {val2};      // error: possible narrowing

    char c4 {24};        // OK: 24 can be represented exactly as a char
    char c5 {264};       // error (assuming 8-bit chars): 264 cannot be represented as a char

    int x4 {2.0};        // error: no double to int value conversion

    // ...
}
```

See §10.5 for the conversion rules for built-in types.

There is no advantage to using {} initialization, and one trap, when using **auto** to get the type determined by the initializer. The trap is that if the initializer is a {}-list, we may not want its type deduced (§6.3.6.2). For example:

```
    auto z1 {99};    // z1 is an initializer_list<int>
    auto z2 = 99;    // z2 is an int
```

So prefer = when using **auto**.

It is possible to define a class so that an object can be initialized by a list of values and alternatively be constructed given a couple of arguments that are not simply values to be stored. The classical example is a **vector** of integers:

```
    vector<int> v1 {99};    // v1 is a vector of 1 element with the value 99
    vector<int> v2(99);     // v2 is a vector of 99 elements each with the default value 0
```

I use the explicit invocation of a constructor, **(99)**, to get the second meaning. Most types do not offer such confusing alternatives – even most **vector**s do not; for example:

```
    vector<string> v1{"hello!"};    // v1 is a vector of 1 element with the value "hello!"
    vector<string> v2("hello!");    // error: no vector constructor takes a string literal
```

So, prefer {} initialization over alternatives unless you have a strong reason not to.

The empty initializer list, {}, is used to indicate that a default value is desired. For example:

```
    int x4 {};           // x4 becomes 0
    double d4 {};        // d4 becomes 0.0
    char* p {};          // p becomes nullptr
    vector<int> v4{};    // v4 becomes the empty vector
    string s4 {};        // s4 becomes ""
```

Most types have a default value. For integral types, the default value is a suitable representation of zero. For pointers, the default value is **nullptr** (§7.2.2). For user-defined types, the default value (if any) is determined by the type's constructors (§17.3.3).

For user-defined types, there can be a distinction between direct initialization (where implicit conversions are allowed) and copy initialization (where they are not); see §16.2.6.

Initialization of particular kinds of objects is discussed where appropriate:

- Pointers: §7.2.2, §7.3.2, §7.4
- References: §7.7.1 (lvalues), §7.7.2 (rvalues)

- Arrays: §7.3.1, §7.3.2
- Constants: §10.4
- Classes: §17.3.1 (not using constructors), §17.3.2 (using constructors), §17.3.3 (default), §17.4 (member and base), §17.5 (copy and move)
- User-defined containers: §17.3.4

6.3.5.1 Missing Initializers

For many types, including all built-in types, it is possible to leave out the initializer. If you do that – and that has unfortunately been common – the situation is more complicated. If you don't like the complications, just initialize consistently. The only really good case for an uninitialized variable is a large input buffer. For example:

```
constexpr int max = 1024*1024;
char buf[max];
some_stream.get(buf,max);    // read at most max characters into buf
```

We could easily have initialized **buf**:

```
char buf[max] {};            // initialize every char to 0
```

By redundantly initializing, we would have suffered a performance hit which just might have been significant. Avoid such low-level use of buffers where you can, and don't leave such buffers uninitialized unless you know (e.g., from measurement) that the optimization compared to using an initialized array is significant.

If no initializer is specified, a global (§6.3.4), namespace (§14.3.1), local **static** (§12.1.8), or **static** member (§16.2.12) (collectively called *static objects*) is initialized to {} of the appropriate type. For example:

```
int a;        // means "int a{};" so that a becomes 0
double d;     // means "double d{};" so that d becomes 0.0
```

Local variables and objects created on the free store (sometimes called *dynamic objects* or *heap objects*; §11.2) are not initialized by default unless they are of user-defined types with a default constructor (§17.3.3). For example:

```
void f()
{
    int x;                   // x does not have a well-defined value
    char buf[1024];          // buf[i] does not have a well-defined value

    int* p {new int};        // *p does not have a well-defined value
    char* q {new char[1024]};  // q[i] does not have a well-defined value

    string s;                // s=="" because of string's default constructor
    vector<char> v;          // v=={} because of vector's default constructor

    string* ps {new string};  // *ps is "" because of string's default constructor
    // ...
}
```

If you want initialization of local variables of built-in type or objects of built-in type created with **new**, use {}. For example:

```
void ff()
{
    int x {};                           // x becomes 0
    char buf[1024]{};                   // buf[i] becomes 0 for all i

    int* p {new int{10}};               // *p becomes 10
    char* q {new char[1024]{}};         // q[i] becomes 0 for all i

    // ...
}
```

A member of an array or a class is default initialized if the array or structure is.

6.3.5.2 Initializer Lists

So far, we have considered the cases of no initializer and one initializer value. More complicated objects can require more than one value as an initializer. This is primarily handled by initializer lists delimited by { and }. For example:

```
int a[] = { 1, 2 };                     // array initializer
struct S { int x, string s };
S s = { 1, "Helios" };                  // struct initializer
complex<double> z = { 0, pi };          // use constructor
vector<double> v = { 0.0, 1.1, 2.2, 3.3 };  // use list constructor
```

For C-style initialization of arrays, see §7.3.1. For C-style structures, see §8.2. For user-defined types with constructors, see §2.3.2 or §16.2.5. For initializer-list constructors, see §17.3.4.

In the cases above, the = is redundant. However, some prefer to add it to emphasize that a set of values are used to initialize a set of member variables.

In some cases, function-style argument lists can also be used (§2.3, §16.2.5). For example:

```
complex<double> z(0,pi);                // use constructor
vector<double> v(10,3.3);               // use constructor: v gets 10 elements initialized to 3.3
```

In a declaration, an empty pair of parentheses, (), always means "function" (§12.1). So, if you want to be explicit about "use default initialization" you need {}. For example:

```
complex<double> z1(1,2);                // function-style initializer (initialization by constructor)
complex<double> f1();                   // function declaration

complex<double> z2 {1,2};               // initialization by constructor to {1,2}
complex<double> f2 {};                  // initialization by constructor to the default value {0,0}
```

Note that initialization using the {} notation does not narrow (§6.3.5).

When using **auto**, a {}-list has its type deduced to **std::initializer_list<T>**. For example:

```
auto x1 {1,2,3,4};                      // x1 is an initializer_list<int>
auto x2 {1.0, 2.25, 3.5 };              // x2 is an initializer_list of<double>
auto x3 {1.0,2};                        // error: cannot deduce the type of {1.0,2} (§6.3.6.2)
```

6.3.6 Deducing a Type: auto and decltype()

The language provides two mechanisms for deducing a type from an expression:
- **auto** for deducing a type of an object from its initializer; the type can be the type of a variable, a **const**, or a **constexpr**.
- **decltype(expr)** for deducing the type of something that is not a simple initializer, such as the return type for a function or the type of a class member.

The deduction done here is very simple: **auto** and **decltype()** simply report the type of an expression already known to the compiler.

6.3.6.1 The auto Type Specifier

When a declaration of a variable has an initializer, we don't need to explicitly specify a type. Instead, we can let the variable have the type of its initializer. Consider:

```
int a1 = 123;
char a2 = 123;
auto a3 = 123;  // the type of a3 is "int"
```

The type of the integer literal **123** is **int**, so **a3** is an **int**. That is, **auto** is a placeholder for the type of the initializer.

There is not much advantage in using **auto** instead of **int** for an expression as simple as **123**. The harder the type is to write and the harder the type is to know, the more useful **auto** becomes. For example:

```
template<class T> void f1(vector<T>& arg)
{
    for (vector<T>::iterator p = arg.begin(); p!=arg.end(); ++p)
        *p = 7;

    for (auto p = arg.begin(); p!=arg.end(); ++p)
        *p = 7;
}
```

The loop using **auto** is the more convenient to write and the easier to read. Also, it is more resilient to code changes. For example, if I changed **arg** to be a **list**, the loop using **auto** would still work correctly whereas the first loop would need to be rewritten. So, unless there is a good reason not to, use **auto** in small scopes.

If a scope is large, mentioning a type explicitly can help localize errors. That is, compared to using a specific type, using **auto** can delay the detection of type errors. For example:

```
void f(double d)
{
    constexpr auto max = d+7;
    int a[max];        // error: array bound not an integer
    // ...
}
```

If **auto** causes surprises, the best cure is typically to make functions smaller, which most often is a good idea anyway (§12.1).

We can decorate a deduced type with specifiers and modifiers (§6.3.1), such as **const** and **&** (reference; §7.7). For example:

```
void f(vector<int>& v)
{
    for (const auto& x : v) {   // x is a const int&
        // ...
    }
}
```

Here, **auto** is determined by the element type of **v**, that is, **int**.

Note that the type of an expression is never a reference because references are implicitly dereferenced in expressions (§7.7). For example:

```
void g(int& v)
{
    auto x = v;     // x is an int (not an int&)
    auto& y = v;    // y is an int&
}
```

6.3.6.2 auto and {}-lists

When we explicitly mention the type of an object we are initializing, we have two types to consider: the type of the object and the type of the initializer. For example:

```
char v1 = 12345;    // 12345 is an int
int v2 = 'c';       // 'c' is a char
T v3 = f();
```

By using the {}-initializer syntax for such definitions, we minimize the chances for unfortunate conversions:

```
char v1 {12345};    // error: narrowing
int v2 {'c'};       // fine: implicit char->int conversion
T v3 {f()};         // works if and only if the type of f() can be implicitly converted to a T
```

When we use **auto**, there is only one type involved, the type of the initializer, and we can safely use the = syntax:

```
auto v1 = 12345;    // v1 is an int
auto v2 = 'c';      // v2 is a char
auto v3 = f();      // v3 is of some appropriate type
```

In fact, it can be an advantage to use the = syntax with **auto**, because the {}-list syntax might surprise someone:

```
auto v1 {12345};    // v1 is a list of int
auto v2 {'c'};      // v2 is a list of char
auto v3 {f()};      // v3 is a list of some appropriate type
```

This is logical. Consider:

```
auto x0 {};        // error: cannot deduce a type
auto x1 {1};       // list of int with one element
auto x2 {1,2};     // list of int with two elements
auto x3 {1,2,3};   // list of int with three elements
```

The type of a homogeneous list of elements of type T is taken to be of type initializer_list<T> (§3.2.1.3, §11.3.3). In particular, the type of x1 is *not* deduced to be int. Had it been, what would be the types of x2 and x3?

Consequently, I recommend using = rather than {} for objects specified auto whenever we don't mean "list."

6.3.6.3 The decltype() Specifier

We can use auto when we have a suitable initializer. But sometimes, we want to have a type deduced without defining an initialized variable. Then, we can use a declaration type specifier: decltype(expr) is the declared type of expr. This is mostly useful in generic programming. Consider writing a function that adds two matrices with potentially different element types. What should be the type of the result of the addition? A matrix, of course, but what might its element type be? The obvious answer is that the element type of the sum is the type of the sum of the elements. So, I can declare:

```
template<class T, class U>
auto operator+(const Matrix<T>& a, const Matrix<U>& b) -> Matrix<decltype(T{}+U{})>;
```

I use the suffix return type syntax (§12.1) to be able to express the return type in terms of the arguments: Matrix<decltype(T{}+U{})>. That is, the result is a Matrix with the element type being what you get from adding a pair of elements from the argument Matrixes: T{}+U{}.

In the definition, I again need decltype() to express Matrix's element type:

```
template<class T, class U>
auto operator+(const Matrix<T>& a, const Matrix<U>& b) -> Matrix<decltype(T{}+U{})>
{
    Matrix<decltype(T{}+U{})> res;
    for (int i=0; i!=a.rows(); ++i)
        for (int j=0; j!=a.cols(); ++j)
            res(i,j) += a(i,j) + b(i,j);
    return res;
}
```

6.4 Objects and Values

We can allocate and use objects that do not have names (e.g., created using new), and it is possible to assign to strange-looking expressions (e.g., *p[a+10]=7). Consequently, we need a name for "something in memory." This is the simplest and most fundamental notion of an object. That is, an *object* is a contiguous region of storage; an *lvalue* is an expression that refers to an object. The word "lvalue" was originally coined to mean "something that can be on the left-hand side of an assignment." However, not every lvalue may be used on the left-hand side of an assignment; an lvalue can refer to a constant (§7.7). An lvalue that has not been declared **const** is often called a *modifiable lvalue*. This simple and low-level notion of an object should not be confused with the notions of class object and object of polymorphic type (§3.2.2, §20.3.2).

6.4.1 Lvalues and Rvalues

To complement the notion of an lvalue, we have the notion of an *rvalue*. Roughly, rvalue means "a value that is not an lvalue," such as a temporary value (e.g., the value returned by a function).

If you need to be more technical (say, because you want to read the ISO C++ standard), you need a more refined view of lvalue and rvalue. There are two properties that matter for an object when it comes to addressing, copying, and moving:

- *Has identity*: The program has the name of, pointer to, or reference to the object so that it is possible to determine if two objects are the same, whether the value of the object has changed, etc.
- *Movable*: The object may be moved from (i.e., we are allowed to move its value to another location and leave the object in a valid but unspecified state, rather than copying; §17.5).

It turns out that three of the four possible combinations of those two properties are needed to precisely describe the C++ language rules (we have no need for objects that do not have identity and cannot be moved). Using "m for movable" and "i for has identity," we can represent this classification of expressions graphically:

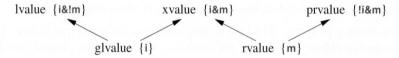

So, a classical lvalue is something that has identity and cannot be moved (because we could examine it after a move), and a classical rvalue is anything that we are allowed to move from. The other alternatives are *prvalue* ("pure rvalue"), *glvalue* ("generalized lvalue"), and *xvalue* ("x" for "extraordinary" or "expert only"; the suggestions for the meaning of this "x" have been quite imaginative). For example:

```
void f(vector<string>& vs)
{
    vector<string>& v2 = std::move(vs);        // move vs to v2
    // ...
}
```

Here, **std::move(vs)** is an xvalue: it clearly has identity (we can refer to it as **vs**), but we have explicitly given permission for it to be moved from by calling **std::move()** (§3.3.2, §35.5.1).

For practical programming, thinking in terms of rvalue and lvalue is usually sufficient. Note that every expression is either an lvalue or an rvalue, but not both.

6.4.2 Lifetimes of Objects

The *lifetime* of an object starts when its constructor completes and ends when its destructor starts executing. Objects of types without a declared constructor, such as an **int**, can be considered to have default constructors and destructors that do nothing.

We can classify objects based on their lifetimes:

- *Automatic*: Unless the programmer specifies otherwise (§12.1.8, §16.2.12), an object declared in a function is created when its definition is encountered and destroyed when its name goes out of scope. Such objects are sometimes called *automatic* objects. In a typical implementation, automatic objects are allocated on the stack; each call of the function gets its own *stack frame* to hold its automatic objects.
- *Static*: Objects declared in global or namespace scope (§6.3.4) and `statics` declared in functions (§12.1.8) or classes (§16.2.12) are created and initialized once (only) and "live" until the program terminates (§15.4.3). Such objects are called *static* objects. A static object has the same address throughout the life of a program execution. Static objects can cause serious problems in a multi-threaded program because they are shared among all threads and typically require locking to avoid data races (§5.3.1, §42.3).
- *Free store*: Using the `new` and `delete` operators, we can create objects whose lifetimes are controlled directly (§11.2).
- *Temporary objects* (e.g., intermediate results in a computation or an object used to hold a value for a reference to `const` argument): their lifetime is determined by their use. If they are bound to a reference, their lifetime is that of the reference; otherwise, they "live" until the end of the full expression of which they are part. A *full expression* is an expression that is not part of another expression. Typically, temporary objects are automatic.
- *Thread-local* objects; that is, objects declared `thread_local` (§42.2.8): such objects are created when their thread is and destroyed when their thread is.

Static and *automatic* are traditionally referred to as *storage classes*.

Array elements and nonstatic class members have their lifetimes determined by the object of which they are part.

6.5 Type Aliases

Sometimes, we need a new name for a type. Possible reasons include:

- The original name is too long, complicated, or ugly (in some programmer's eyes).
- A programming technique requires different types to have the same name in a context.
- A specific type is mentioned in one place only to simplify maintenance.

For example:

```
using Pchar = char*;          // pointer to character
using PF = int(*)(double);    // pointer to function taking a double and returning an int
```

Similar types can define the same name as a member alias:

```
template<class T>
class vector {
    using value_type = T;     // every container has a value_type
    // ...
};
```

```
template<class T>
class list {
    using value_type = T;          // every container has a value_type
    // ...
};
```

For good and bad, type aliases are synonyms for other types rather than distinct types. That is, an alias refers to the type for which it is an alias. For example:

```
Pchar p1 = nullptr;      // p1 is a char*
char* p3 = p1;           // fine
```

People who would like to have distinct types with identical semantics or identical representation should look at enumerations (§8.4) and classes (Chapter 16).

An older syntax using the keyword **typedef** and placing the name being declared where it would have been in a declaration of a variable can equivalently be used in many contexts. For example:

```
typedef int int32_t;        // equivalent to "using int32_t = int;"
typedef short int16_t;      // equivalent to "using int16_t = short;"
typedef void(*PtoF)(int);   // equivalent to "using PtoF = void(*)(int);"
```

Aliases are used when we want to insulate our code from details of the underlying machine. The name **int32_t** indicates that we want it to represent a 32-bit integer. Having written our code in terms of **int32_t**, rather than "plain int," we can port our code to a machine with **sizeof(int)==2** by redefining the single occurrence of **int32_t** in our code to use a longer integer:

```
using int32_t = long;
```

The _t suffix is conventional for aliases ("typedefs"). The **int16_t**, **int32_t**, and other such aliases can be found in **<stdint>** (§43.7). Note that naming a type after its representation rather than its purpose is not necessarily a good idea (§6.3.3).

The **using** keyword can also be used to introduce a **template** alias (§23.6). For example:

```
template<typename T>
    using Vector = std::vector<T, My_allocator<T>>;
```

We cannot apply type specifiers, such as **unsigned**, to an alias. For example:

```
using Char = char;
using Uchar = unsigned Char;    // error
using Uchar = unsigned char;    // OK
```

6.6 Advice

[1]   For the final word on language definition issues, see the ISO C++ standard; §6.1.
[2]   Avoid unspecified and undefined behavior; §6.1.
[3]   Isolate code that must depend on implementation-defined behavior; §6.1.
[4]   Avoid unnecessary assumptions about the numeric value of characters; §6.2.3.2, §10.5.2.1.
[5]   Remember that an integer starting with a **0** is octal; §6.2.4.1.

[6]   Avoid "magic constants"; §6.2.4.1.
[7]   Avoid unnecessary assumptions about the size of integers; §6.2.8.
[8]   Avoid unnecessary assumptions about the range and precision of floating-point types; §6.2.8.
[9]   Prefer plain **char** over **signed char** and **unsigned char**; §6.2.3.1.
[10]   Beware of conversions between signed and unsigned types; §6.2.3.1.
[11]   Declare one name (only) per declaration; §6.3.2.
[12]   Keep common and local names short, and keep uncommon and nonlocal names longer; §6.3.3.
[13]   Avoid similar-looking names; §6.3.3.
[14]   Name an object to reflect its meaning rather than its type; §6.3.3.
[15]   Maintain a consistent naming style; §6.3.3.
[16]   Avoid **ALL_CAPS** names; §6.3.3.
[17]   Keep scopes small; §6.3.4.
[18]   Don't use the same name in both a scope and an enclosing scope; §6.3.4.
[19]   Prefer the {}-initializer syntax for declarations with a named type; §6.3.5.
[20]   Prefer the = syntax for the initialization in declarations using **auto**; §6.3.5.
[21]   Avoid uninitialized variables; §6.3.5.1.
[22]   Use an alias to define a meaningful name for a built-in type in cases in which the built-in type used to represent a value might change; §6.5.
[23]   Use an alias to define synonyms for types; use enumerations and classes to define new types; §6.5.

Pointers, Arrays, and References

*The sublime and the ridiculous
are often so nearly related that
it is difficult to class them separately.*
– Thomas Paine

7.1 Introduction

This chapter deals with the basic language mechanisms for referring to memory. Obviously, we can refer to an object by name, but in C++ (most) objects "have identity." That is, they reside at a specific address in memory, and an object can be accessed if you know its address and its type. The language constructs for holding and using addresses are pointers and references.

7.2 Pointers

For a type T, T∗ is the type "pointer to T." That is, a variable of type T∗ can hold the address of an object of type T. For example:

```
char c = 'a';
char* p = &c;          // p holds the address of c; & is the address-of operator
```

or graphically:

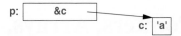

The fundamental operation on a pointer is *dereferencing*, that is, referring to the object pointed to by the pointer. This operation is also called *indirection*. The dereferencing operator is (prefix) unary ∗. For example:

```
char c = 'a';
char* p = &c;     // p holds the address of c; & is the address-of operator
char c2 = *p;     // c2 == 'a'; * is the dereference operator
```

The object pointed to by **c** is **c**, and the value stored in **c** is 'a', so the value of ∗**p** assigned to **c2** is 'a'.

It is possible to perform some arithmetic operations on pointers to array elements (§7.4).

The implementation of pointers is intended to map directly to the addressing mechanisms of the machine on which the program runs. Most machines can address a byte. Those that can't tend to have hardware to extract bytes from words. On the other hand, few machines can directly address an individual bit. Consequently, the smallest object that can be independently allocated and pointed to using a built-in pointer type is a **char**. Note that a **bool** occupies at least as much space as a **char** (§6.2.8). To store smaller values more compactly, you can use the bitwise logical operations (§11.1.1), bit-fields in structures (§8.2.7), or a **bitset** (§34.2.2).

The ∗, meaning "pointer to," is used as a suffix for a type name. Unfortunately, pointers to arrays and pointers to functions need a more complicated notation:

```
int* pi;              // pointer to int
char** ppc;           // pointer to pointer to char
int* ap[15];          // array of 15 pointers to ints
int (*fp)(char*);     // pointer to function taking a char* argument; returns an int
int* f(char*);        // function taking a char* argument; returns a pointer to int
```

See §6.3.1 for an explanation of the declaration syntax and §iso.A for the complete grammar.

Pointers to functions can be useful; they are discussed in §12.5. Pointers to class members are presented in §20.6.

7.2.1 void∗

In low-level code, we occasionally need to store or pass along an address of a memory location without actually knowing what type of object is stored there. A **void**∗ is used for that. You can read **void**∗ as "pointer to an object of unknown type."

A pointer to any type of object can be assigned to a variable of type void∗, but a pointer to function (§12.5) or a pointer to member (§20.6) cannot. In addition, a void∗ can be assigned to another void∗, void∗s can be compared for equality and inequality, and a void∗ can be explicitly converted to another type. Other operations would be unsafe because the compiler cannot know what kind of object is really pointed to. Consequently, other operations result in compile-time errors. To use a void∗, we must explicitly convert it to a pointer to a specific type. For example:

```
void f(int∗ pi)
{
    void∗ pv = pi;   // ok: implicit conversion of int* to void*
    *pv;             // error: can't dereference void*
    ++pv;            // error: can't increment void* (the size of the object pointed to is unknown)

    int∗ pi2 = static_cast<int∗>(pv);            // explicit conversion back to int*

    double∗ pd1 = pv;                            // error
    double∗ pd2 = pi;                            // error
    double∗ pd3 = static_cast<double∗>(pv);      // unsafe (§11.5.2)
}
```

In general, it is not safe to use a pointer that has been converted ("cast") to a type that differs from the type of the object pointed to. For example, a machine may assume that every double is allocated on an 8-byte boundary. If so, strange behavior could arise if pi pointed to an int that wasn't allocated that way. This form of explicit type conversion is inherently unsafe and ugly. Consequently, the notation used, static_cast (§11.5.2), was designed to be ugly and easy to find in code.

The primary use for void∗ is for passing pointers to functions that are not allowed to make assumptions about the type of the object and for returning untyped objects from functions. To use such an object, we must use explicit type conversion.

Functions using void∗ pointers typically exist at the very lowest level of the system, where real hardware resources are manipulated. For example:

```
void∗ my_alloc(size_t n);       // allocate n bytes from my special heap
```

Occurrences of void∗s at higher levels of the system should be viewed with great suspicion because they are likely indicators of design errors. Where used for optimization, void∗ can be hidden behind a type-safe interface (§27.3.1).

Pointers to functions (§12.5) and pointers to members (§20.6) cannot be assigned to void∗s.

7.2.2 nullptr

The literal nullptr represents the null pointer, that is, a pointer that does not point to an object. It can be assigned to any pointer type, but not to other built-in types:

```
int∗ pi = nullptr;
double∗ pd = nullptr;
int i = nullptr;            // error: i is not a pointer
```

There is just one nullptr, which can be used for every pointer type, rather than a null pointer for each pointer type.

Before **nullptr** was introduced, zero (**0**) was used as a notation for the null pointer. For example:

```
int* x = 0; // x gets the value nullptr
```

No object is allocated with the address **0**, and **0** (the all-zeros bit pattern) is the most common representation of **nullptr**. Zero (**0**) is an **int**. However, the standard conversions (§10.5.2.3) allow **0** to be used as a constant of pointer or pointer-to-member type.

It has been popular to define a macro **NULL** to represent the null pointer. For example:

```
int* p = NULL; // using the macro NULL
```

However, there are differences in the definition of **NULL** in different implementations; for example, **NULL** might be **0** or **0L**. In C, **NULL** is typically **(void*)0**, which makes it illegal in C++ (§7.2.1):

```
int* p = NULL; // error: can't assign a void* to an int*
```

Using **nullptr** makes code more readable than alternatives and avoids potential confusion when a function is overloaded to accept either a pointer or an integer (§12.3.1).

7.3 Arrays

For a type **T**, **T[size]** is the type "array of **size** elements of type **T**." The elements are indexed from **0** to **size−1**. For example:

```
float v[3];     // an array of three floats: v[0], v[1], v[2]
char* a[32];    // an array of 32 pointers to char: a[0] .. a[31]
```

You can access an array using the subscript operator, **[]**, or through a pointer (using operator * or operator **[]**; §7.4). For example:

```
void f()
{
    int aa[10];
    aa[6] = 9;      // assign to aa's 7th element
    int x = aa[99]; // undefined behavior
}
```

Access out of the range of an array is undefined and usually disastrous. In particular, run-time range checking is neither guaranteed nor common.

The number of elements of the array, the array bound, must be a constant expression (§10.4). If you need variable bounds, use a **vector** (§4.4.1, §31.4). For example:

```
void f(int n)
{
    int v1[n];          // error: array size not a constant expression
    vector<int> v2(n);  // OK: vector with n int elements
}
```

Multidimensional arrays are represented as arrays of arrays (§7.4.2).

An array is C++'s fundamental way of representing a sequence of objects in memory. If what you want is a simple fixed-length sequence of objects of a given type in memory, an array is the ideal solution. For every other need, an array has serious problems.

An array can be allocated statically, on the stack, and on the free store (§6.4.2). For example:

```
int a1[10];                 // 10 ints in static storage

void f()
{
    int a2 [20];            // 20 ints on the stack
    int*p = new int[40];    // 40 ints on the free store
    // ...
}
```

The C++ built-in array is an inherently low-level facility that should primarily be used inside the implementation of higher-level, better-behaved, data structures, such as the standard-library **vector** or **array**. There is no array assignment, and the name of an array implicitly converts to a pointer to its first element at the slightest provocation (§7.4). In particular, avoid arrays in interfaces (e.g., as function arguments; §7.4.3, §12.2.2) because the implicit conversion to pointer is the root cause of many common errors in C code and C-style C++ code. If you allocate an array on the free store, be sure to **delete[]** its pointer once only and only after its last use (§11.2.2). That's most easily and most reliably done by having the lifetime of the free-store array controlled by a resource handle (e.g., **string** (§19.3, §36.3), **vector** (§13.6, §34.2), or **unique_ptr** (§34.3.1)). If you allocate an array statically or on the stack, be sure never to **delete[]** it. Obviously, C programmers cannot follow these pieces of advice because C lacks the ability to encapsulate arrays, but that doesn't make the advice bad in the context of C++.

One of the most widely used kinds of arrays is a zero-terminated array of **char**. That's the way C stores strings, so a zero-terminated array of **char** is often called a *C-style string*. C++ string literals follow that convention (§7.3.2), and some standard-library functions (e.g., **strcpy()** and **strcmp()**; §43.4) rely on it. Often, a **char**∗ or a **const char**∗ is assumed to point to a zero-terminated sequence of characters.

7.3.1 Array Initializers

An array can be initialized by a list of values. For example:

```
int v1[] = { 1, 2, 3, 4 };
char v2[] = { 'a', 'b', 'c', 0 };
```

When an array is declared without a specific size, but with an initializer list, the size is calculated by counting the elements of the initializer list. Consequently, **v1** and **v2** are of type **int[4]** and **char[4]**, respectively. If a size is explicitly specified, it is an error to give surplus elements in an initializer list. For example:

```
char v3[2] = { 'a', 'b', 0 };       // error: too many initializers
char v4[3] = { 'a', 'b', 0 };       // OK
```

If the initializer supplies too few elements for an array, **0** is used for the rest. For example:

```
int v5[8] = { 1, 2, 3, 4 };
```

is equivalent to

```
int v5[] = { 1, 2, 3, 4 , 0, 0, 0, 0 };
```

There is no built-in copy operation for arrays. You cannot initialize one array with another (not even of exactly the same type), and there is no array assignment:

```
int v6[8] = v5;   // error: can't copy an array (cannot assign an int* to an array)
v6 = v5;          // error: no array assignment
```

Similarly, you can't pass arrays by value. See also §7.4.

When you need assignment to a collection of objects, use a **vector** (§4.4.1, §13.6, §34.2), an **array** (§8.2.4), or a **valarray** (§40.5) instead.

An array of characters can be conveniently initialized by a string literal (§7.3.2).

7.3.2 String Literals

A *string literal* is a character sequence enclosed within double quotes:

```
"this is a string"
```

A string literal contains one more character than it appears to have; it is terminated by the null character, '\0', with the value 0. For example:

```
sizeof("Bohr")==5
```

The type of a string literal is "array of the appropriate number of **const** characters," so **"Bohr"** is of type **const char[5]**.

In C and in older C++ code, you could assign a string literal to a non-**const char***:

```
void f()
{
    char* p = "Plato";   // error, but accepted in pre-C++11-standard code
    p[4] = 'e';          // error: assignment to const
}
```

It would obviously be unsafe to accept that assignment. It was (and is) a source of subtle errors, so please don't grumble too much if some old code fails to compile for this reason. Having string literals immutable is not only obvious but also allows implementations to do significant optimizations in the way string literals are stored and accessed.

If we want a string that we are guaranteed to be able to modify, we must place the characters in a non-**const** array:

```
void f()
{
    char p[] = "Zeno";   // p is an array of 5 char
    p[0] = 'R';          // OK
}
```

A string literal is statically allocated so that it is safe to return one from a function. For example:

```
const char* error_message(int i)
{
    // ...
    return "range error";
}
```

The memory holding "range error" will not go away after a call of error_message().

Whether two identical string literals are allocated as one array or as two is implementation-defined (§6.1). For example:

```
const char* p = "Heraclitus";
const char* q = "Heraclitus";

void g()
{
    if (p == q) cout << "one!\n";        // the result is implementation-defined
    // ...
}
```

Note that == compares addresses (pointer values) when applied to pointers, and not the values pointed to.

The empty string is written as a pair of adjacent double quotes, "", and has the type const char[1]. The one character of the empty string is the terminating '\0'.

The backslash convention for representing nongraphic characters (§6.2.3.2) can also be used within a string. This makes it possible to represent the double quote (") and the escape character backslash (\) within a string. The most common such character by far is the newline character, '\n'. For example:

```
cout<<"beep at end of message\a\n";
```

The escape character, '\a', is the ASCII character BEL (also known as *alert*), which causes a sound to be emitted.

It is not possible to have a "real" newline in a (nonraw) string literal:

```
"this is not a string
but a syntax error"
```

Long strings can be broken by whitespace to make the program text neater. For example:

```
char alpha[] = "abcdefghijklmnopqrstuvwxyz"
               "ABCDEFGHIJKLMNOPQRSTUVWXYZ";
```

The compiler will concatenate adjacent strings, so alpha could equivalently have been initialized by the single string

```
"abcdefghijklmnopqrstuvwxyzABCDEFGHIJKLMNOPQRSTUVWXYZ";
```

It is possible to have the null character in a string, but most programs will not suspect that there are characters after it. For example, the string "Jens\000Munk" will be treated as "Jens" by standard-library functions such as strcpy() and strlen(); see §43.4.

7.3.2.1 Raw Character Strings

To represent a backslash (\) or a double quote (") in a string literal, we have to precede it with a backslash. That's logical and in most cases quite simple. However, if we need a lot of backslashes and a lot of quotes in string literals, this simple technique becomes unmanageable. In particular, in regular expressions a backslash is used both as an escape character and to introduce characters representing character classes (§37.1.1). This is a convention shared by many programming languages, so we can't just change it. Therefore, when you write regular expressions for use with the standard **regex** library (Chapter 37), the fact that a backslash is an escape character becomes a notable source of errors. Consider how to write the pattern representing two words separated by a backslash (\):

> **string s = "\\w\\\\w";**   *// I hope I got that right*

To prevent the frustration and errors caused by this clash of conventions, C++ provides *raw string literals*. A raw string literal is a string literal where a backslash is just a backslash (and a double quote is just a double quote) so that our example becomes:

> **string s = R"(\w\\w)";**   *// I'm pretty sure I got that right*

Raw string literals use the **R"(ccc)"** notation for a sequence of characters **ccc**. The initial **R** is there to distinguish raw string literals from ordinary string literals. The parentheses are there to allow ("unescaped") double quotes. For example:

> **R"("quoted string")"**   *// the string is "quoted string"*

So, how do we get the character sequence)" into a raw string literal? Fortunately, that's a rare problem, but "(and)" is only the default delimiter pair. We can add delimiters before the (and after the) in "(...)". For example:

> **R"***("quoted string containing the usual terminator ("))")"***"**
> *// "quoted string containing the usual terminator ("))"*

The character sequence after the) must be identical to the sequence before the (. This way we can cope with (almost) arbitrarily complicated patterns.

Unless you work with regular expressions, raw string literals are probably just a curiosity (and one more thing to learn), but regular expressions are useful and widely used. Consider a real-world example:

> **"('(?:[^\\\\']|\\\\.)*'|\"(?:[^\\\\"]|\\\\.)*\")|"**   *// Are the five backslashes correct or not?*

With examples like that, even experts easily become confused, and raw string literals provide a significant service.

In contrast to nonraw string literals, a raw string literal can contain a newline. For example:

> **string counts {R"(1**
> **22**
> **333)"};**

is equivalent to

> **string x {"1\n22\n333"};**

7.3.2.2 Larger Character Sets

A string with the prefix **L**, such as **L"angst"**, is a string of wide characters (§6.2.3). Its type is **const wchar_t[]**. Similarly, a string with the prefix **LR**, such as **LR"(angst)"**, is a raw string (§7.3.2.1) of wide characters of type **const wchar_t[]**. Such a string is terminated by a **L'\0'** character.

There are six kinds of character literals supporting Unicode (*Unicode literals*). This sounds excessive, but there are three major encodings of Unicode: UTF-8, UTF-16, and UTF-32. For each of these three alternatives, both raw and "ordinary" strings are supported. All three UTF encodings support all Unicode characters, so which you use depends on the system you need to fit into. Essentially all Internet applications (e.g., browsers and email) rely on one or more of these encodings.

UTF-8 is a variable-width encoding: common characters fit into 1 byte, less frequently used characters (by some estimate of use) into 2 bytes, and rarer characters into 3 or 4 bytes. In particular, the ASCII characters fit into 1 byte with the same encodings (integer values) in UTF-8 as in ASCII. The various Latin alphabets, Greek, Cyrillic, Hebrew, Arabic, and more fit into 2 bytes.

A UTF-8 string is terminated by '\0', a UTF-16 string by u'\0', and a UTF-32 string by U'\0'.

We can represent an ordinary English character string in a variety of ways. Consider a file name using a backslash as the separator:

```
"folder\\file"          // implementation character set string
R"(folder\file)"        // implementation character raw set string
u8"folder\\file"        // UTF-8 string
u8R"(folder\file)"      // UTF-8 raw string
u"folder\\file"         // UTF-16 string
uR"(folder\file)"         // UTF-16 raw string
U"folder\\file"         // UTF-32 string
UR"(folder\file)"         // UTF-32 raw string
```

If printed, these strings will all look the same, but except for the "plain" and UTF-8 strings their internal representations are likely to differ.

Obviously, the real purpose of Unicode strings is to be able to put Unicode characters into them. For example:

```
u8"The official vowels in Danish are: a, e, i, o, u, \u00E6, \u00F8, \u00E5 and y."
```

Printing that string appropriately gives you

The official vowels in Danish are: a, e, i, o, u, æ, ø, å and y.

The hexadecimal number after the \u is a Unicode code point (§iso.2.14.3) [Unicode,1996]. Such a code point is independent of the encoding used and will in fact have different representations (as bits in bytes) in different encodings. For example, u'0430' (Cyrillic lowercase letter "a") is the 2-byte hexadecimal value D0B0 in UTF-8, the 2-byte hexadecimal value 0403 in UTF-16, and the 4-byte hexadecimal value 00000403 in UTF-32. These hexadecimal values are referred to as *universal character names*.

The order of the us and Rs and their cases are significant: RU and Ur are not valid string prefixes.

7.4 Pointers into Arrays

In C++, pointers and arrays are closely related. The name of an array can be used as a pointer to its initial element. For example:

```
int v[] = { 1, 2, 3, 4 };
int* p1 = v;              // pointer to initial element (implicit conversion)
int* p2 = &v[0];          // pointer to initial element
int* p3 = v+4;            // pointer to one-beyond-last element
```

or graphically:

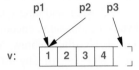

Taking a pointer to the element one beyond the end of an array is guaranteed to work. This is important for many algorithms (§4.5, §33.1). However, since such a pointer does not in fact point to an element of the array, it may not be used for reading or writing. The result of taking the address of the element before the initial element or beyond one-past-the-last element is undefined and should be avoided. For example:

```
int* p4 = v−1;   // before the beginning, undefined: don't do it
int* p5 = v+7;   // beyond the end, undefined: don't do it
```

The implicit conversion of an array name to a pointer to the initial element of the array is extensively used in function calls in C-style code. For example:

```
extern "C" int strlen(const char*);      // from <string.h>

void f()
{
    char v[] = "Annemarie";
    char* p = v;        // implicit conversion of char[] to char*
    strlen(p);
    strlen(v);          // implicit conversion of char[] to char*
    v = p;              // error: cannot assign to array
}
```

The same value is passed to the standard-library function **strlen()** in both calls. The snag is that it is impossible to avoid the implicit conversion. In other words, there is no way of declaring a function so that the array v is copied when the function is called. Fortunately, there is no implicit or explicit conversion from a pointer to an array.

The implicit conversion of the array argument to a pointer means that the size of the array is lost to the called function. However, the called function must somehow determine the size to perform a meaningful operation. Like other C standard-library functions taking pointers to characters, **strlen()** relies on zero to indicate end-of-string; **strlen(p)** returns the number of characters up to and not including the terminating 0. This is all pretty low-level. The standard-library **vector** (§4.4.1, §13.6, §31.4), **array** (§8.2.4, §34.2.1), and **string** (§4.2) don't suffer from this problem. These library types give their number of elements as their **size()** without having to count elements each time.

7.4.1 Navigating Arrays

Efficient and elegant access to arrays (and similar data structures) is the key to many algorithms (see §4.5, Chapter 32). Access can be achieved either through a pointer to an array plus an index or through a pointer to an element. For example:

```
void fi(char v[])
{
    for (int i = 0; v[i]!=0; ++i)
        use(v[i]);
}

void fp(char v[])
{
    for (char* p = v; *p!=0; ++p)
        use(*p);
}
```

The prefix * operator dereferences a pointer so that *p is the character pointed to by p, and ++ increments the pointer so that it refers to the next element of the array.

There is no inherent reason why one version should be faster than the other. With modern compilers, identical code should be (and usually is) generated for both examples. Programmers can choose between the versions on logical and aesthetic grounds.

Subscripting a built-in array is defined in terms of the pointer operations + and *. For every built-in array a and integer j within the range of a, we have:

a[j] == *(&a[0]+j) == *(a+j) == *(j+a) == j[a]

It usually surprises people to find that a[j]==j[a]. For example, 3["Texas"]=="Texas"[3]=='a'. Such cleverness has no place in production code. These equivalences are pretty low-level and do not hold for standard-library containers, such as **array** and **vector**.

The result of applying the arithmetic operators +, −, ++, or −− to pointers depends on the type of the object pointed to. When an arithmetic operator is applied to a pointer p of type T*, p is assumed to point to an element of an array of objects of type T; p+1 points to the next element of that array, and p−1 points to the previous element. This implies that the integer value of p+1 will be sizeof(T) larger than the integer value of p. For example:

```
template<typename T>
int byte_diff(T* p, T* q)
{
    return reinterpret_cast<char*>(q)−reinterpret_cast<char*>(p);
}

void diff_test()
{
    int vi[10];
    short vs[10];
```

```
        cout << vi << ' ' << &vi[1] << ' ' << &vi[1]-&vi[0] << ' ' << byte_diff(&vi[0],&vi[1]) << '\n';
        cout << vs << ' ' << &vs[1] << ' ' << &vs[1]-&vs[0] << ' ' << byte_diff(&vs[0],&vs[1]) << '\n';
}
```

This produced:

```
0x7fffaef0 0x7fffaef4 1 4
0x7fffaedc 0x7fffaede 1 2
```

The pointer values were printed using the default hexadecimal notation. This shows that on my implementation, **sizeof(short)** is **2** and **sizeof(int)** is **4**.

Subtraction of pointers is defined only when both pointers point to elements of the same array (although the language has no fast way of ensuring that is the case). When subtracting a pointer **p** from another pointer **q**, **q-p**, the result is the number of array elements in the sequence **[p:q]** (an integer). One can add an integer to a pointer or subtract an integer from a pointer; in both cases, the result is a pointer value. If that value does not point to an element of the same array as the original pointer or one beyond, the result of using that value is undefined. For example:

```
void f()
{
    int v1[10];
    int v2[10];

    int i1 = &v1[5]-&v1[3];      // i1 = 2
    int i2 = &v1[5]-&v2[3];      // result undefined

    int* p1 = v2+2;              // p1 = &v2[2]
    int* p2 = v2-2;              // *p2 undefined
}
```

Complicated pointer arithmetic is usually unnecessary and best avoided. Addition of pointers makes no sense and is not allowed.

Arrays are not self-describing because the number of elements of an array is not guaranteed to be stored with the array. This implies that to traverse an array that does not contain a terminator the way C-style strings do, we must somehow supply the number of elements. For example:

```
void fp(char v[], int size)
{
    for (int i=0; i!=size; ++i)
        use(v[i]);               // hope that v has at least size elements
    for (int x : v)
        use(x);                  // error: range-for does not work for pointers

    const int N = 7;
    char v2[N];
    for (int i=0; i!=N; ++i)
        use(v2[i]);
    for (int x : v2)
        use(x);                  // range-for works for arrays of known size
}
```

This array concept is inherently low-level. Most advantages of the built-in array and few of the disadvantages can be obtained through the use of the standard-library container **array** (§8.2.4, §34.2.1). Some C++ implementations offer optional range checking for arrays. However, such checking can be quite expensive, so it is often used only as a development aid (rather than being included in production code). If you are not using range checking for individual accesses, try to maintain a consistent policy of accessing elements only in well-defined ranges. That is best done when arrays are manipulated through the interface of a higher-level container type, such as **vector**, where it is harder to get confused about the range of valid elements.

7.4.2 Multidimensional Arrays

Multidimensional arrays are represented as arrays of arrays; a 3-by-5 array is declared like this:

```
int ma[3][5];     // 3 arrays with 5 ints each
```

We can initialize **ma** like this:

```
void init_ma()
{
    for (int i = 0; i!=3; i++)
        for (int j = 0; j!=5; j++)
            ma[i][j] = 10*i+j;
}
```

or graphically:

ma: | 00 | 01 | 02 | 03 | 04 | 10 | 11 | 12 | 13 | 14 | 20 | 21 | 22 | 23 | 24 |

The array **ma** is simply 15 ints that we access as if it were 3 arrays of 5 ints. In particular, there is no single object in memory that is the matrix **ma** – only the elements are stored. The dimensions **3** and **5** exist in the compiler source only. When we write code, it is our job to remember them somehow and supply the dimensions where needed. For example, we might print **ma** like this:

```
void print_ma()
{
    for (int i = 0; i!=3; i++) {
        for (int j = 0; j!=5; j++)
            cout << ma[i][j] << '\t';
        cout << '\n';
    }
}
```

The comma notation used for array bounds in some languages cannot be used in C++ because the comma (,) is a sequencing operator (§10.3.2). Fortunately, most mistakes are caught by the compiler. For example:

```
int bad[3,5];              // error: comma not allowed in constant expression
int good[3][5];            // 3 arrays with 5 ints each
int ouch = good[1,4];      // error: int initialized by int* (good[1,4] means good[4], which is an int*)
int nice = good[1][4];
```

7.4.3 Passing Arrays

Arrays cannot directly be passed by value. Instead, an array is passed as a pointer to its first element. For example:

```
void comp(double arg[10])          // arg is a double*
{
     for (int i=0; i!=10; ++i)
          arg[i]+=99;
}

void f()
{
     double a1[10];
     double a2[5];
     double a3[100];

     comp(a1);
     comp(a2);        // disaster!
     comp(a3);        // uses only the first 10 elements
};
```

This code looks sane, but it is not. The code compiles, but the call **comp(a2)** will write beyond the bounds of **a2**. Also, anyone who guessed that the array was passed by value will be disappointed: the writes to **arg[i]** are writes directly to the elements of **comp()**'s argument, rather than to a copy. The function could equivalently have been written as

```
void comp(double∗ arg)
{
     for (int i=0; i!=10; ++i)
          arg[i]+=99;
}
```

Now the insanity is (hopefully) obvious. When used as a function argument, the first dimension of an array is simply treated as a pointer. Any array bound specified is simply ignored. This implies that if you want to pass a sequence of elements without losing size information, you should not pass a built-in array. Instead, you can place the array inside a class as a member (as is done for **std::array**) or define a class that acts as a handle (as is done for **std::string** and **std::vector**).

If you insist on using arrays directly, you will have to deal with bugs and confusion without getting noticeable advantages in return. Consider defining a function to manipulate a two-dimensional matrix. If the dimensions are known at compile time, there is no problem:

```
void print_m35(int m[3][5])
{
     for (int i = 0; i!=3; i++) {
          for (int j = 0; j!=5; j++)
               cout << m[i][j] << '\t';
          cout << '\n';
     }
}
```

A matrix represented as a multidimensional array is passed as a pointer (rather than copied; §7.4). The first dimension of an array is irrelevant to finding the location of an element; it simply states how many elements (here, 3) of the appropriate type (here, int[5]) are present. For example, look at the layout of ma above and note that by knowing only that the second dimension is 5, we can locate ma[i][5] for any i. The first dimension can therefore be passed as an argument:

```
void print_mi5(int m[][5], int dim1)
{
    for (int i = 0; i!=dim1; i++) {
        for (int j = 0; j!=5; j++)
            cout << m[i][j] << '\t';
        cout << '\n';
    }
}
```

When both dimensions need to be passed, the "obvious solution" does not work:

```
void print_mij(int m[][], int dim1, int dim2)      // doesn't behave as most people would think
{
    for (int i = 0; i!=dim1; i++) {
        for (int j = 0; j!=dim2; j++)
            cout << m[i][j] << '\t';        // surprise!
        cout << '\n';
    }
}
```

Fortunately, the argument declaration m[][] is illegal because the second dimension of a multidimensional array must be known in order to find the location of an element. However, the expression m[i][j] is (correctly) interpreted as *(*(m+i)+j), although that is unlikely to be what the programmer intended. A correct solution is:

```
void print_mij(int* m, int dim1, int dim2)
{
    for (int i = 0; i!=dim1; i++) {
        for (int j = 0; j!=dim2; j++)
            cout << m[i*dim2+j] << '\t'; // obscure
        cout << '\n';
    }
}
```

The expression used for accessing the members in print_mij() is equivalent to the one the compiler generates when it knows the last dimension.

To call this function, we pass a matrix as an ordinary pointer:

```
int test()
{
    int v[3][5] = {
        {0,1,2,3,4}, {10,11,12,13,14}, {20,21,22,23,24}
    };
```

```
            print_m35(v);
            print_mi5(v,3);
            print_mij(&v[0][0],3,5);
    }
```

Note the use of &v[0][0] for the last call; v[0] would do because it is equivalent, but v would be a type error. This kind of subtle and messy code is best hidden. If you must deal directly with multi-dimensional arrays, consider encapsulating the code relying on it. In that way, you might ease the task of the next programmer to touch the code. Providing a multidimensional array type with a proper subscripting operator saves most users from having to worry about the layout of the data in the array (§29.2.2, §40.5.2).

The standard **vector** (§31.4) doesn't suffer from these problems.

7.5 Pointers and const

C++ offers two related meanings of "constant":
- **constexpr**: Evaluate at compile time (§2.2.3, §10.4).
- **const**: Do not modify in this scope (§2.2.3).

Basically, **constexpr**'s role is to enable and ensure compile-time evaluation, whereas **const**'s primary role is to specify immutability in interfaces. This section is primarily concerned with the second role: interface specification.

Many objects don't have their values changed after initialization:
- Symbolic constants lead to more maintainable code than using literals directly in code.
- Many pointers are often read through but never written through.
- Most function parameters are read but not written to.

To express this notion of immutability after initialization, we can add **const** to the definition of an object. For example:

```
const int model = 90;        // model is a const
const int v[] = { 1, 2, 3, 4 };   // v[i] is a const
const int x;                 // error: no initializer
```

Because an object declared **const** cannot be assigned to, it must be initialized.

Declaring something **const** ensures that its value will not change within its scope:

```
void f()
{
    model = 200;    // error
    v[2] = 3;       // error
}
```

Note that **const** modifies a type; it restricts the ways in which an object can be used, rather than specifying how the constant is to be allocated. For example:

```
void g(const X* p)
{
    // can't modify *p here
}
```

```
void h()
{
    X val;        // val can be modified here
    g(&val);
    // ...
}
```

When using a pointer, two objects are involved: the pointer itself and the object pointed to. "Pre-fixing" a declaration of a pointer with **const** makes the object, but not the pointer, a constant. To declare a pointer itself, rather than the object pointed to, to be a constant, we use the declarator operator *const instead of plain *. For example:

```
void f1(char* p)
{
    char s[] = "Gorm";

    const char* pc = s;        // pointer to constant
    pc[3] = 'g';               // error: pc points to constant
    pc = p;                    // OK

    char *const cp = s;        // constant pointer
    cp[3] = 'a';               // OK
    cp = p;                    // error: cp is constant

    const char *const cpc = s; // const pointer to const
    cpc[3] = 'a';              // error: cpc points to constant
    cpc = p;                   // error: cpc is constant
}
```

The declarator operator that makes a pointer constant is *const. There is no const* declarator operator, so a **const** appearing before the * is taken to be part of the base type. For example:

```
char *const cp;        // const pointer to char
char const* pc;        // pointer to const char
const char* pc2;       // pointer to const char
```

Some people find it helpful to read such declarations right-to-left, for example, "**cp** is a **const** pointer to a **char**" and "**pc2** is a pointer to a **char const**."

An object that is a constant when accessed through one pointer may be variable when accessed in other ways. This is particularly useful for function arguments. By declaring a pointer argument **const**, the function is prohibited from modifying the object pointed to. For example:

```
const char* strchr(const char* p, char c);   // find first occurrence of c in p
char* strchr(char* p, char c);               // find first occurrence of c in p
```

The first version is used for strings where the elements mustn't be modified and returns a pointer to **const** that does not allow modification. The second version is used for mutable strings.

You can assign the address of a non-**const** variable to a pointer to constant because no harm can come from that. However, the address of a constant cannot be assigned to an unrestricted pointer because this would allow the object's value to be changed. For example:

```
void f4()
{
    int a = 1;
    const int c = 2;
    const int* p1 = &c;    // OK
    const int* p2 = &a;    // OK
    int* p3 = &c;          // error: initialization of int* with const int*
    *p3 = 7;               // try to change the value of c
}
```

It is possible, but typically unwise, to explicitly remove the restrictions on a pointer to **const** by explicit type conversion (§16.2.9, §11.5).

7.6 Pointers and Ownership

A resource is something that has to be acquired and later released (§5.2). Memory acquired by **new** and released by **delete** (§11.2) and files opened by **fopen()** and closed by **fclose()** (§43.2) are examples of resources where the most direct handle to the resource is a pointer. This can be most confusing because a pointer is easily passed around in a program, and there is nothing in the type system that distinguishes a pointer that owns a resource from one that does not. Consider:

```
void confused(int* p)
{
    // delete p?
}

int global {7};

void f()
{
    X* pn = new int{7};
    int i {7};
    int q = &i;
    confused(pn);
    confused(q);
    confused(&global);
}
```

If **confused()** **deletes** **p** the program will seriously misbehave for the second two calls because we may not **delete** objects not allocated by **new** (§11.2). If **confused()** does not **delete** **p** the program leaks (§11.2.1). In this case, obviously **f()** must manage the lifetime of the object it creates on the free store, but in general keeping track of what needs to be **deleted** in a large program requires a simple and consistent strategy.

It is usually a good idea to immediately place a pointer that represents ownership in a resource handle class, such as **vector**, **string**, and **unique_ptr**. That way, we can assume that every pointer that is not within a resource handle is not an owner and must not be **deleted**. Chapter 13 discusses resource management in greater detail.

7.7 References

A pointer allows us to pass potentially large amounts of data around at low cost: instead of copying the data we simply pass its address as a pointer value. The type of the pointer determines what can be done to the data through the pointer. Using a pointer differs from using the name of an object in a few ways:

- We use a different syntax, for example, *p instead of **obj** and **p–>m** rather than **obj.m**.
- We can make a pointer point to different objects at different times.
- We must be more careful when using pointers than when using an object directly: a pointer may be a **nullptr** or point to an object that wasn't the one we expected.

These differences can be annoying; for example, some programmers find **f(&x)** ugly compared to **f(x)**. Worse, managing pointer variables with varying values and protecting code against the possibility of **nullptr** can be a significant burden. Finally, when we want to overload an operator, say **+**, we want to write **x+y** rather than **&x+&y**. The language mechanism addressing these problems is called a *reference*. Like a pointer, a *reference* is an alias for an object, is usually implemented to hold a machine address of an object, and does not impose performance overhead compared to pointers, but it differs from a pointer in that:

- You access a reference with exactly the same syntax as the name of an object.
- A reference always refers to the object to which it was initialized.
- There is no "null reference," and we may assume that a reference refers to an object (§7.7.4).

A reference is an alternative name for an object, an alias. The main use of references is for specifying arguments and return values for functions in general and for overloaded operators (Chapter 18) in particular. For example:

```
template<class T>
class vector {
    T* elem;
    // ...
public:
    T& operator[](int i) { return elem[i]; }          // return reference to element
    const T& operator[](int i) const { return elem[i]; }   // return reference to const element

    void push_back(const T& a);                       // pass element to be added by reference
    // ...
};

void f(const vector<double>& v)
{
    double d1 = v[1];     // copy the value of the double referred to by v.operator[](1) into d1
    v[2] = 7;             // place 7 in the double referred to by the result of v.operator[](2)

    v.push_back(d1);     // give push_back() a reference to d1 to work with
}
```

The idea of passing function arguments by reference is as old as high-level programming languages (the first version of Fortran used that).

To reflect the lvalue/rvalue and **const**/non-**const** distinctions, there are three kinds of references:
- *lvalue references*: to refer to objects whose value we want to change
- **const** *references*: to refer to objects whose value we do not want to change (e.g., a constant)
- *rvalue references*: to refer to objects whose value we do not need to preserve after we have used it (e.g., a temporary)

Collectively, they are called *references*. The first two are both called *lvalue references*.

7.7.1 Lvalue References

In a type name, the notation **X&** means "reference to **X**." It is used for references to lvalues, so it is often called an *lvalue reference*. For example:

```
void f()
{
    int var = 1;
    int& r {var};     // r and var now refer to the same int
    int x = r;        // x becomes 1

    r = 2;            // var becomes 2
}
```

To ensure that a reference is a name for something (that is, that it is bound to an object), we must initialize the reference. For example:

```
int var = 1;
int& r1 {var};        // OK: r1 initialized
int& r2;              // error: initializer missing
extern int& r3;       // OK: r3 initialized elsewhere
```

Initialization of a reference is something quite different from assignment to it. Despite appearances, no operator operates on a reference. For example:

```
void g()
{
    int var = 0;
    int& rr {var};
    ++rr;             // var is incremented to 1
    int* pp = &rr;    // pp points to var
}
```

Here, **++rr** does not increment the reference **rr**; rather, **++** is applied to the **int** to which **rr** refers, that is, to **var**. Consequently, the value of a reference cannot be changed after initialization; it always refers to the object it was initialized to denote. To get a pointer to the object denoted by a reference **rr**, we can write **&rr**. Thus, we cannot have a pointer to a reference. Furthermore, we cannot define an array of references. In that sense, a reference is not an object.

The obvious implementation of a reference is as a (constant) pointer that is dereferenced each time it is used. It doesn't do much harm to think about references that way, as long as one remembers that a reference isn't an object that can be manipulated the way a pointer is:

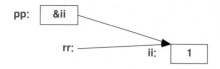

In some cases, the compiler can optimize away a reference so that there is no object representing that reference at run time.

Initialization of a reference is trivial when the initializer is an lvalue (an object whose address you can take; see §6.4). The initializer for a "plain" **T&** must be an lvalue of type **T**.

The initializer for a **const T&** need not be an lvalue or even of type **T**. In such cases:

[1]   First, implicit type conversion to **T** is applied if necessary (see §10.5).
[2]   Then, the resulting value is placed in a temporary variable of type **T**.
[3]   Finally, this temporary variable is used as the value of the initializer.

Consider:

```
double& dr = 1;              // error: lvalue needed
const double& cdr {1};       // OK
```

The interpretation of this last initialization might be:

```
double temp = double{1};     // first create a temporary with the right value
const double& cdr {temp};    // then use the temporary as the initializer for cdr
```

A temporary created to hold a reference initializer persists until the end of its reference's scope.

References to variables and references to constants are distinguished because introducing a temporary for a variable would have been highly error-prone; an assignment to the variable would become an assignment to the – soon-to-disappear – temporary. No such problem exists for references to constants, and references to constants are often important as function arguments (§18.2.4).

A reference can be used to specify a function argument so that the function can change the value of an object passed to it. For example:

```
void increment(int& aa)
{
    ++aa;
}

void f()
{
    int x = 1;
    increment(x);       // x = 2
}
```

The semantics of argument passing are defined to be those of initialization, so when called, **increment**'s argument **aa** became another name for **x**. To keep a program readable, it is often best to avoid functions that modify their arguments. Instead, you can return a value from the function explicitly:

```
int next(int p) { return p+1; }

void g()
{
    int x = 1;
    increment(x);      // x = 2
    x = next(x);       // x = 3
}
```

The increment(x) notation doesn't give a clue to the reader that x's value is being modified, the way x=next(x) does. Consequently, "plain" reference arguments should be used only where the name of the function gives a strong hint that the reference argument is modified.

References can also be used as return types. This is mostly used to define functions that can be used on both the left-hand and right-hand sides of an assignment. A Map is a good example. For example:

```
template<class K, class V>
class Map {          // a simple map class
public:
    V& operator[](const K& v);     // return the value corresponding to the key v

    pair<K,V>* begin() { return &elem[0]; }
    pair<K,V>* end() { return &elem[0]+elem.size(); }
private:
    vector<pair<K,V>> elem;      // {key,value} pairs
};
```

The standard-library map (§4.4.3, §31.4.3) is typically implemented as a red-black tree, but to avoid distracting implementation details, I'll just show an implementation based on linear search for a key match:

```
template<class K, class V>
V& Map<K,V>::operator[](const K& k)
{
    for (auto& x : elem)
        if (k == x.first)
            return x.second;

    elem.push_back({k,V{}});       // add pair at end (§4.4.2)
    return elem.back().second;     // return the (default) value of the new element
}
```

I pass the key argument, k, by reference because it might be of a type that is expensive to copy. Similarly, I return the value by reference because it too might be of a type that is expensive to copy. I use a const reference for k because I don't want to modify it and because I might want to use a literal or a temporary object as an argument. I return the result by non-const reference because the user of a Map might very well want to modify the found value. For example:

```cpp
int main() // count the number of occurrences of each word on input
{
    Map<string,int> buf;

    for (string s; cin>>s;) ++buf[s];

    for (const auto& x : buf)
        cout << x.first << ": " << x.second << '\n';
}
```

Each time around, the input loop reads one word from the standard input stream cin into the string s (§4.3.2) and then updates the counter associated with it. Finally, the resulting table of different words in the input, each with its number of occurrences, is printed. For example, given the input

    aa bb bb aa aa bb aa aa

this program will produce

    aa: 5
    bb: 3

The range- for loop works for this because Map defined begin() and end(), just as is done for the standard-library map.

7.7.2 Rvalue References

The basic idea of having more than one kind of reference is to support different uses of objects:

- A non-const lvalue reference refers to an object, to which the user of the reference can write.
- A const lvalue reference refers to a constant, which is immutable from the point of view of the user of the reference.
- An rvalue reference refers to a temporary object, which the user of the reference can (and typically will) modify, assuming that the object will never be used again.

We want to know if a reference refers to a temporary, because if it does, we can sometimes turn an expensive copy operation into a cheap move operation (§3.3.2, §17.1, §17.5.2). An object (such as a string or a list) that is represented by a small descriptor pointing to a potentially huge amount of information can be simply and cheaply moved if we know that the source isn't going to be used again. The classic example is a return value where the compiler knows that a local variable returned will never again be used (§3.3.2).

An rvalue reference can bind to an rvalue, but not to an lvalue. In that, an rvalue reference is exactly opposite to an lvalue reference. For example:

```cpp
string var {"Cambridge"};
string f();

string& r1 {var};            // lvalue reference, bind r1 to var (an lvalue)
string& r2 {f()};            // lvalue reference, error: f() is an rvalue
string& r3 {"Princeton"};    // lvalue reference, error: cannot bind to temporary
```

```
string&& rr1 {f()};         // rvalue reference, fine: bind rr1 to rvalue (a temporary)
string&& rr2 {var};         // rvalue reference, error: var is an lvalue
string&& rr3 {"Oxford"};    // rr3 refers to a temporary holding "Oxford"

const string cr1& {"Harvard"};// OK: make temporary and bind to cr1
```

The && declarator operator means "rvalue reference." We do *not* use **const** rvalue references; most of the benefits from using rvalue references involve writing to the object to which it refers. Both a **const** lvalue reference and an rvalue reference can bind to an rvalue. However, the purposes will be fundamentally different:

- We use rvalue references to implement a "destructive read" for optimization of what would otherwise have required a copy.
- We use a **const** lvalue reference to prevent modification of an argument.

An object referred to by an rvalue reference is accessed exactly like an object referred to by an lvalue reference or an ordinary variable name. For example:

```
string f(string&& s)
{
    if (s.size())
        s[0] = toupper(s[0]);
    return s;
}
```

Sometimes, a programmer knows that an object won't be used again, even though the compiler does not. Consider:

```
template<class T>
swap(T& a, T& b)            // "old-style swap"
{
    T tmp {a};// now we have two copies of a
    a = b;      // now we have two copies of b
    b = tmp;    // now we have two copies of tmp (aka a)
}
```

If **T** is a type for which it can be expensive to copy elements, such as **string** and **vector**, this **swap()** becomes an expensive operation. Note something curious: we didn't want any copies at all; we just wanted to move the values of **a**, **b**, and **tmp** around. We can tell that to the compiler:

```
template<class T>
void swap(T& a, T& b)       // "perfect swap" (almost)
{
    T tmp {static_cast<T&&>(a)}; // the initialization may write to a
    a = static_cast<T&&>(b);     // the assignment may write to b
    b = static_cast<T&&>(tmp);   // the assignment may write to tmp
}
```

The result value of **static_cast<T&&>(x)** is an rvalue of type **T&&** for **x**. An operation that is optimized for rvalues can now use its optimization for **x**. In particular, if a type **T** has a move constructor (§3.3.2, §17.5.2) or a move assignment, it will be used. Consider **vector**:

```
template<class T> class vector {
    // ...
    vector(const vector& r);    // copy constructor (copy r's representation)
    vector(vector&& r);         // move constructor ("steal" representation from r)
};
```

```
vector<string> s;
vector<string> s2 {s};           // s is an lvalue, so use copy constructor
vector<string> s3 {s+"tail");     // s+"tail" is an rvalue so pick move constructor
```

The use of **static_cast** in **swap()** is a bit verbose and slightly prone to mistyping, so the standard library provides a **move()** function: **move(x)** means **static_cast<X&&>(x)** where **X** is the type of **x**. Given that, we can clean up the definition of **swap()** a bit:

```
template<class T>
void swap(T& a, T& b)       // "perfect swap" (almost)
{
    T tmp {move(a)};        // move from a
    a = move(b);            // move from b
    b = move(tmp);          // move from tmp
}
```

In contrast to the original **swap()**, this latest version need not make any copies; it will use move operations whenever possible.

Since **move(x)** does not move **x** (it simply produces an rvalue reference to **x**), it would have been better if **move()** had been called **rval()**, but by now **move()** has been used for years.

I deemed this **swap()** "almost perfect" because it will swap only lvalues. Consider:

```
void f(vector<int>& v)
{
    swap(v,vector<int>{1,2,3});     // replace v's elements with 1,2,3
    // ...
}
```

It is not uncommon to want to replace the contents of a container with some sort of default value, but this particular **swap()** cannot do that. A solution is to augment it by two overloads:

```
template<class T> void swap(T&& a, T& b);
template<class T> void swap(T& a, T&& b)
```

Our example will be handled by that last version of **swap()**. The standard library takes a different approach by defining **shrink_to_fit()** and **clear()** for **vector**, **string**, etc. (§31.3.3) to handle the most common cases of rvalue arguments to **swap()**:

```
void f(string& s, vector<int>& v)
{
    s.shrink_to_fit();       // make s.capacity()==s.size()
    swap(s,string{s});       // make s.capacity()==s.size()
```

```
        v.clear();              // make v empty
        swap(v.vector<int>{}); // make v empty
        v = {};                 // make v empty
}
```

Rvalue references can also be used to provide perfect forwarding (§23.5.2.1, §35.5.1).

All standard-library containers provide move constructors and move assignment (§31.3.2). Also, their operations that insert new elements, such as **insert()** and **push_back()**, have versions that take rvalue references.

7.7.3 References to References

It you take a reference to a reference to a type, you get a reference to that type, rather than some kind of special reference to reference type. But what kind of reference? Lvalue reference or rvalue reference? Consider:

```
        using rr_i = int&&;
        using lr_i = int&;
        using rr_rr_i = rr_i&&;    // "int && &&" is an int&&
        using lr_rr_i = rr_i&;     // "int && &" is an int&
        using rr_lr_i = lr_i&&;    // "int & &&" is an int&
        using lr_lr_i = lr_i&;     // "int & &" is an int&
```

In other words, lvalue reference always wins. This makes sense: nothing we can do with types can change the fact that an lvalue reference refers to an lvalue. This is sometimes known as *reference collapse*.

The syntax does not allow

```
        int && & r = i;
```

Reference to reference can only happen as the result of an alias (§3.4.5, §6.5) or a template type argument (§23.5.2.1).

7.7.4 Pointers and References

Pointers and references are two mechanisms for referring to an object from different places in a program without copying. We can show this similarity graphically:

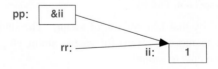

Each has its strengths and weaknesses.

If you need to change which object to refer to, use a pointer. You can use =, +=, -=, ++, and -- to change the value of a pointer variable (§11.1.4). For example:

```
void fp(char* p)
{
    while (*p)
        cout << ++*p;
}

void fr(char& r)
{
    while (r)
        cout << ++r;      // oops: increments the char referred to, not the reference
                          // near-infinite loop!
}

void fr2(char& r)
{
    char* p = &r;         // get a pointer to the object referred to
    while (*p)
        cout << ++*p;
}
```

Conversely, if you want to be sure that a name always refers to the same object, use a reference. For example:

```
template<class T> class Proxy {        // Proxy refers to the object with which it is initialized
    T& m;
public:
    Proxy(T& mm) :m{mm} {}
    // ...
};

template<class T> class Handle {   // Handle refers to its current object
    T* m;
public:
    Proxy(T* mm) :m{mm} {}
    void rebind(T* mm) { m = mm; }
    // ...
};
```

If you want to use a user-defined (overloaded) operator (§18.1) on something that refers to an object, use a reference:

```
Matrix operator+(const Matrix&, const Matrix&);    // OK
Matrix operator–(const Matrix*, const Matrix*);    // error: no user-defined type argument

Matrix y, z;
// ...
Matrix x = y+z;       // OK
Matrix x2 = &y–&z;    // error and ugly
```

It is not possible to (re)define an operator for a pair of built-in types, such as pointers (§18.2.3).

If you want a collection of something that refers to an object, you must use a pointer:

```
int x, y;
string& a1[] = {x, y};          // error: array of references
string* a2[] = {&x, &y};        // OK
vector<string&> s1 = {x , y};   // error: vector of references
vector<string*> s2 = {&x, &y};  // OK
```

Once we leave the cases where C++ leaves no choice for the programmer, we enter the domain of aesthetics. Ideally, we will make our choices so as to minimize the probability of error and in particular to maximize readability of code.

If you need a notion of "no value," pointers offer nullptr. There is no equivalent "null reference," so if you need a "no value," using a pointer may be most appropriate. For example:

```
void fp(X* p)
{
    if (p == nullptr) {
        // no value
    }
    else {
        // use *p
    }
}


void fr(X& r)    // common style
{
    // assume that r is valid and use it
}
```

If you really want to, you can construct and check for a "null reference" for a particular type:

```
void fr2(X& r)
{
    if (&r == &nullX) {    // or maybe r==nullX
        // no value
    }
    else {
        // use r
    }
}
```

Obviously, you need to have suitably defined nullX. The style is not idiomatic and I don't recommend it. A programmer is allowed to assume that a reference is valid. It is possible to create an invalid reference, but you have to go out of your way to do so. For example:

```
char* ident(char * p) { return p; }
```

```
char& r {*ident(nullptr)}; // invalid code
```

This code is not valid C++ code. Don't write such code even if your current implementation doesn't catch it.

7.8 Advice

[1] Keep use of pointers simple and straightforward; §7.4.1.
[2] Avoid nontrivial pointer arithmetic; §7.4.
[3] Take care not to write beyond the bounds of an array; §7.4.1.
[4] Avoid multidimensional arrays; define suitable containers instead; §7.4.2.
[5] Use **nullptr** rather than **0** or **NULL**; §7.2.2.
[6] Use containers (e.g., **vector**, **array**, and **valarray**) rather than built-in (C-style) arrays; §7.4.1.
[7] Use **string** rather than zero-terminated arrays of **char**; §7.4.
[8] Use raw strings for string literals with complicated uses of backslash; §7.3.2.1.
[9] Prefer **const** reference arguments to plain reference arguments; §7.7.3.
[10] Use rvalue references (only) for forwarding and move semantics; §7.7.2.
[11] Keep pointers that represent ownership inside handle classes; §7.6.
[12] Avoid **void**∗ except in low-level code; §7.2.1.
[13] Use **const** pointers and **const** references to express immutability in interfaces; §7.5.
[14] Prefer references to pointers as arguments, except where "no object" is a reasonable option; §7.7.4.

8

Structures, Unions, and Enumerations

Form a more perfect Union.
– The people

- Introduction
- Structures
    struct Layout; struct Names; Structures and Classes; Structures and Arrays; Type Equivalence; Plain Old Data; Fields
- Unions
    Unions and Classes; Anonymous unions
- Enumerations
    enum classes; Plain enums; Unnamed enums
- Advice

8.1 Introduction

The key to effective use of C++ is the definition and use of user-defined types. This chapter introduces the three most primitive variants of the notion of a user-defined type:

- A **struct** (a structure) is a sequence of elements (called *members*) of arbitrary types.
- A **union** is a **struct** that holds the value of just one of its elements at any one time.
- An **enum** (an enumeration) is a type with a set of named constants (called enumerators).
- **enum class** (a scoped enumeration) is an **enum** where the enumerators are within the scope of the enumeration and no implicit conversions to other types are provided.

Variants of these kinds of simple types have existed since the earliest days of C++. They are primarily focused on the representation of data and are the backbone of most C-style programming. The notion of a **struct** as described here is a simple form of a **class** (§3.2, Chapter 16).

8.2 Structures

An array is an aggregate of elements of the same type. In its simplest form, a **struct** is an aggregate of elements of arbitrary types. For example:

```
struct Address {
      const char* name;      // "Jim Dandy"
      int number;            // 61
      const char* street;    // "South St"
      const char* town;      // "New Providence"
      char state[2];         // 'N' 'J'
      const char* zip;       // "07974"
};
```

This defines a type called **Address** consisting of the items you need in order to send mail to someone within the USA. Note the terminating semicolon.

Variables of type **Address** can be declared exactly like other variables, and the individual *members* can be accessed using the . (dot) operator. For example:

```
void f()
{
      Address jd;
      jd.name = "Jim Dandy";
      jd.number = 61;
}
```

Variables of **struct** types can be initialized using the {} notation (§6.3.5). For example:

```
Address jd = {
      "Jim Dandy",
      61, "South St",
      "New Providence",
      {'N','J'}, "07974"
};
```

Note that **jd.state** could not be initialized by the string **"NJ"**. Strings are terminated by a zero character, '\0', so "NJ" has three characters – one more than will fit into **jd.state**. I deliberately use rather low-level types for the members to illustrate how that can be done and what kinds of problems it can cause.

Structures are often accessed through pointers using the -> (**struct** pointer dereference) operator. For example:

```
void print_addr(Address* p)
{
      cout << p->name << '\n'
            << p->number << ' ' << p->street << '\n'
            << p->town << '\n'
            << p->state[0] << p->state[1] << ' ' << p->zip << '\n';
}
```

When **p** is a pointer, p->m is equivalent to (*p).m.

Alternatively, a **struct** can be passed by reference and accessed using the **.** (**struct** member access) operator:

```
void print_addr2(const Address& r)
{
    cout << r.name << '\n'
         << r.number << ' ' << r.street << '\n'
         << r.town << '\n'
         << r.state[0] << r.state[1] << ' ' << r.zip << '\n';
}
```

Argument passing is discussed in §12.2.

Objects of structure types can be assigned, passed as function arguments, and returned as the result from a function. For example:

```
Address current;

Address set_current(Address next)
{
    address prev = current;
    current = next;
    return prev;
}
```

Other plausible operations, such as comparison (== and !=), are not available by default. However, the user can define such operators (§3.2.1.1, Chapter 18).

8.2.1 struct Layout

An object of a **struct** holds its members in the order they are declared. For example, we might store primitive equipment readout in a structure like this:

```
struct Readout {
    char hour;      // [0:23]
    int value;
    char seq; // sequence mark ['a':'z']
};
```

You could imagine the members of a **Readout** object laid out in memory like this:

Members are allocated in memory in declaration order, so the address of **hour** must be less than the address of **value**. See also §8.2.6.

However, the size of an object of a **struct** is not necessarily the sum of the sizes of its members. This is because many machines require objects of certain types to be allocated on architecture-dependent boundaries or handle such objects much more efficiently if they are. For example, integers are often allocated on word boundaries. On such machines, objects are said to have to be properly *aligned* (§6.2.9). This leads to "holes" in the structures. A more realistic layout of a

Readout on a machine with 4-byte **int** would be:

In this case, as on many machines, **sizeof(Readout)** is **12**, and not **6** as one would naively expect from simply adding the sizes of the individual members.

You can minimize wasted space by simply ordering members by size (largest member first). For example:

```
struct Readout {
    int value;
    char hour;     // [0:23]
    char seq; // sequence mark ['a':'z']
};
```

This would give us:

Note that this still leaves a 2-byte "hole" (unused space) in a **Readout** and **sizeof(Readout)==8**. The reason is that we need to maintain alignment when we put two objects next to each other, say, in an array of **Readout**s. The size of an array of 10 **Readout** objects is **10∗sizeof(Readout)**.

It is usually best to order members for readability and sort them by size only if there is a demonstrated need to optimize.

Use of multiple access specifiers (i.e., **public**, **private**, or **protected**) can affect layout (§20.5).

8.2.2 struct **Names**

The name of a type becomes available for use immediately after it has been encountered and not just after the complete declaration has been seen. For example:

```
struct Link {
    Link∗ previous;
    Link∗ successor;
};
```

However, it is not possible to declare new objects of a **struct** until its complete declaration has been seen. For example:

```
struct No_good {
    No_good member;   // error: recursive definition
};
```

This is an error because the compiler is not able to determine the size of **No_good**. To allow two (or more) **struct**s to refer to each other, we can declare a name to be the name of a **struct**. For example:

```
struct List;          // struct name declaration: List to be defined later

struct Link {
    Link* pre;
    Link* suc;
    List* member_of;
    int data;
};

struct List {
    Link* head;
};
```

Without the first declaration of **List**, use of the pointer type **List**∗ in the declaration of **Link** would have been a syntax error.

The name of a **struct** can be used before the type is defined as long as that use does not require the name of a member or the size of the structure to be known. However, until the completion of the declaration of a **struct**, that **struct** is an incomplete type. For example:

```
struct S;  // "S" is the name of some type

extern S a;
S f();
void g(S);
S* h(S*);
```

However, many such declarations cannot be used unless the type **S** is defined:

```
void k(S* p)
{
    S a;            // error: S not defined; size needed to allocate

    f();            // error: S not defined; size needed to return value
    g(a);           // error: S not defined; size needed to pass argument
    p->m = 7;       // error: S not defined; member name not known

    S* q = h(p);    // ok: pointers can be allocated and passed
    q->m = 7;       // error: S not defined; member name not known
}
```

For reasons that reach into the prehistory of C, it is possible to declare a **struct** and a non-**struct** with the same name in the same scope. For example:

```
struct stat { /* ... */ };
int stat(char* name, struct stat* buf);
```

In that case, the plain name (**stat**) is the name of the non-**struct**, and the **struct** must be referred to with the prefix **struct**. Similarly, the keywords **class**, **union** (§8.3), and **enum** (§8.4) can be used as prefixes for disambiguation. However, it is best not to overload names to make such explicit disambiguation necessary.

8.2.3 Structures and Classes

A struct is simply a class where the members are public by default. So, a struct can have member functions (§2.3.2, Chapter 16). In particular, a struct can have constructors. For example:

```
struct Points {
    vector<Point> elem;// must contain at least one Point
    Points(Point p0) { elem.push_back(p0);}
    Points(Point p0, Point p1) { elem.push_back(p0); elem.push_back(p1); }
    // ...
};
```

```
Points x0;                              // error: no default constructor
Points x1{ {100,200} };                 // one Point
Points x1{ {100,200}, {300,400} };      // two Points
```

You do not need to define a constructor simply to initialize members in order. For example:

```
struct Point {
    int x, y;
};
```

```
Point p0;         // danger: uninitialized if in local scope (§6.3.5.1)
Point p1 {};      // default construction: {{},{}}; that is {0.0}
Point p2 {1};     // the second member is default constructed: {1,{}}; that is {1,0}
Point p3 {1,2};   // {1,2}
```

Constructors are needed if you need to reorder arguments, validate arguments, modify arguments, establish invariants (§2.4.3.2, §13.4), etc. For example:

```
struct Address {
    string name;        // "Jim Dandy"
    int number;         // 61
    string street;      // "South St"
    string town;        // "New Providence"
    char state[2];      // 'N' 'J'
    char zip[5];        // 07974

    Address(const string n, int nu, const string& s, const string& t, const string& st, int z);
};
```

Here, I added a constructor to ensure that every member was initialized and to allow me to use a string and an int for the postal code, rather than fiddling with individual characters. For example:

```
Address jd = {
    "Jim Dandy",
    61, "South St",
    "New Providence",
    "NJ", 7974              // (07974 would be octal; §6.2.4.1)
};
```

The Address constructor might be defined like this:

```
Address::Address(const string& n, int nu, const string& s, const string& t, const string& st, int z)
                        // validate postal code
    :name{n},
     number{nu},
     street{s},
     town{t}
{
    if (st.size()!=2)
        error("State abbreviation should be two characters")
    state = {st[0],st[1]};      // store postal code as characters
    ostringstream ost;          // an output string stream; see §38.4.2
    ost << z;                    // extract characters from int
    string zi {ost.str()};
    switch (zi.size()) {
    case 5:
        zip = {zi[0], zi[1], zi[2], zi[3], zi[4]};
        break;
    case 4:   // starts with '0'
        zip = {'0', zi[0], zi[1], zi[2], zi[3]};
        break;
    default:
        error("unexpected ZIP code format");
    }
    // ... check that the code makes sense ...
}
```

8.2.4 Structures and Arrays

Naturally, we can have arrays of **struct**s and **struct**s containing arrays. For example:

```
struct Point {
    int x,y
};

Point points[3] {{1,2},{3,4},{5,6}};
int x2 = points[2].x;

struct Array {
    Point elem[3];
};

Array points2 {{1,2},{3,4},{5,6}};
int y2 = points2.elem[2].y;
```

Placing a built-in array in a **struct** allows us to treat that array as an object: we can copy the **struct** containing it in initialization (including argument passing and function return) and assignment. For example:

```
Array shift(Array a, Point p)
{
    for (int i=0; i!=3; ++i) {
        a.elem[i].x += p.x;
        a.elem[i].y += p.y;
    }
    return a;
}
```

```
Array ax = shift(points2,{10,20});
```

The notation for Array is a bit primitive: Why i!=3? Why keep repeating .elem[i]? Why just elements of type Point? The standard library provides std::array (§34.2.1) as a more complete and elegant development of the idea of a fixed-size array as a struct:

```
template<typename T, size_t N >
struct array {    // simplified (see §34.2.1)
    T elem[N];

    T* begin() noexcept { return elem; }
    const T* begin() const noexcept {return elem; }
    T* end() noexcept { return elem+N; }
    const T* end() const noexcept { return elem+N; }

    constexpr size_t size() noexcept;

    T& operator[](size_t n) { return elem[n]; }
    const T& operator[](size_type n) const { return elem[n]; }

    T * data() noexcept { return elem; }
    const T * data() const noexcept { return elem; }

    // ...
};
```

This array is a template to allow arbitrary numbers of elements of arbitrary types. It also deals directly with the possibility of exceptions (§13.5.1.1) and const objects (§16.2.9.1). Using array, we can now write:

```
struct Point {
    int x,y
};
```

```
using Array = array<Point,3>; // array of 3 Points
```

```
Array points {{1,2},{3,4},{5,6}};
int x2 = points[2].x;
int y2 = points[2].y;
```

```
Array shift(Array a, Point p)
{
    for (int i=0; i!=a.size(); ++i) {
        a[i].x += p.x;
        a[i].y += p.y;
    }
    return a;
}
```

```
Array ax = shift(points,{10,20});
```

The main advantages of **std::array** over a built-in array are that it is a proper object type (has assignment, etc.) and does not implicitly convert to a pointer to an individual element:

```
ostream& operator<<(ostream& os, Point p)
{
    cout << '{' << p[i].x << ',' << p[i].y << '}';
}
```

```
void print(Point a[],int s)  // must specify number of elements
{
    for (int i=0; i!=s; ++i)
        cout << a[i] << '\n';
}
```

```
template<typename T, int N>
void print(array<T,N>& a)
{
    for (int i=0; i!=a.size(); ++i)
        cout << a[i] << '\n';
}
```

```
Point point1[] = {{1,2},{3,4},{5,6}};          // 3 elements
array<Point,3> point2 = {{1,2},{3,4},{5,6}};   // 3 elements
```

```
void f()
{
    print(point1,4);       // 4 is a bad error
    print(point2);
}
```

The disadvantage of **std::array** compared to a built-in array is that we can't deduce the number of elements from the length of the initializer:

```
Point point1[] = {{1,2},{3,4},{5,6}};          // 3 elements
array<Point,3> point2 = {{1,2},{3,4},{5,6}};   // 3 elements
array<Point> point3 = {{1,2},{3,4},{5,6}};     // error: number of elements not given
```

8.2.5 Type Equivalence

Two **struct**s are different types even when they have the same members. For example:

```
struct S1 { int a; };
struct S2 { int a; };
```

S1 and S2 are two different types, so:

```
S1 x;
S2 y = x;  // error: type mismatch
```

A **struct** is also a different type from a type used as a member. For example:

```
S1 x;
int i = x;  // error: type mismatch
```

Every **struct** must have a unique definition in a program (§15.2.3).

8.2.6 Plain Old Data

Sometimes, we want to treat an object as just "plain old data" (a contiguous sequence of bytes in memory) and not worry about more advanced semantic notions, such as run-time polymorphism (§3.2.3, §20.3.2), user-defined copy semantics (§3.3, §17.5), etc. Often, the reason for doing so is to be able to move objects around in the most efficient way the hardware is capable of. For example, copying a 100-element array using 100 calls of a copy constructor is unlikely to be as fast as calling **std::memcpy()**, which typically simply uses a block-move machine instruction. Even if the constructor is inlined, it could be hard for an optimizer to discover this optimization. Such "tricks" are not uncommon, and are important, in implementations of containers, such as **vector**, and in low-level I/O routines. They are unnecessary and should be avoided in higher-level code.

So, a *POD* ("Plain Old Data") is an object that can be manipulated as "just data" without worrying about complications of class layouts or user-defined semantics for construction, copy, and move. For example:

```
struct S0 { };                                  // a POD
struct S1 { int a; };                           // a POD
struct S2 { int a; S2(int aa) : a(aa) { } };    // not a POD (no default constructor)
struct S3 { int a; S3(int aa) : a(aa) { } S3() { } };  // a POD (user-defined default constructor)
struct S4 { int a; S4(int aa) : a(aa) { } S4() = default; };  // a POD
struct S5 { virtual void f(); /* ... */ };      // not a POD (has a virtual function)

struct S6 : S1 { };         // a POD
struct S7 : S0 { int b; };  // a POD
struct S8 : S1 { int b; };  // not a POD (data in both S1 and S8)
struct S9 : S0, S1 {};      // a POD
```

For us to manipulate an object as "just data" (as a POD), the object must

- not have a complicated layout (e.g., with a **vptr**; (§3.2.3, §20.3.2),
- not have nonstandard (user-defined) copy semantics, and
- have a trivial default constructor.

Obviously, we need to be precise about the definition of POD so that we only use such optimizations where they don't break any language guarantees. Formally (§iso.3.9, §iso.9), a POD object must be of

- a *standard layout type*, and
- a *trivially copyable type*,
- a type with a trivial default constructor.

A related concept is a *trivial type*, which is a type with

- a trivial default constructor and
- trivial copy and move operations

Informally, a default constructor is trivial if it does not need to do any work (use **=default** if you need to define one §17.6.1).

A type has standard layout unless it

- has a non-**static** member or a base that is not standard layout,
- has a **virtual** function (§3.2.3, §20.3.2),
- has a **virtual** base (§21.3.5),
- has a member that is a reference (§7.7),
- has multiple access specifiers for non-static data members (§20.5), or
- prevents important layout optimizations
    - by having non-**static** data members in more than one base class or in both the derived class and a base, or
    - by having a base class of the same type as the first non-**static** data member.

Basically, a standard layout type is one that has a layout with an obvious equivalent in C and is in the union of what common C++ Application Binary Interfaces (ABIs) can handle.

A type is trivially copyable unless it has a nontrivial copy operation, move operation, or destructor (§3.2.1.2, §17.6). Informally, a copy operation is trivial if it can be implemented as a bitwise copy. So, what makes a copy, move, or destructor nontrivial?

- It is user-defined.
- Its class has a **virtual** function.
- Its class has a **virtual** base.
- Its class has a base or a member that is not trivial.

An object of built-in type is trivially copyable, and has standard layout. Also, an array of trivially copyable objects is trivially copyable and an array of standard layout objects has standard layout. Consider an example:

```
template<typename T>
    void mycopy(T* to, const T* from, int count);
```

I'd like to optimize the simple case where **T** is a POD. I could do that by only calling **mycopy()** for PODs, but that's error-prone: if I use **mycopy()** can I rely on a maintainer of the code to remember never to call **mycopy()** for non-PODs? Realistically, I cannot. Alternatively, I could call **std::copy()**, which is most likely implemented with the necessary optimization. Anyway, here is the general and optimized code:

```
template<typename T>
void mycopy(T* to, const T* from, int count)
{
    if (is_pod<T>::value)
        memcpy(to,from,count*sizeof(T));
    else
        for (int i=0; i!=count; ++i)
            to[i]=from[i];
}
```

The **is_pod** is a standard-library type property predicate (§35.4.1) defined in **<type_traits>** allowing us to ask the question "Is T a POD?" in our code. The best thing about **is_pod<T>** is that it saves us from remembering the exact rules for what a POD is.

Note that adding or subtracting non-default constructors does not affect layout or performance (that was not true in C++98).

If you feel an urge to become a language lawyer, study the layout and triviality concepts in the standard (§iso.3.9, §iso.9) and try to think about their implications to programmers and compiler writers. Doing so might cure you of the urge before it has consumed too much of your time.

8.2.7 Fields

It seems extravagant to use a whole byte (a **char** or a **bool**) to represent a binary variable – for example, an on/off switch – but a **char** is the smallest object that can be independently allocated and addressed in C++ (§7.2). It is possible, however, to bundle several such tiny variables together as *fields* in a **struct**. A field is often called a *bit-field*. A member is defined to be a field by specifying the number of bits it is to occupy. Unnamed fields are allowed. They do not affect the meaning of the named fields, but they can be used to make the layout better in some machine-dependent way:

```
struct PPN {            // R6000 Physical Page Number
    unsigned int PFN : 22;    // Page Frame Number
    int : 3;                  // unused
    unsigned int CCA : 3;         // Cache Coherency Algorithm
    bool nonreachable : 1;
    bool dirty : 1;
    bool valid : 1;
    bool global : 1;
};
```

This example also illustrates the other main use of fields: to name parts of an externally imposed layout. A field must be of an integral or enumeration type (§6.2.1). It is not possible to take the address of a field. Apart from that, however, it can be used exactly like other variables. Note that a **bool** field really can be represented by a single bit. In an operating system kernel or in a debugger, the type **PPN** might be used like this:

```
void part_of_VM_system(PPN* p)
{
    // ...
```

```
        if (p->dirty) {  // contents changed
              // copy to disk
              p->dirty = 0;
        }
}
```

Surprisingly, using fields to pack several variables into a single byte does not necessarily save space. It saves data space, but the size of the code needed to manipulate these variables increases on most machines. Programs have been known to shrink significantly when binary variables were converted from bit-fields to characters! Furthermore, it is typically much faster to access a **char** or an **int** than to access a field. Fields are simply a convenient shorthand for using bitwise logical operators (§11.1.1) to extract information from and insert information into part of a word.

8.3 Unions

A **union** is a **struct** in which all members are allocated at the same address so that the **union** occupies only as much space as its largest member. Naturally, a **union** can hold a value for only one member at a time. For example, consider a symbol table entry that holds a name and a value:

```
enum Type { str, num };

struct Entry {
        char* name;
        Type t;
        char* s;   // use s if t==str
        int i;     // use i if t==num
};

void f(Entry* p)
{
        if (p->t == str)
              cout << p->s;
        // ...
}
```

The members **s** and **i** can never be used at the same time, so space is wasted. It can be easily recovered by specifying that both should be members of a **union**, like this:

```
union Value {
        char* s;
        int i;
};
```

The language doesn't keep track of which kind of value is held by a **union**, so the programmer must do that:

```
struct Entry {
    char* name;
    Type t;
    Value v;   // use v.s if t==str; use v.i if t==num
};

void f(Entry* p)
{
    if (p->t == str)
        cout << p->s;
    // ...
}
```

To avoid errors, one can encapsulate a **union** so that the correspondence between a type field and access to the **union** members can be guaranteed (§8.3.2).

Unions are sometimes misused for "type conversion." This misuse is practiced mainly by programmers trained in languages that do not have explicit type conversion facilities, so that cheating is necessary. For example, the following "converts" an **int** to an **int*** simply by assuming bitwise equivalence:

```
union Fudge {
    int i;
    int* p;
};

int* cheat(int i)
{
    Fudge a;
    a.i = i;
    return a.p;     // bad use
}
```

This is not really a conversion at all. On some machines, an **int** and an **int*** do not occupy the same amount of space, while on others, no integer can have an odd address. Such use of a **union** is dangerous and nonportable. If you need such an inherently ugly conversion, use an explicit type conversion operator (§11.5.2) so that the reader can see what is going on. For example:

```
int* cheat2(int i)
{
    return reinterpret_cast<int*>(i);     // obviously ugly and dangerous
}
```

Here, at least the compiler has a chance to warn you if the sizes of objects are different and such code stands out like the sore thumb it is.

Use of **unions** can be essential for compactness of data and through that for performance. However, most programs don't improve much from the use of **unions** and **unions** are rather error-prone. Consequently, I consider **unions** an overused feature; avoid them when you can.

8.3.1 Unions and Classes

Many nontrivial **union**s have a member that is much larger than the most frequently used members. Because the size of a **union** is at least as large as its largest member, space is wasted. This waste can often be eliminated by using a set of derived classes (§3.2.2, Chapter 20) instead of a **union**.

Technically, a **union** is a kind of a **struct** (§8.2) which in turn is a kind of a **class** (Chapter 16). However, many of the facilities provided for classes are not relevant for unions, so some restrictions are imposed on **union**s:

[1] A **union** cannot have virtual functions.

[2] A **union** cannot have members of reference type.

[3] A **union** cannot have base classes.

[4] If a **union** has a member with a user-defined constructor, a copy operation, a move operation, or a destructor, then that special function is **deleted** (§3.3.4, §17.6.4) for that **union**; that is, it cannot be used for an object of the **union** type.

[5] At most one member of a **union** can have an in-class initializer (§17.4.4).

[6] A **union** cannot be used as a base class.

These restrictions prevent many subtle errors and simplify the implementation of **union**s. The latter is important because the use of **union**s is often an optimization and we won't want "hidden costs" imposed to compromise that.

The rule that **delete**s constructors (etc.) from a **union** with a member that has a constructor (etc.) keeps simple **union**s simple and forces the programmer to provide complicated operations if they are needed. For example, since **Entry** has no member with constructors, destructors, or assignments, we can create and copy **Entry**s freely. For example:

```
void f(Entry a)
{
      Entry b = a;
};
```

Doing so with a more complicated **union** would cause implementation difficulties or errors:

```
union U {
      int m1;
      complex<double> m2;    // complex has a constructor
      string m3;             // string has a constructor (maintaining a serious invariant)
};
```

To copy a **U** we would have to decide which copy operation to use. For example:

```
void f2(U x)
{
      U u;                   // error: which default constructor?
      U u2 = x;              // error: which copy constructor?
      u.m1 = 1;              // assign to int member
      string s = u.m3;       // disaster: read from string member
      return;                // error: which destructors are called for x, u, and u2?
}
```

It's illegal to write one member and then read another, but people do that nevertheless (usually by mistake). In this case, the **string** copy constructor would be called with an invalid argument. It is fortunate that **U** won't compile. When needed, a user can define a class containing a **union** that properly handles **union** members with constructors, destructors, and assignments (§8.3.2). If desired, such a class can also prevent the error of writing one member and then reading another.

It is possible to specify an in-class initializer for at most one member. If so, this initializer will be used for default initialization. For example:

```
union U2 {
    int a;
    const char* p {""};
};
```

```
U2 x1;          // default initialized to x1.p == ""
U2 x2 {7};      // x2.a == 7
```

8.3.2 Anonymous unions

To see how we can write a class that overcomes the problems with misuse of a **union**, consider a variant of **Entry** (§8.3):

```
class Entry2 { // two alternative representations represented as a union
private:
    enum class Tag { number, text };
    Tag type; // discriminant

    union {    // representation
        int i;
        string s;  // string has default constructor, copy operations, and destructor
    };
public:
    struct Bad_entry { };       // used for exceptions

    string name;

    ˜Entry2();
    Entry2& operator=(const Entry2&);       // necessary because of the string variant
    Entry2(const Entry2&);
    // ...

    int number() const;
    string text() const;

    void set_number(int n);
    void set_text(const string&);
    // ...
};
```

I'm not a fan of get/set functions, but in this case we really need to perform a nontrivial user-specified action on each access. I chose to name the "get" function after the value and use the **set_** prefix for the "set" function. That happens to be my favorite among the many naming conventions.

The read-access functions can be defined like this:

```
int Entry2::number() const
{
    if (type!=Tag::number) throw Bad_entry{};
    return i;
};

string Entry2::text() const
{
    if (type!=Tag::text) throw Bad_entry{};
    return s;
};
```

These access functions check the **type** tag, and if it is the one that correctly corresponds to the access we want, it returns a reference to the value; otherwise, it throws an exception. Such a **union** is often called a *tagged union* or a *discriminated union*.

The write-access functions basically do the same checking of the **type** tag, but note how setting a new value must take the previous value into account:

```
void Entry2::set_number(int n)
{
    if (type==Tag::text) {
        s.˜string();                  // explicitly destroy string (§11.2.4)
        type = Tag::number;
    }
    i = n;
}

void Entry2::set_text(const string& ss)
{
    if (type==Tag::text)
        s = ss;
    else {
        new(&s) string{ss};           // placement new: explicitly construct string (§11.2.4)
        type = Tag::text;
    }
}
```

The use of a **union** forces us to use otherwise obscure and low-level language facilities (explicit construction and destruction) to manage the lifetime of the **union** elements. This is another reason to be wary of using **unions**.

Note that the **union** in the declaration of **Entry2** is not named. That makes it an *anonymous union*. An anonymous **union** is an object, not a type, and its members can be accessed without mentioning an object name. That means that we can use members of an anonymous **union** exactly as we use other members of a class – as long as we remember that **union** members really can be used only one at a time.

Entry2 has a member of a type with a user-defined assignment operator, **string**, so **Entry2**'s assignment operator is **deleted** (§3.3.4, §17.6.4). If we want to assign **Entry2**s, we have to define

Entry2::operator=(). Assignment combines the complexities of reading and writing but is otherwise logically similar to the access functions:

```
Entry2& Entry2::operator=(const Entry2& e)  // necessary because of  the string variant
{
    if (type==Tag::text && e.type==Tag::text) {
        s = e.s;          // usual string assignment
        return *this;
    }

    if (type==Tag::text) s.~string(); // explicit destroy (§11.2.4)

    switch (e.type) {
    case Tag::number:
        i = e.i;
        break;
    case Tag::text:
        new(&s)(e.s);    // placement new: explicit construct (§11.2.4)
        type = e.type;
    }

    return *this;
}
```

Constructors and a move assignment can be defined similarly as needed. We need at least a constructor or two to establish the correspondence between the **type** tag and a value. The destructor must handle the **string** case:

```
Entry2::~Entry2()
{
    if (type==Tag::text) s.~string(); // explicit destroy (§11.2.4)
}
```

8.4 Enumerations

An *enumeration* is a type that can hold a set of integer values specified by the user (§iso.7.2). Some of an enumeration's possible values are named and called *enumerators*. For example:

```
enum class Color { red, green, blue };
```

This defines an enumeration called **Color** with the enumerators **red**, **green**, and **blue**. "An enumeration" is colloquially shortened to "an **enum**."

There are two kinds of enumerations:

[1]   **enum classes**, for which the enumerator names (e.g., **red**) are local to the **enum** and their values do not implicitly convert to other types
[2]   "Plain **enums**," for which the enumerator names are in the same scope as the **enum** and their values implicitly convert to integers

In general, prefer the **enum classes** because they cause fewer surprises.

8.4.1 enum classes

An **enum class** is a scoped and strongly typed enumeration. For example:

```
enum class Traffic_light { red, yellow, green };
enum class Warning { green, yellow, orange, red }; // fire alert levels
```

```
Warning a1 = 7;                        // error: no int->Warning conversion
int a2 = green;                        // error: green not in scope
int a3 = Warning::green;               // error: no Warning->int conversion
Warning a4 = Warning::green;           // OK
```

```
void f(Traffic_light x)
{
    if (x == 9) { /* ... */ }            // error: 9 is not a Traffic_light
    if (x == red) { /* ... */ }          // error: no red in scope
    if (x == Warning::red)  { /* ... */ }  // error: x is not a Warning
    if (x == Traffic_light::red) { /* ... */ }   // OK
}
```

Note that the enumerators present in both **enum**s do not clash because each is in the scope of its own **enum class**.

An enumeration is represented by some integer type and each enumerator by some integer value. We call the type used to represent an enumeration its *underlying type*. The underlying type must be one of the signed or unsigned integer types (§6.2.4); the default is **int**. We could be explicit about that:

```
enum class Warning : int { green, yellow, orange, red }; // sizeof(Warning)==sizeof(int)
```

If we considered that too wasteful of space, we could instead use a **char**:

```
enum class Warning : char { green, yellow, orange, red };     // sizeof(Warning)==1
```

By default, enumerator values are assigned increasing from **0**. Here, we get:

```
static_cast<int>(Warning::green)==0
static_cast<int>(Warning::yellow)==1
static_cast<int>(Warning::orange)==2
static_cast<int>(Warning::red)==3
```

Declaring a variable **Warning** instead of plain **int** can give both the user and the compiler a hint as to the intended use. For example:

```
void f(Warning key)
{
    switch (key) {
    case Warning::green:
        // do something
        break;
    case Warning::orange:
        // do something
        break;
```

```
        case Warning::red:
            // do something
            break;
    }
}
```

A human might notice that **yellow** was missing, and a compiler might issue a warning because only three out of four **Warning** values are handled.

An enumerator can be initialized by a constant expression (§10.4) of integral type (§6.2.1). For example:

```
enum class Printer_flags {
    acknowledge=1,
    paper_empty=2,
    busy=4,
    out_of_black=8,
    out_of_color=16,
    //
};
```

The values for the **Printer_flags** enumerators are chosen so that they can be combined by bitwise operations. An **enum** is a user-defined type, so we can define the | and & operators for it (§3.2.1.1, Chapter 18). For example:

```
constexpr Printer_flags operator|(Printer_flags a, Printer_flags b)
{
    return static_cast<Printer_flags>(static_cast<int>(a)|static_cast<int>(b));
}

constexpr Printer_flags operator&(Printer_flags a, Printer_flags b)
{
    return static_cast<Printer_flags>(static_cast<int>(a)&static_cast<int>(b));
}
```

The explicit conversions are necessary because a **class enum** does not support implicit conversions. Given these definitions of | and & for **Printer_flags**, we can write:

```
void try_to_print(Printer_flags x)
{
    if (x&Printer_flags::acknowledge) {
        // ...
    }
    else if (x&Printer_flags::busy) {
        // ...
    }
    else if (x&(Printer_flags::out_of_black|Printer_flags::out_of_color)) {
        // either we are out of black or we are out of color
        // ...
    }
    // ...
}
```

I defined **operator|()** and **operator&()** to be **constexpr** functions (§10.4, §12.1.6) because someone might want to use those operators in constant expressions. For example:

```
void g(Printer_flags x)
{
    switch (x) {
    case Printer_flags::acknowledge:
        // ...
        break;
    case Printer_flags::busy:
        // ...
        break;
    case Printer_flags::out_of_black:
        // ...
        break;
    case Printer_flags::out_of_color:
        // ...
        break;
    case Printer_flags::out_of_black&Printer_flags::out_of_color:
        // we are out of black *and* out of color
        // ...
        break;
    }

    // ...
}
```

It is possible to declare an **enum class** without defining it (§6.3) until later. For example:

```
enum class Color_code : char;        // declaration
void foobar(Color_code* p);          // use of declaration
// ...
enum class Color_code : char {       // definition
    red, yellow, green, blue
};
```

A value of integral type may be explicitly converted to an enumeration type. The result of such a conversion is undefined unless the value is within the range of the enumeration's underlying type. For example:

```
enum class Flag : char{ x=1, y=2, z=4, e=8 };

Flag f0 {};                          // f0 gets the default value 0
Flag f1 = 5;                         // type error: 5 is not of type Flag
Flag f2 = Flag{5};                   // error: no narrowing conversion to an enum class
Flag f3 = static_cast<Flag>(5);      // brute force
Flag f4 = static_cast<Flag>(999);    // error: 999 is not a char value (maybe not caught)
```

The last assignments show why there is no implicit conversion from an integer to an enumeration; most integer values do not have a representation in a particular enumeration.

Each enumerator has an integer value. We can extract that value explicitly. For example:

```
int i = static_cast<int>(Flag::y);      // i becomes 2
char c = static_cast<char>(Flag::e);    // c becomes 8
```

The notion of a range of values for an enumeration differs from the enumeration notion in the Pascal family of languages. However, bit-manipulation examples that require values outside the set of enumerators to be well defined (e.g., the **Printer_flags** example) have a long history in C and C++.

The **sizeof** an **enum class** is the **sizeof** of its underlying type. In particular, if the underlying type is not explicitly specified, the size is **sizeof(int)**.

8.4.2 Plain enums

A "plain **enum**" is roughly what C++ offered before the **enum class**es were introduced, so you'll find them in lots of C and C++98-style code. The enumerators of a plain **enum** are exported into the **enum**'s scope, and they implicitly convert to values of some integer type. Consider the examples from §8.4.1 with the "**class**" removed:

```
enum Traffic_light { red, yellow, green };
enum Warning { green, yellow, orange, red }; // fire alert levels

// error: two definitions of yellow (to the same value)
// error: two definitions of red (to different values)

Warning a1 = 7;                   // error: no int->Warning conversion
int a2 = green;                   // OK: green is in scope and converts to int
int a3 = Warning::green;          // OK: Warning->int conversion
Warning a4 = Warning::green;      // OK

void f(Traffic_light x)
{
    if (x == 9) { /* ... */ }                 // OK (but Traffic_light doesn't have a 9)
    if (x == red) { /* ... */ }               // error: two reds in scope
    if (x == Warning::red)  { /* ... */ }     // OK (Ouch!)
    if (x == Traffic_light::red) { /* ... */ } // OK
}
```

We were "lucky" that defining **red** in two plain enumerations in a single scope saved us from hard-to-spot errors. Consider "cleaning up" the plain **enum**s by disambiguating the enumerators (as is easily done in a small program but can be done only with great difficulty in a large one):

```
enum Traffic_light { tl_red, tl_yellow, tl_green };
enum Warning { green, yellow, orange, red }; // fire alert levels
```

```
void f(Traffic_light x)
{
    if (x == red) { /* ... */ }                  // OK (ouch!)
    if (x == Warning::red)  { /* ... */ }        // OK (ouch!)
    if (x == Traffic_light::red) { /* ... */ }   // error: red is not a Traffic_light value
}
```

The compiler accepts the **x==red**, which is almost certainly a bug. The injection of names into an enclosing scope (as **enums**, but not **enum class**es or **class**es, do) is *namespace pollution* and can be a major problem in larger programs (Chapter 14).

You can specify the underlying type of a plain enumeration, just as you can for **enum class**es. If you do, you can declare the enumerations without defining them until later. For example:

```
enum Traffic_light : char { tl_red, tl_yellow, tl_green };   // underlying type is char
```

```
enum Color_code : char;          // declaration
void foobar(Color_code* p);      // use of declaration
// ...
enum Color_code : char { red, yellow, green, blue }; // definition
```

If you don't specify the underlying type, you can't declare the **enum** without defining it, and its underlying type is determined by a relatively complicated algorithm: when all enumerators are non-negative, the range of the enumeration is $[0:2^k-1]$ where 2^k is the smallest power of 2 for which all enumerators are within the range. If there are negative enumerators, the range is $[-2^k:2^k-1]$. This defines the smallest bit-field capable of holding the enumerator values using the conventional two's complement representation. For example:

```
enum E1 { dark, light };                // range 0:1
enum E2 { a = 3, b = 9 };               // range 0:15
enum E3 { min = −10, max = 1000000 };   // range -1048576:1048575
```

The rule for explicit conversion of an integer to a plain **enum** is the same as for the **class enum** except that when there is no explicit underlying type, the result of such a conversion is undefined unless the value is within the range of the enumeration. For example:

```
enum Flag { x=1, y=2, z=4, e=8 };   // range 0:15
```

```
Flag f0 {};                         // f0 gets the default value 0
Flag f1 = 5;                        // type error: 5 is not of type Flag
Flag f2 = Flag{5};                  // error: no explicit conversion from int to Flag
Flag f2 = static_cast<Flag>(5);     // OK: 5 is within the range of Flag
Flag f3 = static_cast<Flag>(z|e);   // OK: 12 is within the range of Flag
Flag f4 = static_cast<Flag>(99);    // undefined: 99 is not within the range of Flag
```

Because there is an implicit conversion from a plain **enum** to its underlying type, we don't need to define | to make this example work: **z** and **e** are converted to **int** so that **z|e** can be evaluated. The **sizeof** an enumeration is the **sizeof** its underlying type. If the underlying type isn't explicitly specified, it is some integral type that can hold its range and not larger than **sizeof(int)**, unless an enumerator cannot be represented as an **int** or as an **unsigned int**. For example, sizeof(e1) could be **1** or maybe **4** but not **8** on a machine where sizeof(int)==4.

8.4.3 Unnamed enums

A plain **enum** can be unnamed. For example:

```
enum { arrow_up=1, arrow_down, arrow_sideways };
```

We use that when all we need is a set of integer constants, rather than a type to use for variables.

8.5 Advice

[1] When compactness of data is important, lay out structure data members with larger members before smaller ones; §8.2.1.

[2] Use bit-fields to represent hardware-imposed data layouts; §8.2.7.

[3] Don't naively try to optimize memory consumption by packing several values into a single byte; §8.2.7.

[4] Use **union**s to save space (represent alternatives) and never for type conversion; §8.3.

[5] Use enumerations to represent sets of named constants; §8.4.

[6] Prefer **class enum**s over "plain" enums to minimize surprises; §8.4.

[7] Define operations on enumerations for safe and simple use; §8.4.1.

9

Statements

A programmer is a machine
for turning caffeine into code.
– A programmer

- Introduction
- Statement Summary
- Declarations as Statements
- Selection Statements
    if Statements; **switch** Statements; Declarations in Conditions
- Iteration Statements
    Range-**for** Statements; **for** Statements; **while** Statements; **do** Statements; Loop exit
- **goto** Statements
- Comments and Indentation
- Advice

9.1 Introduction

C++ offers a conventional and flexible set of statements. Basically all that is either interesting or complicated is found in expressions and declarations. Note that a declaration is a statement and that an expression becomes a statement when you add a semicolon at its end.

Unlike an expression, a statement does not have a value. Instead, statements are used to specify the order of execution. For example:

```
a = b+c;        // expression statement
if (a==7)       // if-statement
    b = 9;      // execute if and only if a==9
```

Logically, a=b+c is executed before the if, as everyone would expect. A compiler may reorder code to improve performance as long as the result is identical to that of the simple order of execution.

9.2 Statement Summary

Here is a summary of C++ statements:

statement:
      declaration
      expression$_{opt}$;
      { *statement-list*$_{opt}$ }
      try { *statement-list*$_{opt}$ } *handler-list*

      case *constant-expression* : *statement*
      default : *statement*
      break ;
      continue ;

      return *expression*$_{opt}$;

      goto *identifier* ;
      identifier : *statement*

      selection-statement
      iteration-statement

selection-statement:
      if (*condition*) *statement*
      if (*condition*) *statement* **else** *statement*
      switch (*condition*) *statement*

iteration-statement:
      while (*condition*) *statement*
      do *statement* **while** (*expression*) ;
      for (*for-init-statement condition*$_{opt}$; *expression*$_{opt}$) *statement*
      for (*for-init-declaration* : *expression*) *statement*

statement-list:
      statement statement-list$_{opt}$

condition:
      expression
      type-specifier declarator = *expression*
      type-specifier declarator { *expression* }

handler-list:
      handler handler-list$_{opt}$

handler:
      catch (*exception-declaration*) { *statement-list*$_{opt}$ }

A semicolon is by itself a statement, the *empty statement*.

A (possibly empty) sequence of statements within "curly braces" (i.e., { and }) is called a *block* or a *compound statement*. A name declared in a block goes out of scope at the end of its block (§6.3.4).

A *declaration* is a statement and there is no assignment statement or procedure-call statement; assignments and function calls are expressions.

A *for-init-statement* must be either a declaration or an *expression-statement*. Note that both end with a semicolon.

A *for-init-declaration* must be the declaration of a single uninitialized variable.

The statements for handling exceptions, *try-blocks*, are described in §13.5.

9.3 Declarations as Statements

A declaration is a statement. Unless a variable is declared **static**, its initializer is executed whenever the thread of control passes through the declaration (see also §6.4.2). The reason for allowing declarations wherever a statement can be used (and a few other places; §9.4.3, §9.5.2) is to enable the programmer to minimize the errors caused by uninitialized variables and to allow better locality in code. There is rarely a reason to introduce a variable before there is a value for it to hold. For example:

```
void f(vector<string>& v, int i, const char* p)
{
    if (p==nullptr) return;
    if (i<0 || v.size()<=i)
        error("bad index");
    string s = v[i];
    if (s == p) {
        // ...
    }
    // ...
}
```

The ability to place declarations after executable code is essential for many constants and for single-assignment styles of programming where a value of an object is not changed after initialization. For user-defined types, postponing the definition of a variable until a suitable initializer is available can also lead to better performance. For example:

```
void use()
{
    string s1;
    s1 = "The best is the enemy of the good.";
    // ...
}
```

This requests a default initialization (to the empty string) followed by an assignment. This can be slower than a simple initialization to the desired value:

```
        string s2 {"Voltaire"};
```

The most common reason to declare a variable without an initializer is that it requires a statement to give it its desired value. Input variables are among the few reasonable examples of that:

```
void input()
{
    int buf[max];
    int count = 0;
    for (int i; cin>>i;) {
        if (i<0) error("unexpected negative value");
        if (count==max) error("buffer overflow");
        buf[count++] = i;
    }
    // ...
}
```

I assume that **error()** does not return; if it does, this code may cause a buffer overflow. Often, **push_back()** (§3.2.1.3, §13.6, §31.3.6) provides a better solution to such examples.

9.4 Selection Statements

A value can be tested by either an **if**-statement or a **switch**-statement:

> **if (** *condition* **)** *statement*
> **if (** *condition* **)** *statement* **else** *statement*
> **switch (** *condition* **)** *statement*

A *condition* is either an expression or a declaration (§9.4.3).

9.4.1 if Statements

In an **if**-statement, the first (or only) statement is executed if the condition is **true** and the second statement (if it is specified) is executed otherwise. If a condition evaluates to something different from a Boolean, it is – if possible – implicitly converted to a **bool**. This implies that any arithmetic or pointer expression can be used as a condition. For example, if **x** is an integer, then

> **if (x)** // ...

means

> **if (x != 0)** // ...

For a pointer **p**,

> **if (p)** // ...

is a direct statement of the test "Does **p** point to a valid object (assuming proper initialization)?" and is equivalent to

> **if (p != nullptr)** // ...

Note that a "plain" **enum** can be implicitly converted to an integer and then to a **bool**, whereas an **enum class** cannot (§8.4.1). For example:

```
enum E1 { a, b };
enum class E2 { a, b };

void f(E1 x, E2 y)
{
    if (x)              // OK
        // ...
    if (y)              // error: no conversion to bool
        // ...
    if (y==E2::a)    // OK
        // ...
}
```

The logical operators

&& || !

are most commonly used in conditions. The operators **&&** and **||** will not evaluate their second argument unless doing so is necessary. For example,

```
if (p && 1<p–>count) // ...
```

This tests **1<p–>count** only if **p** is not **nullptr**.

For choosing between two alternatives each of which produces a value, a conditional expression (§11.1.3) is a more direct expression of intent than an **if**-statement. For example:

```
int max(int a, int b)
{
    return (a>b)?a:b;    // return the larger of a and b
}
```

A name can only be used within the scope in which it is declared. In particular, it cannot be used on another branch of an **if**-statement. For example:

```
void f2(int i)
{
    if (i) {
        int x = i+2;
        ++x;
        // ...
    }
    else {
        ++x; // error: x is not in scope
    }
    ++x;        // error: x is not in scope
}
```

A branch of an **if**-statement cannot be just a declaration. If we need to introduce a name in a branch, it must be enclosed in a block (§9.2). For example:

```
void f1(int i)
{
    if (i)
        int x = i+2;        // error: declaration of if-statement branch
}
```

9.4.2 switch **Statements**

A **switch**-statement selects among a set of alternatives (**case**-labels). The expression in the **case** labels must be a constant expression of integral or enumeration type. A value may not be used more than once for **case**-labels in a **switch**-statement. For example:

```
void f(int i)
{
    switch (i) {
    case 2.7: // error: floating point uses for case
        // ...
    case 2:
        // ...
    case 4-2: // error: 2 used twice in case labels
        // ...
    };
```

A **switch**-statement can alternatively be written as a set of **if**-statements. For example:

```
switch (val) {
case 1:
    f();
    break;
case 2:
    g();
    break;
default:
    h();
    break;
}
```

This could be expressed as:

```
if (val == 1)
    f();
else if (val == 2)
    g();
else
    h();
```

The meaning is the same, but the first (**switch**) version is preferred because the nature of the operation (testing a single value against a set of constants) is explicit. This makes the **switch**-statement easier to read for nontrivial examples. It typically also leads to the generation of better code because there is no reason to repeatedly check individual values. Instead, a jump table can be used.

Beware that a case of a switch must be terminated somehow unless you want to carry on executing the next case. Consider:

```
switch (val) {              // beware
case 1:
    cout << "case 1\n";
case 2:
    cout << "case 2\n";
default:
    cout << "default: case not found\n";
}
```

Invoked with val==1, the output will greatly surprise the uninitiated:

```
case 1
case 2
default: case not found
```

It is a good idea to comment the (rare) cases in which a fall-through is intentional so that an uncommented fall-through can be assumed to be an error. For example:

```
switch (action) {              // handle (action,value) pair
case do_and_print:
    act(value);
    // no break: fall through to print
case print:
    print(value);
    break;
// ...
}
```

A **break** is the most common way of terminating a case, but a **return** is often useful (§10.2.1).

When should a **switch**-statement have a **default**? There is no single answer that covers all situations. One use is for the **default** to handle the most common case. Another common use is the exact opposite: the **default**: action is simply a way to catch errors; every valid alternative is covered by the **case**s. However, there is one case where a **default** should not be used: if a **switch** is intended to have one case for each enumerator of an enumeration. If so, leaving out the **default** gives the compiler a chance to warn against a set of **case**s that almost but not quite match the set of enumerators. For example, this is almost certainly an error:

```
enum class Vessel { cup, glass, goblet, chalice };

void problematic(Vessel v)
{
    switch (v) {
    case Vessel::cup:      /* ... */    break;
    case Vessel::glass:    /* ... */    break;
    case Vessel::goblet:   /* ... */    break;
    }
}
```

Such a mistake can easily occur when a new enumerator is added during maintenance.

Testing for an "impossible" enumerator value is best done separately.

9.4.2.1 Declarations in Cases

It is possible, and common, to declare variables within the block of a switch-statement. However, it is not possible to bypass an initialization. For example:

```
void f(int i)
{
    switch (i) {
    case 0:
        int x;          // uninitialized
        int y = 3;      // error: declaration can be bypassed (explicitly initialized)
        string s;       // error: declaration can be bypassed (implicitly initialized)
    case 1:
        ++x;            // error: use of uninitialized object
        ++y;
        s = "nasty!";
    }
}
```

Here, if i==1, the thread of execution would bypass the initializations of y and s, so f() will not compile. Unfortunately, because an int needn't be initialized, the declaration of x is not an error. However, its use is an error: we read an uninitialized variable. Unfortunately, compilers often give just a warning for the use of an uninitialized variable and cannot reliably catch all such misuses. As usual, avoid uninitialized variables (§6.3.5.1).

If we need a variable within a switch-statement, we can limit its scope by enclosing its declaration and its use in a block. For an example, see prim() in §10.2.1.

9.4.3 Declarations in Conditions

To avoid accidental misuse of a variable, it is usually a good idea to introduce the variable into the smallest scope possible. In particular, it is usually best to delay the definition of a local variable until one can give it an initial value. That way, one cannot get into trouble by using the variable before its initial value is assigned.

One of the most elegant applications of these two principles is to declare a variable in a condition. Consider:

```
if (double d = prim(true)) {
    left /= d;
    break;
}
```

Here, d is declared and initialized and the value of d after initialization is tested as the value of the condition. The scope of d extends from its point of declaration to the end of the statement that the condition controls. For example, had there been an else-branch to the if-statement, d would be in scope on both branches.

The obvious and traditional alternative is to declare **d** before the condition. However, this opens the scope (literally) for the use of **d** before its initialization or after its intended useful life:

```
double d;
// ...
d2 = d;    // oops!
// ...
if (d = prim(true)) {
        left /= d;
        break;
}
// ...
d = 2.0;   // two unrelated uses of d
```

In addition to the logical benefits of declaring variables in conditions, doing so also yields the most compact source code.

A declaration in a condition must declare and initialize a single variable or **const**.

9.5 Iteration Statements

A loop can be expressed as a **for-**, **while-**, or **do**-statement:

while (*condition*) *statement*
do *statement* **while** (*expression*) ;
for (*for-init-statement condition*$_{opt}$; *expression*$_{opt}$) *statement*
for (*for-declaration* : *expression*) *statement*

A *for-init-statement* must be either a declaration or an *expression-statement*. Note that both end with a semicolon.

The statement of a **for**-statement (called the *controlled statement* or the *loop body*) is executed repeatedly until the condition becomes **false** or the programmer breaks out of the loop some other way (such as a **break**, a **return**, a **throw**, or a **goto**).

More complicated loops can be expressed as an algorithm plus a lambda expression (§11.4.2).

9.5.1 Range-**for** Statements

The simplest loop is a range-**for**-statement; it simply gives the programmer access to each element of a range. For example:

```
int sum(vector<int>& v)
{
    int s = 0;
    for (int x : v)
        s+=x;
    return s;
}
```

The **for (int x : v)** can be read as "for each element **x** in the range **v**" or just "for each **x** in **v**." The elements of **v** are visited in order from the first to the last.

The scope of the variable naming the element (here, **x**) is the **for**-statement.

The expression after the colon must denote a sequence (a range); that is, it must yield a value for which we can call **v.begin()** and **v.end()** or **begin(v)** and **end(v)** to obtain an iterators (§4.5):

[1]   the compiler first looks for members **begin** and **end** and tries to use those. If a **begin** or an **end** is found that cannot be used as a range (e.g., because a member **begin** is a variable rather than a function), the range-**for** is an error.

[2]   Otherwise, the compiler looks for a **begin/end** member pair in the enclosing scope. If none is found or if what is found cannot be used (e.g., because the **begin** did not take an argument of the sequence's type), the range-**for** is an error.

The compiler uses **v** and **v+N** as **begin(v)** and **end(v)** for a built-in array **T v[N]**. The **<iterator>** header provides **begin(c)** and **end(c)** for built-in arrays and for all standard-library containers. For sequences of our own design, we can define **begin()** and **end()** in the same way as it is done for standard-library containers (§4.4.5).

The controlled variable, **x** in the example, that refers to the current element is equivalent to **∗p** when using an equivalent **for**-statement:

```
int sum2(vector<int>& v)
{
     int s = 0;
     for (auto p = begin(v); p!=end(v); ++p)
          s+=*p;
     return s;
}
```

If you need to modify an element in a range-**for** loop, the element variable should be a reference. For example, we can increment each element of a **vector** like this:

```
void incr(vector<int>& v)
{
     for (int& x : v)
          ++x;
}
```

References are also appropriate for elements that might be large, so that copying them to the element value could be costly. For example:

```
template<class T> T accum(vector<T>& v)
{
     T sum = 0;
     for (const T& x : v)
          sum += x;
     return sum;
}
```

Note that a range-**for** loop is a deliberately simple construct. For example, using it you can't touch two elements at the same time and can't effectively traverse two ranges simultaneously. For that we need a general **for**-statement.

9.5.2 for Statements

There is also a more general **for**-statement allowing greater control of the iteration. The loop variable, the termination condition, and the expression that updates the loop variable are explicitly presented "up front" on a single line. For example:

```
void f(int v[], int max)
{
    for (int i = 0; i!=max; ++i)
        v[i] = i*i;
}
```

This is equivalent to

```
void f(int v[], int max)
{
    int i = 0;         // introduce loop variable
    while (i!=max) {        // test termination condition
        v[i] = i*i;  // execute the loop body
        ++i;         // increment loop variable
    }
}
```

A variable can be declared in the initializer part of a **for**-statement. If that initializer is a declaration, the variable (or variables) it introduced is in scope until the end of the **for**-statement.

It is not always obvious what is the right type to use for a controlled variable in a *for* loop, so **auto** often comes in handy:

```
for (auto p = begin(c); c!=end(c); ++p) {
    // ... use iterator p for elements in container c ...
}
```

If the final value of an index needs to be known after exit from a **for**-loop, the index variable must be declared outside the **for**-loop (e.g., see §9.6).

If no initialization is needed, the initializing statement can be empty.

If the expression that is supposed to increment the loop variable is omitted, we must update some form of loop variable elsewhere, typically in the body of the loop. If the loop isn't of the simple "introduce a loop variable, test the condition, update the loop variable" variety, it is often better expressed as a **while**-statement. However, consider this elegant variant:

```
for (string s; cin>>s;)
    v.push_back(s);
```

Here, the reading and testing for termination and combined in **cin>>s**, so we don't need an explicit loop variable. On the other hand, the use of **for**, rather than **while**, allows us to limit the scope of the "current element," **s**, to the loop itself (the **for**-statement).

A **for**-statement is also useful for expressing a loop without an explicit termination condition:

```
for (;;) {   // "forever"
    // ...
}
```

However, many consider this idiom obscure and prefer to use:

```
while(true) {    // "forever"
    // ...
}
```

9.5.3 while Statements

A while-statement executes its controlled statement until its condition becomes **false**. For example:

```
template<class Iter, class Value>
Iter find(Iter first, Iter last, Value val)
{
    while (first!=last && *first!=val)
        ++first;
    return first;
}
```

I tend to prefer while-statements over for-statements when there isn't an obvious loop variable or where the update of a loop variable naturally comes in the middle of the loop body.

A for-statement (§9.5.2) is easily rewritten into an equivalent while-statement and vice versa.

9.5.4 do Statements

A do-statement is similar to a while-statement except that the condition comes after the body. For example:

```
void print_backwards(char a[], int i)        // i must be positive
{
    cout << '{';
    do {
        cout << a[--i];
    } while (i);
    cout << '}';
}
```

This might be called like this: **print_backwards(s,strlen(s));** but it is all too easy to make a horrible mistake. For example, what if **s** was the empty string?

In my experience, the do-statement is a source of errors and confusion. The reason is that its body is always executed once before the condition is evaluated. However, for the body to work correctly, something very much like the condition must hold even the first time through. More often than I would have guessed, I have found that condition not to hold as expected either when the program was first written and tested or later after the code preceding it has been modified. I also prefer the condition "up front where I can see it." Consequently, I recommend avoiding do-statements.

9.5.5 Loop Exit

If the *condition* of an iteration statement (a for-, while-, or do-statement) is omitted, the loop will not terminate unless the user explicitly exits it by a **break**, **return** (§12.1.4), **goto** (§9.6), **throw** (§13.5), or some less obvious way such as a call of **exit()** (§15.4.3). A **break** "breaks out of" the nearest enclosing *switch-statement* (§9.4.2) or *iteration-statement*. For example:

```
void f(vector<string>& v, string terminator)
{
    char c;
    string s;
    while (cin>>c) {
        // ...
        if (c == '\n') break;
        // ...
    }
}
```

We use a **break** when we need to leave the loop body "in the middle." Unless it warps the logic of a loop (e.g., requires the introduction of an extra varible), it is usually better to have the complete exit condition as the condition of a **while**-statement or a **for**-statement.

Sometimes, we don't want to exit the loop completely, we just want to get to the end of the loop body. A **continue** skips the rest of the body of an *iteration-statement*. For example:

```
void find_prime(vector<string>& v)
{
    for (int i = 0; i!=v.size(); ++i) {
        if (!prime(v[i]) continue;
        return v[i];
    }
}
```

After a **continue**, the increment part of the loop (if any) is executed, followed by the loop condition (if any). So **find_prime()** could equivalently have been written as:

```
void find_prime(vector<string>& v)
{
    for (int i = 0; i!=v.size(); ++i) {
        if (!prime(v[i]) {
            return v[i];
        }
    }
}
```

9.6 goto Statements

C++ possesses the infamous **goto**:

> **goto** *identifier* ;
> *identifier* : *statement*

The **goto** has few uses in general high-level programming, but it can be very useful when C++ code is generated by a program rather than written directly by a person; for example, **goto**s can be used in a parser generated from a grammar by a parser generator.

The scope of a label is the function it is in (§6.3.4). This implies that you can use **goto** to jump both into and out of blocks. The only restriction is that you cannot jump past an initializer or into an exception handler (§13.5).

One of the few sensible uses of **goto** in ordinary code is to break out from a nested loop or **switch**-statement (a **break** breaks out of only the innermost enclosing loop or **switch**-statement). For example:

```
void do_something(int i, int j)
    // do something to a two-dimensional matrix called mn
{
    for (i = 0; i!=n; ++i)
        for (j = 0; j!=m; ++j)
            if (nm[i][j] == a)
                goto found;
    // not found
    // ...
found:
    // nm[i][j] == a
}
```

Note that this **goto** just jumps forward to exit its loop. It does not introduce a new loop or enter a new scope. That makes it the least troublesome and least confusing use of a **goto**.

9.7 Comments and Indentation

Judicious use of comments and consistent use of indentation can make the task of reading and understanding a program much more pleasant. Several different consistent styles of indentation are in use. I see no fundamental reason to prefer one over another (although, like most programmers, I have my preferences, and this book reflects them). The same applies to styles of comments.

Comments can be misused in ways that seriously affect the readability of a program. The compiler does not understand the contents of a comment, so it has no way of ensuring that a comment

- is meaningful,
- describes the program, and
- is up to date.

Most programs contain comments that are incomprehensible, ambiguous, and just plain wrong. Bad comments can be worse than no comments.

If something can be stated *in the language itself*, it should be, and not just mentioned in a comment. This remark is aimed at comments such as these:

```
// variable "v" must be initialized

// variable "v" must be used only by function "f()"

// call function "init()" before calling any other function in this file

// call function "cleanup()" at the end of your program
```

```
// don't use function "weird()"
```

```
// function "f(int ...)" takes two or three arguments
```

Such comments can typically be rendered unnecessary by proper use of C++.

Once something has been stated clearly in the language, it should not be mentioned a second time in a comment. For example:

```
a = b+c;  // a becomes b+c
count++;  // increment the counter
```

Such comments are worse than simply redundant. They increase the amount of text the reader has to look at, they often obscure the structure of the program, and they may be wrong. Note, however, that such comments are used extensively for teaching purposes in programming language textbooks such as this. This is one of the many ways a program in a textbook differs from a real program.

A good comment states what a piece of code is supposed to do (the intent of the code), whereas the code (only) states what it does (in terms of how it does it). Preferably, a comment is expressed at a suitably high level of abstraction so that it is easy for a human to understand without delving into minute details.

My preference is for:

- A comment for each source file stating what the declarations in it have in common, references to manuals, the name of the programmer, general hints for maintenance, etc.
- A comment for each class, template, and namespace
- A comment for each nontrivial function stating its purpose, the algorithm used (unless it is obvious), and maybe something about the assumptions it makes about its environment
- A comment for each global and namespace variable and constant
- A few comments where the code is nonobvious and/or nonportable
- Very little else

For example:

```
//   tbl.c: Implementation of the symbol table.
```

```
/*
   Gaussian elimination with partial pivoting.
   See Ralston: "A first course ..." pg 411.
*/
```

```
//   scan(p,n,c) requires that p points to an array of at least n elements
```

```
// sort(p,q) sorts the elements of the sequence [p:q] using < for comparison.
```

```
// Revised to handle invalid dates. Bjarne Stroustrup, Feb 29 2013
```

A well-chosen and well-written set of comments is an essential part of a good program. Writing good comments can be as difficult as writing the program itself. It is an art well worth cultivating.

Note that /* */ style comments do not nest. For example:

```
/*
    remove expensive check
    if (check(p,q)) error("bad p q") /* should never happen */
*/
```

This nesting should give an error for an unmatched final */.

9.8 Advice

[1]   Don't declare a variable until you have a value to initialize it with; §9.3, §9.4.3, §9.5.2.
[2]   Prefer a **switch**-statement to an **if**-statement when there is a choice; §9.4.2.
[3]   Prefer a range-**for**-statement to a **for**-statement when there is a choice; §9.5.1.
[4]   Prefer a **for**-statement to a **while**-statement when there is an obvious loop variable; §9.5.2.
[5]   Prefer a **while**-statement to a **for**-statement when there is no obvious loop variable; §9.5.3.
[6]   Avoid **do**-statements; §9.5.
[7]   Avoid **goto**; §9.6.
[8]   Keep comments crisp; §9.7.
[9]   Don't say in comments what can be clearly stated in code; §9.7.
[10] State intent in comments; §9.7.
[11] Maintain a consistent indentation style; §9.7.

10

Expressions

Programming is like sex:
It may give some concrete results,
but that is not why we do it.
– apologies to Richard Feynman

10.1 Introduction

This chapter discusses expressions in some detail. In C++, an assignment is an expression, a function call is an expression, the construction of an object is an expression, and so are many other operations that go beyond conventional arithmetic expression evaluation. To give an impression of how expressions are used and to show them in context, I first present a small complete program, a simple "desk calculator." Next, the complete set of operators is listed and their meaning for built-in types is briefly outlined. The operators that require more extensive explanation are discussed in Chapter 11.

10.2 A Desk Calculator

Consider a simple desk calculator program that provides the four standard arithmetic operations as infix operators on floating-point numbers. The user can also define variables. For example, given the input

```
r = 2.5
area = pi * r * r
```

(**pi** is predefined) the calculator program will write

```
2.5
19.635
```

where **2.5** is the result of the first line of input and **19.635** is the result of the second.

The calculator consists of four main parts: a parser, an input function, a symbol table, and a driver. Actually, it is a miniature compiler in which the parser does the syntactic analysis, the input function handles input and lexical analysis, the symbol table holds permanent information, and the driver handles initialization, output, and errors. We could add many features to this calculator to make it more useful, but the code is long enough as it is, and most features would just add code without providing additional insight into the use of C++.

10.2.1 The Parser

Here is a grammar for the language accepted by the calculator:

```
program:
        end                    // end is end-of-input
        expr_list end

expr_list:
        expression print       // print is newline or semicolon
        expression print expr_list

expression:
        expression + term
        expression – term
        term

term:
        term / primary
        term * primary
        primary

primary:
        number                 // number is a floating-point literal
        name                   // name is an identifier
        name = expression
        – primary
        ( expression )
```

In other words, a program is a sequence of expressions separated by semicolons. The basic units of an expression are numbers, names, and the operators *, /, +, – (both unary and binary), and = (assignment). Names need not be declared before use.

I use a style of syntax analysis called *recursive descent*; it is a popular and straightforward top-down technique. In a language such as C++, in which function calls are relatively cheap, it is also efficient. For each production in the grammar, there is a function that calls other functions. Terminal symbols (for example, **end**, **number**, **+**, and **–**) are recognized by a lexical analyzer and nonterminal symbols are recognized by the syntax analyzer functions, **expr()**, **term()**, and **prim()**. As soon as both operands of a (sub)expression are known, the expression is evaluated; in a real compiler, code could be generated at this point.

For input, the parser uses a **Token_stream** that encapsulates the reading of characters and their composition into **Token**s. That is, a **Token_stream** "tokenizes": it turns streams of characters, such as **123.45**, into **Token**s. A **Token** is a {kind-of-token,value} pair, such as {**number,123.45**}, where the **123.45** has been turned into a floating point value. The main parts of the parser need only to know the name of the **Token_stream**, **ts**, and how to get **Token**s from it. To read the next **Token**, it calls **ts.get()**. To get the most recently read **Token** (the "current token"), it calls **ts.current()**. In addition to providing tokenizing, the **Token_stream** hides the actual source of the characters. We'll see that they can come directly from a user typing to **cin**, from a program command line, or from any other input stream (§10.2.7).

The definition of **Token** looks like this:

```
enum class Kind : char {
    name, number, end,
    plus='+', minus='-', mul='*', div='/', print=';', assign='=', lp='(', rp=')'
};

struct Token {
    Kind kind;
    string string_value;
    double number_value;
};
```

Representing each token by the integer value of its character is convenient and efficient and can be a help to people using debuggers. This works as long as no character used as input has a value used as an enumerator – and no current character set I know of has a printing character with a single-digit integer value.

The interface to **Token_stream** looks like this:

```
class Token_stream {
public:
    Token get();            // read and return next token
    const Token& current(); // most recently read token
    // ...
};
```

The implementation is presented in §10.2.2.

Each parser function takes a **bool** (§6.2.2) argument, called **get**, indicating whether the function needs to call **Token_stream::get()** to get the next token. Each parser function evaluates "its" expression and returns the value. The function **expr()** handles addition and subtraction. It consists of a single loop that looks for terms to add or subtract:

```
double expr(bool get)         // add and subtract
{
    double left = term(get);

    for (;;) {                         // "forever"
        switch (ts.current().kind) {
        case Kind::plus:
            left += term(true);
            break;
        case Kind::minus:
            left -= term(true);
            break;
        default:
            return left;
        }
    }
}
```

This function really does not do much itself. In a manner typical of higher-level functions in a large program, it calls other functions to do the work.

The **switch**-statement (§2.2.4, §9.4.2) tests the value of its condition, which is supplied in parentheses after the **switch** keyword, against a set of constants. The **break**-statements are used to exit the **switch**-statement. If the value tested does not match any **case** label, the **default** is chosen. The programmer need not provide a **default**.

Note that an expression such as **2–3+4** is evaluated as **(2–3)+4**, as specified in the grammar.

The curious notation **for(;;)** is a way to specify an infinite loop; you could pronounce it "forever" (§9.5); **while(true)** is an alternative. The **switch**-statement is executed repeatedly until something different from + and – is found, and then the **return**-statement in the default case is executed.

The operators **+=** and **–=** are used to handle the addition and subtraction; **left=left+term(true)** and **left=left–term(true)** could have been used without changing the meaning of the program. However, **left+=term(true)** and **left–=term(true)** are not only shorter but also express the intended operation directly. Each assignment operator is a separate lexical token, so **a + = 1;** is a syntax error because of the space between the + and the =.

C++ provides assignment operators for the binary operators:

$$+ \quad - \quad * \quad / \quad \% \quad \& \quad | \quad \char`^ \quad << \quad >>$$

so that the following assignment operators are possible:

$$= \quad += \quad -= \quad *= \quad /= \quad \%= \quad \&= \quad |= \quad \char`^= \quad <<= \quad >>=$$

The **%** is the modulo, or remainder, operator; **&**, **|**, and **^** are the bitwise logical operators and, or, and exclusive or; **<<** and **>>** are the left shift and right shift operators; §10.3 summarizes the operators and their meanings. For a binary operator **@** applied to operands of built-in types, an expression **x@=y** means **x=x@y**, except that **x** is evaluated once only.

The function **term()** handles multiplication and division in the same way **expr()** handles addition and subtraction:

```cpp
double term(bool get)          // multiply and divide
{
    double left = prim(get);

    for (;;) {
        switch (ts.current().kind) {
        case Kind::mul:
            left *= prim(true);
            break;
        case Kind::div:
            if (auto d = prim(true)) {
                left /= d;
                break;
            }
            return error("divide by 0");
        default:
            return left;
        }
    }
}
```

The result of dividing by zero is undefined and usually disastrous. We therefore test for **0** before dividing and call **error()** if we detect a zero divisor. The function **error()** is described in §10.2.4.

The variable **d** is introduced into the program exactly where it is needed and initialized immediately. The scope of a name introduced in a condition is the statement controlled by that condition, and the resulting value is the value of the condition (§9.4.3). Consequently, the division and assignment **left/=d** are done if and only if **d** is nonzero.

The function **prim()** handling a *primary* is much like **expr()** and **term()**, except that because we are getting lower in the call hierarchy a bit of real work is being done and no loop is necessary:

```cpp
double prim(bool get)          // handle primaries
{
    if (get) ts.get();  // read next token

    switch (ts.current().kind) {
    case Kind::number:         // floating-point constant
    {   double v = ts.current().number_value;
        ts.get();
        return v;
    }
    case Kind::name:
    {   double& v = table[ts.current().string_value];      // find the corresponding
        if (ts.get().kind == Kind::assign) v = expr(true); // '=' seen: assignment
        return v;
    }
```

```
        case Kind::minus:        // unary minus
            return -prim(true);
        case Kind::lp:
    {    auto e = expr(true);
            if (ts.current().kind != Kind::rp) return error("')' expected");
            ts.get();        // eat ')'
            return e;
    }
        default:
            return error("primary expected");
    }
}
```

When a **Token** that is a **number** (that is, an integer or floating-point literal) is seen, its value is placed in its **number_value**. Similarly, when a **Token** that is a **name** (however defined; see §10.2.2 and §10.2.3) is seen, its value is placed in its **string_value**.

Note that **prim()** always reads one more **Token** than it uses to analyze its primary expression. The reason is that it *must* do that in some cases (e.g., to see if a name is assigned to), so for consistency it must do it in all cases. In the cases where a parser function simply wants to move ahead to the next **Token**, it doesn't use the return value from **ts.get()**. That's fine because we can get the result from **ts.current()**. Had ignoring the return value of **get()** bothered me, I'd have either added a **read()** function that just updated **current()** without returning a value or explicitly "thrown away" the result: **void(ts.get())**.

Before doing anything to a name, the calculator must first look ahead to see if it is being assigned to or simply read. In both cases, the symbol table is consulted. The symbol table is a **map** (§4.4.3, §31.4.3):

```
    map<string,double> table;
```

That is, when **table** is indexed by a **string**, the resulting value is the **double** corresponding to the **string**. For example, if the user enters

```
    radius = 6378.388;
```

the calculator will reach **case Kind::name** and execute

```
    double& v = table["radius"];
    // ... expr() calculates the value to be assigned ...
    v = 6378.388;
```

The reference **v** is used to hold on to the **double** associated with **radius** while **expr()** calculates the value **6378.388** from the input characters.

Chapter 14 and Chapter 15 discuss how to organize a program as a set of modules. However, with one exception, the declarations for this calculator example can be ordered so that everything is declared exactly once and before it is used. The exception is **expr()**, which calls **term()**, which calls **prim()**, which in turn calls **expr()**. This loop of calls must be broken somehow. A declaration

```
    double expr(bool);
```

before the definition of **prim()** will do nicely.

10.2.2 Input

Reading input is often the messiest part of a program. To communicate with a person, the program must cope with that person's whims, conventions, and seemingly random errors. Trying to force the person to behave in a manner more suitable for the machine is often (rightly) considered offensive. The task of a low-level input routine is to read characters and compose higher-level tokens from them. These tokens are then the units of input for higher-level routines. Here, low-level input is done by **ts.get()**. Writing a low-level input routine need not be an everyday task. Many systems provide standard functions for this.

First we need to see the complete definition of **Token_stream**:

```
class Token_stream {
public:
    Token_stream(istream& s) : ip{&s}, owns{false} { }
    Token_stream(istream* p) : ip{p}, owns{true} { }

    ~Token_stream() { close(); }

    Token get();        // read and return next token
    Token& current();   // most recently read token

    void set_input(istream& s) { close(); ip = &s; owns=false; }
    void set_input(istream* p) { close(); ip = p; owns = true; }

private:
    void close() { if (owns) delete ip; }

    istream* ip;              // pointer to an input stream
    bool owns;                // does the Token_stream own the istream?
    Token ct {Kind::end} ;    // current token
};
```

We initialize a **Token_stream** with an input stream (§4.3.2, Chapter 38) from which it gets its characters. The **Token_stream** implements the convention that it owns (and eventually deletes; §3.2.1.2, §11.2) an **istream** passed as a pointer, but not an **istream** passed as a reference. This may be a bit elaborate for this simple program, but it is a useful and general technique for classes that hold a pointer to a resource requiring destruction.

A **Token_stream** holds three values: a pointer to its input stream (**ip**), a Boolean (**owns**), indicating ownership of the input stream, and the current token (**ct**).

I gave **ct** a default value because it seemed sloppy not to. People should not call **current()** before **get()**, but if they do, they get a well-defined **Token**. I chose **Kind::end** as the initial value for **ct** so that a program that misuses **current()** will not get a value that wasn't on the input stream.

I present **Token_stream::get()** in two stages. First, I provide a deceptively simple version that imposes a burden on the user. Next, I modify it into a slightly less elegant, but much easier to use, version. The idea for **get()** is to read a character, use that character to decide what kind of token needs to be composed, read more characters when needed, and then return a **Token** representing the characters read.

The initial statements read the first non-whitespace character from ∗**ip** (the stream pointed to by **ip**) into **ch** and check that the read operation succeeded:

```
Token Token_stream::get()
{
     char ch = 0;
     ∗ip>>ch;

     switch (ch) {
     case 0:
          return ct={Kind::end};    // assign and return
```

By default, operator >> skips whitespace (that is, spaces, tabs, newlines, etc.) and leaves the value of **ch** unchanged if the input operation failed. Consequently, **ch==0** indicates end-of-input.

Assignment is an operator, and the result of the assignment is the value of the variable assigned to. This allows me to assign the value **Kind::end** to **curr_tok** and return it in the same statement. Having a single statement rather than two is useful in maintenance. If the assignment and the **return** became separated in the code, a programmer might update the one and forget to update the other.

Note also how the {}-list notation (§3.2.1.3, §11.3) is used on the right-hand side of an assignment. That is, it is an expression. I could have written that **return**-statement as:

```
ct.kind = Kind::end; // assign
return ct;           // return
```

However, I think that assigning a complete object {Kind::end} is clearer than dealing with individual members of **ct**. The {Kind::end} is equivalent to {Kind::end,0,0}. That's good if we care about the last two members of the **Token** and not so good if we are worried about performance. Neither is the case here, but in general dealing with complete objects is clearer and less error-prone than manipulating data members individually. The cases below give examples of the other strategy.

Consider some of the cases separately before considering the complete function. The expression terminator, ';', the parentheses, and the operators are handled simply by returning their values:

```
     case ';':  // end of expression; print
     case '∗':
     case '/':
     case '+':
     case '−':
     case '(':
     case ')':
     case '=':
          return ct={static_cast<Kind>(ch)};
```

The **static_cast** (§11.5.2) is needed because there is no implicit conversion from **char** to **Kind** (§8.4.1); only some characters correspond to **Kind** values, so we have to "certify" that in this case **ch** does.

Numbers are handled like this:

```
     case '0': case '1': case '2': case '3': case '4': case '5': case '6': case '7': case '8': case '9':
     case '.':
```

```
        ip->putback(ch);           // put the first digit (or .) back into the input stream
        *ip >> ct.number_value;  // read the number into ct
        ct.kind=Kind::number;
        return ct;
```

Stacking **case** labels horizontally rather than vertically is generally not a good idea because this arrangement is harder to read. However, having one line for each digit is tedious. Because operator >> is already defined for reading floating-point values into a **double**, the code is trivial. First the initial character (a digit or a dot) is put back into **cin**. Then, the floating-point value can be read into **ct.number_value**.

If the token is not the end of input, an operator, a punctuation character, or a number, it must be a name. A name is handled similarly to a number:

```
    default:                  // name, name =, or error
        if (isalpha(ch)) {
            ip->putback(ch);             // put the first character back into the input stream
            *ip>>ct.string_value;        // read the string into ct
            ct.kind=Kind::name;
            return ct;
        }
```

Finally, we may simply have an error. The simple-minded, but reasonably effective way to deal with an error is the write call an **error()** function and then return a **print** token if **error()** returns:

```
    error("bad token");
    return ct={Kind::print};
```

The standard-library function **isalpha()** (§36.2.1) is used to avoid listing every character as a separate **case** label. Operator >> applied to a string (in this case, **string_value**) reads until it hits whitespace. Consequently, a user must terminate a name by a space before an operator using the name as an operand. This is less than ideal, so we will return to this problem in §10.2.3.

Here, finally, is the complete input function:

```
Token Token_stream::get()
{
    char ch = 0;
    *ip>>ch;

    switch (ch) {
    case 0:
        return ct={Kind::end};       // assign and return
    case ';':   // end of expression; print
    case '*':
    case '/':
    case '+':
    case '-':
    case '(':
    case ')':
    case '=':
        return ct=={static_cast<Kind>(ch)};
```

```
case '0': case '1': case '2': case '3': case '4': case '5': case '6': case '7': case '8': case '9':
case '.':
        ip->putback(ch);              // put the first digit (or .) back into the input stream
        *ip >> ct.number_value;       // read number into ct
        ct.kind=Kind::number;
        return ct;
default:                 // name, name =, or error
        if (isalpha(ch)) {
                ip->putback(ch);              // put the first character back into the input stream
                *ip>>ct.string_value;         // read string into ct
                ct.kind=Kind::name;
                return ct;
        }

        error("bad token");
        return ct={Kind::print};
}
}
```

The conversion of an operator to its **Token** value is trivial because the **kind** of an operator was defined as the integer value of the operator (§10.2.1).

10.2.3 Low-Level Input

Using the calculator as defined so far reveals a few inconveniences. It is tedious to remember to add a semicolon after an expression in order to get its value printed, and having a name terminated by whitespace only is a real nuisance. For example, **x=7** is an identifier – rather than the identifier **x** followed by the operator **=** and the number **7**. To get what we (usually) want, we would have to add whitespace after **x**: **x =7**. Both problems are solved by replacing the type-oriented default input operations in **get()** with code that reads individual characters.

First, we'll make a newline equivalent to the semicolon used to mark the end-of-expression:

```
Token Token_stream::get()
{
        char ch;

        do { // skip whitespace except '\n'
                if (!ip->get(ch)) return ct={Kind::end};
        } while (ch!='\n' && isspace(ch));

        switch (ch) {
        case ';':
        case '\n':
                return ct={Kind::print};
```

Here, I use a **do**-statement; it is equivalent to a **while**-statement except that the controlled statement is always executed at least once. The call **ip->get(ch)** reads a single character from the input stream *ip* into **ch**. By default, **get()** does not skip whitespace the way **>>** does. The test **if (!ip->get(ch))** succeeds if no character can be read from **cin**; in this case, **Kind::end** is returned to terminate the calculator session. The operator **!** (not) is used because **get()** returns **true** in case of success.

The standard-library function **isspace()** provides the standard test for whitespace (§36.2.1); **isspace(c)** returns a nonzero value if **c** is a whitespace character and zero otherwise. The test is implemented as a table lookup, so using **isspace()** is much faster than testing for the individual whitespace characters. Similar functions test if a character is a digit (**isdigit()**), a letter (**isalpha()**), or a digit or letter (**isalnum()**).

After whitespace has been skipped, the next character is used to determine what kind of lexical token is coming.

The problem caused by >> reading into a string until whitespace is encountered is solved by reading one character at a time until a character that is not a letter or a digit is found:

```
default:                // NAME, NAME=, or error
    if (isalpha(ch)) {
        string_value = ch;
        while (ip–>get(ch) && isalnum(ch))
            string_value += ch; // append ch to end of string_value
        ip–>putback(ch);
        return ct={Kind::name};
    }
```

Fortunately, these two improvements could both be implemented by modifying a single local section of code. Constructing programs so that improvements can be implemented through local modifications only is an important design aim.

You might worry that adding characters to the end of a **string** one by one would be inefficient. It would be for very long **strings**, but all modern **string** implementations provide the "small string optimization" (§19.3.3). That means that handling the kind of strings we are likely to use as names in a calculator (or even in a compiler) doesn't involve any inefficient operations. In particular, using a short **string** doesn't require any use of free store. The maximum number of characters for a short **string** is implementation-dependent, but 14 would be a good guess.

10.2.4 Error Handling

It is always important to detect and report errors. However, for this program, a simple error handling strategy suffices. The **error()** function simply counts the errors, writes out an error message, and returns:

```
int no_of_errors;

double error(const string& s)
{
    no_of_errors++;
    cerr << "error: " << s << '\n';
    return 1;
}
```

The stream **cerr** is an unbuffered output stream usually used to report errors (§38.1).

The reason for returning a value is that errors typically occur in the middle of the evaluation of an expression, so we should either abort that evaluation entirely or return a value that is unlikely to cause subsequent errors. The latter is adequate for this simple calculator. Had **Token_stream::get()**

kept track of the line numbers, **error()** could have informed the user approximately where the error occurred. This would be useful when the calculator is used noninteractively.

A more stylized and general error-handling strategy would separate error detection from error recovery. This can be implemented using exceptions (see §2.4.3.1, Chapter 13), but what we have here is quite suitable for a 180-line calculator.

10.2.5 The Driver

With all the pieces of the program in place, we need only a driver to start things. I decided on two functions: **main()** to do setup and error reporting and **calculate()** to handle the actual calculation:

```
Token_stream ts {cin};    // use input from cin

void calculate()
{
    for (;;) {
        ts.get();
        if (ts.current().kind == Kind::end) break;
        if (ts.current().kind == Kind::print) continue;
        cout << expr(false) << '\n';
    }
}

int main()
{
    table["pi"] = 3.1415926535897932385;    // insert predefined names
    table["e"] = 2.7182818284590452354;

    calculate();

    return no_of_errors;
}
```

Conventionally, **main()** returns zero if the program terminates normally and nonzero otherwise (§2.2.1). Returning the number of errors accomplishes this nicely. As it happens, the only initialization needed is to insert the predefined names into the symbol table.

The primary task of the main loop (in **calculate()**) is to read expressions and write out the answer. This is achieved by the line:

```
cout << expr(false) << '\n';
```

The argument **false** tells **expr()** that it does not need to call **ts.get()** to read a token on which to work.

Testing for **Kind::end** ensures that the loop is correctly exited when **ts.get()** encounters an input error or an end-of-file. A **break**-statement exits its nearest enclosing **switch**-statement or loop (§9.5). Testing for **Kind::print** (that is, for '\n' and ';') relieves **expr()** of the responsibility for handling empty expressions. A **continue**-statement is equivalent to going to the very end of a loop.

10.2.6 Headers

The calculator uses standard-library facilities. Therefore, appropriate headers must be **#included** to complete the program:

```
#include<iostream> // I/O
#include<string>   // strings
#include<map>      // map
#include<cctype>   // isalpha(), etc.
```

All of these headers provide facilities in the **std** namespace, so to use the names they provide we must either use explicit qualification with **std::** or bring the names into the global namespace by

using namespace std;

To avoid confusing the discussion of expressions with modularity issues, I did the latter. Chapter 14 and Chapter 15 discuss ways of organizing this calculator into modules using namespaces and how to organize it into source files.

10.2.7 Command-Line Arguments

After the program was written and tested, I found it a bother to first start the program, then type the expressions, and finally quit. My most common use was to evaluate a single expression. If that expression could be presented as a command-line argument, a few keystrokes could be avoided.

A program starts by calling **main()** (§2.2.1, §15.4). When this is done, **main()** is given two arguments specifying the number of arguments, conventionally called **argc**, and an array of arguments, conventionally called **argv**. The arguments are C-style character strings (§2.2.5, §7.3), so the type of **argv** is **char∗[argc+1]**. The name of the program (as it occurs on the command line) is passed as **argv[0]**, so **argc** is always at least **1**. The list of arguments is zero-terminated; that is, **argv[argc]==0**. For example, for the command

dc 150/1.1934

the arguments have these values:

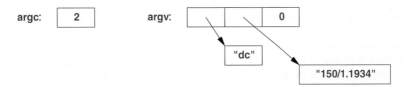

Because the conventions for calling **main()** are shared with C, C-style arrays and strings are used.

The idea is to read from the command string in the same way that we read from the input stream. A stream that reads from a string is unsurprisingly called an **istringstream** (§38.2.2). So to calculate expressions presented on the command line, we simply have to get our **Token_stream** to read from an appropriate **istringstream**:

```
Token_stream ts {cin};

int main(int argc, char* argv[])
{
    switch (argc) {
    case 1:                              // read from standard input
        break;
    case 2:                              // read from argument string
        ts.set_input(new istringstream{argv[1]});
        break;
    default:
        error("too many arguments");
        return 1;
    }

    table["pi"] = 3.1415926535897932385;    // insert predefined names
    table["e"] = 2.7182818284590452354;

    calculate();

    return no_of_errors;
}
```

To use an **istringstream**, include **<sstream>**.

It would be easy to modify **main()** to accept several command-line arguments, but this does not appear to be necessary, especially as several expressions can be passed as a single argument:

```
dc "rate=1.1934;150/rate;19.75/rate;217/rate"
```

I use quotes because ; is the command separator on my UNIX systems. Other systems have different conventions for supplying arguments to a program on startup.

Simple as they are, **argc** and **argv** are still a source of minor, yet annoying, bugs. To avoid those and especially to make it easier to pass around the program arguments, I tend to use a simple function to create a **vector<string>**:

```
vector<string> arguments(int argc, char* argv[])
{
    vector<string> res;
    for (int i = 0; i!=argc; ++i)
        res.push_back(argv[i]);
    return res;
}
```

More elaborate argument parsing functions are not uncommon.

10.2.8 A Note on Style

To programmers unacquainted with associative arrays, the use of the standard-library **map** as the symbol table seems almost like cheating. It is not. The standard library and other libraries are meant to be used. Often, a library has received more care in its design and implementation than a programmer could afford for a handcrafted piece of code to be used in just one program.

Looking at the code for the calculator, especially at the first version, we can see that there isn't much traditional C-style, low-level code presented. Many of the traditional tricky details have been replaced by uses of standard-library classes such as **ostream, string**, and **map** (§4.3.1, §4.2, §4.4.3, §31.4, Chapter 36, Chapter 38).

Note the relative scarcity of loops, arithmetic, and assignments. This is the way things ought to be in code that doesn't manipulate hardware directly or implement low-level abstractions.

10.3 Operator Summary

This section presents a summary of expressions and some examples. Each operator is followed by one or more names commonly used for it and an example of its use. In these tables:

- A *name* is an identifier (e.g., **sum** and **map**), an operator name (e.g., **operator int, operator+**, and **operator"" km**), or the name of a template specialization (e.g., **sort<Record>** and **array<int,10>**), possibly qualified using :: (e.g., **std::vector** and **vector<T>::operator[]**).
- A *class-name* is the name of a class (including **decltype(expr)** where **expr** denotes a class).
- A *member* is a member name (including the name of a destructor or a member template).
- An *object* is an expression yielding a class object.
- A *pointer* is an expression yielding a pointer (including **this** and an object of that type that supports the pointer operation).
- An *expr* is an expression, including a literal (e.g., **17**, **"mouse"**, and **true**)
- An *expr-list* is a (possibly empty) list of expressions.
- An *lvalue* is an expression denoting a modifiable object (§6.4.1).
- A *type* can be a fully general type name (with *, (), etc.) only when it appears in parentheses; elsewhere, there are restrictions (§iso.A).
- A *lambda-declarator* is a (possibly empty, comma-separated) list of parameters optionally followed by the **mutable** specifier, optionally followed by a **noexcept** specifier, optionally followed by a return type (§11.4).
- A *capture-list* is a (possibly empty) list specifying context dependencies (§11.4).
- A *stmt-list* is a (possibly empty) list of statements (§2.2.4, Chapter 9).

The syntax of expressions is independent of operand types. The meanings presented here apply when the operands are of built-in types (§6.2.1). In addition, you can define meanings for operators applied to operands of user-defined types (§2.3, Chapter 18).

A table can only approximate the rules of the grammar. For details, see §iso.5 and §iso.A.

Operator Summary (continues) (§iso.5.1)		
Parenthesized expression	(*expr*)	
Lambda	[*capture-list*] *lambda-declarator* { *stmt-List* }	§11.4
Scope resolution	*class-name* :: *member*	§16.2.3
Scope resolution	*namespace-name* :: *member*	§14.2.1
Global	:: *name*	§14.2.1

Each box holds operators with the same precedence. Operators in higher boxes have higher precedence. For example, **N::x.m** means **(N::m).m** rather than the illegal **N::(x.m)**.

Operator Summary (continued, continues)		
Member selection	*object . member*	§16.2.3
Member selection	*pointer –> member*	§16.2.3
Subscripting	*pointer* [*expr*]	§7.3
Function call	*expr* (*expr-list*)	§12.2
Value construction	*type* { *expr-list* }	§11.3.2
Function-style type conversion	*type* (*expr-list*)	§11.5.4
Post increment	*lvalue* **++**	§11.1.4
Post decrement	*lvalue* **––**	§11.1.4
Type identification	**typeid** (*type*)	§22.5
Run-time type identification	**typeid** (*expr*)	§22.5
Run-time checked conversion	**dynamic_cast** < *type* > (*expr*)	§22.2.1
Compile-time checked conversion	**static_cast** < *type* > (*expr*)	§11.5.2
Unchecked conversion	**reinterpret_cast** < *type* > (*expr*)	§11.5.2
const conversion	**const_cast** < *type* > (*expr*)	§11.5.2
Size of object	**sizeof** *expr*	§6.2.8
Size of type	**sizeof** (*type*)	§6.2.8
Size of parameter pack	**sizeof...** *name*	§28.6.2
Alignment of type	**alignof** (*type*)	§6.2.9
Pre increment	**++** *lvalue*	§11.1.4
Pre decrement	**––** *lvalue*	§11.1.4
Complement	**˜** *expr*	§11.1.2
Not	**!** *expr*	§11.1.1
Unary minus	**–** *expr*	§2.2.2
Unary plus	**+** *expr*	§2.2.2
Address of	**&** *lvalue*	§7.2
Dereference	**∗** *expr*	§7.2
Create (allocate)	**new** *type*	§11.2
Create (allocate and initialize)	**new** *type* (*expr-list*)	§11.2
Create (allocate and initialize)	**new** *type* { *expr-list* }	§11.2
Create (place)	**new** (*expr-list*) *type*	§11.2.4
Create (place and initialize)	**new** (*expr-list*) *type* (*expr-list*)	§11.2.4
Create (place and initialize)	**new** (*expr-list*) *type* { *expr-list* }	§11.2.4
Destroy (deallocate)	**delete** *pointer*	§11.2
Destroy array	**delete** [] *pointer*	§11.2.2
Can expression throw?	**noexcept** (*expr*)	§13.5.1.2
Cast (type conversion)	(*type*) *expr*	§11.5.3
Member selection	*object .∗ pointer-to-member*	§20.6
Member selection	*pointer –>∗ pointer-to-member*	§20.6

For example, postfix **++** has higher precedence than unary ∗, so ∗**p++** means ∗(**p++**), *not* (∗**p**)++.

Operator Summary (continued)		
Multiply	*expr * expr*	§10.2.1
Divide	*expr / expr*	§10.2.1
Modulo (remainder)	*expr % expr*	§10.2.1
Add (plus)	*expr + expr*	§10.2.1
Subtract (minus)	*expr – expr*	§10.2.1
Shift left	*expr << expr*	§11.1.2
Shift right	*expr >> expr*	§11.1.2
Less than	*expr < expr*	§2.2.2
Less than or equal	*expr <= expr*	§2.2.2
Greater than	*expr > expr*	§2.2.2
Greater than or equal	*expr >= expr*	§2.2.2
Equal	*expr == expr*	§2.2.2
Not equal	*expr != expr*	§2.2.2
Bitwise and	*expr & expr*	§11.1.2
Bitwise exclusive-or	*expr ˆ expr*	§11.1.2
Bitwise inclusive-or	*expr | expr*	§11.1.2
Logical and	*expr && expr*	§11.1.1
Logical inclusive or	*expr || expr*	§11.1.1
Conditional expression	*expr ? expr : expr*	§11.1.3
List	*{ expr-list }*	§11.3
Throw exception	**throw** *expr*	§13.5
Simple assignment	*lvalue = expr*	§10.2.1
Multiply and assign	*lvalue *= expr*	§10.2.1
Divide and assign	*lvalue /= expr*	§10.2.1
Modulo and assign	*lvalue %= expr*	§10.2.1
Add and assign	*lvalue += expr*	§10.2.1
Subtract and assign	*lvalue –= expr*	§10.2.1
Shift left and assign	*lvalue <<= expr*	§10.2.1
Shift right and assign	*lvalue >>= expr*	§10.2.1
Bitwise and and assign	*lvalue &= expr*	§10.2.1
Bitwise inclusive-or and assign	*lvalue |= expr*	§10.2.1
Bitwise exclusive-or and assign	*lvalue ˆ= expr*	§10.2.1
comma (sequencing)	*expr , expr*	§10.3.2

For example: a+b*c means a+(b*c) rather than (a+b)*c because * has higher precedence than +.

Unary operators and assignment operators are right-associative; all others are left-associative. For example, a=b=c means a=(b=c) whereas a+b+c means (a+b)+c.

A few grammar rules cannot be expressed in terms of precedence (also known as binding strength) and associativity. For example, a=b<c?d=e:f=g means a=((b<c)?(d=e):(f=g)), but you need to look at the grammar (§iso.A) to determine that.

Before applying the grammar rules, lexical tokens are composed from characters. The longest possible sequence of characters is chosen to make a token. For example, **&&** is a single operator, rather than two **&** operators, and **a+++1** means **(a ++) + 1**. This is sometimes called the *Max Munch rule*.

Token Summary (§iso.2.7)		
Token Class	Examples	Reference
Identifier	**vector, foo_bar, x3**	§6.3.3
Keyword	**int, for, virtual**	§6.3.3.1
Character literal	**'x', \n', 'U'\UFADEFADE'**	§6.2.3.2
Integer literal	**12, 012, 0x12**	§6.2.4.1
Floating-point literal	**1.2, 1.2e–3, 1.2L**	§6.2.5.1
String literal	**"Hello!", R"("World"!)"**	§7.3.2
Operator	**+=, %, <<**	§10.3
Punctuation	**;, „ {, }, (,)**	
Preprocessor notation	**#, ##**	§12.6

Whitespace characters (e.g., space, tab, and newline) can be token separators (e.g., **int count** is a keyword followed by an identifier, rather than **intcount**) but are otherwise ignored.

Some characters from the basic source character set (§6.1.2), such as |, are not convenient to type on some keywords. Also, some programmers find it odd to use of symbols, such as **&&** and ˜, for basic logical operations. Consequently, a set of alternative representation are provided as keywords:

Alternative Representation (§iso.2.12)										
and	and_eq	bitand	bitor	compl	not	not_eq	or	or_eq	xor	xor_eq
&	&=	&	|	˜	!	!=	|	|=	^	^=

For example

```
bool b =  not (x or y) and z;
int x4 = ˜ (x1 bitor x2) bitand x3;
```

is equivalent to

```
bool b = !(x || y) && z;
int x4 = ˜(x1 | x2) & x3;
```

Note that **and=** is not equivalent to **&=**; if you prefer keywords, you must write **and_eq**.

10.3.1 Results

The result types of arithmetic operators are determined by a set of rules known as "the usual arithmetic conversions" (§10.5.3). The overall aim is to produce a result of the "largest" operand type. For example, if a binary operator has a floating-point operand, the computation is done using floating-point arithmetic and the result is a floating-point value. Similarly, if it has a **long** operand, the computation is done using long integer arithmetic, and the result is a **long**. Operands that are smaller than an **int** (such as **bool** and **char**) are converted to **int** before the operator is applied.

The relational operators, ==, <=, etc., produce Boolean results. The meaning and result type of user-defined operators are determined by their declarations (§18.2).

Where logically feasible, the result of an operator that takes an lvalue operand is an lvalue denoting that lvalue operand. For example:

```cpp
void f(int x, int y)
{
    int j = x = y;          // the value of x=y is the value of x after the assignment
    int* p = &++x;          // p points to x
    int* q = &(x++);        // error: x++ is not an lvalue (it is not the value stored in x)
    int* p2 = &(x>y?x:y);   // address of the int with the larger value
    int& r = (x<y)?x:1;     // error: 1 is not an lvalue
}
```

If both the second and third operands of ?: are lvalues and have the same type, the result is of that type and is an lvalue. Preserving lvalues in this way allows greater flexibility in using operators. This is particularly useful when writing code that needs to work uniformly and efficiently with both built-in and user-defined types (e.g., when writing templates or programs that generate C++ code).

The result of **sizeof** is of an unsigned integral type called **size_t** defined in **<cstddef>**. The result of pointer subtraction is of a signed integral type called **ptrdiff_t** defined in **<cstddef>**.

Implementations do not have to check for arithmetic overflow and hardly any do. For example:

```cpp
void f()
{
    int i = 1;
    while (0 < i) ++i;
    cout << "i has become negative!" << i << '\n';
}
```

This will (eventually) try to increase i past the largest integer. What happens then is undefined, but typically the value "wraps around" to a negative number (on my machine **–2147483648**). Similarly, the effect of dividing by zero is undefined, but doing so usually causes abrupt termination of the program. In particular, underflow, overflow, and division by zero do not throw standard exceptions (§30.4.1.1).

10.3.2 Order of Evaluation

The order of evaluation of subexpressions within an expression is undefined. In particular, you cannot assume that the expression is evaluated left-to-right. For example:

```cpp
int x = f(2)+g(3);      // undefined whether f() or g() is called first
```

Better code can be generated in the absence of restrictions on expression evaluation order. However, the absence of restrictions on evaluation order can lead to undefined results. For example:

```cpp
int i = 1;
v[i] = i++; // undefined result
```

The assignment may be evaluated as either v[1]=1 or v[2]=1 or may cause some even stranger behavior. Compilers can warn about such ambiguities. Unfortunately, most do not, so be careful not to write an expression that reads or writes an object more than once, unless it does so using a single operator that makes it well defined, such as **++** and **+=**, or explicitly express sequencing using **,** (comma), **&&**, or **||**.

The operators **,** (comma), **&&** (logical and), and **||** (logical or) guarantee that their left-hand operand is evaluated before their right-hand operand. For example, **b=(a=2,a+1)** assigns **3** to **b**. Examples of the use of **||** and **&&** can be found in §10.3.3. For built-in types, the second operand of **&&** is evaluated only if its first operand is **true**, and the second operand of **||** is evaluated only if its first operand is **false**; this is sometimes called *short-circuit evaluation*. Note that the sequencing operator **,** (comma) is logically different from the comma used to separate arguments in a function call. For example:

```
f1(v[i],i++);        // two arguments
f2( (v[i],i++) );    // one argument
```

The call of **f1** has two arguments, **v[i]** and **i++**, and the order of evaluation of the argument expressions is undefined. So it should be avoided. Order dependence of argument expressions is very poor style and has undefined behavior. The call of **f2** has only one argument, the comma expression **(v[i],i++)**, which is equivalent to **i++**. That is confusing, so that too should be avoided.

Parentheses can be used to force grouping. For example, **a∗b/c** means **(a∗b)/c**, so parentheses must be used to get **a∗(b/c)**; **a∗(b/c)** may be evaluated as **(a∗b)/c** only if the user cannot tell the difference. In particular, for many floating-point computations **a∗(b/c)** and **(a∗b)/c** are significantly different, so a compiler will evaluate such expressions exactly as written.

10.3.3 Operator Precedence

Precedence levels and associativity rules reflect the most common usage. For example:

```
if (i<=0 || max<i) // ...
```

means "if **i** is less than or equal to **0** or if **max** is less than **i**." That is, it is equivalent to

```
if ( (i<=0) || (max<i) ) // ...
```

and not the legal but nonsensical

```
if (i <= (0||max) < i) // ...
```

However, parentheses should be used whenever a programmer is in doubt about those rules. Use of parentheses becomes more common as the subexpressions become more complicated, but complicated subexpressions are a source of errors. Therefore, if you start feeling the need for parentheses, you might consider breaking up the expression by using an extra variable.

There are cases when the operator precedence does not result in the "obvious" interpretation. For example:

```
if (i&mask == 0)     // oops! == expression as operand for &
```

This does not apply a mask to **i** and then test if the result is zero. Because **==** has higher precedence than **&**, the expression is interpreted as **i&(mask==0)**. Fortunately, it is easy enough for a compiler to warn about most such mistakes. In this case, parentheses are important:

```
if ((i&mask) == 0) // ...
```

It is worth noting that the following does not work the way a mathematician might expect:

```
if (0 <= x <= 99) // ...
```

This is legal, but it is interpreted as (0<=x)<=99, where the result of the first comparison is either **true** or **false**. This Boolean value is then implicitly converted to 1 or 0, which is then compared to 99, yielding **true**. To test whether x is in the range 0..99, we might use

```
if (0<=x && x<=99) // ...
```

A common mistake for novices is to use = (assignment) instead of == (equals) in a condition:

```
if (a = 7)   // oops! constant assignment in condition
```

This is natural because = means "equals" in many languages. Again, it is easy for a compiler to warn about most such mistakes – and many do. I do not recommend warping your style to compensate for compilers with weak warnings. In particular, I don't consider this style worthwhile:

```
if (7 == a) // try to protect against misuse of =; not recommended
```

10.3.4 Temporary Objects

Often, the compiler must introduce an object to hold an intermediate result of an expression. For example, for v=x+y*z the result of y*z has to be put somewhere before it is added to x. For built-in types, this is all handled so that a *temporary object* (often referred to as just a *temporary*) is invisible to the user. However, for a user-defined type that holds a resource knowing the lifetime of a temporary can be important. Unless bound to a reference or used to initialize a named object, a temporary object is destroyed at the end of the full expression in which it was created. A *full expression* is an expression that is not a subexpression of some other expression.

The standard-library **string** has a member **c_str()** (§36.3) that returns a C-style pointer to a zero-terminated array of characters (§2.2.5, §43.4). Also, the operator + is defined to mean string concatenation. These are useful facilities for **strings**. However, in combination they can cause obscure problems. For example:

```
void f(string& s1, string& s2, string& s3)
{
    const char* cs = (s1+s2).c_str();
    cout << cs;
    if (strlen(cs=(s2+s3).c_str())<8 && cs[0]=='a') {
        // cs used here
    }
}
```

Probably, your first reaction is "But don't do that!" and I agree. However, such code does get written, so it is worth knowing how it is interpreted.

A temporary **string** object is created to hold s1+s2. Next, a pointer to a C-style string is extracted from that object. Then – at the end of the expression – the temporary object is deleted. However, the C-style string returned by **c_str()** was allocated as part of the temporary object holding s1+s2, and that storage is not guaranteed to exist after that temporary is destroyed. Consequently, **cs** points to deallocated storage. The output operation **cout<<cs** might work as expected, but that would be sheer luck. A compiler can detect and warn against many variants of this problem.

The problem with the if-statement is a bit more subtle. The condition will work as expected because the full expression in which the temporary holding **s2+s3** is created is the condition itself. However, that temporary is destroyed before the controlled statement is entered, so any use of **cs** there is not guaranteed to work.

Please note that in this case, as in many others, the problems with temporaries arose from using a high-level data type in a low-level way. A cleaner programming style yields a more understandable program fragment and avoids the problems with temporaries completely. For example:

```
void f(string& s1, string& s2, string& s3)
{
    cout << s1+s2;
    string s = s2+s3;
    if (s.length()<8 && s[0]=='a') {
        // use s here
    }
}
```

A temporary can be used as an initializer for a **const** reference or a named object. For example:

```
void g(const string&, const string&);

void h(string& s1, string& s2)
{
    const string& s = s1+s2;
    string ss = s1+s2;

    g(s,ss);    // we can use s and ss here
}
```

This is fine. The temporary is destroyed when "its" reference or named object goes out of scope. Remember that returning a reference to a local variable is an error (§12.1.4) and that a temporary object cannot be bound to a non-**const** lvalue reference (§7.7).

A temporary object can also be created explicitly in an expression by invoking a constructor (§11.5.1). For example:

```
void f(Shape& s, int n, char ch)
{
    s.move(string{n,ch});    // construct a string with n copies of ch to pass to Shape::move()
    // ...
}
```

Such temporaries are destroyed in exactly the same way as the implicitly generated temporaries.

10.4 Constant Expressions

C++ offers two related meanings of "constant":

- **constexpr**: Evaluate at compile time (§2.2.3).
- **const**: Do not modify in this scope (§2.2.3, §7.5).

Basically, **constexpr**'s role is to enable and ensure compile-time evaluation, whereas **const**'s primary role is to specify immutability in interfaces. This section is primarily concerned with the first role: compile-time evaluation.

A *constant expression* is an expression that a compiler can evaluate. It cannot use values that are not known at compile time and it cannot have side effects. Ultimately, a constant expression must start out with an integral value (§6.2.1), a floating-point value (§6.2.5), or an enumerator (§8.4), and we can combine those using operators and constexpr functions that in turn produce values. In addition, some addresses can be used in some forms of constant expressions. For simplicity, I discuss those separately in §10.4.5.

There are a variety of reasons why someone might want a named constant rather than a literal or a value stored in a variable:

[1]   Named constants make the code easier to understand and maintain.

[2]   A variable might be changed (so we have to be more careful in our reasoning than for a constant).

[3]   The language requires constant expressions for array sizes, case labels, and template value arguments.

[4]   Embedded systems programmers like to put immutable data into read-only memory because read-only memory is cheaper than dynamic memory (in terms of cost and energy consumption), and often more plentiful. Also, data in read-only memory is immune to most system crashes.

[5]   If initialization is done at compile time, there can be no data races on that object in a multi-threaded system.

[6]   Sometimes, evaluating something once (at compile time) gives significantly better performance than doing so a million times at run time.

Note that reasons [1], [2], [5], and (partly) [4] are logical. We don't just use constant expressions because of an obsession with performance. Often, the reason is that a constant expression is a more direct representation of our system requirements.

As part of the definition of a data item (here, I deliberately avoid the word "variable"), constexpr expresses the need for compile-time evaluation. If the initializer for a constexpr can't be evaluated at compile time, the compiler will give an error. For example:

```
int x1 = 7;
constexpr int x2 = 7;

constexpr int x3 = x1;          // error: initializer is not a constant expression
constexpr int x4 = x2;          // OK

void f()
{
        constexpr int y3 = x1;      // error: initializer is not a constant expression
        constexpr int y4 = x2;      // OK
        // ...
}
```

A clever compiler could deduce that the value of x1 in the initializer for x3 was 7. However, we prefer not to rely on degrees of cleverness in compilers. In a large program, determining the values of variables at compile time is typically either very difficult or impossible.

The expressive power of constant expressions is great. We can use integer, floating-point, and enumeration values. We can use any operator that doesn't modify state (e.g., **+**, **?:**, and **[]**, but not **=** or **++**). We can use **constexpr** functions (§12.1.6) and literal types (§10.4.3) to provide a significant level of type safety and expressive power. It is almost unfair to compare this to what is commonly done with macros (§12.6).

The conditional-expression operator **?:** is the means of selection in a constant expression. For example, we can compute an integer square root at compile time:

```
constexpr int isqrt_helper(int sq, int d, int a)
{
      return sq <= a ? isqrt_helper(sq+d,d+2,a) : d;
}

constexpr int isqrt(int x)
{
      return isqrt_helper(1,3,x)/2 – 1;
}

constexpr int s1 = isqrt(9);        // s1 becomes 3
constexpr int s2 = isqrt(1234);
```

The condition of a **?:** is evaluated and then the selected alternative is evaluated. The alternative not selected is not evaluated and might even not be a constant expression. Similarly, operands of **&&** and **||** that are not evaluated need not be constant expressions. This feature is primarily useful in **constexpr** functions that are sometimes used as constant expressions and sometimes not.

10.4.1 Symbolic Constants

The most important single use of constants (**constexpr** or **const** values) is simply to provide symbolic names for values. Symbolic names should be used systematically to avoid "magic numbers" in code. Literal values scattered freely around in code is one of the nastiest maintenance hazards. If a numeric constant, such as an array bound, is repeated in code, it becomes hard to revise that code because every occurrence of that constant must be changed to update the code correctly. Using a symbolic name instead localizes information. Usually, a numeric constant represents an assumption about the program. For example, **4** may represent the number of bytes in an integer, **128** the number of characters needed to buffer input, and **6.24** the exchange factor between Danish kroner and U.S. dollars. Left as numeric constants in the code, these values are hard for a maintainer to spot and understand. Also, many such values need to change over time. Often, such numeric values go unnoticed and become errors when a program is ported or when some other change violates the assumptions they represent. Representing assumptions as well-commented named (symbolic) constants minimizes such maintenance problems.

10.4.2 consts in Constant Expressions

A **const** is primarily used to express interfaces (§7.5). However, **const** can also be used to express constant values. For example:

```
const int x = 7;
const string s = "asdf";
const int y = sqrt(x);
```

A **const** initialized with a constant expression can be used in a constant expression. A **const** differs from a **constexpr** in that it can be initialized by something that is not a constant expression; in that case, the **const** cannot be used as a constant expression. For example:

```
constexpr int xx = x;          // OK
constexpr string ss = s;       // error: s is not a constant expression
constexpr int yy = y;          // error: sqrt(x) is not a constant expression
```

The reasons for the errors are that **string** is not a literal type (§10.4.3) and **sqrt()** is not a **constexpr** function (§12.1.6).

Usually, **constexpr** is a better choice than **const** for defining simple constants, but **constexpr** is new in C++11, so older code tends to use **const**. In many cases, enumerators (§8.4) are another alternative to **const**s.

10.4.3 Literal Types

A sufficiently simple user-defined type can be used in a constant expression. For example:

```
struct Point {
    int x,y,z;
    constexpr Point up(int d) { return {x,y,z+d}; }
    constexpr Point move(int dx, int dy) { return {x+dx,y+dy}; }
    // ...
};
```

A class with a **constexpr** constructor is called a *literal type*. To be simple enough to be **constexpr**, a constructor must have an empty body and all members must be initialized by potentially constant expressions. For example:

```
constexpr Point origo {0,0};
constexpr int z = origo.x;

constexpr Point a[] = {
    origo, Point{1,1}, Point{2,2}, origo.move(3,3)
};
constexpr int x = a[1].x;         // x becomes 1

constexpr Point xy{0,sqrt(2)};    // error: sqrt(2) is not a constant expression
```

Note that we can have **constexpr** arrays and also access array elements and object members.

Naturally, we can define **constexpr** functions to take arguments of literal types. For example:

```
constexpr int square(int x)
{
    return x*x;
}
```

```
constexpr int radial_distance(Point p)
{
    return isqrt(square(p.x)+square(p.y)+square(p.z));
}


constexpr Point p1 {10,20,30};         // the default constructor is constexpr
constexpr p2 {p1.up(20)};              // Point::up() is constexpr
constexpr int dist = radial_distance(p2);
```

I used int rather than double just because I didn't have a **constexpr** floating-point square root function handy.

For a member function **constexpr** implies **const**, so I did not have to write:

```
constexpr Point move(int dx, int dy) const { return {x+dx,y+dy}; }
```

10.4.4 Reference Arguments

When working with **constexpr**, the key thing to remember is that **constexpr** is all about values. There are no objects that can change values or side effects here: **constexpr** provides a miniature compile-time functional programming language. That said, you might guess that **constexpr** cannot deal with references, but that's only partially true because **const** references refer to values and can therefore be used. Consider the specialization of the general **complex<T>** to a **complex<double>** from the standard library:

```
template<> class complex<double> {
public:
    constexpr complex(double re = 0.0, double im = 0.0);
    constexpr complex(const complex<float>&);
    explicit constexpr complex(const complex<long double>&);

    constexpr double real();       // read the real part
    void real(double);             // set the real part
    constexpr double imag();       // read the imaginary part
    void imag(double);             // set the imaginary part

    complex<double>& operator= (double);
    complex<double>& operator+=(double);
    // ...
};
```

Obviously, operations, such as = and +=, that modify an object cannot be **constexpr**. Conversely, operations that simply read an object, such as **real()** and **imag()**, can be **constexpr** and be evaluated at compile time given a constant expression. The interesting member is the template constructor from another **complex** type. Consider:

```
constexpr complex<float> z1 {1,2};      // note: <float> not <double>
constexpr double re = z1.real();
constexpr double im = z1.imag();
constexpr complex<double> z2 {re,im};   // z2 becomes a copy of z1
constexpr complex<double> z3 {z1};      // z3 becomes a copy of z1
```

The copy constructor works because the compiler recognizes that the reference (the **const com-plex<float>&**) refers to a constant value and we just use that value (rather than trying anything advanced or silly with references or pointers).

Literal types allow for type-rich compile-time programming. Traditionally, C++ compile-time evaluation has been restricted to using integer values (and without functions). This has resulted in code that was unnecessarily complicated and error-prone, as people encoded every kind of information as integers. Some uses of template metaprogramming (Chapter 28) are examples of that. Other programmers have simply preferred run-time evaluation to avoid the difficulties of writing in an impoverished language.

10.4.5 Address Constant Expressions

The address of a statically allocated object (§6.4.2), such as a global variable, is a constant. However, its value is assigned by the linker, rather than the compiler, so the compiler cannot know the value of such an address constant. That limits the range of constant expressions of pointer and reference type. For example:

```
constexpr const char* p1 = "asdf";
constexpr const char* p2 = p1;          // OK
constexpr const char* p2 = p1+2;        // error: the compiler does not know the value of p1
constexpr char c = p1[2];               // OK, c=='d'; the compiler knows the value pointed to by p1
```

10.5 Implicit Type Conversion

Integral and floating-point types (§6.2.1) can be mixed freely in assignments and expressions. Wherever possible, values are converted so as not to lose information. Unfortunately, some value-destroying ("narrowing") conversions are also performed implicitly. A conversion is value-preserving if you can convert a value and then convert the result back to its original type and get the original value. If a conversion cannot do that, it is a *narrowing conversion* (§10.5.2.6). This section provides a description of conversion rules, conversion problems, and their resolution.

10.5.1 Promotions

The implicit conversions that preserve values are commonly referred to as *promotions*. Before an arithmetic operation is performed, *integral promotion* is used to create ints out of shorter integer types. Similarly, *floating-point promotion* is used to create doubles out of floats. Note that these promotions will *not* promote to long (unless the operand is a char16_t, char32_t, wchar_t, or a plain enumeration that is already larger than an int) or long double. This reflects the original purpose of these promotions in C: to bring operands to the "natural" size for arithmetic operations.

The integral promotions are:

- A char, signed char, unsigned char, short int, or unsigned short int is converted to an int if int can represent all the values of the source type; otherwise, it is converted to an unsigned int.
- A char16_t, char32_t, wchar_t (§6.2.3), or a plain enumeration type (§8.4.2) is converted to the first of the following types that can represent all the values of its underlying type: int, unsigned int, long, unsigned long, or unsigned long long.

- A bit-field (§8.2.7) is converted to an int if int can represent all the values of the bit-field; otherwise, it is converted to unsigned int if unsigned int can represent all the values of the bit-field. Otherwise, no integral promotion applies to it.
- A bool is converted to an int; false becomes 0 and true becomes 1.

Promotions are used as part of the usual arithmetic conversions (§10.5.3).

10.5.2 Conversions

The fundamental types can be implicitly converted into each other in a bewildering number of ways (§iso.4). In my opinion, too many conversions are allowed. For example:

```
void f(double d)
{
    char c = d;          // beware: double-precision floating-point to char conversion
}
```

When writing code, you should always aim to avoid undefined behavior and conversions that quietly throw away information ("narrowing conversions").

A compiler can warn about many questionable conversions. Fortunately, many compilers do.

The {}-initializer syntax prevents narrowing (§6.3.5). For example:

```
void f(double d)
{
    char c {d};          // error: double-precision floating-point to char conversion
}
```

If potentially narrowing conversions are unavoidable, consider using some form of run-time checked conversion function, such as narrow_cast<>() (§11.5).

10.5.2.1 Integral Conversions

An integer can be converted to another integer type. A plain enumeration value can be converted to an integer type (§8.4.2) .

If the destination type is unsigned, the resulting value is simply as many bits from the source as will fit in the destination (high-order bits are thrown away if necessary). More precisely, the result is the least unsigned integer congruent to the source integer modulo 2 to the nth, where n is the number of bits used to represent the unsigned type. For example:

```
unsigned char uc = 1023;// binary 1111111111: uc becomes binary 11111111, that is, 255
```

If the destination type is signed, the value is unchanged if it can be represented in the destination type; otherwise, the value is implementation-defined:

```
signed char sc = 1023;   // implementation-defined
```

Plausible results are 127 and –1 (§6.2.3).

A Boolean or plain enumeration value can be implicitly converted to its integer equivalent (§6.2.2, §8.4).

10.5.2.2 Floating-Point Conversions

A floating-point value can be converted to another floating-point type. If the source value can be exactly represented in the destination type, the result is the original numeric value. If the source value is between two adjacent destination values, the result is one of those values. Otherwise, the behavior is undefined. For example:

```
float f = FLT_MAX;        // largest float value
double d = f;             // OK: d == f

double d2 = DBL_MAX;   // largest double value
float f2 = d2;            // undefined if FLT_MAX<DBL_MAX

long double ld = d2;     // OK: ld = d3
long double ld2 = numeric_limits<long double>::max();
double d3 = ld2;          // undefined if sizeof(long double)>sizeof(double)
```

DBL_MAX and **FLT_MAX** are defined in **<climits>**; **numeric_limits** is defined in **<limits>** (§40.2).

10.5.2.3 Pointer and Reference Conversions

Any pointer to an object type can be implicitly converted to a **void**∗ (§7.2.1). A pointer (reference) to a derived class can be implicitly converted to a pointer (reference) to an accessible and unambiguous base (§20.2). Note that a pointer to function or a pointer to member cannot be implicitly converted to a **void**∗.

A constant expression (§10.4) that evaluates to **0** can be implicitly converted to a null pointer of any pointer type. Similarly, a constant expression that evaluates to **0** can be implicitly converted to a pointer-to-member type (§20.6). For example:

```
int∗ p = (1+2)∗(2∗(1−1));   // OK, but weird
```

Prefer **nullptr** (§7.2.2).

A **T**∗ can be implicitly converted to a **const T**∗ (§7.5). Similarly, a **T&** can be implicitly converted to a **const T&**.

10.5.2.4 Pointer-to-Member Conversions

Pointers and references to members can be implicitly converted as described in §20.6.3.

10.5.2.5 Boolean Conversions

Pointer, integral, and floating-point values can be implicitly converted to **bool** (§6.2.2). A nonzero value converts to **true**; a zero value converts to **false**. For example:

```
void f(int∗ p, int i)
{
    bool is_not_zero = p;        // true if p!=0
    bool b2 = i;                 // true if i!=0
    // ...
}
```

The pointer-to-**bool** conversion is useful in conditions, but confusing elsewhere:

```
void fi(int);
void fb(bool);

void ff(int* p, int* q)
{
    if (p) do_something(*p);            // OK
    if (q!=nullptr) do_something(*q);   // OK, but verbose
    // ...
    fi(p);                  // error: no pointer to int conversion
    fb(p);                  // OK: pointer to bool conversion (surprise!?)
}
```

Hope for a compiler warning for **fb(p)**.

10.5.2.6 Floating-Integral Conversions

When a floating-point value is converted to an integer value, the fractional part is discarded. In other words, conversion from a floating-point type to an integer type truncates. For example, the value of **int(1.6)** is **1**. The behavior is undefined if the truncated value cannot be represented in the destination type. For example:

```
int i = 2.7;         // i becomes 2
char b = 2000.7;     // undefined for 8-bit chars: 2000 cannot be represented as an 8-bit char
```

Conversions from integer to floating types are as mathematically correct as the hardware allows. Loss of precision occurs if an integral value cannot be represented exactly as a value of the floating type. For example:

```
int i = float(1234567890);
```

On a machine where both **int**s and **float**s are represented using 32 bits, the value of **i** is **1234567936**.

Clearly, it is best to avoid potentially value-destroying implicit conversions. In fact, compilers can detect and warn against some obviously dangerous conversions, such as floating to integral and **long int** to **char**. However, general compile-time detection is impractical, so the programmer must be careful. When "being careful" isn't enough, the programmer can insert explicit checks. For example:

```
char checked_cast(int i)
{
    char c = i;       // warning: not portable (§10.5.2.1)
    if (i != c) throw std::runtime_error{"int-to-char check failed"};
    return c;
}

void my_code(int i)
{
    char c = checked_cast(i);
    // ...
}
```

A more general technique for expressing checked conversions is presented in §25.2.5.1.

To truncate in a way that is guaranteed to be portable requires the use of **numeric_limits** (§40.2). In initializations, truncation can be avoided by using the {}-initializer notation (§6.3.5).

10.5.3 Usual Arithmetic Conversions

These conversions are performed on the operands of a binary operator to bring them to a common type, which is then used as the type of the result:

[1]   If either operand is of type **long double**, the other is converted to **long double**.
- Otherwise, if either operand is **double**, the other is converted to **double**.
- Otherwise, if either operand is **float**, the other is converted to **float**.
- Otherwise, integral promotions (§10.5.1) are performed on both operands.

[2]   Otherwise, if either operand is **unsigned long long**, the other is converted to **unsigned long long**.
- Otherwise, if one operand is a **long long int** and the other is an **unsigned long int**, then if a **long long int** can represent all the values of an **unsigned long int**, the **unsigned long int** is converted to a **long long int**; otherwise, both operands are converted to **unsigned long long int**. Otherwise, if either operand is **unsigned long long**, the other is converted to **unsigned long long**.
- Otherwise, if one operand is a **long int** and the other is an **unsigned int**, then if a **long int** can represent all the values of an **unsigned int**, the **unsigned int** is converted to a **long int**; otherwise, both operands are converted to **unsigned long int**.
- Otherwise, if either operand is **long**, the other is converted to **long**.
- Otherwise, if either operand is **unsigned**, the other is converted to **unsigned**.
- Otherwise, both operands are **int**.

These rules make the result of converting an unsigned integer to a signed one of possibly larger size implementation-defined. That is yet another reason to avoid mixing unsigned and signed integers.

10.6 Advice

[1]   Prefer the standard library to other libraries and to "handcrafted code"; §10.2.8.
[2]   Use character-level input only when you have to; §10.2.3.
[3]   When reading, always consider ill-formed input; §10.2.3.
[4]   Prefer suitable abstractions (classes, algorithms, etc.) to direct use of language features (e.g., ints, statements); §10.2.8.
[5]   Avoid complicated expressions; §10.3.3.
[6]   If in doubt about operator precedence, parenthesize; §10.3.3.
[7]   Avoid expressions with undefined order of evaluation; §10.3.2.
[8]   Avoid narrowing conversions; §10.5.2.
[9]   Define symbolic constants to avoid "magic constants"; §10.4.1.
[10]   Avoid narrowing conversions; §10.5.2.

11

Select Operations

When someone says
"I want a programming language in which
I need only say what I wish done,"
give him a lollipop.
– Alan Perlis

- Etc. Operators
  Logical Operators; Bitwise Logical Operators; Conditional Expressions; Increment and Decrement
- Free Store
  Memory Management; Arrays; Getting Memory Space; Overloading **new**
- Lists
  Implementation Model; Qualified Lists; Unqualified Lists
- Lambda Expressions
  Implementation Model; Alternatives to Lambdas; Capture; Call and Return; The Type of a Lambda
- Explicit Type Conversion
  Construction; Named Casts; C-Style Cast; Function-Style Cast
- Advice

11.1 Etc. Operators

This section examines a mixed bag of simple operators: logical operators (**&&**, **||**, and **!**), bitwise logical operators (**&**, **|**, **˜**, **<<**, and **>>**), conditional expressions (**?:**), and increment and decrement operators (**++** and **−−**). They have little in common beyond their details not fitting elsewhere in the discussions of operators.

11.1.1 Logical Operators

The logical operators && (and), || (or), and ! (not) take operands of arithmetic and pointer types, convert them to **bool**, and return a **bool** result. The && and || operators evaluate their second argument only if necessary, so they can be used to control evaluation order (§10.3.2). For example:

```
while (p && !whitespace(*p)) ++p;
```

Here, p is not dereferenced if it is the **nullptr**.

11.1.2 Bitwise Logical Operators

The bitwise logical operators & (and), | (or), ^ (exclusive or, xor), ~ (complement), >> (right shift), and << (left shift) are applied to objects of integral types – that is, **char, short, int, long, long long** and their **unsigned** counterparts, and **bool, wchar_t, char16_t,** and **char32_t**. A plain **enum** (but not an **enum class**) can be implicitly converted to an integer type and used as an operand to bitwise logical operations. The usual arithmetic conversions (§10.5.3) determine the type of the result.

A typical use of bitwise logical operators is to implement the notion of a small set (a bit vector). In this case, each bit of an unsigned integer represents one member of the set, and the number of bits limits the number of members. The binary operator & is interpreted as intersection, | as union, ^ as symmetric difference, and ~ as complement. An enumeration can be used to name the members of such a set. Here is a small example borrowed from an implementation of **ostream**:

```
enum ios_base::iostate {
        goodbit=0, eofbit=1, failbit=2, badbit=4
};
```

The implementation of a stream can set and test its state like this:

```
state = goodbit;
// ...
if (state&(badbit|failbit)) // stream not good
```

The extra parentheses are necessary because & has higher precedence than | (§10.3).

A function that reaches the end-of-input might report it like this:

```
state |= eofbit;
```

The |= operator is used to add to the state. A simple assignment, **state=eofbit**, would have cleared all other bits.

These stream state flags are observable from outside the stream implementation. For example, we could see how the states of two streams differ like this:

```
int old = cin.rdstate();     // rdstate() returns the state
// ... use cin ...
if (cin.rdstate()^old) {     // has anything changed?
        // ...
}
```

Computing differences of stream states is not common. For other similar types, computing differences is essential. For example, consider comparing a bit vector that represents the set of interrupts being handled with another that represents the set of interrupts waiting to be handled.

Please note that this bit fiddling is taken from the implementation of iostreams rather than from the user interface. Convenient bit manipulation can be very important, but for reliability, maintainability, portability, etc., it should be kept at low levels of a system. For more general notions of a set, see the standard-library **set** (§31.4.3) and **bitset** (§34.2.2).

Bitwise logical operations can be used to extract bit-fields from a word. For example, one could extract the middle 16 bits of a 32-bit **int** like this:

```
constexpr unsigned short middle(int a)
{
    static_assert(sizeof(int)==4,"unexpected int size");
    static_assert(sizeof(short)==2,"unexpected short size");
    return (a>>8)&0xFFFF;
}

int x = 0xFF00FF00; // assume sizeof(int)==4
short y = middle(x); // y = 0x00FF
```

Using fields (§8.2.7) is a convenient shorthand for such shifting and masking.

Do not confuse the bitwise logical operators with the logical operators: **&&**, **||**, and **!**. The latter return **true** or **false**, and they are primarily useful for writing the test in an **if**-, **while**-, or **for**-statement (§9.4, §9.5). For example, **!0** (not zero) is the value **true**, which converts to **1**, whereas ˜0 (complement of zero) is the bit pattern all-ones, which in two's complement representation is the value –1.

11.1.3 Conditional Expressions

Some **if**-statements can conveniently be replaced by *conditional-expressions*. For example:

```
if (a <= b)
    max = b;
else
    max = a;
```

This is more directly expressed like this:

```
max = (a<=b) ? b : a;
```

The parentheses around the condition are not necessary, but I find the code easier to read when they are used.

Conditional expressions are important in that they can be used in constant expressions (§10.4).

A pair of expressions **e1** and **e2** can be used as alternatives in a conditional expression, **c?e1:e2**, if they are of the same type or if there is a common type **T**, to which they can both be implicitly converted. For arithmetic types, the usual arithmetic conversions (§10.5.3) are used to find that common type. For other types, either **e1** must be implicitly convertible to **e2**'s type or vice versa. In addition, one branch may be a **throw**-expression (§13.5.1). For example:

```
void fct(int* p)
{
    int i = (p) ? *p : std::runtime_error{"unexpected nullptr"};
    // ...
}
```

11.1.4 Increment and Decrement

The ++ operator is used to express incrementing directly, rather than expressing it indirectly using a combination of an addition and an assignment. Provided lvalue has no side effects, ++lvalue means lvalue+=1, which again means lvalue=lvalue+1. The expression denoting the object to be incremented is evaluated once (only). Decrementing is similarly expressed by the −− operator.

The operators ++ and −− can be used both prefix and postfix operators. The value of ++x is the new (that is, incremented) value of x. For example, y=++x is equivalent to y=(x=x+1). The value of x++, however, is the old value of x. For example, y=x++ is equivalent to y=(t=x,x=x+1,t), where t is a variable of the same type as x.

Like adding an int to a pointer, or subtracting it, ++ and −− on a pointer operate in terms of elements of the array into which the pointer points; p++ makes p point to the next element (§7.4.1).

The ++ and −− operators are particularly useful for incrementing and decrementing variables in loops. For example, one can copy a zero-terminated C-style string like this:

```
void cpy(char* p, const char* q)
{
    while (*p++ = *q++) ;
}
```

Like C, C++ is both loved and hated for enabling such terse, expression-oriented coding. Consider:

```
while (*p++ = *q++) ;
```

This is more than a little obscure to non-C programmers, but because the style of coding is not uncommon, it is worth examining more closely. Consider first a more traditional way of copying an array of characters:

```
int length = strlen(q);
for (int i = 0; i<=length; i++)
    p[i] = q[i];
```

This is wasteful. The length of a zero-terminated string is found by reading the string looking for the terminating zero. Thus, we read the string twice: once to find its length and once to copy it. So we try this instead:

```
int i;
for (i = 0; q[i]!=0 ; i++)
    p[i] = q[i];
p[i] = 0;          // terminating zero
```

The variable i used for indexing can be eliminated because p and q are pointers:

```
while (*q != 0) {
    *p = *q;
    p++;           // point to next character
    q++;           // point to next character
}
*p = 0;            // terminating zero
```

Because the post-increment operation allows us first to use the value and then to increment it, we can rewrite the loop like this:

```
    while (*q != 0) {
        *p++ = *q++;
    }
    *p = 0; // terminating zero
```

The value of *p++ = *q++ is *q. We can therefore rewrite the example like this:

```
    while ((*p++ = *q++) != 0) { }
```

In this case, we don't notice that *q is zero until we already have copied it into *p and incremented p. Consequently, we can eliminate the final assignment of the terminating zero. Finally, we can reduce the example further by observing that we don't need the empty block and that the !=0 is redundant because the result of an integral condition is always compared to zero anyway. Thus, we get the version we set out to discover:

```
    while (*p++ = *q++) ;
```

Is this version less readable than the previous versions? Not to an experienced C or C++ programmer. Is this version more efficient in time or space than the previous versions? Except for the first version that called **strlen()**, not really; the performance will be equivalent and often identical code will be generated.

The most efficient way of copying a zero-terminated character string is typically the standard C-style string copy function:

```
    char* strcpy(char*, const char*);    // from <string.h>
```

For more general copying, the standard **copy** algorithm (§4.5, §32.5) can be used. Whenever possible, use standard-library facilities in preference to fiddling with pointers and bytes. Standard-library functions may be inlined (§12.1.3) or even implemented using specialized machine instructions. Therefore, you should measure carefully before believing that some piece of handcrafted code outperforms library functions. Even if it does, the advantage may not exist on some other hardware+compiler combination, and your alternative may give a maintainer a headache.

11.2 Free Store

A named object has its lifetime determined by its scope (§6.3.4). However, it is often useful to create an object that exists independently of the scope in which it was created. For example, it is common to create objects that can be used after returning from the function in which they were created. The operator **new** creates such objects, and the operator **delete** can be used to destroy them. Objects allocated by **new** are said to be "on the *free store*" (also, "on the *heap*" or "in *dynamic memory*").

Consider how we might write a compiler in the style used for the desk calculator (§10.2). The syntax analysis functions might build a tree of the expressions for use by the code generator:

```
    struct Enode {
        Token_value oper;
        Enode* left;
        Enode* right;
        // ...
    };
```

```
Enode* expr(bool get)
{
    Enode* left = term(get);

    for (;;) {
        switch (ts.current().kind) {
        case Kind::plus:
        case Kind::minus:
            left = new Enode {ts.current().kind,left,term(true)};
            break;
        default:
            return left;              // return node
        }
    }
}
```

In cases **Kind::plus** and **Kind::minus**, a new **Enode** is created on the free store and initialized by the value **{ts.current().kind,left,term(true)}**. The resulting pointer is assigned to **left** and eventually returned from **expr()**.

I used the {}-list notation for specifying arguments. Alternatively, I could have used the old-style ()-list notation to specify an initializer. However, trying the = notation for initializing an object created using **new** results in an error:

```
int* p = new int = 7;  // error
```

If a type has a default constructor, we can leave out the initializer, but built-in types are by default uninitialized. For example:

```
auto pc = new complex<double>;   // the complex is initialized to {0,0}
auto pi = new int;               // the int is uninitialized
```

This can be confusing. To be sure to get default initialization, use {}. For example:

```
auto pc = new complex<double>{}; // the complex is initialized to {0,0}
auto pi = new int{};             // the int is initialized to 0
```

A code generator could use the **Enode**s created by **expr()** and delete them:

```
void generate(Enode* n)
{
    switch (n–>oper) {
    case Kind::plus:
        // use n
        delete n;  // delete an Enode from the free store
    }
}
```

An object created by **new** exists until it is explicitly destroyed by **delete**. Then, the space it occupied can be reused by **new**. A C++ implementation does not guarantee the presence of a "garbage collector" that looks out for unreferenced objects and makes them available to **new** for reuse. Consequently, I will assume that objects created by **new** are manually freed using **delete**.

The **delete** operator may be applied only to a pointer returned by **new** or to the **nullptr**. Applying **delete** to the **nullptr** has no effect.

If the deleted object is of a class with a destructor (§3.2.1.2, §17.2), that destructor is called by **delete** before the object's memory is released for reuse.

11.2.1 Memory Management

The main problems with free store are:

- *Leaked objects*: People use **new** and then forget to **delete** the allocated object.
- *Premature deletion*: People **delete** an object that they have some other pointer to and later use that other pointer.
- *Double deletion*: An object is deleted twice, invoking its destructor (if any) twice.

Leaked objects are potentially a bad problem because they can cause a program to run out of space. Premature deletion is almost always a nasty problem because the pointer to the "deleted object" no longer points to a valid object (so reading it may give bad results) and may indeed point to memory that has been reused for another object (so writing to it may corrupt an unrelated object). Consider this example of very bad code:

```
int* p1 = new int{99};
int* p2 = p1;              // potential trouble
delete p1;                 // now p2 doesn't point to a valid object
p1 = nullptr;              // gives a false sense of safety
char* p3 = new char{'x'};  // p3 may now point to the memory pointed to by p2
*p2 = 999;                 // this may cause trouble
cout << *p3 << '\n';       // may not print x
```

Double deletion is a problem because resource managers typically cannot track what code owns a resource. Consider:

```
void sloppy()    // very bad code
{
    int* p = new int[1000];    // acquire memory
    // ... use *p ...
    delete[] p;                // release memory

    // ... wait a while ...

    delete[] p;                // but sloppy() does not own *p
}
```

By the second **delete[]**, the memory pointed to by *p may have been reallocated for some other use and the allocator may get corrupted. Replace **int** with **string** in that example, and we'll see **string**'s destructor trying to read memory that has been reallocated and maybe overwritten by other code, and using what it read to try to **delete** memory. In general, a double deletion is undefined behavior and the results are unpredictable and usually disastrous.

The reason people make these mistakes is typically not maliciousness and often not even simple sloppiness; it is genuinely hard to consistently deallocate every allocated object in a large program (once and at exactly the right point in a computation). For starters, analysis of a localized part of a program will not detect these problems because an error usually involves several separate parts.

As alternatives to using "naked" **news** and **deletes**, I can recommend two general approaches to resource management that avoid such problems:

[1]   Don't put objects on the free store if you don't have to; prefer scoped variables.

[2]   When you construct an object on the free store, place its pointer into a *manager object* (sometimes called a *handle*) with a destructor that will destroy it. Examples are **string**, **vector** and all the other standard-library containers, **unique_ptr** (§5.2.1, §34.3.1), and **shared_ptr** (§5.2.1, §34.3.2). Wherever possible, have that manager object be a scoped variable. Many classical uses of free store can be eliminated by using move semantics (§3.3, §17.5.2) to return large objects represented as manager objects from functions.

This rule [2] is often referred to as RAII ("Resource Acquisition Is Initialization"; §5.2, §13.3) and is the basic technique for avoiding resource leaks and making error handling using exceptions simple and safe.

The standard-library **vector** is an example of these techniques:

```
void f(const string& s)
{
    vector<char> v;
    for (auto c : s)
        v.push_back(c);
    // ...
}
```

The **vector** keeps its elements on the free store, but it handles all allocations and deallocations itself. In this example, **push_back()** does **news** to acquire space for its elements and **deletes** to free space that it no longer needs. However, the users of **vector** need not know about those implementation details and will just rely on **vector** not leaking.

The **Token_stream** from the calculator example is an even simpler example (§10.2.2). There, a user can use **new** and hand the resulting pointer to a **Token_stream** to manage:

```
Token_stream ts{new istringstream{some_string}};
```

We do not need to use the free store just to get a large object out of a function. For example:

```
string reverse(const string& s)
{
    string ss;
    for (int i=s.size()–1; 0<=i; ––i)
        ss.push_back(s[i]);
    return ss;
}
```

Like **vector**, a **string** is really a handle to its elements. So, we simply *move* the **ss** out of **reverse()** rather than copying any elements (§3.3.2).

The resource management "smart pointers" (e.g., **unique_ptr** and **smart_ptr**) are a further example of these ideas (§5.2.1, §34.3.1). For example:

```
void f(int n)
{
    int* p1 = new int[n];                    // potential trouble
    unique_ptr<int[]> p2 {new int[n]};
```

```
        // ...
        if (n%2) throw runtime_error("odd");
        delete[] p1;                    // we may never get here
}
```

For **f(3)** the memory pointed to by **p1** is leaked, but the memory pointed to by **p2** is correctly and implicitly deallocated.

My rule of thumb for the use of **new** and **delete** is "no naked **news**"; that is, **new** belongs in constructors and similar operations, **delete** belongs in destructors, and together they provide a coherent memory management strategy. In addition, **new** is often used in arguments to resource handles.

If everything else fails (e.g., if someone has a lot of old code with lots of undisciplined use of **new**), C++ offers a standard interface to a garbage collector (§34.5).

11.2.2 Arrays

Arrays of objects can also be created using **new**. For example:

```
char* save_string(const char* p)
{
        char* s = new char[strlen(p)+1];
        strcpy(s,p);         // copy from p to s
        return s;
}

int main(int argc, char* argv[])
{
        if (argc < 2) exit(1);
        char* p = save_string(argv[1]);
        // ...
        delete[] p;
}
```

The "plain" operator **delete** is used to delete individual objects; **delete[]** is used to delete arrays.

Unless you really must use a **char*** directly, the standard-library **string** can be used to simplify the **save_string()**:

```
string save_string(const char* p)
{
        return string{p};
}

int main(int argc, char* argv[])
{
        if (argc < 2) exit(1);
        string s = save_string(argv[1]);
        // ...
}
```

In particular, the **new[]** and the **delete[]** vanished.

To deallocate space allocated by new, delete and delete[] must be able to determine the size of the object allocated. This implies that an object allocated using the standard implementation of new will occupy slightly more space than a static object. At a minimum, space is needed to hold the object's size. Usually two or more words per allocation are used for free-store management. Most modern machines use 8-byte words. This overhead is not significant when we allocate many objects or large objects, but it can matter if we allocate lots of small objects (e.g., ints or Points) on the free store.

Note that a vector (§4.4.1, §31.4) is a proper object and can therefore be allocated and deallocated using plain new and delete. For example:

```
void f(int n)
{
    vector<int>* p = new vector<int>(n);    // individual object
    int* q = new int[n];                    // array
    // ...
    delete p;
    delete[] q;
}
```

The delete[] operator may be applied only to a pointer to an array returned by new of an array or to the null pointer (§7.2.2). Applying delete[] to the null pointer has no effect.

However, do not use new to create local objects. For example:

```
void f1()
{
    X* p =new X;
    // ... use *p ...
    delete p;
}
```

That's verbose, inefficient, and error-prone (§13.3). In particular, a return or an exception thrown before the delete will cause a memory leak (unless even more code is added). Instead, use a local variable:

```
void f2()
{
    X x;
    // ... use x ...
}
```

The local variable x is implicitly destroyed upon exit from f2.

11.2.3 Getting Memory Space

The free-store operators new, delete, new[], and delete[] are implemented using functions presented in the <new> header:

```
void* operator new(size_t);      // allocate space for individual object
void operator delete(void* p);   // if (p) deallocate space allocated using operator new()
```

```
void* operator new[](size_t);          // allocate space for array
void operator delete[](void* p);       // if (p) deallocate space allocated using operator new[]()
```

When operator **new** needs to allocate space for an object, it calls **operator new()** to allocate a suitable number of bytes. Similarly, when operator **new** needs to allocate space for an array, it calls **operator new[]()**.

The standard implementations of **operator new()** and **operator new[]()** do not initialize the memory returned.

The allocation and deallocation functions deal in untyped and uninitialized memory (often called "raw memory"), as opposed to typed objects. Consequently, they take arguments or return values of type **void***. The operators **new** and **delete** handle the mapping between this untyped-memory layer and the typed-object layer.

What happens when **new** can find no store to allocate? By default, the allocator throws a standard-library **bad_alloc** exception (for an alternative, see §11.2.4.1). For example:

```
void f()
{
    vector<char*> v;
    try {
        for (;;) {
            char * p = new char[10000];    // acquire some memory
            v.push_back(p);                // make sure the new memory is referenced
            p[0] = 'x';                    // use the new memory
        }
    }
    catch(bad_alloc) {
        cerr << "Memory exhausted!\n";
    }
}
```

However much memory we have available, this will eventually invoke the **bad_alloc** handler. Please be careful: the **new** operator is not guaranteed to throw when you run out of physical main memory. So, on a system with virtual memory, this program can consume a lot of disk space and take a long time doing so before the exception is thrown.

We can specify what **new** should do upon memory exhaustion; see §30.4.1.3.

In addition to the functions defined in **<new>**, a user can define **operator new()**, etc., for a specific class (§19.2.5). Class members **operator new()**, etc., are found and used in preference to the ones from **<new>** according to the usual scope rules.

11.2.4 Overloading **new**

By default, operator **new** creates its object on the free store. What if we wanted the object allocated elsewhere? Consider a simple class:

```
class X {
public:
    X(int);
    // ...
};
```

We can place objects anywhere by providing an allocator function (§11.2.3) with extra arguments and then supplying such extra arguments when using **new**:

```
void* operator new(size_t, void* p) { return p; }    // explicit placement operator
```

```
void* buf = reinterpret_cast<void*>(0xF00F);    // significant address
X* p2 = new(buf) X;                             // construct an X at buf;
                                                // invokes: operator new(sizeof(X),buf)
```

Because of this usage, the **new(buf) X** syntax for supplying extra arguments to **operator new()** is known as the *placement syntax*. Note that every **operator new()** takes a size as its first argument and that the size of the object allocated is implicitly supplied (§19.2.5). The **operator new()** used by the **new** operator is chosen by the usual argument matching rules (§12.3); every **operator new()** has a **size_t** as its first argument.

The ''placement'' **operator new()** is the simplest such allocator. It is defined in the standard header **<new>**:

```
void* operator new (size_t sz, void* p) noexcept;     // place object of size sz at p
void* operator new[](size_t sz, void* p) noexcept;    // place object of size sz at p

void operator delete (void* p, void*) noexcept;       // if (p) make *p invalid
void operator delete[](void* p, void*) noexcept;      // if (p) make *p invalid
```

The ''placement **delete**'' operators do nothing except possibly inform a garbage collector that the deleted pointer is no longer safely derived (§34.5).

The placement **new** construct can also be used to allocate memory from a specific arena:

```
class Arena {
public:
        virtual void* alloc(size_t) =0;
        virtual void free(void*) =0;
        // ...
};
```

```
void* operator new(size_t sz, Arena* a)
{
        return a->alloc(sz);
}
```

Now objects of arbitrary types can be allocated from different **Arena**s as needed. For example:

```
extern Arena* Persistent;
extern Arena* Shared;

void g(int i)
{
        X* p = new(Persistent) X(i);    // X in persistent storage
        X* q = new(Shared) X(i);        // X in shared memory
        // ...
}
```

Placing an object in an area that is not (directly) controlled by the standard free-store manager implies that some care is required when destroying the object. The basic mechanism for that is an explicit call of a destructor:

```
void destroy(X* p, Arena* a)
{
    p->˜X();        // call destructor
    a->free(p);     // free memory
}
```

Note that explicit calls of destructors should be avoided except in the implementation of resource management classes. Even most resource handles can be written using **new** and **delete**. However, it would be hard to implement an efficient general container along the lines of the standard-library **vector** (§4.4.1, §31.3.3) without using explicit destructor calls. A novice should think thrice before calling a destructor explicitly and also should ask a more experienced colleague before doing so.

See §13.6.1 for an example of how placement **new** can interact with exception handling.

There is no special syntax for placement of arrays. Nor need there be, since arbitrary types can be allocated by placement **new**. However, an **operator delete()** can be defined for arrays (§11.2.3).

11.2.4.1 nothrow new

In programs where exceptions must be avoided (§13.1.5), we can use **nothrow** versions of **new** and **delete**. For example:

```
void f(int n)
{
    int* p = new(nothrow) int[n];       // allocate n ints on the free store
    if (p==nullptr) {// no memory available
        // ... handle allocation error ...
    }
    // ...
    operator delete(nothrow,p);         // deallocate *p
}
```

That **nothrow** is the name of an object of the standard-library type **nothrow_t** that is used for disambiguation; **nothrow** and **nothrow_t** are declared in **<new>**.

The functions implementing this are found in **<new>**:

```
void* operator new(size_t sz, const nothrow_t&) noexcept;   // allocate sz bytes;
                                                            // return nullptr if allocation failed
void operator delete(void* p, const nothrow_t&) noexcept;   // deallocate space allocated by new

void* operator new[](size_t sz, const nothrow_t&) noexcept; // allocate sz bytes;
                                                            // return nullptr if allocation failed
void operator delete[](void* p, const nothrow_t&) noexcept; // deallocate space allocated by new
```

These **operator new** functions return **nullptr**, rather than throwing **bad_alloc**, if there is not sufficient memory to allocate.

11.3 Lists

In addition to their use for initializing named variables (§6.3.5.2), {}-lists can be used as expressions in many (but not all) places. They can appear in two forms:

[1] Qualified by a type, T{...}, meaning "create an object of type T initialized by T{...}"; §11.3.2

[2] Unqualified {...}, for which the the type must be determined from the context of use; §11.3.3

For example:

```
struct S { int a, b; };
struct SS { double a, b; };

void f(S);        // f() takes an S

void g(S);
void g(SS);       // g() is overloaded

void h()
{
    f({1,2});     // OK: call f(S{1,2})

    g({1,2});     // error: ambiguous
    g(S{1,2});    // OK: call g(S)
    g(SS{1,2});   // OK: call g(SS)
}
```

As in their use for initializing named variables (§6.3.5), lists can have zero, one, or more elements. A {}-list is used to construct an object of some type, so the number of elements and their types must be what is required to construct an object of that type.

11.3.1 Implementation Model

The implementation model for {}-lists comes in three parts:

- If the {}-list is used as constructor arguments, the implementation is just as if you had used a ()-list. List elements are not copied except as by-value constructor arguments.

- If the {}-list is used to initialize the elements of an aggregate (an array or a class without a constructor), each list element initializes an element of the aggregate. List elements are not copied except as by-value arguments to aggregate element constructors.

- If the {}-list is used to construct an **initializer_list** object each list element is used to initialize an element of the *underlying array* of the **initializer_list**. Elements are typically copied from the **initializer_list** to wherever we use them.

Note that this is the general model that we can use to understand the semantics of a {}-list; a compiler may apply clever optimizations as long as the meaning is preserved.

Consider:

```
vector<double> v = {1, 2, 3.14};
```

The standard-library **vector** has an initializer-list constructor (§17.3.4), so the initializer list

{1,2,3.14} is interpreted as a temporary constructed and used like this:

```
const double temp[] = {double{1}, double{2}, 3.14 } ;
const initializer_list<double> tmp(temp,sizeof(temp)/sizeof(double));
vector<double> v(tmp);
```

That is, the compiler constructs an array containing the initializers converted to the desired type (here, **double**). This array is passed to **vector**s initializer-list constructor as an **initializer_list**. The initializer-list constructor then copies the values from the array into its own data structure for elements. Note that an **initializer_list** is a small object (probably two words), so passing it by value makes sense.

The underlying array is immutable, so there is no way (within the standard's rules) that the meaning of a {}-list can change between two uses. Consider:

```
void f()
{
    initializer_list<int> lst {1,2,3};
    cout << *lst.begin() << '\n';
    *lst.begin() = 2;              // error: lst is immutable
    cout << *lst.begin() << '\n';
}
```

In particular, having a {}-list be immutable implies that a container taking elements from it must use a copy operation, rather than a move operation.

The lifetime of a {}-list (and its underlying array) is determined by the scope in which it is used (§6.4.2). When used to initialize a variable of type **initializer_list<T>**, the list lives as long as the variable. When used in an expression (including as an initializer to a variable of some other type, such as **vector<T>**), the list is destroyed at the end of its full expression.

11.3.2 Qualified Lists

The basic idea of initializer lists as expressions is that if you can initialize a variable **x** using the notation

```
T x {v};
```

then you can create an object with the same value as an expression using **T{v}** or **new T{v}**. Using **new** places the object on the free store and returns a pointer to it, whereas "plain **T{v}**" makes a temporary object in the local scope (§6.4.2). For example:

```
struct S { int a, b; };

void f()
{
    S v {7,8};             // direct initialization of a variable
    v = S{7,8};            // assign using qualified list
    S* p = new S{7,8};     // construct on free store using qualified list
}
```

The rules constructing an object using a qualified list are those of direct initialization (§16.2.6).

One way of looking at a qualified initializer list with one element is as a conversion from one type to another. For example:

```
template<class T>
T square(T x)
{
    return x*x;
}

void f(int i)
{
    double d = square(double{i});
    complex<double> z = square(complex<double>{i});
}
```

That idea is explored further in §11.5.1.

11.3.3 Unqualified Lists

A unqualified list is used where an expected type is unambiguously known. It can be used as an expression only as:

- A function argument
- A return value
- The right-hand operand of an assignment operator (=, +=, *=, etc.)
- A subscript

For example:

```
int f(double d, Matrix& m)
{
    int v {7};              // initializer (direct initialization)
    int v2 = {7};           // initializer (copy initialization)
    int v3 = m[{2,3}];      // assume m takes value pairs as subscripts

    v = {8};                // right-hand operand of assignment
    v += {88};              // right-hand operand of assignment
    {v} = 9;                // error: not left-hand operand of assignment
    v = 7+{10};             // error: not an operand of a non-assignment operator
    f({10.0});              // function argument
    return {11};            // return value
}
```

The reason that an unqualified list is not allowed on the left-hand side of assignments is primarily that the C++ grammar allows { in that position for compound statements (blocks), so that readability would be a problem for humans and ambiguity resolution would be tricky for compilers. This is not an insurmountable problem, but it was decided not to extend C++ in that direction.

When used as the initializer for a named object without the use of a = (as for v above), an unqualified {}-list performs direct initialization (§16.2.6). In all other cases, it performs copy initialization (§16.2.6). In particular, the otherwise redundant = in an initializer restricts the set of initializations that can be performed with a given {}-list.

The standard-library type initializer_list<T> is used to handle variable-length {}-lists (§12.2.3). Its most obvious use is to allow initializer lists for user-defined containers (§3.2.1.3), but it can also be used directly; for example:

```
int high_value(initializer_list<int> val)
{
    int high = numeric_traits<int>lowest();
    if (val.size()==0) return high;

    for (auto x : val)
        if (x>high) high = x;

    return high;
}

int v1 = high_value({1,2,3,4,5,6,7});
int v2 = high_value({-1,2,v1,4,-9,20,v1});
```

A {}-list is the simplest way of dealing with homogeneous lists of varying lengths. However, beware that zero elements can be a special case. If so, that case should be handled by a default constructor (§17.3.3).

The type of a {}-list can be deduced (only) if all elements are of the same type. For example:

```
auto x0 = {};        // error (no element type)
auto x1 = {1};       // initializer_list<int>
auto x2 = {1,2};     // initializer_list<int>
auto x3 = {1,2,3};   // initializer_list<int>
auto x4 = {1,2.0};   // error: nonhomogeneous list
```

Unfortunately, we do not deduce the type of an unqualified list for a plain template argument. For example:

```
template<typename T>
void f(T);

f({});        // error: type of initializer is unknown
f({1});       // error: an unqualified list does not match "plain T"
f({1,2});     // error: an unqualified list does not match "plain T"
f({1,2,3});   // error: an unqualified list does not match "plain T"
```

I say "unfortunately" because this is a language restriction, rather than a fundamental rule. It would be technically possible to deduce the type of those {}-lists as initializer_list<int>, just like we do for auto initializers.

Similarly, we do not deduce the element type of a container represented as a template. For example:

```
template<class T>
void f2(const vector<T>&);

f2({1,2,3});            // error: cannot deduce T
f2({"Kona","Sidney"});  // error: cannot deduce T
```

This too is unfortunate, but it is a bit more understandable from a language-technical point of view: nowhere in those calls does it say **vector**. To deduce **T** the compiler would first have to decide that the user really wanted a **vector** and then look into the definition of **vector** to see if it has a constructor that accepts {1,2,3}. In general, that would require an instantiation of **vector** (§26.2). It would be possible to handle that, but it could be costly in compile time, and the opportunities for ambiguities and confusion if there were many overloaded versions of f2() are reasons for caution. To call f2(), be more specific:

```
f2(vector<int>{1,2,3});            // OK
f2(vector<string>{"Kona","Sidney"});   // OK
```

11.4 Lambda Expressions

A *lambda expression*, sometimes also referred to as a *lambda function* or (strictly speaking incorrectly, but colloquially) as a *lambda*, is a simplified notation for defining and using an anonymous function object. Instead of defining a named class with an **operator()**, later making an object of that class, and finally invoking it, we can use a shorthand. This is particularly useful when we want to pass an operation as an argument to an algorithm. In the context of graphical user interfaces (and elsewhere), such operations are often referred to as *callbacks*. This section focuses on technical aspects of lambdas; examples and techniques for the use of lambdas can be found elsewhere (§3.4.3, §32.4, §33.5.2).

A lambda expression consists of a sequence of parts:
*   A possibly empty *capture list*, specifying what names from the definition environment can be used in the lambda expression's body, and whether those are copied or accessed by reference. The capture list is delimited by [] (§11.4.3).
*   An optional *parameter list*, specifying what arguments the lambda expression requires. The parameter list is delimited by () (§11.4.4).
*   An optional **mutable** specifier, indicating that the lambda expression's body may modify the state of the lambda (i.e., change the lambda's copies of variables captured by value) (§11.4.3.4).
*   An optional **noexcept** specifier.
*   An optional return type declaration of the form –> *type* (§11.4.4).
*   A *body*, specifying the code to be executed. The body is delimited by {} (§11.4.3).

The details of passing arguments, returning results, and specifying the body are those of functions and are presented in Chapter 12. The notion of "capture" of local variables is not provided for functions. This implies that a lambda can act as a local function even though a function cannot.

11.4.1 Implementation Model

Lambda expressions can be implemented in a variety of ways, and there are some rather effective ways of optimizing them. However, I find it useful to understand the semantics of a lambda by considering it a shorthand for defining and using a function object. Consider a relatively simple example:

```
void print_modulo(const vector<int>& v, ostream& os, int m)
    // output v[i] to os if v[i]%m==0
{
    for_each(begin(v),end(v),
        [&os,m](int x) { if (x%m==0) os << x << '\n'; }
    );
}
```

To see what this means, we can define the equivalent function object:

```
class Modulo_print {
    ostream& os;   // members to hold the capture list
    int m;
public:
    Modulo_print(ostream& s, int mm) :os(s), m(mm) {}       // capture
    void operator()(int x) const
        { if (x%m==0) os << x << '\n'; }
};
```

The capture list, [&os,m], becomes two member variables and a constructor to initialize them. The **&** before **os** means that we should store a reference, and the absence of a **&** for **m** means that we should store a copy. This use of **&** mirrors its use in function argument declarations.

The body of the lambda simply becomes the body of the **operator()()**. Since the lambda doesn't return a value, the **operator()()** is **void**. By default, **operator()()** is **const**, so that the lambda body doesn't modify the captured variables. That's by far the most common case. Should you want to modify the state of a lambda from its body, the lambda can be declared **mutable** (§11.4.3.4). This corresponds to an **operator()()** *not* being declared **const**.

An object of a class generated from a lambda is called a *closure object* (or simply a *closure*). We can now write the original function like this:

```
void print_modulo(const vector<int>& v, ostream& os, int m)
    // output v[i] to os if v[i]%m==0
{
    for_each(begin(v),end(v),Modulo_print{os,m});
}
```

If a lambda potentially captures every local variable by reference (using the capture list [&]), the closure may be optimized to simply contain a pointer to the enclosing stack frame.

11.4.2 Alternatives to Lambdas

That final version of **print_modulo()** is actually quite attractive, and naming nontrivial operations is generally a good idea. A separately defined class also leaves more room for comments than does a lambda embedded in some argument list.

However, many lambdas are small and used only once. For such uses, the realistic equivalent involves a local class defined immediately before its (only) use. For example:

```
void print_modulo(const vector<int>& v, ostream& os, int m)
    // output v[i] to os if v[i]%m==0
{
    class Modulo_print {
        ostream& os;   // members to hold the capture list
        int m;
    public:
        Modulo_print (ostream& s, int mm) :os(s), m(mm) {}      // capture
        void operator()(int x) const
            { if (x%m==0) os << x << '\n'; }
    };

    for_each(begin(v),end(v),Modulo_print{os,m});
}
```

Compared to that, the version using the lambda is a clear winner. If we really want a name, we can just name the lambda:

```
void print_modulo(const vector<int>& v, ostream& os, int m)
    // output v[i] to os if v[i]%m==0
{
    auto Modulo_print = [&os,m] (int x) { if (x%m==0) os << x << '\n'; };

    for_each(begin(v),end(v),Modulo_print);
}
```

Naming the lambda is often a good idea. Doing so forces us to consider the design of the operation a bit more carefully. It also simplifies code layout and allows for recursion (§11.4.5).

Writing a **for**-loop is an alternative to using a lambda with a **for_each()**. Consider:

```
void print_modulo(const vector<int>& v, ostream& os, int m)
    // output v[i] to os if v[i]%m==0
{
    for (auto x : v)
        if (x%m==0) os << x << '\n';
}
```

Many would find this version much clearer than any of the lambda versions. However, **for_each** is a rather special algorithm, and **vector<int>** is a very specific container. Consider generalizing **print_modulo()** to handle arbitrary containers:

```
template<class C>
void print_modulo(const C& v, ostream& os, int m)
    // output v[i] to os if v[i]%m==0
{
    for (auto x : v)
        if (x%m==0) os << x << '\n';
}
```

This version works nicely for a **map**. The C++ range-for-statement specifically caters to the special case of traversing a sequence from its beginning to its end. The STL containers make such traversals easy and general. For example, using a **for**-statement to traverse a **map** gives a depth-first traversal. How would we do a breadth-first traversal? The **for**-loop version of **print_modulo()** is not amenable to change, so we have to rewrite it to an algorithm. For example:

```
template<class C>
void print_modulo(const C& v, ostream& os, int m)
    // output v[i] to os if v[i]%m==0
{
    breadth_first(begin(v),end(v),
        [&os,m](int x) { if (x%m==0) os << x << '\n'; }
    );
}
```

Thus, a lambda can be used as "the body" for a generalized loop/traversal construct represented as an algorithm. Using **for_each** rather than **breadth_first** would give depth-first traversal.

The performance of a lambda as an argument to a traversal algorithm is equivalent (typically identical) to that of the equivalent loop. I have found that to be quite consistent across implementations and platforms. The implication is that we have to base our choice between "algorithm plus lambda" and "**for**-statement with body" on stylistic grounds and on estimates of extensibility and maintainability.

11.4.3 Capture

The main use of lambdas is for specifying code to be passed as arguments. Lambdas allow that to be done "inline" without having to name a function (or function object) and use it elsewhere. Some lambdas require no access to their local environment. Such lambdas are defined with the empty lambda introducer []. For example:

```
void algo(vector<int>& v)
{
    sort(v.begin(),v.end());    // sort values
    // ...
    sort(v.begin(),v.end(),[](int x, int y) { return abs(x)<abs(y); });    // sort absolute values
    // ...
}
```

If we want to access local names, we have to say so or get an error:

```
void f(vector<int>& v)
{
    bool sensitive = true;
    // ...
    sort(v.begin(),v.end(),
        [](int x, int y) { return sensitive ? x<y : abs(x)<abs(y); }    // error: can't access sensitive
    );
}
```

I used the *lambda introducer* []. This is the simplest lambda introducer and does not allow the lambda to refer to names in the calling environment. The first character of a lambda expression is always [. A lambda introducer can take various forms:

- []: an empty capture list. This implies that no local names from the surrounding context can be used in the lambda body. For such lambda expressions, data is obtained from arguments or from nonlocal variables.
- [&]: implicitly capture by reference. All local names can be used. All local variables are accessed by reference.
- [=]: implicitly capture by value. All local names can be used. All names refer to copies of the local variables taken at the point of call of the lambda expression.
- [*capture-list*]: explicit capture; the *capture-list* is the list of names of local variables to be captured (i.e., stored in the object) by reference or by value. Variables with names preceded by & are captured by reference. Other variables are captured by value. A capture list can also contain this and names followed by ... as elements.
- [&, *capture-list*]: implicitly capture by reference all local variables with names not mentioned in the list. The capture list can contain this. Listed names cannot be preceded by &. Variables named in the capture list are captured by value.
- [=, *capture-list*]: implicitly capture by value all local variables with names not mentioned in the list. The capture list cannot contain this. The listed names must be preceded by &. Variables named in the capture list are captured by reference.

Note that a local name preceded by & is always captured by reference and a local name not preceded by & is always captured by value. Only capture by reference allows modification of variables in the calling environment.

The *capture-list* cases are used for fine-grained control over what names from the call environment are used and how. For example:

```
void f(vector<int>& v)
{
    bool sensitive = true;
    // ...
    sort(v.begin(),v.end()
        [sensitive](int x, int y) { return sensitive ? x<y : abs(x)<abs(y); }
    );
}
```

By mentioning sensitive in the capture list, we make it accessible from within the lambda. By not specifying otherwise, we ensure that the capture of sensitive is done "by value"; just as for argument passing, passing a copy is the default. Had we wanted to capture sensitive "by reference," we could have said so by adding a & before sensitive in the capture list: [&sensitive].

The choice between capturing by value and by reference is basically the same as the choice for function arguments (§12.2). We use a reference if we need to write to the captured object or if it is large. However, for lambdas, there is the added concern that a lambda might outlive its caller (§11.4.3.1). When passing a lambda to another thread, capturing by value ([=]) is typically best: accessing another thread's stack through a reference or a pointer can be most disruptive (to performance or correctness), and trying to access the stack of a terminated thread can lead to extremely difficult-to-find errors.

If you need to capture a variadic template (§28.6) argument, use .... For example:

```
template<typename... Var>
void algo(int s, Var... v)
{
    auto helper = [&s,&v...] { return s*(h1(v...)+h2(v...)); }
    // ...
}
```

Beware that is it easy to get too clever about capture. Often, there is a choice between capture and argument passing. When that's the case, capture is usually the least typing but has the greatest potential for confusion.

11.4.3.1 Lambda and Lifetime

A lambda might outlive its caller. This can happen if we pass a lambda to a different thread or if the callee stores away the lambda for later use. For example:

```
void setup(Menu& m)
{
    // ...
    Point p1, p2, p3;
    // compute positions of p1, p2, and p3
    m.add("draw triangle",[&]{ m.draw(p1,p2,p3); });    // probable disaster
    // ...
}
```

Assuming that **add()** is an operation that adds a (name,action) pair to a menu and that the **draw()** operation makes sense, we are left with a time bomb: the **setup()** completes and later – maybe minutes later – a user presses the **draw triangle** button and the lambda tries to access the long-gone local variables. A lambda that wrote to a variable caught by reference would be even worse in that situation.

If a lambda might outlive its caller, we must make sure that all local information (if any) is copied into the closure object and that values are returned through the **return** mechanism (§12.1.4) or through suitable arguments. For the **setup()** example, that is easily done:

```
m.add("draw triangle",[=]{ m.draw(p1,p2,p3); });
```

Think of the capture list as the initializer list for the closure object and [=] and [&] as short-hand notation (§11.4.1).

11.4.3.2 Namespace Names

We don't need to "capture" namespace variables (including global variables) because they are always accessible (provided they are in scope). For example:

```
template<typename U, typename V>
ostream& operator<<(ostream& os, const pair<U,V>& p)
{
    return os << '{' << p.first << ',' << p.second << '}';
}
```

```
void print_all(const map<string,int>& m, const string& label)
{
    cout << label << ":\n{\n";
    for_each(m.begin(),m.end(),
        [](const pair<string,int>& p) { cout << p << '\n'; }
    );
    cout << "}\n";
}
```

Here, we don't need to capture **cout** or the output operator for **pair**.

11.4.3.3 Lambda and this

How do we access members of a class object from a lambda used in a member function? We can include class members in the set of names potentially captured by adding **this** to the capture list. This is used when we want to use a lambda in the implementation of a member function. For example, we might have a class for building up requests and retrieving results:

```
class Request {
    function<map<string,string>(const map<string,string>&)> oper;    // operation
    map<string,string> values;                   // arguments
    map<string,string> results;                  // targets
public:
    Request(const string& s);                    // parse and store request

    void execute()
    {
        [this]() { results=oper(values); }       // do oper to values yielding results
    }
};
```

Members are always captured by reference. That is, **[this]** implies that members are accessed through **this** rather than copied into the lambda. Unfortunately, **[this]** and **[=]** are incompatible. This implies that incautious use can lead to race conditions in multi-threaded programs (§42.4.6).

11.4.3.4 mutable Lambdas

Usually, we don't want to modify the state of the function object (the closure), so by default we can't. That is, the **operator()()** for the generated function object (§11.4.1) is a **const** member function. In the unlikely event that we want to modify the state (as opposed to modifying the state of some variable captured by reference; §11.4.3), we can declare the lambda **mutable**. For example:

```
void algo(vector<int>& v)
{
    int count = v.size();
    std::generate(v.begin(),v.end(),
        [count]()mutable{ return --count; }
    );
}
```

The **--count** decrements the copy of **v**'s size stored in the closure.

11.4.4 Call and Return

The rules for passing arguments to a lambda are the same as for a function (§12.2), and so are the rules for returning results (§12.1.4). In fact, with the exception of the rules for capture (§11.4.3) most rules for lambdas are borrowed from the rules for functions and classes. However, two irregularities should be noted:

[1] If a lambda expression does not take any arguments, the argument list can be omitted. Thus, the minimal lambda expression is []{}.

[2] A lambda expression's return type can be deduced from its body. Unfortunately, that is not also done for a function.

If a lambda body does not have a **return**-statement, the lambda's return type is **void**. If a lambda body consists of just a single **return**-statement, the lambda's return type is the type of the **return**'s expression. If neither is the case, we have to explicitly supply a return type. For example:

```
void g(double y)
{
    [&]{ f(y); }                                  // return type is void
    auto z1 = [=](int x){ return x+y; }           // return type is double
    auto z2 = [=,y]{ if (y) return 1; else return 2; }    // error: body too complicated
                                                  // for return type deduction
    auto z3 =[y]() { return 1 : 2; }              // return type is int
    auto z4 = [=,y]()->int { if (y) return 1; else return 2; }   // OK: explicit return type
}
```

When the suffix return type notation is used, we cannot omit the argument list.

11.4.5 The Type of a Lambda

To allow for optimized versions of lambda expressions, the type of a lambda expression is not defined. However, it is defined to be the type of a function object in the style presented in §11.4.1. This type, called the *closure type*, is unique to the lambda, so no two lambdas have the same type. Had two lambdas had the same type, the template instantiation mechanism might have gotten confused. A lambda is of a local class type with a constructor and a **const** member function **operator()()**. In addition to using a lambda as an argument, we can use it to initialize a variable declared **auto** or **std::function<R(AL)>** where **R** is the lambda's return type and **AL** is its argument list of types (§33.5.3).

For example, I might try to write a lambda to reverse the characters in a C-style string:

```
auto rev = [&rev](char∗ b, char∗ e)
            { if (1<e−b) { swap(∗b,∗−−e); rev(++b,e); } };      // error
```

However, that's not possible because I cannot use an **auto** variable before its type has been deduced. Instead, I can introduce a name and then use it:

```
void f(string& s1, string& s2)
{
    function<void(char∗ b, char∗ e)> rev =
        [&](char∗ b, char∗ e) { if (1<e−b) { swap(∗b,∗−−e); rev(++b,e); } };
```

```
        rev(&s1[0],&s1[0]+s1.size());
        rev(&s2[0],&s2[0]+s2.size());
}
```

Now, the type of **rev** is specified before it is used.

If we just want to name a lambda, rather than using it recursively, **auto** can simplify things:

```
void g(vector<string>& vs1, vector<string>& vs2)
{
        auto rev = [&](char* b, char* e) { while (1<e–b) swap(*b++,*––e); };

        rev(&s1[0],&s1[0]+s1.size());
        rev(&s2[0],&s2[0]+s2.size());
}
```

A lambda that captures nothing can be assigned to a pointer to function of an appropriate type. For example:

```
double (*p1)(double) = [](double a) { return sqrt(a); };
double (*p2)(double) = [&](double a) { return sqrt(a); };      // error: the lambda captures
double (*p3)(int) = [](int a) { return sqrt(a); };             // error: argument types do not match
```

11.5 Explicit Type Conversion

Sometimes, we have to convert a value of one type into a value of another. Many (arguably too many) such conversions are done implicitly according to the language rules (§2.2.2, §10.5). For example:

```
double d = 1234567890;   // integer to floating-point
int i = d;               // floating-point to integer
```

In other cases, we have to be explicit.

For logical and historical reasons, C++ offers explicit type conversion operations of varying convenience and safety:

- Construction, using the {} notation, providing type-safe construction of new values (§11.5.1)
- Named conversions, providing conversions of various degrees of nastiness:
  - **const_cast** for getting write access to something declared **const** (§7.5)
  - **static_cast** for reversing a well-defined implicit conversion (§11.5.2)
  - **reinterpret_cast** for changing the meaning of bit patterns (§11.5.2)
  - **dynamic_cast** for dynamically checked class hierarchy navigation (§22.2.1)
- C-style casts, providing any of the named conversions and some combinations of those (§11.5.3)
- Functional notation, providing a different notation for C-style casts (§11.5.4)

I have ordered these conversions in my order of preference and safety of use.

Except for the {} construction notation, I can't say I like any of those, but at least **dynamic_cast** is run-time checked. For conversion between two scalar numeric types, I tend to use a homemade explicit conversion function, **narrow_cast**, where a value might be narrowed:

```
template<class Target, class Source>
Target narrow_cast(Source v)
{
    auto r = static_cast<Target>(v);        // convert the value to the target type
    if (static_cast<Source>(r)!=v)
        throw runtime_error("narrow_cast<>() failed");
    return r;
}
```

That is, if I can convert a value to the target type, convert the result back to the source type, and get back the original value, I'm happy with the result. That is a generalization of the rule the language applies to values in {} initialization (§6.3.5.2). For example:

```
void test(double d, int i, char* p)
{
    auto c1 = narrow_cast<char>(64);
    auto c2 = narrow_cast<char>(-64);       // will throw if chars are unsigned
    auto c3 = narrow_cast<char>(264);       // will throw if chars are 8-bit and signed

    auto d1 = narrow_cast<double>(1/3.0F); // OK
    auto f1 = narrow_cast<float>(1/3.0);    // will probably throw

    auto c4 = narrow_cast<char>(i);         // may throw
    auto f2 = narrow_cast<float>(d);        // may throw

    auto p1 = narrow_cast<char*>(i);        // compile-time error
    auto i1 = narrow_cast<int>(p);          // compile-time error

    auto d2 = narrow_cast<double>(i);       // may throw (but probably will not)
    auto i2 = narrow_cast<int>(d);          // may throw
}
```

Depending on your use of floating-point numbers, it may be worthwhile to use a range test for floating-point conversions, rather than !=. That is easily done using specializations (§25.3.4.1) or type traits (§35.4.1).

11.5.1 Construction

The construction of a value of type T from a value e can be expressed by the notation T{e} (§iso.8.5.4). For example:

```
auto d1 = double{2};        // d1==2.0
double d2 {double{2}/4};     // d1==0.5
```

Part of the attraction of the T{v} notation is that it will perform only "well-behaved" conversions. For example:

```
void f(int);
void f(double);

void g(int i, double d)
{
    f(i);                                // call f(int)
    f(double{i});                        // error: {} doesn't do int to floating conversion

    f(d);                                // call f(double)
    f(int{d});                           // error: {} doesn't truncate
    f(static_cast<int>(d));              // call f(int) with a truncated value

    f(round(d));                         // call f(double) with a rounded value
    f(static_cast<int>(lround(d)));      // call f(int) with a rounded value
                                         // if the d is overflows the int, this still truncates
}
```

I don't consider truncation of floating-point numbers (e.g., **7.9** to **7**) "well behaved," so having to be explicit when you want it is a good thing. If rounding is desirable, we can use the standard-library function **round()**; it performs "conventional 4/5 rounding," such as **7.9** to **8** and **7.4** to **7**.

It sometimes comes as a surprise that {}-construction doesn't allow **int** to **double** conversion, but if (as is not uncommon) the size of an **int** is the same as the size of a **double**, then some such conversions must lose information. Consider:

```
static_assert(sizeof(int)==sizeof(double),"unexpected sizes");

int x = numeric_limits<int>::max(); // largest possible integer
double d = x;
int y = x;
```

We will not get **x==y**. However, we can still initialize a **double** with an integer literal that can be represented exactly. For example:

```
double d { 1234 };    // fine
```

Explicit qualification with the desired type does not enable ill-behaved conversions. For example:

```
void g2(char* p)
{
    int x = int{p};         // error: no char* to int conversion
    using Pint = int*;
    int* p2 = Pint{p};      // error: no char* to int* conversion
    // ...
}
```

For **T{v}**, "reasonably well behaved" is defined as having a "non-narrowing" (§10.5) conversion from **v** to **T** or having an appropriate constructor for **T** (§17.3).

The constructor notation **T{}** is used to express the default value of type **T**. For example:

```
template<class T> void f(const T&);

void g3()
{
    f(int{});                    // default int value
    f(complex<double>{});        // default complex value
    // ...
}
```

The value of an explicit use of the constructor for a built-in type is **0** converted to that type (§6.3.5). Thus, **int{}** is another way of writing **0**. For a user-defined type **T**, **T{}** is defined by the default constructor (§3.2.1.1, §17.6), if any, otherwise by default construction, **MT{}**, of each member.

Explicitly constructed unnamed objects are temporary objects, and (unless bound to a reference) their lifetime is limited to the full expression in which they are used (§6.4.2). In this, they differ from unnamed objects created using **new** (§11.2).

11.5.2 Named Casts

Some type conversions are not well behaved or easy to type check; they are not simple constructions of values from a well-defined set of argument values. For example:

```
IO_device* d1 = reinterpret_cast<IO_device*>(0Xff00);  // device at 0Xff00
```

There is no way a compiler can know whether the integer **0Xff00** is a valid address (of an I/O device register). Consequently, the correctness of the conversions is completely in the hands of the programmer. Explicit type conversion, often called *casting*, is occasionally essential. However, traditionally it is seriously overused and a major source of errors.

Another classical example of the need for explicit type conversion is dealing with "raw memory," that is, memory that holds or will hold objects of a type not known to the compiler. For example, a memory allocator (such as **operator new()**; §11.2.3) may return a **void*** pointing to newly allocated memory:

```
void* my_allocator(size_t);

void f()
{
    int* p = static_cast<int*>(my_allocator(100));     // new allocation used as ints
    // ...
}
```

A compiler does not know the type of the object pointed to by the **void***.

The fundamental idea behind the named casts is to make type conversion more visible and to allow the programmer to express the intent of a cast:

- **static_cast** converts between related types such as one pointer type to another in the same class hierarchy, an integral type to an enumeration, or a floating-point type to an integral type. It also does conversions defined by constructors (§16.2.6, §18.3.3, §iso.5.2.9) and conversion operators (§18.4).

- **reinterpret_cast** handles conversions between unrelated types such as an integer to a pointer or a pointer to an unrelated pointer type (§iso.5.2.10).
- **const_cast** converts between types that differ only in **const** and **volatile** qualifiers (§iso.5.2.11).
- **dynamic_cast** does run-time checked conversion of pointers and references into a class hierarchy (§22.2.1, §iso.5.2.7).

These distinctions among the named casts allow the compiler to apply some minimal type checking and make it easier for a programmer to find the more dangerous conversions represented as **reinterpret_casts**. Some **static_casts** are portable, but few **reinterpret_casts** are. Hardly any guarantees are made for **reinterpret_cast**, but generally it produces a value of a new type that has the same bit pattern as its argument. If the target has at least as many bits as the original value, we can **reinterpret_cast** the result back to its original type and use it. The result of a **reinterpret_cast** is guaranteed to be usable only if its result is converted back to the exact original type. Note that **reinterpret_cast** is the kind of conversion that must be used for pointers to functions (§12.5). Consider:

```
char x = 'a';
int* p1 = &x;                            // error: no implicit char* to int* conversion
int* p2 = static_cast<int*>(&x);         // error: no implicit char* to int* conversion
int* p3 = reinterpret_cast<int*>(&x);    // OK: on your head be it

struct B { /* ... */ };
struct D : B { /* ... */ };              // see §3.2.2 and §20.5.2

B* pb = new D;                           // OK: implicit conversion from D* to B*
D* pd = pb;                              // error: no implicit conversion from B* to D*
D* pd = static_cast<D*>(pb);            // OK
```

Conversions among class pointers and among class reference types are discussed in §22.2.

If you feel tempted to use an explicit type conversion, take the time to consider if it is *really* necessary. In C++, explicit type conversion is unnecessary in most cases when C needs it (§1.3.3) and also in many cases in which earlier versions of C++ needed it (§1.3.2, §44.2.3). In many programs, explicit type conversion can be completely avoided; in others, its use can be localized to a few routines.

11.5.3 C-Style Cast

From C, C++ inherited the notation (T)e, which performs any conversion that can be expressed as a combination of **static_casts**, **reinterpret_casts**, **const_casts** to make a value of type T from the expression e (§44.2.3). Unfortunately, the C-style cast can also cast from a pointer to a class to a pointer to a private base of that class. Never do that, and hope for a warning from the compiler if you do it by mistake. This C-style cast is far more dangerous than the named conversion operators because the notation is harder to spot in a large program and the kind of conversion intended by the programmer is not explicit. That is, (T)e might be doing a portable conversion between related types, a nonportable conversion between unrelated types, or removing the **const** modifier from a pointer type. Without knowing the exact types of T and e, you cannot tell.

11.5.4 Function-Style Cast

The construction of a value of type **T** from a value **e** can be expressed by the functional notation
T(e). For example:

```
void f(double d)
{
    int i = int(d);              // truncate d
    complex z = complex(d); // make a complex from d
    // ...
}
```

The **T(e)** construct is sometimes referred to as a *function-style cast*. Unfortunately, for a built-in
type **T**, **T(e)** is equivalent to **(T)e** (§11.5.3). This implies that for many built-in types **T(e)** is not safe.

```
void f(double d, char* p)
{
    int a = int(d);    // truncates
    int b = int(p);    // not portable
    // ...
}
```

Even explicit conversion of a longer integer type to a shorter (such as **long** to **char**) can result in
nonportable implementation-defined behavior.

Prefer **T{v}** conversions for well-behaved construction and the named casts (e.g., **static_cast**) for
other conversions.

11.6 Advice

[1]   Prefer prefix ++ over suffix ++; §11.1.4.
[2]   Use resource handles to avoid leaks, premature deletion, and double deletion; §11.2.1.
[3]   Don't put objects on the free store if you don't have to; prefer scoped variables; §11.2.1.
[4]   Avoid "naked **new**" and "naked **delete**"; §11.2.1.
[5]   Use RAII; §11.2.1.
[6]   Prefer a named function object to a lambda if the operation requires comments; §11.4.2.
[7]   Prefer a named function object to a lambda if the operation is generally useful; §11.4.2.
[8]   Keep lambdas short; §11.4.2.
[9]   For maintainability and correctness, be careful about capture by reference; §11.4.3.1.
[10]   Let the compiler deduce the return type of a lambda; §11.4.4.
[11]   Use the **T{e}** notation for construction; §11.5.1.
[12]   Avoid explicit type conversion (casts); §11.5.
[13]   When explicit type conversion is necessary, prefer a named cast; §11.5.
[14]   Consider using a run-time checked cast, such as **narrow_cast<>()**, for conversion between
        numeric types; §11.5.

12

Functions

Death to all fanatics!
– Paradox

12.1 Function Declarations

The main way of getting something done in a C++ program is to call a function to do it. Defining a function is the way you specify how an operation is to be done. A function cannot be called unless it has been previously declared.

A function declaration gives the name of the function, the type of the value returned (if any), and the number and types of the arguments that must be supplied in a call. For example:

```cpp
Elem* next_elem();          // no argument; return an Elem*
void exit(int);             // int argument; return nothing
double sqrt(double);        // double argument; return a double
```

The semantics of argument passing are identical to the semantics of copy initialization (§16.2.6). Argument types are checked and implicit argument type conversion takes place when necessary. For example:

```
double s2 = sqrt(2);          // call sqrt() with the argument double{2}
double s3 = sqrt("three");    // error: sqrt() requires an argument of type double
```

The value of such checking and type conversion should not be underestimated.

A function declaration may contain argument names. This can be a help to the reader of a program, but unless the declaration is also a function definition, the compiler simply ignores such names. As a return type, **void** means that the function does not return a value (§6.2.7).

The type of a function consists of the return type and the argument types. For class member functions (§2.3.2, §16.2), the name of the class is also part of the function type. For example:

```
double f(int i, const Info&);      // type: double(int,const Info&)
char& String::operator[](int);     // type: char& String::(int)
```

12.1.1 Why Functions?

There is a long and disreputable tradition of writing very long functions – hundreds of lines long. I once encountered a single (handwritten) function with more than 32,768 lines of code. Writers of such functions seem to fail to appreciate one of the primary purposes of functions: to break up complicated computations into meaningful chunks and name them. We want our code to be comprehensible, because that is the first step on the way to maintainability. The first step to comprehensibility is to break computational tasks into comprehensible chunks (represented as functions and classes) and name those. Such functions then provide the basic vocabulary of computation, just as the types (built-in and user-defined) provide the basic vocabulary of data. The C++ standard algorithms (e.g., **find**, **sort**, and **iota**) provide a good start (Chapter 32). Next, we can compose functions representing common or specialized tasks into larger computations.

The number of errors in code correlates strongly with the amount of code and the complexity of the code. Both problems can be addressed by using more and shorter functions. Using a function to do a specific task often saves us from writing a specific piece of code in the middle of other code; making it a function forces us to name the activity and document its dependencies. Also, function call and return saves us from using error-prone control structures, such as **goto**s (§9.6) and **contin-ue**s (§9.5.5). Unless they are very regular in structure, nested loops are an avoidable source of errors (e.g., use a dot product to express a matrix algorithm rather than nesting loops; §40.6).

The most basic advice is to keep a function of a size so that you can look at it in total on a screen. Bugs tend to creep in when we can view only part of an algorithm at a time. For many programmers that puts a limit of about 40 lines on a function. My ideal is a much smaller size still, maybe an average of 7 lines.

In essentially all cases, the cost of a function call is not a significant factor. Where that cost could be significant (e.g., for frequently used access functions, such as vector subscripting) inlining can eliminate it (§12.1.5). Use functions as a structuring mechanism.

12.1.2 Parts of a Function Declaration

In addition to specifying a name, a set of arguments, and a return type, a function declaration can contain a variety of specifiers and modifiers. In all we can have:

- The name of the function; required
- The argument list, which may be empty (); required
- The return type, which may be **void** and which may be prefix or suffix (using **auto**); required
- **inline**, indicating a desire to have function calls implemented by inlining the function body (§12.1.5)
- **constexpr**, indicating that it should be possible to evaluate the function at compile time if given constant expressions as arguments (§12.1.6)
- **noexcept**, indicating that the function may not throw an exception (§13.5.1.1)
- A linkage specification, for example, **static** (§15.2)
- **[[noreturn]]**, indicating that the function will not return using the normal call/return mechanism (§12.1.4)

In addition, a member function may be specified as:

- **virtual**, indicating that it can be overridden in a derived class (§20.3.2)
- **override**, indicating that it must be overriding a virtual function from a base class (§20.3.4.1)
- **final**, indicating that it cannot be overriden in a derived class (§20.3.4.2)
- **static**, indicating that it is not associated with a particular object (§16.2.12)
- **const**, indicating that it may not modify its object (§3.2.1.1, §16.2.9.1)

If you feel inclined to give readers a headache, you may write something like:

```
struct S {
    [[noreturn]] virtual inline auto f(const unsigned long int *const) -> void const noexcept;
};
```

12.1.3 Function Definitions

Every function that is called must be defined somewhere (once only; §15.2.3). A function definition is a function declaration in which the body of the function is presented. For example:

```
void swap(int*, int*);          // a declaration

void swap(int* p, int* q)       // a definition
{
    int t = *p;
    *p = *q;
    *q = t;
}
```

The definition and all declarations for a function must specify the same type. Unfortunately, to preserve C compatibility, a **const** is ignored at the highest level of an argument type. For example, this is two declarations of the same function:

```
void f(int);            // type is void(int)
void f(const int);      // type is void(int)
```

That function, f(), could be defined as:

```
void f(int x) { /*we can modify x here */ }
```

Alternatively, we could define f() as:

```
void f(const int x) { /*we cannot modify x here */ }
```

In either case, the argument that f() can or cannot modify is a copy of what a caller provided, so there is no danger of an obscure modification of the calling context.

Function argument names are not part of the function type and need not be identical in different declarations. For example:

```
int& max(int& a, int& b, int& c); // return a reference to the larger of a, b, and c

int& max(int& x1, int& x2, int& x3)
{
        return (x1>x2)? ((x1>x3)?x1:x3) : ((x2>x3)?x2:x3);
}
```

Naming arguments in declarations that are not definitions is optional and commonly used to simplify documentation. Conversely, we can indicate that an argument is unused in a function definition by not naming it. For example:

```
void search(table* t, const char* key, const char*)
{
        // no use of the third argument
}
```

Typically, unnamed arguments arise from the simplification of code or from planning ahead for extensions. In both cases, leaving the argument in place, although unused, ensures that callers are not affected by the change.

In addition to functions, there are a few other things that we can call; these follow most rules defined for functions, such as the rules for argument passing (§12.2):

- *Constructors* (§2.3.2, §16.2.5) are technicallly not functions; in particular, they don't return a value, can initialize bases and members (§17.4), and can't have their address taken.
- *Destructors* (§3.2.1.2, §17.2) can't be overloaded and can't have their address taken.
- *Function objects* (§3.4.3, §19.2.2) are not functions (they are objects) and can't be overloaded, but their operator()s are functions.
- *Lambda expressions* (§3.4.3, §11.4) are basically a shorthand for defining function objects.

12.1.4 Returning Values

Every function declaration contains a specification of the function's *return type* (except for constructors and type conversion functions). Traditionally, in C and C++, the return type comes first in a function declaration (before the name of the function). However, a function declaration can also be written using a syntax that places the return type after the argument list. For example, the following two declarations are equivalent:

```
string to_string(int a);            // prefix return type
auto to_string(int a) -> string;    // suffix return type
```

That is, a prefix **auto** indicates that the return type is placed after the argument list. The suffix return type is preceded by –>.

The essential use for a suffix return type comes in function template declarations in which the return type depends on the arguments. For example:

```
template<class T, class U>
auto product(const vector<T>& x, const vector<U>& y) -> decltype(x*y);
```

However, the suffix return syntax can be used for any function. There is an obvious similarity between the suffix return syntax for a function and the lambda expression syntax (§3.4.3, §11.4); it is a pity those two constructs are not identical.

A function that does not return a value has a "return type" of **void**.

A value must be returned from a function that is not declared **void** (however, **main()** is special; see §2.2.1). Conversely, a value cannot be returned from a **void** function. For example:

```
int f1() { }            // error: no value returned
void f2() { }           // OK

int f3() { return 1; }  // OK
void f4() { return 1; } // error: return value in void function

int f5() { return; }    // error: return value missing
void f6() { return; }   // OK
```

A return value is specified by a **return**-statement. For example:

```
int fac(int n)
{
    return (n>1) ? n*fac(n–1) : 1;
}
```

A function that calls itself is said to be *recursive*.

There can be more than one **return**-statement in a function:

```
int fac2(int n)
{
    if (n > 1)
        return n*fac2(n–1);
    return 1;
}
```

Like the semantics of argument passing, the semantics of function value return are identical to the semantics of copy initialization (§16.2.6). A **return**-statement initializes a variable of the returned type. The type of a return expression is checked against the type of the returned type, and all standard and user-defined type conversions are performed. For example:

```
double f() { return 1; }     // 1 is implicitly converted to double{1}
```

Each time a function is called, a new copy of its arguments and local (automatic) variables is created. The store is reused after the function returns, so a pointer to a local non-**static** variable should never be returned. The contents of the location pointed to will change unpredictably:

```
int* fp()
{
    int local = 1;
    // ...
    return &local;  // bad
}
```

An equivalent error can occur when using references:

```
int& fr()
{
    int local = 1;
    // ...
    return local;   // bad
}
```

Fortunately, a compiler can easily warn about returning references to local variables (and most do).

There are no **void** values. However, a call of a **void** function may be used as the return value of a **void** function. For example:

```
void g(int* p);

void h(int* p)
{
    // ...
    return g(p);    // OK: equivalent to "g(p); return;"
}
```

This form of return is useful to avoid special cases when writing template functions where the return type is a template parameter.

A **return**-statement is one of five ways of exiting a function:

- Executing a **return**-statement.
- "Falling off the end" of a function; that is, simply reaching the end of the function body. This is allowed only in functions that are not declared to return a value (i.e., **void** functions) and in **main()**, where falling off the end indicates successful completion (§12.1.4).
- Throwing an exception that isn't caught locally (§13.5).
- Terminating because an exception was thrown and not caught locally in a **noexcept** function (§13.5.1.1).
- Directly or indirectly invoking a system function that doesn't return (e.g., **exit()**; §15.4).

A function that does not return normally (i.e., through a **return** or "falling off the end") can be marked [[noreturn]] (§12.1.7).

12.1.5 inline Functions

A function can be defined to be **inline**. For example:

```
inline int fac(int n)
{
    return (n<2) ? 1 : n*fac(n–1);
}
```

The inline specifier is a hint to the compiler that it should attempt to generate code for a call of fac() inline rather than laying down the code for the function once and then calling through the usual function call mechanism. A clever compiler can generate the constant 720 for a call fac(6). The possibility of mutually recursive inline functions, inline functions that recurse or not depending on input, etc., makes it impossible to guarantee that every call of an inline function is actually inlined. The degree of cleverness of a compiler cannot be legislated, so one compiler might generate 720, another 6∗fac(5), and yet another an un-inlined call fac(6). If you want a guarantee that a value is computed at compile time, declare it constexpr and make sure that all functions used in its evaluation are constexpr (§12.1.6).

To make inlining possible in the absence of unusually clever compilation and linking facilities, the definition – and not just the declaration – of an inline function must be in scope (§15.2). An inline specifier does not affect the semantics of a function. In particular, an inline function still has a unique address, and so do static variables (§12.1.8) of an inline function.

If an inline function is defined in more than one translation unit (e.g., typically because it was defined in a header; §15.2.2), its definition in the different translation units must be identical (§15.2.3).

12.1.6 constexpr Functions

In general, a function cannot be evaluated at compile time and therefore cannot be called in a constant expression (§2.2.3, §10.4). By specifying a function constexpr, we indicate that we want it to be usable in constant expressions if given constant expressions as arguments. For example:

```
constexpr int fac(int n)
{
    return (n>1) ? n∗fac(n−1) : 1;
}

constexpr int f9 = fac(9);        // must be evaluated at compile time
```

When constexpr is used in a function definition, it means "should be usable in a constant expression when given constant expressions as arguments." When used in an object definition, it means "evaluate the initializer at compile time." For example:

```
void f(int n)
{
    int f5 = fac(5);              // may be evaluated at compile time
    int fn = fac(n);              // evaluated at run time (n is a variable)

    constexpr int f6 = fac(6);    // must be evaluated at compile time
    constexpr int fnn = fac(n);   // error: can't guarantee compile-time evaluation (n is a variable)

    char a[fac(4)];               // OK: array bounds must be constants and fac() is constexpr
    char a2[fac(n)];              // error: array bounds must be constants and n is a variable

    // ...
}
```

To be evaluated at compile time, a function must be suitably simple: a constexpr function must consist of a single **return**-statement; no loops and no local variables are allowed. Also, a **constexpr** function may not have side effects. That is, a **constexpr** function is a pure function. For example:

```
int glob;

constexpr void bad1(int a)      // error: constexpr function cannot be void
{
      glob = a;                 // error: side effect in constexpr function
}

constexpr int bad2(int a)
{
      if (a>=0) return a; else return –a;    // error: if-statement in constexpr function
}

constexpr int bad3(int a)
{
      sum = 0;                              // error: local variable in constexpr function
      for (int i=0; i<a; +=i) sum +=fac(i); // error: loop in constexpr function
      return sum;
}
```

The rules for a **constexpr** constructor are suitably different (§10.4.3); there, only simple initialization of members is allowed.

A **constexpr** function allows recursion and conditional expressions. This implies that you can express just about anything as a **constexpr** function if you really want to. However, you'll find the debugging gets unnecessarily difficult and compile times longer than you would like unless you restrict the use of **constexpr** functions to the relatively simple tasks for which they are intended.

By using literal types (§10.4.3), **constexpr** functions can be defined to use user-defined types.

Like inline functions, **constexpr** functions obey the ODR ("one-definition rule"), so that definitions in the different translation units must be identical (§15.2.3). You can think of **constexpr** functions as a restricted form of inline functions (§12.1.5).

12.1.6.1 constexpr and References

A **constexpr** function cannot have side effects, so writing to nonlocal objects is not possible. However, a **constexpr** function can refer to nonlocal objects as long as it does not write to them.

```
constexpr int ftbl[] { 1, 2, 3, 5, 8, 13 };

constexpr int fib(int n)
{
      return (n<sizeof(ftbl)/sizeof(*ftbl)) ? ftbl[n] : fib(n);
}
```

A **constexpr** function can take reference arguments. Of course, it cannot write through such references, but **const** reference parameters are as useful as ever. For example, in the standard library (§40.4) we find:

```
template<> class complex<float> {
public:
// ...
    explicit constexpr complex(const complex<double>&);
    // ...
};
```

This allows us to write:

```
constexpr complex<float> z {2.0};
```

The temporary variable that is logically constructed to hold the **const** reference argument simply becomes a value internal to the compiler.

It is possible for a **constexpr** function to return a reference or a pointer. For example:

```
constexpr const int* addr(const int& r) { return &r; }     // OK
```

However, doing so brings us away from the fundamental role of **constexpr** functions as parts of constant expression evaluation. In particular, it can be quite tricky to determine whether the result of such a function is a constant expression. Consider:

```
static const int x = 5;
constexpr const int* p1 = addr(x);        // OK
constexpr int xx = *p1;                    // OK

static int y;
constexpr const int* p2 = addr(y);        // OK
constexpr int yy = *y;                     // error: attempt to read a variable

constexpr const int* tp = addr(5);        // error: address of temporary
```

12.1.6.2 Conditional Evaluation

A branch of a conditional expression that is not taken in a **constexpr** function is not evaluated. This implies that a branch not taken can require run-time evaluation. For example:

```
constexpr int check(int i)
{
    return (low<=i && i<high) ? i : throw out_of_range();
}

constexpr int low = 0;
constexpr int  high = 99;


// ...
constexpr int val = check(f(x,y,z));
```

You might imagine **low** and **high** to be configuration parameters that are known at compile time, but not at design time, and that **f(x,y,z)** computes some implementation-dependent value.

12.1.7 [[noreturn]] Functions

A construct [[...]] is called an *attribute* and can be placed just about anywhere in the C++ syntax. In general, an attribute specifies some implementation-dependent property about the syntactic entity that precedes it. In addition, an attribute can be placed in front of a declaration. There are only two standard attributes (§iso.7.6), and [[noreturn]] is one of them. The other is [[carries_dependency]] (§41.3).

Placing [[noreturn]] at the start of a function declaration indicates that the function is not expected to return. For example:

```
[[noreturn]] void exit(int);       // exit will never return
```

Knowing that a function does not return is useful for both comprehension and code generation. What happens if the function returns despite a [[noreturn]] attribute is undefined.

12.1.8 Local Variables

A name defined in a function is commonly referred to as a *local name*. A local variable or constant is initialized when a thread of execution reaches its definition. Unless declared **static**, each invocation of the function has its own copy of the variable. If a local variable is declared **static**, a single, statically allocated object (§6.4.2) will be used to represent that variable in all calls of the function. It will be initialized only the first time a thread of execution reaches its definition. For example:

```
void f(int a)
{
    while (a--) {
        static int n = 0;       // initialized once
        int x = 0;              // initialized 'a' times in each call of f()

        cout << "n == " << n++ << ", x == " << x++ << '\n';
    }
}

int main()
{
    f(3);
}
```

This prints:

```
n == 0, x == 0
n == 1, x == 0
n == 2, x == 0
```

A **static** local variable allows the function to preserve information between calls without introducing a global variable that might be accessed and corrupted by other functions (see also §16.2.12).

Initialization of a **static** local variable does not lead to a data race (§5.3.1) unless you enter the function containing it recursively or a deadlock occurs (§iso.6.7). That is, the C++ implementation must guard the initialization of a local **static** variable with some kind of lock-free construct (e.g., a call_once; §42.3.3). The effect of initializing a local **static** recursively is undefined. For example:

```
int fn(int n)
{
    static int n1 = n;          // OK
    static int n2 = fn(n–1)+1;  // undefined
    return n;
}
```

A **static** local variable is useful for avoiding order dependencies among nonlocal variables (§15.4.1).

There are no local functions; if you feel you need one, use a function object or a lambda expression (§3.4.3, §11.4).

The scope of a label (§9.6), should you be foolhardy enough to use one, is the complete function, independent of which nested scope it may be in.

12.2 Argument Passing

When a function is called (using the suffix (), known as the *call operator* or *application operator*), store is set aside for its *formal arguments* (also known as its *parameters*), and each formal argument is initialized by its corresponding actual argument. The semantics of argument passing are identical to the semantics of initialization (copy initialization, to be precise; §16.2.6). In particular, the type of an actual argument is checked against the type of the corresponding formal argument, and all standard and user-defined type conversions are performed. Unless a formal argument (parameter) is a reference, a copy of the actual argument is passed to the function. For example:

```
int* find(int* first, int* last, int v)   // find x in [first:last)
{
    while (first!=last && *first!=v)
            ++first;
    return first;
}

void g(int* p, int* q)
{
    int* pp = find(p,q,'x');
    // ...
}
```

Here, the caller's copy of the argument, **p**, is not modified by the operations on **find()**'s copy, called **first**. The pointer is passed by value.

There are special rules for passing arrays (§12.2.2), a facility for passing unchecked arguments (§12.2.4), and a facility for specifying default arguments (§12.2.5). The use of initializer lists is described in §12.2.3 and the ways of passing arguments to template functions in §23.5.2 and §28.6.2.

12.2.1 Reference Arguments

Consider:

```
void f(int val, int& ref)
{
    ++val;
    ++ref;
}
```

When f() is called, ++val increments a local copy of the first actual argument, whereas ++ref increments the second actual argument. Consider:

```
void g()
{
    int i = 1;
    int j = 1;
    f(i,j);
}
```

The call f(i,j) will increment j but not i. The first argument, i, is passed *by value*; the second argument, j, is passed *by reference*. As mentioned in §7.7, functions that modify call-by-reference arguments can make programs hard to read and should most often be avoided (but see §18.2.5). It can, however, be noticeably more efficient to pass a large object by reference than to pass it by value. In that case, the argument might be declared a **const** reference to indicate that the reference is used for efficiency reasons only and not to enable the called function to change the value of the object:

```
void f(const Large& arg)
{
    // the value of "arg" cannot be changed
    // (except by using explicit type conversion; §11.5)
}
```

The absence of **const** in the declaration of a reference argument is taken as a statement of intent to modify the variable:

```
void g(Large& arg);        // assume that g() modifies arg
```

Similarly, declaring a pointer argument **const** tells readers that the value of an object pointed to by that argument is not changed by the function. For example:

```
int strlen(const char*);              // number of characters in a C-style string
char* strcpy(char* to, const char* from);    // copy a C-style string
int strcmp(const char*, const char*);    // compare C-style strings
```

The importance of using **const** arguments increases with the size of a program.

Note that the semantics of argument passing are different from the semantics of assignment. This is important for **const** arguments, reference arguments, and arguments of some user-defined types.

Following the rules for reference initialization, a literal, a constant, and an argument that requires conversion can be passed as a **const T&** argument, but not as a plain (non-**const**) **T&** argument. Allowing conversions for a **const T&** argument ensures that such an argument can be given exactly the same set of values as a T argument by passing the value in a temporary, if necessary. For example:

```
float fsqrt(const float&);   // Fortran-style sqrt taking a reference argument

void g(double d)
{
    float r = fsqrt(2.0f);    // pass reference to temp holding 2.0f
    r = fsqrt(r);             // pass reference to r
    r = fsqrt(d);             // pass reference to temp holding static_cast<float>(d)
}
```

Disallowing conversions for non-**const** reference arguments (§7.7) avoids the possibility of silly mistakes arising from the introduction of temporaries. For example:

```
void update(float& i);

void g(double d, float r)
{
    update(2.0f);    // error: const argument
    update(r);       // pass reference to r
    update(d);       // error: type conversion required
}
```

Had these calls been allowed, **update()** would quietly have updated temporaries that immediately were deleted. Usually, that would come as an unpleasant surprise to the programmer.

If we wanted to be precise, pass-by-reference would be pass-by-lvalue-reference because a function can also take rvalue references. As described in §7.7, an rvalue can be bound to an rvalue reference (but not to an lvalue reference) and an lvalue can be bound to an lvalue reference (but not to an rvalue reference). For example:

```
void f(vector<int>&);          // (non-const) lvalue reference argument
void f(const vector<int>&);    // const lvalue reference argument
void f(vector<int>&&);         // rvalue reference argument

void g(vector<int>& vi, const vector<int>& cvi)
{
    f(vi);                  // call f(vector<int>&)
    f(cvi);                 // call f(const vector<int>&)
    f(vector<int>{1,2,3,4}); // call f(vector<int>&&);
}
```

We must assume that a function will modify an rvalue argument, leaving it good only for destruction or reassignment (§17.5). The most obvious use of rvalue references is to define move constructors and move assignments (§3.3.2, §17.5.2). I'm sure someone will find a clever use for **const**-rvalue-reference arguments, but so far, I have not seen a genuine use case.

Please note that for a template argument T, the template argument type deduction rules give **T&&** a significantly different meaning from **X&&** for a type **X** (§23.5.2.1). For template arguments, an rvalue reference is most often used to implement "perfect forwarding" (§23.5.2.1, §28.6.3).

How do we choose among the ways of passing arguments? My rules of thumb are:

[1]   Use pass-by-value for small objects.

[2]   Use pass-by-**const**-reference to pass large values that you don't need to modify.

[3]   Return a result as a **return** value rather than modifying an object through an argument.

[4]   Use rvalue references to implement move (§3.3.2, §17.5.2) and forwarding (§23.5.2.1).

[5]   Pass a pointer if "no object" is a valid alternative (and represent "no object" by **nullptr**).

[6]   Use pass-by-reference only if you have to.

The "when you have to" in the last rule of thumb refers to the observation that passing pointers is often a less obscure mechanism for dealing with objects that need modification (§7.7.1, §7.7.4) than using references.

12.2.2 Array Arguments

If an array is used as a function argument, a pointer to its initial element is passed. For example:

```
int strlen(const char*);

void f()
{
    char v[] = "Annemarie";
    int i = strlen(v);
    int j = strlen("Nicholas");
}
```

That is, an argument of type **T[]** will be converted to a **T*** when passed as an argument. This implies that an assignment to an element of an array argument changes the value of an element of the argument array. In other words, arrays differ from other types in that an array is not passed by value. Instead, a pointer is passed (by value).

A parameter of array type is equivalent to a parameter of pointer type. For example:

```
void odd(int* p);
void odd(int a[]);
void odd(int buf[1020]);
```

These three declarations are equivalent and declare the same function. As usual, the argument names do not affect the type of the function (§12.1.3). The rules and techniques for passing multi-dimensional arrays can be found in §7.4.3.

The size of an array is not available to the called function. This is a major source of errors, but there are several ways of circumventing this problem. C-style strings are zero-terminated, so their size can be computed (e.g., by a potentially expensive call of **strlen()**; §43.4). For other arrays, a second argument specifying the size can be passed. For example:

```
void compute1(int* vec_ptr, int vec_size);    // one way
```

At best, this is a workaround. It is usually preferable to pass a reference to some container, such as **vector** (§4.4.1, §31.4), **array** (§34.2.1), or **map** (§4.4.3, §31.4.3).

If you really want to pass an array, rather than a container or a pointer to the first element of an array, you can declare a parameter of type reference to array. For example:

```
void f(int(&r)[4]);

void g()
{
    int a1[] = {1,2,3,4};
    int a2[] = {1,2};

    f(a1);      // OK
    f(a2);      // error : wrong number of elements
}
```

Note that the number of elements is part of a reference-to-array type. That makes such references far less flexible than pointers and containers (such as **vector**). The main use of references to arrays is in templates, where the number of elements is then deduced. For example:

```
template<class T, int N> void f(T(&r)[N])
{
    // ...
}

int a1[10];
double a2[100];

void g()
{
    f(a1);      // T is int; N is 10
    f(a2);      // T is double; N is 100
}
```

This typically gives rise to as many function definitions as there are calls to f() with distinct array types.

Multidimensional arrays are tricky (see §7.3), but often arrays of pointers can be used instead, and they need no special treatment. For example:

```
const char* day[] = {
    "mon", "tue", "wed", "thu", "fri", "sat", "sun"
};
```

As ever, **vector** and similar types are alternatives to the built-in, low-level arrays and pointers.

12.2.3 List Arguments

A {}-delimited list can be used as an argument to a parameter of:

[1]   Type **std::initializer_list<T>**, where the values of the list can be implicitly converted to **T**

[2]   A type that can be initialized with the values provided in the list

[3]   A reference to an array of **T**, where the values of the list can be implicitly converted to **T**

Technically, case [2] covers all examples, but I find it easier to think of the three cases separately. Consider:

```
template<class T>
void f1(initializer_list<T>);

struct S {
     int a;
     string s;
};
void f2(S);

template<class T, int N>
void f3(T (&r)[N]);

void f4(int);

void g()
{
     f1({1,2,3,4});    // T is int and the initializer_list has size() 4
     f2({1,"MKS"});    // f2(S{1,"MKS"})
     f3({1,2,3,4});    // T is int and N is 4
     f4({1});          // f4(int{1});
}
```

If there is a possible ambiguity, an **initializer_list** parameter takes priority. For example:

```
template<class T>
void f(initializer_list<T>);

struct S {
     int a;
     string s;
};
void f(S);

template<class T, int N>
void f(T (&r)[N]);

void f(int);

void g()
{
     f({1,2,3,4});    // T is int and the initializer_list has size() 4
     f({1,"MKS"});    // calls f(S)
     f({1});          // T is int and the initializer_list has size() 1
}
```

The reason that a function with an **initializer_list** argument take priority is that it could be very confusing if different functions were chosen based on the number of elements of a list. It is not possible to eliminate every form of confusion in overload resolution (for example, see §4.4, §17.3.4.1), but giving **initializer_list** parameters priority for {}-list arguments seems to minimize confusion.

If there is a function with an initializer-list argument in scope, but the argument list isn't a match for that, another function can be chosen. The call f({1,"MKS"}) was an example of that.

Note that these rules apply to std::initializer_list<T> arguments only. There are no special rules for std::initializer_list<T>& or for other types that just happen to be called initializer_list (in some other scope).

12.2.4 Unspecified Number of Arguments

For some functions, it is not possible to specify the number and type of all arguments expected in a call. To implement such interfaces, we have three choices:

[1] Use a variadic template (§28.6): this allows us to handle an arbitrary number of arbitrary types in a type-safe manner by writing a small template metaprogram that interprets the argument list to determine its meaning and take appropriate actions.

[2] Use an initializer_list as the argument type (§12.2.3). This allows us to handle an arbitrary number of arguments of a single type in a type-safe manner. In many contexts, such homogeneous lists are the most common and important case.

[3] Terminate the argument list with the ellipsis (...), which means "and maybe some more arguments." This allows us to handle an arbitrary number of (almost) arbitrary types by using some macros from <cstdarg>. This solution is *not* inherently type-safe and can be hard to use with sophisticated user-defined types. However, this mechanism has been used from the earliest days of C.

The first two mechanisms are described elsewhere, so I describe only the third mechanism (even though I consider it inferior to the others for most uses). For example:

```
int printf(const char* ...);
```

This specifies that a call of the standard-library function printf() (§43.3) must have at least one argument, a C-style string, but may or may not have others. For example:

```
printf("Hello, world!\n");
printf("My name is %s %s\n", first_name, second_name);
printf("%d + %d = %d\n",2,3,5);
```

Such a function must rely on information not available to the compiler when interpreting its argument list. In the case of printf(), the first argument is a format string containing special character sequences that allow printf() to handle other arguments correctly; %s means "expect a char* argument" and %d means "expect an int argument." However, the compiler cannot in general ensure that the expected arguments are really provided in a call or that an argument is of the expected type. For example:

```
#include <cstdio>

int main()
{
    std::printf("My name is %s %s\n",2);
}
```

This is not valid code, but most compilers will not catch this error. At best, it will produce some strange-looking output (try it!).

Clearly, if an argument has not been declared, the compiler does not have the information needed to perform the standard type checking and type conversion for it. In that case, a **char** or a **short** is passed as an **int** and a **float** is passed as a **double**. This is not necessarily what the programmer expects.

A well-designed program needs at most a few functions for which the argument types are not completely specified. Overloaded functions, functions using default arguments, functions taking **initializer_list** arguments, and variadic templates can be used to take care of type checking in most cases when one would otherwise consider leaving argument types unspecified. Only when both the number of arguments *and* the types of arguments vary *and* a variadic template solution is deemed undesirable is the ellipsis necessary.

The most common use of the ellipsis is to specify an interface to C library functions that were defined before C++ provided alternatives:

```
int fprintf(FILE*, const char* ...);      // from <cstdio>
int execl(const char* ...);               // from UNIX header
```

A standard set of macros for accessing the unspecified arguments in such functions can be found in **<cstdarg>**. Consider writing an error function that takes one integer argument indicating the severity of the error followed by an arbitrary number of strings. The idea is to compose the error message by passing each word as a separate C-style string argument. The list of string arguments should be terminated by the null pointer:

```
extern void error(int ...);
extern char* itoa(int, char[]);   // int to alpha

int main(int argc, char* argv[])
{
    switch (argc) {
    case 1:
        error(0,argv[0],nullptr);
        break;
    case 2:
        error(0,argv[0],argv[1],nullptr);
        break;
    default:
        char buffer[8];
        error(1,argv[0],"with",itoa(argc–1,buffer),"arguments",nullptr);
    }
    // ...
}
```

The function **itoa()** returns a C-style string representing its **int** argument. It is popular in C, but not part of the C standard.

I always pass **argv[0]** because that, conventionally, is the name of the program.

Note that using the integer **0** as the terminator would not have been portable: on some implementations, the integer 0 and the null pointer do not have the same representation (§6.2.8). This illustrates the subtleties and extra work that face the programmer once type checking has been suppressed using the ellipsis.

The **error()** function could be defined like this:

```
#include <cstdarg>

void error(int severity ...) // "severity" followed by a zero-terminated list of char*s
{
    va_list ap;
    va_start(ap,severity);      // arg startup

    for (;;) {
        char* p = va_arg(ap,char*);
        if (p == nullptr) break;
        cerr << p << ' ';
    }

    va_end(ap);                 // arg cleanup

    cerr << '\n';
    if (severity) exit(severity);
}
```

First, a **va_list** is defined and initialized by a call of **va_start()**. The macro **va_start** takes the name of the **va_list** and the name of the last formal argument as arguments. The macro **va_arg()** is used to pick the unnamed arguments in order. In each call, the programmer must supply a type; **va_arg()** assumes that an actual argument of that type has been passed, but it typically has no way of ensuring that. Before returning from a function in which **va_start()** has been used, **va_end()** must be called. The reason is that **va_start()** may modify the stack in such a way that a return cannot successfully be done; **va_end()** undoes any such modifications.

Alternatively, **error()** could have been defined using a standard-library **initializer_list**:

```
void error(int severity, initializer_list<string> err)
{
    for (auto& s : err)
        cerr << s << ' ';
    cerr << '\n';
    if (severity) exit(severity);
}
```

It would then have to be called using the list notation. For example:

```
switch (argc) {
case 1:
    error(0,{argv[0]});
    break;
case 2:
    error(0,{argv[0],argv[1]});
    break;
default:
    error(1,{argv[0],"with",to_string(argc–1),"arguments"});
}
```

The int-to-string conversion function to_string() is provided by the standard library (§36.3.5).

If I didn't have to mimic C style, I would further simplify the code by passing a container as a single argument:

```
void error(int severity, const vector<string>& err)  // almost as before
{
    for (auto& s : err)
        cerr << s << ' ';
    cerr << '\n';
    if (severity) exit(severity);
}

vector<string> arguments(int argc, char* argv[]) // package arguments
{
    vector<string> res;
    for (int i = 0; i!=argc; ++i)
        res.push_back(argv[i]);
    return res
}

int main(int argc, char* argv[])
{
    auto args = arguments(argc,argv);
    error((args.size()<2)?0:1,args);
    // ...
}
```

The helper function, arguments(), is trivial, and main() and error() are simple. The interface between main() and error() is more general in that it now passes all arguments. That would allow later improvements of error(). The use of the vector<string> is far less error-prone than any use of an unspecified number of arguments.

12.2.5 Default Arguments

A general function often needs more arguments than are necessary to handle simple cases. In particular, functions that construct objects (§16.2.5) often provide several options for flexibility. Consider class complex from §3.2.1.1:

```
class complex {
    double re, im;
public:
    complex(double r, double i) :re{r}, im{i} {}      // construct complex from two scalars
    complex(double r) :re{r}, im{0} {}                 // construct complex from one scalar
    complex() :re{0}, im{0} {}
// default complex: {0,0}
    // ...
};
```

The actions of complex's constructors are quite trivial, but logically there is something odd about having three functions (here, constructors) doing essentially the same task. Also, for many classes, constructors do more work and the repetitiveness is common. We could deal with the repetitiveness by considering one of the constructors "the real one" and forward to that (§17.4.3):

```
complex(double r, double i) :re{r}, im{i} {}     // construct complex from two scalars
complex(double r) :complex{2,0} {}               // construct complex from one scalar
complex() :complex{0,0} {}                        // default complex: {0,0}
```

Say we wanted to add some debugging, tracing, or statistics-gathering code to **complex**; we now have a single place to do so. However, this can be abbreviated further:

```
complex(double r ={}, double i ={}) :re{r}, im{i} {}   // construct complex from two scalars
```

This makes it clear that if a user supplies fewer than the two arguments needed, the default is used. The intent of having a single constructor plus some shorthand notation is now explicit.

A default argument is type checked at the time of the function declaration and evaluated at the time of the call. For example:

```
class X {
public:
    static int def_arg;
    void f(int =def_arg);
    // ...
};

int X::def_arg = 7;

void g(X& a)
{
    a.f();           // maybe f(7)
    a.def_arg = 9;
    a.f();           // f(9)
}
```

Default arguments that can change value are most often best avoided because they introduce subtle context dependencies.

Default arguments may be provided for trailing arguments only. For example:

```
int f(int, int =0, char* =nullptr);// OK
int g(int =0, int =0, char*);        // error
int h(int =0, int, char* =nullptr);  // error
```

Note that the space between the ∗ and the = is significant (∗= is an assignment operator; §10.3):

```
int nasty(char*=nullptr);            // syntax error
```

A default argument cannot be repeated or changed in a subsequent declaration in the same scope. For example:

```
void f(int x = 7);
void f(int = 7);                     // error: cannot repeat default argument
void f(int = 8);                     // error: different default arguments
```

```
void g()
{
    void f(int x = 9);      // OK: this declaration hides the outer one
    // ...
}
```

Declaring a name in a nested scope so that the name hides a declaration of the same name in an outer scope is error-prone.

12.3 Overloaded Functions

Most often, it is a good idea to give different functions different names, but when different functions conceptually perform the same task on objects of different types, it can be more convenient to give them the same name. Using the same name for operations on different types is called *overloading*. The technique is already used for the basic operations in C++. That is, there is only one name for addition, +, yet it can be used to add values of integer and floating-point types and combinations of such types. This idea is easily extended to functions defined by the programmer. For example:

```
void print(int);         // print an int
void print(const char*);  // print a C-style string
```

As far as the compiler is concerned, the only thing functions of the same name have in common is that name. Presumably, the functions are in some sense similar, but the language does not constrain or aid the programmer. Thus, overloaded function names are primarily a notational convenience. This convenience is significant for functions with conventional names such as **sqrt**, **print**, and **open**. When a name is semantically significant, this convenience becomes essential. This happens, for example, with operators such as +, *, and <<, in the case of constructors (§16.2.5, §17.1), and in generic programming (§4.5, Chapter 32).

Templates provide a systematic way of defining sets of overloaded functions (§23.5).

12.3.1 Automatic Overload Resolution

When a function **fct** is called, the compiler must determine which of the functions named **fct** to invoke. This is done by comparing the types of the actual arguments with the types of the parameters of all functions in scope called **fct**. The idea is to invoke the function that is the best match to the arguments and give a compile-time error if no function is the best match. For example:

```
void print(double);
void print(long);

void f()
{
    print(1L);       // print(long)
    print(1.0);      // print(double)
    print(1);        // error, ambiguous: print(long(1)) or print(double(1))?
}
```

To approximate our notions of what is reasonable, a series of criteria are tried in order:

[1] Exact match; that is, match using no or only trivial conversions (for example, array name to pointer, function name to pointer to function, and **T** to **const T**)

[2] Match using promotions; that is, integral promotions (**bool** to **int**, **char** to **int**, **short** to **int**, and their **unsigned** counterparts; §10.5.1) and **float** to **double**

[3] Match using standard conversions (e.g., **int** to **double**, **double** to **int**, **double** to **long double**, **Derived**∗ to **Base**∗ (§20.2), **T**∗ to **void**∗ (§7.2.1), **int** to **unsigned int** (§10.5))

[4] Match using user-defined conversions (e.g., **double** to **complex<double>**; §18.4)

[5] Match using the ellipsis ... in a function declaration (§12.2.4)

If two matches are found at the highest level where a match is found, the call is rejected as ambiguous. The resolution rules are this elaborate primarily to take into account the elaborate C and C++ rules for built-in numeric types (§10.5). For example:

```
void print(int);
void print(const char∗);
void print(double);
void print(long);
void print(char);

void h(char c, int i, short s, float f)
{
     print(c);      // exact match: invoke print(char)
     print(i);      // exact match: invoke print(int)
     print(s);      // integral promotion: invoke print(int)
     print(f);      // float to double promotion: print(double)

     print('a');    // exact match: invoke print(char)
     print(49);     // exact match: invoke print(int)
     print(0);      // exact match: invoke print(int)
     print("a");    // exact match: invoke print(const char*)
     print(nullptr); // nullptr_t to const char* promotion: invoke print(cost char*)
}
```

The call **print(0)** invokes **print(int)** because **0** is an **int**. The call **print('a')** invokes **print(char)** because 'a' is a **char** (§6.2.3.2). The reason to distinguish between conversions and promotions is that we want to prefer safe promotions, such as **char** to **int**, over unsafe conversions, such as **int** to **char**. See also §12.3.5.

Overload resolution is independent of the order of declaration of the functions considered.

Function templates are handled by applying the overload resolution rules to the result of specialization based on a set of arguments (§23.5.3). There are separate rules for overloading when a {}-list is used (initializer lists take priority; §12.2.3, §17.3.4.1) and for rvalue reference template arguments (§23.5.2.1).

Overloading relies on a relatively complicated set of rules, and occasionally a programmer will be surprised which function is called. So, why bother? Consider the alternative to overloading. Often, we need similar operations performed on objects of several types. Without overloading, we must define several functions with different names:

```
void print_int(int);
void print_char(char);
void print_string(const char*);        // C-style string

void g(int i, char c, const char* p, double d)
{
    print_int(i);         // OK
    print_char(c);        // OK
    print_string(p);      // OK

    print_int(c);         // OK? calls print_int(int(c)), prints a number
    print_char(i);        // OK? calls print_char(char(i)), narrowing
    print_string(i);      // error
    print_int(d);         // OK? calls print_int(int(d)), narrowing
}
```

Compared to the overloaded **print()**, we have to remember several names and remember to use those correctly. This can be tedious, defeats attempts to do generic programming (§4.5), and generally encourages the programmer to focus on relatively low-level type issues. Because there is no overloading, all standard conversions apply to arguments to these functions. It can also lead to errors. In the previous example, this implies that only one of the four calls with doubtful semantics is caught by the compiler. In particular, two calls rely on error-prone narrowing (§2.2.2, §10.5). Thus, overloading can increase the chances that an unsuitable argument will be rejected by the compiler.

12.3.2 Overloading and Return Type

Return types are not considered in overload resolution. The reason is to keep resolution for an individual operator (§18.2.1, §18.2.5) or function call context-independent. Consider:

```
float sqrt(float);
double sqrt(double);

void f(double da, float fla)
{
    float fl = sqrt(da);    // call sqrt(double)
    double d = sqrt(da);    // call sqrt(double)
    fl = sqrt(fla);         // call sqrt(float)
    d = sqrt(fla);          // call sqrt(float)
}
```

If the return type were taken into account, it would no longer be possible to look at a call of **sqrt()** in isolation and determine which function was called.

12.3.3 Overloading and Scope

Overloading takes place among the members of an overload set. By default, that means the functions of a single scope; functions declared in different non-namespace scopes do not overload. For example:

```
    void f(int);

    void g()
    {
        void f(double);
        f(1);               // call f(double)
    }
```

Clearly, **f(int)** would have been the best match for **f(1)**, but only **f(double)** is in scope. In such cases, local declarations can be added or subtracted to get the desired behavior. As always, intentional hiding can be a useful technique, but unintentional hiding is a source of surprises.

A base class and a derived class provide different scopes so that overloading between a base class function and a derived class function doesn't happen by default. For example:

```
    struct Base {
        void f(int);
    };

    struct Derived : Base {
        void f(double);
    };

    void g(Derived& d)
    {
        d.f(1);        // call Derived::f(double);
    }
```

When overloading across class scopes (§20.3.5) or namespace scopes (§14.4.5) is wanted, **using**-declarations or **using**-directives can be used (§14.2.2). Argument-dependent lookup (§14.2.4) can also lead to overloading across namespaces.

12.3.4 Resolution for Multiple Arguments

We can use the overload resolution rules to select the most appropriate function when the efficiency or precision of computations differs significantly among types. For example:

```
    int pow(int, int);
    double pow(double, double);
    complex pow(double, complex);
    complex pow(complex, int);
    complex pow(complex, complex);

    void k(complex z)
    {
        int i = pow(2,2);           // invoke pow(int,int)
        double d = pow(2.0,2.0);    // invoke pow(double,double)
        complex z2 = pow(2,z);      // invoke pow(double,complex)
        complex z3 = pow(z,2);      // invoke pow(complex,int)
        complex z4 = pow(z,z);      // invoke pow(complex,complex)
    }
```

In the process of choosing among overloaded functions with two or more arguments, a best match is found for each argument using the rules from §12.3. A function that is the best match for one argument and a better or equal match for all other arguments is called. If no such function exists, the call is rejected as ambiguous. For example:

```
void g()
{
    double d = pow(2.0,2);    // error: pow(int(2.0),2) or pow(2.0,double(2))?
}
```

The call is ambiguous because **2.0** is the best match for the first argument of **pow(double,double)** and **2** is the best match for the second argument of **pow(int,int)**.

12.3.5 Manual Overload Resolution

Declaring too few (or too many) overloaded versions of a function can lead to ambiguities. For example:

```
void f1(char);
void f1(long);

void f2(char*);
void f2(int*);

void k(int i)
{
    f1(i);      // ambiguous: f1(char) or f1(long)?
    f2(0);      // ambiguous: f2(char*) or f2(int*)?
}
```

Where possible, consider the set of overloaded versions of a function as a whole and see if it makes sense according to the semantics of the function. Often the problem can be solved by adding a version that resolves ambiguities. For example, adding

```
inline void f1(int n) { f1(long(n)); }
```

would resolve all ambiguities similar to **f1(i)** in favor of the larger type **long int**.

One can also add an explicit type conversion to resolve a specific call. For example:

```
f2(static_cast<int*>(0));
```

However, this is most often simply an ugly stopgap. Soon another similar call will be made and have to be dealt with.

Some C++ novices get irritated by the ambiguity errors reported by the compiler. More experienced programmers appreciate these error messages as useful indicators of design errors.

12.4 Pre- and Postconditions

Every function has some expectations on its arguments. Some of these expectations are expressed in the argument types, but others depend on the actual values passed and on relationships among argument values. The compiler and linker can ensure that arguments are of the right types, but it is up to the programmer to decide what to do about "bad" argument values. We call logical criteria that are supposed to hold when a function is called *preconditions*, and logical criteria that are supposed to hold when a function returns its *postconditions*. For example:

```
int area(int len, int wid)
/*
      calculate the area of a rectangle

      precondition: len and wid are positive

      postcondition: the return value is positive

      postcondition: the return value is the area of a rectangle with sides len and wid
*/
{
      return len*wid;
}
```

Here, the statements of the pre- and postconditions are longer than the function body. This may seem excessive, but the information provided is useful to the implementer, to the users of **area()**, and to testers. For example, we learn that **0** and **−12** are not considered valid arguments. Furthermore, we note that we could pass a couple of huge values without violating the precondition, but if **len*wid** overflows either or both of the postconditions are not met.

What should we do about a call **area(numeric_limits<int>::max(),2)**?

[1]   Is it the caller's task to avoid it? Yes, but what if the caller doesn't?

[2]   Is it the implementer's task to avoid it? If so, how is an error to be handled?

There are several possible answers to these questions. It is easy for a caller to make a mistake and fail to establish a precondition. It is also difficult for an implementer to cheaply, efficiently, and completely check preconditions. We would like to rely on the caller to get the preconditions right, but we need a way to test for correctness. For now, just note that some pre- and postconditions are easy to check (e.g., **len** is positive and **len*wid** is positive). Others are semantic in nature and hard to test directly. For example, how do we test "the return value is the area of a rectangle with sides **len** and **wid**"? This is a semantic constraint because we have to know the meaning of "area of a rectangle," and just trying to multiply **len** and **wid** again with a precision that precluded overflow could be costly.

It seems that writing out the pre- and postconditions for **area()** uncovered a subtle problem with this very simple function. This is not uncommon. Writing out pre- and postconditions is a great design tool and provides good documentation. Mechanisms for documenting and enforcing conditions are discussed in §13.4.

If a function depends only on its arguments, its preconditions are on its arguments only. However, we have to be careful about functions that depend on non-local values (e.g., a member function that depends on the state of its object). In essence, we have to consider every nonlocal value read as an implicit argument to a function. Similarly, the postcondition of a function without side effects simply states that a value is correctly computed, but if a function writes to nonlocal objects, its effect must be considered and documented.

The writer of a function has several alternatives, including:
[1]   Make sure that every input has a valid result (so that we don't have a precondition).
[2]   Assume that the precondition holds (rely on the caller not to make mistakes).
[3]   Check that the precondition holds and throw an exception if it does not.
[4]   Check that the precondition holds and terminate the program if it does not.
If a postconditon fails, there was either an unchecked precondition or a programming error. §13.4 discusses ways to represent alternative strategies for checking.

12.5 Pointer to Function

Like a (data) object, the code generated for a function body is placed in memory somewhere, so it has an address. We can have a pointer to a function just as we can have a pointer to an object. However, for a variety of reasons – some related to machine architecture and others to system design – a pointer to function does not allow the code to be modified. There are only two things one can do to a function: call it and take its address. The pointer obtained by taking the address of a function can then be used to call the function. For example:

```
void error(string s) { /* ... */ }

void (*efct)(string);        // pointer to function taking a string argument and returning nothing

void f()
{
    efct = &error;           // efct points to error
    efct("error");           // call error through efct
}
```

The compiler will discover that **efct** is a pointer and call the function pointed to. That is, dereferencing a pointer to function using * is optional. Similarly, using **&** to get the address of a function is optional:

```
void (*f1)(string) = &error;     // OK: same as = error
void (*f2)(string) = error;      // OK: same as = &error

void g()
{
    f1("Vasa");                  // OK: same as (*f1)("Vasa")
    (*f1)("Mary Rose");          // OK: as f1("Mary Rose")
}
```

Pointers to functions have argument types declared just like the functions themselves. In pointer assignments, the complete function type must match exactly. For example:

```
void (*pf)(string);     // pointer to void(string)
void f1(string);        // void(string)
int f2(string);         // int(string)
void f3(int*);          // void(int*)
```

```
void f()
{
    pf = &f1;            // OK
    pf = &f2;            // error: bad return type
    pf = &f3;            // error: bad argument type

    pf("Hera");          // OK
    pf(1);               // error: bad argument type

    int i = pf("Zeus");  // error: void assigned to int
}
```

The rules for argument passing are the same for calls directly to a function and for calls to a function through a pointer.

You can convert a pointer to function to a different pointer-to-function type, but you must cast the resulting pointer back to its original type or strange things may happen:

```
using P1 = int(*)(int*);
using P2 = void(*)(void);

void f(P1 pf)
{
    P2 pf2 = reinterpret_cast<P2>(pf)
    pf2();                              // likely serious problem
    P1 pf1 = reinterpret_cast<P1>(pf2); // convert pf2 "back again"
    int x = 7;
    int y = pf1(&x);                    // OK
    // ...
}
```

We need the nastiest of casts, **reinterpret_cast**, to do conversion of pointer-to-function types. The reason is that the result of using a pointer to function of the wrong type is so unpredictable and system-dependent. For example, in the example above, the called function may write to the object pointed to by its argument, but the call **pf2()** didn't supply any argument!

Pointers to functions provide a way of parameterizing algorithms. Because C does not have function objects (§3.4.3) or lambda expressions (§11.4), pointers to functions are widely used as function arguments in C-style code. For example, we can provide the comparison operation needed by a sorting function as a pointer to function:

```
using CFT = int(const void*, const void*);

void ssort(void* base, size_t n, size_t sz, CFT cmp)
/*
    Sort the "n" elements of vector "base" into increasing order
    using the comparison function pointed to by "cmp".
    The elements are of size "sz".

    Shell sort (Knuth, Vol3, pg84)
*/
```

```
    {
        for (int gap=n/2; 0<gap; gap/=2)
            for (int i=gap; i!=n; i++)
                for (int j=i-gap; 0<=j; j-=gap) {
                    char* b = static_cast<char*>(base);        // necessary cast
                    char* pj = b+j*sz;                          // &base[j]
                    char* pjg = b+(j+gap)*sz;                   // &base[j+gap]
                    if (cmp(pjg,pj)<0) {                        // swap base[j] and base[j+gap]:
                        for (int k=0; k!=sz; k++) {
                            char temp = pj[k];
                            pj[k] = pjg[k];
                            pjg[k] = temp;
                        }
                    }
                }
    }
```

The **ssort()** routine does not know the type of the objects it sorts, only the number of elements (the array size), the size of each element, and the function to call to perform a comparison. The type of **ssort()** was chosen to be the same as the type of the standard C library sort routine, **qsort()**. Real programs use **qsort()**, the C++ standard-library algorithm **sort** (§32.6), or a specialized sort routine. This style of code is common in C, but it is not the most elegant way of expressing this algorithm in C++ (see §23.5, §25.3.4.1).

Such a sort function could be used to sort a table such as this:

```
struct User {
    const char* name;
    const char* id;
    int dept;
};

vector<User> heads = {
    "Ritchie D.M.",      "dmr",     11271,
    "Sethi R.",          "ravi",    11272,
    "Szymanski T.G.",    "tgs",     11273,
    "Schryer N.L.",      "nls",     11274,
    "Schryer N.L.",      "nls",     11275,
    "Kernighan B.W.",    "bwk",     11276
};

void print_id(vector<User>& v)
{
    for (auto& x : v)
        cout << x.name << '\t' << x.id << '\t' << x.dept << '\n';
}
```

To be able to sort, we must first define appropriate comparison functions. A comparison function must return a negative value if its first argument is less than the second, zero if the arguments are equal, and a positive number otherwise:

```
int cmp1(const void* p, const void* q)   // Compare name strings
{
    return strcmp(static_cast<const User*>(p)->name,static_cast<const User*>(q)->name);
}

int cmp2(const void* p, const void* q)   // Compare dept numbers
{
    return static_cast<const User*>(p)->dept – static_cast<const User*>(q)->dept;
}
```

There is no implicit conversion of argument or return types when pointers to functions are assigned or initialized. This means that you cannot avoid the ugly and error-prone casts by writing:

```
int cmp3(const User* p, const User* q)   // Compare ids
{
    return strcmp(p->id,q->id);
}
```

The reason is that accepting **cmp3** as an argument to **ssort()** would violate the guarantee that **cmp3** will be called with arguments of type **const User*** (see also §15.2.6).

This program sorts and prints:

```
int main()
{
    cout << "Heads in alphabetical order:\n";
    ssort(heads,6,sizeof(User),cmp1);
    print_id(heads);
    cout << '\n';

    cout << "Heads in order of department number:\n";
    ssort(heads,6,sizeof(User),cmp2);
    print_id(heads);
}
```

To compare, we can equivalently write:

```
int main()
{
    cout << "Heads in alphabetical order:\n";
    sort(heads.begin(), head.end(),
        [](const User& x, const User& y) { return x.name<y.name; }
    );
    print_id(heads);
    cout << '\n';

    cout << "Heads in order of department number:\n";
    sort(heads.begin(), head.end(),
        [](const User& x, const User& y) { return x.dept<y.dept; }
    );
    print_id(heads);
}
```

No mention of sizes is needed nor any helper functions. If the explicit use of **begin()** and **end()** is annoying, it can be eliminated by using a version of **sort()** that takes a container (§14.4.5):

```
sort(heads,[](const User& x, const User& y) { return x.name<y.name; });
```

You can take the address of an overloaded function by assigning to or initializing a pointer to function. In that case, the type of the target is used to select from the set of overloaded functions. For example:

```
void f(int);
int f(char);

void (*pf1)(int) = &f;      // void f(int)
int (*pf2)(char) = &f;      // int f(char)
void (*pf3)(char) = &f;     // error: no void f(char)
```

It is also possible to take the address of member functions (§20.6), but a pointer to member function is quite different from a pointer to (nonmember) function.

A pointer to a **noexcept** function can be declared **noexcept**. For example:

```
void f(int) noexcept;
void g(int);

void (*p1)(int) = f;             // OK: but we throw away useful information
void (*p2)(int) noexcept = f;    // OK: we preserve the noexcept information
void (*p3)(int) noexcept = g;    // error: we don't know that g doesn't throw
```

A pointer to function must reflect the linkage of a function (§15.2.6). Neither linkage specification nor **noexcept** may appear in type aliases:

```
using Pc = extern "C" void(int);     // error: linkage specification in alias
using Pn = void(int) noexcept;       // error: noexcept in alias
```

12.6 Macros

Macros are very important in C but have far fewer uses in C++. The first rule about macros is: don't use them unless you have to. Almost every macro demonstrates a flaw in the programming language, in the program, or in the programmer. Because they rearrange the program text before the compiler proper sees it, macros are also a major problem for many programming support tools. So when you use macros, you should expect inferior service from tools such as debuggers, cross-reference tools, and profilers. If you must use macros, please read the reference manual for your own implementation of the C++ preprocessor carefully and try not to be too clever. Also, to warn readers, follow the convention to name macros using lots of capital letters. The syntax of macros is presented in §iso.16.3.

I recommend using macros only for conditional compilation (§12.6.1) and in particular for include guards (§15.3.3).

A simple macro is defined like this:

```
#define NAME rest of line
```

Where **NAME** is encountered as a token, it is replaced by **rest of line**. For example:

> **named = NAME**

will expand into

> **named = rest of line**

A macro can also be defined to take arguments. For example:

> **#define MAC(x,y) argument1: x argument2: y**

When **MAC** is used, two argument strings must be presented. They will replace **x** and **y** when **MAC()** is expanded. For example:

> **expanded = MAC(foo bar, yuk yuk)**

will be expanded into

> **expanded = argument1: foo bar argument2: yuk yuk**

Macro names cannot be overloaded, and the macro preprocessor cannot handle recursive calls:

> **#define PRINT(a,b) cout<<(a)<<(b)**
> **#define PRINT(a,b,c) cout<<(a)<<(b)<<(c)**   */* trouble?: redefines, does not overload */*
>
> **#define FAC(n) (n>1)?n∗FAC(n−1):1**   */* trouble: recursive macro */*

Macros manipulate character strings and know little about C++ syntax and nothing about C++ types or scope rules. Only the expanded form of a macro is seen by the compiler, so an error in a macro will be reported when the macro is expanded, not when it is defined. This leads to very obscure error messages.

Here are some plausible macros:

> **#define CASE break;case**
> **#define FOREVER for(;;)**

Here are some completely unnecessary macros:

> **#define PI 3.141593**
> **#define BEGIN {**
> **#define END }**

Here are some dangerous macros:

> **#define SQUARE(a) a∗a**
> **#define INCR_xx (xx)++**

To see why they are dangerous, try expanding this:

> **int xx = 0;**   */ global counter*
>
> **void f(int xx)**
> **{**
>   **int y = SQUARE(xx+2);**   */ y=xx+2*xx+2; that is, y=xx+(2*xx)+2*
>   **INCR_xx;**   */ increments argument xx (not the global xx)*
> **}**

If you must use a macro, use the scope resolution operator, ::, when referring to global names (§6.3.4) and enclose occurrences of a macro argument name in parentheses whenever possible. For example:

```
#define MIN(a,b) (((a)<(b))?(a):(b))
```

This handles the simpler syntax problems (which are often caught by compilers), but not the problems with side effects. For example:

```
int x = 1;
int y = 10;
int z = MIN(x++,y++);          // x becomes 3; y becomes 11
```

If you must write macros complicated enough to require comments, it is wise to use /* */ comments because old C preprocessors that do not know about // comments are sometimes used as part of C++ tools. For example:

```
#define M2(a) something(a)     /* thoughtful comment */
```

Using macros, you can design your own private language. Even if you prefer this "enhanced language" to plain C++, it will be incomprehensible to most C++ programmers. Furthermore, the preprocessor is a very simple-minded macro processor. When you try to do something nontrivial, you are likely to find it either impossible or unnecessarily hard to do. The **auto, constexpr, const, decltype, enum, inline**, lambda expressions, **namespace**, and **template** mechanisms can be used as better-behaved alternatives to many traditional uses of preprocessor constructs. For example:

```
const int answer = 42;

template<class T>
inline const T& min(const T& a, const T& b)
{
    return (a<b)?a:b;
}
```

When writing a macro, it is not unusual to need a new name for something. A string can be created by concatenating two strings using the ## macro operator. For example:

```
#define NAME2(a,b) a##b

int NAME2(hack,cah)();
```

will produce

```
int hackcah();
```

A single # before a parameter name in a replacement string means a string containing the macro argument. For example:

```
#define printx(x) cout << #x " = " << x << '\n';

int a = 7;
string str = "asdf";
```

```
void f()
{
    printx(a);      // cout << "a" << " = " << a << '\n';
    printx(str);    // cout << "str" << " = " << str << '\n';
}
```

Writing #x " = " rather than #x << " = " is obscure "clever code" rather than an error. Adjacent string literals are concatenated (§7.3.2).

The directive

#undef X

ensures that no macro called **X** is defined – whether or not one was before the directive. This affords some protection against undesired macros. However, it is not always easy to know what the effects of **X** on a piece of code were supposed to be.

The argument list ("replacement list") of a macro can be empty:

```
#define EMPTY() std::cout<<"empty\n"
EMPTY();        // print "empty\n"
EMPTY;          // error: macro replacement list missing
```

I have a hard time thinking of uses of an empty macro argument list that are not error-prone or malicious.

Macros can even be variadic. For example:

```
#define err_print(...) fprintf(stderr,"error: %s %d\n", __VA_ARGS__)
err_print("The answer",54);
```

The ellipsis (...) means that **__VA_ARGS__** represents the arguments actually passed as a string, so the output is:

error: The answer 54

12.6.1 Conditional Compilation

One use of macros is almost impossible to avoid. The directive

#ifdef IDENTIFIER

does nothing if **IDENTIFIER** is defined, but if it is not, the directive causes all input to be ignored until a #endif directive is seen. For example:

```
int f(int a
#ifdef arg_two
,int b
#endif
);
```

Unless a macro called **arg_two** has been **#defined** , this produces:

```
int f(int a
);
```

This example confuses tools that assume sane behavior from the programmer.

Most uses of **#ifdef** are less bizarre, and when used with restraint, **#ifdef** and its complement **#ifn-def** do little harm. See also §15.3.3.

Names of the macros used to control **#ifdef** should be chosen carefully so that they don't clash with ordinary identifiers. For example:

```
struct Call_info {
    Node* arg_one;
    Node* arg_two;
    // ...
};
```

This innocent-looking source text will cause some confusion should someone write:

```
#define arg_two x
```

Unfortunately, common and unavoidable headers contain many dangerous and unnecessary macros.

12.6.2 Predefined Macros

A few macros are predefined by the compiler (§iso.16.8, §iso.8.4.1):

- __cplusplus: defined in a C++ compilation (and not in a C compilation). Its value is **201103L** in a C++11 program; previous C++ standards have lower values.
- __DATE__: date in "yyyy:mm:dd" format.
- __TIME__: time in "hh:mm:ss" format.
- __FILE__: name of current source file.
- __LINE__: source line number within the current source file.
- __FUNC__: an implementation-defined C-style string naming the current function.
- __STDC_HOSTED__: **1** if the implementation is hosted (§6.1.1); otherwise **0**.

In addition, a few macros are conditionally defined by the implementation:

- __STDC__: defined in a C compilation (and not in a C++ compilation)
- __STDC_MB_MIGHT_NEQ_WC__: **1** if, in the encoding for **wchar_t**, a member of the basic character set (§6.1) might have a code value that differs from its value as an ordinary character literal
- __STDCPP_STRICT_POINTER_SAFETY__: **1** if the implementation has strict pointer safety (§34.5); otherwise undefined.
- __STDCPP_THREADS__: **1** if a program can have more than one thread of execution; otherwise undefined.

For example:

```
cout << __FUNC__ << "() in file " << __FILE__ << " on line " << __LINE__ << "\n";
```

In addition, most C++ implementations allow a user to define arbitrary macros on the command line or in some other form of compile-time environment. For example, **NDEBUG** is defined unless the compilation is done in (some implementation-specific) "debug mode" and is used by the **assert()** macro (§13.4). This can be useful, but it does imply that you can't be sure of the meaning of a program just by reading its source text.

12.6.3 Pragmas

Implementations often provide facilities that differ from or go beyond what the standard offers. Obviously, the standard cannot specify how such facilities are provided, but one standard syntax is a line of tokens prefixed with the preprocessor directive **#pragma**. For example:

    #pragma foo bar 666 foobar

If possible, **#pragma**s are best avoided.

12.7 Advice

[1] "Package" meaningful operations as carefully named functions; §12.1.
[2] A function should perform a single logical operation; §12.1.
[3] Keep functions short; §12.1.
[4] Don't return pointers or references to local variables; §12.1.4.
[5] If a function may have to be evaluated at compile time, declare it **constexpr**; §12.1.6.
[6] If a function cannot return, mark it **[[noreturn]]**; §12.1.7.
[7] Use pass-by-value for small objects; §12.2.1.
[8] Use pass-by-**const**-reference to pass large values that you don't need to modify; §12.2.1.
[9] Return a result as a **return** value rather than modifying an object through an argument; §12.2.1.
[10] Use rvalue references to implement move and forwarding; §12.2.1.
[11] Pass a pointer if "no object" is a valid alternative (and represent "no object" by **nullptr**); §12.2.1.
[12] Use pass-by-non-**const**-reference only if you have to; §12.2.1.
[13] Use **const** extensively and consistently; §12.2.1.
[14] Assume that a **char∗** or a **const char∗** argument points to a C-style string; §12.2.2.
[15] Avoid passing arrays as pointers; §12.2.2.
[16] Pass a homogeneous list of unknown length as an **initializer_list<T>** (or as some other container); §12.2.3.
[17] Avoid unspecified numbers of arguments (...); §12.2.4.
[18] Use overloading when functions perform conceptually the same task on different types; §12.3.
[19] When overloading on integers, provide functions to eliminate common ambiguities; §12.3.5.
[20] Specify preconditions and postconditions for your functions; §12.4.
[21] Prefer function objects (including lambdas) and virtual functions to pointers to functions; §12.5.
[22] Avoid macros; §12.6.
[23] If you must use macros, use ugly names with lots of capital letters; §12.6.

13

Exception Handling

*Don't interrupt me
while I'm interrupting.
– Winston S. Churchill*

- Error Handling
    Exceptions; Traditional Error Handling; Muddling Through; Alternative Views of Exceptions; When You Can't Use Exceptions; Hierarchical Error Handling; Exceptions and Efficiency
- Exception Guarantees
- Resource Management
    Finally
- Enforcing Invariants
- Throwing and Catching Exceptions
    Throwing Exceptions; Catching Exceptions; Exceptions and Threads
- A **vector** Implementation
    A Simple **vector**; Representing Memory Explicitly; Assignment; Changing Size
- Advice

13.1 Error Handling

This chapter presents error handling using exceptions. For effective error handling, the language mechanisms must be used based on a strategy. Consequently, this chapter presents the *exception-safety guarantees* that are central to recovery from run-time errors and the *Resource Acquisition Is Initialization* (RAII) technique for resource management using constructors and destructors. Both the exception-safety guarantees and RAII depend on the specification of *invariants*, so mechanisms for enforcement of assertions are presented.

The language facilities and techniques presented here address problems related to the handling of errors in software; the handling of asynchronous events is a different topic.

The discussion of errors focuses on errors that cannot be handled locally (within a single small function), so that they require separation of error-handling activities into different parts of a program. Such parts of a program are often separately developed. Consequently, I often refer to a part of a program that is invoked to perform a task as "a library." A library is just ordinary code, but in the context of a discussion of error handling it is worth remembering that a library designer often cannot even know what kind of programs the library will become part of:

- The author of a library can detect a run-time error but does not in general have any idea what to do about it.
- The user of a library may know how to cope with a run-time error but cannot easily detect it (or else it would have been handled in the user's code and not left for the library to find).

The discussion of exceptions focuses on problems that need to be handled in long-running systems, systems with stringent reliability requirements, and libraries. Different kinds of programs have different requirements, and the amount of care and effort we expend should reflect that. For example, I would not apply every technique recommended here to a two-page program written just for myself. However, many of the techniques presented here simplify code, so I would use those.

13.1.1 Exceptions

The notion of an *exception* is provided to help get information from the point where an error is detected to a point where it can be handled. A function that cannot cope with a problem *throws* an exception, hoping that its (direct or indirect) caller can handle the problem. A function that wants to handle a kind of problem indicates that by *catch*ing the corresponding exception (§2.4.3.1):

- A calling component indicates the kinds of failures that it is willing to handle by specifying those exceptions in a **catch**-clause of a **try**-block.
- A called component that cannot complete its assigned task reports its failure to do so by throwing an exception using a **throw**-expression.

Consider a simplified and stylized example:

```
void taskmaster()
{
    try {
        auto result = do_task();
        // use result
    }
    catch (Some_error) {
        // failure to do_task: handle problem
    }
}

int do_task()
{
    // ...
    if (/* could perform the task */)
        return result;
    else
        throw Some_error{};
}
```

The **taskmaster()** asks **do_task()** to do a job. If **do_task()** can do that job and return a correct result, all is fine. Otherwise, **do_task()** must report a failure by throwing some exception. The **taskmaster()** is prepared to handle a **Some_error**, but some other kind of exception may be thrown. For example, **do_task()** may call other functions to do a lot of subtasks, and one of those may throw because it can't do its assigned subtask. An exception different from **Some_error** indicates a failure of **taskmaster()** to do its job and must be handled by whatever code invoked **taskmaster()**.

A called function cannot just return with an indication that an error happened. If the program is to continue working (and not just print an error message and terminate), the returning function must leave the program in a good state and not leak any resources. The exception-handling mechanism is integrated with the constructor/destructor mechanisms and the concurrency mechanisms to help ensure that (§5.2). The exception-handling mechanism:

- Is an alternative to the traditional techniques when they are insufficient, inelegant, or error-prone
- Is complete; it can be used to handle all errors detected by ordinary code
- Allows the programmer to explicitly separate error-handling code from "ordinary code," thus making the program more readable and more amenable to tools
- Supports a more regular style of error handling, thus simplifying cooperation between separately written program fragments

An exception is an object **thrown** to represent the occurrence of an error. It can be of any type that can be copied, but it is strongly recommended to use only user-defined types specifically defined for that purpose. That way, we minimize the chances of two unrelated libraries using the same value, say **17**, to represent different errors, thereby throwing our recovery code into chaos.

An exception is caught by code that has expressed interest in handling a particular type of exception (a **catch**-clause). Thus, the simplest way of defining an exception is to define a class specifically for a kind of error and throw that. For example:

```
struct Range_error {};

void f(int n)
{
    if (n<0 || max<n) throw Range_error {};
    // ...
}
```

If that gets tedious, the standard library defines a small hierarchy of exception classes (§13.5.2).

An exception can carry information about the error it represents. Its type represents the kind of error, and whatever data it holds represents the particular occurrence of that error. For example, the standard-library exceptions contain a string value, which can be used to transmit information such as the location of the throw (§13.5.2).

13.1.2 Traditional Error Handling

Consider the alternatives to exceptions for a function detecting a problem that cannot be handled locally (e.g., an out-of-range access) so that an error must be reported to a caller. Each conventional approach has problems, and none are general:

- *Terminate the program.* This is a pretty drastic approach. For example:

      if (something_wrong) exit(1);

  For most errors, we can and must do better. For example, in most situations we should at least write out a decent error message or log the error before terminating. In particular, a library that doesn't know about the purpose and general strategy of the program in which it is embedded cannot simply **exit()** or **abort()**. A library that unconditionally terminates cannot be used in a program that cannot afford to crash.

- *Return an error value.* This is not always feasible because there is often no acceptable "error value." For example:

      int get_int();   *// get next integer from input*

  For this input function, *every* **int** is a possible result, so there can be no integer value representing an input failure. At a minimum, we would have to modify **get_int()** to return a pair of values. Even where this approach is feasible, it is often inconvenient because every call must be checked for the error value. This can easily double the size of a program (§13.1.7). Also, callers often ignore the possibility of errors or simply forget to test a return value. Consequently, this approach is rarely used systematically enough to detect all errors. For example, **printf()** (§43.3) returns a negative value if an output or encoding error occurred, but programmers essentially never test for that. Finally, some operations simply do not have return values; a constructor is the obvious example.

- *Return a legal value and leave the program in an "error state."* This has the problem that the calling function may not notice that the program has been put in an error state. For example, many standard C library functions set the nonlocal variable **errno** to indicate an error (§43.4, §40.3):

      double d = sqrt(–1.0);

  Here, the value of **d** is meaningless and **errno** is set to indicate that **–1.0** isn't an acceptable argument for a floating-point square root function. However, programs typically fail to set and test **errno** and similar nonlocal state consistently enough to avoid consequential errors caused by values returned from failed calls. Furthermore, the use of nonlocal variables for recording error conditions doesn't work well in the presence of concurrency.

- *Call an error-handler function.* For example:

      if (something_wrong) something_handler();   *// and possibly continue here*

  This must be some other approach in disguise because the problem immediately becomes "What does the error-handling function do?" Unless the error-handling function can completely resolve the problem, the error-handling function must in turn either terminate the program, return with some indication that an error had occurred, set an error state, or throw an exception. Also, if the error-handling function can handle the problem without bothering the ultimate caller, why do we consider it an error?

Traditionally, an unsystematic combination of these approached co-exists in a program.

13.1.3 Muddling Through

One aspect of the exception-handling scheme that will appear novel to some programmers is that the ultimate response to an unhandled error (an uncaught exception) is to terminate the program. The traditional response has been to muddle through and hope for the best. Thus, exception handling makes programs more "brittle" in the sense that more care and effort must be taken to get a program to run acceptably. This is preferable, though, to getting wrong results later in the development process – or after the development process is considered complete and the program is handed over to innocent users. Where termination is unacceptable, we can catch all exceptions (§13.5.2.2). Thus, an exception terminates a program only if a programmer allows it to terminate. Typically, this is preferable to the unconditional termination that happens when a traditional incomplete recovery leads to a catastrophic error. Where termination is an acceptable response, an uncaught exception will achieve that because it turns into a call of **terminate()** (§13.5.2.5). Also, a **noexcept** specifier (§13.5.1.1) can make that desire explicit.

Sometimes, people try to alleviate the unattractive aspects of "muddling through" by writing out error messages, putting up dialog boxes asking the user for help, etc. Such approaches are primarily useful in debugging situations in which the user is a programmer familiar with the structure of the program. In the hands of nondevelopers, a library that asks the (possibly absent) user/operator for help is unacceptable. A good library doesn't "blabber" in this way. If a user has to be informed, an exception handler can compose a suitable message (e.g., in Finnish for Finnish users or in XML for an error-logging system). Exceptions provide a way for code that detects a problem from which it cannot recover to pass the problem on to a part of the system that might be able to recover. Only a part of the system that has some idea of the context in which the program runs has any chance of composing a meaningful error message.

Please recognize that error handling will remain a difficult task and that the exception-handling mechanism – although more formalized than the techniques it replaces – is still relatively unstructured compared with language features involving only local control flow. The C++ exception-handling mechanism provides the programmer with a way of handling errors where they are most naturally handled, given the structure of a system. Exceptions make the complexity of error handling visible. However, exceptions are not the cause of that complexity. Be careful not to blame the messenger for bad news.

13.1.4 Alternative Views of Exceptions

"Exception" is one of those words that means different things to different people. The C++ exception-handling mechanism is designed to support handling of errors that cannot be handled locally ("exceptional conditions"). In particular, it is intended to support error handling in programs composed of independently developed components. Given that there is nothing particularly exceptional about a part of a program being unable to perform its given task, the word "exception" may be considered a bit misleading. Can an event that happens most times a program is run be considered exceptional? Can an event that is planned for and handled be considered an error? The answer to both questions is "yes." "Exceptional" does not mean "almost never happens" or "disastrous."

13.1.4.1 Asynchronous Events

The mechanism is designed to handle only synchronous exceptions, such as array range checks and I/O errors. Asynchronous events, such as keyboard interrupts and power failures, are not necessarily exceptional and are not handled directly by this mechanism. Asynchronous events require mechanisms fundamentally different from exceptions (as defined here) to handle them cleanly and efficiently. Many systems offer mechanisms, such as signals, to deal with asynchrony, but because these tend to be system-dependent, they are not described here.

13.1.4.2 Exceptions That Are Not Errors

Think of an exception as meaning "some part of the system couldn't do what it was asked to do" (§13.1.1, §13.2).

Exception **throw**s should be infrequent compared to function calls or the structure of the system has been obscured. However, we should expect most large programs to **throw** and **catch** at least some exceptions in the course of a normal and successful run.

If an exception is expected and caught so that it has no bad effects on the behavior of the program, then how can it be an error? Only because the programmer thinks of it as an error and of the exception-handling mechanisms as tools for handling errors. Alternatively, one might think of the exception-handling mechanisms as simply another control structure, an alternative way of returning a value to a caller. Consider a binary tree search function:

```
void fnd(Tree* p, const string& s)
{
    if (s == p->str) throw p;        // found s
    if (p->left) fnd(p->left,s);
    if (p->right) fnd(p->right,s);
}

Tree* find(Tree* p, const string& s)
{
    try {
        fnd(p,s);
    }
    catch (Tree* q) {        // q->str==s
        return q;
    }
    return 0;
}
```

This actually has some charm, but it should be avoided because it is likely to cause confusion and inefficiencies. When at all possible, stick to the "exception handling is error handling" view. When this is done, code is clearly separated into two categories: ordinary code and error-handling code. This makes code more comprehensible. Furthermore, the implementations of the exception mechanisms are optimized based on the assumption that this simple model underlies the use of exceptions.

Error handling is inherently difficult. Anything that helps preserve a clear model of what is an error and how it is handled should be treasured.

13.1.5 When You Can't Use Exceptions

Use of exceptions is the only fully general and systematic way of dealing with errors in a C++ program. However, we must reluctantly conclude that there are programs that for practical and historical reasons cannot use exceptions. For example:

- A time-critical component of an embedded system where an operation must be guaranteed to complete in a specific maximum time. In the absence of tools that can accurately estimate the maximum time for an exception to propagate from a **throw** to a **catch**, alternative error-handling methods must be used.
- A large old program in which resource management is an ad hoc mess (e.g., free store is unsystematically "managed" using "naked" pointers, **new**s, and **delete**s), rather than relying on some systematic scheme, such as resource handles (e.g., **string** and **vector**; §4.2, §4.4).

In such cases, we are thrown back onto "traditional" (pre-exception) techniques. Because such programs arise in a great variety of historical contexts and in response to a variety of constraints, I cannot give a general recommendation for how to handle them. However, I can point to two popular techniques:

- To mimic RAII, give every class with a constructor an **invalid()** operation that returns some **error_code**. A useful convention is for **error_code==0** to represent success. If the constructor fails to establish the class invariant, it ensures that no resource is leaked and **invalid()** returns a nonzero **error_code**. This solves the problem of how to get an error condition out of a constructor. A user can then systematically test **invalid()** after each construction of an object and engage in suitable error handling in case of failure. For example:

```
void f(int n)
{
    my_vector<int> x(n);
    if (x.invalid()) {
        // ... deal with error ...
    }
    // ...
}
```

- To mimic a function either returning a value or throwing an exception, a function can return a **pair<Value,Error_code>** (§5.4.3). A user can then systematically test the **error_code** after each function call and engage in suitable error handling in case of failure. For example:

```
void g(int n)
{
    auto v = make_vector(n); // return a pair
    if (v.second) {
        // ... deal with error ...
    }
    auto val = v.first;
    // ...
}
```

Variations of this scheme have been reasonably successful, but they are clumsy compared to using exceptions in a systematic manner.

13.1.6 Hierarchical Error Handling

The purpose of the exception-handling mechanisms is to provide a means for one part of a program to inform another part that a requested task could not be performed (that an "exceptional circumstance" has been detected). The assumption is that the two parts of the program are written independently and that the part of the program that handles the exception often can do something sensible about the error.

To use handlers effectively in a program, we need an overall strategy. That is, the various parts of the program must agree on how exceptions are used and where errors are dealt with. The exception-handling mechanisms are inherently nonlocal, so adherence to an overall strategy is essential. This implies that the error-handling strategy is best considered in the earliest phases of a design. It also implies that the strategy must be simple (relative to the complexity of the total program) and explicit. Something complicated would not be consistently adhered to in an area as inherently tricky as error recovery.

Successful fault-tolerant systems are multilevel. Each level copes with as many errors as it can without getting too contorted and leaves the rest to higher levels. Exceptions support that view. Furthermore, **terminate()** supports this view by providing an escape if the exception-handling mechanism itself is corrupted or if it has been incompletely used, thus leaving exceptions uncaught. Similarly, **noexcept** provides a simple escape for errors where trying to recover seems infeasible.

Not every function should be a firewall. That is, not every function can test its preconditions well enough to ensure that no errors could possibly stop it from meeting its postcondition. The reasons that this will not work vary from program to program and from programmer to programmer. However, for larger programs:

[1]   The amount of work needed to ensure this notion of "reliability" is too great to be done consistently.

[2]   The overhead in time and space is too great for the system to run acceptably (there will be a tendency to check for the same errors, such as invalid arguments, over and over again).

[3]   Functions written in other languages won't obey the rules.

[4]   This purely local notion of "reliability" leads to complexities that actually become a burden to overall system reliability.

However, separating the program into distinct subsystems that either complete successfully or fail in well-defined ways is essential, feasible, and economical. Thus, major libraries, subsystems, and key interface functions should be designed in this way. Furthermore, in most systems, it is feasible to design every function to ensure that it always either completes successfully or fails in a well-defined manner.

Usually, we don't have the luxury of designing all of the code of a system from scratch. Therefore, to impose a general error-handling strategy on all parts of a program, we must take into account program fragments implemented using strategies different from ours. To do this we must address a variety of concerns relating to the way a program fragment manages resources and the state in which it leaves the system after an error. The aim is to have the program fragment appear to follow the general error-handling strategy even if it internally follows a different strategy.

Occasionally, it is necessary to convert from one style of error reporting to another. For example, we might check **errno** and possibly throw an exception after a call to a C library or, conversely, catch an exception and set **errno** before returning to a C program from a C++ library:

```
void callC()      // Call a C function from C++; convert errno to a throw
{
    errno = 0;
    c_function();
    if (errno) {
        // ... local cleanup, if possible and necessary ...
        throw C_blewit(errno);
    }
}

extern "C" void call_from_C() noexcept        // Call a C++ function from C; convert a throw to errno
{
    try {
        c_plus_plus_function();
    }
    catch (...) {
        // ... local cleanup, if possible and necessary ...
        errno = E_CPLPLFCTBLEWIT;
    }
}
```

In such cases, it is important to be systematic enough to ensure that the conversion of error-reporting styles is complete. Unfortunately, such conversions are often most desirable in "messy code" without a clear error-handling strategy and therefore difficult to be systematic about.

Error handling should be – as far as possible – hierarchical. If a function detects a run-time error, it should not ask its caller for help with recovery or resource acquisition. Such requests set up cycles in the system dependencies. That in turn makes the program hard to understand and introduces the possibility of infinite loops in the error-handling and recovery code.

13.1.7 Exceptions and Efficiency

In principle, exception handling can be implemented so that there is no run-time overhead when no exception is thrown. In addition, this can be done so that throwing an exception isn't all that expensive compared to calling a function. Doing so without adding significant memory overhead while maintaining compatibility with C calling sequences, debugger conventions, etc., is possible, but hard. However, please remember that the alternatives to exceptions are not free either. It is not unusual to find traditional systems in which half of the code is devoted to error handling.

Consider a simple function f() that appears to have nothing to do with exception handling:

```
void f()
{
    string buf;
    cin>>buf;
    // ...
    g(1);
    h(buf);
}
```

However, g() or h() may throw an exception, so f() must contain code ensuring that buf is destroyed correctly in case of an exception.

Had g() not thrown an exception, it would have had to report its error some other way. Consequently, the comparable code using ordinary code to handle errors instead of exceptions isn't the plain code above, but something like:

```
bool g(int);
bool h(const char*);
char* read_long_string();

bool f()
{
    char* s = read_long_string();
    // ...
    if (g(1)) {
        if (h(s)) {
            free(s);
            return true;
        }
        else {
            free(s);
            return false;
        }
    }
    else {
        free(s);
        return false;
    }
}
```

Using a local buffer for s would simplify the code by eliminating the calls to free(), but then we'd have range-checking code instead. Complexity tends to move around rather than just disappear.

People don't usually handle errors this systematically, though, and it is not always critical to do so. However, when careful and systematic handling of errors is necessary, such housekeeping is best left to a computer, that is, to the exception-handling mechanisms.

The noexcept specifier (§13.5.1.1) can be most helpful in improving generated code. Consider:

```
void g(int) noexcept;
void h(const string&) noexcept;
```

Now, the code generated for f() can possibly be improved.

No traditional C function throws an exception, so most C functions can be declared noexcept. In particular, a standard-library implementer knows that only a few standard C library functions (such as atexit() and qsort()) can throw, and can take advantage of that fact to generate better code.

Before declaring a "C function" noexcept, take a minute to consider if it could possibly throw an exception. For example, it might have been converted to use the C++ operator new, which can throw bad_alloc, or it might call a C++ library that throws an exception.

As ever, discussions about efficiency are meaningless in the absence of measurements.

13.2 Exception Guarantees

To recover from an error – that is, to catch an exception and continue executing a program – we need to know what can be assumed about the state of the program before and after the attempted recovery action. Only then can recovery be meaningful. Therefore, we call an operation *exception-safe* if that operation leaves the program in a valid state when the operation is terminated by throwing an exception. However, for that to be meaningful and useful, we have to be precise about what we mean by "valid state." For practical design using exceptions, we must also break down the overly general "exception-safe" notion into a few specific guarantees.

When reasoning about objects, we assume that a class has a class invariant (§2.4.3.2, §17.2.1). We assume that this invariant is established by its constructor and maintained by all functions with access to the object's representation until the object is destroyed. So, by *valid state* we mean that a constructor has completed and the destructor has not yet been entered. For data that isn't easily viewed as an object, we must reason similarly. That is, if two pieces of nonlocal data are assumed to have a specific relationship, we must consider that an invariant and our recovery action must preserve it. For example:

```
namespace Points {        // (vx[i],vy[i]) is a point for all i
    vector<int> vx;
    vector<int> vy;
};
```

Here it is assumed that **vx.size()==vy.size()** is (always) true. However, that was only stated in a comment, and compilers do not read comments. Such implicit invariants can be very hard to discover and maintain.

Before a **throw**, a function must place all constructed objects in valid states. However, such a valid state may be one that doesn't suit the caller. For example, a **string** may be left as the empty string or a container may be left unsorted. Thus, for complete recovery, an error handler may have to produce values that are more appropriate/desirable for the application than the (valid) ones existing at the entry to a **catch**-clause.

The C++ standard library provides a generally useful conceptual framework for design for exception-safe program components. The library provides one of the following guarantees for every library operation:

- The *basic guarantee* for all operations: The basic invariants of all objects are maintained, and no resources, such as memory, are leaked. In particular, the basic invariants of every built-in and standard-library type guarantee that you can destroy an object or assign to it after every standard-library operation (§iso.17.6.3.1).
- The *strong guarantee* for key operations: in addition to providing the basic guarantee, either the operation succeeds, or it has no effect. This guarantee is provided for key operations, such as **push_back()**, single-element **insert()** on a **list**, and **uninitialized_copy()**.
- The *nothrow guarantee* for some operations: in addition to providing the basic guarantee, some operations are guaranteed not to throw an exception. This guarantee is provided for a few simple operations, such as **swap()** of two containers and **pop_back()**.

Both the basic guarantee and the strong guarantee are provided on the condition that
- user-supplied operations (such as assignments and **swap()** functions) do not leave container elements in invalid states,
- user-supplied operations do not leak resources, and
- destructors do not throw exceptions (§iso.17.6.5.12).

Violating a standard-library requirement, such as having a destructor exit by throwing an exception, is logically equivalent to violating a fundamental language rule, such as dereferencing a null pointer. The practical effects are also equivalent and often disastrous.

Both the basic guarantee and the strong guarantee require the absence of resource leaks. This is necessary for every system that cannot afford resource leaks. In particular, an operation that throws an exception must not only leave its operands in well-defined states but must also ensure that every resource that it acquired is (eventually) released. For example, at the point where an exception is thrown, all memory allocated must be either deallocated or owned by some object, which in turn must ensure that the memory is properly deallocated. For example:

```
void f(int i)
{
    int* p = new int[10];
    // ...
    if (i<0) {
        delete[] p;      // delete before the throw or leak
        throw Bad();
    }
    // ...
}
```

Remember that memory isn't the only kind of resource that can leak. I consider anything that has to be acquired from another part of the system and (explicitly or implicitly) given back to be a resource. Files, locks, network connections, and threads are examples of system resources. A function may have to release those or hand them over to some resource handler before throwing an exception.

The C++ language rules for partial construction and destruction ensure that exceptions thrown while constructing subobjects and members will be handled correctly without special attention from standard-library code (§17.2.3). This rule is an essential underpinning for all techniques dealing with exceptions.

In general, we must assume that every function that can throw an exception will throw one. This implies that we must structure our code so that we don't get lost in a rat's nest of complicated control structures and brittle data structures. When analyzing code for potential errors, simple, highly structured, "stylized" code is the ideal; §13.6 includes a realistic example of such code.

13.3 Resource Management

When a function acquires a resource – that is, it opens a file, allocates some memory from the free store, acquires a mutex, etc. – it is often essential for the future running of the system that the resource be properly released. Often that "proper release" is achieved by having the function that acquired it release it before returning to its caller. For example:

```
void use_file(const char* fn)   // naive code
{
    FILE* f = fopen(fn,"r");

    // ... use f ...

    fclose(f);
}
```

This looks plausible until you realize that if something goes wrong after the call of **fopen()** and before the call of **fclose()**, an exception may cause **use_file()** to be exited without **fclose()** being called. Exactly the same problem can occur in languages that do not support exception handling. For example, the standard C library function **longjmp()** can cause the same problem. Even an ordinary **return**-statement could exit **use_file** without closing **f**.

A first attempt to make **use_file()** fault-tolerant looks like this:

```
void use_file(const char* fn)   // clumsy code
{
    FILE* f = fopen(fn,"r");
    try {
        // ... use f ...
    }
    catch (...) {              // catch every possible exception
        fclose(f);
        throw;
    }
    fclose(f);
}
```

The code using the file is enclosed in a **try**-block that catches every exception, closes the file, and rethrows the exception.

The problem with this solution is that it is verbose, tedious, and potentially expensive. Worse still, such code becomes significantly more complex when several resources must be acquired and released. Fortunately, there is a more elegant solution. The general form of the problem looks like this:

```
void acquire()
{
    // acquire resource 1
    // ...
    // acquire resource n

    // ... use resources ...

    // release resource n
    // ...
    // release resource 1
}
```

It is typically important that resources are released in the reverse order of their acquisition. This strongly resembles the behavior of local objects created by constructors and destroyed by destructors. Thus, we can handle such resource acquisition and release problems using objects of classes with constructors and destructors. For example, we can define a class **File_ptr** that acts like a **FILE**∗:

```
class File_ptr {
    FILE* p;
public:
    File_ptr(const char* n, const char* a)     // open file n
        : p{fopen(n,a)}
    {
        if (p==nullptr) throw runtime_error{"File_ptr: Can't open file"};
    }

    File_ptr(const string& n, const char* a)  // open file n
        :File_ptr{n.c_str(),a}
    {}

    explicit File_ptr(FILE* pp)                // assume ownership of pp
        :p{pp}
    {
        if (p==nullptr) throw runtime_error("File_ptr: nullptr"};
    }

    // ... suitable move and copy operations ...

    ˜File_ptr() { fclose(p); }

    operator FILE*() { return p; }
};
```

We can construct a **File_ptr** given either a **FILE**∗ or the arguments required for **fopen()**. In either case, a **File_ptr** will be destroyed at the end of its scope and its destructor will close the file. **File_ptr** throws an exception if it cannot open a file because otherwise every operation on the file handle would have to test for **nullptr**. Our function now shrinks to this minimum:

```
void use_file(const char* fn)
{
    File_ptr f(fn,"r");
    // ... use f ...
}
```

The destructor will be called independently of whether the function is exited normally or exited because an exception is thrown. That is, the exception-handling mechanisms enable us to remove the error-handling code from the main algorithm. The resulting code is simpler and less error-prone than its traditional counterpart.

This technique for managing resources using local objects is usually referred to as "Resource Acquisition Is Initialization" (RAII; §5.2). This is a general technique that relies on the properties of constructors and destructors and their interaction with exception handling.

It is often suggested that writing a "handle class" (a RAII class) is tedious so that providing a nicer syntax for the catch(...) action would provide a better solution. The problem with that approach is that you need to remember to "catch and correct" the problem wherever a resource is acquired in an undisciplined way (typically dozens or hundreds of places in a large program), whereas the handler class need be written only once.

An object is not considered constructed until its constructor has completed. Then and only then will stack unwinding (§13.5.1) call the destructor for the object. An object composed of subobjects is constructed to the extent that its subobjects have been constructed. An array is constructed to the extent that its elements have been constructed (and only fully constructed elements are destroyed during unwinding).

A constructor tries to ensure that its object is completely and correctly constructed. When that cannot be achieved, a well-written constructor restores – as far as possible – the state of the system to what it was before creation. Ideally, a well-designed constructor always achieves one of these alternatives and doesn't leave its object in some "half-constructed" state. This can be simply achieved by applying the RAII technique to the members.

Consider a class X for which a constructor needs to acquire two resources: a file x and a mutex y (§5.3.4). This acquisition might fail and throw an exception. Class X's constructor must never complete having acquired the file but not the mutex (or the mutex and not the file, or neither). Furthermore, this should be achieved without imposing a burden of complexity on the programmer. We use objects of two classes, File_ptr and std::unique_lock (§5.3.4), to represent the acquired resources. The acquisition of a resource is represented by the initialization of the local object that represents the resource:

```
class Locked_file_handle {
    File_ptr p;
    unique_lock<mutex> lck;
public:
    X(const char* file, mutex& m)
        : p{file,"rw"},        // acquire "file"
          lck{m}               // acquire "m"
    {}
    // ...
};
```

Now, as in the local object case, the implementation takes care of all of the bookkeeping. The user doesn't have to keep track at all. For example, if an exception occurs after p has been constructed but before lck has been, then the destructor for p but not for lck will be invoked.

This implies that where this simple model for acquisition of resources is adhered to, the author of the constructor need not write explicit exception-handling code.

The most common resource is memory, and string, vector, and the other standard containers use RAII to implicitly manage acquisition and release. Compared to ad hoc memory management using new (and possibly also delete), this saves lots of work and avoids lots of errors.

When a pointer to an object, rather than a local object, is needed, consider using the standard-library types unique_ptr and shared_ptr (§5.2.1, §34.3) to avoid leaks.

13.3.1 Finally

The discipline required to represent a resource as an object of a class with a destructor have bothered some. Again and again, people have invented "finally" language constructs for writing arbitrary code to clean up after an exception. Such techniques are generally inferior to RAII because they are ad hoc, but if you really want ad hoc, RAII can supply that also. First, we define a class that will execute an arbitrary action from its destructor.

```
template<typename F>
struct Final_action {
    Final_action(F f): clean{f} {}
    ~Final_action() { clean(); }
    F clean;
};
```

The "finally action" is provided as an argument to the constructor.

Next, we define a function that conveniently deduces the type of an action:

```
template<class F>
Final_action<F> finally(F f)
{
    return Final_action<F>(f);
}
```

Finally, we can test finally():

```
void test()
    // handle undiciplined resource acquisition
    // demonstrate that arbitrary actions are possible
{
    int* p = new int{7};                        // probably should use a unique_ptr (§5.2)
    int* buf = (int*)malloc(100*sizeof(int));   // C-style allocation

    auto act1 = finally([&]{    delete p;
                                free(buf);       // C-style deallocation
                                cout<< "Goodby, Cruel world!\n";
                           }
                         );

    int var = 0;
    cout << "var = " << var << '\n';

    // nested block:
    {
        var = 1;
        auto act2 = finally([&]{ cout<< "finally!\n"; var=7; });
        cout << "var = " << var << '\n';
    } // act2 is invoked here

    cout << "var = " << var << '\n';
} // act1 is invoked here
```

This produced:

```
var = 0
var = 1
finally!
var = 7
Goodby, Cruel world!
```

In addition, the memory allocated and pointed to by **p** and **buf** is appropriately **deleted** and **free()**d.

It is generally a good idea to place a guard close to the definition of whatever it is guarding. That way, we can at a glance see what is considered a resource (even if ad hoc) and what is to be done at the end of its scope. The connection between **finally()** actions and the resources they manipulate is still ad hoc and implicit compared to the use of RAII for resource handles, but using **finally()** is far better than scattering cleanup code around in a block.

Basically, **finally()** does for a block what the increment part of a **for**-statement does for the **for**-statement (§9.5.2): it specifies the final action at the top of a block where it is easy to be seen and where it logically belongs from a specification point of view. It says what is to be done upon exit from a scope, saving the programmer from trying to write code at each of the potentially many places from which the thread of control might exit the scope.

13.4 Enforcing Invariants

When a precondition for a function (§12.4) isn't met, the function cannot correctly perform its task. Similarly, when a constructor cannot establish its class invariant (§2.4.3.2, §17.2.1), the object is not usable. In those cases, I typically throw exceptions. However, there are programs for which throwing an exception is not an option (§13.1.5), and there are people with different views of how to deal with the failure of a precondition (and similar conditions):

- *Just don't do that:* It is the caller's job to meet preconditions, and if the caller doesn't do that, let bad results occur – eventually those errors will be eliminated from the system through improved design, debugging, and testing.
- *Terminate the program:* Violating a precondition is a serious design error, and the program must not proceed in the presence of such errors. Hopefully, the total system can recover from the failure of one component (that program) – eventually such failures may be eliminated from the system through improved design, debugging, and testing.

Why would anyone choose one of these alternatives? The first approach often relates to the need for performance: systematically checking preconditions can lead to repeated tests of logically unnecessary conditions (for example, if a caller has correctly validated data, millions of tests in thousands of called functions may be logically redundant). The cost in performance can be significant. It may be worthwhile to suffer repeated crashes during testing to gain that performance. Obviously, this assumes that you eventually get all critical precondition violations out of the system. For some systems, typically systems completely under the control of a single organization, that can be a realistic aim.

The second approach tends to be used in systems where complete and timely recovery from a precondition failure is considered infeasible. That is, making sure that recovery is complete imposes unacceptable complexity on the system design and implementation. On the other hand, termination of a program is considered acceptable. For example, it is not unreasonable to consider program termination acceptable if it is easy to rerun the program with inputs and parameters that make repeated failure unlikely. Some distributed systems are like this (as long as the program that terminates is only a part of the complete system), and so are many of the small programs we write for our own consumption.

Realistically, many systems use a mix of exceptions and these two alternative approaches. All three share a common view that preconditions should be defined and obeyed; what differs is how enforcement is done and whether recovery is considered feasible. Program structure can be radically different depending on whether (localized) recovery is an aim. In most systems, some exceptions are thrown without real expectation of recovery. For example, I often throw an exception to ensure some error logging or to produce a decent error message before terminating or re-initializing a process (e.g., from a **catch(...)** in **main()**).

A variety of techniques are used to express checks of desired conditions and invariants. When we want to be neutral about the logical reason for the check, we typically use the word *assertion*, often abbreviated to an *assert*. An assertion is simply a logical expression that is assumed to be **true**. However, for an assertion to be more than a comment, we need a way of expressing what happens if it is **false**. Looking at a variety of systems, I see a variety of needs when it comes to expressing assertions:

- We need to choose between compile-time asserts (evaluated by the compiler) and run-time asserts (evaluated at run time).
- For run-time asserts we need a choice of throw, terminate, or ignore.
- No code should be generated unless some logical condition is **true**. For example, some run-time asserts should not be evaluated unless the logical condition is **true**. Usually, the logical condition is something like a debug flag, a level of checking, or a mask to select among asserts to enforce.
- Asserts should not be verbose or complicated to write (because they can be very common).

Not every system has a need for or supports every alternative.

The standard offers two simple mechanisms:

- In **<cassert>**, the standard library provides the **assert(A)** macro, which checks its assertion, **A**, at run time if and only if the macro **NDEBUG** (''not debugging'') is not defined (§12.6.2). If the assertion fails, the compiler writes out an error message containing the (failed) assertion, the source file name, and the source file line number and terminates the program.
- The language provides **static_assert(A,message)**, which unconditionally checks its assertion, **A**, at compile time (§2.4.3.3). If the assertion fails, the compiler writes out the **message** and the compilation fails.

Where **assert()** and **static_assert()** are insufficient, we could use ordinary code for checking. For example:

```
void f(int n)
    // n should be in [1:max)
{
    if (2<debug_level && (n<=0 || max<n))
        throw Assert_error("range problem");
    // ...
}
```

However, using such "ordinary code" tends to obscure what is being tested. Are we:
- Evaluating the conditions under which we test? (Yes, the **2<debug_level** part.)
- Evaluating a condition that is expected to be true for some calls and not for others? (No, because we are throwing an exception – unless someone is trying to use exceptions as simply another return mechanism; §13.1.4.2.)
- Checking a precondition which should never fail? (Yes, the exception is simply our chosen response.)

Worse, the precondition testing (or invariant testing) can easily get dispersed in other code and thus be harder to spot and easier to get wrong. What we would like is a recognizable mechanism for checking assertions. What follows here is a (possibly slightly overelaborate) mechanism for expressing a variety of assertions and a variety of responses to failures. First, I define mechanisms for deciding when to test and deciding what to do if an assertion fails:

```
namespace Assert {
    enum class Mode { throw_, terminate_, ignore_ };
    constexpr Mode current_mode = CURRENT_MODE;
    constexpr int current_level = CURRENT_LEVEL;
    constexpr int default_level = 1;

    constexpr bool level(int n)
        { return n<=current_level; }

    struct Error : runtime_error {
        Error(const string& p) :runtime_error(p) {}
    };

    // ...
}
```

The idea is to test whenever an assertion has a "level" lower than or equal to **current_level**. If an assertion fails, **current_mode** is used to choose among three alternatives. The **current_level** and **current_mode** are constants because the idea is to generate no code whatsoever for an assertion unless we have made a decision to do so. Imagine **CURRENT_MODE** and **CURRENT_LEVEL** to be set in the build environment for a program, possibly as compiler options.

The programmer will use **Assert::dynamic()** to make assertions:

```
namespace Assert {
    // ...

    string compose(const char* file, int line, const string& message)
        // compose message including file name and line number
    {
        ostringstream os ("(");
        os << file << "," << line << "):" << message;
        return os.str();
    }
}
```

```
template<bool condition =level(default_level), class Except = Error>
void dynamic(bool assertion, const string& message ="Assert::dynamic failed")
{
    if (assertion)
        return;
    if (current_mode == Assert_mode::throw_)
        throw Except{message};
    if (current_mode == Assert_mode::terminate_)
        std::terminate();
}

template<>
void dynamic<false,Error>(bool, const string&)      // do nothing
{
}

void dynamic(bool b, const string& s)          // default action
{
    dynamic<true,Error>(b,s);
}

void dynamic(bool b)                           // default message
{
    dynamic<true,Error>(b);
}
}
```

I chose the name **Assert::dynamic** (meaning "evaluate at run time") to contrast with **static_assert** (meaning "evaluate at compile time"; §2.4.3.3).

Further implementation trickery could be used to minimize the amount of code generated. Alternatively, we could do more of the testing at run time if more flexibility is needed. This **Assert** is not part of the standard and is presented primarily as an illustration of the problems and the implementation techniques. I suspect that the demands on an assertion mechanism vary too much for a single one to be used everywhere.

We can use **Assert::dynamic** like this:

```
void f(int n)
    // n should be in [1:max)
{
    Assert::dynamic<Assert::level(2),Assert::Error>(
        (n<=0 || max<n), Assert::compose(__FILE__,__LINE__,"range problem");
    // ...
}
```

The **__FILE__** and **__LINE__** are macros that expand at their point of appearance in the source code (§12.6.2). I can't hide them from the user's view by placing them inside the implementation of **Assert** where they belong.

Assert::Error is the default exception, so we need not mention it explicitly. Similarly, if we are willing to use the default assertion level, we don't need to mention the level explicitly:

```
void f(int n)
      // n should be in [1:max]
{
      Assert::dynamic((n<=0 || max<n),Assert::compose(__FILE__,__LINE__,"range problem"));
      // ...
}
```

I do not recommend obsessing about the amount of text needed to express an assertion, but by using a namespace directive (§14.2.3) and the default message, we can get to a minimum:

```
void f(int n)
      // n should be in [1:max]
{
      dynamic(n<=0||max<n);
      // ...
}
```

It is possible to control the testing done and the response to testing through build options (e.g., controlling conditional compilation) and/or through options in the program code. That way, you can have a debug version of a system that tests extensively and enters the debugger and a production version that does hardly any testing.

I personally favor leaving at least some tests in the final (shipping) version of a program. For example, with **Assert** the obvious convention is that assertions marked as level zero will always be checked. We never find the last bug in a large program under continuous development and maintenance. Also, even if all else works perfectly, having a few "sanity checks" left to deal with hardware failures can be wise.

Only the builder of the final complete system can decide whether a failure is acceptable or not. The writer of a library or reusable component usually does not have the luxury of terminating unconditionally. I interpret that to mean that for general library code, reporting an error – preferably by throwing an exception – is essential.

As usual, destructors should not throw, so don't use a throwing **Assert()** in a destructor.

13.5 Throwing and Catching Exceptions

This section presents exceptions from a language-technical point of view.

13.5.1 Throwing Exceptions

We can **throw** an exception of any type that can be copied or moved. For example:

```
class No_copy {
      No_copy(const No_copy&) = delete;      // prohibit copying (§17.6.4)
};

class My_error {
      // ...
};
```

```
void f(int n)
{
    switch (n) {
    case 0:    throw My_error{};        // OK
    case 1:    throw No_copy{};         // error: can't copy a No_copy
    case 2:    throw My_error;          // error: My_error is a type, rather than an object
    }
}
```

The exception object caught (§13.5.2) is in principle a copy of the one thrown (though an optimizer is allowed to minimize copying); that is, a **throw x;** initializes a temporary variable of **x**'s type with **x**. This temporary may be further copied several times before it is caught: the exception is passed (back) from called function to calling function until a suitable handler is found. The type of the exception is used to select a handler in the **catch**-clause of some **try**-block. The data in the exception object – if any – is typically used to produce error messages or to help recovery. The process of passing the exception "up the stack" from the point of throw to a handler is called *stack unwinding*. In each scope exited, the destructors are invoked so that every fully constructed object is properly destroyed. For example:

```
void f()
{
    string name {"Byron"};
    try {
        string s = "in";
        g();
    }
    catch (My_error) {
        // ...
    }
}

void g()
{
    string s = "excess";
    {
        string s = "or";
        h();
    }
}

void h()
{
    string s = "not";
    throw My_error{};
    string s2 = "at all";
}
```

After the throw in h(), all the **strings** that were constructed are destroyed in the reverse order of their construction: "**not**", "**or**", "**excess**", "**in**", but not "**at all**", which the thread of control never reached, and not "**Byron**", which was unaffected.

Because an exception is potentially copied several times before it is caught, we don't usually put huge amounts of data in it. Exceptions containing a few words are very common. The semantics of exception propagation are those of initialization, so objects of types with move semantics (e.g., **strings**) are not expensive to throw. Some of the most common exceptions carry no information; the name of the type is sufficient to report the error. For example:

```
struct Some_error { };

void fct()
{
    // ...
    if (something_wrong)
        throw Some_error{};
}
```

There is a small standard-library hierarchy of exception types (§13.5.2) that can be used either directly or as base classes. For example:

```
struct My_error2 : std::runtime_error {
    const char* what() const noexcept { return "My_error2"; }
};
```

The standard-library exception classes, such as **runtime_error** and **out_of_range**, take a string argument as a constructor argument and have a virtual function **what()** that will regurgitate that string. For example:

```
void g(int n)     // throw some exception
{
    if (n)
        throw std::runtime_error{"I give up!"};
    else
        throw My_error2{};
}

void f(int n)     // see what exception g() throws
{
    try {
        void g(n);
    }
    catch (std::exception& e) {
        cerr << e.what() << '\n';
    }
}
```

13.5.1.1 noexcept Functions

Some functions don't throw exceptions and some really shouldn't. To indicate that, we can declare such a function **noexcept**. For example:

```
double compute(double) noexcept; // may not throw an exception
```

Now no exception will come out of **compute()**.

Declaring a function **noexcept** can be most valuable for a programmer reasoning about a program and for a compiler optimizing a program. The programmer need not worry about providing **try**-clauses (for dealing with failures in a **noexcept** function) and an optimizer need not worry about control paths from exception handling.

However, **noexcept** is not completely checked by the compiler and linker. What happens if the programmer "lied" so that a **noexcept** function deliberately or accidentally threw an exception that wasn't caught before leaving the **noexcept** function? Consider:

```
double compute(double x) noexcept;
{
    string s = "Courtney and Anya";
    vector<double> tmp(10);
    // ...
}
```

The **vector** constructor may fail to acquire memory for its ten **double**s and throw a **std::bad_alloc**. In that case, the program terminates. It terminates unconditionally by invoking **std::terminate()** (§30.4.1.3). It does not invoke destructors from calling functions. It is implementation-defined whether destructors from scopes between the **throw** and the **noexcept** (e.g., for **s** in **compute()**) are invoked. The program is just about to terminate, so we should not depend on any object anyway. By adding a **noexcept** specifier, we indicate that our code was not written to cope with a **throw**.

13.5.1.2 The noexcept Operator

It is possible to declare a function to be conditionally **noexcept**. For example:

```
template<typename T>
void my_fct(T& x) noexcept(Is_pod<T>());
```

The **noexcept(Is_pod<T>())** means that **My_fct** may not throw if the predicate **Is_pod<T>()** is **true** but may throw if it is **false**. I may want to write this if **my_fct()** copies its argument. I know that copying a POD does not throw, whereas other types (e.g., a **string** or a **vector**) may.

The predicate in a **noexcept()** specification must be a constant expression. Plain **noexcept** means **noexcept(true)**.

The standard library provides many type predicates that can be useful for expressing the conditions under which a function may throw an exception (§35.4).

What if the predicate we want to use isn't easily expressed using type predicates only? For example, what if the critical operation that may or may not throw is a function call **f(x)**? The **noexcept()** operator takes an expression as its argument and returns **true** if the compiler "knows" that it cannot throw and **false** otherwise. For example:

```
template<typename T>
void call_f(vector<T>& v) noexcept(noexcept(f(v[0]))
{
    for (auto x : v)
        f(x);
}
```

The double mention of **noexcept** looks a bit odd, but **noexcept** is not a common operator.

The operand of **noexcept()** is not evaluated, so in the example we do not get a run-time error if we pass **call_f()** with an empty **vector**.

A **noexcept(expr)** operator does not go to heroic lengths to determine whether **expr** can throw; it simply looks at every operation in **expr** and if they *all* have **noexcept** specifications that evaluate to **true**, it returns **true**. A **noexcept(expr)** does not look inside definitions of operations used in **expr**.

Conditional **noexcept** specifications and the **noexcept()** operator are common and important in standard-library operations that apply to containers. For example (§iso.20.2.2):

```
template<class T, size_t N>
void swap(T (&a)[N], T (&b)[N]) noexcept(noexcept(swap(*a, *b)));
```

13.5.1.3 Exception Specifications

In older C++ code, you may find *exception specifications*. For example:

```
void f(int) throw(Bad,Worse);   // may only throw Bad or Worse exceptions
void g(int) throw();            // may not throw
```

An empty exception specification **throw()** is defined to be equivalent to **noexcept** (§13.5.1.1). That is, if an exception is thrown, the program terminates.

The meaning of a nonempty exception specification, such as **throw(Bad,Worse)**, is that if the function (here **f()**) throws any exception that is not mentioned in the list or publicly derived from an exception mentioned there, an *unexpected handler* is called. The default effect of an unexpected exception is to terminate the program (§30.4.1.3). A nonempty **throw** specification is hard to use well and implies potentially expensive run-time checks to determine if the right exception is thrown. This feature has not been a success and is deprecated. Don't use it.

If you want to dynamically check which exceptions are thrown, use a **try**-block.

13.5.2 Catching Exceptions

Consider:

```
void f()
{
    try {
        throw E{};
    }
    catch(H) {
        // when do we get here?
    }
}
```

The handler is invoked:

[1]   If **H** is the same type as **E**
[2]   If **H** is an unambiguous public base of **E**
[3]   If **H** and **E** are pointer types and [1] or [2] holds for the types to which they refer
[4]   If **H** is a reference and [1] or [2] holds for the type to which **H** refers

In addition, we can add **const** to the type used to catch an exception in the same way that we can add it to a function parameter. This doesn't change the set of exceptions we can catch; it only restricts us from modifying the exception caught.

In principle, an exception is copied when it is thrown (§13.5). The implementation may apply a wide variety of strategies for storing and transmitting exceptions. It is guaranteed, however, that there is sufficient memory to allow **new** to throw the standard out-of-memory exception, **bad_alloc** (§11.2.3).

Note the possibility of catching an exception by reference. Exception types are often defined as part of class hierarchies to reflect relationships among the kinds of errors they represent. For examples, see §13.5.2.3 and §30.4.1.1. The technique of organizing exception classes into hierarchies is common enough for some programmers to prefer to catch every exception by reference.

The {} in both the **try**-part and a **catch**-clause of a **try**-block are real scopes. Consequently, if a name is to be used in both parts of a **try**-block or outside it, that name must be declared outside the **try**-block. For example:

```
void g()
{
    int x1;

    try {
        int x2 = x1;
        // ...
    }
    catch (Error) {
        ++x1;       // OK
        ++x2;       // error: x2 not in scope
        int x3 = 7;
        // ...
    }
    catch(...) {
        ++x3;       // error: x3 not in scope
        // ...
    }

    ++x1;           // OK
    ++x2;           // error: x2 not in scope
    ++x3;           // error: x3 not in scope
}
```

The "catch everything" clause, **catch(...)**, is explained in §13.5.2.2.

13.5.2.1 Rethrow

Having caught an exception, it is common for a handler to decide that it can't completely handle the error. In that case, the handler typically does what can be done locally and then throws the exception again. Thus, an error can be handled where it is most appropriate. This is the case even when the information needed to best handle the error is not available in a single place, so that the recovery action is best distributed over several handlers. For example:

```
void h()
{
    try {
        // ... code that might throw an exception ...
    }
    catch (std::exception& err) {
        if (can_handle_it_completely) {
            // ... handle it ...
            return;
        }
        else {
            // ... do what can be done here ...
            throw;       // rethrow the exception
        }
    }
}
```

A rethrow is indicated by a **throw** without an operand. A rethrow may occur in a **catch**-clause or in a function called from a **catch**-clause. If a rethrow is attempted when there is no exception to rethrow, **std::terminate()** (§13.5.2.5) will be called. A compiler can detect and warn about some, but not all, such cases.

The exception rethrown is the original exception caught and not just the part of it that was accessible as an **exception**. For example, had an **out_of_range** been thrown, **h()** would catch it as a plain **exception**, but **throw**; would still rethrow it as an **out_of_range**. Had I written **throw err**; instead of the simpler **throw**;, the exception would have been sliced (§17.5.1.4) and **h()**'s caller could not have caught it as an **out_of_range**.

13.5.2.2 Catch Every Exception

In **<stdexcept>**, the standard library provides a small hierarchy of exception classes with a common base **exception** (§30.4.1.1). For example:

```
void m()
{
    try {
        // ... do something ...
    }
    catch (std::exception& err) {        // handle every standard-library exception
        // ... cleanup ...
        throw;
    }
}
```

This catches every standard-library exception. However, the standard-library exceptions are just one set of exception types. Consequently, you cannot catch every exception by catching **std::exception**. If someone (unwisely) threw an **int** or an exception from some application-specific hierarchy, it would not be caught by the handler for **std::exception&**.

However, we often need to deal with every kind of exception. For example, if **m()** is supposed to leave some pointers in the state in which it found them, then we can write code in the handler to give them acceptable values. As for functions, the ellipsis, ..., indicates "any argument" (§12.2.4), so **catch(...)** means "catch any exception." For example:

```
void m()
{
    try {
        // ... something ...
    }
    catch (...) {          // handle every exception
        // ... cleanup ...
        throw;
    }
}
```

13.5.2.3 Multiple Handlers

A **try**-block may have multiple **catch**-clauses (handlers). Because a derived exception can be caught by handlers for more than one exception type, the order in which the handlers are written in a **try**-statement is significant. The handlers are tried in order. For example:

```
void f()
{
    try {
        // ...
    }
    catch (std::ios_base::failure) {
        // ... handle any iostream error (§30.4.1.1) ...
    }
    catch (std::exception& e) {
        // ... handle any standard-library exception (§30.4.1.1) ...
    }
    catch (...) {
        // ... handle any other exception (§13.5.2.2) ...
    }
}
```

The compiler knows the class hierarchy, so it can warn about many logical mistakes. For example:

```
void g()
{
    try {
        // ...
    }
    catch (...) {
        // ... handle every exception (§13.5.2.2) ...
    }
    catch (std::exception& e) {
        // ...handle any standard library exception (§30.4.1.1) ...
    }
```

```
    catch (std::bad_cast) {
        // ... handle dynamic_cast failure (§22.2.1) ...
    }
}
```

Here, the **exception** is never considered. Even if we removed the "catch-all" handler, **bad_cast** wouldn't be considered because it is derived from **exception**. Matching exception types to **catch**-clauses is a (fast) run-time operation and is not as general as (compile-time) overload resolution.

13.5.2.4 Function **try**-Blocks

The body of a function can be a **try**-block. For example:

```
int main()
try
{
    // ... do something ...
}
catch (...) {
    // ... handle exception ...
}
```

For most functions, all we gain from using a function **try**-block is a bit of notational convenience. However, a **try**-block allows us to deal with exceptions thrown by base-or-member initializers in constructors (§17.4). By default, if an exception is thrown in a base-or-member initializer, the exception is passed on to whatever invoked the constructor for the member's class. However, the constructor itself can catch such exceptions by enclosing the complete function body – including the member initializer list – in a **try**-block. For example:

```
class X {
    vector<int> vi;
    vector<string> vs;

    // ...
public:
    X(int,int);
    // ...
};

X::X(int sz1, int sz2)
try
    :vi(sz1),   // construct vi with sz1 ints
     vs(sz2),   // construct vs with sz2 strings
{
    // ...
}
catch (std::exception& err) { // exceptions thrown for vi and vs are caught here
    // ...
}
```

So, we can catch exceptions thrown by member constructors. Similarly, we can catch exceptions thrown by member destructors in a destructor (though a destructor should never throw). However, we cannot "repair" the object and return normally as if the exception had not happened: an exception from a member constructor means that the member may not be in a valid state. Also, other member objects will either not be constructed or already have had their destructors invoked as part of the stack unwinding.

The best we can do in a **catch**-clause of a function **try**-block for a constructor or destructor is to throw an exception. The default action is to rethrow the original exception when we "fall off the end" of the **catch**-clause (§iso.15.3).

There are no such restrictions for the **try**-block of an ordinary function.

13.5.2.5 Termination

There are cases where exception handling must be abandoned for less subtle error-handling techniques. The guiding principles are:
*   Don't throw an exception while handling an exception.
*   Don't throw an exception that can't be caught.
If the exception-handling implementation catches you doing either, it will terminate your program.

If you managed to have two exceptions active at one time (in the same thread, which you can't), the system would have no idea which of the exceptions to try to handle: your new one or the one it was already trying to handle. Note that an exception is considered handled immediately upon entry into a **catch**-clause. Rethrowing an exception (§13.5.2.1) or throwing a new exception from within a **catch**-clause is considered a new throw done after the original exception has been handled. You can throw an exception from within a destructor (even during stack unwinding) as long as you catch it before it leaves the destructor.

The specific rules for calling **terminate()** are (§iso.15.5.1)
*   When no suitable handler was found for a thrown exception
*   When a **noexcept** function tries to exit with a **throw**
*   When a destructor invoked during stack unwinding tries to exit with a **throw**
*   When code invoked to propagate an exception (e.g., a copy constructor) tries to exit with a **throw**
*   When someone tries to rethrow (**throw;**) when there is no current exception being handled
*   When a destructor for a statically allocated or thread-local object tries to exit with a **throw**
*   When an initializer for a statically allocated or thread-local object tries to exit with a **throw**
*   When a function invoked as an **atexit()** function tries to exit with a **throw**
In such cases, the function **std::terminate()** is called. In addition, a user can call **terminate()** if less drastic approaches are infeasible.

By "tries to exit with a **throw**," I mean that an exception is thrown somewhere and not caught so that the run-time system tries to propagate it from a function to its caller.

By default, **terminate()** will call **abort()** (§15.4.3). This default is the correct choice for most users – especially during debugging. If that is not acceptable, the user can provide a *terminate handler* function by a call **std::set_terminate()** from **<exception>**:

```
using terminate_handler = void(*)();        // from <exception>

[[noreturn]] void my_handler()              // a terminate handler cannot return
{
        // handle termination my way
}

void dangerous()     // very!
{
        terminate_handler old = set_terminate(my_handler);
        // ...
        set_terminate(old);  // restore the old terminate handler
}
```

The return value is the previous function given to **set_terminate()**.

For example, a terminate handler could be used to abort a process or maybe to re-initialize a system. The intent is for **terminate()** to be a drastic measure to be applied when the error recovery strategy implemented by the exception-handling mechanism has failed and it is time to go to another level of a fault tolerance strategy. If a terminate handler is entered, essentially nothing can be assumed about a program's data structures; they must be assumed to be corrupted. Even writing an error message using **cerr** must be assumed to be hazardous. Also, note that as **dangerous()** is written, it is not exception-safe. A **throw** or even a **return** before **set_terminate(old)** will leave **my_handler** in place when it wasn't meant to be. If you must mess with **terminate()**, at least use RAII (§13.3).

A terminate handler cannot return to its caller. If it tries to, **terminate()** will call **abort()**.

Note that **abort()** indicates abnormal exit from the program. The function **exit()** can be used to exit a program with a return value that indicates to the surrounding system whether the exit is normal or abnormal (§15.4.3).

It is implementation-defined whether destructors are invoked when a program is terminated because of an uncaught exception. On some systems, it is essential that the destructors are not called so that the program can be resumed from the debugger. On other systems, it is architecturally close to impossible *not* to invoke the destructors while searching for a handler.

If you want to ensure cleanup when an otherwise uncaught exception happens, you can add a catch-all handler (§13.5.2.2) to **main()** in addition to handlers for exceptions you really care about. For example:

```
int main()
try {
        // ...
}
catch (const My_error& err) {
        // ... handle my error ...
}
catch (const std::range_error&)
{
        cerr << "range error: Not again!\n";
}
```

```
catch (const std::bad_alloc&)
{
      cerr << "new ran out of memory\n";
}
catch (...) {
      // ...
}
```

This will catch every exception, except those thrown by construction and destruction of namespace and thread-local variables (§13.5.3). There is no way of catching exceptions thrown during initialization or destruction of namespace and thread-local variables. This is another reason to avoid global variables whenever possible.

When an exception is caught, the exact point where it was thrown is generally not known. This represents a loss of information compared to what a debugger might know about the state of a program. In some C++ development environments, for some programs, and for some people, it might therefore be preferable *not* to catch exceptions from which the program isn't designed to recover.

See **Assert** (§13.4) for an example of how one might encode the location of a **throw** into the thrown exception.

13.5.3 Exceptions and Threads

If an exception is not caught on a **thread** (§5.3.1, §42.2), **std::terminate()** (§13.5.2.5) is called. So, if we don't want an error in a thread to stop the whole program, we must catch all errors from which we would like to recover and somehow report them to a part of the program that is interested in the results of the thread. The "catch-all" construct **catch(...)** (§13.5.2.2) comes in handy for that.

We can transfer an exception thrown on one thread to a handler on another thread using the standard-library function **current_exception()** (§30.4.1.2). For example:

```
try {
      // ... do the work ...
}
catch(...) {
      prom.set_exception(current_exception());
}
```

This is the basic technique used by **packaged_task** to handle exceptions from user code (§5.3.5.2).

13.6 A **vector** Implementation

The standard **vector** provides splendid examples of techniques for writing exception-safe code: its implementation illustrates problems that occur in many contexts and solutions that apply widely.

Obviously, a **vector** implementation relies on many language facilities provided to support the implementation and use of classes. If you are not (yet) comfortable with C++'s classes and templates, you may prefer to delay studying this example until you have read Chapter 16, Chapter 25, and Chapter 26. However, a good understanding of the use of exceptions in C++ requires a more extensive example than the code fragments so far in this chapter.

The basic tools available for writing exception-safe code are:
- The **try**-block (§13.5).
- The support for the "Resource Acquisition Is Initialization" technique (§13.3).

The general principles to follow are to
- Never let go of a piece of information before its replacement is ready for use.
- Always leave objects in valid states when throwing or rethrowing an exception.

That way, we can always back out of an error situation. The practical difficulty in following these principles is that innocent-looking operations (such as <, =, and **sort()**) might throw exceptions. Knowing what to look for in an application takes experience.

When you are writing a library, the ideal is to aim at the strong exception-safety guarantee (§13.2) and always to provide the basic guarantee. When writing a specific program, there may be less concern for exception safety. For example, if I write a simple data analysis program for my own use, I'm usually quite willing to have the program terminate in the unlikely event of memory exhaustion.

Correctness and basic exception safety are closely related. In particular, the techniques for providing basic exception safety, such as defining and checking invariants (§13.4), are similar to the techniques that are useful to get a program small and correct. It follows that the overhead of providing the basic exception-safety guarantee (§13.2) – or even the strong guarantee – can be minimal or even insignificant.

13.6.1 A Simple vector

A typical implementation of **vector** (§4.4.1, §31.4) will consist of a handle holding pointers to the first element, one-past-the-last element, and one-past-the-last allocated space (§31.2.1) (or the equivalent information represented as a pointer plus offsets):

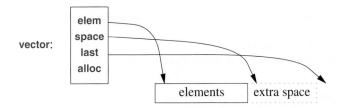

In addition, it holds an allocator (here, **alloc**), from which the **vector** can acquire memory for its elements. The default allocator (§34.4.1) uses **new** and **delete** to acquire and release memory.

Here is a declaration of **vector** simplified to present only what is needed to discuss exception safety and avoidance of resource leaks:

```
template<class T, class A = allocator<T>>
class vector {
private:
    T* elem;        // start of allocation
    T* space;       // end of element sequence, start of space allocated for possible expansion
    T* last;        // end of allocated space
    A alloc;        // allocator
```

```
public:
      using size_type = unsigned int;              // type used for vector sizes

      explicit vector(size_type n, const T& val = T(), const A& = A());

      vector(const vector& a);                     // copy constructor
      vector& operator=(const vector& a);          // copy assignment

      vector(vector&& a);                          // move constructor
      vector& operator=(vector&& a);               // move assignment

      ˜vector();

      size_type size() const { return space−elem; }
      size_type capacity() const { return last−elem; }
      void reserve(size_type n);                   // increase capacity to n

      void resize(size_type n, const T& = {});     // increase size to n
      void push_back(const T&);                    // add an element at the end

      // ...
};
```

Consider first a naive implementation of the constructor that initializes a **vector** to n elements initialized to **val**:

```
template<class T, class A>
vector<T,A>::vector(size_type n, const T& val, const A& a)  // warning: naive implementation
      :alloc{a}                     // copy the allocator
{
      elem = alloc.allocate(n);     // get memory for elements (§34.4)
      space = last = elem+n;
      for (T* p = elem; p!=last; ++p)
            a.construct(p,val);     // construct copy of val in *p (§34.4)
}
```

There are two potential sources of exceptions here:

[1]   allocate() may throw an exception if no memory is available.

[2]   T's copy constructor may throw an exception if it can't copy **val**.

What about the copy of the allocator? We can imagine that it throws, but the standard specifically requires that it does not do that (§iso.17.6.3.5). Anyway, I have written the code so that it wouldn't matter if it did.

In both cases of a **throw**, no **vector** object is created, so **vector**'s destructor is not called (§13.3).

When allocate() fails, the **throw** will exit before any resources are acquired, so all is well.

When T's copy constructor fails, we have acquired some memory that must be freed to avoid memory leaks. Worse still, the copy constructor for T might throw an exception after correctly constructing a few elements but before constructing them all. These T objects may own resources that then would be leaked.

To handle this problem, we could keep track of which elements have been constructed and destroy those (and only those) in case of an error:

```
template<class T, class A>
vector<T,A>::vector(size_type n, const T& val, const A& a)        // elaborate implementation
     :alloc{a}                              // copy the allocator
{
     elem = alloc.allocate(n);              // get memory for elements

     iterator p;

     try {
         iterator end = elem+n;
         for (p=elem; p!=end; ++p)
              alloc.construct(p,val);        // construct element (§34.4)
         last = space = p;
     }
     catch (...) {
         for (iterator q = elem; q!=p; ++q)
              alloc.destroy(q);              // destroy constructed elements
         alloc.deallocate(elem,n);           // free memory
         throw;                              // rethrow
     }
}
```

Note that the declaration of **p** is outside the **try**-block; otherwise, we would not be able to access it in both the **try**-part and the **catch**-clause.

The overhead here is the overhead of the **try**-block. In a good C++ implementation, this overhead is negligible compared to the cost of allocating memory and initializing elements. For implementations where entering a **try**-block incurs a cost, it may be worthwhile to add a test **if (n)** before the **try** to explicitly handle the (very common) empty **vector** case.

The main part of this constructor is a repeat of the implementation of **std::uninitialized_fill()**:

```
template<class For, class T>
void uninitialized_fill(For beg, For end, const T& x)
{
     For p;
     try {
         for (p=beg; p!=end; ++p)
              ::new(static_cast<void*>(&*p)) T(x);    // construct copy of x in *p (§11.2.4)
     }
     catch (...) {
         for (For q = beg; q!=p; ++q)
              (&*q)->~T();                            // destroy element (§11.2.4)
         throw;                                       // rethrow (§13.5.2.1)
     }
}
```

The curious construct **&*p** takes care of iterators that are not pointers. In that case, we need to take the address of the element obtained by dereference to get a pointer. Together with the explicitly global ::new, the explicit cast to **void**∗ ensures that the standard-library placement function (§17.2.4) is used to invoke the constructor, and not some user-defined **operator new()** for **T**∗s. The calls to **alloc.construct()** in the **vector** constructors are simply syntactic sugar for this placement **new**. Similarly, the **alloc.destroy()** call simply hides explicit destruction (like **(&∗q)->˜T()**). This code is operating at a rather low level where writing truly general code can be difficult.

Fortunately, we don't have to invent or implement **uninitialized_fill()**, because the standard library provides it (§32.5.6). It is often essential to have initialization operations that either complete successfully, having initialized every element, or fail, leaving no constructed elements behind. Consequently, the standard library provides **uninitialized_fill()**, **uninitialized_fill_n()**, and **uninitialized_copy()** (§32.5.6), which offer the strong guarantee (§13.2).

The **uninitialized_fill()** algorithm does not protect against exceptions thrown by element destructors or iterator operations (§32.5.6). Doing so would be prohibitively expensive and probably impossible.

The **uninitialized_fill()** algorithm can be applied to many kinds of sequences. Consequently, it takes a forward iterator (§33.1.2) and cannot guarantee to destroy elements in the reverse order of their construction.

Using **uninitialized_fill()**, we can simplify our constructor:

```
template<class T, class A>
vector<T,A>::vector(size_type n, const T& val, const A& a)      // still a bit messy
    :alloc(a)                              // copy the allocator
{
    elem = alloc.allocate(n);              // get memory for elements
    try {
        uninitialized_fill(elem,elem+n,val); // copy elements
        space = last = elem+n;
    }
    catch (...) {
        alloc.deallocate(elem,n);          // free memory
        throw;                             // rethrow
    }
}
```

This is a significant improvement on the first version of this constructor, but the next section demonstrates how to further simplify it.

The constructor rethrows a caught exception. The intent is to make **vector** transparent to exceptions so that the user can determine the exact cause of a problem. All standard-library containers have this property. Exception transparency is often the best policy for templates and other "thin" layers of software. This is in contrast to major parts of a system ("modules") that generally need to take responsibility for all exceptions thrown. That is, the implementer of such a module must be able to list every exception that the module can throw. Achieving this may involve grouping exceptions into hierarchies (§13.5.2) and using **catch(...)** (§13.5.2.2).

13.6.2 Representing Memory Explicitly

Experience shows that writing correct exception-safe code using explicit **try**-blocks is more difficult than most people expect. In fact, it is unnecessarily difficult because there is an alternative: The

"Resource Acquisition Is Initialization" technique (§13.3) can be used to reduce the amount of code that must be written and to make the code more stylized. In this case, the key resource required by the **vector** is memory to hold its elements. By providing an auxiliary class to represent the notion of memory used by a **vector**, we can simplify the code and decrease the chances of accidentally forgetting to release it:

```
template<class T, class A = allocator<T> >
struct vector_base {                        // memory structure for vector
    A alloc;        // allocator
    T* elem;        // start of allocation
    T* space;       // end of element sequence, start of space allocated for possible expansion
    T* last;        // end of allocated space

    vector_base(const A& a, typename A::size_type n)
        : alloc{a}, elem{alloc.allocate(n)}, space{elem+n}, last{elem+n} { }
    ~vector_base() { alloc.deallocate(elem,last−elem); }

    vector_base(const vector_base&) = delete;           // no copy operations
    vector_base& operator=(const vector_base&) = delete;

    vector_base(vector_base&&);                          // move operations
    vector_base& operator=(vector_base&&);
};
```

As long as **elem** and **last** are correct, **vector_base** can be destroyed. Class **vector_base** deals with memory for a type **T**, not objects of type **T**. Consequently, a user of **vector_base** must construct all objects explicitly in the allocated space and later destroy all constructed objects in a **vector_base** before the **vector_base** itself is destroyed.

The **vector_base** is designed exclusively to be part of the implementation of **vector**. It is always hard to predict where and how a class will be used, so I made sure that a **vector_base** can't be copied and also that a move of a **vector_base** properly transfers ownership of the memory allocated for elements:

```
template<class T, class A>
vector_base<T,A>::vector_base(vector_base&& a)
    : alloc{a.alloc},
      elem{a.elem},
      space{a.space},
      last{a.space}
{
    a.elem = a.space = a.last = nullptr; // no longer owns any memory
}

template<class T, class A>
vector_base<T,A>::& vector_base<T,A>::operator=(vector_base&& a)
{
    swap(*this,a);
    return *this;
}
```

This definition of the move assignment uses **swap()** to transfer ownership of any memory allocated for elements. There are no objects of type **T** to destroy: **vector_base** deals with memory and leaves concerns about objects of type **T** to **vector**.

Given **vector_base**, **vector** can be defined like this:

```
template<class T, class A = allocator<T> >
class vector {
        vector_base<T,A> vb;                    // the data is here
        void destroy_elements();
public:
        using size_type = unsigned int;

        explicit vector(size_type n, const T& val = T(), const A& = A());

        vector(const vector& a);                // copy constructor
        vector& operator=(const vector& a);     // copy assignment

        vector(vector&& a);                     // move constructor
        vector& operator=(vector&& a);          // move assignment

        ˜vector() { destroy_elements(); }

        size_type size() const { return vb.space–vb.elem; }
        size_type capacity() const { return vb.last–vb.elem; }

        void reserve(size_type);                // increase capacity

        void resize(size_type, T = {});         // change the number of elements
        void clear() { resize(0); }             // make the vector empty
        void push_back(const T&);               // add an element at the end

        // ...
};
```

```
template<class T, class A>
void vector<T,A>::destroy_elements()
{
        for (T* p = vb.elem; p!=vb.space; ++p)
                p->˜T();                        // destroy element (§17.2.4)
        vb.space=vb.elem;
}
```

The **vector** destructor explicitly invokes the **T** destructor for every element. This implies that if an element destructor throws an exception, the **vector** destruction fails. This can be a disaster if it happens during stack unwinding caused by an exception and **terminate()** is called (§13.5.2.5). In the case of normal destruction, throwing an exception from a destructor typically leads to resource leaks and unpredictable behavior of code relying on reasonable behavior of objects. There is no really good way to protect against exceptions thrown from destructors, so the library makes no guarantees if an element destructor throws (§13.2).

Now the constructor can be simply defined:

```
template<class T, class A>
vector<T,A>::vector(size_type n, const T& val, const A& a)
    :vb{a,n}        // allocate space for n elements
{
    uninitialized_fill(vb.elem,vb.elem+n,val); // make n copies of val
}
```

The simplification achieved for this constructor carries over to every **vector** operation that deals with initialization or allocation. For example, the copy constructor differs mostly by using **uninitialized_copy()** instead of **uninitialized_fill()**:

```
template<class T, class A>
vector<T,A>::vector(const vector<T,A>& a)
    :vb{a.alloc,a.size()}
{
    uninitialized_copy(a.begin(),a.end(),vb.elem);
}
```

This style of constructor relies on the fundamental language rule that when an exception is thrown from a constructor, subobjects (including bases) that have already been completely constructed will be properly destroyed (§13.3). The **uninitialized_fill()** algorithm and its cousins (§13.6.1) provide the equivalent guarantee for partially constructed sequences.

The move operations are even simpler:

```
template<class T, class A>
vector<T,A>::vector(vector&& a)                         // move constructor
    :vb{move(a.vb)}        // transfer ownership
{
}
```

The **vector_base** move constructor will set the argument's representation to "empty."

For the move assignment, we must take care of the old value of the target:

```
template<class T, class A>
vector<T,A>::& vector<T,A>::operator=(vector&& a)          // move assignment
{
    clear();            // destroy elements
    swap(*this,a);      // transfer ownership
}
```

The **clear()** is strictly speaking redundant because I could assume that the rvalue **a** would be destroyed immediately after the assignment. However, I don't know if some programmer has been playing games with **std::move()**.

13.6.3 Assignment

As usual, assignment differs from construction in that an old value must be taken care of. First consider a straightforward implementation:

```
template<class T, class A>
vector<T,A>& vector<T,A>::operator=(const vector& a)        // offers the strong guarantee (§13.2)
{
        vector_base<T,A> b(alloc,a.size());           // get memory
        uninitialized_copy(a.begin(),a.end(),b.elem); // copy elements
        destroy_elements();                           // destroy old elements
        swap(vb,b);                                   // transfer ownership
        return *this;                                 // implicitly destroy the old value
}
```

This **vector** assignment provides the strong guarantee, but it repeats a lot of code from constructors
and destructors. We can avoid repetition:

```
template<class T, class A>
vector<T,A>& vector<T,A>::operator=(const vector& a)        // offers the strong guarantee (§13.2)
{
        vector temp {a};                // copy allocator
        std::swap(*this,temp);          // swap representations
        return *this;
}
```

The old elements are destroyed by **temp**'s destructor, and the memory used to hold them is deallocated by **temp**'s **vector_base**'s destructor.

The reason that the standard-library **swap()** (§35.5.2) works for **vector_base**s is that we defined
vector_base move operations for **swap()** to use.

The performance of the two versions ought to be equivalent. Essentially, they are just two different ways of specifying the same set of operations. However, the second implementation is
shorter and doesn't replicate code from related **vector** functions, so writing the assignment that way
ought to be less error-prone and lead to simpler maintenance.

Note that I did not test for self-assignment, such as **v=v**. This implementation of = works by
first constructing a copy and then swapping representations. This obviously handles self-assignment correctly. I decided that the efficiency gained from the test in the rare case of self-assignment
was more than offset by its cost in the common case where a different **vector** is assigned.

In either case, two potentially significant optimizations are missing:

[1]   If the capacity of the **vector** assigned to is large enough to hold the assigned **vector**, we
       don't need to allocate new memory.
[2]   An element assignment may be more efficient than an element destruction followed by an
       element construction.

Implementing these optimizations, we get:

```
template<class T, class A>
vector<T,A>& vector<T,A>::operator=(const vector& a)        // optimized, basic guarantee (§13.2) only
{
        if (capacity() < a.size()) {  // allocate new vector representation:
                vector temp {a};              // copy allocator
                swap(*this,temp);             // swap representations
                return *this;                 // implicitly destroy the old value
        }
}
```

```
        if (this == &a) return *this;                          // optimize self assignment

        size_type sz = size();
        size_type asz = a.size();
        vb.alloc = a.vb.alloc;                                 // copy the allocator
        if (asz<=sz) {
            copy(a.begin(),a.begin()+asz,vb.elem);
            for (T* p = vb.elem+asz; p!=vb.space; ++p)         // destroy surplus elements (§16.2.6)
                p->~T();
        }
        else {
            copy(a.begin(),a.begin()+sz,vb.elem);
            uninitialized_copy(a.begin()+sz,a.end(),vb.space); // construct extra elements
        }
        vb.space = vb.elem+asz;
        return *this;
    }
```

These optimizations are not free. Obviously, the complexity of the code is far higher. Here, I also test for self-assignment. However, I do so mostly to show how it is done because here it is only an optimization.

The **copy()** algorithm (§32.5.1) does *not* offer the strong exception-safety guarantee. Thus, if **T::operator=()** throws an exception during **copy()**, the **vector** being assigned to need not be a copy of the **vector** being assigned, and it need not be unchanged. For example, the first five elements might be copies of elements of the assigned **vector** and the rest unchanged. It is also plausible that an element – the element that was being copied when **T::operator=()** threw an exception – ends up with a value that is neither the old value nor a copy of the corresponding element in the **vector** being assigned. However, if **T::operator=()** leaves its operands in valid states before it throws (as it should), the **vector** is still in a valid state – even if it wasn't the state we would have preferred.

The standard-library **vector** assignment offers the (weaker) basic exception-safety guarantee of this last implementation – and its potential performance advantages. If you need an assignment that leaves the **vector** unchanged if an exception is thrown, you must either use a library implementation that provides the strong guarantee or provide your own assignment operation. For example:

```
template<class T, class A>
void safe_assign(vector<T,A>& a, const vector<T,A>& b)      // simple a = b
{
    vector<T,A> temp{b};            // copy the elements of b into a temporary
    swap(a,temp);
}
```

Alternatively, we could simply use call-by-value (§12.2):

```
template<class T, class A>
void safe_assign(vector<T,A>& a, vector<T,A> b)            // simple a = b (note: b is passed by value)
{
    swap(a,b);
}
```

I never can decide if this last version is simply beautiful or too clever for real (maintainable) code.

13.6.4 Changing Size

One of the most useful aspects of **vector** is that we can change its size to suit our needs. The most popular functions for changing size are **v.push_back(x)**, which adds an **x** at the end of **v**, and **v.resize(s)**, which makes **s** the number of elements in **v**.

13.6.4.1 reserve()

The key to a simple implementation of such functions is **reserve()**, which adds free space at the end for the **vector** to grow into. In other words, **reserve()** increases the **capacity()** of a **vector**. If the new allocation is larger than the old, **reserve()** needs to allocate new memory and move the elements into it. We could try the trick from the unoptimized assignment (§13.6.3):

```
template<class T, class A>
void vector<T,A>::reserve(size_type newalloc)        // flawed first attempt
{
      if (newalloc<=capacity()) return;              // never decrease allocation
      vector<T,A> v(capacity());                     // make a vector with the new capacity
      copy(elem,elem+size(),v.begin())               // copy elements
      swap(*this,v);                                 // install new value
} // implicitly release old value
```

This has the nice property of providing the strong guarantee. However, not all types have a default value, so this implementation is flawed. Furthermore, looping over the elements twice, first to default construct and then to copy, is a bit odd. So let us optimize:

```
template<class T, class A>
void vector<T,A>::reserve(size_type newalloc)
{
      if (newalloc<=capacity()) return;              // never decrease allocation
      vector_base<T,A> b {vb.alloc,newalloc};        // get new space
      uninitialized_move(elem,elem+size(),b.elem);   // move elements
      swap(vb,b);                                    // install new base
} // implicitly release old space
```

The problem is that the standard library doesn't offer **uninitialized_move()**, so we have to write it:

```
template<typename In, typename Out>
Out uninitialized_move(In b, In e, Out oo)
{
      for (; b!=e; ++b,++oo) {
            new(static_cast<void*>(&*oo)) T{move(*b)};  // move construct
            b->~T();                                    // destroy
      }
      return b;
}
```

In general, there is no way of recovering the original state from a failed move, so I don't try to. This **uninitialized_move()** offers only the basic guarantee. However, it is simple and for the vast majority of cases it is fast. Also, the standard-library **reserve()** only offers the basic guarantee.

Whenever **reserve()** may have moved the elements, any iterators into the **vector** may have been invalidated (§31.3.3).

Remember that a move operation should not throw. In the rare cases where the obvious implementation of a move might throw, we typically go out of our way to avoid that. A throw from a move operation is rare, unexpected, and damaging to normal reasoning about code. If at all possible avoid it. The standard-library **move_if_noexcept()** operations may be of help here (§35.5.1).

The explicit use of **move()** is needed because the compiler doesn't know that **elem[i]** is just about to be destroyed.

13.6.4.2 resize()

The **vector** member function **resize()** changes the number of elements. Given **reserve()**, the implementation **resize()** is fairly simple. If the number of elements increases, we must construct the new elements. Conversely, if the number of elements decrease, we must destroy the surplus elements:

```
template<class T, class A>
void vector<T,A>::resize(size_type newsize, const T& val)
{
    reserve(newsize);
    if (size()<newsize)
        uninitialized_fill(elem+size(),elem+newsize,val);   // construct new elements: [size():newsize)
    else
        destroy(elem.size(),elem+newsize);                  // destroy surplus elements: [newsize:size())
    vb.space = vb.last = vb.elem+newsize;
}
```

There is no standard **destroy()**, but that easily written:

```
template<typename In>
void destroy(In b, In e)
{
    for (; b!=e; ++b)      // destroy [b:e)
        b->~T();
}
```

13.6.4.3 push_back()

From an exception-safety point of view, **push_back()** is similar to assignment in that we must take care that the **vector** remains unchanged if we fail to add a new element:

```
template< class T, class A>
void vector<T,A>::push_back(const T& x)
{
    if (capacity()==size())                     // no more free space; relocate:
        reserve(sz?2*sz:8);                     // grow or start with 8
    vb.alloc.construct(&vb.elem[size()],val);   // add val at end
    ++vb.space;                                 // increment size
}
```

Naturally, the copy constructor used to initialize *space* might throw an exception. If that happens, the value of the **vector** remains unchanged, with **space** left unincremented. However, **reserve()** may already have reallocated the existing elements.

This definition of **push_back()** contains two "magic numbers" (**2** and **8**). An industrial-strength implementation would not do that, but it would still have values determining the size of the initial allocation (here, **8**) and the rate of growth (here, **2**, indicating a doubling in size each time the **vector** would otherwise overflow). As it happens, these are not unreasonable or uncommon values. The assumption is that once we have seen one **push_back()** for a **vector**, we will almost certainly see many more. The factor two is larger than the mathematically optimal factor to minimize average memory use (**1.618**), so as to give better run-time performance for systems where memories are not tiny.

13.6.4.4 Final Thoughts

Note the absence of **try**-blocks in the **vector** implementation (except for the one hidden inside **uninitialized_copy()**). The changes in state were done by carefully ordering the operations so that if an exception is thrown, the **vector** remains unchanged or at least valid.

The approach of gaining exception safety through ordering and the RAII technique (§13.3) tends to be more elegant and more efficient than explicitly handling errors using **try**-blocks. More problems with exception safety arise from a programmer ordering code in unfortunate ways than from lack of specific exception-handling code. The basic rule of ordering is not to destroy information before its replacement has been constructed and can be assigned without the possibility of an exception.

Exceptions introduce possibilities for surprises in the form of unexpected control flows. For a piece of code with a simple local control flow, such as the **reserve()**, **safe_assign()**, and **push_back()** examples, the opportunities for surprises are limited. It is relatively simple to look at such code and ask, "Can this line of code throw an exception, and what happens if it does?" For large functions with complicated control structures, such as complicated conditional statements and nested loops, this can be hard. Adding **try**-blocks increases this local control structure complexity and can therefore be a source of confusion and errors (§13.3). I conjecture that the effectiveness of the ordering approach and the RAII approach compared to more extensive use of **try**-blocks stems from the simplification of the local control flow. Simple, stylized code is easier to understand, easier to get right, and easier to generate good code for.

This **vector** implementation is presented as an example of the problems that exceptions can pose and of techniques for addressing those problems. The standard does not require an implementation to be exactly like the one presented here. However, the standard does require the exception-safety guarantees as provided by the example.

13.7 Advice

[1]   Develop an error-handling strategy early in a design; §13.1.
[2]   Throw an exception to indicate that you cannot perform an assigned task; §13.1.1.
[3]   Use exceptions for error handling; §13.1.4.2.
[4]   Use purpose-designed user-defined types as exceptions (not built-in types); §13.1.1.

[5]   If you for some reason cannot use exceptions, mimic them; §13.1.5.

[6]   Use hierarchical error handling; §13.1.6.

[7]   Keep the individual parts of error handling simple; §13.1.6.

[8]   Don't try to catch every exception in every function; §13.1.6.

[9]   Always provide the basic guarantee; §13.2, §13.6.

[10] Provide the strong guarantee unless there is a reason not to; §13.2, §13.6.

[11] Let a constructor establish an invariant, and throw if it cannot; §13.2.

[12] Release locally owned resources before throwing an exception; §13.2.

[13] Be sure that every resource acquired in a constructor is released when throwing an exception in that constructor; §13.3.

[14] Don't use exceptions where more local control structures will suffice; §13.1.4.

[15] Use the "Resource Acquisition Is Initialization" technique to manage resources; §13.3.

[16] Minimize the use of **try**-blocks; §13.3.

[17] Not every program needs to be exception-safe; §13.1.

[18] Use "Resource Acquisition Is Initialization" and exception handlers to maintain invariants; §13.5.2.2.

[19] Prefer proper resource handles to the less structured **finally**; §13.3.1.

[20] Design your error-handling strategy around invariants; §13.4.

[21] What can be checked at compile time is usually best checked at compile time (using **static_assert**); §13.4.

[22] Design your error-handling strategy to allow for different levels of checking/enforcement; §13.4.

[23] If your function may not throw, declare it **noexcept**; §13.5.1.1

[24] Don't use exception specification; §13.5.1.3.

[25] Catch exceptions that may be part of a hierarchy by reference; §13.5.2.

[26] Don't assume that every exception is derived from class **exception**; §13.5.2.2.

[27] Have **main()** catch and report all exceptions; §13.5.2.2, §13.5.2.4.

[28] Don't destroy information before you have its replacement ready; §13.6.

[29] Leave operands in valid states before throwing an exception from an assignment; §13.2.

[30] Never let an exception escape from a destructor; §13.2.

[31] Keep ordinary code and error-handling code separate; §13.1.1, §13.1.4.2.

[32] Beware of memory leaks caused by memory allocated by **new** not being released in case of an exception; §13.3.

[33] Assume that every exception that can be thrown by a function will be thrown; §13.2.

[34] A library shouldn't unilaterally terminate a program. Instead, throw an exception and let a caller decide; §13.4.

[35] A library shouldn't produce diagnostic output aimed at an end user. Instead, throw an exception and let a caller decide; §13.1.3.

14

Namespaces

The year is 787!
A.D.?
– Monty Python

- Composition Problems
- Namespaces
    Explicit Qualification; **using**-Declarations; **using**-Directives; Argument-Dependent Lookup;
    Namespaces Are Open
- Modularization and Interfaces
    Namespaces as Modules; Implementations; Interfaces and Implementations
- Composition Using Namespaces
    Convenience vs. Safety; Namespace Aliases; Namespace Composition; Composition and
    Selection; Namespaces and Overloading; Versioning; Nested Namespaces; Unnamed Name-
    spaces; C Headers
- Advice

14.1 Composition Problems

Any realistic program consists of a number of separate parts. Functions (§2.2.1, Chapter 12) and
classes (§3.2, Chapter 16) provide relatively fine-grained separation of concerns, whereas
"libraries," source files, and translation units (§2.4, Chapter 15) provide coarser grain. The logical
ideal is *modularity*, that is, to keep separate things separate and to allow access to a "module" only
through a well-specified interface. C++ does not provide a single language feature supporting the
notion of a module; there is no module construct. Instead, modularity is expressed through combinations of other language facilities, such as functions, classes, and namespaces, and source code
organization.

   This chapter and the next deal with the coarse structure of a program and its physical representation as source files. That is, these two chapters are more concerned with programming in the

large than with the elegant expression of individual types, algorithms, and data structures.

Consider some of the problems that can arise when people fail to design for modularity. For example, a graphics library may provide different kinds of graphical **Shape**s and functions to help use them:

```
// Graph_lib:

class Shape { /* ... */ };
class Line : public Shape { /* ... */ };
class Poly_line: public Shape { /* ... */ };    // connected sequence of lines
class Text : public Shape { /* ... */ };        // text label

Shape operator+(const Shape&, const Shape&);    // compose

Graph_reader open(const char*);                 // open file of Shapes
```

Now someone comes along with another library, providing facilities for text manipulation:

```
// Text_lib:

class Glyph { /* ... */ };
class Word { /* ... */ };        // sequence of Glyphs
class Line { /* ... */ };        // sequence of Words
class Text { /* ... */ };        // sequence of Lines

File* open(const char*);                         // open text file

Word operator+(const Line&, const Line&);    // concatenate
```

For the moment, let us ignore the specific design issues for graphics and text manipulation and just consider the problems of using **Graph_lib** and **Text_lib** together in a program.

Assume (realistically enough) that the facilities of **Graph_lib** are defined in a header (§2.4.1), **Graph_lib.h**, and the facilities of **Text_lib** are defined in another header, **Text_lib.h**. Now, I can "innocently" **#include** both and try to use facilities from the two libraries:

```
#include "Graph_lib.h"
#include "Text_lib.h"
// ...
```

Just **#include**ing those headers causes a slurry of error messages: **Line**, **Text**, and **open()** are defined twice in ways that a compiler cannot disambiguate. Trying to use the libraries would give further error messages.

There are many techniques for dealing with such *name clashes*. For example, some such problems can be addressed by placing all the facilities of a library inside a few classes, by using supposedly uncommon names (e.g., **Text_box** rather than **Text**), or by systematically using a prefix for names from a library (e.g., **gl_shape** and **gl_line**). Each of these techniques (also known as "workarounds" and "hacks") works in some cases, but they are not general and can be inconvenient to use. For example, names tend to become long, and the use of many different names inhibits generic programming (§3.4).

14.2 Namespaces

The notion of a *namespace* is provided to directly represent the notion of a set of facilities that directly belong together, for example, the code of a library. The members of a namespace are in the same scope and can refer to each other without special notation, whereas access from outside the namespace requires explicit notation. In particular, we can avoid name clashes by separating sets of declarations (e.g., library interfaces) into namespaces. For example, we might call the graph library Graph_lib:

```
namespace Graph_lib {
    class Shape { /* ... */ };
    class Line : public Shape { /* ... */ };
    class Poly_line: public Shape { /* ... */ };        // connected sequence of lines
    class Text : public Shape { /* ... */ };            // text label

    Shape operator+(const Shape&, const Shape&);    // compose

    Graph_reader open(const char*);                 // open file of Shapes
}
```

Similarly, the obvious name for our text library is Text_lib:

```
namespace Text_lib {
    class Glyph { /* ... */ };
    class Word { /* ... */ };            // sequence of Glyphs
    class Line { /* ... */ };            // sequence of Words
    class Text { /* ... */ };            // sequence of Lines

    File* open(const char*);             // open text file

    Word operator+(const Line&, const Line&);    // concatenate
}
```

As long as we manage to pick distinct namespace names, such as Graph_lib and Text_lib (§14.4.2), we can now compile the two sets of declarations together without name clashes.

A namespace should express some logical structure: the declarations within a namespace should together provide facilities that unite them in the eyes of their users and reflect a common set of design decisions. They should be seen as a logical unit, for example, "the graphics library" or "the text manipulation library," similar to the way we consider the members of a class. In fact, the entities declared in a namespace are referred to as the members of the namespace.

A namespace is a (named) scope. You can access members defined earlier in a namespace from later declarations, but you cannot (without special effort) refer to members from outside the namespace. For example:

```
class Glyph { /* ... */ };
class Line { /* ... */ };

namespace Text_lib {
    class Glyph { /* ... */ };
    class Word { /* ... */ };         // sequence of Glyphs
```

```
        class Line { /* ... */ }; // sequence of Words
        class Text { /* ... */ }; // sequence of Lines

        File* open(const char*);                    // open text file

        Word operator+(const Line&, const Line&);   // concatenate
    }

    Glyph glyph(Line& ln, int i);    // ln[i]
```

Here, the **Word** and **Line** in the declaration of **Text_lib::operator+()** refer to **Text_lib::Word** and **Text_lib::Line**. That local name lookup is not affected by the global **Line**. Conversely, the **Glyph** and **Line** in the declaration of the global **glyph()** refer to the global **::Glyph** and **::Line**. That (nonlocal) lookup is not affected by **Text_lib**'s **Glyph** and **Line**.

To refer to members of a namespace, we can use its fully qualified name. For example, if we want a **glyph()** that uses definitions from **Text_lib**, we can write:

```
    Text_lib::Glyph glyph(Text_lib::Line& ln, int i);    // ln[i]
```

Other ways of referring to members from outside their namespace are **using**-declarations (§14.2.2), **using**-directives (§14.2.3), and argument-dependent lookup (§14.2.4).

14.2.1 Explicit Qualification

A member can be declared within a namespace definition and defined later using the *namespace-name* :: *member-name* notation.

Members of a namespace must be introduced using this notation:

```
    namespace namespace–name {
        // declaration and definitions
    }
```

For example:

```
    namespace Parser {
        double expr(bool);       // declaration
        double term(bool);
        double prim(bool);
    }

    double val = Parser::expr();    // use

    double Parser::expr(bool b)     // definition
    {
        // ...
    }
```

We cannot declare a new member of a namespace outside a namespace definition using the qualifier syntax (§iso.7.3.1.2). The idea is to catch errors such as misspellings and type mismatches, and also to make it reasonably easy to find all names in a namespace declaration. For example:

```
void Parser::logical(bool);      // error: no logical() in Parser
double Parser::trem(bool);       // error: no trem() in Parser (misspelling)
double Parser::prim(int);        // error: Parser::prim() takes a bool argument (wrong type)
```

A namespace is a scope. The usual scope rules hold for namespaces. Thus, "namespace" is a very fundamental and relatively simple concept. The larger a program is, the more useful namespaces are to express logical separations of its parts. The global scope is a namespace and can be explicitly referred to using ::. For example:

```
int f();          // global function

int g()
{
     int f;       // local variable; hides the global function
     f();          // error: we can't call an int
     ::f();        // OK: call the global function
}
```

Classes are namespaces (§16.2).

14.2.2 using-Declarations

When a name is frequently used outside its namespace, it can be a bother to repeatedly qualify it with its namespace name. Consider:

```
#include<string>
#include<vector>
#include<sstream>

std::vector<std::string> split(const std::string& s)
     // split s into its whitespace-separated substrings
{
     std::vector<std::string> res;
     std::istringstream iss(s);
     for (std::string buf; iss>>buf;)
          res.push_back(buf);
     return res;
}
```

The repeated qualification std is tedious and distracting. In particular, we repeat **std::string** four times in this small example. To alleviate that we can use a **using**-declaration to say that in this code **string** means **std::string**:

```
using std::string;   // use "string" to mean "std::string"

std::vector<string> split(const string& s)
     // split s into its whitespace-separated substrings
{
     std::vector<string> res;
     std::istringstream iss(s);
```

```
        for (string buf; iss>>buf;)
            res.push_back(buf);
        return res;
    }
```

A **using**-declaration introduces a synonym into a scope. It is usually a good idea to keep local synonyms as local as possible to avoid confusion.

When used for an overloaded name, a **using**-declaration applies to all the overloaded versions. For example:

```
namespace N {
    void f(int);
    void f(string);
};

void g()
{
    using N::f;
    f(789);            // N::f(int)
    f("Bruce");        // N::f(string)
}
```

For the use of **using**-declarations within class hierarchies, see §20.3.5.

14.2.3 using-Directives

In the **split()** example (§14.2.2), we still had three uses of **std::** left after introducing a synonym for **std::string**. Often, we like to use every name from a namespace without qualification. That can be achieved by providing a **using**-declaration for each name from the namespace, but that's tedious and requires extra work each time a new name is added to or removed from the namespace. Alternatively, we can use a **using**-directive to request that every name from a namespace be accessible in our scope without qualification. For example:

```
using namespace std;     // make every name from std accessible

vector<string> split(const string& s)
    // split s into its whitespace-separated substrings
{
    vector<string> res;
    istringstream iss(s);
    for (string buf; iss>>buf;)
        res.push_back(buf);
    return res;
}
```

A **using**-directive makes names from a namespace available almost as if they had been declared outside their namespace (see also §14.4). Using a **using**-directive to make names from a frequently used and well-known library available without qualification is a popular technique for simplifying code. This is the technique used to access standard-library facilities throughout this book. The standard-library facilities are defined in namespace **std**.

Within a function, a **using**-directive can be safely used as a notational convenience, but care should be taken with global **using**-directives because overuse can lead to exactly the name clashes that namespaces were introduced to avoid. For example:

```
namespace Graph_lib {
     class Shape { /* ... */ };
     class Line : Shape { /* ... */ };
     class Poly_line: Shape { /* ... */ };      // connected sequence of lines
     class Text : Shape { /* ... */ };          // text label

     Shape operator+(const Shape&, const Shape&);    // compose

     Graph_reader open(const char*);   // open file of Shapes
}

namespace Text_lib {
     class Glyph { /* ... */ };
     class Word { /* ... */ };         // sequence of Glyphs
     class Line { /* ... */ };         // sequence of Words
     class Text { /* ... */ };         // sequence of Lines

     File* open(const char*);  // open text file

     Word operator+(const Line&, const Line&);    // concatenate
}

using namespace Graph_lib;
using namespace Text_lib;

Glyph gl;               // Text_lib::Glyph
vector<Shape*> vs;      // Graph_lib::Shape
```

So far, so good. In particular, we can use names that do not clash, such as **Glyph** and **Shape**. However, name clashes now occur as soon as we use one of the names that clash – exactly as if we had not used namespaces. For example:

```
Text txt;                                  // error: ambiguous
File* fp = open("my_precious_data");       // error: ambiguous
```

Consequently, we must be careful with **using**-directives in the global scope. In particular, don't place a **using**-directive in the global scope in a header file except in very specialized circumstances (e.g., to aid transition) because you never know where a header might be **#include**d.

14.2.4 Argument-Dependent Lookup

A function taking an argument of user-defined type **X** is more often than not defined in the same namespace as **X**. Consequently, if a function isn't found in the context of its use, we look in the namespaces of its arguments. For example:

```
namespace Chrono {
    class Date { /* ... */ };

    bool operator==(const Date&, const std::string&);

    std::string format(const Date&);      // make string representation
    // ...
}

void f(Chrono::Date d, int i)
{
    std::string s = format(d);      // Chrono::format()
    std::string t = format(i);      // error: no format() in scope
}
```

This lookup rule (called *argument-dependent lookup* or simply ADL) saves the programmer a lot of typing compared to using explicit qualification, yet it doesn't pollute the namespace the way a **using**-directive (§14.2.3) can. It is especially useful for operator operands (§18.2.5) and template arguments (§26.3.5), where explicit qualification can be quite cumbersome.

Note that the namespace itself needs to be in scope and the function must be declared before it can be found and used.

Naturally, a function can take arguments from more than one namespace. For example:

```
void f(Chrono::Date d, std::string s)
{
    if (d == s) {
        // ...
    }
    else if (d == "August 4, 1914") {
        // ...
    }
}
```

In such cases, we look for the function in the scope of the call (as ever) and in the namespaces of every argument (including each argument's class and base classes) and do the usual overload resolution (§12.3) of all functions we find. In particular, for the call **d==s**, we look for **operator==** in the scope surrounding **f()**, in the **std** namespace (where **==** is defined for **string**), and in the **Chrono** namespace. There is a **std::operator==()**, but it doesn't take a **Date** argument, so we use **Chrono::operator==()**, which does. See also §18.2.5.

When a class member invokes a named function, other members of the same class and its base classes are preferred over functions potentially found based on the argument types (operators follow a different rule; §18.2.1, §18.2.5). For example:

```
namespace N {
    struct S { int i };
    void f(S);
    void g(S);
    void h(int);
}
```

```
struct Base {
    void f(N::S);
};

struct D : Base {
    void mf();

    void g(N::S x)
    {
        f(x);       // call Base::f()
        mf(x);      // call D::mf()
        h(1);       // error: no h(int) available
    }
};
```

In the standard, the rules for argument-dependent lookup are phrased in terms of *associated name-spaces* (§iso.3.4.2). Basically:

- If an argument is a class member, the associated namespaces are the class itself (including its base classes) and the class's enclosing namespaces.
- If an argument is a member of a namespace, the associated namespaces are the enclosing namespaces.
- If an argument is a built-in type, there are no associated namespaces.

Argument-dependent lookup can save a lot of tedious and distracting typing, but occasionally it can give surprising results. For example, the search for a declaration of a function f() does not have a preference for functions in a **namespace** in which f() is called (the way it does for functions in a **class** in which f() is called):

```
namespace N {
    template<class T>
        void f(T, int);    // N::f()
    class X { };
}

namespace N2 {
    N::X x;

    void f(N::X, unsigned);

    void g()
    {
        f(x,1);     // calls N::f(X,int)
    }
}
```

It may seem obvious to choose N2::f(), but that is not done. Overload resolution is applied and the best match is found: N::f() is the best match for f(x,1) because 1 is an **int** rather than an **unsigned**. Conversely, examples have been seen where a function in the caller's namespace is chosen but the programmer expected a better function from a known namespace to be used (e.g., a standard-library function from **std**). This can be most confusing. See also §26.3.6.

14.2.5 Namespaces Are Open

A namespace is open; that is, you can add names to it from several separate namespace declarations. For example:

```
namespace A {
        int f();      // now A has member f()
}

namespace A {
        int g();    // now A has two members, f() and g()
}
```

That way, the members of a namespace need not be placed contiguously in a single file. This can be important when converting older programs to use namespaces. For example, consider a header file written without the use of namespaces:

```
// my header:

        void mf();      // my function
        void yf();      // your function
        int mg();       // my function
        // ...
```

Here, we have (unwisely) just added the declarations needed without concerns of modularity. This can be rewritten without reordering the declarations:

```
// my header:

        namespace Mine {
                void mf();      // my function
                // ...
        }

        void yf();              // your function (not yet put into a namespace)

        namespace Mine {
                int mg();       // my function
                // ...
        }
```

When writing new code, I prefer to use many smaller namespaces (see §14.4) rather than putting really major pieces of code into a single namespace. However, that is often impractical when converting major pieces of software to use namespaces.

Another reason to define the members of a namespace in several separate namespace declarations is that sometimes we want to distinguish parts of a namespace used as an interface from parts used to support easy implementation; §14.3 provides an example.

A namespace alias (§14.4.2) cannot be used to re-open a namespace.

14.3 Modularization and Interfaces

Any realistic program consists of a number of separate parts. For example, even the simple "Hello, world!" program involves at least two parts: the user code requests Hello, world! to be printed, and the I/O system does the printing.

Consider the desk calculator example from §10.2. It can be viewed as composed of five parts:

[1]   The parser, doing syntax analysis: expr(), term(), and prim()
[2]   The lexer, composing tokens out of characters: Kind, Token, Token_stream, and ts
[3]   The symbol table, holding (string,value) pairs: table
[4]   The driver: main() and calculate()
[5]   The error handler: error() and number_of_errors

This can be represented graphically:

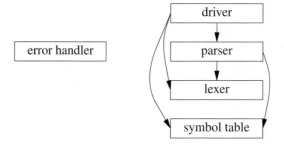

where an arrow means "using." To simplify the picture, I have not represented the fact that every part relies on error handling. In fact, the calculator was conceived as three parts, with the driver and error handler added for completeness.

When one module uses another, it doesn't need to know everything about the module used. Ideally, most of the details of a module are unknown to its users. Consequently, we make a distinction between a module and its interface. For example, the parser directly relies on the lexer's interface (only), rather than on the complete lexer. The lexer simply implements the services advertised in its interface. This can be presented graphically like this:

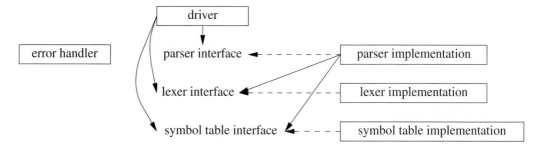

A dashed line means "implements." I consider this to be the real structure of the program, and our job as programmers is to represent this faithfully in code. That done, the code will be simple, efficient, comprehensible, maintainable, etc., because it will directly reflect our fundamental design.

The following subsections show how the logical structure of the desk calculator program can be made clear, and §15.3 shows how the program source text can be physically organized to take advantage of it. The calculator is a tiny program, so in "real life" I wouldn't bother using namespaces and separate compilation (§2.4.1, §15.1) to the extent done here. Making the structure of the calculator explicit is simply an illustration of techniques useful for larger programs without drowning in code. In real programs, each "module" represented by a separate namespace will often have hundreds of functions, classes, templates, etc.

Error handling permeates the structure of a program. When breaking up a program into modules or (conversely) when composing a program out of modules, we must take care to minimize dependencies between modules caused by error handling. C++ provides exceptions to decouple the detection and reporting of errors from the handling of errors (§2.4.3.1, Chapter 13).

There are many more notions of modularity than the ones discussed in this chapter and the next. For example, we might use concurrently executing and communicating tasks (§5.3, Chapter 41) or processes to represent important aspects of modularity. Similarly, the use of separate address spaces and the communication of information between address spaces are important topics not discussed here. I consider these notions of modularity largely independent and orthogonal. Interestingly, in each case, separating a system into modules is easy. The hard problem is to provide safe, convenient, and efficient communication across module boundaries.

14.3.1 Namespaces as Modules

A namespace is a mechanism for expressing logical grouping. That is, if some declarations logically belong together according to some criteria, they can be put in a common namespace to express that fact. So we can use namespaces to express the logical structure of our calculator. For example, the declarations of the parser from the desk calculator (§10.2.1) may be placed in a namespace Parser:

```
namespace Parser {
    double expr(bool);
    double prim(bool get) { /* ... */ }
    double term(bool get) { /* ... */ }
    double expr(bool get) { /* ... */ }
}
```

The function expr() must be declared first and then later defined to break the dependency loop described in §10.2.1.

The input part of the desk calculator could also be placed in its own namespace:

```
namespace Lexer {
    enum class Kind : char { /* ... */ };
    class Token { /* ... */ };
    class Token_stream { /* ... */ };

    Token_stream ts;
}
```

The symbol table is extremely simple:

```
namespace Table {
    map<string,double> table;
}
```

The driver cannot be completely put into a namespace because the language rules require **main()** to be a global function:

```
namespace Driver {
    void calculate() { /* ... */ }
}

int main() { /* ... */ }
```

The error handler is also trivial:

```
namespace Error {
    int no_of_errors;
    double error(const string& s) { /* ... */ }
}
```

This use of namespaces makes explicit what the lexer and the parser provide to a user. Had I included the source code for the functions, this structure would have been obscured. If function bodies are included in the declaration of a realistically sized namespace, you typically have to wade through screenfuls of information to find what services are offered, that is, to find the interface.

An alternative to relying on separately specified interfaces is to provide a tool that extracts an interface from a module that includes implementation details. I don't consider that a good solution. Specifying interfaces is a fundamental design activity, a module can provide different interfaces to different users, and often an interface is designed long before the implementation details are made concrete.

Here is a version of the **Parser** with the interface separated from the implementation:

```
namespace Parser {
    double prim(bool);
    double term(bool);
    double expr(bool);
}

double Parser::prim(bool get) { /* ... */ }
double Parser::term(bool get) { /* ... */ }
double Parser::expr(bool get) { /* ... */ }
```

Note that as a result of separating the implementation from the interface, each function now has exactly one declaration and one definition. Users will see only the interface containing declarations. The implementation – in this case, the function bodies – will be placed "somewhere else" where a user need not look.

Ideally, every entity in a program belongs to some recognizable logical unit ("module"). Therefore, every declaration in a nontrivial program should ideally be in some namespace named to indicate its logical role in the program. The exception is **main()**, which must be global in order for the compiler to recognize it as special (§2.2.1, §15.4).

14.3.2 Implementations

What will the code look like once it has been modularized? That depends on how we decide to access code in other namespaces. We can always access names from "our own" namespace exactly as we did before we introduced namespaces. However, for names in other namespaces, we have to choose among explicit qualification, **using**-declarations, and **using**-directives.

Parser::prim() provides a good test case for the use of namespaces in an implementation because it uses each of the other namespaces (except **Driver**). If we use explicit qualification, we get:

```
double Parser::prim(bool get)        // handle primaries
{
    if (get) Lexer::ts.get();

    switch (Lexer::ts.current().kind) {
    case Lexer::Kind::number:              // floating-point constant
    {   double v = Lexer::ts.current().number_value;
        Lexer::ts.get();
        return v;
    }
    case Lexer::Kind::name:
    {   double& v = Table::table[Lexer::ts.current().string_value];
        if (Lexer::ts.get().kind == Lexer::Kind::assign) v = expr(true);  // '=' seen: assignment
        return v;
    }
    case Lexer::Kind::minus:       // unary minus
        return –prim(true);
    case Lexer::Kind::lp:
    {   double e = expr(true);
        if (Lexer::ts.current().kind != Lexer::Kind::rp) return Error::error(" ')' expected");
        Lexer::ts.get();      // eat ')'
        return e;
    }
    default:
        return Error::error("primary expected");
    }
}
```

I count 14 occurrences of **Lexer::**, and (despite theories to the contrary) I don't think the more explicit use of modularity has improved readability. I didn't use **Parser::** because that would be redundant within namespace **Parser**.

If we use **using**-declarations, we get:

```
using Lexer::ts;          // saves eight occurrences of "Lexer::"
using Lexer::Kind;        // saves six occurrences of "Lexer::"
using Error::error;       // saves two occurrences of "Error::"
using Table::table;       // saves one occurrence of "Table::"
```

```
double prim(bool get)     // handle primaries
{
    if (get) ts.get();

    switch (ts.current().kind) {
    case Kind::number:        // floating-point constant
    {   double v = ts.current().number_value;
        ts.get();
        return v;
    }
    case Kind::name:
    {   double& v = table[ts.current().string_value];
        if (ts.get().kind == Kind::assign) v = expr(true);     // '=' seen: assignment
        return v;
    }
    case Kind::minus:         // unary minus
        return –prim(true);
    case Kind::lp:
    {   double e = expr(true);
        if (ts.current().kind != Kind::rp) return error("')' expected");
        ts.get();         // eat ')'
        return e;
    }
    default:
        return error("primary expected");
    }
}
```

My guess is that the **using**-declarations for **Lexer::** were worth it, but that the value of the others was marginal.

If we use **using**-directives, we get:

```
using namespace Lexer;     // saves fourteen occurrences of "Lexer::"
using namespace Error;     // saves two occurrences of "Error::"
using namespace Table;     // saves one occurrence of "Table::"

double prim(bool get)              // handle primaries
{
    // as before
}
```

The **using**-declarations for **Error** and **Table** don't buy much notationally, and it can be argued that they obscure the origins of the formerly qualified names.

So, the tradeoff among explicit qualification, **using**-declarations, and **using**-directives must be made on a case-by-case basis. The rules of thumb are:

[1]   If some qualification is really common for several names, use a **using**-directive for that namespace.

[2]   If some qualification is common for a particular name from a namespace, use a **using**-declaration for that name.

[3]   If a qualification for a name is uncommon, use explicit qualification to make it clear from where the name comes.

[4]   Don't use explicit qualification for names in the same namespace as the user.

14.3.3 Interfaces and Implementations

It should be clear that the namespace definition we used for **Parser** is not the ideal interface for **Parser** to present to its users. Instead, that **Parser** declares the set of declarations that is needed to write the individual parser functions conveniently. The **Parser**'s interface to its users should be far simpler:

```
namespace Parser {// user interface
    double expr(bool);
}
```

We see the namespace **Parser** used to provide two things:

[1]   The common environment for the functions implementing the parser

[2]   The external interface offered by the parser to its users

Thus, the driver code, **main()**, should see only the user interface.

The functions implementing the parser should see whichever interface we decided on as the best for expressing those functions' shared environment. That is:

```
namespace Parser {              // implementer interface
    double prim(bool);
    double term(bool);
    double expr(bool);

    using namespace Lexer;       // use all facilities offered by lexer
    using Error::error;
    using Table::table;
}
```

or graphically:

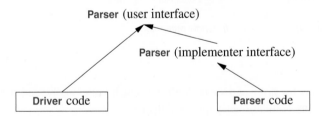

The arrows represent "relies on the interface provided by" relations.

We could give the user's interface and the implementer's interface different names, but (because namespaces are open; §14.2.5) we don't have to. The lack of separate names need not lead to confusion because the physical layout of the program (see §15.3.2) naturally provides separate (file) names. Had we decided to use a separate implementation namespace, the design would not have looked different to users:

```
namespace Parser {// user interface
    double expr(bool);
}

namespace Parser_impl {                    // implementer interface
    using namespace Parser;

    double prim(bool);
    double term(bool);
    double expr(bool);

    using namespace Lexer; // use all facilities offered by Lexer
    using Error::error;
    using Table::table;
}
```

or graphically:

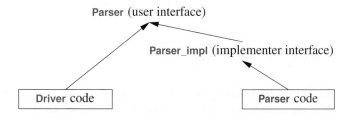

For larger programs, I lean toward introducing _impl interfaces.

The interface offered to implementers is larger than the interface offered to users. Had this interface been for a realistically sized module in a real system, it would change more often than the interface seen by users. It is important that the users of a module (in this case, **Driver** using **Parser**) be insulated from such changes.

14.4 Composition Using Namespaces

In larger programs, we tend to use many namespaces. This section examines technical aspects of composing code out of namespaces.

14.4.1 Convenience vs. Safety

A **using**-declaration adds a name to a local scope. A **using**-directive does not; it simply renders names accessible in the scope in which they were declared. For example:

```
namespace X {
    int i, j, k;
}
```

```
int k;

void f1()
{
    int i = 0;
    using namespace X;      // make names from X accessible
    i++;                    // local i
    j++;                    // X::j
    k++;                    // error: X's k or the global k?
    ::k++;                  // the global k
    X::k++;                 // X's k
}

void f2()
{
    int i = 0;
    using X::i;      // error: i declared twice in f2()
    using X::j;
    using X::k;      // hides global k

    i++;
    j++;             // X::j
    k++;             // X::k
}
```

A locally declared name (declared either by an ordinary declaration or by a using-declaration) hides nonlocal declarations of the same name, and any illegal overloading of the name is detected at the point of declaration.

Note the ambiguity error for k++ in f1(). Global names are not given preference over names from namespaces made accessible in the global scope. This provides significant protection against accidental name clashes, and – importantly – ensures that there are no advantages to be gained from polluting the global namespace.

When libraries declaring *many* names are made accessible through using-directives, it is a significant advantage that clashes of unused names are not considered errors.

14.4.2 Namespace Aliases

If users give their namespaces short names, the names of different namespaces will clash:

```
namespace A {// short name, will clash (eventually)
    // ...
}

A::String s1 = "Grieg";
A::String s2 = "Nielsen";
```

However, long namespace names can be impractical in real code:

```
namespace American_Telephone_and_Telegraph {      // too long
    // ...
}


American_Telephone_and_Telegraph::String s3 = "Grieg";
American_Telephone_and_Telegraph::String s4 = "Nielsen";
```

This dilemma can be resolved by providing a short alias for a longer namespace name:

```
// use namespace alias to shorten names:

namespace ATT = American_Telephone_and_Telegraph;

ATT::String s3 = "Grieg";
ATT::String s4 = "Nielsen";
```

Namespace aliases also allow a user to refer to ''the library'' and have a single declaration defining what library that really is. For example:

```
namespace Lib = Foundation_library_v2r11;

// ...

Lib::set s;
Lib::String s5 = "Sibelius";
```

This can immensely simplify the task of replacing one version of a library with another. By using **Lib** rather than **Foundation_library_v2r11** directly, you can update to version ''v3r02'' by changing the initialization of the alias **Lib** and recompiling. The recompile will catch source-level incompatibilities. On the other hand, overuse of aliases (of any kind) can lead to confusion.

14.4.3 Namespace Composition

Often, we want to compose an interface out of existing interfaces. For example:

```
namespace His_string {
    class String { /* ... */ };
    String operator+(const String&, const String&);
    String operator+(const String&, const char*);
    void fill(char);
    // ...
}

namespace Her_vector {
    template<class T>
        class Vector { /* ... */ };
    // ...
}
```

```
namespace My_lib {
    using namespace His_string;
    using namespace Her_vector;
    void my_fct(String&);
}
```

Given this, we can now write the program in terms of **My_lib**:

```
void f()
{
    My_lib::String s = "Byron";      // finds My_lib::His_string::String
    // ...
}

using namespace My_lib;

void g(Vector<String>& vs)
{
    // ...
    my_fct(vs[5]);
    // ...
}
```

If an explicitly qualified name (such as **My_lib::String**) isn't declared in the namespace mentioned, the compiler looks in namespaces mentioned in **using**-directives (such as **His_string**).

Only if we need to define something do we need to know the real namespace of an entity:

```
void My_lib::fill(char c)         // error: no fill() declared in My_lib
{
    // ...
}

void His_string::fill(char c)     // OK: fill() declared in His_string
{
    // ...
}

void My_lib::my_fct(String& v)// OK: String is My_lib::String, meaning His_string::String
{
    // ...
}
```

Ideally, a namespace should

[1]   express a logically coherent set of features,

[2]   not give users access to unrelated features, and

[3]   not impose a significant notational burden on users.

Together with the **#include** mechanism (§15.2.2), the composition techniques presented here and in the following subsections provide strong support for this.

14.4.4 Composition and Selection

Combining composition (by **using**-directives) with selection (by **using**-declarations) yields the flexibility needed for most real-world examples. With these mechanisms, we can provide access to a variety of facilities in such a way that we resolve name clashes and ambiguities arising from their composition. For example:

```
namespace His_lib {
    class String { /* ... */ };
    template<class T>
        class Vector { /* ... */ };
    // ...
}

namespace Her_lib {
    template<class T>
        class Vector { /* ... */ };
    class String { /* ... */ };
    // ...
}

namespace My_lib {
    using namespace His_lib;        // everything from His_lib
    using namespace Her_lib;        // everything from Her_lib

    using His_lib::String;          // resolve potential clash in favor of His_lib
    using Her_lib::Vector;          // resolve potential clash in favor of Her_lib

    template<class T>
        class List { /* ... */ };   // additional stuff
    // ...
}
```

When looking into a namespace, names explicitly declared there (including names declared by **using**-declarations) take priority over names made accessible in another scope by a **using**-directive (see also §14.4.1). Consequently, a user of **My_lib** will see the name clashes for **String** and **Vector** resolved in favor of **His_lib::String** and **Her_lib::Vector**. Also, **My_lib::List** will be used by default independently of whether **His_lib** or **Her_lib** is providing a **List**.

Usually, I prefer to leave a name unchanged when including it into a new namespace. Then, I don't have to remember two different names for the same entity. However, sometimes a new name is needed or simply nice to have. For example:

```
namespace Lib2 {
    using namespace His_lib;        // everything from His_lib
    using namespace Her_lib;        // everything from Her_lib

    using His_lib::String;          // resolve potential clash in favor of His_lib
    using Her_lib::Vector;          // resolve potential clash in favor of Her_lib
```

```
        using Her_string = Her_lib::String;              // rename
        template<class T>
            using His_vec = His_lib::Vector<T>;     // rename

        template<class T>
            class List { /* ... */ };        // additional stuff
        // ...
    }
```

There is no general language mechanism for renaming, but for types and templates, we can introduce aliases with **using** (§3.4.5, §6.5).

14.4.5 Namespaces and Overloading

Function overloading (§12.3) works across namespaces. This is essential to allow us to migrate
existing libraries to use namespaces with minimal source code changes. For example:

```
    // old A.h:
        void f(int);
        // ...

    // old B.h:
        void f(char);
        // ...

    // old user.c:
        #include "A.h"
        #include "B.h"

        void g()
        {
            f('a'); // calls the f() from B.h
        }
```

This program can be upgraded to a version using namespaces without changing the actual code:

```
    // new A.h:

        namespace A {
            void f(int);
            // ...
        }

    // new B.h:

        namespace B {
            void f(char);
            // ...
        }
```

```
// new user.c:

    #include "A.h"
    #include "B.h"

    using namespace A;
    using namespace B;

    void g()
    {
        f('a');        // calls the f() from B.h
    }
```

Had we wanted to keep user.c completely unchanged, we would have placed the using-directives in the header files. However, it is usually best to avoid using-directives in header files, because putting them there greatly increases the chances of name clashes.

This overloading rule also provides a mechanism for extending libraries. For example, people often wonder why they have to explicitly mention a sequence to manipulate a container using a standard-library algorithm. For example:

```
    sort(v.begin(),v.end());
```

Why not write:

```
    sort(v);
```

The reason is the need for generality (§32.2), but manipulating a container is by far the most common case. We can accommodate that case like this:

```
    #include<algorithm>

    namespace Estd {
        using namespace std;
        template<class C>
            void sort(C& c) { std::sort(c.begin(),c.end()); }
        template<class C, class P>
            void sort(C& c, P p) { std::sort(c.begin(),c.end(),p); }
    }
```

Estd (my "extended std") provides the frequently wanted container versions of sort(). Those are of course implemented using std::sort() from <algorithm>. We can use it like this:

```
    using namespace Estd;

    template<class T>
    void print(const vector<T>& v)
    {
        for (auto& x : v)
            cout << v << ' ';
        cout << '\n';
    }
```

```
void f()
{
    std::vector<int> v {7, 3, 9, 4, 0, 1};

    sort(v);
    print(v);
    sort(v,[](int x, int y) { return x>y; });
    print(v);
    sort(v.begin(),v.end());
    print(v);
    sort(v.begin(),v.end(),[](int x, int y) { return x>y; });
    print(v);
}
```

The namespace lookup rules and the overloading rules for templates ensure that we find and invoke the correct variants of sort() and get the expected output:

```
0 1 3 4 7 9
9 7 4 3 1 0
0 1 3 4 7 9
9 7 4 3 1 0
```

If we removed the using namespace std; from Estd, this example would still work because std's sort()s would be found by argument-dependent lookup (§14.2.4). However, we would then not find the standard sort()s for our own containers defined outside std.

14.4.6 Versioning

The toughest test for many kinds of interfaces is to cope with a sequence of new releases (versions). Consider a widely used interface, say, an ISO C++ standard header. After some time, a new version is defined, say, the C++11 version of the C++98 header. Functions may have been added, classes renamed, proprietary extensions (that should never have been there) removed, types changed, templates modified. To make life "interesting" for the implementer, hundreds of millions of lines of code are "out there" using the old header, and the implementer of the new version cannot ever see or modify them. Needless to say, breaking such code will cause howls of outrage, as will the absence of a new and better version. The namespace facilities described so far can be used to handle this problem with very minor exceptions, but when large amounts of code are involved, "very minor" still means a lot of code. Consequently, there is a way of selecting between two versions that simply and obviously guarantees that a user sees exactly one particular version. This is called an *inline namespace*:

```
namespace Popular {

    inline namespace V3_2 { // V3_2 provides the default meaning of Popular
        double f(double);
        int f(int);
        template<class T>
            class C { /* ... */ };
    }
```

```
namespace V3_0 {
    // ...
}
namespace V2_4_2 {
    double f(double);
    template<class T>
        class C { /* ... */ };
}
}
```

Here, **Popular** contains three subnamespaces, each defining a version. The **inline** specifies that **V3_2** is the default meaning of **Popular**. So we can write:

```
using namespace Popular;

void f()
{
    f(1);              // Popular::V3_2::f(int)
    V3_0::f(1);            // Popular::V3_0::f(double)
    V2_4_2::f(1);    // Popular::V2_4_2::f(double)
}

template<class T>
Popular::C<T*> { /* ... */ };
```

This **inline namespace** solution is intrusive; that is, to change which version (subnamespace) is the default requires modification of the header source code. Also, naively using this way of handling versioning would involve a lot of replication (of common code in the different versions). However, that replication can be minimized using **#include** tricks. For example:

```
// file V3_common:
    // ... lots of declarations ...
```

```
// file V3_2:

    namespace V3_2 {  // V3_2 provides the default meaning of Popular
        double f(double);
        int f(int);
        template<class T>
            class C { /* ... */ };
        #include "V3_common"
    }
```

```
// file V3_0.h:

    namespace V3_0 {
        #include "V3_common"
    }
```

```
// file Popular.h:

    namespace Popular {
        inline
        #include "V3_2.h"
        #include "V3_0.h"
        #include "V2_4_2.h"
    }
```

I do not recommend such intricate use of header files unless it is really necessary. The example above repeatedly violates the rules against including into a nonlocal scope and against having a syntactic construct span file boundaries (the use of **inline**); see §15.2.2. Sadly, I have seen worse.

In most cases, we can achieve versioning by less intrusive means. The only example I can think of that is completely impossible to do by other means is the specialization of a template explicitly using the namespace name (e.g., **Popular::C<T∗>**). However, in many important cases "in most cases" isn't good enough. Also, a solution based on a combination of other techniques is less obviously completely right.

14.4.7 Nested Namespaces

One obvious use of namespaces is to wrap a complete set of declarations and definitions in a separate namespace:

```
namespace X {
    // ... all my declarations ...
}
```

The list of declarations will, in general, contain namespaces. Thus, nested namespaces are allowed. This is allowed for practical reasons, as well as for the simple reason that constructs ought to nest unless there is a strong reason for them not to. For example:

```
void h();

namespace X {
    void g();
    // ...
    namespace Y {
        void f();
        void ff();
        // ...
    }
}
```

The usual scope and qualification rules apply:

```
void X::Y::ff()
{
    f(); g(); h();
}
```

```
void X::g()
{
    f();         // error: no f() in X
    Y::f();      // OK
}

void h()
{
    f();             // error: no global f()
    Y::f();          // error: no global Y
    X::f();          // error: no f() in X
    X::Y::f();       // OK
}
```

For examples of nested namespaces in the standard library, see **chrono** (§35.2) and **rel_ops** (§35.5.3).

14.4.8 Unnamed Namespaces

It is sometimes useful to wrap a set of declarations in a namespace simply to protect against the possibility of name clashes. That is, the aim is to preserve locality of code rather than to present an interface to users. For example:

```
#include "header.h"
namespace Mine {
    int a;
    void f() { /* ... */ }
    int g() { /* ... */ }
}
```

Since we don't want the name **Mine** to be known outside a local context, it simply becomes a bother to invent a redundant global name that might accidentally clash with someone else's names. In that case, we can simply leave the namespace without a name:

```
#include "header.h"
namespace {
    int a;
    void f() { /* ... */ }
    int g() { /* ... */ }
}
```

Clearly, there has to be some way of accessing members of an unnamed namespace from outside the unnamed namespace. Consequently, an unnamed namespace has an implied **using**-directive. The previous declaration is equivalent to

```
namespace $$$ {
    int a;
    void f() { /* ... */ }
    int g() { /* ... */ }
}
using namespace $$$;
```

where $$$ is some name unique to the scope in which the namespace is defined. In particular, unnamed namespaces in different translation units are different. As desired, there is no way of naming a member of an unnamed namespace from another translation unit.

14.4.9 C Headers

Consider the canonical first C program:

```
#include <stdio.h>

int main()
{
    printf("Hello, world!\n");
}
```

Breaking this program wouldn't be a good idea. Making standard libraries special cases isn't a good idea either. Consequently, the language rules for namespaces are designed to make it relatively easy to take a program written without namespaces and turn it into a more explicitly structured one using namespaces. In fact, the calculator program (§10.2) is an example of this.

One way to provide the standard C I/O facilities in a namespace would be to place the declarations from the C header stdio.h in a namespace std:

```
// cstdio:

namespace std {
    int printf(const char* ... );
    // ...
}
```

Given this <cstdio>, we could provide backward compatibility by adding a using-directive:

```
// stdio.h:

#include<cstdio>
using namespace std;
```

This <stdio.h> makes the Hello, world! program compile. Unfortunately, the using-directive makes every name from namespace std accessible in the global namespace. For example:

```
#include<vector>      // carefully avoids polluting the global namespace
vector v1;            // error: no "vector" in global scope
#include<stdio.h>     // contains a "using namespace std;"
vector v2;            // oops: this now works
```

So the standard requires that <stdio.h> place only names from <cstdio> in the global scope. This can be done by providing a using-declaration for each declaration in <cstdio>:

```
// stdio.h:

#include<cstdio>
using std::printf;
// ...
```

Another advantage is that the **using**-declaration for **printf()** prevents a user from (accidentally or deliberately) defining a nonstandard **printf()** in the global scope. I consider nonlocal **using**-directives primarily a transition tool. I also use them for essential foundation libraries, such as the ISO C++ standard library (**std**). Most code referring to names from other namespaces can be expressed more clearly with explicit qualification and **using**-declarations.

The relationship between namespaces and linkage is described in §15.2.5.

14.5 Advice

[1]   Use namespaces to express logical structure; §14.3.1.
[2]   Place every nonlocal name, except **main()**, in some namespace; §14.3.1.
[3]   Design a namespace so that you can conveniently use it without accidentally gaining access to unrelated namespaces; §14.3.3.
[4]   Avoid very short names for namespaces; §14.4.2.
[5]   If necessary, use namespace aliases to abbreviate long namespace names; §14.4.2.
[6]   Avoid placing heavy notational burdens on users of your namespaces; §14.2.2, §14.2.3.
[7]   Use separate namespaces for interfaces and implementations; §14.3.3.
[8]   Use the **Namespace::member** notation when defining namespace members; §14.4.
[9]   Use **inline** namespaces to support versioning; §14.4.6.
[10] Use **using**-directives for transition, for foundational libraries (such as **std**), or within a local scope; §14.4.9.
[11] Don't put a **using**-directive in a header file; §14.2.3.

15

Source Files and Programs

Form must follow function.
– Le Corbusier

- Separate Compilation
- Linkage
    File-Local Names; Header Files; The One-Definition Rule; Standard-Library Headers; Linkage to Non-C++ Code; Linkage and Pointers to Functions
- Using Header Files
    Single-Header Organization; Multiple-Header Organization; Include Guards
- Programs
    Initialization of Nonlocal Variables; Initialization and Concurrency; Program Termination
- Advice

15.1 Separate Compilation

Any realistic program consists of many logically separate components (e.g., namespaces; Chapter 14). To better manage these components, we can represent the program as a set of (source code) files where each file contains one or more logical components. Our task is to devise a physical structure (set of files) for the program that represents the logical components in a consistent, comprehensible, and flexible manner. In particular, we aim for a clean separation of interfaces (e.g., function declarations) and implementations (e.g., function definitions). A file is the traditional unit of storage (in a file system) and the traditional unit of compilation. There are systems that do not store, compile, and present C++ programs to the programmer as sets of files. However, the discussion here will concentrate on systems that employ the traditional use of files.

Having a complete program in one file is usually impossible. In particular, the code for the standard libraries and the operating system is typically not supplied in source form as part of a user's program. For realistically sized applications, even having all of the user's own code in a single file is both impractical and inconvenient. The way a program is organized into files can help emphasize its logical structure, help a human reader understand the program, and help the compiler enforce that logical structure. Where the unit of compilation is a file, all of the file must be recompiled whenever a change (however small) has been made to it or to something on which it depends. For even a moderately sized program, the amount of time spent recompiling can be significantly reduced by partitioning the program into files of suitable size.

A user presents a *source file* to the compiler. The file is then preprocessed; that is, macro processing (§12.6) is done and #include directives bring in headers (§2.4.1, §15.2.2). The result of preprocessing is called a *translation unit*. This unit is what the compiler proper works on and what the C++ language rules describe. In this book, I differentiate between source file and translation unit only where necessary to distinguish what the programmer sees from what the compiler considers.

To enable separate compilation, the programmer must supply declarations providing the type information needed to analyze a translation unit in isolation from the rest of the program. The declarations in a program consisting of many separately compiled parts must be consistent in exactly the same way the declarations in a program consisting of a single source file must be. Your system has tools to help ensure this. In particular, the linker can detect many kinds of inconsistencies. The *linker* is the program that binds together the separately compiled parts. A linker is sometimes (confusingly) called a *loader*. Linking can be done completely before a program starts to run. Alternatively, new code can be added to the running program ("dynamically linked") later.

The organization of a program into source files is commonly called the *physical structure* of a program. The physical separation of a program into separate files should be guided by the logical structure of the program. The same dependency concerns that guide the composition of programs out of namespaces guide its composition into source files. However, the logical and physical structures of a program need not be identical. For example, it can be helpful to use several source files to store the functions from a single namespace, to store a collection of namespace definitions in a single file, or to scatter the definition of a namespace over several files (§14.3.3).

Here, we will first consider some technicalities relating to linking and then discuss two ways of breaking the desk calculator (§10.2, §14.3.1) into files.

15.2 Linkage

Names of functions, classes, templates, variables, namespaces, enumerations, and enumerators must be used consistently across all translation units unless they are explicitly specified to be local.

It is the programmer's task to ensure that every namespace, class, function, etc., is properly declared in every translation unit in which it appears and that all declarations referring to the same entity are consistent. For example, consider two files:

```
// file1.cpp:
    int x = 1;
    int f() { /* do something */ }
```

```
// file2.cpp:
    extern int x;
    int f();
    void g() { x = f(); }
```

The x and f() used by g() in **file2.cpp** are the ones defined in **file1.cpp**. The keyword **extern** indicates that the declaration of x in **file2.cpp** is (just) a declaration and not a definition (§6.3). Had x been initialized, **extern** would simply be ignored because a declaration with an initializer is always a definition. An object must be defined exactly once in a program. It may be declared many times, but the types must agree exactly. For example:

```
// file1.cpp:
    int x = 1;
    int b = 1;
    extern int c;
```

```
// file2.cpp:
    int x;              // means "int x = 0;"
    extern double b;
    extern int c;
```

There are three errors here: x is defined twice, b is declared twice with different types, and c is declared twice but not defined. These kinds of errors (linkage errors) cannot be detected by a compiler that looks at only one file at a time. Many, however, are detectable by the linker. For example, all implementations I know of correctly diagnose the double definition of x. However, the inconsistent declarations of b are uncaught on popular implementations, and the missing definition of c is typically only caught if c is used.

Note that a variable defined without an initializer in the global or a namespace scope is initialized by default (§6.3.5.1). This is *not* the case for non-static local variables or objects created on the free store (§11.2).

Outside a class body, an entity must be declared before it is used (§6.3.4). For example:

```
// file1.cpp:
    int g() { return f()+7; }    // error: f() not (yet) declared
    int f() { return x; }        // error: x not (yet) declared
    int x;
```

A name that can be used in translation units different from the one in which it was defined is said to have *external linkage*. All the names in the previous examples have external linkage. A name that can be referred to only in the translation unit in which it is defined is said to have *internal linkage*. For example:

```
static int x1 = 1;       // internal linkage: not accessible from other translation units
const char x2 = 'a';     // internal linkage: not accessible from other translation units
```

When used in namespace scope (including the global scope; §14.2.1), the keyword **static** (somewhat illogically) means "not accessible from other source files" (i.e., internal linkage). If you wanted x1 to be accessible from other source files ("have external linkage"), you should remove the **static**. The keyword **const** implies default internal linkage, so if you wanted x2 to have external linkage, you need to precede its definitions with **extern**:

```
int x1 = 1;                      // external linkage: accessible from other translation units
extern const char x2 = 'a';      // external linkage: accessible from other translation units
```

Names that a linker does not see, such as the names of local variables, are said to have *no linkage*.

An inline function (§12.1.3, §16.2.8) must be defined identically in every translation unit in which it is used (§15.2.3). Consequently, the following example isn't just bad taste; it is illegal:

```
// file1.cpp:
        inline int f(int i) { return i; }
```

```
// file2.cpp:
        inline int f(int i) { return i+1; }
```

Unfortunately, this error is hard for an implementation to catch, and the following – otherwise perfectly logical – combination of external linkage and inlining is banned to make life simpler for compiler writers:

```
// file1.cpp:
        extern inline int g(int i);
        int h(int i) { return g(i); }    // error: g() undefined in this translation unit
```

```
// file2.cpp:
        extern inline int g(int i) { return i+1; }
        // ...
```

We keep inline function definitions consistent by using header files(§15.2.2). For example:

```
// h.h:
        inline int next(int i) { return i+1; }
```

```
// file1.cpp:
        #include "h.h"
        int h(int i) { return next(i); }      // fine
```

```
// file2.cpp:
        #include "h.h"
        // ...
```

By default, const objects (§7.5), constexpr objects (§10.4), type aliases (§6.5), and anything declared static (§6.3.4) in a namespace scope have internal linkage. Consequently, this example is legal (although potentially confusing):

```
// file1.cpp:
        using T = int;
        const int x = 7;
        constexpr T c2 = x+1;
```

```
// file2.cpp:
        using T = double;
        const int x = 8;
        constexpr T c2 = x+9;
```

To ensure consistency, place aliases, **consts**, **constexprs**, and **inlines** in header files (§15.2.2).

A **const** can be given external linkage by an explicit declaration:

```
// file1.cpp:
    extern const int a = 77;
```

```
// file2.cpp:
    extern const int a;

    void g()
    {
        cout << a << '\n';
    }
```

Here, **g()** will print **77**.

The techniques for managing template definitions are described in §23.7.

15.2.1 File-Local Names

Global variables are in general best avoided because they cause maintenance problems. In particular, it is hard to know where in a program they are used, and they can be a source of data races in multi-threaded programs (§41.2.4), leading to very obscure bugs.

Placing variables in a namespace helps a bit, but such variables are still subject to data races.

If you must use global variables, at least restrict their use to a single source file. This restriction can be achieved in one of two ways:

[1]   Place declarations in an unnamed namespace.

[2]   Declare an entity **static**.

An unnamed namespace (§14.4.8) can be used to make names local to a compilation unit. The effect of an unnamed namespace is very similar to that of internal linkage. For example:

```
// file 1.cpp:
    namespace {
        class X { /* ... */ };
        void f();
        int i;
        // ...
    }
```

```
// file2.cpp:
    class X { /* ... */ };
    void f();
    int i;
    // ...
```

The function **f()** in **file1.cpp** is not the same function as the **f()** in **file2.cpp**. Having a name local to a translation unit and also using that same name elsewhere for an entity with external linkage is asking for trouble.

The keyword **static** (confusingly) means "use internal linkage" (§44.2.3). That's an unfortunate leftover from the earliest days of C.

15.2.2 Header Files

The types in all declarations of the same object, function, class, etc., must be consistent. Consequently, the source code submitted to the compiler and later linked together must be consistent. One imperfect but simple method of achieving consistency for declarations in different translation units is to #include *header files* containing interface information in source files containing executable code and/or data definitions.

The #include mechanism is a text manipulation facility for gathering source program fragments together into a single unit (file) for compilation. Consider:

```
#include "to_be_included"
```

The #include-directive replaces the line in which the #include appears with the contents of the file to_be_included. The content of to_be_included should be C++ source text because the compiler will proceed to read it.

To include standard-library headers, use the angle brackets, < and >, around the name instead of quotes. For example:

```
#include <iostream>      // from standard include directory
#include "myheader.h"    // from current directory
```

Unfortunately, spaces are significant within the < > or " " of an include directive:

```
#include < iostream >    // will not find <iostream>
```

It seems extravagant to recompile a source file each time it is included somewhere, but the text can be a reasonably dense encoding for program interface information, and the compiler need only analyze details actually used (e.g., template bodies are often not completely analyzed until instantiation time; §26.3). Furthermore, most modern C++ implementations provide some form of (implicit or explicit) precompiling of header files to minimize the work needed to handle repeated compilation of the same header.

As a rule of thumb, a header may contain:

Named namespaces	namespace N { /* ... */ }
inline namespaces	inline namespace N { /* ... */ }
Type definitions	struct Point { int x, y; };
Template declarations	template<class T> class Z;
Template definitions	template<class T> class V { /* ... */ };
Function declarations	extern int strlen(const char∗);
inline function definitions	inline char get(char∗ p) { /* ... */ }
constexpr function definitions	constexpr int fac(int n) { return (n<2) ? 1 : fac(n−1); }
Data declarations	extern int a;
const definitions	const float pi = 3.141593;
constexpr definitions	constexpr float pi2 = pi∗pi;
Enumerations	enum class Light { red, yellow, green };
Name declarations	class Matrix;
Type aliases	using value_type = long;

Compile-time assertions	static_assert(4<=sizeof(int),"small ints");
Include directives	#include<algorithm>
Macro definitions	#define VERSION 12.03
Conditional compilation directives	#ifdef __cplusplus
Comments	/* check for end of file */

This rule of thumb for what may be placed in a header is not a language requirement. It is simply a reasonable way of using the #include mechanism to express the physical structure of a program. Conversely, a header should never contain:

Ordinary function definitions	char get(char* p) {return *p++; }
Data definitions	int a;
Aggregate definitions	short tbl[] = { 1, 2, 3 };
Unnamed namespaces	namespace { /* ... */ }
using-directives	using namespace Foo;

Including a header containing such definitions will lead to errors or (in the case of the using-directive) to confusion. Header files are conventionally suffixed by .h, and files containing function or data definitions are suffixed by .cpp. They are therefore often referred to as ".h files" and ".cpp files," respectively. Other conventions, such as .c, .C, .cxx, .cc, .hh, and hpp are also found. The manual for your compiler will be quite specific about this issue.

The reason for recommending that the definition of simple constants, but not the definition of aggregates, be placed in header files is that it is hard for implementations to avoid replication of aggregates presented in several translation units. Furthermore, the simple cases are far more common and therefore more important for generating good code.

It is wise not to be too clever about the use of #include. My recommendations are:
- #include only as headers (don't #include "ordinary source code containing variable definitions and non-inline functions").
- #include only complete declarations and definitions.
- #include only in the global scope, in linkage specification blocks, and in namespace definitions when converting old code (§15.2.4).
- Place all #includes before other code to minimize unintended dependencies.
- Avoid macro magic.
- Minimize the use of names (especially aliases) not local to a header in a header.

One of my least favorite activities is tracking down an error caused by a name being macro-substituted into something completely different by a macro defined in an indirectly #included header that I have never even heard of.

15.2.3 The One-Definition Rule

A given class, enumeration, and template, etc., must be defined exactly once in a program.

From a practical point of view, this means that there must be exactly one definition of, say, a class residing in a single file somewhere. Unfortunately, the language rule cannot be that simple. For example, the definition of a class may be composed through macro expansion (ugh!), and a definition of a class may be textually included in two source files by #include directives (§15.2.2).

Worse, a "file" isn't a concept that is part of the C++ language definition; there exist implementations that do not store programs in source files.

Consequently, the rule in the standard that says that there must be a unique definition of a class, template, etc., is phrased in a somewhat more complicated and subtle manner. This rule is commonly referred to as *the one-definition rule* ("the ODR"). That is, two definitions of a class, template, or inline function are accepted as examples of the same unique definition if and only if

[1]   they appear in different translation units, and

[2]   they are token-for-token identical, and

[3]   the meanings of those tokens are the same in both translation units.

For example:

```
// file1.cpp:
    struct S { int a; char b; };
    void f(S*);
```

```
// file2.cpp:
    struct S { int a; char b; };
    void f(S* p) { /* ... */ }
```

The ODR says that this example is valid and that S refers to the same class in both source files. However, it is unwise to write out a definition twice like that. Someone maintaining file2.cpp will naturally assume that the definition of S in file2.cpp is the only definition of S and so feel free to change it. This could introduce a hard-to-detect error.

The intent of the ODR is to allow inclusion of a class definition in different translation units from a common source file. For example:

```
// s.h:
    struct S { int a; char b; };
    void f(S*);
```

```
// file1.cpp:
    #include "s.h"
    // use f() here
```

```
// file2.cpp:
    #include "s.h"
    void f(S* p) { /* ... */ }
```

or graphically:

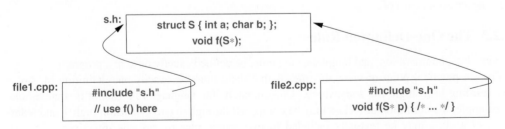

Here are examples of the three ways of violating the ODR:

```
// file1.cpp:
    struct S1 { int a; char b; };

    struct S1 { int a; char b; };      // error: double definition
```

This is an error because a **struct** may not be defined twice in a single translation unit.

```
// file1.cpp:
    struct S2 { int a; char b; };
```

```
// file2.cpp:
    struct S2 { int a; char bb; };     // error
```

This is an error because **S2** is used to name classes that differ in a member name.

```
// file1.cpp:
    typedef int X;
    struct S3 { X a; char b; };
```

```
// file2.cpp:
    typedef char X;
    struct S3 { X a; char b; }; // error
```

Here the two definitions of **S3** are token-for-token identical, but the example is an error because the meaning of the name **X** has sneakily been made to differ in the two files.

Checking against inconsistent class definitions in separate translation units is beyond the ability of most C++ implementations. Consequently, declarations that violate the ODR can be a source of subtle errors. Unfortunately, the technique of placing shared definitions in headers and #includeing them doesn't protect against this last form of ODR violation. Local type aliases and macros can change the meaning of #included declarations:

```
// s.h:
    struct S { Point a; char b; };
```

```
// file1.cpp:
    #define Point int
    #include "s.h"
    // ...
```

```
// file2.cpp:
    class Point { /* ... */ };
    #include "s.h"
    // ...
```

The best defense against this kind of hackery is to make headers as self-contained as possible. For example, if class **Point** had been declared in the **s.h** header, the error would have been detected.

A template definition can be #included in several translation units as long as the ODR is adhered to. This applies even to function template definitions and to class templates containing member function definitions.

15.2.4 Standard-Library Headers

The facilities of the standard library are presented through a set of standard headers (§4.1.2, §30.2). No suffix is needed for standard-library headers; they are known to be headers because they are included using the #include<...> syntax rather than #include"...". The absence of a .h suffix does not imply anything about how the header is stored. A header such as <map> is usually stored as a text file called map.h in some standard directory. On the other hand, standard headers are not required to be stored in a conventional manner. An implementation is allowed to take advantage of knowledge of the standard-library definition to optimize the standard-library implementation and the way standard headers are handled. For example, an implementation might have knowledge of the standard math library (§40.3) built in and treat #include<cmath> as a switch that makes the standard math functions available without actually reading any file.

For each C standard-library header <X.h>, there is a corresponding standard C++ header <cX>. For example, #include<cstdio> provides what #include<stdio.h> does. A typical **stdio.h** will look something like this:

```
#ifdef __cplusplus        // for C++ compilers only (§15.2.5)
namespace std {           // the standard library is defined in namespace std (§4.1.2)
extern "C" {              // stdio functions have C linkage (§15.2.5)
#endif
    /* ... */
    int printf(const char*, ...);
    /* ... */
#ifdef __cplusplus
}
}
// ...
using std::printf;    // make printf available in global namespace
// ...
#endif
```

That is, the actual declarations are (most likely) shared, but linkage and namespace issues must be addressed to allow C and C++ to share a header. The macro __cplusplus is defined by the C++ compiler (§12.6.2) and can be used to distinguish C++ code from code intended for a C compiler.

15.2.5 Linkage to Non-C++ Code

Typically, a C++ program contains parts written in other languages (e.g., C or Fortran). Similarly, it is common for C++ code fragments to be used as parts of programs written mainly in some other language (e.g., Python or Matlab). Cooperation can be difficult between program fragments written in different languages and even between fragments written in the same language but compiled with different compilers. For example, different languages and different implementations of the same language may differ in their use of machine registers to hold arguments, the layout of arguments put on a stack, the layout of built-in types such as strings and integers, the form of names passed by the compiler to the linker, and the amount of type checking required from the linker. To help, one can specify a *linkage* convention to be used in an **extern** declaration. For example, this declares the C and C++ standard-library function **strcpy()** and specifies that it should be linked according to the (system-specific) C linkage conventions:

```
extern "C" char* strcpy(char*, const char*);
```

The effect of this declaration differs from the effect of the "plain" declaration

```
extern char* strcpy(char*, const char*);
```

only in the linkage convention used for calling strcpy().

The extern "C" directive is particularly useful because of the close relationship between C and C++. Note that the C in extern "C" names a linkage convention and not a language. Often, extern "C" is used to link to Fortran and assembler routines that happen to conform to the conventions of a C implementation.

An extern "C" directive specifies the linkage convention (only) and does not affect the semantics of calls to the function. In particular, a function declared extern "C" still obeys the C++ type-checking and argument conversion rules and not the weaker C rules. For example:

```
extern "C" int f();

int g()
{
        return f(1);            // error: no argument expected
}
```

Adding extern "C" to a lot of declarations can be a nuisance. Consequently, there is a mechanism to specify linkage to a group of declarations. For example:

```
extern "C" {
        char* strcpy(char*, const char*);
        int strcmp(const char*, const char*);
        int strlen(const char*);
        // ...
}
```

This construct, commonly called a *linkage block*, can be used to enclose a complete C header to make a header suitable for C++ use. For example:

```
extern "C" {
#include <string.h>
}
```

This technique is commonly used to produce a C++ header from a C header. Alternatively, conditional compilation (§12.6.1) can be used to create a common C and C++ header:

```
#ifdef __cplusplus
extern "C" {
#endif
        char* strcpy(char*, const char*);
        int strcmp(const char*, const char*);
        int strlen(const char*);
        // ...
#ifdef __cplusplus
}
#endif
```

The predefined macro name __cplusplus (§12.6.2) is used to ensure that the C++ constructs are edited out when the file is used as a C header.

Any declaration can appear within a linkage block:

```
extern "C" {        // any declaration here, for example:
    int g1;         // definition
    extern int g2;  // declaration, not definition
}
```

In particular, the scope and storage class (§6.3.4, §6.4.2) of variables are not affected, so g1 is still a global variable – and is still defined rather than just declared. To declare but not define a variable, you must apply the keyword extern directly in the declaration. For example:

```
extern "C" int g3;        // declaration, not definition
extern "C" { int g4; }    // definition
```

This looks odd at first glance. However, it is a simple consequence of keeping the meaning unchanged when adding "C" to an extern-declaration and the meaning of a file unchanged when enclosing it in a linkage block.

A name with C linkage can be declared in a namespace. The namespace will affect the way the name is accessed in the C++ program, but not the way a linker sees it. The printf() from std is a typical example:

```
#include<cstdio>

void f()
{
    std::printf("Hello, ");    // OK
    printf("world!\n");        // error: no global printf()
}
```

Even when called std::printf, it is still the same old C printf() (§43.3).

Note that this allows us to include libraries with C linkage into a namespace of our choice rather than polluting the global namespace. Unfortunately, the same flexibility is not available to us for headers defining functions with C++ linkage in the global namespace. The reason is that linkage of C++ entities must take namespaces into account so that the object files generated will reflect the use or lack of use of namespaces.

15.2.6 Linkage and Pointers to Functions

When mixing C and C++ code fragments in one program, we sometimes want to pass pointers to functions defined in one language to functions defined in the other. If the two implementations of the two languages share linkage conventions and function call mechanisms, such passing of pointers to functions is trivial. However, such commonality cannot in general be assumed, so care must be taken to ensure that a function is called the way it expects to be called.

When linkage is specified for a declaration, the specified linkage applies to all function types, function names, and variable names introduced by the declaration(s). This makes all kinds of strange – and occasionally essential – combinations of linkage possible. For example:

```
typedef int (*FT)(const void*, const void*);          // FT has C++ linkage

extern "C" {
    typedef int (*CFT)(const void*, const void*);     // CFT has C linkage
    void qsort(void* p, size_t n, size_t sz, CFT cmp); // cmp has C linkage
}

void isort(void* p, size_t n, size_t sz, FT cmp);     // cmp has C++ linkage
void xsort(void* p, size_t n, size_t sz, CFT cmp);    // cmp has C linkage
extern "C" void ysort(void* p, size_t n, size_t sz, FT cmp); // cmp has C++ linkage

int compare(const void*, const void*);                 // compare() has C++ linkage
extern "C" int ccmp(const void*, const void*);         // ccmp() has C linkage

void f(char* v, int sz)
{
    qsort(v,sz,1,&compare); // error
    qsort(v,sz,1,&ccmp);         // OK

    isort(v,sz,1,&compare);  // OK
    isort(v,sz,1,&ccmp);      // error
}
```

An implementation in which C and C++ use the same calling conventions might accept the declarations marked *error* as a language extension. However, even for compatible C and C++ implementations, `std::function` (§33.5.3) or lambdas with any form of capture (§11.4.3) cannot cross the language barrier.

15.3 Using Header Files

To illustrate the use of headers, I present a few alternative ways of expressing the physical structure of the calculator program (§10.2, §14.3.1).

15.3.1 Single-Header Organization

The simplest solution to the problem of partitioning a program into several files is to put the definitions in a suitable number of .cpp files and to declare the types, functions, classes, etc., needed for them to cooperate in a single .h file that each .cpp file #includes. That's the initial organization I would use for a simple program for my own use; if something more elaborate turned out to be needed, I would reorganize later.

For the calculator program, we might use five .cpp files – lexer.cpp, parser.cpp, table.cpp, error.cpp, and main.cpp – to hold function and data definitions. The header dc.h holds the declarations of every name used in more than one .cpp file:

```
// dc.h:

#include <map>
#include<string>
#include<iostream>

namespace Parser {
    double expr(bool);
    double term(bool);
    double prim(bool);
}

namespace Lexer {
    enum class Kind : char {
        name, number, end,
        plus='+', minus='-', mul='*', div='/', print=';', assign='=', lp='(', rp=')'
    };

    struct Token {
        Kind kind;
        string string_value;
        double number_value;
    };

    class Token_stream {
    public:
        Token(istream& s) : ip{&s}, owns(false), ct{Kind::end} { }
        Token(istream* p) : ip{p}, owns{true}, ct{Kind::end} { }

        ~Token() { close(); }

        Token get();        // read and return next token
        Token& current();   // most recently read token

        void set_input(istream& s) { close(); ip = &s; owns=false; }
        void set_input(istream* p) { close(); ip = p; owns = true; }
    private:
        void close() { if (owns) delete ip; }

        istream* ip;        // pointer to an input stream
        bool owns;          // does the Token_stream own the istream?
        Token ct {Kind::end};   // current_token
    };

    extern Token_stream ts;
}
```

```
namespace Table {
    extern map<string,double> table;
}

namespace Error {
    extern int no_of_errors;
    double error(const string& s);
}

namespace Driver {
    void calculate();
}
```

The keyword **extern** is used for every variable declaration to ensure that multiple definitions do not occur as we **#include dc.h** in the various **.cpp** files. The corresponding definitions are found in the appropriate **.cpp** files.

I added standard-library headers as needed for the declarations in **dc.h**, but I did not add declarations (such as **using**-declarations) needed only for the convenience of an individual **.cpp** file.

Leaving out the actual code, **lexer.cpp** will look something like this:

```
// lexer.cpp:

#include "dc.h"
#include <cctype>
#include <iostream>        // redundant: in dc.h

Lexer::Token_stream ts;

Lexer::Token Lexer::Token_stream::get() { /* ... */ }
Lexer::Token& Lexer::Token_stream::current() { /* ... */ }
```

I used explicit qualification, **Lexer::**, for the definitions rather that simply enclosing them all in

```
namespace Lexer { /* ... */ }
```

That avoids the possibility of accidentally adding new members to **Lexer**. On the other hand, had I wanted to add members to **Lexer** that were not part of its interface, I would have had to reopen the namespace (§14.2.5).

Using headers in this manner ensures that every declaration in a header will at some point be included in the file containing its definition. For example, when compiling **lexer.cpp** the compiler will be presented with:

```
namespace Lexer {  // from dc.h
    // ...
    class Token_stream {
    public:
        Token get();
        // ...
    };
}
```

// ...

```
Lexer::Token Lexer::Token_stream::get() { /* ... */ }
```

This ensures that the compiler will detect any inconsistencies in the types specified for a name. For example, had **get()** been declared to return a **Token**, but defined to return an **int**, the compilation of **lexer.cpp** would have failed with a type-mismatch error. If a definition is missing, the linker will catch the problem. If a declaration is missing, some **.cpp** files will fail to compile.

File **parser.cpp** will look like this:

```
// parser.cpp:

#include "dc.h"

double Parser::prim(bool get) { /* ... */ }
double Parser::term(bool get) { /* ... */ }
double Parser::expr(bool get) { /* ... */ }
```

File **table.cpp** will look like this:

```
// table.cpp:

#include "dc.h"

std::map<std::string,double> Table::table;
```

The symbol table is a standard-library **map**.

File **error.cpp** becomes:

```
// error.cpp:

#include "dg.h"
// any more #includes or declarations

int Error::no_of_errors;
double Error::error(const string& s) { /* ... */ }
```

Finally, file **main.cpp** will look like this:

```
// main.cpp:

#include "dc.h"
#include <sstream>
#include <iostream>        // redundant: in dc.h

void Driver::calculate() { /* ... */ }

int main(int argc, char* argv[]) { /* ... */ }
```

To be recognized as *the* **main()** of the program, **main()** must be a global function (§2.2.1, §15.4), so no namespace is used here.

The physical structure of the system can be presented like this:

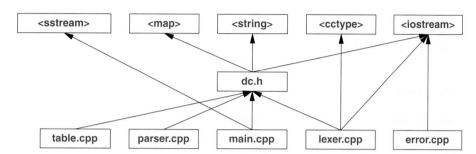

The headers on the top are all headers for standard-library facilities. For many forms of program analysis, these libraries can be ignored because they are well known and stable. For tiny programs, the structure can be simplified by moving all **#include** directives to the common header. Similarly, for a small program, separating out **error.cpp** and **table.cpp** from **main.cpp** would often be excessive.

This single-header style of physical partitioning is most useful when the program is small and its parts are not intended to be used separately. Note that when namespaces are used, the logical structure of the program is still represented within **dc.h**. If namespaces are not used, the structure is obscured, although comments can be a help.

For larger programs, the single-header-file approach is unworkable in a conventional file-based development environment. A change to the common header forces recompilation of the whole program, and updates of that single header by several programmers are error-prone. Unless strong emphasis is placed on programming styles relying heavily on namespaces and classes, the logical structure deteriorates as the program grows.

15.3.2 Multiple-Header Organization

An alternative physical organization lets each logical module have its own header defining the facilities it provides. Each **.cpp** file then has a corresponding **.h** file specifying what it provides (its interface). Each **.cpp** file includes its own **.h** file and usually also other **.h** files that specify what it needs from other modules in order to implement the services advertised in the interface. This physical organization corresponds to the logical organization of a module. The interface for users is put into its **.h** file, the interface for implementers is put into a file suffixed **_impl.h**, and the module's definitions of functions, variables, etc., are placed in **.cpp** files. In this way, the parser is represented by three files. The parser's user interface is provided by **parser.h**:

// parser.h:

```
namespace Parser {         // interface for users
    double expr(bool get);
}
```

The shared environment for the functions **expr()**, **prim()**, and **term()**, implementing the parser is presented by **parser_impl.h**:

```
// parser_impl.h:

#include "parser.h"
#include "error.h"
#include "lexer.h"

using Error::error;
using namespace Lexer;

namespace Parser {           // interface for implementers
    double prim(bool get);
    double term(bool get);
    double expr(bool get);
}
```

The distinction between the user interface and the interface for implementers would be even clearer had we used a **Parser_impl** namespace (§14.3.3).

The user's interface in header **parser.h** is #included to give the compiler a chance to check consistency (§15.3.1).

The functions implementing the parser are stored in **parser.cpp** together with #include directives for the headers that the **Parser** functions need:

```
// parser.cpp:

#include "parser_impl.h"
#include "table.h"

using Table::table;

double Parser::prim(bool get) { /* ... */ }
double Parser::term(bool get) { /* ... */ }
double Parser::expr(bool get) { /* ... */ }
```

Graphically, the parser and the driver's use of it look like this:

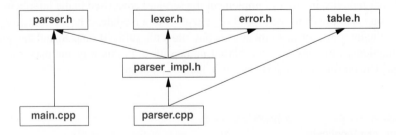

As intended, this is a rather close match to the logical structure described in §14.3.1. To simplify this structure, we could have #included **table.h** in **parser_impl.h** rather than in **parser.cpp**. However, **table.h** is an example of something that is not necessary to express the shared context of the parser functions; it is needed only by their implementation. In fact, it is used by just one function, **prim()**, so if we were really keen on minimizing dependencies we could place prim() in its own .cpp file and #include table.h there only:

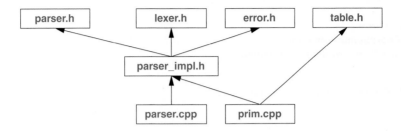

Such elaboration is not appropriate except for larger modules. For realistically sized modules, it is common to #include extra files where needed for individual functions. Furthermore, it is not uncommon to have more than one _impl.h, since different subsets of the module's functions need different shared contexts.

Please note that the _impl.h notation is not a standard or even a common convention; it is simply the way I like to name things.

Why bother with this more complicated scheme of multiple header files? It clearly requires far less thought simply to throw every declaration into a single header, as was done for dc.h.

The multiple-header organization scales to modules several magnitudes larger than our toy parser and to programs several magnitudes larger than our calculator. The fundamental reason for using this type of organization is that it provides a better localization of concerns. When analyzing and modifying a large program, it is essential for a programmer to focus on a relatively small chunk of code. The multiple-header organization makes it easy to determine exactly what the parser code depends on and to ignore the rest of the program. The single-header approach forces us to look at every declaration used by any module and decide if it is relevant. The simple fact is that maintenance of code is invariably done with incomplete information and from a local perspective. The multiple-header organization allows us to work successfully "from the inside out" with only a local perspective. The single-header approach – like every other organization centered around a global repository of information – requires a top-down approach and will forever leave us wondering exactly what depends on what.

The better localization leads to less information needed to compile a module, and thus to faster compiles. The effect can be dramatic. I have seen compile times drop by a factor of 1000 as the result of a simple dependency analysis leading to a better use of headers.

15.3.2.1 Other Calculator Modules

The remaining calculator modules can be organized similarly to the parser. However, those modules are so small that they don't require their own _impl.h files. Such files are needed only where the implementation of a logical module consists of many functions that need a shared context (in addition to what is provided to users).

The error handler provides its interface in error.h:

```
// error.h:

#include<string>

namespace Error {
    int Error::number_of_errors;
    double Error::error(const std::string&);
}
```

The implementation is found in **error.cpp**:

```
// error.cpp:

#include "error.h"

int Error::number_of_errors;
double Error::error(const std::string&) { /* ... */ }
```

The lexer provides a rather large and messy interface:

```
// lexer.h:

#include<string>
#include<iostream>

namespace Lexer {

    enum class Kind : char {/* ... */ };

    class Token { /* ... */ };
    class Token_stream { /* ... */ };

    extern Token_stream is;
}
```

In addition to **lexer.h**, the implementation of the lexer depends on **error.h** and on the character-classification functions in **<cctype>** (§36.2):

```
// lexer.cpp:

#include "lexer.h"
#include "error.h"
#include <iostream>       // redundant: in lexer.h
#include <cctype>

Lexer::Token_stream is; // defaults to "read from cin"

Lexer::Token Lexer::Token_stream::get() { /* ... */ };
Lexer::Token& Lexer::Token_stream::current() { /* ... */ };
```

We could have factored out the #include directive for **error.h** as the **Lexer**'s **_impl.h** file. However, I considered that excessive for this tiny program.

As usual, we #include the interface offered by the module – in this case, lexer.h – in the module's implementation to give the compiler a chance to check consistency.

The symbol table is essentially self-contained, although the standard-library header <map> could drag in all kinds of interesting stuff to implement an efficient map template class:

```
// table.h:

#include <map>
#include <string>

namespace Table {
    extern std::map<std::string,double> table;
}
```

Because we assume that every header may be #included in several .cpp files, we must separate the declaration of table from its definition:

```
// table.cpp:

#include "table.h"

std::map<std::string,double> Table::table;
```

I just stuck the driver into main.cpp:

```
// main.cpp:

#include "parser.h"
#include "lexer.h"    // to be able to set ts
#include "error.h"
#include "table.h"    // to be able to predefine names
#include <sstream> // to be able to put main()'s arguments into a string stream

namespace Driver {
    void calculate() { /* ... */ }
}

int main(int argc, char* argv[]) { /* ... */ }
```

For a larger system, it is usually worthwhile to separate out the driver and minimize what is done in main(). That way main() calls a driver function placed in a separate source file. This is particularly important for code intended to be used as a library. Then, we cannot rely on code in main() and must be prepared for the driver to be called from a variety of functions.

15.3.2.2 Use of Headers

The number of headers to use for a program is a function of many factors. Many of these factors have more to do with the way files are handled on your system than with C++. For example, if your editor/IDE does not make it convenient to look at several files simultaneously, then using many headers becomes less attractive.

A word of caution: a few dozen headers plus the standard headers for the program's execution environment (which can often be counted in the hundreds) are usually manageable. However, if you partition the declarations of a large program into the logically minimal-size headers (putting each structure declaration in its own file, etc.), you can easily get an unmanageable mess of hundreds of files even for minor projects. I find that excessive.

For large projects, multiple headers are unavoidable. In such projects, hundreds of files (not counting standard headers) are the norm. The real confusion starts when they begin to be counted in the thousands. At that scale, the basic techniques discussed here still apply, but their management becomes a Herculean task. Tools, such as dependency analysers, can be of great help, but there is little they can do for compiler and linker performance if the program is an unstructured mess. Remember that for realistically sized programs, the single-header style is not an option. Such programs will have multiple headers. The choice between the two styles of organization occurs (repeatedly) for the parts that make up the program.

The single-header style and the multiple-header style are not really alternatives. They are complementary techniques that must be considered whenever a significant module is designed and must be reconsidered as a system evolves. It's crucial to remember that one interface doesn't serve all equally well. It is usually worthwhile to distinguish between the implementers' interface and the users' interface. In addition, many larger systems are structured so that providing a simple interface for the majority of users and a more extensive interface for expert users is a good idea. The expert users' interfaces ("complete interfaces") tend to #include many more features than the average user would ever want to know about. In fact, the average users' interface can often be identified by eliminating features that require the inclusion of headers that define facilities that would be unknown to the average user. The term "average user" is not derogatory. In the fields in which I don't *have* to be an expert, I strongly prefer to be an average user. In that way, I minimize hassles.

15.3.3 Include Guards

The idea of the multiple-header approach is to represent each logical module as a consistent, self-contained unit. Viewed from the program as a whole, many of the declarations needed to make each logical module complete are redundant. For larger programs, such redundancy can lead to errors, as a header containing class definitions or inline functions gets #included twice in the same compilation unit (§15.2.3).

We have two choices. We can

[1]   reorganize our program to remove the redundancy, or

[2]   find a way to allow repeated inclusion of headers.

The first approach – which led to the final version of the calculator – is tedious and impractical for realistically sized programs. We also need that redundancy to make the individual parts of the program comprehensible in isolation.

The benefits of an analysis of redundant #includes and the resulting simplifications of the program can be significant both from a logical point of view and by reducing compile times. However, it can rarely be complete, so some method of allowing redundant #includes must be applied. Preferably, it must be applied systematically, since there is no way of knowing how thorough an analysis a user will find worthwhile.

The traditional solution is to insert *include guards* in headers. For example:

// error.h:

```
#ifndef CALC_ERROR_H
#define CALC_ERROR_H

namespace Error {
    // ...
}

#endif    // CALC_ERROR_H
```

The contents of the file between the **#ifndef** and **#endif** are ignored by the compiler if **CALC_ERROR_H** is defined. Thus, the first time error.h is seen during a compilation, its contents are read and **CALC_ERROR_H** is given a value. Should the compiler be presented with error.h again during the compilation, the contents are ignored. This is a piece of macro hackery, but it works and it is pervasive in the C and C++ worlds. The standard headers all have include guards.

Header files are included in essentially arbitrary contexts, and there is no namespace protection against macro name clashes. Consequently, I choose rather long and ugly names for my include guards.

Once people get used to headers and include guards, they tend to include *lots* of headers directly and indirectly. Even with C++ implementations that optimize the processing of headers, this can be undesirable. It can cause unnecessarily long compile time, and it can bring *lots* of declarations and macros into scope. The latter might affect the meaning of the program in unpredictable and adverse ways. Headers should be included only when necessary.

15.4 Programs

A program is a collection of separately compiled units combined by a linker. Every function, object, type, etc., used in this collection must have a unique definition (§6.3, §15.2.3). A program must contain exactly one function called main() (§2.2.1). The main computation performed by the program starts with the invocation of the global function main() and ends with a return from main(). The return type of main() is int, and the following two versions of main() are supported by all implementations:

```
int main() { /* ... */ }
int main(int argc, char* argv[]) { /* ... */ }
```

A program can only provide one of those two alternatives. In addition, an implementation can allow other versions of main(). The argc, argv version is used to transmit arguments from the program's environment; see §10.2.7.

The int returned by main() is passed to whatever system invoked main() as the result of the program. A nonzero return value from main() indicates an error.

This simple story must be elaborated on for programs that contain global variables (§15.4.1) or that throw an uncaught exception (§13.5.2.5).

15.4.1 Initialization of Nonlocal Variables

In principle, a variable defined outside any function (that is, global, namespace, and class **static** variables) is initialized before **main()** is invoked. Such nonlocal variables in a translation unit are initialized in their definition order. If such a variable has no explicit initializer, it is by default initialized to the default for its type (§17.3.3). The default initializer value for built-in types and enumerations is 0. For example:

```
double x = 2;        // nonlocal variables
double y;
double sqx = sqrt(x+y);
```

Here, x and y are initialized before sqx, so sqrt(2) is called.

There is no guaranteed order of initialization of global variables in different translation units. Consequently, it is unwise to create order dependencies between initializers of global variables in different compilation units. In addition, it is not possible to catch an exception thrown by the initializer of a global variable (§13.5.2.5). It is generally best to minimize the use of global variables and in particular to limit the use of global variables requiring complicated initialization.

Several techniques exist for enforcing an order of initialization of global variables in different translation units. However, none are both portable and efficient. In particular, dynamically linked libraries do not coexist happily with global variables that have complicated dependencies.

Often, a function returning a reference is a good alternative to a global variable. For example:

```
int& use_count()
{
    static int uc = 0;
    return uc;
}
```

A call **use_count()** now acts as a global variable except that it is initialized at its first use (§7.7). For example:

```
void f()
{
    cout << ++use_count();   // read and increment
    // ...
}
```

Like other uses of **static**, this technique is not thread-safe. The initialization of a local **static** is thread-safe (§42.3.3). In this case, the initialization is even with a constant expression (§10.4), so that it is done at link time and not subject to data races (§42.3.3). However, the **++** can lead to a data race.

The initialization of nonlocal (statically allocated) variables is controlled by whatever mechanism an implementation uses to start up a C++ program. This mechanism is guaranteed to work properly only if **main()** is executed. Consequently, one should avoid nonlocal variables that require run-time initialization in C++ code intended for execution as a fragment of a non-C++ program.

Note that variables initialized by constant expressions (§10.4) cannot depend on the value of objects from other translation units and do not require run-time initialization. Such variables are therefore safe to use in all cases.

15.4.2 Initialization and Concurrency

Consider:

```
int x = 3;
int y = sqrt(++x);
```

What could be the values of x and y? The obvious answer is "3 and 2!" Why? The initialization of a statically allocated object with a constant expression is done at link time, so x becomes 3. However, y's initializer is not a constant expression (sqrt() is no constexpr), so y is not initialized until run time. However, the order of initialization of statically allocated objects in a single translation unit is well defined: they are initialized in definition order (§15.4.1). So, y becomes 2.

The flaw in this argument is that if multiple threads are used (§5.3.1, §42.2), each will do the run-time initialization. No mutual exclusion is implicitly provided to prevent a data race. Then, sqrt(++x) in one thread may happen before or after the other thread manages to increment x. So, the value of y may be sqrt(4) or sqrt(5).

To avoid such problems, we should (as usual):

* Minimize the use of statically allocated objects and keep their initialization as simple as possible.
* Avoid dependencies on dynamically initialized objects in other translation units (§15.4.1).

In addition, to avoid data races in initialization, try these techniques in order:

[1] Initialize using constant expressions (note that built-in types without initializers are initialized to zero and that standard containers and strings are initialized to empty by link-time initialization).

[2] Initialize using expressions without side effects.

[3] Initialize in a known single-threaded "startup phase" of computation.

[4] Use some form of mutual exclusion (§5.3.4, §42.3).

15.4.3 Program Termination

A program can terminate in several ways:

[1] By returning from main()

[2] By calling exit()

[3] By calling abort()

[4] By throwing an uncaught exception

[5] By violating noexcept

[6] By calling quick_exit()

In addition, there are a variety of ill-behaved and implementation-dependent ways of making a program crash (e.g., dividing a double by zero).

If a program is terminated using the standard-library function exit(), the destructors for constructed static objects are called (§15.4.1, §16.2.12). However, if the program is terminated using the standard-library function abort(), they are not. Note that this implies that exit() does not terminate a program immediately. Calling exit() in a destructor may cause an infinite recursion. The type of exit() is:

```
void exit(int);
```

Like the return value of **main()** (§2.2.1), **exit()**'s argument is returned to "the system" as the value of the program. Zero indicates successful completion.

Calling **exit()** means that the local variables of the calling function and its callers will not have their destructors invoked. Throwing an exception and catching it ensures that local objects are properly destroyed (§13.5.1). Also, a call of **exit()** terminates the program without giving the caller of the function that called **exit()** a chance to deal with the problem. It is therefore often best to leave a context by throwing an exception and letting a handler decide what to do next. For example, **main()** may catch every exception (§13.5.2.2).

The C (and C++) standard-library function **atexit()** offers the possibility to have code executed at program termination. For example:

```
void my_cleanup();

void somewhere()
{
    if (atexit(&my_cleanup)==0) {
        // my_cleanup will be called at normal termination
    }
    else {
        // oops: too many atexit functions
    }
}
```

This strongly resembles the automatic invocation of destructors for global variables at program termination (§15.4.1, §16.2.12). An argument to **atexit()** cannot take arguments or return a result, and there is an implementation-defined limit to the number of atexit functions. A nonzero value returned by **atexit()** indicates that the limit is reached. These limitations make **atexit()** less useful than it appears at first glance. Basically, **atexit()** is a C workaround for the lack of destructors.

The destructor of a constructed statically allocated object (§6.4.2) created before a call of **atexit(f)** will be invoked after **f** is invoked. The destructor of such an object created after a call of **atexit(f)** will be invoked before **f** is invoked.

The **quick_exit()** function is like **exit()** except that it does not invoke any destructors. You register functions to be invoked by **quick_exit()** using **at_quick_exit()**.

The **exit()**, **abort()**, **quick_exit()**, **atexit()**, and **at_quick_exit()** functions are declared in **<cstdlib>**.

15.5 Advice

[1]   Use header files to represent interfaces and to emphasize logical structure; §15.1, §15.3.2.
[2]   **#include** a header in the source file that implements its functions; §15.3.1.
[3]   Don't define global entities with the same name and similar-but-different meanings in different translation units; §15.2.
[4]   Avoid non-inline function definitions in headers; §15.2.2.
[5]   Use **#include** only at global scope and in namespaces; §15.2.2.
[6]   **#include** only complete declarations; §15.2.2.
[7]   Use include guards; §15.3.3.

[8] #include C headers in namespaces to avoid global names; §14.4.9, §15.2.4.
[9] Make headers self-contained; §15.2.3.
[10] Distinguish between users' interfaces and implementers' interfaces; §15.3.2.
[11] Distinguish between average users' interfaces and expert users' interfaces; §15.3.2.
[12] Avoid nonlocal objects that require run-time initialization in code intended for use as part of non-C++ programs; §15.4.1.

Part III

Abstraction Mechanisms

This part describes C++'s facilities for defining and using new types. Techniques commonly called *object-oriented programming* and *generic programming* are presented.

Chapters

"... there is nothing more difficult to carry out, nor more doubtful of success, nor more dangerous to handle, than to initiate a new order of things. For the reformer makes enemies of all those who profit by the old order, and only lukewarm defenders in all those who would profit by the new order..."

— Niccolò Machiavelli ("The Prince" §vi)

16

Classes

Those types are not "abstract";
they are as real as int *and* float.
– Doug McIlroy

16.1 Introduction

C++ classes are a tool for creating new types that can be used as conveniently as the built-in types. In addition, derived classes (§3.2.4, Chapter 20) and templates (§3.4, Chapter 23) allow the programmer to express (hierachical and parametric) relationships among classes and to take advantage of such relationships.

A type is a concrete representation of a concept (an idea, a notion, etc.). For example, the C++ built-in type float with its operations +, –, *, etc., provides a concrete approximation of the mathematical concept of a real number. A class is a user-defined type. We design a new type to provide a definition of a concept that has no direct counterpart among the built-in types. For example, we might provide a type Trunk_line in a program dealing with telephony, a type Explosion for a video game, or a type list<Paragraph> for a text-processing program. A program that provides types that closely match the concepts of the application tends to be easier to understand, easier to reason about, and easier to modify than a program that does not. A well-chosen set of user-defined types also makes a program more concise. In addition, it makes many sorts of code analysis feasible. In particular, it enables the compiler to detect illegal uses of objects that would otherwise be found only through exhaustive testing.

The fundamental idea in defining a new type is to separate the incidental details of the implementation (e.g., the layout of the data used to store an object of the type) from the properties essential to the correct use of it (e.g., the complete list of functions that can access the data). Such a separation is best expressed by channeling all uses of the data structure and its internal housekeeping routines through a specific interface.

This chapter focuses on relatively simple "concrete" user-defined types that logically don't differ much from built-in types:

§16.2 *Class Basics* introduces the basic facilities for defining a class and its members.

§16.3 *Concrete Classes* discusses the design of elegant and efficient concrete classes.

The following chapters go into greater detail and presents abstract classes and class hierarchies:

Chapter 17   *Construction, Cleanup, Copy, and Move* presents the variety of ways to control initialization of objects of a class, how to copy and move objects, and how to provide "cleanup actions" to be performed when an object is destroyed (e.g., goes out of scope).

Chapter 18   *Operator Overloading* explains how to define unary and binary operators (such as **+**, **∗**, and **!**) for user-defined types and how to use them.

Chapter 19   *Special Operators* considers how to define and use operators (such as **[]**, **()**, **->**, **new**) that are "special" in that they are commonly used in ways that differ from arithmetic and logical operators. In particular, this chapter shows how to define a string class.

Chapter 20   *Derived Classes* introduces the basic language features supporting object-oriented programming. Base and derived classes, virtual functions, and access control are covered.

Chapter 21   *Class Hierarchies* focuses on the use of base and derived classes to effectively organize code around the notion of class hierarchies. Most of this chapter is devoted to discussion of programming techniques, but technical aspects of multiple inheritance (classes with more than one base class) are also covered.

Chapter 22   *Run-Time Type Information* describes the techniques for explicitly navigating class hierarchies. In particular, the type conversion operations **dynamic_cast** and **static_cast** are presented, as is the operation for determining the type of an object given one of its base classes (**typeid**).

16.2 Class Basics

Here is a very brief summary of classes:

- A class is a user-defined type.
- A class consists of a set of members. The most common kinds of members are data members and member functions.
- Member functions can define the meaning of initialization (creation), copy, move, and cleanup (destruction).

- Members are accessed using . (dot) for objects and –> (arrow) for pointers.
- Operators, such as +, !, and [], can be defined for a class.
- A class is a namespace containing its members.
- The **public** members provide the class's interface and the **private** members provide implementation details.
- A **struct** is a **class** where members are by default **public**.

For example:

```
class X {
private:                    // the representation (implementation) is private
    int m;
public:                     // the user interface is public
    X(int i =0) :m{i} { }   // a constructor (initialize the data member m)

    int mf(int i)           // a member function
    {
        int old = m;
        m = i;              // set a new value
        return old;         // return the old value
    }
};

X var {7};  // a variable of type X, initialized to 7

int user(X var, X* ptr)
{
    int x = var.mf(7);      // access using . (dot)
    int y = ptr–>mf(9);     // access using –> (arrow)
    int z = var.m;          // error: cannot access private member
}
```

The following sections expand on this and give rationale. The style is tutorial: a gradual development of ideas, with details postponed until later.

16.2.1 Member Functions

Consider implementing the concept of a date using a **struct** (§2.3.1, §8.2) to define the representation of a **Date** and a set of functions for manipulating variables of this type:

```
struct Date {         // representation
    int d, m, y;
};

void init_date(Date& d, int, int, int);   // initialize d
void add_year(Date& d, int n);            // add n years to d
void add_month(Date& d, int n);           // add n months to d
void add_day(Date& d, int n);             // add n days to d
```

There is no explicit connection between the data type, **Date**, and these functions. Such a connection can be established by declaring the functions as members:

```
struct Date {
    int d, m, y;

    void init(int dd, int mm, int yy);      // initialize
    void add_year(int n);                   // add n years
    void add_month(int n);                  // add n months
    void add_day(int n);                    // add n days
};
```

Functions declared within a class definition (a **struct** is a kind of class; §16.2.4) are called *member functions* and can be invoked only for a specific variable of the appropriate type using the standard syntax for structure member access (§8.2). For example:

```
Date my_birthday;

void f()
{
    Date today;

    today.init(16,10,1996);
    my_birthday.init(30,12,1950);

    Date tomorrow = today;
    tomorrow.add_day(1);
    // ...
}
```

Because different structures can have member functions with the same name, we must specify the structure name when defining a member function:

```
void Date::init(int dd, int mm, int yy)
{
    d = dd;
    m = mm;
    y = yy;
}
```

In a member function, member names can be used without explicit reference to an object. In that case, the name refers to that member of the object for which the function was invoked. For example, when **Date::init()** is invoked for **today**, **m=mm** assigns to **today.m**. On the other hand, when **Date::init()** is invoked for **my_birthday**, **m=mm** assigns to **my_birthday.m**. A class member function "knows" for which object it was invoked. But see §16.2.12 for the notion of a **static** member.

16.2.2 Default Copying

By default, objects can be copied. In particular, a class object can be initialized with a copy of an object of its class. For example:

```
Date d1 = my_birthday;   // initialization by copy
Date d2 {my_birthday};   // initialization by copy
```

By default, the copy of a class object is a copy of each member. If that default is not the behavior wanted for a class x, a more appropriate behavior can be provided (§3.3, §17.5).

Similarly, class objects can by default be copied by assignment. For example:

```
void f(Date& d)
{
    d = my_birthday;
}
```

Again, the default semantics is memberwise copy. If that is not the right choice for a class x, the user can define an appropriate assignment operator (§3.3, §17.5).

16.2.3 Access Control

The declaration of Date in the previous subsection provides a set of functions for manipulating a Date. However, it does not specify that those functions should be the only ones to depend directly on Date's representation and the only ones to directly access objects of class Date. This restriction can be expressed by using a class instead of a struct:

```
class Date {
    int d, m, y;
public:
    void init(int dd, int mm, int yy);      // initialize

    void add_year(int n);                    // add n years
    void add_month(int n);                   // add n months
    void add_day(int n);                     // add n days
};
```

The public label separates the class body into two parts. The names in the first, *private*, part can be used only by member functions. The second, *public*, part constitutes the public interface to objects of the class. A struct is simply a class whose members are public by default (§16.2.4); member functions can be defined and used exactly as before. For example:

```
void Date::add_year(int n)
{
    y += n;
}
```

However, nonmember functions are barred from using private members. For example:

```
void timewarp(Date& d)
{
    d.y -= 200;            // error: Date::y is private
}
```

The init() function is now essential because making the data private forces us to provide a way of initializing members. For example:

```
Date dx;
dx.m = 3;                  // error: m is private
dx.init(25,3,2011);        // OK
```

There are several benefits to be obtained from restricting access to a data structure to an explicitly declared list of functions. For example, any error causing a **Date** to take on an illegal value (for example, December 36, 2016) must be caused by code in a member function. This implies that the first stage of debugging – localization – is completed before the program is even run. This is a special case of the general observation that any change to the behavior of the type **Date** can and must be effected by changes to its members. In particular, if we change the representation of a class, we need only change the member functions to take advantage of the new representation. User code directly depends only on the public interface and need not be rewritten (although it may need to be recompiled). Another advantage is that a potential user need examine only the definitions of the member functions in order to learn to use a class. A more subtle, but most significant, advantage is that focusing on the design of a good interface simply leads to better code because thoughts and time otherwise devoted to debugging are expended on concerns related to proper use.

The protection of private data relies on restriction of the use of the class member names. It can therefore be circumvented by address manipulation (§7.4.1) and explicit type conversion (§11.5). But this, of course, is cheating. C++ protects against accident rather than deliberate circumvention (fraud). Only hardware can offer perfect protection against malicious use of a general-purpose language, and even that is hard to do in realistic systems.

16.2.4 class and struct

The construct .

```
class X { ... };
```

is called a *class definition*; it defines a type called **X**. For historical reasons, a class definition is often referred to as a *class declaration*. Also, like declarations that are not definitions, a class definition can be replicated in different source files using **#include** without violating the one-definition rule (§15.2.3).

By definition, a **struct** is a class in which members are by default public; that is,

```
struct S { /* ... */ };
```

is simply shorthand for

```
class S { public: /* ... */ };
```

These two definitions of **S** are interchangeable, though it is usually wise to stick to one style. Which style you use depends on circumstances and taste. I tend to use **struct** for classes that I think of as "just simple data structures." If I think of a class as "a proper type with an invariant," I use **class**. Constructors and access functions can be quite useful even for **structs**, but as a shorthand rather than guarantors of invariants (§2.4.3.2, §13.4).

By default, members of a **class** are private:

```
class Date1 {
        int d, m, y;          // private by default
    public:
        Date1(int dd, int mm, int yy);
        void add_year(int n);      // add n years
};
```

However, we can also use the access specifier **private:** to say that the members following are private, just as **public:** says that the members following are public:

```
struct Date2 {
private:
    int d, m, y;
public:
    Date2(int dd, int mm, int yy);
    void add_year(int n);        // add n years
};
```

Except for the different name, **Date1** and **Date2** are equivalent.

It is not a requirement to declare data first in a class. In fact, it often makes sense to place data members last to emphasize the functions providing the public user interface. For example:

```
class Date3 {
public:
    Date3(int dd, int mm, int yy);
    void add_year(int n);        // add n years
private:
    int d, m, y;
};
```

In real code, where both the public interface and the implementation details typically are more extensive than in tutorial examples, I usually prefer the style used for **Date3**.

Access specifiers can be used many times in a single class declaration. For example:

```
class Date4 {
public:
    Date4(int dd, int mm, int yy);
private:
    int d, m, y;
public:
    void add_year(int n);        // add n years
};
```

Having more than one public section, as in **Date4**, tends to be messy, though, and might affect the object layout (§20.5). So does having more than one private section. However, allowing many access specifiers in a class is useful for machine-generated code.

16.2.5 Constructors

The use of functions such as init() to provide initialization for class objects is inelegant and error-prone. Because it is nowhere stated that an object must be initialized, a programmer can forget to do so – or do so twice (often with equally disastrous results). A better approach is to allow the programmer to declare a function with the explicit purpose of initializing objects. Because such a function constructs values of a given type, it is called a *constructor*. A constructor is recognized by having the same name as the class itself. For example:

```
class Date {
    int d, m, y;
public:
    Date(int dd, int mm, int yy);        // constructor
    // ...
};
```

When a class has a constructor, all objects of that class will be initialized by a constructor call. If the constructor requires arguments, these arguments must be supplied:

```
Date today = Date(23,6,1983);
Date xmas(25,12,1990);        // abbreviated form
Date my_birthday;             // error: initializer missing
Date release1_0(10,12);       // error: third argument missing
```

Since a constructor defines initialization for a class, we can use the {}-initializer notation:

```
Date today = Date {23,6,1983};
Date xmas {25,12,1990};       // abbreviated form
Date release1_0 {10,12};      // error: third argument missing
```

I recommend the {} notation over the () notation for initialization because it is explicit about what is being done (initialization), avoids some potential mistakes, and can be used consistently (§2.2.2, §6.3.5). There are cases where () notation must be used (§4.4.1, §17.3.2.1), but they are rare.

By providing several constructors, we can provide a variety of ways of initializing objects of a type. For example:

```
class Date {
    int d, m, y;
public:
    // ...

    Date(int, int, int);        // day, month, year
    Date(int, int);             // day, month, today's year
    Date(int);                  // day, today's month and year
    Date();                     // default Date: today
    Date(const char*);          // date in string representation
};
```

Constructors obey the same overloading rules as do ordinary functions (§12.3). As long as the constructors differ sufficiently in their argument types, the compiler can select the correct one for a use:

```
Date today {4};               // 4, today.m, today.y
Date july4 {"July 4, 1983"};
Date guy {5,11};              // 5, November, today.y
Date now;                     // default initialized as today
Date start {};                // default initialized as today
```

The proliferation of constructors in the **Date** example is typical. When designing a class, a programmer is always tempted to add features just because somebody might want them. It takes more thought to carefully decide what features are really needed and to include only those. However, that extra thought typically leads to smaller and more comprehensible programs. One way of reducing the number of related functions is to use default arguments (§12.2.5). For **Date**, each argument can be given a default value interpreted as "pick the default: **today**."

```
class Date {
    int d, m, y;
public:
    Date(int dd =0, int mm =0, int yy =0);
    // ...
};

Date::Date(int dd, int mm, int yy)
{
    d = dd ? dd : today.d;
    m = mm ? mm : today.m;
    y = yy ? yy : today.y;

    // check that the Date is valid
}
```

When an argument value is used to indicate "pick the default," the value chosen must be outside the set of possible values for the argument. For **day** and **month**, this is clearly so, but for **year**, zero may not be an obvious choice. Fortunately, there is no year zero on the European calendar; 1AD (**year==1**) comes immediately after 1BC (**year==–1**).

Alternatively, we could use the default values directly as default arguments:

```
class Date {
    int d, m, y;
public:
    Date(int dd =today.d, int mm =today.m, int yy =today.y);
    // ...
};

Date::Date(int dd, int mm, int yy)
{
    // check that the Date is valid
}
```

However, I chose to use **0** to avoid building actual values into **Date**'s interface. That way, we have the option to later improve the implementation of the default.

Note that by guaranteeing proper initialization of objects, the constructors greatly simplify the implementation of member functions. Given constructors, other member functions no longer have to deal with the possibility of uninitialized data (§16.3.1).

16.2.6 explicit Constructors

By default, a constructor invoked by a single argument acts as an implicit conversion from its argument type to its type. For example:

```
complex<double> d {1};        // d=={1,0} (§5.6.2)
```

Such implicit conversions can be extremely useful. Complex numbers are an example: if we leave out the imaginary part, we get a complex number on the real axis. That's exactly what mathematics requires. However, in many cases, such conversions can be a significant source of confusion and errors. Consider Date:

```
void my_fct(Date d);

void f()
{
    Date d {15};    // plausible: x becomes {15,today.m,today.y}
    // ...
    my_fct(15);     // obscure
    d = 15;         // obscure
    // ...
}
```

At best, this is obscure. There is no clear logical connection between the number 15 and a Date independently of the intricacies of our code.

Fortunately, we can specify that a constructor is not used as an *implicit* conversion. A constructor declared with the keyword explicit can only be used for initialization and explicit conversions. For example:

```
class Date {
    int d, m, y;
public:
    explicit Date(int dd =0, int mm =0, int yy =0);
    // ...
};
```

```
Date d1 {15};            // OK: considered explicit
Date d2 = Date{15};      // OK: explicit
Date d3 = {15};          // error: = initialization does not do implicit conversions
Date d4 = 15;            // error: = initialization does not do implicit conversions

void f()
{
    my_fct(15);          // error: argument passing does not do implicit conversions
    my_fct({15});        // error: argument passing does not do implicit conversions
    my_fct(Date{15});    // OK: explicit
    // ...
}
```

An initialization with an = is considered a *copy initialization*. In principle, a copy of the initializer is placed into the initialized object. However, such a copy may be optimized away (elided), and a move operation (§3.3.2, §17.5.2) may be used if the initializer is an rvalue (§6.4.1). Leaving out the = makes the initialization explicit. Explicit initialization is known as *direct initialization*.

By default, declare a constructor that can be called with a single argument explicit. You need a good reason not to do so (as for complex). If you define an implicit constructor, it is best to document your reason or a maintainer may suspect that you were forgetful (or ignorant).

If a constructor is declared `explicit` and defined outside the class, that `explicit` cannot be repeated:

```
class Date {
    int d, m, y;
public:
    explicit Date(int dd);
    // ...
};


Date::Date(int dd) { /* ... */ }            // OK
explicit Date::Date(int dd) { /* ... */ }   // error
```

Most examples where `explicit` is important involve a single constructor argument. However, `explicit` can also be useful for constructors with zero or more than one argument. For example:

```
struct X {
    explicit X();
    explicit X(int,int);
};


X x1 = {};          // error: implicit
X x2 = {1,2};       // error: implicit


X x3 {};            // OK: explicit
X x4 {1,2};         // OK: explicit


int f(X);


int i1 = f({});         // error: implicit
int i2 = f({1,2});      // error: implicit


int i3 = f(X{});        // OK: explicit
int i4 = f(X{1,2});     // OK: explicit
```

The distinction between direct and copy initialization is maintained for list initialization (§17.3.4.3).

16.2.7 In-Class Initializers

When we use several constructors, member initialization can become repetitive. For example:

```
class Date {
    int d, m, y;
public:
    Date(int, int, int);        // day, month, year
    Date(int, int);             // day, month, today's year
    Date(int);                  // day, today's month and year
    Date();                     // default Date: today
    Date(const char*);          // date in string representation
    // ...
};
```

We can deal with that by introducing default arguments to reduce the number of constructors (§16.2.5). Alternatively, we can add initializers to data members:

```
class Date {
    int d {today.d};
    int m {today.m};
    int y {today.y};
public:
    Date(int, int, int);        // day, month, year
    Date(int, int);             // day, month, today's year
    Date(int);                  // day, today's month and year
    Date();                     // default Date: today
    Date(const char*);          // date in string representation
    // ...
```

Now, each constructor has the d, m, and y initialized unless it does it itself. For example:

```
Date::Date(int dd)
    :d{dd}
{
    // check that the Date is valid
}
```

This is equivalent to:

```
Date::Date(int dd)
    :d{dd}, m{today.m}, y{today.y}
{
    // check that the Date is valid
}
```

16.2.8 In-Class Function Definitions

A member function defined within the class definition – rather than simply declared there – is taken to be an inline (§12.1.5) member function. That is, in-class definition of member functions is for small, rarely modified, frequently used functions. Like the class definition it is part of, a member function defined in-class can be replicated in several translation units using #include. Like the class itself, the member function's meaning must be the same wherever it is #included (§15.2.3).

A member can refer to another member of its class independently of where that member is defined (§6.3.4). Consider:

```
class Date {
public:
    void add_month(int n) { m+=n; }     // increment the Date's m
    // ...
private:
    int d, m, y;
};
```

That is, function and data member declarations are order independent. I could equivalently have written:

```
class Date {
public:
        void add_month(int n) { m+=n; }      // increment the Date's m
        // ...
private:
        int d, m, y;
};


inline void Date::add_month(int n)  // add n months
{
        m+=n;       // increment the Date's m
}
```

This latter style is often used to keep class definitions simple and easy to read. It also provides a textual separation of a class's interface and implementation.

Obviously, I simplified the definition of **Date::add_month**; just adding n and hoping to hit a good date is too naive (§16.3.1).

16.2.9 Mutability

We can define a named object as a constant or as a variable. In other words, a name can refer to an object that holds an *immutable* or a *mutable* value. Since the precise terminology can be a bit clumsy, we end up referring to some variables as being constant or briefer still to **const** variables. However odd that may sound to a native English speaker, the concept is useful and deeply embedded in the C++ type system. Systematic use of immutable objects leads to more comprehensible code, to more errors being found early, and sometimes to improved performance. In particular, immutability is a most useful property in a multi-threaded program (§5.3, Chapter 41).

To be useful beyond the definition of simple constants of built-in types, we must be able to define functions that operate on **const** objects of user-defined types. For freestanding functions that means functions that take **const T&** arguments. For classes it means that we must be able to define member functions that work on **const** objects.

16.2.9.1 Constant Member Functions

The **Date** as defined so far provides member functions for giving a **Date** a value. Unfortunately, we didn't provide a way of examining the value of a **Date**. This problem can easily be remedied by adding functions for reading the day, month, and year:

```
class Date {
        int d, m, y;
public:
        int day() const { return d; }
        int month() const { return m; }
        int year() const;

        void add_year(int n);       // add n years
        // ...
};
```

The **const** after the (empty) argument list in the function declarations indicates that these functions do not modify the state of a **Date**.

Naturally, the compiler will catch accidental attempts to violate this promise. For example:

```
int Date::year() const
{
        return ++y;     // error: attempt to change member value in const function
}
```

When a **const** member function is defined outside its class, the **const** suffix is required:

```
int Date::year()        // error: const missing in member function type
{
        return y;
}
```

In other words, **const** is part of the type of **Date::day()**, **Date::month()**, and **Date::year()**.

A **const** member function can be invoked for both **const** and non-**const** objects, whereas a non-**const** member function can be invoked only for non-**const** objects. For example:

```
void f(Date& d, const Date& cd)
{
        int i = d.year();       // OK
        d.add_year(1);          // OK

        int j = cd.year();      // OK
        cd.add_year(1);         // error: cannot change value of a const Date
}
```

16.2.9.2 Physical and Logical Constness

Occasionally, a member function is logically **const**, but it still needs to change the value of a member. That is, to a user, the function appears not to change the state of its object, but some detail that the user cannot directly observe is updated. This is often called *logical constness*. For example, the **Date** class might have a function returning a string representation. Constructing this representation could be a relatively expensive operation. Therefore, it would make sense to keep a copy so that repeated requests would simply return the copy, unless the **Date**'s value had been changed. Caching values like that is more common for more complicated data structures, but let's see how it can be achieved for a **Date**:

```
class Date {
public:
        // ...
        string string_rep() const;     // string representation
private:
        bool cache_valid;
        string cache;
        void compute_cache_value(); // fill cache
        // ...
};
```

From a user's point of view, **string_rep** doesn't change the state of its **Date**, so it clearly should be a **const** member function. On the other hand, the **cache** and **cache_valid** members must change occasionally for the design to make sense.

Such problems could be solved through brute force using a cast, for example, a **const_cast** (§11.5.2). However, there are also reasonably elegant solutions that do not involve messing with type rules.

16.2.9.3 mutable

We can define a member of a class to be **mutable**, meaning that it can be modified even in a **const** object:

```
class Date {
public:
    // ...
    string string_rep() const;          // string representation
private:
    mutable bool cache_valid;
    mutable string cache;
    void compute_cache_value() const;   // fill (mutable) cache
    // ...
};
```

Now we can define **string_rep()** in the obvious way:

```
string Date::string_rep() const
{
    if (!cache_valid) {
        compute_cache_value();
        cache_valid = true;
    }
    return cache;
}
```

We can now use **string_rep()** for both **const** and non-**const** objects. For example:

```
void f(Date d, const Date cd)
{
    string s1 = d.string_rep();
    string s2 = cd.string_rep();        // OK!
    // ...
}
```

16.2.9.4 Mutability through Indirection

Declaring a member **mutable** is most appropriate when only a small part of a representation of a small object is allowed to change. More complicated cases are often better handled by placing the changing data in a separate object and accessing it indirectly. If that technique is used, the string-with-cache example becomes:

```
struct cache {
    bool valid;
    string rep;
};

class Date {
public:
    // ...
    string string_rep() const;              // string representation
private:
    cache* c;                               // initialize in constructor
    void compute_cache_value() const;       // fill what cache refers to
    // ...
};

string Date::string_rep() const
{
    if (!c–>valid) {
        compute_cache_value();
        c–>valid = true;
    }
    return c–>rep;
}
```

The programming techniques that support a cache generalize to various forms of lazy evaluation.

Note that **const** does not apply (transitively) to objects accessed through pointers or references. The human reader may consider such an object as "a kind of subobject," but the compiler does not know such pointers or references to be any different from any others. That is, a member pointer does not have any special semantics that distinguish it from other pointers.

16.2.10 Self-Reference

The state update functions **add_year()**, **add_month()**, and **add_day()** (§16.2.3) were defined not to return values. For such a set of related update functions, it is often useful to return a reference to the updated object so that the operations can be chained. For example, we would like to write:

```
void f(Date& d)
{
    // ...
    d.add_day(1).add_month(1).add_year(1);
    // ...
}
```

to add a day, a month, and a year to **d**. To do this, each function must be declared to return a reference to a **Date**:

```
class Date {
    // ...
```

```
Date& add_year(int n);      // add n years
Date& add_month(int n);  // add n months
Date& add_day(int n);       // add n days
};
```

Each (non-static) member function knows for which object it was invoked and can explicitly refer
to it. For example:

```
Date& Date::add_year(int n)
{
    if (d==29 && m==2 && !leapyear(y+n)) {  // beware of February 29
        d = 1;
        m = 3;
    }
    y += n;
    return *this;
}
```

The expression *this refers to the object for which a member function is invoked.

In a non-static member function, the keyword this is a pointer to the object for which the function was invoked. In a non-const member function of class X, the type of this is X*. However, this is considered an rvalue, so it is not possible to take the address of this or to assign to this. In a const member function of class X, the type of this is const X* to prevent modification of the object itself (see also §7.5).

Most uses of this are implicit. In particular, every reference to a non-static member from within a class relies on an implicit use of this to get the member of the appropriate object. For example, the add_year function could equivalently, but tediously, have been defined like this:

```
Date& Date::add_year(int n)
{
    if (this->d==29 && this->m==2 && !leapyear(this->y+n)) {
        this->d = 1;
        this->m = 3;
    }
    this->y += n;
    return *this;
}
```

One common explicit use of this is in linked-list manipulation. For example:

```
struct Link {
    Link* pre;
    Link* suc;
    int data;

    Link* insert(int x)    // insert x before this
    {
        return pre = new Link{pre,this,x};
    }
}
```

```
    void remove()  // remove and destroy this
    {
        if (pre) pre->suc = suc;
        if (suc) suc->pre = pre;
        delete this;
    }

    // ...
};
```

Explicit use of this is required for access to members of base classes from a derived class that is a template (§26.3.7).

16.2.11 Member Access

A member of a class **X** can be accessed by applying the . (dot) operator to an object of class **X** or by applying the -> (arrow) operator to a pointer to an object of class **X**. For example:

```
struct X {
    void f();
    int m;
};

void user(X x, X* px)
{
    m = 1;          // error: there is no m in scope
    x.m = 1;        // OK
    x->m = 1;       // error: x is not a pointer
    px->m = 1;      // OK
    px.m = 1;       // error: px is a pointer
}
```

Obviously, there is a bit of redundancy here: the compiler knows whether a name refers to an **X** or to an **X***, so a single operator would have been sufficient. However, a programmer might be confused, so from the first days of C the rule has been to use separate operators.

From inside a class no operator is needed. For example:

```
void X::f()
{
    m = 1;          // OK: "this->m = 1;" (§16.2.10)
}
```

That is, an unqualified member name acts as if it had been prefixed by this->. Note that a member function can refer to the name of a member before it has been declared:

```
struct X {
    int f() { return m; }   // fine: return this X's m
    int m;
};
```

If we want to refer to a member in general, rather than to a member of a particular object, we qualify by the class name followed by ::. For example:

```
struct S {
    int m;
    int f();
    static int sm;
};
```

```
int X::f() { return m; }          // X's f
int X::sm {7};                    // X's static member sm (§16.2.12)
int (S::*) pmf() {&S::f};         // X's member f
```

That last construct (a pointer to member) is fairly rare and esoteric; see §20.6. I mention it here just to emphasize the generality of the rule for ::.

16.2.12 [static] Members

The convenience of a default value for **Date**s was bought at the cost of a significant hidden problem. Our **Date** class became dependent on the global variable **today**. This **Date** class can be used only in a context in which **today** is defined and correctly used by every piece of code. This is the kind of constraint that causes a class to be useless outside the context in which it was first written. Users get too many unpleasant surprises trying to use such context-dependent classes, and maintenance becomes messy. Maybe "just one little global variable" isn't too unmanageable, but that style leads to code that is useless except to its original programmer. It should be avoided.

Fortunately, we can get the convenience without the encumbrance of a publicly accessible global variable. A variable that is part of a class, yet is not part of an object of that class, is called a **static** member. There is exactly one copy of a **static** member instead of one copy per object, as for ordinary non-**static** members (§6.4.2). Similarly, a function that needs access to members of a class, yet doesn't need to be invoked for a particular object, is called a **static** member function.

Here is a redesign that preserves the semantics of default constructor values for **Date** without the problems stemming from reliance on a global:

```
class Date {
    int d, m, y;
    static Date default_date;
public:
    Date(int dd =0, int mm =0, int yy =0);
    // ...
    static void set_default(int dd, int mm, int yy); // set default_date to Date(dd,mm,yy)
};
```

We can now define the **Date** constructor to use **default_date** like this:

```
Date::Date(int dd, int mm, int yy)
{
    d = dd ? dd : default_date.d;
    m = mm ? mm : default_date.m;
    y = yy ? yy : default_date.y;

    // ... check that the Date is valid ...

}
```

Using set_default(), we can change the default date when appropriate. A static member can be referred to like any other member. In addition, a static member can be referred to without mentioning an object. Instead, its name is qualified by the name of its class. For example:

```
void f()
{
    Date::set_default(4,5,1945);    // call Date's static member set_default()
}
```

If used, a static member – a function or data member – must be defined somewhere. The keyword static is not repeated in the definition of a static member. For example:

```
Date Date::default_date {16,12,1770};      // definition of Date::default_date

void Date::set_default(int d, int m, int y)    // definition of Date::set_default
{
    default_date = {d,m,y};                // assign new value to default_date
}
```

Now, the default value is Beethoven's birth date – until someone decides otherwise.

Note that Date{} serves as a notation for the value of Date::default_date. For example:

```
Date copy_of_default_date = Date{};

void f(Date);

void g()
{
    f(Date{});
}
```

Consequently, we don't need a separate function for reading the default date. Furthermore, where the target type is unambiguously a Date, plain {} is sufficient. For example:

```
void f1(Date);

void f2(Date);
void f2(int);

void g()
{
    f1({});         // OK: equivalent to f1(Date{})
    f2({}):         // error: ambiguous: f2(int) or f2(Date)?
    f2(Date{});     // OK
```

In multi-threaded code, static data members require some kind of locking or access discipline to avoid race conditions (§5.3.4, §41.2.4). Since multi-threading is now very common, it is unfortunate that use of static data members was quite popular in older code. Older code tends to use static members in ways that imply race conditions.

16.2.13 Member Types

Types and type aliases can be members of a class. For example:

```
template<typename T>
class Tree {
    using value_type = T;                    // member alias
    enum Policy { rb, splay, treeps };       // member enum
    class Node {                             // member class
        Node* right;
        Node* left;
        value_type value;
    public:
        void f(Tree*);
    };
    Node* top;
public:
    void g(const T&);
    // ...
};
```

A *member class* (often called a *nested class*) can refer to types and **static** members of its enclosing class. It can only refer to non-**static** members when it is given an object of the enclosing class to refer to. To avoid getting into the intricacies of binary trees, I use purely technical "f() and g()"-style examples.

A nested class has access to members of its enclosing class, even to **private** members (just as a member function has), but has no notion of a current object of the enclosing class. For example:

```
template<typename T>
void Tree::Node::f(Tree* p)
{
    top = right;                 // error: no object of type Tree specified
    p->top = right;              // OK
    value_type v = left->value;  // OK: value_type is not associated with an object
}
```

A class does not have any special access rights to the members of its nested class. For example:

```
template<typename T>
void Tree::g(Tree::Node* p)
{
    value_type val = right->value;      // error: no object of type Tree::Node
    value_type v = p->right->value;     // error: Node::right is private
    p->f(this);                         // OK
}
```

Member classes are more a notational convenience than a feature of fundamental importance. On the other hand, member aliases are important as the basis of generic programming techniques relying on associated types (§28.2.4, §33.1.3). Member **enums** are often an alternative to **enum classes** when it comes to avoiding polluting an enclosing scope with the names of enumerators (§8.4.1).

16.3 Concrete Classes

The previous section discussed bits and pieces of the design of a **Date** class in the context of introducing the basic language features for defining classes. Here, I reverse the emphasis and discuss the design of a simple and efficient **Date** class and show how the language features support this design.

Small, heavily used abstractions are common in many applications. Examples are Latin characters, Chinese characters, integers, floating-point numbers, complex numbers, points, pointers, coordinates, transforms, (*pointer,offset*) pairs, dates, times, ranges, links, associations, nodes, (*value,unit*) pairs, disk locations, source code locations, currency values, lines, rectangles, scaled fixed-point numbers, numbers with fractions, character strings, vectors, and arrays. Every application uses several of these. Often, a few of these simple concrete types are used heavily. A typical application uses a few directly and many more indirectly from libraries.

C++ directly supports a few of these abstractions as built-in types. However, most are not, and cannot be, directly supported by the language because there are too many of them. Furthermore, the designer of a general-purpose programming language cannot foresee the detailed needs of every application. Consequently, mechanisms must be provided for the user to define small concrete types. Such types are called *concrete types* or *concrete classes* to distinguish them from abstract classes (§20.4) and classes in class hierarchies (§20.3, §21.2).

A class is called *concrete* (or *a concrete class*) if its representation is part of its definition. This distinguishes it from abstract classes (§3.2.2, §20.4) which provide an interface to a variety of implementations. Having the representation available allows us:

- To place objects on the stack, in statically allocated memory, and in other objects
- To copy and move objects (§3.3, §17.5)
- To refer directly to named objects (as opposed to accessing through pointers and references)

This makes concrete classes simple to reason about and easy for the compiler to generate optimal code for. Thus, we prefer concrete classes for small, frequently used, and performance-critical types, such as complex numbers (§5.6.2), smart pointers (§5.2.1), and containers (§4.4).

It was an early explicit aim of C++ to support the definition and efficient use of such user-defined types very well. They are a foundation of elegant programming. As usual, the simple and mundane is statistically far more significant than the complicated and sophisticated. In this light, let us build a better **Date** class:

```
namespace Chrono {

    enum class Month { jan=1, feb, mar, apr, may, jun, jul, aug, sep, oct, nov, dec };

    class Date {
    public:          // public interface:
        class Bad_date { }; // exception class

        explicit Date(int dd ={}, Month mm ={}, int yy ={});        // {} means "pick a default"
```

```
        // nonmodifying functions for examining the Date:
            int day() const;
            Month month() const;
            int year() const;

            string string_rep() const;                  // string representation
            void char_rep(char s[], in max) const;      // C-style string representation

        // (modifying) functions for changing the Date:
            Date& add_year(int n);                       // add n years
            Date& add_month(int n);                      // add n months
            Date& add_day(int n);                        // add n days
        private:
            bool is_valid();                             // check if this Date represents a date
            int d, m, y;                                 // representation
        };

        bool is_date(int d, Month m, int y);             // true for valid date
        bool is_leapyear(int y);                         // true if y is a leap year

        bool operator==(const Date& a, const Date& b);
        bool operator!=(const Date& a, const Date& b);

        const Date& default_date();                      // the default date

        ostream& operator<<(ostream& os, const Date& d); // print d to os
        istream& operator>>(istream& is, Date& d);       // read Date from is into d
    } // Chrono
```

This set of operations is fairly typical for a user-defined type:

[1]   A constructor specifying how objects/variables of the type are to be initialized (§16.2.5).

[2]   A set of functions allowing a user to examine a **Date**. These functions are marked **const** to indicate that they don't modify the state of the object/variable for which they are called.

[3]   A set of functions allowing the user to modify **Dates** without actually having to know the details of the representation or fiddle with the intricacies of the semantics.

[4]   Implicitly defined operations that allow **Dates** to be freely copied (§16.2.2).

[5]   A class, **Bad_date**, to be used for reporting errors as exceptions.

[6]   A set of useful helper functions. The helper functions are not members and have no direct access to the representation of a **Date**, but they are identified as related by the use of the namespace **Chrono**.

I defined a **Month** type to cope with the problem of remembering the month/day order, for example, to avoid confusion about whether the 7th of June is written {6,7} (American style) or {7,6} (European style).

I considered introducing separate types **Day** and **Year** to cope with possible confusion of **Date{1995,Month::jul,27}** and **Date{27,Month::jul,1995}**. However, these types would not be as useful as the **Month** type. Almost all such errors are caught at run time anyway – the 26th of July year 27 is not a common date in my work. Dealing with historical dates before year 1800 or so is a tricky issue best left to expert historians. Furthermore, the day of the month can't be properly checked in isolation from its month and year.

To save the user from having to explicitly mention year and month even when they are implied by context, I added a mechanism for providing a default. Note that for **Month** the {} gives the (default) value **0** just as for integers even though it is not a valid **Month** (§8.4). However, in this case, that's exactly what we want: an otherwise illegal value to represent "pick the default." Providing a default (e.g., a default value for **Date** objects) is a tricky design problem. For some types, there is a conventional default (e.g., **0** for integers); for others, no default makes sense; and finally, there are some types (such as **Date**) where the question of whether to provide a default is nontrivial. In such cases, it is best – at least initially – not to provide a default value. I provide one for **Date** primarily to be able to discuss how to do so.

I omitted the cache technique from §16.2.9 as unnecessary for a type this simple. If needed, it can be added as an implementation detail without affecting the user interface.

Here is a small – and contrived – example of how **Date**s can be used:

```
void f(Date& d)
{
    Date lvb_day {16,Month::dec,d.year()};

    if (d.day()==29 && d.month()==Month::feb) {
        // ...
    }

    if (midnight()) d.add_day(1);

    cout << "day after:" << d+1 << '\n';

    Date dd;    // initialized to the default date
    cin>>dd;
    if (dd==d) cout << "Hurray!\n";
}
```

This assumes that the addition operator, +, has been declared for **Date**s. I do that in §16.3.3.

Note the use of explicit qualification of **dec** and **feb** by **Month**. I used an **enum class** (§8.4.1) specifically to be able to use short names for the months, yet also ensure that their use would not be obscure or ambiguous.

Why is it worthwhile to define a specific type for something as simple as a date? After all, we could just define a simple data structure:

```
struct Date {
    int day, month, year;
};
```

Each programmer could then decide what to do with it. If we did that, though, every user would either have to manipulate the components of **Date**s directly or provide separate functions for doing so. In effect, the notion of a date would be scattered throughout the system, which would make it hard to understand, document, or change. Inevitably, providing a concept as only a simple structure causes extra work for every user of the structure.

Also, even though the Date type seems simple, it takes some thought to get right. For example, incrementing a Date must deal with leap years, with the fact that months are of different lengths, and so on. Also, the day-month-and-year representation is rather poor for many applications. If we decided to change it, we would need to modify only a designated set of functions. For example, to represent a Date as the number of days before or after January 1, 1970, we would need to change only Date's member functions.

To simplify, I decided to eliminate the notion of changing the default date. Doing so eliminates some opportunities for confusion and the likelihood of race conditions in a multi-threaded program (§5.3.1). I seriously considered eliminating the notion of a default date altogether. That would have forced users to consistently explicitly initialize their Dates. However, that can be inconvenient and surprising, and more importantly common interfaces used for generic code require default construction (§17.3.3). That means that I, as the designer of Date, have to pick the default date. I chose January 1, 1970, because that is the starting point for the C and C++ standard-library time routines (§35.2, §43.6). Obviously, eliminating set_default_date() caused some loss of generality of Date. However, design – including class design – is about making decisions, rather than just deciding to postpone them or to leave all options open for users.

To preserve an opportunity for future refinement, I declared default_date() as a helper function:

```
const Date& Chrono::default_date();
```

That doesn't say anything about how the default date is actually set.

16.3.1 Member Functions

Naturally, an implementation for each member function must be provided somewhere. For example:

```
Date::Date(int dd, Month mm, int yy)
    :d{dd}, m{mm}, y{yy}
{
    if (y == 0) y = default_date().year();
    if (m == Month{}) m = default_date().month();
    if (d == 0) d = default_date().day();

    if (!is_valid()) throw Bad_date();
}
```

The constructor checks that the data supplied denotes a valid Date. If not, say, for {30,Month::feb,1994}, it throws an exception (§2.4.3.1, Chapter 13), which indicates that something went wrong. If the data supplied is acceptable, the obvious initialization is done. Initialization is a relatively complicated operation because it involves data validation. This is fairly typical. On the other hand, once a Date has been created, it can be used and copied without further checking. In other words, the constructor establishes the invariant for the class (in this case, that it denotes a valid date). Other member functions can rely on that invariant and must maintain it. This design technique can simplify code immensely (see §2.4.3.2, §13.4).

I'm using the value Month{} – which doesn't represent a month and has the integer value 0 – to represent "pick the default month." I could have defined an enumerator in Month specifically to represent that. But I decided that it was better to use an obviously anomalous value to represent "pick the default month" rather than give the appearance that there were 13 months in a year. Note that Month{}, meaning 0, can be used because it is within the range guaranteed for the enumeration Month (§8.4).

I use the member initializer syntax (§17.4) to initialize the members. After that, I check for 0 and modify the values as needed. This clearly does not provide optimal performance in the (hopefully rare) case of an error, but the use of member initializers leaves the structure of the code obvious. This makes the style less error-prone and easier to maintain than alternatives. Had I aimed at optimal performance, I would have used three separate constructors rather than a single constructor with default arguments.

I considered making the validation function is_valid() public. However, I found the resulting user code more complicated and less robust than code relying on catching the exception:

```
void fill(vector<Date>& aa)
{
    while (cin) {
        Date d;
        try {
            cin >> d;
        }
        catch (Date::Bad_date) {
            // ... my error handling ...
            continue;
        }
        aa.push_back(d);    // see §4.4.2
    }
}
```

However, checking that a {d,m,y} set of values is a valid date is not a computation that depends on the representation of a Date, so I implemented is_valid() in terms of a helper function:

```
bool Date::is_valid()
{
    return is_date(d,m,y);
}
```

Why have both is_valid() and is_date()? In this simple example, we could manage with just one, but I can imagine systems where is_date() (as here) checks that a (d,m,y)-tuple represents a valid date and where is_valid() does an additional check on whether that date can be reasonably represented. For example, is_valid() might reject dates from before the modern calendar became commonly used.

As is common for such simple concrete types, the definitions of Date's member functions vary between the trivial and the not-too-complicated. For example:

```
inline int Date::day() const
{
    return d;
}
```

```
Date& Date::add_month(int n)
{
    if (n==0) return *this;

    if (n>0) {
        int delta_y = n/12;                        // number of whole years
        int mm = static_cast<int>(m)+n%12;         // number of months ahead
        if (12 < mm) {                             // note: dec is represented by 12
            ++delta_y;
            mm -= 12;
        }

        // ... handle the cases where the month mm doesn't have day d ...

        y += delta_y;
        m = static_cast<Month>(mm);
        return *this;
    }

    // ... handle negative n ...

    return *this;
}
```

I wouldn't call the code for **add_month()** pretty. In fact, if I added all the details, it might even approach the complexity of relatively simple real-world code. This points to a problem: adding a month is conceptually simple, so why is our code getting complicated? In this case, the reason is that the **d,m,y** representation isn't as convenient for the computer as it is for us. A better representation (for many purposes) would be simply a number of days since a defined "day zero" (e.g., January 1, 1970). That would make computation on **Date**s simple at the expense of complexity in providing output fit for humans.

Note that assignment and copy initialization are provided by default (§16.2.2). Also, **Date** doesn't need a destructor because a **Date** owns no resources and requires no cleanup when it goes out of scope (§3.2.1.2).

16.3.2 Helper Functions

Typically, a class has a number of functions associated with it that need not be defined in the class itself because they don't need direct access to the representation. For example:

```
int diff(Date a, Date b);     // number of days in the range [a,b) or [b,a)

bool is_leapyear(int y);
bool is_date(int d, Month m, int y);

const Date& default_date();
Date next_weekday(Date d);
Date next_saturday(Date d);
```

Defining such functions in the class itself would complicate the class interface and increase the number of functions that would potentially need to be examined when a change to the representation was considered.

How are such functions "associated" with class **Date**? In early C++, as in C, their declarations were simply placed in the same file as the declaration of class **Date**. Users who needed **Date**s would make them all available by including the file that defined the interface (§15.2.2). For example:

```
#include "Date.h"
```

In addition (or alternatively), we can make the association explicit by enclosing the class and its helper functions in a namespace (§14.3.1):

```
namespace Chrono {          // facilities for dealing with time

    class Date { /* ... */};

    int diff(Date a, Date b);
    bool is_leapyear(int y);
    bool is_date(int d, Month m, int y);
    const Date& default_date();
    Date next_weekday(Date d);
    Date next_saturday(Date d);
    // ...
}
```

The **Chrono** namespace would naturally also contain related classes, such as **Time** and **Stopwatch**, and their helper functions. Using a namespace to hold a single class is usually an overelaboration that leads to inconvenience.

Naturally, the helper function must be defined somewhere:

```
bool Chrono::is_date(int d, Month m, int y)
{
    int ndays;

    switch (m) {
    case Month::feb:
        ndays = 28+is_leapyear(y);
        break;
    case Month::apr: case Month::jun: case Month::sep: case Month::nov:
        ndays = 30;
        break;
    case Month::jan: case Month::mar: case Month::may: case Month::jul:
    case Month::aug: case Month::oct: case Month::dec:
        ndays = 31;
        break;
    default:
        return false;
    }

    return 1<=d && d<=ndays;
}
```

I'm deliberately being a bit paranoid here. A **Month** shouldn't be outside the **jan** to **dec** range, but it is possible (someone might have been sloppy with a cast), so I check.

The troublesome **default_date** finally becomes:

```
const Date& Chrono::default_date()
{
    static Date d {1,Month::jan,1970};
    return d;
}
```

16.3.3 Overloaded Operators

It is often useful to add functions to enable conventional notation. For example, **operator==()** defines the equality operator, **==**, to work for **Dates**:

```
inline bool operator==(Date a, Date b)          // equality
{
    return a.day()==b.day() && a.month()==b.month() && a.year()==b.year();
}
```

Other obvious candidates are:

```
bool operator!=(Date, Date);          // inequality
bool operator<(Date, Date);           // less than
bool operator>(Date, Date);           // greater than
// ...

Date& operator++(Date& d) { return d.add_day(1); }          // increase Date by one day
Date& operator––(Date& d) { return d.add_day(–1); }         // decrease Date by one day

Date& operator+=(Date& d, int n) { return d.add_day(n); }   // add n days
Date& operator–=(Date& d, int n) { return d.add_day(–n); }  // subtract n days

Date operator+(Date d, int n) { return d+=n; }              // add n days
Date operator–(Date d, int n) { return d+=n; }              // subtract n days

ostream& operator<<(ostream&, Date d);          // output d
istream& operator>>(istream&, Date& d);         // read into d
```

These operators are defined in **Chrono** together with **Date** to avoid overload problems and to benefit from argument-dependent lookup (§14.2.4).

For **Date**, these operators can be seen as mere conveniences. However, for many types – such as complex numbers (§18.3), vectors (§4.4.1), and function-like objects (§3.4.3, §19.2.2) – the use of conventional operators is so firmly entrenched in people's minds that their definition is almost mandatory. Operator overloading is discussed in Chapter 18.

For **Date**, I was tempted to provide **+=** and **–=** as member functions instead of **add_day()**. Had I done so, I would have followed a common idiom (§3.2.1.1).

Note that assignment and copy initialization are provided by default (§16.3, §17.3.3).

16.3.4 The Significance of Concrete Classes

I call simple user-defined types, such as Date, *concrete types* to distinguish them from abstract classes (§3.2.2) and class hierarchies (§20.4), and also to emphasize their similarity to built-in types such as int and char. Concrete classes are used just like built-in types. Concrete types have also been called *value types* and their use *value-oriented programming*. Their model of use and the "philosophy" behind their design are quite different from what is often called object-oriented programming (§3.2.4, Chapter 21).

The intent of a concrete type is to do a single, relatively simple thing well and efficiently. It is not usually the aim to provide the user with facilities to modify the behavior of a concrete type. In particular, concrete types are not intended to display run-time polymorphic behavior (see §3.2.3, §20.3.2).

If you don't like some detail of a concrete type, you build a new one with the desired behavior. If you want to "reuse" a concrete type, you use it in the implementation of your new type exactly as you would have used an int. For example:

```
class Date_and_time {
private:
    Date d;
    Time t;
public:
    Date_and_time(Date d, Time t);
    Date_and_time(int d, Date::Month m, int y, Time t);
    // ...
};
```

Alternatively, the derived class mechanism discussed in Chapter 20 can be used to define new types from a concrete class by describing the desired differences. The definition of Vec from vector (§4.4.1.2) is an example of this. However, derivation from a concrete class should be done with care and only rarely because of the lack of virtual functions and run-time type information (§17.5.1.4, Chapter 22).

With a reasonably good compiler, a concrete class such as Date incurs no hidden overhead in time or space. In particular, no indirection through pointers is necessary for access to objects of concrete classes, and no "housekeeping" data is stored in objects of concrete classes. The size of a concrete type is known at compile time so that objects can be allocated on the run-time stack (that is, without free-store operations). The layout of an object is known at compile time so that inlining of operations is trivially achieved. Similarly, layout compatibility with other languages, such as C and Fortran, comes without special effort.

A good set of such types can provide a foundation for applications. In particular, they can be used to make interfaces more specific and less error-prone. For example:

```
Month do_something(Date d);
```

This is far less likely to be misunderstood or misused than:

```
int do_something(int d);
```

Lack of concrete types can lead to obscure programs and time wasted when each programmer writes code to directly manipulate "simple and frequently used" data structures represented as simple aggregates of built-in types. Alternatively, lack of suitable "small efficient types" in an application can lead to gross run-time and space inefficiencies when overly general and expensive classes are used.

16.4 Advice

[1]   Represent concepts as classes; §16.1.

[2]   Separate the interface of a class from its implementation; §16.1.

[3]   Use public data (**structs**) only when it really is just data and no invariant is meaningful for the data members; §16.2.4.

[4]   Define a constructor to handle initialization of objects; §16.2.5.

[5]   By default declare single-argument constructors **explicit**; §16.2.6.

[6]   Declare a member function that does not modify the state of its object **const**; §16.2.9.

[7]   A concrete type is the simplest kind of class. Where applicable, prefer a concrete type over more complicated classes and over plain data structures; §16.3.

[8]   Make a function a member only if it needs direct access to the representation of a class; §16.3.2.

[9]   Use a namespace to make the association between a class and its helper functions explicit; §16.3.2.

[10] Make a member function that doesn't modify the value of its object a **const** member function; §16.2.9.1.

[11] Make a function that needs access to the representation of a class but needn't be called for a specific object a **static** member function; §16.2.12.

Construction, Cleanup, Copy, and Move

Ignorance more frequently begets confidence
than does knowledge.
– Charles Darwin

17.1 Introduction

This chapter focuses on technical aspects of an object's "life cycle": How do we create an object, how do we copy it, how do we move it around, and how do we clean up after it when it goes away? What are proper definitions of "copy" and "move"? For example:

```
string ident(string arg)        // string passed by value (copied into arg)
{
        return arg;             // return string (move the value of arg out of ident() to a caller)
}

int main ()
{
        string s1 {"Adams"};    // initialize string (construct in s1).
        s1 = indet(s1);         // copy s1 into ident()
                                // move the result of ident(s1) into s1;
                                // s1's value is "Adams".
        string s2 {"Pratchett"};// initialize string (construct in s2)
        s1 = s2;                // copy the value of s2 into s1
                                // both s1 and s2 have the value "Pratchett".
}
```

Clearly, after the call of **ident()**, the value of **s1** ought to be **"Adams"**. We copy the value of **s1** into the argument **arg**, then we move the value of **arg** out of the function call and (back) into **s1**. Next, we construct **s2** with the value **"Prachett"** and copy it into **s1**. Finally, at the exit from **main()** we destroy the variables **s1** and **s2**. The difference between *move* and *copy* is that after a copy two objects must have the same value, whereas after a move the source of the move is not required to have its original value. Moves can be used when the source object will not be used again. They are particularly useful for implementing the notion of moving a resource (§3.2.1.2, §5.2).

Several functions are used here:

- A constructor initializing a **string** with a string literal (used for **s1** and **s2**)
- A copy constructor copying a **string** (into the function argument **arg**)
- A move constructor moving the value of a **string** (from **arg** out of **ident()** into a temporary variable holding the result of **ident(s1)**)
- A move assignment moving the value of a **string** (from the temporary variable holding the result of **ident(s1)** into **s1**)
- A copy assignment copying a **string** (from **s2** into **s1**)
- A destructor releasing the resources owned by **s1**, **s2**, and the temporary variable holding the result of **ident(s1)**

An optimizer can eliminate some of this work. For example, in this simple example the temporary variable is typically eliminated. However, in principle, these operations are executed.

Constructors, copy and move assignment operations, and destructors directly support a view of lifetime and resource management. An object is considered an object of its type after its constructor completes, and it remains an object of its type until its destructor starts executing. The interaction between object lifetime and errors is explored further in §13.2 and §13.3. In particular, this chapter doesn't discuss the issue of half-constructed and half-destroyed objects.

Construction of objects plays a key role in many designs. This wide variety of uses is reflected in the range and flexibility of the language features supporting initialization.

Constructors, destructors, and copy and move operations for a type are not logically separate. We must define them as a matched set or suffer logical or performance problems. If a class **X** has a destructor that performs a nontrivial task, such as free-store deallocation or lock release, the class is likely to need the full complement of functions:

```
class X {
    X(Sometype);         // "ordinary constructor": create an object
    X();                 // default constructor
    X(const X&);         // copy constructor
    X(X&&);              // move constructor
    X& operator=(const X&); // copy assignment: clean up target and copy
    X& operator=(X&&);   // move assignment: clean up target and move
    ~X();                // destructor: clean up
    // ...
};
```

There are five situations in which an object is copied or moved:

- As the source of an assignment
- As an object initializer
- As a function argument
- As a function return value
- As an exception

In all cases, the copy or move constructor will be applied (unless it can be optimized away).

In addition to the initialization of named objects and objects on the free store, constructors are used to initialize temporary objects (§6.4.2) and to implement explicit type conversion (§11.5).

Except for the "ordinary constructor," these special member functions can be generated by the compiler; see §17.6.

This chapter is full of rules and technicalities. Those are necessary for a full understanding, but most people just learn the general rules from examples.

17.2 Constructors and Destructors

We can specify how an object of a class is to be initialized by defining a constructor (§16.2.5, §17.3). To complement constructors, we can define a destructor to ensure "cleanup" at the point of destruction of an object (e.g., when it goes out of scope). Some of the most effective techniques for resource management in C++ rely on constructor/destructor pairs. So do other techniques relying on a pair of actions, such as do/undo, start/stop, before/after, etc. For example:

```
struct Tracer {
    string mess;
    Tracer(const string& s) :mess{s} { clog << mess; }
    ~Tracer() {clog << "~" << mess; }
};

void f(const vector<int>& v)
{
    Tracer tr {"in f()\n"};
    for (auto x : v) {
        Tracer tr {string{"v loop "}+to<string>(x)+'\n'};  // §25.2.5.1
        // ...
    }
}
```

We could try a call:

```
f({2,3,5});
```

This would print to the logging stream:

```
in_f()
v loop 2
˜v loop 2
v loop 3
˜v loop 3
v loop 5
˜v loop 5
˜in_f()
```

17.2.1 Constructors and Invariants

A member with the same name as its class is called a *constructor*. For example:

```
class Vector {
public:
        Vector(int s);
        // ...
};
```

A constructor declaration specifies an argument list (exactly as for a function) but has no return type. The name of a class cannot be used for an ordinary member function, data member, member type, etc., within the class. For example:

```
struct S {
        S();                    // fine
        void S(int);            // error: no type can be specified for a constructor
        int S;                  // error: the class name must denote a constructor
        enum S { foo, bar };    // error: the class name must denote a constructor
};
```

A constructor's job is to initialize an object of its class. Often, that initialization must establish a *class invariant*, that is, something that must hold whenever a member function is called (from outside the class). Consider:

```
class Vector {
public:
        Vector(int s);
        // ...
private:
        double* elem; // elem points to an array of sz doubles
        int sz;       // sz is non-negative
};
```

Here (as is often the case), the invariant is stated as comments: "**elem** points to an array of **sz** doubles" and "**sz** is non-negative." The constructor must make that true. For example:

```
Vector::Vector(int s)
{
    if (s<0) throw Bad_size{s};
    sz = s;
    elem = new double[s];
}
```

This constructor tries to establish the invariant and if it cannot, it throws an exception. If the constructor cannot establish the invariant, no object is created and the constructor must ensure that no resources are leaked (§5.2, §13.3). A resource is anything we need to acquire and eventually (explicitly or implicitly) give back (release) once we are finished with it. Examples of resources are memory (§3.2.1.2), locks (§5.3.4), file handles (§13.3), and thread handles (§5.3.1).

Why would you define an invariant?

- To focus the design effort for the class (§2.4.3.2)
- To clarify the behavior of the class (e.g., under error conditions; §13.2)
- To simplify the definition of member functions (§2.4.3.2, §16.3.1)
- To clarify the class's management of resources (§13.3)
- To simplify the documentation of the class

On average, the effort to define an invariant ends up saving work.

17.2.2 Destructors and Resources

A constructor initializes an object. In other words, it creates the environment in which the member functions operate. Sometimes, creating that environment involves acquiring a resource – such as a file, a lock, or some memory – that must be released after use (§5.2, §13.3). Thus, some classes need a function that is guaranteed to be invoked when an object is destroyed in a manner similar to the way a constructor is guaranteed to be invoked when an object is created. Inevitably, such a function is called a *destructor*. The name of a destructor is ˜ followed by the class name, for example ˜**Vector**(). One meaning of ˜ is "complement" (§11.1.2), and a destructor for a class complements its constructors. A destructor does not take an argument, and a class can have only one destructor. Destructors are called implicitly when an automatic variable goes out of scope, an object on the free store is deleted, etc. Only in very rare circumstances does the user need to call a destructor explicitly (§17.2.4).

Destructors typically clean up and release resources. For example:

```
class Vector {
public:
    Vector(int s) :elem{new double[s]}, sz{s} { };    // constructor: acquire memory
    ˜Vector() { delete[] elem; }                       // destructor: release memory
    // ...
private:
    double* elem;  // elem points to an array of sz doubles
    int sz;        // sz is non-negative
};
```

For example:

```
Vector* f(int s)
{
    Vector v1(s);
    // ...
    return new Vector(s+s);
}

void g(int ss)
{
    Vector* p = f(ss);
    // ...
    delete p;
}
```

Here, the Vector v1 is destroyed upon exit from f(). Also, the Vector created on the free store by f() using new is destroyed by the call of delete. In both cases, Vector's destructor is invoked to free (deallocate) the memory allocated by the constructor.

What if the constructor failed to acquire enough memory? For example, s*sizeof(double) or (s+s)*sizeof(double) may be larger than the amount of available memory (measured in bytes). In that case, an exception std::bad_alloc (§11.2.3) is thrown by new and the exception-handling mechanism invokes the appropriate destructors so that all memory that has been acquired (and only that) is freed (§13.5.1).

This style of constructor/destructor-based resource management is called *Resource Acquisition Is Initialization* or simply *RAII* (§5.2, §13.3).

A matching constructor/destructor pair is the usual mechanism for implementing the notion of a variably sized object in C++. Standard-library containers, such as vector and unordered_map, use variants of this technique for providing storage for their elements.

A type that has no destructor declared, such as a built-in type, is considered to have a destructor that does nothing.

A programmer who declares a destructor for a class must also decide if objects of that class can be copied or moved (§17.6).

17.2.3 Base and Member Destructors

Constructors and destructors interact correctly with class hierarchies (§3.2.4, Chapter 20). A constructor builds a class object "from the bottom up":

[1]   first, the constructor invokes its base class constructors,

[2]   then, it invokes the member constructors, and

[3]   finally, it executes its own body.

A destructor "tears down" an object in the reverse order:

[1]   first, the destructor executes its own body,

[2]   then, it invokes its member destructors, and

[3]   finally, it invokes its base class destructors.

In particular, a virtual base is constructed before any base that might use it and destroyed after all such bases (§21.3.5.1). This ordering ensures that a base or a member is not used before it has been initialized or used after it has been destroyed. The programmer can defeat this simple and essential rule, but only through deliberate circumvention involving passing pointers to uninitialized variables as arguments. Doing so violates language rules and the results are usually disastrous.

Constructors execute member and base constructors in declaration order (not the order of initializers): if two constructors used a different order, the destructor could not (without serious overhead) guarantee to destroy in the reverse order of construction. See also §17.4.

If a class is used so that a default constructor is needed, and if the class does not have other constructors, the compiler will try to generate a default constructor. For example:

```
struct S1 {
    string s;
};
```

```
S1 x;      // OK: x.s is initialized to ""
```

Similarly, memberwise initialization can be used if initializers are needed. For example:

```
struct X { X(int); };
```

```
struct S2 {
    X x;
};
```

```
S2 x1;     // error:
S2 x2 {1}; // OK: x2.x is initialized with 1
```

See also §17.3.1.

17.2.4 Calling Constructors and Destructors

A destructor is invoked implicitly upon exit from a scope or by **delete**. It is typically not only unnecessary to explicitly call a destructor; doing so would lead to nasty errors. However, there are rare (but important) cases where a destructor must be called explicitly. Consider a container that (like **std::vector**) maintains a pool of memory into which it can grow and shrink (e.g., using **push_back()** and **pop_back()**). When we add an element, the container must invoke its constructor for a specific address:

```
void C::push_back(const X& a)
{
    // ...
    new(p) X{a};    // copy construct an X with the value a in address p
    // ...
}
```

This use of a constructor is known as "placement **new**" (§11.2.4).

Conversely, when we remove an element, the container needs to invoke its destructor:

```
void C::pop_back()
{
    // ...
    p->~X();   // destroy the X in address p
}
```

The **p->˜X()** notation invokes **X**'s destructor for *p. That notation should never be used for an object that is destroyed in the normal way (by its object going out of scope or being **delete**d).

For a more complete example of explicit management of objects in a memory area, see §13.6.1.

If declared for a class **X**, a destructor will be implicitly invoked whenever an **X** goes out of scope or is **delete**d. This implies that we can prevent destruction of an **X** by declaring its destructor **=delete** (§17.6.4) or **private**.

Of the two alternatives, using **private** is the more flexible. For example, we can create a class for which objects can be explicitly destroyed, but not implicitly:

```cpp
class Nonlocal {
public:
    // ...
    void destroy() { this->˜Nonlocal(); }       // explicit destruction
private:
    // ...
    ˜Nonlocal();                                 // don't destroy implicitly
};

void user()
{
    Nonlocal x;              // error: cannot destroy a Nonlocal
    X* p = new Nonlocal;     // OK
    // ...
    delete p;                // error: cannot destroy a Nonlocal
    p.destroy();             // OK
}
```

17.2.5 virtual Destructors

A destructor can be declared to be **virtual**, and usually should be for a class with a virtual function. For example:

```cpp
class Shape {
public:
    // ...
    virtual void draw() = 0;
    virtual ˜Shape();
};

class Circle {
public:
    // ...
    void draw();
    ˜Circle();        // overrides ˜Shape()
    // ...
};
```

The reason we need a **virtual** destructor is that an object usually manipulated through the interface provided by a base class is often also **delete**d through that interface:

```
void user(Shape* p)
{
    p->draw();      // invoke the appropriate draw()
    // ...
    delete p;       // invoke the appropriate destructor
};
```

Had **Shape**'s destructor not been **virtual** that **delete** would have failed to invoke the appropriate derived class destructor (e.g., ˜**Circle()**). That failure would cause the resources owned by the deleted object (if any) to be leaked.

17.3 Class Object Initialization

This section discusses how to initialize objects of a class with and without constructors. It also shows how to define constructors to accept arbitrarily sized homogeneous initializer lists (such as {1,2,3} and {1,2,3,4,5,6}).

17.3.1 Initialization Without Constructors

We cannot define a constructor for a built-in type, yet we can initialize it with a value of suitable type. For example:

```
int a {1};
char* p {nullptr};
```

Similarly, we can initialize objects of a class for which we have not defined a constructor using
- memberwise initialization,
- copy initialization, or
- default initialization (without an initializer or with an empty initializer list).

For example:

```
struct Work {
    string author;
    string name;
    int year;
};

Work s9 { "Beethoven",
        "Symphony No. 9 in D minor, Op. 125; Choral",
        1824
    };                              // memberwise initialization

Work currently_playing { s9 };      // copy initialization
Work none {};                       // default initialization
```

The three members of **currently_playing** are copies of those of **s9**.

The default initialization of using {} is defined as initialization of each member by {}. So, **none** is initialized to {{},{},{}}, which is {"","",0} (§17.3.3).

Where no constructor requiring arguments is declared, it is also possible to leave out the initializer completely. For example:

```
Work alpha;

void f()
{
    Work beta;
    // ...
}
```

For this, the rules are not as clean as we might like. For statically allocated objects (§6.4.2), the rules are exactly as if you had used {}, so the value of alpha is {"","",0}. However, for local variables and free-store objects, the default initialization is done only for members of class type, and members of built-in type are left uninitialized, so the value of beta is {"","",unknown}.

The reason for this complication is to improve performance in rare critical cases. For example:

```
struct Buf {
    int count;
    char buf[16*1024];
};
```

You can use a Buf as a local variable without initializing it before using it as a target for an input operation. Most local variable initializations are not performance critical, and uninitialized local variables are a major source of errors. If you want guaranteed initialization or simply dislike surprises, supply an initializer, such as {}. For example:

```
Buf buf0;        // statically allocated, so initialized by default

void f()
{
    Buf buf1;            // leave elements uninitialized
    Buf buf2 {};         // I really want to zero out those elements

    int* p1 = new int;    // *p1 is uninitialized
    int* p2 = new int{};  // *p2 == 0
    int* p3 = new int{7}; // *p3 == 7
    // ...
}
```

Naturally, memberwise initialization works only if we can access the members. For example:

```
template<class T>
class Checked_pointer { // control access to T* member
public:
    T& operator*();       // check for nullptr and return value
    // ...
};

Checked_pointer<int> p {new int{7}};      // error: can't access p.p
```

If a class has a private non-static data member, it needs a constructor to initialize it.

17.3.2 Initialization Using Constructors

Where memberwise copy is not sufficient or desirable, a constructor can be defined to initialize an object. In particular, a constructor is often used to establish an invariant for its class and to acquire resources necessary to do that (§17.2.1).

If a constructor is declared for a class, some constructor will be used for every object. It is an error to try to create an object without a proper initializer as required by the constructors. For example:

```
struct X {
      X(int);
};
```

```
X x0;            // error: no initializer
X x1 {};         // error: empty initializer
X x2 {2};        // OK
X x3 {"two"};    // error: wrong initializer type
X x4 {1,2};      // error: wrong number of initializers
X x5 {x4};       // OK: a copy constructor is implicitly defined (§17.6)
```

Note that the default constructor (§17.3.3) disappears when you define a constructor requiring arguments; after all, X(int) states that an int is required to construct an X. However, the copy constructor does not disappear (§17.3.3); the assumption is that an object can be copied (once properly constructed). Where the latter might cause problems (§3.3.1), you can specifically disallow copying (§17.6.4).

I used the {} notation to make explicit the fact that I am initializing. I am not (just) assigning a value, calling a function, or declaring a function. The {} notation for initialization can be used to provide arguments to a constructor wherever an object can be constructed. For example:

```
struct Y : X {
      X m {0};                   // provide default initializer for member m
      Y(int a) :X{a}, m{a} { };  // initialize base and member (§17.4)
      Y() : X{0} { };            // initialize base and member
};
```

```
X g {1};    // initialize global variable
```

```
void f(int a)
{
      X def {};                  // error: no default value for X
      Y de2 {};                  // OK: use default constructor
      X∗ p {nullptr};
      X var {2};                 // initialize local variable
      p = new X{4};              // initialize object on free store
      X a[] {1,2,3};             // initialize array elements
      vector<X> v {1,2,3,4};     // initialize vector elements
}
```

For this reason, {} initialization is sometimes referred to as *universal* initialization: the notation can be used everywhere. In addition, {} initialization is *uniform*: wherever you initialize an object of type **X** with a value **v** using the **{v}** notation, the same value of type **X** (**X{v}**) is created.

The = and () notations for initialization (§6.3.5) are not universal. For example:

```
struct Y : X {
    X m;
    Y(int a) : X(a), m=a { };    // syntax error: can't use = for member initialization
};


X g(1);    // initialize global variable


void f(int a)
{
    X def();                    // function returning an X (surprise!?)
    X* p {nullptr};
    X var = 2;                  // initialize local variable
    p = new X=4;               // syntax error: can't use = for new
    X a[](1,2,3);              // error: can't use () for array initialization
    vector<X> v(1,2,3,4);      // error: can't use () for list elements
}
```

The = and () notations for initialization are not uniform either, but fortunately the examples of that are obscure. If you insist on using = or () initialization, you have to remember where they are allowed and what they mean.

The usual overload resolution rules (§12.3) apply for constructors. For example:

```
struct S {
    S(const char*);
    S(double*);
};


S s1 {"Napier"};              // S::S(const char*)
S s2 {new double{1.0}};       // S::S(double*);
S s3 {nullptr};               // ambiguous: S::S(const char*) or S::S(double*)?
```

Note that the {}-initializer notation does not allow narrowing (§2.2.2). That is another reason to prefer the {} style over () or =.

17.3.2.1 Initialization by Constructors

Using the () notation, you can request to use a constructor in an initialization. That is, you can ensure that for a class, you will get initialization by constructor and not get the memberwise initialization or initializer-list initialization (§17.3.4) that the {} notation also offers. For example:

```
struct S1 {
    int a,b;                   // no constructor
};
```

```
struct S2 {
    int a,b;
    S2(int a = 0, int b = 0) : a(aa), b(bb) {}        // constructor
};
```

```
S1 x11(1,2);    // error: no constructor
S1 x12 {1,2};   // OK: memberwise initialization
```

```
S1 x13(1);      // error: no constructor
S1 x14 {1};     // OK: x14.b becomes 0
```

```
S2 x21(1,2);    // OK: use constructor
S2 x22 {1,2};   // OK: use constructor
```

```
S2 x23(1);      // OK: use constructor and one default argument
S2 x24 {1};     // OK: use constructor and one default argument
```

The uniform use of {} initialization only became possible in C++11, so older C++ code uses () and = initialization. Consequently, the () and = may be more familiar to you. However, I don't know any logical reason to prefer the () notation except in the rare case where you need to distinguish between initialization with a list of elements and a list of constructor arguments. For example:

```
vector<int> v1 {77};    // one element with the value 77
vector<int> v2(77);     // 77 elements with the default value 0
```

This problem – and the need to choose – can occur when a type with an initializer-list constructor (§17.3.4), typically a container, also has an "ordinary constructor" accepting arguments of the element type. In particular, we occasionally must use ()initialization for **vector**s of integers and floating-point numbers but never need to for **vector**s of strings of pointers:

```
vector<string> v1 {77};       // 77 elements with the default value ""
                              // (vector<string>(std::initializer_list<string>) doesn't accept {77})
vector<string> v2(77);        // 77 elements with the default value ""
```

```
vector<string> v3 {"Booh!"};  // one element with the value "Booh!"
vector<string> v4("Booh!");   // error: no constructor takes a string argument
```

```
vector<int*> v5 {100,0};      // 100 int*'s initialized to nullptr (100 is not an int*)
```

```
vector<int*> v6 {0,0};        // 2 int*'s initialized to nullptr
vector<int*> v7(0,0);         // empty vector (v7.size()==0)
vector<int*> v8;              // empty vector (v7.size()==0)
```

The **v6** and **v7** examples are only of interest to language lawyers and testers.

17.3.3 Default Constructors

A constructor that can be invoked without an argument is called a *default constructor*. Default constructors are very common. For example:

```
class Vector {
public:
    Vector();   // default constructor: no elements
    // ...
};
```

A default constructor is used if no arguments are specified or if an empty initializer list is provided:

```
Vector v1;      // OK
Vector v2 {};   // OK
```

A default argument (§12.2.5) can make a constructor that takes arguments into a default constructor. For example:

```
class String {
public:
    String(const char* p = "");   // default constructor: empty string
    // ...
};
```

```
String s1;      // OK
String s2 {};   // OK
```

The standard-library **vector** and **string** have such default constructors (§36.3.2, §31.3.2).

The built-in types are considered to have default and copy constructors. However, for a built-in type the default constructor is not invoked for uninitialized non-**static** variables (§17.3). The default value of a built-in type is **0** for integers, **0.0** for floating-point types, and **nullptr** for pointers. For example:

```
void f()
{
    int a0;         // uninitialized
    int a1();       // function declaration (intended?)

    int a {};       // a becomes 0
    double d {};    // d becomes 0.0
    char* p {};     // p becomes nullptr

    int* p1 = new int;    // uninitialized int
    int* p2 = new int{};  // the int is initialized to 0
}
```

Constructors for built-in types are most often used for template arguments. For example:

```
template<class T>
struct Handle {
    T* p;
    Handle(T* pp = new T{}) :p{pp} { }
    // ...
};
```

```
Handle<int> px;   // will generate int{}
```

The generated int will be initialized to 0.

References and consts must be initialized (§7.7, §7.5). Therefore, a class containing such members cannot be default constructed unless the programmer supplies in-class member initializers (§17.4.4) or defines a default constructor that initializes them (§17.4.1). For example:

```
int glob {9};

struct X {
    const int a1 {7};      // OK
    const int a2;          // error: requires a user-defined constructor
    const int& r {9};      // OK
    int& r1 {glob};        // OK
    int& r2;               // error: requires a user-defined constructor
};

X x;        // error: no default constructor for X
```

An array, a standard-library vector, and similar containers can be declared to allocate a number of default-initialized elements. In such cases, a default constructor is obviously required for a class used as the element type of a vector or array. For example:

```
struct S1 { S1(); };           // has default constructor
struct S2 { S2(string); };     // no default constructor

S1 a1[10];                     // OK: 10 default elements
S2 a2[10];                     // error: cannot initialize elements
S2 a3[] { "alpha", "beta" };   // OK: two elements: S2{"alpha"}, S2{"beta"}

vector<S1> v1(10);             // OK: 10 default elements
vector<S2> v2(10);             // error: cannot initialize elements
vector<S2> v3 { "alpha", "beta" };  // OK: two elements: S2{"alpha"}, S2{"beta"}

vector<S2> v2(10,"");          // OK: 10 elements each initialized to S2{""}
vector<S2> v4;                 // OK: no elements
```

When should a class have a default constructor? A simple-minded technical answer is "when you use it as the element type for an array, etc." However, a better question is "For what types does it make sense to have a default value?" or even "Does this type have a 'special' value we can 'naturally' use as a default?" String has the empty string, "", containers have the empty set, {}, and numeric values have zero. The trouble with deciding on a default Date (§16.3) arose because there is no "natural" default date (the Big Bang is too far in the past and not precisely associated with our everyday dates). It is a good idea not to be too clever when inventing default values. For example, the problem with containers of elements without default values is often best solved by not allocating elements until you have proper values for them (e.g., using push_back()).

17.3.4 Initializer-List Constructors

A constructor that takes a single argument of type std::initializer_list is called an *initializer-list constructor*. An initializer-list constructor is used to construct objects using a {}-list as its initializer value. Standard-library containers (e.g., **vector** and **map**) have initializer-list constructors, assignments, etc. (§31.3.2, §31.4.3). Consider:

```
vector<double> v = { 1, 2, 3.456, 99.99 };

list<pair<string,string>> languages = {
    {"Nygaard","Simula"}, {"Richards","BCPL"}, {"Ritchie","C"}
};

map<vector<string>,vector<int>> years = {
    { {"Maurice","Vincent", "Wilkes"},{1913, 1945, 1951, 1967, 2000} },
    { {"Martin", "Richards"} {1982, 2003, 2007} },
    { {"David", "John", "Wheeler"}, {1927, 1947, 1951, 2004} }
};
```

The mechanism for accepting a {}-list is a function (often a constructor) taking an argument of type **std::initializer_list<T>**. For example:

```
void f(initializer_list<int>);

f({1,2});
f({23,345,4567,56789});
f({});       // the empty list

f{1,2};      // error: function call () missing

years.insert({{"Bjarne","Stroustrup"},{1950, 1975, 1985}});
```

The initializer list can be of arbitrary length but must be homogeneous. That is, all elements must be of the template argument type, **T**, or implicitly convertible to **T**.

17.3.4.1 initializer_list Constructor Disambiguation

When you have several constructors for a class, the usual overload resolution rules (§12.3) are used to select the right one for a given set of arguments. For selecting a constructor, default and initializer lists take precedence. Consider:

```
struct X {
    X(initializer_list<int>);
    X();
    X(int);
};

X x0 {};    // empty list: default constructor or initializer-list constructor? (the default constructor)
X x1 {1};   // one integer: an int argument or a list of one element? (the  initializer-list constructor)
```

The rules are:

- If either a default constructor or an initializer-list constructor could be invoked, prefer the default constructor.
- If both an initializer-list constructor and an "ordinary constructor" could be invoked, prefer the initializer-list constructor.

The first rule, "prefer the default constructor," is basically common sense: pick the simplest constructor when you can. Furthermore, if you define an initializer-list constructor to do something with an empty list that differs from what the default constructor does, you probably have a design error on your hands.

The second rule, "prefer the initializer-list constructor," is necessary to avoid different resolutions based on different numbers of elements. Consider **std::vector** (§31.4):

```
vector<int> v1 {1};        // one element
vector<int> v2 {1,2};      // two elements
vector<int> v3 {1,2,3};    // three elements

vector<string> vs1 {"one"};
vector<string> vs2 {"one", "two"};
vector<string> vs3 {"one", "two", "three"};
```

In every case, the initializer-list constructor is used. If we really want to invoke the constructor taking one or two integer arguments, we must use the () notation:

```
vector<int> v1(1);   // one element with the default value (0)
vector<int> v2(1,2); // one element with the value 2
```

17.3.4.2 Use of initializer_lists

A function with an initializer_list<T> argument can access it as a sequence using the member functions begin(), end(), and size(). For example:

```
void f(initializer_list<int> args)
{
    for (int i = 0; i!=args.size(); ++i)
        cout << args.begin()[i] << "\n";
}
```

Unfortunately, initializer_list doesn't provide subscripting.

An initializer_list<T> is passed by value. That is required by the overload resolution rules (§12.3) and does not impose overhead because an initializer_list<T> object is just a small handle (typically two words) to an array of Ts.

That loop could equivalently have been written:

```
void f(initializer_list<int> args)
{
    for (auto p=args.begin(); p!=args.end(); ++p)
        cout << *p << "\n";
}
```

or:

```
void f(initializer_list<int> args)
{
    for (auto x : args)
        cout << x << "\n";
}
```

To explicitly use an **initializer_list** you must **#include** the header file in which it is defined: **<initializer_list>**. However, since **vector**, **map**, etc., use **initializer_list**s, their headers (**<vector>**, **<map>**, etc.) already **#include <initializer_list>**, so you rarely have to do so directly.

The elements of an **initializer_list** are immutable. Don't even think about trying to modify their values. For example:

```
int f(std::initializer_list<int> x, int val)
{
        *x.begin() = val;          // error: attempt to change the value of an initializer-list element
        return *x.begin();   // OK
}


void g()
{
        for (int i=0; i!=10; ++i)
                cout << f({1,2,3},i) << '\n';
}
```

Had the assignment in **f()** succeeded, it would have appeared that the value of **1** (in **{1,2,3}**) could change. That would have done serious damage to some of our most fundamental concepts. Because **initializer_list** elements are immutable, we cannot apply a move constructor (§3.3.2, §17.5.2) to them.

A container might implement an initializer-list constructor like this:

```
template<class E>
class Vector {
public:
        Vector(std::initializer_list<E> s); // initializer-list constructor
        // ...
private:
        int sz;
        E* elem;
};


template<class E>
Vector::Vector(std::initializer_list<E> s)
        :sz{s.size()}                           // set vector size
{
        reserve(sz);                            // get the right amount of space
        uninitialized_copy(s.begin(), s.end(), elem);    // initialize elements in elem[0:s.size())
}
```

The initializer lists are part of the universal and uniform initialization design (§17.3).

17.3.4.3 Direct and Copy Initialization

The distinction between direct initialization and copy initialization (§16.2.6) is maintained for {} initialization. For a container, this implies that the distinction is applied to both the container and its elements:

- The container's initializer-list constructor can be **explicit** or not.
- The constructor of the element type of the initializer list can be **explicit** or not.

For a **vector<vector<double>>**, we can see the direct initialization vs. copy initialization distinction applied to elements. For example:

```
vector<vector<double>> vs = {
    {10,11,12,13,14},         // OK: vector of five elements
    {10},                     // OK: vector of one element
    10,                       // error: vector<double>(int) is explicit

    vector<double>{10,11,12,13}, // OK: vector of five elements
    vector<double>{10},       // OK: vector of one element with value 10.0
    vector<double>(10),       // OK:  vector of 10 elements with value 0.0
};
```

A container can have some constructors explicit and some not. The standard-library **vector** is an example of that. For example, **std::vector<int>(int)** is **explicit**, but **std::vector<int>(initialize_list<int>)** is not:

```
vector<double> v1(7);     // OK: v1 has 7 elements; note: uses () rather than {}
vector<double> v2 = 9;    // error: no conversion from int to vector

void f(const vector<double>&);
void g()
{
    v1 = 9;               // error: no conversion from int to vector
    f(9);                 // error: no conversion from int to vector
}
```

By replacing () with {} we get:

```
vector<double> v1 {7};    // OK: v1 has one element (with the value 7)
vector<double> v2 = {9};  // OK: v2 has one element (with the value 9)

void f(const vector<double>&);
void g()
{
    v1 = {9};             // OK: v1 now has one element (with the value 9)
    f({9});               // OK: f is called with the list {9}
}
```

Obviously, the results are dramatically different.

This example was carefully crafted to give an example of the most confusing cases. Note that the apparent ambiguities (in the eyes of the human reader but not the compiler) do not emerge for longer lists. For example:

```
vector<double> v1 {7,8,9};    // OK: v1 has three elements with values {7,8,9}
vector<double> v2 = {9,8,7};  // OK: v2 has three elements with values {9,8,7}
```

```
void f(const vector<double>&);
void g()
{
    v1 = {9,10,11};        // OK: v1 now has three elements with values {9,10,11}
    f({9,8,7,6,5,4});      // OK: f is called with the list {9,8,7,6,5,4}
}
```

Similarly, the potential ambiguities do not occur for lists of elements of nonintegral types:

```
vector<string> v1 { "Anya"};        // OK: v1 has one element (with the value "Anya")
vector<string> v2 = {"Courtney"};   // OK: v2 has one element (with the value "Courtney")

void f(const vector<string>&);
void g()
{
    v1 = {"Gavin"};        // OK: v1 now has one element (with the value "Gavin")
    f({"Norah"});          // OK: f is called with the list {"Norah"}
}
```

17.4 Member and Base Initialization

Constructors can establish invariants and acquire resources. Generally, they do that by initializing class members and base classes.

17.4.1 Member Initialization

Consider a class that might be used to hold information for a small organization:

```
class Club {
    string name;
    vector<string> members;
    vector<string> officers;
    Date founded;
    // ...
    Club(const string& n, Date fd);
};
```

The Club's constructor takes the name of the club and its founding date as arguments. Arguments for a member's constructor are specified in a *member initializer list* in the definition of the constructor of the containing class. For example:

```
Club::Club(const string& n, Date fd)
    : name{n}, members{}, officers{}, founded{fd}
{
    // ...
}
```

The member initializer list starts with a colon, and the individual member initializers are separated by commas.

The members' constructors are called before the body of the containing class's own constructor is executed (§17.2.3). The constructors are called in the order in which the members are declared in the class rather than the order in which the members appear in the initializer list. To avoid confusion, it is best to specify the initializers in the member declaration order. Hope for a compiler warning if you don't get the order right. The member destructors are called in the reverse order of construction after the body of the class's own destructor has been executed.

If a member constructor needs no arguments, the member need not be mentioned in the member initializer list. For example:

```
Club::Club(const string& n, Date fd)
    : name{n}, founded{fd}
{
    // ...
}
```

This constructor is equivalent to the previous version. In each case, **Club::officers** and **Club::members** are initialized to a **vector** with no elements.

It is usually a good idea to be explicit about initializing members. Note that an "implicitly initialized" member of a built-in type is left uninitialized (§17.3.1).

A constructor can initialize members and bases of its class, but not members or bases of its members or bases. For example:

```
struct B { B(int); /* ... */};
struct BB : B { /* ... */ };
struct BBB : BB {
    BBB(int i) : B(i) { };   // error: trying to initialize base's base
    // ...
};
```

17.4.1.1 Member Initialization and Assignment

Member initializers are essential for types for which the meaning of initialization differs from that of assignment. For example:

```
class X {
    const int i;
    Club cl;
    Club& rc;
    // ...
    X(int ii, const string& n, Date d, Club& c) : i{ii}, cl{n,d}, rc{c} { }
};
```

A reference member or a **const** member must be initialized (§7.5, §7.7, §17.3.3). However, for most types the programmer has a choice between using an initializer and using an assignment. In that case, I usually prefer to use the member initializer syntax to make it explicit that initialization is being done. Often, there also is an efficiency advantage to using the initializer syntax (compared to using an assignment). For example:

```
class Person {
    string name;
    string address;
    // ...
    Person(const Person&);
    Person(const string& n, const string& a);
};

Person::Person(const string& n, const string& a)
    : name{n}
{
    address = a;
}
```

Here **name** is initialized with a copy of **n**. On the other hand, **address** is first initialized to the empty string and then a copy of **a** is assigned.

17.4.2 Base Initializers

Bases of a derived class are initialized in the same way non-data members are. That is, if a base requires an initializer, it must be provided as a base initializer in a constructor. If we want to, we can explicitly specify default construction. For example:

```
class B1 { B1(); };    // has default constructor
class B2 { B2(int); } // no default constructor

struct D1 : B1, B2 {
    D1(int i) :B1{}, B2{i} {}
};

struct D2 : B1, B2 {
    D2(int i) :B2{i} {}          // B1{} is used implicitly
};

struct D1 : B1, B2 {
    D1(int i) { }                // error: B2 requires an int initializer
};
```

As with members, the order of initialization is the declaration order, and it is recommended to specify base initializers in that order. Bases are initialized before members and destroyed after members (§17.2.3).

17.4.3 Delegating Constructors

If you want two constructors to do the same action, you can repeat yourself or define "an **init()** function" to perform the common action. Both "solutions" are common (because older versions of C++ didn't offer anything better). For example:

```
class X {
    int a;
    validate(int x) { if (0<x && x<=max) a=x; else throw Bad_X(x); }
public:
    X(int x) { validate(x); }
    X() { validate(42); }
    X(string s) { int x = to<int>(s); validate(x); }     // §25.2.5.1
    // ...
};
```

Verbosity hinders readability and repetition is error-prone. Both get in the way of maintainability. The alternative is to define one constructor in terms of another:

```
class X {
    int a;
public:
    X(int x) { if (0<x && x<=max) a=x; else throw Bad_X(x); }
    X() :X{42} { }
    X(string s) :X{to<int>(s)} { }          // §25.2.5.1
    // ...
};
```

That is, a member-style initializer using the class's own name (its constructor name) calls another constructor as part of the construction. Such a constructor is called a *delegating constructor* (and occasionally a *forwarding constructor*).

You cannot both delegate and explicitly initialize a member. For example:

```
class X {
    int a;
public:
    X(int x) { if (0<x && x<=max) a=x; else throw Bad_X(x); }
    X() :X{42}, a{56} { }        // error
    // ...
};
```

Delegating by calling another constructor in a constructor's member and base initializer list is very different from explicitly calling a constructor in the body of a constructor. Consider:

```
class X {
    int a;
public:
    X(int x) { if (0<x && x<=max) a=x; else throw Bad_X(x); }
    X() { X{42}; }    // likely error
    // ...
};
```

The X{42} simply creates a new unnamed object (a temporary) and does nothing with it. Such use is more often than not a bug. Hope for a compiler warning.

An object is not considered constructed until its constructor completes (§6.4.2). When using a delegating constructor, the object is not considered constructed until the delegating constructor completes – just completing the delegated-to constructor is not sufficient. A destructor will not be called for an object unless its original constructor completed.

If all you need is to set a member to a default value (that doesn't depend on a constructor argument), a member initializer (§17.4.4) may be simpler.

17.4.4 In-Class Initializers

We can specify an initializer for a non-**static** data member in the class declaration. For example:

```
class A {
public:
        int a {7};
        int b = 77;
};
```

For pretty obscure technical reasons related to parsing and name lookup, the {} and = initializer notations can be used for in-class member initializers, but the () notation cannot.

By default, a constructor will use such an in-class initializer, so that example is equivalent to:

```
class A {
public:
        int a;
        int b;
        A() : a{7}, b{77} {}
};
```

Such use of in-class initializers can save a bit of typing, but the real benefits come in more complicated classes with multiple constructors. Often, several constructors use the same initializer for a member. For example:

```
class A {
public:
        A() :a{7}, b{5}, algorithm{"MD5"}, state{"Constructor run"} {}
        A(int a_val) :a{a_val}, b{5}, algorithm{"MD5"}, state{"Constructor run"} {}
        A(D d) :a{7}, b{g(d)}, algorithm{"MD5"}, state{"Constructor run"} {}
        // ...
private:
        int a, b;
        HashFunction algorithm;      // cryptographic hash to be applied to all As
        string state;                // string indicating state in object life cycle
};
```

The fact that **algorithm** and **state** have the same value in all constructors is lost in the mess of code and can easily become a maintenance problem. To make the common values explicit, we can factor out the unique initializer for data members:

```
class A {
public:
        A() :a{7}, b{5} {}
        A(int a_val) :a{a_val}, b{5} {}
        A(D d) :a{7}, b{g(d)} {}
        // ...
```

```
private:
    int a, b;
    HashFunction algorithm {"MD5"};        // cryptographic hash to be applied to all As
    string state {"Constructor run"};      // string indicating state in object life cycle
};
```

If a member is initialized by both an in-class initializer and a constructor, only the constructor's initialization is done (it "overrides" the default). So we can simplify further:

```
class A {
public:
    A() {}
    A(int a_val) :a{a_val} {}
    A(D d) :b{g(d)} {}
    // ...
private:
    int a {7};                             // the meaning of 7 for a is ...
    int b {5};                             // the meaning of 5 for b is ...
    HashFunction algorithm {"MD5"};        // Cryptographic hash to be applied to all As
    string state {"Constructor run"};      // String indicating state in object lifecycle
};
```

As shown, default in-class initializers provide an opportunity for documentation of common cases.

An in-class member initializer can use names that are in scope at the point of their use in the member declaration. Consider the following headache-inducing technical example:

```
int count = 0;
int count2 = 0;

int f(int i) { return i+count; }

struct S {
    int m1 {count2};      // that is, ::count2
    int m2 {f(m1)};       // that is, this->m1+::count; that is, ::count2+::count
    S() { ++count2; }     // very odd constructor
};

int main()
{
    S s1;        // {0,0}
    ++count;
    S s2;        // {1,2}
}
```

Member initialization is done in declaration order (§17.2.3), so first **m1** is initialized to the value of a global variable **count2**. The value of the global variable is obtained at the point where the constructor for a new **S** object is run, so it can (and in this example does) change. Next, **m2** is initialized by a call to the global **f()**.

It is a bad idea to hide subtle dependencies on global data in member initializers.

17.4.5 static Member Initialization

A **static** class member is statically allocated rather than part of each object of the class. Generally, the **static** member declaration acts as a declaration for a definition outside the class. For example:

```
class Node {
    // ...
    static int node_count;          // declaration
};

int Node::node_count = 0;           // definition
```

However, for a few simple special cases, it is possible to initialize a **static** member in the class declaration. The **static** member must be a **const** of an integral or enumeration type, or a **constexpr** of a literal type (§10.4.3), and the initializer must be a *constant-expression*. For example:

```
class Curious {
public:
    static const int c1 = 7;        // OK
    static int c2 = 11;             // error: not const
    const int c3 = 13;              // OK, but not static (§17.4.4)
    static const int c4 = sqrt(9);  // error: in-class initializer not constant
    static const float c5 = 7.0;    // error: in-class not integral (use constexpr rather than const)
    // ...
};
```

If (and only if) you use an initialized member in a way that requires it to be stored as an object in memory, the member must be (uniquely) defined somewhere. The initializer may not be repeated:

```
const int Curious::c1;              // don't repeat initializer here
const int* p = &Curious::c1;        // OK: Curious::c1 has been defined
```

The main use of member constants is to provide symbolic names for constants needed elsewhere in the class declaration. For example:

```
template<class T, int N>
class Fixed {   // fixed-size array
public:
    static constexpr int max = N;
    // ...
private:
    T a[max];
};
```

For integers, enumerators (§8.4) offer an alternative for defining symbolic constants within a class declaration. For example:

```
class X {
    enum { c1 = 7, c2 = 11, c3 = 13, c4 = 17 };
    // ...
};
```

17.5 Copy and Move

When we need to transfer a value from **a** to **b**, we usually have two logically distinct options:

- *Copy* is the conventional meaning of **x=y**; that is, the effect is that the values of **x** and **y** are both equal to **y**'s value before the assignment.
- *Move* leaves **x** with **y**'s former value and **y** with some *moved-from state*. For the most interesting cases, containers, that moved-from state is "empty."

This simple logical distinction is confounded by tradition and by the fact that we use the same notation for both move and copy.

Typically, a move cannot throw, whereas a copy might (because it may need to acquire a resource), and a move is often more efficient than a copy. When you write a move operation, you should leave the source object in a valid but unspecified state because it will eventually be destroyed and the destructor cannot destroy an object left in an invalid state. Also, standard-library algorithms rely on being able to assign to (using move or copy) a moved-from object. So, design your moves not to throw, and to leave their source objects in a state that allows destruction and assignment.

To save us from tedious repetitive work, copy and move have default definitions (§17.6.2).

17.5.1 Copy

Copy for a class **X** is defined by two operations:

- Copy constructor: **X(const X&)**
- Copy assignment: **X& operator=(const X&)**

You can define these two operations with more adventurous argument types, such as **volatile X&**, but don't; you'll just confuse yourself and others. A copy constructor is supposed to make a copy of an object without modifying it. Similarly, you can use **const X&** as the return type of the copy assignment. My opinion is that doing so causes more confusion than it is worth, so my discussion of copy assumes that the two operations have the conventional types.

Consider a simple two-dimensional **Matrix**:

```
template<class T>
class Matrix {
      array<int,2> dim;       // two dimensions
      T* elem;                // pointer to dim[0]*dim[1] elements of type T
public:
      Matrix(int d1, int d2) :dim{d1,d2}, elem{new T[d1*d2]} {}      // simplified (no error handling)
      int size() const { return dim[0]*dim[1]; }

      Matrix(const Matrix&);             // copy constructor
      Matrix& operator=(const Matrix&);  // copy assignment

      Matrix(Matrix&&);                  // move constructor
      Matrix& operator=(Matrix&&);       // move assignment

      ~Matrix() { delete[] elem; }
      // ...
};
```

First we note that the default copy (copy the members) would be disastrously wrong: the **Matrix** elements would not be copied, the **Matrix** copy would have a pointer to the same elements as the source, and the **Matrix** destructor would delete the (shared) elements twice (§3.3.1).

However, the programmer can define any suitable meaning for these copy operations, and the conventional one for a container is to copy the contained elements:

```
template<class T>
Matrix:: Matrix(const Matrix& m)          // copy constructor
    : dim{m.dim},
      elem{new T[m.size()]}
{
    uninitialized_copy(m.elem,m.elem+m.size(),elem);        // copy elements
}

template<class T>
Matrix& Matrix::operator=(const Matrix& m)          // copy assignment
{
    if (dim[0]!=m.dim[0] || dim[1]!=m.dim[1])
        throw runtime_error("bad size in Matrix =");
    copy(m.elem,m.elem+m.size(),elem);     // copy elements
}
```

A copy constructor and a copy assignment differ in that a copy constructor initializes uninitialized memory, whereas the copy assignment operator must correctly deal with an object that has already been constructed and may own resources.

The **Matrix** copy assignment operator has the property that if a copy of an element throws an exception, the target of the assignment may be left with a mixture of its old value and the new. That is, that **Matrix** assignment provided the basic guarantee, but not the strong guarantee (§13.2). If that is not considered acceptable, we can avoid it by the fundamental technique of first making a copy and then swapping representations:

```
Matrix& Matrix::operator=(const Matrix& m)          // copy assignment
{
    Matrix tmp {m};           // make a copy
    swap(tmp,*this);          // swap tmp's representation with *this's
    return *this;
}
```

The **swap()** will be done only if the copy was successful. Obviously, this **operator=()** works only if the implementation **swap()** does not use assignment (**std::swap()** does not); see §17.5.2.

Usually a copy constructor must copy every non-**static** member (§17.4.1). If a copy constructor cannot copy an element (e.g., because it needs to acquire an unavailable resource to do so), it can throw an exception.

Note that I did not protect **Matrix**'s copy assignment against self-assignment, **m=m**. The reason I did not test is that self-assignment of the members is already safe: both my implementations of **Matrix**'s copy assignment will work correctly and reasonably efficiently for **m=m**. Also, self-assignment is rare, so test for self-assignment in a copy assignment only if you are sure that you need to.

17.5.1.1 Beware of Default Constructors

When writing a copy operation, be sure to copy every base and member. Consider:

```
class X {
    string s;
    string s2;
    vector<string> v;

    X(const X&)          // copy constructor
        :s{a.s}, v{a.v}  // probably sloppy and probably wrong
    {
    }
    // ...
};
```

Here, I "forgot" to copy **s2**, so it gets default initialized (to ""). This is unlikely to be right. It is also unlikely that I would make this mistake for a simple class. However, for larger classes the chances of forgetting go up. Worse, when someone long after the initial design adds a member to a class, it is easy to forget to add it to the list of members to be copied. This is one reason to prefer the default (compiler-generated) copy operations (§17.6).

17.5.1.2 Copy of Bases

For the purposes of copying, a base is just a member: to copy an object of a derived class you have to copy its bases. For example:

```
struct B1 {
    B1();
    B1(const B1&);
    // ...
};

struct B2 {
    B2(int);
    B2(const B2&);
    // ...
};

struct D : B1, B2 {
    D(int i) :B1{}, B2{i}, m1{}, m2{2*i} {}
    D(const D& a) :B1{a}, B2{a}, m1{a.m1}, m2{a.m2} {}
    B1 m1;
    B2 m2;
};

D d {1};    // construct with int argument
D dd {d};   // copy construct
```

The order of initialization is the usual (base before member), but for copying the order had better not matter.

A **virtual** base (§21.3.5) may appear as a base of several classes in a hierarchy. A default copy constructor (§17.6) will correctly copy it. If you define your own copy constructor, the simplest technique is to repeatedly copy the **virtual** base. Where the base object is small and the **virtual** base occurs only a few times in a hierarchy, that can be more efficient than techniques for avoiding the replicated copies.

17.5.1.3 The Meaning of Copy

What does a copy constructor or copy assignment have to do to be considered "a proper copy operation"? In addition to be declared with a correct type, a copy operation must have the proper copy semantics. Consider a copy operation, **x=y**, of two objects of the same type. To be suitable for value-oriented programming in general (§16.3.4), and for use with the standard library in particular (§31.2.2), the operation must meet two criteria:

- *Equivalence*: After **x=y**, operations on **x** and **y** should give the same result. In particular, if **==** is defined for their type, we should have **x==y** and **f(x)==f(y)** for any function **f()** that depends only on the values of **x** and **y** (as opposed to having its behavior depend on the addresses of **x** and **y**).
- *Independence*: After **x=y**, operations on **x** should not implicitly change the state of **y**, that is **f(x)** does not change the value of **y** as long as **f(x)** doesn't refer to **y**.

This is the behavior that **int** and **vector** offer. Copy operations that provide equivalence and independence lead to simpler and more maintainable code. This is worth stating because code that violate these simple rules is not uncommon, and programmers don't always realize that such violations are the root cause of some of their nastier problems. A copy that provides equivalence and independence is part of the notion of a regular type (§24.3.1).

First consider the requirement of equivalence. People rarely violate this requirement deliberately, and the default copy operations do not violate it; they do memberwise copy (§17.3.1, §17.6.2). However, tricks, such as having the meaning of copy depend on "options," occasionally appear and typically cause confusion. Also, it is not uncommon for an object to contain members that are not considered part of its value. For example, a copy of a standard container does not copy its allocator because the allocator is considered part of the container, rather than part of its value. Similarly, counters for statistics gathering and cached values are sometimes not simply copied. Such "non-value" parts of an object's state should not affect the result of comparison operators. In particular, **x=y** should imply **x==y**. Furthermore, slicing (§17.5.1.4) can lead to "copies" that behave differently, and is most often a bad mistake.

Now consider the requirement of independence. Most of the problems related to (lack of) independence have to do with objects that contain pointers. The default meaning of copy is memberwise copy. A default copy operation copies a pointer member, but does not copy the object (if any) that it points to. For example:

```
struct S {
    int* p;    // a pointer
};

S x {new int{0}};
```

```
void f()
{
    S y {x};            // "copy" x

    *y.p = 1;           // change y; affects x
    *x.p = 2;           // change x; affects y
    delete y.p;         // affects x and y
    y.p = new int{3};   // OK: change y; does not affect x
    *x.p = 4;           // oops: write to deallocated memory
}
```

Here I violated the rule of independence. After the "copy" of **x** into **y**, we can manipulate part of **x**'s state through **y**. This is sometimes called *shallow copy* and (too) often praised for "efficiency." The obvious alternative of copying the complete state of an object is called *deep copy*. Often, the better alternative to deep copy is not a shallow copy, but a move operation, which minimizes copying without adding complexity (§3.3.2, §17.5.2).

A shallow copy leaves two objects (here, **x** and **y**) with a *shared state*, and has a huge potential for confusion and errors. We say that the objects **x** and **y** have become *entangled* when the requirement of independence have been violated. It is not possible to reason about an entangled object in isolation. For example, it is not obvious from the source code that the two assignments to *∗x.p* can have dramatically different effects.

We can represent two entangled objects graphically:

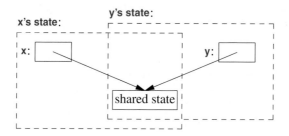

Note that entanglement can arise in a variety of ways. Often, it is not obvious that entanglement has happened until probems arise. For example, a type like **S** may incautiously be used as a member of an otherwise well-behaved class. The original author of **S** may be aware of the entanglement and prepared to cope with it, but someone naively assuming that copying an **S** meant copying its complete value could be surprised, and someone who finds an **S** deeply nested in other classes could be very surprised.

We can address problems related to the lifetime of a shared subobject by introducing a form of garbage collection. For example:

```
struct S2 {
    shared_ptr<int> p;
};

S2 x {new int{0}};
```

```
void f()
{
    S2 y {x};                // "copy" x

    *y.p = 1;                // change y, affects x
    *x.p = 2;                // change x; affects y
    y.p.reset(new int{3});   // change y; affects x
    *x.p = 4;                // change x; affects y
}
```

In fact, shallow copy and such entangled objects are among the sources of demands for garbage collection. Entangled objects lead to code that is very hard to manage without some form of garbage collection (e.g., **shared_ptrs**).

However, a **shared_ptr** is still a pointer, so we cannot consider objects containing a **shared_ptr** in isolation. Who can update the pointed-to object? How? When? If we are running in a multi-threaded system, is synchronization needed for access to the shared data? How can we be sure? Entangled objects (here, resulting from a shallow copy) is a source of complexity and errors that is at best partially solved by garbage collection (in any form).

Note that an immutable shared state is not a problem. Unless we compare addresses, we cannot tell whether two equal values happen to be represented as one or two copies. This is a useful observation because many copies are never modified. For example, objects passed by value are rarely written to. This observation leads to the notion of *copy-on-write*. The idea is that a copy doesn't actually need independence until a shared state is written to, so we can delay the copying of the shared state until just before the first write to it. Consider:

```
class Image {
public:
    // ...
    Image(const Image& a);          // copy constructor
    // ...
    void write_block(Descriptor);
    // ...
private:
    Representation* clone();        // copy *rep
    Representation* rep;
    bool shared;
};
```

Assume that a **Representation** can be huge and that a **write_block()** is expensive compared to testing a **bool**. Then, depending on the use of **Image**s, it can make sense to implement the copy constructor as a shallow copy:

```
Image::Image(const Image& a)    // do shallow copy and prepare for copy-on-write
    :rep{a.rep},
     shared{true}
{
}
```

We protect the argument to that copy constructor by copying the **Representation** before a write:

```
    void write_block(Descriptor d)
    {
        if (shared) {
            rep =clone();          // make a copy of *rep
            shared = false;        // no more sharing
        }
        // ... now we can safely write to our own copy of rep ...
    }
```

Like any other technique, copy-on-write is not a panacea, but it can be an effective combination of the simplicity of true copy and the efficiency of shallow copy.

17.5.1.4 Slicing

A pointer to a derived class implicitly converts to a pointer to its public base class. When applied to a copy operation, this simple and necessary rule (§3.2.4, §20.2) leads to a trap for the unwary. Consider:

```
    struct Base {
        int b;
        Base(const Base&);
        // ...
    };

    struct Derived : Base {
        int d;
        Derived(const Derived&);
        // ...
    };

    void naive(Base* p)
    {
        B b2 = *p;      // may slice: invokes Base::Base(const Base&)
        // ...
    }

    void user()
    {
        Derived d;
        naive(&d);
        Base bb = d;    // slices: invokes Base::Base(const Base&), not Derived::Derived(const Derived&)
        // ...
    }
```

The variables `b2` and `bb` contain copies of the `Base` part of `d`, that is, a copy of `d.b`. The member `d.d` is not copied. This phenomenon is called *slicing*. It may be exactly what you intended (e.g., see the copy constructor for `D` in §17.5.1.2 where we pass selected information to a base class), but typically it is a subtle bug. If you don't want slicing, you have two major tools to prevent it:

[1]   Prohibit copying of the base class: **delete** the copy operations (§17.6.4).

[2]   Prevent conversion of a pointer to a derived to a pointer to a base: make the base class a **private** or **protected** base (§20.5).

The former would make the initializations of **b2** and **bb** errors; the latter would make the call of **naive()** and the initialization of **bb** errors.

17.5.2 Move

The traditional way of getting a value from **a** to **b** is to copy it. For an integer in a computer's memory, that's just about the only thing that makes sense: that's what the hardware can do with a single instruction. However, from a general and logical point of view that's not so. Consider the obvious implementation of **swap()** exchanging the value of two objects:

```
template<class T>
void swap(T& a, T& b)
{
        const T tmp = a;        // put a copy of a into tmp
        a = b;                  // put a copy of b into a
        b = tmp;                // put a copy of tmp into b
};
```

After the initialization of **tmp**, we have two copies of **a**'s value. After the assignment to **tmp**, we have two copies of **b**'s value. After the assignment to **b**, we have two copies of **tmp**'s value (that is, the original value of **a**). Then we destroy **tmp**. That sounds like a lot of work, and it can be. For example:

```
void f(string& s1, string& s2,
       vector<string>& vs1, vector<string>& vs2,
       Matrix& m1, Matrix& m2)
{
       swap(s1,s2);
       swap(vs1.vs2);
       swap(m1,m2);
}
```

What if **s1** has a thousand characters? What if **vs2** has a thousand elements each of a thousand characters? What if **m1** is a 1000∗1000 matrix of **doubles**? The cost of copying those data structures could be significant. In fact, the standard-library **swap()** has always been carefully designed to avoid such overhead for **string** and **vector**. That is, effort has been made to avoid copying (taking advantage of the fact that **string** and **vector** objects really are just handles to their elements). Similar work must be done to avoid a serious performance problem for **swap()** of **Matrix**es. If the only operation we have is copy, similar work must be done for huge numbers of functions and data structures that are not part of the standard.

The fundamental problem is that we really didn't want to do any copying at all: we just wanted to exchange pairs of values.

We can also look at the issue of copying from a completely different point of view: we don't usually copy physical things unless we absolutely have to. If you want to borrow my phone, I pass my phone to you rather than making you your own copy. If I lend you my car, I give you a key and you drive away in my car, rather than in your freshly made copy of my car. Once I have given you an object, you have it and I no longer do. Consequently, we talk about "giving away," "handing over," "transferring ownership of," and "moving" physical objects. Many objects in a computer resemble physical objects (which we don't copy without need and only at considerable cost) more than integer values (which we typically copy because that's easier and cheaper than alternatives). Examples are locks, sockets, file handles, threads, long strings, and large vectors.

To allow the user to avoid the logical and performance problems of copying, C++ directly supports the notion of *moving* as well as the notion of *copying*. In particular, we can define *move constructors* and *move assignments* to move rather than copy their argument. Consider again the simple two-dimensional **Matrix** from §17.5.1:

```
template<class T>
class Matrix {
    std::array<int,2> dim;
    T* elem;    // pointer to sz elements of type T

    Matrix(int d1, int d2) :dim{d1,d2}, elem{new T[d1*d2]} {}
    int size() const { return dim[0]*dim[1]; }

    Matrix(const Matrix&);          // copy constructor
    Matrix(Matrix&&);               // move constructor

    Matrix& operator=(const Matrix&); // copy assignment
    Matrix& operator=(Matrix&&);      // move assignment

    ˜Matrix(); // destructor
    // ...
};
```

The **&&** indicates an rvalue reference (§7.7.2).

The idea behind a move assignment is to handle lvalues separately from rvalues: copy assignment and copy constructors take lvalues whereas move assignment and move constructors take rvalues. For a **return** value, the move constructor is chosen.

We can define **Matrix**'s move constructor to simply take the representation from its source and replace it with an empty **Matrix** (which is cheap to destroy). For example:

```
template<class T>
Matrix<T>::Matrix(Matrix&& a)        // move constructor
    :dim{a.dim}, elem{a.elem}        // grab a's representation
{
    a.dim = {0,0};                   // clear a's representation
    a.elem = nullptr;
}
```

For the move assignment, we can simply do a swap. The idea behind using a swap to implement a move assignment is that the source is just about to be destroyed, so we can just let the destructor for the source do the necessary cleanup work for us:

```
template<class T>
Matrix<T>& Matrix<T>::operator=(Matrix&& a)              // move assignment
{
    swap(dim,a.dim);             // swap representations
    swap(elem,a.elem);
    return *this;
}
```

Move constructors and move assignments take non-**const** (rvalue) reference arguments: they can, and usually do, write to their argument. However, the argument of a move operation must always be left in a state that the destructor can cope with (and preferably deal with very cheaply and easily).

For resource handles, move operations tend to be significantly simpler and more efficient than copy operations. In particular, move operations typically do not throw exceptions; they don't acquire resources or do complicated operations, so they don't need to. In this, they differ from many copy operations (§17.5).

How does the compiler know when it can use a move operation rather than a copy operation? In a few cases, such as for a return value, the language rules say that it can (because the next action is defined to destroy the element). However, in general we have to tell it by giving an rvalue reference argument. For example:

```
template<class T>
void swap(T& a, T& b)     // "perfect swap" (almost)
{
    T tmp = std::move(a);
    a = std::move(b);
    b = std::move(tmp);
}
```

The **move()** is a standard-library function returning an rvalue reference to its argument (§35.5.1): **move(x)** means "give me an rvalue reference to x." That is, **std::move(x)** does not move anything; instead, it allows a user to move **x**. It would have been better if **move()** had been called **rval()**, but the name **move()** has been used for this operation for years.

Standard-library containers have move operations (§3.3.2, §35.5.1) and so have other standard-library types, such as **pair** (§5.4.3, §34.2.4.1) and **unique_ptr** (§5.2.1, §34.3.1). Furthermore, operations that insert new elements into standard-library containers, such as **insert()** and **push_back()**, have versions that take rvalue references (§7.7.2). The net result is that the standard containers and algorithms deliver better performance than they would have been able to if they had to copy.

What if we try to swap objects of a type that does not have a move constructor? We copy and pay the price. In general, a programmer is responsible for avoiding excessive copying. It is not the compiler's job to decide what is excessive and what is necessary. To get the copy-to-move optimization for your own data structures, you have to provide move operations (either explicitly or implicitly; see §17.6).

Built-in types, such as **int** and **double**∗, are considered to have move operations that simply copy. As usual, you have to be careful about data structures containing pointers (§3.3.1). In particular, don't assume that a moved-from pointer is set to **nullptr**.

Having move operations affects the idiom for returning large objects from functions. Consider:

```
Matrix operator+(const Matrix& a, const Matrix& b)
    // res[i][j] = a[i][j]+b[i][j] for each i and j
{
    if (a.dim[0]!=b.dim[0] || a.dim[1]!=b.dim[1])
        throw std::runtime_error("unequal Matrix sizes in +");

    Matrix res{a.dim[0],a.dim[1]};
    constexpr auto n = a.size();
    for (int i = 0; i!=n; ++i)
        res.elem[i] = a.elem[i]+b.elem[i];
    return res;
}
```

Matrix has a move constructor so that "return by value" is simple and efficient as well as "natural." Without move operations, we have performance problems and must resort to workarounds. We might have considered:

```
Matrix& operator+(const Matrix& a, const Matrix& b)    // beware!
{
    Matrix& res = *new Matrix;    // allocate on free store
    // res[i][j] = a[i][j]+b[i][j] for each i and j
    return res;
}
```

The use of new within operator+() is not obvious and forces the user of + to deal with tricky memory management issues:

- How does the object created by new get deleted?
- Do we need a garbage collector?
- Should we use a pool of Matrixes rather than the general new?
- Do we need use-counted Matrix representations?
- Should we redesign the interface of our Matrix addition?
- Must the caller of operator+() remember to delete the result?
- What happens to the newly allocated memory if the computation throws an exception?

None of the alternatives are elegant or general.

17.6 Generating Default Operations

Writing conventional operations, such as a copy and a destructor, can be tedious and error-prone, so the compiler can generate them for us as needed. By default, a class provides:

- A default constructor: X()
- A copy constructor: X(const X&)
- A copy assignment: X& operator=(const X&)
- A move constructor: X(X&&)
- A move assignment: X& operator=(X&&)
- A destructor: ~X()

By default, the compiler generates each of these operations if a program uses it. However, if the programmer takes control by defining one or more of those operations, the generation of related operations is suppressed:

- If the programmer declares any constructor for a class, the default constructor is not generated for that class.
- If the programmer declares a copy operation, a move operation, or a destructor for a class, no copy operation, move operation, or destructor is generated for that class.

Unfortunately, the second rule is only incompletely enforced: for backward compatibility, copy constructors and copy assignments are generated even if a destructor is defined. However, that generation is deprecated in the ISO standard (§iso.D), and you should expect a modern compiler to warn against it.

If necessary, we can be explicit about which functions are generated (§17.6.1) and which are not (§17.6.4).

17.6.1 Explicit Defaults

Since the generation of otherwise default operations can be suppressed, there has to be a way of getting back a default. Also, some people prefer to see a complete list of operations in the program text even if that complete list is not needed. For example, we can write:

```
class gslice {
    valarray<size_t> size;
    valarray<size_t> stride;
    valarray<size_t> d1;
public:
    gslice() = default;
    ~gslice() = default;
    gslice(const gslice&) = default;
    gslice(gslice&&) = default;
    gslice& operator=(const gslice&) = default;
    gslice& operator=(gslice&&) = default;
    // ...
};
```

This fragment of the implementation of **std::gslice** (§40.5.6) is equivalent to:

```
class gslice {
    valarray<size_t> size;
    valarray<size_t> stride;
    valarray<size_t> d1;
public:
    // ...
};
```

I prefer the latter, but I can see the point of using the former in code bases maintained by less experienced C++ programmers: what you don't see, you might forget about.

Using =**default** is always better than writing your own implementation of the default semantics. Someone assuming that it is better to write something, rather than nothing, might write:

```
class gslice {
    valarray<size_t> size;
    valarray<size_t> stride;
    valarray<size_t> d1;
public:
    // ...
    gslice(const gslice& a);
};

gslice::gslice(const gslice& a)
    : size{a.size },
      stride{a.stride},
      d1{a.d1}
{
}
```

This is not only verbose, making it harder to read the definition of **gslice**, but also opens the opportunity for making mistakes. For example, I might forget to copy one of the members and get it default initialized (rather than copied). Also, when the user provides a function, the compiler no longer knows the semantics of that function and some optimizations become inhibited. For the default operations, those optimizations can be significant.

17.6.2 Default Operations

The default meaning of each generated operation, as implemented when the compiler generates it, is to apply the operation to each base and non-**static** data member of the class. That is, we get memberwise copy, memberwise default construction, etc. For example:

```
struct S {
    string a;
    int b;
};

S f(S arg)
{
    S s0 {};    // default construction: {"",0}
    S s1 {s0};// copy construction
    s1 = arg; // copy assignment
    return s1;// move construction
}
```

The copy construction of **s1** copies **s0.a** and **s0.b**. The **return** of **s1** moves **s1.a** and **s1.b**, leaving **s1.a** as the empty string and **s1.b** unchanged.

Note that the value of a moved-from object of a built-in type is unchanged. That's the simplest and fastest thing for the compiler to do. If we want something else done for a member of a class, we have to write our move operations for that class.

The default moved-from state is one for which the default destructor and default copy assignment work correctly. It is not guaranteed (or required) that an arbitrary operation on a moved-from object will work correctly. If you need stronger guarantees, write your own operations.

17.6.3 Using Default Operations

This section presents a few examples demonstrating how copy, move, and destructors are logically linked. If they were not linked, errors that are obvious when you think about them would not be caught by the compiler.

17.6.3.1 Default Constructors

Consider:

```
struct X {
       X(int);        // require an int to initialize an X
};
```

By declaring a constructor that requires an integer argument, the programmer clearly states that a user needs to provide an **int** to initialize an **X**. Had we allowed the default constructor to be generated, that simple rule would have been violated. We have:

```
X a {1};    // OK
X b {};     // error: no default constructor
```

If we also want the default constructor, we can define one or declare that we want the default generated by the compiler. For example:

```
struct Y {
       string s;
       int n;
       Y(const string& s); // initialize Y with a string
       Y() = default;         // allow default initialization with the default meaning
};
```

The default (i.e., generated) default constructor default constructs each member. Here, **Y()** sets **s** to the empty string. The "default initialization" of a built-in member leaves that member uninitialized. Sigh! Hope for a compiler warning.

17.6.3.2 Maintaining Invariants

Often, a class has an invariant. If so, we want copy and move operations to maintain it and the destructor to free any resources involved. Unfortunately, the compiler cannot in every case know what a programmer considers an invariant. Consider a somewhat far-fetched example:

```
struct Z { // invariant:
              // my_favorite is the index of my favorite element of elem
              // largest points to the element with the highest value in elem
       vector<int> elem;
       int my_favorite;
       int* largest;
};
```

The programmer stated an invariant in the comment, but the compiler doesn't read comments. Furthermore, the programmer did not leave a hint about how that invariant is to be established and maintained. In particular, there are no constructors or assignments declared. That invariant is implicit. The result is that a **Z** can be copied and moved using the default operations:

```
Z v0;                        // no initialization (oops! possibility of undefined values)
Z val {{1,2,3},1,&val[2]};   // OK, but ugly and error-prone
Z v2 = val;                  // copies: v2.largest points into val
Z v3 = move(val);            // moves: val.elem becomes empty; v3.my_favorite is out of range
```

This is a mess. The root problem is that **Z** is badly designed because critical information is "hidden" in a comment or completely missing. The rules for the generation of default operations are heuristic intended to catch common mistakes and to encourage a systematic approach to construction, copy, move, and destruction. Wherever possible

[1]   Establish an invariant in a constructor (including possibly resource acquisition).
[2]   Maintain the invariant with copy and move operations (with the usual names and types).
[3]   Do any needed cleanup in the destructor (incl. possibly resource release).

17.6.3.3 Resource Invariants

Many of the most critical and obvious uses of invariants relate to resource management. Consider a simple **Handle**:

```
template<class T> class Handle {
    T* p;
public:
    Handle(T* pp) :p{pp} { }
    T& operator*() { return *p; }
    ~Handle() { delete p; }
};
```

The idea is that you construct a **Handle** given a pointer to an object allocated using **new**. The **Handle** provides access to the object pointed to and eventually **delete**s that object. For example:

```
void f1()
{
    Handle<int> h {new int{99}};
    // ...
}
```

Handle declares a constructor that takes an argument: this suppresses the generation of the default constructor. That's good because a default constructor could leave **Handle<T>::p** uninitialized:

```
void f2()
{
    Handle<int> h; // error: no default constructor
    // ...
}
```

The absence of a default constructor saves us from the possibility of a **delete** with a random memory address.

Also, **Handle** declares a destructor: this suppresses the generation of copy and move operations. Again, that saves us from a nasty problem. Consider:

```
void f3()
{
    Handle<int> h1 {new int{7}};
    Handle<int> h2 {h1};         // error: no copy constructor
    // ...
}
```

Had `Handle` had a default copy constructor, both `h1` and `h2` would have had a copy of the pointer and both would have `deleted` it. The results would be undefined and most likely disastrous (§3.3.1). Caveat: the generation of copy operations is only deprecated, not banned, so if you ignore warnings, you might get this example past the compiler. In general, if a class has a pointer member, the default copy and move operations should be considered suspicious. If that pointer member represents ownership, memberwise copy is wrong. If that pointer member does not represent ownership and memberwise copy *is* appropriate, explicit `=default` and a comment are most likely a good idea.

If we wanted copy construction, we could define something like:

```
template<class T>
class Handle {
    // ...
    Handle(const T& a) :p{new T{*a.p}} { }        // clone
};
```

17.6.3.4 Partially Specified Invariants

Troublesome examples that rely on invariants but only partially express them through constructors or destructors are rarer but not unheard of. Consider:

```
class Tic_tac_toe {
public:
    Tic_tac_toe(): pos(9) {}    // always 9 positions

    Tic_tac_toe& operator=(const Tic_tac_toe& arg)
    {
        for(int i = 0; i<9; ++i)
            pos.at(i) = arg.pos.at(i);
        return *this;
    }

    // ... other operations ...

    enum State { empty, nought, cross };
private:
    vector<State> pos;
};
```

This was reported to have been part of a real program. It uses the "magic number" 9 to implement a copy assignment that accesses its argument `arg` without checking that the argument actually has nine elements. Also, it explicitly implements the copy assignment, but not the copy constructor. This is not what I consider good code.

We defined copy assignment, so we must also define the destructor. That destructor can be =default because all it needs to do is to ensure that the member pos is destroyed, which is what would have been done anyway had the copy assignment not been defined. At this point, we notice that the user-defined copy assignment is essentially the one we would have gotten by default, so we can =default that also. Add a copy constructor for completeness and we get:

```
class Tic_tac_toe {
public:
        Tic_tac_toe(): pos(9) {}    // always 9 positions
        Tic_tac_toe(const Tic_tac_toe&) = default;
        Tic_tac_toe& operator=(const Tic_tac_toe& arg) = default;
        ~Tic_tac_toe() = default;

        // ... other operations ...

        enum State { empty, nought, cross };
private:
        vector<State> pos;
};
```

Looking at this, we realize that the net effect of these =defaults is just to eliminate move operations. Is that what we want? Probably not. When we made the copy assignment =default, we eliminated the nasty dependence on the magic constant 9. Unless other operations on Tic_tac_toe, not mentioned so far, are also "hardwired with magic numbers," we can safely add move operations. The simplest way to do that is to remove the explicit =defaults, and then we see that Tic_tac_toe is really a perfectly ordinary type:

```
class Tic_tac_toe {
public:
        // ... other operations ...
        enum State { empty, nought, cross };
private:
        vector<State> pos {Vector<State>(9)};        // always 9 positions
};
```

One conclusion that I draw from this and other examples where an "odd combination" of the default operations is defined is that we should be highly suspicious of such types: their irregularity often hides design flaws. For every class, we should ask:

[1] Is a default constructor needed (because the default one is not adequate or has been suppressed by another constructor)?

[2] Is a destructor needed (e.g., because some resource needs to be released)?

[3] Are copy operations needed (because the default copy semantics is not adequate, e.g., because the class is meant to be a base class or because it contains pointers to objects that must be deleted by the class)?

[4] Are move operations needed (because the default semantics is not adequate, e.g., because an empty object doesn't make sense)?

In particular, we should never just consider one of these operations in isolation.

17.6.4 deleted Functions

We can "delete" a function; that is, we can state that a function does not exist so that it is an error to try to use it (implicitly or explicitly). The most obvious use is to eliminate otherwise defaulted functions. For example, it is common to want to prevent the copying of classes used as bases because such copying easily leads to slicing (§17.5.1.4):

```
class Base {
      // ...
      Base& operator=(const Base&) = delete;// disallow copying
      Base(const Base&) = delete;

      Base& operator=(Base&&) = delete;          // disallow moving
      Base(Base&&) = delete;
};


Base x1;
Base x2 {x1};   // error: no copy constructor
```

Enabling and disabling copy and move is typically more conveniently done by saying what we want (using =default; §17.6.1) rather than saying what we don't want (using =delete). However, we can **delete** any function that we can declare. For example, we can eliminate a specialization from the set of possible specializations of a function template:

```
template<class T>
T* clone(T* p) // return copy of *p
{
      return new T{*p};
};

Foo* clone(Foo*) = delete;          // don't try to clone a Foo

void f(Shape* ps, Foo* pf)
{
      Shape* ps2 = clone(ps);       // fine
      Foo* pf2 = clone(pf);         // error: clone(Foo*) deleted
}
```

Another application is to eliminate an undesired conversion. For example:

```
struct Z {
      // ...
      Z(double);          // can initialize with a double
      Z(int) = delete;    // but not with an integer
};

void f()
{
      Z z1 {1};       // error: Z(int) deleted
      Z z2 {1.0};     // OK
}
```

A further use is to control where a class can be allocated:

```
class Not_on_stack {
    // ...
    ~Not_on_stack() = delete;
};

class Not_on_free_store {
    // ...
    void* operator new(size_t) = delete;
};
```

You can't have a local variable that can't be destroyed (§17.2.2), and you can't allocate an object on the free store when you have =deleted its class's memory allocation operator (§19.2.5). For example:

```
void f()
{
    Not_on_stack v1;            // error: can't destroy
    Not_on_free_store v2;       // OK

    Not_on_stack* p1 = new Not_on_stack;            // OK
    Not_on_free_store* p2 = new Not_on_free_store;  // error: can't allocate
}
```

However, we can never **delete** that **Not_on_stack** object. The alternative technique of making the destructor **private** (§17.2.2) can address that problem.

Note the difference between a =deleted function and one that simply has not been declared. In the former case, the compiler notes that the programmer has tried to use the **delete**d function and gives an error. In the latter case, the compiler looks for alternatives, such as not invoking a destructor or using a global **operator new()**.

17.7 Advice

[1] Design constructors, assignments, and the destructor as a matched set of operations; §17.1.
[2] Use a constructor to establish an invariant for a class; §17.2.1.
[3] If a constructor acquires a resource, its class needs a destructor to release the resource; §17.2.2.
[4] If a class has a virtual function, it needs a virtual destructor; §17.2.5.
[5] If a class does not have a constructor, it can be initialized by memberwise initialization; §17.3.1.
[6] Prefer {} initialization over = and () initialization; §17.3.2.
[7] Give a class a default constructor if and only if there is a "natural" default value; §17.3.3.
[8] If a class is a container, give it an initializer-list constructor; §17.3.4.
[9] Initialize members and bases in their order of declaration; §17.4.1.
[10] If a class has a reference member, it probably needs copy operations (copy constructor and copy assignment); §17.4.1.1.

[11] Prefer member initialization over assignment in a constructor; §17.4.1.1.

[12] Use in-class initializers to provide default values; §17.4.4.

[13] If a class is a resource handle, it probably needs copy and move operations; §17.5.

[14] When writing a copy constructor, be careful to copy every element that needs to be copied (beware of default initializers); §17.5.1.1.

[15] A copy operations should provide equivalence and independence; §17.5.1.3.

[16] Beware of entangled data structures; §17.5.1.3.

[17] Prefer move semantics and copy-on-write to shallow copy; §17.5.1.3.

[18] If a class is used as a base class, protect against slicing; §17.5.1.4.

[19] If a class needs a copy operation or a destructor, it probably needs a constructor, a destructor, a copy assignment, and a copy constructor; §17.6.

[20] If a class has a pointer member, it probably needs a destructor and non-default copy operations; §17.6.3.3.

[21] If a class is a resource handle, it needs a constructor, a destructor, and non-default copy operations; §17.6.3.3.

[22] If a default constructor, assignment, or destructor is appropriate, let the compiler generate it (don't rewrite it yourself); §17.6.

[23] Be explicit about your invariants; use constructors to establish them and assignments to maintain them; §17.6.3.2.

[24] Make sure that copy assignments are safe for self-assignment; §17.5.1.

[25] When adding a new member to a class, check to see if there are user-defined constructors that need to be updated to initialize the member; §17.5.1.

18

Operator Overloading

*When **I** use a word it means just what*
I choose it to mean – neither more nor less.
– Humpty Dumpty

- Introduction
- Operator Functions
  Binary and Unary Operators; Predefined Meanings for Operators; Operators and User-Defined Types; Passing Objects; Operators in Namespaces
- A Complex Number Type
  Member and Nonmember Operators; Mixed-Mode Arithmetic; Conversions; Literals; Accessor Functions; Helper Functions
- Type Conversion
  Conversion Operators; **explicit** Conversion Operators; Ambiguities
- Advice

18.1 Introduction

Every technical field – and most nontechnical fields – has developed conventional shorthand notation to make convenient the presentation and discussion involving frequently used concepts. For example, because of long acquaintance,

x+y*z

is clearer to us than

multiply y by z and add the result to x

It is hard to overestimate the importance of concise notation for common operations.

Like most languages, C++ supports a set of operators for its built-in types. However, most concepts for which operators are conventionally used are not built-in types in C++, so they must be represented as user-defined types. For example, if you need complex arithmetic, matrix algebra, logic signals, or character strings in C++, you use classes to represent these notions. Defining operators for such classes sometimes allows a programmer to provide a more conventional and convenient notation for manipulating objects than could be achieved using only the basic functional notation. Consider:

```
class complex {                  // very simplified complex
        double re, im;
public:
        complex(double r, double i) :re{r}, im{i} { }
        complex operator+(complex);
        complex operator*(complex);
};
```

This defines a simple implementation of the concept of complex numbers. A complex is represented by a pair of double-precision floating-point numbers manipulated by the operators + and *. The programmer defines complex::operator+() and complex::operator*() to provide meanings for + and *, respectively. For example, if b and c are of type complex, b+c means b.operator+(c). We can now approximate the conventional interpretation of complex expressions:

```
void f()
{
        complex a = complex{1,3.1};
        complex b {1.2, 2};
        complex c {b};

        a = b+c;
        b = b+c*a;
        c = a*b+complex(1,2);
}
```

The usual precedence rules hold, so the second statement means b=b+(c*a), not b=(b+c)*a.

Note that the C++ grammar is written so that the {} notation can only be used for initializers and on the right-hand side of an assignment:

```
void g(complex a, complex b)
{
        a = {1,2};          // OK: right hand side of assignment
        a += {1,2};         // OK: right hand side of assignment
        b = a+{1,2};        // syntax error
        b = a+complex{1,2}; // OK
        g(a,{1,2});         // OK: a function argument is considered an initializer
        {a,b} = {b,a};      // syntax error
}
```

There seems to be no fundamental reason not to use {} in more places, but the technical problems of writing a grammar allowing {} everywhere in an expression (e.g., how would you know if a { after a semicolon was the start of an expression or a block?) and also giving good error messages led to a more limited use of {} in expressions.

Many of the most obvious uses of operator overloading are for numeric types. However, the usefulness of user-defined operators is not restricted to numeric types. For example, the design of general and abstract interfaces often leads to the use of operators such as ->, [], and ().

18.2 Operator Functions

Functions defining meanings for the following operators (§10.3) can be declared:

+	–	*	/	%	^	&
|	~	!	=	<	>	+=
–=	*=	/=	%=	^=	&=	|=
<<	>>	>>=	<<=	==	!=	<=
>=	&&	||	++	––	->*	,
->	[]	()	new	new[]	delete	delete[]

The following operators cannot be defined by a user:

::	scope resolution (§6.3.4, §16.2.12)
.	member selection (§8.2)
.*	member selection through pointer to member (§20.6)

They take a name, rather than a value, as their second operand and provide the primary means of referring to members. Allowing them to be overloaded would lead to subtleties [Stroustrup,1994]. The named "operators"cannot be overloaded because they report fundamental facts about their operands:

sizeof	size of object (§6.2.8)
alignof	alignment of object (§6.2.9)
typeid	type_info of an object (§22.5)

Finally, the ternary conditional expression operator cannot be overloaded (for no particularly fundamental reason):

?:	conditional evaluation (§9.4.1)

In addition, user-defined literals (§19.2.6) are defined by using the **operator**"" notation. This is a kind of syntactic subterfuge because there is no operator called "". Similarly, **operator T**() defines a conversion to a type **T** (§18.4).

It is not possible to define new operator tokens, but you can use the function call notation when this set of operators is not adequate. For example, use **pow**(), not **. These restrictions may seem Draconian, but more flexible rules can easily lead to ambiguities. For example, defining an operator ** to mean exponentiation may seem an obvious and easy task, but think again. Should ** bind to the left (as in Fortran) or to the right (as in Algol)? Should the expression **a**p** be interpreted as **a*(*p)** or as **(a)**(p)**? There are solutions to all such technical questions. However, it is most uncertain if applying subtle technical rules will lead to more readable and maintainable code. If in doubt, use a named function.

The name of an operator function is the keyword **operator** followed by the operator itself, for example, **operator<<**. An operator function is declared and can be called like any other function. A use of the operator is only a shorthand for an explicit call of the operator function. For example:

```
void f(complex a, complex b)
{
    complex c = a + b;          // shorthand
    complex d = a.operator+(b);  // explicit call
}
```

Given the previous definition of **complex**, the two initializers are synonymous.

18.2.1 Binary and Unary Operators

A binary operator can be defined by either a non-**static** member function taking one argument or a nonmember function taking two arguments. For any binary operator @, aa@bb can be interpreted as either **aa.operator@(bb)** or **operator@(aa,bb)**. If both are defined, overload resolution (§12.3) determines which, if any, interpretation is used. For example:

```
class X {
public:
    void operator+(int);
    X(int);
};

void operator+(X,X);
void operator+(X,double);

void f(X a)
{
    a+1;      // a.operator+(1)
    1+a;      // ::operator+(X(1),a)
    a+1.0;    // ::operator+(a,1.0)
}
```

A unary operator, whether prefix or postfix, can be defined by either a non-**static** member function taking no arguments or a nonmember function taking one argument. For any prefix unary operator @, @aa can be interpreted as either **aa.operator@()** or **operator@(aa)**. If both are defined, overload resolution (§12.3) determines which, if any, interpretation is used. For any postfix unary operator @, aa@ can be interpreted as either **aa.operator@(int)** or **operator@(aa,int)**. This is explained further in §19.2.4. If both are defined, overload resolution (§12.3) determines which, if any, interpretation is used. An operator can be declared only for the syntax defined for it in the grammar (§iso.A). For example, a user cannot define a unary % or a ternary +. Consider:

```
class X {
public:        // members (with implicit this pointer):

    X* operator&();     // prefix unary & (address of)
    X operator&(X);     // binary & (and)
    X operator++(int);  // postfix increment (see §19.2.4)
    X operator&(X,X);   // error: ternary
    X operator/();      // error: unary /
};
```

```
// nonmember functions :

X operator-(X);         // prefix unary minus
X operator-(X,X);       // binary minus
X operator--(X&,int);   // postfix decrement
X operator-();          // error: no operand
X operator-(X,X,X);     // error: ternary
X operator%(X);         // error: unary %
```

Operator [] is described in §19.2.1, operator () in §19.2.2, operator -> in §19.2.3, operators ++ and -- in §19.2.4, and the allocation and deallocation operators in §11.2.4 and §19.2.5.

The operators **operator=** (§18.2.2), **operator[]** (§19.2.1), **operator()** (§19.2.2), and **operator->** (§19.2.3) must be non-**static** member functions.

The default meaning of **&&**, **||**, and **,** (comma) involves sequencing: the first operand is evaluated before the second (and for **&&** and **||** the second operand is not always evaluated). This special rule does not hold for user-defined versions of **&&**, **||**, and **,** (comma); instead these operators are treated exactly like other binary operators.

18.2.2 Predefined Meanings for Operators

The meanings of some built-in operators are defined to be equivalent to some combination of other operators on the same arguments. For example, if **a** is an int, **++a** means **a+=1**, which in turn means **a=a+1**. Such relations do not hold for user-defined operators unless the user defines them to. For example, a compiler will not generate a definition of **Z::operator+=()** from the definitions of **Z::operator+()** and **Z::operator=()**.

The operators **=** (assignment), **&** (address-of), and **,** (sequencing; §10.3.2) have predefined meanings when applied to class objects. These predefined meanings can be eliminated ("deleted"; §17.6.4):

```
class X {
public:
    // ...
    void operator=(const X&) = delete;
    void operator&() = delete;
    void operator,(const X&) = delete;
    // ...
};

void f(X a, X b)
{
    a = b;      // error: no operator=()
    &a;         // error: no operator&()
    a,b;        // error: no operator,()
}
```

Alternatively, they can be given new meanings by suitable definitions.

18.2.3 Operators and User-Defined Types

An operator function must either be a member or take at least one argument of a user-defined type (functions redefining the **new** and **delete** operators need not). This rule ensures that a user cannot change the meaning of an expression unless the expression contains an object of a user-defined type. In particular, it is not possible to define an operator function that operates exclusively on pointers. This ensures that C++ is extensible but not mutable (with the exception of operators =, &, and , for class objects).

An operator function intended to accept a built-in type (§6.2.1) as its first operand cannot be a member function. For example, consider adding a complex variable **aa** to the integer **2**: **aa+2** can, with a suitably declared member function, be interpreted as **aa.operator+(2)**, but **2+aa** cannot because there is no class **int** for which to define + to mean **2.operator+(aa)**. Even if there were, two different member functions would be needed to cope with **2+aa** and **aa+2**. Because the compiler does not know the meaning of a user-defined +, it cannot assume that the operator is commutative and so interpret **2+aa** as **aa+2**. This example is trivially handled using one or more nonmember functions (§18.3.2, §19.4).

Enumerations are user-defined types so that we can define operators for them. For example:

```
enum Day { sun, mon, tue, wed, thu, fri, sat };

Day& operator++(Day& d)
{
        return d = (sat==d) ? sun : static_cast<Day>(d+1);
}
```

Every expression is checked for ambiguities. Where a user-defined operator provides a possible interpretation, the expression is checked according to the overload resolution rules in §12.3.

18.2.4 Passing Objects

When we define an operator, we typically want to provide a conventional notation, for example, **a=b+c**. Consequently, we have limited choices of how to pass arguments to the operator function and how it returns its value. For example, we cannot require pointer arguments and expect programmers to use the address-of operator or return a pointer and expect the user to dereference it: ***a=&b+&c** is not acceptable.

For arguments, we have two main choices (§12.2):

- Pass-by-value
- Pass-by-reference

For small objects, say, one to four words, call-by-value is typically a viable alternative and often the one that gives the best performance. However, performance of argument passing and use depends on machine architecture, compiler interface conventions (Application Binary Interfaces; ABIs), and the number of times an argument is accessed (it almost always is faster to access an argument passed by value than one passed by reference). For example, assume that a **Point** is represented as a pair of ints:

```
void Point::operator+=(Point delta);     // pass-by-value
```

Larger objects, we pass by reference. For example, because a **Matrix** (a simple matrix of **double**s; §17.5.1) is most likely larger than a few words, we use pass-by-reference:

```
Matrix operator+(const Matrix&, const Matrix&);    // pass-by-const-reference
```

In particular, we use **const** references to pass large objects that are not meant to be modified by the called function (§12.2.1).

Typically, an operator returns a result. Returning a pointer or a reference to a newly created object is usually a very bad idea: using a pointer gives notational problems, and referring to an object on the free store (whether by a pointer or by a reference) results in memory management problems. Instead, return objects by value. For large objects, such as a **Matrix**, define move operations to make such transfers of values efficient (§3.3.2, §17.5.2). For example:

```
Matrix operator+(const Matrix& a, const Matrix& b)    // return-by-value
{
    Matrix res {a};
    return res+=b;
}
```

Note that operators that return one of their argument objects can – and usually do – return a reference. For example, we could define **Matrix**'s operator += like this:

```
Matrix& Matrix::operator+=(const Matrix& a)    // return-by-reference
{
    if (dim[0]!=a.dim[0] || dim[1]!=a.dim[1])
        throw std::exception("bad Matrix += argument");

    double* p = elem;
    double* q = a.elem;
    double* end = p+dim[0]*dim[1];
    while(p!=end)
        *p++ += *q++

    return *this;
}
```

This is particularly common for operator functions that are implemented as members.

If a function simply passes an object to another function, an rvalue reference argument should be used (§17.4.3, §23.5.2.1, §28.6.3).

18.2.5 Operators in Namespaces

An operator is either a member of a class or defined in some namespace (possibly the global namespace). Consider this simplified version of string I/O from the standard library:

```
namespace std {          // simplified std

    class string {
        // ...
    };
```

```
        class ostream {
            // ...
            ostream& operator<<(const char*);              // output C-style string
        };


        extern ostream cout;


        ostream& operator<<(ostream&, const string&);     // output std::string
    } // namespace std

    int main()
    {
        const char* p = "Hello";
        std::string s = "world";
        std::cout << p << ", " << s << "!\n";
    }
```

Naturally, this writes out **Hello, world!**. But why? Note that I didn't make everything from **std** accessible by writing:

```
    using namespace std;
```

Instead, I used the **std::** prefix for **string** and **cout**. In other words, I was on my best behavior and didn't pollute the global namespace or in other ways introduce unnecessary dependencies.

The output operator for C-style strings is a member of **std::ostream**, so by definition

```
    std::cout << p
```

means

```
    std::cout.operator<<(p)
```

However, **std::ostream** doesn't have a member function to output a **std::string**, so

```
    std::cout << s
```

means

```
    operator<<(std::cout,s)
```

Operators defined in namespaces can be found based on their operand types just as functions can be found based on their argument types (§14.2.4). In particular, **cout** is in namespace **std**, so **std** is considered when looking for a suitable definition of **<<**. In that way, the compiler finds and uses:

```
    std::operator<<(std::ostream&, const std::string&)
```

Consider a binary operator **@**. If **x** is of type **X** and **y** is of type **Y**, **x@y** is resolved like this:
- If **X** is a class, look for **operator@** as a member of **X** or as a member of a base of **X**; and
- look for declarations of **operator@** in the context surrounding **x@y**; and
- if **X** is defined in namespace **N**, look for declarations of **operator@** in **N**; and
- if **Y** is defined in namespace **M**, look for declarations of **operator@** in **M**.

Declarations for several **operator@**s may be found and overload resolution rules (§12.3) are used to find the best match, if any. This lookup mechanism is applied only if the operator has at least one operand of a user-defined type. Therefore, user-defined conversions (§18.3.2, §18.4) will be considered. Note that a type alias is just a synonym and not a separate user-defined type (§6.5).

Unary operators are resolved analogously.

Note that in operator lookup no preference is given to members over nonmembers. This differs from lookup of named functions (§14.2.4). The lack of hiding of operators ensures that built-in operators are never inaccessible and that users can supply new meanings for an operator without modifying existing class declarations. For example:

```
X operator!(X);

struct Z {
    Z operator!();              // does not hide ::operator!()
    X f(X x) { /* ... */ return !x; }     // invoke ::operator!(X)
    int f(int x) { /* ... */ return !x; } // invoke the built-in ! for ints
};
```

In particular, the standard **iostream** library defines << member functions to output built-in types, and a user can define << to output user-defined types without modifying class **ostream** (§38.4.2).

18.3 A Complex Number Type

The implementation of complex numbers presented in §18.1 is too restrictive to please anyone. For example, we would expect this to work:

```
void f()
{
    complex a {1,2};
    complex b {3};
    complex c {a+2.3};
    complex d {2+b};
    b = c*2*c;
}
```

In addition, we would expect to be provided with a few additional operators, such as == for comparison and << for output, and a suitable set of mathematical functions, such as sin() and sqrt().

Class **complex** is a concrete type, so its design follows the guidelines from §16.3. In addition, users of complex arithmetic rely so heavily on operators that the definition of **complex** brings into play most of the basic rules for operator overloading.

The **complex** type developed in this section uses **double** for its scalars and is roughly equivalent to the standard-library **complex<double>** (§40.4).

18.3.1 Member and Nonmember Operators

I prefer to minimize the number of functions that directly manipulate the representation of an object. This can be achieved by defining only operators that inherently modify the value of their first argument, such as +=, in the class itself. Operators that simply produce a new value based on the values of their arguments, such as +, are then defined outside the class and use the essential operators in their implementation:

```
class complex {
    double re, im;
public:
    complex& operator+=(complex a);  // needs access to representation
    // ...
};

complex operator+(complex a, complex b)
{
    return a += b;  // access representation through +=
}
```

The arguments to this **operator+()** are passed by value, so **a+b** does not modify its operands.

Given these declarations, we can write:

```
void f(complex x, complex y, complex z)
{
    complex r1 {x+y+z}; // r1 = operator+(operator+(x,y),z)

    complex r2 {x};      // r2 = x
    r2 += y;             // r2.operator+=(y)
    r2 += z;             // r2.operator+=(z)
}
```

Except for possible efficiency differences, the computations of **r1** and **r2** are equivalent.

Composite assignment operators such as **+=** and **∗=** tend to be simpler to define than their "simple" counterparts **+** and **∗**. This surprises most people at first, but it follows from the fact that three objects are involved in a **+** operation (the two operands and the result), whereas only two objects are involved in a **+=** operation. In the latter case, run-time efficiency is improved by eliminating the need for temporary variables. For example:

```
inline complex& complex::operator+=(complex a)
{
    re += a.re;
    im += a.im;
    return *this;
}
```

This does not require a temporary variable to hold the result of the addition and is simple for a compiler to inline perfectly.

A good optimizer will generate close to optimal code for uses of the plain **+** operator also. However, we don't always have a good optimizer, and not all types are as simple as **complex**, so §19.4 discusses ways of defining operators with direct access to the representation of classes.

18.3.2 Mixed-Mode Arithmetic

To cope with **2+z**, where **z** is a **complex**, we need to define operator **+** to accept operands of different types. In Fortran terminology, we need *mixed-mode arithmetic*. We can achieve that simply by adding appropriate versions of the operators:

```
class complex {
    double re, im;
public:
    complex& operator+=(complex a)
    {
        re += a.re;
        im += a.im;
        return *this;
    }

    complex& operator+=(double a)
    {
        re += a;
        return *this;
    }

    // ...
};
```

The three variants of **operator+()** can be defined outside **complex**:

```
complex operator+(complex a, complex b)
{
    return a += b;   // calls complex::operator+=(complex)
}

complex operator+(complex a, double b)
{
    return {a.real()+b,a.imag()};
}

complex operator+(double a, complex b)
{
    return {a+b.real(),b.imag()};
}
```

The access functions **real()** and **imag()** are defined in §18.3.6.

Given these declarations of **+**, we can write:

```
void f(complex x, complex y)
{
    auto r1 = x+y;   // calls operator+(complex,complex)
    auto r2 = x+2;   // calls operator+(complex,double)
    auto r3 = 2+x;   // calls operator+(double,complex)
    auto r4 = 2+3;   // built-in integer addition
}
```

I added the integer addition for completeness.

18.3.3 Conversions

To cope with assignments and initialization of **complex** variables with scalars, we need a conversion of a scalar (integer or floating-point number) to a **complex**. For example:

```
complex b {3}; // should mean b.re=3, b.im=0

void comp(complex x)
{
    x = 4;     // should mean x.re=4, x.im=0
    // ...
}
```

We can achieve that by providing a constructor that takes a single argument. A constructor taking a single argument specifies a conversion from its argument type to the constructor's type. For example:

```
class complex {
    double re, im;
public:
    complex(double r) :re{r}, im{0} { }   // build a complex from a double
    // ...
};
```

The constructor specifies the traditional embedding of the real line in the complex plane.

A constructor is a prescription for creating a value of a given type. The constructor is used when a value of a type is expected and when such a value can be created by a constructor from the value supplied as an initializer or assigned value. Thus, a constructor requiring a single argument need not be called explicitly. For example:

```
complex b {3};
```

means

```
complex b {3,0};
```

A user-defined conversion is implicitly applied only if it is unique (§12.3). If you don't want a constructor to be used implicitly, declare it **explicit** (§16.2.6).

Naturally, we still need the constructor that takes two **double**s, and a default constructor initializing a **complex** to {0,0} is also useful:

```
class complex {
    double re, im;
public:
    complex() : re{0}, im{0} { }
    complex(double r) : re{r}, im{0} { }
    complex(double r, double i) : re{r}, im{i} { }
    // ...
};
```

Using default arguments, we can abbreviate:

```
class complex {
    double re, im;
public:
    complex(double r =0, double i =0) : re{r}, im{i} { }
    // ...
};
```

By default, copying **complex** values is defined as copying the real and imaginary parts (§16.2.2). For example:

```
void f()
{
    complex z;
    complex x {1,2};
    complex y {x};  // y also has the value {1,2}
    z = x;          // z also has the value {1,2}
}
```

18.3.3.1 Conversions of Operands

We defined three versions of each of the four standard arithmetic operators:

```
complex operator+(complex,complex);
complex operator+(complex,double);
complex operator+(double,complex);
// ...
```

This can get tedious, and what is tedious easily becomes error-prone. What if we had three alternatives for the type of each argument for each function? We would need three versions of each single-argument function, nine versions of each two-argument function, 27 versions of each three-argument function, etc. Often these variants are very similar. In fact, almost all variants involve a simple conversion of arguments to a common type followed by a standard algorithm.

The alternative to providing different versions of a function for each combination of arguments is to rely on conversions. For example, our **complex** class provides a constructor that converts a **double** to a **complex**. Consequently, we could simply declare only one version of the equality operator for **complex**:

```
bool operator==(complex,complex);

void f(complex x, complex y)
{
    x==y;   // means operator==(x,y)
    x==3;   // means operator==(x,complex(3))
    3==y;   // means operator==(complex(3),y)
}
```

There can be reasons for preferring to define separate functions. For example, in some cases the conversion can impose overhead, and in other cases, a simpler algorithm can be used for specific argument types. Where such issues are not significant, relying on conversions and providing only the most general variant of a function – plus possibly a few critical variants – contain the combinatorial explosion of variants that can arise from mixed-mode arithmetic.

Where several variants of a function or an operator exist, the compiler must pick "the right" variant based on the argument types and the available (standard and user-defined) conversions. Unless a best match exists, an expression is ambiguous and is an error (see §12.3).

An object constructed by explicit or implicit use of a constructor in an expression is automatic and will be destroyed at the first opportunity (see §10.3.4).

No implicit user-defined conversions are applied to the left-hand side of a . (or a ->). This is the case even when the . is implicit. For example:

```
void g(complex z)
{
    3+z;                    // OK: complex(3)+z
    3.operator+=(z);        // error: 3 is not a class object
    3+=z;                   // error: 3 is not a class object
}
```

Thus, you can approximate the notion that an operator requires an lvalue as its left-hand operand by making that operator a member. However, that is only an approximation because it is possible to access a temporary with a modifying operation, such as **operator+=()**:

```
complex x {4,5}
complex z {sqrt(x)+={1,2}};      // like tmp=sqrt(x), tmp+={1,2}
```

If we don't want implicit conversions, we can use **explicit** to suppress them (§16.2.6, §18.4.2).

18.3.4 Literals

We have literals of built-in types. For example, **1.2** and **12e3** are literals of type **double**. For **complex**, we can come pretty close to that by declaring constructors **constexpr** (§10.4). For example:

```
class complex {
public:
    constexpr complex(double r =0, double i =0) : re{r}, im{i} { }
    // ...
}
```

Given that, a **complex** can be constructed from its constituent parts at compile time just like a literal from a built-in type. For example:

```
complex z1 {1.2,12e3};
constexpr complex z2 {1.2,12e3};   // guaranteed compile-time initialization
```

When constructors are simple and inline, and especially when they are **constexpr**, it is quite reasonable to think of constructor invocations with literal arguments as literals.

It is possible to go further and introduce a user-defined literal (§19.2.6) in support of our **complex** type. In particular, we could define i to be a suffix meaning "imaginary." For example:

```
constexpr complex<double> operator "" i(long double d)    // imaginary literal
{
    return {0,d};     // complex is a literal type
}
```

This would allow us to write:

```
complex z1 {1.2+12e3i};

complex f(double d)
{
    auto x {2.3i};
    return x+sqrt(d+12e3i)+12e3i;
}
```

This user-defined literal gives us one advantage over what we get from **constexpr** constructors: we can use user-defined literals in the middle of expressions where the {} notation can only be used when qualified by a type name. The example above is roughly equivalent to:

```
complex z1 {1.2,12e3};

complex f(double d)
{
    complex x {0,2.3};
    return x+sqrt(complex{d,12e3})+complex{0,12e3};
}
```

I suspect that the choice of style of literal depends on your sense of aesthetics and the conventions of your field of work. The standard-library **complex** uses **constexpr** constructors rather than a user-defined literal.

18.3.5 Accessor Functions

So far, we have provided class **complex** with constructors and arithmetic operators only. That is not quite sufficient for real use. In particular, we often need to be able to examine and change the value of the real and imaginary parts:

```
class complex {
    double re, im;
public:
    constexpr double real() const { return re; }
    constexpr double imag() const { return im; }

    void real(double r) { re = r; }
    void imag(double i) { im = i; }
    // ...
};
```

I don't consider it a good idea to provide individual access to all members of a class; in general, it is not. For many types, individual access (sometimes referred to as *get-and-set functions*) is an invitation to disaster. If we are not careful, individual access could compromise an invariant, and it typically complicates changes to the representation. For example, consider the opportunities for misuse from providing getters and setters for every member of the **Date** from §16.3 or (even more so) for the **String** from §19.3. However, for **complex**, **real()** and **imag()** are semantically significant: some algorithms are most cleanly written if they can set the real and imaginary parts independently.

For example, given **real()** and **imag()**, we can simplify simple, common, and useful operations, such as ==, as nonmember functions (without compromising performance):

```
inline bool operator==(complex a, complex b)
{
    return a.real()==b.real() && a.imag()==b.imag();
}
```

18.3.6 Helper Functions

If we put all the bits and pieces together, the **complex** class becomes:

```
class complex {
    double re, im;
public:
    constexpr complex(double r =0, double i =0) : re(r), im(i) { }

    constexpr double real() const { return re; }
    constexpr double imag() const { return im; }

    void real(double r) { re = r; }
    void imag(double i) { im = i; }

    complex& operator+=(complex);
    complex& operator+=(double);

    // -=, *=, and /=
};
```

In addition, we must provide a number of helper functions:

```
complex operator+(complex,complex);
complex operator+(complex,double);
complex operator+(double,complex);

// binary -, *, and /

complex operator-(complex); // unary minus
complex operator+(complex); // unary plus

bool operator==(complex,complex);
bool operator!=(complex,complex);

istream& operator>>(istream&,complex&);    // input
ostream& operator<<(ostream&,complex);     // output
```

Note that the members **real()** and **imag()** are essential for defining the comparisons. The definitions of most of the following helper functions similarly rely on **real()** and **imag()**.

We might provide functions to allow users to think in terms of polar coordinates:

```
complex polar(double rho, double theta);
complex conj(complex);

double abs(complex);
double arg(complex);
double norm(complex);

double real(complex);        // for notational convenience
double imag(complex);        // for notational convenience
```

Finally, we must provide an appropriate set of standard mathematical functions:

```
complex acos(complex);
complex asin(complex);
complex atan(complex);
// ...
```

From a user's point of view, the **complex** type presented here is almost identical to the **complex<double>** found in **<complex>** in the standard library (§5.6.2, §40.4).

18.4 Type Conversion

Type conversion can be accomplished by
- A constructor taking a single argument (§16.2.5)
- A conversion operator (§18.4.1)

In either case the conversion can be
- **explicit**; that is, the conversion is only performed in a direct initialization (§16.2.6), i.e., as an initializer not using a =.
- Implicit; that is, it will be applied wherever it can be used unambiguously (§18.4.3), e.g., as a function argument.

18.4.1 Conversion Operators

Using a constructor taking a single argument to specify type conversion is convenient but has implications that can be undesirable. Also, a constructor cannot specify

   [1]   an implicit conversion from a user-defined type to a built-in type (because the built-in types are not classes), or

   [2]   a conversion from a new class to a previously defined class (without modifying the declaration for the old class).

These problems can be handled by defining a *conversion operator* for the source type. A member function X::operator T(), where T is a type name, defines a conversion from X to T. For example, we could define a 6-bit non-negative integer, Tiny, that can mix freely with integers in arithmetic operations. Tiny throws Bad_range if its operations overflow or underflow:

```
class Tiny {
    char v;
    void assign(int i) { if (i&~077) throw Bad_range(); v=i; }
public:
    class Bad_range { };

    Tiny(int i) { assign(i); }
    Tiny& operator=(int i) { assign(i); return *this; }

    operator int() const { return v; }      // conversion to int function
};
```

The range is checked whenever a **Tiny** is initialized by an **int** and whenever an **int** is assigned to one. No range check is needed when we copy a **Tiny**, so the default copy constructor and assignment are just right.

To enable the usual integer operations on **Tiny** variables, we define the implicit conversion from **Tiny** to int, **Tiny::operator int()**. Note that the type being converted to is part of the name of the operator and cannot be repeated as the return value of the conversion function:

```
Tiny::operator int() const { return v; }        // right
int Tiny::operator int() const { return v; }     // error
```

In this respect also, a conversion operator resembles a constructor.

Whenever a **Tiny** appears where an **int** is needed, the appropriate **int** is used. For example:

```
int main()
{
    Tiny c1 = 2;
    Tiny c2 = 62;
    Tiny c3 = c2-c1;      // c3 = 60
    Tiny c4 = c3;         // no range check (not necessary)
    int i = c1+c2;        // i = 64

    c1 = c1+c2;           // range error: c1 can't be 64
    i = c3-64;            // i = -4
    c2 = c3-64;           // range error: c2 can't be -4
    c3 = c4;              // no range check (not necessary)
}
```

Conversion functions appear to be particularly useful for handling data structures when reading (implemented by a conversion operator) is trivial, while assignment and initialization are distinctly less trivial.

The **istream** and **ostream** types rely on a conversion function to enable statements such as:

```
while (cin>>x)
    cout<<x;
```

The input operation **cin>>x** returns an **istream&**. That value is implicitly converted to a value indicating the state of **cin**. This value can then be tested by the **while** (see §38.4.4). However, it is typically *not* a good idea to define an implicit conversion from one type to another in such a way that information is lost in the conversion.

In general, it is wise to be sparing in the introduction of conversion operators. When used in excess, they lead to ambiguities. Such ambiguities are caught by the compiler, but they can be a nuisance to resolve. Probably the best idea is initially to do conversions by named functions, such as **X::make_int()**. If such a function becomes popular enough to make explicit use inelegant, it can be replaced by a conversion operator **X::operator int()**.

If both user-defined conversions and user-defined operators are defined, it is possible to get ambiguities between the user-defined operators and the built-in operators. For example:

```
int operator+(Tiny,Tiny);

void f(Tiny t, int i)
{
    t+i;   // error, ambiguous: "operator+(t,Tiny(i))" or "int(t)+i"?
}
```

It is therefore often best to rely on user-defined conversions or user-defined operators for a given type, but not both.

18.4.2 explicit Conversion Operators

Conversion operators tend to be defined so that they can be used everywhere. However, it is possible to declare a conversion operator **explicit** and have it apply only for direct initialization (§16.2.6), where an equivalent **explicit** constructor would have been used. For example, the standard-library **unique_ptr** (§5.2.1, §34.3.1) has an explicit conversion to **bool**:

```
template <typename T, typename D = default_delete<T>>
class unique_ptr {
public:
    // ...
    explicit operator bool() const noexcept;      // does *this hold a pointer (that is not nullptr)?
    // ...
};
```

The reason to declare this conversion operator **explicit** is to avoid its use in surprising contexts. Consider:

```
void use(unique_ptr<Record> p, unique_ptr<int> q)
{
    if (!p)        // OK: we want this use
        throw Invalid_uninque_ptr{};

    bool b = p;    // error; suspicious use
    int x = p+q;   // error; we definitly don't want this
}
```

Had **unique_ptr**'s conversion to bool not been **explicit**, the last two definitions would have compiled. The value of **b** would have become **true** and the value of **x** would have become **1** or **2** (depending on whether **q** was valid or not).

18.4.3 Ambiguities

An assignment of a value of type **V** to an object of class **X** is legal if there is an assignment operator **X::operator=(Z)** so that **V** is **Z** or there is a unique conversion of **V** to **Z**. Initialization is treated equivalently.

In some cases, a value of the desired type can be constructed by repeated use of constructors or conversion operators. This must be handled by explicit conversions; only one level of user-defined implicit conversion is legal. In some cases, a value of the desired type can be constructed in more than one way; such cases are illegal. For example:

```
class X { /* ... */ X(int); X(const char*); };
class Y { /* ... */ Y(int); };
class Z { /* ... */ Z(X); };


X f(X);
Y f(Y);


Z g(Z);


void k1()
{
    f(1);               // error: ambiguous f(X(1)) or f(Y(1))?
    f(X{1});            // OK
    f(Y{1});            // OK

    g("Mack");          // error: two user-defined conversions needed; g(Z{X{"Mack"}}) not tried
    g(X{"Doc"});        // OK: g(Z{X{"Doc"}})
    g(Z{"Suzy"});       // OK: g(Z{X{"Suzy"}})
}
```

User-defined conversions are considered only if a call cannot be resolved without them (i.e., using only built-in conversions). For example:

```
class XX { /* ... */ XX(int); };

void h(double);
void h(XX);

void k2()
{
    h(1); // h(double{1}) or h(XX{1})? h(double{1})!
}
```

The call **h(1)** means **h(double(1))** because that alternative uses only a standard conversion rather than a user-defined conversion (§12.3).

The rules for conversion are neither the simplest to implement, nor the simplest to document, nor the most general that could be devised. They are, however, considerably safer, and the resulting resolutions are typically less surprising than alternatives. It is far easier to manually resolve an ambiguity than to find an error caused by an unsuspected conversion.

The insistence on strict bottom-up analysis implies that the return type is not used in overloading resolution. For example:

```
class Quad {
public:
     Quad(double);
     // ...
};

Quad operator+(Quad,Quad);

void f(double a1, double a2)
{
     Quad r1 = a1+a2;        // double-precision floating-point add
     Quad r2 = Quad{a1}+a2;  // force quad arithmetic
}
```

The reason for this design choice is partly that strict bottom-up analysis is more comprehensible and partly that it is not considered the compiler's job to decide which precision the programmer might want for the addition.

Once the types of both sides of an initialization or assignment have been determined, both types are used to resolve the initialization or assignment. For example:

```
class Real {
public:
     operator double();
     operator int();
     // ...
};

void g(Real a)
{
     double d = a;   // d = a.double();
     int i = a;      // i = a.int();

     d = a;          // d = a.double();
     i = a;          // i = a.int();
}
```

In these cases, the type analysis is still bottom-up, with only a single operator and its argument types considered at any one time.

18.5 Advice

[1]   Define operators primarily to mimic conventional usage; §18.1.
[2]   Redefine or prohibit copying if the default is not appropriate for a type; §18.2.2.
[3]   For large operands, use **const** reference argument types; §18.2.4.
[4]   For large results, use a move constructor; §18.2.4.

[5]   Prefer member functions over nonmembers for operations that need access to the representation; §18.3.1.

[6]   Prefer nonmember functions over members for operations that do not need access to the representation; §18.3.2.

[7]   Use namespaces to associate helper functions with "their" class; §18.2.5.

[8]   Use nonmember functions for symmetric operators; §18.3.2.

[9]   Use member functions to express operators that require an lvalue as their left-hand operand; §18.3.3.1.

[10]   Use user-defined literals to mimic conventional notation; §18.3.4.

[11]   Provide "**set()** and **get()** functions" for a data member only if the fundamental semantics of a class require them; §18.3.5.

[12]   Be cautious about introducing implicit conversions; §18.4.

[13]   Avoid value-destroying ("narrowing") conversions; §18.4.1.

[14]   Do not define the same conversion as both a constructor and a conversion operator; §18.4.3.

19

Special Operators

We are all special cases.
– Albert Camus

- Introduction
- Special Operators
    Subscripting; Function Call; Dereferencing; Increment and Decrement; Allocation and De-
    allocation; User-Defined Literals
- A String Class
    Essential Operations; Access to Characters; Representation; Member Functions; Helper
    Functions; Using Our String
- Friends
    Finding Friends; Friends and Members
- Advice

19.1 Introduction

Overloading is not just for arithmetic and logical operations. In fact, operators are crucial in the design of containers (e.g., **vector** and **map**; §4.4), "smart pointers" (e.g., **unique_ptr** and **shared_ptr**; §5.2.1), iterators (§4.5), and other classes concerned with resource management.

19.2 Special Operators

The operators

    [] () -> ++ -- **new delete**

are special only in that the mapping from their use in the code to a programmer's definition differs slightly from that used for conventional unary and binary operators, such as +, <, and ˜ (§18.2.3). The [] (subscript) and () (call) operators are among the most useful user-defined operators.

19.2.1 Subscripting

An **operator[]** function can be used to give subscripts a meaning for class objects. The second argument (the subscript) of an **operator[]** function may be of any type. This makes it possible to define
vectors, associative arrays, etc.

As an example, we can define a simple associative array type like this:

```
struct Assoc {
    vector<pair<string,int>> vec;  // vector of {name,value} pairs

    const int& operator[] (const string&) const;
    int& operator[](const string&);
};
```

An **Assoc** keeps a vector of **std::pair**s. The implementation uses the same trivial and inefficient
search method as in §7.7:

```
int& Assoc::operator[](const string& s)
    // search for s; return a reference to its value if found;
    // otherwise, make a new pair {s,0} and return a reference to its value
{
    for (auto x : vec)
        if (s == x.first) return x.second;

    vec.push_back({s,0});          // initial value: 0

    return vec.back().second;      // return last element (§31.2.2)
}
```

We can use **Assoc** like this:

```
int main()       // count the occurrences of each word on input
{
    Assoc values;
    string buf;
    while (cin>>buf) ++values[buf];
    for (auto x : values.vec)
        cout << '{' << x.first << ',' << x.second << "}\n";
}
```

The standard-library **map** and **unordered_map** are further developments of the idea of an associative
array (§4.4.3, §31.4.3) with less naive implementations.

An **operator[]()** must be a non-**static** member function.

19.2.2 Function Call

Function call, that is, the notation *expression(expression-list),* can be interpreted as a binary operation with the *expression* as the left-hand operand and the *expression-list* as the right-hand operand.
The call operator, (), can be overloaded in the same way as other operators can. For example:

```
struct Action {
    int operator()(int);
    pair<int,int> operator()(int,int);
    double operator()(double);
    // ...
};

void f(Action act)
{
    int x = act(2);
    auto y = act(3,4);
    double z = act(2.3);
    // ...
};
```

An argument list for an **operator()()** is evaluated and checked according to the usual argument-passing rules. Overloading the function call operator seems to be useful primarily for defining types that have only a single operation and for types for which one operation is predominant. The *call operator* is also known as the *application operator*.

The most obvious and also the most important, use of the () operator is to provide the usual function call syntax for objects that in some way behave like functions. An object that acts like a function is often called a *function-like object* or simply a *function object* (§3.4.3). Such function objects allow us to write code that takes nontrivial operations as parameters. In many cases, it is essential that function objects can hold data needed to perform their operation. For example, we can define a class with an **operator()()** that adds a stored value to its argument:

```
class Add {
    complex val;
public:
    Add(complex c) :val{c} { }                          // save a value
    Add(double r, double i) :val{{r,i}} { }

    void operator()(complex& c) const { c += val; }     // add a value to argument
};
```

An object of class **Add** is initialized with a complex number, and when invoked using (), it adds that number to its argument. For example:

```
void h(vector<complex>& vec, list<complex>& lst, complex z)
{
    for_each(vec.begin(),vec.end(),Add{2,3});
    for_each(lst.begin(),lst.end(),Add{z});
}
```

This will add **complex{2,3}** to every element of the **vector** and **z** to every element of the **list**. Note that **Add{z}** constructs an object that is used repeatedly by **for_each()**: **Add{z}**'s **operator()()** is called for each element of the sequence.

This all works because **for_each** is a template that applies () to its third argument without caring exactly what that third argument really is:

```
template<typename Iter, typename Fct>
Fct for_each(Iter b, Iter e, Fct f)
{
    while (b != e) f(*b++);
    return f;
}
```

At first glance, this technique may look esoteric, but it is simple, efficient, and extremely useful (§3.4.3, §33.4).

Note that a lambda expression (§3.4.3, §11.4) is basically a syntax for defining a function object. For example, we could have written:

```
void h2(vector<complex>& vec, list<complex>& lst, complex z)
{
    for_each(vec.begin(),vec.end(),[](complex& a){ a+={2,3}; });
    for_each(lst.begin(),lst.end(),[](complex& a){ a+=z; });
}
```

In this case, each of the lambda expressions generates the equivalent of the function object **Add**.

Other popular uses of **operator()()** are as a substring operator and as a subscripting operator for multidimensional arrays (§29.2.2, §40.5.2).

An **operator()()** must be a non-**static** member function.

Function call operators are often templates (§29.2.2, §33.5.3).

19.2.3 Dereferencing

The dereferencing operator, -> (also known as the *arrow* operator), can be defined as a unary postfix operator. For example:

```
class Ptr {
    // ...
    X* operator->();
};
```

Objects of class **Ptr** can be used to access members of class **X** in a very similar manner to the way pointers are used. For example:

```
void f(Ptr p)
{
    p->m = 7;       // (p.operator->())->m = 7
}
```

The transformation of the object **p** into the pointer **p.operator->()** does not depend on the member **m** pointed to. That is the sense in which **operator->()** is a unary postfix operator. However, there is no new syntax introduced, so a member name is still required after the ->. For example:

```
void g(Ptr p)
{
    X* q1 = p->;            // syntax error
    X* q2 = p.operator->(); // OK
}
```

Overloading -> is primarily useful for creating "smart pointers," that is, objects that act like pointers and in addition perform some action whenever an object is accessed through them. The standard-library "smart pointers" **unique_ptr** and **shared_ptr** (§5.2.1) provide operator ->.

As an example, we could define a class **Disk_ptr** for accessing objects stored on disk. **Disk_ptr**'s constructor takes a name that can be used to find the object on disk, **Disk_ptr::operator->()** brings the object into main memory when accessed through its **Disk_ptr**, and **Disk_ptr**'s destructor eventually writes the updated object back out to disk:

```
template<typename T>
class Disk_ptr {
    string identifier;
    T* in_core_address;
    // ...
public:
    Disk_ptr(const string& s) : identifier{s}, in_core_address{nullptr} { }
    ~Disk_ptr() { write_to_disk(in_core_address,identifier); }

    T* operator->()
    {
        if (in_core_address == nullptr)
            in_core_address = read_from_disk(identifier);
        return in_core_address;
    }
};
```

Disk_ptr might be used like this:

```
struct Rec {
    string name;
    // ...
};

void update(const string& s)
{
    Disk_ptr<Rec> p {s};          // get Disk_ptr for s

    p->name = "Roscoe";           // update s; if necessary, first retrieve from disk
    // ...
}                                 // p's destructor writes back to disk
```

Naturally, a realistic program would contain error-handling code and use a less naive way of interacting with the disk.

For ordinary pointers, use of -> is synonymous with some uses of unary * and []. Given a class **Y** for which ->, *, and [] have their default meaning and a **Y*** called **p**, then:

```
p->m == (*p).m         // is true
(*p).m == p[0].m       // is true
p->m == p[0].m         // is true
```

As usual, no such guarantee is provided for user-defined operators. The equivalence can be provided where desired:

```
template<typename T>
class Ptr {
    Y* p;
public:
    Y* operator->() { return p; }        // dereference to access member
    Y& operator*() { return *p; }        // dereference to access whole object
    Y& operator[](int i) { return p[i]; } // dereference to access element
    // ...
};
```

If you provide more than one of these operators, it might be wise to provide the equivalence, just as it is wise to ensure that ++x and x+=1 have the same effect as x=x+1 for a simple variable x of some class X if ++, +=, =, and + are provided.

The overloading of -> is important to a class of interesting programs and is not just a minor curiosity. The reason is that *indirection* is a key concept and that overloading -> provides a clean, direct, and efficient way of representing indirection in a program. Iterators (Chapter 33) provide an important example of this.

Operator -> must be a non-**static** member function. If used, its return type must be a pointer or an object of a class to which you can apply ->. The body of a template class member function is only checked if the function is used (§26.2.1), so we can define **operator->()** without worrying about types, such as **Ptr<int>**, for which -> does not make sense.

Despite the similarity between -> and . (dot), there is no way of overloading operator . (dot).

19.2.4 Increment and Decrement

Once people invent "smart pointers," they often decide to provide the increment operator ++ and the decrement operator -- to mirror these operators' use for built-in types. This is especially obvious and necessary where the aim is to replace an ordinary pointer type with a "smart pointer" type that has the same semantics, except that it adds a bit of run-time error checking. For example, consider a troublesome traditional program:

```
void f1(X a)        // traditional use
{
    X v[200];
    X* p = &v[0];
    p--;
    *p = a;    // oops: p out of range, uncaught
    ++p;
    *p = a;    // OK
}
```

Here, we might want to replace the **X*** with an object of a class **Ptr<X>** that can be dereferenced only if it actually points to an **X**. We would also like to ensure that p can be incremented and decremented only if it points to an object within an array and the increment and decrement operations yield an object within that array. That is, we would like something like this:

```
void f2(Ptr<X> a)          // checked
{
    X v[200];
    Ptr<X> p(&v[0],v);
    p--;
    *p = a;      // run-time error: p out of range
    ++p;
    *p = a;      // OK
}
```

The increment and decrement operators are unique among C++ operators in that they can be used as both prefix and postfix operators. Consequently, we must define prefix and postfix increment and decrement for Ptr<T>. For example:

```
template<typename T>
class Ptr {
    T* ptr;
    T* array;
    int sz;
public:
    template<int N>
        Ptr(T* p, T(&a)[N]);      // bind to array a, sz==N, initial value p
    Ptr(T* p, T* a, int s);       // bind to array a of size s, initial value p
    Ptr(T* p);                    // bind to single object, sz==0, initial value p

    Ptr& operator++();            // prefix
    Ptr operator++(int);          // postfix

    Ptr& operator--();            // prefix
    Ptr operator--(int);          // postfix

    T& operator*();               // prefix
};
```

The int argument is used to indicate that the function is to be invoked for postfix application of ++. This int is never used; the argument is simply a dummy used to distinguish between prefix and postfix application. The way to remember which version of an operator++ is prefix is to note that the version without the dummy argument is prefix, exactly like all the other unary arithmetic and logical operators. The dummy argument is used only for the "odd" postfix ++ and --.

Consider omitting postfix ++ and -- in a design. They are not only odd syntactically, they tend to be marginally harder to implement than the postfix versions, less efficient, and less frequently used. For example:

```
template<typename T>
Ptr& Ptr<T>::operator++()         // return the current object after incrementing
{
    // ... check that ptr+1 can be pointed to ...
    return *++ptr;
}
```

```
template<typename T>
Ptr Ptr<T>::operator++(int)              // increment and return a Ptr with the old value
{
    // ... check that ptr+1 can be pointed to ...
    Ptr<T> old {ptr,array,sz};
    ++ptr;
    return old;
}
```

The pre-increment operator can return a reference to its object. The post-increment operator must make a new object to return.

Using **Ptr**, the example is equivalent to:

```
void f3(T a)          // checked
{
    T v[200];
    Ptr_to_T p(&v[0],v,200);
    p.operator--(0);          // suffix: p--
    p.operator*() = a;        // run-time error: p out of range
    p.operator++();           // prefix: ++p
    p.operator*() = a;        // OK
}
```

Completing class **Ptr** is left as an exercise. A pointer template that behaves correctly with respect to inheritance is presented in §27.2.2.

19.2.5 Allocation and Deallocation

Operator **new** (§11.2.3) acquires its memory by calling an **operator new()**. Similarly, operator **delete** frees its memory by calling an **operator delete()**. A user can redefine the global **operator new()** and **operator delete()** or define **operator new()** and **operator delete()** for a particular class.

Using the standard-library type alias **size_t** (§6.2.8) for sizes, the declarations of the global versions look like this:

```
void* operator new(size_t);           // use for individual object
void* operator new[](size_t);         // use for array
void operator delete(void*, size_t);  // use for individual object
void operator delete[](void*, size_t); // use for array

// for more versions, see §11.2.4
```

That is, when **new** needs memory on the free store for an object of type **X**, it calls **operator new(sizeof(X))**. Similarly, when **new** needs memory on the free store for an array of **N** objects of type **X**, it calls **operator new[](N*sizeof(X))**. A **new** expression may ask for more memory than is indicated by **N*sizeof(X)**, but it will always do so in terms of a number of characters (i.e., a number of bytes). Replacing the global **operator new()** and **operator delete()** is not for the fainthearted and not recommended. After all, someone else might rely on some aspect of the default behavior or might even have supplied other versions of these functions.

A more selective, and often better, approach is to supply these operations for a specific class. This class might be the base for many derived classes. For example, we might like to have a class **Employee** provide a specialized allocator and deallocator for itself and all of its derived classes:

```
class Employee {
public:
    // ...

    void* operator new(size_t);
    void operator delete(void*, size_t);

    void* operator new[](size_t);
    void operator delete[](void*, size_t);
};
```

Member **operator new()**s and **operator delete()**s are implicitly **static** members. Consequently, they don't have a **this** pointer and do not modify an object. They provide storage that a constructor can initialize and a destructor can clean up.

```
void* Employee::operator new(size_t s)
{
    // allocate s bytes of memory and return a pointer to it
}

void Employee::operator delete(void* p, size_t s)
{
    if (p) {        // delete only if p!=0; see §11.2, §11.2.3
        // assume p points to s bytes of memory allocated by Employee::operator new()
        // and free that memory for reuse
    }
}
```

The use of the hitherto mysterious **size_t** argument now becomes obvious. It is the size of the object being **deleted**. Deleting a "plain" **Employee** gives an argument value of **sizeof(Employee)**; deleting a **Manager** derived from **Employee** that does not have its own **operator delete()** gives an argument value of **sizeof(Manager)**. This allows a class-specific allocator to avoid storing size information with each allocation. Naturally, a class-specific allocator can store such information (as a general-purpose allocator must) and ignore the **size_t** argument to **operator delete()**. However, doing so makes it harder to improve significantly on the speed and memory consumption of a general-purpose allocator.

How does a compiler know how to supply the right size to **operator delete()**? The type specified in the **delete** operation matches the type of the object being **deleted**. If we **delete** an object through a pointer to a base class, that base class must have a **virtual** destructor (§17.2.5) for the correct size to be given:

```
Employee* p = new Manager;  // potential trouble (the exact type is lost)
// ...
delete p;                   // hope Employee has a virtual destructor
```

In principle, deallocation is then done by the destructor (which knows the size of its class).

19.2.6 User-defined Literals

C++ provides literals for a variety of built-in types (§6.2.6):

```
123         // int
1.2         // double
1.2F        // float
'a'         // char
1ULL        // unsigned long long
0xD0        // hexadecimal unsigned
"as"        // C-style string (const char[3])
```

In addition, we can define literals for user-defined types and new forms of literals for built-in types. For example:

```
"Hi!"s                              // string, not "zero-terminated array of char"
1.2i                                // imaginary
101010111000101b                    // binary
123s                                // seconds
123.56km                            // not miles! (units)
12345678901234567890123456789012345678901234567890x   // extended-precision
```

Such *user-defined literals* are supported through the notion of *literal operators* that map literals with a given suffix into a desired type. The name of a literal operator is **operator""** followed by the suffix. For example:

```
constexpr complex<double> operator"" i(long double d)      // imaginary literal
{
        return {0,d};   // complex is a literal type
}

std::string operator"" s(const char* p, size_t n)    // std::string literal
{
        return string{p,n};   // requires free-store allocation
}
```

These two operators define suffixes **i** and **s**, respectively. I use **constexpr** to enable compile-time evaluation. Given those, we can write:

```
template<typename T> void f(const T&);

void g()
{
        f("Hello");      // pass pointer to char*
        f("Hello"s);     // pass (five-character) string object
        f("Hello\n"s);   // pass (six-character) string object

        auto z = 2+1i;   // complex{2,1}
}
```

The basic (implementation) idea is that after parsing what could be a literal, the compiler always checks for a suffix. The user-defined literal mechanism simply allows the user to specify a new suffix and define what is to be done with the literal before it. It is not possible to redefine the meaning of a built-in literal suffix or to augment the syntax of literals.

There are four kinds of literals that can be suffixed to make a user-defined literal (§iso.2.14.8):

- An integer literal (§6.2.4.1): accepted by a literal operator taking an **unsigned long long** or a **const char∗** argument or by a template literal operator, for example, **123m** or **12345678901234567890X**
- A floating-point literal (§6.2.5.1): accepted by a literal operator taking a **long double** or a **const char∗** argument or by a template literal operator, for example, **12345678901234567890.976543210x** or **3.99s**
- A string literal (§7.3.2): accepted by a literal operator taking a (**const char∗, size_t**) pair of arguments, for example, **"string"s** and **R"(Foo\bar)"_path**
- A character literal (§6.2.3.2): accepted by a literal operator taking a character argument of type **char, wchar_t, char16_t,** or **char32_t**, for example, **'f'_runic** or **u'BEEF'_w**.

For example, we could define a literal operator to collect digits for integer values that cannot be represented in any of the built-in integer types:

```
Bignum operator"" x(const char∗ p)
{
    return Bignum(p);
}


void f(Bignum);


f(12345678901234567890123456789012345678901234567890123456789012345x);
```

Here, the C-style string **"12345678901234567890123456789012345678901234567890123456789012345"** is passed to **operator"" x()**. Note that I did not put those digits in double quotes. I requested a C-style string for my operator, and the compiler delivered it from the digits provided.

To get a C-style string from the program source text into a literal operator, we request both the string and its number of characters. For example:

```
string operator"" s(const char∗ p, size_t n);


string s12 = "one two"s;         // calls operator ""("one two",7)
string s22 = "two\ntwo"s;        // calls operator ""("two\ntwo",7)
string sxx = R"(two\ntwo)"s;     // calls operator ""("two\\ntwo",8)
```

In the raw string (§7.3.2.1), "\n" represents the two characters '\' and 'n'.

The rationale for requiring the number of characters is that if we want to have "a different kind of string," we almost always want to know the number of characters anyway.

A literal operator that takes just a **const char∗** argument (and no size) can be applied to integer and floating-point literals. For example:

```
string operator"" SS(const char∗ p);         // warning: this will not work as expected


string s12 = "one two"SS;                    // error: no applicable literal operator
string s13 = 13SS;                           // OK, but why would anyone do that?
```

A literal operator converting numerical values to strings could be quite confusing.

A *template literal operator* is a literal operator that takes its argument as a template parameter pack, rather than as a function argument. For example:

```
template<char...>
constexpr int operator"" _b3();            // base 3, i.e., ternary
```

Given that, we get:

```
201_b3    // means operator"" b3<'2','0','1'>(); so 9*2+0*3+1 == 19
241_b3    // means operator"" b3<'2','4','1'>(); so error: 4 isn't a ternary digit
```

The variadic template techniques (§28.6) can be disconcerting, but it is the only way of assigning nonstandard meanings to digits at compile time.

To define **operator"" _b3()**, we need some helper functions:

```
constexpr int ipow(int x, int n) // x to the nth power for n>=0
{
    return (n>0) ? x*ipow(n–1) : 1;
}


template<char c>        // handle the single ternary digit case
constexpr int b3_helper()
{
    static_assert(c<'3',"not a ternary digit");
    return c;
}


template<char c, char... tail>   // peel off one ternary digit
constexpr int b3_helper()
{
    static_assert(c<'3',"not a ternary digit");
    return ipow(3,sizeof...(tail))*(c–'0')+b3_helper(tail...);
}
```

Given that, we can define our base 3 literal operator:

```
template<char... chars>
constexpr int operator"" _b3()        // base 3, i.e., ternary
{
    return b3_helper(chars...);
}
```

Many suffixes will be short (e.g., **s** for **std::string**, **i** for imaginary, **m** for meter (§28.7.3), and **x** for extended), so different uses could easily clash. Use namespaces to prevent clashes:

```
namespace Numerics {
    // ...

    class Bignum { /* ... */ };

    namespace literals {
        Bignum operator"" x(char const*);
    }
```

```
        // ...
}
```

```
using namespace Numerics::literals;
```

The standard library reserves all suffixes not starting with an initial underscore, so define your suffixes starting with an underscore or risk your code breaking in the future:

```
123km          // reserved by the standard library
123_km         // available for your use
```

19.3 A String Class

The relatively simple string class presented in this section illustrates several techniques that are useful for the design and implementation of classes using conventionally defined operators. This **String** is a simplified version of the standard-library **string** (§4.2, Chapter 36). **String** provides value semantics, checked and unchecked access to characters, stream I/O, support for range-**for** loops, equality operations, and concatenation operators. I also added a **String** literal, which **std::string** does not (yet) have.

To allow simple interoperability with C-style strings (including string literals (§7.3.2)), I represent strings as zero-terminated arrays of characters. For realism, I implement the *short string optimization*. That is, a **String** with only a few characters stores those characters in the class object itself, rather than on the free store. This optimizes string usage for small strings. Experience shows that for a huge number of applications most strings are short. This optimization is particularly important in multi-threaded systems where sharing through pointers (or references) is infeasible and free-store allocation and deallocation relatively expensive.

To allow **String**s to efficiently "grow" by adding characters at the end, I implement a scheme for keeping extra space for such growth similar to the one used for **vector** (§13.6.1). This makes **String** a suitable target for various forms of input.

Writing a better string class and/or one that provides more facilities is a good exercise. That done, we can throw away our exercises and use **std::string** (Chapter 36).

19.3.1 Essential Operations

Class **String** provides the usual set of constructors, a destructor, and assignment operations (§17.1):

```
class String {
public:
    String();                               // default constructor: x{""}

    explicit String(const char* p);         // constructor from C-style string: x{"Euler"}

    String(const String&);                  // copy constructor
    String& operator=(const String&);       // copy assignment
```

```
        String(String&& x);                      // move constructor
        String& operator=(String&& x);           // move assignment

        ˜String() { if (short_max<sz) delete[] ptr; }    // destructor

        // ...
    };
```

This **String** has value semantics. That is, after an assignment **s1=s2**, the two strings **s1** and **s2** are fully distinct, and subsequent changes to one have no effect on the other. The alternative would be to give **String** pointer semantics. That would be to let changes to **s2** after **s1=s2** also affect the value of **s1**. Where it makes sense, I prefer value semantics; examples are **complex**, **vector**, **Matrix**, and **string**. However, for value semantics to be affordable, we need to pass **String**s by reference when we don't need copies and to implement move semantics (§3.3.2, §17.5.2) to optimize **return**s.

The slightly nontrivial representation of **String** is presented in §19.3.3. Note that it requires user-defined versions of the copy and move operations.

19.3.2 Access to Characters

The design of access operators for a string is a difficult topic because ideally access is by conventional notation (that is, using []), maximally efficient, and range checked. Unfortunately, you cannot have all of these properties simultaneously. Here, I follow the standard library by providing efficient unchecked operations with the conventional [] subscript notation plus range-checked **at()** operations:

```
    class String {
    public:
        // ...

        char& operator[](int n) { return ptr[n]; }         // unchecked element access
        char operator[](int n) const { return ptr[n]; }

        char& at(int n) { check(n); return ptr[n]; }        // range-checked element access
        char at(int n) const { check(n); return ptr[n]; }

        String& operator+=(char c);                         // add c at end

        const char* c_str() { return ptr; }                 // C-style string access
        const char* c_str() const { return ptr; }

        int size() const { return sz; }                     // number of elements
        int capacity() const                                // elements plus available space
            { return (sz<=short_max) ? short_max : sz+space; }

        // ...
    };
```

The idea is to use [] for ordinary use. For example:

```
int hash(const String& s)
{
    int h {s[0]};
    for (int i {1}; i!=s.size(); i++) h ˆ= s[i]>>1;        // unchecked access to s
    return h;
}
```

Here, using the checked **at()** would be redundant because we correctly access **s** only from **0** to **s.size()–1**.

We can use **at()** where we see a possibility of mistakes. For example:

```
void print_in_order(const String& s,const vector<int>& index)
{
    for (x : index) cout << s.at(x) << '\n';
}
```

Unfortunately, assuming that people will use **at()** consistently where mistakes can be made is overly optimistic, so some implementations of **std::string** (from which the **[]/at()** convention is borrowed) also check **[]**. I personally prefer a checked **[]** at least during development. However, for serious string manipulation tasks, a range check on each character access could impose quite noticeable overhead.

I provide **const** and non-**const** versions of the access functions to allow them to be used for **const** as well as other objects.

19.3.3 Representation

The representation for **String** was chosen to meet three goals:

- To make it easy to convert a C-style string (e.g., a string literal) to a **String** and to allow easy access to the characters of a **String** as a C-style string
- To minimize the use of the free store
- To make adding characters to the end of a **String** efficient

The result is clearly messier than a simple {pointer,size} representation, but much more realistic:

```
class String {
/*
    A simple string that implements the short string optimization

    size()==sz is the number of elements
    if size()<= short_max, the characters are held in the String object itself;
    otherwise the free store is used.

    ptr points to the start of the character sequence
    the character sequence is kept zero-terminated: ptr[size()]==0;
    this allows us to use C library string functions and to easily return a C-style string: c_str()

    To allow efficient addition of characters at end, String grows by doubling its allocation;
    capacity() is the amount of space available for characters
    (excluding the terminating 0): sz+space
*/
```

```
public:
    // ...
private:
    static const int short_max = 15;
    int sz;                        // number of characters
    char* ptr;
    union {
        int space;                 // unused allocated space
        char ch[short_max+1];      // leave space for terminating 0
    };

    void check(int n) const        // range check
    {
        if (n<0 || sz<=n)
            throw std::out_of_range("String::at()");
    }

    // ancillary member functions:
    void copy_from(const String& x);
    void move_from(String& x);
};
```

This supports what is known as the *short string optimization* by using two string representations:

- If sz<=short_max, the characters are stored in the String object itself, in the array named ch.
- If !(sz<=short_max), the characters are stored on the free store and we may allocate extra space for expansion. The member named space is the number of such characters.

In both cases, the number of elements is kept in sz and we look at sz, to determine which implementation scheme is used for a given string.

In both cases, ptr points to the elements. This is essential for performance: the access functions do not need to test which representation is used; they simply use ptr. Only the constructors, assignments, moves, and the destructor (§19.3.4) must care about the two alternatives.

We use the array ch only if sz<=short_max and the integer space only if !(sz<=short_max). Consequently, it would be a waste to allocate space for both ch and space in a String object. To avoid such waste, I use a union (§8.3). In particular, I used a form of union called an *anonymous union* (§8.3.2), which is specifically designed to allow a class to manage alternative representations of objects. All members of an anonymous union are allocated in the same memory, starting at the same address. Only one member may be used at any one time, but otherwise they are accessed and used exactly as if they were separate members of the scope surrounding the anonymous union. It is the programmer's job to make sure that they are never misused. For example, all member functions of String that use space must make sure that it really was space that was set and not ch. That is done by looking at sz<=short_max. In other words, Shape is (among other things) a discriminated union with sz<=short_max as the discriminant.

19.3.3.1 Ancillary Functions

In addition to functions intended for general use, I found that my code became cleaner when I provided three ancillary functions as "building blocks" to help me with the somewhat tricky representation and to minimize code replication. Two of those need to access the representation of **String**, so I made them members. However, I made them **private** members because they don't represent operations that are generally useful and safe to use. For many interesting classes, the implementation is not just the representation plus the **public** functions. Ancillary functions can lead to less duplication of code, better design, and improved maintainability.

The first such function moves characters into newly allocated memory:

```cpp
char* expand(const char* ptr, int n)     // expand into free store
{
    char* p = new char[n];
    strcpy(p,ptr);                   // §43.4
    return p;
}
```

This function does not access the **String** representation, so I did not make it a member.

The second implementation function is used by copy operations to give a **String** a copy of the members of another:

```cpp
void String::copy_from(const String& x)
    // make *this a copy of x
{
    if (x.sz<=short_max) {           // copy *this
        memcpy(this,&x,sizeof(x));   // §43.5
        ptr = ch;
    }
    else {                           // copy the elements
        ptr = expand(x.ptr,x.sz+1);
        sz = x.sz;
        space = 0;
    }
}
```

Any necessary cleanup of the target **String** is the task of callers of **copy_from()**; **copy_from()** unconditionally overwrites its target. I use the standard-library **memcpy()** (§43.5) to copy the bytes of the source into the target. That's a low-level and sometimes pretty nasty function. It should be used only where there are no objects with constructors or destructors in the copied memory because **memcpy()** knows nothing about types. Both **String** copy operations use **copy_from()**.

The corresponding function for move operations is:

```cpp
void String::move_from(String& x)
{
    if (x.sz<=short_max) {           // copy *this
        memcpy(this,&x,sizeof(x));   // §43.5
        ptr = ch;
    }
```

```
    else {                   // grab the elements
        ptr = x.ptr;
        sz = x.sz;
        space = x.space;
        x.ptr = x.ch;        // x = ""
        x.sz = 0;
        x.ch[0]=0;
    }
}
```

It too unconditionally makes its target a copy of its argument. However, it does not leave its argument owning any free store. I could also have used **memcpy()** in the long string case, but since a long string representation uses only part of **String**'s representation, I decided to copy the used members individually.

19.3.4 Member Functions

The default constructor defines a **String** to be empty:

```
String::String()             // default constructor: x{""}
        : sz{0}, ptr{ch}     // ptr points to elements, ch is an initial location (§19.3.3)
    {
        ch[0] = 0;           // terminating 0
    }
```

Given **copy_from()** and **move_from()**, the constructors, moves, and assignments are fairly simple to implement. The constructor that takes a C-style string argument must determine the number of characters and store them appropriately:

```
String::String(const char* p)
        :sz{strlen(p)},
        ptr{(sz<=short_max) ? ch : new char[sz+1]},
        space{0}
    {
        strcpy(ptr,p);   // copy characters into ptr from p
    }
```

If the argument is a short string, **ptr** is set to point to **ch**; otherwise, space is allocated on the free store. In either case, the characters are copied from the argument string into the memory managed by **String**.

The copy constructor simply copies the representation of its arguments:

```
String::String(const String& x)     // copy constructor
    {
        copy_from(x);  // copy representation from x
    }
```

I didn't bother trying to optimize the case where the size of the source equals the size of the target (as was done for **vector**; §13.6.3). I don't know if that would be worthwhile.

Similarly, the move constructor moves the representation from its source (and possibly sets it argument to be the empty string):

```
String::String(String&& x)        // move constructor
{
    move_from(x);
}
```

Like the copy constructor, the copy assignment uses **copy_from()** to clone its argument's representation. In addition, it has to **delete** any free store owned by the target and make sure it does not get into trouble with self-assignment (e.g., **s=s**):

```
String& String::operator=(const String& x)
{
    if (this==&x) return *this;        // deal with self-assignment
    char* p = (short_max<sz) ? ptr : 0;
    copy_from(x);
    delete[] p;
    return *this;
}
```

The **String** move assignment deletes its target's free store (if there is any) and then moves:

```
String& String::operator=(String&& x)
{
    if (this==&x) return *this;        // deal with self-assignment (x = move(x) is insanity)
    if (short_max<sz) delete[] ptr;    // delete target
    move_from(x);                      // does not throw
    return *this;
}
```

It is logically possible to move a source into itself (e.g., **s=std::move(s)**), so again we have to protect against self-assignment (however unlikely).

The logically most complicated **String** operation is **+=**, which adds a character to the end of the string, increasing its size by one:

```
String& String::operator+=(char c)
{
    if (sz==short_max) {          // expand to long string
        int n = sz+sz+2;          // double the allocation (+2 because of the terminating 0)
        ptr = expand(ptr,n);
        space = n-sz-2;
    }
    else if (short_max<sz) {
        if (space==0) {                  // expand in free store
            int n = sz+sz+2;             // double the allocation (+2 because of the terminating 0)
            char* p = expand(ptr,n);
            delete[] ptr;
            ptr = p;
            space = n-sz-2;
        }
        else
            --space;
    }
```

```
        ptr[sz] = c;          // add c at end
        ptr[++sz] = 0;        // increase size and set terminator

        return *this;
}
```

There is a lot going on here: **operator+=()** has to keep track of which representation (short or long) is used and whether there is extra space available to expand into. If more space is needed, **expand()** is called to allocate that space and move the old characters into the new space. If there was an old allocation that needs deleting, it is returned, so that += can delete it. Once enough space is available, it is trivial to put the new character **c** into it and to add the terminating **0**.

Note the calculation of available memory for **space**. Of all the **String** implementation that took the longest to get right: its a messy little calculation prone to off-by-one errors. That repeated constant **2** feels awfully like a "magic constant."

All **String** members take care not to modify a new representation before they are certain that a new one can be put in place. In particular, they don't **delete** until after any possible **new** operations have been done. In fact, the **String** members provide the strong exception guarantee (§13.2).

If you don't like the kind of fiddly code presented as part of the implementation of **String**, simply use **std::string**. To a large extent, the standard-library facilities exist to save us from programming at this low level most of the time. Stronger: writing a string class, a vector class, or a map is an excellent exercise. However, once the exercise is done, one outcome should be an appreciation of what the standard offers and a desire not to maintain your own version.

19.3.5 Helper Functions

To complete class **String**, I provide a set of useful functions, stream I/O, support for range-**for** loops, comparison, and concatenation. These all mirror the design choices used for **std::string**. In particular, << just prints the characters without added formatting, and >> skips initial whitespace before reading until it finds terminating whitespace (or the end of the stream):

```
ostream& operator<<(ostream& os, const String& s)
{
        return os << s.c_str();    // §36.3.3
}

istream& operator>>(istream& is, String& s)
{
        s = "";        // clear the target string
        is>>ws;        // skip whitespace (§38.4.5.1)
        char ch = ' ';
        while(is.get(ch) && !isspace(ch))
                s += ch;
        return is;
}
```

I provide == and != for comparison:

```
bool operator==(const String& a, const String& b)
{
    if (a.size()!=b.size())
        return false;
    for (int i = 0; i!=a.size(); ++i)
        if (a[i]!=b[i])
            return false;
    return true;
}

bool operator!=(const String& a, const String& b)
{
    return !(a==b);
}
```

Adding <, etc., would be trivial.

To support the range-**for** loop, we need **begin()** and **end()** (§9.5.1). Again, we can provide those as freestanding (nonmember) functions without direct access to the **String** implementation:

```
char* begin(String& x)        // C-string-style access
{
    return x.c_str();
}

char* end(String& x)
{
    return x.c_str()+x.size();
}

const char* begin(const String& x)
{
    return x.c_str();
}

const char* end(const String& x)
{
    return x.c_str()+x.size();
}
```

Given the member function += that adds a character at the end, concatenation operators are easily provided as nonmember functions:

```
String& operator+=(String& a, const String& b)    // concatenation
{
    for (auto x : b)
        a+=x;
    return a;
}
```

```
String operator+(const String& a, const String& b)// concatenation
{
    String res {a};
    res += b;
    return res;
}
```

I feel that I may have slightly "cheated" here. Should I have provided a member += that added a C-style string to the end? The standard-library **string** does, but without it, concatenation with a C-style string still works. For example:

```
String s = "Njal ";
s += "Gunnar";        // concatenate: add to the end of s
```

This use of += is interpreted as **operator+=(s,String("Gunnar"))**. My guess is that I could provide a more efficient **String::operator+=(const char∗)**, but I have no idea if the added performance would be worthwhile in real-world code. In such cases, I try to be conservative and deliver the minimal design. Being able to do something is not by itself a good reason for doing it.

Similarly, I do not try to optimize += by taking the size of a source string into account.

Adding _s as a string literal suffix meaning **String** is trivial:

```
String operator"" _s(const char∗ p, size_t)
{
    return String{p};
}
```

We can now write:

```
void f(const char∗);        // C-style string
void f(const String&);      // our string

void g()
{
    f("Madden's");              // f(const char*)
    f("Christopher's"_s);       // f(const String&);
}
```

19.3.6 Using Our String

The main program simply exercises the **String** operators a bit:

```
int main()
{
    String s ("abcdefghij");
    cout << s << '\n';
    s += 'k';
    s += 'l';
    s += 'm';
    s += 'n';
    cout << s << '\n';
```

```
String s2 = "Hell";
s2 += " and high water";
cout << s2 << '\n';

String s3 = "qwerty";
s3 = s3;
String s4 ="the quick brown fox jumped over the lazy dog";
s4 = s4;
cout << s3 << " " << s4 << "\n";
cout << s + ". " + s3 + String(". ") + "Horsefeathers\n";

String buf;
while (cin>>buf && buf!="quit")
    cout << buf << " " << buf.size() << " " << buf.capacity() << '\n';
}
```

This String lacks many features that you might consider important or even essential. However, for what it does it closely resembles std::string (Chapter 36) and illustrates techniques used for the implementation of the standard-library string.

19.4 Friends

An ordinary member function declaration specifies three logically distinct things:

[1] The function can access the private part of the class declaration.

[2] The function is in the scope of the class.

[3] The function must be invoked on an object (has a this pointer).

By declaring a member function static (§16.2.12), we can give it the first two properties only. By declaring a nonmember function a friend, we can give it the first property only. That is, a function declared friend is granted access to the implementation of a class just like a member function but is otherwise independent of that class.

For example, we could define an operator that multiplies a Matrix by a Vector. Naturally, Vector and Matrix hide their respective representations and provide a complete set of operations for manipulating objects of their type. However, our multiplication routine cannot be a member of both. Also, we don't really want to provide low-level access functions to allow every user to both read and write the complete representation of both Matrix and Vector. To avoid this, we declare the operator* a friend of both:

```
constexpr rc_max {4};      // row and column size

class Matrix;

class Vector {
    float v[rc_max];
    // ...
    friend Vector operator*(const Matrix&, const Vector&);
};
```

```
class Matrix {
    Vector v[rc_max];
    // ...
    friend Vector operator*(const Matrix&, const Vector&);
};
```

Now **operator*()** can reach into the implementation of both **Vector** and **Matrix**. That would allow sophisticated implementation techniques, but a simple implementation would be:

```
Vector operator*(const Matrix& m, const Vector& v)
{
    Vector r;
    for (int i = 0; i!=rc_max; i++) {        // r[i] = m[i] * v;
        r.v[i] = 0;
        for (int j = 0; j!=rc_max; j++)
            r.v[i] += m.v[i].v[j] * v.v[j];
    }
    return r;
}
```

A **friend** declaration can be placed in either the private or the public part of a class declaration; it does not matter where. Like a member function, a friend function is explicitly declared in the declaration of the class of which it is a friend. It is therefore as much a part of that interface as is a member function.

A member function of one class can be the friend of another. For example:

```
class List_iterator {
    // ...
    int* next();
};
```

```
class List {
    friend int* List_iterator::next();
    // ...
};
```

There is a shorthand for making all functions of one class friends of another. For example:

```
class List {
    friend class List_iterator;
    // ...
};
```

This **friend** declaration makes all of **List_iterator**'s member functions friends of **List**.

Declaring a class a **friend** grants access to every function of that class. That implies that we cannot know the set of functions that can access the granting class's representation just by looking at the class itself. In this, a friend class declaration differs from the declaration of a member function and a friend function. Clearly, friend classes should be used with caution and only to express closely connected concepts.

It is possible to make a template argument a **friend**:

```
template<typename T>
class X {
    friend T;
    friend class T;   // redundant "class"
    // ...
};
```

Often, there is a choice between making a class a member (a nested class) or a nonmember friend (§18.3.1).

19.4.1 Finding Friends

A friend must be previously declared in an enclosing scope or defined in the non-class scope immediately enclosing the class that is declaring it to be a **friend**. Scopes outside the innermost enclosing namespace scope are not considered for a name first declared as a **friend** (§iso.7.3.1.2). Consider a technical example:

```
class C1 { };     // will become friend of N::C
void f1();        // will become friend of N::C

namespace N {
    class C2 { };         // will become friend of C
    void f2() { }         // will become friend of C

    class C {
        int x;
    public:
        friend class C1;      // OK (previously defined)
        friend void f1();

        friend class C3;      // OK (defined in enclosing namespace)
        friend void f3();
        friend class C4;      // First declared in N and assumed to be in N
        friend void f4();
    };

    class C3 {};          // friend of C
    void f3() {  C x; x.x = 1; } // OK: friend of C
} // namespace N

class C4 { };                   // not friend of N::C
void f4() { N::C x; x.x = 1; }   // error: x is private and f4() is not a friend of N::C
```

A friend function can be found through its arguments (§14.2.4) even if it was not declared in the immediately enclosing scope. For example:

```
void f(Matrix& m)
{
    invert(m);      // Matrix's friend invert()
}
```

Thus, a friend function should be explicitly declared in an enclosing scope or take an argument of its class or a class derived from that. If not, the friend cannot be called. For example:

```
// no f() in this scope

class X {
    friend void f();           // useless
    friend void h(const X&);   // can be found through its argument
};

void g(const X& x)
{
    f();       // no f() in scope
    h(x);      // X's friend h()
}
```

19.4.2 Friends and Members

When should we use a friend function, and when is a member function the better choice for specifying an operation? First, we try to minimize the number of functions that access the representation of a class and try to make the set of access functions as appropriate as possible. Therefore, the first question is not "Should it be a member, a **static** member, or a friend?" but rather "Does it really need access?" Typically, the set of functions that need access is smaller than we are willing to believe at first. Some operations must be members – for example, constructors, destructors, and virtual functions (§3.2.3, §17.2.5) – but typically there is a choice. Because member names are local to the class, a function that requires direct access to the representation should be a member unless there is a specific reason for it to be a nonmember.

Consider a class **X** supplying alternative ways of presenting an operation:

```
class X {
    // ...
    X(int);

    int m1();              // member
    int m2() const;

    friend int f1(X&);     // friend, not member
    friend int f2(const X&);
    friend int f3(X);
};
```

Member functions can be invoked for objects of their class only; no user-defined conversions are applied to the leftmost operand of a . or –> (but see §19.2.3). For example:

```
void g()
{
    99.m1();   // error: X(99).m1() not tried
    99.m2();   // error: X(99).m2() not tried
}
```

The global function f1() has a similar property because implicit conversions are not used for non-**const** reference arguments (§7.7). However, conversions may be applied to the arguments of f2() and f3():

```
void h()
{
    f1(99);     // error: f1(X(99)) not tried: non-const X& argument
    f2(99);     // OK: f2(X(99)); const X& argument
    f3(99);     // OK: f3(X(99)); X argument
}
```

An operation modifying the state of a class object should therefore be a member or a function taking a non-**const** reference argument (or a non-**const** pointer argument).

Operators that modify an operand (e.g., =, *=, and ++) are most naturally defined as members for user-defined types. Conversely, if implicit type conversion is desired for all operands of an operation, the function implementing it must be a nonmember function taking a **const** reference argument or a non-reference argument. This is often the case for the functions implementing operators that do not require lvalue operands when applied to fundamental types (e.g., +, −, and ||). However, such operators often need access to the representations of their operand class. Consequently, binary operators are the most common source of friend functions.

Unless type conversions are defined, there appears to be no compelling reason to choose a member over a friend taking a reference argument, or vice versa. In some cases, the programmer may have a preference for one call syntax over another. For example, most people seem to prefer the notation m2=inv(m) for producing a inverted **Matrix** from m to the alternative m2=m.inv(). On the other hand, if inv() inverts m itself, rather than producing a new **Matrix** that is the inverse of **m**, it should be a member.

All other things considered equal, implement operations that need direct access to a representation as member functions:

- It is not possible to know if someone someday will define a conversion operator.
- The member function call syntax makes it clear to the user that the object may be modified; a reference argument is far less obvious.
- Expressions in the body of a member can be noticeably shorter than the equivalent expressions in a global function; a nonmember function must use an explicit argument, whereas the member can use **this** implicitly.
- Member names are local to a class, so they tend to be shorter than the names of nonmember functions.
- If we have defined a member f() and we later feel the need for a nonmember f(x), we can simply define it to mean x.f().

Conversely, operations that do not need direct access to a representation are often best represented as nonmember functions, possibly in a namespace that makes their relationship with the class explicit (§18.3.6).

19.5 Advice

[1]   Use **operator[]()** for subscripting and for selection based on a single value; §19.2.1.

[2]   Use **operator()()** for call semantics, for subscripting, and for selection based on multiple values; §19.2.2.

[3]   Use **operator–>()** to dereference "smart pointers"; §19.2.3.

[4]   Prefer prefix **++** over suffix **++**; §19.2.4.

[5]   Define the global **operator new()** and **operator delete()** only if you really have to; §19.2.5.

[6]   Define member **operator new()** and member **operator delete()** to control allocation and deallocation of objects of a specific class or hierarchy of classes; §19.2.5.

[7]   Use user-defined literals to mimic conventional notation; §19.2.6.

[8]   Place literal operators in separate namespaces to allow selective use; §19.2.6.

[9]   For nonspecialized uses, prefer the standard **string** (Chapter 36) to the result of your own exercises; §19.3.

[10]   Use a friend function if you need a nonmember function to have access to the representation of a class (e.g., to improve notation or to access the representation of two classes); §19.4.

[11]   Prefer member functions to friend functions for granting access to the implementation of a class; §19.4.2.

20

Derived Classes

Do not multiply objects without necessity.
– William Occam

20.1 Introduction

From Simula, C++ borrowed the ideas of classes and class hierarchies. In addition, it borrowed the design idea that classes should be used to model concepts in the programmer's and the application's world. C++ provides language constructs that directly support these design notions. Conversely, using the language features in support of design ideas distinguishes effective use of C++. Using language constructs as just notational props for traditional types of programming is to miss key strengths of C++.

A concept (idea, notion, etc.) does not exist in isolation. It coexists with related concepts and derives much of its power from relationships with other concepts. For example, try to explain what a car is. Soon you'll have introduced the notions of wheels, engines, drivers, pedestrians, trucks, ambulances, roads, oil, speeding tickets, motels, etc. Since we use classes to represent concepts, the issue becomes how to represent relationships among concepts. However, we can't express arbitrary relationships directly in a programming language. Even if we could, we wouldn't want to. To be useful, our classes should be more narrowly defined than our everyday concepts – and more precise.

The notion of a derived class and its associated language mechanisms are provided to express hierarchical relationships, that is, to express commonality between classes. For example, the concepts of a circle and a triangle are related in that they are both shapes; that is, they have the concept of a shape in common. Thus, we explicitly define class **Circle** and class **Triangle** to have class **Shape** in common. In that case, the common class, here **Shape**, is referred to as the *base* class or *superclass* and classes derived from that, here **Circle** and **Triangle**, are referred to as *derived* classes or *subclasses*. Representing a circle and a triangle in a program without involving the notion of a shape would be to miss something essential. This chapter is an exploration of the implications of this simple idea, which is the basis for what is commonly called *object-oriented programming*. The language features support building new classes from existing ones:

- *Implementation inheritance*: to save implementation effort by sharing facilities provided by a base class
- *Interface inheritance*: to allow different derived classes to be used interchangeably through the interface provided by a common base class

Interface inheritance is often referred to as *run-time polymorphism* (or *dynamic polymorphism*). In contrast, the uniform use of classes not related by inheritance provided by templates (§3.4, Chapter 23) is often referred to as *compile-time polymorphism* (or *static polymorphism*).

The discussion of class hierarchies is organized into three chapters:

- *Derived Classes* (Chapter 20): This chapter introduces the basic language features supporting object-oriented programming. Base and derived classes, virtual functions, and access control are covered.
- *Class Hierarchies* (Chapter 21): This chapter focuses on the use of base and derived classes to effectively organize code around the notion of class hierarchies. Most of this chapter is devoted to discussion of programming techniques, but technical aspects of multiple inheritance (classes with more than one base class) are also covered.
- *Run-time Type Identification* (Chapter 22): This chapter describes the techniques for explicitly navigating class hierarchies. In particular, the type conversion operations **dynamic_cast** and **static_cast** are presented, as is the operation for determining the type of an object given one of its base classes (**typeid**).

A brief introduction to the basic idea of hierarchical organization of types can be found in Chapter 3: base and derived classes (§3.2.2) and virtual functions (§3.2.3). These chapters examine these fundamental features and their associated programming and design techniques in greater detail.

20.2 Derived Classes

Consider building a program dealing with people employed by a firm. Such a program might have a data structure like this:

```
struct Employee {
    string first_name, family_name;
    char middle_initial;
    Date hiring_date;
    short department;
    // ...
};
```

Next, we might try to define a manager:

```
struct Manager {
    Employee emp;             // manager's employee record
    list<Employee*> group;    // people managed
    short level;
    // ...
};
```

A manager is also an employee; the **Employee** data is stored in the **emp** member of a **Manager** object. This may be obvious to a human reader – especially a careful reader – but there is nothing that tells the compiler and other tools that **Manager** is also an **Employee**. A **Manager**∗ is not an **Employee**∗, so one cannot simply use one where the other is required. In particular, one cannot put a **Manager** onto a list of **Employee**s without writing special code. We could either use explicit type conversion on a **Manager**∗ or put the address of the **emp** member onto a list of **employee**s. However, both solutions are inelegant and can be quite obscure. The correct approach is to explicitly state that a **Manager** *is* an **Employee**, with a few pieces of information added:

```
struct Manager : public Employee {
    list<Employee*> group;
    short level;
    // ...
};
```

The **Manager** is *derived* from **Employee**, and conversely, **Employee** is a *base class* for **Manager**. The class **Manager** has the members of class **Employee** (**first_name**, **department**, etc.) in addition to its own members (**group**, **level**, etc.).

Derivation is often represented graphically by a pointer from the derived class to its base class indicating that the derived class refers to its base (rather than the other way around):

A derived class is often said to inherit properties from its base, so the relationship is also called *inheritance*. A base class is sometimes called a *superclass* and a derived class a *subclass*. This terminology, however, is confusing to people who observe that the data in a derived class object is a superset of the data of an object of its base class. A derived class is typically larger (and never smaller) than its base class in the sense that it holds more data and provides more functions.

A popular and efficient implementation of the notion of derived classes has an object of the derived class represented as an object of the base class, with the information belonging specifically to the derived class added at the end. For example:

Employee: Manager:

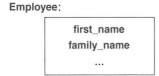

No memory overhead is implied by deriving a class. The space required is just the space required by the members.

Deriving **Manager** from **Employee** in this way makes **Manager** a subtype of **Employee**, so that a **Manager** can be used wherever an **Employee** is acceptable. For example, we can now create a list of **Employee**s, some of whom are **Manager**s:

```
void f(Manager m1, Employee e1)
{
    list<Employee*> elist {&m1,&e1};
    // ...
}
```

A **Manager** is (also) an **Employee**, so a **Manager**∗ can be used as an **Employee**∗. Similarly, a **Manager&** can be used as an **Employee&**. However, an **Employee** is not necessarily a **Manager**, so an **Employee**∗ cannot be used as a **Manager**∗. In general, if a class **Derived** has a public base class (§20.5) **Base**, then a **Derived**∗ can be assigned to a variable of type **Base**∗ without the use of explicit type conversion. The opposite conversion, from **Base**∗ to **Derived**∗, must be explicit. For example:

```
void g(Manager mm, Employee ee)
{
    Employee* pe = &mm;        // OK: every Manager is an Employee
    Manager* pm = &ee;         // error: not every Employee is a Manager

    pm->level = 2;             // disaster: ee doesn't have a level

    pm = static_cast<Manager*>(pe);  // brute force: works because pe points
                                     // to the Manager mm

    pm->level = 2;             // fine: pm points to the Manager mm that has a level
}
```

In other words, an object of a derived class can be treated as an object of its base class when manipulated through pointers and references. The opposite is not true. The use of **static_cast** and **dynamic_cast** is discussed in §22.2.

Using a class as a base is equivalent to defining an (unnamed) object of that class. Consequently, a class must be defined in order to be used as a base (§8.2.2):

```
class Employee;      // declaration only, no definition

class Manager : public Employee { // error: Employee not defined
    // ...
};
```

20.2.1 Member Functions

Simple data structures, such as **Employee** and **Manager**, are really not that interesting and often not particularly useful. We need to provide a proper type with a suitable set of operations, and we need to do so without being tied to the details of a particular representation. For example:

```
class Employee {
public:
    void print() const;
    string full_name() const { return first_name + ' ' + middle_initial + ' ' + family_name; }
    // ...
private:
    string first_name, family_name;
    char middle_initial;
    // ...
};

class Manager : public Employee {
public:
    void print() const;
    // ...
};
```

A member of a derived class can use the public – and protected (see §20.5) – members of a base class as if they were declared in the derived class itself. For example:

```
void Manager::print() const
{
    cout << "name is " << full_name() << '\n';
    // ...
}
```

However, a derived class cannot access private members of a base class:

```
void Manager::print() const
{
    cout << " name is " << family_name << '\n';        // error!
    // ...
}
```

This second version of **Manager::print()** will not compile because **family_name** is not accessible to **Manager::print()**.

This comes as a surprise to some, but consider the alternative: that a member function of a derived class could access the private members of its base class. The concept of a private member would be rendered meaningless by allowing a programmer to gain access to the private part of a class simply by deriving a new class from it. Furthermore, one could no longer find all uses of a private name by looking at the functions declared as members and friends of that class. One would have to examine every source file of the complete program for derived classes, then examine every function of those classes, then find every class derived from those classes, etc. This is, at best, tedious and often impractical. Where it is acceptable, protected – rather than private – members can be used (§20.5).

Typically, the cleanest solution is for the derived class to use only the public members of its base class. For example:

```
void Manager::print() const
{
    Employee::print();    // print Employee information
    cout << level;        // print Manager-specific information
    // ...
}
```

Note that :: must be used because print() has been redefined in **Manager**. Such reuse of names is typical. The unwary might write this:

```
void Manager::print() const
{
    print();    // oops!
    // print Manager-specific information
}
```

The result is a sequence of recursive calls ending with some form of program crash.

20.2.2 Constructors and Destructors

As usual, constructors and destructors are as essential:

- Objects are constructed from the bottom up (base before member and member before derived) and destroyed top-down (derived before member and member before base); §17.2.3.
- Each class can initialize its members and bases (but not directly members or bases of its bases); §17.4.1.
- Typically, destructors in a hierarchy need to be **virtual**; §17.2.5.
- Copy constructors of classes in a hierarchy should be used with care (if at all) to avoid slicing; §17.5.1.4.
- The resolution of a virtual function call, a **dynamic_cast**, or a **typeid()** in a constructor or destructor reflects the stage of construction and destruction (rather than the type of the yet-to-be-completed object); §22.4.

In computer science "up" and "down" can get very confused. In source text, definitions of base classes must occur before the definitions of their derived classes. This implies that for small examples, the bases appear above the derived classes on a screen. Furthermore, we tend to draw trees with the root on top. However, when I talk about constructing objects from the bottom up, I mean starting with the most fundamental (e.g., base classes) and building what depends on that (e.g., derived classes) later. We build from the roots (base classes) toward the leaves (derived classes).

20.3 Class Hierarchies

A derived class can itself be a base class. For example:

```
class Employee { /* ... */ };
class Manager : public Employee { /* ... */ };
class Director : public Manager { /* ... */ };
```

Such a set of related classes is traditionally called a *class hierarchy*. Such a hierarchy is most often a tree, but it can also be a more general graph structure. For example:

```
class Temporary { /* ... */ };
class Assistant : public Employee { /* ... */ };
class Temp : public Temporary, public Assistant { /* ... */ };
class Consultant : public Temporary, public Manager { /* ... */ };
```

or graphically:

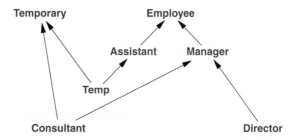

Thus, as is explained in detail in §21.3, C++ can express a directed acyclic graph of classes.

20.3.1 Type Fields

To use derived classes as more than a convenient shorthand in declarations, we must solve the following problem: Given a pointer of type **Base**∗, to which derived type does the object pointed to really belong? There are four fundamental solutions:

[1] Ensure that only objects of a single type are pointed to (§3.4, Chapter 23).
[2] Place a type field in the base class for the functions to inspect.
[3] Use **dynamic_cast** (§22.2, §22.6).
[4] Use virtual functions (§3.2.3, §20.3.2).

Unless you have used **final** (§20.3.4.2), solution 1 relies on more knowledge about the types involved than is available to the compiler. In general, it is not a good idea to try to be smarter than the type system, but (especially in combination with the use of templates) it can be used to implement homogeneous containers (e.g., the standard-library **vector** and **map**) with unsurpassed performance. Solutions [2], [3], and [4] can be used to build heterogeneous lists, that is, lists of (pointers to) objects of several different types. Solution [3] is a language-supported variant of solution [2].

Solution [4] is a special type-safe variation of solution [2]. Combinations of solutions [1] and [4] are particularly interesting and powerful; in almost all situations, they yield cleaner code than do solutions [2] and [3].

Let us first examine the simple type-field solution to see why it is typically best avoided. The manager/employee example could be redefined like this:

```
struct Employee {
    enum Empl_type { man, empl };
    Empl_type type;

    Employee() : type{empl} { }

    string first_name, family_name;
    char middle_initial;

    Date hiring_date;
    short department;
    // ...
};

struct Manager : public Employee {
    Manager() { type = man; }

    list<Employee*> group;   // people managed
    short level;
    // ...
};
```

Given this, we can now write a function that prints information about each **Employee**:

```
void print_employee(const Employee* e)
{
    switch (e->type) {
    case Employee::empl:
        cout << e->family_name << '\t' << e->department << '\n';
        // ...
        break;
    case Employee::man:
    {   cout << e->family_name << '\t' << e->department << '\n';
        // ...
        const Manager* p = static_cast<const Manager*>(e);
        cout << " level " << p->level << '\n';
        // ...
        break;
    }
    }
}
```

and use it to print a list of **Employee**s, like this:

```
void print_list(const list<Employee*>& elist)
{
    for (auto x : elist)
        print_employee(x);
}
```

This works fine, especially in a small program maintained by a single person. However, it has a fundamental weakness in that it depends on the programmer manipulating types in a way that cannot be checked by the compiler. This problem is usually made worse because functions such as **print_employee()** are often organized to take advantage of the commonality of the classes involved:

```
void print_employee(const Employee* e)
{
    cout << e->family_name << '\t' << e->department << '\n';
    // ...
    if (e->type == Employee::man) {
        const Manager* p = static_cast<const Manager*>(e);
        cout << " level " << p->level << '\n';
        // ...
    }
}
```

Finding all such tests on the type field buried in a large function that handles many derived classes can be difficult. Even when they have been found, understanding what is going on can be difficult. Furthermore, any addition of a new kind of **Employee** involves a change to all the key functions in a system – the ones containing the tests on the type field. The programmer must consider every function that could conceivably need a test on the type field after a change. This implies the need to access critical source code and the resulting necessary overhead of testing the affected code. The use of an explicit type conversion is a strong hint that improvement is possible.

In other words, use of a type field is an error-prone technique that leads to maintenance problems. The problems increase in severity as the size of the program increases because the use of a type field causes a violation of the ideals of modularity and data hiding. Each function using a type field must know about the representation and other details of the implementation of every class derived from the one containing the type field.

It also seems that any common data accessible from every derived class, such as a type field, tempts people to add more such data. The common base thus becomes the repository of all kinds of "useful information." This, in turn, gets the implementation of the base and derived classes intertwined in ways that are most undesirable. In a large class hierarchy, accessible (not **private**) data in a common base class becomes the "global variables" of the hierarchy. For clean design and simpler maintenance, we want to keep separate issues separate and avoid mutual dependencies.

20.3.2 Virtual Functions

Virtual functions overcome the problems with the type-field solution by allowing the programmer to declare functions in a base class that can be redefined in each derived class. The compiler and linker will guarantee the correct correspondence between objects and the functions applied to them. For example:

```
class Employee {
public:
     Employee(const string& name, int dept);
     virtual void print() const;
     // ...
private:
     string first_name, family_name;
     short department;
     // ...
};
```

The keyword **virtual** indicates that **print()** can act as an interface to the **print()** function defined in this class and **print()** functions defined in classes derived from it. Where such **print()** functions are defined in derived classes, the compiler ensures that the right **print()** for the given **Employee** object is invoked in each case.

To allow a virtual function declaration to act as an interface to functions defined in derived classes, the argument types specified for a function in a derived class cannot differ from the argument types declared in the base, and only very slight changes are allowed for the return type (§20.3.6). A virtual member function is sometimes called a *method*.

A virtual function *must* be defined for the class in which it is first declared (unless it is declared to be a pure virtual function; see §20.4). For example:

```
void Employee::print() const
{
     cout << family_name << '\t' << department << '\n';
     // ...
}
```

A virtual function can be used even if no class is derived from its class, and a derived class that does not need its own version of a virtual function need not provide one. When deriving a class, simply provide an appropriate function if it is needed. For example:

```
class Manager : public Employee {
public:
     Manager(const string& name, int dept, int lvl);
     void print() const;
     // ...
private:
     list<Employee*> group;
     short level;
     // ...
};

void Manager::print() const
{
     Employee::print();
     cout << "\tlevel " << level << '\n';
     // ...
}
```

A function from a derived class with the same name and the same set of argument types as a virtual function in a base is said to *override* the base class version of the virtual function. Furthermore, it is possible to override a virtual function from a base with a more derived return type (§20.3.6).

Except where we explicitly say which version of a virtual function is called (as in the call Employee::print()), the overriding function is chosen as the most appropriate for the object for which it is called. Independently of which base class (interface) is used to access an object, we always get the same function when we use the virtual function call mechanism.

The global function print_employee() (§20.3.1) is now unnecessary because the print() member functions have taken its place. A list of Employees can be printed like this:

```
void print_list(const list<Employee*>& s)
{
    for (auto x : s)
        x->print();
}
```

Each Employee will be written out according to its type. For example:

```
int main()
{
    Employee e {"Brown",1234};
    Manager m {"Smith",1234,2};

    print_list({&e,&m});
}
```

produced:

```
Smith 1234
    level 2
Brown 1234
```

Note that this will work even if print_list() was written and compiled before the specific derived class Manager was even conceived of! This is a key aspect of classes. When used properly, it becomes the cornerstone of object-oriented designs and provides a degree of stability to an evolving program.

Getting "the right" behavior from Employee's functions independently of exactly what kind of Employee is actually used is called *polymorphism*. A type with virtual functions is called a *polymorphic type* or (more precisely) a *run-time polymorphic type*. To get runtime polymorphic behavior in C++, the member functions called must be virtual and objects must be manipulated through pointers or references. When manipulating an object directly (rather than through a pointer or reference), its exact type is known by the compiler so that run-time polymorphism is not needed.

By default, a function that overrides a virtual function itself becomes virtual. We can, but do not have to, repeat virtual in a derived class. I don't recommend repeating virtual. If you want to be explicit, use override (§20.3.4.1).

Clearly, to implement polymorphism, the compiler must store some kind of type information in each object of class Employee and use it to call the right version of the virtual function print(). In a typical implementation, the space taken is just enough to hold a pointer (§3.2.3): the usual implementation technique is for the compiler to convert the name of a virtual function into an index into a table of pointers to functions. That table is usually called *the virtual function table* or simply the **vtbl**. Each class with virtual functions has its own **vtbl** identifying its virtual functions. This can be represented graphically like this:

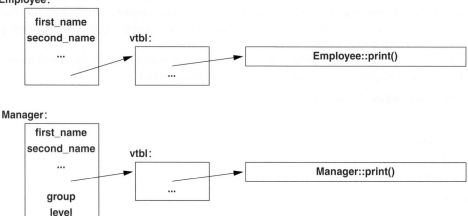

The functions in the **vtbl** allow the object to be used correctly even when the size of the object and the layout of its data are unknown to the caller. The implementation of a caller need only know the location of the **vtbl** in an **Employee** and the index used for each virtual function. This virtual call mechanism can be made almost as efficient as the "normal function call" mechanism (within 25%), so efficiency concerns should not deter anyone from using a virtual function where an ordinary function call would be acceptably efficient. Its space overhead is one pointer in each object of a class with virtual functions plus one **vtbl** for each such class. You pay this overhead only for objects of a class with a virtual function. You choose to pay this overhead only if you need the added functionality virtual functions provide. Had you chosen to use the alternative type-field solution, a comparable amount of space would have been needed for the type field.

A virtual function invoked from a constructor or a destructor reflects that the object is partially constructed or partially destroyed (§22.4). It is therefore typically a bad idea to call a virtual function from a constructor or a destructor.

20.3.3 Explicit Qualification

Calling a function using the scope resolution operator, ::, as is done in **Manager::print()** ensures that the **virtual** mechanism is not used:

```
void Manager::print() const
{
    Employee::print();   // not a virtual call
    cout << "\tlevel " << level << '\n';
    // ...
}
```

Otherwise, **Manager::print()** would suffer an infinite recursion. The use of a qualified name has another desirable effect. That is, if a virtual function is also **inline** (as is not uncommon), then inline substitution can be used for calls specified using ::. This provides the programmer with an efficient way to handle some important special cases in which one virtual function calls another for the same object. The **Manager::print()** function is an example of this. Because the type of the object is determined in the call of **Manager::print()**, it need not be dynamically determined again for the resulting call of **Employee::print()**.

20.3.4 Override Control

If you declare a function in a derived class that has exactly the same name and type as a virtual function in a base class, then the function in the derived class overrides the one in the base class. That's a simple and effective rule. However, for larger class hierarchies it can be difficult to be sure that you actually override the function you meant to override. Consider:

```
struct B0 {
    void f(int) const;
    virtual void g(double);
};

struct B1 : B0 { /* ... */ };
struct B2 : B1 { /* ... */ };
struct B3 : B2 { /* ... */ };
struct B4 : B3 { /* ... */ };
struct B5 : B4 { /* ... */ };

struct D : B5 {
    void f(int) const;      // override f() in base class
    void g(int);            // override g() in base class
    virtual int h();        // override h() in base class
};
```

This illustrates three errors that are far from obvious when they appear in a real class hierarchy where the classes **B0**...**B5** have many members each and are scattered over many header files. Here:

- **B0::f()** is not **virtual**, so you can't override it, only hide it (§20.3.5).
- **D::g()** doesn't have the same argument type as **B0::g()**, so if it overrides anything it's not the virtual function **B0::g()**. Most likely, **D::g()** just hides **B0::g()**.
- There is no function called **h()** in **B0**, if **D::h()** overrides anything, it is not a function from **B0**. Most likely, it is introducing a brand-new virtual function.

I didn't show you what was in **B1**...**B5**, so maybe something completely different is going on because of declarations in those classes. I personally don't (redundantly) use **virtual** for a function that's meant to override. For smaller programs (especially with a compiler with decent warnings against common mistakes) getting overriding done correctly isn't hard. However, for larger hierarchies more specific controls are useful:

- **virtual**: The function may be overridden (§20.3.2).
- **=0**: The function must be **virtual** and must be overridden (§20.4).

- **override**: The function is meant to override a virtual function in a base class (§20.3.4.1).
- **final**: The function is not meant to be overridden (§20.3.4.2).

In the absence of any of these controls, a non-**static** member function is virtual if and only if it overrides a **virtual** function in a base class (§20.3.2).

A compiler can warn against inconsistent use of explicit override controls. For example, a class declaration that uses **override** for seven out of nine virtual base class functions could be confusing to maintainers.

20.3.4.1 override

We can be explicit about our desire to override:

```
struct D : B5 {
    void f(int) const override;      // error: B0::f() is not virtual
    void g(int) override;            // error: B0::f() takes a double argument
    virtual int h() override;        // error: no function h() to override
};
```

Given this definition (and assuming that the intermediate base classes **B1**...**B5** do not provide relevant functions), all three declarations give errors.

In a large or complicated class hierarchy with many virtual functions, it is best to use **virtual** only to introduce a new virtual function and to use **override** on all functions intended as overriders. Using **override** is a bit verbose but clarifies the programmer's intent.

The **override** specifier comes last in a declaration, after all other parts. For example:

```
void f(int) const noexcept override; // OK (if there is a suitable f() to override)
override void f(int) const noexcept; // syntax error
void f(int) override const noexcept; // syntax error
```

And yes, it's illogical that **virtual** is a prefix and **override** is a suffix. This is part of the price we pay for compatibility and stability over decades.

An **override** specifier is not part of the type of a function and cannot be repeated in an out-of-class definition. For example:

```
class Derived : public Base {
    void f() override;      // OK if Base has a virtual f()
    void g() override;      // OK if Base has a virtual g()
};

void Derived::f() override     // error: override out of class
{
    // ...
}

void g()                       // OK
{
    // ...
}
```

Curiously, **override** is not a keyword; it is what is called a *contextual keyword*. That is, **override** has a special meaning in a few contexts but can be used as an identifier elsewhere. For example:

```
int override = 7;

struct Dx : Base {
    int override;

    int f() override
    {
        return override + ::override;
    }
};
```

Don't indulge in such cleverness; it complicates maintenance. The only reason that **override** is a contextual keyword, rather than an ordinary keyword, is that there exists a significant amount of code that has used **override** as an ordinary identifier for decades. The other contextual keyword is **final** (§20.3.4.2).

20.3.4.2 final

When we declare a member function, we have a choice between **virtual** and not **virtual** (the default). We use **virtual** for functions we want writers of derived classes to be able to define or redefine. We base our choice on the meaning (semantics) of our class:

- Can we imagine the need for further derived classes?
- Does a designer of a derived class need to redefine the function to achieve a plausible aim?
- Is overriding a function error-prone (i.e., is it hard for an overriding function to provide the expected semantics of a virtual function)?

If the answer is "no" to all three questions, we can leave the function non-**virtual** to gain simplicity of design and occasionally some performance (mostly from inlining). The standard library is full of examples of this.

Far more rarely, we have a class hierarchy that starts out with virtual functions, but after the definition of a set of derived classes, one of the answers becomes "no." For example, we can imagine an abstract syntax tree for a language where all language constructs have been defined as concrete node classes derived from a few interfaces. We only need to derive a new class if we change the language. In that case, we might want to prevent our users from overriding virtual functions because the only thing such overrides could do would be to change the semantics of our language. That is, we might want to close our design to modification from its users. For example:

```
struct Node {   // interface class
    virtual Type type() = 0;
    // ...
};

class If_statement : public Node {
public:
    Type type() override final;      // prevent further overriding
    // ...
};
```

In a realistic class hierarchy, there would be several intermediate classes between the general interface (here, **Node**) and the derived class representing a specific language construct (here, **If_state-
ment**). However, the key point about this example is that **Node::type()** is meant to be overridden
(that's why it's declared **virtual**) and its overrider **If_statement::type()** is not (that's why it's declared
final). After using **final** for a member function, it can no longer be overridden and an attempt to do
so is an error. For example:

```
class Modified_if_statement : public If_statement {
public:
    Type type() override;       // error: If_statement::type() is final
    // ...
};
```

We can make every **virtual** member function of a class **final**; just add **final** after the class name. For
example:

```
class For_statement final : public Node {
public:
    Type type() override;
    // ...
};
```

```
class Modified_for_statement : public For_statement {       // error: For_statement is final
    Type type() override;
    // ...
};
```

For good and bad, adding **final** to the class not only prevents overriding, it also prevents further
derivation from a class. There are people who use **final** to try to gain performance – after all, a non-
virtual function is faster than a **virtual** one (by maybe 25% on a modern implementation) and offers
greater opportunities for inlining (§12.1.5). However, do not blindly use **final** as an optimization
aid; it affects the class hierarchy design (often negatively), and the performance improvements are
rarely significant. Do some serious measurements before claiming efficiency improvements. Use
final where it clearly reflects a class hierarchy design that you consider proper. That is, use **final** to
reflect a semantic need.

A **final** specifier is not part of the type of a function and cannot be repeated in an out-of-class
definition. For example:

```
class Derived : public Base {
    void f() final;       // OK if Base has a virtual f()
    void g() final;       // OK if Base has a virtual g()
    // ...
};
```

```
void Derived::f() final       // error: final out of class
{
    // ...
}
```

```
void g() final              // OK
{
    // ...
}
```

Like **override** (§20.3.4.1), **final** is a contextual keyword. That is, **final** has a special meaning in a few contexts but can be used as an ordinary identifier elsewhere. For example:

```
int final = 7;

struct Dx : Base {
    int final;

    int f() final
    {
        return final + ::final;
    }
};
```

Don't indulge in such cleverness; it complicates maintenance. The only reason that **final** is a contextual keyword, rather than an ordinary keyword, is that there exist a significant amount of code that has used **final** as an ordinary identifier for decades. The other contextual keyword is **override** (§20.3.4.1).

20.3.5 using Base Members

Functions do not overload across scopes (§12.3.3). For example:

```
struct Base {
    void f(int);
};

struct Derived : Base {
    void f(double);
};

void use(Derived d)
{
    d.f(1);         // call Derived::f(double)
    Base& br = d
    br.f(1);        // call Base::f(int)
}
```

This can surprise people, and sometimes we want overloading to ensure that the best matching member function is used. As for namespaces, **using**-declarations can be used to add a function to a scope. For example:

```
struct D2 : Base {
    using Base::f;      // bring all fs from Base into D2
    void f(double);
};
```

```
void use2(D2 d)
{
    d.f(1);           // call D2::f(int), that is, Base::f(int)
    Base& br = d
    br.f(1);          // call Base::f(int)
}
```

This is a simple consequence of a class also being considered a namespace (§16.2).

Several **using**-declarations can bring in names from multiple base classes. For example:

```
struct B1 {
    void f(int);
};

struct B2 {
    void f(double);
};

struct D : B1, B2 {
    using B1::f;
    using B2::f;
    void f(char);
};

void use(D d)
{
    d.f(1);     // call D::f(int), that is, B1::f(int)
    d.f('a');   // call D::f(char)
    d.f(1.0);   // call D::f(double), that is, B2::f(double)
}
```

We can bring constructors into a derived class scope; see §20.3.5.1. A name brought into a derived class scope by a **using**-declaration has its access determined by the placement of the **using**-declaration; see §20.5.3. We cannot use **using**-directives to bring all members of a base class into a derived class.

20.3.5.1 Inheriting Constructors

Say I want a vector that's just like **std::vector**, but with guaranteed range checking. I can try this:

```
template<class T>
struct Vector : std::vector<T> {
    T& operator[](size_type i) { check(i); return this–>elem(i); }
    const T& operator[](size_type i) const { check(i); return this–>elem(i); }

    void check(size_type i) { if (this–>size()<i) throw range_error{"Vector::check() failed"}; }
};
```

Unfortunately, we would soon find out that this definition is rather incomplete. For example:

```
Vector<int> v { 1, 2, 3, 5, 8 };    // error: no initializer-list constructor
```

A quick check will show that **Vector** failed to inherit any constructors from **std::vector**.

That's not an unreasonable rule: if a class adds data members to a base or requires a stricter class invariant, it would be a disaster to inherit constructors. However, **Vector** did not do anything like that.

We solve the problem by simply saying that the constructors should be inherited:

```
template<class T>
struct Vector : std::vector<T> {
        using vector<T>::vector;        // inherit constructors

        T& operator=[](size_type i) { check(i); return this->elem(i); }
        const T& operator=(size_type i) const { check(i); return this->elem(i); }

        void check(size_type i) { if (this->size()<i) throw Bad_index(i); }
};
```

```
Vector<int> v { 1, 2, 3, 5, 8 };        // OK: use initializer-list constructor from std::vector
```

This use of **using** is exactly equivalent to its use for ordinary functions (§14.4.5, §20.3.5).

If you so choose, you can shoot yourself in the foot by inheriting constructors in a derived class in which you define new member variables needing explicit initialization:

```
struct B1 {
        B1(int) { }
};

struct D1 : B1 {
        using B1::B1;   // implicitly declares D1(int)
        string s;        // string has a default constructor
        int x;           // we "forgot" to provide for initialization of x
};

void test()
{
        D1 d {6};        // oops: d.x is not initialized
        D1 e;            // error: D1 has no default constructor
}
```

The reason that **D1::s** is initialized and **D1::x** is not is that the inheriting constructor is equivalent to a constructor that simply initializes the base. In this case, we might equivalently have written:

```
struct D1 : B1 {
        D1(int i) : B1(i) { }
        string s;        // string has a default constructor
        int x;           // we "forgot" to provide for initialization of x
};
```

One way to remove the bullet from your foot is by adding an in-class member initializer (§17.4.4):

```
struct D1 : B1 {
    using B1::B1;   // implicitly declares D1(int)
    int x {0};      // note: x is initialized
};

void test()
{
    D1 d {6};  // d.x is zero
}
```

Most often it is best to avoid being clever and restrict the use of inheriting constructors to the simple cases where no data members are added.

20.3.6 Return Type Relaxation

There is a relaxation of the rule that the type of an overriding function must be the same as the type of the virtual function it overrides. That is, if the original return type was **B***, then the return type of the overriding function may be **D***, provided **B** is a public base of **D**. Similarly, a return type of **B&** may be relaxed to **D&**. This is sometimes called the *covariant return* rule.

This relaxation applies only to return types that are pointers or references, and not to "smart pointers" such as **unique_ptr** (§5.2.1). In particular, there is not a similar relaxation of the rules for argument types because that would lead to type violations.

Consider a class hierarchy representing different kinds of expressions. In addition to the operations for manipulating expressions, the base class **Expr** would provide facilities for making new expression objects of the various expression types:

```
class Expr {
public:
    Expr();                  // default constructor
    Expr(const Expr&);       // copy constructor
    virtual Expr* new_expr() =0;
    virtual Expr* clone() =0;
    // ...
};
```

The idea is that **new_expr()** makes a default object of the type of the expression and **clone()** makes a copy of the object. Both will return an object of some specific class derived from **Expr**. They can never just return a "plain **Expr**" because **Expr** was deliberately and appropriately declared to be an abstract class.

A derived class can override **new_expr()** and/or **clone()** to return an object of its own type:

```
class Cond : public Expr {
public:
    Cond();
    Cond(const Cond&);
    Cond* new_expr() override { return new Cond(); }
    Cond* clone() override { return new Cond(*this); }
    // ...
};
```

This means that given an object of class **Expr**, a user can create a new object of "just the same type." For example:

```
void user(Expr* p)
{
    Expr* p2 = p->new_expr();
    // ...
}
```

The pointer assigned to **p2** is declared to point to a "plain **Expr**," but it will point to an object of a type derived from **Expr**, such as **Cond**.

The return type of **Cond::new_expr()** and **Cond::clone()** is **Cond∗** rather than **Expr∗**. This allows a **Cond** to be cloned without loss of type information. Similarly, a derived class **Addition** would have a **clone()** returning a **Addition∗**. For example:

```
void user2(Cond* pc, Addition* pa)
{
    Cond* p1 = pc->clone();
    Addition* p2 = pa->clone();
    // ...
}
```

If we use **clone()** for an **Expr** we only know that the result is an **Expr∗**:

```
void user3(Cond* pc, Expr* pe)
{
    Cond* p1 = pc->clone();
    Cond* p2 = pe->clone();      // error: Expr::clone() returns an Expr*
    // ...
}
```

Because functions such as **new_expr()** and **clone()** are **virtual** and they (indirectly) construct objects, they are often called *virtual constructors*. Each simply uses a constructor to create a suitable object.

To make an object, a constructor needs the exact type of the object it is to create. Consequently, a constructor cannot be **virtual**. Furthermore, a constructor is not quite an ordinary function. In particular, it interacts with memory management routines in ways ordinary member functions don't. So, you cannot take a pointer to a constructor and pass that to an object creation function.

Both of these restrictions can be circumvented by defining a function that calls a constructor and returns a constructed object. This is fortunate because creating a new object without knowing its exact type is often useful. The **Ival_box_maker** (§21.2.4) is an example of a class designed specifically to do that.

20.4 Abstract Classes

Many classes resemble class **Employee** in that they are useful as themselves, as interfaces for derived classes, and as part of the implementation of derived classes. For such classes, the techniques described in §20.3.2 suffice. However, not all classes follow that pattern. Some classes, such as a class **Shape**, represent abstract concepts for which objects cannot exist. A **Shape** makes sense only as the base of some class derived from it. This can be seen from the fact that it is not possible to provide sensible definitions for its virtual functions:

```
class Shape {
public:
    virtual void rotate(int) { throw runtime_error{"Shape::rotate"}; }    // inelegant
    virtual void draw() const { throw runtime_error{"Shape::draw"}; }
    // ...
};
```

Trying to make a shape of this unspecified kind is silly but legal:

```
Shape s;  // silly: "shapeless shape"
```

It is silly because every operation on **s** will result in an error.

A better alternative is to declare the virtual functions of class **Shape** to be *pure virtual functions*. A virtual function is "made pure" by the "pseudo initializer" = **0**:

```
class Shape {        // abstract class
public:
    virtual void rotate(int) = 0;      // pure virtual function
    virtual void draw() const = 0;     // pure virtual function
    virtual bool is_closed() const = 0; // pure virtual function
    // ...
    virtual ˜Shape();                  // virtual
};
```

A class with one or more pure virtual functions is an *abstract class*, and no objects of that abstract class can be created:

```
Shape s;  // error: variable of abstract class Shape
```

An abstract class is intended as an interface to objects accessed through pointers and references (to preserve polymorphic behavior). Consequently, it is usually important for an abstract class to have a virtual destructor (§3.2.4, §21.2.2). Because the interface provided by an abstract class cannot be used to create objects using a constructor, abstract classes don't usually have constructors.

An abstract class can be used only as an interface to other classes. For example:

```
class Point { /* ... */ };

class Circle : public Shape {
public:
    void rotate(int) override { }
    void draw() const override;
    bool is_closed() const override { return true; }

    Circle(Point p, int r);
private:
    Point center;
    int radius;
};
```

A pure virtual function that is not defined in a derived class remains a pure virtual function, so the derived class is also an abstract class. This allows us to build implementations in stages:

```
class Polygon : public Shape {            // abstract class
public:
      bool is_closed() const override { return true; }
      // ... draw and rotate not overridden ...
};

      Polygon b {p1,p2,p3,p4};      // error: declaration of object of abstract class Polygon
```

Polygon is still abstract because we did not override **draw()** and **rotate()**. Only when that is done do we have a class from which we can create objects:

```
class Irregular_polygon : public Polygon {
      list<Point> lp;
public:
      Irregular_polygon(initializer_list<Point>);

      void draw() const override;
      void rotate(int) override;
      // ...
};

      Irregular_polygon poly {p1,p2,p3,p4};    // assume that p1 .. p4 are Points defined somewhere
```

An abstract class provides an interface without exposing implementation details. For example, an operating system might hide the details of its device drivers behind an abstract class:

```
class Character_device {
public:
      virtual int open(int opt) = 0;
      virtual int close(int opt) = 0;
      virtual int read(char* p, int n) = 0;
      virtual int write(const char* p, int n) = 0;
      virtual int ioctl(int ...) = 0;          // device I/O control

      virtual ~Character_device() { }      // virtual destructor
};
```

We can then specify drivers as classes derived from **Character_device** and manipulate a variety of drivers through that interface.

The design style supported by abstract classes is called *interface inheritance* in contrast to the *implementation inheritance* supported by base classes with state and/or defined member functions. Combinations of the two approaches are possible. That is, we can define and use base classes with both state and pure virtual functions. However, such mixtures of approaches can be confusing and require extra care.

With the introduction of abstract classes, we have the basic facilities for writing a complete program in a modular fashion using classes as building blocks.

20.5 Access Control

A member of a class can be **private**, **protected**, or **public**:

- If it is **private**, its name can be used only by member functions and friends of the class in which it is declared.
- If it is **protected**, its name can be used only by member functions and friends of the class in which it is declared and by member functions and friends of classes derived from this class (see §19.4).
- If it is **public**, its name can be used by any function.

This reflects the view that there are three kinds of functions accessing a class: functions implementing the class (its friends and members), functions implementing a derived class (the derived class's friends and members), and other functions. This can be presented graphically:

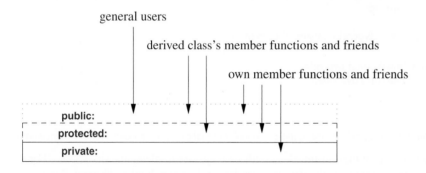

The access control is applied uniformly to names. What a name refers to does not affect the control of its use. This means that we can have **private** member functions, types, constants, etc., as well as **private** data members. For example, an efficient nonintrusive list class often requires data structures to keep track of elements. A list is *nonintrusive* if it does not require modification to its elements (e.g., by requiring element types to have link fields). The information and data structures used to organize the list can be kept **private**:

```
template<class T>
class List {
public:
    void insert(T);
    T get();
    // ...
private:
    struct Link { T val; Link* next; };

    struct Chunk {
        enum { chunk_size = 15 };
        Link v[chunk_size];
        Chunk* next;
    };
```

```
        Chunk* allocated;
        Link* free;
        Link* get_free();
        Link* head;
};
```

The definitions of the public functions are pretty strainghtforward:

```
template<class T>
void List<T>::insert(T val)
{
    Link* lnk = get_free();
    lnk->val = val;
    lnk->next = head;
    head = lnk;
}

template<class T>
T List<T>::get()
{
    if (head == 0)
            throw Underflow{};  // Underflow is my exception class

    Link* p= head;
    head = p->next;
    p->next = free;
    free = p;
    return p->val;
}
```

As is common, the definition of the supporting (here, private) functions are a bit more tricky:

```
template<class T>
typename List<T>::Link* List<T>::get_free()
{
    if (free == 0) {
            // ... allocate a new chunk and place its Links on the free list ...
    }
    Link* p = free;
    free = free->next;
    return p;
}
```

The **List\<T\>** scope is entered by saying **List\<T\>::** in a member function definition. However, because the return type of **get_free()** is mentioned before the name **List\<T\>::get_free()** is mentioned, the full name **List\<T\>::Link** must be used instead of the abbreviation **Link**. The alternative is to use the suffix notation for return types (§12.1.4):

```
template<class T>
auto List<T>::get_free() -> Link*
{
    // ...
}
```

Nonmember functions (except friends) do not have such access:

```
template<typename T>
void would_be_meddler(List<T>* p)
{
    List<T>::Link* q = 0;                    // error: List<T>::Link is private
    // ...
    q = p->free;                             // error: List<T>::free is private
    // ...
    if (List<T>::Chunk::chunk_size > 31) {   // error: List<T>::Chunk::chunk_size is private
        // ...
    }
}
```

In a **class**, members are by default **private**; in a **struct**, members are by default **public** (§16.2.4).

The obvious alternative to using a member type is to place the type in the surrounding namespace. For example:

```
template<class T>
struct Link2 {
    T val;
    Link2* next;
};

template<class T>
class List {
private:
    Link2<T>* free;
    // ...
};
```

Link is implicitly parameterized with **List<T>**'s parameter **T**. For **Link2**, we must make that explicit.

If a member type does not depend on all the template class's parameters, the nonmember version can be preferable; see §23.4.6.3.

If the nested class is not generally useful by itself and the enclosing class needs access to its representation, declaring the member class a **friend** (§19.4.2) may be a good idea:

```
template<class T> class List;

template<class T>
class Link3 {
    friend class List<T>;      // only List<T> can access Link<T>
    T val;
    Link3* next;
};
```

```
template<class T>
class List {
private:
    Link3<T>* free;
    // ...
};
```

A compiler may reorder sections of a class with separate access specifiers (§8.2.6). For example:

```
class S {
public:
    int m1;
public:
    int m2;
};
```

The compiler may decide for m2 to precede m1 in the layout of an S object. Such reordering could come as a surprise to the programmer and is implementation-dependent, so don't use multiple access specifiers for data members without good reason.

20.5.1 protected Members

When designing a class hierarchy, we sometimes provide functions designed to be used by implementers of derived classes but not by the general user. For example, we may provide an (efficient) unchecked access function for derived class implementers and (safe) checked access for others. Declaring the unchecked version **protected** achieves that. For example:

```
class Buffer {
public:
    char& operator[](int i);    // checked access
    // ...
protected:
    char& access(int i);        // unchecked access
    // ...
};

class Circular_buffer : public Buffer {
public:
    void reallocate(char* p, int s);        // change location and size
    // ...
};

void Circular_buffer::reallocate(char* p, int s)// change location and size
{
    // ...
    for (int i=0; i!=old_sz; ++i)
        p[i] = access(i);       // no redundant checking
    // ...
}
```

```
void f(Buffer& b)
{
    b[3] = 'b';          // OK (checked)
    b.access(3) = 'c';   // error: Buffer::access() is protected
}
```

For another example, see **Window_with_border** in §21.3.5.2.

A derived class can access a base class's protected members only for objects of its own type:

```
class Buffer {
protected:
    char a[128];
    // ...
};

class Linked_buffer : public Buffer {
    // ...
};

class Circular_buffer : public Buffer {
    // ...
    void f(Linked_buffer* p)
    {
        a[0] = 0;        // OK: access to Circular_buffer's own protected member
        p->a[0] = 0;     // error: access to protected member of different type
    }
};
```

This prevents subtle errors that would otherwise occur when one derived class corrupts data belonging to other derived classes.

20.5.1.1 Use of protected Members

The simple private/public model of data hiding serves the notion of concrete types (§16.3) well. However, when derived classes are used, there are two kinds of users of a class: derived classes and "the general public." The members and friends that implement the operations on the class operate on the class objects on behalf of these users. The private/public model allows the programmer to distinguish clearly between the implementers and the general public, but it does not provide a way of catering specifically to derived classes.

Members declared **protected** are far more open to abuse than members declared **private**. In particular, declaring data members **protected** is usually a design error. Placing significant amounts of data in a common class for all derived classes to use leaves that data open to corruption. Worse, protected data, like public data, cannot easily be restructured because there is no good way of finding every use. Thus, protected data becomes a software maintenance problem.

Fortunately, you don't have to use protected data; **private** is the default in classes and is usually the better choice. In my experience, there have always been alternatives to placing significant amounts of information in a common base class for derived classes to use directly.

However, none of these objections are significant for protected member *functions*; **protected** is a fine way of specifying operations for use in derived classes. The **Ival_slider** in §21.2.2 is an example of this. Had the implementation class been **private** in this example, further derivation would have been infeasible. On the other hand, making bases providing implementation details **public** invites mistakes and misuse.

20.5.2 Access to Base Classes

Like a member, a base class can be declared **private**, **protected**, or **public**. For example:

```
class X : public B { /* ... */ };
class Y : protected B { /* ... */ };
class Z : private B { /* ... */ };
```

The different access specifiers serve different design needs:
- **public** derivation makes the derived class a subtype of its base. For example, **X** is a kind of **B**. This is the most common form of derivation.
- **private** bases are most useful when defining a class by restricting the interface to a base so that stronger guarantees can be provided. For example, **B** is an implementation detail of **Z**. The **Vector** of pointers template that adds type checking to its **Vector<void∗>** base from §25.3 is a good example.
- **protected** bases are useful in class hierarchies in which further derivation is the norm. Like **private** derivation, **protected** derivation is used to represent implementation details. The **Ival_slider** from §21.2.2 is a good example.

The access specifier for a base class can be left out. In that case, the base defaults to a private base for a **class** and a public base for a **struct**. For example:

```
class XX : B { /* ... */ };    // B is a private base
struct YY : B { /* ... */ };   // B is a public base
```

People expect base classes to be **public** (that is, to express a subtype relationship), so the absence of an access specifier for a base is likely to be surprising for a **class** but not for a **struct**.

The access specifier for a base class controls the access to members of the base class and the conversion of pointers and references from the derived class type to the base class type. Consider a class **D** derived from a base class **B**:
- If **B** is a **private** base, its public and protected members can be used only by member functions and friends of **D**. Only friends and members of **D** can convert a **D∗** to a **B∗**.
- If **B** is a **protected** base, its public and protected members can be used only by member functions and friends of **D** and by member functions and friends of classes derived from **D**. Only friends and members of **D** and friends and members of classes derived from **D** can convert a **D∗** to a **B∗**.
- If **B** is a **public** base, its public members can be used by any function. In addition, its protected members can be used by members and friends of **D** and members and friends of classes derived from **D**. Any function can convert a **D∗** to a **B∗**.

This basically restates the rules for member access (§20.5). When designing a class, we choose access for bases in the same way as we do for members. For an example, see **Ival_slider** in §21.2.2.

20.5.2.1 Multiple Inheritance and Access Control

If the name of a base class can be reached through multiple paths in a multiple-inheritance lattice
(§21.3), it is accessible if it is accessible through any path. For example:

```
struct B {
    int m;
    static int sm;
    // ...
};

class D1 : public virtual B { /* ... */ } ;
class D2 : public virtual B { /* ... */ } ;
class D12 : public D1, private D2 { /* ... */ };

D12* pd = new D12;
B* pb = pd;          // OK: accessible through D1
int i1 = pd–>m;      // OK: accessible through D1
```

If a single entity is reachable through several paths, we can still refer to it without ambiguity. For
example:

```
class X1 : public B { /* ... */ } ;
class X2 : public B { /* ... */ } ;
class XX : public X1, public X2 { /* ... */ };

XX* pxx = new XX;
int i1 = pxx–>m;     // error, ambiguous: XX::X1::B::m or XX::X2::B::m?
int i2 = pxx–>sm;    // OK: there is only one B::sm in an XX (sm is a static member)
```

20.5.3 using-Declarations and Access Control

A **using**-declaration (§14.2.2, §20.3.5) cannot be used to gain access to additional information. It is
simply a mechanism for making accessible information more convenient to use. On the other hand,
once access is available, it can be granted to other users. For example:

```
class B {
private:
    int a;
protected:
    int b;
public:
    int c;
};

class D : public B {
public:
    using B::a;       // error: B::a is private
    using B::b;       // make B::b publicly available through D
};
```

When a **using**-declaration is combined with private or protected derivation, it can be used to specify interfaces to some, but not all, of the facilities usually offered by a class. For example:

```
class BB : private B {      // give access to B::b and B::c, but not B::a
public:
    using B::b;
    using B::c;
};
```

See also §20.3.5.

20.6 Pointers to Members

A pointer to member is an offset-like construct that allows a programmer to indirectly refer to a member of a class. The operators ->* and .* are arguably the most specialized and least used C++ operators. Using ->, we can access a member of a class, **m**, by naming it: **p->m**. Using ->*, we can access a member that (conceptually) has its name stored in a pointer to member, **ptom**: **p->*ptom**. This allows us to access members with their names passed as arguments. In both cases, **p** must be a pointer to an object of an appropriate class.

A pointer to member cannot be assigned to a **void**∗ or any other ordinary pointer. A null pointer (e.g., **nullptr**) can be assigned to a pointer to member and then represents "no member."

20.6.1 Pointers to Function Members

Many classes provide simple, very general interfaces intended to be invoked in several different ways. For example, many "object-oriented" user interfaces define a set of requests to which every object represented on the screen should be prepared to respond. In addition, such requests can be presented directly or indirectly from programs. Consider a simple variant of this idea:

```
class Std_interface {
public:
    virtual void start() = 0;
    virtual void suspend() = 0;
    virtual void resume() = 0;
    virtual void quit() = 0;
    virtual void full_size() = 0;
    virtual void small() = 0;

    virtual ~Std_interface() {}
};
```

The exact meaning of each operation is defined by the object on which it is invoked. Often, there is a layer of software between the person or program issuing the request and the object receiving it. Ideally, such intermediate layers of software should not have to know anything about the individual operations such as **resume()** and **full_size()**. If they did, the intermediate layers would have to be updated each time an operation changed. Consequently, such intermediate layers simply transmit data representing the operation to be invoked from the source of the request to its recipient.

One simple way of doing that is to send a **string** representing the operation to be invoked. For example, to invoke **suspend()** we could send the string **"suspend"**. However, someone has to create that string and someone has to decode it to determine to which operation it corresponds – if any. Often, that seems indirect and tedious. Instead, we might simply send an integer representing the operation. For example, **2** might be used to mean **suspend()**. However, while an integer may be convenient for machines to deal with, it can get pretty obscure for people. We still have to write code to determine that **2** means **suspend()** and to invoke **suspend()**.

However, we can use a pointer to member to indirectly refer to a member of a class. Consider **Std_interface**. If I want to invoke **suspend()** for some object without mentioning **suspend()** directly, I need a pointer to member referring to **Std_interface::suspend()**. I also need a pointer or reference to the object I want to suspend. Consider a trivial example:

```
using Pstd_mem = void (Std_interface::*)();   // pointer-to-member type

void f(Std_interface* p)
{
        Pstd_mem s = &Std_interface::suspend;     // pointer to suspend()
        p->suspend();                             // direct call
        p->*s();                                  // call through pointer to member
}
```

A *pointer to member* can be obtained by applying the address-of operator, **&**, to a fully qualified class member name, for example, **&Std_interface::suspend**. A variable of type "pointer to member of class **X**" is declared using a declarator of the form **X::***.

The use of an alias to compensate for the lack of readability of the C declarator syntax is typical. However, please note how the **X::*** declarator matches the traditional ***** declarator exactly.

A pointer to member **m** can be used in combination with an object. The operators **–>*** and **.*** allow the programmer to express such combinations. For example, **p->*m** binds **m** to the object pointed to by **p**, and **obj.*m** binds **m** to the object **obj**. The result can be used in accordance with **m**'s type. It is not possible to store the result of a **–>*** or a **.*** operation for later use.

Naturally, if we knew which member we wanted to call, we would invoke it directly rather than mess with pointers to members. Just like ordinary pointers to functions, pointers to member functions are used when we need to refer to a function without having to know its name. However, a pointer to member isn't a pointer to a piece of memory the way a pointer to a variable or a pointer to a function is. It is more like an offset into a structure or an index into an array, but of course an implementation takes into account the differences between data members, virtual functions, non-virtual functions, etc. When a pointer to member is combined with a pointer to an object of the right type, it yields something that identifies a particular member of a particular object.

The **p->*s()** call can be represented graphically like this:

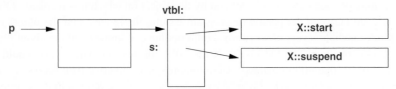

Because a pointer to a virtual member (**s** in this example) is a kind of offset, it does not depend on an object's location in memory. A pointer to a virtual member can therefore be passed between different address spaces as long as the same object layout is used in both. Like pointers to ordinary functions, pointers to non-virtual member functions cannot be exchanged between address spaces.

Note that the function invoked through the pointer to function can be **virtual**. For example, when we call **suspend()** through a pointer to function, we get the right **suspend()** for the object to which the pointer to function is applied. This is an essential aspect of pointers to functions.

When writing an interpreter, we might use pointers to members to invoke functions presented as strings:

```
map<string,Std_interface*> variable;
map<string,Pstd_mem> operation;

void call_member(string var, string oper)
{
    (variable[var]->*operation[oper])(); // var.oper()
}
```

A **static** member isn't associated with a particular object, so a pointer to a **static** member is simply an ordinary pointer. For example:

```
class Task {
    // ...
    static void schedule();
};

void (*p)() = &Task::schedule;          // OK
void (Task::* pm)() = &Task::schedule;  // error: ordinary pointer assigned
                                        // to pointer to member
```

Pointers to data members are described in §20.6.2.

20.6.2 Pointers to Data Members

Naturally, the notion of pointer to member applies to data members and to member functions with arguments and return types. For example:

```
struct C {
    const char* val;
    int i;

    void print(int x) { cout << val << x << '\n'; }
    int f1(int);
    void f2();
    C(const char* v) { val = v; }
};

using Pmfi = void (C::*)(int);   // pointer to member function of C taking an int
using Pm = const char* C::*;     // pointer to char* data member of C
```

```
void f(C& z1, C& z2)
{
    C* p = &z2;
    Pmfi pf = &C::print;
    Pm pm = &C::val;

    z1.print(1);
    (z1.*pf)(2);
    z1.*pm = "nv1 ";
    p->*pm = "nv2 ";
    z2.print(3);
    (p->*pf)(4);

    pf = &C::f1;      // error: return type mismatch
    pf = &C::f2;      // error: argument type mismatch
    pm = &C::i;       // error: type mismatch
    pm = pf;          // error: type mismatch
}
```

The type of a pointer to function is checked just like any other type.

20.6.3 Base and Derived Members

A derived class has at least the members that it inherits from its base classes. Often it has more. This implies that we can safely assign a pointer to a member of a base class to a pointer to a member of a derived class, but not the other way around. This property is often called *contravariance*. For example:

```
class Text : public Std_interface {
public:
    void start();
    void suspend();
    // ...
    virtual void print();
private:
    vector s;
};

void (Std_interface::* pmi)() = &Text::print;    // error
void (Text::*pmt)() = &Std_interface::start;     // OK
```

This contravariance rule appears to be the opposite of the rule that says we can assign a pointer to a derived class to a pointer to its base class. In fact, both rules exist to preserve the fundamental guarantee that a pointer may never point to an object that doesn't at least have the properties that the pointer promises. In this case, **Std_interface::*** can be applied to any **Std_interface**, and most such objects presumably are not of type **Text**. Consequently, they do not have the member **Text::print** with which we tried to initialize **pmi**. By refusing the initialization, the compiler saves us from a run-time error.

20.7 Advice

[1]   Avoid type fields; §20.3.1.
[2]   Access polymorphic objects through pointers and references; §20.3.2.
[3]   Use abstract classes to focus design on the provision of clean interfaces; §20.4.
[4]   Use **override** to make overriding explicit in large class hierarchies; §20.3.4.1.
[5]   Use **final** only sparingly; §20.3.4.2.
[6]   Use abstract classes to specify interfaces; §20.4.
[7]   Use abstract classes to keep implementation details out of interfaces; §20.4.
[8]   A class with a virtual function should have a virtual destructor; §20.4.
[9]   An abstract class typically doesn't need a constructor; §20.4.
[10]   Prefer **private** members for implementation details; §20.5.
[11]   Prefer **public** members for interfaces; §20.5.
[12]   Use **protected** members only carefully when really needed; §20.5.1.1.
[13]   Don't declare data members **protected**; §20.5.1.1.

21

Class Hierarchies

Abstraction is selective ignorance.
– Andrew Koenig

- Introduction
- Design of Class Hierarchies
    Implementation Inheritance; Interface Inheritance; Alternative Implementations; Localizing
    Object Creation
- Multiple Inheritance
    Multiple Interfaces; Multiple Implementation Classes; Ambiguity Resolution; Repeated Use
    of a Base Class; Virtual Base Classes; Replicated vs. Virtual Bases
- Advice

21.1 Introduction

The primary focus of this chapter is design techniques, rather than language features. The examples are taken from user-interface design, but I avoid the topic of event-driven programming as commonly used for graphical user interface (GUI) systems. A discussion of exactly how an action on the screen is transformed into a call of a member function would add little to the issues of class hierarchy design and has a huge potential for distraction: it is an interesting and important topic in its own right. For an understanding of GUI, have a look at one of the many C++ GUI libraries.

21.2 Design of Class Hierarchies

Consider a simple design problem: Provide a way for a program ("an application") to get an integer value from a user. This can be done in a bewildering number of ways. To insulate our program from this variety, and also to get a chance to explore the possible design choices, let us start by defining our program's model of this simple input operation.

The idea is to have a class **Ival_box** ("integer value input box") that knows what range of input values it will accept. A program can ask an **Ival_box** for its value and ask it to prompt the user if necessary. In addition, a program can ask an **Ival_box** if a user changed the value since the program last looked at it:

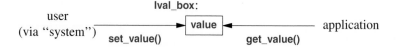

Because there are many ways of implementing this basic idea, we must assume that there will be many different kinds of **Ival_box**es, such as sliders, plain boxes in which a user can type a number, dials, and voice interaction.

The general approach is to build a "virtual user-interface system" for the application to use. This system provides some of the services provided by existing user-interface systems. It can be implemented on a wide variety of systems to ensure the portability of application code. Naturally, there are other ways of insulating an application from a user-interface system. I chose this approach because it is general, because it allows me to demonstrate a variety of techniques and design tradeoffs, because those techniques are also the ones used to build "real" user-interface systems, and – most important – because these techniques are applicable to problems far beyond the narrow domain of interface systems.

In addition to ignoring the topic of how to map user actions (events) to library calls, I also ignore the need for locking in a multi-threaded GUI system.

21.2.1 Implementation Inheritance

Our first solution is a class hierarchy using implementation inheritance (as is commonly found in older programs).

Class **Ival_box** defines the basic interface to all **Ival_box**es and specifies a default implementation that more specific kinds of **Ival_box**es can override with their own versions. In addition, we declare the data needed to implement the basic notion:

```
class Ival_box {
protected:
    int val;
    int low, high;
    bool changed {false};         // changed by user using set_value()
public:
    Ival_box(int ll, int hh) :val{ll}, low{ll}, high{hh} { }

    virtual int get_value() { changed = false; return val; }      // for application
    virtual void set_value(int i) { changed = true; val = i; }     // for user
    virtual void reset_value(int i) { changed = false; val = i; }  // for application
    virtual void prompt() { }
    virtual bool was_changed() const { return changed; }

    virtual ~Ival_box() {};
};
```

The default implementation of the functions is pretty sloppy and is provided here primarily to illustrate the intended semantics. A realistic class would, for example, provide some range checking.

A programmer might use these "ival classes" like this:

```
void interact(Ival_box* pb)
{
    pb->prompt(); // alert user
    // ...
    int i = pb->get_value();
    if (pb->was_changed()) {
        // ... new value; do something ...
    }
    else {
        // ... do something else ...
    }
}

void some_fct()
{
    unique_ptr<Ival_box> p1 {new Ival_slider{0,5}};     // Ival_slider derived from Ival_box
    interact(p1.get());

    unique_ptr<Ival_box> p2 {new Ival_dial{1,12}};
    interact(p2.get());
}
```

Most application code is written in terms of (pointers to) plain **Ival_box**es the way **interact()** is. That way, the application doesn't have to know about the potentially large number of variants of the **Ival_box** concept. The knowledge of such specialized classes is isolated in the relatively few functions that create such objects. This isolates users from changes in the implementations of the derived classes. Most code can be oblivious to the fact that there are different kinds of **Ival_box**es.

I use **unique_ptr** (§5.2.1, §34.3.1) to avoid forgetting to **delete** the ival_boxes.

To simplify the discussion, I do not address issues of how a program waits for input. Maybe the program really does wait for the user in **get_value()** (e.g., using a **get()** on a **future**; §5.3.5.1), maybe the program associates the **Ival_box** with an event and prepares to respond to a callback, or maybe the program spawns a thread for the **Ival_box** and later inquires about the state of that thread. Such decisions are crucial in the design of user-interface systems. However, discussing them here in any realistic detail would simply distract from the presentation of programming techniques and language facilities. The design techniques described here and the language facilities that support them are not specific to user interfaces. They apply to a far greater range of problems.

The different kinds of **Ival_box**es are defined as classes derived from **Ival_box**. For example:

```
class Ival_slider : public Ival_box {
private:
    // ... graphics stuff to define what the slider looks like, etc. ...
public:
    Ival_slider(int, int);
```

```
        int get_value() override;  // get value from user and deposit it in val
        void prompt() override;
};
```

The data members of **Ival_box** were declared **protected** to allow access from derived classes. Thus, **Ival_slider::get_value()** can deposit a value in **Ival_box::val**. A **protected** member is accessible from a class's own members and from members of derived classes, but not to general users (see §20.5).

In addition to **Ival_slider**, we would define other variants of the **Ival_box** concept. These could include **Ival_dial**, which lets you select a value by turning a knob; **Flashing_ival_slider**, which flashes when you ask it to **prompt()**; and **Popup_ival_slider**, which responds to **prompt()** by appearing in some prominent place, thus making it hard for the user to ignore.

From where would we get the graphics stuff? Most user-interface systems provide a class defining the basic properties of being an entity on the screen. So, if we use the system from "Big Bucks Inc.," we would have to make each of our **Ival_slider**, **Ival_dial**, etc., classes a kind of **BBwidget**. This would most simply be achieved by rewriting our **Ival_box** so that it derives from **BBwidget**. In that way, all our classes inherit all the properties of a **BBwidget**. For example, every **Ival_box** can be placed on the screen, obey the graphical style rules, be resized, be dragged around, etc., according to the standard set by the **BBwidget** system. Our class hierarchy would look like this:

```
class Ival_box : public BBwidget { /* ... */ };      // rewritten to use BBwidget
class Ival_slider : public Ival_box { /* ... */ };
class Ival_dial : public Ival_box { /* ... */ };
class Flashing_ival_slider : public Ival_slider { /* ... */ };
class Popup_ival_slider : public Ival_slider { /* ... */ };
```

or graphically:

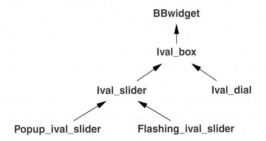

21.2.1.1 Critique

This design works well in many ways, and for many problems this kind of hierarchy is a good solution. However, there are some awkward details that could lead us to look for alternative designs.

We retrofitted **BBwidget** as the base of **Ival_box**. This is not quite right (even if this style is common in real-world systems). The use of **BBwidget** isn't part of our basic notion of an **Ival_box**; it is an implementation detail. Deriving **Ival_box** from **BBwidget** elevated an implementation detail to a first-level design decision. That can be right. For example, using the environment defined by "Big Bucks Inc." may be a key decision based on how our organization conducts its business. However, what if we also wanted to have implementations of our **Ival_boxes** for systems from "Imperial

Bananas," "Liberated Software," and "Compiler Whizzes"? We would have to maintain four distinct versions of our program:

```
class Ival_box : public BBwidget { /* ... */ };    // BB version
class Ival_box : public CWwidget { /* ... */ };    // CW version
class Ival_box : public IBwidget { /* ... */ };    // IB version
class Ival_box : public LSwindow { /* ... */ };    // LS version
```

Having many versions could result in a version control nightmare.

In reality, we are unlikely to find a simple, coherent, two-letter prefix scheme. More likely, the libraries from different purveyors would be in different namespaces and use different terminologies for similar concepts, such as **BigBucks::Widget**, **Wizzies::control**, and **LS::window**. But that does not affect our class hierarchy design discussion, so to simplify I ignore naming and namespace issues.

Another problem is that every derived class shares the basic data declared in **Ival_box**. That data is, of course, an implementation detail that also crept into our **Ival_box** interface. From a practical point of view, it is also the wrong data in many cases. For example, an **Ival_slider** doesn't need the value stored specifically. It can easily be calculated from the position of the slider when someone executes **get_value()**. In general, keeping two related, but different, sets of data is asking for trouble. Sooner or later someone will get them out of sync. Also, experience shows that novice programmers tend to mess with protected data in ways that are unnecessary and that cause maintenance problems. Data members are better kept private so that writers of derived classes cannot mess with them. Better still, data should be in the derived classes, where it can be defined to match requirements exactly and cannot complicate the life of unrelated derived classes. In almost all cases, a protected interface should contain only functions, types, and constants.

Deriving from **BBwidget** gives the benefit of making the facilities provided by **BBwidget** available to users of **Ival_box**. Unfortunately, it also means that changes to class **BBwidget** may force users to recompile or even rewrite their code to recover from such changes. In particular, the way most C++ implementations work implies that a change in the size of a base class requires a recompilation of all derived classes.

Finally, our program may have to run in a mixed environment in which windows of different user-interface systems coexist. This could happen either because two systems somehow share a screen or because our program needs to communicate with users on different systems. Having our user-interface systems "wired in" as the one and only base of our one and only **Ival_box** interface just isn't flexible enough to handle those situations.

21.2.2 Interface Inheritance

So, let's start again and build a new class hierarchy that solves the problems presented in the critique of the traditional hierarchy:

[1]   The user-interface system should be an implementation detail that is hidden from users who don't want to know about it.
[2]   The **Ival_box** class should contain no data.
[3]   No recompilation of code using the **Ival_box** family of classes should be required after a change of the user-interface system.
[4]   **Ival_box**es for different interface systems should be able to coexist in our program.

Several alternative approaches can be taken to achieve this. Here, I present one that maps cleanly into the C++ language.

First, I specify class **lval_box** as a pure interface:

```
class lval_box {
public:
        virtual int get_value() = 0;
        virtual void set_value(int i) = 0;
        virtual void reset_value(int i) = 0;
        virtual void prompt() = 0;
        virtual bool was_changed() const = 0;
        virtual ~lval_box() { }
};
```

This is much cleaner than the original declaration of **lval_box**. The data is gone and so are the simplistic implementations of the member functions. Gone, too, is the constructor, since there is no data for it to initialize. Instead, I added a virtual destructor to ensure proper cleanup of the data that will be defined in the derived classes.

The definition of **lval_slider** might look like this:

```
class lval_slider : public lval_box, protected BBwidget {
public:
        lval_slider(int,int);
        ~lval_slider() override;

        int get_value() override;
        void set_value(int i) override;
        // ...
protected:
        // ... functions overriding BBwidget virtual functions
        // e.g., BBwidget::draw(), BBwidget::mouse1hit() ...
private:
        // ... data needed for slider ...
};
```

The derived class **lval_slider** inherits from an abstract class (**lval_box**) that requires it to implement the base class's pure virtual functions. It also inherits from **BBwidget** which provides it with the means of doing so. Since **lval_box** provides the interface for the derived class, it is derived using **public**. Since **BBwidget** is only an implementation aid, it is derived using **protected** (§20.5.2). This implies that a programmer using **lval_slider** cannot directly use facilities defined by **BBwidget**. The interface provided by **lval_slider** is the one inherited from **lval_box**, plus what **lval_slider** explicitly declares. I used **protected** derivation instead of the more restrictive (and usually safer) **private** derivation to make **BBwidget** available to classes derived from **lval_slider**. I used explicit **override** because this "widget hierarchy" is exactly the kind of large, complicated hierarchy where being explicit can help minimize confusion.

Deriving directly from more than one class is usually called *multiple inheritance* (§21.3). Note that **lval_slider** must override functions from both **lval_box** and **BBwidget**. Therefore, it must be derived directly or indirectly from both. As shown in §21.2.1.1, deriving **lval_slider** indirectly from **BBwidget** by making **BBwidget** a base of **lval_box** is possible, but doing so has undesirable side effects. Similarly, making the "implementation class" **BBwidget** a member of **Ival_box** is not a solution because a class cannot override virtual functions of its members. Representing the window by a **BBwidget**∗ member in **Ival_box** leads to a completely different design with a separate set of tradeoffs.

To some people, the words "multiple inheritance" indicate something complicated and scary. However, the use of one base class for implementation details and another for interface (the abstract class) is common to all languages supporting inheritance and compile-time checked interfaces. In particular, the use of the abstract class **Ival_box** is almost identical to the use of an interface in Java or C#.

Interestingly, this declaration of **Ival_slider** allows application code to be written exactly as before. All we have done is to restructure the implementation details in a more logical way.

Many classes require some form of cleanup for an object before it goes away. Since the abstract class **Ival_box** cannot know if a derived class requires such cleanup, it must assume that it does require some. We ensure proper cleanup by defining a virtual destructor **Ival_box::˜Ival_box()** in the base and overriding it suitably in derived classes. For example:

```
void f(Ival_box∗ p)
{
    // ...
    delete p;
}
```

The **delete** operator explicitly destroys the object pointed to by **p**. We have no way of knowing exactly to which class the object pointed to by **p** belongs, but thanks to **Ival_box**'s virtual destructor, proper cleanup as (optionally) defined by that class' destructor will be done.

The **Ival_box** hierarchy can now be defined like this:

```
class Ival_box { /* ... */ };
class Ival_slider
    : public Ival_box, protected BBwidget { /* ... */ };
class Ival_dial
    : public Ival_box, protected BBwidget { /* ... */ };
class Flashing_ival_slider
    : public Ival_slider { /* ... */ };
class Popup_ival_slider
    : public Ival_slider { /* ... */ };
```

or graphically:

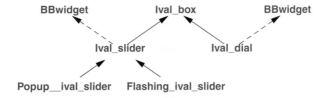

I used a dashed line to represent protected inheritance (§20.5.1). General users cannot access the protected bases because they are (correctly) considered part of the implementation.

21.2.3 Alternative Implementations

This design is cleaner and more easily maintainable than the traditional one – and no less efficient. However, it still fails to solve the version control problem:

```
class Ival_box { /* ... */ }; // common
class Ival_slider
    : public Ival_box, protected BBwidget { /* ... */ }; // for BB
class Ival_slider
    : public Ival_box, protected CWwidget { /* ... */ }; // for CW
// ...
```

There is no way of having the **Ival_slider** for **BBwidget**s coexist with the **Ival_slider** for **CWwidget**s, even if the two user-interface systems could themselves coexist. The obvious solution is to define several different **Ival_slider** classes with separate names:

```
class Ival_box { /* ... */ };
class BB_ival_slider
    : public Ival_box, protected BBwidget { /* ... */ };
class CW_ival_slider
    : public Ival_box, protected CWwidget { /* ... */ };
// ...
```

or graphically:

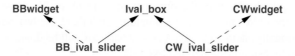

To further insulate our application-oriented **Ival_box** classes from implementation details, we can derive an abstract **Ival_slider** class from **Ival_box** and then derive the system-specific **Ival_slider**s from that:

```
class Ival_box { /* ... */ };
class Ival_slider
    : public Ival_box { /* ... */ };
class BB_ival_slider
    : public Ival_slider, protected BBwidget { /* ... */ };
class CW_ival_slider
    : public Ival_slider, protected CWwidget { /* ... */ };
// ...
```

or graphically:

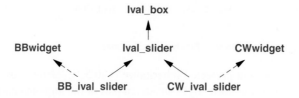

Usually, we can do better yet by utilizing more specific classes in the implementation hierarchy. For example, if the "Big Bucks Inc." system has a slider class, we can derive our **Ival_slider** directly from the **BBslider**:

```
class BB_ival_slider
    : public Ival_slider, protected BBslider { /* ... */ };
class CW_ival_slider
    : public Ival_slider, protected CWslider { /* ... */ };
```

or graphically:

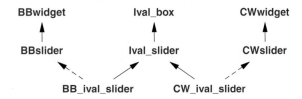

This improvement becomes significant where – as is not uncommon – our abstractions are not too different from the ones provided by the system used for implementation. In that case, programming is reduced to mapping between similar concepts. Derivation from general base classes, such as **BBwidget**, is then done only rarely.

The complete hierarchy will consist of our original application-oriented conceptual hierarchy of interfaces expressed as derived classes:

```
class Ival_box { /* ... */ };
class Ival_slider
    : public Ival_box { /* ... */ };
class Ival_dial
    : public Ival_box { /* ... */ };
class Flashing_ival_slider
    : public Ival_slider { /* ... */ };
class Popup_ival_slider
    : public Ival_slider { /* ... */ };
```

followed by the implementations of this hierarchy for various graphical user interface systems, expressed as derived classes:

```
class BB_ival_slider
    : public Ival_slider, protected BBslider { /* ... */ };
class BB_flashing_ival_slider
    : public Flashing_ival_slider, protected BBwidget_with_bells_and_whistles { /* ... */ };
class BB_popup_ival_slider
    : public Popup_ival_slider, protected BBslider { /* ... */ };
class CW_ival_slider
    : public Ival_slider, protected CWslider { /* ... */ };
// ...
```

Using obvious abbreviations, this hierarchy can be represented graphically like this:

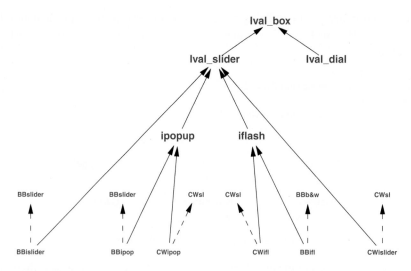

The original **lval_box** class hierarchy appears unchanged surrounded by implementation classes.

21.2.3.1 Critique

The abstract class design is flexible and almost as simple to deal with as the equivalent design that relies on a common base defining the user-interface system. In the latter design, the windows class is the root of a tree. In the former, the original application class hierarchy appears unchanged as the root of classes that supply its implementations. From the application's point of view, these designs are equivalent in the strong sense that almost all code works unchanged and in the same way in the two cases. In either case, you can look at the **lval_box** family of classes without bothering with the window-related implementation details most of the time. For example, we would not need to re-write **interact()** from §21.2.1 if we switched from one class hierarchy to the other.

In either case, the implementation of each **lval_box** class must be rewritten when the public interface of the user-interface system changes. However, in the abstract class design, almost all user code is protected against changes to the implementation hierarchy and requires no recompilation after such a change. This is especially important when the supplier of the implementation hierarchy issues a new "almost compatible" release. In addition, users of the abstract class hierarchy are in less danger of being locked into a proprietary implementation than are users of a classical hierarchy. Users of the **lval_box** abstract class application hierarchy cannot accidentally use facilities from the implementation because only facilities explicitly specified in the **lval_box** hierarchy are accessible; nothing is implicitly inherited from an implementation-specific base class.

The logical conclusion of this line of thought is a system represented to users as a hierarchy of abstract classes and implemented by a classical hierarchy. In other words:

- Use abstract classes to support interface inheritance (§3.2.3, §20.1).
- Use base classes with implementations of virtual functions to support implementation inheritance (§3.2.3, §20.1).

21.2.4 Localizing Object Creation

Most of an application can be written using the Ival_box interface. Further, should the derived interfaces evolve to provide more facilities than plain Ival_box, then most of an application can be written using the Ival_box, Ival_slider, etc., interfaces. However, the creation of objects must be done using implementation-specific names such as CW_ival_dial and BB_flashing_ival_slider. We would like to minimize the number of places where such specific names occur, and object creation is hard to localize unless it is done systematically.

As usual, the solution is to introduce an indirection. This can be done in many ways. A simple one is to introduce an abstract class to represent the set of creation operations:

```
class Ival_maker {
public:
    virtual Ival_dial* dial(int, int) =0;                // make dial
    virtual Popup_ival_slider* popup_slider(int, int) =0;   // make popup slider
    // ...
};
```

For each interface from the Ival_box family of classes that a user should know about, class Ival_maker provides a function that makes an object. Such a class is sometimes called a *factory*, and its functions are (somewhat misleadingly) sometimes called *virtual constructors* (§20.3.6).

We now represent each user-interface system by a class derived from Ival_maker:

```
class BB_maker : public Ival_maker {        // make BB versions
public:
    Ival_dial* dial(int, int) override;
    Popup_ival_slider* popup_slider(int, int) override;
    // ...
};
```

```
class LS_maker : public Ival_maker {        // make LS versions
public:
    Ival_dial* dial(int, int) override;
    Popup_ival_slider* popup_slider(int, int) override;
    // ...
};
```

Each function creates an object of the desired interface and implementation type. For example:

```
Ival_dial* BB_maker::dial(int a, int b)
{
    return new BB_ival_dial(a,b);
}
```

```
Ival_dial* LS_maker::dial(int a, int b)
{
    return new LS_ival_dial(a,b);
}
```

Given an Ival_maker, a user can now create objects without having to know exactly which user-interface system is used. For example:

```
void user(lval_maker& im)
{
    unique_ptr<lval_box> pb {im.dial(0,99)};        // create appropriate dial
    // ...
}

BB_maker BB_impl;        // for BB users
LS_maker LS_impl;        // for LS users

void driver()
{
    user(BB_impl);        // use BB
    user(LS_impl);        // use LS
}
```

Passing arguments to such "virtual constructors" is a bit tricky. In particular, we cannot override the base class functions that represent the interface with different arguments in different derived classes. This implies that a fair bit of foresight is required to design the factory class's interface.

21.3 Multiple Inheritance

As described in §20.1, inheritance aims to provide one of two benefits:

- *Shared interfaces*: leading to less replication of code using classes and making such code more uniform. This is often called *run-time polymorphism* or *interface inheritance*.
- *Shared implementation*: leading to less code and more uniform implementation code. This is often called *implementation inheritance*.

A class can combine aspects of these two styles.

Here, we explore more general uses of multiple base classes and examine more technical issues related to combining and accessing features from multiple base classes.

21.3.1 Multiple Interfaces

An abstract class (e.g., lval_box; §21.2.2) is the obvious way to represent an interface. For an abstract class without mutable state, there really is little difference between single and multiple uses of a base class in a class hierarchy. The resolution of potential ambiguities is discussed in §21.3.3, §21.3.4, and §21.3.5. In fact, any class without mutable state can be used as an interface in a multiple-inheritance lattice without significant complications and overhead. The key observation is that a class without mutable state can be replicated if necessary or shared if that is desired.

The use of multiple abstract classes as interfaces is almost universal in object-oriented designs (in any language with a notion of an interface).

21.3.2 Multiple Implementation Classes

Consider a simulation of bodies orbiting the Earth in which orbiting objects are represented as object of class Satellite. A Satellite object would contain orbital, size, shape, albedo, density parameters, etc., and provide operations for orbital calculations, modifying attributes, etc. Examples of satellites would be rocks, debris from old space vehicles, communication satellites, and the International Space Station. These kinds of satellites would be objects of classes derived from **Satellite**. Such derived classes would add data members and functions and would override some of **Satellite**'s virtual functions to adjust their meaning suitably.

Now assume that I want to display the results of these simulations graphically and that I had available a graphics system that used the (not uncommon) strategy of deriving objects to be displayed from a common base class holding graphical information. This graphics class would provide operations for placement on the screen, scaling, etc. For generality, simplicity, and to hide the details of the actual graphics system, I will refer to the class providing graphical (or in fact alternatively nongraphical) output **Display**.

We can now define a class of simulated communication satellites, class **Comm_sat**:

```
class Comm_sat : public Satellite, public Displayed {
public:
        // ...
};
```

or graphically:

In addition to whatever operations are defined specifically for a **Comm_sat**, the union of operations on **Satellite** and **Displayed** can be applied. For example:

```
void f(Comm_sat& s)
{
        s.draw();              // Displayed::draw()
        Pos p = s.center();    // Satellite::center()
        s.transmit();          // Comm_sat::transmit()
}
```

Similarly, a **Comm_sat** can be passed to a function that expects a **Satellite** and to a function that expects **Displayed**. For example:

```
void highlight(Displayed*);
Pos center_of_gravity(const Satellite*);

void g(Comm_sat* p)
{
        highlight(p);                   // pass a pointer to the Displayed part of the Comm_sat
        Pos x = center_of_gravity(p);   // pass a pointer to the Satellite part of the Comm_sat
}
```

The implementation of this clearly involves some (simple) compiler technique to ensure that functions expecting a **Satellite** see a different part of a **Comm_sat** than do functions expecting a **Displayed**. Virtual functions work as usual. For example:

```
class Satellite {
public:
        virtual Pos center() const = 0;        // center of gravity
        // ...
};

class Displayed {
public:
        virtual void draw() = 0;
        // ...
};

class Comm_sat : public Satellite, public Displayed {
public:
        Pos center() const override;    // override Satellite::center()
        void draw() override;           // override Displayed::draw()
        // ...
};
```

This ensures that **Comm_sat::center()** and **Displayed::draw()** will be called for a **Comm_sat** treated as a **Comm_sat** and a **Displayed**, respectively.

Why didn't I just keep the **Satellite** and **Displayed** parts of a **Comm_sat** completely separate? I could have defined **Comm_sat** to have a **Satellite** member and a **Displayed** member. Alternatively, I could have defined **Comm_sat** to have a **Satellite**∗ member and a **Displayed**∗ member and let its constructor set up the proper connections. For many design problems, I would do just that. However, the system that inspired this example was built on the idea of a **Satellite** class with virtual functions and a (separately designed) **Displayed** class with virtual functions. You provided your own satellites and your own displayed objects through derivation. In particular, you had to override **Satellite** virtual member functions and **Displayed** virtual member functions to specify the behavior of your own objects. That is the situation in which multiple inheritance of base classes with state and implementation is hard to avoid. Workarounds can be painful and hard to maintain.

The use of multiple inheritance to "glue" two otherwise unrelated classes together as part of the implementation of a third class is crude, effective, and relatively important, but not very interesting. Basically, it saves the programmer from writing a lot of forwarding functions (to compensate for the fact that we can only override functions defined in bases). This technique does not affect the overall design of a program significantly and can occasionally clash with the wish to keep implementation details hidden. However, a technique doesn't have to be clever to be useful.

I generally prefer to have a single implementation hierarchy and (where needed) several abstract classes providing interfaces. This is typically more flexible and leads to systems that are easier to evolve. However, you can't always get that – especially if you need to use existing classes that you don't want to modify (e.g., because they are parts of someone else's library).

Note that with single inheritance (only), the programmer's choices for implementing the classes **Displayed**, **Satellite**, and **Comm_sat** would be limited. A **Comm_sat** could be a **Satellite** or a **Displayed**, but not both (unless **Satellite** was derived from **Displayed** or vice versa). Either alternative involves a loss of flexibility.

Why would anyone want a class **Comm_sat**? Contrary to some people's conjectures, the **Satellite** example is real. There really was – and maybe there still is – a program constructed along the lines used to describe multiple implementation inheritance here. It was used to study the design of communication systems involving satellites, ground stations, etc. In fact, **Satellite** was derived from an early notion of a concurrent task. Given such a simulation, we can answer questions about communication traffic flow, determine proper responses to a ground station that is being blocked by a rainstorm, consider tradeoffs between satellite connections and Earth-bound connections, etc.

21.3.3 Ambiguity Resolution

Two base classes may have member functions with the same name. For example:

```
class Satellite {
public:
    virtual Debug_info get_debug();
    // ...
};

class Displayed {
public:
    virtual Debug_info get_debug();
    // ...
};
```

When a **Comm_sat** is used, these functions must be disambiguated. This can be done simply by qualifying a member name by its class name:

```
void f(Comm_sat& cs)
{
    Debug_info di = cs.get_debug();      // error: ambiguous
    di = cs.Satellite::get_debug();      // OK
    di = cs.Displayed::get_debug();      // OK
}
```

However, explicit disambiguation is messy, so it is usually best to resolve such problems by defining a new function in the derived class:

```
class Comm_sat : public Satellite, public Displayed {
public:
    Debug_info get_debug() // override Comm_sat::get_debug() and Displayed::get_debug()
    {
        Debug_info di1 = Satellite::get_debug();
        Debug_info di2 = Displayed::get_debug();
        return merge_info(di1,di2);
    }
    // ...
};
```

A function declared in a derived class overrides *all* functions of the same name and type in its base classes. Typically, that is exactly the right thing to do because it is generally a bad idea to use the same name for operations with different semantics in a single class. The ideal for **virtual** is for a call to have the same effect independently of which interface was used to find the function (§20.3.2).

In the implementation of an overriding function, it is often necessary to explicitly qualify the name to get the right version from a base class. A qualified name, such as **Telstar::draw**, can refer to a **draw** declared either in **Telstar** or in one of its base classes. For example:

```
class Telstar : public Comm_sat {
public:
    void draw()
    {
        Comm_sat::draw();          // finds Displayed::draw
        // ... own stuff ...
    }
    // ...
};
```

or graphically:

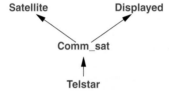

If **Comm_sat::draw** doesn't resolve to a **draw** declared in **Comm_sat**, the compiler recursively looks in its base classes; that is, it looks for **Satellite::draw** and **Displayed::draw**, and if necessary looks in their base classes. If exactly one match is found, that name will be used. Otherwise, **Comm_sat::draw** is either not found or is ambiguous.

If, in **Telstar::draw()**, I had said plain **draw()**, the result would have been an "infinite" recursive call of **Telstar::draw()**.

I could have said **Displayed::draw()**, but now the code would be subtly broken if someone added a **Comm_sat::draw()**; it is generally better to refer to a direct base class than to an indirect base class. I could have said **Comm_sat::Displayed::draw()**, but that would have been redundant. Had I said **Satellite::draw()**, the result would have been an error because the **draw** is over on the **Displayed** branch of the class hierarchy.

The **get_debug()** example basically assumes that at least some parts of **Satellite** and **Displayed** have been designed together. Getting an exact match of names, return types, argument types, and semantics by accident is extremely unlikely. It is far more likely that similar functionality is provided in different ways so that it takes effort to merge it into something that can be used together. We might originally have been presented with two classes **SimObj** and **Widget** that we could not modify, didn't exactly provide what we needed, and where they did provide what we needed, did so through incompatible interfaces. In that case, we might have designed **Satellite** and **Displayed** as our interface classes, providing a "mapping layer" for our higher-level classes to use:

```
class Satellite : public SimObj {
    // map SimObj facilities to something easier to use for Satellite simulation
public:
    virtual Debug_info get_debug();     // call SimObj::DBinf() and extract information
    // ...
};
```

```
class Displayed : public Widget {
    // map Widget facilities to something easier to use to display Satellite simulation results
public:
    virtual Debug_info get_debug();     // read Widget data and compose Debug_info
    // ...
};
```

or graphically:

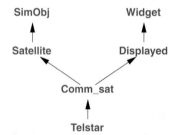

Interestingly enough, this is exactly the technique we would use to disambiguate in the unlikely case where two base classes provided operations with exactly the same name, but with different semantics: add an interface layer. Consider the classical (but mostly hypothetical/theoretical) example of a class of a **draw()** member function in a video game involving cowboys:

```
class Window {
public:
    void draw();     // display image
    // ...
};
```

```
class Cowboy {
public:
    void draw();     // pull gun from holster
    // ...
};
```

```
class Cowboy_window : public Cowboy, public Window {
    // ...
};
```

How do we override **Cowboy::draw()** and **Window::draw()**? These two functions have radically different meanings (semantics) but are identical in name and type; we need to override them by two separate functions. There is no direct language solution to this (exotic) problem, but adding inter-mediate classes will do:

```
struct WWindow : Window {
    using Window::Window;              // inherit constructors
    virtual void win_draw() = 0;       // force derived class to override
    void draw() override final { win_draw(); }   // display image
};

struct CCowboy : Cowboy{
    using Cowboy::Cowboy;              // inherit constructors
    virtual void cow_draw() = 0;       // force derived class to override
    void draw() override final { cow_draw(); }   // pull gun from holster
};

class Cowboy_window : public CCowboy, public WWindow {
public:
    void cow_draw() override;
    void win_draw() override;
    // ...
};
```

Or graphically:

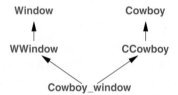

Had the designer of Window been a bit more careful and specified draw() to be const, the whole problem would have evaporated. I find that fairly typical.

21.3.4 Repeated Use of a Base Class

When each class has only one direct base class, the class hierarchy will be a tree, and a class can only occur once in the tree. When a class can have multiple base classes, a class can appear multiple times in the resulting hierarchy. Consider a class providing facilities for storing state in a file (e.g., for breakpointing, debug information, or persistence) and restoring it later:

```
struct Storable {      // persistent storage
    virtual string get_file() = 0;
    virtual void read() = 0;
    virtual void write() = 0;

    virtual ~Storable() { }
};
```

Such a useful class will naturally be used in several places in a class hierarchy. For example:

```
class Transmitter : public Storable {
public:
    void write() override;
    // ...
};

class Receiver : public Storable {
public:
    void write() override;
    // ...
};

class Radio : public Transmitter, public Receiver {
public:
    string get_file() override;
    void read() override;
    void write() override;
    // ...
};
```

Given that, we could imagine two cases:

[1]   A **Radio** object has two subobjects of class **Storable** (one for **Transmitter** and one for **Receiver**).

[2]   A **Radio** object has one subobject of class **Storable** (shared by **Transmitter** and **Receiver**).

The default, provided for the example as written, is two subobjects. Unless you state otherwise, you get one copy for each time you mention a class as a base. Graphically, we can represent that like this:

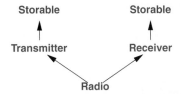

A virtual function of a replicated base class can be overridden by a (single) function in a derived class. Typically, an overriding function calls its base class versions and then does the work specific to the derived class:

```
void Radio::write()
{
    Transmitter::write();
    Receiver::write();
    // ... write radio-specific information ...
}
```

Casting from a replicated base class to a derived class is discussed in §22.2. For a technique for overriding each of the **write()** functions with separate functions from derived classes, see §21.3.3.

21.3.5 Virtual Base Classes

The **Radio** example in the previous subsection works because class **Storable** can be safely, conveniently, and efficiently replicated. The reason for that is simply that **Storable** is an abstract class providing a pure interface. A **Storable** object holds no data of its own. This is the simplest case and the one that offers the best separation of interface and implementation concerns. In fact, a class could not without some difficulty determine that there were two **Storable** subobjects on a **Radio**.

What if **Storable** did hold data and it was important that it should not be replicated? For example, we might define **Storable** to hold the name of the file to be used for storing the object:

```
class Storable {
public:
    Storable(const string& s);      // store in file named s
    virtual void read() = 0;
    virtual void write() = 0;
    virtual ˜Storable();
protected:
    string file_name;

    Storable(const Storable&) = delete;
    Storable& operator=(const Storable&) = delete;
};
```

Given this apparently minor change to **Storable**, we must change the design of **Radio**. All parts of an object must share a single copy of **Storable**. Otherwise, we could get two parts of something derived from **Storable** multiple times using different files. We avoid replication by declaring a base **virtual**: every **virtual** base of a derived class is represented by the same (shared) object. For example:

```
class Transmitter : public virtual Storable {
public:
    void write() override;
    // ...
};

class Receiver : public virtual Storable {
public:
    void write() override;
    // ...
};

class Radio : public Transmitter, public Receiver {
public:
    void write() override;
    // ...
};
```

Or graphically:

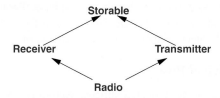

Compare this diagram with the drawing of the **Storable** object in §21.3.4 to see the difference between ordinary inheritance and virtual inheritance. In an inheritance graph, every base class of a given name that is specified to be **virtual** will be represented by a single object of that class. On the other hand, each base class not specified **virtual** will have its own subobject representing it.

Why would someone want to use a virtual base containing data? I can think of three obvious ways for two classes in a class hierarchy to share data:

[1]   Make the data nonlocal (outside the class as a global or namespace variable).

[2]   Put the data in a base class.

[3]   Allocate an object somewhere and give each of the two classes a pointer.

Option [1], nonlocal data, is usually a poor choice because we cannot control what code accesses the data and how. It breaks all notions of encapsulation and locality.

Option [2], put the data in a base class, is usually the simplest. However, for single inheritance that solution makes useful data (and functions) "bubble up" to a common base class; often it "bubbles" all the way to the root of an inheritance tree. This means that every member of the class hierarchy gets access. That is logically very similar to using nonlocal data and suffers from the same problems. So we need a common base that is not the root of a tree – that is, a virtual base.

Option [3], sharing an object accessed through pointers, makes sense. However, then constructor(s) need to set aside memory for that shared object, initialize it, and provide pointers to the shared object to objects needing access. That is roughly what constructors do to implement a virtual base.

If you don't need sharing, you can do without virtual bases, and your code is often better and typically simpler for it. However, if you do need sharing within a general class hierarchy, you basically have a choice between using a virtual base and laboriously constructing your own variants of the idea.

We can represent an object of a class with a virtual base like this:

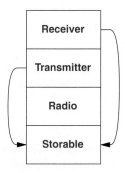

The "pointers" to the shared object representing the virtual base, **Storable**, will be offsets, and often one of those can be optimized away by placing **Storable** in a fixed position relative to either the **Receiver** or the **Transmitter** subobject. Expect a storage overhead of one word for each virtual base.

21.3.5.1 Constructing Virtual Bases

Using virtual bases you can create complicated lattices. Naturally, we would prefer to keep the lattices simple, but however complicated we make them, the language ensures that a constructor of a virtual base is called exactly once. Furthermore, the constructor of a base (whether virtual or not) is called before its derived classes. Anything else would cause chaos (that is, an object might be used before it had been initialized). To avoid such chaos, the constructor of every virtual base is invoked (implicitly or explicitly) from the constructor for the complete object (the constructor for the most derived class). In particular, this ensures that a virtual base is constructed exactly once even if it is mentioned in many places in the class hierarchy. For example:

```
struct V {
    V(int i);
    // ...
};

struct A {
    A();        // default constructor
    // ...
};

struct B : virtual V, virtual A {
    B() :V{1} { /* ... */ };   // default constructor; must initialize base V
    // ...
};

class C : virtual V {
public:
    C(int i) : V{i} { /* ... */ };    // must initialize base V
    // ...
};

class D : virtual public B, virtual public C {
    // implicitly gets the virtual base V from B and C
    // implicitly gets virtual base A from B
public:
    D() { /* ... */ }                   // error: no default constructor for C or V
    D(int i) :C{i} { /* ... */ };       // error: no default constructor for V
    D(int i, int j) :V{i}, C{j} { /* ... */ }    // OK
    // ...
};
```

Note that **D** can and must provide an initializer for **V**. The fact that **V** wasn't explicitly mentioned as a base of **D** is irrelevant. Knowledge of a virtual base and the obligation to initialize it "bubbles up" to the most derived class. A virtual base is always considered a direct base of its most derived class. The fact that both **B** and **C** initialized **V** is irrelevant because the compiler has no idea which of those two initializers to prefer. Thus, only the initializer provided by the most derived class is used.

The constructor for a virtual base is called before the constructors for its derived classes.

In practice, this is not quite as localized as we would prefer. In particular, if we derive another class, **DD**, from **D**, then **DD** has to do work to initialize the virtual bases. Unless we can simply inherit **D**'s constructors (§20.3.5.1), that can be a nuisance. That ought to encourage us not to overuse virtual base classes.

This logical problem with constructors does not exist for destructors. They are simply invoked in reverse order of construction (§20.2.2). In particular, a destructor for a virtual base is invoked exactly once.

21.3.5.2 Calling a Virtual Class Member Once Only

When defining the functions for a class with a virtual base, the programmer in general cannot know whether the base will be shared with other derived classes. This can be a problem when implementing a service that requires a base class function to be called exactly once for each call of a derived function. Where needed, the programmer can simulate the scheme used for constructors by calling a virtual base class function only from the most derived class. For example, assume we have a basic **Window** class that knows how to draw its contents:

```
class Window {
public:
    // basic stuff
    virtual void draw();
};
```

In addition, we have various ways of decorating a window and adding facilities:

```
class Window_with_border : public virtual Window {
    // border stuff
protected:
    void own_draw();    // display the border
public:
    void draw() override;
};

class Window_with_menu : public virtual Window {
    // menu stuff
protected:
    void own_draw();    // display the menu
public:
    void draw() override;
};
```

The **own_draw()** functions need not be **virtual** because they are meant to be called from within a virtual **draw()** function that "knows" the type of the object for which it was called.

From this, we can compose a plausible **Clock** class:

```
class Clock : public Window_with_border, public Window_with_menu {
    // clock stuff
protected:
    void own_draw();    // display the clock face and hands
public:
    void draw() override;
};
```

or graphically:

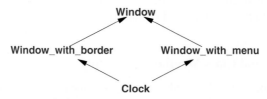

The **draw()** functions can now be defined using the **own_draw()** functions, so that a caller of any **draw()** gets **Window::draw()** invoked exactly once. This is done independently of the kind of **Window** for which **draw()** is invoked:

```
void Window_with_border::draw()
{
    Window::draw();
    own_draw();    // display the border
}

void Window_with_menu::draw()
{
    Window::draw();
    own_draw();    // display the menu
}

void Clock::draw()
{
    Window::draw();
    Window_with_border::own_draw();
    Window_with_menu::own_draw();
    own_draw();    // display the clock face and hands
}
```

Note that a qualified call, such as **Window::draw()**, does not use the virtual call mechanism. Instead, it directly calls the explicitly named function, thus avoiding nasty infinite recursion.

Casting from a virtual base class to a derived class is discussed in §22.2.

21.3.6 Replicated vs. Virtual Bases

Using multiple inheritance to provide implementations for abstract classes representing pure interfaces affects the way a program is designed. Class **BB_ival_slider** (§21.2.3) is an example:

```
class BB_ival_slider
    : public Ival_slider,      // interface
        protected BBslider     // implementation
{
    // implementation of functions required by Ival_slider and BBslider, using facilities from BBslider
};
```

In this example, the two base classes play logically distinct roles. One base is a public abstract class providing the interface, and the other is a protected concrete class providing implementation "details." These roles are reflected in both the style of the classes and in the access control (§20.5) provided. The use of multiple inheritance is close to essential here because the derived class needs to override virtual functions from both the interface and the implementation.

For example, consider again the **Ival_box** classes from §21.2.1. In the end (§21.2.2), I made all the **Ival_box** classes abstract to reflect their role as pure interfaces. Doing that allowed me to place all implementation details in specific implementation classes. Also, all sharing of implementation details was done in the classical hierarchy of the windows system used for the implementation.

When using an abstract class (without any shared data) as an interface, we have a choice:

- Replicate the interface class (one object per mention in the class hierarchy).
- Make the interface class **virtual** to share a simple object among all classes in the hierarchy that mention it.

Using **Ival_slider** as a virtual base gives us:

```
class BB_ival_slider
    : public virtual Ival_slider, protected BBslider { /* ... */ };
class Popup_ival_slider
    : public virtual Ival_slider { /* ... */ };
class BB_popup_ival_slider
    : public virtual Popup_ival_slider, protected BB_ival_slider { /* ... */ };
```

or graphically:

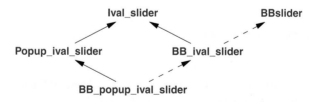

It is easy to imagine further interfaces derived from **Popup_ival_slider** and further implementation classes derived from such classes and **BB_popup_ival_slider**.

However, we also have this alternative using replicated **Ival_slider** objects:

```
class BB_ival_slider
    : public Ival_slider, protected BBslider { /* ... */ };
class Popup_ival_slider
    : public Ival_slider { /* ... */ };
class BB_popup_ival_slider
    : public Popup_ival_slider, protected BB_ival_slider { /* ... */ };
```

or graphically:

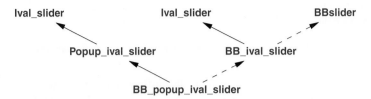

Surprisingly, there are no fundamental run-time or space advantages to one design over the other. There are logical differences, though. In the replicated **Ival_slider** design, a **BB_popup_ival_slider** can't be implicitly converted to an **Ival_slider** (because that would be ambiguous):

```
void f(Ival_slider* p);

void g(BB_popup_ival_slider* p)
{
        f(p); // error: Popup_ival_slider::Ival_slider or BB_ival_slider::Ival_slider?
}
```

On the other hand, it is possible to construct plausible scenarios where the sharing implied in the virtual base design causes ambiguities for casts *from* the base class (§22.2). However, such ambiguities are easily dealt with.

How do we choose between virtual base classes and replicated base classes for our interfaces? Most often, of course, we don't get a choice because we have to conform to an existing design. When we do have a choice, we can take into account that (surprisingly) the replicated base solution tends to lead to slightly smaller objects (because there is no need for data structures supporting sharing) and that we often get our interface objects from "virtual constructors" or "factory functions" (§21.2.4). For example:

```
Popup_ival_slider* popup_slider_factory(args)
{
        // ...
        return new BB_popup_ival_slider(args);
        // ...
}
```

No explicit conversion is needed to get from an implementation (here, **BB_popup_ival_slider**) to its direct interfaces (here, **Popup_ival_slider**).

21.3.6.1 Overriding Virtual Base Functions

A derived class can override a virtual function of its direct or indirect virtual base class. In particular, two different classes might override different virtual functions from the virtual base. In that way, several derived classes can contribute implementations to the interface presented by a virtual base class. For example, the **Window** class might have functions **set_color()** and **prompt()**. In that case, **Window_with_border** might override **set_color()** as part of controlling the color scheme, and **Window_with_menu** might override **prompt()** as part of its control of user interactions:

```
class Window {
    // ...
    virtual void set_color(Color) = 0;        // set background color
    virtual void prompt() = 0;
};

class Window_with_border : public virtual Window {
    // ...
    void set_color(Color) override;           // control background color
};

class Window_with_menu : public virtual Window {
    // ...
    void prompt() override;                    // control user interactions
};

class My_window : public Window_with_menu, public Window_with_border {
    // ...
};
```

What if different derived classes override the same function? This is allowed if and only if some overriding class is derived from every other class that overrides the function. That is, one function must override all others. For example, **My_window** could override **prompt()** to improve on what **Window_with_menu** provides:

```
class My_window : public Window_with_menu, public Window_with_border {
    // ...
    void prompt() override;   // don't leave user interactions to base
};
```

or graphically:

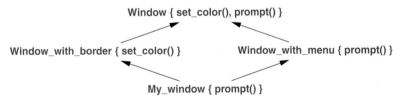

If two classes override a base class function, but neither overrides the other, the class hierarchy is an error. The reason is that no single function can be used to give a consistent meaning for all calls independently of which class they use as an interface. Or, using implementation terminology, no virtual function table can be constructed because a call to that function on the complete object would be ambiguous. For example, had **Radio** in §21.3.5 not declared **write()**, the declarations of **write()** in **Receiver** and **Transmitter** would have caused an error when defining **Radio**. As with **Radio**, such a conflict is resolved by adding an overriding function to the most derived class.

A class that provides some – but not all – of the implementation for a virtual base class is often called a *mixin*.

21.4 Advice

[1]   Use **unique_ptr** or **shared_ptr** to avoid forgetting to **delete** objects created using **new**; §21.2.1.
[2]   Avoid date members in base classes intended as interfaces; §21.2.1.1.
[3]   Use abstract classes to express interfaces; §21.2.2.
[4]   Give an abstract class a virtual destructor to ensure proper cleanup; §21.2.2.
[5]   Use **override** to make overriding explicit in large class hierarchies; §21.2.2.
[6]   Use abstract classes to support interface inheritance; §21.2.2.
[7]   Use base classes with data members to support implementation inheritance; §21.2.2.
[8]   Use ordinary multiple inheritance to express a union of features; §21.3.
[9]   Use multiple inheritance to separate implementation from interface; §21.3.
[10]   Use a virtual base to represent something common to some, but not all, classes in a hierarchy; §21.3.5.

22

Run-Time Type Information

Premature optimization
is the root of all evil.
– Donald Knuth

On the other hand,
we cannot ignore efficiency.
– Jon Bentley

22.1 Introduction

In general, a class is constructed from a lattice of base classes. Such a *class lattice* is often called a *class hierarchy*. We try to design classes so that users need not be unduly concerned about the way a class is composed out of other classes. In particular, the virtual call mechanism ensures that when we call a function f() on an object, the same function is called whichever class in the hierarchy provided the declaration of f() used for the call and whichever class defined it. This chapter explains how to gain information about the total object given only the interface provided by a base class.

22.2 Class Hierarchy Navigation

A plausible use of the **Ival_box**es defined in §21.2 would be to hand them to a system that controlled a screen and have that system hand objects back to the application program whenever some activity had occurred. We will refer to the combination of GUI library and operating system facilities that control the screen as *the system*. Objects passed back and forth between the system and the application are commonly referred to as *widgets* or *controls*. This is how many user interfaces work. From a language point of view, it is important that the system does not know about our **Ival_box**es. The system's interfaces are specified in terms of the system's own classes and objects rather than our application's classes. This is necessary and proper. However, it does have the unpleasant effect that we lose information about the type of objects passed to the system and later returned to us.

Recovering the "lost" type of an object requires us to somehow ask the object to reveal its type. Any operation on an object requires us to have a pointer or reference of a suitable type for the object. Consequently, the most obvious and useful operation for inspecting the type of an object at run time is a type conversion operation that returns a valid pointer if the object is of the expected type and a null pointer if it isn't. The **dynamic_cast** operator does exactly that. For example, assume that "the system" invokes **my_event_handler()** with a pointer to a **BBwindow**, where an activity has occurred. I then might invoke my application code using **Ival_box**'s **do_something()**:

```
void my_event_handler(BBwindow* pw)
{
    if (auto pb = dynamic_cast<Ival_box*>(pw)) { // does pw point to an Ival_box?
        // ...
        int x = pb->get_value();  // use the Ival_box
        // ...
    }
    else {
        // ... oops! cope with unexpected event ...
    }
}
```

One way of explaining what is going on here is that **dynamic_cast** translates from the implementation-oriented language of the user-interface system to the language of the application. It is important to note what is *not* mentioned in this example: the actual type of the object. The object will be a particular kind of **Ival_box**, say, an **Ival_slider**, implemented by a particular kind of **BBwindow**, say, a **BBslider**. It is neither necessary nor desirable to make the actual type of the object explicit in this interaction between "the system" and the application. An interface exists to represent the essentials of an interaction. In particular, a well-designed interface hides inessential details.

Graphically, the action of **pb=dynamic_cast<Ival_box*>(pw)** can be represented like this:

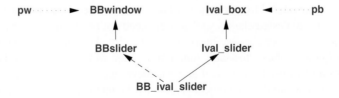

The arrows from **pw** and **pb** represent the pointers into the object passed, whereas the rest of the arrows represent the inheritance relationships between the different parts of the object passed.

The use of type information at run time is conventionally referred to as "run-time type information," often abbreviated to RTTI.

Casting from a base class to a derived class is often called a *downcast* because of the convention of drawing inheritance trees growing from the root down. Similarly, a cast from a derived class to a base is called an *upcast*. A cast that goes from a base to a sibling class, like the cast from **BBwindow** to **lval_box**, is called a *crosscast*.

22.2.1 dynamic_cast

The **dynamic_cast** operator takes two operands: a type bracketed by < and >, and a pointer or reference bracketed by (and). Consider first the pointer case:

```
dynamic_cast<T*>(p)
```

If **p** is of type **T**∗ or of a type **D**∗ where **T** is a base class of **D**, the result is exactly as if we had simply assigned **p** to a **T**∗. For example:

```
class BB_ival_slider : public lval_slider, protected BBslider {
    // ...
};

void f(BB_ival_slider* p)
{
    lval_slider* pi1 = p;                                    // OK
    lval_slider* pi2 = dynamic_cast<lval_slider*>(p);       // OK

    BBslider* pbb1 = p;                                     // error: BBslider is a protected base
    BBslider* pbb2 = dynamic_cast<BBslider*>(p);           // OK: pbb2 becomes nullptr
}
```

This (the upcast) is the uninteresting case. However, it is reassuring to know that **dynamic_cast** doesn't allow accidental violation of the protection of private and protected base classes. Since a **dynamic_cast** used as an upcast is *exactly* like a simple assignment, it implies no overhead and is sensitive to its lexical context.

The purpose of **dynamic_cast** is to deal with the case in which the correctness of the conversion cannot be determined by the compiler. In that case, **dynamic_cast<T*>(p)** looks at the object pointed to by **p** (if any). If that object is of class **T** or has a unique base class of type **T**, then **dynamic_cast** returns a pointer of type **T**∗ to that object; otherwise, **nullptr** is returned. If the value of **p** is **nullptr**, **dynamic_cast<T*>(p)** returns **nullptr**. Note the requirement that the conversion must be to a uniquely identified object. It is possible to construct examples where the conversion fails and **nullptr** is returned because the object pointed to by **p** has more than one subobject representing bases of type **T** (§22.2).

A **dynamic_cast** requires a pointer or a reference to a polymorphic type in order to do a downcast or a crosscast. For example:

```
class My_slider: public Ival_slider {        // polymorphic base (Ival_slider has virtual functions)
    // ...
};

class My_date : public Date {                // base not polymorphic (Date has no virtual functions)
    // ...
};

void g(Ival_box* pb, Date* pd)
{
    My_slider* pd1 = dynamic_cast<My_slider*>(pb);       // OK
    My_date* pd2 = dynamic_cast<My_date*>(pd);           // error: Date not polymorphic
}
```

Requiring the pointer's type to be polymorphic simplifies the implementation of **dynamic_cast** because it makes it easy to find a place to hold the necessary information about the object's type. A typical implementation will attach a "type information object" (§22.5) to an object by placing a pointer to the type information in the virtual function table for the object's class (§3.2.3). For example:

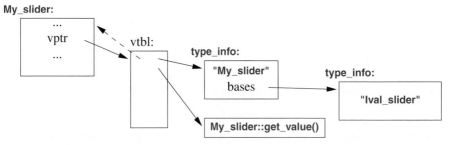

The dashed arrow represents an offset that allows the start of the complete object to be found given only a pointer to a polymorphic subobject. It is clear that **dynamic_cast** can be efficiently implemented. All that is involved are a few comparisons of **type_info** objects representing base classes; no expensive lookups or string comparisons are needed.

Restricting **dynamic_cast** to polymorphic types also makes sense from a logical point of view. That is, if an object has no virtual functions, it cannot safely be manipulated without knowledge of its exact type. Consequently, care should be taken not to get such an object into a context in which its type isn't known. If its type *is* known, we don't need to use **dynamic_cast**.

The target type of **dynamic_cast** need not be polymorphic. This allows us to wrap a concrete type in a polymorphic type, say, for transmission through an object I/O system (§22.2.4), and then "unwrap" the concrete type later. For example:

```
class Io_obj {              // base class for object I/O system
    virtual Io_obj* clone() = 0;
};
```

```
class lo_date : public Date, public lo_obj { };

void f(lo_obj* pio)
{
    Date* pd = dynamic_cast<Date*>(pio);
    // ...
}
```

A **dynamic_cast** to **void*** can be used to determine the address of the beginning of an object of polymorphic type. For example:

```
void g(Ival_box* pb, Date* pd)
{
    void* pb2 = dynamic_cast<void*>(pb);   // OK
    void* pd2 = dynamic_cast<void*>(pd);   // error: Date not polymorphic
}
```

The object representing a base class, such as **Ival_box**, in a derived class object is not necessarily the first subobject in that object of the most derived class. So, **pb** does not necessarily hold the same address as **pb2**.

Such casts are only useful for interaction with very low-level functions (only such functions deal with **void***s). There is no **dynamic_cast** from **void*** (because there would be no way of knowing where to find the **vptr**; §22.2.3).

22.2.1.1 dynamic_cast to Reference

To get polymorphic behavior, an object must be manipulated through a pointer or a reference. When a **dynamic_cast** is used for a pointer type, a **nullptr** indicates failure. That is neither feasible nor desirable for references.

Given a pointer result, we must consider the possibility that the result is **nullptr**, that is, that the pointer doesn't point to an object. Consequently, the result of a **dynamic_cast** of a pointer should always be explicitly tested. For a pointer **p**, **dynamic_cast<T*>(p)** can be seen as the question "Is the object pointed to by **p**, if any, of type **T**?" For example:

```
void fp(Ival_box* p)
{
    if (Ival_slider* is = dynamic_cast<Ival_slider*>(p)) {     // does p point to an Ival_slider?
        // ... use is ...
    }
    else {
        // ... *p not a slider; handle alternatives ...
    }
}
```

On the other hand, we may legitimately assume that a reference refers to an object (§7.7.4). Consequently, **dynamic_cast<T&>(r)** of a reference **r** is not a question but an assertion: "The object referred to by **r** is of type **T**." The result of a **dynamic_cast** for a reference is implicitly tested by the implementation of **dynamic_cast** itself. If the operand of a **dynamic_cast** to a reference isn't of the expected type, a **bad_cast** exception is thrown. For example:

```
void fr(lval_box& r)
{
      lval_slider& is = dynamic_cast<lval_slider&>(r);          // r references an lval_slider!
      // ... use is ...
}
```

The difference in results of a failed dynamic pointer cast and a failed dynamic reference cast reflects a fundamental difference between references and pointers. If a user wants to protect against bad casts to references, a suitable handler must be provided. For example:

```
void g(BB_ival_slider& slider, BB_ival_dial& dial)
{
      try {
            fp(&slider);       // pointer to BB_ival_slider passed as lval_box*
            fr(slider);        // reference to BB_ival_slider passed as lval_box&
            fp(&dial);         // pointer to BB_ival_dial passed as lval_box*
            fr(dial);          // dial passed as lval_box
      }
      catch (bad_cast) {  // §30.4.1.1
            // ...
      }
}
```

The calls to **fp()** and the first call to **fr()** will return normally (assuming that **fp()** really can cope with a **BB_ival_dial**), but the second call of **fr()** will cause a **bad_cast** exception that will be caught by **g()**.

Explicit tests against **nullptr** can easily be accidentally omitted. If that worries you, you can write a conversion function that throws an exception instead of returning **nullptr** in case of failure.

22.2.2 Multiple Inheritance

When only single inheritance is used, a class and its base classes constitute a tree rooted in a single base class. This is simple but often constraining. When multiple inheritance is used, there is no single root. In itself, this doesn't complicate matters much. However, if a class appears more than once in a hierarchy, we must be a bit careful when we refer to the object or objects that represent that class.

Naturally, we try to keep hierarchies as simple as our application allows (and no simpler). However, once a nontrivial hierarchy has been constructed, we sometimes need to navigate it to find a specific class to use. This need occurs in two variants:

- Sometimes, we want to explicitly name a base class for use as an interface, for example, to resolve an ambiguity or to call a specific function without relying on the virtual function mechanism (an explicitly qualified call; §21.3.3).
- Sometimes, we want to obtain a pointer to a subobject of a hierarchy given a pointer to another, for example, to get a pointer to the complete derived class object from a pointer to a base (a downcast; §22.2.1) or to get a pointer to a base class object from a pointer to another base (a crosscast; §22.2.4).

Here, we consider how to navigate a class hierarchy using type conversions (casts) to gain a pointer of the desired type. To illustrate the mechanisms available and the rules that guide them, consider a lattice containing both a replicated base and a virtual base:

```
class Component
    : public virtual Storable { /* ... */ };
class Receiver
    : public Component { /* ... */ };
class Transmitter
    : public Component { /* ... */ };
class Radio
    : public Receiver, public Transmitter { /* ... */ };
```

or graphically:

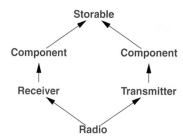

Here, a **Radio** object has two subobjects of class **Component**. Consequently, a **dynamic_cast** from **Storable** to **Component** within a **Radio** will be ambiguous and return a **0**. There is simply no way of knowing which **Component** the programmer wanted:

```
void h1(Radio& r)
{
    Storable* ps = &r;   // a Radio has a unique Storable
    // ...
    Component* pc = dynamic_cast<Component*>(ps);          // pc = 0; a Radio has two Components
    // ...
}
```

In general – and typically – a programmer (and a compiler looking at a single translation unit) does not know the complete class lattice. Instead, code is written with the knowledge of some sublattice. For example, a programmer might know only about the **Transmitter** part of a **Radio** and write:

```
void h2(Storable* ps)        // ps might or might not point to a Component
{
    if (Component* pc = dynamic_cast<Component*>(ps)) {
        // we have a component!
    }
    else {
        // it wasn't a Component
    }
}
```

The ambiguity for a pointer to a **Radio** object is not in general detectable at compile time.

This kind of run-time ambiguity detection is needed only for virtual bases. For ordinary bases, there is always a unique subobject of a given cast (or none) when downcasting (that is, toward a derived class; §22.2). The equivalent ambiguity for virtual bases occurs when upcasting (that is, toward a base), but such ambiguities are caught at compile time.

22.2.3 static_cast and dynamic_cast

A **dynamic_cast** can cast from a polymorphic virtual base class to a derived class or a sibling class (§22.2.1). A **static_cast** (§11.5.2) does not examine the object it casts from, so it cannot:

```
void g(Radio& r)
{
    Receiver* prec = &r;                        // Receiver is an ordinary base of Radio
    Radio* pr = static_cast<Radio*>(prec);      // OK, unchecked
    pr = dynamic_cast<Radio*>(prec);            // OK, run-time checked

    Storable* ps = &r;                          // Storable is a virtual base of Radio
    pr = static_cast<Radio*>(ps);               // error: cannot cast from virtual base
    pr = dynamic_cast<Radio*>(ps);              // OK, run-time checked
}
```

The **dynamic_cast** requires a polymorphic operand because there is no information stored in a non-polymorphic object that can be used to find the objects for which it represents a base. In particular, an object of a type with layout constraints determined by some other language – such as Fortran or C – may be used as a virtual base class. For objects of such types, only static type information will be available. However, the information needed to provide run-time type identification includes the information needed to implement the **dynamic_cast**.

Why would anyone want to use a **static_cast** for class hierarchy navigation? There is a run-time cost associated with the use of a **dynamic_cast** (§22.2.1). More significantly, there are millions of lines of code that were written before **dynamic_cast** became available. This code relies on alternative ways of making sure that a cast is valid, so the checking done by **dynamic_cast** is seen as redundant. However, such code is typically written using the C-style cast (§11.5.3); often obscure errors remain. Where possible, use the safer **dynamic_cast**.

The compiler cannot assume anything about the memory pointed to by a **void***. This implies that **dynamic_cast** – which must look into an object to determine its type – cannot cast from a **void***. For that, a **static_cast** is needed. For example:

```
Radio* f1(void* p)
{
    Storable* ps = static_cast<Storable*>(p);   // trust the programmer
    return dynamic_cast<Radio*>(ps);
}
```

Both **dynamic_cast** and **static_cast** respect **const** and access controls. For example:

```
class Users : private set<Person> { /* ... */ };

void f2(Users* pu, const Receiver* pcr)
{
    static_cast<set<Person>*>(pu);              // error: access violation
    dynamic_cast<set<Person>*>(pu);             // error: access violation
```

```
        static_cast<Receiver*>(pcr);           // error: can't cast away const
        dynamic_cast<Receiver*>(pcr);          // error: can't cast away const

        Receiver* pr = const_cast<Receiver*>(pcr);   // OK
        // ...
    }
```

It is not possible to cast to a private base class using **static_cast** or **reinterpret_cast**, and "casting away **const**" (or **volatile**) requires a **const_cast** (§11.5.2). Even then, using the result is safe only provided the object wasn't originally declared **const** (or **volatile**) (§16.2.9).

22.2.4 Recovering an Interface

From a design perspective, **dynamic_cast** (§22.2.1) can be seen as a mechanism for asking an object if it provides a given interface.

As an example, consider a simple object I/O system. Users want to read objects from a stream, determine that they are of the expected types, and then use them. For example:

```
    void user()
    {
        // ... open file assumed to hold shapes, and attach ss as an istream for that file ...

        unique_ptr<Io_obj> p {get_obj(ss)}; // read object from stream

        if (auto sp = dynamic_cast<Shape*>(p.get())) {
            sp->draw();     // use the Shape
            // ...
        }
        else {
            // oops: non-shape in Shape file
        }
    }
```

The function **user()** deals with shapes exclusively through the abstract class **Shape** and can therefore use every kind of shape. The use of **dynamic_cast** is essential because the object I/O system can deal with many other kinds of objects, and the user may accidentally have opened a file containing perfectly good objects of classes that the user has never heard of.

I used **unique_ptr<Io_obj>** (§5.2.1, §34.3.1) so that I would not forget to delete the object allocated by **get_obj()**.

This object I/O system assumes that every object read or written is of a class derived from **Io_obj**. Class **Io_obj** must be a polymorphic type to allow the user of **get_obj()** to use **dynamic_cast** to recover the "true type" of a returned object. For example:

```
    class Io_obj {
    public:
        virtual Io_obj* clone() const =0;    // polymorphic
        virtual ~Io_obj() {}
    };
```

The critical function in the object I/O system is **get_obj()**, which reads data from an **istream** and creates class objects based on that data. Assume that the data representing an object on an input stream is prefixed by a string identifying the object's class. The job of **get_obj()** is to read that string and call a function capable of reading and creating an object of the right class. For example:

```
using Pf = Io_obj*(istream&);          // pointer to function returning an Io_obj*

map<string,Pf> io_map;                 // maps strings to creation functions

string get_word(istream& is);          // read a word from is; throw Read_error if the read failed

Io_obj* get_obj(istream& is)
{
        string str = get_word(is);     // read initial word
        if (auto f = io_map[str])      // look up str to get function
                return f(is);          // call function
        throw Unknown_class{};         // no match for str
}
```

The **map** called **io_map** holds pairs of name strings and functions that can construct objects of the class with that name.

We could derive class **Shape** from **Io_obj** as needed by **user()**:

```
class Shape : public Io_obj {
        // ...
};
```

However, it would be more interesting (and in many cases more realistic) to use an already defined **Shape** (§3.2.4) unchanged:

```
struct Io_circle : Circle, Io_obj {
        Io_circle(istream&);                                            // initialize from input stream
        Io_circle* clone() const { return new Io_circle{*this}; }       // use copy constructor
        static Io_obj* new_circle(istream& is) { return new Io_circle{is}; } // for io_map
};
```

This is an example of how a class can be fitted into a hierarchy using an abstract class with less foresight than would have been required to build it as a node class in the first place (§21.2.2).

The **Io_circle(istream&)** constructor initializes an object with data from its **istream** argument. The **new_circle()** function is the one put into the **io_map** to make the class known to the object I/O system. For example:

```
io_map["Io_circle"]=&Io_circle::new_circle;  // somewhere
```

Other shapes are constructed in the same way:

```
class Io_triangle : public Triangle, public Io_obj {
        // ...
};
```

```
io_map["Io_triangle"]=&Io_circle::new_triangle;  // somewhere
```

If the provision of the object I/O scaffolding becomes tedious, a template might help:

```
template<class T>
struct Io : T, Io_obj {
public:
    Io(istream&);                                          // initialize from input stream
    Io* clone() const override { return new Io{*this}; }
    static Io* new_io(istream& is) { return new Io{is}; }  // for io_map
};
```

Given this, we can define Io_circle:

```
using Io_circle = Io<Circle>;
```

We still need to define Io<Circle>::Io(istream&) explicitly, though, because it needs to know about the details of Circle. Note that Io<Circle>::Io(istream&) does not have access to T's private or protected data. The idea is that the transmission format for a type X is what is needed to construct an X using one of X's constructors. The information of the stream is not necessarily the sequence of X's member values.

The Io template is an example of a way to fit concrete types into a class hierarchy by providing a handle that is a node in that hierarchy. It derives from its template parameter to allow casting from Io_obj. For example:

```
void f(Io<Shape>& ios)
{
    Shape* ps = &ios;
    // ...
}
```

Unfortunately, deriving from the template argument precludes using Io for a built-in type:

```
using Io_date = Io<Date>;      // wrap concrete type
using Io_int = Io<int>;        // error: cannot derive from built-in type
```

This problem can be handled by making the user's object a member of Io_obj:

```
template<class T>
struct Io :Io_obj {
    T val;

    Io(istream&);                                          // initialize from input stream
    Io* clone() const override { return new Io{*this}; }
    static Io* new_io(istream& is) { return new Io{is}; }  // for io_map
};
```

Now we can handle

```
using Io_int = Io<int>;        // wrap built-in type
```

Having made the value a member rather than a base, we can no longer directly cast an Io_obj<X> to an X, so we provide a function to do that:

```
template<typename T>
T* get_val<T>(lo_obj* p)
{
    if (auto pp = dynamic_cast<lo<T>*>(p))
        return &pp->val;
    return nullptr;
}
```

The user() function now becomes:

```
void user()
{
    // ... open file assumed to hold shapes, and attach ss as an istream for that file ...

    unique_ptr<lo_obj> p {get_obj(ss)}; // read object from stream

    if (auto sp = get_val<Shape>(p.get())) {
        sp->draw();    // use the Shape
        // ...
    }
    else {
        // ... oops: cope with non-shape in Shape file ...
    }
}
```

This simple object I/O system does not do everything anyone ever wanted, but it almost fits on a single page and the key mechanisms have many uses. It is a blueprint for the "receiver end" of a system for transmitting arbitrary objects across a communication channel in a type-safe manner. More generally, these techniques can be used to invoke a function based on a string supplied by a user and to manipulate objects of unknown type through interfaces discovered through run-time type identification.

In general, the sender part of such an object I/O system will also use RTTI. Consider:

```
class Face : public Shape {
public:
    Shape* outline;
    array<Shape*> eyes;
    Shape* mouth;

    // ...
};
```

To correctly write out the **Shape** pointed to by **outline**, we need to figure out which kind of **Shape** it is. That's a job for **typeid()** (§22.5). In general, we must also keep a table of (pointer,unique identifier) pairs to be able to transmit linked data structures and to avoid duplicating objects pointed to by more than one pointer (or reference).

22.3   Double Dispatch and Visitors

Classical object-oriented programming is based on selecting a virtual function based on the dynamic type (the type of the most derived class) of an object given only a pointer or a reference to an interface (a base class). In particular, C++ can do this run-time lookup (also called a *dynamic dispatch*) for one type at a time. In this, C++ resembles Simula and Smalltalk and more recent languages, such as Java and C#. Not being able to select a function based on two dynamic types can be a serious limitation. Also, a virtual function must be a member function. This implies that we cannot add a virtual function to a class hierarchy without modifying the base class(es) that provides the interface and all derived classes that should be affected. This too can be a serious problem. This section describes the basic workarounds for these problems:

§22.3.1   *Double Dispatch* shows how to select a virtual function based on two types.

§22.3.2   *Visitors* shows how to use double dispatch to add multiple functions to a class hierarchy with only a single additional virtual function in the hierarchy.

Most realistic examples of these techniques occur when we deal with data structures, such as vectors or graphs or pointers to objects of polymorphic types. In such cases, the actual type of an object (e.g., a vector element or a graph node) can only be known dynamically by (implicitly or explicitly) inspecting the interface provided by a base class.

22.3.1   Double Dispatch

Consider how to select a function based on two arguments. For example:

```
void do_someting(Shape& s1, Shape& s2)
{
    if (s1.intersect(s2)) {
        // the two shapes overlap
    }
    // ...
}
```

We would like this to work for any two classes in the class hierarchy rooted in **Shape**, such as **Circle** and **Triangle**.

The basic strategy is to do a virtual function call to select the right function for **s1** and then do a second call to select the right function for **s2**. To simplify, I will leave out the calculation of whether the two shapes actually intersect and just write the code skeleton for selecting the right functions. First we define **Shape** with a function for intersection:

```
class Circle;
class Triangle;

class Shape {
public:
    virtual bool intersect(const Shape&) const =0;
    virtual bool intersect(const Circle&) const =0;
    virtual bool intersect(const Triangle&) const =0;
};
```

Next we need to define **Circle** and **Triangle** to override those virtual functions:

```
class Circle : public Shape {
public:
     bool intersect(const Shape&) const override;
     virtual bool intersect(const Circle&) const override;
     virtual bool intersect(const Triangle&) const override
};

class Triangle : public Shape {
public:
     bool intersect(const Shape&) const override;
     virtual bool intersect(const Circle&) const override;
     virtual bool intersect(const Triangle&) const override;
};
```

Now each class can handle all possible classes in the **Shape** hierarchy, so we just have to decide what should be done for each combination:

```
bool Circle::intersect(const Shape& s) const { return s.intersect(*this); }
bool Circle::intersect(const Circle&) const { cout <<"intersect(circle,circle)\n"; return true; }
bool Circle::intersect(const Triangle&) const { cout <<"intersect(circle,triangle)\n"; return true; }

bool Triangle::intersect(const Shape& s) const { return s.intersect(*this); }
bool Triangle::intersect(const Circle&) const { cout <<"intersect(triangle,circle)\n"; return true; }
bool Triangle::intersect(const Triangle&) const { cout <<"intersect(triangle,triangle)\n"; return true; }
```

The interesting functions here are **Circle::intersect(const Shape&)** and **Triangle::intersect(const Shape&)**. These need to handle a **Shape&** argument because that argument must refer to a derived class. The trick/technique is to simply do a virtual call with the arguments in the reverse order. That done, we are in one of the four functions that can actually do an intersection calculation.

We can test this by making a **vector** of all pairs of **Shape∗** values and calling **intersect()** for those:

```
void test(Triangle& t, Circle& c)
{
     vector<pair<Shape*,Shape*>> vs { {&t,&t}, {&t,&c}, {&c,&t}, {&c,&c} };
     for (auto p : vs)
          p.first->intersect(*p.second);
}
```

Using **Shape∗**s ensures that we rely on run-time resolution of the types. We get:

```
intersect(triangle,triangle)
intersect(triangle,circle)
intersect(circle,triangle)
intersect(circle,circle)
```

If you consider this elegant, you need to raise your standards, but it gets the task done. As the class hierarchy grows, the need for virtual functions grows exponentially. That is not acceptable in most cases. Expanding this to three or more arguments is trivial, but tedious. Worst of all, each new operation and each new derived class require a modification to every class in the hierarchy: this double-dispatch technique is highly intrusive. Ideally, I would have preferred a simple **inter-cept(Shape&,Shape&)** function with overriders specified for the desired combinations of particular shapes. That is possible [Pirkelbauer,2009], but not in C++11.

The awkwardness of double dispatch does not make the problem it is trying to address less important. It is not unusual to want an action, such as **intersect(x,y)**, that depends on the types of two (or more) operands. Workarounds abound. For example, finding the intersection of rectangles is simple and efficient. So, for many applications, people have found it sufficient to define a "bounding box" for each shape and then calculate intersections on bounding boxes. For example:

```
class Shape {
public:
        virtual Rectangle box() const = 0;        // the rectangle encloses the shape
        // ...
};

class Circle : public Shape {
public:
        Rectangle box() const override;
        // ...
};

class Triangle : public Shape {
public:
        Rectangle box() const override;
        // ...
};

bool intersect(const Rectangle&, const Rectangle&);        // simple to calculate

bool intersect(const Shape& s1, const Shape& s2)
{
        return intersect(s1.box(),s2.box());
}
```

Another technique is to precompute a lookup table for combinations of types [Stroustrup,1994]:

```
bool intersect(const Shape& s1, const Shape& s2)
{
        auto i = index(type_id(s1),type_id(s2));
        return intersect_tbl[i](s1,s2);
}
```

Variations of this idea are widely used. Many variants use precomputed values stored in objects to speed up type identification (§27.4.2).

22.3.2 Visitors

The visitor pattern [Gamma,1994] is a partial solution to the exponential growth of virtual functions and overriders and the unpleasant intrusiveness of the (too) simple double-dispatch technique.

Consider how to apply two (or more) operations to every class in a class hierarchy. Basically, we will do a double dispatch for a hierarchy of nodes and a hierarchy of operations to select the correct operation for the correct node. The operations are called *visitors*; here they are defined in classes derived from class **Visitor**. The nodes are a hierarchy of classes with a virtual function **accept()** that takes **Visitor&**s. For this example, I use a hierarchy of **Node**s that describe language constructs, as is common in tools based on abstract syntax trees (ASTs):

```
class Visitor;

class Node {
public:
     virtual void accept(Visitor&) = 0;
};

class Expr : public Node {
public:
     void accept(Visitor&) override;
};

class Stmt : public Node {
public:
     void accept(Visitor&) override;
};
```

So far, so good: the **Node** hierarchy simply provides a virtual function **accept()** that takes a **Visitor&** argument representing what should be done to a **Node** of a given type.

I do not use **const** here, because in general an operation from a **Visitor** may update either the **Node** "visited" or the **Visitor** itself.

Now the **Node**'s **accept()** performs the double-dispatch trick and passes the **Node** itself to the **Visitor**'s **accept()**:

```
void Expr::accept(Visitor& v) { v.accept(*this); }
void Stmt::accept(Visitor& v) { v.accept(*this); }
```

The **Visitor** declares a set of operations:

```
class Visitor {
public:
     virtual void accept(Expr&) = 0;
     virtual void accept(Stmt&) = 0;
};
```

We can then define sets of operations by deriving from **Visitor** and overriding its **accept()** functions. For example:

```
class Do1_visitor : public Visitor {
     void accept(Expr&) { cout << "do1 to Expr\n"; }
     void accept(Stmt&) { cout << "do1 to Stmt\n"; }
};

class Do2_visitor : public Visitor {
     void accept(Expr&) { cout << "do2 to Expr\n"; }
     void accept(Stmt&) { cout << "do2 to Stmt\n"; }
};
```

We can test by making a **vector** of **pairs** of pointers to ensure that run-time type resolution is used:

```
void test(Expr& e, Stmt& s)
{
    vector<pair<Node∗,Visitor∗>> vn {&e,&do1}, {&s,&do1}, {&e,&do2}, {&s,&do2}};
    for (auto p : vn)
        p.first−>accept(∗p.second);
}
```

We get:

```
do1 to Expr
do1 to Stmt
do2 to Expr
do2 to Stmt
```

As opposed to the simple double dispatch, the visitor pattern is heavily used in real-world programming. It is only mildly intrusive (the **accept()** function), and many variations on the basic idea are used. However, many operations on class hierarchies are hard to express as visitors. For example, an operation that needs access to multiple nodes of different types in a graph cannot be trivially implemented as a visitor. So, I consider the visitor pattern an inelegant workaround. Alternatives exist, for example, [Solodkyy,2012], but not in plain C++11.

Most alternatives to visitors in C++ are based on the idea of explicit iteration over a homogeneous data structure (e.g., a vector or a graph of nodes containing pointers to polymorphic types). At each element or node, a call of a virtual function can perform the desired operation, or some optimization based on stored data can be applied (e.g., see §27.4.2).

22.4 Construction and Destruction

A class object is more than simply a region of memory (§6.4). A class object is built from "raw memory" by its constructors, and it reverts to "raw memory" as its destructors are executed. Construction is bottom-up, destruction is top-down, and a class object is an object to the extent that it has been constructed or destroyed. This order is necessary to ensure that an object is not accessed before it has been initialized. It is unwise to try to access base and member objects early or out of order through "clever" pointer manipulation (§17.2.3). The order of construction and destruction is reflected in the rules for RTTI, exception handling (§13.3), and virtual functions (§20.3.2).

It is unwise to rely on details of the order of construction and destruction, but you can observe that order by calling virtual functions, **dynamic_cast** (§22.2), or **typeid** (§22.5) at a point where the object isn't complete. At such a point in a constructor, the (dynamic) type of the object reflects only what is constructed so far. For example, if the constructor for **Component** in the hierarchy from §22.2.2 calls a virtual function, it will invoke a version defined for **Storable** or **Component**, but not one from **Receiver**, **Transmitter**, or **Radio**. At that point of construction, the object isn't yet a **Radio**. Similarly, calling a virtual function from a destructor will reflect only what is still not destroyed. It is best to avoid calling virtual functions during construction and destruction.

22.5 Type Identification

The **dynamic_cast** operator serves most needs for information about the type of an object at run time. Importantly, it ensures that code written using it works correctly with classes derived from those explicitly mentioned by the programmer. Thus, **dynamic_cast** preserves flexibility and extensibility in a manner similar to virtual functions.

However, it is occasionally essential to know the exact type of an object. For example, we might like to know the name of the object's class or its layout. The **typeid** operator serves this purpose by yielding an object representing the type of its operand. Had **typeid()** been a function, its declaration would have looked something like this:

```
class type_info;
const type_info& typeid(expression);    // pseudo declaration
```

That is, **typeid()** returns a reference to a standard-library type called **type_info** defined in **<typeinfo>**:

- Given the name of a type as its operand, **typeid(type_name)** returns a reference to a **type_info** that represents the **type_name**; **type_name** must be a completely defined type (§8.2.2).
- Given an *expression* as its operand, **typeid(expr)** returns a reference to a **type_info** that represents the type of the object denoted by the **expr**; the **expr** must refer to a completely defined type (§8.2.2). If the value of **expr** is **nullptr**, **typeid(expr)** throws a **std::bad_typeid**.

A **typeid()** can find the type of an object referred to by a reference or a pointer:

```
void f(Shape& r, Shape* p)
{
    typeid(r);      // type of the object referred to by r
    typeid(*p);     // type of the object pointed to by p
    typeid(p);      // type of the pointer, that is, Shape* (uncommon, except as a mistake)
}
```

If the operand of **typeid()** is a pointer or a reference of a polymorphic type with the value **nullptr**, **typeid()** throws a **std::bad_typeid**. If the operand of **typeid()** has a nonpolymorphic type or is not an lvalue, the result is determined at compile time without evaluating the operand expression.

If the object denoted by a dereferenced pointer or a reference to a polymorphic type, the **type_info** returned is that of the most derived class for the object, that is, the type used when the object was defined. For example:

```
struct Poly {    // polymorphic base class
    virtual void f();
    // ...
};

struct Non_poly { /* ... */ }; // no virtual functions

struct D1
    : Poly { /* ... */ };
struct D2
    : Non_poly { /* ... */ };
```

```
void f(Non_poly& npr, Poly& pr)
{
     cout << typeid(npr).name() << '\n';  // writes something like "Non_poly"
     cout << typeid(pr).name() << '\n';   // name of Poly or a class derived from Poly
}

void g()
{
     D1 d1;
     D2 d2;
     f(d2,d1);  // writes "Non_poly D1"
     f(*static_cast<Poly*>(nullptr),*static_cast<Null_poly*>(nullptr));  // oops!
}
```

That last call will print just **Non_poly** (because **typeid(npr)** is not evaluated) before throwing a **bad_typeid**.

The definition of **type_info** looks like this:

```
class type_info {
     // data
public:
     virtual ~type_info();                                  // is polymorphic

     bool operator==(const type_info&) const noexcept;      // can be compared
     bool operator!=(const type_info&) const noexcept;

     bool before(const type_info&) const noexcept;          // ordering
     size_t hash_code() const noexcept;                     // for use by unordered_map and the like
     const char* name() const noexcept;                     // name of type

     type_info(const type_info&) = delete;                  // prevent copying
     type_info& operator=(const type_info&) = delete;       // prevent copying
};
```

The **before()** function allows **type_info**s to be sorted. In particular, it allows **type_id**s to be used as keys for ordered containers (such as **map**). There is no relation between the relationships defined by **before** and inheritance relationships. The **hash_code()** function allows **type_id**s be used as keys for hash tables (such as **unordered_map**).

It is *not* guaranteed that there is only one **type_info** object for each type in the system. In fact, where dynamically linked libraries are used, it can be hard for an implementation to avoid duplicate **type_info** objects. Consequently, we should use **==** on **type_info** objects to test equality, rather than **==** on pointers to such objects.

We sometimes want to know the exact type of an object so as to perform some service on the whole object (and not just on one of its bases). Ideally, such services are presented as virtual functions so that the exact type needn't be known. In some cases, no common interface can be assumed for every object manipulated, so the detour through the exact type becomes necessary (§22.5.1). Another, much simpler use has been to obtain the name of a class for diagnostic output:

```
#include<typeinfo>

void g(Component* p)
{
    cout << typeid(*p).name();
}
```

The character representation of a class's name is implementation-defined. This C-style string resides in memory owned by the system, so the programmer should not attempt to **delete[]** it.

22.5.1 Extended Type Information

A **type_info** object contains only minimal information. Therefore, finding the exact type of an object is often just the first step to acquiring and using more detailed information about that type.

Consider how an implementation or a tool could make information about types available to users at run time. Suppose I have a tool that generates descriptions of object layouts for each class used. I can put these descriptors into a **map** to allow user code to find the layout information:

```
#include <typeinfo>

map<string, Layout> layout_table;

void f(B* p)
{
    Layout& x = layout_table[typeid(*p).name()];  // find the Layout based on *p's name
    // ... use x ...
}
```

The resulting data structure looks like this:

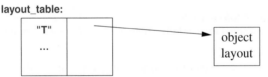

Someone else might provide a completely different kind of information:

```
unordered_map<type_index,Icon> icon_table;        // §31.4.3.2

void g(B* p)
{
    Icon& i = icon_table[type_index{typeid(*p)}];
    // ... use i ...
}
```

The **type_index** is a standard-library type for comparing and hashing **type_info** objects (§35.5.4).

The resulting data structure looks like this:

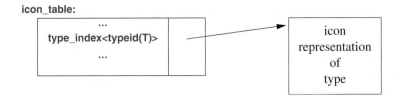

icon_table:

Associating **typeid**s with information without modifying system headers allows several people or tools to associate different information with types independently of each other. This is important because the likelihood that someone can come up with a single set of information that satisfies every user is close to zero.

22.6 Uses and Misuses of RTTI

We should use explicit run-time type information only when necessary. Static (compile-time) checking is safer, implies less overhead, and – where applicable – leads to better-structured programs. Interfaces based on virtual functions combine static type checking with a run-time lookup in a way that gives both type safety and flexibility. However, programmers sometimes overlook these alternatives and use RTTI where it is unsuitable. For example, RTTI can be used to write thinly disguised **switch**-statements:

```
// misuse of run-time type information:

void rotate(const Shape& r)
{
    if (typeid(r) == typeid(Circle)) {
        // do nothing
    }
    else if (typeid(r) == typeid(Triangle)) {
        // ... rotate triangle ...
    }
    else if (typeid(r) == typeid(Square)) {
        // ... rotate square ...
    }
    // ...
}
```

Using **dynamic_cast** rather than **typeid** would improve this code only marginally. Either way, this code is syntactically ugly and also inefficient in that it performs an expensive operation repeatedly.

Unfortunately, this is not a strawman example; such code really does get written. For many people trained in languages without equivalents to class hierachies and virtual functions, there is an almost irresistible urge to organize software as a set of **switch**-statements. This urge should usually be resisted. Use virtual functions (§3.2.3, §20.3.2) rather than RTTI to handle most cases when run-time discrimination based on type is needed.

Many examples of proper use of RTTI arise when some service code is expressed in terms of one class and a user wants to add functionality through derivation. The use of **lval_box** in §22.2 is an example of this. If the user is willing and able to modify the definitions of the library classes, say **BBwindow**, then the use of RTTI can be avoided; otherwise, it is needed. Even if the user is willing to modify the base classes (e.g., to add a virtual function), such modification may cause its own problems. For example, it may be necessary to introduce dummy implementations of virtual functions in classes for which those functions are not needed or not meaningful. A use of RTTI to implement a simple object I/O system can be found in §22.2.4.

For people with a background in languages that rely heavily on dynamic type checking, such as Smalltalk, pre-generics Java, or Lisp, it is tempting to use RTTI in conjunction with overly general types. Consider:

```
// misuse of run-time type information:

class Object { // polymorphic
    // ...
};

class Container : public Object {
public:
    void put(Object*);
    Object* get();
    // ...
};

class Ship : public Object { /* ... */ };

Ship* f(Ship* ps, Container* c)
{
    c->put(ps);                              // put the Ship into the container
    // ...
    Object* p = c->get();                    // retrieve an Object from the container
    if (Ship* q = dynamic_cast<Ship*>(p)) {  // run-time check that the Object is a Ship
        return q;
    }
    else {
        // ... do something else (typically, error handling) ...
    }
}
```

Here, class **Object** is an unnecessary implementation artifact. It is overly general because it does not correspond to an abstraction in the application domain and forces the application programmer to use an implementation-level abstraction (**Object**). Problems of this kind are often better solved by using container templates that hold only a single kind of pointer:

```
Ship* f(Ship* ps, vector<Ship*>& c)
{
    c.push_back(ps);       // put the Ship into the container
    // ...
    return c.pop_back();   // retrieve a Ship from the container
}
```

This style of code is less error-prone (better statically type checked) and less verbose than a pure-**Object**-based alternative. Combined with the use of virtual functions, this technique handles most cases. In a template, a template argument **T** takes the place of **Object** and enables static type checking (§27.2).

22.7 Advice

[1]   Use virtual functions to ensure that the same operation is performed independently of which interface is used for an object; §22.1.

[2]   Use **dynamic_cast** where class hierarchy navigation is unavoidable; §22.2.

[3]   Use **dynamic_cast** for type-safe explicit navigation of a class hierarchy; §22.2.1.

[4]   Use **dynamic_cast** to a reference type when failure to find the required class is considered a failure; §22.2.1.1.

[5]   Use **dynamic_cast** to a pointer type when failure to find the required class is considered a valid alternative; §22.2.1.1.

[6]   Use double dispatch or the visitor pattern to express operations on two dynamic types (unless you need an optimized lookup); §22.3.1.

[7]   Don't call virtual functions during construction or destruction; §22.4.

[8]   Use **typeid** to implement extended type information; §22.5.1.

[9]   Use **typeid** to find the type of an object (and not to find an interface to an object); §22.5.

[10] Prefer virtual functions to repeated **switch**-statements based on **typeid** or **dynamic_cast**; §22.6.

23

Templates

Your quote here.
– B. Stroustrup

23.1 Introduction and Overview

Templates provide direct support for generic programming (§3.4) in the form of programming using types as parameters. The C++ template mechanism allows a type or a value to be a parameter in the definition of a class, a function, or a type alias. Templates provide a straightforward way to represent a wide range of general concepts and simple ways to combine them. The resulting classes and functions can match handwritten, less general code in run-time and space efficiency.

A template depends only on the properties that it actually uses from its parameter types and does not require types used as arguments to be explicitly related. In particular, the argument types used for a template need not be part of an inheritance hierarchy. Built-in types are acceptable and very common as template arguments.

The composition offered by templates is type-safe (no object can be implicitly used in a way that disagrees with its definition), but unfortunately, a template's requirements on its arguments cannot be simply and directly stated in code (§24.3).

Every major standard-library abstraction is represented as a template (for example, **string**, **ostream**, **regex**, **complex**, **list**, **map**, **unique_ptr**, **thread**, **future**, **tuple**, and **function**), and so are the key operations (for example, **string** comparisons, the output operator **<<**, **complex** arithmetic operations, **list** insertions and deletions, and **sort()**). This makes the library chapters (Part IV) of this book a rich source of examples of templates and programming techniques relying on them.

Here, templates are introduced with the primary focus on techniques needed for the design, implementation, and use of the standard library. The standard library requires a greater degree of generality, flexibility, and efficiency than does most software. Consequently, techniques that can be used in the design and implementation of the standard library are effective and efficient in the design of solutions to a wide variety of problems. These techniques enable an implementer to hide sophisticated implementations behind simple interfaces and to expose complexity to the user when the user has a specific need for it.

Templates and the fundamental techniques for using them are the focus of this and the following six chapters. This chapter focuses on the most basic template facilities and fundamental programming techniques for using them:

§23.2 *A Simple String Template*: The basic mechanisms for defining and using class templates are introduced through the example of a string template.

§23.3 *Type Checking*: The basic rules of type equivalence and type checking as they apply to templates.

§23.4 *Class Template Members*: How members of a class template are defined and used.

§23.5 *Function Templates*: How to define and use function templates. How overloading is resolved for function templates and ordinary functions.

§23.6 *Template Aliases*: Template aliases provide a powerful mechanism for hiding implementation details and cleaning up the notation used for templates.

§23.7 *Source Code Organization*: How to organize templates into source files.

Chapter 24, *Generic Programming*, presents the basic technique of generic programming, and the fundamental idea of *concepts* (requirements on template arguments) is explored:

§24.2 *Algorithms and Lifting*: An example of the basic technique for developing a *generic* algorithm from *concrete* examples.

§24.3 *Concepts*: Introduces and discusses the fundamental notion of a *concept*, that is, a set of requirements that a template can impose on its template arguments.

§24.4 *Making Concepts Concrete*: Presents techniques for using concepts expressed as compile-time predicates.

Chapter 25, *Specialization*, discusses template argument passing and the notion of specialization:

§25.2 *Template Parameters and Arguments*: What can be a template argument: types, values, and templates. How to specify and use default template arguments.

§25.3 *Specialization*: Special versions, called *specializations*, of a template for a specific set of template arguments can be generated from the templates by the compiler or be provided by the programmer.

Chapter 26, *Instantiation*, presents issues related to generation of template specialization (instances) and name binding:

    §26.2   *Template Instantiation*: The rules for when and how a compiler generates specializations from a template definition and how to specify them manually.

    §26.3   *Name Binding*: The rules for determining to which entity a name used in a template definition refers.

Chapter 27, *Templates and Hierarchies*, discusses the relation between the generic programming techniques supported by templates and the object-oriented techniques supported by class hierarchies. The emphasis is on how to use them in combination:

    §27.2   *Parameterization and Hierarchy*: Templates and class hierarchies are two ways of representing sets of related abstractions. How do we choose between them?

    §27.3   *Hierarchies of Class Templates*: Why it is usually a bad idea simply to add template parameters to an existing class hierarchy?

    §27.4   *Template Parameters as Base Classes*: Presents techniques for composing interfaces and data structures for type safety and performance.

Chapter 28, *Metaprogramming*, concentrates on the use of templates as a means of generating functions and classes:

    §28.2   *Type Functions*: Functions that take types as arguments or return types as results.

    §28.3   *Compile-time Control Structures*: How to express selection and recursion for type functions, and some rules of thumb for their use.

    §28.4   *Conditional Definition:* `enable_if`: How to conditionally define functions and overload templates using (almost) arbitrary predicates.

    §28.5   *A Compile-time List:* `Tuple`: How to build and access lists with elements of (almost) arbitrary types.

    §28.6   *Variadic templates*: How (in a statically type-safe manner) to define templates that take arbitrary numbers of template arguments of arbitrary types.

    §28.7   *SI Units Example*: This example uses simple metaprogramming techniques in combination with other programming techniques to provide a library for computations that are (at compile time) checked for correct use of the meters, kilograms, and seconds system of units.

Chapter 29, *A Matrix Design*, demonstrates how various template features can be used in combination to address a challenging design task:

    §29.2   *A* `Matrix` *Template*: How to define an N-dimensional matrix with flexible and type-safe initialization, subscription, and submatrices.

    §29.3   `Matrix` *Arithmetic Operations*: How to provide simple arithmetic operations on an N-dimensional matrix.

    §29.4   `Matrix` *Implementation*: Some useful implementation techniques.

    §29.5   *Solving Linear Equations*: An example of simple matrix use.

Templates were introduced early (§3.4.1, §3.4.2) and used throughout this book, so I assume that you have some familiarity with them.

23.2 A Simple String Template

Consider a string of characters. A string is a class that holds characters and provides operations such as subscripting, concatenation, and comparison that we usually associate with the notion of a "string." We would like to provide that behavior for many different kinds of characters. For example, strings of signed characters, of unsigned characters, of Chinese characters, of Greek characters, etc., are useful in various contexts. Thus, we want to represent the notion of "string" with minimal dependence on a specific kind of character. The definition of a string relies on the fact that a character can be copied, and little else (§24.3). Thus, we can make a more general string type by taking the string of **char** from §19.3 and making the character type a parameter:

```
template<typename C>
class String {
public:
    String();
    explicit String(const C*);
    String(const String&);
    String operator=(const String&);
    // ...
    C& operator[](int n) { return ptr[n]; }      // unchecked element access
    String& operator+=(C c);                     // add c at end
    // ...
private:
    static const int short_max = 15;             // for the short string optimization
    int sz;
    C* ptr;     // ptr points to sz Cs
};
```

The **template<typename C>** prefix specifies that a template is being declared and that a type argument **C** will be used in the declaration. After its introduction, **C** is used exactly like other type names. The scope of **C** extends to the end of the declaration prefixed by **template<typename C>**. You may prefer the shorter and equivalent form **template<class C>**. In either case, **C** is a *type* name; it need not be the name of a *class*. Mathematicians will recognize **template<typename C>** as a variant of the traditional "for all C" or more specifically "for all types C" or even "for all C, such that C is a type." If you think along those lines, you will note that C++ lacks a fully general mechanism for specifying the required properties of a template parameter **C**. That is, we can't say "for all C, such that ..." where the "..." is a set of requirements for **C**. In other words, C++ does not offer a direct way to say what kind of type a template argument **C** is supposed to be (§24.3).

The name of a class template followed by a type bracketed by < > is the name of a class (as defined by the template) and can be used exactly like other class names. For example:

```
String<char> cs;
String<unsigned char> us;
String<wchar_t> ws;

struct Jchar { /* ... */ };     // Japanese character

String<Jchar> js;
```

Except for the special syntax of its name, **String<char>** works exactly as if it had been defined using the definition of class **String** in §19.3. Making **String** a template allows us to provide the facilities we had for **String** of **char** for **String**s of any kind of character. For example, if we use the standard-library **map** and the **String** template, the word-counting example from §19.2.1 becomes:

```
int main() // count the occurrences of each word on input
{
    map<String<char>,int> m;
    for (String<char> buf; cin>>buf;)
        ++m[buf];
    // ... write out result ...
}
```

The version for our Japanese-character type **Jchar** would be:

```
int main() // count the occurrences of each word on input
{
    map<String<Jchar>,int> m;
    for (String<Jchar> buf; cin>>buf;)
        ++m[buf];
    // ... write out result ...
}
```

The standard library provides the template class **basic_string** that is similar to the templatized **String** (§19.3, §36.3). In the standard library, **string** is a synonym for **basic_string<char>** (§36.3):

```
using string = std::basic_string<char>;
```

This allows us to write the word-counting program like this:

```
int main() // count the occurrences of each word on input
{
    map<string,int> m;
    for (string buf; cin>>buf;)
        ++m[buf];
    // ... write out result ...
}
```

In general, type aliases (§6.5) are useful for shortening the long names of classes generated from templates. Also, we often prefer not to know the details of how a type is defined, and an alias allows us to hide the fact that a type is generated from a template.

23.2.1 Defining a Template

A class generated from a class template is a perfectly ordinary class. Thus, use of a template does not imply any run-time mechanisms beyond what is used for an equivalent "handwritten" class. In fact, using a template can lead to a decrease of code generated because code for a member function of a class template is only generated if that member is used (§26.2.1).

In addition to class templates, C++ offers function templates (§3.4.2, §23.5). I will introduce most of the "mechanics" of templates in the context of class templates and postpone detailed discussion of function templates to §23.5. A template is a specification of how to generate something given suitable template arguments; the language mechanisms for doing that generation (instantiation (§26.2) and specialization (§25.3)) don't care much whether a class or a function is generated. So, unless otherwise stated, the rules for templates apply equally to class templates and function templates. Templates can also be defined as aliases (§23.6), but other plausible constructs, such as namespace templates, are not provided.

There are people who make semantic distinctions between the terms *class template* and *template class*. I don't; that would be too subtle: please consider those terms interchangeable. Similarly, I consider *function template* interchangeable with *template function*.

When designing a class template, it is usually a good idea to debug a particular class, such as **String**, before turning it into a template such as **String<C>**. By doing so, we handle many design problems and most of the code errors in the context of a concrete example. This kind of debugging is familiar to all programmers, and most people cope better with a concrete example than with an abstract concept. Later, we can deal with any problems that might arise from generalization without being distracted by more conventional errors. Similarly, when trying to understand a template, it is often useful to imagine its behavior for a particular type argument such as **char** before trying to comprehend the template in its full generality. This also fits with the philosophy that a generic component should be developed as a generalization of one or more concrete examples, rather than simply being designed from first principles (§24.2).

Members of a class template are declared and defined exactly as they would have been for a non-template class. A template member need not be defined within the template class itself. In that case, its definition must be provided somewhere else, just as for non-template class members (§16.2.1). Members of a template class are themselves templates parameterized by the parameters of their template class. When such a member is defined outside its class, it must explicitly be declared a template. For example:

```
template<typename C>
String<C>::String() // String<C>'s constructor
     :sz{0}, ptr{ch}
{
     ch[0] = {}; // terminating 0 of the appropriate character type
}


template<typename C>
String& String<C>::operator+=(C c)
{
     // ... add c to the end of this string ...
     return *this;
}
```

A template parameter, such as **C**, is a parameter rather than the name of a specific type. However, that doesn't affect the way we write the template code using the name. Within the scope of **String<C>**, qualification with **<C>** is redundant for the name of the template itself, so **String<C>::String** is the name for the constructor.

Just as there can be only one function defining a class member function in a program, there can be only one function template defining a class template member function in a program. However, specialization (§25.3) enables us to provide alternative implementations for a template given

specific template arguments. For functions, we can also use overloading to provide different definitions for different argument types (§23.5.3).

It is not possible to overload a class template name, so if a class template is declared in a scope,
no other entity can be declared there with the same name. For example:

```
template<typename T>
class String { /* ... */ };
```

```
class String { /* ... */ };    // error: double definition
```

A type used as a template argument must provide the interface expected by the template. For
example, a type used as an argument to **String** must provide the usual copy operations (§17.5,
§36.2.2). Note that there is no requirement that different arguments for the same template parameter should be related by inheritance. See also §25.2.1 (template type parameters), §23.5.2 (template
parameter deduction), and §24.3 (requirements on template arguments).

23.2.2 Template Instantiation

The process of generating a class or a function from a template plus a template argument list is
often called *template instantiation* (§26.2). A version of a template for a specific template argument list is called a *specialization*.

In general, it is the implementation's job – *not* the programmer's – to ensure that specializations
of a template are generated for each template argument list used. For example:

```
String<char> cs;
```

```
void f()
{
    String<Jchar> js;

    cs = "It's the implementation's job to figure out what code needs to be generated";
}
```

For this, the implementation generates declarations for classes **String<char>** and **String<Jchar>**, for
their destructors and default constructors, and for **String<char>::operator=(char∗)**. Other member
functions are not used and will not be generated. Generated classes are perfectly ordinary classes
that obey all the usual rules for classes. Similarly, generated functions are ordinary functions that
obey all the usual rules for functions.

Obviously, templates provide a powerful way of generating lots of code from relatively short
definitions. Consequently, a certain amount of caution is in order to avoid flooding memory with
almost identical function definitions (§25.3). On the other hand, templates can be written to enable
otherwise unachievable quality of generated code. In particular, composition using templates combined with simple inlining can be used to eliminate many direct and indirect function calls. For
example, that is how simple operations on critical data structures (such as < in a **sort()** and + for
scalars in a matrix computation) are reduced to single machine instructions in heavily parameterized libraries. Thus, incautious use of templates leading to the generation of very similar large
functions can cause code bloat, whereas use of templates to enable inlining of tiny functions can
lead to significant code shrinkage (and speedup) compared to alternatives. In particular, the code

generated for a simple < or [] is often a single machine instruction, which is both much faster than any function call and smaller than the code needed to invoke a function and receive its result.

23.3 Type Checking

Template instantiation takes a template plus a set of template arguments and generates code from them. Because so much information is available at instantiation time, weaving together the information from the template definition and the template argument types provides wonderful degrees of flexibility and can yield unparalleled run-time performance. Unfortunately, this flexibility also implies complexity of type checking and difficulties for accurate reporting of type errors.

Type checking is done on the code generated by template instantiation (exactly as if the programmer had expanded the templates by hand). This generated code may contain much that the user of a template has never heard of (such as names of details of a template implementation) and often happens uncomfortably late in the build process. This mismatch between what the programmer sees/writes and what the compiler type checks can be a major problem, and we need to design our programs to minimize its consequences.

The fundamental weakness of the template mechanism is that it is not possible to directly express requirements on a template argument. For example, we cannot say:

```
template<Container Cont, typename Elem>
    requires Equal_comparable<Cont::value_type,Elem>()  // requirements for types Cont and Elem
int find_index(Cont& c, Elem e);                        // find the index of e in c
```

That is, we have no way in C++ itself to directly say that **Cont** should be a type that can act as a container and that the type **Elem** should be a type that allows us to compare a value to an element of **Cont**. Work is being done to make this possible in future versions of C++ (without loss of flexibility, without loss of run-time performance, and without significant increases in compile time [Sutton,2011]), but for now we will have to do without.

The first step in dealing effectively with problems related to template argument passing is to establish a framework and vocabulary for discussing requirements. Think of a set of requirements on template arguments as a predicate. For example, we can think of "**C** must be a container" as a predicate that takes a type, **C**, as an argument and returns **true** if **C** is a container (however we may have defined "container") and **false** if it is not. For example, **Container<vector<int>>()** and **Container<list<string>>()** should be true whereas **Container<int>()** and **Container<shared_ptr<string>>()** should be false. We call such a predicate a *concept*. A concept is not (yet) a language construct in C++; it is a notion that we can use to reason about requirements on template arguments, use in comments, and sometimes support with our own code (§24.3).

For starters, think of a concept as a design tool: specify **Container<T>()** as a set of comments saying what properties a type **T** must have for **Container<T>()** to be true. For example:

- **T** must have a subscript operator ([]).
- **T** must have a **size()** member function.
- **T** must have a member type **value_type** which is the type of its elements.

Note that this list is incomplete (e.g., what does [] take as an argument and what does it return?) and fails to address most semantic issues (e.g., what does [] actually do?). However, even a partial set of requirements can be useful; even something very simple allows us to hand-check our uses and catch obvious errors. For example, Container<int>() is obviously false because int does not have a subscript operator. I will return to the design of concepts (§24.3), consider techniques for supporting concepts in code (§24.4), and give an example of a set of useful concepts (§24.3.2). For now, just note that C++ does not directly support concepts, but that does not mean that concepts don't exist: for every working template, the designer had some concepts in mind for its arguments. Dennis Ritchie famously said, "C is a strongly typed, weakly checked language." You could say the same about C++'s templates, except that the checking of template argument requirements (concepts) is actually done, but it is done too late in the compilation process and at an unhelpfully low level of abstraction.

23.3.1 Type Equivalence

Given a template, we can generate types by supplying template arguments. For example:

```
String<char> s1;
String<unsigned char> s2;
String<int> s3;

using Uchar = unsigned char;
using uchar = unsigned char;

String<Uchar> s4;
String<uchar> s5;
String<char> s6;

template<typename T, int N>        // §25.2.2
    class Buffer;
Buffer<String<char>,10> b1;
Buffer<char,10> b2;
Buffer<char,20–10> b3;
```

When using the same set of template arguments for a template, we always refer to the same generated type. However, what does "the same" mean in this context? Aliases do not introduce new types, so String<Uchar> and String<uchar> are the same type as String<unsigned char>. Conversely, because char and unsigned char are different types (§6.2.3), String<char> and String<unsigned char> are different types.

The compiler can evaluate constant expressions (§10.4), so Buffer<char,20–10> is recognized to be the same type as Buffer<char,10>.

Types generated from a single template by different template arguments are different types. In particular, generated types from related arguments are not automatically related. For example, assume that a Circle is a kind of Shape:

```
Shape* p {new Circle(p,100)};              // Circle* converts to Shape*
vector<Shape>* q {new vector<Circle>{}};   // error: no vector<Circle>* to vector<Shape>* conversion
vector<Shape> vs {vector<Circle>{}};       // error: no vector<Circle> to vector<Shape> conversion
vector<Shape*> vs {vector<Circle*>{}};     // error: no vector<Circle*> to vector<Shape*> conversion
```

Had such conversions been allowed, type errors would have resulted (§27.2.1). If conversions between generated classes are needed, the programmer can define them (§27.2.2).

23.3.2 Error Detection

A template is defined and then later used in combination with a set of template arguments. When the template is defined, the definition is checked for syntax errors and possibly also for other errors that can be detected in isolation from a particular set of template arguments. For example:

```
template<typename T>
struct Link {
    Link* pre;
    Link* suc              // syntax error: missing semicolon
    T val;
};

template<typename T>
class List {
    Link<T>* head;
public:
    List() :head{7} { }                            // error: pointer initialized with int
    List(const T& t) : head{new Link<T>{0,o,t}} { }  // error: undefined identifier o
    // ...
    void print_all() const;
};
```

A compiler can catch simple semantic errors at the point of definition or later at the point of use. Users generally prefer early detection, but not all "simple" errors are easy to detect. Here, I made three "mistakes":

- *A simple syntax error*: Leaving out a semicolon at the end of a declaration.
- *A simple type error*: Independently of what the template parameter is, a pointer cannot be initialized by the integer **7**.
- *A name lookup error*: The identifier **o** (a mistyped **0**, of course) cannot be an argument to **Link<T>**'s constructor because there is no such name in scope.

A name used in a template definition must either be in scope or in some reasonably obvious way depend on a template parameter (§26.3). The most common and obvious ways of depending on a template parameter **T** are to explicitly use the name **T**, to use a member of a **T**, and to take an argument of type **T**. For example:

```
template<typename T>
void List<T>::print_all() const
{
    for (Link<T>* p = head; p; p=p–>suc)   // p depends on T
        cout << *p;                         // << depends on T
}
```

Errors that relate to the use of template parameters cannot be detected until the template is used. For example:

```
class Rec {
    string name;
    string address;
};
```

```
void f(const List<int>& li, const List<Rec>& lr)
{
    li.print_all();
    lr.print_all();
}
```

The **li.print_all()** checks out fine, but **lr.print_all()** gives a type error because there is no **<<** output operator defined for **Rec**. The earliest that errors relating to a template parameter can be detected is at the first point of use of the template for a particular template argument. That point is called the first *point of instantiation* (§26.3.3). The implementation is allowed to postpone essentially all checking until the program is linked, and for some errors link time is also the earliest point when complete checking is possible. Independently of when checking is done, the same set of rules is checked. Naturally, users prefer early checking.

23.4 Class Template Members

Exactly like a class, a template class can have members of several kinds:
- Data members (variable and constant); §23.4.1
- Member functions; §23.4.2
- Member type aliases; §23.6
- **static** members (function and data); §23.4.4
- Member types (e.g., a member class); §23.4.5
- Member templates (e.g., a member class template); §23.4.6.3

In addition, a class template can declare **friend**s, just as an "ordinary class" can; §23.4.7.

The rules for class template members are those for their generated classes. That is, if you want to know what the rules of a template member are, just look for the rules for a member of an ordinary class (Chapter 16, Chapter 17, and Chapter 20); that will answer most questions.

23.4.1 Data Members

As for an "ordinary class," a class template can have data members of any type. A non-**static** data member can be initialized in its definition (§17.4.4) or in a constructor (§16.2.5). For example:

```
template<typename T>
struct X {
    int m1 = 7;
    T m2;
    X(const T& x) :m2{x} { }
};

X<int> xi {9};
X<string> xs {"Rapperswil"};
```

Non-**static** data members can be **const**, but unfortunately not **constexpr**.

23.4.2 Member Functions

As for an "ordinary class," a non-**static** member function of a class template can be defined in-class or outside the class. For example:

```
template<typename T>
struct X {
    void mf1() { /* ... */ }      // defined in-class
    void mf2();
};


template<typename T>
void X<T>::mf2() { /* ... */ }    // defined out of class
```

Similarly, a member function of a template can be **virtual** or not. However, a virtual member function cannot also be a member function template (§23.4.6.2).

23.4.3 Member Type Aliases

Member type aliases, whether introduced using **using** or **typedef** (§6.5), play a major role in the design of class templates. They define related types of a class in a way that is easy to access from outside the class. For example, we specify a container's iterator and element types as aliases:

```
template<typename T>
class Vector {
public:
    using value_type = T;
    using iterator = Vector_iter<T>;     // Vector_iter is defined elsewhere
    // ...
};
```

The template argument name, **T**, is only accessible to the template itself, so for other code to refer to the element type, we must provide an alias.

Type aliases play a major role in generic programming by allowing the designer of classes to provide common names for types in different classes (and class templates) with common semantics. Type names as member aliases are often referred to as *associated types*. The **value_type** and **iterator** names are borrowed from the standard library's container design (§33.1.3). If a class is missing a desired member alias, a trait can be used to compensate (§28.2.4).

23.4.4 static Members

A **static** data or function member that is not defined in-class must have a unique definition in a program. For example:

```
template<typename T>
struct X {
    static constexpr Point p {100,250}; // Point must be a literal type (§10.4.3)
    static const int m1 = 7;
    static int m2 = 8;                 // error: not const
```

```
        static int m3;
        static void f1() { /* ... */ }
        static void f2();
};

template<typename T> int X<T>::m1 = 88;          // error: two initializers
template<typename T> int X<T>::m3 = 99;

template<typename T> void X::<T>::f2() { /* ... */ }
```

As for non-template classes, a **const** or **conexpr static** data member of literal type can be initialized in-class and need not be defined outside the class (§17.4.5, §iso.9.2).

A **static** member need only be defined if it is used (§iso.3.2, §iso.9.4.2, §16.2.12). For example:

```
template<typename T>
struct X {
    static int a;
    static int b;
};

int* p = &X<int>::a;
```

If this is all the mention of X<int> in a program, we will get a "not defined" error for X<int>::a, but not for X<int>::b.

23.4.5 Member Types

As for an "ordinary class," we can define types as members. As usual, such a type can be a class or an enumeration. For example:

```
template<typename T>
struct X {
    enum E1 { a, b };
    enum E2;            // error: underlying type not known
    enum class E3;
    enum E4 : char;

    struct C1 { /* ... */ };
    struct C2;
};

template<typename T>
enum class X<T>::E3 { a, b };              // needed

template<typename T>
enum class X<T>::E4 : char { x, y };       // needed

template<typename T>
struct X<T>::C2 { /* ... */ };             // needed
```

The out-of-class definition of a member enumeration is only allowed for an enumeration for which we know the underlying type (§8.4).

As usual, the enumerators of a non-**class enum** are placed in the scope of the enumeration; that is, for a member enumeration, the enumerators are in the scope of its class.

23.4.6 Member Templates

A class or a class template can have members that are themselves templates. This allows us to represent related types with a pleasing degree of control and flexibility. For example, complex numbers are best represented as pairs of values of some scalar type:

```
template<typename Scalar>
class complex {
    Scalar re, im;
public:
    complex() :re{}, im{} {}                    // default constructor
    template<typename T>
    complex(T rr, T ii =0) :re{rr}, im{ii} { }

    complex(const complex&) = default;          // copy constructor
    template<typename T>
        complex(const complex<T>& c) : re{c.real()}, im{c.imag()} { }
    // ...
};
```

This allows mathematically meaningful conversions among complex types, while prohibiting the undesirable narrowing conversions (§10.5.2.6):

```
complex<float> cf;                  // default value
complex<double> cd {cf};            // OK: uses float to double conversion
complex<float> cf2 {cd};            // error: no implicit double->float conversion

complex<float> cf3 {2.0,3.0};       // error: no implicit double->float conversion
complex<double> cd2 {2.0F,3.0F};    // OK: uses float to double conversion

class Quad {
    // no conversion to int
};

complex<Quad> cq;
complex<int> ci {cq};               // error: no Quad to int conversion
```

Given this definition of **complex**, we can construct a **complex<T1>** from a **complex<T2>** or from a pair of **T2** values if and only if we can construct a **T1** from a **T2**. That seems reasonable.

Be warned that the narrowing error in the **complex<double>** to **complex<float>** case will not be caught until the instantiation of **complex<float>**'s template constructors and then only because I used the {} initialization syntax (§6.3.5) in the constructor's member initializers. That syntax does not allow narrowing.

Using the (old) () syntax would leave us open to narrowing errors. For example:

```
template<typename Scalar>
class complex {                              // old style
    Scalar re, im;
public:
    complex() :re(0), im(0) { }
    template<typename T>
    complex(T rr, T ii =0) :re(rr), im(ii) { }

    complex(const complex&) = default;       // copy constructor
    template<typename T>
        complex(const complex<T>& c) : re(c.real()), im(c.imag()) { }
    // ...
};

complex<float> cf4 {2.1,2.9};    // ouch! narrows
complex<float> cf5 {cd};         // ouch! narrows
```

I consider this yet another reason to be consistent in the use of the {} notation for initialization.

23.4.6.1 Templates and Constructors

To minimize the chances of confusion, I explicitly added a default copy constructor. Leaving it out would not change the meaning of the definition: **complex** would still get a default copy constructor. For technical reasons, a template constructor is never used to generate a copy constructor, so without the explicitly declared copy constructor, a default copy constructor would have been generated. Similarly, copy assignments, move constructors, and move assignments (§17.5.1, §17.6, §19.3.1) must be defined as non-template operators or the default versions will be generated.

23.4.6.2 Templates and virtual

A member template cannot be **virtual**. For example:

```
class Shape {
    // ...
    template<typename T>
        virtual bool intersect(const T&) const =0;     // error: virtual template
};
```

This must be illegal. If it were allowed, the traditional virtual function table technique for implementing virtual functions (§3.2.3) could not be used. The linker would have to add a new entry to the virtual table for class **Shape** each time someone called **intersect()** with a new argument type. Complicating the implementation of the linker in this way was considered unacceptable. In particular, handling dynamic linking would require implementation techniques rather different from what is most commonly used.

23.4.6.3 Use of Nesting

In general, it is a good idea to keep information as local as possible. That way, a name is easier to find and less likely to interfere with anything else in a program. This line of thinking leads to types being defined as members. Doing so is often a good idea. However, for members of class templates we must consider if the parameterization is appropriate for a member type. Formally, a member of a template depends on all of a template's arguments. That can have unfortunate side effects in cases where the behavior of the member does not in fact use every template argument. A famous example is a link type of a linked list. Consider:

```
template<typename T, typename Allocator>
class List {
private:
    struct Link {
        T val;
        Link* succ;
        Link* prev;
    };
    // ...
};
```

Here, **Link** is an implementation detail of **List**. Thus, it seems a perfect example of a type best defined in the scope of **List** and even kept **private**. This has been a popular design and generally works very well. But surprisingly, it can imply performance cost compared to using a nonlocal **Link** type. Assume that no member of **Link** depends on the **Allocator** parameter, and that we need **List<double,My_allocator>** and **List<double,Your_allocator>**. Now **List<double,My_allocator>::Link** and **List<double,Your_allocator>::Link** are different types, so code using them cannot (without clever optimizers) be identical. That is, making **Link** a member when it uses only one of **List**'s two template parameters implies some code bloat. This leads us to consider a design where **Link** isn't a member:

```
template<typename T, typename Allocator>
class List;

template<typename T>
class Link {
    template<typename U, typename A>
        friend class List;
    T val;
    Link* succ;
    Link* prev;
};

template<typename T, typename Allocator>
class List {
    // ...
};
```

I made all members of **Link private** and granted **List** access. Except for making the name **Link** nonlocal, this preserves the design intent that **Link** is an implementation detail of **List**.

But what if a nested class is *not* considered an implementation detail? That is, what if we need an associated type that is meant for a variety of users? Consider:

```
template<typename T, typename A>
class List {
public:
    class Iterator {
        Link<T>* current_position;
    public:
        // ... usual iterator operations ...
    };

    Iterator<T,A> begin();
    Iterator<T,A> end();
    // ...
};
```

Here, the member type **List<T,A>::Iterator** (obviously) does not use the second template argument **A**. However, because **Iterator** is a member and therefore formally depends on **A** (the compiler doesn't know anything to the contrary), we can't write a function to process **List**s independently of how they were constructed using allocators:

```
void fct(List<int>::Iterator b, List<int>::Iterator e)   // error: List takes two arguments
{
    auto p = find(b,e,17);
    // ...
}


void user(List<int,My_allocator>& lm, List<int,Your_allocator>& ly)
{
    fct(lm.begin(),lm.end());
    fct(ly.begin(),ly.end());

}
```

Instead, we need to write a function template with a dependence on the allocator argument:

```
void fct(List<int,My_allocator>::Iterator b, List<int,My_allocator>::Iterator e)
{

    auto p = find(b,e,17);
    // ...
}
```

However, that breaks our **user()**:

```
void user(List<int,My_allocator>& lm, List<int,Your_allocator>& ly)
{
    fct(lm.begin(),lm.end());
    fct(ly.begin(),ly.end());                // error: fct takes List<int,My_allocator>::Iterators
}
```

We could make **fct** a template and generate separate specializations for each allocator. However, that would generate a new specialization for every use of **Iterator**, so this could lead to significant code bloat [Tsafrir,2009]. Again, we solve the problem by moving **Link** out of the class template:

```
template<typename T>
struct Iterator {
    Link<T>* current_position;
};

template<typename T, typename A>
class List {
public:
    Iterator<T> begin();
    Iterator<T> end();
    // ...
};
```

This makes iterators for every **List** with the same first template argument interchangeable as far as their types are concerned. In this case, that was exactly what we wanted. Our **user()** now works as defined. Had **fct()** been defined to be a function template, there would have been only one copy (instantiation) of the definition of **fct()**. My rule of thumb is "Avoid nested types in templates unless they genuinely rely on every template parameter." This is a special case of the general rule to avoid unnecessary dependencies in code.

23.4.7 Friends

As shown in §23.4.6.3, a template class can designate functions as **friend**s. Consider the **Matrix** and **Vector** example from §19.4. Typically, both **Matrix** and **Vector** will be templates:

```
template<typename T> class Matrix;

template<typename T>
class Vector {
    T v[4];
public:
    friend Vector operator*<>(const Matrix<T>&, const Vector&);
    // ...
};

template<typename T>
class Matrix {
    Vector<T> v[4];
public:
    friend Vector<T> operator*<>(const Matrix&, const Vector<T>&);
    // ...
};
```

The **<>** after the name of the friend function is needed to make clear that the friend is a template function. Without the **<>**, a non-template function would be assumed. The multiplication operator can then be defined to access data from **Vector** and **Matrix** directly:

```
template<typename T>
Vector<T> operator*(const Matrix<T>& m, const Vector<T>& v)
{
    Vector<T> r;
    // ... use m.v[i] and v.v[i] for direct access to elements ...
    return r;
}
```

Friends do not affect the scope in which the template class is defined, nor do they affect the scope in which the template is used. Instead, friend functions and operators are found using a lookup based on their argument types (§14.2.4, §18.2.5, §iso.11.3). Like a member function, a friend function is instantiated only if it is used (§26.2.1).

Like other classes, a class template can designate other classes as **friend**s. For example:

```
class C;
using C2 = C;

template<typename T>
class My_class {
    friend C;               // OK: C is a class
    friend C2;              // OK: C2 is an alias for a class
    friend C3;              // error: no class C3 in scope
    friend class C4;        // OK: introduces a new class C4
};
```

Naturally, the interesting cases are those where the friend depends on a template argument. For example:

```
template<typename T>
class my_other_class {
    friend T;               // my argument is my friend!
    friend My_class<T>;     // My_class with the corresponding argument is my friend
    friend class T;         // error: redundant "class"
};
```

As ever, friendship is neither inherited nor transitive (§19.4). For example, **C** has not become a friend of **My_other_class<int>** even though **My_class<int>** is a friend and **C** is a friend of **My_class<int>**.

We cannot directly make a template a friend of a class, but we can make a friend declaration a template. For example:

```
template<typename T, typename A>
class List;

template<typename T>
class Link {
    template<typename U, typename A>
        friend class List;
    // ...
};
```

Unfortunately, there is no way of saying that **Link<X>** should only be a friend of **List<X>**.

Friend classes are designed to allow the representation of small clusters of closely related concepts. A complicated pattern of friendship is almost certainly a design error.

23.5 Function Templates

For many people, the first and most obvious use of templates is to define and use container classes such as **vector** (§31.4), **list** (§31.4.2), and **map** (§31.4.3). Soon after, the need for function templates to manipulate such containers arises. Sorting a **vector** is a simple example:

```
template<typename T> void sort(vector<T>&);        // declaration

void f(vector<int>& vi, vector<string>& vs)
{
    sort(vi);   // sort(vector<int>&);
    sort(vs);   // sort(vector<string>&);
}
```

When a function template is called, the types of the function arguments determine which version of the template is used; that is, the template arguments are deduced from the function arguments (§23.5.2).

Naturally, the function template must be defined somewhere (§23.7):

```
template<typename T>
void sort(vector<T>& v)                    // definition
    // Shell sort (Knuth, Vol. 3, pg. 84)
{
    const size_t n = v.size();

    for (int gap=n/2; 0<gap; gap/=2)
        for (int i=gap; i<n; i++)
            for (int j=i–gap; 0<=j; j–=gap)
                if (v[j+gap]<v[j]) {    // swap v[j] and v[j+gap]
                    T temp = v[j];
                    v[j] = v[j+gap];
                    v[j+gap] = temp;
                }
}
```

Please compare this definition to the **sort()** defined in §12.5. This templatized version is cleaner and shorter because it can rely on more information about the type of the elements it sorts. Typically, it is also faster because it doesn't rely on a pointer to function for the comparison. This implies that no indirect function calls are needed and that inlining a simple < is easy.

A further simplification is to use the standard-library template **swap()** (§35.5.2) to reduce the action to its natural form:

```
if (v[j+gap]<v[j])
    swap(v[j],v[j+gap]);
```

This does not introduce any new overhead. Better yet, the standard-library **swap()** uses move semantics, so we may see a speedup (§35.5.2).

In this example, operator < is used for comparison. However, not every type has a < operator. This limits the use of this version of sort(), but the limitation is easily avoided by adding an argument (see §25.2.3). For example:

```
template<typename T, typename Compare = std::less<T>>
void sort(vector<T>& v)                        // definition
    // Shell sort (Knuth, Vol. 3, pg. 84)
{
        Compare cmp;                  // make a default Compare object
        const size_t n = v.size();

        for (int gap=n/2; 0<gap; gap/=2)
            for (int i=gap; i<n; i++)
                for (int j=i–gap; 0<=j; j–=gap)
                    if (cmp(v[j+gap],v[j]))
                        swap(v[j],v[j+gap]);
}
```

We can now sort using the default comparison operation (<) or supply our own:

```
struct No_case {
        bool operator()(const string& a, const string& b) const;       // compare case insensitive
};

void f(vector<int>& vi, vector<string>& vs)
{
        sort(vi);                           // sort(vector<int>&)
        sort<int,std::greater<int>>(vi);    // sort(vector<int>&) using greater

        sort(vs);                           // sort(vector<string>&)
        sort<string,No_case>(vs);           // sort(vector<string>&) using No_case
}
```

Unfortunately, the rule that only trailing template arguments can be specified leads us to have to specify (rather than deduce) the element type when we specify the comparison operations.

The explicit specification of function template arguments is explained in §23.5.2.

23.5.1 Function Template Arguments

Function templates are essential for writing generic algorithms to be applied to a wide variety of container types (§3.4.2, §32.2). The ability to deduce template arguments for a call from the function arguments is crucial.

A compiler can deduce type and non-type arguments from a call, provided the function argument list uniquely identifies the set of template arguments. For example:

```
template<typename T, int max>
struct Buffer {
    T buf[max];
public:
    // ...
};

template<typename T, int max>
T& lookup(Buffer<T,max>& b, const char* p);

Record& f(Buffer<string,128>& buf, const char* p)
{
    return lookup(buf,p); // use the lookup() where T is string and i is 128
}
```

Here, lookup()'s T is deduced to be string and max is deduced to be 128.

Note that class template parameters are never deduced. The reason is that the flexibility provided by several constructors for a class would make such deduction impossible in many cases and obscure in many more. Instead, specialization (§25.3) provides a mechanism for implicitly choosing between alternative definitions of a template. If we need to create an object of a deduced type, we can often do that by calling a function to do the deduction (and creation). For example, consider a simple variant of the standard library's make_pair() (§34.2.4.1):

```
template<typename T1, typename T2>
pair<T1,T2> make_pair(T1 a, T2 b)
{
    return {a,b};
}

auto x = make_pair(1,2);                    // x is a pair<int,int>
auto y = make_pair(string("New York"),7.7); // y is a pair<string,double>
```

If a template argument cannot be deduced from the function arguments (§23.5.2), we must specify it explicitly. This is done in the same way that template arguments are explicitly specified for a template class (§25.2, §25.3). For example:

```
template<typename T>
T* create();              // make a T and return a pointer to it

void f()
{
    vector<int> v;                // class, template argument int
    int* p = create<int>();       // function, template argument int
    int* q = create();            // error: can't deduce template argument
}
```

This use of explicit specification to provide a return type for a function template is very common. It allows us to define families of object creation functions (e.g., create()) and conversion functions (e.g., §27.2.2). The syntax for static_cast, dynamic_cast, etc. (§11.5.2, §22.2.1), matches the explicitly qualified function template syntax.

Default template arguments can be used to simplify explicit qualification in some cases
(§25.2.5.1).

23.5.2 Function Template Argument Deduction

A compiler can deduce a type template argument, T or TT, and a non-type template argument, I,
from a template function argument with a type composed of the following constructs
(§iso.14.8.2.1):

T	const T	volatile T
T∗	T&	T[constant_expression]
type[I]	class_template_name<T>	class_template_name<I>
TT<T>	T<I>	T<>
T type::∗	T T::∗	type T::∗
T (∗)(args)	type (T::∗)(args)	T (type::∗)(args)
type (type::∗)(args_TI)	T (T::∗)(args_TI)	type (T::∗)(args_TI)
T (type::∗)(args_TI)	type (∗)(args_TI)	

Here, args_TI is a parameter list from which a T or an I can be determined by recursive application
of these rules, and args is a parameter list that does not allow deduction. If not all parameters can
be deduced in this way, a call is ambiguous. For example:

```
template<typename T, typename U>
void f(const T∗, U(∗)(U));

int g(int);

void h(const char∗ p)
{
      f(p,g);     // T is char, U is int
      f(p,h);     // error: can't deduce U
}
```

Looking at the arguments of the first call of f(), we easily deduce the template arguments. Looking
at the second call of f(), we see that h() doesn't match the pattern U(∗)(U) because h()'s argument and
return types differ.

If a template parameter can be deduced from more than one function argument, the same type
must be the result of each deduction. Otherwise, the call is an error. For example:

```
template<typename T>
void f(T i, T∗ p);

void g(int i)
{
      f(i,&i);                // OK
      f(i,"Remember!");       // error, ambiguous: T is int or T is const char?
}
```

23.5.2.1 Reference Deduction

It can be useful to have different actions taken for lvalues and rvalues. Consider a class for holding an {integer,pointer} pair:

```
template<typename T>
class Xref {
public:
    Xref(int i, T* p)        // store a pointer: Xref is the owner
        :index{i}, elem{p}, owner{true}
    { }

    Xref(int i, T& r)        // store a pointer to r, owned by someone else
        :index{i}, elem{&r}, owner{false}
    { }

    Xref(int i, T&& r)       // move r into Xref, Xref is the owner
        :index{i}, elem{new T{move(r)}}, owner{true}
    { }

    ~Xref()
    {
        if(owned) delete elem;
    }
    // ...
private:
    int index;
    T* elem;
    bool owned;
};
```

So:

```
string x {"There and back again"};

Xref<string> r1 {7,"Here"};              // r1 owns a copy of string{"Here"}
Xref<string> r2 {9,x};                   // r2 just refers to x
Xref<string> r3 {3,new string{"There"}}; // r3 owns the string{"There"}
```

Here, r1 picks **Xref(int,string&&)** because **x** is an rvalue. Similarly, **r2** picks **Xref(int,string&)** because **x** is an lvalue.

Lvalues and rvalues are distinguished by template argument deduction: an lvalue of type **X** is deduced as an **X&** and an rvalue as **X**. This differs from the binding of values to non-template argument rvalue references (§12.2.1) but is especially useful for argument forwarding (§35.5.1). Consider writing a factory function that make **Xref**s on the free store and returns **unique_ptr**s to them:

```
template<typename T>
    T&& std::forward(typename remove_reference<T>::type& t) noexcept; // §35.5.1
template<typename T>
    T&& std::forward(typename remove_reference<T>::type&& t) noexcept;
```

```
template<typename TT, typename A>
unique_ptr<TT> make_unique(int i, A&& a)     // simple variant of make_shared (§34.3.2)
{
     return unique_ptr<TT>{new TT{i,forward<A>(a)}};
}
```

We want **make_unique<T>(arg)** to construct a **T** from an **arg** without making any spurious copies. To do that, it is essential that the lvalue/rvalue distinction is maintained. Consider:

```
auto p1 = make_unique<Xref<string>>(7,"Here");
```

"Here" is an rvalue, so **forward(string&&)** is called, passing along an rvalue, so that **Xref(int,string&&)** is called to move from the **string** holding **"Here"**.

The more interesting (subtle) case is:

```
auto p2 = make_unique<Xref<string>>(9,x);
```

Here, **x** is an lvalue, so **forward(string&)** is called, passing along an lvalue: **forward()**'s **T** is deduced to **string&** so that the return value becomes **string& &&**, which means **string&** (§7.7.3). Thus, **Xref(int,string&)** is called for the lvalue **x**, so that **x** is copied.

Unfortunately, **make_unique()** is not part of the standard library, but it is widely supported nevertheless. Defining a **make_unique()** that can take arbitrary arguments is relatively easy using a variadic template for forwarding (§28.6.3).

23.5.3 Function Template Overloading

We can declare several function templates with the same name and even declare a combination of function templates and ordinary functions with the same name. When an overloaded function is called, overload resolution is necessary to find the right function or function template to invoke. For example:

```
template<typename T>
     T sqrt(T);
template<typename T>
     complex<T> sqrt(complex<T>);
double sqrt(double);

void f(complex<double> z)
{
     sqrt(2);     // sqrt<int>(int)
     sqrt(2.0);   // sqrt(double)
     sqrt(z);     // sqrt<double>(complex<double>)
}
```

In the same way that a function template is a generalization of the notion of a function, the rules for resolution in the presence of function templates are generalizations of the function overload resolution rules. Basically, for each template we find the specialization that is best for the set of function arguments. Then, we apply the usual function overload resolution rules to these specializations and all ordinary functions (§iso.14.8.3):

[1]   Find the set of function template specializations (§23.2.2) that will take part in overload resolution. Do this by considering each function template and deciding which template arguments, if any, would be used if no other function templates or functions of the same name were in scope. For the call **sqrt(z)**, this makes **sqrt<double>(complex<double>)** and **sqrt<complex<double>>(complex<double>)** candidates. See also §23.5.3.2.

[2]   If two function templates can be called and one is more specialized than the other (§25.3.3), consider only the most specialized template function in the following steps. For the call **sqrt(z)**, this means that **sqrt<double>(complex<double>)** is preferred over **sqrt<complex<double>>(complex<double>)**: any call that matches **sqrt<T>(complex<T>)** also matches **sqrt<T>(T)**.

[3]   Do overload resolution for this set of functions, plus any ordinary functions, as for ordinary functions (§12.3). If a function template's argument has been determined by template argument deduction (§23.5.2), that argument cannot also have promotions, standard conversions, or user-defined conversions applied. For **sqrt(2)**, **sqrt<int>(int)** is an exact match, so it is preferred over **sqrt(double)**.

[4]   If a function and a specialization are equally good matches, the function is preferred. Consequently, **sqrt(double)** is preferred over **sqrt<double>(double)** for **sqrt(2.0)**.

[5]   If no match is found, the call is an error. If we end up with two or more equally good matches, the call is ambiguous and is an error.

For example:

```
template<typename T>
T max(T,T);

const int s = 7;

void k()
{
      max(1,2);       // max<int>(1,2)
      max('a','b');   // max<char>('a','b')
      max(2.7,4.9);   // max<double>(2.7,4.9)
      max(s,7);       // max<int>(int{s},7) (trivial conversion used)

      max('a',1);     // error: ambiguous: max<char,char>() or max<int,int>()?
      max(2.7,4);     // error: ambiguous: max<double,double>() or max<int,int>()?
}
```

The problem with the last two calls is that we don't apply promotions and standard conversions until after template parameters have been uniquely determined. There is no rule telling the compiler to prefer one resolution over the other. In most cases, it is probably good that the language rules leave subtle decisions in the hands of the programmer. The alternative to surprising ambiguity errors is surprising results from unexpected resolutions. People's "intuitions" about overload resolution differ dramatically, so it is impossible to design a perfectly intuitive set of overload resolution rules.

23.5.3.1 Ambiguity Resolution

We could resolve the two ambiguities by explicit qualification:

```
void f()
{
    max<int>('a',1);          // max<int>(int('a'),1)
    max<double>(2.7,4);       // max<double>(2.7,double(4))
}
```

Alternatively, we could add suitable declarations:

```
inline int max(int i, int j) { return max<int>(i,j); }
inline double max(int i, double d) { return max<double>(i,d); }
inline double max(double d, int i) { return max<double>(d,i); }
inline double max(double d1, double d2) { return max<double>(d1,d2); }

void g()
{
    max('a',1);      // max(int('a'),1)
    max(2.7,4);      // max(2.7,4)
}
```

For ordinary functions, ordinary overloading rules (§12.3) apply, and the use of **inline** ensures that no extra overhead is imposed.

The definition of **max()** is trivial, so we could have implemented the comparison directly rather than calling a specialization of **max()**. However, using an explicit specialization of the template is an easy way of defining such resolution functions and can help maintenance by avoiding almost identical code in several functions.

23.5.3.2 Argument Substitution Failure

When looking for a best match for a set of arguments for a function template, the compiler considers whether the argument can be used in the way required by the complete function template declaration (including the return type). For example:

```
template<typename Iter>
typename Iter::value_type mean(Iter first, Iter last);

void f(vector<int>& v, int* p, int n)
{
    auto x = mean(v.begin(),v.end());     // OK
    auto y = mean(p,p+n);                 // error
}
```

Here, the initialization of **x** succeeds because the arguments match and **vector<int>::iterator** has a member called **value_type**. The initialization of **y** fails because even though the arguments match, **int*** does not have a member called **value_type**, so we cannot say:

```
int*::value_type mean(int*,int*);         // int* does not have a member called value_type
```

However, what if there were another definition of **mean()**?

```
template<typename Iter>
typename Iter::value_type mean(Iter first, Iter last);        // #1

template<typename T>
T mean(T*,T*);                                                // #2

void f(vector<int>& v, int* p, int n)
{
    auto x = mean(v.begin(),v.end());      // OK: call #1
    auto y = mean(p,p+n);                  // OK: call #2
}
```

This works: both initializations succeed. But why didn't we get an error when trying to match mean(p,p+n) with the first template definition? The arguments match perfectly, but by substituting in the actual template argument (int*), we get the function declaration:

```
int*::value_type mean(int*,int*);     // int* does not have a member called value_type
```

That is garbage, of course: a pointer does not have a member value_type. Fortunately, considering this possible declaration is not by itself an error. There is a language rule (§iso.14.8.2) that says that such a *substitution failure* is not an error. It simply causes the template to be ignored; that is, the template does not contribute a specialization to the overload set. That done, mean(p,p+n) matches declaration #2, which is called.

Without the "substitution error is not a failure" rule, we would get compile-time errors even when error-free alternatives (such as #2) are available. More, this rule gives us a general tool for selecting among templates. Techniques based on this rule are described in §28.4. In particular, the standard library provides enable_if to simplify conditional definition of templates (§35.4.2).

The rule is known under the unpronounceable acronym SFINAE (*Substitution Failure Is Not An Error*). SFINAE is often used as a verb with the "F" pronounced as a "v": "I SFINAEd away that constructor." That sounds quite impressive, but I tend to avoid this jargon. "The constructor was eliminated by a substitution failure" is clearer for most people and does less violence to the English language.

So, if – in the process of generating a candidate function to resolve a function call – the compiler finds itself generating a template specialization that would be nonsensical, that candidate is not entered into the overloading set. A template specialization is considered nonsensical if it would lead to a type error. In this, we consider only a declaration; template function definitions and the definition of class members are not considered (or generated) unless they are actually used. For example:

```
template<typename Iter>
Iter mean(Iter first, Iter last)                 // #1
{
    typename Iter::value_type = *first;
    // ...
}

template<typename T>
T* mean(T*,T*);                                  // #2
```

```
void f(vector<int>& v, int* p, int n)
{
    auto x = mean(v.begin(),v.end());     // OK: call #1
    auto y = mean(p,p+n);                 // error: ambiguous
}
```

The declaration of mean() #1 is fine for mean(p,p+n). The compiler does not start to instantiate the body of that mean() and eliminate it because of the type error.

Here, the result is an ambiguity error. Had mean() #2 not been present, declaration #1 would have been chosen and we would have suffered an instantiation-time error. Thus, a function may be chosen as the best match yet still fail to compile.

23.5.3.3 Overloading and Derivation

The overload resolution rules ensure that function templates interact properly with inheritance:

```
template<typename T>
    class B { /* ... */ };
template<typename T>
    class D : public B<T> { /* ... */ };

template<typename T> void f(B<T>*);

void g(B<int>* pb, D<int>* pd)
{
    f(pb);          // f<int>(pb) of course
    f(pd);          // f<int>(static_cast<B<int>*>(pd));
                    // standard conversion D<int>* to B<int>* used
}
```

In this example, the function template f() accepts a B<T>* for any type T. We have an argument of type D<int>*, so the compiler easily deduces that by choosing T to be int, the call can be uniquely resolved to a call of f(B<int>*).

23.5.3.4 Overloading and Non-Deduced Parameters

A function argument that is not involved in the deduction of a template parameter is treated exactly as an argument of a non-template function. In particular, the usual conversion rules hold. Consider:

```
template<typename T, typename C>
T get_nth(C& p, int n);     // get the nth element
```

This function presumably returns the value of the nth element of a container of type C. Because C has to be deduced from an actual argument of get_nth() in a call, conversions are not applicable to the first argument. However, the second argument is perfectly ordinary, so the full range of possible conversions is considered. For example:

```
struct Index {
    operator int();
    // ...
};

void f(vector<int>& v, short s, Index i)
{
    int i1 = get_nth<int>(v,2); // exact match
    int i2 = get_nth<int>(v,s); // standard conversion: short to int
    int i3 = get_nth<int>(v,i); // user-defined conversion: Index to int
}
```

This notation is sometimes called *explicit specialization* (§23.5.1).

23.6 Template Aliases

We can define an alias for a type with the **using** syntax or with the **typedef** syntax (§6.5). The **using** syntax is more general in the important sense that it can be used to define an alias for a template with some of its arguments bound. Consider:

```
template<typename T, typename Allocator = allocator<T>> vector;

using Cvec = vector<char>;                  // both arguments are bound

Cvec vc = {'a', 'b', 'c'};                  // vc is a vector<char,allocator<char>>

template<typename T>
using Vec = vector<T,My_alloc<T>>;          // vector using my allocator (2nd argument is bound)

Vec<int> fib = {0, 1, 1, 2, 3, 5, 8, 13};   // fib is a vector<int,My_alloc<int>>
```

In general, if we bind all arguments of a template, we get a type, but if we bind only some, we get a template. Note that what we get from **using** in an alias definition is always an alias. That is, when we use the alias, it is completely equivalent to a use of the original template. For example:

```
vector<char,alloc<char>> vc2 = vc;          // vc2 and vc are of the same type
vector<int,My_alloc<int>> verbose = fib;    // verbose and fib are of the same type
```

The equivalence of the alias and the original template implies that if you specialize the template, you (correctly) get the specializations when you use the alias. For example:

```
template<int>
struct int_exact_traits {   // idea: int_exact_traits<N>::type is a type with exactly N bits
    using type = int;
};

template<>
struct int_exact_traits<8> {
    using type = char;
};
```

```
template<>
struct int_exact_traits<16> {
    using type = short;
};

template<int N>
using int_exact = typename int_exact_traits<N>::type;  // define alias for convenient notation

int_exact<8> a = 7;   // int_exact<8> is an int with 8 bits
```

If specializations did not get used through the alias, we couldn't claim that **int_exact** was simply an alias for **int_exact_traits<N>::type**; they would behave differently. On the other hand, you cannot define a specialization of an alias. If you had been able to, it would have been rather easy for a human reader to get confused about what was specialized, so no syntax is provided for specializing an alias.

23.7 Source Code Organization

There are three reasonably obvious ways of organizing code using templates:
- [1]   Include template definitions before their use in a translation unit.
- [2]   Include template declarations (only) before their use in a translation unit. Include definitions of templates later in the translation unit (potentially after their use).
- [3]   Include template declarations (only) before their use in a translation unit. Define the templates in some other translation unit.

For technical and historical reasons, option [3], the separate compilation of template definitions and their uses, is not offered. By far the most common approach is to include (usually **#include**) the definition of the templates you use in every translation unit in which you use them and rely on your implementation to optimize compile times and eliminate object code duplication. For example, I might provide a template **out()** in a header **out.h**:

```
// file out.h:

    #include<iostream>

    template<typename T>
    void out(const T& t)
    {
        std::cerr << t;
    }
```

We would **#include** this header wherever **out()** was needed. For example:

```
// file user1.cpp:

    #include "out.h"
    // use out()
```

and

```
// file user2.cpp:

        #include "out.h"
        // use out()
```

That is, the definition of **out()** and all declarations on which it depends are **#include**d in several different compilation units. It is up to the compiler to generate code when needed (only) and to optimize the process of reading redundant definitions. This strategy treats template functions the same way as inline functions.

An obvious problem with this strategy is that users may accidentally come to depend on declarations included only for the benefit of the definition of **out()**. This danger can be limited by taking approach [2] "include template definitions later," by using namespaces, by avoiding macros, and generally by reducing the amount of information included. The ideal is to minimize a template definition's dependency on its environment.

To use the "include template definitions later" approach for our simple **out()** example, we first split **out.h** into two. The declarations go into a **.h** file:

```
// file outdecl.h:

        template<typename T>
        void out(const T& t);
```

The definitions go into **out.cpp**:

```
// file out.cpp:

        #include<iostream>

        template<typename T>
        void out(const T& t)
        {
                std::cerr << t;
        }
```

A user now **#include**s both:

```
// file user3.cpp:

        #include "out.h"
        // use out()
        #include "out.cpp"
```

This minimizes the chances of the implementation of the templates having undesirable effects on the user code. Unfortunately, it also increases the chances that something in the user code (say, a macro) will have an undesirable effect on the template definitions.

As ever, non-**inline**, non-template functions and **static** members (§16.2.12) must have a unique definition in some compilation unit. This implies that such members are best not used for templates that are otherwise included in many translation units. As shown with **out()**, the definition of a template function may be replicated in different translation units, so beware of contexts that might subtly change the meaning of a definition:

```
// file user1.cpp:

    #include "out.h"
    // use out()
```

and

```
// file user4.cpp:

    #define std MyLib
    #include "out.c"
    // use out()
```

This sneaky and error-prone use of a macro changes the definition of **out** so that **user4.cpp**'s definition differs from **user1.cpp**'s. This is an error, but it is an error that an implementation may not catch. This kind of error can be very hard to detect in large programs, so be careful to minimize context dependencies of templates and be very suspicious about macros (§12.6).

If you need more control over the context of instantiation, you can use explicit instantiation and **extern templates** (§26.2.2).

23.7.1 Linkage

The rules for linkage of templates are the rules for linkage of the generated classes and functions (§15.2, §15.2.3). This implies that if the layout of a class template or the definition of an inline function template changes, all code that uses that class or function must be recompiled.

For templates defined in header files and included "everywhere" this can imply a lot of recompilation because templates tend to include a lot of information in header files, more than non-template code using **.cpp** files. In particular, if dynamically linked libraries are used, care has to be taken that all uses of a template are consistently defined.

Sometimes, it is possible to minimize the exposure to changes in complicated template libraries by encapsulating their use in functions with non-template interfaces. For example, I might like to implement some computations using a general numerical library supporting a wide variety of types (e.g., Chapter 29, §40.4, §40.5, §40.6). However, I often know the type used for my calculations. For example, in a program I may consistently use **double**s and **vector<double>**. In that case, I could define:

```
double accum(const vector<double>& v)
{
    return accumulate(v.begin(),v.end(),0.0);
}
```

Given that, I can use the simple non-templated declaration of **accum()** in my code:

```
double accum(const vector<double>& v);
```

The dependence on **std::accumulate** has disappeared into a **.cpp** file that is not seen by the rest of my code. Also, I suffer the compilation-time overhead of a **#include<numeric>** only in that **.cpp** file.

Note that I took the opportunity to simplify the interface to **accum()** compared to **std::accumu-late()**. The generality that is a key attribute of good template libraries can be seen as a source of complexity in a particular application.

I suspect that I would not use this technique for standard-library templates. Those are stable over years and known to the implementations. In particular, I did not bother to try to encapsulate **vector<double>**. However, for more complex, esoteric, or frequently changing template libraries, such encapsulation can be useful.

23.8 Advice

[1]   Use templates to express algorithms that apply to many argument types; §23.1.
[2]   Use templates to express containers; §23.2.
[3]   Note that **template<class T>** and **template<typename T>** are synonymous; §23.2.
[4]   When defining a template, first design and debug a non-template version; later generalize by adding parameters; §23.2.1.
[5]   Templates are type-safe, but checking happens too late; §23.3.
[6]   When designing a template, carefully consider the concepts (requirements) assumed for its template arguments; §23.3.
[7]   If a class template should be copyable, give it a non-template copy constructor and a non-template copy assignment; §23.4.6.1.
[8]   If a class template should be movable, give it a non-template move constructor and a non-template move assignment; §23.4.6.1.
[9]   A virtual function member cannot be a template member function; §23.4.6.2.
[10]   Define a type as a member of a template only if it depends on all the class template's arguments; §23.4.6.3.
[11]   Use function templates to deduce class template argument types; §23.5.1.
[12]   Overload function templates to get the same semantics for a variety of argument types; §23.5.3.
[13]   Use argument substitution failure to provide just the right set of functions for a program; §23.5.3.2.
[14]   Use template aliases to simplify notation and hide implementation details; §23.6.
[15]   There is no separate compilation of templates: **#include** template definitions in every translation unit that uses them; §23.7.
[16]   Use ordinary functions as interfaces to code that cannot deal with templates; §23.7.1.
[17]   Separately compile large templates and templates with nontrivial context dependencies; §23.7.

24

Generic Programming

*Now is a good time to put your work
on a firm theoretical basis.*
– Sam Morgan

- Introduction
- Algorithms and Lifting
- Concepts
    Discovering a Concept; Concepts and Constraints
- Making Concepts Concrete
    Axioms; Multi-argument Concepts; Value Concepts; Constraints Checks; Template Definition Checking
- Advice

24.1 Introduction

What are templates for? In other words, what programming techniques are effective when you use templates? Templates offer:
- The ability to pass types (as well as values and templates) as arguments without loss of information. This implies excellent opportunities for inlining, of which current implementations take great advantage.
- Delayed type checking (done at instantiation time). This implies opportunities to weave together information from different contexts.
- The ability to pass constant values as arguments. This implies the ability to do compile-time computation.

In other words, templates provide a powerful mechanism for compile-time computation and type manipulation that can lead to very compact and efficient code. Remember that types (classes) can contain both code and values.

The first and most common use of templates is to support *generic programming*, that is, programming focused on the design, implementation, and use of general algorithms. Here, "general" means that an algorithm can be designed to accept a wide variety of types as long as they meet the algorithm's requirements on its arguments. The template is C++'s main support for generic programming. Templates provide (compile-time) parametric polymorphism.

There are many definitions of "generic programming." Thus, the term can be confusing. However, in the context of C++, "generic programming" implies an emphasis on the design of general algorithms implemented using templates.

Focusing more on generative techniques (seeing templates as type and function generators) and relying on type functions to express compile-time computation are called *template metaprogramming*, which is the subject of Chapter 28.

The type checking provided for templates checks the use of arguments in the template definition rather than against an explicit interface (in a template declaration). This provides a compile-time variant of what is often called *duck typing* ("If it walks like a duck and it quacks like a duck, it's a duck"). Or – using more technical terminology – we operate on values, and the presence and meaning of an operation depend solely on its operand values. This differs from the alternative view that objects have types, which determine the presence and meaning of operations. Values "live" in objects. This is the way objects (e.g., variables) work in C++, and only values that meet an object's requirements can be put into it. What is done at compile time using templates does not involve objects, only values. In particular, there are no variables at compile time. Thus, template programming resembles programming in dynamically-typed programming languages, but the run-time cost is zero, and errors that in a run-time typed language manifest themselves as exceptions become compile-time errors in C++.

A key aspect of generic programming, metaprogramming, and probably all uses of templates is the uniform handling of built-in types and user-defined types. For example, an **accumulate()** operation does not care whether the types of values it adds up are **int**s, **complex<double>**s, or **Matrix**es. What it cares about is that they can be added using the + operator. The use of a type as a template argument does not imply or require the use of a class hierarchy or any form of run-time self-identification of the type of an object. This is logically pleasing and essential for high-performance applications.

This section focuses on two aspects of generic programming:

- *Lifting*: generalizing an algorithm to allow the greatest (reasonable) range of argument types (§24.2), that is, to limit an algorithm's (or a class's) dependency on properties to what is essential
- *Concepts*: carefully and precisely specifying the requirements of an algorithm (or a class) on its arguments (§24.3)

24.2 Algorithms and Lifting

A function template is a generalization of an ordinary function in the sense that it can perform its actions on a variety of data types and use a variety of operations passed as arguments to implement those actions. An *algorithm* is a procedure or formula for solving a problem: a finite series of computation steps to produce a result. Thus, a function template is often called an algorithm.

How do we get from a function doing specific operations on specific data to an algorithm doing more general operations on a variety of data types? The most effective way of getting a good algorithm is to generalize from one – and preferably more – concrete example. Such generalization is called *lifting*: that is, lifting a general algorithm from specific functions. It is important to go from the concrete to the abstract while maintaining performance and keeping an eye on what is reasonable. Overly clever programmers can generalize to an absurd extent to try to cover every eventuality. Thus, trying to abstract from first principles in the absence of concrete examples typically leads to bloated, hard-to-use code.

I will illustrate the process of lifting by a concrete example. Consider:

```
double add_all(double* array, int n)
    // one concrete algorithm on array of doubles
{
    double s {0};
    for (int i = 0; i<n; ++i)
        s = s + array[i];
    return s;
}
```

Obviously, this computes the sum of the **double**s in the argument array. Also consider:

```
struct Node {
    Node* next;
    int data;
};

int sum_elements(Node* first, Node* last)
    // another concrete algorithm on list of ints
{
    int s = 0;
    while (first!=last) {
        s += first->data;
        first = first->next;
    }
    return s;
}
```

This computes the sum of the **int**s in the singly-linked list implemented by the **Node**s.

These two code fragments differ in detail and in style, but an experienced programmer will immediately say, "Well, this is just two implementations of the accumulate algorithm." This is a popular algorithm. Like most popular algorithms, it has many names, including reduce, fold, sum, and aggregate. However, let us try to develop a general algorithm from the two concrete examples in stages, so as to get a feel for the process of lifting. First we try to abstract away the data types so that we don't have to be specific about

- **double** vs. **int**, or
- array vs. linked list.

To do so, I write some pseudo code:

```
// pseudo code:

T sum(data)
      // somehow parameterize by the value type and the container type
{
      T s = 0
      while (not at end) {
                  s = s + current value
                  get next data element
      }
      return s
}
```

To make this concrete, we need three operations to access the "container" data structure:
- Not at end
- Get current value
- Get next data element

For the actual data, we also need three operations:
- Initialize to zero
- Add
- Return the result

Obviously, this is rather imprecise, but we can turn it into code:

```
// concrete STL-like code:

template<typename Iter, typename Val>
Val sum(Iter first, Iter last)
{
      Val s = 0;
      while (first!=last) {
            s = s + *first;
            ++first;
      }
      return s;
}
```

Here, I took advantage of knowing the usual STL way of representing a sequence of values (§4.5). The sequence is represented as a pair of iterators supporting three operations:
- * for accessing the current value
- ++ for moving forward to the next element
- != for comparing iterators to check if we are at the end of a sequence

We now have an algorithm (a function template) that can be used for both arrays and linked lists and for both **ints** and **doubles**. The array example works immediately because **double*** is an example of an iterator:

```
double ad[] = {1,2,3,4};
double s = sum<double*>(ad,ad+4);
```

To use the handcrafted singly-linked list, we need to provide an iterator for it. Given a few operations, a **Node*** can be the iterator:

```
struct Node { Node* next; int data; };

Node* operator++(Node* p) { return p->next; }
int operator*(Node* p) { return p->data; }
Node* end(lst) { return nullptr; }

void test(Node* lst)
{
    int s = sum<int*>(lst,end(lst));
}
```

I use the **nullptr** as the end iterator. I use an explicit template argument (here, **<int>**) to allow a caller to specify the type to use for the accumulator variable.

What we have so far is more general than a lot of real-world code. For example, **sum()** would work for lists of floating-point numbers (of all precisions), for arrays of integers (of all ranges), and for many other types, such as a **vector<char>**. Importantly, **sum()** is as efficient as the handcrafted functions we started from. We do not want to achieve generality at the cost of performance.

The experienced programmer will note that **sum()** can be generalized further. In particular, the use of an extra template argument is awkward, and we required the initial value **0**. We can solve that by letting the caller supply an initial value and then deduce **Val**:

```
template<typename Iter, typename Val>
Val accumulate(Iter first, Iter last, Val s)
{
    while (first!=last) {
        s = s + *first;
        ++first;
    }
    return s;
}

double ad[] = {1,2,3,4};
double s1 = accumulate(ad,ad+4,0.0);   // accumulate in a double
double s2 = accumulate(ad,ad+4,0);     // accumulate in an int
```

But why +? We sometimes want to multiply elements. In fact, there seem to be quite a few operations we might want to apply to the elements of a sequence. This leads to a further generalization:

```
template<typename Iter, typename Val, typename Oper>
Val accumulate(Iter first, Iter last, Val s, Oper op)
{
    while (first!=last) {
        s = op(s,*first);
        ++first;
    }
    return s;
}
```

We now use the argument **op** to combine element values with the accumulator. For example:

```
double ad[] = {1,2,3,4};
double s1 = accumulate(ad,ad+4,0.0,std::plus<double>);        // as before
double s2 = accumulate(ad,ad+4,1.0,std::multiply<double>);
```

The standard library provides common operations, such as **plus** and **multiply**, as function objects to be used as arguments. Here, we see the utility of having the caller supply the initial value: **0** and ∗ don't go well together for accumulation. The standard library offers a further generalization of **accumulate()** that allows a user to provide an alternative to = for combining the result of the "addition" and the accumulator (§40.6).

Lifting is a skill that requires knowledge of an application domain and some experience. The most important single guide for designing algorithms is to lift them from concrete examples without adding features (notation or run-time cost) that would impair their use. The standard-library algorithms are the results of lifting done with great attention to performance issues.

24.3 Concepts

What are a template's requirements for its arguments? In other words, what does the template code assume about its argument types? Or conversely, what must a type provide to be acceptable as an argument to a template? The possibilities are infinite because we can build classes and templates with arbitrary properties, for example:

- Types that provide – but not +
- Types that can copy but not move values
- Types for which copy operations does not copy (§17.5.1.3)
- Types for which == compares equality and others for which **compare()** does that
- Types that define addition as a member function **plus()** and others that define it as a non-member function **operator+()**

In that direction lies chaos. If every class has a unique interface, it becomes difficult to write templates that can take many different types. Conversely, if each template's requirements are unique, it becomes difficult to define types that can be used with many templates. We would have to remember and keep track of a multitude of interfaces; that's feasible for a tiny program, but unmanageable for real-world libraries and programs. What we need to do is to identify a small number of *concepts* (sets of requirements) that can be used for many templates and many types as arguments. The ideal is a kind of "plug compatibility" as we know it from the physical world, with a small number of standard plug designs.

24.3.1 Discovering a Concept

As an example, consider the **String** class template from §23.2:

```
template<typename C>
class String {
    // ...
};
```

What is required of a type, **X**, for it to be used as an argument to **String**: **String<X>**? More generally, what does it take to be a character in such a character string class? An experienced designer will have a small number of likely answers to that question and start the design based on those. However, let us consider how we might answer it from first principles. We proceed through three stages of analysis:

[1]   First, we look at our (initial) implementation and determine which properties (operations, functions, member types, etc.) it uses from its parameter types (and the meaning of those operations). The resulting list is the minimal requirements for that particular template implementation.

[2]   Next, we look at plausible alternative template implementations and list their requirements on their template arguments. Doing so, we may decide that we should place more or stricter requirements on the template arguments to allow for alternative implementations. Alternatively, we might decide to prefer an implementation that makes fewer and/or simpler requirements.

[3]   Finally, we look at the resulting list (or lists) of required properties and compare it to lists of requirements (concepts) that we have used for other templates. We try to find simple, preferably common, concepts that can express what would otherwise be many long lists of requirements. The aim here is to make our design benefit from general work on classification. The resulting concepts are easier to give meaningful names and easier to remember. They should also maximize the degree of interoperability of templates and types by limiting variations in concepts to what is essential.

The first two steps are – for fundamental reasons – very similar to the way we generalize ("lift") concrete algorithms into generic algorithms (§24.2). The last step counteracts the temptation to provide each algorithm with a set of argument requirements that exactly match its implementation. Such requirement lists are overspecialized and not stable: each change to the implementation would imply changes to the requirements documented as part of the algorithm's interface.

For String<C>, first consider the operations actually performed on the parameter C by the implementation of String (§19.3). That will be the minimal set of requirements for that implementation of String:

[1]   Cs are copied by copy assignment and copy initialization.
[2]   String compares Cs using == and !=.
[3]   String makes arrays of Cs (that implies default construction of Cs).
[4]   String takes the address of Cs.
[5]   Cs are destroyed when a String is destroyed.
[6]   String has >> and << operators that somehow must read and write Cs.

Requirements [4] and [5] are technical requirements that we usually assume for all data types, and I will not discuss types that fail to meet them; such types are almost all overly clever artifacts. The first requirement – that values can be copied – is not true for a few important types, such as std::unique_ptr, that represent real resources (§5.2.1, §34.3.1). However, it is true for almost all "ordinary types," so we require it. The ability to invoke a copy operation goes together with the semantic requirement that a copy really is a copy of the original, that is, that – except for taking the address – the two copies behave identically. Therefore, the ability to copy usually (as for our String) goes together with the requirement to provide == with the usual semantics.

By requiring assignment, we imply that a const type cannot be used as a template argument. For example, String<const char> is not guaranteed to work. That's fine in this case, as in most cases. Having assignment means that an algorithm can use temporary variables of its argument type, create containers of objects of an argument type, etc. It does not imply that we cannot use **const** to specify interfaces. For example:

```
template<typename T>
bool operator==(const String<T>& s1, const String<T>& s2)
{
    if (s1.size()!=s2.size()) return false;
    for (auto i = 0; i!=s1.size(); ++i)
        if (s1[i]!=s2[i]) return false;
    return true;
}
```

For **String<X>** we require that objects of type **X** can be copied. Independently, through the **const**s in its argument types, **operator==()** promises not to write to the **X** elements.

Should we require a move for an element type **C**? After all, we provide move operations for **String<C>**. We could, but it's not essential: what we do with a **C** can be handled by copying, and if some copy is implicitly turned into a move (e.g., when we returned a **C**), so much the better. In particular, potentially important examples, such as **String<String<char>>**, will work fine (correctly and efficiently) without adding move operations to the requirements.

So far, so good, but the last requirement (that we can read and write **C**s using **>>** and **<<**) seems excessive. Do we really read and write every kind of string? Maybe it would be better to say that *if* we read and write a **String<X>**, then **X** must provide **>>** and **<<**? That is, instead of placing a requirement on **C** for the whole **String**, we require it (only) for **String**s that we actually read and write.

This is an important and fundamental design choice: we can place a requirement on class template arguments (so that they apply to all class members) or just to template arguments on individual class function members. The latter is more flexible, but also more verbose (we have to express the requirement for each function that needs it) and harder for a programmer to remember.

Looking at the list of requirements so far, I note the absence of a couple of operations that are common for "ordinary characters" in "ordinary strings":

[1]   No ordering (e.g., **<**)

[2]   No conversion to an integer value

After this initial analysis we can consider which "well-known concepts" (§24.3.2) our lists of requirements relate to. The central concept for "ordinary types" is *regular*. A *regular type* is a type that

- you can copy (using assignment or initialization) with the proper copy semantics (§17.5.1.3),
- you can default construct,
- doesn't have problems with various minor technical requirements (such as taking the address of a variable),
- you can compare for equality (using **==** and **!=**).

That seems an excellent choice for our **String** template arguments. I considered leaving out the equality comparisons but decided that copying without equality is rarely useful. Typically, **Regular** is the safe bet, and thinking about the meaning of **==** can help avoid errors in the definition of copying. All the built-in types are regular.

But does it make sense to leave out ordering (<) for **String**? Consider how we use strings. The desired use of a template (such as **String**) should determine its requirements on its arguments. We do compare strings extensively, and in addition we use comparisons indirectly when we sort sequences of strings, we put strings into sets, etc. Also, the standard-library **string** does provide <. It is usually a good idea to look to the standard for inspiration. So, we require not just **Regular** for our **String**, but also ordering. That's the concept **Ordered**.

Interestingly, there has been quite some debate on whether **Regular** should require < or not. It seems that most types related to numbers have a natural order. For example, characters are encoded in bit patterns that can be interpreted as integers, and any sequence of values can be lexicographically ordered. However, many types do not have a natural order (e.g., complex numbers and images) even though we could define one. Other types have several natural orderings, but no unique best ordering (e.g., records may be ordered by name or by address). Finally, some (reasonable) types simply don't have an order. For example, consider:

```
enum class rsp { rock, scissors, paper };
```

The rock-scissors-and-paper game critically depends on
- scissors<rock,
- rock<paper, and
- paper<scissors.

However, our **String** is not supposed to take an arbitrary type as its character type; it is supposed to take a type that supports string operations (such as comparisons, sorting, and I/O), so I decided to require ordering.

Adding a default constructor and the == and < operator, to our requirements for **String**'s template argument allows us to provide several useful operations for **String**. In fact, the more we require of a template argument type, the easier the various tasks become for the template implementer and the more services the template can offer to its users. On the other hand, it is important not to load down a template with requirements that are only used rarely and by specific operations: each requirement places a burden on the implementer of argument types and limits the set of types that can be used as arguments. So, for **String<X>** we require:
- Ordered<X>
- >> and << for X (only) if we use **String<X>**'s >> and <<
- Convertibility to an integer (only) if we define and use a conversion operation from **X**

So far, we have expressed our requirement of a character type for **String** in terms of syntactic properties, such as X must provide copy operations, ==, and <. In addition, we must require that these operations have the right semantics; for example, a copy operation makes a copy, == (equality) compares for equality, and < (less than) provides ordering. Often, this semantics involves relations among the operations. For example, for the standard library, we have (§31.2.2.1):
- The result of a copy compares equal to anything the original compares equal to (**a==b** implies T{a}==T{b}) and the copy is independent of its source (§17.5.1.3).
- A less-than comparison (e.g., <) provides a strict weak order (§31.2.2.1).

The semantics are defined in English text or (better still) mathematics, but unfortunately we have no way of expressing semantic requirements in C++ itself (but see §24.4.1). For the standard library, you can find the semantic requirements written in formalized English in the ISO standard.

24.3.2 Concepts and Constraints

A concept is not an arbitrary collection of properties. Most lists of properties of a type (or a set of types) do not define a coherent and useful concept. To be useful as a concept, a list of requirements has to reflect the needs of a set of algorithms or a set of operations of a template class. In many fields of endeavor, people have designed or discovered concepts describing the fundamental concepts of the field (the technical use of the word "concept" in C++ was chosen with this common usage in mind). There seem to be surprisingly few concepts that make sense. For example, algebra builds on concepts such as monad, field, and ring, whereas the STL relies on concepts such as forward iterator, bidirectional iterator, and random-access iterator. Finding a new concept in a field is a major accomplishment; it is not something you should expect to do every year. Mostly, you find concepts by examining the foundational texts of a field of study or an application domain. The set of concepts used in this book are described in §24.4.4.

"Concepts" is a very general idea that does not inherently have anything to do with templates. Even K&R C [Kernighan,1978] had concepts in the sense that *signed integral type* is the language's generalization of the idea of an integer in memory. Our requirements on template arguments are concepts (however expressed), so most interesting issues related to concepts come in the context of templates.

I see a concept as a carefully crafted entity that reflects fundamental properties of an application domain. Consequently, there should be only few concepts, and these can act as a guideline for the design of algorithms and types. The analogy is with physical plugs and sockets; we want the minimal number to simplify our lives and to keep design and construction costs down. This ideal can conflict with the ideal of minimal requirements for each individual generic algorithm (§24.2) and each individual parameterized class. Furthermore, the ideal can conflict with the ideal of providing absolutely minimal interfaces to classes (§16.2.3) and even with what some programmers regard as their right to write their code "exactly as they like." However, we don't get plug compatibility without effort and some form of standard.

I set the bar for being a concept very high: I require generality, some stability, usability across many algorithms, semantic consistency, and more. In fact, many simple constraints that we'd like for template arguments don't qualify as concepts according to my criteria. I think that is unavoidable. In particular, we write many templates that do not reflect general algorithms or widely applicable types. Instead, they are implementation details, and their arguments only have to reflect the necessary details of a template intended for a single use in a single implementation of something. I call requirements for such template arguments *constraints* or (if you must) *ad hoc concepts*. One way to look at constraints is to consider them incomplete (partial) specifications of an interface. Often, a partial specification can be useful and much better than no specification.

As an example, consider a library for experimenting with balancing strategies for balanced binary trees. The tree takes a **Balancer** as a template argument:

```
template<typename Node, typename Balance>
struct node_base {  // base of balanced tree
    // ...
}
```

A balancer is simply a class that provides three operations on nodes. For example:

```
struct Red_black_balance {
    // ...
    template<typename Node> static void add_fixup(Node* x);
    template<typename Node> static void touch(Node* x);
    template<typename Node> static void detach(Node* x);
};
```

Obviously, we'd like to say what's required of node_base's arguments, but a balancer is not meant to be a widely used and easily understood interface; it's meant to be used only as a detail of a particular implementation of balanced trees. This idea of a balancer (I hesitate to use the word "concept") is unlikely to be used elsewhere or even to survive a major rewrite of the balanced tree implementation unchanged. It would be hard to pin down the exact semantics of a balancer. For starters, the semantics of Balancer would critically depend on the semantics of Node. In those aspects, a Balancer differs from a proper concept, such as Random_access_iterator. We can, however, still use the minimal specification of a balancer, "provides those three functions on nodes," as a constraint on arguments to a node_base.

Note the way "semantics" keep cropping up in the discussion of concepts. I find that "Can I write out a semiformal semantics?" to be the question that is most helpful when it comes to deciding whether something is a concept or simply an ad hoc collection of constraints on a type (or set of types). If I can write out a meaningful semantic specification, I have a concept. If not, what I have is a constraint that may be useful but shouldn't be expected to be stable or widely useful.

24.4 Making Concepts Concrete

Unfortunately, C++ does not have specific language facilities for directly expressing concepts. However, handling "concepts" as a design notion only and presenting them informally as comments is not ideal. For starters, compilers do not understand comments, so requirements expressed only as comments must be checked by the programmer and cannot help the compiler provide good error messages. Experience shows that even though concepts cannot be represented perfectly without direct language support, we can approximate them using code that performs compile-time checks of template argument properties.

A concept is a predicate; that is, we think of a concept as a compile-time function that looks at a set of template arguments and returns true if they meet the concept's requirements and false if they don't. So, we implement a concept as a constexpr function. Here, I will use the term *constraints check* to refer to a call of a constexpr predicate that checks a concept for a set of types and values. In contrast to proper concepts, a constraints check does not deal with semantic issues; it simply checks assumptions about syntactic properties.

Consider our String; its character type argument is supposed to be Ordered:

```
template<typename C>
class String {
    static_assert(Ordered<C>(),"String's character type is not ordered");
    // ...
};
```

When String<X> is instantiated for a type X, the static_assert will be executed by the compiler. If

Ordered<X>() returns true, the compilation proceeds, generating exactly the code it would have done without the assert. Otherwise, the error message is produced.

At first glance, this looks rather reasonable for a workaround. I'd rather have said:

```
template<Ordered C>
class String {
    // ...
};
```

However, that is for the future, so let us see how to define the predicate Ordered<T>():

```
template<typename T>
constexpr bool Ordered()
{
    return Regular<T>() && Totally_ordered<T>();
}
```

That is, a type is Ordered if it is both Regular and Totally_ordered. Let us "dig down" to see what that means:

```
template<typename T>
constexpr bool Totally_ordered()
{
    return Equality_comparable<T>()    // has == and !=
        && Has_less<T>()&& Boolean<Less_result<T>>()
        && Has_greater<T>() && Boolean<Greater_result<T>>()
        && Has_less_equal<T>() && Boolean<Less_equal_result<T>>()
        && Has_greater_equal<T>() && Boolean<Greater_equal_result<T>>();
}
```

```
template<typename T>
constexpr bool Equality_comparable()
{
    return Has_equal<T>() && Boolean<Equal_result<T>>()
        && Has_not_equal<T>() && Boolean<Not_equal_result<T>>();
}
```

So, a type T is ordered if it is regular and provides the usual six comparison operations. The comparison operations have to deliver results that can be converted to bool. The comparison operators are also supposed to have their proper mathematical meaning. The C++ standard precisely specifies what that means (§31.2.2.1, §iso.25.4).

Has_equals is implemented using enable_if and the techniques described in §28.4.4.

I capitalize my constraints names (e.g., Regular) even though doing so violates my "house style" of capitalizing type and template names, but not functions. However, concepts are even more fundamental than types, so I feel a need to emphasize them. I also keep them in a separate namespace (Estd) in the hope that very similar names will eventually become part of the language or the standard library.

Digging a bit further into the set of useful concepts, we can define Regular:

```
template<typename T>
constexpr bool Regular()
{
    return Semiregular<T>() && Equality_comparable<T>();
}
```

Equality_comparable gives us **==** and **!=**. **Semiregular** is the concept that express the notion of a type that doesn't have unusual technical restrictions:

```
template<typename T>
constexpr bool Semiregular()
{
    return Destructible<T>()
        && Default_constructible<T>()
        && Move_constructible<T>()
        && Move_assignable<T>()
        && Copy_constructible<T>()
        && Copy_assignable<T>();
}
```

A **Semiregular** can be both moved and copied. That describes most types, but there are examples of types that cannot be copied, such as **unique_ptr**. However, I don't know of useful types that can be copied but not moved. Types that can neither be moved nor copied, such as **type_info** (§22.5), are very rare and tend to reflect system properties.

We can also use constraints checks for functions; for example:

```
template<typename C>
ostream& operator<<(ostream& out, String<C>& s)
{
    static_assert(Streamable<C>(),"String's character not streamable");
    out << '"';
    for (int i=0; i!=s.size(); ++i) cout << s[i];
    out << '"';
}
```

The concept **Streamable** needed by **String**'s output operator **<<** requires its argument **C** to provide the output operator **<<**:

```
template<typename T>
constexpr bool Streamable()
{
    return Input_streamable<T>() && Output_streamable<T>();
}
```

That is, **Streamable** tests that we can use the standard stream I/O (§4.3, Chapter 38) for a type.

Checking concepts through constraints-check templates has obvious weaknesses:

- Constraints checks are placed in definitions, but they really belong in declarations. That is, a concept is part of the interface to an abstraction, but a constraints check can be used only in its implementation.
- The checking of constraints occurs as part of the instantiation of the constraints-check template. Therefore, the checking may occur later than we would like. In particular, we would

have preferred for a constraints check to be guaranteed to be done by the compiler at the point of the first call, but that is impossible without language changes.

- We can forget to insert a constraints check (especially for a function template).
- The compiler does not check that a template implementation uses only the properties speci-fied in its concepts. Thus, a template implementation may pass the constraints check, yet still fail to type check.
- We do not specify semantic properties in a way that a compiler can understand (e.g., we use comments).

Adding constraints checks makes the requirements on template arguments explicit, and if a con-straints check is well designed, it leads to more comprehensible error messages. If we forget to insert constraints checks, we are back to the ordinary type checking of the code generated by tem-plate instantiation. That can be unfortunate, but it is not disastrous. These constraints checks are a technique for making checking of designs based on concepts more robust, rather than an integral part of the type system.

If we want to, we can place constraints checks almost anywhere. For example, to guarantee that a particular type is checked against a particular concept, we could place constraints checks in a namespace scope (e.g., the global scope). For example:

```
static_assert(Ordered<std::string>,"std::string is not Ordered");      // will succeed
static_assert(Ordered<String<char>>,"String<char> is not Ordered");  // will fail
```

The first **static_assert** checks if the standard **string** is **Ordered** (it is, because it provides ==, !=, and <). The second checks if our **String** is **Ordered** (it is not, because I "forgot" to define <). Using such a global check will perform the constraints check independently of whether we actually use that particular specialization of a template in the program. Depending on our aims, that can be an advantage or a bother. Such a check forces type checking to be done at a specific point in the pro-gram; that is usually good for error isolation. Also, such checks can help unit testing. However, for programs using a number of libraries, explicit checks quickly become unmanageable.

Being **Regular** is an ideal for a type. We can copy objects of regular types, put them into **vector**s and arrays, compare them, etc. If a type is **Ordered**, we can also use its objects in sets, sort sequences of such objects, etc. So, we go back and improve our **String** to make it **Ordered**. In par-ticular, we add < to provide a lexicographical ordering:

```
template<typename C>
bool operator<(const String<C>& s1, const String<C>& s2)
{
    static_assert(Ordered<C>(),"String's character type not ordered");
    bool eq = true;
    for (int i=0; i!=s1.size() && i!=s2.size(); ++i) {
        if (s2[i]<s1[i]) return false;
        if (s1[i]<s2[i]) eq = false;             // not s1==s2
    }
    if (s2.size()<s1.size()) return false;       // s2 is shorter than s1
    if (s1.size()==s2.size() && eq) return false;   // s1==s2
    return true;
}
```

24.4.1 Axioms

As in mathematics, an *axiom* is something we can't prove. It is something we assume to be true. In the context of requirements for template arguments, we use "axiom" in that sense to refer to semantic properties. We use an axiom to state what a class or an algorithm assumes about its set of inputs. An axiom, however expressed, represents an algorithm's or class's expectations of (assumptions about) its arguments. We cannot in general test to see whether an axiom holds for values of a type (that is one reason we refer to them as axioms). Furthermore, an axiom is only required to hold for the values actually used by an algorithm. For example, an algorithm can carefully avoid dereferencing null pointers or copying a floating-point NaN. If so, it could have axioms that require pointers to be dereferenceable and floating-point values to be copyable. Alternatively, axioms can be written with the general assumption that singular values (e.g., NaN and **nullptr**) violate some precondition, so that they need not be considered.

C++ does not (currently) have any way of expressing axioms, but as for concepts, we can make our idea of a concept a bit more concrete than a comment or some text in a design document.

Consider how we might express some of the key semantic requirements for a type to be regular:

```
template<typename T>
bool Copy_equality(T x)                    // semantics of copy construction
{
    return T{x}==x;      // a copy compares equal to what it is a copy of
}


template<typename T>
bool Copy_assign_equality(T x, T& y)       // semantics of assignment
{
    return (y=x, y==x);  // the result of an assignment compares equal to the source of the assignment
}
```

In other words, copy operations make copies.

```
template<typename T>
bool Move_effect(T x, T& y)                // semantics of move
{
    return (x==y ? T{std::move(x)}==y) : true) && can_destroy(y);
}


template<typename T>
bool Move_assign_effect(T x, T& y, T& z)   // semantics of move assignment
{
    return (y==z ? (x=std::move(y), x==z)) : true) && can_destroy(y);
}
```

In other words, a move operation yields a value that compares equal to whatever the source of the move operation compared equal to, and the source of the move can be destroyed.

These axioms are represented as executable code. We might use them for testing, but most importantly, we have to think harder to express them than we would have to simply write a comment. The resulting axioms are more precisely stated than would have been the case in "ordinary English." Basically, we can express such pseudo axioms using first-order predicate logic.

24.4.2 Multi-argument Concepts

When looking at a single-argument concept and applying it to a type, it looks very much as if we are doing conventional type checking and that the concept is the type of a type. That's part of the story, but only a part. Often, we find that relationships among argument types are essential for correct specification and use. Consider the standard-library find() algorithm:

```
template<typename Iter, typename Val>
Iter find(Iter b, Iter e, Val x);
```

The Iter template argument must be an input iterator, and we can (relatively) easily define a constraints-check template for that concept.

So far, so good, but find() depends critically on comparing x to elements of the sequence [b:e]. We need to specify that comparison is required; that is, we need to state that Val and and the value type of the input iterator are equality comparable. That requires a two-argument version of Equality_comparable:

```
template<typename A, typename B>
constexpr bool Equality_comparable(A a, B b)
{
    return Common<T, U>()
            && Totally_ordered<T>()
            && Totally_ordered<U>()
            && Totally_ordered<Common_type<T,U>>()
            && Has_less<T,U>() && Boolean<Less_result<T,U>>()
            && Has_less<U,T>() && Boolean<Less_result<U,T>>()
            && Has_greater<T,U>() && Boolean<Greater_result<T,U>>()
            && Has_greater<U,T>() && Boolean<Greater_result<U,T>>()
            && Has_less_equal<T,U>() && Boolean<Less_equal_result<T,U>>()
            && Has_less_equal<U,T>() && Boolean<Less_equal_result<U,T>>()
            && Has_greater_equal<T,U>() && Boolean<Greater_equal_result<T,U>>()
            && Has_greater_equal<U,T>() && Boolean<Greater_equal_result<U,T>>();
};
```

This is rather verbose for a simple concept. However, I wanted to be explicit about all of the operators and about the symmetry of their use rather than burying the complexity in a generalization.

Given that, we can define find():

```
template<typename Iter, typename Val>
Iter find(Iter b, Iter e, Val x)
{
    static_assert(Input_iterator<Iter>(),"find() requires an input iterator");
    static_assert(Equality_comparable<Value_type<Iter>,Val>(),
                      "find()'s iterator and value arguments must match");

    while (b!=e) {
        if (*b==x) return b;
        ++b;
    }
    return b;
}
```

Multi-argument concepts are particularly common and useful when specifying generic algorithms. This is also the area where you find the greatest number of concepts and the greatest need to specify new concepts (as opposed to picking "standard ones" from a catalog of common concepts). The variations among well-defined types appear to be somewhat more limited than the variations among algorithms' requirements on their arguments.

24.4.3 Value Concepts

Concepts can express arbitrary (syntactic) requirements on a set of template arguments. In particular, a template argument can be an integer value, so concepts can take integer arguments. For example, we can write a constraints check to test that a value template argument is small:

```
template<int N>
constexpr bool Small_size()
{
    return N<=8;
}
```

A more realistic example would be a concept for which the numeric argument was just one among others. For example:

```
constexpr int stack_limit = 2048;

template<typename T,int N>
constexpr bool Stackable()      // T is regular and N elements of T can fit on a small stack
{
    return Regular<T>() && sizeof(T)*N<=stack_limit;
}
```

This implements a notion of "small enough to be stack allocated." It might be used like this:

```
template<typename T, int N>
struct Buffer {
    // ...
};

template<typename T, int N>
void fct()
{
    static_assert(Stackable<T,N>(),"fct() buffer won't fit on stack");
    Buffer<T,N> buf;
    // ...
}
```

Compared to the fundamental concepts for types, value concepts tend to be small and ad hoc.

24.4.4 Constraints Checks

The constraints checks used in this book can be found on the book's support site. They are not part of a standard, and I hope that in the future they will be replaced by a proper language mechanism. However, they can be useful for thinking about template and type design and reflect the de facto concepts in the standard library. They should go in a separate namespace to avoid interfering with possible future language features and alternative implementations of the idea of concepts. I use namespace **Estd**, but that may be an alias (§14.4.2). Here are a few constraints checks that you might find useful:

- **Input_iterator<X>**: **X** is an iterator that we can use only once to traverse a sequence (forward using ++), reading each element once only.
- **Output_iterator<X>**: **X** is an iterator that we can use only once to traverse a sequence (forward using ++), writing each element once only.
- **Forward_iterator<X>**: **X** is an iterator that we can use to traverse a sequence (forward using ++). This is what a singly-linked list (e.g., **forward_list**) naturally supports.
- **Bidirectional_iterator<X>**: **X** is an iterator that we can move both forward (using ++) and backward (using --). This is what a doubly-linked list (e.g., **list**) naturally supports.
- **Random_access_iterator<X>**: **X** is an iterator that we can use to traverse a sequence (forward and backward) and to randomly access elements using subscripting and positioning using += and -=. This is what an array naturally supports.
- **Equality_comparable<X,Y>**: An **X** can be compared with a **Y** using == and !=.
- **Totally_ordered<X,Y>**: **X** and **Y** are **Equality_comparable** and an **X** can be compared with a **Y** using <, <=, > and >=.
- **Semiregular<X>**: **X**s can be copied, default constructed, allocated on the free store, and are free of minor annoying technical restrictions.
- **Regular<X>**: **X**s are **Semiregular** and can be compared using equality. The standard-library containers require their elements to be regular.
- **Ordered<X>**: **X**s are **Regular** and **Totally_ordered**. The standard-library associative containers require their elements to be ordered unless you explicitly provide a comparison operation.
- **Assignable<X,Y>**: A **Y** can be assigned to an **X** using =.
- **Predicate<F,X>**: An **F** can be called for an **X** yielding a **bool**.
- **Streamable<X>**: An **X** can be read and written using iostreams.
- **Movable<X>**: An **X** can be moved; that is, it has a move constructor and a move assignment. In addition, an **X** is addressable and destructible.
- **Copyable<X>**: An **X** is **Movable** and can also be copied.
- **Convertible<X,Y>**: An **X** can be implicitly converted to a **Y**.
- **Common<X,Y>**: An **X** and a **Y** can unambiguously be converted to a common type called **Common_type<X,Y>**. This is a formalization of the language rule for compatibility of operands to **?:** (§11.1.3). For example, **Common_type<Base∗,Derived∗>** is **Base∗** and **Common_type<int,long>** is **long**.
- **Range<X>**: An **X** that can be used by a range-**for** (§9.5.1), that is, **X** must provide members, **x.begin()** and **x.end()**, or nonmember equivalents, **begin(x)** and **end(x)**, with the required semantics.

Obviously, these definitions are informal. In most cases, these concepts are based on standard-library type predicates (§35.4.1), and the ISO C++ standard provides formal definitions (e.g., §iso.17.6.3).

24.4.5 Template Definition Checking

A constraints-check template ensures that a type provides the properties required by the concept. If the implementation of a template in fact uses more properties than its concepts guarantee, we may get type errors. For example, the standard-library **find()** requires a pair of input iterators as arguments, but we might (incautiously) have defined it like this:

```
template<typename Iter, typename Val>
Iter find(Iter b, Iter e, Val x)
{
    static_assert(Input_iterator<Iter>(),"find(): Iter is not a Forward iterator");
    static_assert(Equality_comparable<Value_type<Iter>,Val>),
                  "find(): value type doesn't match iterator");

    while (b!=e) {
        if (*b==x) return b;
        b = b+1;                    // note: not ++b
    }
    return b;
}
```

Now, **b+1** is an error unless **b** is a random-access iterator (and not just a forward iterator as ensured by the constraints check). However, the constraints check does not help us detect that problem. For example:

```
void f(list<int>& lst, vector<string>& vs)
{
    auto p = find(lst.begin(),lst.end(),1209);        // error: list does not provide +
    auto q = find(vs.begin(),vs.end(),"Cambridge");   // OK: vector provides +
    // ...
}
```

The call of **find()** for the **list** will fail (because **+** is not defined for the forward iterator provided by **list**) and the call for the **vector** will succeed (because **b+1** is fine for **vector<string>::iterator**).

Constraints checks primarily provide a service to the user of a template: the actual template arguments are checked against the template's requirements. On the other hand, constraints checks do not help a template writer who would like to be sure that the implementation doesn't use any properties beyond those specified in the concepts. Ideally, the type system would ensure that, but that requires language features that are still in the future. So, how do we test the implementation of a parameterized class or a generic algorithm?

Concepts provide a strong guideline: the implementation should use no property of an argument that isn't specified by the concepts, so we should test the implementation with arguments that provide the properties specified by the implementation's concepts, and only those. Such a type is sometimes called an *archetype*.

So, for the **find()** example, we look at **Forward_iterator** and **Equality_comparable** or at the standard's definition of the forward-iterator and equal-comparable concepts (§iso.17.6.3.1, §iso.24.2.5). Then, we decide that we need an **Iterator** type that provides at least:

- A default constructor
- A copy constructor and a copy assignment
- Operators == and !=
- A prefix operator ++
- A type **Value_type<Iterator>**
- A prefix operator *
- The ability to assign the result of * to a **Value_type<Iterator>**
- The ability to assign a **Value_type<Iterator>** to the result of *

This is slightly simplified from the standard-library forward iterator, but sufficient for **find()**. Constructing that list by looking at the concepts is easy.

Given this list, we need to find or define a type that provides only the desired features. For a forward iterator, as needed by **find()**, the standard-library **forward_list** fits the bill perfectly. This is because "forward iterator" was defined to express the idea of something that allows us to iterate through a singly-linked list. It is not uncommon that a popular type is an archetype for a popular concept. If we decide to use an existing type, we have to be careful, though, not to pick a type that is more flexible than required. For example, the typical mistake when testing algorithms, such as **find()**, is to use a **vector**. However, the very generality and flexibility that make **vector** so popular make it unusable as an archetype for many simple algorithms.

If we can't find an existing type that fits our needs, we must define one ourselves. That is done by going through the list of requirements and defining suitable members:

```
template<typename Val>
struct Forward {          // for checking find()
    Forward();
    Forward(const Forward&);
    Forward operator=(const Forward&);
    bool operator==(const Forward&);
    bool operator!=(const Forward&);
    void operator++();
    Val& operator*();     // simplified: does not handle a proxy for Val
};

template<typename Val>
using Value_type<Forward<Val>> = Val;     // simplified; see §28.2.4

void f()
{
    Forward<int> p = find(Forward<int>{},Forward<int>{},7);
}
```

At this level of testing, we need not check that these operations actually implement the right semantics. We just check that the template implementation does not rely on properties that it should not.

Here, I have simplified the testing by not introducing an archetype for the **Val** argument. Instead, I simply used **int**. Testing nontrivial conversions between an archetype for **Val** and an archetype for **Iter** would be significantly more work and most likely not particularly useful.

Writing a test harness that checks the implementation of **find()** against **std::forward_list** or **X** is not trivial, but it is not among the most difficult tasks facing a designer of generic algorithms.

Using a relatively small and well-specified set of concepts makes the task manageable. The tests can and should be completely compile-time.

Note that this simple specification and checking strategy leads to find() requiring its iterator argument to have a Value_type type function (§28.2). That allows pointers to be used as iterators. For many template parameters it is important that built-in types can be used as well as user-defined types (§1.2.2, §25.2.1).

24.5 Advice

[1]   A template can pass argument types without loss of information; §24.1.
[2]   Templates provide a general mechanism for compile-time programming; §24.1.
[3]   Templates provide compile-time "duck typing"; §24.1.
[4]   Design generic algorithms by "lifting" from concrete examples; §24.2.
[5]   Generalize algorithms by specifying template argument requirements in terms of concepts; §24.3.
[6]   Do not give unconventional meaning to conventional notation; §24.3.
[7]   Use concepts as a design tool; §24.3.
[8]   Aim for "plug compatibility" among algorithms and argument type by using common and regular template argument requirements; §24.3.
[9]   Discover a concept by minimizing an algorithm's requirements on its template arguments and then generalizing for wider use; §24.3.1.
[10] A concept is not just a description of the needs of a particular implementation of an algorithm; §24.3.1.
[11] If possible, choose a concept from a list of well-known concepts; §24.3.1, §24.4.4.
[12] The default concept for a template argument is Regular; §24.3.1.
[13] Not all template argument types are Regular; §24.3.1.
[14] A concept requires a semantic aspect; it is not primarily a syntactic notion; §24.3.1, §24.3.2, §24.4.1.
[15] Make concepts concrete in code; §24.4.
[16] Express concepts as compile-time predicates (constexpr functions) and test them using static_assert() or enable_if<>; §24.4.
[17] Use axioms as a design tool; §24.4.1.
[18] Use axioms as a guide for testing; §24.4.1.
[19] Some concepts involve two or more template arguments; §24.4.2.
[20] Concepts are not just types of types; §24.4.2.
[21] Concepts can involve numeric values; §24.4.3.
[22] Use concepts as a guide for testing template definitions; §24.4.5.

Specialization

> *It ain't what you don't know that gets you into trouble.*
> *It's what you know for sure that just ain't so.*
> *– Mark Twain*

25.1 Introduction

Over the last two decades, templates have developed from a relatively simple idea to the backbone of most advanced C++ programming. In particular, templates are key to techniques for
- improving type safety (e.g., by eliminating the use of casts; §12.5);
- raising the general level of abstraction of programs (e.g., by using standard containers and algorithms; §4.4, §4.5, §7.4.3, Chapter 31, Chapter 32); and
- providing more flexible, type-safe, and efficient parameterization of types and algorithms (§25.2.3).

These techniques all critically rely on the ability of template code to use template arguments without overhead and in a type-safe manner. Most techniques also rely on the type deduction mechanisms offered by templates (sometimes called *compile-time polymorphism*; §27.2). These techniques are the backbone of C++ use in performance-critical areas, such as high-performance numerical computing and embedded systems programming. For mature examples, see the standard library (Part IV).

This chapter and the following two present simple examples of the advanced and/or specialized language features supporting techniques aimed at uncompromised flexibility and performance. Many of these techniques are primarily developed for and used by library implementers. Like most programmers, I prefer to forget about the more advanced techniques most of the time. Where I can, I keep my code simple and rely on libraries so that I can benefit from the use of advanced features in the hands of experts in a given application domain.

Templates are introduced in §3.4. This chapter is part of a sequence presenting templates and their uses:

- Chapter 23 gives a more detailed introduction to templates.
- Chapter 24 discusses generic programming, the most common use of templates.
- Chapter 25 (this chapter) shows how to specialize a template with a set of arguments.
- Chapter 26 focuses on template implementation issues related to name binding.
- Chapter 27 discusses the relation between templates and class hierarchies.
- Chapter 28 focuses on templates as a language for generating classes and functions.
- Chapter 29 presents a larger example of template-based programming techniques.

25.2 Template Parameters and Arguments

A template can take parameters:

- *Type parameters* of "type type"
- *Value parameters* of built-in types such as ints (§25.2.2) and pointers to functions (§25.2.3)
- *Template parameters* of "type template" (§25.2.4)

Type parameters are by far the most common, but value parameters are essential for many important techniques (§25.2.2, §28.3).

A template can take a fixed number of parameters or a variable number. The discussion of variadic templates is postponed until §28.6.

Note that it is common to use short names with initial uppercase letters as names of template type arguments, for example, **T**, **C**, **Cont**, and **Ptr**. This is acceptable because such names tend to be conventional and restricted to a relatively small scope (§6.3.3). However, when using **ALL_CAPS**, there is always a chance of clashing with macros (§12.6), so don't use names that are long enough to clash with likely macro names.

25.2.1 Types as Arguments

A template argument is defined to be a *type parameter* by prefixing it with **typename** or **class**. The result of using either is completely equivalent. Every type (built-in or user-defined) is syntactically acceptable to a template declared to take a type parameter. For example:

```
template<typename T>
void f(T);

template<typename T>
class X {
    // ...
};
```

```
f(1);                           // T deduced to be int
f<double>(1);                   // T is double
f<complex<double>>(1);          // T is complex<double>

X<double> x1;                   // T is double
X<complex<double>> x2;          // T is complex<double>
```

A type argument is unconstrained; that is, there is nothing in the interface of a class that constrains it to be a certain kind of type or part of a class hierarchy. The validity of an argument type depends exclusively on its use in the templates, providing a form of duck typing (§24.1). You can implement general constraints as concepts (§24.3).

User-defined and built-in types are handled equivalently when used as template arguments. This is essential for allowing us to define templates that work identically for user-defined and built-in types. For example:

```
vector<double> x1;                  // vector of doubles
vector<complex<double>> x2;         // vector of complex<double>
```

In particular, there is no space or time overhead implied by using either compared to the other:

- Values of built-in types are not "boxed" into special container objects.
- Values of all types are retrieved directly from a **vector** without use of potentially expensive (e.g., virtual) "**get()** functions."
- Values of user-defined types are not implicitly accessed through references.

To be used as a template argument, a type must be in scope and accessible. For example:

```
class X {
    class M { /* ... */ };
    // ...
    void mf();
};

void f()
{
    struct S { /* ... */ };
    vector<S> vs;               // OK
    vector<X::M> vm;            // error: X::M is private
    // ...
}

void M::mf()
{
    vector<S> vs;              // error: no S in scope
    vector<M> vm;              // OK
    // ...
};
```

25.2.2 Values as Arguments

A template parameter that is not a type or a template is called a *value parameter* and an argument passed to it a *value argument*. For example, integer arguments come in handy for supplying sizes and limits:

```
template<typename T, int max>
class Buffer {
    T v[max];
public:
    Buffer() { }
    // ...
};


Buffer<char,128> cbuf;
Buffer<int,5000> ibuf;
Buffer<Record,8> rbuf;
```

Simple and constrained containers such as **Buffer** can be important where run-time efficiency and compactness are paramount. They avoid the use of free store implied by the use of a more general **string** or **vector** while not suffering from the implicit conversions to a pointer like a built-in array (§7.4). The standard-library **array** (§34.2.1) implements this idea.

An argument for a template value parameter can be (§iso.14.3.2):

- An integral constant expression (§10.4)
- A pointer or a reference to an object or a function with external linkage (§15.2)
- A nonoverloaded pointer to member (§20.6)
- A null pointer (§7.2.2)

A pointer used as a template argument must be of the form **&of**, where **of** is the name of an object or a function, or of the form **f**, where **f** is the name of a function. A pointer to member must be of the form **&X::of**, where **of** is the name of a member. In particular, a string literal is *not* acceptable as a template argument:

```
template<typename T, char* label>
class X {
    // ...
};


X<int,"BMW323Ci"> x1;       // error: string literal as template argument
char lx2[] = "BMW323Ci";
X<int,lx2> x2;              // OK: lx2 has external linkage
```

This restriction, like the one against floating-point template value arguments, exists to simplify implementation of separately compiled translation units. It is best to think of template value arguments as a mechanism for passing integers and pointers to functions. Resist the temptation to try something more clever. Unfortunately (for no fundamental reason), literal types (§10.4.3) cannot be used as template value parameters. The value template arguments are the mechanism for some more advanced compile-time computation techniques (Chapter 28).

An integer template argument must be a constant. For example:

```
constexpr int max = 200;

void f(int i)
{
    Buffer<int,i> bx;        // error: constant expression expected
    Buffer<int,max> bm;      // OK: constant expression
    // ...
}
```

Conversely, a value template parameter is a constant within the template so that an attempt to change the value of a parameter is an error. For example:

```
template<typename T, int max>
class Buffer {
    T v[max];
public:
    Buffer(int i) { max = i; }   // error: attempt to assign to template value argument
    // ...
};
```

A type template parameter can be used as a type later in a template parameter list. For example:

```
template<typename T, T default_value>
class Vec {
    // ...
};


Vec<int,42> c1;
Vec<string,""> c2;
```

This becomes particularly useful when combined with a default template argument (§25.2.5); for example:

```
template<typename T, T default_value = T{}>
class Vec {
    // ...
};


Vec<int,42> c1;
Vec<int> c11;                   // default_value is int{}, that is, 0
Vec<string,"fortytwo"> c2;
Vec<string> c22;                // default_value is string{}; that is, ""
```

25.2.3 Operations as Arguments

Consider a slightly simplified version of the standard-library **map** (§31.4.3):

```
template<typename Key, Class V>
class map {
    // ...
};
```

How do we supply comparison criteria for **Keys**?

- We can't hardwire a comparison criterion into the container because the container can't (in general) impose its needs on the element types. For example, by default, the **map** uses < for comparison, but not all **Keys** have a < that we would want to use.
- We can't hardwire an ordering criterion into the **Key** type because (in general) there are many different ways of ordering elements based on a key. For example, one of the most common **Key** types is **string** and **strings** can be ordered based on a variety of criteria (e.g., case sensitive and case insensitive).

Consequently, a sorting criterion is not built into the container type or into the element type. In principle, the notion of sorting criteria for a **map** could be represented as:

[1]   A template value argument (e.g., a pointer to a comparison function)

[2]   A template type argument to the **map** template determining the type of a comparison object

At first glance, the first solution (pass a comparison object of a specific type) seems simpler. For example:

```
template<typename Key, typename V, bool(*cmp)(const Key&, const Key&)>
class map {
public:
    map();
    // ...
};
```

This **map** requires a user to supply the comparison as a function:

```
bool insensitive(const string& x, const string& y)
{
    // compare case insensitive (e.g., "hello" equals "HellO")
}


    map<string,int,insensitive> m;          // compare using insensitive()
```

However, this is not very flexible. In particular, the designer of **map** will have to decide whether to compare the (unknown) **Key** type using a pointer to function or a function object of some specific type. Also, because the argument types of the comparison operator must depend on the **Key** type, it can be hard to provide a default comparison criterion.

Consequently, the second alternative (pass the type of the comparison as a template type parameter) is the more common and the one used in the standard library. For example:

```
template<typename Key, Class V, typename Compare = std::less<Key>>
class map {
public:
    map() { /* ... */ }                     // use the default comparison
    map(Compare c) :cmp{c} { /* ... */ }    // override the default
    // ...
    Compare cmp {};                         // default comparison
};
```

The most common case, comparing using less-than, is the default. If we want a different comparison criterion, we can supply it as a function object (§3.4.3):

```
map<string,int> m1;                          // use the default comparison (less<string>)

map<string,int,std::greater<string>> m2;     // compare using greater<string>()
```

Function objects can carry state. For example:

```
Complex_compare f3 {"French",3};             // make a comparison object (§25.2.5)
map<string,int,Complex_compare> m3 {f3};     // compare using f3()
```

We can also use pointers to functions, including lambdas that can convert to a pointer to function (§11.4.5). For example:

```
using Cmp = bool(*)(const string&,const string&);
map<string,int,Cmp> m4 {insensitive};        // compare using a pointer to function

map<string,int,Cmp> m4 {[](const string& a, const string b) { return a>b; } };
```

Passing the comparison operations as a function object has significant benefits compared to passing pointers to functions:

- A simple class member function defined in-class is trivial to inline, whereas inlining a call through a pointer to function requires exceptional attention from a compiler.
- A function object with no data members can be passed with no run-time cost.
- Several operations can be passed as a single object with no additional run-time cost.

The comparison criterion for a **map** is just an example. However, the technique used to pass it is general and very widely used to parameterize classes and functions with "policies." Examples include actions for algorithms (§4.5.4, §32.4), allocators for containers (§31.4, §34.4), and deleters for **unique_ptr** (§34.3.1). We have the same design alternatives when we need to specify arguments for a function template, such as **sort()**, and the standard library chooses alternative [2] for those cases also (e.g., see §32.4).

If we had only one use of a comparison criterion in our program, it might make sense to use a lambda to express the function object version a bit more tersely:

```
map<string,int,Cmp> c3 {[](const string& x, const string& y) const { return x<y; }}; // error
```

Unfortunately, that doesn't work because there is no conversion of a lambda to a function object type. We could name the lambda and then use that name:

```
auto cmp = [](const string& x, const string& y) const { return x<y; }
map<string,int,decltype(cmp)> c4 {cmp};
```

I find naming operations useful from a design and maintenance point of view. Also, anything named and declared nonlocally might find other uses.

25.2.4 Templates as Arguments

Sometimes it is useful to pass templates – rather than classes or values – as template arguments. For example:

```
template<typename T, template<typename> class C>
class Xrefd {
    C<T> mems;
    C<T*> refs;
    // ...
};
```

```
template<typename T>
    using My_vec = vector<T>;          // use default allocator
```

```
Xrefd<Entry,My_vec> x1;         // store cross references for Entrys in a vector
```

```
template<typename T>
class My_container {
    // ...
};
```

```
Xrefd<Record,My_container> x2;   // store cross references for Records in a My_container
```

To declare a template as a template parameter, we must specify its required arguments. For example, we specify that **Xrefd**'s template parameter **C** is a template class that takes a single type argument. If we didn't, we wouldn't be able to use specializations of **C**. The point of using a template as a template parameter is usually that we want to instantiate it with a variety of argument types (such as **T** and **T**∗ in the previous example). That is, we want to express the member declarations of a template in terms of another template, but we want that other template to be a parameter so that it can be specified by users.

Only class templates can be template arguments.

The common case in which a template needs only a container or two is often better handled by passing the container types (§31.5.1). For example:

```
template<typename C, typename C2>
class Xrefd2 {
    C mems;
    C2 refs;
    // ...
};
```

```
Xrefd2<vector<Entry>,set<Entry*>> x;
```

Here, the value types of **C** and **C2** can be obtained by a simple type function (§28.2) for obtaining the type of elements of a container, for example, **Value_type<C>**. This is the technique used for the standard-library container adaptors, such as **queue** (§31.5.2).

25.2.5 Default Template Arguments

Explicitly specifying the comparison criterion for each use of **map** is tedious – especially as **less<Key>** is typically the best choice. We can specify **less<Key>** to be the default type for the **Compare** template argument, so that only uncommon comparison criteria have to be explicitly specified:

```
template<typename Key, Class V, typename Compare = std::less<Key>>
class map {
public:
    explicit map(const Compare& comp ={});
    // ...
};


map<string,int> m1;              // will use less<string> for comparisons
map<string,int,less<string>> m2;  // same type as m1

struct No_case {
    // define operator()() to do case-insensitive string comparison
};


map<string,int,No_case> m3;      // m3 is of a different type from m1 and m2
```

Note how the default **map** constructor creates a default comparison object, **Compare{}**. That's the common case. If we want a more elaborate construction, we must do so explicitly. For example:

```
map<string,int,Complex_compare> m {Complex_compare{"French",3}};
```

The semantic checking of a default argument for a template parameter is done only if that default argument is actually used. In particular, as long as we refrain from using the default template argument **less<Key>**, we can **compare()** values of a type **X** for which **less<X>** wouldn't compile. This point is crucial in the design of the standard containers (e.g., **std::map**), which rely on a template argument to specify default values (§31.4).

Just as for default function arguments (§12.2.5), the default template arguments can be specified and supplied for trailing arguments only:

```
void f1(int x = 0, int y);       // error: default argument not trailing
void f2(int x = 0, int y = 1);   // OK

f2(,2);     // syntax error
f2(2);      // call f(2,1);

template<typename T1 = int, typename T2>
class X1 {          // error: default argument not trailing
    // ...
};

template<typename T1 = int, typename T2 = double>
class X2 {     // OK
    // ...
};

X2<,float> v1;  // syntax error
X2<float> v2;   // v2 is an X2<float,double>
```

Not allowing an "empty" argument to mean "use the default" was a deliberate tradeoff between flexibility and the opportunity for obscure errors.

The technique of supplying a policy through a template argument and then defaulting that argument to supply the most common policy is almost universal in the standard library (e.g., §32.4). Curiously enough, it is not used for **basic_string** (§23.2, Chapter 36) comparisons. Instead, the standard-library string relies on **char_traits** (§36.2.2). Similarly, the standard algorithms rely on **iterator_traits** (§33.1.3) and the standard-library containers rely on **allocators** (§34.4). The use of traits is presented in §28.2.4.

25.2.5.1 Default Function Template Arguments

Naturally, default template arguments can also be useful for function templates. For example:

```
template<typename Target =string, typename Source =string>
Target to(Source arg)                 // convert Source to Target
{
    stringstream interpreter;
    Target result;

    if (!(interpreter << arg)                // write arg into stream
        || !(interpreter >> result)          // read result from stream
        || !(interpreter >> std::ws).eof())  // stuff left in stream?
        throw runtime_error{"to<>() failed"};

    return result;
}
```

A function template argument needs to be explicitly mentioned only if it cannot be deduced or if there is no default, so we can write:

```
auto x1 = to<string,double>(1.2);   // very explicit (and verbose)
auto x2 = to<string>(1.2);          // Source is deduced to double
auto x3 = to<>(1.2);                // Target is defaulted to string; Source is deduced to double
auto x4 = to(1.2);                  // the <> is redundant
```

If all function template arguments are defaulted, the <> can be left out (exactly as in function template specializations; §25.3.4.1).

This implementation of **to()** is a bit heavyweight for combinations of simple types, such as **to<double>(int)**, but improved implementations can be supplied as specializations (§25.3). Note that **to<char>(int)** will not work because **char** and **int** do not share a **string** representation. For conversion among scalar numeric types, I tend to prefer **narrow_cast<>()** (§11.5).

25.3 Specialization

By default, a template gives a single definition to be used for every template argument (or combination of template arguments) that a user can think of. This doesn't always make sense for someone writing a template. I might want to say, "If the template argument is a pointer, use this implementation; if it is not, use that implementation," or "Give an error unless the template argument is a pointer derived from class **My_base**." Many such design concerns can be addressed by providing alternative definitions of the template and having the compiler choose between them based on the template arguments provided where they are used. Such alternative definitions of a template are called *user-defined specializations*, or simply *user specializations*. Consider likely uses of a **Vector**:

```
template<typename T>
class Vector {  // general vector type
    T* v;
    int sz;
public:
    Vector();
    explicit Vector(int);

    T& elem(int i) { return v[i]; }
    T& operator[](int i);

    void swap(Vector&);
    // ...
};

Vector<int> vi;
Vector<Shape*> vps;
Vector<string> vs;
Vector<char*> vpc;
Vector<Node*> vpn;
```

In such code, most **Vector**s will be **Vector**s of some pointer type. There are several reasons for this, but the primary reason is that to preserve run-time polymorphic behavior, we must use pointers (§3.2.2, §20.3.2). That is, anyone who practices object-oriented programming and uses type-safe containers (such as the standard-library containers) will end up with a lot of containers of pointers.

The default behavior of most C++ implementations is to replicate the code for template functions. This is usually good for run-time performance, but unless care is taken, it leads to code bloat in critical cases such as the **Vector** example.

Fortunately, there is an obvious solution. Containers of pointers can share a single implementation. This can be expressed through specialization. First, we define a version (a specialization) of **Vector** for pointers to **void**:

```
template<>
class Vector<void*> {          // complete specialization
    void** p;
    // ...
    void*& operator[](int i);
};
```

This specialization can then be used as the common implementation for all **Vector**s of pointers. Another use would be to implement **unique_ptr<T>** based on a single shared implementation class storing a **void**∗.

The **template<>** prefix says that this is a specialization that can be specified without a template parameter. The template arguments for which the specialization is to be used are specified in <> brackets after the name. That is, the **<void*>** says that this definition is to be used as the implementation of every **Vector** for which **T** is **void**∗.

The **Vector<void∗>** is a *complete specialization*. That is, there is no template parameter to specify or deduce when we use the specialization; **Vector<void∗>** is used for **Vector**s declared like this:

```
Vector<void∗> vpv;
```

To define a specialization that is used for every **Vector** of pointers and only for **Vector**s of pointers,
we can write:

```
template<typename T>
class Vector<T∗> : private Vector<void∗> {    // partial specialization
public:
    using Base = Vector<void∗>;

    Vector() {}
    explicit Vector(int i) : Base(i) {}

    T∗& elem(int i) { return reinterpret_cast<T∗&>(Base::elem(i)); }
    T∗& operator[](int i) { return reinterpret_cast<T∗&>(Base::operator[](i)); }

    // ...
};
```

The specialization pattern **<T∗>** after the name says that this specialization is to be used for every
pointer type; that is, this definition is to be used for every **Vector** with a template argument that can
be expressed as **T∗**. For example:

```
Vector<Shape∗> vps;    // <T*> is <Shape*> so T is Shape
Vector<int∗∗> vppi;    // <T*> is <int**> so T is int*
```

A specialization with a pattern containing a template parameter is called a *partial specialization* in
contrast to *complete specializations* (as in the definition of **vector<void∗>**), where "the pattern" is
simply a specific type.

Note that when a partial specialization is used, a template parameter is deduced from the specialization pattern; the template parameter is not simply the actual template argument. In particular, for **Vector<Shape∗>**, **T** is **Shape** and not **Shape∗**.

Given this partial specialization of **Vector**, we have a shared implementation for all **Vector**s of
pointers. The **Vector<T∗>** class is simply an interface to **Vector<void∗>** implemented exclusively
through derivation and inline expansion.

It is important that this refinement of the implementation of **Vector** be achieved without affecting the interface presented to users. Specialization is a way of specifying alternative implementations for different uses of a common interface. Naturally, we could have given the general **Vector**
and the **Vector** of pointers different names. However, when I tried that, many people who should
have known better forgot to use the pointer classes and found their code much larger than expected.
In this case, it is much better to hide the crucial implementation details behind a common interface.

This technique proved successful in curbing code bloat in real use. People who do not use a
technique like this (in C++ or in other languages with similar facilities for type parameterization)
have found that replicated code can cost megabytes of code space even in moderately sized programs. By eliminating the time needed to compile those additional versions of the **Vector** operations, this technique can also cut compile and link times dramatically. Using a single specialization

to implement all lists of pointers is an example of the general technique of minimizing code bloat by maximizing the amount of shared code.

Some compilers are getting smart enough to perform this particular optimization without help from the programmer, but the technique is generally applicable and useful.

Variants of the technique of using a single run-time representation for values of a number of types and relying on the (static) type system to ensure that they are used only according to their declared type has been called *type erasure*. In the context of C++, it was first documented in the original template paper [Stroustrup,1988].

25.3.1 Interface Specialization

Sometimes, a specialization is not an algorithmic optimization, but a modification of an interface (or even a representation). For example, the standard library **complex** uses specializations to adjust the set of constructors and the argument types for important operations for important specializations (such as **complex<float>** and **complex<double>**). The general (primary) template (§25.3.1.1) looks like this:

```
template<typename T>
class complex {
public:
    complex(const T& re = T{}, const T& im = T{});
    complex(const complex&);                    // copy constructor
    template<typename X>
        complex(const complex<X>&);             // conversion from complex<X> to complex<T>

    complex& operator=(const complex&);
    complex<T>& operator=(const T&);
    complex<T>& operator+=(const T&);
    // ...
    template<typename X>
        complex<T>& operator=(const complex<X>&);
    template<typename X>
        complex<T>& operator+=(const complex<X>&);
    // ...
};
```

Note that the scalar assignment operators take reference arguments. That's not efficient for **floats**, so **complex<float>** passes those by value:

```
template<>
class complex<float> {
public:
    // ...
    complex<float>& operator= (float);
    complex<float>& operator+=(float);
    // ...
    complex<float>& operator=(const complex<float>&);
    // ...
};
```

For **complex<double>**, that same optimization applies. In addition, conversions from **complex<float>** and **complex<long double>** are provided (as described in §23.4.6):

```
template<>
class complex<double> {
public:
    constexpr complex(double re = 0.0, double im = 0.0);
    constexpr complex(const complex<float>&);
    explicit constexpr complex(const complex<long double>&);
    // ...
};
```

Note that these specialized constructors are **constexpr**, making **complex<double>** a literal type. We could not do that for the general **complex<T>**. Also, this definition takes advantage of the knowledge that conversion from **complex<float>** to **complex<double>** is safe (it never narrows), so that we can have an implicit constructor from **complex<float>**. However, the constructor from **complex<long double>** is explicit to make narrowing less likely.

25.3.1.1 Implementation Specialization

Specialization can be used to provide alternative implementations of a class template for a specific set of template parameters. In that case, a specialization can even provide a representation that differs from that of the general template. For example:

```
template<typename T, int N>
class Matrix;          // N-dimensional Matrix of Ts

template<typename T,0>
class Matrix {          // specialization for N==1
    T val;
    // ...
};

template<typename T,1>
class Matrix {          // specialization for N=1
    T* elem;
    int sz;      // number of elements
    // ...
};

template<typename T,2>
class Matrix {          // specialization for N=2
    T* elem;
    int dim1; // number of rows
    int dim2; // number of columns
    // ...
};
```

25.3.2 The Primary Template

When we have both a general definition of a template and specializations defining implementations for specific sets of template arguments, we refer to the most general template as the *primary template*. The primary template defines the interface for all specializations (§iso.14.5.5). That is, the primary template is the one used to determine if a use is valid and takes part in overload resolution. Only after a primary template has been chosen are specializations considered.

The primary template must be declared before any specialization. For example:

```
template<typename T>
class List<T*> {
    // ...
};

template<typename T>
class List {                    // error: primary template after specialization
    // ...
};
```

The critical information supplied by the primary template is the set of template parameters that the user must supply to use it or any of its specializations. If we have defined a constraints check for a template (§24.4), the primary template is where it belongs because concepts are something a user cares about and must understand to use the template. For example:

```
template<typename T>
class List {
    static_assert(Regular<T>(),"List<T>: T must be Regular");
    // ...
};
```

For technical reasons (because the language doesn't recognize constraints checks for what they are), a constraints check needs to be replicated in every specialization.

A declaration of the primary template is sufficient to allow the definition of a specialization:

```
template<typename T>
class List;                 // not a definition

template<typename T>
class List<T*> {
    // ...
};
```

If used, the primary template must be defined somewhere (§23.7). If the primary template is never instantiated, it need not be defined. This can be used to define a template for which only a fixed set of alternative arguments are accepted. If a user specializes a template, that specialization must be in scope for every use of the template with the type for which it was specialized. For example:

```
template<typename T>
class List {
    // ...
};
```

```
List<int*> li;

template<typename T>
class List<T*> {          // error: specialization used before defined
    // ...
};
```

Here, **List** was specialized for **int*** after **List<int*>** had been used.

It is essential that every use of a template for a given set of template arguments be implemented by the same specialization. If not, the type system is broken, so that identical uses of a template in different places may yield different results and objects created in different parts of a program may not be compatible. Clearly that would be disastrous, so a programmer must take care that explicit specialization is consistent throughout a program. In principle, implementations are capable of detecting inconsistent specialization, but the standard does not require them to and some don't.

All specializations of a template must be declared in the same namespace as the primary template. If used, a specialization that is explicitly declared (as opposed to generated from a more general template) must also be explicitly defined somewhere (§23.7). In other words, explicitly specializing a template implies that no (other) definition is generated for that specialization.

25.3.3 Order of Specialization

One specialization is *more specialized* than another if every argument list that matches its specialization pattern also matches the other, but not vice versa. For example:

```
template<typename T>
    class Vector;            // general; the primary template
template<typename T>
    class Vector<T*>;        // specialized for any pointer
template<>
    class Vector<void*>;     // specialized for void*
```

Every type can be used as a template argument for the most general **Vector**, but only pointers can be used for **Vector<T*>** and only **void*** s can be used for **Vector<void*>**.

The most specialized version will be preferred over the others in declarations of objects, pointers, etc. (§25.3).

A specialization pattern can be specified in terms of types composed using the constructs allowed for template parameter deduction (§23.5.2).

25.3.4 Function Template Specialization

Specialization is also useful for template functions (§25.2.5.1). However, we can overload functions, so we see less specialization. Furthermore, C++ supports only complete specialization for functions (§iso.14.7), so we use overloading where we might have tried partial specialization.

25.3.4.1 Specialization and Overloading

Consider the Shell sort from §12.5 and §23.5. Those versions compare elements using < and swap elements using detailed code. A better definition would be:

```
template<typename T>
bool less(T a, T b)
{
     return a<b;
}


template<typename T>
void sort(Vector<T>& v)
{
     const size_t n = v.size();

     for (int gap=n/2; 0<gap; gap/=2)
          for (int i=gap; i!=n; ++i)
               for (int j=i–gap; 0<=j; j–=gap)
                    if (less(v[j+gap],v[j]))
                         swap(v[j],v[j+gap]);
}
```

This does not improve the algorithm itself, but it allows improvements to its implementation. We now have **less** and **swap** as named entities for which we can provide improved versions. Such names are often referred to as *customization points*.

As written, **sort()** will not sort a **Vector<char∗>** correctly because < will compare the two **char∗**s. That is, it will compare the addresses of the first **char** in each string. Instead, we would like it to compare the characters pointed to. A simple specialization of **less()** for **const char∗** will take care of that:

```
template<>
bool less<const char∗>(const char∗ a, const char∗ b)
{
     return strcmp(a,b)<0;
}
```

As for classes (§25.3), the **template<>** prefix says that this is a specialization that can be specified without a template parameter. The **<const char∗>** after the template function name means that this specialization is to be used in cases where the template argument is **const char∗**. Because the template argument can be deduced from the function argument list, we need not specify it explicitly. So, we can simplify the definition of the specialization:

```
template<>
bool less<>(const char∗ a, const char∗ b)
{
     return strcmp(a,b)<0;
}
```

Given the **template<>** prefix, the second empty <> is redundant, so we would typically simply write:

```
template<>
bool less(const char* a, const char* b)
{
     return strcmp(a,b)<0;
}
```

I prefer this shorter form of declaration. We can go further still. With this last version the distinction between specialization and overloading has become razor thin and largely irrelevant, so we can simply write:

```
bool less(const char* a, const char* b)
{
     return strcmp(a,b)<0;
}
```

Now that we have "specialized" **less()** to a version that is semantically correct, we can consider what we might do for **swap()**. The standard-library **swap()** is correct for our use and has already been optimized for every type that has efficient move operations. Therefore, when we used **swap()** instead of the three potentially expensive copy operations, we improved performance for a large number of argument types.

Specialization comes in handy when an irregularity of an argument type causes the general algorithm to give an undesired result (such as **less()** for C-style strings). These "irregular types" are often the built-in pointer and array types.

25.3.4.2 Specialization That Is Not Overloading

How does a specialization differ from overloading? From a technical point of view, they differ because individual functions take part in overloading whereas only the primary template takes part in specialization (§25.3.1.1). However, I can't think of an example where that makes a practical difference.

There are a few uses of function specializations. For example, we can select among functions taking no arguments:

```
template<typename T> T max_value();    // no definition

template<> constexpr int max_value<int>() { return INT_MAX; }
template<> constexpr char max_value<char>() { return CHAR_MAX; }
//...

template<typename Iter>
Iter my_algo(Iter p)
{
     auto x = max_value<Value_type<Iter>>();       // works for types with specialized max_value()
     // ...
}
```

I used the type function **Value_type<>** to get the type of the object pointed to by an **Iter** (§24.4.2).

To get a roughly equivalent effect with overloading, we would have to pass a dummy (unused) argument. For example:

```
int max2(int) { return INT_MAX; }
char max2(char) { return INT_MAX; }

template<typename Iter>
Iter my_algo2(Iter p)
{
    auto x = max2(Value_type<Iter>{});      // works for the types for which we overload max2()
    // ...
}
```

25.4 Advice

[1]   Use templates to improve type safety; §25.1.

[2]   Use templates to raise the level of abstraction of code; §25.1.

[3]   Use templates to provide flexible and efficient parameterization of types and algorithms; §25.1.

[4]   Remember that value template arguments must be compile-time constants; §25.2.2.

[5]   Use function objects as type arguments to parameterize types and algorithms with "policies"; §25.2.3.

[6]   Use default template arguments to provide simple notation for simple uses; §25.2.5.

[7]   Specialize templates for irregular types (such as arrays); §25.3.

[8]   Specialize templates to optimize for important cases; §25.3.

[9]   Define the primary template before any specialization; §25.3.1.1.

[10]   A specialization must be in scope for every use; §25.3.1.1.

26

Instantiation

For every complex problem,
there is an answer that is
clear, simple, and wrong.
– H. L. Mencken

- Introduction
- Template Instantiation
    When Is Instantiation Needed?; Manual Control of Instantiation
- Name Binding
    Dependent Names; Point-of-Definition Binding; Point-of-Instantiation Binding; Multiple Instantiation Points; Templates and Namespaces; Overaggressive ADL; Names from Base Classes
- Advice

26.1 Introduction

One of the great strengths of templates is that they are an extremely flexible mechanism for composition of code. To produce impressive code quality, a compiler combines code (information) from
- the template definition and its lexical environment,
- the template arguments and their lexical environment, and
- the environment of the template's use.

The key to the resulting performance is that the compiler is able to look at code from those contexts simultaneously and weave it together in ways that use all information available. The problem with this is that code in a template definition isn't as localized as we would prefer (all other things being equal). Sometimes, we can get confused about what a name used in a template definition refers to:
- Is it a local name?
- Is it a name associated with a template argument?

- Is it a name from a base class in a hierarchy?
- Is it a name from a named namespace?
- Is it a global name?

This chapter discusses such questions related to *name binding* and considers their implications for programming styles.

- Templates were introduced in §3.4.1 and §3.4.2.
- Chapter 23 gives a detailed introduction to templates and the use of template arguments.
- Chapter 24 introduces generic programming and the key notion of concepts.
- Chapter 25 presents details of class templates and function templates and introduces the notion of specialization.
- Chapter 27 discusses the relationship between templates and class hierarchies (supporting generic and object-oriented programming).
- Chapter 28 focuses on templates as a language for generating classes and functions.
- Chapter 29 presents a larger example of how the language facilities and programming techniques can be used in combination.

26.2   Template Instantiation

Given a template definition and a use of that template, it is the implementation's job to generate correct code. From a class template and a set of template arguments, the compiler needs to generate the definition of a class and the definitions of those of its member functions that were used in the program (and only those; §26.2.1). From a template function and a set of template arguments, a function needs to be generated. This process is commonly called *template instantiation*.

The generated classes and functions are called *specializations*. When we need to distinguish between generated specializations and specializations explicitly written by the programmer (§25.3), we refer to *generated specializations* and *explicit specializations*, respectively. An explicit specialization is often referred to as a *user-defined specialization*, or simply a *user specialization*.

To use templates in nontrivial programs, a programmer must understand the basics of how names used in a template definition are bound to declarations and how source code can be organized (§23.7).

By default, the compiler generates classes and functions from the templates used in accordance with the name-binding rules (§26.3). That is, a programmer need not state explicitly which versions of which templates must be generated. This is important because it is not easy for a programmer to know exactly which versions of a template are needed. Often, templates that the programmer hasn't even heard of are used in the implementation of libraries, and sometimes templates that the programmer does know of are used with unknown template argument types. For example, the standard-library **map** (§4.4.3, §31.4.3) is implemented in terms of a red-black tree template with data types and operations unknown to all but the most curious user. In general, the set of generated functions needed can be known only by recursive examination of the templates used in application code libraries. Computers are better suited than humans for doing such analysis.

On the other hand, it is sometimes important for a programmer to be able to state specifically where code should be generated from a template (§26.2.2). By doing so, the programmer gains detailed control over the context of the instantiation.

26.2.1 When Is Instantiation Needed?

It is necessary to generate a specialization of a class template only if the class's definition is needed (§iso.14.7.1). In particular, to declare a pointer to some class, the actual definition of a class is not needed. For example:

```
class X;
X* p;        // OK: no definition of X needed
X a;         // error: definition of X needed
```

When defining template classes, this distinction can be crucial. A template class is *not* instantiated unless its definition is actually needed. For example:

```
template<typename T>
class Link {
    Link* suc;        // OK: no definition of Link needed (yet)
    // ...
};

Link<int>* pl;        // no instantiation of Link<int> needed (yet)

Link<int> lnk;        // now we need to instantiate Link<int>
```

A place where a template is used defines a point of instantiation (§26.3.3).

An implementation instantiates a template function only if that function has been used. By "used" we mean "called or had its address taken." In particular, instantiation of a class template does not imply the instantiation of all of its member functions. This allows the programmer an important degree of flexibility when defining a template class. Consider:

```
template<typename T>
class List {
    // ...
    void sort();
};

class Glob {
    // ... no comparison operators ...
};

void f(List<Glob>& lb, List<string>& ls)
{
    ls.sort();
    // ... use operations on lb, but not lb.sort() ...
}
```

Here, **List<string>::sort()** is instantiated, but **List<Glob>::sort()** isn't. This both reduces the amount of code generated and saves us from having to redesign the program. Had **List<Glob>::sort()** been generated, we would have had to either add the operations needed by **List::sort()** to **Glob**, redefine **sort()** so that it wasn't a member of **List** (the better design anyway), or use some other container for **Glob**s.

26.2.2 Manual Control of Instantiation

The language does not require any explicit user action to achieve template instantiation. However, it does provide two mechanisms to help the user take control when needed. The need sometimes arises from a wish to

- optimize the compile-and-link process by eliminating redundant replicated instantiations, or
- know exactly which point of instantiation is used to eliminate surprises from complicated name-binding contexts.

An explicit instantiation request (often simply called an *explicit instantiation*) is a declaration of a specialization prefixed by the keyword **template** (not followed by <):

```
template class vector<int>;              // class
template int& vector<int>::operator[](int);    // member function
template int convert<int,double>(double);      // nonmember function
```

A template declaration starts with **template<**, whereas plain **template** starts an instantiation request. Note that **template** prefixes a complete declaration; just stating a name is not sufficient:

```
template vector<int>::operator[];    // syntax error
template convert<int,double>;        // syntax error
```

As in template function calls, the template arguments that can be deduced from the function arguments can be omitted (§23.5.1). For example:

```
template int convert<int,double>(double);    // OK (redundant)
template int convert<int>(double);           // OK
```

When a class template is explicitly instantiated, every member function is also instantiated.

The link-time and recompilation efficiency impact of instantiation requests can be significant. I have seen examples in which bundling most template instantiations into a single compilation unit cut the compile time from a number of hours to the equivalent number of minutes.

It is an error to have two definitions for the same specialization. It does not matter if such multiple specializations are user-defined (§25.3), implicitly generated (§23.2.2), or explicitly requested. However, a compiler is not required to diagnose multiple instantiations in separate compilation units. This allows a smart implementation to ignore redundant instantiations and thereby avoid problems related to composition of programs from libraries using explicit instantiation. However, implementations are not required to be smart. Users of "less smart" implementations must avoid multiple instantiations. The worst that will happen if they don't is that their program won't link; there will be no silent changes of meaning.

To complement explicit instantiation requests, the language provides explicit requests *not* to instantiate (usually called **extern template**s). The obvious use is to have one explicit instantiation for a specialization and use **extern template**s for its use in other translation units. This mirrors the classical use of one definition and many declarations (§15.2.3). For example:

```
#include "MyVector.h"

extern template class MyVector<int>;    // suppresses implicit instantiation
                                        // explicitly instantiate elsewhere
```

```
void foo(MyVector<int>& v)
{
    // ... use the vector in here ...
}
```

The "elsewhere" might look something like this:

```
#include "MyVector.h"

template class MyVector<int>;      // instantiate in this translation unit; use this point of instantiation
```

In addition to generating specializations for all members of a class, the explicit instantiation also determines a single point of instantiation so that other points of instantiation (§26.3.3) can be ignored. One use of this is to place the explicit instantiation in a shared library.

26.3 Name Binding

Define template functions to minimize dependencies on nonlocal information. The reason is that a template will be used to generate functions and classes based on unknown types and in unknown contexts. Every subtle context dependency is likely to surface as a problem for somebody – and that somebody is unlikely to want to know the implementation details of the template. The general rule of avoiding global names as much as possible should be taken especially seriously in template code. Thus, we try to make template definitions as self-contained as possible and to supply much of what would otherwise have been global context in the form of template arguments (e.g., traits; §28.2.4, §33.1.3). Use concepts to document dependencies on template arguments (§24.3).

However, it is not unusual that some nonlocal names must be used to achieve the most elegant formulation of a template. In particular, it is more common to write a set of cooperating template functions than to write just one self-contained function. Sometimes, such functions can be class members, but not always. Sometimes, nonlocal functions are the best choice. Typical examples of that are **sort()**'s calls to **swap()** and **less()** (§25.3.4). The standard-library algorithms are a large-scale example (Chapter 32). When something needs to be nonlocal, prefer a named namespace to the global scope. Doing so preserves some locality.

Operations with conventional names and semantics, such as **+**, **∗**, **[]**, and **sort()**, are another source of nonlocal name use in a template definition. Consider:

```
bool tracing;

template<typename T>
T sum(std::vector<T>& v)
{
    T t {};
    if (tracing)
        cerr << "sum(" << &v << ")\n";
    for (int i = 0; i!=v.size(); i++)
        t = t + v[i];
    return t;
}
```

```
// ...

#include<quad.h>

void f(std::vector<Quad>& v)
{
    Quad c = sum(v);
}
```

The innocent-looking template function **sum()** depends on several names that are not explicitly specified in its definition, such as **tracing**, **cerr**, and the + operator. In this example, + is defined in **<quad.h>**:

```
Quad operator+(Quad,Quad);
```

Importantly, nothing related to **Quad** is in scope when **sum()** is defined, and the writer of **sum()** cannot be assumed to know about class **Quad**. In particular, the + may be defined later than **sum()** in the program text, and even later in time.

The process of finding the declaration for each name explicitly or implicitly used in a template is called *name binding*. The general problem with template name binding is that three contexts are involved in a template instantiation and they cannot be cleanly separated:

[1]   The context of the template definition
[2]   The context of the argument type declaration
[3]   The context of the use of the template

When defining a function template, we want to assure that enough context is available for the template definition to make sense in terms of its actual arguments without picking up "accidental stuff" from the environment of a point of use. To help with this, the language separates names used in a template definition into two categories:

[1]   *Dependent names*: names that depend on a template parameter. Such names are bound at a point of instantiation (§26.3.3). In the **sum()** example, the definition of + can be found in the instantiation context because it takes operands of the template argument type.

[2]   *Nondependent names*: names that don't depend on a template parameter. Such names are bound at the point of definition of the template (§26.3.2). In the **sum()** example, the template **vector** is defined in the standard header **<vector>**, and the Boolean **tracing** is in scope when the definition of **sum()** is encountered by the compiler.

To be considered, both dependent and independent names must either be in scope at their point of use or be found by argument-dependent lookup (ADL; §14.2.4).

The following subsections go into considerable technical detail about how dependent and nondependent names in a template definition are bound for a specialization. For complete details, see §iso.14.6.

26.3.1 Dependent Names

The simplest definition of "**N** depends on a template parameter **T**" would be "**N** is a member of **T**." Unfortunately, this doesn't quite suffice; addition of **Quad**s (§26.3) is a counter-example.

Consequently, a function call is said to *depend on* a template argument if and only if one of these conditions holds:

[1]   The type of the actual argument depends on a template parameter **T** according to the type deduction rules (§23.5.2), for example, **f(T(1))**, **f(t)**, **f(g(t))**, and **f(&t)**, assuming that **t** is a **T**.

[2]   The function called has a parameter that depends on **T** according to the type deduction rules (§23.5.2), for example, **f(T)**, **f(list<T>&)**, and **f(const T∗)**.

Basically, the name of a called function is dependent if it is obviously dependent by looking at its arguments or at its formal parameters. For example:

```
template<typename T>
T f(T a)
{
        return g(a);      // OK: a is a dependent name and therefore so is g
}

class Quad { /* ... */ };
void g(Quad);

int z = f(Quad{2});           // f's g is bound to g(Quad)
```

A call that by coincidence has an argument that matches an actual template parameter type is not dependent. For example:

```
class Quad { /* ... */ };

template<typename T>
T ff(T a)
{
        return gg(Quad{1});        // error: no gg() in scope and gg(Quad{1}) doesn't depend on T
}

int gg(Quad);

int zz = ff(Quad{2});
```

Had **gg(Quad{1})** been considered dependent, its meaning would have been most mysterious to a reader of the template definition. If a programmer wants **gg(Quad)** to be called, **gg(Quad)**'s declaration should be placed before the definition of **ff()** so that **gg(Quad)** is in scope when **ff()** is analyzed. This is exactly the same rule as for non-template function definitions (§26.3.2).

By default, a dependent name is assumed to name something that is not a type. So, to use a dependent name as a type, you have to say so, using the keyword **typename**. For example:

```
template<typename Container>
void fct(Container& c)
{
        Container::value_type v1 = c[7];    // syntax error: value_type is assumed to be a non-type name
        typename Container::value_type v2 = c[9];     // OK: value_type assumed to name a type
        auto v3 = c[11];                              // OK: let the compiler figure it out
        // ...
}
```

We can avoid such awkward use of **typename** by introducing a type alias (§23.6). For example:

```
template<typename T>
using Value_type<T> = typename T::value_type;

template<typename Container>
void fct2(Container& c)
{
    Value_type<Container> v1 = c[7];   // OK
    // ...
}
```

Naming a member template after a . (dot), ->, or :: requires similar use of the keyword **template**. For example:

```
class Pool {     // some allocator
public:
    template<typename T> T* get();
    template<typename T> void release(T*);
    // ...
};

template<typename Alloc>
void f(Alloc& all)
{
    int* p1 = all.get<int>();                   // syntax error: get is assumed to name a non-template
    int* p2 = all.template get<int>();          // OK: get() is assumed to be a template
    // ...
}

void user(Pool& pool){
    f(pool);
    // ...
}
```

Compared to the use of **typename** to explicitly state that a name is assumed to name a type, the use of **template** to explicitly state that a name is assumed to name a template is rare. Note the difference in the placement of the disambiguating keyword: **typename** appears before the qualified name and **template** immediately before the template name.

26.3.2 Point-of-Definition Binding

When the compiler sees a template definition, it determines which names are dependent (§26.3.1). If a name is dependent, looking for its declaration is postponed until instantiation time (§26.3.3).

   Names that do not depend on a template argument are treated like names that are not in templates; they must be in scope (§6.3.4) at the point of definition. For example:

```
int x;
```

```
template<typename T>
T f(T a)
{
    ++x;        // OK: x is in scope
    ++y;        // error: no y in scope, and y doesn't depend on T
    return a;   // OK: a is dependent
}

int y;

int z = f(2);
```

If a declaration is found, that declaration is used even if a "better" declaration might be found later. For example:

```
void g(double);
void g2(double);

template<typename T>
int ff(T a)
{
    g2(2);      // call g2(double);
    g3(2);      // error: no g3() in scope
    g(2);       // call g(double); g(int) is not in scope
    // ...
}

void g(int);
void g3(int);

int x = ff(a);
```

Here, **ff()** will call **g(double)**. The definition of **g(int)** comes too late to be considered – just as if **ff()** had not been a template or if **g** had named a variable.

26.3.3 Point-of-Instantiation Binding

The context used to determine the meaning of a dependent name (§26.3.1) is determined by the use of a template with a given set of arguments. This is called a *point of instantiation* for that specialization (§iso.14.6.4.1). Each use of a template for a given set of template arguments defines a point of instantiation. For a function template, that point is in the nearest global or namespace scope enclosing its use, just after the declaration that contains that use. For example:

```
void g(int);

template<typename T>
void f(T a)
{
    g(a);       // g is bound at a point of instantiation
}
```

```
void h(int i)
{
     extern void g(double);
     f(i);
}
// point of declaration for f<int>
```

The point of instantiation for **f<int>()** is *outside* **h()**. This is essential to ensure that the **g()** called in
f() is the global **g(int)** rather than the local **g(double)**. An unqualified name used in a template definition can never be bound to a local name. Ignoring local names is essential to prevent a lot of nasty
macro-like behavior.

To enable recursive calls, the point of declaration for a function template is *after* the declaration
that instantiates it. For example:

```
void g(int);

template<typename T>
void f(T a)
{
     g(a);              // g is bound at a point of instantiation
     if (i) h(a−1);     // h is bound at a point of instantiation
}

void h(int i)
{
     extern void g(double);
     f(i);
}
// point of declaration for f<int>
```

Here, having the point of instantiation *after* the definition of **h()** is necessary to allow the (indirectly
recursive) call **h(a−1)**.

For a template class or a class member, the point of instantiation is just *before* the declaration
containing its use.

```
template<typename T>
class Container {
     vector<T> v;    // elements
     // ...
public:
     void sort();    // sort elements
     // ...
};

// point of instantiation of Container<int>
void f()
{
     Container<int> c;    // point of use
     c.sort();
}
```

Had the point of instantiation been after **f()** the call **c.sort()** would have failed to find the definition of **Container<int>**.

Relying on template arguments to make dependencies explicit simplifies our thinking about the template code and even allows us to access local information. For example:

```
void fff()
{
    struct S { int a,b; };
    vector<S> vs;
    // ...
}
```

Here, **S** is a local name, but since we use it as an explicit argument, rather than trying to bury its name in the definition of **vector**, we have no potentially surprising subtleties.

So why don't we completely avoid nonlocal names in template definitions? That would certainly solve the technical problem with name lookup, but – as for ordinary function and class definitions – we want to be able to use "other functions and types" freely in our code. Turning every dependency into an argument can lead to very messy code. For example:

```
template<typename T>
void print_sorted(vector<T>& v)
{
    sort(v.begin(),v.end());
    for (const auto T& x : v)
        cout << x << '\n';
}

void use(vector<string>& vec)
{
    // ...
    print_sorted(vec);   // sort using std::sort, then print using std::cout
}
```

Here, we are using just two nonlocal names (**sort** and **cout**, both from the standard library). To eliminate those we would need to add parameters:

```
template<typename T, typename S>
void print_sorted(vector<T>& v, S sort, ostream& os)
{
    sort(v.begin(),v.end());
    for (const auto T& x : v)
        os << x << '\n';
}

void fct(vector<string>& vec)
{
    // ...
    using Iter = decltype(vs.begin());   // vec's iterator type
    print_sorted(some_vec,std::sort<Iter>,std::cout);
}
```

In this trivial case, there is a lot to be said for removing the dependence on the global name **cout**. However, in general, as illustrated by **sort()**, adding parameters can make the code much more verbose without necessarily making it easier to understand.

Also, if the name-binding rules for templates were radically more restrictive than the rules for non-template code, writing template code would be a completely separate skill from writing non-template code. Templates and non-template code would no longer interoperate simply and freely.

26.3.4 Multiple Instantiation Points

A template specialization may be generated
- at any point of instantiation (§26.3.3),
- at any point subsequent to that in a translation unit,
- or in a translation unit specifically created for generating specializations.

This reflects three obvious strategies an implementation can use for generating specializations:

[1]   Generate a specialization the first time a call is seen.

[2]   At the end of a translation unit, generate all specializations needed for it.

[3]   Once every translation unit of a program has been seen, generate all specializations needed for the program.

All three strategies have strengths and weaknesses, and combinations of these strategies are also possible.

So, a template used several times with the same set of template arguments has several points of instantiation. A program is illegal if it is possible to construct two different meanings by choosing different points of instantiation. That is, if the bindings of a dependent or a nondependent name can differ, the program is illegal. For example:

```
void f(int);                         // here, I take care of ints

namespace N {
    class X { };
    char g(X,int);
}

template<typename T>
void ff(T t, double d)
{
    f(d);           // f is bound to f(int)
    return g(t,d);  // g might be bound to g(X,int)
}

auto x1 = ff(N::X{},1.1);            // ff<N::X,double>; may bind g to N::g(X,int), narrowing 1.1 to 1


Namespace N {                        // reopen N to take care of doubles
    double g(X,double);
}

auto x2 = ff(N::X,2.2);              // ff<N::X,double>; binds g to N::g(X,double); the best match
```

For ff() we have two instantiation points. For the first call, we could generate the specialization at the initialization of x1 and get g(N::X,int) called. Alternatively, we could wait and generate the specialization at the end of the translation unit and get g(N::X,char) called. Consequently, the call ff(N::X{},1.1) is an error.

It is sloppy programming to call an overloaded function between two of its declarations. However, looking at a large program, a programmer would have no reason to suspect a problem. In this particular case, a compiler could catch the ambiguity. However, similar problems can occur in separate translation units, and then detection becomes much harder (for both compilers and programmers). An implementation is not obliged to catch problems of this kind.

To avoid surprising name bindings, try to limit context dependencies in templates.

26.3.5 Templates and Namespaces

When a function is called, its declaration can be found even if it is not in scope, provided it is declared in the same namespace as one of its arguments (§14.2.4). This is important for functions called in template definitions because it is the mechanism by which dependent functions are found during instantiation. The binding of dependent names is done (§iso.14.6.4.2) by looking at

[1]   the names in scope at the point where the template is defined, plus

[2]   the names in the namespace of an argument of a dependent call (§14.2.4).

For example:

```
namespace N {
      class A { /* ... */ };
      char f(A);
}

char f(int);

template<typename T>
char g(T t)
{
      return f(t);        // choose f() depending on what T is
}

char f(double);

char c1 = g(N::A());       // causes N::f(N::A) to be called
char c2 = g(2);            // causes f(int) to be called
char c3 = g(2.1);          // causes f(int) to be called; f(double) not considered
```

Here, f(t) is clearly dependent, so we can't bind f at the point of definition. To generate a specialization for g<N::A>(N::A), the implementation looks in namespace N for functions called f() and finds N::f(N::A).

The f(int) is found because it is in scope at the point of definition of the template. The f(double) is not found because it is not in scope at the point of definition of the template (§iso.14.6.4.1), and argument-dependent lookup (§14.2.4) does not find a global function that takes only arguments of built-in types. I find it easy to forget that.

26.3.6 Overaggressive ADL

Argument-dependent lookup (often referred to as ADL) is very useful to avoid verbosity (§14.2.4). For example:

```
#include <iostream>

int main()
{
        std::cout << "Hello, world" << endl;// OK because of ADL
}
```

Without argument-dependent lookup, the **endl** manipulator would not be found. As it is, the compiler notices that the first argument to **<<** is an **ostream** defined in **std**. Therefore, it looks for **endl** in **std** and finds it (in **<iostream>**).

However, ADL can be "too aggressive" when combined with unconstrained templates. Consider:

```
#include<vector>
#include<algorithm>
// ...

namespace User {
        class Customer { /* ... */ };
        using Index = std::vector<Customer*>;

        void copy(const Index&, Index&, int deep);     // deep or shallow copy depending on the value of deep

        void algo(Index& x, Index& y)
        {
                // ...
                copy(x,y,false);// error
        }
}
```

It would be a good guess that the author of **User** meant for **User::alg()** to call **User::copy()**. However, that's not what happens. The compiler notices that **Index** really is a **vector** defined in **std** and looks to see if a relevant function is available in **std**. In **<algorithm>**, it finds:

```
template<typename In, typename Out>
Out copy(In,In,Out);
```

Obviously, this general template is a perfect match for **copy(x,y,false)**. On the other hand, the **copy()** in **User** can be called only with a **bool**-to-**int** conversion. For this example, as for equivalent examples, the compiler's resolution is a surprise to most programmers and a source of very obscure bugs. Using ADL to find fully general templates is arguably a language design error. After all, **std::copy()** requires a pair of iterators (not just two arguments of the same type, such as the two **Index**es). The standard says so, but the code does not. Many such problems can be solved by the use of concepts (§24.3, §24.3.2). For example, had the compiler known that **std::copy()** required two iterators, a nonobscure error would have been the result.

```
template<typename In, typename Out>
Out copy(In p1, In p2, Out q)
{
        static_assert(Input_iterator<In>(), "copy(): In is not an input iterator");
        static_assert(Output_iterator<Out>(), "copy(): Out is not an output iterator");
        static_assert(Assignable<Value_type<Out>,Value_type<In>>(), "copy(): value type mismatch");
        // ...
}
```

Better still, the compiler would have noticed that **std::copy()** wasn't even a valid candidate for that call and **User::copy()** would have been invoked. For example (§28.4):

```
template<typename In, typename Out,
         typename = enable_if(Input_iterator<In>()
                              && Output_iterator<Out>()
                              && Assignable<Value_type<Out>,Value_type<In>>())>
Out copy(In p1, In p2, Out q)
{
        // ...
}
```

Unfortunately, many such templates are in libraries that a user cannot modify (e.g., the standard library).

It is a good idea to avoid fully general (completely unconstrained) function templates in headers that also contain type definitions, but that's hard to avoid. If you need one, protecting it with a constraints check is often worthwhile.

What can a user do if a library has trouble-causing unconstrained templates? Often, we know which namespace our function should come from, so we can be specific about that. For example:

```
void User::algo(Index& x, Index& y)
{
        User::copy(x,y,false);    // OK
        // ...
        std::swap(*x[i],*x[j]);   // OK: only std::swap is considered
}
```

If we don't want to be specific about which namespace to use, but want to make sure that a particular version of a function is considered by function overloading, we can use a **using**-declaration (§14.2.2). For example:

```
template<typename Range, typename Op>
void apply(const Range& r, Op f)
{
        using std::begin;
        using std::end;
        for (auto& x : r)
                f(x);
}
```

Now, the standard **begin()** and **end()** are in the overload set used by the range-**for** to traverse the **Range** (unless **Range** has members **begin()** and **end()**; §9.5.1).

26.3.7 Names from Base Classes

When a class template has a base class, it can access names from that base. As for other names, there are two distinct possibilities:

- The base class depends on a template argument.
- The base class does not depend on a template argument.

The latter case is simple and treated just like base classes in classes that are not templates. For example:

```
void g(int);

struct B {
    void g(char);
    void h(char);
};

template<typename T>
class X : public B {
public:
    void h(int);
    void f()
    {
        g(2);       // call B::g(char)
        h(2);       // call X::h(int)
    }
    // ...
};
```

As ever, local names hide other names, so h(2) binds to X::h(int) and B::h(char) is never considered. Similarly, the call g(2) is bound to B::g(char) without any concern for functions declared outside X. That is, the global g() is never considered.

For base classes that depend on a template parameter, we have to be a bit more careful and explicit about what we want. Consider:

```
void g(int);

struct B {
    void g(char);
    void h(char);
};

template<typename T>
class X : public T {
public:
    void f()
    {
        g(2);       // call ::g(int)
    }
    // ...
};
```

```
    void h(X<B> x)
    {
        x.f();
    }
```

Why doesn't **g(2)** call **B::g(char)** (as in the previous example)? Because **g(2)** isn't dependent on the template parameter **T**. It is therefore bound at the point of definition; names from the template argument **T** (which happens to be used as a base class) are not (yet) known and therefore not considered. If we want to have names from a dependent class considered, we must make the dependency clear. We have three ways of doing that:

* Qualify a name with a dependent type (e.g., **T::g**).
* Say that the name refers an object of this class (e.g., **this–>g**).
* Bring the name into scope with a **using**-declaration (e.g., **using T::g**).

For example:

```
    void g(int);
    void g2(int);

    struct B {
        using Type = int;
        void g(char);
        void g2(char)
    };

    template<typename T>
    class X : public T {
    public:
        typename T::Type m;      // OK
        Type m2;                 // error (no Type in scope)

        using T::g2();           // bring T::g2() into scope

        void f()
        {
            this–>g(2);          // call T::g
            g(2);                // call ::g(int); surprise?
            g2(2);               // call T::g2
        }
        // ...
    };

    void h(X<B> x)
    {
        x.f();
    }
```

Only at the point of instantiation can we know if the argument used for the parameter **T** (here **B**) has the required names.

It is easy to forget to qualify names from a base, and the qualified code often looks a bit verbose and messy. However, the alternative would be that a name in a template class would sometimes bind to a base class member and sometimes to a global entity depending on the template argument. That is not ideal either, and the language rule supports the rule of thumb that a template definition should be as self-contained as possible (§26.3).

Qualifying access to dependent base members of a template can be a nuisance. However, explicit qualifications help maintainers, so the initial author shouldn't grumble too much about the extra typing. A common occurrence of this problem is when a whole class hierarchy is templatized. For example:

```
template<typename T>
class Matrix_base {        // memory for matrices, operations of all elements
    // ...
    int size() const { return sz; }
protected:
    int sz;      // number of elements
    T* elem;  // matrix elements
};

template<typename T, int N>
class Matrix : public Matrix_base<T> {   // N-dimensional matrix
    // ...
    T* data()  // return pointer to element storage
    {
        return this–>elem;
    }
};
```

Here, the **this–>** qualification is required.

26.4 Advice

[1]   Let the compiler/implementation generate specializations as needed; §26.2.1.
[2]   Explicitly instantiate if you need exact control of the instantiation environment; §26.2.2.
[3]   Explicitly instantiate if you optimize the time needed to generate specializations; §26.2.2.
[4]   Avoid subtle context dependencies in a template definition; §26.3.
[5]   Names must be in scope when used in a template definition or findable through argument-dependent lookup (ADL); §26.3, §26.3.5.
[6]   Keep the binding context unchanged between instantiation points; §26.3.4.
[7]   Avoid fully general templates that can be found by ADL; §26.3.6.
[8]   Use concepts and/or **static_assert** to avoid using inappropriate templates; §26.3.6.
[9]   Use **using**-declarations to limit the reach of ADL; §26.3.6.
[10]   Qualify names from a template base class with –> or T:: as appropriate; §26.3.7.

27

Templates and Hierarchies

Euclid's and Beethoven's Fifth;
knowing just one of them marks you as semi-educated.
– Stan Kelley-Bootle

- Introduction
- Parameterization and Hierarchy
    Generated Types; Template Conversions
- Hierarchies of Class Templates
    Templates as Interfaces
- Template Parameters as Base Classes
    Composing Data Structures; Linearizing Class Hierarchies
- Advice

27.1 Introduction

Templates and derivation are mechanisms for building new types out of existing ones, for specifying interfaces, and generally for writing useful code that exploits various forms of commonality:

- A template class defines an interface. The template's own implementation and those of its specializations can be accessed through that interface. The source code implementing the template (in the template definition) is identical for all parameter types. The implementations of different specializations can be very different, but they should all implement the semantics specified for the primary template. A specialization can add functionality to what the primary template offers.
- A base class defines an interface. The class's own implementation and those of its derived classes can (using virtual functions) be accessed through that interface. The implementations of different derived classes can be very different, but they should all implement the semantics specified for the base class. A derived class can add functionality to what the base class offers.

From a design perspective, the two approaches are close enough to deserve a common name. Since both allow an algorithm to be expressed once and applied to a variety of types, people refer to both as *polymorphic* (from Greek "many shapes"). To distinguish them, what virtual functions provide is called *run-time polymorphism*, and what templates offer is called *compile-time polymorphism* or *parametric polymorphism*.

The rough duality of the generic and object-oriented approaches can be deceptive. Object-oriented programmers tend to focus on the design of hierarchies of classes (types) with an interface being an individual class (Chapter 21). Generic programmers tend to focus on the design of algorithms with the concepts for template arguments providing an interface that can accommodate many types (Chapter 24). The ideal for a programmer should be mastery of both techniques to the point where either can be used where most appropriate. In many cases, the optimal design contains elements of both. For example **vector<Shape∗>** is a compile-time polymorphic (generic) container holding elements from a run-time polymorphic (object-oriented) hierarchy (§3.2.4).

Generally, good object-oriented programming requires more foresight than good generic programming because all types in a hierarchy must explicitly share an interface defined as a base class. A template will accept any type that meets its concept as an argument, even if there is no explicitly declared commonality among those types. For example **accumulate()** (§3.4.2, §24.2, §40.6.1) will accept **vector**s of **int**s and **list**s of **complex<double>** even though there are no declared relationship between the two element types and no declared relationship between the two sequence types.

27.2 Parameterization and Hierarchy

As shown in §4.4.1 and §27.2.2, combinations of templates and class hierarchies are the basis for many useful techniques. So:

- When do we choose to use a class template?
- When do we rely on a class hierarchy?

Consider these questions from a slightly simplified and abstract point of view:

```
template<typename X>
class Ct {          // interface expressed in terms of the parameter
    X mem;
public:
    X f();
    int g();
    void h(X);
};


template<>
class Ct<A> {       // specialization (for A)
    A∗ mem;         // the representation can differ from that of the primary template
public:
    A f();
    int g();
    void h(A);
    void k(int);    // added functionality
};
```

```
Ct<A> cta;          // specialization for A
Ct<B> ctb;          // specialization for B
```

Given that, we can use f(), g(), and h() on the variables **cta** and **ctb**, using the implementations of
Ct<A> and **Ct<B>**, respectively. I used an explicit specialization (§23.5.3.4) to show that implemen-
tations can vary from what the primary template offers and that it is possible to add functionality.
The simpler case – without added functionality – is by far the more common.

The rough equivalent using a hierarchy is:

```
class X {
        // ...
};

class Cx {                    // interface expressed in terms of types in scope
        X mem;
public:
        virtual X& f();
        virtual int g();
        virtual void h(X&);
};

Class DA : public Cx {    // derived class
public:
        X& f();
        int g();
        void h(X&);
};

Class DB : public Cx {    // derived class
        DB* p;                // representation can be more extensive than what the base provides
public:
        X& f();
        int g();
        void h(X&);
        void k(int);          // added functionality

};

Cx& cxa {*new DA}; // cxa is an interface to a DA
Cx& cxb {*new DB}; // cxb is an interface to a DB
```

Given that, we can use f(), g(), and h() on the variables **cxa** and **cxb**, using the implementations of **DA**
and **DB**, respectively. I use references in the hierarchical version to reflect that we must manipulate
derived class objects through pointers or references to preserve run-time polymorphic behavior.

In either case, we manipulate objects that share a common set of operations. From this simplified and abstract point of view we can observe:

- If the types in the interface to the generated or derived classes need to differ, templates have
  an advantage. To gain access to differing interfaces for derived classes through a base, we
  must use some form of explicit casting (§22.2).

- If the implementations of generated or derived classes differ only through a parameter or differ only in a few special cases, templates have an advantage. Irregular implementations can be expressed through derived classes or specializations.
- If the actual types of objects used cannot be known at compile time, a class hierarchy is essential.
- If a hierarchical relationship is required between generated or derived types, hierarchies have an advantage. The base class provides a common interface. Conversions among template specializations must be explicitly defined by the programmer (§27.2.2).
- If explicit use of free store (§11.2) is undesirable, templates have an advantage.
- If run-time efficiency is at such a premium that inlining of operations is essential, templates should be used (because effective use of hierarchy requires the use of pointers or references, which inhibit inlining).

Keeping base classes minimal and type-safe can be a struggle. Expressing the interface in terms of existing types that cannot vary for derived classes can be a struggle. Often the result is a compromise that either overconstrains the base class interface (e.g., we pick a class **X** with a "rich interface" which must be implemented by all derived classes and "for all time") or underconstrains (e.g., we use **void**∗ or a minimal **Object**∗).

The combination of templates and class hierarchies provides design choices and flexibility beyond what either can offer by itself. For example, a pointer to a base class can be used as a template argument to provide run-time polymorphism (§3.2.4), and a template parameter can be used to specify a base class interface to provide type safety (§26.3.7, §27.3.1).

It is not possible to have a **virtual** function template (§23.4.6.2).

27.2.1 Generated Types

A class template is usefully understood as a specification of how particular types are to be created. In other words, the template implementation is a mechanism that generates types when needed based on a specification. Consequently, a class template is sometimes called a *type generator*.

As far as the C++ language rules are concerned, there is no relationship between two classes generated from a single class template. For example:

```
class Shape {
    // ...
};

class Circle : public Shape {
{
    // ...
};
```

Given these declarations, people sometimes think that there must be an inheritance relationship between **set<Circle>** and **set<Shape>** or at least between **set<Circle**∗**>** and **set<Shape**∗**>**. This is a serious logical error based on a flawed argument: "A **Circle** is a **Shape**, so a set of **Circle**s is also a set of **Shape**s; therefore, I should be able to use a set of **Circle**s as a set of **Shape**s." The "therefore" part of this argument doesn't hold. The reason is that a set of **Circle**s guarantees that the members of the set are **Circle**s; a set of **Shape**s does not provide that guarantee. For example:

```
class Triangle : public Shape {
    // ...
};

void f(set<Shape*>& s)
{
    // ...
    s.insert(new Triangle{p1,p2,p3});
}

void g(set<Circle*>& s)
{
    f(s); // error, type mismatch: s is a set<Circle*>, not a set<Shape*>
}
```

This won't compile because there is no built-in conversion from **set<Circle*>&** to **set<Shape*>&**. Nor should there be. The guarantee that the members of a **set<Circle*>** are **Circle**s allows us to safely and efficiently apply **Circle**-specific operations, such as determining the radius, to members of the set. If we allowed a **set<Circle*>** to be treated as a **set<Shape*>**, we could no longer maintain that guarantee. For example, **f()** inserts a **Triangle*** into its **set<Shape*>** argument. If the **set<Shape*>** could have been a **set<Circle*>**, the fundamental guarantee that a **set<Circle*>** contains **Circle***s only would have been violated.

Logically, we could treat an immutable **set<Circle*>** as an immutable **set<Shape*>** because the problem of inserting an inappropriate element into the set cannot occur when we cannot change the set. That is, we could provide a conversion from **const set<const Circle*>** to **const set<const Shape*>**. The language doesn't do so by default, but the designer of **set** could.

The combination of an array and a base class is particularly nasty because a built-in array does not offer the type safety provided by containers. For example:

```
void maul(Shape* p, int n)        // Danger!
{
    for (int i=0; i!=n; ++i)
        p[i].draw();              // looks innocent; it is not
}

void user()
{
    Circle image[10];             // an image is composed of 10 Circles
    // ...
    maul(image,10);               // "maul" 10 Circles
    // ...
}
```

How can we call **maul()** with **image**? First, **image**'s type is converted (decays) from **Circle[]** to **Circle***. Next, **Circle*** is converted to **Shape***. The implicit conversion of an array name to a pointer to the array's first element is fundamental to C-style programming. Similarly, implicit conversion of a pointer to a derived class to a pointer to its base class is fundamental to object-oriented programming. In combination, they offer the opportunity of disaster.

In the example above, assume that a **Shape** is an abstract class with size **4** and that **Circle** adds a center and a radius. Then **sizeof(Circle)>sizeof(Shape)** and when we look at the layout of **image** we find something like this:

user() view:	image[0]				image[1]		image[2]		image[3]	
maul() view:	p[0]	p[1]	p[2]	p[3]						

When **maul()** tries to invoke a virtual function on **p[1]**, there is no virtual function pointer where it is expected and the call hopefully fails instantly.

Note that no explicit cast was needed to get this disaster:

- Prefer containers over built-in arrays.
- Consider interfaces such as **void f(T* p, int count)** highly suspect; when **T** can be a base class and **count** is an element count, trouble awaits.
- Consider . (dot) suspect when applied to something that is supposed to be run-time polymorphic unless it is obviously applied to a reference.

27.2.2 Template Conversions

There cannot be any *default* relationship between classes generated from the same template (§27.2.1). However, for some templates we would like to express such a relationship. For example, when we define a pointer template, we would like to reflect inheritance relationships among the objects pointed to. Member templates (§23.4.6) allow us to specify many such relationships where desired. Consider:

```
template<typename T>
class Ptr {        // pointer to T
    T* p;
public:
    Ptr(T*);
    Ptr(const Ptr&);                       // copy constructor
    template<typename T2>
        explicit operator Ptr<T2>();       // convert Ptr<T> to Ptr<T2>
    // ...
};
```

We would like to define the conversion operators to provide the inheritance relationships we are accustomed to for built-in pointers for these user-defined **Ptr**s. For example:

```
void f(Ptr<Circle> pc)
{
    Ptr<Shape> ps {pc};      // should work
    Ptr<Circle> pc2 {ps};    // should give error
}
```

We want to allow the first initialization if and only if **Shape** really is a direct or indirect public base class of **Circle**. In general, we need to define the conversion operator so that the **Ptr<T>** to **Ptr<T2>** conversion is accepted if and only if a **T*** can be assigned to a **T2***. That can be done like this:

```
template<typename T>
    template<typename T2>
        Ptr<T>::operator Ptr<T2>()
        {
            return Ptr<T2>{p};
        }
```

The **return**-statement will compile if and only if **p** (which is a **T**∗) can be an argument to the **Ptr<T2>(T2**∗**)** constructor. Therefore, if **T**∗ can be implicitly converted into a **T2**∗, the **Ptr<T>** to **Ptr<T2>** conversion will work. For example, we can now write:

```
void f(Ptr<Circle> pc)
{
    Ptr<Shape> ps {pc};        // OK: can convert Circle* to Shape*
    Ptr<Circle> pc2 {ps};      // error: cannot convert Shape* to Circle*
}
```

Be careful to define logically meaningful conversions only. If in doubt, use a named conversion function, rather than a conversion operator. A named conversion function offers fewer opportunities for ambiguities.

The template parameter lists of a template and one of its template members cannot be combined. For example:

```
template<typename T, typename T2>    // error
Ptr<T>::operator Ptr<T2>()
{
    return Ptr<T2>(p);
}
```

An alternative solution to this problem uses type traits and **enable_if()** (§28.4).

27.3 Hierarchies of Class Templates

Using object-oriented techniques, a base class is often used to provide a common interface to a set of derived classes. A template can be used to parameterize such an interface, and when that is done it is tempting to parameterize the whole hierarchy of derived classes with the same template parameters. For example, we could parameterize the classical shape example (§3.2.4) with types used to provide an abstraction of the target output "device":

```
template<typename Color_scheme, typename Canvas>    // questionable example
class Shape {
    // ...
};

template<typename Color_scheme, typename Canvas>
class Circle : public Shape {
    // ...
};
```

```
template<typename Color_scheme, typename Canvas>
class Triangle : public Shape {
     // ...
};

void user()
{
     auto p = new Triangle<RGB,Bitmapped>{{0,0},{0,60},{30,sqrt(60*60–30*30)}};
     // ...
}
```

Something along this line is often the first idea (after seeing something like **vector<T>**) that a programmer used to object-oriented programming considers. However, caution is recommended when mixing object-oriented and generic techniques.

As written, this parameterized shape hierarchy is too verbose for real use. That could be addressed using default template arguments (§25.2.5). However, the verbosity is not the main problem. If only one combination of **Color_scheme** and **Canvas** is used in a program, the amount of code generated is almost exactly the same as would have been generated for the unparameterized equivalent. The "almost" comes because the compiler will suppress code generation for the definitions of unused non-virtual member functions of a class template. However, if N combinations of **Color_scheme** and **Canvas** are used in a program, the code for every virtual function will be replicated N times. Because a graphics hierarchy is likely to have many derived classes, many member functions, and many complicated functions, the result is likely to be massive code bloat. In particular, the compiler cannot know whether a virtual function is used or not, so it must generate code for all such functions and for all functions called by such functions. Parameterizing a huge class hierarchy with many virtual member functions is typically a poor idea.

For this shape example, the **Color_scheme** and **Canvas** parameters are unlikely to affect the interface much: most member functions will not have them as part of their function type. These parameters are an "implementation detail" that escaped into the interface – with likely serious performance implications. It is not really the whole hierarchy that needs those parameters; it is a few configuration functions and (most likely) a few lower-level drawing/rendering functions. It is generally not a good idea to "overparameterize" (§23.4.6.3): try to avoid parameters that affect only a few members. If only a few member functions are affected by a parameter, try to make those function templates with that parameter. For example:

```
class Shape {
     template<typename Color_scheme, typename Canvas>
          void configure(const Color_scheme&, const Canvas&);
     // ...
};
```

How to share the configuration information among different classes and different objects is a separate issue. Clearly, we cannot simply store a **Color_scheme** and **Canvas** in the **Shape** without parameterizing **Shape** itself with **Color_scheme** and **Canvas**. One solution would be for **configure()** to "translate" the information in **Color_scheme** and **Canvas** into a standard set of configuration parameters (e.g., a set of integers). Another solution is to give a **Shape** a **Configuration**∗ member, where **Configuration** is a base class providing a general interface to configuration information.

27.3.1 Templates as Interfaces

A template class can be used to provide a flexible and type-safe interface to a common implementation. The vector from §25.3 is a good example of this:

```
template<typename T>
class Vector<T*>
    : private Vector<void*>
{
    // ...
};
```

In general, this technique can be used to provide type-safe interfaces and for localizing casts to implementations, rather than forcing users to write them.

27.4 Template Parameters as Base Classes

In classical object-oriented programming using class hierarchies, we place information that can be different for different classes in derived classes and access it through virtual functions in a base class (§3.2.4, §21.2.1). That way, we can write common code without worrying about variations in the implementations. However, this technique does not allow us to vary the types used in the interface (§27.2). Also, those virtual function calls can be expensive compared to a simple operation from an inlined function. To compensate, we might pass the specialized information and operations to the base class as template arguments. In fact, a template argument can be used as a base class.

The general problem addressed by the following two subsections is "How can we combine separately specified information into a single compact object with a well-specified interface?" This is a fundamental question and the solutions are of general importance.

27.4.1 Composing Data Structures

Consider writing a balanced binary tree library. Since we are providing a library to be used by many different users, we can't build the type of the user's (application's) data into our tree nodes. We have many alternatives:

- We could put the user's data in a derived class and access it using virtual functions. But the virtual function calls (or equivalently, run-time resolved and checked solutions) are relatively expensive, and our interface to the user's data is not expressed in terms of the user's type, so we still need to use casts to access it.
- We could put a **void*** in our nodes and let the user use that to refer to data allocated outside our nodes. But that could double the number of allocations, add many (potentially expensive) pointer dereferences, and add the space overhead of a pointer in each node. We would also need to use a cast to access our user data using its correct type. That cast can't be type checked.
- We could put a **Data*** into our nodes, where **Data** is a "universal base class" for our data structures. That would solve the type-checking problem, but that combines the cost and inconvenience of the previous two approaches.

There are more alternatives, but consider:

```cpp
template<typename N>
struct Node_base {         // doesn't know about Val (the user data)
    N* left_child;
    N* right_child;

    Node_base();

    void add_left(N* p)
    {
        if (left_child==nullptr)
            left_child = p;
        else
            // ...
    }
    // ...
};

template<typename Val>
struct Node : Node_base<Node<Val>> {         // use derived class as part of its own base
    Val v;
    Node(Val vv);
    // ...
};
```

Here, we pass the derived class `Node<Val>` as a template argument to its own base (`Node_base`). That allows `Node_base` to use `Node<Val>` in its interfaces without even knowing its real name!

Note that the layout of a `Node` is compact. For example, a `Node<double>` will look roughly equivalent to this:

```cpp
struct Node_base_double {
    double val;
    Node_base_double* left_child;
    Node_base_double* right_child;
};
```

Unfortunately, with this design, a user has to be aware of `Node_base`'s operations and the structure of the resulting tree. For example:

```cpp
using My_node = Node<double>;

void user(const vector<double>& v)
{
    My_node root;
    int i = 0;

    for (auto x : v) {
        auto p = new My_node{x};
```

```
            if (i++%2)                    // choose where to insert
                    root.add_left(p);
            else
                    root.add_right(p);
    }
}
```

However, it is not easy for a user to keep the structure of a tree reasonable. Typically, we would like to let the tree take care of that by implementing a tree-balancing algorithm. However, to balance a tree so that you can search it efficiently, the balancer needs to know the user's values.

How do we add a balancer to our design? We could hardwire the balancing strategy into **Node_base** and let **Node_base** "peek" at the user data. For example, a balanced tree implementation, such as the standard-library **map**, (by default) requires that a value type provides a less-than operation. That way, the **Node_base** operations can simply use <:

```
template<typename N>
struct Node_base {
    static_assert(Totally_ordered<N>(), "Node_base: N must have a <");

    N* left_child;
    N* right_child;
    Balancing_info bal;

    Node_base();

    void insert(N& n)
    {
        if (n<left_child)
                // ... do something ...
        else
                // ... do something else ...
    }
    // ...
};
```

This works nicely. In fact, the more information about nodes we build into the **Node_base**, the simpler the implementation becomes. In particular, we could parameterize the **Node_base** with a value type rather than a node type (as is done for **std::map**), and we would have the tree in a single compact package. However, doing so doesn't address the fundamental question we are trying to address here: how to combine information from several separately specified sources. Writing everything in one place dodges that problem.

So let us assume that the user will want to manipulate **Node**s (e.g., move a node from one tree to another), so that we can't simply store user data into an anonymous node. Let us further assume that we would like to be able to use a variety of balancing algorithms, so that we need to make the balancer an argument. These assumptions force us to face the fundamental question. The simplest solution is to let **Node** combine the value type with a balancer type. However, **Node** doesn't need to use the balancer, so it just passes it on to **Node_base**:

```
template<typename Val, typename Balance>
struct Search_node : public Node_base<Search_node<Val, Balance>, Balance>
{
    Val val;          // user data
    search_node(Val v): val(v) {}
};
```

Balance is mentioned twice here because it is part of the node type and because **Node_base** needs to make an object of type **Balance**:

```
template<typename N, typename Balance>
struct Node_base : Balance {
    N∗ left_child;
    N∗ right_child;

    Node_base();

    void insert(N& n)
    {
        if (this–>compare(n,left_child))      // use compare() from Balance
            // ... do something ...
        else
            // ... do something else ...
    }
    // ...
};
```

I could have used **Balance** to define a member, rather than using it as a base. However, some important balancers require no per-node data, so by making **Balance** a base, I benefit from the *empty-base optimization*. The language guarantees that if a base class has no non-**static** data members, no memory will be allocated for it in an object of derived class (§iso.1.8). Also, this design is with minor stylistic differences that of a real binary tree framework [Austern,2003]. We might use these classes like this:

```
struct Red_black_balance {
    // data and operations needed to implement red-black trees
};

template<typename T>
using Rbnode = Search_node<T,Red_black_balance>;  // type alias for red-black trees

Rbnode<double> my_root;        // a red-black tree of doubles

using My_node = Rb_node<double>;

void user(const vector<double>& v)
{
    for (auto x : v)
        root.insert(∗new My_node{x});
}
```

The layout of a node is compact, and we can easily inline all performance-critical functions. What we achieved by the slightly elaborate set of definitions was type safety and ease of composition. This elaboration delivers a performance advantage compared to every approach that introduces a **void**∗ into the data structure or function interfaces. Such a use of **void**∗ disables valuable type-based optimization techniques. Choosing a low-level (C-style) programming technique in the key parts of a balanced binary tree implementation implies a significant run-time cost.

We passed the balancer as a separate template argument:

```
template<typename N, typename Balance>
struct Node_base : Balance {
        // ...
};


template<typename Val, typename Balance>
struct Search_node
    : public Node_base<Search_node<Val, Balance>, Balance>
{
    // ...
};
```

Some find this clear, explicit, and general; others find it verbose and confusing. The alternative is to make the balancer an implicit argument in the form of an associated type (a member type of **Search_node**):

```
template<typename N>
struct Node_base : N::balance_type {    // use N's balance_type
        // ...
};


template<typename Val, typename Balance>
struct Search_node
    : public Node_base<Search_node<Val,Balance>>
{
    using balance_type = Balance;
    // ...
};
```

This technique is heavily used in the standard library to minimize explicit template arguments.

The technique of deriving from a base class is very old. It was mentioned in the ARM (1989) and is sometimes referred to as *the Barton-Nackman trick* after an early use in mathematical software [Barton,1994]. Jim Coplien called it *the curiously recurring template pattern* (CRTP) [Coplien,1995].

27.4.2 Linearizing Class Hierarchies

The **Search_node** example from §27.4.1 uses its template to compress its representation and to avoid using **void**∗. The techniques are general and very useful. In particular, many programs that deal with trees rely on it for type safety and performance. For example, the "Internal Program Representation" (IPR) [DosReis,2011] is a general and systematic representation of C++ code as typed abstract syntax trees. It uses template parameters as base classes extensively, both as an implementation aid (implementation inheritance) and to provide abstract interfaces in the classical object-oriented way (interface inheritance). The design addresses a difficult set of criteria, including compactness of nodes (there can be many millions of nodes), optimized memory management, access speed (don't introduce unnecessary indirections or nodes), type safety, polymorphic interfaces, and generality.

The users see a hierarchy of abstract classes providing perfect encapsulation and clean functional interfaces representing the semantics of a program. For example, a variable is a declaration, which is a statement, which is an expression, which is a node:

Var –> Decl –> Stmt –> Expr –> Node

Clearly, some generalization has been done in the design of the IPR because in ISO C++ statements cannot be used as expressions.

In addition, there is a parallel hierarchy of concrete classes providing compact and efficient implementations of the classes in the interface hierarchy:

impl::Var –> impl::Decl –> impl::Stmt –> impl::Expr –> impl::Node

In all, there are about 80 leaf classes (such as **Var**, **If_stmt**, and **Multiply**) and about 20 generalizations (such as **Decl**, **Unary**, and **impl::Stmt**).

The first attempt of a design was a classical multiple-inheritance "diamond" hierarchy (using solid arrows to represent interface inheritance and dotted arrows for implementation inheritance):

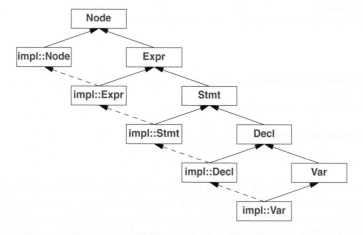

That worked but led to excessive memory overhead: the nodes were too large because of data needed to navigate the virtual bases. In addition, programs were seriously slowed down by the many indirections to access the many virtual bases in each object (§21.3.5).

The solution was to linearize the dual hierarchy so that no virtual bases were used:

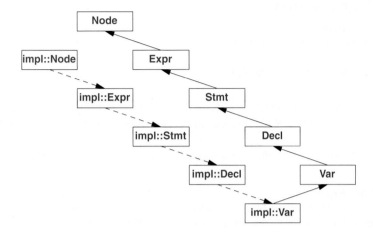

For the full set of classes the chain of derivation becomes:

```
impl::Var ->
    impl::Decl<impl::Var> ->
        impl::Stmt<impl::Var> ->
            impl::Expr<impl::Var> ->
                impl::Node<impl::Var> ->
                    ipr::Var ->
                        ipr::Decl ->
                            ipr::Stmt ->
                                ipr::Expr ->
                                    ipr::Node
```

This is represented as a compact object with no internal "management data" except the single **vptr** (§3.2.3, §20.3.2).

I will show how that is done. The interface hierarchy, defined in namespace **ipr** is described first. Starting from the bottom, a **Node** holds data used to optimize traversal and **Node** type identification (the **code_category**) and to ease storage of IPR graphs in files (the **node_id**). These are fairly typical "implementation details" hidden from the users. What a user will know is that every node in an IPR graph has a unique base of type **Node** and that this can be used to implement operations using the *visitor pattern* [Gamma,1994] (§22.3):

```
struct ipr::Node {
    const int node_id;
    const Category_code category;

    virtual void accept(Visitor&) const = 0;   // hook for visitor classes
protected:
    Node(Category_code);
};
```

Node is meant to be used as a base class only, so its constructor is **protected**. It also has a pure virtual function, so it cannot be instantiated except as a base class.

An expression (**Expr**) is a **Node** that has a type:

```
struct ipr::Expr : Node {
    virtual const Type& type() const = 0;
protected:
    Expr(Category_code c) : Node(c) { }
};
```

Obviously, this is quite a generalization of C++ because it implies that even statements and types have types: it is an aim of the IPR to represent all of C++ without implementing all of C++'s irregularities and limitations.

A statement (**Stmt**) is an **Expr** that has a source file location and can be annotated with various information:

```
struct ipr::Stmt : Expr {
    virtual const Unit_location& unit_location() const = 0;      // line in file
    virtual const Source_location& source_location() const = 0;  // file

    virtual const Sequence<Annotation>& annotation() const = 0;
protected:
    Stmt(Category_code c) : Expr(c) { }
};
```

A declaration (**Decl**) is a **Stmt** that introduces a name:

```
struct ipr::Decl : Stmt {
    enum Specifier { /* storage class, virtual, access control, etc. */ };

    virtual Specifier specifiers() const = 0;
    virtual const Linkage& lang_linkage() const = 0;

    virtual const Name& name() const = 0;

    virtual const Region& home_region() const = 0;
    virtual const Region& lexical_region() const = 0;

    virtual bool has_initializer() const = 0;
    virtual const Expr& initializer() const = 0;

        // ...
protected:
    Decl(Category_code c) : Stmt(c) { }
};
```

As you might expect, **Decl** is one of the central notions when it comes to representing C++ code. This is where you find scope information, storage classes, access specifiers, initializers, etc.

Finally, we can define a class to represent a variable (**Var**) as a leaf class (most derived class) of our interface hierarchy:

```
struct ipr::Var : Category<var_cat, Decl> {
};
```

Basically, **Category** is a notational aid with the effect of deriving **Var** from **Decl** and giving the **Category_code** used to optimize **Node** type identification:

```
template<Category_code Cat, typename T = Expr>
struct Category : T {
protected:
    Category() : T(Cat) { }
};
```

Every data member is a **Var**. That includes global, namespace, local, and class **static** variables and constants.

Compared to representations you find in compilers, this interface is tiny. Except for some data for optimizations in **Node**, this is just a set of classes with pure virtual functions. Note that it is a single hierarchy with no virtual base classes. It is a straightforward object-oriented design. However, implementing this simply, efficiently, and maintainably is not easy, and IPR's solution is certainly not what an experienced object-oriented designer would first think of.

For each IPR interface class (in **ipr**), there is a corresponding implementation class (in **impl**). For example:

```
template<typename T>
struct impl::Node : T {
    using Interface = T; // make the template argument type available to users
    void accept(ipr::Visitor& v) const override { v.visit(*this); }
};
```

The "trick" is to establish the correspondence between the **ipr** nodes and the **impl** nodes. In particular, the **impl** nodes must provide the necessary data members and override the abstract virtual functions in the **ipr** nodes. For **impl::Node**, we can see that if **T** is an **ipr::Node** or any class derived from **ipr::Node**, then the **accept()** function is properly overridden.

Now, we can proceed to provide implementation classes for the rest of the **ipr** interface classes:

```
template<typename Interface>
struct impl::Expr : impl::Node<Interface> {
    const ipr::Type* constraint;        // constraint is the type of the expression

    Expr() : constraint(0) { }

    const ipr::Type& type() const override { return *util::check(constraint); }
};
```

If the **Interface** argument is an **ipr::Expr** or any class derived from **ipr::Expr**, then **impl::Expr** is an implementation for **ipr::Expr**. We can make sure of that. Since **ipr::Expr** is derived from **ipr::Node**, this implies that **impl::Node** gets the **ipr::Node** base class that it needs.

In other words, we have managed to provide implementations for two (different) interface classes. We can proceed in this manner:

```
template<typename S>
struct impl::Stmt : S {
        ipr::Unit_location unit_locus;          // logical position in translation unit
        ipr::Source_location src_locus;         // source file, line, and column
        ref_sequence<ipr::Annotation> notes;

        const ipr::Unit_location& unit_location() const override { return unit_locus; }
        const ipr::Source_location& source_location() const override { return src_locus; }
        const ipr::Sequence<ipr::Annotation>& annotation() const override { return notes; }
};
```

That is, **impl:Stmt** provides the three data items needed to implement **ipr::Stmt**'s interface and overrides **ipr::Stmt**'s three virtual functions to do so.

Basically, all **impl** classes follow **Stmt**'s pattern:

```
template<typename D>
struct impl::Decl : Stmt<Node<D> > {
        basic_decl_data<D> decl_data;
        ipr::Named_map* pat;
        val_sequence<ipr::Substitution> args;

        Decl() : decl_data(0), pat(0) { }

        const ipr::Sequence<ipr::Substitution>& substitutions() const { return args; }
        const ipr::Named_map& generating_map() const override { return *util::check(pat); }
        const ipr::Linkage& lang_linkage() const override;
        const ipr::Region& home_region() const override;
};
```

Finally, we can define the leaf class **impl::Var**:

```
struct Var : impl::Decl<ipr::Var> {
        const ipr::Expr* init;
        const ipr::Region* lexreg;

        Var();

        bool has_initializer() const override;
        const ipr::Expr& initializer() const override;
        const ipr::Region& lexical_region() const override;
};
```

Note that **Var** is not a template; it is a user-level abstraction in our application. The implementation of **Var** is an example of generic programming, but its use is classical object-oriented programming.

The combination of inheritance and parameterization is powerful. This expressive power can lead to confusion for beginners and occasionally even for experienced programmers when faced with a new application area. However, the benefits of the combination are concrete: type safety, performance, and minimal source code size. The extensibility offered by class hierarchies and virtual functions is not compromised.

27.5 Advice

[1]   When having to express a general idea in code, consider whether to represent it as a template or as a class hierachy; §27.1.

[2]   A template usually provides common code for a variety of arguments; §27.1.

[3]   An abstract class can completely hide implementation details from users; §27.1.

[4]   Irregular implementations are usually best represented as derived classes; §27.2.

[5]   If explicit use of free store is undesirable, templates have an advantage over class hierarchies; §27.2.

[6]   Templates have an advantage over abstract classes where inlining is important; §27.2.

[7]   Template interfaces are easily expressed in terms of template argument types; §27.2.

[8]   If run-time resolution is needed, class hierarchies are necessary; §27.2.

[9]   The combination of templates and class hierarchies is often superior to either without the other; §27.2.

[10]   Think of templates as type generators (and function generators); §27.2.1.

[11]   There is no default relation between two classes generated from the same template; §27.2.1.

[12]   Do not mix class hierarchies and arrays; §27.2.1.

[13]   Do not naively templatize large class hierarchies; §27.3.

[14]   A template can be used to provide a type-safe interface to a single (weakly typed) implementation; §27.3.1.

[15]   Templates can be used to compose type-safe and compact data structures; §27.4.1.

[16]   Templates can be used to linearize a class hierarchy (minimizing space and access time); §27.4.2.

28

Metaprogramming

Trips to fairly unknown regions should be made twice;
once to make mistakes and once to correct them.
— John Steinbeck

28.1 Introduction

Programming that manipulates program entities, such as classes and functions, is commonly called
metaprogramming. I find it useful to think of templates as generators: they are used to make
classes and functions. This leads to the notion of template programming as an exercise in writing
programs that compute at compile time and generate programs. Variations of this idea have been
called *two-level programming*, *multilevel programming*, *generative programming*, and – more commonly – *template metaprogramming*.

There are two main reasons for using metaprogramming techniques:

- *Improved type safety*: We can compute the exact types needed for a data structure or algorithm so that we don't need to directly manipulate low-level data structures (e.g., we can eliminate many uses of explicit type conversion).
- *Improved run-time performance*: We can compute values at compile time and select functions to be called at run time. That way, we don't need to do those computations at run time (e.g., we can resolve many examples of polymorphic behavior to direct function calls). In particular, by taking advantage of the type system, we can dramatically improve the opportunities for inlining. Also, by using compact data structures (possibly generated; §27.4.2, §28.5), we make better use of memory with positive effects on both the amount of data we can handle and the execution speed.

Templates were designed to be very general and able to generate optimal code [Stroustrup,1994]. They provide arithmetic, selection, and recursion. In fact, they constitute a complete compile-time functional programming language [Veldhuizen,2003]. That is, templates and their template instantiation mechanism are Turing complete. One demonstration of this was that Eisenecker and Czarnecki wrote a Lisp interpreter in only a few pages using templates [Czarnecki,2000]. The C++ compile-time mechanisms provide a *pure* functional programming language: You can create values of various types, but there are no variables, assignments, increment operators, etc. The Turing completeness implies the possibility of infinite compilations, but that's easily taken care of by translation limits (§iso.B). For example, an infinite recursion will be caught by running out of some compile-time resource, such as the number of recursive **constexpr** calls, the number of nested classes, or the number of recursively nested template instantiations.

Where should we draw the line between generic programming and template metaprogramming? The extreme positions are:

- It is all template metaprogramming: after all, any use of compile-time parameterization implies instantiation that generates "ordinary code."
- It is all generic programming: after all, we are just defining and using generic types and algorithms.

Both of these positions are useless because they basically define generic programming and template metaprogramming as synonyms. I think there is a useful distinction to be made. A distinction helps us decide between alternative approaches to problems and to focus on what is important for a given problem. When I write a generic type or algorithm, I don't feel that I am writing a compile-time program. I am not using my programming skills for the compile-time part of my program. Instead, I am focusing on defining requirements on arguments (§24.3). Generic programming is primarily a design philosophy – a programming paradigm, if you must (§1.2.1).

In contrast, metaprogramming is programming. The emphasis is on computation, often involving selection and some form of iteration. Metaprogramming is primarily a set of implementation techniques. I can think of four levels of implementation complexity:

[1]   No computation (just pass type and value arguments)
[2]   Simple computation (on types or values) not using compile-time tests or iteration, for example, **&&** of Booleans (§24.4) or addition of units (§28.7.1)
[3]   Computation using explicit compile-time tests, for example, a compile-time **if** (§28.3).
[4]   Computation using compile-time iteration (in the form of recursion; §28.3.2).

The ordering indicates the level of complexity, with implications for the difficulty of the task, the difficulty of debugging, and the likelihood of error.

So, metaprogramming is a combination of "meta" and programming: *a metaprogram is a compile-time computation yielding types or functions to be used at run time.* Note that I don't say "template metaprogramming" because the computation may be done using **constexpr** functions. Note also that you can rely on other people's metaprogramming without actually doing metaprogramming yourself: calling a **constexpr** function hiding a metaprogram (§28.2.2) or extracting the type from a template type function (§28.2.4) is not in itself metaprogramming; it just uses a metaprogram.

Generic programming usually falls into the first, "no computation" category, but it is quite possible to support generic programming using metaprogramming techniques. When doing so, we have to be careful that our interface specifications are precisely defined and correctly implemented. Once we use (meta)programming as part of an interface, the possibility of programming errors creeps in. Without programming, the meaning is directly defined by the language rules.

Generic programming focuses on interface specification, whereas metaprogramming is programming, usually with types as the values.

Overenthusiastic use of metaprogramming can lead to debugging problems and excessive compile times that render some uses unrealistic. As ever, we have to apply common sense. There are many simple uses of metaprogramming that lead to better code (better type safety, lower memory footprint, and lower run time) without exceptional compile-time overhead. Many standard-library components, such as **function** (§33.5.3), **thread** (§5.3.1, §42.2.2), and **tuple** (§34.2.4.2), are examples of relatively simple application of metaprogramming techniques.

This chapter explores the basic metaprogramming techniques and presents the basic building blocks of metaprograms. Chapter 29 offers a more extensive example.

28.2 Type Functions

A *type function* is a function that either takes at least one type argument or produces at least one type as a result. For example, **sizeof(T)** is a built-in type function that given a type argument **T** returns the size of an object (measured in **char**s; §6.2.8).

Type functions don't have to look like conventional functions. In fact, most don't. For example, the standard library's **is_polymorphic<T>** takes its argument as a template argument and returns its result as a member called **value**:

```
if (is_polymorphic<int>::value) cout << "Big surprise!";
```

The **value** member of **is_polymorphic** is either **true** or **false**. Similarly, the standard-library convention is that a type function that returns a type does so by a member called **type**. For example:

```
enum class Axis : char { x, y, z };
enum flags { off, x=1, y=x<<1, z=x<<2, t=x<<3 };

typename std::underlying_type<Axis>::type x;      // x is a char
typename std::underlying_type<Axis>::type y;      // y is probably an int (§8.4.2)
```

A type function can take more than one argument and return several result values. For example:

```
template<typename T, int N>
struct Array_type {
    using type = T;
    static const int dim = N;
    // ...
};
```

This `Array_type` is not a standard-library function or even a particularly useful function. I just used it as an excuse to show how to write a simple multi-argument, multi-return-value type function. It can be used like this:

```
using Array = Array_type<int,3>;

Array::type x;              // x is an int
constexpr int s = Array::dim;  // s is 3
```

Type functions are compile-time functions. That is, they can only take arguments (types and values) that are known at compile time and produce results (types and values) that can be used at compile time.

Most type functions take at least one type argument, but there are useful ones that don't. For example, here is a type function that returns an integer type of the appropriate number of bytes:

```
template<int N>
struct Integer {
    using Error = void;
    using type = Select<N,Error,signed char,short,Error,int,Error,Error,Error,long>;
};

typename Integer<4>::type i4 = 8;   // 4-byte integer
typename Integer<1>::type i1 = 9;   // 1-byte integer
```

`Select` is defined and explained in §28.3.1.3. It is of course possible to write templates that take values only and produce values only. I don't consider those type functions. Also, `constexpr` functions (§12.1.6) are usually a better way of expressing compile-time computations on values. I can compute a square root at compile time using templates, but why would I want to when I can express the algorithm more cleanly using `constexpr` functions (§2.2.3, §10.4, §28.3.2)?

So, C++ type functions are mostly templates. They can perform very general computations using types and values. They are the backbone of metaprogramming. For example, we might want to allocate an object on the stack provided that it is small and on the free store otherwise:

```
constexpr int on_stack_max = sizeof(std::string); // max size of object we want on the stack

template<typename T>
struct Obj_holder {
    using type = typename std::conditional<(sizeof(T)<=on_stack_max),
                                Scoped<T>,        // first alternative
                                On_heap<T>        // second alternative
                    >::type;
};
```

The standard-library template **conditional** is a compile-time selector between two alternatives. If its first argument evaluates to **true**, the result (presented as the member **type**) is the second argument; otherwise, the result is the third argument. §28.3.1.1 shows how **conditional** is implemented. In this case, **Obj_holder<X>**'s **type** is defined to be **Scoped<X>** if an object of **X** is small and **On_heap<X>** if it is large. **Obj_holder** can be used like this:

```
void f()
{
    typename Obj_holder<double>::type v1;                // the double goes on the stack
    typename Obj_holder<array<double,200>>::type v2;     // the array goes on the free store
    // ...
    *v1 = 7.7;      // Scoped provides pointer-like access (* and [])
    v2[77] = 9.9;   // On_heap provides pointer-like access (* and [])
    // ...
}
```

The **Obj_holder** example is not hypothetical. For example, the C++ standard contains the following comment in its definition of the **function** type (§33.5.3) for holding function-like entities: "Implementations are encouraged to avoid the use of dynamically allocated memory for small callable objects, for example, where f's target is an object holding only a pointer or reference to an object and a member function pointer" (§iso.20.8.11.2.1). It would be hard to follow that advice without something like **Obj_holder**.

How are **Scoped** and **On_heap** implemented? Their implementations are trivial and do not involve any metaprogramming, but here they are:

```
template<typename T>
struct On_heap {
    On_heap() :p(new T) { }     // allocate
    ~On_heap() { delete p; }    // deallocate

    T& operator*() { return *p; }
    T* operator->() { return p; }

    On_heap(const On_heap&) = delete;            // prevent copying
    On_heap operator=(const On_heap&) = delete;
private:
    T* p;        // pointer to object on the free store
};

template<typename T>
struct Scoped {
    T& operator*() { return x; }
    T* operator->() { return &x; }

    Scoped(const Scoped&) = delete;           // prevent copying
    Scoped operator=(const Scoped&) = delete;
private:
    T x;        // the object
};
```

On_heap and **Scoped** provide good examples of how generic programming and template metaprogramming require us to devise uniform interfaces to different implementations of a general idea (here, the idea of allocation of an object).

Both **On_heap** and **Scoped** can be used as members as well as local variables. **On_heap** always places its object on the free store, whereas **Scoped** contains its object.

§28.6 shows how we can implement versions of **On_heap** and **Scoped** for types that take constructor arguments.

28.2.1 Type Aliases

Note how the implementation details of **Obj_holder** (as for **Int**) shine through when we use **typename** and **::type** to extract the member type. This is a consequence of the way the language is specified and used, this is the way template metaprogramming code has been written for the last 15 years, and this is the way it appears in the C++11 standard. I consider it insufferable. It reminds me of the bad old days in C, where every occurrence of a user-defined type had to be prefixed with the **struct** keyword. By introducing a template alias (§23.6), we can hide the **::type** implementation details and make a type function look much more like a function returning a type (or like a type). For example:

```
template<typename T>
using Holder = typename Obj_holder<T>::type;

void f2()
{
    Holder<double> v1;
        // the double goes on the stack
    Holder<array<double,200>> v2;      // the array goes on the free store
    // ...
    *v1 = 7.7;        // Scoped provides pointer-like access (* and [])
    v2[77] = 9.9;     // On_heap provides pointer-like access (* and [])
    // ...
}
```

Except when explaining an implementation or what the standard specifically offers, I use such type aliases systematically. When the standard provides a type function (called something like "type property predicate" or "composite type category predicate"), such as **conditional**, I define a corresponding type alias (§35.4.1):

```
template<typename C, typename T, typename F>
using Conditional = typename std::conditional<C,T,F>::type;
```

Please note that these aliases are unfortunately not part of the standard.

28.2.1.1 When Not to Use an Alias

There is one case in which it is significant to use **::type** directly, rather than an alias. If only one of the alternatives is supposed to be a valid type, we should not use an alias. Consider first a simple analogy:

```
if (p) {
    p–>f(7);
    // ...
}
```

It is important that we don't enter the block if **p** is the **nullptr**. We are using the test to see if **p** is valid. Similarly, we might want to test to see if a type is valid. For example:

```
conditional<
    is_integral<T>::value,
    make_unsigned<T>,
    Error<T>
>::type
```

Here, we test if **T** is an integral type (using the **std::is_integral** type predicate) and make the unsigned variant of that type if it is (using the **std::make_unsigned** type function). If that succeeds, we have an unsigned type; otherwise, we will have to deal with the **Error** indicator.

Had we written **Make_unsigned<T>** meaning

```
typename make_unsigned<T>::type
```

and tried to use it for a nonintegral type, say **std::string**, we would have tried to make a nonexistent type (**make_unsigned<std::string>::type**). The result would have been a compile-time error.

In the rare cases where we can't use aliases consistently to hide **::type**, we can fall back on the more explicit, implementation-oriented **::type** style. Alternatively, we can introduce a **Delay** type function to delay evaluation of a type function until its use:

```
Conditional<
    is_integral<T>::value,
    Delay<Make_unsigned,T>,
    Error<T>
>
```

The implementation of a perfect **Delay** function is nontrivial, but for many uses this will do:

```
template<template<typename...> class F, typename... Args>
using Delay = F<Args...>;
```

This uses a template template argument (§25.2.4) and variadic templates (§28.6).

Independently of which solution we choose to avoid the undesired instantiation, this is the kind of expert territory that I enter only with some trepidation.

28.2.2 Type Predicates

A predicate is a function that returns a Boolean value. If you want to write functions that take arguments that are types, it seems obvious that you'll like to ask questions about the arguments' types. For example: Is this a signed type? Is this type polymorphic (i.e., does it have at least one virtual function)? Is this type derived from that type?

The answers to many such questions are known to the compiler and exposed to the programmer through a set of standard-library type predicates (§35.4.1). For example:

```
template<typename T>
void copy(T* p, const T* q, int n)
{
    if (std::is_pod<T>::value)
        memcpy(p,q,n);              // use optimized memory copy
    else
        for (int i=0; i!=n; ++i)
            p[i] = q[i];            // copy individual values
}
```

Here, we try to optimize the copy by using the (supposedly optimal) standard-library function **memcpy()** when we can treat the objects as "plain old data" (POD; §8.2.6). If not, we copy the objects one by one (potentially) using their copy constructor. We determine whether the template argument type is a POD by the standard-library type predicate **is_pod**. The result is presented by the member **value**. This standard-library convention is similar to the way type functions present their result as a member **type**.

The **std::is_pod** predicate is one of the many provided by the standard library (§35.4.1). Since the rules for being a POD are tricky, **is_pod** is most likely a compiler intrinsic rather than implemented in the library as C++ code.

Like the **::type** convention, the value **::value** causes verbosity and is a departure from conventional notation that lets implementation details shine through: a function returning a **bool** should be called using ():

```
template<typename T>
void copy(T* p, const T* q, int n)
{
    if (is_pod<T>())
    // ...
}
```

Fortunately, the standard supports that for all standard-library type predicates. Unfortunately, for language-technical reasons, this resolution is not available in the context of a template argument. For example:

```
template<typename T>
void do_something()
{
    Conditional<is_pod<T>(),On_heap<T>,Scoped<Y>) x;    // error: is_pod<T>() is a type
    // ..
}
```

In particular, **is_pod<T>** is interpreted as the type of a function taking no argument and returning an **is_pod<T>** (§iso.14.3[2]).

My solution is to add functions to provide the conventional notation in all contexts:

```
template<typename T>
constexpr bool Is_pod()
{
    return std::is_pod<T>::value;
}
```

I capitalize the names of these type functions to avoid confusion with the standard-library versions. In addition, I keep them in a separate namespace (**Estd**).

We can define our own type predicates. For example:

```
template<typename T>
constexpr bool Is_big()
{
        return 100<sizeof(T);
}
```

We could use this (rather crude) notion of "big" like this:

```
template<typename T>
using Obj_holder = Conditional<(Is_big<T>()), Scoped<T>, On_heap<T>>;
```

It is rarely necessary to define predicates that directly reflect basic properties of types because the standard library provides many of those. Examples are **is_integral**, **is_pointer**, **is_empty**, **is_polymorphic**, and **is_move_assignable** (§35.4.1). When we have to define such predicates, we have rather powerful techniques available. For example, we can define a type function to determine whether a class has a member of a given name and of an appropriate type (§28.4.4).

Naturally, type predicates with more than one argument can also be useful. In particular, this is how we represent relations between two types, such as **is_same**, **is_base_of**, and **is_convertible**. These are also from the standard library.

I use **Is_∗ constexpr** functions to support the usual () calling syntax for all of these **is_∗** functions.

28.2.3 Selecting a Function

A function object is an object of some type, so the techniques for selecting types and values can be used to select a function. For example:

```
struct X { // write X
        void operator()(int x) { cout <<"X" << x << "!"; }
        // ...
};

struct Y { // write Y
        void operator()(int y) { cout <<"Y" << y << "!"; }
        // ...
};

void f()
{
        Conditional<(sizeof(int)>4),X,Y>{}(7);     // make an X or a Y and call it

        using Z = Conditional<(Is_polymorphic<X>()),X,Y>;
        Z zz;        // make an X or a Y
        zz(7);       // call an X or a Y
}
```

As shown, a selected function object type can be used immediately or "remembered" for later use.

Classes with member functions computing some value are the most general and flexible mechanism for computation in template metaprogramming.

Conditional is a mechanism for compile-time programming. In particular, this means that the condition must be a constant expression. Note the parentheses around **sizeof(int)>4**; without those, we would have gotten a syntax error because the compiler would have interpreted the > as the end of the template argument list. For that reason (and others), I prefer to use < (less than) rather than > (greater than). Also, I sometimes use parentheses around conditions for readability.

28.2.4 Traits

The standard library relies heavily on *traits*. A trait is used to associate properties with a type. For example, the properties of an iterator are defined by its **iterator_traits** (§33.1.3):

```
template<typename Iterator>
struct iterator_traits {
    using difference_type = typename Iterator::difference_type;
    using value_type = typename Iterator::value_type;
    using pointer = typename Iterator::pointer;
    using reference = typename Iterator::reference;
    using iterator_category = typename Iterator::iterator_category;
};
```

You can see a trait as a type function with many results or as a bundle of type functions.

The standard library provides **allocator_traits** (§34.4.2), **char_traits** (§36.2.2), **iterator_traits** (§33.1.3), **regex_traits** (§37.5), **pointer_traits** (§34.4.3). In addition, it provides **time_traits** (§35.2.4) and **type_traits** (§35.4.1), which confusingly are simple type functions.

Given **iterator_traits** for a pointer, we can talk about the **value_type** and the **difference_type** of a pointer even though pointers don't have members:

```
template<typename Iter>
Iter search(Iter p, Iter q, typename iterator_traits<Iter>::value_type val)
{
    typename iterator_traits<Iter>::difference_type m = q−p;
    // ...
}
```

This is a most useful and powerful technique, but:

- It is verbose.
- It often bundles otherwise weakly related type functions.
- It exposes implementation details to users.

Also, people sometimes throw in type aliases "just in case," leading to unneccesary complexity. Consequently, I prefer to use simple type functions:

```
template<typename T>
    using Value_type = typename std::iterator_trait<T>::value_type;


template<typename T>
    using Difference_type = typename std::iterator_trait<T>::difference_type;
```

```
template<typename T>
    using Iterator_category= typename std::iterator_trait<T>::iterator_category;
```

The example cleans up nicely:

```
template<typename Iter>
Iter search(Iter p, iter q, Value_type<Iter> val)
{
    Difference_type<Iter> m = q−p;
    // ...
}
```

I suspect that traits are currently overused. Consider how to write the previous example without any mention of traits or other type functions:

```
template<typename Iter, typename Val>
Iter search(Iter p, iter q, Val val)
{
    auto x = ∗p;                             // if we don't need to name *p's type
    auto m = q−p;                            // if we don't need to name q-p's type

    using value_type = decltype(∗p);         // if we want to name *p's type
    using difference_type = decltype(q−p);   // if we want to name q-p's type

    // ...
}
```

Of course, decltype() is a type function, so all I did was to eliminate user-defined and standard-library type functions. Also, auto and decltype are new in C++11, so older code could not have been written this way.

We need a trait (or equivalent, such as decltype()) to associate a type with another type, such as a value_type with a T∗. For that, a trait (or an equivalent) is indispensable for non-intrusively adding type names needed for generic programming or metaprogramming. When a trait is used simply to provide a name for something that already has a perfectly good name, such as pointer for value_type∗ and reference for value_type&, the utility is less clear and the potential for confusion greater. Don't blindly define traits for everything "just in case."

28.3 Control Structures

To do general computation at compile time, we need selection and recursion.

28.3.1 Selection

In addition to what is trivially done using ordinary constant expressions (§10.4), I use:
- Conditional: a way of choosing between two types (an alias for std::conditional)
- Select: a way of choosing among several types (defined in §28.3.1.3)

These type functions return types. If you want to choose among values, ?: is sufficient; Conditional and **Select** are for selecting types. They are not simply compile-time equivalents to **if** and **switch** even though they can appear to be when they are used to choose among function objects (§3.4.3, §19.2.2).

28.3.1.1 Selecting between Two Types

It is surprisingly simple to implement **Conditional**, as used in §28.2. The **conditional** template is part of the standard library (in **<type_traits>**), so we don't have to implement it, but it illustrates an important technique:

```
template<bool C, typename T, typename F>    // general template
struct conditional {
    using type = T;
};

template<typename T, typename F>            // specialization for false
struct conditional<false,T,F> {
    using type = F;
};
```

The primary template (§25.3.1.1) simply defines its **type** to be **T** (the first template parameter after the condition). If the condition is not **true**, the specialization for **false** is chosen and **type** is defined to be **F**. For example:

```
typename conditional<(std::is_polymorphic<T>::value),X,Y>::type z;
```

Obviously, the syntax leaves a bit to be desired (§28.2.2), but the underlying logic is beautiful.

Specialization is used to separate the general case from one or more specialized ones (§25.3). In this example, the primary template takes care of exactly half of the functionality, but that fraction can vary from nothing (every nonerroneous case is handled by a specialization; §25.3.1.1) to all but a single terminating case (§28.5). This form of selection is completely compile-time and doesn't cost a byte or a cycle at run time.

To improve the syntax, I introduce a type alias:

```
template<bool B, typename T, typename F>
using Conditional = typename std::conditional<B,T,F>::type;
```

Given that, we can write:

```
Conditional<(Is_polymorphic<T>()),X,Y> z;
```

I consider that a significant improvement.

28.3.1.2 Compile Time vs. Run Time

Looking at something like

```
Conditional<(std::is_polymorphic<T>::value),X,Y> z;
```

for the first time, it is not uncommon for people to think, "Why don't we just write a normal **if**?" Consider having to choose between two alternatives, **Square** and **Cube**:

```
struct Square {
    constexpr int operator()(int i) { return i*i; }
};

struct Cube {
    constexpr int operator()(int i) { return i*i*i; }
};
```

We might try the familiar if-statement:

```
if (My_cond<T>())
    using Type = Square;     // error: declaration as if-statement branch
else
    using Type = Cube;       // error: declaration as if-statement branch

Type x;    // error: Type is not in scope
```

A declaration cannot be the only statement of a branch of an if-statement (§6.3.4, §9.4.1), so this will not work even though `My_cond<T>()` is computed at compile time. Thus, an ordinary if-statement is useful for ordinary expressions, but not for type selection.

Let us try an example that doesn't involve defining a variable:

```
Conditional<My_cond<T>(),Square,Cube>{}(99);    // invoke Square{}(99) or Cube{}(99)
```

That is, select a type, construct a default object of that type, and call it. That works. Using "conventional control structures," this would become:

```
((My_cond<T>())?Square:Cube){}(99);
```

This example doesn't work because `Square{}(99)` and `Cube{}(99)` do not yield types, rather than values of types that are compatible in a conditional expression (§11.1.3). We could try

```
(My_cond<T>()?Square{}:Cube{})(99);    // error: incompatible arguments for ?:
```

Unfortunately, this version still suffers from the problem that `Square{}` and `Cube{}` are not of compatible types acceptable as alternatives in a ?: expression. The restriction to compatible types is often unacceptable in metaprogramming because we need to choose between types that are not explicitly related.

Finally, this works:

```
My_cond<T>()?Square{}(99):Cube{}(99);
```

Furthermore, it is not significantly more readable than

```
Conditional<My_cond<T>(),Square,Cube>{}(99);
```

28.3.1.3 Selecting among Several Types

Selecting among N alternatives is very similar to choosing between two. Here is a type function returning its Nth argument type:

```
class Nil {};

template<int I, typename T1 =Nil, typename T2 =Nil, typename T3 =Nil, typename T4 =Nil>
struct select;

template<int I, typename T1 =Nil, typename T2 =Nil, typename T3 =Nil, typename T4 =Nil>
using Select = typename select<I,T1,T2,T3,T4>::type;

// Specializations for 0-3:

template<typename T1, typename T2, typename T3, typename T4>
struct select<0,T1,T2,T3,T4> { using type = T1; };   // specialize for N==0

template<typename T1, typename T2, typename T3, typename T4>
struct select<1,T1,T2,T3,T4> { using type = T2; };   // specialize for N==1

template<typename T1, typename T2, typename T3, typename T4>
struct select<2,T1,T2,T3,T4> { using type = T3; };   // specialize for N==2

template<typename T1, typename T2, typename T3, typename T4>
struct select<3,T1,T2,T3,T4> { using type = T4; };   // specialize for N==3
```

The general version of **select** should never be used, so I didn't define it. I chose zero-based numbering to match the rest of C++. This technique is perfectly general: such specializations can present any aspect of the template arguments. We don't really want to pick a maximum number of alternatives (here, four), but that problem can be addressed using variadic templates (§28.6). The result of picking a nonexisting alternative is to use the primary (general) template. For example:

```
Select<5,int,double,char> x;
```

In this case, that would lead to an immediate compile-time error as the general **Select** isn't defined.

A realistic use would be to select the type for a function returning the Nth element of a tuple:

```
template<int N, typename T1, typename T2, typename T3, typename T4>
Select<N,T1,T2,T3,T4> get(Tuple<T1,T2,T3,T4>& t);       // see §28.5.2

auto x = get<2>(t);   // assume that t is a Tuple
```

Here, the type of **x** will be whatever **T3** is for the **Tuple** called **t**. Indexing into tuples is zero-based. Using variadic templates (§28.6), we can provide a far simpler and more general **select**:

```
template<unsigned N, typename... Cases>     // general case; never instantiated
struct select;

template<unsigned N, typename T, typename... Cases>
struct select<N,T,Cases...> :select<N–1,Cases...> {
};
```

```
template<typename T, typename... Cases>    // final case: N==0
struct select<0,T,Cases...> {
    using type = T;
};

template<unsigned N, typename... Cases>
using Select = typename select<N,Cases...>::type;
```

28.3.2 Iteration and Recursion

The basic techniques for calculating a value at compile time can be illustrated by a factorial function template:

```
template<int N>
constexpr int fac()
{
    return N*fac<N–1>();
}}

template<>
constexpr int fac<1>()
{
    return 1;
}

constexpr int x5 = fac<5>();
```

The factorial is implemented using recursion, rather than using a loop. Since we don't have variables at compile time (§10.4), that makes sense. In general, if we want to iterate over a set of values at compile time, we use recursion.

Note the absence of a condition: there is no N==1 or N<2 test. Instead, the recursion is terminated when the call of **fac()** selects the specialization for N==1. In template metaprogramming (as in functional programming), the idiomatic way of working your way through a sequence of values is to recurse until you reach a terminating specialization.

In this case, we could also do the computation in the more conventional way:

```
constexpr int fac(int i)
{
    return (i<2)?1:fac(i–1);
}

constexpr int x6 = fac(6);
```

I find this clearer than the function template expression of the idea, but tastes vary and there are algorithms that are best expressed by separating the terminating case from the general case. The non-template version is marginally easier for a compiler to handle. The run-time performance will, of course, be identical.

The **constexpr** version can be used for both compile-time and run-time evaluation. The template (metaprogramming) version is for compile-time use only.

28.3.2.1 Recursion Using Classes

Iteration involving more complicated state or more elaborate parameterization can be handled using classes. For example, the factorial program becomes:

```
template<int N>
struct Fac {
      static const int value = N*Fac<N–1>::value;
};

template<>
struct Fac<1> {
      static const int value = 1;
};

constexpr int x7 = Fac<7>::value;
```

For a more realistic example, see §28.5.2.

28.3.3 When to Use Metaprogramming

Using the control structures described here, you can compute absolutely everything at compile time (translation limits permitting). The question remains: Why would you want to? We should use these techniques if and when they yield cleaner, better-performing, and easier-to-maintain code than alternative techniques. The most obvious constraint on metaprogramming is that code depending on complicated uses of templates can be hard to read and very hard to debug. Nontrivial uses of templates can also impact compile times. If you have a hard time understanding what is going on in code requiring complicated patterns of instantiation, so might the compiler. Worse still, so may the programmer who gets to maintain your code.

Template metaprogramming attracts clever people:

- Partly, that's because metaprogramming allows us to express things that simply can't be done at the same level of type safety and run-time performance. When the improvements are significant and the code maintainable, these are good – sometimes even compelling – reasons.
- Partly, that's because metaprogramming allows us to show off our cleverness. Obviously, that is to be avoided.

How would you know that you have gone too far with metaprogramming? One warning sign that I use is an urge to use macros (§12.6) to hide "details" that have become too ugly to deal with directly. Consider:

```
#define IF(c,x,y) typename std::conditional<(c),x,y>::type
```

Is this going too far? It allows us to write

```
IF(cond,Cube,Square) z;
```

rather than

```
typename std::conditional<(cond),Cube,Square>::type z;
```

I have biased the question by using the very short name **IF** and the long form **std::conditional**.

Similarly, a more complex condition would almost equalize the number of characters used. The fundamental difference is that I have to write **typename** and **::type** to use the standard's terminology. That exposes the template implementation technique. I would like to hide that, and the macro does. However, if many people need to collaborate and programs get large, a bit of verbosity is preferable to a divergence of notations.

Another serious argument against the **IF** macro is that its name is misleading: **conditional** is not a "drop-in replacement" for a conventional **if**. That **::type** represents a significant difference: **conditional** selects between types; it does not directly alter control flow. Sometimes it is used to select a function and thus represent a branch in a computation; sometimes it is not. The **IF** macro hides an essential aspect of its function. Similar objections can be leveled at many other "sensible" macros: they are named for some programmer's particular idea of their use, rather than reflecting fundamental functionality.

In this case, the problems of verbosity, of the implementation details leaking out, and of poor naming are easily handled by a type alias (**Conditional**; §28.2.1). In general, look hard for ways to clean up the syntax presented to users without inventing a private language. Prefer systematic techniques, such as specialization and the use of aliases, to macro hackery. Prefer **constexpr** functions to templates for compile-time computation, and hide template metaprogramming implementation details in **constexpr** functions whenever feasible (§28.2.2).

Alternatively, we can look at the fundamental complexity of what we are trying to do:

[1]   Does it require explicit tests?
[2]   Does it require recursion?
[3]   Can we write concepts (§24.3) for our template arguments?

If the answer to question [1] or [2] is "yes" or the answer to question [3] is "no," we should consider whether there may be maintenance problems. Maybe some form of encapsulation is possible? Remember that complexities of a template implementation become visible to users ("leak out") whenever an instantiation fails. Also, many programmers do look into header files where every detail of a metaprogram is immediately exposed.

28.4 Conditional Definition: Enable_if

When we write a template, we sometimes want to provide an operation for some template arguments, but not for others. For example:

```
template<typename T>
class Smart_pointer {
    // ...
    T& operator*();        // return reference to whole object
    T* operator->();       // select a member (for classes only)
    // ...
}
```

If **T** is a class, we should provide **operator->()**, but if **T** is a built-in type, we simply cannot do so (with the usual semantics). Therefore, we want a language mechanism for saying, "If this type has this property, define the following." We might try the obvious:

```
template<typename T>
class Smart_pointer {
    // ...
    T& operator*();                         // return reference to whole object
    if (Is_class<T>()) T* operator->();   // syntax error
    // ...
}
```

However, that does not work. C++ does not provide an **if** that can select among definitions based on a general condition. But, as with **Conditional** and **Select** (§28.3.1), there is a way. We can write a somewhat curious type function to make the definition of **operator->()** conditional. The standard library (in **<type_traits>**) provides **enable_if** for that. The **Smart_pointer** example becomes:

```
template<typename T>
class Smart_pointer {
    // ...
    T& operator*();                                 // return reference to whole object
    Enable_if<Is_class<T>(),T>* operator->();   // select a member (for classes only)
    // ...
}
```

As usual, I have used type aliases and **constexpr** functions to simplify the notation:

```
template<bool B, typename T>
using Enable_if = typename std::enable_if<B,T>::type;

template<typename T> bool Is_class()
{
    return std::is_class<T>::value;
}
```

If **Enable_if**'s condition evaluates to **true**, its result is its second argument (here, **T**). If **Enable_if**'s condition evaluates to **false**, the whole function declaration of which it is part is completely ignored. In this case, if **T** is a class, we get a definition of **operator->()** returning a **T***, and if it is not, we don't declare anything.

Given the definition of **Smart_pointer** using **Enable_if**, we get:

```
void f(Smart_pointer<double> p, Smart_pointer<complex<double>> q)
{
    auto d0 = *p;           // OK
    auto c0 = *q;           // OK
    auto d1 = q->real();    // OK
    auto d2 = p->real();    // error: p doesn't point to a class object
    // ...
}
```

You may consider **Smart_pointer** and **operator->()** exotic, but providing (defining) operations conditionally is very common. The standard library provides many examples of conditional definition, such as **Alloc::size_type** (§34.4.2) and **pair** being movable if both of their elements are (§34.2.4.1). The language itself defines **->** only for pointers to class objects (§8.2).

In this case, the elaboration of the declaration of operator->() with Enable_if simply changes the kind of error we get from examples, such as p->real():

- If we unconditionally declare operator->(), we get a "-> used on a non-class pointer" error at instantiation time for the definition of Smart_pointer<double>::operator->().
- If we conditionally declare operator->() using Enable_if, if we use -> on a smart_ptr<double>, we get a "Smart_ptr<double>::operator->() not defined" error at the point of use of Smart_ptr<double>::operator->().

In either case, we do not get an error unless we use -> on a smart_ptr<T> where T is not a class.

We have moved the error detection and reporting from the implementation of smart_pointer<T>::operator->() to its declaration. Depending on the compiler and especially on how deep in a nest of template instantiations the error happens, this can make a significant difference. In general, it is preferable to specify templates precisely so as to detect errors early rather than relying on bad instantiations being caught. In this sense, we can see Enable_if as a variant of the idea of a concept (§24.3): it allows a more precise specification of the requirements of a template.

28.4.1 Use of Enable_if

For many uses, the functionality of enable_if is pretty ideal. However, the notation we have to use is often awkward. Consider:

```
Enable_if<Is_class<T>(),T>* operator->();
```

The implementation shows through rather dramatically. However, what is actually expressed is pretty close to the minimal ideal:

```
declare_if (Is_class<T>()) T* operator->();    // not C++
```

However, C++ does not have a declare_if construct for selecting declarations.

Using Enable_if to decorate the return type places it up front where you can see it and where it logically belongs, because it affects the whole declaration (not just the return type). However, some declarations do not have a return type. Consider two of vector's constructors:

```
template<typename T>
class vector<T> {
public:
    vector(size_t n, const T& val); // n elements of type T with value val

    template<typename Iter>
        vector(Iter b, Iter e); // initialize from [b:e]
    // ...
};
```

This looks innocent enough, but the constructor taking a number of elements wrecks its usual havoc. Consider:

```
vector<int> v(10,20);
```

Is that 10 elements with the value 20 or an attempt to initialize from [10:20]? The standard requires the former, but the code above would naively pick the latter because an int-to-size_t conversion is required for the first constructor whereas the pair of ints is a perfect match for the template constructor. The problem is that I "forgot" to tell the compiler that the **Iter** type should be an iterator. However, that can be done:

```
template<typename T>
class vector<T> {
public:
      vector(size_t n, const T& val);        // n elements of type T with value val

      template<typename Iter, typename =Enable_if<Input_iterator<Iter>(),Iter>>
          vector(Iter b, Iter e);        // initialize from [b:e]
      // ...
};
```

That (unused) default template argument will be instantiated because we certainly can't deduce that unused template parameter. This implies that the declaration of **vector(Iter,Iter)** will fail unless **Iter** is an **Input_iterator** (§24.4.4).

I introduced the **Enable_if** as a default template argument because that is the most general solution. It can be used for templates without arguments and/or without return types. However, in this case, we could alternatively apply it to the constructor argument type:

```
template<typename T>
class vector<T> {
public:
      vector(size_t n, const T& val);        // n elements of type T with value val

      template<typename Iter>
          vector(Enable_if<Input_iterator<Iter>(),Iter>> b, Iter e);        // initialize from [b:e]
      // ...
};
```

The **Enable_if** techniques work for template functions (including member functions of class templates and specializations) only. The implementation and use of **Enable_if** rely on a detail in the rules for overloading function templates (§23.5.3.2). Consequently, it cannot be used to control declarations of classes, variables, or non-template functions. For example:

```
Enable_if<(version2_2_3<config),M_struct>* make_default() // error: not a template
{
      return new Mystruct{};
}


template<typename T>
void f(const T& x)
{
      Enable_if<(20<sizeof<T>),T> tmp = x;                // error: tmp is not a function
      Enable_if<!(20<sizeof<T>),T&> tmp = *new T{x};   // error: tmp is not a function
      // ...
}
```

For **tmp**, using **Holder** (§28.2) would almost certainly be cleaner anyway: if you had managed to construct that free-store object, how would you **delete** it?

28.4.2 Implementing Enable_if

The implementation of **Enable_if** is almost trivial:

```
template<bool B, typename T = void>
struct std::enable_if {
    typedef T type;
};

template<typename T>
struct std::enable_if<false, T> {};        // no ::type if B==false

template<bool B, typename T = void>
using Enable_if = typename std::enable_if<B,T>::type;
```

Note that we can leave out the type argument and get **void** by default.

For a language-technical explanation of how these simple declarations become useful as a fundamental construct see §23.5.3.2.

28.4.3 Enable_if and Concepts

We can use **Enable_if** for a wide variety of predicates, including many tests of type properties (§28.3.1.1). Concepts are among the most general and useful predicates we have. Ideally, we would like to overload based on concepts, but lacking language support for concepts, the best we can do is to use **Enable_if** to select based on constraints. For example:

```
template<typename T>
Enable_if<Ordered<T>()> fct(T*,T*);        // optimized implementation

template<typename T>
Enable_if<!Ordered<T>()> fct(T*,T*);       // nonoptimized implementation
```

Note that **Enable_if** defaults to **void**, so **fct()** is a **void** function. I'm not sure that using that default increases readability, but we can use **fct()** like this:

```
void f(vector<int>& vi, vector<complex<int>>& vc)
{
    if (vi.size()==0 || vc.size()==0) throw runtime_error("bad fct arg");
    fct(&vi.front(),&vi.back());           // call optimized
    fct(&vc.front(),&vc.back());           // call nonoptimized
}
```

These calls are resolved as described because we can use < for an **int** but not for a **complex<int>**. **Enable_if** resolves to **void** if we don't provide a type argument.

28.4.4 More Enable_if Examples

When using **Enable_if**, sooner or later we want to ask if a class has a member with a specific name and an appropriate type. For many of the standard operations, such as constructors and assignments, the standard library provides a type property predicate, such as **is_copy_assignable** and **is_default_constructible** (§35.4.1). However, we can build our own predicates. Consider the question "Can we call f(x) if x is of type X?" Defining has_f to answer that question gives an opportunity to demonstrate some of the techniques used and some of the scaffolding/boilerplate code provided internally in many template metaprogramming libraries (including parts of the standard library). First, define the usual class plus specialization to represent an alternative:

```
struct substitution_failure { }; // represent a failure to declare something

template<typename T>
struct substitution_succeeded : std::true_type
{ };

template<>
struct substitution_succeeded<substitution_failure> : std::false_type
{ };
```

Here, substitution_failure is used to represent a substitution failure (§23.5.3.2). We derive from std::true_type unless the argument type is substitution_failure. Obviously, std::true_type and std::false_type are types that represent the values true and false, respectively:

```
std::true_type::value == true
std::false_type::value == false
```

We use substitution_succeeded to define the type functions we really want. For example, we might be looking for a function f that we can call as f(x). For that, we can define has_f:

```
template<typename T>
struct has_f
  : substitution_succeeded<typename get_f_result<T>::type>
{ };
```

So, if get_f_result<T> yields a proper type (presumably the return type of a call of f), has_f::value is true_type::value, which is true. If get_f_result<T> doesn't compile, it returns substitution_failure and has_f::value is false.

So far, so good, but how do we get get_f_result<T> to be substitution_failure if somehow f(x) doesn't compile for a value x of type X? The definition that achieves that looks innocent enough:

```
template<typename T>
struct get_f_result {
private:
    template<typename X>
        static auto check(X const& x) -> decltype(f(x));    // can call f(x)
        static substitution_failure check(...);             // cannot call f(x)
public:
        using type = decltype(check(std::declval<T>()));
};
```

We simply declare a function check so that check(x) has the same return type as f(x). Obviously, that won't compile unless we can call f(x). So, that declaration of check fails if we can't call f(x). In that case, because substitution failure is not an error (SFINAE; §23.5.3.2), we get the second definition of check(), which has substitution_failure as its return type. And, yes, this elaborate piece of trickery fails if our function f was declared to return a substitution_failure.

Note that decltype() does not evaluate its operand.

We managed to turn what looked like a type error into the value false. It would have been simpler if the language had provided a primitive (built-in) operation for doing that conversion; for example:

```
is_valid());      // can f(x) be compiled?
```

However, a language cannot provide everything as a language primitive. Given the scaffolding code, we just have to provide conventional syntax:

```
template<typename T>
constexpr bool Has_f()
{
    return has_f<T>::value;
}
```

Now, we can write:

```
template<typename T>
class X {
    // ...
    Enable_if<Has_f<T>()> use_f(const T&)
    {
        // ...
        f(t);
        // ...
    }
    // ...
};
```

X<T> has a member use_f() if and only if f(t) can be called for a T value t.

Note that we cannot simply write:

```
if (Has_f<decltype(t)>()) f(t);
```

The call f(t) will be type checked (and fail type checking) even if Has_f<decltype(t)>() returns false.

Given the technique used to define Has_f, we can define Has_foo for any operation or member foo we can think of. The scaffolding is 14 lines of code for each foo. This can get repetitive but is not difficult.

This implies that Enable_if<> allows us to choose among overloaded templates based on just about any logical criteria for argument types. For example, we can define a Has_not_equals() type function to check if != is available and use it like this:

```
template<typename Iter, typename Val>
Enable_if<Has_not_equals<Iter>(),Iter> find(Iter first, Iter last, Val v)
{
    while (first!=last && !(*first==v))
        ++first;
    return first;
}
```

```
template<typename Iter, typename Val>
Enable_if<!Has_not_equals<Iter>(),Iter> find(Iter first, Iter last, Val v)
{
      while (!(first==last) && !(*first==v))
            ++first;
      return first;
}
```

Such ad hoc overloading easily gets messy and unmanageable. For example, try adding versions that use != for the value comparison (that is, *first!=v, rather than !(*first==v)), when possible. Consequently, I recommend relying on the more structured standard overloading rules (§12.3.1) and specialization rules (§25.3) when there is a choice. For example:

```
template<typename T>
auto operator!=(const T& a, const T& b) –> decltype(!(a==b))
{
      return !(a==b);
}
```

The rules ensure that if a specific != has already been defined for a type **T** (as a template or as a non-template function), this definition will not be instantiated. I use **decltype()** partly to show how in general to derive the return type from a previously defined operator, and partly to handle the rare cases where != returns something different from **bool**.

Similarly, we can conditionally define >, <=, >=, etc., given a <.

28.5 A Compile-Time List: Tuple

Here, I'll demonstrate the basic template metaprogramming techniques in a single simple, but realistic, example. I will define a **Tuple** with an associated access operation and an output operation. **Tuples** defined like this have been used industrially for more than a decade. The more elegant and more general **std::tuple** is presented in §28.6.4 and §34.2.4.2.

The idea is to allow code like this:

```
Tuple<double, int, char> x {1.1, 42, 'a'};
cout << x << "\n";
cout << get<1>(x) << "\n";
```

The resulting output is:

```
{ 1.1, 42, 'a'};
42
```

The definition of **Tuple** is fundamentally simple:

```
template<typename T1=Nil, typename T2=Nil, typename T3=Nil, typename T4=Nil>
struct Tuple : Tuple<T2, T3, T4> {    // layout: {T2,T3,T4} before T1
      T1 x;

      using Base = Tuple<T2, T3, T4>;
```

```
Base* base() { return static_cast<Base*>(this); }
const Base* base() const { return static_cast<const Base*>(this); }

Tuple(const T1& t1, const T2& t2, const T3& t3, const T4& t4) :Base{t2,t3,t4}, x{t1} { }
};
```

So, a **Tuple** of four elements (often referred to as a 4-tuple) is a **Tuple** of three elements (a 3-tuple) followed by a fourth element.

We construct a **Tuple** of four elements with a constructor that takes four values (potentially of four different types). It uses its last three elements (its tail) to initialize its base 3-tuple and the first (its head) to initialize its member **x**.

Manipulation of the tail of a **Tuple** – that is of the base class of the **Tuple** – is important and common in the implementation of the **Tuple**. Consequently, I provided an alias **Base** and a pair of member functions **base()** to simplify manipulation of the base/tail.

Obviously, this definition handles only tuples that really have four elements. Furthermore, it leaves much of the work to the 3-tuple. Tuples with fewer than four elements are defined as specializations:

```
template<>
struct Tuple<> { Tuple() {} };          // 0-tuple

template<typename T1>
struct Tuple<T1> : Tuple<> {            // 1-tuple
    T1 x;

    using Base = Tuple<>;
    Base* base() { return static_cast<Base*>(this); }
    const Base* base() const { return static_cast<const Base*>(this); }

    Tuple(const T1& t1) :Base{}, x{t1} { }
};

template<typename T1, typename T2>
struct Tuple<T1, T2> : Tuple<T2> {      // 2-tuple, layout: T2 before T1
    T1 x;

    using Base = Tuple<T2>;
    Base* base() { return static_cast<Base*>(this); }
    const Base* base() const { return static_cast<const Base*>(this); }

    Tuple(const T1& t1, const T2& t2) :Base{t2}, x{t1} { }
};

template<typename T1, typename T2, typename T3>
struct Tuple<T1, T2, T3> : Tuple<T2, T3> {    // 3-tuple, layout: {T2,T3} before T1
    T1 x;
```

```
    using Base = Tuple<T2, T3>;
    Base* base() { return static_cast<Base*>(this); }
    const Base* base() const { return static_cast<const Base*>(this); }

    Tuple(const T1& t1, const T2& t2, const T3& t3) :Base{t2, t3}, x{t1} { }
};
```

These declarations are rather repetitive and follow the simple pattern of the first Tuple (the 4-tuple). That definition of a 4-tuple, Tuple, is the primary template and provides the interface to Tuples of all sizes (0, 1, 2, 3, and 4). That is why I had to provide those Nil default template arguments. In fact, they will never be used. Specialization will choose one of the simpler Tuples rather than use Nil.

The way I defined Tuple as a "stack" of derived classes is fairly conventional (e.g., std::tuple is defined similarly; §28.5). It has the curious effect that the first element of a Tuple will (given the usual implementation techniques) get the highest address and that the last element will have the same address as the whole Tuple. For example:

```
    tuple<double,string,int,char>{3.14,string{"Bob"},127,'c'}
```

can be graphically represented like this:

char	int	string	double
'c'	127	"Bob"	3.14

This opens some interesting optimization possibilities. Consider:

```
    class FO { /* function object with no data members */ };

    typedef Tuple<int*, int*> T0;
    typedef Tuple<int*,FO> T1;
    typedef Tuple<int*, FO, FO> T2;
```

On my implementation, I got sizeof(T0)==8, sizeof(T1)==4, and sizeof(T2)==4 as the compiler optimizes away the empty base classes. This is called the *empty-base optimization* and is guaranteed by the language (§27.4.1).

28.5.1 A Simple Output Function

The definition of Tuple has a nice regular, recursive structure that we can use to define a function for displaying the list of elements. For example:

```
    template<typename T1, typename T2, typename T3, typename T4>
    void print_elements(ostream& os, const Tuple<T1,T2,T3,T4>& t)
    {
        os  << t.x << ", ";                  // t's x
        print_elements(os,*t.base());
    }
```

```
template<typename T1, typename T2, typename T3>
void print_elements(ostream& os, const Tuple<T1,T2,T3>& t)
{
    os  << t.x << ", ";
    print_elements(os,*t.base());
}


template<typename T1, typename T2>
void print_elements(ostream& os, const Tuple<T1,T2>& t)
{
    os  << t.x << ", ";
    print_elements(os,*t.base());
}


template<typename T1>
void print_elements(ostream& os, const Tuple<T1>& t)
{
    os << t.x;
}


template<>
void print_elements(ostream& os, const Tuple<>& t)
{
    os << " ";
}
```

The similarity of the print_elements() for the 4-tuple, 3-tuple, and 2-tuple hints at a better solution (§28.6.4), but for now I'll just use these print_elements() to define a << for Tuples:

```
template<typename T1, typename T2, typename T3, typename T4>
ostream& operator<<(ostream& os, const Tuple<T1,T2,T3,T4>& t)
{
    os << "{ ";
    print_elements(os,t);
    os << " }";
    return os;
}
```

We can now write:

```
Tuple<double, int, char> x {1.1, 42, 'a'};
cout << x << "\n";

cout << Tuple<double,int,int,int>{1.2,3,5,7} << "\n";
cout << Tuple<double,int,int>{1.2,3,5} << "\n";
cout << Tuple<double,int>{1.2,3} << "\n";
cout << Tuple<double>{1.2} << "\n";
cout << Tuple<>{} << "\n";
```

Unsurprisingly, the output is:

```
{ 1.1 42, a }
{ 1.2,3,5,7 }
{ 1.2,3,5 }
{ 1.2,3 }
{ 1.2 }
{  }
```

28.5.2 Element Access

As defined, **Tuple** has a variable number of elements of potentially differing types. We would like
to access those elements efficiently and without the possibility of type system violations (i.e., without using casts). We can imagine a variety of schemes, such as naming the elements, numbering
the elements, and accessing elements by recursing though the elements until we reach a desired element. The last alternative is what we will use to implement the most common access strategy:
index the elements. In particular, I want to implement a way to subscript a tuple. Unfortunately, I
am unable to implement an appropriate **operator[]**, so I use a function template **get()**:

```cpp
Tuple<double, int, char> x {1.1, 42, 'a'};

cout << "{ "
    << get<0>(x) << ", "
    << get<1>(x) << ", "
    << get<2>(x) << " }\n";     // write { 1.1, 42, a }

auto xx = get<0>(x); // xx is a double
```

The idea is to index the elements, starting from 0, in such a way that the element selection is done
at compile time and we preserve all type information.

The **get()** function constructs an object of type **getNth<T,int>**. The job of **getNth<X,N>** is to return
a reference to the **N**th element, which is assumed to have type **X**. Given such a helper, we can
define **get()**:

```cpp
template<int N, typename T1, typename T2, typename T3, typename T4>
Select<N, T1, T2, T3, T4>& get(Tuple<T1, T2, T3, T4>& t)
{
    return getNth<Select<N, T1, T2, T3, T4>,N>::get(t);
}
```

The definition of **getNth** is a variant of the usual recursion from **N** down to the specialization for **0**:

```cpp
template<typename Ret, int N>
struct getNth {              // getNth() remembers the type (Ret) of the Nth element
    template<typename T>
    static Ret& get(T& t)        // get the value element N from t's Base
    {
        return getNth<Ret,N–1>::get(*t.base());
    }
};
```

```
template<typename Ret>
struct getNth<Ret,0> {
    template<typename T>
    static Ret& get(T& t)
    {
        return t.x;
    }
};
```

Basically, **getNth** is a special-purpose **for**-loop, implemented by recursing **N–1** times. The member functions are **static** because we don't really want any objects of class **getNth**. That class is only used as a place to hold **Ret** and **N** in a way that allows the compiler to use them.

This is quite a bit of scaffolding to index into a **Tuple**, but at least the resulting code is type-safe and efficient. By "efficient," I mean that given a reasonably good compiler (as is common), there is no run-time overhead for accessing a **Tuple** member.

Why must we write **get<2>(x)** rather than just **x[2]**? We could try:

```
template<typename T>
constexpr auto operator[](T t,int N)
{
    return get<N>(t);
}
```

Unfortunately, this does not work:

- **operator[]()** must be a member, but we could handle that by defining it within **Tuple**.
- Inside **operator[]()**, the argument **N** is not known to be a constant expression.
- I "forgot" that only lambdas can deduce their result type from their **return**-statement (§11.4.4), but that could be handled by adding a **–>decltype(get<N>(t))**.

To get that, we need some language lawyering and for now we have to make do with **get<2>(x)**.

28.5.2.1 const **Tuples**

As defined, **get()** works for non-**const Tuple** elements and can be used on the left-hand side of assignments. For example:

```
Tuple<double, int, char> x {1.1, 42, 'a'};
```

```
get<2>(x) = 'b';       // OK
```

However, it can't be used for **const**s:

```
const Tuple<double, int, char> xx {1.1, 42, 'a'};
```

```
get<2>(xx) = 'b';        // error: xx is const
char cc = get<2>(xx);    // error: xx is const (surprise?)
```

The problem is that **get()** takes its argument by non-**const** reference. But **xx** is a **const**, so it is not an acceptable argument.

Naturally, we also want to be able to have **const Tuple**s. For example:

```
const Tuple<double, int, char> xx {1.1, 422, 'a'};
char cc = get<2>(xx);              // OK: reading from const
cout << "xx: " << xx << "\n";
get<2>(xx) = 'x';                  // error: xx is const
```

To handle **const Tuples**, we have to add **const** versions of **get()** and **getNth**'s **get()**. For example:

```
template<typename Ret, int N>
struct getNth {              // getNth() remembers the type (Ret) of the Nth element
    template<typename T>
    static Ret& get(T& t)      //  get the value element N from t's Base
    {
        return getNth<Ret,N–1>::get(*t.base());
    }

    template<typename T>
    static const Ret& get(const T& t)          //  get the value element N from t's Base
    {
        return getNth<Ret,N–1>::get(*t.base());
    }
};

template<typename Ret>
struct getNth<Ret,0> {
    template<typename T> static Ret& get(T& t) { return t.x; }
    template<typename T> static const Ret& get(const T& t) { return t.x; }
};

template<int N, typename T1, typename T2, typename T3, typename T4>
Select<N, T1, T2, T3, T4>& get(Tuple<T1, T2, T3, T4>& t)
{
    return getNth<Select<N, T1, T2, T3, T4>,N>::get(t);
}

template<int N, typename T1, typename T2, typename T3>
const Select<N, T1, T2, T3>& get(const Tuple<T1, T2, T3>& t)
{
    return getNth<Select<N, T1, T2, T3>,N>::get(t);
}
```

Now, we can handle both **const** and non-**const** arguments.

28.5.3 make_tuple

A class template cannot deduce its template arguments, but a function template can deduce them
from its function arguments. This implies that we can make a **Tuple** type implicit in code by having
a function construct it for us:

```
template<typename T1, typename T2, typename T3, typename T4>
Tuple<T1, T2, T3, T4> make_tuple(const T1& t1, const T2& t2, const T3& t3, const T4& t4)
{
    return Tuple<T1, T2, T3, T4>{t1, t2, t3,t4};
}
```

// ... and the other four make_Tuples ...

Given **make_tuple()**, we can write:

```
auto xxx = make_Tuple(1.2,3,'x',1223);
cout << "xxx: " << xxx << "\n";
```

Other useful functions, such as **head()** and **tail()**, are easily implemented. The standard-library **tuple** provides a few such utility functions (§28.6.4).

28.6 Variadic Templates

Having to deal with an unknown number of elements is a common problem. For example, an error-reporting function may take between zero and ten arguments, a matrix may have between one and ten dimensions, and a tuple can have zero to ten elements. Note that in the first and the last example, the elements may not necessarily be of the same type. In most cases, we would prefer not to deal with each case separately. Ideally, a single piece of code should handle the cases for one element, two elements, three elements, etc. Also, I pulled the number ten out of a hat: ideally, there should be no fixed upper limit on the number of elements.

Over the years, many solutions have been found. For example, default arguments (§12.2.5) can be used to allow a single function to accept a variable number of arguments, and function overloading (§12.3) can be used to provide a function for each number of arguments. Passing a single list of elements (§11.3) can be an alternative to having a variable number of arguments as long as the elements are all of the same type. However, to elegantly handle the case of an unknown number of arguments of unknown (and possibly differing) types, some additional language support is needed. That language feature is called a *variadic template*.

28.6.1 A Type-Safe printf()

Consider the archetypical example of a function needing an unknown number of arguments of a variety of types: **printf()**. As provided by the C and C++ standard libraries, **printf()** is flexible and performs nicely (§43.3). However, it is not extensible to user-defined types and not type-safe, and it is a popular target for hackers.

The first argument to **printf()** is a C-style string interpreted as a "format string." Additional arguments are used as required by the format string. Format specifiers, such as **%g** for floating-point and **%s** for zero-terminated arrays of characters, control the interpretation of the additional arguments. For example:

```
printf("The value of %s is %g\n","x",3.14);
```

```
string name = "target";
printf("The value of %s is %P\n",name,Point{34,200});

printf("The value of %s is %g\n",7);
```

The first call of **printf()** works as intended, but the second call has two problems: the format specification **%s** refers to C-style strings, and **printf()** will not interpret the **std::string** argument correctly. Furthermore, there is no **%P** format and in general no direct way of printing values of user-defined types, such as **Point**. In the third call of **printf()**, I provided an **int** as the argument for **%s** and I "forgot" to provide an argument for **%g**. In general, a compiler is not able to compare the number and types of arguments required by the format string with the number and types of arguments provided by the programmer. The output of that last call (if any) would not be pretty.

Using variadic templates, we can implement an extensible and type-safe variant of **printf()**. As is common for compile-time programming, the implementation has two parts:

[1]   Handle the case where there is just one argument (the format string).
[2]   Handle the case where there is at least one "additional" argument that, suitably formatted, needs to output at an appropriate point indicated by the format string.

The simplest case is the one with only one argument, the format string:

```
void printf(const char* s)
{
        if (s==nullptr) return;

        while (*s) {
                if (*s=='%' && *++s!='%') // make sure no more arguments are expected
                                        // %% represents plain % in a format string
                        throw runtime_error("invalid format: missing arguments");
                std::cout << *s++;
        }
}
```

That prints out the format string. If a format specifier is found, this **printf()** throws an exception because there is no argument to be formatted. A format specifier is defined to be a % not followed by another % (%% is **printf()**'s notation for a % that does not start a type specifier). Note that *++s does not overflow even if a % is the last character in a string. In that case, *++s refers to the terminating zero.

That done, we must handle **printf()** with more arguments. Here is where a template, and in particular a variadic template, comes into play:

```
template<typename T, typename... Args>      // variadic template argument list: one or more arguments
void printf(const char* s, T value, Args... args)      // function argument list: two or more arguments
{
        while (s && *s) {
                if (*s=='%' && *++s!='%') {      // a format specifier (ignore which one it is)
                        std::cout << value;      // use first non-format argument
                        return printf(++s, args...);      // do a recursive call with the tail of the argument list
                }
}
```

```
            std::cout << *s++;
        }
        throw std::runtime_error("extra arguments provided to printf");
    }
```

This **printf()** finds and prints the first non-format argument, "peels off" that argument, and then calls itself recursively. When there are no more non-format arguments, it calls the first (simpler) **printf()**. Ordinary characters (i.e., not % formal specifiers) are simply printed.

The overloading of << replaces the use of the (possibly erroneous) "hint" in the format specifier. If an argument has a type for which << is defined, that argument is printed; otherwise, that call does not type check and the program will never run. A formatting character after a % is not used. I can imagine type-safe uses for such characters, but the purpose of this example is not to design the perfect **printf()** but to explain variadic templates.

The **Args...** defines what is called a *parameter pack*. A parameter pack is a sequence of (type/value) pairs from which you can "peel off" arguments starting with the first. When **printf()** is called with two or more arguments

```
    void printf(const char* s, T value, Args... args);
```

is chosen, with the first argument as **s**, the second as **value**, and the rest (if any) bundled into the parameter pack **args** for later use. In the call **printf(++s,args...)** the parameter pack **args** is expanded so that the first element of **args** is selected as **value** and **args** is one element shorter than in the previous call. This carries on until **args** is empty, so that we call:

```
    void printf(const char*);
```

If we really wanted to, we could check **printf()** format directives, such as **%s**. For example:

```
    template<typename T, typename... Args>      // variadic template argument list: one or more arguments
    void printf(const char* s, T value, Args... args)       // function argument list: two or more arguments
    {
        while (s && *s) {
            if (*s=='%') {   // a format specifier or %%
                switch (*++s) {
                case '%':         // not format specifier
                    break;
                case 's':
                    if (!Is_C_style_string<T>() && !Is_string<T>())
                        throw runtime_error("Bad printf() format");
                    break;
                case 'd':
                    if (!Is_integral<T>()) throw runtime_error("Bad printf() format");
                    break;
                case 'g':
                    if (!Is_floating_point<T>()) throw runtime_error("Bad printf() format");
                    break;
                }
```

```
            std::cout << value;          // use first non-format argument
            return printf(++s, args...);  // do a recursive call with the tail of the argument list
        }
        std::cout << *s++;
    }
    throw std::runtime_error("extra arguments provided to printf");
}
```

The standard library provides **std::is_integral** and **std::is_floating_point**, but you'd have to craft **Is_C_style_string** yourself.

28.6.2 Technical Details

If you are familiar with functional programming, you should find the **printf()** example (§28.6) an unusual notation for a pretty standard technique. If not, here are minimal technical examples that might help. First, we can declare and use a simple variadic template function:

```
template<typename... Types>
void f(Types... args);      // variadic template function
```

That is, **f()** is a function that can be called with an arbitrary number of arguments of arbitrary types:

```
f();                  // OK: args contains no arguments
f(1);                 // OK: args contains one argument: int
f(2, 1.0);            // OK: args contains two arguments: int and double
f(2, 1.0, "Hello");   // OK: args contains three arguments: int, double, and const char*
```

A variadic template is defined with the ... notation:

```
template<typename... Types>
void f(Types... args);      // variadic template function
```

The **typename...** in the declaration of **Types** specifies that **Types** is a *template parameter pack*. The ... in the type of **args** specifies that **args** is a *function parameter pack*. The type of each **args** function argument is the corresponding **Types** template argument. We can use **class...** with the same meaning as **typename...**. The ellipsis (...) is a separate lexical token, so you can place whitespace before or after it. That ellipsis can appear in many different places in the grammar, but it always means "zero or more occurrences of something"). Think of a parameter pack as a sequence of values for which the compiler has remembered the types. For example, we could graphically represent a parameter pack for {'c',127,string{"Bob"},3.14}:

char	int	string	double
'c'	127	"Bob"	3.14

This is typically called a *tuple*. The memory layout is not specified by the C++ standard. For example, it might be the reverse of what is shown here (last element at the lowest memory address; §28.5). However, it is a dense, not a linked, representation. To get to a value, we need to start from the beginning and work our way through to what we want. The implementation of **Tuple** demonstrates that technique (§28.5). We can find the type of the first element and access it using that, then we can (recursively) proceed to the next argument. If we want to, we can give the appearance of indexed access using something like **get<N>** for **Tuple** (and for **std::tuple**; §28.6.4), but unfortunately there is no direct language support for that.

If you have a parameter pack, you can expand it into its sequence of elements by placing a ... after it. For example:

```
template<typename T, typename... Args>
void printf(const char* s, T value, Args... args)
{
    // ...
    return printf(++s, args...);        // do a recursive call with the elements of args as arguments
    // ...
}
```

Expansion of a parameter pack into its elements is not restricted to function calls. For example:

```
template<typename... Bases>
class X : public Bases... {
public:
    X(const Bases&... b) : Bases(b)... { }
};


X<> x0;
X<Bx> x1(1);
X<Bx,By> x2(2,3);
X<Bx,By,Bz> x3(2,3,4);
```

Here, **Bases...** says that **X** has zero or more bases. When it comes to initializing an **X**, the constructor requires zero or more values of types specified in the **Bases** variadic template argument. One by one those values are passed to the corresponding base initializer.

We can use the ellipsis to mean "zero or more elements of something" in most places where a list of elements is required (§iso.14.5.3), such as in:

- A template argument list
- A function argument list
- An initializer list
- A base specifier list
- A base or member initializer list
- A **sizeof...** expression

A **sizeof...** expression is used to obtain the number of elements in a parameter pack. For example, we can define a constructor for a **tuple** given a **pair** provided the number of **tuple** elements is two:

```
template<typename... Types>
class tuple {
    // ...
    template<typename T, typename U, typename = Enable_if<sizeof...(Types)==2>
        tuple(const pair<T,U>>&);
};
```

28.6.3 Forwarding

One of the major uses of variadic templates is forwarding from one function to another. Consider how to write a function that takes as arguments something to be called and a possibly empty list of arguments to give to the "something" as arguments:

```
template<typename F, typename... T>
void call(F&& f, T&&... t)
{
        f(forward<T>(t)...);
}
```

That is pretty simple and not a hypothetical example. The standard-library **thread** has constructors using this technique (§5.3.1, §42.2.2). I use pass-by-rvalue-reference of a deduced template argument type to be able to correctly distinguish between rvalues and lvalues (§23.5.2.1) and **std::forward()** to take advantage of that (§35.5.1). The ... in **T&&...** is read as "accept zero or more **&&** arguments, each of the type of the corresponding **T**." The ... in **forward<T>(t)...** is read "forward the zero or more arguments from **t**."

I used a template argument for the type of the "something" to be called, so that **call()** can accept functions, pointers to functions, function objects, and lambdas.

We can test **call()**:

```
void g0()
{
        cout << "g0()\n";
}

template<typename T>
void g1(const T& t)
{
        cout << "g1(): " << t << '\n';
}

void g1d(double t)
{
        cout << "g1d(): " << t << '\n';
}

template<typename T, typename T2>
void g2(const T& t, T2&& t2)
{
        cout << "g2(): " << t << ' ' << t2 << '\n';
}

void test()
{
        call(g0);
        call(g1);                       // error: too few arguments
```

```
        call(g1<int>,1);
        call(g1<const char*>,"hello");
        call(g1<double>,1.2);
        call(g1d,1.2);
        call(g1d,"No way!");              // error: wrong argument type for g1d()
        call(g1d,1.2,"I can't count");    // error: too many arguments for g1d()
        call(g2<double,string>,1,"world!");

        int i = 99;                        // testing with lvalues
        const char* p = "Trying";
        call(g2<double,string>,i,p);

        call([](){ cout <<"l1()\n";  });
        call([](int i){ cout <<"l0(): " << i << "\n";},17);
        call([i](){ cout <<"l1(): " << i << "\n";  });
}
```

I have to be specific about which specialization of a template function to pass because **call()** cannot deduce which one to use from the types of the other arguments.

28.6.4 The Standard-Library **tuple**

The simple **Tuple** in §28.5 has an obvious weakness: it can handle at most four elements. This section presents the definition of the standard-library **tuple** (from **<tuple>**; §34.2.4.2) and explains the techniques used to implement it. The key difference between **std::tuple** and our simple **Tuple** is that the former uses variadic templates to remove the limitation on the number of elements. Here are the key definitions:

```
template<typename Head, typename... Tail>
class tuple<Head, Tail...>
        : private tuple<Tail...> {    // here is the recursion
/*
        Basically, a tuple stores its head (first (type,value) pairs)
        and derives from the tuple of its tail (the rest of the (type/value) pairs).
        Note that the type is encoded in the type, not stored as data
*/
        typedef tuple<Tail...> inherited;
public:
        constexpr tuple() { }// default: the empty tuple

        // Construct tuple from separate arguments:
        tuple(Add_const_reference<Head> v, Add_const_reference<Tail>... vtail)
                : m_head(v), inherited(vtail...) { }

        // Construct tuple from another tuple:
        template<typename... VValues>
        tuple(const tuple<VValues...>& other)
                : m_head(other.head()), inherited(other.tail()) { }
```

```
        template<typename... VValues>
        tuple& operator=(const tuple<VValues...>& other)  // assignment
        {
            m_head = other.head();
            tail() = other.tail();
            return *this;
        }
        // ...

    protected:
        Head m_head;
    private:
        Add_reference<Head> head() { return m_head; }
        Add_const_reference<const Head> head() const { return m_head; }

        inherited& tail() { return *this; }
        const inherited& tail() const { return *this; }
    };
```

There is no guarantee that **std::tuple** is implemented as hinted here. In fact, several popular implementations derive from a helper class (also a variadic class template), so as to get the element layout in memory to be the same as a **struct** with the same member types.

The "add reference" type functions add a reference to a type if it isn't a reference already.
They are used to avoid copying (§35.4.1).

Curiously, **std::tuple** does not provide **head()** and **tail()** functions, so I made them private. In fact,
tuple does not provide any member functions for accessing an element. If you want to access an
element of a **tuple**, you must (directly or indirectly) call a function that splits it into a value and ....
If I want **head()** and **tail()** for the standard-library **tuple**, I can write them:

```
    template<typename Head, typename... Tail>
    Head head(tuple<Head,Tail...>& t)
    {
        return std::get<0>(t);      // get first element of t (§34.2.4.2)
    }

    template<typename Head, typename... Tail>
    tuple<T&...> tail(tuple<Head, Tail...>& t)
    {
        return /* details */;
    }
```

The "details" of the definition of **tail()** are ugly and complicated. If the designers of **tuple** had
meant for us to use **tail()** on a **tuple**, they would have provided it as a member.

Given **tuple**, we can make tuples and copy and manipulate them:

```
    tuple<string,vector,double> tt("hello",{1,2,3,4},1.2);
    string h = head(tt.head);                   // "hello"
    tuple<vector<int>,double> t2 = tail(tt.tail);   // {{1,2,3,4},1.2};
```

It can get tedious to mention all of those types. Instead, we can deduce them from argument types, for example, using the standard-library make_tuple():

```
template<typename... Types>
tuple<Types...> make_tuple(Types&&... t)        // simplified (§iso.20.4.2.4)
{
    return tuple<Types...>(t...);
}


string s = "Hello";
vector<int> v = {1,22,3,4,5};
auto x = make_tuple(s,v,1.2);
```

The standard-library **tuple** has many more members than listed in the implementation above (hence the // ...). In addition, the standard provides several helper functions. For example, **get()** is provided for element access (like **get()** from §28.5.2), so we can write:

```
auto t = make_tuple("Hello tuple", 43, 3.15);
double d = get<2>(t);          // d becomes 3.15
```

So **std::get()** provides compile-time zero-based subscripting of **std::tuples**.

Every member of **std::tuple** is useful to someone and most are useful to many, but none adds to our understanding of variadic templates, so I do not go into details. There are constructors and assignments from the same type (copy and move), from other tuple types (copy and move), and from pairs (copy and move). The operations taking a **std::pair** argument use **sizeof...** (§28.6.2) to ensure that their target **tuples** have exactly two elements. There are (nine) constructors and assignments taking allocators (§34.4) and a **swap()** (§35.5.2).

Unfortunately, the standard library does not offer << or >> for **tuple**. Worse, writing a << for **std::tuple** is amazingly complicated because there is no simple and general way of iterating through the elements of a standard-library **tuple**. First we need a helper; it is a **struct** with two **print()** functions. One **print()** recurses through a list printing elements, and the other stops the recursion when there is no more elements to print:

```
template<size_t N> // print element N and following elements
struct print_tuple {
    template<typename... T>
    typename enable_if<(N<sizeof...(T))>::type
    print(ostream& os, const tuple<T...>& t) const       // nonempty tuple
    {
        os << ", " << get<N>(t);        // print an element
        print_tuple<N+1>()(os,t);       // print the rest of the elements
    }

    template<typename... T>
    typename enable_if<!(N<sizeof...(T))>::type                // empty tuple
    print(ostream&, const tuple<T...>&) const
    {
    }
};
```

The pattern is that of a recursive function with a terminating overload (like **printf()** from §28.6.1).

However, note how it wastefully lets **get\<N>()** count from **0** to **N**.

We can now write a **<<** for **tuple**:

```
std::ostream& operator << (ostream& os, const tuple<>&)     // the empty tuple
{
   return os << "{}";
}


template<typename T0, typename ...T>
ostream& operator<<(ostream& os, const tuple<T0, T...>& t) // a nonempty tuple
{
   os << '{' << std::get<0>(t);     // print first element
   print_tuple<1>::print(os,t);  // print the rest of the elements
   return os << '}';
}
```

We can now print a **tuple**:

```
void user()
{
    cout << make_tuple() << '\n';
    cout << make_tuple("One meatball!") << '\n';
    cout << make_tuple(1,1.2,"Tail!") << '\n';
}
```

28.7 SI Units Example

Using **constexpr** and templates, we can compute just about anything at compile time. Providing input for such computations can be tricky, but we can always **#include** data into the program text. However, I prefer simpler examples that in my opinion stand a better chance when it comes to maintenance. Here, I will show an example that provides a reasonable tradeoff between implementation complexity and utility. The compilation overhead is minimal and there is no run-time overhead. The example is to provide a small library for computations using units, such as meters, kilograms, and seconds. These MKS units are a subset of the international standard (SI) units used universally in science. The example is chosen to show how the simplest metaprogramming techniques can be used in combination with other language features and techniques.

We want to attach units to our values, so as to avoid meaningless computations. For example:

```
auto distance = 10_m;          // 10 meters
auto time = 20_s;              // 20 seconds
auto speed = distance/time;    // .5 m/s (meters per second)

if (speed == 20)              // error: 20 is dimensionless
// ...
if (speed == distance)        // error: can't compare m to m/s
// ...
```

```
if (speed == 10_m/20_s)        // OK: the units match
// ...
Quantity<MpS2> acceleration = distance/square(time);  // MpS2 means m/(s*s)

cout << "speed==" << speed << " acceleration==" << acceleration << "\n";
```

Units provide a type system for physical values. As shown, we can use **auto** to hide types when we want to (§2.2.2), user-defined literals to introduce typed values (§19.2.6), and a type **Quantity** for use when we want to be explicit about **Units**. A **Quantity** is a numeric value with a **Unit**.

28.7.1 Units

First, I will define **Unit**:

```
template<int M, int K, int S>
struct Unit {
    enum { m=M, kg=K, s=S };
};
```

A **Unit** has components representing the three units of measurement that we are interested in:

- Meters for length
- Kilograms for mass
- Seconds for time

Note that the unit values are encoded in the type. A **Unit** is meant for compile-time use.

We can provide more conventional notation for the most common units:

```
using M = Unit<1,0,0>;        // meters
using Kg = Unit<0,1,0>;       // kilograms
using S = Unit<0,0,1>;        // seconds
using MpS = Unit<1,0,-1>;     // meters per second (m/s)
using MpS2 = Unit<1,0,-2>;    // meters per square second (m/(s*s))
```

Negative unit values indicate division by a quantity with that unit. This three-value representation of a unit is very flexible. We can represent the proper unit of any computation involving distance, mass, and time. I doubt we will find much use for **Quantity<123,–15,1024>**, that is, **123** distances multiplied, divided by **15** masses multiplied, and then multiplied by **1024** time measurements multiplied – but it is nice to know that the system is general. **Unit<0,0,0>** indicates a dimensionless entity, a value without a unit.

When we multiply two quantities, their units are added. Thus, addition of **Units** is useful:

```
template<typename U1, typename U2>
struct Uplus {
    using type = Unit<U1::m+U2::m, U1::kg+U2::kg, U1::s+U2::s>;
};

template<typename U1, U2>
using Unit_plus = typename Uplus<U1,U2>::type;
```

Similarly, when we divide two quantities, their units are subtracted:

```
template<typename U1, typename U2>
struct Uminus {
    using type = Unit<U1::m–U2::m, U1::kg–U2::kg, U1::s–U2::s>;
};

template<typename U1, U2>
using Unit_minus = typename Uminus<U1,U2>::type;
```

Unit_plus and Unit_minus are simple type functions (§28.2) on Units.

28.7.2 Quantitys

A Quantity is a value with an associated Unit:

```
template<typename U>
struct Quantity {
    double val;
    explicit Quantity(double d) : val{d} {}
};
```

A further refinement would have made the type used to represent the value a template parameter, possibly defaulted to double. We can define Quantitys with a variety of units:

```
Quantity<M> x {10.5};    // x is 10.5 meters
Quantity<S> y {2};       // y is 2 seconds
```

I made the Quantity constructor explicit to make it less likely to get implicit conversions from dimensionless entities, such as plain C++ floating-point literals:

```
Quantity<MpS> s = 7;     // error: attempt to convert an int to meters/second

Quantity<M> comp(Quantity<M>);
// ...
Quantity<M> n = comp(7);    // error: comp() requires a distance
```

Now we can start thinking about computations. What do we do to physical measurements? I'm not going to review a whole physics textbook, but certainly we need addition, subtraction, multiplication, and division. You can only add and subtract values with the same units:

```
template<typename U>
Quantity<U> operator+(Quantity<U> x, Quantity<U> y) // same dimension
{
    return Quantity<U>{x.val+y.val};
}

template<typename U>
Quantity<U> operator–(Quantity<U> x, Quantity<U> y) // same dimension
{
    return Quantity<U>{x.val–y.val};
}
```

Quantity's constructor is explicit, so we have to convert the resulting double value back to Quantity.

Multiplication **Quantity**s require addition of their **Unit**s. Similarly, division of **Quantity**s subtraction of their **Unit**s. For example:

```
template<typename U1, typename U2>
Quantity<Unit_plus<U1,U2>> operator*(Quantity<U1> x, Quantity<U2> y)
{
    return Quantity<Unit_plus<U1,U2>>{x.val*y.val};
}

template<typename U1, typename U2>
Quantity<Unit_minus<U1,U2>> operator/(Quantity<U1> x, Quantity<U2> y)
{
    return Quantity<Unit_minus<U1,U2>>{x.val/y.val};
}
```

Given these arithmetic operations, we can express most computations. However, we find that real-world computations contain a fair number of scaling operations, that is, multiplications and divisions by dimensionless values. We could use **Quantity<Unit<0,0,0>>** but that gets tedious:

```
Quantity<MpS> speed {10};
auto double_speed = Quantity<Unit<0,0,0>>{2}*speed;
```

To eliminate that verbosity, we can either provide an implicit conversion from **double** to **Quantity<Unit<0,0,0>>** or add a couple of variants to the arithmetic operations. I chose the latter:

```
template<typename U>
Quantity<U> operator*(Quantity<U> x, double y)
{
    return Quantity<U>{x.val*y};
}

template<typename U>
Quantity<U> operator*(double x, Quantity<U> y)
{
    return Quantity<U>{x*y.val};
}
```

We can now write:

```
Quantity<MpS> speed {10};
auto double_speed = 2*speed;
```

The main reason I do not define an implicit conversion from **double** to **Quantity<Unit<0,0,0>>** is that we do not want that conversion for addition or subtraction:

```
Quantity<MpS> speed {10};
auto increased_speed = 2.3+speed;        // error: can't add a dimensionless scalar to a speed
```

It is nice to have the detailed requirement for the code precisely dictated by the application domain.

28.7.3 Unit Literals

Thanks to the type aliases for the most common units, we can now write:

```
auto distance = Quantity<M>{10};   // 10 meters
auto time = Quantity<S>{20};       // 20 seconds
auto speed = distance/time;        // .5 m/s (meters per second)
```

That's not bad, but it is still verbose compared to code that conventionally simply leaves the units in the heads of the programmers:

```
auto distance = 10.0;      // 10 meters
double time = 20;          // 20 seconds
auto speed = distance/time;  // .5 m/s (meters per second)
```

We needed the .0 or the explicit double to ensure that the type is double (and get the correct result for the division).

The code generated for the two examples should be identical, and we can do better still notationally. We can introduce user-defined literals (UDLs; §19.2.6) for the Quantity types:

```
constexpr Quantity<M> operator"" _m(double d) { return Quantity<M>{d}; }
constexpr Quantity<Kg> operator"" _kg(double d) { return Quantity<Kg>{d}; }
constexpr Quantity<S> operator"" _s(double d) { return Quantity<S>{d}; }
```

That gives us the literals from our original example:

```
auto distance = 10_m;      // 10 meters
auto time = 20_s;          // 20 seconds
auto speed = distance/time;  // .5 m/s (meters per second)

if (speed == 20)           // error: 20 is dimensionless
// ...
if (speed == distance)     // error: can't compare m to m/s
// ...
if (speed == 10_m/20_s)    // OK: the units match
```

I defined * and / for combinations of Quantitys and dimensionless values, so we can scale the units using multiplication or division. However, we could also provide more of the conventional units as user-defined literals:

```
constexpr Quantity<M> operator"" _km(double d) { return 1000*d; }
constexpr Quantity<Kg> operator"" _g(double d) { return d/1000; }
constexpr Quantity<Kg> operator"" _mg(double d) { return d/10000000; }      // milligram
constexpr Quantity<S> operator"" _ms(double d) { return d/1000; }           // milliseconds
constexpr Quantity<S> operator"" _us(double d) { return d/1000; }           // microseconds
constexpr Quantity<S> operator"" _ns(double d) { return d/1000000000; }     // nanoseconds
// ...
```

Obviously, this could really get out of control through overuse of nonstandard suffixes (e.g., us is suspect even though it is widely used because u looks a bit like a Greek μ).

I could have provided the various magnitudes as more types (as is done for std::ratio; §35.3) but thought it simpler to keep the Unit types simple and focused on doing their primary task well.

I use underscores in my units _s and _m so as not to get in the way of the standard library providing the shorter and nicer s and m suffixes.

28.7.4 Utility Functions

To finish the job (as defined by the initial example), we need the utility function **square()**, the equality operator, and the output operator. Defining **square()** is trivial:

```
template<typename U>
Quantity<Unit_plus<U,U>> square(Quantity<U> x)
{
    return Quantity<Unit_plus<U,U>>(x.val*x.val);
}
```

That basically shows how to write arbitrary computational functions. I could have constructed the **Unit** right there in the return value definition, but using the existing type function was easier. Alternatively, we could easily have defined a type function **Unit_double**.

The **==** looks more or less like all **==**s. It is defined for values of the same **Units** only:

```
template<typename U>
bool operator==(Quantity<U> x, Quantity<U> y)
{
    return x.val==y.val;
}

template<typename U>
bool operator!=(Quantity<U> x, Quantity<U> y)
{
    return x.val!=y.val;
}
```

Note that I pass **Quantitys** by value. At run time, they are represented as **doubles**.

The output functions just do conventional character manipulation:

```
string suffix(int u, const char* x)    // helper function
{
    string suf;
    if (u) {
        suf += x;
        if (1<u) suf += '0'+u;

        if (u<0) {
            suf += '-';
            suf += '0'-u;
        }
    }
    return suf;
}
```

```
template<typename U>
ostream& operator<<(ostream& os, Quantity<U> v)
{
    return os << v.val << suffix(U::m,"m") << suffix(U::kg,"kg") << suffix(U::s,"s");
}
```

Finally, we can write:

```
auto distance = 10_m;        // 10 meters
auto time = 20_s;            // 20 seconds
auto speed = distance/time;   // .5 m/s (meters per second)

if (speed == 20)             // error: 20 is dimensionless
// ...
if (speed == distance)        // error: can't compare m to m/s
// ...
if (speed == 10_m/20_s)      // OK: the units match
// ...

Quantity<MpS2> acceleration = distance/square(time);  // MpS2 means m/(s*s)

cout << "speed==" << speed << " acceleration==" << acceleration << "\n";
```

Such code will, given a reasonable compiler, generate exactly the same code as would have been generated using **doubles** directly. However, it is "type checked" (at compile time) according to the rules for physical units. It is an example of how we can add a whole new set of application-specific types with their own checking rules to a C++ program.

28.8 Advice

[1]   Use metaprogramming to improve type safety; §28.1.
[2]   Use metaprogramming to improve performance by moving computation to compile time; §28.1.
[3]   Avoid using metaprogramming to an extent where it significantly slows down compilation; §28.1.
[4]   Think in terms of compile-time evaluation and type functions; §28.2.
[5]   Use template aliases as the interfaces to type functions returning types; §28.2.1.
[6]   Use **constexpr** functions as the interfaces to type functions returning (non-type) values; §28.2.2.
[7]   Use traits to nonintrusively associate properties with types; §28.2.4.
[8]   Use **Conditional** to choose between two types; §28.3.1.1.
[9]   Use **Select** to choose among several alternative types; §28.3.1.3.
[10] Use recursion to express compile-time iteration; §28.3.2.
[11] Use metaprogramming for tasks that cannot be done well at run time; §28.3.3.
[12] Use **Enable_if** to selectively declare function templates; §28.4.
[13] Concepts are among the most useful predicates to use with **Enable_if**; §28.4.3.

[14] Use variadic templates when you need a function that takes a variable number of arguments of a variety of types; §28.6.

[15] Don't use variadic templates for homogeneous argument lists (prefer initializer lists for that); §28.6.

[16] Use variadic templates and **std::move()** where forwarding is needed; §28.6.3.

[17] Use simple metaprogramming to implement efficient and elegant unit systems (for fine-grained type checking); §28.7.

[18] Use user-defined literals to simplify the use of units; §28.7.

29

A Matrix Design

*Never express yourself more clearly
than you are able to think.*
– Niels Bohr

29.1 Introduction

A language feature in isolation is boring and useless. This chapter demonstrates how features can be used in combination to address a challenging design task: a general N-dimensional matrix.

I have never seen a perfect matrix class. In fact, given the wide variety of uses of matrices, it is doubtful whether one could exist. Here, I present the programming and design techniques needed to write a simple N-dimensional dense matrix. If nothing else, this **Matrix** is far easier to use, and just as compact and fast, as anything a programmer would have time to write using **vector**s or built-in arrays directly. The design and programming techniques used for **Matrix** are widely applicable.

29.1.1 Basic Matrix Uses

Matrix<T,N> is an **N**-dimensional matrix of some value type **T**. It can be used like this:

```
Matrix<double,0> m0 {1};             // zero dimensions: a scalar
Matrix<double,1> m1 {1,2,3,4};       // one dimension: a vector (4 elements)
Matrix<double,2> m2 {               // two dimensions (4*3 elements)
    {00,01,02,03},      // row 0
    {10,11,12,13},      // row 1
    {20,21,22,23}       // row 2
};
Matrix<double,3> m3(4,7,9);          // three dimensions (4*7*9 elements), all 0-initialized
Matrix<complex<double>,17> m17; // 17 dimensions (no elements so far)
```

The element type must be something we can store. We do not require every property that we have for a floating-point number from every element type. For example:

```
Matrix<double,2> md;        // OK
Matrix<string,2> ms;        // OK: just don't try arithmetic operations

Matrix<Matrix<int,2>,2> mm { // 3-by-2 matrix of 2-by-2 matrices
                             // a matrix is a plausible "number"
    { // row 0
        {{1, 2}, {3, 4}}, // col 0
        {{4, 5}, {6, 7}}, // col 1
    },
    { // row 1
        {{8, 9}, {0, 1}}, // col 0
        {{2, 3}, {4, 5}}, // col 1
    },
    { // row 2
        {{1, 2}, {3, 4}}, // col 0
        {{4, 5}, {6, 7}}, // col 1
    }
};
```

Matrix arithmetic doesn't have exactly the same mathematical properties as integer or floating-point arithmetic (e.g., matrix multiplication is not commutative), so we must be careful how we use such a matrix.

As for **vector**, we use () to specify sizes and {} to specify element values (§17.3.2.1, §17.3.4.1). The number rows must match the specified number of dimensions and the number of elements in each dimension (each column) must match. For example:

```
Matrix<char,2> mc1(2,3,4);       // error: too many dimension sizes
Matrix<char,2> mc2 {
    {'1','2','3'}                 // error: initializer missing for second dimension
};
Matrix<char,2> mc2 {
    {'1','2','3'},
    {'4','5'}                     // error: element missing for third column
};
```

Matrix<T,N> has its number of dimensions (its **order()**) specified as a template argument (here, **N**). Each dimension has a number of elements (its **extent()**) deduced from the initializer list or specified as a **Matrix** constructor argument using the **()** notation. The total number of elements is referred to as its **size()**. For example:

```
Matrix<double,1> m1(100);        // one dimension: a vector (100 elements)
Matrix<double,2> m2(50,6000);    // two dimensions: 50*6000 elements

auto d1 = m1.order();            // 1
auto d2 = m2.order();            // 2

auto e1 = m1.extent(0);          // 100
auto e1 = m1.extent(1);          // error: m1 is one-dimensional

auto e2 = m2.extent(0);          // 50
auto e2 = m2.extent(1);          // 6000

auto s1 = m1.size();             // 100
auto s2 = m2.size();             // 50*6000
```

We can access **Matrix** elements by several forms of subscripting. For example:

```
Matrix<double,2> m {             // two dimensions (4*3 elements)
    {00,01,02,03},  // row 0
    {10,11,12,13},  // row 1
    {20,21,22,23}   // row 2
};

double d1 = m(1,2);              // d==12
double d2 = m[1][2];             // d==12
Matrix<double,1> m1 = m[1];      // row 1: {10,11,12,13}
double d3 = m1[2];               // d==12
```

We can define an output function for use in debugging like this:

```
template<typename M>
    Enable_if<Matrix_type<M>(),ostream&>
operator<<(ostream& os, const M& m)
{
    os << '{';
    for (size_t i = 0; i!=rows(m); ++i) {
        os << m[i];
        if (i+1!=rows(m)) os << ',';
    }
    return os << '}';
}
```

Here, **Matrix_type** is a concept (§24.3). **Enable_if** is an alias for **enable_if**'s type (§28.4), so this **operator<<()** returns an **ostream&**.

Given that, **cout<<m** prints: {{0,1,2,3},{10,11,12,13},{20,21,22,23}}.

29.1.2 Matrix **Requirements**

Before proceeding with an implementation, consider what properties we might like to have:

- N dimensions, where N is a parameter that can vary from 0 to many, without specialized code for every dimension.
- N-dimensional storage is useful in general, so the element type can be anything we can store (like a **vector** element).
- The mathematical operations should apply to any type that can reasonably be described as a number, including a **Matrix**.
- Fortran-style subscripting using one index per dimension, for example, m(1,2,3) for a 3-D **Matrix**, yielding an element.
- C-style subscripting, for example, m[7], yielding a row (a row is an N–1-D sub-**Matrix** of an N-D **Matrix**).
- Subscripting should be potentially fast and potentially range checked.
- Move assignment and move constructor to ensure efficient passing of **Matrix** results and to eliminate expensive temporaries.
- Some mathematical matrix operations, such as + and ∗=.
- A way to read, write, and pass around references to submatrices, **Matrix_refs**, for use for both reading and writing elements.
- The absence of resource leaks in the form of the basic guarantee (§13.2).
- Fused critical operations, for example, m∗v+v2 as a single function call.

This is a relatively long and ambitious list, but it does not add up to "everything for everybody." For example, I did not list:

- Many more mathematical matrix operations
- Specialized matrices (e.g., diagonal and triangular matrices)
- Sparse **Matrix** support
- Support for parallel execution of **Matrix** operations

However valuable those properties are, they go beyond what is needed to present basic programming techniques.

To provide this, I use a combination of several language features and programming techniques:

- Classes (of course)
- Parameterization with numbers and types
- Move constructors and assignments (to minimize copying)
- RAII (relying on constructors and destructors)
- Variadic templates (for specifying extents and for indexing)
- Initializer lists
- Operator overloading (to get conventional notation)
- Function objects (to carry information about subscripting)
- Some simple template metaprogramming (e.g., for checking initializer lists and for distinguishing reading and writing for **Matrix_refs**)
- Implementation inheritance for minimizing code replication.

Obviously, a **Matrix** like this could be a built-in type (as it is in many languages), but the point here is exactly that in C++ it is *not* built in. Instead, facilities are provided for users to make their own.

29.2 A Matrix Template

To give an overview, here is the declaration of Matrix with its most interesting operations:

```
template<typename T, size_t N>
class Matrix {
public:
    static constexpr size_t order = N;
    using value_type = T;
    using iterator = typename std::vector<T>::iterator;
    using const_iterator = typename std::vector<T>::const_iterator;

    Matrix() = default;
    Matrix(Matrix&&) = default;                                     // move
    Matrix& operator=(Matrix&&) = default;
    Matrix(Matrix const&) = default;                               // copy
    Matrix& operator=(Matrix const&) = default;
    ~Matrix() = default;

    template<typename U>
        Matrix(const Matrix_ref<U,N>&);                           // construct from Matrix_ref
    template<typename U>
        Matrix& operator=(const Matrix_ref<U,N>&);                // assign from Matrix_ref

    template<typename... Exts>                                     // specify the extents
        explicit Matrix(Exts... exts);

    Matrix(Matrix_initializer<T,N>);                              // initialize from list
    Matrix& operator=(Matrix_initializer<T,N>);                  // assign from list

    template<typename U>
        Matrix(initializer_list<U>) = delete;                    // don't use {} except for elements
    template<typename U>
        Matrix& operator=(initializer_list<U>) = delete;

    static constexpr size_t order() { return N; }                // number of dimensions
    size_t extent(size_t n) const { return desc.extents[n]; }    // #elements in the nth dimension
    size_t size() const { return elems.size(); }                 // total number of elements
    const Matrix_slice<N>& descriptor() const { return desc; }   // the slice defining subscripting

    T* data() { return elems.data(); }                           // "flat" element access
    const T* data() const { return elems.data(); }

    // ...

private:
    Matrix_slice<N> desc;       // slice defining extents in the N dimensions
    vector<T> elems;            // the elements
};
```

Using a **vector<T>** to hold the elements relieves us from concerns of memory management and exception safety. A **Matrix_slice** holds the sizes necessary to access the elements as an **N**-dimensional matrix (§29.4.2). Think of it as a **gslice** (§40.5.6) specialized for our **Matrix**.

A **Matrix_ref** (§29.4.3) behaves just like a **Matrix** except that it refers to a **Matrix**, typically a sub-**Matrix** such as a row or a column, rather than owning its own elements. Think of it as a reference to a sub-**Matrix**.

A **Matrix_initializer<T,N>** is a suitably nested initializer list for a **Matrix<T,N>** (§29.4.4).

29.2.1 Construction and Assignment

The default copy and move operations have just the right semantics: memberwise copy or move of the **desc** (slice descriptor defining subscripting) and the **elements**. Note that for management of the storage for elements, **Matrix** gets all the benefits from **vector**. Similarly, the default constructor and destructor have just the right semantics.

The constructor that takes extents (numbers of elements in dimensions) is a fairly trivial example of a variadic template (§28.6):

```
template<typename T, size_t N>
    template<typename... Exts>
    Matrix<T,N>::Matrix(Exts... exts)
        :desc{exts...},        // copy extents
        elems(desc.size)       // allocate desc.size elements and default initialize them
    {}
```

The constructor that takes an initializer list requires a bit of work:

```
template<typename T, size_t N>
Matrix<T, N>::Matrix(Matrix_initializer<T,N> init)
{
    Matrix_impl::derive_extents(init,desc.extents);    // deduce extents from initializer list (§29.4.4)
    elems.reserve(desc.size);                          // make room for slices
    Matrix_impl::insert_flat(init,elems);              // initialize from initializer list (§29.4.4)
    assert(elems.size() == desc.size);
}
```

The **Matrix_initializer** is a suitably nested **initializer_list** (§29.4.4). The extents are deduced by the **Matrix_slice** constructor, checked, and stored in **desc**. Then, the elements are stored in **elems** by insert_flat() from the **Matrix_impl** namespace.

To ensure that {} initialization is only used for lists of elements, I =deleted the simple **initializer_list** constructor. This is to enforce the use of () initialization for extents. For example:

```
enum class Piece { none, cross, naught };

Matrix<Piece,2> board1 {
    {Piece::none, Piece::none, Piece::none},
    {Piece::none, Piece::none, Piece::none},
    {Piece::none, Piece::none, Piece::cross}
};
Matrix<Piece,2> board2(3,3);  // OK
Matrix<Piece,2> board3 {3,3}; // error: constructor from initializer_list<int> deleted
```

Without that =delete, that last definition would have been accepted.

Finally, we have to be able to construct from a **Matrix_ref**, that is, from a reference to a **Matrix** or a part of a **Matrix** (a submatrix):

```
template<typename T, size_t N>
    template<typename U>
    Matrix<T,N>::Matrix(const Matrix_ref<U,N>& x)
        :desc{x.desc}, elems{x.begin(),x.end()}   // copy desc and elements
    {
        static_assert(Convertible<U,T>(),"Matrix constructor: incompatible element types");
    }
```

The use of a template allows us to construct from a **Matrix** with a compatible element type.

As usual, the assignments resemble the constructors. For example:

```
template<typename T, size_t N>
    template<typename U>
    Matrix<T,N>& Matrix<T,N>::operator=(const Matrix_ref<U,N>& x)
    {
        static_assert(Convertible<U,T>(),"Matrix =: incompatible element types");

        desc = x.desc;
        elems.assign(x.begin(),x.end());
        return *this;
    }
```

That is, we copy the members of **Matrix**.

29.2.2 Subscripting and Slicing

A **Matrix** can be accessed through subscripting (to elements or rows), through rows and columns, or through slices (parts of rows or columns).

Matrix<T,N> **Access**	
m.row(i)	Row i of m; a Matrix_ref<T,N–1>
m.column(i)	Column i of m; a Matrix_ref<T,N–1>
m[i]	C-style subscripting: m.row(i)
m(i,j)	Fortran-style element access: m[i][j]; a T&; the number of subscripts must be N
m(slice(i,n),slice(j))	Submatrix access with slicing: a Matrix_ref<T,N>; slice(i,n) is elements [i:i+n] of the subscript's dimension; slice(j) is elements [i:max) of the subscript's dimension; max is the dimension's extent; the number of subscripts must be N

These are all member functions:

```
template<typename T, size_t N>
class Matrix {
public:
    // ...
```

```
template<typename... Args>                                          // m(i,j,k) subscripting with integers
    Enable_if<Matrix_impl::Requesting_element<Args...>(), T&>
    operator()(Args... args);
template<typename... Args>
    Enable_if<Matrix_impl::Requesting_element<Args...>(), const T&>
    operator()(Args... args) const;
template<typename... Args>                                          // m(s1,s2,s3) subscripting with slices
    Enable_if<Matrix_impl::Requesting_slice<Args...>(), Matrix_ref<T, N>>
    operator()(const Args&... args);
template<typename... Args>
    Enable_if<Matrix_impl::Requesting_slice<Args...>(), Matrix_ref<const T,N>>
    operator()(const Args&... args) const;

Matrix_ref<T,N–1> operator[](size_t i) { return row(i); }          // m[i] row access
Matrix_ref<const T,N–1> operator[](size_t i) const { return row(i); }

Matrix_ref<T,N–1> row(size_t n);                                   // row access
Matrix_ref<const T,N–1> row(size_t n) const;

Matrix_ref<T,N–1> col(size_t n);                                   // column access
Matrix_ref<const T,N–1> col(size_t n) const;

    // ...
};
```

C-style subscripting is done by **m[i]** selecting and returning the ith row:

```
template<typename T, size_t N>
Matrix_ref<T,N–1> Matrix<T,N>::operator[](size_t n)
{
    return row(n);     // §29.4.5
}
```

Think of a **Matrix_ref** (§29.4.3) as a reference to a sub-**Matrix**.

Matrix_ref<T,0> is specialized so that it refers to a single element (§29.4.6).

Fortran-style subscripting is done by listing an index for each dimension, for example, **m(i,j,k)**, yielding a scalar:

```
Matrix<int,2> m2 {
    {01,02,03},
    {11,12,13}
};

m(1,2) = 99;        // overwrite the element in row 1 column 2; that is 13
auto d1 = m(1);     // error: too few subscripts
auto d2 = m(1,2,3); // error: too many subscripts
```

In addition to subscripting with integers, we can subscript with **slices**. A **slice** describes a subset of the elements of a dimension (§40.5.4). In particular, **slice{i,n}** refers to elements [i:i+n] of the dimension to which it applies. For example:

```
Matrix<int> m2 {
    {01,02,03},
    {11,12,13},
    {21,22,23}
};
```

```
auto m22 = m(slice{1,2},slice{0,3});
```

Now **m22** is a **Matrix<int,2>** with the value

```
{
    {11,12,13},
    {21,22,23}
}
```

The first (row) subscript **slice{1,2}** selects the last two rows, and the second (column) subscript **slice{0,3}** selects all elements in the columns.

The return type for a () with **slice** subscripts is a **Matrix_ref**, so we can use it as the target of an assignment. For example:

```
m(slice{1,2},slice{0,3}) = {
    {111,112,113},
    {121,122,123}
}
```

Now **m** has the value

```
{
    {01,02,03},
    {111,112,113},
    {121,122,123}
}
```

Selecting all elements from a point onward is so common that there is a shorthand: **slice{i}** means **slice{i,max}** where **max** is larger than the largest subscript in the dimension. So, we can simplify **m(slice{1,2},slice{0,3})** to the equivalent **m(slice{1,2},slice{0})**.

The other simple common case is to select all elements of a single row or column, so a plain integer subscript **i** among a set of **slice** subscripts is interpreted as **slice{i,1}**. For example:

```
Matrix<int> m3 {
    {01,02,03},
    {11,12,13},
    {21,22,23}
};
```

```
auto m31 = m(slice{1,2},1);        // m31 becomes {{12},{22}}
auto m32 = m(slice{1,2},0);        // m33 becomes {{11},{21}}
auto x = m(1,2);                   // x == 13
```

The notion of slicing subscripts is supported in essentially all languages used for numeric programming, so hopefully it is not too unfamiliar.

The implementations of **row()**, **column()**, and **operator()()** are presented in §29.4.5. The implementations of **const** versions of these functions are basically the same as those of their non-**const** versions. The key difference is that **const** versions return results with **const** elements.

29.3 Matrix **Arithmetic Operations**

So, we can create **Matrixes**, copy them, access their elements and rows. However, what we often want is to have mathematical operations that save us from expressing our algorithms in terms of accesses to individual elements (scalars). For example:

```
Matrix<int,2> mi {{1,2,3}, {4,5,6 }};      // 2-by-3
Matrix<int,2> m2 {mi};                      // copy
mi*=2;                                       // scale: {{2,4,6},{8,10,12}}
Matrix<int,2> m3 = mi+m2;                    // add: {{3,6,9},{12,15,18}}
Matrix<int,2> m4 {{1,2}, {3,4}, {5,6}};      // 3-by-2
Matrix<int,1> v = mi*m4;                     // multiply: {{18,24,30},{38,52,66},{58,80,102}}
```

The mathematical operations are defined like this:

```
template<typename T, size_t N>
class Matrix {
    // ...

    template<typename F>
        Matrix& apply(F f);                  // f(x) for every element x

    template<typename M, typename F>
        Matrix& apply(const M& m, F f);      // f(x,mx) for corresponding elements

    Matrix& operator=(const T& value);       // assignment with scalar

    Matrix& operator+=(const T& value);      // scalar addition
    Matrix& operator-=(const T& value);      // scalar subtraction
    Matrix& operator*=(const T& value);      // scalar multiplication
    Matrix& operator/=(const T& value);      // scalar division
    Matrix& operator%=(const T& value);      // scalar modulo

    template<typename M>                     // matrix addition
        Matrix& operator+=(const M& x);
    template<typename M>                     // matrix subtraction
        Matrix& operator-=(const M& x);

    // ...
};

// Binary +, -, * are provided as nonmember functions
```

29.3.1 Scalar Operations

A scalar arithmetic operation simply applies its operation and right-hand operand to each element. For example:

```
template<typename T, size_t N>
Matrix<T,N>& Matrix<T,N>::operator+=(const T& val)
{
    return apply([&](T& a) { a+=val; } ); // using a lambda (§11.4)
}
```

This **apply()** applies a function (or a function object) to each element of its **Matrix**:

```
template<typename T, size_t N>
    template<typename F>
    Matrix<T,N>& Matrix<T,N>::apply(F f)
    {
        for (auto& x : elems) f(x);        // this loop uses stride iterators
        return *this;
    }
```

As usual, returning *this enables chaining. For example:

```
m.apply(abs).apply(sqrt);      // m[i] = sqrt(abs(m[i])) for all i
```

As usual (§3.2.1.1, §18.3), we can define the "plain operators," such as +, outside the class using the assignment operators, such as +=. For example:

```
template<typename T, size_t N>
Matrix<T,N> operator+(const Matrix<T,N>& m, const T& val)
{
    Matrix<T,N> res = m;
    res+=val;
    return res;
}
```

Without the move constructor, this return type would be a bad performance bug.

29.3.2 Addition

Addition of two **Matrixes** is very similar to the scalar versions:

```
template<typename T, size_t N>
    template<typename M>
    Enable_if<Matrix_type<M>(),Matrix<T,N>&> Matrix<T,N>::operator+=(const M& m)
    {
        static_assert(m.order()==N,"+=: mismatched Matrix  dimensions");
        assert(same_extents(desc,m.descriptor()));       // make sure sizes match

        return apply(m, [](T& a,Value_type<M>&b) { a+=b; });
    }
```

Matrix::apply(m,f) is the two-argument version of **Matrix::apply(f)**. It applies its **f** to its two **Matrixes** (**m** and *this):

```
template<typename T, size_t N>
    template<typename M, typename F>
    Enable_if<Matrix_type<M>(),Matrix<T,N>&> Matrix<T,N>::apply(M& m, F f)
    {
        assert(same_extents(desc,m.descriptor()));        // make sure sizes match
        for (auto i = begin(), j = m.begin(); i!=end(); ++i, ++j)
            f(*i,*j);
        return *this;
    }
```

Now **operator+()** is easily defined:

```
template<typename T, size_t N>
Matrix<T,N> operator+(const Matrix<T,N>& a, const Matrix<T,N>& b)
{
    Matrix<T,N> res = a;
    res+=b;
    return res;
}
```

This defines + for two **Matrixes** of the same type yielding a result of that type. We could generalize:

```
template<typename T, typename T2, size_t N,
    typename RT = Matrix<Common_type<Value_type<T>,Value_type<T2>>,N>
Matrix<RT,N> operator+(const Matrix<T,N>& a, const Matrix<T2,N>& b)
{
    Matrix<RT,N> res = a;
    res+=b;
    return res;
}
```

If, as is common, **T** and **T2** are the same type, **Common_type** is that type. The **Common_type** type function is derived from **std::common_type** (§35.4.2). For built-in types it, like **?:**, gives a type that best preserves values of arithmetic operations. If **Common_type** is not defined for a pair of types we want to use in combination, we can define it. For example:

```
template<>
struct common_type<Quad,long double> {
    using type = Quad;
};
```

Now **Common_type<Quad,long double>** is Quad.

We also need operations involving **Matrix_refs** (§29.4.3). For example:

```
template<typename T, size_t N>
Matrix<T,N> operator+(const Matrix_ref<T,N>& x, const T& n)
{
    Matrix<T,N> res = x;
    res+=n;
    return res;
}
```

Such operations look exactly like their **Matrix** equivalents. There is no difference between **Matrix** and **Matrix_ref** element access: the difference between **Matrix** and **Matrix_ref** is in the initialization and ownership of elements.

Subtraction, multiplication, etc., by scalars and the handling of **Matrix_refs** are just repetition of the techniques used for addition.

29.3.3 Multiplication

Matrix multiplication is not as simple as addition: the product of an N-by-M matrix and a M-by-P matrix is an N-by-P matrix. For **M==1** we get that the product of two vectors is a matrix, and from **P==1** we get that the product of a matrix and a vector is a vector. We can generalize matrix multiplication into higher dimensions, but to do that we have to introduce tensors [Kolecki,2002], and I don't want to divert this discussion of programming techniques and how to use language features into a physics and engineering math lesson. So, I'll stick to one and two dimensions.

Treating one **Matrix<T,1>** as an N-by-1 matrix and another as a 1-by-M matrix, we get:

```
template<typename T>
Matrix<T,2> operator*(const Matrix<T,1>& u, const Matrix<T,1>& v)
{
    const size_t n = u.extent(0);
    const size_t m = v.extent(0);
    Matrix<T,2> res(n,m);               // an n-by-m matrix
    for (size_t i = 0; i!=n; ++i)
        for (size_t j = 0; j!=m; ++j)
            res(i,j) = u[i]*v[j];
    return res;
}
```

This is the simplest case: matrix element **res(i,j)** is **u[i]*v[j]**. I have not tried to generalize to handle the cases where the element types of the vectors are different. If necessary, the techniques discussed for addition can be used.

Note that I'm writing to each element of **res** twice: once to initialize to **T{}** and once to assign **u[i]*v[j]**. This roughly doubles the cost of the multiplication. If that bothers you, write a multiplication without that overhead and see if the difference matters in your program.

Next, we can multiply an N-by-M matrix with a vector seen as an M-by-1 matrix. The result is an N-by-1 matrix:

```
template<typename T>
Matrix<T,1> operator*(const Matrix<T,2>& m, const Matrix<T,1>& v)
{
    assert(m.extent(1)==v.extent(0));

    const size_t n = m.extent(0);
    Matrix<T,1> res(n);
    for (size_t i = 0; i!=n; ++i)
        for (size_t j = 0; j!=n; ++j)
            res(i) += m(i,j)*v(j);
    return res;
}
```

Note that the declaration of **res** initializes its elements to **T{}**, which is zero for numeric types, so that the **+=** starts out from zero.

The N-by-M matrix times M-by-P matrix is handled similarly:

```
template<typename T>
Matrix<T,2> operator*(const Matrix<T,2>& m1, const Matrix<T,2>& m2)
{
    const size_t n = m1.extent(0);
    const size_t m = m1.extent(1);
    assert(m==m2.extent(0));        // columns must match rows

    const size_t p = m2.extent(1);
    Matrix<T,2> res(n,p);
    for (size_t i = 0; i!=n; ++i)
        for (size_t j = 0; j!=m; ++j)
            for (size_t k = 0; k!=p; ++k)
                res(i,j) = m1(i,k)*m2(k,j);
    return res;
}
```

There are numerous ways of optimizing this important operation.

That innermost loop could be more elegantly expressed as:

```
res(i,j) = dot_product(m1[i],m2.column(j))
```

Here, **dot_product()** is simply an interface to the standard-library **inner_product()** (§40.6.2):

```
template<typename T>
T dot_product(const Matrix_ref<T,1>& a, const Matrix_ref<T,1>& b)
{
    return inner_product(a.begin(),a.end(),b.begin(),0.0);
}
```

29.4 Matrix Implementation

So far, I have delayed the presentation of the most complicated (and for some programmers the most interesting) "mechanical" parts of the **Matrix** implementation. For example: What is a **Matrix_ref**? What is a **Matrix_slice**? How do you initialize a **Matrix** from a nest of **initializer_list**s and make sure the dimensions are reasonable? How do we ensure that we don't instantiate a **Matrix** with an unsuitable element type?

The easiest way to present this code is to place all of **Matrix** in a header file. In that case, add **inline** the definition of every nonmember function.

The definitions of functions that are not members of **Matrix**, **Matrix_ref**, **Matrix_slice**, or part of the general interface are placed in namespace **Matrix_impl**.

29.4.1 slice()

A simple **slice** as used for **slice** subscripting describes a mapping from an integer (subscript) to an element location (index) in terms of three values:

```
struct slice {
    slice() :start(-1), length(-1), stride(1) { }
    explicit slice(size_t s) :start(s), length(-1), stride(1) { }
    slice(size_t s, size_t l, size_t n = 1) :start(s), length(l), stride(n) { }

    size_t operator()(size_t i) const { return start+i*stride; }

    static slice all;

    size_t start;       // first index
    size_t length;      // number of indices included (can be used for range checking)
    size_t stride;      // distance between elements in sequence
};
```

There is a standard-library version of **slice**; see §40.5.4 for a more thorough discussion. This version provides notational convenience (e.g., the default values provided by the constructors).

29.4.2 Matrix Slices

A **Matrix_slice** is the part of the **Matrix** implementation that maps a set of subscripts to the location of an element. It uses the idea of generalized slices (§40.5.6):

```
template<size_t N>
struct Matrix_slice {
    Matrix_slice() = default;                                   // an empty matrix: no elements

    Matrix_slice(size_t s, initializer_list<size_t> exts); // extents
    Matrix_slice(size_t s, initializer_list<size_t> exts, initializer_list<size_t> strs);// extents and strides

    template<typename... Dims>                                  // N extents
        Matrix_slice(Dims... dims);

    template<typename... Dims,
            typename = Enable_if<All(Convertible<Dims,size_t>()...)>>
        size_t operator()(Dims... dims) const;     // calculate index from a set of subscripts

    size_t size;                    // total number of elements
    size_t start;                   // starting offset
    array<size_t,N> extents;        // number of elements in each dimension
    array<size_t,N> strides;        // offsets between elements in each dimension
};
```

In other words, a **Matrix_slice** describes what is considered rows and columns in a region of memory. In the usual C/C++ row-major layout of a matrix, the elements of rows are contiguous, and the elements of a column are separated by a fixed number of elements (a stride). A **Matrix_slice** is a function object, and its **operator()()** does a stride calculation (§40.5.6):

```
template<size_t N>
    template<typename... Dims>
    size_t Matrix_slice<N>::operator()(Dims... dims) const
    {
        static_assert(sizeof...(Dims) == N, "");

        size_t args[N] { size_t(dims)... };    // Copy arguments into an array

        return inner_product(args,args+N,strides.begin(),size_t(0));
    }
```

Subscripting must be efficient. This is a simplified algorithm that needs to be optimized. If nothing else, specialization can be used to eliminate the simplifying copy of subscripts out of the variadic template's parameter pack. For example:

```
template<>
struct Matrix_slice<1> {

    // ...

    size_t operator()(size_t i) const
    {
        return i;
    }
}

template<>
struct Matrix_slice<2> {

    // ...

    size_t operator()(size_t i, size_t j) const
    {
        return i*stides[0]+j;
    }
}
```

The Matrix_slice is fundamental for defining the shape of a Matrix (its extents) and for implementing N-dimensional subscripting. However, it is also useful for defining submatrices.

29.4.3 Matrix_ref

A Matrix_ref is basically a clone of the Matrix class used to represent sub-Matrixes. However, a Matrix_ref does not own its elements. It is constructed from a Matrix_slice and a pointer to elements:

```
template<typename T, size_t N>
class Matrix_ref {
public:
    Matrix_ref(const Matrix_slice<N>& s, T* p) :desc{s}, ptr{p} {}
    // ... mostly like Matrix ...
```

```
private:
    Matrix_slice<N> desc;         // the shape of the matrix
    T* ptr;                       // the first element in the matrix
};
```

A `Matrix_ref` simply points to the elements of "its" `Matrix`. Obviously, a `Matrix_ref` should not out-live its `Matrix`. For example:

```
Matrix_ref<double,1> user()
{
    Matrix<double,2> m = {{1,2}, {3,4}, {5,6}};
    return m.row(1);
}
```

```
auto mr = user();        // trouble
```

The great similarity between `Matrix` and `Matrix_ref` leads to duplication. If that becomes a bother, we can derive both from a common base:

```
template<typename T, size_t N>
class Matrix_base {
    // ... common stuff ...
};
```

```
template<typename T, size_t N>
class Matrix : public Matrix_base<T,N> {
    // ... special to Matrix ...
private:
    Matrix_slice<N> desc;         // the shape of the matrix
    vector<T> elements;
};
```

```
template<typename T, size_t N>
class Matrix_ref : public Matrix_base<T,N> {
    // ... special to Matrix_ref ...
private:
    Matrix_slice<N> desc;         // the shape of the matrix
    T* ptr;
};
```

29.4.4 **Matrix** List Initialization

The `Matrix` constructor that constructs from an `initializer_list` takes as its argument type the alias `Matrix_initializer`:

```
template<typename T, size_t N>
using Matrix_initializer = typename Matrix_impl::Matrix_init<T, N>::type;
```

`Matrix_init` describes the structure of a nested `initializer_list`.

Matrix_init<T,N> simply has Matrix_init<T,N–1> as its member type:

```
template<typename T, size_t N>
struct Matrix_init {
    using type = initializer_list<typename Matrix_init<T,N–1>::type>;
};
```

The N==1 is special. That is where we get to the (most deeply nested) initializer_list<T>:

```
template<typename T>
struct Matrix_init<T,1> {
    using type = initializer_list<T>;
};
```

To avoid surprises, we define N=0 to be an error:

```
template<typename T>
struct Matrix_init<T,0>;    // undefined on purpose
```

We can now complete the Matrix constructor that takes a Matrix_initializer:

```
template<typename T, size_t N>
Matrix<T, N>::Matrix(Matrix_initializer<T,N> init)
{
    Matrix_impl::derive_extents(init,desc.extents);     // deduce extents from initializer list (§29.4.4)
    elems.reserve(desc.size);                           // make room for slices
    Matrix_impl::insert_flat(init,elems);               // initialize from initializer list (§29.4.4)
    assert(elems.size() == desc.size());
}
```

To do so, we need two operations that recurse down a tree of initializer_lists for a Matrix<T,N>:

- derive_extents() determines the shape of the Matrix:
    - Checks that the tree really is N deep
    - Checks that each row (sub-initialize_list) has the same number of elements
    - Sets the extent of each row
- insert_flat() copies the elements of the tree of initializer_list<T>s into the elems of a Matrix.

The derived_extents() called from a Matrix constructor to initialize its desc looks like this:

```
template<size_t N, typename List>
array<size_t, N> derive_extents(const List& list)
{
    array<size_t,N> a;
    auto f = a.begin();
    add_extents<N>(f,list);    // put extents from list into f[]
    return a;
}
```

You give it an initializer_list and it returns an array of extents.

The recursion is done from N to the final 1 where the initializer_list is an initializer_list<T>.

```
template<size_t N, typename I, typename List>
Enable_if<(N>1),void> add_extents(I& first, const List& list)
{
    assert(check_non_jagged(list));
    *first = list.size();
    add_extents<N-1>(++first,*list.begin());
}

template<size_t N, typename I, typename List>
Enable_if<(N==1),void> add_extents(I& first, const List& list)
{
    *first++ = list.size();      // we reached the deepest nesting
}
```

The check_non_jagged() function checks that all rows have the same number of elements:

```
template<typename List>
bool check_non_jagged(const List& list)
{
    auto i = list.begin();
    for (auto j = i+1; j!=list.end(); ++j)
        if (i->size()!=j->size())
            return false;
    return true;
}
```

We need insert_flat() to take a possibly nested initializer list and present its elements to Matrix<T> as a vector<T>. It takes the initializer_list given to a Matrix as the Matrix_initializer and provides the elements as the target:

```
template<typename T, typename Vec>
void insert_flat(initializer_list<T> list, Vec& vec)
{
    add_list(list.begin(),list.end(),vec);
}
```

Unfortunately, we can't rely on the elements being allocated contiguously in memory, so we need to build the vector through a set of recursive calls. If we have a list of initializer_lists, we recurse through each:

```
template<typename T, typename Vec>    // nested initializer_lists
void add_list(const initializer_list<T>* first, const initializer_list<T>* last, Vec& vec)
{
    for (;first!=last;++first)
        add_list(first->begin(),first->end(),vec);
}
```

When we reach a list with non-initializer_list elements, we insert those elements into our vector:

```
template<typename T, typename Vec>
void add_list(const T* first, const T* last, Vec& vec)
{
        vec.insert(vec.end(),first,last);
}
```

I use **vec.insert(vec.end(),first,last)** because there is no **push_back()** that takes a sequence argument.

29.4.5 Matrix Access

A **Matrix** provides access by row, column, slice (§29.4.1), and element (§29.4.3). A **row()** or **column()** operation returns a **Matrix_ref<T,N–1>**, the () subscript operation with integers returns a **T&**, and the () subscript operation with **slices** returns a **Matrix<T,N>**.

The row of a **Matrix<T,N>** is a **Matrix_ref<T,N–1>** as long as **1<N**:

```
template<typename T, size_t N>
Matrix_ref<T,N–1> Matrix<T,N>::row(size_t n)
{
        assert(n<rows());
        Matrix_slice<N–1> row;
        Matrix_impl::slice_dim<0>(n,desc,row);
        return {row,data()};
}
```

We need specializations for **N==1** and **N==0**:

```
template<typename T>
T& Matrix<T,1>::row(size_t i)
{
        return &elems[i];
}
```

```
template<typename T>
T& Matrix<T,0>::row(size_t n) = delete;
```

Selecting a **column()** is essentially the same as selecting a **row()**. The difference is simply in the construction of the **Matrix_slice**:

```
template<typename T, size_t N>
Matrix_ref<T,N–1> Matrix<T,N>::column(size_t n)
{
        assert(n<cols());
        Matrix_slice<N–1> col;
        Matrix_impl::slice_dim<1>(n,desc,col);
        return {col,data()};
}
```

The **const** versions are equivalent.

Requesting_element() and **Requesting_slice()** are concepts for a set of integers used for subscripting with a set of integers and subscripting by a slice, respectively (§29.4.5). They check that a sequence of access-function arguments are of suitable types for use as subscripts.

Subscripting with integers is defined like this:

```
template<typename T, size_t N>          // subscripting with integers
    template<typename... Args>
    Enable_if<Matrix_impl::Requesting_element<Args...>(),T&>
    Matrix<T,N>::operator()(Args... args)
    {
        assert(Matrix_impl::check_bounds(desc, args...));
        return *(data() + desc(args...));
    }
```

The **check_bounds()** predicate checks that the number of subscripts equals the number of dimensions and that the subscripts are within bounds:

```
template<size_t N, typename... Dims>
bool check_bounds(const Matrix_slice<N>& slice, Dims... dims)
{
    size_t indexes[N] {size_t(dims)...};
    return equal(indexes, indexes+N, slice.extents, less<size_t> {});
}
```

The actual location of the element in the **Matrix** is calculated by invoking the **Matrix**'s **Matrix_slice**'s generalized slice calculation presented as a function object: **desc(args...)**. Add that to the start of the data (**data()**) and we have our location:

```
return *(data() + desc(args...));
```

This leaves the most mysterious part of the declaration for last. The specification of **operator()()**'s return type looks like this:

```
Enable_if<Matrix_impl::Requesting_element<Args...>(),T&>
```

So the return type is **T&** provided that

```
Matrix_impl::Requesting_element<Args...>()
```

is **true** (§28.4). This predicate simply checks that every subscript can be converted to the required **size_t** by using a concept version of the standard-library predicate **is_convertible** (§35.4.1):

```
template<typename... Args>
constexpr bool Requesting_element()
{
    return All(Convertible<Args,size_t>()...);
}
```

All() simply applies its predicate to every element of a variadic template:

```
constexpr bool All() { return true; }

template<typename... Args>
constexpr bool All(bool b, Args... args)
{
    return b && All(args...);
}
```

The reason for using a predicate (Requesting_element) and the Enable_if() "hidden" within Request is to choose between the element and the slice subscript operators. The predicate used by the slice subscript operator looks like this:

```
template<typename... Args>
constexpr bool Requesting_slice()
{
        return All((Convertible<Args,size_t>() || Same<Args,slice>())...)
                    && Some(Same<Args,slice>()...);
}
```

That is, if there is at least one slice argument and if all arguments are either convertible to slice or size_t, we have something that can be used to describe a Matrix<T,N>:

```
template<typename T, size_t N>       // subscripting with slices
    template<typename... Args>
            Enable_if<Matrix_impl::Requesting_slice<Args...>(), Matrix_ref<T,N>>
    Matrix<T,N>::operator()(const Args&... args)
    {
            matrix_slice<N> d;
            d.start = matrix_impl::do_slice(desc,d,args...);
            return {d,data()};
    }
```

The slices represented as extents and strides in a Matrix_slice and used for slice subscripting are computed like this:

```
template<size_t N, typename T, typename... Args>
size_t do_slice(const Matrix_slice<N>& os, Matrix_slice<N>& ns, const T& s, const Args&... args)
{
        size_t m = do_slice_dim<sizeof...(Args)+1>(os,ns,s);
        size_t n = do_slice(os,ns,args...);
        return m+n;
}
```

As usual, the recursion is terminated by a simple function:

```
template<size_t N>
size_t do_slice(const Matrix_slice<N>& os, Matrix_slice<N>& ns)
{
        return 0;
}
```

The do_slice_dim() is a tricky bit of computation (to get the slice values right) but illustrates no new programming techniques.

29.4.6 Zero-Dimensional Matrix

The Matrix code contains a lot of occurrences of N−1 where N is the number of dimensions. Thus, N==0 could easily become a nasty special case (for the programming as well as for the mathematics). Here, we solve the problem by defining a specialization:

```
template<typename T>
class Matrix<T,0> {
public:
    static constexpr size_t order = 0;
    using value_type = T;

    Matrix(const T& x) : elem(x) { }
    Matrix& operator=(const T& value) { elem = value; return *this; }

    T& operator()() { return elem; }
    const T& operator()() const { return elem; }

    operator T&() { return elem; }
    operator const T&() { return elem; }
private:
    T elem;
};
```

Matrix<T,0> is not really a matrix. It stores a single element of type T and can only be converted to a reference to that type.

29.5 Solving Linear Equations

The code for a numerical computation makes sense if you understand the problem being solved and the math used to express the solution and tends to appear to be utter nonsense if you don't. The example used here should be rather trivial if you have learned basic linear algebra; if not, just see it as an example of transcribing a textbook solution into code with minimal rewording.

The example here is chosen to demonstrate a reasonably realistic and important use of Matrixes. We will solve a set (any set) of linear equations of this form:

$$a_{1,1}x_1 + \cdots + a_{1,n}x_n = b_1$$
$$\cdots$$
$$a_{n,1}x_1 + \cdots + a_{n,n}x_n = b_n$$

Here, the xs designate the n unknowns; as and bs are given constants. For simplicity, we assume that the unknowns and the constants are floating-point values. The goal is to find values for the unknowns that simultaneously satisfy the n equations. These equations can compactly be expressed in terms of a matrix and two vectors:

Ax =b

Here, A is the square n-by-n matrix defined by the coefficients:

$$\mathbf{A} = \begin{bmatrix} a_{1,1} & \cdots & a_{1,n} \\ \cdots & \cdots & \cdots \\ a_{n,1} & \cdots & a_{n,n} \end{bmatrix}$$

The vectors x and b are the vectors of unknowns and constants, respectively:

$$\mathbf{x} = \begin{bmatrix} x_1 \\ \cdots \\ x_n \end{bmatrix}, \text{ and } \mathbf{b} = \begin{bmatrix} b_1 \\ \cdots \\ b_n \end{bmatrix}$$

This system may have zero, one, or an infinite number of solutions, depending on the coefficients of the matrix **A** and the vector **b**. There are various methods for solving linear systems. We use a classic scheme, called Gaussian elimination [Freeman,1992], [Stewart,1998], [Wood,1999]. First, we transform **A** and **b** so that **A** is an upper-triangular matrix. By "upper-triangular," we mean all the coefficients below the diagonal of **A** are zero. In other words, the system looks like this:

$$\begin{bmatrix} a_{1,1} & \cdots & a_{1,n} \\ 0 & \cdots & \cdots \\ 0 & 0 & a_{n,n} \end{bmatrix} \begin{bmatrix} x_1 \\ \cdots \\ x_n \end{bmatrix} = \begin{bmatrix} b_1 \\ \cdots \\ b_n \end{bmatrix}$$

This is easily done. A zero for position **a(i,j)** is obtained by multiplying the equation for row **i** by a constant so that **a(i,j)** equals another element in column **j**, say **a(k,j)**. That done, we just subtract the two equations, and **a(i,j)==0** and the other values in row **i** change appropriately.

If we can get all the diagonal coefficients to be nonzero, then the system has a unique solution, which can be found by "back substitution." The last equation is easily solved:

$$a_{n,n} x_n = b_n$$

Obviously, **x[n]** is **b[n]/a(n,n)**. That done, eliminate row **n** from the system and proceed to find the value of **x[n−1]**, and so on, until the value for **x[1]** is computed. For each **n**, we divide by **a(n,n)** so the diagonal values must be nonzero. If that does not hold, the back substitution method fails, meaning that the system has zero or an infinite number of solutions.

29.5.1 Classical Gaussian Elimination

Now let us look at the C++ code to express this. First, we'll simplify our notation by convention-ally naming the two **Matrix** types that we are going to use:

```
using Mat2d = Matrix<double,2>;
using Vec = Matrix<double,1>;
```

Next, we will express our desired computation:

```
Vec classical_gaussian_elimination(Mat2d A, Vec b)
{
    classical_elimination(A, b);
    return back_substitution(A, b);
}
```

That is, we make copies of our inputs **A** and **b** (using call-by-value), call a function to solve the system, and then calculate the result to return by back substitution. The point is that our breakdown of the problem and our notation for the solution are right out of the textbook. To complete our solution, we have to implement **classical_elimination()** and **back_substitution()**. Again, the solution is in the textbook:

```
void classical_elimination(Mat2d& A, Vec& b)
{
    const size_t n = A.dim1();

    // traverse from 1st column to the next-to-last, filling zeros into all elements under the diagonal:
    for (size_t j = 0; j!=n–1; ++j) {
        const double pivot = A(j, j);
        if (pivot==0) throw Elim_failure(j);
        // fill zeros into each element under the diagonal of the ith row:
        for (size_t i = j+1; i!=n; ++i) {
            const double mult = A(i,j) / pivot;
            A[i](slice(j)) = scale_and_add(A[j](slice(j)), –mult,A[i](slice(j)));
            b(i) –= mult*b(j); // make the corresponding change to b
        }
    }
}
```

The *pivot* is the element that lies on the diagonal of the row we are currently dealing with. It must be nonzero because we need to divide by it; if it is zero, we give up by throwing an exception:

```
Vec back_substitution(const Mat2d& A, const Vec& b)
{
    const size_t n = A.dim1();
    Vec x(n);

    for (size_t i = n–1; i>=0; ––i) {
        double s = b(i)–dot_product(A[i](slice(i+1)),x(slice(i+1)));
        if (double m = A(i,i))
            x(i) = s/m;
        else
            throw Back_subst_failure(i);
    }
    return x;
}
```

29.5.2 Pivoting

We can avoid the divide-by-zero problem and also achieve a more robust solution by sorting the rows to get zeros and small values away from the diagonal. By "more robust" we mean less sensitive to rounding errors. However, the values change as we go along placing zeros under the diagonal, so we have to also reorder to get small values away from the diagonal (that is, we can't just reorder the matrix and then use the classical algorithm):

```
void elim_with_partial_pivot(Mat2d& A, Vec& b)
{
    const size_t n = A.dim1();

    for (size_t j = 0; j!=n; ++j) {
        size_t pivot_row = j;
```

```
// look for a suitable pivot:
    for (size_t k = j+1; k!=n; ++k)
        if (abs(A(k,j)) > abs(A(pivot_row,j)))
            pivot_row = k;

    // swap the rows if we found a better pivot:
    if (pivot_row!=j) {
        A.swap_rows(j,pivot_row);
        std::swap(b(j),b(pivot_row));
    }

    // elimination:
    for (size_t i = j+1; i!=n; ++i) {
        const double pivot = A(j,j);
        if (pivot==0) error("can't solve: pivot==0");
        const double mult = A(i,j)/pivot;
        A[i].slice(j) = scale_and_add(A[j].slice(j), –mult, A[i].slice(j));
        b(i) –= mult*b(j);
    }
    }
}
```

We use **swap_rows()** and **scale_and_multiply()** to make the code more conventional and to save us from writing an explicit loop.

29.5.3 Testing

Obviously, we have to test our code. Fortunately, there is a simple way to do that:

```
void solve_random_system(size_t n)
{
    Mat2d A = random_matrix(n);  // generate random Mat2d
    Vec b = random_vector(n);    // generate random Vec

    cout << "A = " << A << endl;
    cout << "b = " << b << endl;

    try {
        Vec x = classical_gaussian_elimination(A, b);
        cout << "classical elim solution is x = " << x << endl;
            Vec v = A * x;
        cout << " A * x = " << v << endl;
    }
    catch(const exception& e) {
        cerr << e.what() << endl;
    }
}
```

We can get to the **catch**-clause in three ways:

- A bug in the code (but, being optimists, we don't think there are any)
- An input that trips up classical_elimination() (using elim_with_partial_pivot() would minimize the chances of that)
- Rounding errors

However, our test is not as realistic as we'd like because genuinely random matrices are unlikely to cause problems for classical_elimination().

To verify our solution, we print out A∗x, which had better equal b (or close enough for our purpose, given rounding errors). The likelihood of rounding errors is the reason we didn't just do:

```
if (A∗x!=b) error("substitution failed");
```

Because floating-point numbers are just approximations to real numbers, we have to accept approximately correct answers. In general, using == and != on the result of a floating-point computation is best avoided: floating-point is inherently an approximation. Had I felt the need for a machine check, I would have defined an equal() function with a notion of which error ranges to consider acceptable and then written:

```
if (equal(A∗x,b)) error("substitution failed");
```

The random_matrix() and random_vector() are simple uses of random numbers and are left as simple exercises for the reader.

29.5.4 Fused Operations

In addition to providing efficient primitive operations, a general matrix class must handle three related problems to satisfy performance-conscious users:

[1] The number of temporaries must be minimized.
[2] Copying of matrices must be minimized.
[3] Multiple loops over the same data in composite operations must be minimized.

Consider U=M∗V+W, where U, V, and W are vectors (Matrix<T,1>) and M is a Matrix<T,2>. A naive implementation introduces temporary vectors for M∗V and M∗V+W and copies the results of M∗V and M∗V+W. A smart implementation calls a function mul_add_and_assign(&U,&M,&V,&W) that introduces no temporaries, copies no vectors, and touches each element of the matrices the minimum number of times.

The move constructor helps: the temporary used for M∗V is used for (M∗V)+W. If we had written

```
Matrix<double,1> U=M∗V+W;
```

we would have eliminated all element copies: the elements allocated in the local variable in M∗V are the ones ending up in U.

That leaves the problem of merging the loops: *loop fusion*. This degree of optimization is rarely necessary for more than a few kinds of expressions, so a simple solution to efficiency problems is to provide functions such as mul_add_and_assign() and let the user call those where it matters. However, it is possible to design a Matrix so that such optimizations are applied automatically for expressions of the right form. That is, we can treat U=M∗V+W as a use of a single operator with four operands. The basic technique was demonstrated for ostream manipulators (§38.4.5.2). In general, it can be used to make a combination of n binary operators act like an (n+1)-ary operator. Handling U=M∗V+W requires the introduction of two auxiliary classes. However, the technique can result in impressive speedups (say, 30 times) on some systems by enabling more powerful optimization techniques. First, for simplicity, let us restrict ourselves to two-dimensional matrices of double-precision floating-point numbers:

```
using Mat2d = Matrix<double,2>;
using Vec = Matrix<double,1>;
```

We define the result of multiplying a Mat2d by a Vec:

```
struct MVmul {
    const Mat2d& m;
    const Vec& v;

    MVmul(const Mat2d& mm, const Vec &vv) :m{mm}, v{vv} { }

    operator Vec(); // evaluate and return result
};

inline MVmul operator*(const Mat2d& mm, const Vec& vv)
{
    return MVmul(mm,vv);
}
```

This "multiplication" should replace the one from §29.3 and does nothing except store references to its operands; the evaluation of M*V is deferred. The object produced by * is closely related to what is called a *closure* in many technical communities. Similarly, we can deal with what happens if we add a Vec:

```
struct MVmulVadd {
    const Mat2d& m;
    const Vec& v;
    const Vec& v2;

    MVmulVadd(const MVmul& mv, const Vec& vv) :m(mv.m), v(mv.v), v2(vv) { }

    operator Vec(); // evaluate and return result
};

inline MVmulVadd operator+(const MVmul& mv, const Vec& vv)
{
    return MVmulVadd(mv,vv);
}
```

This defers the evaluation of M*V+W. We now have to ensure that it all gets evaluated using a good algorithm when it is assigned to a Vec:

```
template<>
class Matrix<double,1> {        // specialization (just for this example)
    // ...
```

```
    public:
        Matrix(const MVmulVadd& m)                    // initialize by result of m
        {
            // allocate elements, etc.
            mul_add_and_assign(this,&m.m,&m.v,&m.v2);
        }


        Matrix& operator=(const MVmulVadd& m)         // assign the result of m to *this
        {
            mul_add_and_assign(this,&m.m,&m.v,&m.v2);
            return *this;
        }
        // ...
};
```

Now **U=M∗V+W** is automatically expanded to

> **U.operator=(MVmulVadd(MVmul(M,V),W))**

which because of inlining resolves to the desired simple call

> **mul_add_and_assign(&U,&M,&V,&W)**

Clearly, this eliminates the copying and the temporaries. In addition, we might write **mul_add_and_assign()** in an optimized fashion. However, if we just wrote it in a fairly simple and unoptimized fashion, it would still be in a form that offered great opportunities to an optimizer.

The importance of this technique is that most really time-critical vector and matrix computations are done using a few relatively simple syntactic forms. Typically, there is no real gain in optimizing expressions of half a dozen operators. For that we typically want to write a function anyway.

This technique is based on the idea of using compile-time analysis and closure objects to transfer evaluation of a subexpression into an object representing a composite operation. It can be applied to a variety of problems with the common attribute that several pieces of information need to be gathered into one function before evaluation can take place. I refer to the objects generated to defer evaluation as *composition closure objects*, or simply *compositors*.

If this composition technique is used to delay execution of all operations, it is referred to as *expression templates* [Vandevoorde,2002] [Veldhuizen,1995]. Expression templates systematically use function objects to represent expressions as abstract syntax trees (ASTs).

29.6 Advice

[1] List basic use cases; §29.1.1.
[2] Always provide input and output operations to simplify simple testing (e.g., unit testing); §29.1.1.
[3] Carefully list the properties a program, class, or library ideally should have; §29.1.2.
[4] List the properties of a program, class, or library that are considered beyond the scope of the project; §29.1.2.

[5]   When designing a container template, carefully consider the requirements on the element type; §29.1.2.

[6]   Consider how the design might accommodate run-time checking (e.g., for debugging); §29.1.2.

[7]   If possible, design a class to mimic existing professional notation and semantics; §29.1.2.

[8]   Make sure that the design does not leak resources (e.g., have a unique owner for each resource and use RAII); §29.2.

[9]   Consider how a class can be constructed and copied; §29.1.1.

[10]   Provide complete, flexible, efficient, and semantically meaningful access to elements; §29.2.2, §29.3.

[11]   Place implementation details in their own _impl namespace; §29.4.

[12]   Provide common operations that do not require direct access to the representation as helper functions; §29.3.2, §29.3.3.

[13]   For fast access, keep data compact and use accessor objects to provide necessary nontrivial access operations; §29.4.1,§29.4.2, §29.4.3.

[14]   The structure of data can often be expressed as nested initializer lists; §29.4.4.

[15]   When dealing with numbers, aways consider "end cases," such as zero and "many"; §29.4.6.

[16]   In addition to unit testing and testing that the code meets its requirements, test the design through examples of real use; §29.5.

[17]   Consider how the design might accommodate unusually stringent performance requirements; §29.5.4

Part IV

The Standard Library

This part describes the C++ standard library. The aim is to provide an understanding of how to use the library, to demonstrate generally useful design and programming techniques, and to show how to extend the library in the ways in which it was intended to be extended.

Chapters

"... I am just now beginning to discover the difficulty of expressing one's ideas on paper. As long as it consists solely of description it is pretty easy; but where reasoning comes into play, to make a proper connection, a clearness & a moderate fluency, is to me, as I have said, a difficulty of which I had no idea ..."

– Charles Darwin

Standard-Library Overview

Many secrets of art and nature
are thought by the unlearned to be magical.
– Roger Bacon

- Introduction
      Standard-Library Facilities; Design Constraints; Description Style
- Headers
- Language Support
      initializer_list Support; Range-for Support
- Error Handling
      Exceptions; Assertions; system_error
- Advice

30.1 Introduction

The standard library is the set of components specified by the ISO C++ standard and shipped with identical behavior (modulo performance) by every C++ implementation. For portability and long-term maintainability, I strongly recommend using the standard library whenever feasible. Maybe you can design and implement a better alternative for your application, but:

- How easy will it be for some future maintainer to learn that alternative design?
- How likely is the alternative to be available on a yet unknown platform ten years from now?
- How likely is the alternative to be useful for future applications?
- How likely is it that your alternative will be interoperable with code written using the standard library?
- How likely is it that you can spend as much effort optimizing and testing your alternative as was done for the standard library?

And, of course, if you use an alternative, you (or your organization) will be responsible for the maintenance and evolution of the alternative "forever." In general: try not to reinvent the wheel.

The standard library is rather large: its specification in the ISO C++ standard is 785 dense pages. And that is without describing the ISO C standard library, which is a part of the C++ standard library (another 139 pages). To compare, the C++ language specification is 398 pages. Here, I summarize, relying heavily on tables, and give a few examples. Details can be found elsewhere, including online copies of the standard, complete online documentation of implementations, and (if you like to read code) open source implementations. Rely on the references to the standard for complete details.

The standard-library chapters are not intended to be read in their order of presentation. Each chapter and typically each major subsection can be read in isolation. Rely on cross-references and the index if you encounter something unknown.

30.1.1 Standard-Library Facilities

What ought to be in the standard C++ library? One ideal is for a programmer to be able to find every interesting, significant, and reasonably general class, function, template, etc., in a library. However, the question here is not "What ought to be in *some* library?" but "What ought to be in the *standard* library?" "Everything!" is a reasonable first approximation to an answer to the former question but not to the latter. A standard library is something that every implementer must supply so that every programmer can rely on it.

The C++ standard library provides:

- Support for language features, such as memory management (§11.2), the range-**for** statement (§9.5.1), and run-time type information (§22.2).
- Information about implementation-defined aspects of the language, such as the largest finite **float** value (§40.2).
- Primitive operations that cannot be easily or efficiently implemented in the language itself, such as **is_polymorphic**, **is_scalar**, and **is_nothrow_constructible** (§35.4.1).
- Facilities for low-level ("lock-free") concurrent programming (§41.3).
- Support for thread-based concurrency (§5.3, §42.2).
- Minimal support for task-based concurrency, such as **future** and **async()** (§42.4).
- Functions that most programmers cannot easily implement optimally and portably, such as **uninitialized_fill()** (§32.5) and **memmove()** (§43.5).
- Minimal support for (optional) reclamation of unused memory (garbage collection), such as **declare_reachable()** (§34.5).
- Nonprimitive foundational facilities that a programmer can rely on for portability, such as **lists** (§31.4), **maps** (§31.4.3), **sort()** (§32.6), and I/O streams (Chapter 38).
- Frameworks for extending the facilities it provides, such as conventions and support facilities that allow a user to provide I/O of a user-defined type in the style of I/O for built-in types (Chapter 38) and the STL (Chapter 31).

A few facilities are provided by the standard library simply because it is conventional and useful to do so. Examples are the standard mathematical functions, such as **sqrt()** (§40.3), random number generators (§40.7), **complex** arithmetic (§40.4), and regular expressions (Chapter 37).

The standard library aims to be the common foundation for other libraries. In particular, combinations of its facilities allow the standard library to play three supporting roles:

- A foundation for portability
- A set of compact and efficient components that can be used as the foundation for performance-sensitive libraries and applications
- A set of components enabling intra-library communications

The design of the library is primarily determined by these three roles. These roles are closely related. For example, portability is commonly an important design criterion for a specialized library, and common container types such as lists and maps are essential for convenient communication between separately developed libraries.

The last role is especially important from a design perspective because it helps limit the scope of the standard library and places constraints on its facilities. For example, string and list facilities are provided in the standard library. If they were not, separately developed libraries could communicate only by using built-in types. However, advanced linear algebra and graphics facilities are not provided. Such facilities are obviously widely useful, but they are rarely directly involved in communication between separately developed libraries.

Unless a facility is somehow needed to support these roles, it can be left to some library outside the standard. For good and bad, leaving something out of the standard library opens the opportunity for different libraries to offer competing realizations of an idea. Once a library proves itself widely useful in a variety of computing environments and application domains, it becomes a candidate for the standard library. The regular expression library (Chapter 37) is an example of this.

A reduced standard library is available for freestanding implementations, that is, implementations running with minimal or no operating system support (§6.1.1).

30.1.2 Design Constraints

The roles of a standard library impose several constraints on its design. The facilities offered by the C++ standard library are designed to be:

- Valuable and affordable to essentially every student and professional programmer, including the builders of other libraries.
- Used directly or indirectly by every programmer for everything within the library's scope.
- Efficient enough to provide genuine alternatives to hand-coded functions, classes, and templates in the implementation of further libraries.
- Either policy free or with an option to supply policies as arguments.
- Primitive in the mathematical sense. That is, a component that serves two weakly related roles will almost certainly suffer overhead compared to individual components designed to perform only a single role.
- Convenient, efficient, and reasonably safe for common uses.
- Complete in what they do. The standard library may leave major functions to other libraries, but if it takes on a task, it must provide enough functionality so that individual users or implementers need not replace it to get the basic job done.
- Easy to use with built-in types and operations.
- Type safe by default, and therefore in principle checkable at run time.
- Supportive of commonly accepted programming styles.
- Extensible to deal with user-defined types in ways similar to the way built-in types and standard-library types are handled.

For example, building the comparison criteria into a sort function is unacceptable because the same data can be sorted according to different criteria. This is why the C standard-library **qsort()** takes a comparison function as an argument rather than relying on something fixed, say, the < operator (§12.5). On the other hand, the overhead imposed by a function call for each comparison compromises **qsort()** as a building block for further library building. For almost every data type, it is easy to do a comparison without imposing the overhead of a function call.

Is that overhead serious? In most cases, probably not. However, the function call overhead can dominate the execution time for some algorithms and cause users to seek alternatives. The technique described in §25.2.3 of supplying comparison criteria through a template argument solves that problem for **sort()** and many other standard-library algorithms. The sort example illustrates the tension between efficiency and generality. It is also an example of how such tensions can be resolved. A standard library is not merely required to perform its tasks. It must also perform them so efficiently that users are not tempted to supply their own alternatives to what the standard offers. Otherwise, implementers of more advanced features are forced to bypass the standard library in order to remain competitive. This would add a burden to the library developer and seriously complicate the lives of users wanting to stay platform-independent or to use several separately developed libraries.

The requirements of "primitiveness" and "convenience of common uses" can conflict. The former requirement precludes exclusively optimizing the standard library for common cases. However, components serving common, but nonprimitive, needs can be included in the standard library in addition to the primitive facilities, rather than as replacements. The cult of orthogonality must not prevent us from making life convenient for the novice and the casual user. Nor should it cause us to leave the default behavior of a component obscure or dangerous.

30.1.3 Description Style

A full description of even a simple standard-library operation, such as a constructor or an algorithm, can take pages. Consequently, I use an extremely abbreviated style of presentation. Sets of related operations are typically presented in tables:

Some Operations	
p=op(b,e,x)	op does something to the range [b:e) and x, returning p
foo(x)	foo does something to x but returns no result
bar(b,e,x)	Does x have something to do with [b:e)?

I try to be mnemonic when choosing identifiers, so **b** and **e** will be iterators specifying a range, **p** a pointer or an iterator, and **x** some value, all depending on context. In this notation, only the commentary distinguishes no result from a Boolean result, so you can confuse those if you try hard enough. For an operation returning a Boolean, the explanation usually ends with a question mark. Where an algorithm follows the usual pattern of returning the end of an input sequence to indicate "failure," "not found," etc. (§4.5.1, §33.1.1), I do not mention that explicitly.

Usually, such an abbreviated description is accompanied with a reference to the ISO C++ standard, some further explanation, and examples.

30.2 Headers

The facilities of the standard library are defined in the **std** namespace and presented as a set of headers. The headers identify the major parts of the library. Thus, listing them gives an overview of the library.

The rest of this subsection is a list of headers grouped by function, accompanied by brief explanations and annotated by references to where they are discussed. The grouping is chosen to match the organization of the standard.

A standard header with a name starting with the letter **c** is equivalent to a header in the C standard library. For every header **<X.h>** defining part of the C standard library in the global namespace and also in namespace **std**, there is a header **<cX>** defining the same names. Ideally, the names from a **<cX>** header do not pollute the global namespace (§15.2.4), but unfortunately (due to complexities of maintaining multilanguage, multi-operating-system environments) most do.

Containers		
<vector>	One-dimensional resizable array	§31.4.2
<deque>	Double-ended queue	§31.4.2
<forward_list>	Singly-linked list	§31.4.2
<list>	Doubly-linked list	§31.4.2
<map>	Associative array	§31.4.3
<set>	Set	§31.4.3
<unordered_map>	Hashed associative array	§31.4.3.2
<unordered_set>	Hashed set	§31.4.3.2
<queue>	Queue	§31.5.2
<stack>	Stack	§31.5.1
<array>	One-dimensional fixed-size array	§34.2.1
<bitset>	Array of **bool**	§34.2.2

The associative containers **multimap** and **multiset** can be found in **<map>** and **<set>**, respectively. The **priority_queue** (§31.5.3) is declared in **<queue>**.

General Utilities		
<utility>	Operators and pairs	§35.5, §34.2.4.1
<tuple>	Tuples	§34.2.4.2
<type_traits>	Type traits	§35.4.1
<typeindex>	Use a **type_info** as a key or a hash code	§35.5.4
<functional>	Function objects	§33.4
<memory>	Resource management pointers	§34.3
<scoped_allocator>	Scoped allocators	§34.4.4
<ratio>	Compile-time rational arithmetic	§35.3
<chrono>	Time utilities	§35.2
<ctime>	C-style date and time	§43.6
<iterator>	Iterators and iterator support	§33.1

Iterators provide the mechanism to make standard algorithms generic (§3.4.2, §33.1.4).

Algorithms		
<algorithm>	General algorithms	§32.2
<cstdlib>	bsearch(), qsort()	§43.7

A typical general algorithm can be applied to any sequence (§3.4.2, §32.2) of any type of element. The C standard library functions **bsearch()** and **qsort()** apply to built-in arrays with elements of types without user-defined copy constructors and destructors only (§12.5).

Diagnostics		
<exception>	Exception class	§30.4.1.1
<stdexcept>	Standard exceptions	§30.4.1.1
<cassert>	Assert macro	§30.4.2
<cerrno>	C-style error handling	§13.1.2
<system_error>	System error support	§30.4.3

Assertions using exceptions are described in §13.4.

Strings and Characters		
<string>	String of **T**	Chapter 36
<cctype>	Character classification	§36.2.1
<cwctype>	Wide-character classification	§36.2.1
<cstring>	C-style string functions	§43.4
<cwchar>	C-style wide-character string functions	§36.2.1
<cstdlib>	C-style allocation functions	§43.5
<cuchar>	C-style multibyte characters	
<regex>	Regular expression matching	Chapter 37

The <cstring> header declares the **strlen()**, **strcpy()**, etc., family of functions. The <cstdlib> declares **atof()** and **atoi()** which convert C-style strings to numeric values.

Input/Output		
<iosfwd>	Forward declarations of I/O facilities	§38.1
<iostream>	Standard **iostream** objects and operations	§38.1
<ios>	iostream bases	§38.4.4
<streambuf>	Stream buffers	§38.6
<istream>	Input stream template	§38.4.1
<ostream>	Output stream template	§38.4.2
<iomanip>	Manipulators	§38.4.5.2
<sstream>	Streams to/from strings	§38.2.2
<cctype>	Character classification functions	§36.2.1
<fstream>	Streams to/from files	§38.2.1
<cstdio>	printf() family of I/O	§43.3
<cwchar>	printf()-style I/O of wide characters	§43.3

Manipulators are objects used to manipulate the state of a stream (§38.4.5.2).

Localization		
<locale>	Represent cultural differences	Chapter 39
<clocale>	Represent cultural differences C-style	
<codecvt>	Code conversion facets	§39.4.6

A **locale** localizes differences such as the output format for dates, the symbol used to represent currency, and string collation criteria that vary among different natural languages and cultures.

Language Support		
<limits>	Numeric limits	§40.2
<climits>	C-style numeric scalar-limit macros	§40.2
<cfloat>	C-style numeric floating-point limit macros	§40.2
<cstdint>	Standard integer type names	§43.7
<new>	Dynamic memory management	§11.2.3
<typeinfo>	Run-time type identification support	§22.5
<exception>	Exception-handling support	§30.4.1.1
<initializer_list>	initializer_list	§30.3.1
<cstddef>	C library language support	§10.3.1
<cstdarg>	Variable-length function argument lists	§12.2.4
<csetjmp>	C-style stack unwinding	
<cstdlib>	Program termination	§15.4.3
<ctime>	System clock	§43.6
<csignal>	C-style signal handling	

The <cstddef> header defines the type of values returned by **sizeof()**, **size_t**, the type of the result of pointer subtraction and of array subscripts, **ptrdiff_t** (§10.3.1), and the infamous **NULL** macro (§7.2.2).

C-style stack unwinding (using **setjmp** and **longjmp** from <csetjmp>) is incompatible with the use of destructors and with exception handling (Chapter 13, §30.4) and is best avoided. C-style stack unwinding and signals are not discussed in this book.

Numerics		
<complex>	Complex numbers and operations	§40.4
<valarray>	Numeric vectors and operations	§40.5
<numeric>	Generalized numeric operations	§40.6
<cmath>	Standard mathematical functions	§40.3
<cstdlib>	C-style random numbers	§40.7
<random>	Random number generators	§40.7

For historical reasons, **abs()** and **div()** are found in <cstdlib> rather than in <cmath> with the rest of the mathematical functions (§40.3).

Concurrency		
<atomic>	Atomic types and operations	§41.3
<condition_variable>	Waiting for an action	§42.3.4
<future>	Asynchronous task	§42.4.4
<mutex>	Mutual exclusion classes	§42.3.1
<thread>	Threads	§42.2

C provides standard-library facilities of varying relevance to C++ programmers. The C++ standard library provides access to all such facilities:

C Compatibility		
<cinttypes>	Aliases for common integer types	§43.7
<cstdbool>	C bool	
<ccomplex>	<complex>	
<cfenv>	Floating-point environment	
<cstdalign>	C alignment	
<ctgmath>	C "type generic math": <complex> and <cmath>	

The <cstdbool> header will not define macros **bool**, **true**, or **false**. The <cstdalign> header will not define a macro **alignas**. The **.h** equivalents to <cstdbool>, <ccomplex>, <calign>, and <ctgmath> approximate C++ facilities for C. Avoid them if you can.

The <cfenv> header provides types (such as **fenv_t** and **fexcept_t**), floating-point status flags, and control modes describing an implementation's floating-point environment.

A user or a library implementer is not allowed to add or subtract declarations from the standard headers. Nor is it acceptable to try to change the contents of a header by defining macros to change the meaning of declarations in a header (§15.2.3). Any program or implementation that plays such games does not conform to the standard, and programs that rely on such tricks are not portable. Even if they work today, the next release of any part of an implementation may break them. Avoid such trickery.

For a standard-library facility to be used, its header must be included. Writing out the relevant declarations yourself is *not* a standards-conforming alternative. The reason is that some implementations optimize compilation based on standard header inclusion, and others provide optimized implementations of standard-library facilities triggered by the headers. In general, implementers use standard headers in ways programmers cannot predict and shouldn't have to know about.

A programmer can, however, specialize utility templates, such as **swap()** (§35.5.2), for non-standard-library, user-defined types.

30.3 Language Support

A small but essential part of the standard library is language support, that is, facilities that must be present for a program to run because language features depend on them.

Library Supported Language Features		
<new>	new and delete	§11.2
<typeinfo>	typeid() and type_info	§22.5
<iterator>	Range-for	§30.3.2
<initializer_list>	initializer_list	§30.3.1

30.3.1 initializer_list Support

A {}-list is converted into an object of type **std::initializer_list<X>** according to the rules described in §11.3. In **<initializer_list>**, we find **initializer_list**:

```
template<typename T>
class initializer_list {      // §iso.18.9
public:
    using value_type = T;
    using reference = const T&;          // note const: initializer_list elements are immutable
    using const_reference = const T&;
    using size_type = size_t;
    using iterator = const T*;
    using const_iterator = const T*;

    initializer_list() noexcept;

    size_t size() const noexcept;        // number of elements
    const T* begin() const noexcept;     // first element
    const T* end() const noexcept;       // one-past-last element
};

template<typename T>
    const T* begin(initializer_list<T> lst) noexcept { return lst.begin(); }
template<typename T>
    const T* end(initializer_list<T> lst) noexcept { return lst.end(); }
```

Unfortunately, **initializer_list** does not offer a subscript operator. If you want to use [] rather than *, subscript a pointer:

```
void f(initializer_list<int> lst)
{
    for(int i=0; i<lst.size(); ++i)
        cout << lst[i] << '\n';         // error

    const int* p = lst.begin();
    for(int i=0; i<lst.size(); ++i)
        cout << p[i] << '\n';           // OK
}
```

Naturally, an **initializer_list** can also be used by a range-**for**. For example:

```
void f2(initializer_list<int> lst)
{
        for (auto x : lst)
                cout << x << '\n';
}
```

30.3.2 Range-for Support

A range-for statement is mapped to a for-statement using an iterator as described in §9.5.1.

In <iterator>, the standard library provides std::begin() and std::end() functions for built-in arrays and for every type that provides member begin() and end(); see §33.3.

All standard-library containers (e.g., vector and unordered_map) and strings support iteration using range-for; container adaptors (such as stack and priority_queue) do not. The container headers, such as <vector>, include<initializer_list>, so the user rarely has to do so directly.

30.4 Error Handling

The standard library consists of components developed over a period of almost 40 years. Thus, their style and approaches to error handling are not consistent:

- C-style libraries consist of functions, many of which set errno to indicate that an error happened; see §13.1.2 and §40.3.
- Many algorithms operating on a sequence of elements return an iterator to the one-past-the-last element to indicate "not found" or "failure"; see §33.1.1.
- The I/O streams library relies on a state in each stream to reflect errors and may (if the user requests it) throw exceptions to indicate errors; see §38.3.
- Some standard-library components, such as vector, string, and bitset, throw exceptions to indicate errors.

The standard library is designed so that all facilities obey "the basic guarantee" (§13.2); that is, even if an exception is thrown, no resource (such as memory) is leaked and no invariant for a standard-library class is broken.

30.4.1 Exceptions

Some standard-library facilities report errors by throwing exceptions:

Standard-Library Exceptions (continues)	
bitset	Throws invalid_argument, out_of_range, overflow_error
iostream	Throws ios_base::failure if exceptions are enabled
regex	Throws regex_error
string	Throws length_error, out_of_range
vector	Throws out_of_range

Standard-Library Exceptions (continued)	
new T	Throws **bad_alloc** if it cannot allocate memory for a **T**
dynamic_cast<T>(r)	Throws **bad_cast** if it cannot convert the reference r to a **T**
typeid()	Throws **bad_typeid** if it cannot deliver a **type_info**
thread	Throws **system_error**
call_once()	Throws **system_error**
mutex	Throws **system_error**
condition_variable	Throws **system_error**
async()	Throws **system_error**
packaged_task	Throws **system_error**
future and promise	Throws **future_error**

These exceptions may be encountered in any code that directly or indirectly uses these facilities. In addition, any operation that manipulates an object that may throw an exception must be assumed to throw (that exception) unless care has been taken to avoid that. For example, a **packaged_task** will throw an exception if the function it is required to execute throws.

Unless you know that no facility is used in a way that could throw an exception, it is a good idea to always catch one of the root classes of the standard-library exception hierarchy (such as **exception**) as well as any exception (...) somewhere (§13.5.2.3), for example, in **main()**.

30.4.1.1 The Standard exception Hierarchy

Do not throw built-in types, such as **int** and C-style strings. Instead, throw objects of types specifically defined to be used as exceptions.

This hierarchy of standard exception classes provides a classification of exceptions:

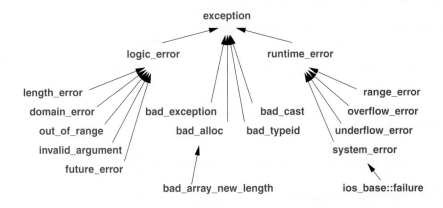

This hierarchy attempts to provide a framework for exceptions beyond the ones defined by the standard library. Logic errors are errors that in principle could be caught either before the program starts executing or by tests of arguments to functions and constructors. Run-time errors are all other errors. The **system_error** is described in §30.4.3.3.

The standard-library exception hierarchy is rooted in class **exception**:

```
class exception {
public:
    exception();
    exception(const exception&);
    exception& operator=(const exception&);
    virtual ˜exception();
    virtual const char∗ what() const;
};
```

The **what()** function can be used to obtain a string that is supposed to indicate something about the error that caused the exception.

A programmer can define an exception by deriving from a standard-library exception like this:

```
struct My_error : runtime_error {
    My_error(int x) :runtime_error{"My_error"}, interesting_value{x} { }
    int interesting_value;
};
```

Not all exceptions are part of the standard-library **exception** hierarchy. However, all exceptions thrown by the standard library are from the **exception** hierarchy.

Unless you know that no facility is used in a way that could throw an exception, it is a good idea to somewhere catch all exceptions. For example:

```
int main()
try {
    // ...
}
catch (My_error& me) {        // a My_error happened
    // we can use me.interesting_value and me.what()
}
catch (runtime_error& re) {    // a runtine_error happened
    // we can use re.what()
}
catch (exception& e) {        // some standard-library exception happened
    // we can use e.what()
}
catch (...) {                 // Some unmentioned exception happened
    // we can do local cleanup
}
```

As for function arguments, we use references to avoid slicing (§17.5.1.4).

30.4.1.2 Exception Propagation

In **<exception>**, the standard library provides facilities for making propagation of exceptions accessible to programmers:

Exception Propagation (§iso.18.8.5)	
exception_ptr	Unspecified type used to point to exceptions
ep=current_exception()	ep is an exception_ptr to the current exception, or to no exception if there is no currently active exception; noexcept
rethrow_exception(ep)	Re-throw the exception pointed to by ep; ep's contained pointer must not be nullptr; noreturn (§12.1.7)
ep=make_exception_ptr(e)	ep is an exception_ptr to exception e; noexcept

An exception_ptr can point to any exception, not just exceptions from the exception hierarchy. Think of exception_ptr as a smart pointer (like shared_ptr) that keeps its exception alive for as long as an exception_ptr points to it. That way, we can pass an exception_pointer to an exception out of a function that caught it and re-throw elsewhere. In particular, an exception_ptr can be used to implement a re-throw of an exception in a different thread from the one in which the exception was caught. This is what promise and future (§42.4) rely on. Use of rethrow_exception() on an exception_ptr (from different threads) does not introduce a data race.

The make_exception_ptr() could be implemented as:

```
template<typename E>
exception_ptr make_exception_ptr(E e) noexcept;
try {
    throw e;
}
catch(...) {
    return current_exception();
}
```

A nested_exception is class that stores an exception_ptr obtained from a call of current_exception():

nested_exception (§iso.18.8.6)	
nested_exception ne {};	Default constructor: ne holds an exception_ptr to the current_exception(); noexcept
nested_exception ne {ne2};	Copy constructor: both ne and ne2 hold an exception_ptr to the stored exception
ne2=ne	Copy assignment: both ne and ne2 hold an exception_ptr to the stored exception
ne.˜nested_exception()	Destructor; virtual
ne.rethrow_nested()	Rethrow ne's stored exception; terminate() if no exception is stored in ne; noreturn
ep=ne.nested_ptr()	ep is an exception_ptr pointing to ne's stored exception; noexcept
throw_with_nested(e)	Throw an exception of type derived from nested_exception and e's type; e must not be derived from nested_exception; noreturn
rethrow_if_nested(e)	dynamic_cast<const nested_exception&>(e).rethrow_nested(); e's type must be derived from nested_exception

The intended use of **nested_exception** is as a base class for a class used by an exception handler to pass some information about the local context of an error together with a **exception_ptr** to the exception that caused it to be called. For example:

```
struct My_error : runtime_error {
    My_error(const string&);
    // ...
};

void my_code()
{
    try {
        // ...
    }
    catch (...) {
        My_error err {"something went wrong in my_code()"};
        // ...
        throw_with_nested(err);
    }
}
```

Now **My_error** information is passed along (rethrown) together with a **nested_exception** holding an **exception_ptr** to the exception caught.

Further up the call chain, we might want to look at the nested exception:

```
void user()
{
    try {
        my_code();
    }
    catch(My_error& err) {

    // ... clear up My_error problems ...

        try {
            rethrow_if_nested(err);   // re-throw the nested exception, if any
        }
        catch (Some_error& err2) {
            // ... clear up Some_error problems ...
        }
    }
}
```

This assumes that we know that **some_error** might be nested with **My_error**.

An exception cannot propagate out of a **noexcept** function (§13.5.1.1).

30.4.1.3 terminate()

In **<exception>**, the standard library provides facilities for dealing with unexpected exceptions:

terminate (§iso.18.8.3, §iso.18.8.4)	
h=get_terminate()	h is the current terminate handler; noexcept
h2=set_terminate(h)	h becomes the current terminate handler;
	h2 is the previous terminate handler; noexcept
terminate()	Terminate the program; noreturn; noexcept
uncaught_exception()	Has an exception been thrown on the current thread
	and not yet been caught? noexcept

Avoid using these functions, except very occasionally **set_terminate()** and **terminate()**. A call of **terminate()** terminates a program by calling a terminate handler set by a call of **set_terminate()**. The – almost always correct – default is to immediately terminate the program. For fundamental operating system reasons, it is implementation-defined whether destructors for local objects are invoked when **terminate()** is called. If **terminate()** is invoked as the result of a **noexcept** violation, the system is allowed (important) optimizations that imply that the stack may even be partially unwound (§iso.15.5.1).

It is sometimes claimed that **uncaught_exception()** can be useful for writing destructors that behave differently depending on whether a function is exited normally or by an exception. However, **uncaught_exception()** is also true during stack unwinding (§13.5.1) after the initial exception has been caught. I consider **uncaught_exception()** too subtle for practical use.

30.4.2 Assertions

The standard provides:

Assertions (§iso.7)	
static_assert(e,s)	Evaluate e at compile time; give s as a compiler error message if !e
assert(e)	If the macro **NDBUG** is not defined, evaluate e at run time
	and if !e, write a message to **cerr** and **abort()**; if **NDBUG** is defined, do nothing

For example:

```
template<typename T>
void draw_all(vector<T*>& v)
{
    static_assert(Is_base_of<Shape,T>(),"non-Shape type for draw_all()");

    for (auto p : v) {
        assert(p!=nullptr);
        // ...
    }
}
```

The **assert()** is a macro found in **<cassert>**. The error message produced by **assert()** is implementation-defined but should contain the source file name (**__FILE__**), and the source line number (**__LINE__**) containing the **assert()**.

Asserts are (as they should be) used more frequently in production code than in small illustrative textbook examples.

The name of the function (__func__) may also be included in the message. It can be a serious mistake to assume that the **assert()** is evaluated when it is not. For example, given a usual compiler setup, **assert(p!=nullptr)** will catch an error during debugging, but not in the final shipped product.

For a way to manage assertions, see §13.4.

30.4.3 system_error

In **<system_error>**, the standard library provides a framework for reporting errors from the operating system and lower-level system components. For example, we may write a function to check a file name and then open a file like this:

```
ostream& open_file(const string& path)
{
    auto dn = split_into_directory_and_name(path);        // split into {path,name}

    error_code err {does_directory_exist(dn.first)};      // ask "the system" about the path
    if (err) {    // err!=0 means error

        // ... see if anything can be done ...

        if (cannot_handle_err)
            throw system_error(err);
    }

    // ...
    return ofstream{path};
}
```

Assuming that "the system" doesn't know about C++ exceptions, we have no choice about whether to deal with error codes or not; the only questions are "where?" and "how?" In **<system_error>**, the standard library provides facilities for classifying error codes, for mapping system-specific error codes into more portable ones, and for mapping error codes into exceptions:

System Error Types	
error_code	Holds a value identifying an error and the category of that error; system-specific (§30.4.3.1)
error_category	A base class for types used to identify the source and encoding of a particular kind (category) of error code (§30.4.3.2)
system_error	A runtime_error exception containing an error_code (§30.4.3.3)
error_condition	Holds a value identifying an error and the category of that error; potentially portable (§30.4.3.4)
errc	enum class with enumerators for error codes from <cerrno> (§40.3); basically POSIX error codes
future_errc	enum class with enumerators for error codes from <future> (§42.4.4)
io_errc	enum class with enumerators for error codes from <ios> (§38.4.4)

30.4.3.1 Error Codes

When an error "bubbles up" from a lower level as an error code, we must handle the error it represents or turn it into an exception. But first we must classify it: different systems use different error codes for the same problem, and different systems simply have different kinds of errors.

error_code (§iso.19.5.2)	
error_code ec {};	Default constructor: ec={0,&generic_category}; noexcept
error_code ec {n,cat};	ec={n,cat}; cat is an error_category
	and n is an int representing an error in cat; noexcept
error_code ec {n};	ec={n,&generic_category};
	n represents an error; n is a value of type EE for which
	is_error_code_enum<EE>::value==true; noexcept
ec.assign(n,cat)	ec={n,cat}; cat is an error_category;
	n represents an error; n is a value of type EE for which
	is_error_code_enum<EE>::value==true; noexcept
ec=n	ec={n,&generic_category}: ec=make_error_code(n);
	n represets an error; n is a value of type EE for which
	is_error_code_enum<EE>::value==true; noexcept
ec.clear()	ec={0,&generic_category()}; noexcept
n=ec.value()	n is ec's stored value; noexcept
cat=ec.category()	cat is a reference to ec's stored category; noexcept
s=ec.message()	s is a string representing ec potentially used as
	an error message: ec.category().message(ec.value())
bool b {ec};	Convert ec to bool; b is true if ec represents
	an error; that is, b==false means "no error"; explicit
ec==ec2	Either or both of ec and ec2 can be an error_code;
	to compare equal ec and ec2 must have equivalent
	category()s and equivalent value()s; if ec and ec2 are
	of the same type, equivalence is defined by ==;
	if not, equivalence is defined by category().equivalent().
ec!=ec2	!(ec==ec2)
ec<ec2	An order ec.category()<ec2.category()
	|| (ec.category()==ec2.category() && ec.value()<ec2.value())
e=ec.default_error_condition()	e is a reference to an error_condition:
	e=ec.category().default_error_condition(ec.value())
os<<ec	Write ec.name() to the ostream os
ec=make_error_code(e)	e is an errc;
	ec=error_code(static_cast<int>(e),&generic_category())

For a type representing the simple idea of an error code, error_code provides a lot of members. It is basically as simple map from an integer to a pointer to an error_category:

```
class error_code {
public:
        // representation: {value,category} of type {int,const error_category*}
};
```

An **error_category** is an interface to an object of a class derived from **error_category**. Therefore, an **error_category** is passed by reference and stored as a pointer. Each separate **error_category** is represented by a unique object.

Consider again the **open_file()** example:

```
ostream& open_file(const string& path)
{
        auto dn = split_into_directory_and_name(path);          // split into {path,name}

        if (error_code err {does_directory_exist(dn.first)}) {   // ask "the system" about the path
            if (err==errc::permission_denied) {
                // ...
            }
            else if (err==errc::not_a_directory) {
                // ...
            }
            throw system_error(err); // can't do anything locally
        }

        // ...
        return ofstream{path};
}
```

The **errc** error codes are described in §30.4.3.6. Note that I used an if-then-else chain rather than the more obvious **switch**-statement. The reason is that **==** is defined in terms of equivalence, taking both the error **category()** and the error **value()** into account.

The operations on **error_code**s are system-specific. In some cases, **error_code**s can be mapped into **error_condition**s (§30.4.3.4) using the mechanisms described in §30.4.3.5. An **error_condition** is extracted from an **error_code** using **default_error_condition()**. An **error_condition** typically contains less information than an **error_code**, so it is usually a good idea to keep the **error_code** available and only extract its **error_condition** when needed.

Manipulating **error_code**s does not change the value of **errno** (§13.1.2, §40.3). The standard library leaves the error states provided by other libraries unchanged.

30.4.3.2 Error Categories

An **error_category** represents a classification of errors. Specific errors are represented by a class derived from class **error_category**:

```
class error_category {
public:
        // ... interface to specific categories derived from error_category ...
};
```

error_category (§iso.19.5.1.1)	
cat.˜error_category()	Destructor; virtual; noexcept
s=cat.name()	s is the name of **cat**; **s** is a C-style string; virtual; noexcept
ec=cat.default_error_condition(n)	ec is the **error_condition** for n in **cat**; virtual; noexcept
cat.equivalent(n,ec)	Is ec.category()==cat and ec.value()==n? ec is an **error_condition**; virtual; noexcept
cat.equivalent(ec,n)	Is ec.category()==cat and ec.value()==n? ec is an **error_code**; virtual; noexcept
s=cat.message(n)	s is a **string** describing the error n in **cat**; virtual
cat==cat2	Is **cat** the same category as **cat2**? noexcept
cat!=cat2	!(cat==cat2); noexcept
cat<cat2	Is cat<cat2 in an order based on **error_category** addresses: **std::less<const error_category∗>()(cat, cat2)**? noexcept

Because **error_category** is designed to be used as a base class, no copy or move operations are provided. Access an **error_category** through pointers or references.

There are four named standard-library categories:

Standard-library Error Categories (§iso.19.5.1.1)	
ec=generic_category()	ec.name()=="generic"; ec is a reference to an **error_category**
ec=system_category()	ec.name()=="system" ec is a reference to an **error_category**; represents system errors: if **ec** corresponds to a POSIX error then ec.value() equals that error's errno
ec=future_category()	ec.name()=="future"; ec is a reference to an **error_category**; represents errors from **<future>**
iostream_category()	ec.name()=="iostream"; ec is a reference to an **error_category**; represents errors from the **iostream** library

These categories are necessary because a simple integer error code can have different meanings in different contexts (**categorys**). For example, **1** means "operation not permitted" (**EPERM**) in POSIX, is a generic code (**state**) for all errors as an **iostream** error, and means "future already retrieved" (**future_already_retrieved**) as a **future** error.

30.4.3.3 Exception system_error

A **system_error** is used to report errors that ultimately originate in the parts of the standard library that deal with the operating system. It passes along an **error_code** and optionally an error-message string:

```
class system_error : public runtime_error {
public:
    // ...
};
```

Exception Class system_error (§iso.19.5.6)	
system_error se {ec,s};	se holds {ec,s}; ec is an error_code; s is a string or a C-style string intended as part of an error message
system_error se {ec};	se holds {ec}; ec is an error_code
system_error se {n,cat,s};	se holds {error_code{n,cat},s}; cat is an error_category and n is an int representing an error in cat; s is a string or a C-style string intended as part of an error message
system_error se {n,cat};	se holds error_code{n,cat}; cat is an error_category and n is an int representing an error in cat
ec=se.code()	ec is a reference to se's error_code; noexcept
p=se.what()	p is a C-style string version of se's error string; noexcept

Code catching a system_error has its error_code available. For example:

```
try {
    // something
}
catch (system_error& err) {
    cout << "caught system_error " << err.what() <<'\n';      // error message

    auto ec = err.code();
    cout << "category: " << ec.category().what() <<'\n';
    cout << "value: " << ec.value() <<'\n';
    cout << "message: " << ec.message() <<'\n';
}
```

Naturally, system_errors can be used by code that is not part of the standard library. A system-specific error_code is passed, rather than a potentially portable error_condition (§30.4.3.4). To get an error_condition from an error_code use default_error_condition() (§30.4.3.1).

30.4.3.4 Potentially Portable Error Conditions

Potentially portable error codes (error_conditions) are represented almost identically to the system-specific error_codes:

```
class error_condition {   // potentially portable (§iso.19.5.3)
public:
    // like error_code but
    // no output operator (<<) and
    // no default_error_condition()
};
```

The general idea is that each system has a set of specific ("native") codes that are mapped into the potentially portable ones for the convenience of programmers of programs (often libraries) that need to work on multiple platforms.

30.4.3.5 Mapping Error Codes

Making an **error_category** with a set of **error_codes** and at least one **error_condition** starts with defining an enumeration with the desired **error_code** values. For example:

```
enum class future_errc {
    broken_promise = 1,
    future_already_retrieved,
    promise_already_satisfied,
    no_state
};
```

The meaning of these values is completely category-specific. The integer values of these enumerators are implementation-defined.

The **future** error category is part of the standard, so you can find it in your standard library. The details are likely to differ from what I describe.

Next, we need to define a suitable category for our error codes:

```
class future_cat : error_category {          // to be returned from future_category()
public:
    const char* name() const noexcept override { return "future"; }

    string message(int ec) const override;
};


const error_category& future_category() noexcept
{
    static future_cat obj;
    return &obj;
}
```

The mapping from integer values to error **message()** strings is a bit tedious. We have to invent a set of messages that are likely to be meaningful to a programmer. Here, I'm not trying to be clever:

```
string future_error::message(int ec) const
{
    switch (ec) {
    default:                                 return "bad future_error code";
    future_errc::broken_promise:             return "future_error: broken promise";
    future_errc::future_already_retrieved:   return "future_error: future already retrieved";
    future_errc::promise_already_satisfied:  return "future_error: promise already satisfied";
    future_errc::no_state:                   return "future_error: no state";
    }
}
```

We can now make an **error_code** out of a **future_errc**:

```
error_code make_error_code(future_errc e) noexcept
{
    return error_code{int(e),future_category()};
}
```

For the **error_code** constructor and assignment that take a single error value, it is required that the argument be of the appropriate type for the **error_category**. For example, an argument intended to become the **value()** of an **error_code** of **future_category()** must be a **future_errc**. In particular, we can't just use any **int**. For example:

```
error_code ec1 {7};                         // error
error_code ec2 {future_errc::no_state};     // OK

ec1 = 9;                                     // error
ec2 = future_errc::promise_already_satisfied;   // OK
ec2 = errc::broken_pipe;                     // error: wrong error category
```

To help the implementer of **error_code**, we specialize the trait **is_error_code_enum** for our enumeration:

```
template<>
struct is_error_code_enum<future_errc> : public true_type { };
```

The standard already provides the general template:

```
template<typename>
struct is_error_code_enum : public false_type { };
```

This states that anything we don't deem an error code value isn't. For **error_condition** to work for our category, we must repeat what we did for **error_code**. For example:

```
error_condition make_error_condition(future_errc e) noexcept;

template<>
struct is_error_condition_enum<future_errc> : public true_type { };
```

For a more interesting design, we could use a separate **enum** for the **error_condition** and have **make_error_condition()** implement a mapping from **future_errc** to that.

30.4.3.6 errc Error Codes

Standard **error_code**s for the **system_category()** are defined by **enum class errc** with values equivalent to the POSIX-derived contents of **<cerrno>**:

enum class errc **Enumerators** (§iso.19.5) (continues)	
address_family_not_supported	EAFNOSUPPORT
address_in_use	EADDRINUSE
address_not_available	EADDRNOTAVAIL
already_connected	EISCONN
argument_list_too_long	E2BIG
argument_out_of_domain	EDOM
bad_address	EFAULT
bad_file_descriptor	EBADF
bad_message	EBADMSG

enum class errc **Enumerators (§iso.19.5) (continued, continues)**	
broken_pipe	EPIPE
connection_aborted	ECONNABORTED
connection_already_in_progress	EALREADY
connection_refused	ECONNREFUSED
connection_reset	ECONNRESET
cross_device_link	EXDEV
destination_address_required	EDESTADDRREQ
device_or_resource_busy	EBUSY
directory_not_empty	ENOTEMPTY
executable_format_error	ENOEXEC
file_exists	EEXIST
file_too_large	EFBIG
filename_too_long	ENAMETOOLONG
function_not_supported	ENOSYS
host_unreachable	EHOSTUNREACH
identifier_removed	EIDRM
illegal_byte_sequence	EILSEQ
inappropriate_io_control_operation	ENOTTY
interrupted	EINTR
invalid_argument	EINVAL
invalid_seek	ESPIPE
io_error	EIO
is_a_directory	EISDIR
message_size	EMSGSIZE
network_down	ENETDOWN
network_reset	ENETRESET
network_unreachable	ENETUNREACH
no_buffer_space	ENOBUFS
no_child_process	ECHILD
no_link	ENOLINK
no_lock_available	ENOLCK
no_message	ENOMSG
no_message_available	ENODATA
no_protocol_option	ENOPROTOOPT
no_space_on_device	ENOSPC
no_stream_resources	ENOSR
no_such_device	ENODEV
no_such_device_or_address	ENXIO
no_such_file_or_directory	ENOENT
no_such_process	ESRCH
not_a_directory	ENOTDIR

enum class errc **Enumerators (§iso.19.5) (continued)**	
not_a_socket	ENOTSOCK
not_a_stream	ENOSTR
not_connected	ENOTCONN
not_enough_memory	ENOMEM
not_supported	ENOTSUP
operation_canceled	ECANCELED
operation_in_progress	EINPROGRESS
operation_not_permitted	EPERM
operation_not_supported	EOPNOTSUPP
operation_would_block	EWOULDBLOCK
owner_dead	EOWNERDEAD
permission_denied	EACCES
protocol_error	EPROTO
protocol_not_supported	EPROTONOSUPPORT
read_only_file_system	EROFS
resource_deadlock_would_occur	EDEADLK
resource_unavailable_try_again	EAGAIN
result_out_of_range	ERANGE
state_not_recoverable	ENOTRECOVERABLE
stream_timeout	ETIME
text_file_busy	ETXTBSY
timed_out	ETIMEDOUT
too_many_files_open	EMFILE
too_many_files_open_in_system	ENFILE
too_many_links	EMLINK
too_many_symbolic_link_levels	ELOOP
value_too_large	EOVERFLOW
wrong_protocol_type	EPROTOTYPE

These codes are valid for the "**system**" category: **system_category()**. For systems supporting POSIX-like facilities, they are also valid for the "**generic**" category: **generic_category()**.

The POSIX macros are integers whereas the **errc** enumerators are of type **errc**. For example:

```
void problem(errc e)
{
    if (e==EPIPE) {              // error: no conversion of errc to int
        // ...
    }

    if (e==broken_pipe) {        // error: broken_pipe not in scope
        // ...
    }
```

```
        if (e==errc::broken_pipe) {      // OK
             // ...
        }
  }
```

30.4.3.7 future_errc **Error Codes**

Standard **error_code**s for the **future_category()** are defined by **enum class future_errc**:

enum class future_errc **Enumerators (§iso.30.6.1)**	
broken_promise	1
future_already_retrieved	2
promise_already_satisfied	3
no_state	4

These codes are valid for the "**future**" category: **future_category()**.

30.4.3.8 io_errc **Error Codes**

Standard **error_code**s for the **iostream_category()** are defined by **enum class io_errc**:

enum class io_errc **Enumerator (§iso.27.5.1)**	
stream	1

This code is valid for the "**iostream**" category: **iostream_category()**.

30.5 Advice

[1]   Use standard-library facilities to maintain portability; §30.1, §30.1.1.
[2]   Use standard-library facilities to minimize maintenance costs; §30.1.
[3]   Use standard-library facilities as a base for more extensive and more specialized libraries; §30.1.1.
[4]   Use standard-library facilities as a model for flexible, widely usable software; §30.1.1.
[5]   The standard-library facilities are defined in namespace **std** and found in standard-library headers; §30.2.
[6]   A C standard-library header **X.h** is presented as a C++ standard-library header in **<cX>**; §30.2.
[7]   Do not try to use a standard-library facility without #**include**ing its header; §30.2.
[8]   To use a range-**for** on a built-in array, #**include<iterator>**; §30.3.2.
[9]   Prefer exception-based error handling over return-code-based error handling; §30.4.
[10] Always catch **exception&** (for standard-library and language support exceptions) and ... (for unexpected exceptions); §30.4.1.
[11] The standard-library **exception** hierarchy can be (but does not have to be) used for a user's own exceptions; §30.4.1.1.
[12] Call **terminate()** in case of serious trouble; §30.4.1.3.

[13] Use **static_assert()** and **assert()** extensively; §30.4.2.

[14] Do not assume that **assert()** is always evaluated; §30.4.2.

[15] If you can't use exceptions, consider **<system_error>**; §30.4.3.

31

STL Containers

It was new.
It was singular.
It was simple.
It must succeed!
– H. Nelson

31.1 Introduction

The STL consists of the iterator, container, algorithm, and function object parts of the standard library. The rest of the STL is presented in Chapter 32 and Chapter 33.

31.2 Container Overview

A container holds a sequence of objects. This section summarizes the types of containers and briefly outlines their properties. Operations on containers are summarized in §31.3.

Containers can be categorized like this:

- *Sequence containers* provide access to (half-open) sequences of elements.
- *Associative containers* provide associative lookup based on a key.

In addition, the standard library provides types of objects that hold elements while not offering all of the facilities of sequence containers or associative containers:

- *Container adaptors* provide specialized access to underlying containers.
- *Almost containers* are sequences of elements that provide most, but not all, of the facilities of a container.

The STL containers (the sequence and associative containers) are all resource handles with copy and move operations (§3.3.1). All operations on containers provide the basic guarantee (§13.2) to ensure that they interact properly with exception-based error handling.

Sequence Containers	
vector<T,A>	A contiguously allocated sequence of Ts; the default choice of container
list<T,A>	A doubly-linked list of T; use when you need to insert and delete elements without moving existing elements
forward_list<T,A>	A singly-linked list of T; ideal for empty and very short sequences
deque<T,A>	A double-ended queue of T; a cross between a vector and a list; slower than one or the other for most uses

The **A** template argument is the allocator that the container uses to acquire and release memory (§13.6.1, §34.4). For example:

```
template<typename T, typename A = allocator<T>>
class vector {
    // ...
};
```

A is defaulted to **std::allocator<T>** (§34.4.1) which uses **operator new()** and **operator delete()** when it needs to acquire or release memory for its elements.

These containers are defined in **<vector>**, **<list>**, and **<deque>**. The sequence containers are contiguously allocated (e.g., **vector**) or linked lists (e.g., **forward_list**) of elements of their **value_type** (**T** in the notation used above). A **deque** (pronounced "deck") is a mixture of linked-list and contiguous allocation.

Unless you have a solid reason not to, use a **vector**. Note that **vector** provides operations for inserting and erasing (removing) elements, allowing a **vector** to grow and shrink as needed. For sequences of small elements, a **vector** can be an excellent representation for a data structure requiring list operations.

When inserting and erasing elements of a **vector**, elements may be moved. In contrast, elements of a list or an associative container do not move when new elements are inserted or other elements are erased.

A **forward_list** (a singly-linked list) is basically a list optimized for empty and very short lists. An empty **forward_list** takes up only one word. There are surprisingly many uses for lists where most are empty (and the rest are very short).

Ordered Associative Containers (§iso.23.4.2)	
C is the type of the comparison; A is the allocator type	
map<K,V,C,A>	An ordered map from K to V; a sequence of (K,V) pairs
multimap<K,V,C,A>	An ordered map from K to V; duplicate keys allowed
set<K,C,A>	An ordered set of K
multiset<K,C,A>	An ordered set of K; duplicate keys allowed

These containers are usually implemented as balanced binary trees (usually red-black trees).

The default ordering criterion for a key, K, is std::less<K> (§33.4).

As for sequence containers, the A template argument is the *allocator* that the container uses to acquire and release memory (§13.6.1, §34.4). The A template argument is defaulted to std::allocator<std::pair<const K,T>> (§31.4.3) for maps and std::allocator<K> for sets.

Unordered Associative Containers (§iso.23.5.2)	
H is the hash function type; E is the equality test; A is the allocator type	
unordered_map<K,V,H,E,A>	An unordered map from K to V
unordered_multimap<K,V,H,E,A>	An unordered map from K to V; duplicate keys allowed
unordered_set<K,H,E,A>	An unordered set of K
unordered_multiset<K,H,E,A>	An unordered set of K; duplicate keys allowed

These containers are implemented as hash tables with linked overflow. The default hash function type, H, for a type K is std::hash<K> (§31.4.3.2). The default for the equality function type, E, for a type K is std::equal_to<K> (§33.4); the equality function is used to decide whether two objects with the same hash code are equal.

The associative containers are linked structures (trees) with nodes of their value_type (in the notation used above, pair<const K,V> for maps and K for sets). The sequence of a set, map, or multimap is ordered by its key value (K). An unordered container need not have an ordering relation for its elements (e.g., <) and uses a hash function instead (§31.2.2.1). The sequence of an unordered container does not have a guaranteed order. A multimap differs from a map in that a key value may occur many times.

Container adaptors are containers providing specialized interfaces to other containers:

Container Adaptors	
C is the container type	
priority_queue<T,C,Cmp>	Priority queue of Ts; Cmp is the priority function type
queue<T,C>	Queue of Ts with push() and pop()
stack<T,C>	Stack of Ts with push() and pop()

The default for a priority_queue's priority function, Cmp, is std::less<T>. The default for the container type, C, is std::deque<T> for queue and std::vector<T> for stack and priority_queue. See §31.5.

Some data types provide much of what is required of a standard container, but not all. We sometimes refer to those as "almost containers." The most interesting of those are:

"Almost Containers"	
T[N]	A fixed-size built-in array: **N** contiguous elements of type **T**; no **size()** or other member functions
array<T,N>	A fixed-size array of **N** contiguous elements of type **T**; like the built-in array, but with most problems solved
basic_string<C,Tr,A>	A contiguously allocated sequence of characters of type **C** with text manipulation operations, e.g., concatenation (**+** and **+=**); **basic_string** is typically optimized not to require free store for short strings (§19.3.3)
string	basic_string<char>
u16string	basic_string<char16_t>
u32string	basic_string<char32_t>
wstring	basic_string<wchar_t>
valarray<T>	A numerical vector with vector operations, but with restrictions to encourage high-performance implementations; use only if you do a lot of vector arithmetic
bitset<N>	A set of **N** bits with set operations, such as **&** and **|**
vector<bool>	A specialization of **vector<T>** with compactly stored bits

For **basic_string**, **A** is the allocator (§34.4) and **Tr** is the character traits (§36.2.2).

Prefer a container, such as **vector**, **string**, or **array**, over an array when you have a choice. The implicit array-to-pointer conversion and the need to remember the size for a built-in array are major sources of errors (e.g., see §27.2.1).

Prefer the standard strings to other strings and to C-style strings. The pointer semantics of C-style strings imply an awkward notation and extra work for the programmer, and they are a major source of errors (such as memory leaks) (§36.3.1).

31.2.1 Container Representation

The standard doesn't prescribe a particular representation for a standard container. Instead, the standard specifies the container interfaces and some complexity requirements. Implementers will choose appropriate and often cleverly optimized implementations to meet the general requirements and common uses. In addition to what is needed to manipulate elements, such a "handle" will hold an allocator (§34.4).

For a **vector**, the element data structure is most likely an array:

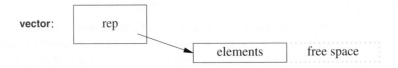

The **vector** will hold a pointer to an array of elements, the number of elements, and the capacity (the number of allocated, currently unused slots) or equivalent (§13.6).

A **list** is most likely represented by a sequence of links pointing to the elements and the number of elements:

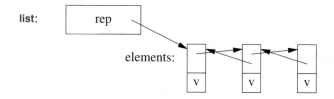

A **forward_list** is most likely represented by a sequence of links pointing to the elements:

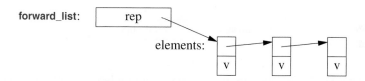

A **map** is most likely implemented as a (balanced) tree of nodes pointing to (key,value) pairs:

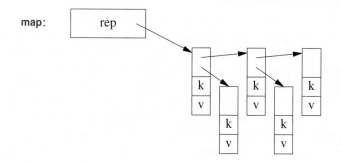

An **unordered_map** is most likely implemented as a hash table:

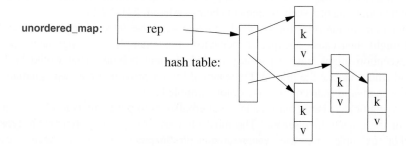

A **string** might be implemented as outlined in §19.3 and §23.2; that is, for short **strings** the characters are stored in the **string** handle itself, and for longer **strings** the elements are stored contiguously
on the free-store (like **vector** elements). Like **vector**, a string can grow into "free space" allocated
to avoid repeated reallocations:

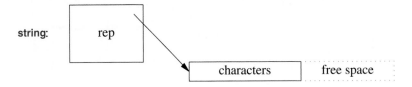

Like a built-in array (§7.3), an **array** is simply a sequence of elements, with no handle:

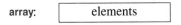

This implies that a local **array** does not use any free store (unless it is allocated there) and that an
array member of a class does not imply any free store operations.

31.2.2 Element Requirements

To be an element of a container, an object must be of a type that allows the container implementation to copy or move it, and to swap elements. If a container copies an element using a copy constructor or copy assignment, the result of the copy must be an equivalent object. This roughly
means that any test for equality that you can devise on the value of the objects must deem the copy
equal to the original. In other words, copying an element must work much like an ordinary copy of
an **int**. Similarly, a move constructor and a move assignment must have the conventional definitions
and move semantics (§17.5.1). In addition, it must be possible to **swap()** elements with the usual
semantics. If a type has copy or move, the standard-library **swap()** will work.

The details of the element requirements are scattered over the standard and quite hard to read
(§iso.23.2.3, §iso.23.2.1, §iso.17.6.3.2), but basically a container can hold elements of a type that
has conventional copy or move operations. Many basic algorithms, such as **copy()**, **find()**, and **sort()**
will work as long as the requirements for being a container element are met as well as the algorithm's specific requirements (such as elements being ordered; §31.2.2.1).

Some violations of the rules for standard containers can be detected by a compiler, but others
cannot and might then cause unexpected behavior. For example, an assignment operation that
throws an exception might leave a partially copied element behind. That would be bad design
(§13.6.1) and would violate the rules of the standard by not providing the basic guarantee (§13.2).
An element in an invalid state could cause serious trouble later.

When copying objects is not reasonable, an alternative is to put pointers to objects into containers instead of the objects themselves. The most obvious example is polymorphic types (§3.2.2,
§20.3.2). For example, we use **vector<unique_ptr<Shape>>** or **vector<Shape*>** rather than
vector<Shape> to preserve polymorphic behavior.

31.2.2.1 Comparisons

Associative containers require that their elements can be ordered. So do many operations that can be applied to containers (e.g., **sort()** and **merge()**). By default, the < operator is used to define the order. If < is not suitable, the programmer must provide an alternative (§31.4.3, §33.4). The ordering criterion must define a *strict weak ordering*. Informally, this means that both less-than and equality (if defined) must be transitive. That is, for an ordering criterion **cmp** (think of it as "less than") we require:

[1]   Irreflexivity: **cmp(x,x)** is false.
[2]   Antisymmetry: **cmp(x,y)** implies **!cmp(y,x)**.
[3]   Transitivity: If **cmp(x,y)** and **cmp(y,z)**, then **cmp(x,z)**.
[4]   Transitivity of equivalence: Define **equiv(x,y)** to be **!(cmp(x,y)||cmp(y,x))**. If **equiv(x,y)** and **equiv(y,z)**, then **equiv(x,z)**.

The last rule is the one that allows us to define equality (**x==y**) as **!(cmp(x,y)||cmp(y,x))** if we need **==**.

Standard-library operations that require a comparison come in two versions. For example:

```
template<typename Ran>
     void sort(Ran first, Ran last);            // use < for comparison
template<typename Ran, typename Cmp>
     void sort(Ran first, Ran last, Cmp cmp); // use cmp
```

The first version uses < and the second uses a user-supplied comparison **cmp**. For example, we might decide to sort **fruit** using a comparison that isn't case sensitive. We do that by defining a function object (§3.4.3, §19.2.2) that does the comparison when invoked for a pair of **string**s:

```
class Nocase {       // case-insensitive string compare
public:
     bool operator()(const string&, const string&) const;
};

bool Nocase::operator()(const string& x, const string& y) const
     // return true if x is lexicographically less than y, not taking case into account
{
     auto p = x.begin();
     auto q = y.begin();

     while (p!=x.end() && q!=y.end() && toupper(*p)==toupper(*q)) {
          ++p;
          ++q;
     }
     if (p == x.end()) return q != y.end();
     if (q == y.end()) return false;
     return toupper(*p) < toupper(*q);
}
```

We can call **sort()** using that comparison criterion. Consider:

```
fruit:
     apple  pear  Apple  Pear  lemon
```

Sorting using **sort(fruit.begin(),fruit.end(),Nocase())** would yield something like

> **fruit:**
>   **Apple apple lemon Pear pear**

Assuming a character set in which uppercase letters precede lowercase letters, plain **sort(fruit.begin(),fruit.end())** would give:

> **fruit:**
>   **Apple Pear apple lemon pear**

Beware that < on C-style strings (i.e., **const char∗**s) compares pointer values (§7.4). Thus, associative containers will not work as most people would expect them to if C-style strings are used as keys. To make them work properly, a less-than operation that compares based on lexicographical order must be used. For example:

```
struct Cstring_less {
    bool operator()(const char∗ p, const char∗ q) const { return strcmp(p,q)<0; }
};

map<char∗,int,Cstring_less> m;        // map that uses strcmp() to compare const char* keys
```

31.2.2.2 Other Relational Operators

By default, containers and algorithms use < when they need to do a less-than comparison. When the default isn't right, a programmer can supply a comparison criterion. However, no mechanism is provided for also passing an equality test. Instead, when a programmer supplies a comparison **cmp**, equality is tested using two comparisons. For example:

> **if (x == y)**   // not done where the user supplied a comparison
>
> **if (!cmp(x,y) && !cmp(y,x))**   // done where the user supplied a comparison cmp

This saves the user from having to provide an equality operation for every type used as the value type for an associative container or by an algorithm using a comparison. It may look expensive, but the library doesn't check for equality very often, in about 50% of the cases only a single call of **cmp()** is needed, and often the compiler can optimize away the double check.

Using an equivalence relationship defined by less-than (by default <) rather than equality (by default ==) also has practical uses. For example, associative containers (§31.4.3) compare keys using an equivalence test !(cmp(x,y)||cmp(y,x)). This implies that equivalent keys need not be equal. For example, a **multimap** (§31.4.3) that uses case-insensitive comparison as its comparison criterion will consider the strings **Last**, **last**, **lAst**, **laSt**, and **lasT** equivalent, even though == for strings deems them different. This allows us to ignore differences we consider insignificant when sorting.

If equals (by default ==) always gives the same result as the equivalence test !(cmp(x,y)||cmp(y,x)) (by default **cmp()** is <), we say that we have a *total order*.

Given < and ==, we can easily construct the rest of the usual comparisons. The standard library defines them in the namespace **std::rel_ops** and presents them in <utility> (§35.5.3).

31.3 Operations Overview

The operations and types provided by the standard containers can be summarized like this:

Container:

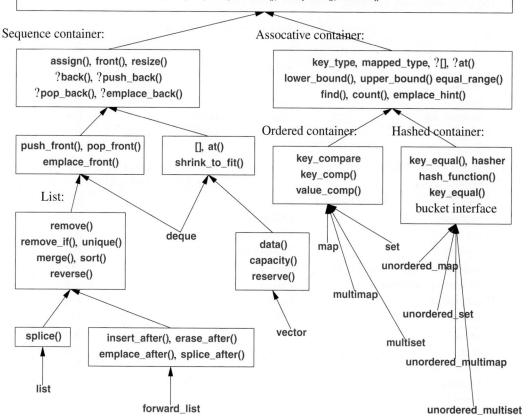

An arrow indicates that a set of operations is provided for a container; it is not an inheritance operation. A question mark (?) indicates a simplification: I have included operations that are provided for only some of the containers. In particular:

- A **multi**∗ associative container or a set does not provide [] or **at()**.
- A **forward_list** does not provide **insert()**, **erase()**, or **emplace()**; instead, it provides the ∗_**after** operations.
- A **forward_list** does not provide **back()**, **push_back()**, **pop_back()**, or **emplace_back()**.
- A **forward_list** does not provide **reverse_iterator**, **const_reverse_iterator**, **rbegin()**, **rend()**, **crbegin()**, **crend()**, or **size()**.
- A **unordered_**∗ associative container does not provide **<**, **<=**, **>**, or **>=**.

The [] and **at()** operations are replicated simply to reduce the number of arrows.

The bucket interface is described in §31.4.3.2.

Where meaningful, an access operation exists in two versions: one for **const** and one for non-**const** objects.

The standard-library operations have complexity guarantees:

Standard Container Operation Complexity					
	[] §31.2.2	List §31.3.7	Front §31.4.2	Back §31.3.6	Iterators §33.1.2
vector	const	O(n)+		const+	Ran
list		const	const	const	Bi
forward_list		const	const		For
deque	const	O(n)	const	const	Ran
stack				const	
queue			const	const	
priority_queue			O(log(n))	O(log(n))	
map	O(log(n))	O(log(n))+			Bi
multimap		O(log(n))+			Bi
set		O(log(n))+			Bi
multiset		O(log(n))+			Bi
unordered_map	const+	const+			For
unordered_multimap		const+			For
unordered_set		const+			For
unordered_multiset		const+			For
string	const	O(n)+	O(n)+	const+	Ran
array	const				Ran
built-in array	const				Ran
valarray	const				Ran
bitset	const				

"Front" operations refer to insertion and deletion before the first element. Similarly, "Back" operations refer to insertion and deletion after the last element, and "List" operations refer to insertion and deletion not necessarily at the ends of a container.

In the *Iterators* column, "Ran" means "random-access iterator," "For" means "forward iterator," and "Bi" means "bidirectional iterator" (§33.1.4).

Other entries are measures of the efficiency of the operations. A **const** entry means the operation takes an amount of time that does not depend on the number of elements in the container; another conventional notation for *constant time* is **O(1)**. **O(n)** means the operation takes time proportional to the number of elements involved. A **+** suffix indicates that occasionally a significant extra cost is incurred. For example, inserting an element into a **list** has a fixed cost (so it is listed as **const**), whereas the same operation on a **vector** involves moving the elements following the insertion point (so it is listed as **O(n)**). Occasionally, all elements of a **vector** must be relocated (so I added a **+**). The "big O" notation is conventional. I added the **+** for the benefit of programmers who care about predictability in addition to average performance. A conventional term for **O(n)+** is *amortized linear time*.

Naturally, if a constant is large, it can dwarf a small cost proportional to the number of elements. However, for large data structures **const** tends to mean "cheap," **O(n)** to mean "expensive," and **O(log(n))** to mean "fairly cheap." For even moderately large values of n, **O(log(n))**, where **log** is the binary logarithm, is far closer to constant time than to **O(n)**. For example:

Logarithm Examples					
n	16	128	1,024	16,384	1,048,576
log(n)	4	7	10	14	20
n*n	256	802,816	1,048,576	268,435,456	1.1e+12

People who care about cost must take a closer look. In particular, they must understand what elements are counted to get the **n**. However, the message is clear: don't mess with quadratic algorithms for larger values of **n**.

The measures of complexity and cost are upper bounds. The measures exist to give users some guidance as to what they can expect from implementations. Naturally, implementers will try to do better in important cases.

Note that the "Big O" complexity measures are asymptotic; that is, it could require a lot of elements before complexity differences matter. Other factors, such as the cost of an individual operation on an element, may dominate. For example, traversing a **vector** and a **list** both have complexity **O(n)**. However, given modern machine architectures, getting to the next element through a link (in a **list**) can be very much more expensive than getting to the next element of a **vector** (where the elements are contiguous). Similarly, a linear algorithm may take significantly more or significantly less than ten times as long for ten times as many elements because of the details of memory and processor architecture. Don't just trust your intuition about cost and your complexity measures; measure. Fortunately, the container interfaces are so similar that comparisons are easy to code.

The **size()** operation is constant time for all operations. Note that **forward_list** does not have **size()**, so if you want to know the number of elements, you must count them yourself (at the cost of **O(n)**). A **forward_list** is optimized for space and does not store its size or a pointer to its last element.

The **string** estimates are for longer strings. The "short string optimization" (§19.3.3) makes all operations of short strings (e.g., less than 14 characters) constant time.

The entries for **stack** and **queue** reflect the cost for the default implementation using a **deque** as the underlying container (§31.5.1, §31.5.2).

31.3.1 Member Types

A container defines a set of member types:

Member types (§iso.23.2, §iso.23.3.6.1)	
value_type	Type of element
allocator_type	Type of memory manager
size_type	Unsigned type of container subscripts, element counts, etc.
difference_type	Signed type of difference between iterators
iterator	Behaves like value_type*
const_iterator	Behaves like const_value_type*
reverse_iterator	Behaves like value_type*
const_reverse_iterator	Behaves like const_value_type*
reference	value_type&
const_reference	const_value_type&
pointer	Behaves like value_type*
const_pointer	Behaves like const_value_type*
key_type	Type of key; associative containers only
mapped_type	Type of mapped value; associative containers only
key_compare	Type of comparison criterion; ordered containers only
hasher	Type of hash function; unordered containers only
key_equal	Type of equivalence function; unordered containers only
local_iterator	Type of bucket iterator; unordered containers only
const_local_iterator	Type of bucket iterator; unordered containers only

Every container and "almost container" provides most of these member types. However, they don't provide types that are not meaningful. For example, array does not have an allocator_type and vector does not have a key_type.

31.3.2 Constructors, Destructor, and Assignments

Containers provide a variety of constructors and assignment operations. For a container called C (e.g., vector<double> or map<string,int>) we have:

Constructors, Destructor, and Assignment (continues)	
C is a container; by default, a C uses the default allocator C::allocator_type{}	
C c {};	Default constructor: c is an empty container
C c {a};	Default construct c; use allocator a
C c(n);	c initialized with n elements with the value value_type{}; not for associative containers
C c(n,x);	Initialize c with n copies of x; not for associative containers
C c(n,x,a);	Initialize c with n copies of x; use allocator a; not for associative containers

Constructors, Destructor, and Assignment (continued)	
C is a container; by default, a C uses the default allocator C::allocator_type{}	
C c {elem};	Initialize c from elem;
	if C has an initializer-list constructor, prefer that;
	otherwise, use another constructor
C c {c2};	Copy constructor: copy c2's elements and allocator into c
C c {move(c2)};	Move constructor: move c2's elements and allocator into c
C c {{elem},a};	Initialize c from the initializer_list {elem}; use allocator a
C c {b,e};	Initialize c with elements from [b:e)
C c {b,e,a};	Initialize c with elements from [b:e); use allocator a
c.~C()	Destructor: destroy c's elements and release all resources
c2=c	Copy assignment: copy c's elements into c2
c2=move(c)	Move assignment: move c's elements into c2
c={elem}	Assign to c from initializer_list {elem}
c.assign(n,x)	Assign n copies of x; not for associative containers
c.assign(b,e)	Assign to c from [b:e)
c.assign({elem})	Assign to c from initializer_list {elem}

Additional constructors for associative containers are described in §31.4.3.

Note that an assignment does not copy or move allocators. A target container gets a new set of elements but retains its old container, which it uses to allocate space for the new elements (if any). Allocators are described in §34.4.

Remember that a constructor or an element copy may throw an exception to indicate that it cannot perform its tasks.

The potential ambiguities for initializers are discussed in §11.3.3 and §17.3.4.1. For example:

```
void use()
{
    vector<int> vi {1,3,5,7,9};          // vector initialized by five ints
    vector<string> vs(7);                // vector initialized by seven empty strings

    vector<int> vi2;
    vi2 = {2,4,6,8};                     // assign sequence of four ints to vi2
    vi2.assign(&vi[1],&vi[4]);           // assign the sequence 3,5,7 to vi2

    vector<string> vs2;
    vs2 = {"The Eagle", "The Bird and Baby"};        // assign two strings to vs2
    vs2.assign("The Bear", "The Bull and Vet");      // run-time error
}
```

The error in the assignment to vs2 is that a pair of pointers are passed (not an initializer_list) and the two pointers do not point into the same array. Use () for size initializers and {} for every other kind of iterator.

Containers are often large, so we almost always pass them by reference. However, because they are resource handles (§31.2.1), we can return them (implicitly using move) efficiently. Similarly, we can move them as arguments when we don't want aliasing. For example:

```
void task(vector<int>&& v);

vector<int> user(vector<int>& large)
{
    vector<int> res;
    // ...
    task(move(large));    // transfer ownership of data to task()
    // ...
    return res;
}
```

31.3.3 Size and Capacity

The size is the number of elements in the container; the capacity is the number of elements that a container can hold before allocating more memory:

Size and Capacity	
x=c.size()	x is the number of elements of c
c.empty()	Is c empty?
x=c.max_size()	x is the largest possible number of elements of c
x=c.capacity()	x is the space allocated for c; vector and string only
c.reserve(n)	Reserve space for n elements for c; vector and string only
c.resize(n)	Change size of c to n; use the default element value for added elements; sequence containers only (and string)
c.resize(n,v)	Change size of c to n; use v for added elements; sequence containers only (and string)
c.shrink_to_fit()	Make c.capacity() equal to c.size(); vector, deque, and string only
c.clear()	Erase all elements of c

When changing the size or the capacity, the elements may be moved to new storage locations. That implies that iterators (and pointers and references) to elements may become invalid (i.e., point to the old element locations). For an example, see §31.4.1.1.

An iterator to an element of an associative container (e.g., a map) is only invalidated if the element to which it points is removed from the container (erase()d; §31.3.7). To contrast, an iterator to an element of a sequence container (e.g., a vector) is invalidated if the elements are relocated (e.g., by a resize(), reserve(), or push_back()) or if the element to which it points is moved within the container (e.g., by an erase() or insert() of an element with a lower index).

It is tempting to assume that reserve() improves performance, but the standard growth strategies for vector (§31.4.1.1) are so effective that performance is rarely a good reason to use reserve(). Instead, see reserve() as a way of increasing the predictability of performance and for avoiding invalidation of iterators.

31.3.4 Iterators

A container can be viewed as a sequence either in the order defined by the containers iterator or in the reverse order. For an associative container, the order is based on the containers comparison criterion (by default <):

Iterators	
p=c.begin()	p points to first element of **c**
p=c.end()	p points to one-past-last element of **c**
cp=c.cbegin()	p points to constant first element of **c**
p=c.cend()	p points to constant one-past-last element of **c**
p=c.rbegin()	p points to first element of reverse sequence of **c**
p=c.rend()	p points to one-past-last element of reverse sequence of **c**
p=c.crbegin()	p points to constant first element of reverse sequence of **c**
p=c.crend()	p points to constant one-past-last element of reverse sequence of **c**

The most common form of iteration over elements is to traverse a container from its beginning to its end. The simplest way of doing that is by a range-**for** (§9.5.1) which implicitly uses **begin()** and **end()**. For example:

```
for (auto& x : v)            // implicit use of v.begin() and v.end()
    cout << x << '\n';
```

When we need to know the position of an element in a container or if we need to refer to more than one element at a time, we use iterators directly. In such cases, **auto** is useful to minimize source code size and eliminate opportunities for typos. For example, assuming a random-access iterator:

```
for (auto p = v.begin(); p!=end(); ++p) {
    if (p!=v.begin() && *(p−1)==*p)
        cout << "duplicate " << *p << '\n';
}
```

When we don't need to modify elements, **cbegin()** and **cend()** are appropriate. That is, I should have written:

```
for (auto p = v.cbegin(); p!=cend(); ++p) {        // use const iterators
    if (p!=v.cbegin() && *(p−1)==*p)
        cout << "duplicate " << *p << '\n';
}
```

For most containers and most implementations, using **begin()** and **end()** repeatedly is not a performance problem, so I did not bother to complicate the code like this:

```
auto beg = v.cbegin();
auto end = v.cend();

for (auto p = beg; p!=end; ++p) {
    if (p!=beg && *(p−1)==*p)
        cout << "duplicate " << *p << '\n';
}
```

31.3.5 Element Access

Some elements can be accessed directly:

Element Access	
c.front()	Reference to first element of c; not for associative containers
c.back()	Reference to last element of c; not for forward_list or associative containers
c[i]	Reference to the ith element of c; unchecked access; not for lists or associative containers
c.at(i)	Reference to the ith element of c; throw an out_of_range if i is out of range; not for lists or associative containers
c[k]	Reference to the element with key k of c; insert (k,mapped_type{}) if not found; for map and unordered_map only
c.at(k)	Reference to the ith element of c; throw an out_of_range if k is not found; for map and unordered_map only

Some implementations – especially debug versions – always do range checking, but you cannot portably rely on that for correctness or on the absence of checking for performance. Where such issues are important, examine your implementations.

The associative containers map and unordered_map have [] and at() that take arguments of the key type, rather than positions (§31.4.3).

31.3.6 Stack Operations

The standard vector, deque, and list (but not forward_list or the associative containers) provide efficient operations at the end (back) of their sequence of elements:

Stack Operations	
c.push_back(x)	Add x to c (using copy or move) after the last element
c.pop_back()	Remove the last element from c
c.emplace_back(args)	Add an object constructed from args to c after the last element

A c.push_back(x) moves or copies x into c, increasing c's size by one. If we run out of memory or x's copy constructor throws an exception, c.push_back(x) fails. A failed push_back() has no effect on the container: the strong guarantee is offered (§13.2).

Note that pop_back() does not return a value. Had it done so, a copy constructor throwing an exception could seriously complicate the implementation.

In addition, list and deque provide the equivalent operations on the start (front) of their sequences (§31.4.2). So does forward_list.

The push_back() is a perennial favorite for growing a container without preallocation or chance of overflow, but emplace_back() can be used similarly. For example:

```
vector<complex<double>> vc;
for (double re,im; cin>>re>>im; )          // read two doubles
    vc.emplace_back(re,im);                // add complex<double>{re,im} at the end
```

31.3.7 List Operations

Containers provide list operations:

List Operations	
q=c.insert(p,x)	Add x before p; use copy or move
q=c.insert(p,n,x)	Add n copies of x before p; if c is an associative container, p is a hint of where to start searching
q=c.insert(p,first,last)	Add elements from [first:last) before p; not for associative containers
q=c.insert(p,{elem})	Add elements from initializer_list {elem} before p; p is a hint of where to start searching for a place to put the new element; for ordered associative containers only
q=c.emplace(p,args)	Add element constructed from args before p; not for associative containers
q=c.erase(p)	Remove element at p from c
q=c.erase(first,last)	Erase [first:last) of c
c.clear()	Erase all elements of c

For insert() functions, the result, q, points to the last element inserted. For erase() functions, q points to the element that followed the last element erased.

For containers with contiguous allocation, such as vector and deque, inserting and erasing an element can cause elements to be moved. An iterator pointing to a moved element becomes invalid. An element is moved if its position is after the insertion/deletion point or if all elements are moved because the new size exceeds the previous capacity. For example:

```
vector<int> v {4,3,5,1};
auto p = v.begin()+2;              // points to v[2], that is, the 5
v.push_back(6);                    // p becomes invalid; v == {4,3,5,1,6}
p = v.begin()+2;                   // points to v[2], that is, the 5
auto p2 = v.begin()+4;             // p2 points to v[4], that is, the 6
v.erase(v.begin()+3);             // v == {4,3,5,6}; p is still valid; p2 is invalid
```

Any operation that adds an element to a vector may cause every element to be reallocated (§13.6.4).

The emplace() operation is used when it is notationally awkward or potentially inefficient to first create an object and then copy (or move) it into a container. For example:

```
void user(list<pair<string,double>>& lst)
{
     auto p = lst.begin();
     while (p!=lst.end()&& p->first!="Denmark")        // find an insertion point
          /* do nothing */ ;
     p=lst.emplace(p,"England",7.5);                    // nice and terse
     p=lst.insert(p,make_pair("France",9.8));           // helper function
     p=lst.insert(p,pair<string,double>>{"Greece",3.14});   // verbose
}
```

The forward_list does not provide operations, such as insert(), that operate before an element identified by an iterator. Such an operation could not be implemented because there is no general way of finding the previous element in a **forward_list** given only an iterator. Instead, **forward_iterator** provides operations, such as **insert_after()**, that operate after an element identified by an iterator. Similarly, unordered containers use **emplace_hint()** to provide a hint rather than "plain" **emplace()**.

31.3.8 Other Operations

Containers can be compared and swapped:

Comparisons and Swap	
c1==c2	Do all corresponding elements of **c1** and **c2** compare equal?
c1!=c2	!(c1==c2)
c1<c2	Is **c1** lexicographically before **c2**?
c1<=c2	!(c2<c1)
c1>c2	c2<c1
c1>=c2	!(c1<c2)
c1.swap(c2)	Exchanges values of **c1** and **c2**; noexcept
swap(c1,c2)	c1.swap(c2)

When comparing containers with an operator (e.g., **<=**), the elements are compared using the equivalent element operator generated from **==** or **<** (e.g., **a>b** is done using **!(b<a)**).

The **swap()** operations exchange both elements and allocators.

31.4 Containers

This section goes into more detail about:
- **vector**, the default container (§31.4.1)
- The linked lists: **list** and **forward_list** (§31.4.2)
- The associative containers, such as **map** and **unordered_map** (§31.4.3)

31.4.1 vector

The STL **vector** is the default container. Use it unless you have a good reason not to. If your suggested alternative is a list or a built-in array, think twice.

§31.3 describes the operations on **vector** and implicitly contrasts them with what is provided for other containers. However, given the importance of **vector**, this section takes a second look with more emphasis on how the operations are provided.

The **vector**'s template argument and member types are defined like this:

```
template<typename T, typename Allocator = allocator<T>>
class vector {
public:
    using reference = value_type&;
    using const_reference = const value_type&;
    using iterator = /* implementation-defined */;
    using const_iterator = /* implementation-defined */;
```

```
using size_type = /* implementation-defined */;
using difference_type = /* implementation-defined */;
using value_type = T;
using allocator_type = Allocator;
using pointer = typename allocator_traits<Allocator>::pointer;
using const_pointer = typename allocator_traits<Allocator>::const_pointer;
using reverse_iterator = std::reverse_iterator<iterator>;
using const_reverse_iterator = std::reverse_iterator<const_iterator>;

// ...
};
```

31.4.1.1 vector and Growth

Consider the layout of a **vector** object (as described in §13.6):

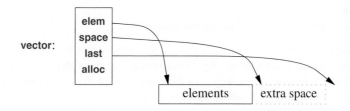

The use of both a size (number of elements) and a capacity (the number of available slots for elements without reallocation) makes growth through **push_back()** reasonably efficient: there is not an allocation operation each time we add an element, but only every time we exceed capacity (§13.6). The standard does not specify by how much capacity is increased when it is exceeded, but adding half the size is common. I used to be careful about using **reserve()** when I was reading into a **vector**. I was surprised to find that for essentially all of my uses, calling **reserve()** did not measurably affect performance. The default growth strategy worked just as well as my estimates, so I stopped trying to improve performance using **reserve()**. Instead, I use it to increase predictability of reallocation delays and to prevent invalidation of pointers and iterators.

The notion of capacity allows for iterators into a **vector** to be valid unless a reallocation actually happens. Consider reading letters into a buffer and keeping track of word boundaries:

```
vector<char> chars;          // input "buffer" for characters
constexpr int max = 20000;
chars.reserve(max);
vector<char*> words;         // pointers to start of words

bool in_word = false;
for (char c; cin.get(c)) {
    if (isalpha(c)) {
        if (!in_word) {              // found beginning of word
            in_word = true;
```

```
                chars.push_back(0);        // end of previous word
                chars.push_back(c);
                words.push_back(&chars.back());
            }
            else
                chars.push_back(c);
        }
        else
            in_word = false;
    }
    if (in_word)
        chars.push_back(0);        // terminate last word

    if (max<chars.size()) {    // oops: chars grew beyond capacity; the words are invalid
        // ...
    }
    chars.shrink_to_fit();      // release any surplus capacity
```

Had I not used **reserve()** here, the pointers in **words** would have been invalidated if **chars.push_back()** caused a relocation. By "invalidated," I mean that any use of those pointers would be undefined behavior. They may – or may not – point to an element, but almost certainly not to the elements they pointed to before the relocation.

The ability to grow a **vector** using **push_back()** and related operations implies that low-level C-style use of **malloc()** and **realloc()** (§43.5) is as unnecessary as it is tedious and error-prone.

31.4.1.2 vector and Nesting

A **vector** (and similar contiguously allocated data structures) has three major advantages compared to other data structures:

- The elements of a **vector** are compactly stored: there is no per-element memory overhead. The amount of memory consumed by a **vec** of type **vector<X>** is roughly **sizeof(vector<X>)+vec.size()*sizeof(X)**. The **sizeof(vector<X>)** is about 12 bytes, which is insignificant for larger vectors.
- Traversal of a **vector** is very fast. To get to the next element, the code does not have to indirect through a pointer, and modern machines are optimized for consecutive access through a **vector**-like structure. This makes linear scans of **vector** elements, as in **find()** and **copy()**, close to optimal.
- **vector** supports simple and efficient random access. This is what makes many algorithms on **vectors**, such as **sort()** and **binary_search()**, efficient.

It is easy to underestimate these benefits. For example, a doubly-linked list, such as **list**, usually incurs a four-words-per-element memory overhead (two links plus a free-store allocation header), and traversing it can easily be an order of magnitude more expensive than traversing a **vector** containing equivalent data. The effect can be so spectacular and surprising that I suggest you test it yourself [Stroustrup,2012a].

The benefits of compactness and efficiency of access can be unintentionally compromised. Consider how to represent a two-dimensional matrix. There are two obvious alternatives:

- A **vector** of **vectors**: **vector<vector<double>>** accessed by C-style double subscripting: **m[i][j]**
- A specific matrix type, **Matrix<2,double>** (Chapter 29), that stores elements contiguously (e.g., in a **vector<double>**) and computes locations in that **vector** from a pair of indices: **m(i,j)**

The memory layout for a 3-by-4 **vector<vector<double>>** looks like this:

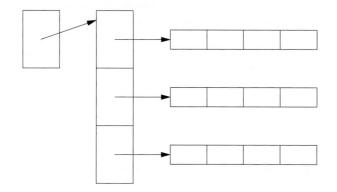

The memory layout for **Matrix<2,double>** looks like this:

To construct the **vector<vector<double>>**, we need four constructor calls with four free-store allocation operations. To access an element, we need to do a double indirection.

To construct the **Matrix<2,double>**, we need one constructor call with one free-store allocation. To access an element, we need a single indirection.

Once we reach an element of a row, we don't need a further indirection to access its successor, so access to the **vector<vector<double>>** is not always twice as costly as access to **Matrix<2,double>**. However, for algorithms that require high performance, the allocation, deallocation, and access costs implied by the linked structure of **vector<vector<double>>** could be a problem.

The **vector<vector<double>>** solution implies the possiblity of the row having different sizes. There are cases where that is an advantage, but more often it is simply an opportunity for errors and a burden for testing.

The problems and overhead get worse when we need higher dimensions: compare the number of added indirections and allocations for a **vector<vector<vector<double>>>** and a **Matrix<3,double>**.

In summary, I note that the importance of compactness of data structures is often underestimated or compromised. The advantages are logical as well as performance related. Combine this with a tendency to overuse pointers and **new** and we have a widespread problem. For example, consider the development complexities, run-time costs, memory costs, and opportunities for errors in an implementation of a two-dimensional structure when the rows are implemented as independent objects on the free store: **vector<vector<double>*>**.

31.4.1.3 vector **and Arrays**

A **vector** is a resource handle. This is what allows it to be resized and enables efficient move semantics. However, that occasionally puts it at a disadvantage compared to data structures (such as built-in arrays and **array**) that do not rely on storing elements separately from a handle. Keeping a sequence of elements on the stack or in another object can give a performance advantage, just as it can be a disadvantage.

A **vector** deals with properly initialized objects. This is what allows us to use them simply and rely on proper destruction of elements. However, that occasionally puts it at a disadvantage compared to data structures (such as built-in arrays and **array**) that allow uninitialized elements.

As an example, we need not initialize array elements before reading into them:

```
void read()
{
    array<int,MAX]> a;
    for (auto& x : a)
        cin.get(&x);
}
```

For **vector**, we might use **emplace_back()** to achieve a similar effect (without having to specify a **MAX**).

31.4.1.4 vector **and** string

A **vector<char>** is a resizable, contiguous sequence of **chars**, and so is a **string**. So how do we choose between the two?

A **vector** is a general mechanism for storing values. It makes no assumptions about the relationships among the values stored in it. To a **vector<char>**, the string **Hello, World!** is just a sequence of 13 elements of type **char**. Sorting them into **!,HWdellloor** (preceded by a space) makes sense. To contrast, a **string** is intended to hold character sequences. The relationships among the characters are assumed to be important. So, for example, we rarely sort the characters in a **string** because that destroys meaning. Some **string** operations reflect that (e.g., **c_str()**, **>>**, and **find()** "know" that C-style strings are zero-terminated). The implementations of **string** reflect assumptions about the way we use **strings**. For example, the short-string optimization (§19.3.3) would be a pure pessimization if it wasn't for the fact that we use many short strings, so that minimizing free-store use becomes worthwhile.

Should there be a "short-**vector** optimization"? I suspect not, but it would require a massive empirical study to be sure.

31.4.2 Lists

The STL provides two linked-list types:
- **list**: a doubly-linked list
- **forward_list**: a singly-linked list

A **list** is a sequence optimized for insertion and deletion of elements. When you insert into a **list** or delete an element from a **list**, the locations of other elements of the **list** are not affected. In particular, iterators referring to other elements are not affected.

Compared to **vector**, subscripting could be painfully slow, so subscripting is not provided for lists. If necessary, use **advance()** and similar operations to navigate lists (§33.1.4). A list can be traversed using iterators: **list** provides bidirectional iterators (§33.1.2) and **forward_list** provides forward iterators (hence the name of that type of list).

By default, **list** elements are individually allocated in memory and include predecessor and successor pointers (§11.2.2). Compared to a **vector**, a **list** uses more memory per element (usually at least four words more per element), and traversals (iteration) are significantly slower because they involve indirection through pointers rather than simple consecutive access.

A **forward_list** is a singly-linked list. Think of it as a data structure optimized for empty or very short lists that you typically traverse starting from the beginning. For compactness, **forward_list** doesn't even provide a **size()**; an empty **forward_list** takes up just one word of memory. If you need to know the number of elements of a **forward_list**, just count them. If there are enough elements to make counting them expensive, maybe you should use a different container.

With the exception of subscripting, capacity management, and **size()** for **forward_list**, the STL lists provide the member types and operations offered by **vector** (§31.4). In addition, **list** and **forward_list** provide specific list member functions:

Operations for Both list<T> and forward_list<T> (§iso.23.3.4.5, §iso.23.3.5.4)	
lst.push_front(x)	Add x to lst (using copy or move) before the first element
lst.pop_front()	Remove the first element from lst
lst.emplace_front(args)	Add T{args} to lst before the first element
lst.remove(v)	Remove all elements of lst with value v
lst.remove_if(f)	Remove all elements of lst for which f(x)==true
lst.unique()	Remove adjacent duplicate elements of lst
lst.unique(f)	Remove adjacent duplicate elements of lst using f for equality
lst.merge(lst2)	Merge the ordered lists lst and lst2 using < as the order; lst2 is merged into lst and emptied in the process
lst.merge(lst2,f)	Merge the ordered lists lst and lst2 using f as the order; lst2 is merged into lst and emptied in the process
lst.sort()	Sort lst using < as the order
lst.sort(f)	Sort lst using f as the order
lst.reverse()	Reverse the order of the elements of lst; noexcept

As opposed to the general **remove()** and **unique()** algorithms (§32.5), the member algorithms really do affect the size of a list. For example:

```
void use()
{
    list<int> lst {2,3,2,3,5};
    lst.remove(3);              // lst is now {2,2,5}
    lst.unique();               // lst is now {2,5}
    cout << lst.size() << '\n'; // writes 2
}
```

The **merge()** algorithm is stable; that is, equivalent elements keep their relative order.

Operations for list<T> **(§iso.23.3.5.5)**

p points to an element of lst or lst.end()

lst.splice(p,lst2)	Insert the elements of lst2 before p; lst2 becomes empty
lst.splice(p,lst2,p2)	Insert the element pointed to by p2 in lst2 before p; the element pointed to by p2 is removed from lst2
lst.splice(p,lst2,b,e)	Insert the elements [b:e) from lst2 before p; the elements [b:e) are removed from lst2

A **splice()** operation does not copy element values and does not invalidate iterators to elements. For example:

```
list<int> lst1 {1,2,3};
list<int> lst2 {5,6,7};

auto p = lst1.begin();
++p;                        // p points to 2

auto q = lst2.begin();
++q;                        // q points to 6

lst1.splice(p,lst2);        // lst1 is now {1,5,6,7,2,3}; lst2 is now {}
                            // p still points to 2 and q still points to 6
```

A **forward_list** cannot access the element before one pointed to by an iterator (it does not have a predecessor link), so its **emplace()**, **insert()**, **erase()**, and **splice()** operations operate on the position after an iterator:

Operations for forward_list<T> **(§iso.23.3.4.6)**

p2=lst.emplace_after(p,args)	Emplace element constructed from **args** after p; p2 points to the new element
p2=lst.insert_after(p,x)	Insert **x** after p; p2 points to the new element
p2=lst.insert_after(p,n,x)	Insert n copies of **x** after p; p2 points to the last new element
p2=lst.insert_after(p,b,e)	Insert [b:e) after p; p2 points to the last new element
p2=lst.insert_after(p,{elem})	Insert {elem} after p; p2 points to the last new element; elem is an initializer_list
p2=lst.erase_after(p)	Erase the element after p; p2 points to the element after p or lst.end()
p2=lst.erase_after(b,e)	Erase [b:e); p2=e
lst.splice_after(p,lst2)	Splice in lst2 after p
lst.splice_after(p,b,e)	Splice in [b:e) after p
lst.splice_after(p,lst2,p2)	Splice in p2 after p; remove p2 from lst2
lst.splice_after(p,lst2,b,e)	Splice in [b:e) after p; remove [b:e) from lst2

These **list** operations are all *stable*; that is, they preserve the relative order of elements that have equivalent values.

31.4.3 Associative Containers

Associative containers provide lookup based on keys. They come in two variants:
- *Ordered associative containers* do lookup based on an ordering criterion, by default < (less than). They are implemented as balanced binary trees, usually red-black trees.
- *Unordered associative containers* do lookup based on a hash function. They are implemented as hash tables with linked overflow.

Both come as
- **map**s: sequences of {key,value} pairs
- **set**s: **map**s without values (or you could say that the key is also the value)

Finally, maps and sets, whether ordered or unordered, come in two variants:
- "Plain" sets or maps with a unique entry for each key
- "Multi" sets or maps for which multiple entries can exist for each key

The name of an associate container indicates its place in this 3-dimensional space: {set|map, plain|unordered, plain|multi}. "Plain" is never spelled out, so the associative containers are:

Associative Containers (§iso.23.4.1, §iso.23.5.1)			
set	multiset	unordered_set	unordered_multiset
map	multimap	unordered_map	unordered_multimap

Their template arguments are described in §31.4.

Internally, a **map** and an **unordered_map** are very different. See §31.2.1 for graphical representations. In particular, **map** uses its comparison criterion (typically <) on a key to search through a balanced tree (an **O(log(n))** operation), whereas **unordered_map** applies a hash function on a key to find a slot in a hash table (an **O(1)** operation for a good hash function).

31.4.3.1 Ordered Associative Containers

Here are the template arguments and member types for **map**:

```
template<typename Key,
    typename  T,
    typename  Compare = less<Key>,
    typename  Allocator = allocator<pair<const Key, T>>>
class map {
public:
    using key_type = Key;
    using mapped_type = T;
    using value_type = pair<const Key, T>;
    using key_compare = Compare;
    using allocator_type = Allocator;
    using reference = value_type&;
    using const_reference = const value_type&;
    using iterator = /* implementation-defined */ ;
    using const_iterator = /* implementation-defined */ ;
    using size_type = /* implementation-defined */ ;
    using difference_type = /* implementation-defined */ ;
```

```
using pointer = typename allocator_traits<Allocator>::pointer;
using const_pointer = typename allocator_traits<Allocator>::const_pointer;
using reverse_iterator = std::reverse_iterator<iterator>;
using const_reverse_iterator = std::reverse_iterator<const_iterator>;

class value_compare { /* operator()(k1,k2)  does a key_compare()(k1,k2) */ };
// ...
};
```

In addition to the constructors mentioned in §31.3.2, the associative containers have constructors allowing a programmer to supply a comparator:

map<K,T,C,A> Constructors (§iso.23.4.4.2)	
map m {cmp,a};	Construct m to use comparator cmp and allocator a; explicit
map m {cmp};	map m {cmp, A{}}; explicit
map m {};	map m {C{}}; explicit
map m {b,e,cmp,a};	Construct m to use comparator cmp and allocator a; initialize with the elements from [b:e)
map m {b,e,cmp};	map m {b,e,cmp, A{}};
map m {b,e};	map m {b,e,C{}};
map m {m2};	Copy and move constructors
map m {a};	Construct default map; use allocator a; explicit
map m {m2,a};	Copy or move construct m from m2; use allocator a
map m {{elem},cmp,a};	Construct m to use comparator cmp and allocator a; initialize with the elements from initializer_list {elem}
map m {{elem},cmp};	map m {{elem},cmp,A{}};
map m {{elem}};	map m {{elem},C{}};

For example:

```
map<string,pair<Coordinate,Coordinate>> locations
    {
        {"Copenhagen",{"55:40N","12:34E"}},
        {"Rome",{"41:54N","12:30E"}},
        {"New York",{"40:40N","73:56W"}
    };
```

The associative containers offer a variety of insertion and lookup operations:

Associative Container Operations (§iso.23.4.4.1)	
v=c[k]	v is a reference to the element with key k; if k is not found, {k,mapped_type{}} is inserted into c; only for map and unordered_map
v=c.at(k)	v is a reference to the element with key k; if k is not found, an out_of_range is thrown; only for map and unordered_map

Associative Container Operations (continued) (§iso.23.4.4.1)	
p=c.find(k)	p points to the first element with key **k** or **c.end()**
p=c.lower_bound(k)	p points to the first element with key >=**k** or **c.end()**; ordered containers only
p=c.upper_bound(k)	p points to the first element with key >**k** or **c.end()**; ordered containers only
pair(p1,p2)=c.equal_range(k)	p1=c.lower_bound(k); p2=c.upper_bound(k)
pair(p,b)=c.insert(x)	x is a **value_type** or something that can be copied into a **value_type** (e.g., a two-element **tuple**); b is **true** if **x** was inserted and **false** if there already was an entry with **x**'s key; p points to the (possibly new) element with **x**'s key
p2=c.insert(p,x)	x is a **value_type** or something that can be copied into a **value_type** (e.g., a two-element **tuple**); p is a hint of where to start looking for an element with **x**'s key; p2 points to the (possibly new) element with **x**'s key
c.insert(b,e)	c.insert(∗p) for every **p** in [**b**:**e**)
c.insert({args})	Insert each element of the **initializer_list args**; an element is of type **pair<key_type,mapped_type>**
p=c.emplace(args)	p points to an object of **c**'s **value_type** constructed from **args** and inserted into **c**
p=c.emplace_hint(h,args)	p points to an object of **c**'s **value_type** constructed from **args** and inserted into **c**; h is an iterator into **c**, possibly used as a hint of where to start to search for a place for the new entry
r=c.key_comp()	r is a copy of the key comparison object; ordered containers only
r=c.value_comp()	r is a copy of the value comparison object; ordered containers only
n=c.count(k)	n is the number of elements with key **k**

Operations specific to unordered containers are presented in §31.4.3.5.

If a key, **k**, is not found by a subscript operation, **m[k]**, a default value is inserted. For example:

```
map<string,string> dictionary;

dictionary["sea"]="large body of water";     // insert or assign to element

cout << dictionary["seal"];                   // read value
```

If **seal** is not in the dictionary, nothing is printed: the empty string was entered as the value for **seal** and returned as the result of the lookup.

If that is not the desired behavior, we can use find() and insert() directly:

```
auto q = dictionary.find("seal");          // lookup; don't insert

if (q==dictionary.end()) {
    cout << "entry not found";
    dictionary.insert(make_pair("seal","eats fish"));
}
else
    cout q->second;
```

In fact, [] is little more than a convenient notation for insert(). The result of m[k] is equivalent to the result of (∗(m.insert(make_pair(k,V{})).first)).second, where V is the mapped type.

The insert(make_pair()) notation is rather verbose. Instead, we could use emplace():

```
dictionary.emplace("sea cow","extinct");
```

Depending on the quality of the optimizer, this may also be more efficient.

If you try to insert a value into a map and there already is an element with its key, the map is unchanged. If you want to have more than one value for a single key, use a multimap.

The first iterator of the pair (§34.2.4.1) returned by equal_range() is lower_bound() and the second upper_bound(). You can print the value of all elements with the key "apple" in a multimap<string,int> like this:

```
multimap<string,int> mm {{"apple",2}, { "pear",2}, {"apple",7}, {"orange",2}, {"apple",9}};

const string k {"apple"};
auto pp = mm.equal_range(k);
if (pp.first==pp.second)
    cout << "no element with value '" << k << "'\n";
else {
    cout << "elements with value '" << k << "':\n";
    for (auto p=pp.first; p!=pp.second; ++p)
        cout << p->second << ' ';
}
```

This prints 2 7 9.

I could equivalently have written:

```
auto pp = make_pair(m.lower_bound(),m.upper_bound());
// ...
```

However, that would imply an extra traversal of the map. The equal_range(), lower_bound(), and upper_bound() are also provided for sorted sequences (§32.6).

I tend to think of a set as a map with no separate value_type. For a set, the value_type is also the key_type. Consider:

```
struct Record {
    string label;
    int value;
};
```

To have a **set<Record>**, we need to provide a comparison function. For example:

```
bool operator<(const Record& a, const Record& b)
{
    return a.label<b.label;
}
```

Given that, we can write:

```
set<Record> mr {{"duck",10}, {"pork",12}};

void read_test()
{
    for (auto& r : mr) {
        cout << '{' << r.label << ':' << r.value << '}';
    }
    cout << endl;
}
```

The key of an element in an associative container is immutable (§iso.23.2.4). Therefore, we cannot change the values of a **set**. We cannot even change a member of an element that takes no part in the comparison. For example:

```
void modify_test()
{
    for (auto& r : mr)
        ++r.value;        // error: set elements are immutable
}
```

If you need to modify an element, use a **map**. Don't try to modify a key: if you were to succeed, the underlying mechanism for finding elements would break.

31.4.3.2 Unordered Associative Containers

The unordered associative containers (**unordered_map**, **unordered_set**, **unordered_multimap**, **unordered_multiset**) are hash tables. For simple uses, there are few differences from (ordered) containers because the associative containers share most operations (§31.4.3.1). For example:

```
unordered_map<string,int> score1 {
    {"andy", 7}, {"al",9}, {"bill",-3}, {"barbara",12}
};

map<string,int> score2 {
    {"andy", 7}, {"al",9}, {"bill",-3}, {"barbara",12}
};

template<typename X, typename Y>
ostream& operator<<(ostream& os, pair<X,Y>& p)
{
    return os << '{' << p.first << ',' << p.second << '}';
}
```

```
void user()
{
    cout <<"unordered: ";
    for (const auto& x : score1)
        cout << x << ", ";

    cout << "\nordered: ";
    for (const auto& x : score2)
        cout << x << ", ";
}
```

The visible difference is that iteration through a **map** is ordered and for an **unordered_map** it is not:

    unordered: {andy,7}, {al,9}, {bill,–3}, {barbara,12},
    ordered: {al,9}, {andy, 7}, {barbara,12}, {bill,–3},

Iteration over an **unordered_map** depends on the order of insertion, the hash function, and the load factor. In particular, there is no guarantee that elements are printed in the order of their insertion.

31.4.3.3 Constructing unordered_maps

The **unordered_map** has a lot of template arguments and member type aliases to match:

```
template<typename Key,
         typename  T,
         typename  Hash = hash<Key>,
         typename  Pred = std::equal_to<Key>,
         typename  Allocator = std::allocator<std::pair<const Key, T>>>
class unordered_map {
public:
    using key_type = Key;
    using value_type = std::pair<const Key, T>;
    using mapped_type = T;
    using hasher = Hash;
    using key_equal = Pred;
    using allocator_type = Allocator;
    using pointer = typename allocator_traits<Allocator>::pointer;
    using const_pointer= typename allocator_traits<Allocator>::const_pointer;
    using reference = value_type&;
    using const_reference = const value_type&
    using size_type = /* implementation-defined */;
    using difference_type = /* implementation-defined */;
    using iterator = /* implementation-defined */;
    using const_iterator = /* implementation-defined */;
    using local_iterator = /* implementation-defined */;
    using const_local_iterator = /* implementation-defined */;

    // ...
};
```

By default, an **unordered_map<X>** uses **hash<X>** for hashing and **equal_to<X>** to compare keys.

The default **equal_to<X>** (§33.4) simply compares **X** values using ==.

The general (primary) template **hash** doesn't have a definition. It is up to users of a type **X** to define **hash<X>** if needed. For common types, such as **string**, standard **hash** specializations are provided, so the user need not provide them:

Types with hash<T> (§iso.20.8.12) Supplied by the Standard Library			
string	u16string	u32string	wstring
C-style string	bool	characters	integers
floating-point types	pointers	type_index	thread::id
error_code	bitset<N>	unique_ptr<T,D>	shared_ptr<T>

A hash function (e.g., a specialization of **hash** for a type **T** or a pointer to function) must be callable with an argument of type **T** and return a **size_t** (§iso.17.6.3.4). Two calls of a hash function for the same value must give the same result, and ideally such results are uniformly distributed over the set of **size_t** values so as to minimize the chances that h(x)==h(y) if x!=y.

There is a potentially bewildering set of combinations of template argument types, constructors, and defaults for an unordered container. Fortunately, there is a pattern:

unordered_map<K,T,H,E,A> **Constructors** (§iso.23.5.4)	
unordered_map m {n,hf,eql,a};	Construct m with n buckets, the hash function hf, the equality function eql, and the allocator a; explicit
unordered_map m {n,hf,eql};	unordered_map m{n,hf,eql,allocator_type{}}; explicit
unordered_map m {n,hf};	unordered_map m {n,hf,key_eql{}}; explicit
unordered_map m {n};	unordered_map m {n,hasher{}}; explicit
unordered_map m {};	unordered_map m {N}; the bucket count N is implementation-defined; explicit

Here, **n** is an element count for an otherwise empty **unordered_map**.

unordered_map<K,T,H,E,A> **Constructors** (§iso.23.5.4)	
unordered_map m {b,e,n,hf,eql,a};	Construct m with n buckets from the elems of [b:e), using hash function hf, the equality function eql, and the allocator a;
unordered_map m {b,e,n,hf,eql};	unordered_map m {b,e,n,hf,eql,allocator_type{}};
unordered_map m {b,e,n,hf};	unordered_map m {b,e,n,hf,key_equal{}};
unordered_map m {b,e,n};	unordered_map m {b,e,n,hasher{}};
unordered_map m {b,e};	unordered_map m {b,e,N}; the bucket count N is implementation-defined

Here, we get the initial elements from a sequence [b:e). The number of elements will be then number of elements in [b:e), distance(b,e).

unordered_map<K,T,H,E,A> Constructors (§iso.23.5.4)	
unordered_map m {{elem},n,hf,eql,a};	Construct m from the elems of an initializer_list, using n buckets, the hash function hf, the equality function eql, and the allocator a
unordered_map m {{elem},n,hf,eql};	unordered_map m {{elem},n,hf,eql,allocator_type{}};
unordered_map m {{elem},n,hf};	unordered_map m {{elem},n,hf,key_equal{}};
unordered_map m {{elem},n};	unordered_map m {{elem},n,hasher{}};
unordered_map m {{elem}};	unordered_map m {{elem},N}; the bucket count N is implementation-defined

Here, we get the initial elements from a sequence from a {}-delimited initializer list of elements. The number of elements in the **unordered_map** will be the number of elements in the initializer list.

Finally, **unordered_map** has copy and move constructors, and also equivalent constructors that supply allocators:

unordered_map<K,T,H,E,A> Constructors (§iso.23.5.4)	
unordered_map m {m2};	Copy and move constructors: construct m from m2
unordered_map m {a};	Default construct m and give it allocator a; explicit
unordered_map m {m2,a};	Construct m from m2 and give it allocator a

Be careful when constructing an **unordered_map** with one or two arguments. There are many possible combinations of types, and mistakes can lead to strange error messages. For example:

```
map<string,int> m {My_comparator};          // OK
unordered_map<string,int> um {My_hasher};    // error
```

A single constructor argument must be another **unordered_map** (for a copy or move constructor), a bucket count, or an allocator. Try something like:

```
unordered_map<string,int> um {100,My_hasher}; // OK
```

31.4.3.4 Hash and Equality Functions

Naturally, a user can define a hash function. In fact, there are several ways to do that. Different techniques serve different needs. Here, I present several versions, starting with the most explicit and ending with the simplest. Consider a simple **Record** type:

```
struct Record {
    string name;
    int val;
};
```

I can define **Record** hash and equality operations like this:

```
struct Nocase_hash {
    int d = 1;       // shift code d number of bits in each iteration
```

```
            size_t operator()(const Record& r) const
            {
                size_t h = 0;
                for (auto x : r.name) {
                    h <<= d;
                    h ^= toupper(x);
                }

                return h;
            }
        };

        struct Nocase_equal {
            bool operator()(const Record& r,const Record& r2) const
            {
                if (r.name.size()!=r2.name.size()) return false;
                for (int i = 0; i<r.name.size(); ++i)
                    if (toupper(r.name[i])!=toupper(r2.name[i]))
                        return false;
                return true;
            }
        };
```

Given that, I can define and use an unordered_set of Records:

```
        unordered_set<Record,Nocase_hash,Nocase_equal> m {
            { {"andy", 7}, {"al",9}, {"bill",−3}, {"barbara",12} },
            Nocase_hash{2},
            Nocase_equal{}
        };

        for (auto r : m)
            cout << "{" << r.name << ',' << r.val << "}\n";
```

If, as is most common, I wanted to use the default values for my hash and equality functions, I could do that by simply not mentioning them as constructor arguments. By default, the unordered_set uses the default versions:

```
        unordered_set<Record,Nocase_hash,Nocase_equal> m {
            {"andy", 7}, {"al",9}, {"bill",−3}, {"barbara",12}
            // use Nocase_hash{} and Nocase_equal{}
        };
```

Often, the easiest way of writing a hash function is to use the standard-library hash functions provided as specializations of hash (§31.4.3.2). For example:

```
        size_t hf(const Record& r) { return hash<string>()(r.name)^hash<int>()(r.val); };

        bool eq (const Record& r, const Record& r2) { return r.name==r2.name && r.val==r2.val; };
```

Combining hash values using exclusive OR (^) preserves their distributions over the set of values of type size_t (§3.4.5, §10.3.1).

Given this hash function and equality function, we can define an `unordered_set`:

```
unordered_set<Record,decltype(&hf),decltype(&eq)> m {
    { {"andy", 7}, {"al",9}, {"bill",–3}, {"barbara",12} },
    hf,
    eq
};

for (auto r : m)
    cout << "{" << r.name << ',' << r.val << "}\n";
}
```

I used `decltype` to avoid having to explicitly repeat the types of `hf` and `eq`.

If we don't have an initializer list handy, we can give an initial size instead:

```
unordered_set<Record,decltype(&hf),decltype(&eq)> m {10,hf,eq};
```

That also makes it a bit easier to focus on the hash and equality operations.

If we wanted to avoid separating the definitions of `hf` and `eq` from their point of use, we could try lambdas:

```
unordered_set<Record,                              // value type
        function<size_t(const Record&)>,           // hash type
        function<bool(const Record&,const Record&)>   // equal type
    > m { 10,
    [](const Record& r) { return hash<string>{}(r.name)^hash<int>{}(r.val); },
    [](const Record& r, const Record& r2) { return r.name==r2.name && r.val==r2.val; }
};
```

The point about using (named or unnamed) lambdas instead of functions is that they can be defined locally in a function, next to their use.

However, here, `function` may incur overhead that I would prefer to avoid if the `unordered_set` was heavily used. Also, I consider that version messy and prefer to name the lambdas:

```
auto hf = [](const Record& r) { return hash<string>()(r.name)^hash<int>()(r.val); };
auto eq = [](const Record& r, const Record& r2) { return r.name==r2.name && r.val==r2.val; };

unordered_set<Record,decltype(hf),decltype(eq)> m {10,hf,eq};
```

Finally, we may prefer to define the meaning of hash and equality once for all `unordered` containers of `Record` by specializing the standard-library `hash` and `equal_to` templates used by `unordered_map`:

```
namespace std {
    template<>
    struct hash<Record>{
        size_t operator()(const Record &r) const
        {
            return hash<string>{}(r.name)^hash<int>{}(r.val);
        }
    };
```

```
        template<>
        struct equal_to<Record> {
            bool operator()(const Record& r, const Record& r2) const
            {
                return r.name==r2.name && r.val==r2.val;
            }
        };
    }

    unordered_set<Record> m1;
    unordered_set<Record> m2;
```

The default `hash` and hashes obtained from it by using exclusive-or are often pretty good. Don't rush to use homemade hash functions without experimentation.

31.4.3.5 Load and Buckets

Significant parts of the implementation of an unordered container are made visible to the programmer. Keys with the same hash value are said to be "in the same bucket" (see §31.2.1). A programmer can examine and set the size of the hash table (known as "the number of buckets"):

Hash Policy (§iso.23.2.5)	
h=c.hash_function()	h is c's hash function
eq=c.key_eq()	eq is c's equality test
d=c.load_factor()	d is the number of elements divided by the number of buckets: double(c.size())/c.bucket_count(); noexcept
d=c.max_load_factor()	d is the maximum load factor for c; noexcept
c.max_load_factor(d)	Set c's maximum load factor to d; if c's load factor gets close to its maximum load factor, c will resize the hash table (increase the number of buckets)
c.rehash(n)	Make c's bucket count >= n
c.reserve(n)	Make room for n entries (taking the load factor into account): c.rehash(ceil(n/c.max_load_factor()))

The *load factor* of an unordered associative container is simply the fraction of the capacity that has been used. For example, if the `capacity()` is 100 elements and the `size()` is 30, the `load_factor()` is 0.3.

Note that setting the `max_load_factor`, calling `rehash()`, or calling `reserve()` can be very expensive operations (worst case $O(n*n)$) because they can – and in realistic scenarios typically do – cause rehashing of all elements. These functions are used to ensure that rehashing takes place at relatively convenient times in a program's execution. For example:

```
    unordered_set<Record,[](const Record& r) { return hash(r.name); }> people;
    // ...
    constexpr int expected = 1000000;        // expected maximum number of elements
    people.max_load_factor(0.7);             // at most 70% full
    people.reserve(expected);                // about 1,430,000 buckets
```

You need to experiment to find a suitable load factor for a given set of elements and a particular hash function, but 70% (**0.7**) is often a good choice.

Bucket Interface (§iso.23.2.5)	
n=c.bucket_count()	n is the number of buckets in **c** (the size of the hash table); noexcept
n=c.max_bucket_count()	n is the largest possible number of elements in a bucket; noexcept
m=c.bucket_size(n)	m is the number of elements in the nth bucket
i=c.bucket(k)	An element with key **k** would be in the **i**th bucket
p=c.begin(n)	p points to the first element in bucket n
p =c.end(n)	p points to the one-past-the-last element in bucket n
p=c.cbegin(n)	p points to the first element in bucket n; p is a **const** iterator
p =c.cend(n)	p points to the one-past-the-last element in bucket n; p is a **const** iterator

Use of an **n** for which **c.max_bucket_count()<=n** as an index into a bucket is undefined (and probably disastrous).

One use for the bucket interface is to allow experimentation with hash functions: a poor hash function will lead to large **bucket_count()**s for some key values. That is, it will lead to many keys being mapped to the same hash value.

31.5 Container Adaptors

A *container adaptor* provides a different (typically restricted) interface to a container. Container adaptors are intended to be used only through their specialized interfaces. In particular, the STL container adaptors do not offer direct access to their underlying container. They do not offer iterators or subscripting.

The techniques used to create a container adaptor from a container are generally useful for non-intrusively adapting the interface of a class to the needs of its users.

31.5.1 stack

The **stack** container adaptor is defined in **<stack>**. It can be described by a partial implementation:

```
template<typename T, typename C = deque<T>>
class stack {          // §iso.23.6.5.2
public:
    using value_type = typename C::value_type;
    using reference = typename C::reference;
    using const_reference = typename C::const_reference;
    using size_type = typename C::size_type;
    using container_type = C;
```

```
public:
        explicit stack(const C&); // copy from container
        explicit stack(C&& = C{});        // move from container

    // default copy, move, assignment, destructor

    template<typename A>
        explicit stack(const A& a);             // default container, allocator a
    template<typename A>
        stack(const C& c, const A& a);          // elements from c, allocator a
    template<typename A>
        stack(C&&, const A&);
    template<typename A>
        stack(const stack&, const A&);
    template<typename A>
        stack(stack&&, const A&);

    bool empty() const { return c.empty(); }
    size_type size() const { return c.size(); }
    reference top() { return c.back(); }
    const_reference top() const { return c.back(); }
    void push(const value_type& x) { c.push_back(x); }
    void push(value_type&& x) { c.push_back(std::move(x)); }
    void pop() { c.pop_back(); }            // pop the last element

    template<typename... Args>
    void emplace(Args&&... args)
    {
        c.emplace_back(std::forward<Args>(args)...);
    }

    void swap(stack& s) noexcept(noexcept(swap(c, s.c)))
    {
        using std::swap;      // be sure to use the standard swap()
        swap(c,s.c);
    }
protected:
    C c;
};
```

That is, a **stack** is an interface to a container of the type passed to it as a template argument. A **stack** eliminates the non-stack operations on its container from the interface, and provides the conventional names: **top()**, **push()**, and **pop()**.

In addition, **stack** provides the usual comparison operators (**==**, **<**, etc.) and a nonmember **swap()**.

By default, a **stack** makes a **deque** to hold its elements, but any sequence that provides **back()**, **push_back()**, and **pop_back()** can be used. For example:

```
stack<char> s1;                   // uses a deque<char> to store elements
stack<int,vector<int>> s2;        // uses a vector<int> to store elements
```

Often, **vector** is faster than **deque** and uses less memory.

Elements are added to a **stack** using **push_back()** on the underlying container. Consequently, a **stack** cannot "overflow" as long as there is memory available on the machine for the container to acquire. On the other hand, a **stack** can underflow:

```
void f()
{
    stack<int> s;
    s.push(2);
    if (s.empty()) {            // underflow is preventable
        // don't pop
    }
    else {                      // but not impossible
        s.pop();            // fine: s.size() becomes 0
        s.pop();            // undefined effect, probably bad
    }
}
```

We do not **pop()** an element to use it. Instead, the **top()** is accessed and then **pop()**ed when it is no longer needed. This is not too inconvenient, can be more efficient when a **pop()** is not necessary, and greatly simplifies the implementation of exception guarantees. For example:

```
void f(stack<char>& s)
{
    if (s.top()=='c') s.pop();   // optionally remove optional initial 'c'
    // ...
}
```

By default, a **stack** relies on the allocator from its underlying container. If that's not enough, there are a handful of constructors for supplying another.

31.5.2 queue

Defined in **<queue>**, a **queue** is an interface to a container that allows the insertion of elements at the **back()** and the extraction of elements at the **front()**:

```
template<typename T, typename C = deque<T> >
class queue {           //§iso.23.6.3.1
    // ... like stack ...
    void pop() { c.pop_front(); }           // pop the first element
};
```

Queues seem to pop up somewhere in every system. One might define a server for a simple message-based system like this:

```
void server(queue<Message>& q, mutex& m)
{
    while (!q.empty()) {
        Message mess;
        {   lock_guard<mutex> lck(m);       // lock while extracting message
            if (q.empty()) return;          // somebody else got the message
```

```
                    mess = q.front();
                    q.pop();
                }
                // serve request
        }
    }
```

31.5.3 priority_queue

A **priority_queue** is a queue in which each element is given a priority that controls the order in which the elements get to be the **top()**. The declaration of **priority_queue** is much like the declaration of **queue** with additions to deal with a comparison object and a couple of constructors initializing from a sequence:

```
template<typename T, typename C = vector<T>, typename Cmp = less<typename C::value_type>>
class priority_queue {          // §iso.23.6.4
protected:
    C c;
    Cmp comp;
public:
    priority_queue(const Cmp& x, const C&);
    explicit priority_queue(const Cmp& x = Cmp{}, C&& = C{});
    template<typename In>
        priority_queue(In b, In e, const Cmp& x, const C& c);    // insert [b:e) into c
    // ...
};
```

The declaration of **priority_queue** is found in **<queue>**.

By default, the **priority_queue** simply compares elements using the < operator, and **top()** returns the largest element:

```
struct Message {
    int priority;
    bool operator<(const Message& x) const { return priority < x.priority; }
    // ...
};

void server(priority_queue<Message>& q, mutex& m)
{
    while (!q.empty()) {
        Message mess;
        {    lock_guard<mutex> lck(m);      // hold lock while extracting message
             if (q.empty()) return;          // somebody else got the message
             mess = q.top();
             q.pop();
        }
        // serve highest priority request
    }
}
```

This differs from the **queue** version (§31.5.2) in that **Messages** with higher priority will get served first. The order in which elements with equal priority come to the head of the queue is not defined. Two elements are considered of equal priority if neither has higher priority than the other (§31.2.2.1).

Keeping elements in order isn't free, but it needn't be expensive either. One useful way of implementing a **priority_queue** is to use a tree structure to keep track of the relative positions of elements. This gives an **O(log(n))** cost of both **push()** and **pop()**. A **priority_queue** is almost certainly implemented using a **heap** (§32.6.4).

31.6 Advice

[1]   An STL container defines a sequence; §31.2.

[2]   Use **vector** as your default container; §31.2, §31.4.

[3]   Insertion operators, such as **insert()** and **push_back()** are often more efficient on a **vector** than on a **list**; §31.2, §31.4.1.1.

[4]   Use **forward_list** for sequences that are usually empty; §31.2, §31.4.2.

[5]   When it comes to performance, don't trust your intuition: measure; §31.3.

[6]   Don't blindly trust asymptotic complexity measures; some sequences are short and the cost of individual operations can vary dramatically; §31.3.

[7]   STL containers are resource handles; §31.2.1.

[8]   A **map** is usually implemented as a red-black tree; §31.2.1, §31.4.3.

[9]   An **unordered_map** is a hash table; §31.2.1, §31.4.3.2.

[10]   To be an element type for a STL container, a type must provide copy or move operations; §31.2.2.

[11]   Use containers of pointers or smart pointers when you need to preserve polymorphic behavior; §31.2.2.

[12]   Comparison operations should implement a strict weak order; §31.2.2.1.

[13]   Pass a container by reference and return a container by value; §31.3.2.

[14]   For a container, use the ()-initializer syntax for sizes and the {}-initializer syntax for lists of elements; §31.3.2.

[15]   For simple traversals of a container, use a range-**for** loop or a begin/end pair of iterators; §31.3.4.

[16]   Use **const** iterators where you don't need to modify the elements of a container; §31.3.4.

[17]   Use **auto** to avoid verbosity and typos when you use iterators; §31.3.4.

[18]   Use **reserve()** to avoid invalidating pointers and iterators to elements; §31.3.3, §31.4.1.

[19]   Don't assume performance benefits from **reserve()** without measurement; §31.3.3.

[20]   Use **push_back()** or **resize()** on a container rather than **realloc()** on an array; §31.3.3, §31.4.1.1.

[21]   Don't use iterators into a resized **vector** or **deque**; §31.3.3.

[22]   When necessary, use **reserve()** to make performance predictable; §31.3.3.

[23]   Do not assume that [] range checks; §31.2.2.

[24]   Use **at()** when you need guaranteed range checks; §31.2.2.

[25]   Use **emplace()** for notational convenience; §31.3.7.

[26] Prefer compact and contiguous data structures; §31.4.1.2.

[27] Use **emplace()** to avoid having to pre-initialize elements; §31.4.1.3.

[28] A **list** is relatively expensive to traverse; §31.4.2.

[29] A **list** usually has a four-word-per-element memory overhead; §31.4.2.

[30] The sequence of an ordered container is defined by its comparison object (by default <); §31.4.3.1.

[31] The sequence of an unordered container (a hashed container) is not predictably ordered; §31.4.3.2.

[32] Use unordered containers if you need fast lookup for large amounts of data; §31.3.

[33] Use unordered containers for element types with no natural order (e.g., no reasonable <); §31.4.3.

[34] Use ordered associative containers (e.g., **map** and **set**) if you need to iterate over their elements in order; §31.4.3.2.

[35] Experiment to check that you have an acceptable hash function; §31.4.3.4.

[36] Hash function obtained by combining standard hash functions for elements using exclusive or are often good; §31.4.3.4.

[37] **0.7** is often a reasonable load factor; §31.4.3.5.

[38] You can provide alternative interfaces for containers; §31.5.

[39] The STL adaptors do not offer direct access to their underlying containers; §31.5.

32

STL Algorithms

> *Form is liberating.*
> *– Engineer´s proverb*

32.1 Introduction

This chapter presents the STL algorithms. The STL consists of the iterator, container, algorithm, and function object parts of the standard library. The rest of the STL is presented in Chapter 31 and Chapter 33.

32.2 Algorithms

There are about 80 standard algorithms defined in <algorithm>. They operate on *sequences* defined by a pair of iterators (for inputs) or a single iterator (for outputs). When copying, comparing, etc., two sequences, the first is represented by a pair of iterators, [b:e), but the second by just a single iterator, **b2**, which is considered the start of a sequence holding sufficient elements for the algorithm, for example, as many elements as the first sequence: [**b2:b2+(e–b)**]. Some algorithms, such as **sort()**, require random-access iterators, whereas many, such as **find()**, only read their elements in order so that they can make do with a forward iterator. Many algorithms follow the usual convention of returning the end of a sequence to represent "not found" (§4.5). I don't mention that for each algorithm.

Algorithms, both the standard-library algorithms and the users' own ones, are important:

- Each names a specific operation, documents an interface, and specifies semantics.
- Each can be widely used and known by many programmers.

For correctness, maintainability, and performance, these can be immense advantages compared to "random code" with less well-specified functions and dependencies. If you find yourself writing a piece of code with several loops, local variables that don't seem to relate to each other, or complicated control structures, consider if the code could be simplified by making a part into a function/algorithm with a descriptive name, a well-defined purpose, a well-defined interface, and well-defined dependencies.

Numerical algorithms in the style of the STL algorithms are presented in §40.6.

32.2.1 Sequences

The ideal for a standard-library algorithm is to provide the most general and flexible interface to something that can be implemented optimally. The iterator-based interfaces are a good, but not perfect, approximation to that ideal (§33.1.1). For example, an iterator-based interface does not directly represent the notion of a sequence, leading to the possibility of confusion and difficulties in detecting some range errors:

```
void user(vector<int>& v1, vector<int>& v2)
{
        copy(v1.begin(),v1.end(),v2.begin());        // may overflow v2
        sort(v1.begin(),v2.end());                    // oops!
}
```

Many such problems can be alleviated by providing container versions of the standard-library algorithms. For example:

```
template<typename Cont>
void sort(Cont& c)
{
        static_assert(Range<Cont>(), "sort(): Cont argument not a Range");
        static_assert(Sortable<Iterator<Cont>>(), "sort(): Cont argument not Sortable");

        std::sort(begin(c),end(c));
}

template<typename Cont1, typename Cont2>
void copy(const Cont1& source, Cont2& target)
{
        static_assert(Range<Cont1>(), "copy(): Cont1 argument not a Range");
        static_assert(Range<Cont2>(), "copy(): Cont2 argument not a Range");
```

```
        if (target.size()<source.size()) throw out_of_range{"copy target too small"};

        std::copy(source.begin(),source.end(),target.begin());
    }
```

This would simplify the definition of **user()**, make the second error impossible to express, and catch the first at run time:

```
    void user(vector<int>& v1, vector<int>& v2)
    {
        copy(v1,v2);    // overflows will be caught
        sort(v1);
    }
```

However, the container versions are also less general than the versions that use iterators directly. In particular, you cannot use the container **sort()** to sort half a container, and you cannot use the container **copy()** to write to an output stream.

A complementary approach is to define a "range" or "sequence" abstraction that allows us to define sequences when needed. I use the concept **Range** to denote anything with **begin()** and **end()** iterators (§24.4.4). That is, there is no **Range** class holding data – exactly as there is no **Iterator** class or **Container** class in the STL. So, in the "container **sort()**" and "container **copy()**" examples, I called the template argument **Cont** (for "container"), but they will accept any sequence with a **begin()** and an **end()** that meets the rest of the requirements for the algorithm.

The standard-library containers mostly return iterators. In particular, they do not return containers of results (except in a few rare examples, a **pair**). One reason for that is that when the STL was designed, there was no direct support for move semantics. So, there was no obvious and efficient way to return a lot of data from an algorithm. Some programmers used explicit indirection (e.g., a pointer, reference, or iterator) or some clever trickery. Today, we can do better:

```
    template<typename Cont, typename Pred>
    vector<Value_type<Cont>*>
    find_all(Cont& c, Pred p)
    {
        static_assert(Range<Cont>(), "find_all(): Cont argument not a Range");
        static_assert(Predicate<Pred>(), "find_all(): Pred argument not a Predicate");

        vector<Value_type<Cont>*> res;
        for (auto& x : c)
            if (p(x)) res.push_back(&x);
        return res;
    }
```

In C++98, this **find_all()** would have been a bad performance bug whenever the number of matches was large. If the choice of standard-library algorithms seems restrictive or insufficient, extension with new versions of STL algorithms or new algorithms is often a viable and superior alternative to just writing "random code" to work around the problem.

Note that whatever an STL algorithm returns, it cannot be an argument container. The arguments to STL algorithms are iterators (Chapter 33), and an algorithm has no knowledge of the data structure those iterators point into. Iterators exist primarily to isolate algorithms from the data structure on which they operate, and vice versa.

32.3   Policy Arguments

Most standard-library algorithms come in two versions:
- A "plain" version that performs its action using conventional operations, such as < and ==
- A version that takes key operations as arguments

For example:

```
template<class Iter>
void sort(Iter first, Iter last)
{
        // ... sort using e1<e2 ...
}


template<class Iter, class Pred>
void sort(Iter first, Iter last, Pred pred)
{
        // ... sort using pred(e1,e2) ...
}
```

This greatly increases the flexibility of the standard library and its range of uses.

The usual two versions of an algorithm can be implemented as two (overloaded) function templates or as a single function template with a default argument. For example:

```
template<typename Ran, typename Pred = less<Value_type<Ran>>>   // use a default template argument
sort(Ran first, Ran last, Pred pred ={})
{
        // ... use pred(x,y) ...
}
```

The difference between having two functions and having one with a default argument can be observed by someone taking pointers to functions. However, thinking of many of the variants of the standard algorithms as simply "the version with the default predicate" roughly halves the number of template functions you need to remember.

In some cases, an argument could be interpreted as either a predicate or a value. For example:

```
bool pred(int);
```

```
auto p = find(b,e,pred);   // find element pred or apply predicate'pred()? (the latter)
```

In general, a compiler cannot disambiguate such examples, and programmers would get confused even in the cases where the compiler could disambiguate.

To simplify the task for the programmer, the _if suffix is often used to indicate that an algorithm takes a predicate. The reason to distinguish by using two names is to minimize ambiguities and confusion. Consider:

```
using Predicate = bool(*)(int);
```

```
void f(vector<Predicate>& v1, vector<int>& v2)
{
    auto p1 = find(v1.begin(),v1.end(),pred);      // find element with the value pred
    auto p2 = find_if(v2.begin(),v2.end(),pred);   // count elements for which pred() returns true
}
```

Some operations passed as arguments to an algorithm are meant to modify the element to which they are applied (e.g., some operations passed to **for_each()**; §32.4.1), but most are predicates (e.g., a comparison object for **sort()**). Unless otherwise stated, assume that a policy argument passed to an algorithm should not modify an element. In particular, do not try to modify elements through predicates:

```
int n_even(vector<int>& v)                         // don't do this
    // count the number of even values in v
{
    return find_if(v.begin(),v.end(),[](int& x) {++x; return x&1; });
}
```

Modifying an element through a predicate obscures what is being done. If you are really sneaky, you could even modify the sequence (e.g., by inserting or removing an element using the name of a container being iterated over), so that the iteration would fail (probably in obscure ways). To avoid accidents, you may pass arguments to predicates by **const** reference.

Similarly, a predicate should not carry state that changes the meaning of its operation. The implementation of an algorithm may copy a predicate, and we rarely want repeated uses of a predicate on the same value to give different results. Some function objects passed to algorithms, such as random number generators, do carry mutable state. Unless you are really sure that an algorithm doesn't copy, keep a function object argument's mutable state in another object and access it through a pointer or a reference.

The **==** and **<** operations on pointer elements are rarely appropriate for an STL algorithm: they compare machine addresses rather than the values pointed to. In particular, do not sort or search containers of C-style strings using the default **==** and **<** (§32.6).

32.3.1 Complexity

As for containers (§31.3), the complexity of algorithms is specified by the standard. Most algorithms are linear, **O(n)**, for some **n**, which is usually the length of an input sequence.

Algorithm Complexity (§iso.25)	
O(1)	**swap()**, **iter_swap()**
O(log(n))	**lower_bound()**, **upper_bund()**, **equal_range()**, **binary_search()**, **push_heap()**, **pop_heap()**
O(n∗log(n))	**inplace_merge()** (worst case), **stable_partition()** (worst case),
	sort(), **stable_sort()**, **partial_sort()**, **partial_sort_copy()**, **sort_heap()**
O(n∗n)	**find_end()**, **find_first_of()**, **search()**, **search_n()**
O(n)	All the rest

As ever, these are asymptotic complexities, and you have to know what **n** measures to have an idea of the implications. For example, if **n<3**, a quadratic algorithm may be the best choice. The cost of each iteration can vary dramatically. For example, traversing a list can be much slower than traversing a vector, even though the complexity in both cases is linear (**O(n)**). Complexity measures are not a substitute for common sense and actual time measurements; they are one tool among many to ensure quality code.

32.4 Nonmodifying Sequence Algorithms

A nonmodifying algorithm just reads the values of elements of its input sequences; it does not rearrange the sequence and does not change the values of the elements. Typically, user-supplied operations to an algorithm don't change the values of elements either; they tend to be predicates (which may not modify their arguments).

32.4.1 for_each()

The simplest algorithm is **for_each()**, which just applies an operation to each element of a sequence:

for_each (§iso.25.2.4)
f=for_each(b,e,f)   Do f(x) for each **x** in [b:e); return **f**

When possible, prefer a more specific algorithm.

The operation passed to **for_each()** may modify elements. For example:

```
void increment_all(vector<int>& v) // increment each element of v
{
     for_each(v.begin(),v.end(), [](int& x) {++x;});
}
```

32.4.2 Sequence Predicates

Sequence Predicates (§iso.25.2.1)	
all_of(b,e,f)	Is f(x) true for all **x** in [b:e)?
any_of(b,e,f)	Is f(x) true for any **x** in [b:e)?
none_of(b,e,f)	Is f(x) false for all **x** in [b:e)?

For example:

```
vector<double> scale(const vector<double>& val, const vector<double>& div)
{
     assert(val.size()<div.size());
     assert(all_of(div.begin(),div.end(),[](double x){ return 0<x; });

     vector res(val.size());
     for (int i = 0; i<val.size(); ++i)
          res[i] = val[i]/div[i];
     return res;
}
```

When one of these sequence predicates fails, it does not tell which element caused the failure.

32.4.3 count()

count (§iso.25.2.9)	
x=count(b,e,v)	x is the number of elements *p in [b:e) such that v==*p
x=count_if(b,e,v,f)	x is the number of elements *p in [b:e) such that f(*p)

For example:

```
void f(const string& s)
{
    auto n_space = count(s.begin(),s.end(),' ');
    auto n_whitespace = count_if(s.begin(),s.end(),isspace);
    // ...
}
```

The isspace() predicate (§36.2) lets us count all whitespace characters, rather than just space.

32.4.4 find()

The find() family of algorithms do linear searches for some element or predicate match:

The find Family (§iso.25.2.5)	
p=find(b,e,v)	p points to the first element in [b:e) such that *p==v
p=find_if(b,e,f)	p points to the first element in [b:e) such that f(*p)
p=find_if_not(b,e,f)	p points to the first element in [b:e) such that !f(*p)
p=find_first_of(b,e,b2,e2)	p points to the first element in [b:e) such that *p==*q for some q in [b2:e2)
p=find_first_of(b,e,b2,e2,f)	p points to the first element in [b:e) such that f(*p,*q) for some q in [b2:e2)
p=adjacent_find(b,e)	p points to the first element in [b:e) such that *p==*(p+1)
p=adjacent_find(b,e,f)	p points to the first element in [b:e) such that f(*p,*(p+1))
p=find_end(b,e,b2,e2)	p points to the last *p in [b:e) such that *p==*q for an element *q in [b2:e2)
p=find_end(b,e,b2,e2,f)	p points to the last *p in [b:e) such that f(*p,*q) for an element *q in [b2:e2)

The algorithms find() and find_if() return an iterator to the first element that matches a value and a predicate, respectively.

```
void f(const string& s)
{
    auto p_space = find(s.begin(),s.end(),' ');
    auto p_whitespace = find_if(s.begin(),s.end(), isspace);
    // ...
}
```

The find_first_of() algorithms find the first occurrence in a sequence of an element from another sequence. For example:

```
array<int> x = {1,3,4 };
array<int> y = {0,2,3,4,5};

void f()
{
    auto p = find_first_of(x.begin(),x.end(),y.begin(),y.end);        // p = &x[1]
    auto q = find_first_of(p+1,x.end(),y.begin(),y.end());           // q = &x[2]
}
```

The iterator **p** will point to **x[1]** because **3** is the first element of **x** with a match in **y**. Similarly, **q** will point to **x[2]**.

32.4.5 equal() and mismatch()

The **equal()** and **mismatch()** algorithms compare pairs of sequences:

equal **and** mismatch() (§iso.25.2.11, §iso.25.2.10)	
equal(b,e,b2)	Is **v==v2** for all corresponding elements of [b:e) and [b2:b2+(e–b))?
equal(b,e,b2,f)	Is **f(v,v2)** for all corresponding elements of [b:e) and [b2:b2+(e–b))?
pair(p1,p2)=mismatch(b,e,b2)	**p1** points to the first element in [b:e) and **p2** points to the first element in [b2:b2+(e–b)) such that !(∗p1==∗p2) or p1==e
pair(p1,p2)=mismatch(b,e,b2,f)	**p1** points to the first element in [b:e) and **p2** points to the first element in [b2:b2+(e–b)) such that !f(∗p1,∗p2) or p1==e

The **mismatch()** looks for the first pair of elements of two sequences that compare unequal and returns iterators to those elements. No end is specified for the second sequence; that is, there is no **last2**. Instead, it is assumed that there are at least as many elements in the second sequence as in the first, and **first2+(last–first)** is used as **last2**. This technique is used throughout the standard library, where pairs of sequences are used for operations on pairs of elements. We could implement **mismatch()** like this:

```
template<class In, class In2, class Pred = equal_to<Value_type<In>>>
pair<In, In2> mismatch(In first, In last, In2 first2, Pred p ={})
{
    while (first != last && p(∗first,∗first2)) {
        ++first;
        ++first2;
    }
    return {first,first2};
}
```

I used the standard function object **equal_to** (§33.4) and the type function **Value_type** (§28.2.1).

32.4.6 search()

The **search()** and **search_n()** algorithms find one sequence as a subsequence in another:

Searching for Sequences (§iso.25.2.13)	
p=search(b,e,b2,e2)	**p** points to the first *p in [**b**:**e**) such that [**p**:**p**+(**e**−**b**)) equals [**b2**:**e2**)
p=search(b.e,b2,e2,f)	**p** points to the first *p in [**b**:**e**) such that [**p**:**p**+(**e**−**b**)) equals [**b2**:**e2**), using **f** for element comparison
p=search_n(b,e,n,v)	**p** points to the first element of [**b**:**e**) such that each element of [**p**:**p**+**n**) has the value **v**
p=search_n(b,e,n,v,f)	**p** points to the first element of [**b**:**e**) such that for each element *q in [**p**:**p**+**n**) we have **f**(*p,v)

The **search()** algorithm looks for its second sequence as a subsequence of its first. If that second sequence is found, an iterator for the first matching element in the first sequence is returned. As usual, the end of the sequence is used to represent "not found." For example:

```
string quote {"Why waste time learning, when ignorance is instantaneous?"};

bool in_quote(const string& s)
{
    auto p = search(quote.begin(),quote.end(),s.begin(),s.end()); // find s in quote
    return p!=quote.end();
}

void g()
{
    bool b1 = in_quote("learning");    // b1 = true
    bool b2 = in_quote("lemming");     // b2 = false
}
```

Thus, **search()** is a useful algorithm for finding a substring generalized to all sequences.

Use **find()** or **binary_search()** (§32.6) to look for just a single element.

32.5 Modifying Sequence Algorithms

The modifying algorithms (also called *mutating sequence algorithms*) can (and often do) modify elements of their argument sequences.

transform (§iso.25.3.4)	
p=transform(b,e,out,f)	Apply *q=f(*p1) to every *p1 in [**b**:**e**), writing to the corresponding *q in [**out**:**out**+(**e**−**b**)); p=out+(e−b)
p=transform(b,e,b2,out,f)	Apply *q=f(*p1,*p2) to every element in *p1 in [**b**:**e**) and the corresponding *p2 in [**b2**:**b2**+(**e**−**b**)), writing to the corresponding *q in [**out**:**out**+(**e**−**b**)); p=out+(e−b)

Somewhat confusingly, **transform()** doesn't necessarily change its input. Instead, it produces an output that is a transformation of its input based on a user-supplied operation. The one-input-sequence version of **transform()** may be defined like this:

```
template<class In, class Out, class Op>
Out transform(In first, In last, Out res, Op op)
{
    while (first!=last)
        *res++ = op(*first++);
    return res;
}
```

The output sequence may be the same as the input sequence:

```
void toupper(string& s)   // remove case
{
    transform(s.begin(),s.end(),s.begin(),toupper);
}
```

This really transforms the input **s**.

32.5.1 copy()

The **copy()** family of algorithms copy elements from one sequence into another. The following sections list versions of **copy()** combined with other algorithms, such as **replace_copy()** (§32.5.3).

The copy Family (§iso.25.3.1)	
p=copy(b,e,out)	Copy all elements in [b:e) to [out:p); p=out+(e−b)
p=copy_if(b,e,out,f)	Copy elements x in [b:e) for which f(x) to [out:p)
p=copy_n(b,n,out)	Copy the first n elements in [b:b+n) to [out:p); p=out+n
p=copy_backward(b,e,out)	Copy all elements in [b:e) to [out:p), starting with its last element; p=out+(e−b)
p=move(b,e,out)	Move all elements in [b:e) to [out:p); p=out+(e−b)
p=move_backward(b,e,out)	Move all elements in [b:e) to [out:p), starting with its last element; p=out+(e−b)

The target of a copy algorithm need not be a container. Anything that can be described by an output iterator (§38.5) will do. For example:

```
void f(list<Club>& lc, ostream& os)
{
    copy(lc.begin(),lc.end(),ostream_iterator<Club>(os));
}
```

To read a sequence, we need a pair of iterators describing where to begin and where to end. To write, we need only an iterator describing where to write to. However, we must take care not to write beyond the end of the target. One way to ensure that we don't do this is to use an inserter (§33.2.2) to grow the target as needed. For example:

```
    void f(const vector<char>& vs, vector<char>& v)
    {
        copy(vs.begin(),vs.end(),v.begin());            // might overwrite end of v
        copy(vs.begin(),vs.end(),back_inserter(v));     // add elements from vs to end of v
    }
```

The input sequence and the output sequence may overlap. We use **copy()** when the sequences do not overlap or if the end of the output sequence is in the input sequence.

We use **copy_if()** to copy only elements that fulfill some criterion. For example:

```
    void f(list<int>&ld, int n, ostream& os)
    {
        copy_if(ld.begin(),ld.end(),
            ostream_iterator<int>(os),
            [](int x) { return x>n); });
    }
```

See also **remove_copy_if()**.

32.5.2 unique()

The **unique()** algorithm removes adjacent duplicate elements from a sequence:

The unique Family (§iso.25.3.9)	
p=unique(b,e)	Move elements in [**b**:**e**) such that [**b**:**p**) has no adjacent duplicates
p=unique(b,e,f)	Move elements in [**b**:**e**) such that [**b**:**p**) has no adjacent duplicates; f(∗**p**,∗(**p**+1)) defines ''duplicate''
p=unique_copy(b,e,out)	Copy [**b**:**e**) to [**out**:**p**); don't copy adjacent duplicates
p=unique_copy(b,e,out,f)	Copy [**b**:**e**) to [**out**:**p**); don't copy adjacent duplicates; f(∗**p**,∗(**p**+1)) defines ''duplicate''

The **unique()** and **unique_copy()** algorithms eliminate adjacent duplicate values. For example:

```
    void f(list<string>& ls, vector<string>& vs)
    {
        ls.sort();          // list sort (§31.4.2)
        unique_copy(ls.begin(),ls.end(),back_inserter(vs));
    }
```

This copies **ls** to **vs**, eliminating duplicates in the process. I used **sort()** to get equal strings adjacent.

Like other standard algorithms, **unique()** operates on iterators. It does not know which container these iterators point into, so it cannot modify that container. It can only modify the values of the elements. This implies that **unique()** does not eliminate duplicates from its input sequence in the way we naively might expect. Therefore, this does not eliminate duplicates in a **vector**:

```
    void bad(vector<string>& vs)               // warning: doesn't do what it appears to do!
    {
        sort(vs.begin(),vs.end());             // sort vector
        unique(vs.begin(),vs.end());           // eliminate duplicates (no it doesn't!)
    }
```

Rather, **unique()** moves unique elements toward the front (head) of a sequence and returns an iterator to the end of the subsequence of unique elements. For example:

```
int main()
{
    string s ="abbcccde";

    auto p = unique(s.begin(),s.end());
    cout << s << ' ' << p–s.begin() << '\n';
}
```

produces

```
abcdecde 5
```

That is, **p** points to the second **c** (that is, the first of the duplicates).

Algorithms that might have removed elements (but can't) generally come in two forms: the
"plain" version that reorders elements in a way similar to **unique()** and a _copy version that produces a new sequence in a way similar to **unique_copy()**.

To eliminate duplicates from a container, we must explicitly shrink it:

```
template<class C>
void eliminate_duplicates(C& c)
{
    sort(c.begin(),c.end());              // sort
    auto p = unique(c.begin(),c.end());  // compact
    c.erase(p,c.end());                   // shrink
}
```

I could equivalently have written **c.erase(unique(c.begin(),c.end()),c.end())**, but I don't think such
terseness improves readability or maintainability.

32.5.3 remove() and replace()

The **remove()** algorithm "removes" elements to the end of a sequence:

remove (§iso.25.3.8)	
p=remove(b,e,v)	Remove elements with value **v** from [**b**:**e**), such that [**b**:**p**) becomes the elements for which !(*q==v)
p=remove_if(b,e,v,f)	Remove elements *q from [**b**:**e**), such that [**b**:**p**) becomes the elements for which !f(*q)
p=remove_copy(b,e,out,v)	Copy elements from [**b**:**e**) for which !(*q==v) to [**out**:**p**)
p=remove_copy_if(b,e,out,f)	Copy elements from [**b**:**e**) for which !f(*q) to [**out**:**p**)
reverse(b,e)	Reverse the order of elements in [**b**:**e**)
p=reverse_copy(b,e,out)	Copy [**b**:**e**) into [**out**:**p**) in reverse order

The **replace()** algorithm assigns new values to selected elements:

replace (§iso.25.3.5)	
replace(b,e,v,v2)	Replace elements *p in [b:e) for which *p==v with **v2**
replace_if(b,e,f,v2)	Replace elements *p in [b:e) for which f(*p) with **v2**
p=replace_copy(b,e,out,v,v2)	Copy [b:e) to [out:p), replacing elements for which *p==v with **v2**
p=replace_copy_if(b,e,out,f,v2)	Copy [b:e) to [out:p), replacing elements for which f(*p,v) with **v2**

These algorithms cannot change the size of their input sequence, so even **remove()** leaves the size of its input sequence unchanged. Like **unique()**, it "removes" by moving elements to the left. For example:

```
string s {"*CamelCase*IsUgly*"};
cout << s << '\n';                                  // *CamelCase*IsUgly*
auto p = remove(s.begin(),s.end(),'*');
copy(s.begin(),p,ostream_iterator<char>{cout});    // CamelCaseIsUgly
cout << s << '\n';                                  // CamelCaseIsUglyly*
```

32.5.4 rotate(), random_shuffle(), and partition()

The **rotate()**, **random_shuffle()**, and **partition()** algorithms provide systematic ways of moving elements around in a sequence:

rotate() (§iso.25.3.11)	
p=rotate(b,m,e)	Left-rotate elements: treat [b:e) as a circle with the first element right after the last; move *(b+i) to *((b+(i+(e−m))%(e−b)); note: *b moves to *m; p=b+(e−m)
p=rotate_copy(b,m,e,out)	Copy [b:e) into a rotated sequence [out:p)

The movement of elements done by **rotate()** (and by the shuffle and partition algorithms) is done using **swap()**.

random_shuffle() (§iso.25.3.12)	
random_shuffle(b,e)	Shuffle elements of [b:e), using the default random number generator
random_shuffle(b,e,f)	Shuffle elements of [b:e), using the random number generator **f**
shuffle(b,e,f)	Shuffle elements of [b:e), using the uniform random number generator **f**

A shuffle algorithm shuffles its sequence much in the way we would shuffle a pack of cards. That is, after a shuffle, the elements are in a random order, where "random" is defined by the distribution produced by the random number generator.

By default, **random_shuffle()** shuffles its sequence using a uniform distribution random number generator. That is, it chooses a permutation of the elements of the sequence so that each permutation has the same chances of being chosen. If you want a different distribution or a better random number generator, you can supply one. For a call **random_shuffle(b,e,r)**, the generator is called with the number of elements in the sequence (or a subsequence) as its argument. For example, for a call **r(e–b)** the generator must return a value in the range **[0,e–b)**. If **My_rand** is such a generator, we might shuffle a deck of cards like this:

```
void f(deque<Card>& dc, My_rand& r)
{
    random_shuffle(dc.begin(),dc.end(),r);
    // ...
}
```

The partition algorithm separates a sequence into two parts based on a partition criterion:

partition() (§iso.25.3.13)	
p=partition(b,e,f)	Place elements for which f(∗p1) in [b:p) and other elements in [p:e)
p=stable_partition(b,e,f)	Place elements for which f(∗p1) in [b:p) and other elements in [p:e); preserve relative order
pair(p1,p2)=partition_copy(b,e,out1,out2,f)	Copy elements of [b:e) for which f(∗p) into [out1:p1) and elements of [b:e) for which !f(∗p) into [out2:p2)
p=partition_point(b,e,f)	For [b:e) p is the point such that all_of(b,p,f) and none_of(p,e,f)
is_partitioned(b,e,f)	Does every element of [b:e) for which f(∗p) precede every element for which !f(∗p)?

32.5.5 Permutations

The permutation algorithms provide a systematic way of generating all permutations of a sequence.

Permutations (§iso.25.4.9, §iso.25.2.12)	
x is **true** if the **next_∗** operation succeeded, otherwise **false**	
x=next_permutation(b,e)	Make [b:e) the next permutation in lexicographical order
x=next_permutation(b,e,f)	Make [b:e) the next permutation, using f for comparison
x=prev_permutation(b,e)	Make [b:e) the previous permutation in lexicographical order
x=prev_permutation(b,e,f)	Make [b:e) the previous permutation, using f for comparison
is_permutation(b,e,b2)	Is there a permutation of [b2:b2+(e–b)) that compares equal to [b,e)?
is_permutation(b,e,b2,f)	Is there a permutation of [b2:b2+(e–b)) that compares equal to [b,e), using f(∗p,∗q) as the element comparison?

Permutations are used to generate combinations of elements of a sequence. For example, the permutations of **abc** are **acb**, **bac**, **bca**, **cab**, and **cba**.

The **next_permutation()** takes a sequence [b:e) and transforms it into the next permutation. The next permutation is found by assuming that the set of all permutations is lexicographically sorted. If such a permutation exists, **next_permutation()** returns **true**; otherwise, it transforms the sequence into the smallest permutation, that is, the ascendingly sorted one (**abc** in the example), and returns **false**. So, we can generate the permutations of **abc** like this:

```
vector<char> v {'a','b','c'};
while(next_permutation(v.begin(),v.end()))
     cout << v[0] << v[1] << v[2] << ' ';
```

Similarly, the return value for **prev_permutation()** is **false** if [b:e) already contains the first permutation (**abc** in the example); in that case, it returns the last permutation (**cba** in the example).

32.5.6 fill()

The **fill()** family of algorithms provide ways of assigning to and initializing elements of a sequence:

The fill **Family (§iso.25.3.6, §iso.25.3.7, §iso.20.6.12)**	
fill(b,e,v)	Assign **v** to each element of [b:e)
p=fill_n(b,n,v)	Assign **v** to each element of [b:b+n); p=b+n
generate(b,e,f)	Assign f() to each element of [b:e)
p=generate_n(b,n,f)	Assign f() to each element of [b:b+n); p=b+n
uninitialized_fill(b,e,v)	Initialize each element in [b:e) with v
p=uninitialized_fill_n(b,n,v)	Initialize each element in [b:b+n) with v; p=b+n
p=uninitialized_copy(b,e,out)	Initialize each element of [out:out+(e–b)); p=b+n with its corresponding element from [b:e)
p=uninitialized_copy_n(b,n,out)	Initialize each element of [out:out+n) with its corresponding element from [b:b+n); p=b+n

The **fill()** algorithm repeatedly assigns the specified value, whereas **generate()** assigns values obtained by calling its function argument repeatedly. For example, using the random number generators **Randint** and **Urand** from §40.7:

```
int v1[900];
array<int,900> v2;
vector v3;

void f()
{
     fill(begin(v1),end(v1),99);                         // set all elements of v1 to 99
     generate(begin(v2),end(v2),Randint{});              // set to random values (§40.7)

     // output 200 random integers in the interval [0:100):
     generate_n(ostream_iterator<int>{cout},200,Urand{100});    // see §40.7

     fill_n(back_inserter{v3},20,99);                     // add 20 elements with the value 99 to v3
}
```

The **generate()** and **fill()** functions assign rather than initialize. If you need to manipulate raw storage, say, to turn a region of memory into objects of well-defined type and state, you use one of the **uninitialized_** versions (presented in **<memory>**).

Uninitialized sequences should only occur at the lowest level of programming, usually inside the implementation of containers. Elements that are targets of **uninitialized_fill()** or **uninitial- ized_copy()** must be of built-in type or uninitialized. For example:

```
vector<string> vs {"Breugel","El Greco","Delacroix","Constable"};
vector<string> vs2 {"Hals","Goya","Renoir","Turner"};
copy(vs.begin(),vs.end(),vs2.begin());                    // OK
uninitialized_copy(vs.begin(),vs.end(),vs2.begin());      // leaks!
```

A few more facilities for dealing with uninitialized memory are described in §34.6.

32.5.7 swap()

A **swap()** algorithm exchanges the values of two objects:

The swap Family (§iso.25.3.3)	
swap(x,y)	Exchange the values of **x** and **y**
p=swap_ranges(b,e,b2)	swap(v,v2) corresponding elements in [b:e) and [b2,b2+(e–b))
iter_swap(p,q)	swap(∗p,∗q)

for example:

```
void use(vector<int>& v, int* p)
{
    swap_ranges(v.begin(),v.end(),p);   // exchange values
}
```

The pointer **p** had better point to an array with at least **v.size()** elements.

The **swap()** algorithm is possibly the simplest and arguably the most crucial algorithm in the standard library. It is used as part of the implementaton of many of the most widely used algo- rithms. Its implementation is used as an example in §7.7.2 and the standard-library version is pre- sented in §35.5.2.

32.6 Sorting and Searching

Sorting and searching in sorted sequences are fundamental, and the needs of programmers are quite varied. Comparison is by default done using the < operator, and equivalence of values **a** and **b** is determined by !(a<b)&&!(b<a) rather than requiring operator ==.

The sort Family (§iso.25.4.1) (continues)	
sort(b,e)	Sort [b:e)
sort(b,e,f)	Sort [b:e), using **f**(∗p,∗q) as the sorting criterion

In addition to the "plain sort" there are many variants:

The sort Family (continued)(§iso.25.4.1)	
stable_sort(b,e)	Sort [b:e) maintaining order of equal elements
stable_sort(b,e,f)	Sort [b:e), using f(*p,*q) as the sorting criterion, maintaining order of equal elements
partial_sort(b,m,e)	Sort enough of [b:e) to get [b:m) into order; [m:e) need not be sorted
partial_sort(b,m,e,f)	Sort enough of [b:e) to get [b:m) into order, using f(*p,*q) as the sorting criterion; [m:e) need not be sorted
p=partial_sort_copy(b,e,b2,e2)	Sort enough of [b:e) to copy the first e2–b2 elements into [b2:e2); p is the smaller of b2 and b2+(e–b)
p=partial_sort_copy(b,e,b2,e2,f)	Sort enough of [b:e) to copy the first e2–b2 elements into [b2:e2), using f for comparison; p is the smaller of b2 and b2+(e–b)
is_sorted(b,e)	Is [b:e) sorted?
is_sorted(b,e,f)	Is [b:e) sorted, using f for comparison?
p=is_sorted_until(b,e)	p points to the first element in [b:e) that is not in order
p=is_sorted_until(b,e,f)	p points to the first element in [b:e) that is not in order, using f for comparison
nth_element(b,n,e)	*n is in the position it would be in if [b:e) was sorted; elements in [b:n) are <= *n and *n <= elements in [n:e)
nth_element(b,n,e,f)	*n is in the position it would be in if [b:e) was sorted; elements in [b:n) are <= *n and *n <= elements in [n:e), using f for comparison

The **sort()** algorithms require random-access iterators (§33.1.2).

Despite its name, **is_sorted_until()** returns an iterator, rather than a **bool**.

The standard **list** (§31.3) does not provide random-access iterators, so **lists** should be sorted using the specific **list** operations (§31.4.2) or by copying their elements into a **vector**, sorting that **vector**, and then copying the elements back into the **list**:

```
template<typename List>
void sort_list(List& lst)
{
        vector v {lst.begin(),lst.end()};       // initialize from lst
        sort(v);                                // use container sort (§32.2)
        copy(v,lst);
}
```

The basic **sort()** is efficient (on average **N∗log(N)**). If a stable sort is required, **stable_sort()** should be used, that is, an **N∗log(N)∗log(N)** algorithm that improves toward **N∗log(N)** when the system has sufficient extra memory. The **get_temporary_buffer()** function may be used for getting such extra memory (§34.6). The relative order of elements that compare equal is preserved by **stable_sort()** but not by **sort()**.

Sometimes, only the first elements of a sorted sequence are needed. In that case, it makes sense to sort the sequence only as far as is needed to get the first part in order, that is, a partial sort. The plain **partial_sort(b,m,e)** algorithms put the elements in the range [b:m) in order. The **partial_sort_copy()** algorithms produce N elements, where N is the lower of the number of elements in the output sequence and the number of elements in the input sequence. We need to specify both the start and the end of the result sequence because that's what determines how many elements we need to sort. For example:

```
void f(const vector<Book>& sales) // find the top ten books
{
    vector<Book> bestsellers(10);
    partial_sort_copy(sales.begin(),sales.end(),
            bestsellers.begin(),bestsellers.end(),
            [](const Book& b1, const Book& b2) { return b1.copies_sold()>b2.copies_sold(); });
    copy(bestsellers.begin(),bestsellers.end(),ostream_iterator<Book>{cout,"\n"});
}
```

Because the target of **partial_sort_copy()** must be a random-access iterator, we cannot sort directly to **cout**.

If the number of elements desired to be sorted by a **partial_sort()** is small compared to the total number of elements, these algorithms can be significantly faster than a complete **sort()**. Then, their complexity approaches O(N) compared to **sort()**'s O(N∗log(N)).

The **nth_element()** algorithm sorts only as far as is necessary to get the Nth element to its proper place with no element comparing less than the Nth element placed after it in the sequence. For example:

```
vector<int> v;
for (int i=0; i<1000; ++i)
    v.push_back(randint(1000));        // §40.7
constexpr int n = 30;
nth_element(v.begin(), v.begin()+n, v.end());
cout << "nth: " << v[n] < '\n';
for (int i=0; i<n; ++i)
    cout << v[i] << ' ';
```

This produces:

```
nth: 24
10 8 15 19 21 15 8 7 6 17 21 2 18 8 1 9 3 21 20 18 10 7 3 3 8 11 11 22 22 23
```

The **nth_element()** differs from **partial_sort()** in that the elements before n are not necessarily sorted, just all less than the nth element. Replacing **nth_element** with **partial_sort** in that example (and using the same seed for the random number generator to get the same sequence), I got:

```
nth: 995
1 2 3 3 3 6 7 7 8 8 8 8 9 10 10 11 11 15 15 17 18 18 19 20 21 21 21 22 22 23
```

The **nth_element()** algorithm is particularly useful for people – such as economists, sociologists, and teachers – who need to look for medians, percentiles, etc.

Sorting C-style strings requires an explicit sorting criterion. The reason is that C-style strings are simply pointers with a set of conventions for their use, so < on pointers compares machine addresses rather than character sequences. For example:

```
vector<string> vs = {"Helsinki","Copenhagen","Oslo","Stockholm"};
vector<char*> vcs = {"Helsinki","Copenhagen","Oslo","Stockholm"};

void use()
{
    sort(vs);   // I have defined a range version of sort()
    sort(vcs);

    for (auto& x : vs)
        cout << x << ' '
    cout << '\n';
    for (auto& x : vcs)
        cout << x << ' ';
```

This prints:

Copenhagen Helsinki Stockholm Oslo
Helsinki Copenhagen Oslo Stockholm

Naively, we might have expected the same output from both **vectors**. However, to sort C-style strings by string value rather than by address we need a proper sort predicate. For example:

```
sort(vcs, [](const char* p, const char* q){ return strcmp(p,q)<0; });
```

The standard-library function **strcmp()** is described in §43.4.

Note that I did not have to supply a == to sort C-style strings. To simplify the user interface, the standard library uses **!(x<y>||y<x)** rather than **x==y** to compare elements (§31.2.2.2).

32.6.1 Binary Search

The **binary_search()** family of algorithms provide binary searches of ordered (sorted) sequences:

Binary Search (§iso.25.4.3)	
p=lower_bound(b,e,v)	p points to the first occurrence of v in [b:e)
p=lower_bound(b,e,v,f)	p points to the first occurrence of v in [b:e), using f for comparison
p=upper_bound(b,e,v)	p points to the first value larger than v in [b:e)
p=upper_bound(b,e,v,f)	p points to the first value larger than v in [b:e), using f for comparison
binary_search(b,e,v)	Is v in the sorted sequence [b:e)?
binary_search(b,e,v,f)	Is v in the sorted sequence [b:e), using f for comparison?
pair(p1,p2)=equal_range(b,e,v)	[p1,p2) is the subsequence of [b:e) with the value v; basically, a binary search for v
pair(p1,p2)=equal_range(b,e,v,f)	[p1,p2) is the subsequence of [b:e) with the value v, using f for comparison; basically, a binary search for v

A sequential search such as **find()** (§32.4) is terribly inefficient for large sequences, but it is about the best we can do without sorting or hashing (§31.4.3.2). Once a sequence is sorted, however, we can use a binary search to determine whether a value is in a sequence. For example:

```
void f(vector<int>& c)
{
    if (binary_search(c.begin(),c.end(),7)) {   // is 7 in c?
        // ...
    }
    // ...
}
```

A **binary_search()** returns a **bool** indicating whether a value is present. As with **find()**, we often also want to know where the elements with that value are in that sequence. However, there can be many elements with a given value in a sequence, and we often need to find either the first or all such elements. Consequently, algorithms are provided for finding a range of equal elements, **equal_range()**, and algorithms for finding the **lower_bound()** and **upper_bound()** of that range. These algorithms correspond to the operations on **multimaps** (§31.4.3). We can think of **lower_bound()** as a fast **find()** and **find_if()** for sorted sequences. For example:

```
void g(vector<int>& c)
{
    auto p = find(c.begin(),c.end(),7);            // probably slow: O(N); c needn't be sorted
    auto q = lower_bound(c.begin(),c.end(),7);     // probably fast: O(log(N)); c must be sorted
    // ...
}
```

If **lower_bound(first,last,k)** doesn't find **k**, it returns an iterator to the first element with a key greater than **k**, or **last** if no such greater element exists. This way of reporting failure is also used by **upper_bound()** and **equal_range()**. This means that we can use these algorithms to determine where to insert a new element into a sorted sequence so that the sequence remains sorted: just insert before the **second** of the returned **pair**.

Curiously enough, the binary search algorithms do not require random-access iterators: a forward iterator suffices.

32.6.2 merge()

The **merge** algorithms combine two ordered (sorted) sequences into one:

The merge Family (§iso.25.4.4)	
p=merge(b,e,b2,e2,out)	Merge two sorted sequences [b2:e2) and [b:e) into [out:p)
p=merge(b,e,b2,e2,out,f)	Merge two sorted sequences [b2:e2) and [b:e) into [out,out+p), using f as the comparison
inplace_merge(b,m,e)	Merge two sorted subsequences [b:m) and [m:e) into a sorted sequence [b:e)
inplace_merge(b,m,e,f)	Merge two sorted subsequences [b:m) and [m:e) into a sorted sequence [b:e), using f as the comparison

The **merge()** algorithm can take different kinds of sequences and elements of different types. For example:

```
vector<int> v {3,1,4,2};
list<double> lst {0.5,1.5,2,2.5};          // lst is in order

sort(v.begin(),v.end());                   // put v in order

vector<double> v2;
merge(v.begin(),v.end(),lst.begin(),lst.end(),back_inserter(v2));   // merger v and lst into v2
for (double x : v2)
     cout << x << ", ";
```

For inserters, see §33.2.2. The output is:

0.5, 1, 1.5, 2, 2, 2.5, 3, 4,

32.6.3 Set Algorithms

These algorithms treat a sequence as a set of elements and provide the basic set operations. The input sequences are supposed to be sorted and the output sequences are also sorted.

Set Algorithms (§iso.25.4.5)	
includes(b,e,b2,e2)	Are all elements of [b:e) also in [b2:e2)?
includes(b,e,b2,e2,f)	Are all elements of [b:e) also in [b2:e2), using f for comparison?
p=set_union(b,e,b2,e2,out)	Construct a sorted sequence [out:p) of elements that are in either [b:e) or [b2:e2)
p=set_union(b,e,b2,e2,out,f)	Construct a sorted sequence [out:p) of elements that are in either [b:e) or [b2:e2), using f for comparison
p=set_intersection(b,e,b2,e2,out)	Construct a sorted sequence [out:p) of elements that are in both [b:e) and [b2:e2)
p=set_intersection(b,e,b2,e2,out,f)	Construct a sorted sequence [out:p) of elements that are in both [b:e) and [b2:e2), using f for comparison
p=set_difference(b,e,b2,e2,out)	Construct a sorted sequence [out:p) of elements that are in [b:e) but not in [b2:e2)
p=set_difference(b,e,b2,e2,out,f)	Construct a sorted sequence [out:p) of elements that are in [b:e) but not in [b2:e2), using f for comparison
p=set_symmetric_difference(b,e,b2,e2,out)	Construct a sorted sequence [out:p) of elements that are in [b:e) or [b2:e2) but not in both
p=set_symmetric_difference(b,e,b2,e2,out,f)	Construct a sorted sequence [out:p) of elements that are in [b:e) or [b2:e2) but not in both, using f for comparison

For example:

```
string s1 = "qwertyasdfgzxcvb";
string s2 = "poiuyasdfg/.,mnb";
sort(s1.begin(),s1.end());              // the set algorithms require sorted sequences
sort(s2.begin(),s2.end());

string s3(s1.size()+s2.size(),'*');     // set aside enough space for the largest possible result
cout << s3 << '\n';
auto up = set_union(s1.begin(),s1.end(),s2.begin(),s2.end(),s3.begin());
cout << s3 << '\n';
for (auto p = s3.begin(); p!=up; ++p)
     cout << *p;
cout << '\n';

s3.assign(s1.size()+s2.size(),'+');
up = set_difference(s1.begin(),s1.end(),s2.begin(),s2.end(),s3.begin());
cout << s3 << '\n';
for (auto p = s3.begin(); p!=up; ++p)
     cout << *p;
cout << '\n';
```

This little test produces:

```
******************************
,./abcdefgimnopqrstuvxyz
ceqrtvwxz+++++++++++++++++++++
ceqrtvwxz
```

32.6.4 Heaps

A heap is a compact data structure that keeps the element with the highest value first. Think of a heap as a representation of a binary tree. The heap algorithms allow a programmer to treat a random-access sequence as a heap:

Heap Operations (§iso.25.4.6)	
make_heap(b,e)	Make [b:e) ready to be used as a heap
make_heap(b,e,f)	Make [b:e) ready to be used as a heap, using f for comparison
push_heap(b,e)	Add *(e−1) to the heap [b:e−1); afterward [b:e) is a heap
push_heap(b,e,f)	Add an element to the heap [b:e−1), using f for comparison
pop_heap(b,e)	Remove *(e−1) from the heap [b:e); afterward, [b:e−1) is a heap
pop_heap(b,e,f)	Remove element from the heap [b:e), using f for comparison
sort_heap(b,e)	Sort the heap [b:e)
sort_heap(b,e,f)	Sort the heap [b:e), using f for comparison
is_heap(b,e)	Is [b:e) a heap?
is_heap(b,e,f)	Is [b:e) a heap, using f for comparison?
p=is_heap_until(b,e)	p is the largest p such that [b:p) is a heap
p=is_heap_until(b,e,f)	p is the largest p such that [b:p) is a heap, using f for comparison

Think of the end, **e**, of a heap **[b:e]** as a pointer, which it decremented by **pop_heap()** and incremented by **push_heap()**. The largest element is extracted by reading through **b** (e.g., **x=∗b**) and then doing a **pop_heap()**. A new element is inserted by writing through **e** (e.g., **∗e=x**) and then doing a **push_heap()**. For example:

```
string s = "herewego";
make_heap(s.begin(),s.end());          // rogheeew
pop_heap(s.begin(),s.end());           // rogheeew
pop_heap(s.begin(),s.end()–1);         // ohgeeerw
pop_heap(s.begin(),s.end()–2);         // hegeeorw

∗(s.end()–3)='f';
push_heap(s.begin(),s.end()–2);        // hegeefrw
∗(s.end()–2)='x';
push_heap(s.begin(),s.end()–1);        // xeheefge
∗(s.end()–1)='y';
push_heap(s.begin(),s.end());          // yxheefge
sort_heap(s.begin(),s.end());          // eeefghxy
reverse(s.begin(),s.end());            // yxhgfeee
```

The way to understand the changes to **s** is that a user reads only **s[0]** and writes only **s[x]** where **x** is the index of the current end of the heap. The heap removes an element (always **s[0]**) by swapping it with **s[x]**.

The point of a heap is to provide fast addition of elements and fast access to the element with the highest value. The main use of heaps is to implement priority queues.

32.6.5 lexicographical_compare()

A lexicographical compare is the rule we use to order words in dictionaries.

Lexicographical Compare (§iso.25.4.8)	
lexicographical_compare(b,e,b2,e2)	Is [b:e)<[b2:e2)?
lexicographical_compare(b,e,b2,e2,f)	Is [b:e)<[b2:e2), using f for element comparison?

We might implement **lexicographical_compare(b,e,b2,e2)** like this:

```
template<class In, class In2>
bool lexicographical_compare(In first, In last, In2 first2, In2 last2)
{
     for (; first!=last && first2!=last2; ++first,++last) {
          if (∗first<∗first2)
                  return true;    // [first:last)<[first2:last2)
          if (∗first2<∗first)
                  return false;   // [first2:last2)<[first:last)
     }
     return first==last && first2!=last2;  // [first:last)<[first2:last2) if [first:last) is shorter
}
```

That is, a string compares as a sequence of characters. For example:

```
string n1 {"10000"};
string n2 {"999"};

bool b1 = lexicographical_compare(n1.begin(),n1.end(),n2.begin(),n2.end());        // b1 == true

n1 = "Zebra";
n2 = "Aardvark";
bool b2 = lexicographical_compare(n1.begin(),n1.end(),n2.begin(),n2.end());        // b2 == false
```

32.7 Min and Max

Value comparisons are useful in many contexts:

The min and max Family (§iso.25.4.7)	
x=min(a,b)	x is the smaller of a and b
x=min(a,b,f)	x is the smaller of a and b, using f for comparison
x=min({elem})	x is the smallest element in {elem}
x=min({elem},f)	x is the smallest element in {elem}, using f for the element comparison
x=max(a,b)	x is the larger of a and b
x=max(a,b,f)	x is the larger of a and b, using f for comparison
x=max({elem})	x is the largest element in {elem}
x=max({elem},f)	x is the largest element in {elem}, using f for the element comparison
pair(x,y)=minmax(a,b)	x is min(a,b) and y is max(a,b)
pair(x,y)=minmax(a,b,f)	x is min(a,b,f) and y is max(a,b,f)
pair(x,y)=minmax({elem})	x is min({elem}) and y is max({elem})
pair(x,y)=minmax({elem},f)	x is min({elem},f) and y is max({elem},f)
p=min_element(b,e)	p points to the smallest element of [b:e) or e
p=min_element(b,e,f)	p points to the smallest element of [b:e) or e, using f for the element comparison
p=max_element(b,e)	p points to the largest element of [b:e) or e
p=max_element(b,e,f)	p points to the largest element of [b:e) or e, using f for the element comparison
pair(x,y)=minmax_element(b,e)	x is min_element(b,e) and y is max_element(b,e)
pair(x,y)=minmax_element(b,e,f)	x is min_element(b,e,f) and y is max_element(b,e,f)

If we compare two lvalues, the result is a reference to the result; otherwise, an rvalue is returned. Unfortunately, the versions that take lvalues take **const** lvalues, so you can never modify the result of one of these functions. For example:

```
int x = 7;
int y = 9;
```

```
++min(x,y);      // the result of min(x,y) is a const int&
++min({x,y});    // error: the result of min({x,y}) is an rvalue (an initializer_list is immutable)
```

The _element functions return iterators and the **minmax** function returns **pairs**, so we can write:

```
string s = "Large_Hadron_Collider";
auto p = minmax_element(s.begin(),s.end(),
                        [](char c1,char c2) { return toupper(c1)<toupper(c2); });
cout << "min==" << *(p.first) << ' ' << "max==" << *(p.second) << '\n';
```

With the ACSII character set on my machine, this little test produces:

```
min==a max==_
```

32.8 Advice

[1]   An STL algorithm operates on one or more sequences; §32.2.

[2]   An input sequence is half-open and defined by a pair of iterators; §32.2.

[3]   When searching, an algorithm usually returns the end of the input sequence to indicate "not found"; §32.2.

[4]   Prefer a carefully specified algorithm to "random code"; §32.2.

[5]   When writing a loop, consider whether it could be expressed as a general algorithm; §32.2.

[6]   Make sure that a pair of iterator arguments really do specify a sequence; §32.2.

[7]   When the pair-of-iterators style becomes tedious, introduce a container/range algorithm; §32.2.

[8]   Use predicates and other function objects to give standard algorithms a wider range of meanings; §32.3.

[9]   A predicate must not modify its argument; §32.3.

[10]   The default == and < on pointers are rarely adequate for standard algorithms; §32.3.

[11]   Know the complexity of the algorithms you use, but remember that a complexity measure is only a rough guide to performance; §32.3.1.

[12]   Use **for_each()** and **transform()** only when there is no more-specific algorithm for a task; §32.4.1.

[13]   Algorithms do not directly add or subtract elements from their argument sequences; §32.5.2, §32.5.3.

[14]   If you have to deal with uninitialized objects, consider the **uninitialized_*** algorithms; §32.5.6.

[15]   An STL algorithm uses an equality comparison generated from its ordering comparison, rather than ==; §32.6.

[16]   Note that sorting and searching C-style strings requires the user to supply a string comparison operation; §32.6.

33

STL Iterators

The reason that STL containers
and algorithms work so well together
is that they know nothing of each other.
– Alex Stepanov

33.1 Introduction

This chapter presents the STL iterators and utilities, notably standard-library function objects. The STL consists of the iterator, container, algorithm, and function object parts of the standard library. The rest of the STL is presented in Chapter 31 and Chapter 32.

Iterators are the glue that ties standard-library algorithms to their data. Conversely, you can say that iterators are the mechanism used to minimize an algorithm's dependence on the data structures on which it operates:

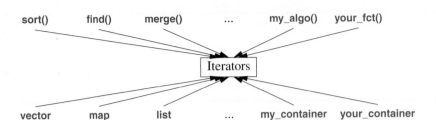

33.1.1 Iterator Model

An iterator is akin to a pointer in that it provides operations for indirect access (e.g., ∗ for derefer-encing) and for moving to point to a new element (e.g., ++ for moving to the next element). A *sequence* is defined by a pair of iterators defining a half-open range [begin:end):

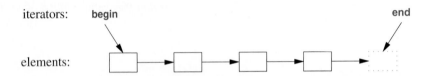

That is, **begin** points to the first element of the sequence, and **end** points to the one-beyond-the-last element of the sequence. Never read from or write to ∗**end**. Note that the empty sequence has **begin==end**; that is, [p:p) is the empty sequence for any iterator **p**.

To read a sequence, an algorithm usually takes a pair of iterators **(b,e)** and iterates using ++ until the end is reached:

```
while (b!=e) {        // use != rather than <
    // do something
    ++b;  // go to next element
}
```

The reason to use != rather than < for testing whether we have reached the end is partially because that is the more precise statement of what we are testing for and partially because only random-access iterators support <.

Algorithms that search for something in a sequence usually return the end of the sequence to indicate "not found"; for example:

```
auto p = find(v.begin(),v.end(),x);        // look for x in v

if (p!=v.end()) {
    // x found at p
}
else {
    // x not found in [v.begin():v.end())
}
```

Algorithms that write to a sequence often are given only an iterator to its first element. In that case, it is the programmer's responsibility not to write beyond the end of that sequence. For example:

```
template<typename Iter>
void forward(Iter p, int n)
{
    while (n>0)
            *p++ = --n;
}

void user()
{
    vector<int> v(10);
    forward(v.begin(),v.size());     // OK
    forward(v.begin(),1000);         // big trouble
}
```

Some standard-library implementations range check – that is, throw an exception for that last call of **forward()** – but you can't rely on that for portable code: many implementations don't check. For a simple and safe alternative use an insert iterator (§33.2.2).

33.1.2 Iterator Categories

The standard library provides five kinds of iterators (five *iterator categories*):

- *Input iterator*: We can iterate forward using ++ and read each element (repeatedly) using ∗. We can compare input iterators using == and !=. This is the kind of iterator that **istream** offers; see §38.5.
- *Output iterator*: We can iterate forward using ++ and write an element once only using ∗. This is the kind of iterator that **ostream** offers; see §38.5.
- *Forward iterator*: We can iterate forward repeatedly using ++ and read and write (unless the elements are **const**) elements repeatedly using ∗. If a forward iterator points to a class object, we can use -> to refer to a member. We can compare forward iterators using == and !=. This is the kind of iterator **forward_list** offers (§31.4).
- *Bidirectional iterator*: We can iterate forward (using ++) and backward (using --) and read and write (unless the elements are **const**) elements repeatedly using ∗. If a bidirectional iterator points to a class object, we can use -> to refer to a member. We can compare bidirectional iterators using == and !=. This is the kind of iterator that **list**, **map**, and **set** offer (§31.4).
- *Random-access iterator*: We can iterate forward (using ++ or +=) and backward (using - or -=) and read and write (unless the elements are **const**) elements repeatedly using ∗ or []. If a random-access iterator points to a class object, we can use -> to refer to a member. We can subscript a random-access iterator using [], add an integer using +, and subtract an integer using -. We can find the distance between two random-access iterators to the same sequence by subtracting one from the other. We can compare random-access iterators using ==, !=, <, <=, >, and >=. This is the kind of iterator that **vector** offers (§31.4).

Logically, these iterators are organized in a hierarchy (§iso.24.2):

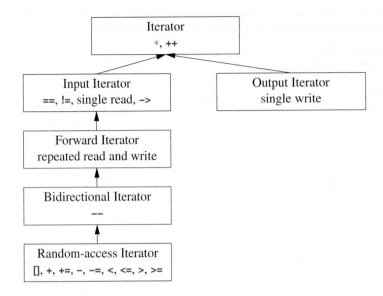

The iterator categories are concepts (§24.3) rather than classes, so this hierarchy is not a class hierarchy implemented using derivation. If you need to do something advanced with iterator categories, use iterator_traits (directly or indirectly).

33.1.3 Iterator Traits

In <iterator>, the standard library provides a set of type functions that allow us to write code specialized for specific properties of an iterator:

Iterator Traits (§iso.24.4.1)	
iterator_traits<Iter>	Traits type for a non-pointer Iter
iterator_traits<T*>	Traits type for a pointer T*
iterator<Cat,T,Dist,Ptr,Re>	Simple class defining the basic iterator member types
input_iterator_tag	Category for input iterators
output_iterator_tag	Category for output iterators
forward_iterator_tag	Category for forward iterators; derived from input_iterator_tag; provided for forward_list, unordered_set, unordered_multiset, unordered_map, and unordered_multimap
bidirectional_iterator_tag	Category for bidirectional iterators; derived from forward_iterator_tag; provided for list, set, multiset, map, multimap
random_access_iterator_tag	Category for random-access iterators; derived from bidirectional_iterator_tag; provided for vector, deque, array, built-in arrays, and string

The iterator tags are types used to select among algorithms based on the type of an iterator. For example, a random-access iterator can go directly to an element:

```
template<typename Iter>
void advance_helper(Iter p, int n, random_access_iterator_tag)
{
    p+=n;
}
```

On the other hand, a forward iterator must get to the nth element by moving one step at a time (e.g., following links on a list):

```
template<typename Iter>
void advance_helper(Iter p, int n, forward_iterator_tag)
{
    if (0<n)
        while (n--) ++p;
    else if (n<0)
        while (n++) --p;
}
```

Given these helpers, **advance()** can consistently use the optimal algorithm:

```
template<typename Iter>
void advance(Iter p, int n)         // use the optimal algorithm
{
    advance_helper(p,n,typename iterator_traits<Iter>::iterator_category{});
}
```

Typically, **advance()** and/or **advance_helper()** will be inlined to ensure that no run-time overhead is introduced by this *tag dispatch* technique. Variants of this technique are pervasive in the STL.

The key properties of an iterator are described by the aliases in **iterator_traits**:

```
template<typename Iter>
struct iterator_traits {
    using value_type = typename Iter::value_type;
    using difference_type = typename Iter::difference_type;
    using pointer = typename Iter::pointer;              // pointer type
    using reference = typename Iter::reference;          // reference type
    using iterator_category = typename Iter::iterator_category;  // (tag)
};
```

For an iterator that does not have these member types (e.g., an **int**∗), we provide a specialization of iterator_traits:

```
template<typename T>
struct iterator_traits<T∗> {                 // specialization for pointers
    using difference_type = ptrdiff_t;
    using value_type = T;
    using pointer = T∗;
    using reference = T& reference;
    using iterator_category = random_access_iterator_tag;
};
```

We cannot in general say:

```
template<typename Iter>
typename Iter::value_type read(Iter p, int n)          // not general
{
      // ... do some checking ...
      return p[n];
{
```

This is an error waiting to happen. Calling this **read()** with a pointer argument would be an error.
The compiler would catch it, but the error messages might be voluminous and obscure. Instead, we
can write:

```
template<typename Iter>
typename iterator_traits<Iter>::value_type read(Iter p, int n)       // more general
{
      // ... do some checking ...
      return p[n];
{
```

The idea is that to find a property of an iterator, you look in its **iterator_traits** (§28.2.4), rather than
at the iterator itself. To avoid directly referring to the **iterator_traits**, which after all is just an implementation detail, we can define an alias. For example:

```
template<typename Iter>
using Category<Iter> = typename std::iterator_traits<Iter>::iterator_category;

template<typename Iter>
using Difference_type<Iter> = typename std::iterator_traits<Iter>::difference_type;
```

So, if we want to know the type of the difference between two iterators (pointing to the same
sequence), we have some choices:

```
tempate<typename Iter>
void f(Iter p, Iter q)
{
      Iter::difference_type d1 = distance(p,q);            // syntax error: "typename" missing

      typename Iter::difference_type d2 = distance(p,q); // doesn't work for pointers, etc.

      typename iterator_traits<Iter>::distance_type d3 = distance(p,q);    // OK, but ugly
      Distance_type<Iter> d4 = distance(p,q);                             // OK, much better

      auto d5 = distance(p,q);      // OK, if you don't need to mention the type explicitly
      // ...
}
```

I recommend the last two alternatives.

The **iterator** template simply bundles the key properties of an iterator into a **struct** for the convenience of iterator implementers and provides a few defaults:

```
template<typename Cat, typename T, typename Dist = ptrdiff_t, typename Ptr = T*, typename Ref = T&>
struct iterator {
    using value_type = T;
    using difference_type = Dist ;        // type used by distance()
    using pointer = Ptr;                  // pointer type
    using reference = Ref;                // reference type
    using iterator_category = Cat;        // category (tag)
};
```

33.1.4 Iterator Operations

Depending on its category (§33.1.2), an iterator provides some or all of these operations:

Iterator Operations (§iso.24.2.2)	
++p	Pre-increment (advance one element): make **p** refer to the next element or to the one-beyond-the-last element; the resulting value is the incremented value
p++	Post-increment (advance one element): make **p** refer to the next element or to the one-beyond-the-last element; the resulting value is **p**'s value before the increment
*p	Access (dereference): *p refers to the element pointed to by **p**
--p	Pre-decrement (go back one element): make **p** point to the previous element; the resulting value is the decremented value
p--	Post-decrement (go back one element): make **p** point to the previous element; the resulting value is **p**'s value before the decrement
p[n]	Access (subscripting): **p[n]** refers to the element pointed to by **p+n**; equivalent to *(p+n)
p->n	Access (member access): equivalent to (*p).m
p==q	Equality: Do **p** and **q** point to the same element or do both point to the one-beyond-the-last element?
p!=q	Inequality: !(p==q)
p<q	Does **p** point to an element before the one **q** points to?
p<=q	p<q ∥ p==q
p>q	Does **p** point to an element after the one **q** points to?
p>=q	p>q ∥ p==q
p+=n	Advance n: make **p** point to the nth element after the one to which it points
p-=n	Advance –n: make **p** point to the nth element before the one to which it points
q=p+n	**q** points to the nth element after the one **p** points to
q=p-n	**q** points to the nth element before the one **p** points to

A **++p** returns a reference to **p**, whereas **p++** must return a copy of **p** holding the old value. Thus, for more complicated iterators, **++p** is likely to be more efficient than **p++**.

The following operations work for every iterator for which they can be implemented, but they may work more efficiently for random-access iterators (see §33.1.2):

Iterator Operations (§iso.24.4.4)	
advance(p)	Like p+=n; p must be at least an input iterator
x=distance(p,q)	Like x=q–p; p must be at least an input iterator
q=next(p,n)	Like q=p+n; p must be at least a forward iterator
q=next(p)	q=next(p,1)
q=prev(p,n)	Like q=p–n; p must be at least a bidirectional iterator
q=prev(p)	q=prev(p,1)

In each case, if **p** is not a random-access iterator, the algorithm will take **n** steps.

33.2 Iterator Adaptors

In **<iterator>**, the standard library provides adaptors to generate useful related iterator types from a given iterator type:

Iterator Adaptors		
reverse_iterator	Iterate backward	§33.2.1
back_insert_iterator	Insert at end	§33.2.2
front_insert_iterator	Insert at beginning	§33.2.2
insert_iterator	Insert anywhere	§33.2.2
move_iterator	Move rather than copy	§33.2.3
raw_storage_iterator	Write to uninitialized storage	§34.6.2.

Iterators for **iostreams** are described in §38.5.

33.2.1 Reverse Iterator

Using an iterator we can traverse a sequence [**b**:**e**) from **b** to **e**. If the sequence allows bidirectional access, we can also traverse the sequence in reverse order, from **e** to **b**. An iterator that does that is called a **reverse_iterator**. A **reverse_iterator** iterates from the end of the sequence defined by its underlying iterator to the beginning of that sequence. To get a half-open sequence, we must consider **b–1** as one past the end and **e–1** as the start of the sequence: [**e–1**,**b–1**). Thus, the fundamental relation between a reverse iterator and its corresponding iterator is **&∗(reverse_iterator(p))==&∗(p–1)**. In particular, if **v** is a **vector**, **v.rbegin()** points to its last element, **v[v.size()–1]**. Consider:

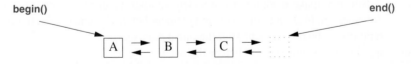

This sequence can be viewed like this using a **reverse_iterator**:

The definition of **reverse_iterator** looks something like this:

```
template<typename Iter>
class reverse_iterator
    : public iterator<Iterator_category<Iter>,
                    Value_type<Iter>,
                    Difference_type<Iter>,
                    Pointer<Iter>,
                    Reference<Iter>> {
public:
    using iterator_type = Iter;

    reverse_iterator(): current{} { }
    explicit reverse_iterator(Iter p): current{p} { }
    template<typename Iter2>
        reverse_iterator(const reverse_iterator<Iter2>& p) :current(p.base()) { }

    Iter base() const { return current; } // current iterator value

    reference operator*() const { tmp = current; return *--tmp; }
    pointer operator->() const;
    reference operator[](difference_type n) const;

    reverse_iterator& operator++() { --current; return *this; }     // note: not ++
    reverse_iterator operator++(int) { reverse_iterator t = current; --current;  return t; }
    reverse_iterator& operator--() { ++current; return *this; }     // note: not --
    reverse_iterator operator--(int) { reverse_iterator t = current; ++current;  return t; }

    reverse_iterator operator+(difference_type n) const;
    reverse_iterator& operator+=(difference_type n);
    reverse_iterator operator-(difference_type n) const;
    reverse_iterator& operator-=(difference_type n);
    // ...
protected:
    Iterator current;          // current points to the element after the one *this refers to
private:
    // ...
    iterator tmp;              // for temporaries that need to outlive a function scope
};
```

A **reverse_iterator<Iter>** has the same member types and operations as **Iter**. In particular, if **Iter** is a random-access operator, its **reverse_iterator<Iter>** has [], +, and <. For example:

```
void f(vector<int>& v, list<char>& lst)
{
    v.rbegin()[3] = 7;              // OK: random-access iterator
    lst.rbegin()[3] = '4';         // error: bidirectional iterator doesn't support []
    *(next(lst.rbegin(),3)) = '4'; // OK!
}
```

I use **next()** to move the iterator because (like **[]**) **+** wouldn't work for a bidirectional iterator, such as **list<char>::iterator**.

Reverse iterators allow us to use algorithms in a way that views a sequence in the reverse order. For example, to find the last occurrence of an element in a sequence, we can apply **find()** to its reverse sequence:

```
auto ri = find(v.rbegin(),v.rend(),val);      // last occurrence
```

Note that **C::reverse_iterator** is not the same type as **C::iterator**. So, if I wanted to write a **find_last()** algorithm using a reverse sequence, I would have to decide which type of iterator to return:

```
template<typename C, typename Val>
auto find_last(C& c, Val v) -> decltype(c.begin())       // use C's iterator in the interface
{
    auto ri = find(c.rbegin(),c.rend(),v);
    if (ri == c.rend()) return c.end();                  // use c.end() to indicate "not found"
    return prev(ri.base());
}
```

For a **reverse_iterator**, **ri.base()** returns an **iterator** pointing one beyond the position pointed to by **ri**. So, to get an iterator pointing to the same element as the reverse iterator **ri**, I have to return **ri.base()–1**. However, my container may be a **list** that does not support **–** for its iterators, so I use **prev()** instead.

A reverse iterator is a perfectly ordinary iterator, so I could write the loop explicitly:

```
template<typename C, Val v>
auto find_last(C& c, Val v) -> decltype(c.begin())
{
    for (auto p = c.rbegin(); p!=c.rend(); ++p)       // view sequence in reverse order
        if (*p==v) return --p.base();
    return c.end();                                    // use c.end() to indicate "not found"
}
```

The equivalent code searching backward using a (forward) iterator is:

```
template<typename C>
auto find_last(C& c, Val v) -> decltype(c.begin())
{
    for (auto p = c.end(); p!=c.begin(); )            // search backward from end
        if (*--p==v) return p;
    return c.end();                                    // use c.end() to indicate "not found"
}
```

As for the earlier definitions of **find_last()**, this version requires at least a bidirectional iterator.

33.2.2 Insert Iterators

Producing output through an iterator into a container implies that elements following the one pointed to by the iterator can be overwritten. This implies the possibility of overflow and consequent memory corruption. For example:

```
void f(vector<int>& vi)
{
    fill_n(vi.begin(),200,7);        // assign 7 to vi[0]..[199]
}
```

If **vi** has fewer than **200** elements, we are in trouble.

In **<iterator>**, the standard library provides a solution in the form of an *inserter*: when written to, an inserter inserts a new element into a sequence rather than overwriting an existing element. For example:

```
void g(vector<int>& vi)
{
    fill_n(back_inserter(vi),200,7);     // add 200 7s to the end of vi
}
```

When writing to an element through an insert iterator, the iterator inserts its value rather than overwriting the element pointed to. So, a container grows by one element each time a value is written to it through an insert iterator. Inserters are as simple and efficient as they are useful.

There are three insert iterators:

- **insert_iterator** inserts before the element pointed to using **insert()**.
- **front_insert_iterator** inserts before the first element of a sequence using **push_front()**.
- **back_insert_iterator** inserts after the last element of the sequence using **push_back()**.

An inserter is usually constructed by a call to a helper function:

Inserter Construction Functions (§iso.24.5.2)	
ii=inserter(c,p)	ii is an **insert_iterator** pointing to p in container **c**
ii=back_inserter(c)	ii is a **back_insert_iterator** pointing to **back()** in container **c**
ii=front_inserter(c)	ii is a **front_insert_iterator** pointing to **front()** in container **c**

The iterator passed to **inserter()** must be an iterator into the container. For a sequence container, that implies that it must be a bidirectional iterator (so that you can insert before it). For example, you can't use **inserter()** to make an iterator to insert into a **forward_list**. For an associative container, where that iterator is only used as a hint for where to insert, a forward iterator (e.g., as provided by an **unordered_set**) can be acceptable.

An inserter is an output iterator:

insert_iterator<C> Operations (§iso.24.5.2) (continues)	
insert_iterator p {c,q};	Inserter for container **c** pointing to *q; **q** must point into **c**
insert_iterator p {q};	Copy constructor: **p** is a copy of **q**
p=q	Copy assignment: **p** is a copy of **q**
p=move(q)	Move assignment: **p** points to what **q** pointed to

insert_iterator<C> **Operations (continued) (§iso.24.5.2)**	
++p	Make **p** point to the next element; the value is **p**'s new value
p++	Make **p** point to the next element; the value is **p**'s old value
*p=x	Insert **x** before **p**
*p++=x	Insert **x** before **p**, then increment **p**

The front_insert_iterator and back_insert_iterator differ in that their constructors don't require an iterator. For example:

```
vector<string> v;
back_insert_iterator<v> p;
```

You cannot read through an inserter.

33.2.3 Move Iterator

A move iterator is an iterator where reading from the pointed-to element moves rather than copies. We usually make a move iterator from another iterator using a helper function:

Move Iterator Construction Function	
mp=make_move_iterator(p)	mp is a **move_iterator** pointing to the same element as **p**; **p** must be an input iterator

A move iterator has the same operations as the iterator from which it is made. For example, we can do --p if the move iterator **p** was made from a bidirectional iterator. A move iterator's **operator*()** simply returns an rvalue reference (§7.7.2) to the element pointed to: **std::move(q)**. For example:

```
vector<string> read_strings(istream&);
auto vs = read_strings(cin);                    // get some strings

vector<string> vs2;
copy(vs,back_inserter(vs2));                     // copy strings from vs into vs2

vector<string> vs3;
copy(vs2,make_move_iterator(back_inserter(vs3)));   // move strings from vs2 into vs3
```

This assumes that a container version of **std::copy()** has been defined.

33.3 Range Access Functions

In <iterator>, the standard library provides a nonmember **begin()** and **end()** functions for containers:

begin() and end() (§iso.24.6.5)	
p=begin(c)	**p** is an iterator for the first element of **c**; **c** is a built-in array or has **c.begin()**
p=end(c)	**p** is an iterator for the one-past-the-end of **c**; **c** is a built-in array or has **c.end()**

These functions are very simple:

```
template<typename C>
    auto begin(C& c) -> decltype(c.begin());
template<typename C>
    auto begin(const C& c) -> decltype(c.begin());
template<typename C>
    auto end(C& c) -> decltype(c.end());
template<typename C>
    auto end(const C& c) -> decltype(c.end());

template<typename T, size_t N>              // for built-in arrays
    auto begin(T (&array)[N]) -> T*;
template<typename T, size_t N>
    auto end(T (&array)[N]) -> T*;
```

These functions are used by the range-**for**-statement (§9.5.1) but can of course also be used directly by users. For example:

```
template<typename Cont>
void print(Cont& c)
{
    for(auto p=begin(c); p!=end(c); ++p)
        cout << *p << '\n';
}

void f()
{
    vector<int> v {1,2,3,4,5};
    print(v);

    int a[] {1,2,3,4,5};
    print(a);
}
```

Had I said **c.begin()** and **c.end()**, the call **print(a)** would have failed.

A user-defined container with member **begin()** and **end()** automatically gets nonmember versions when **<iterator>** is #included. To provide nonmember **begin()** and **end()** for a container, **My_container**, that doesn't have them, I have to write something like:

```
template<typename T>
Iterator<My_container<T>> begin(My_container<T>& c)
{
    return Iterator<My_container<T>>{&c[0]};           // iterator to first element
}

template<typename T>
Iterator<My_container<T>> end(My_container<T>& c)
{
    return Iterator<My_container<T>>{&c[0]+c.size()};   // iterator to last element
}
```

Here, I assume that passing the address of the first element is a way to create an iterator to the first element of **My_container** and that **My_container** has a **size()**.

33.4 Function Objects

Many of the standard algorithms take function objects (or functions) as arguments to control the way they work. Common uses are comparison criteria, predicates (functions returning **bool**), and arithmetic operations. In **<functional>**, the standard library supplies a few common function objects:

Predicates (§iso.20.8.5, §iso.20.8.6, §iso.20.8.7)	
p=equal_to<T>(x,y)	p(x,y) means x==y when x and y are of type T
p=not_equal_to<T>(x,y)	p(x,y) means x!=y when x and y are of type T
p=greater<T>(x,y)	p(x,y) means x>y when x and y are of type T
p=less<T>(x,y)	p(x,y) means x<y when x and y are of type T
p=greater_equal<T>(x,y)	p(x,y) means x>=y when x and y are of type T
p=less_equal<T>(x,y)	p(x,y) means x<=y when x and y are of type T
p=logical_and<T>(x,y)	p(x,y) means x&&y when x and y are of type T
p=logical_or<T>(x,y)	p(x,y) means x||y when x and y are of type T
p=logical_not<T>(x)	p(x) means !x when x is of type T
p=bit_and<T>(x,y)	p(x,y) means x&y when x and y are of type T
p=bit_or<T>(x,y)	p(x,y) means x|y when x and y are of type T
p=bit_xor<T>(x,y)	p(x,y) means xˆy when x and y are of type T

For example:

```
vector<int> v;
// ...
sort(v.begin(),v.end(),greater<int>{});          // sort v into decreasing order
```

Such predicates are roughly equivalent to simple lambdas. For example:

```
vector<int> v;
// ...
sort(v.begin(),v.end(),[](int a, int b) { return a>b; });     // sort v into decreasing order
```

Note that **logical_and** and **logical_or** always evaluate both their arguments (**&&** and **||** do not).

Arithmetic Operations (§iso.20.8.4)	
f=plus<T>(x,y)	f(x,y) means x+y when x and y are of type T
f=minus<T>(x,y)	f(x,y) means x–y when x and y are of type T
f=multiplies<T>(x,y)	f(x,y) means x∗y when x and y are of type T
f=divides<T>(x,y)	f(x,y) means x/y when x and y are of type T
f=modulus<T>(x,y)	f(x,y) means x%y when x and y are of type T
f=negate<T>(x)	f(x) means –x when x is of type T

33.5 Function Adaptors

A function adaptor takes a function as argument and returns a function object that can be used to invoke the original function.

Adaptors (§iso.20.8.9, §iso.20.8.10, §iso.20.8.8)	
g=bind(f,args)	g(args2) is equivalent to f(args3) where args3 is obtained by replacing placeholders in args with arguments from args2 for the use of placeholders, such as _1, _2, and _3
g=mem_fn(f)	g(p,args) means p–>f(args) if p is a pointer and p.mf(args) if p is not; args is a (possibly empty) list of arguments
g=not1(f)	g(x) means !f(x)
g=not2(f)	g(x,y) means !f(x,y)

The bind() and mem_fn() adaptors do argument binding, also called *Currying* or *partial evaluation*. These binders, and their deprecated predecessors (such as bind1st(), mem_fun(), and mem_fun_ref()), were heavily used in the past, but most uses seem to be more easily expressed using lambdas (§11.4).

33.5.1 bind()

Given a function and a set of arguments, bind() produces a function object that can be called with "the remaining" arguments, if any, of the function. For example:

```
double cube(double);

auto cube2 = bind(cube,2);
```

A call cube2() will invoke cube with the argument 2, that is, cube(2). We don't have to bind every argument of a function. For example:

```
using namespace placeholders;

void f(int,const string&);
auto g = bind(f,2,_1);        // bind f()'s first argument to 2
f(2,"hello");
g("hello");                   // also calls f(2,"hello");
```

The curious _1 argument to the binder is a placeholder telling bind() where arguments to the resulting function object should go. In this case, g()'s (first) argument is used as f()'s second argument.

The placeholders are found in the (sub)namespace std::placeholders that is part of <functional>. The placeholder mechanism is very flexible. Consider:

```
f(2,"hello");
bind(f)(2,"hello");          // also calls f(2,"hello");
bind(f,_1,_2)(2,"hello");    // also calls f(2,"hello");
bind(f,_2,_1)("hello",2);    // reverse order of arguments: also calls f(2,"hello");

auto g = [](const string& s, int i) { f(i,s); } // reverse order of arguments
g("hello",2);                              // also calls f(2,"hello");
```

To bind arguments for an overloaded function, we have to explicitly state which version of the function we want to bind:

```
int pow(int,int);
double pow(double,double);   // pow() is overloaded

auto pow2 = bind(pow,_1,2);                                  // error: which pow()?
auto pow2 = bind((double(*)(double,double))pow,_1,2); // OK (but ugly)
```

Note that **bind()** takes ordinary expressions as arguments. This implies that references are dereferenced before **bind()** gets to see them. For example:

```
void incr(int& i)
{
    ++i;
}

void user()
{
    int i = 1;
    incr(i);                     // i becomes 2
    auto inc = bind(incr,_1);
    inc(i);                      // i stays 2; inc(i) incremented a local copy of i
}
```

To deal with that, the standard library provides yet another pair of adaptors:

reference_wrapper<T> (§iso.20.8.3)	
r=ref(t)	r is a **reference_wrapper** for **T& t**; noexcept
r=cref(t)	r is a **reference_wrapper** for a **const T& t**; noexcept

This solves the "reference problem" for **bind()**:

```
void user()
{
    int i = 1;
    incr(i);                     // i becomes 2
    auto inc = bind(incr,_1);
    inc(ref(i));                 // i becomes 3
}
```

This **ref()** is needed to pass references as arguments to **thread**s because **thread** constructors are variadic templates (§42.2.2).

So far, I either used the result of **bind()** immediately or assigned it to a variable declared using **auto**. This saves me the bother of specifying the return type of a call of **bind()**. That can be useful because the return type of **bind()** varies with the type of function to be called and the argument values stored. In particular, the returned function object is larger when it has to hold values of bound parameters. However, we sometimes want to be specific about the types of the arguments required and the type of result returned. If so, we can specify them for a **function** (§33.5.3).

33.5.2 mem_fn()

The function adaptor **mem_fn(mf)** produces a function object that can be called as a nonmember function. For example:

```
void user(Shape* p)
{
    p->draw();
    auto draw = mem_fn(&Shape::draw);
    draw(p);
}
```

The major use of **mem_fn()** is when an algorithm requires an operation to be called as a nonmember function. For example:

```
void draw_all(vector<Shape*>& v)
{
    for_each(v.begin(),v.end(),mem_fn(&Shape::draw));
}
```

Thus, **mem_fn()** can be seen as a mapping from the object-oriented calling style to the functional one.

Often, lambdas provide a simple and general alternative to binders. For example:

```
void draw_all(vector<Shape*>& v)
{
    for_each(v.begin(),v.end(),[](Shape* p) { p->draw(); });
}
```

33.5.3 function

A **bind()** can be used directly, and it can be used to initialize an **auto** variable. In that, **bind()** resembles a lambda.

If we want to assign the result of **bind()** to a variable with a specific type, we can use the standard-library type **function**. A **function** is specified with a specific return type and a specific argument type.

function<R(Argtypes...)> (§iso.20.8.11.2) (continues)	
function f {};	f is an empty **function**; noexcept
function f {nullptr};	f is an empty **function**; noexcept
function f {g};	f is a **function** holding g; g can be anything that can be invoked with f's argument types
function f {allocator_arg_t,a};	f is an empty **function**; use allocator a; noexcept
function f {allocator_arg_t,a,nullptr_t};	f is an empty function; use allocator a; noexcept
function f {allocator_arg_t,a,g};	f is a function holding g; use allocator a; noexcept
f2=f	f2 is a copy of f
f=nullptr	f becomes empty

function<R(Argtypes...)> **(continued)**(§iso.20.8.11.2)	
f.swap(f2)	Swap the contents of f and f2; f and f2 must be of the same **function** type; noexcept
f.assign(f2,a)	f gets a copy of f2 and the allocator **a**
bool b {f};	conversion of f to **bool**; b is **true** if f is nonempty; explicit; noexcept
r=f(args)	Invoke the contained function with **args**; the argument types must match f's
ti=f.target_type()	ti is the **type_info** for f; if f doesn't contain something callable ti==**typid(void)**; noexcept
p=f.target<F>()	If f.target_type()==typeid(F), p points to the contained object, otherwise, p==**nullptr**; noexcept
f==nullptr	Is f empty? noexcept
nullptr==f	f==nullptr
f!=nullptr	!(f==nullptr)
nullptr!=f	!(f==nullptr)
swap(f,f2)	f.swap(f2)

For example:

```
int f(double);
function<int(double)> fct {f};   // initialize to f
int g(int);

void user()
{
    fct = [](double d) { return round(d); };    // assign lambda to fct
    fct = f;                                      // assign function to fct
    fct = g;                                      // error: incorrect return type
}
```

The target functions are provided for the rare cases where someone wants to examine a **function**, rather than simply call it as usually intended.

The standard-library **function** is a type that can hold any object you can invoke using the call operator () (§2.2.1, §3.4.3, §11.4, §19.2.2). That is, an object of type **function** is a function object. For example:

```
int round(double x) { return static_cast<double>(floor(x+0.5)); }   // conventional 4/5 rounding

function<int(double)> f;   // f can hold anything that can be called with a double and return an int

enum class Round_style { truncate, round };

struct Round {        // function object carrying a state
    Round_style s;
    Round(Round_style ss) :s(ss) { }
    int operator()(double x) const { return (s==Round_style::round) ? (x+0.5) : x; };
};
```

```
void t1()
{
    f = round;
    cout << f(7.6) << '\n';                          // call through f to the function round

    f = Round(Round_style::truncate);
    cout << f(7.6) << '\n';                          // call the function object

    Round_style style = Round_style::round;
    f = [style] (double x){ return (style==Round_style::round) ? x+0.5 : x; };

    cout << f(7.6) << '\n';                          // call the lambda

    vector<double> v {7.6};
    f = Round(Round_style::round);
    std::transform(v.begin(),v.end(),v.begin(),f);   // pass to algorithm

    cout << v[0] << '\n';                            // transformed by the lambda
}
```

We get **8**, **8**, **7**, and **8**.

Obviously, **function**s are useful for callbacks, for passing operations as arguments, etc.

33.6 Advice

[1] An input sequence is defined by a pair of iterators; §33.1.1.
[2] An output sequence is defined by a single iterator; avoid overflow; §33.1.1.
[3] For any iterator **p**, [**p**:**p**] is the empty sequence; §33.1.1.
[4] Use the end of a sequence to indicate "not found"; §33.1.1.
[5] Think of iterators as more general and often better behaved pointers; §33.1.1.
[6] Use iterator types, such as **list<char>::iterator**, rather than pointers to refer to elements of a container; §33.1.1.
[7] Use **iterator_traits** to obtain information about iterators; §33.1.3.
[8] You can do compile-time dispatch using **iterator_traits**; §33.1.3.
[9] Use **iterator_traits** to select an optimal algorithm based on an iterator's category; §33.1.3.
[10] **iterator_traits** are an implementation detail; prefer to use them implicitly; §33.1.3.
[11] Use **base()** to extract an **iterator** from a **reverse_iterator**; §33.2.1.
[12] You can use an insert iterator to add elements to a container; §33.2.2.
[13] A **move_iterator** can be used to make copy operations into move operations; §33.2.3.
[14] Make sure that your containers can be traversed using a range-**for**; §33.3.
[15] Use **bind()** to create variants of functions and function objects; §33.5.1.
[16] Note that **bind()** dereferences references early; use **ref()** if you want to delay dereferencing; §33.5.1.

[17]   A **mem_fn()** or a lambda can be used to convert the **p–>f(a)** calling convention into **f(p,a)**;
       §33.5.2.

[18]   Use **function** when you need a variable that can hold a variety of callable objects; §33.5.3.

34

Memory and Resources

> *Anyone can have an idea;*
> *it´s what you do with the idea*
> *that´s the important thing.*
> *– Terry Pratchett*

- Introduction
- "Almost Containers"
    array; **bitset**; **vector<bool>**; Tuples
- Resource Management Pointers
    unique_ptr; **shared_ptr**; **weak_ptr**
- Allocators
    The Default Allocator; Allocator Traits; Pointer Traits; Scoped Allocators
- The Garbage Collection Interface
- Uninitialized Memory
    Temporary Buffers; **raw_storage_iterator**
- Advice

34.1 Introduction

The STL (Chapter 31, Chapter 32, Chapter 33) is the most highly structured and general part standard-library facilities for the management and manipulation of data. This chapter presents facilities
that are more specialized or deal with raw memory (as opposed to typed objects).

34.2 "Almost Containers"

The standard library provides several containers that don't fit perfectly into the STL framework
(§31.4, §32.2, §33.1). Examples are built-in arrays, **array**, and **string**. I sometimes refer to those as

"almost containers" (§31.4), but that is not quite fair: they hold elements, so they are containers, but each has restrictions or added facilities that make them awkward in the context of the STL. Describing them separately also simplifies the description of the STL.

"Almost Containers"	
T[N]	Built-in array: a fixed-size continuously allocated sequence of N elements of type T; implicitly converts to a T*
array<T,N>	A fixed-size continuously allocated sequence of N elements of type T; like the built-in array, but with most problems solved
bitset<N>	A fixed-size sequence of N bits
vector<bool>	A sequence of bits compactly stored in a specialization of vector
pair<T,U>	Two elements of types T and U
tuple<T...>	A sequence of an arbitrary number of elements of arbitrary types
basic_string<C>	A sequence of characters of type C; provides string operations
valarray<T>	An array of numeric values of type T; provides numeric operations

Why does the standard library provide so many containers? They serve common but different (often overlapping) needs. If the standard library didn't provide them, many people would have to design and implement their own. For example:

- pair and tuple are heterogeneous; all other containers are homogeneous (all elements are of the same type).
- array, vector, and tuple elements are contiguously allocated; forward_list and map are linked structures.
- bitset and vector<bool> hold bits and access them through proxy objects; all other standard-library containers can hold a variety of types and access elements directly.
- basic_string requires its elements to be some form of character and to provide string manipulation, such as concatenation and locale-sensitive operations (Chapter 39) and valarray requires its elements to be numbers and to provide numerical operations.

All of these containers can be seen as providing specialized services needed by large communities of programmers. No single container could serve all of these needs because some needs are contradictory, for example, "ability to grow" vs. "guaranteed to be allocated in a fixed location," and "elements do not move when elements are added" vs. "contiguously allocated." Furthermore, a very general container would imply overhead deemed unacceptable for individual containers.

34.2.1 array

An array, defined in <array>, is a fixed-size sequence of elements of a given type where the number of elements is specified at compile time. Thus, an array can be allocated with its elements on the stack, in an object, or in static storage. The elements are allocated in the scope where the array is defined. An array is best understood as a built-in array with its size firmly attached, without implicit, potentially surprising conversions to pointer types, and with a few convenience functions provided. There is no overhead (time or space) involved in using an array compared to using a built-in array. An array does *not* follow the "handle to elements" model of STL containers. Instead, an array directly contains its elements:

```
template<typename T, size_t N>          // an array of N Ts (§iso.23.3.2)
struct array {
/*
        types and operations like vector's (§31.4),
        except operations that change the container size, constructors, and assign() functions
*/
        void fill(const T& v);// assign N copies of v
        void swap(array&) noexcept(noexcept(swap(declval<T&>(), declval<T&>())));

        T __elem[N];    // implementation detail
};
```

No "management information" (e.g., a size) is stored in an **array**. This implies that moving (§17.5) an **array** is no more efficient than copying it (unless the **array**'s elements are resource handles with efficient moves). An **array** does not have a constructor or an allocator (because it does not directly allocate anything).

The number of elements and subscript values for **array** are of an **unsigned** type (**size_t**), just like **vector**'s, but different from the built-in array's. So, **array<int,–1>** might be accepted by an inattentive compiler. Hope for a warning.

An **array** can be initialized by an initializer list:

```
array<int,3> a1 = { 1, 2, 3 };
```

The number of elements in the initializer must be equal to or less than the number of elements specified for the **array**. As usual, if the initializer list provides values for some but not all elements, the remainder is initialized with the appropriate default value. For example:

```
void f()
{
        array<string, 4> aa = {"Churchill", "Clare"};
        //
}
```

The last two elements will be empty strings.

The element count is not optional:

```
array<int> ax = { 1, 2, 3 }; // error size not specified
```

To save us from a special case, the number of elements can be zero:

```
int<int,0> a0;
```

The element count must be a constant expression:

```
void f(int n)
{
        array<string,n> aa = {"John's", "Queens' "};           // error: size not a constant expression
        //
}
```

If you need the element count to be variable, use **vector**. On the other hand, since **array**'s element count is known at compile time, **array**'s **size()** is a **constexpr** function.

There is no constructor for **array** that copies an argument value (as there is for **vector**; §31.3.2). Instead, a **fill()** operation is provided:

```
void f()
{
    array<int,8> aa;        // uninitialized, so far
    aa.fill(99);            // assign eight copies of 99
    // ...
}
```

Because an **array** doesn't follow the "handle to elements" model, **swap()** has to actually swap elements so that swapping two **array<T,N>**s applies **swap()** to N pairs of Ts. The declaration of **array<T,N>::swap()** basically says that if a **swap()** of Ts can throw, then so can a **swap()** of an **array<T,N>**. Obviously, throwing **swap()**s should be avoided like the plague.

When necessary, an **array** can be explicitly passed to a C-style function that expects a pointer. For example:

```
void f(int* p, int sz); // C-style interface

void g()
{
    array<int,10> a;

    f(a,a.size());              // error: no conversion
    f(&a[0],a.size());          // C-style use
    f(a.data(),a.size());       // C-style use

    auto p = find(a.begin(),a.end(),777);       // C++/STL-style use
    // ...
}
```

Why would we use an **array** when **vector** is so much more flexible? Because an **array** is less flexible, it is simpler. Occasionally, there is a significant performance advantage to be had by directly accessing elements allocated on the stack rather than allocating elements on the free store, accessing them indirectly through the **vector** (a handle), and then deallocating them. On the other hand, the stack is a limited resource (especially on some embedded systems), and stack overflow is nasty.

Why would we use an **array** when we could use a built-in array? An **array** knows its size, so it is easy to use with standard-library algorithms, and it can be copied (using = or initialization). However, my main reason to prefer **array** is that it saves me from surprising nasty conversions to pointers. Consider:

```
void h()
{
    Circle a1[10];
    array<Circle,10> a2;
    // ...
    Shape* p1 = a1;         // OK: disaster waiting to happen
    Shape* p2 = a2;         // error: no conversion of array<Circle,10> to Shape*
    p1[3].draw();           // disaster
}
```

The "disaster" comment assumes that **sizeof(Shape)<sizeof(Circle)**, so that subscripting a **Circle[]** through a **Shape**∗ gives a wrong offset (§27.2.1, §17.5.1.4). All standard containers provide this advantage over built-in arrays.

An **array** can be seen as a **tuple** (§34.2.4) where all elements are of the same type. The standard library provides support for that view. The **tuple** helper type functions **tuple_size** and **tuple_element** can be applied to **array**s:

```
tuple_size<array<T,N>>::value              // N
tuple_element<S,array<T,N>>::type          // T
```

We can also use a **get<i>** function to access the ith element:

```
template<size_t index, typename T, size_t N>
    T& get(array<T,N>& a) noexcept;
template<size_t index, typename T, size_t N>
    T&& get(array<T,N>&& a) noexcept;
template<size_t index, typename T, size_t N>
    const T& get(const array<T,N>& a) noexcept;
```

For example:

```
array<int,7> a = {1,2,3,5,8,13,25};
auto x1 = get<5>(a);                               // 13
auto x2 = a[5];                                    // 13
auto sz = tuple_size<decltype(a)>::value;          // 7
typename tuple_element<5,decltype(a)>::type x3 = 13;  // x3 is an int
```

These type functions are for people writing code that expects **tuple**s.

Use a **constexpr** function (§28.2.2) and a type alias (§28.2.1) to improve readability:

```
auto sz = Tuple_size<decltype(a)>();          // 7

Tuple_element<5,decltype(a)> x3 = 13;   // x3 is an int
```

The **tuple** syntax is meant for use in generic code.

34.2.2 bitset

Aspects of a system, such as the state of an input stream (§38.4.5.1), are often represented as a set of flags indicating binary conditions such as good/bad, true/false, and on/off. C++ supports the notion of small sets of flags efficiently through bitwise operations on integers (§11.1.1). Class **bitset<N>** generalizes this notion and offers greater convenience by providing operations on a sequence of **N** bits [0:N), where **N** is known at compile time. For sets of bits that don't fit into a **long long int**, using a **bitset** is much more convenient than using integers directly. For smaller sets, **bitset** is usually optimized. If you want to name the bits, rather than numbering them, the alternatives are to use a **set** (§31.4.3), an enumeration (§8.4), or a bit-field (§8.2.7).

A **bitset<N>** is an array of **N** bits. It is presented in **<bitset>**. A **bitset** differs from a **vector<bool>** (§34.2.3) by being of fixed size, from **set** (§31.4.3) by having its bits indexed by integers rather than associatively by value, and from both **vector<bool>** and **set** by providing operations to manipulate the bits.

It is not possible to address a single bit directly using a built-in pointer (§7.2). Consequently, **bitset** provides a reference-to-bit (proxy) type. This is actually a generally useful technique for addressing objects for which a built-in pointer for some reason is unsuitable:

```
template<size_t N>
class bitset {
public:
    class reference {             // reference to a single bit:
        friend class bitset;
        reference() noexcept;
    public:                       // support zero-based subscripting in [0:b.size())
        ˜reference() noexcept;
        reference& operator=(bool x) noexcept;              // for b[i] = x;
        reference& operator=(const reference&) noexcept;    // for b[i] = b[j];
        bool operator˜() const noexcept;                    // return ˜b[i]
        operator bool() const noexcept;                     // for x = b[i];
        reference& flip() noexcept;                         // b[i].flip();
    };
    // ...
};
```

For historical reasons, **bitset** differs in style from other standard-library classes. For example, if an index (also known as a *bit position*) is out of range, an **out_of_range** exception is thrown. No iterators are provided. Bit positions are numbered from right to left in the same way bits often are in a word, so the value of **b[i]** is **pow(2,i)**. Thus, a bitset can be thought of as an **N**-bit binary number:

position:	9	8	7	6	5	4	3	2	1	0
bitset<10>(989):	1	1	1	1	0	1	1	1	0	1

34.2.2.1 Constructors

A **bitset** can be constructed with a specified number of zeros, from the bits in an **unsigned long long int**, or from a **string**:

bitset<N> Constructors (§iso.20.5.1) (continues)	
bitset bs {};	N zero bits
bitset bs {n};	Bits from n; n is an **unsigned long long**
bitset bs {s,i,n,z,o};	n bits [i:i+n) of s; s is a **basic_string<C,Tr,A>**;
	z is the character of type **C** used for zero;
	o is the character of type **C** used for one; explicit
bitset bs {s,i,n,z};	bitset bs {s,i,n,z,C{'1'}};
bitset bs {s,i,n};	bitset bs {s,i,n,C{'0'},C{'1'}};}
bitset bs {s,i};	bitset bs {s,i,npos,C{'0'},C{'1'}};
bitset bs {s};	bitset bs {s,0,npos,C{'0'},C{'1'}};

bitset<N> Constructors (continued) (§iso.20.5.1)	
bitset bs {p,n,z,o};	n bits [p:p+n); p is a C-style string of type C∗;
	z is the character of type C used for zero;
	o is the character of type C used for one; explicit
bitset bs {p,n,z};	bitset bs {p,n,z,C{'0'}};
bitset bs {p,n};	bitset bs {p,n,C{'1'},C{'0'}};
bitset bs {p};	bitset bs {p,npos,C{'1'},C{'0'}};

The position **npos** is **string<C>**'s "beyond the end" position, meaning "all characters until the end" (§36.3).

When an **unsigned long long int** argument is supplied, each bit in the integer is used to initialize the corresponding bit in the **bitset** (if any). A **basic_string** (§36.3) argument does the same, except that the character '0' gives the bit value 0, the character '1' gives the bit value 1, and other characters cause an **invalid_argument** exception to be thrown. For example:

```
void f()
{
    bitset<10> b1;  // all 0

    bitset<16> b2 = 0xaaaa;                        // 1010101010101010
    bitset<32> b3 = 0xaaaa;                        // 00000000000000001010101010101010

    bitset<10> b4 {"1010101010"};                 // 1010101010
    bitset<10> b5 {"10110111011110",4};           // 0111011110

    bitset<10> b6 {string{"1010101010"}};         // 1010101010
    bitset<10> b7 {string{"10110111011110"},4};    // 0111011110
    bitset<10> b8 {string{"10110111011110"},2,8};  // 0011011101

    bitset<10> b9 {string{"n0g00d"}};             // invalid_argument thrown
    bitset<10> b10 = string{"101001"};            // error: no implicit string to bitset conversion
}
```

A key idea in the design of **bitset** is that an optimized implementation can be provided for **bitset**s that fit in a single word. The interface reflects this assumption.

34.2.2.2 bitset Operations

A **bitset** provides the operators for accessing individual bits and for manipulating all bits in the set:

bitset<N> Operations (§iso.20.5) (continues)	
bs[i]	The ith bit of bs
bs.test(i)	The ith bit of bs; throw **out_of_range** if i is not in [0:bs.size())
bs&=bs2	Bitwise and
bs|=bs2	Bitwise or
bs^=bs2	Bitwise exclusive or

bitset<N> **Operations (continued) (§iso.20.5)**	
bs<<=n	Logical left shift (fill with zeros)
bs>>=n	Logical right shift (fill with zeros)
bs.set()	Set every bit of **bs** to 1
bs.set(i,v)	bs[i]=v
bs.reset()	Set every bit of **bs** to 0
bs.reset(i)	b[i]=0;
bs.flip()	bs[i]=˜bs[i] for every bit in **bs**
bs.flip(i)	bs[i]=˜bs[i]
bs2=˜bs	Make complement set: bs2=bs, bs2.flip()
bs2=bs<<n	Make left-shifted set: bs2=bs, bs2<<=n
bs2=bs>>n	Make right-shifted set: bs2=bs, bs2>>=n
bs3=bs&bs2	Bitwise and: bs3[i]=bs[i]&bs2[i] for each bit in **bs**
bs3=bs|bs2	Bitwise or: bs3[i]=bs[i]|bs2[i] for each bit in **bs**
bs3=bs˜bs2	Bitwise exclusive or: bs3[i]=bs[i]˜bs2[i] for each bit in **bs**
is>>bs	Read from **is** into **bs**; **is** is an **istream**
os<<bs	Write **bs** to **os**; **os** is an **ostream**

The >> and << are I/O operators when their first operand is an **iostream**; otehwise, they are shift operators and their second operand must be an integer. For example:

```
bitset<9> bs ("110001111"};
cout << bs << '\n';        // write "110001111" to cout
auto bs2 = bs<<3;          // bs2 == "001111000";
cout << bs2 << '\n';       // write "001111000" to cout
cin >> bs;                 // read from cin
bs2 = bs>>3;               // bs2 == "000110001" if the input were "110001111"
cout << bs2 << '\n';       // write "000110001" to cout
```

When bits are shifted, a logical (rather than cyclic) shift is used. That implies that some bits "fall off the end" and that some positions get the default value 0. Note that because size_t is an unsigned type, it is not possible to shift by a negative number. It does, however, imply that b<<−1 shifts by a very large positive value, thus leaving every bit of the bitset b with the value 0. Your compiler should warn against this.

A bitset also supports common operations such as size(), ==, I/O, etc.:

More bitset<N> **Operations (§iso.20.5)** C, Tr, and A have defaults for basic_string<C,Tr,A>	
n=bs.to_ulong()	n is the **unsigned long** corresponding to **bs**
n=bs.to_ullong()	n is the **unsigned long long** corresponding to **bs**
s=bs.to_string<C,Tr,A>(c0,c1)	s[i]=(b[i])?c1:c0; s is a basic_string<C,Tr,A>
s=bs.to_string<C,Tr,A>(c0)	s=bs.template to_string<C,Tr,A>(c0,C{'1'})
s=bs.to_string<C,Tr,A>()	s=bs.template to_string<C,Tr,A>(C{'0'},C{'1'})

More bitset<N> Operations (continued) (§iso.20.5)	
C, Tr, and A have defaults for basic_string<C,Tr,A>	
n=bs.count()	n is the number of bits with value 1 in bs
n=bs.size()	n is the number of bits in bs
bs==bs2	Do bs and b2 have the same value?
bs!=bs2	!(bs==bs2)
bs.all()	Do all bits in bs have the value 1?
bs.any()	Does any bit in bs have the value 1?
bs.none()	Does no bit in bs have the value 1?
hash<bitset<N>>	Specialization of hash for bitset<N>

The operations to_ullong() and to_string() provide the inverse operations to the constructors. To avoid nonobvious conversions, named operations were preferred over conversion operators. If the value of the bitset has so many significant bits that it cannot be represented as an unsigned long, to_ulong() throws overflow_error; so does to_ullong() if its bitset argument doesn't fit.

Fortunately, the template arguments for the basic_string returned by to_string are defaulted. For example, we could write out the binary representation of an int:

```
void binary(int i)
{
        bitset<8*sizeof(int)> b = i;             // assume 8-bit byte (see also §40.2)

        cout << b.to_string<char,char_traits<char>,allocator<char>>() << '\n';   // general and verbose
        cout << b.to_string<char>() << '\n'; // use default traits and allocator
        cout << b.to_string<>() << '\n';         // use all defaults
        cout << b.to_string() << '\n';           // use all defaults
}
```

This prints the bits represented as 1s and 0s from left to right, with the most significant bit leftmost, so that argument 123 would give the output

```
00000000000000000000000001111011
00000000000000000000000001111011
00000000000000000000000001111011
00000000000000000000000001111011
```

For this example, it is simpler to directly use the bitset output operator:

```
void binary2(int i)
{
        bitset<8*sizeof(int)> b = i;     // assume 8-bit byte (see also §40.2)
        cout << b << '\n';
}
```

34.2.3 vector<bool>

The vector<bool> from <vector> is a specialization of vector (§31.4) providing compact storage of bits (bools):

```
template<typename A>
class vector<bool,A> {    // specialization of vector<T,A> (§31.4)
public:
    using const_reference = bool;
    using value_type = bool;
    // like vector<T,A>

    class reference {    // support zero-based subscripting in [0:v.size())
        friend class vector;
        reference() noexcept;
    public:
        ˜reference();
        operator bool() const noexcept;
        reference& operator=(const bool x) noexcept;        // v[i] = x
        reference& operator=(const reference& x) noexcept;  // v[i] = v[j]
        void flip() noexcept;                               // flip the bit: v[i]=˜v[i]
    };

    void flip() noexcept;// flip all bits of v

    // ...
};
```

The similarity to **bitset** is obvious, but, unlike **bitset** but like **vector<T>**, **vector<bool>** has an allocator and can have its size changed.

As in a **vector<T>**, elements of a **vector<bool>** with higher indices have higher addresses:

position:	0	1	2	3	4	5	6	7	8	9
vector<bool>:	1	1	1	1	0	1	1	1	0	1

This is exactly the opposite of the layout in a **bitset**. Also, there is no direct support for converting integers and strings to and from a **vector<bool>**.

Use **vector<bool>** as you would any other **vector<T>**, but expect operations on a single bit to be less efficient than the equivalent operations on a **vector<char>**. Also, it is impossible in C++ to completely faithfully mimic the behavior of a (built-in) reference with a proxy, so don't try to be subtle about rvalue/lvalue distinctions when using a **vector<bool>**.

34.2.4 Tuples

The standard library provides two ways of grouping values of arbitrary types into a single object:
- A **pair** (§34.2.4.1) holds two values.
- A **tuple** (§34.2.4) holds zero or more values.

We use **pair** when it is useful to know (statically) that we have exactly two values. With **tuple**, we always have to deal with all possible numbers of values.

34.2.4.1 pair

In **<utility>**, the standard library provides class **pair** for manipulating pairs of values:

```
template<typename T, typename U>
struct pair {
    using first_type = T;      // the type of the first element
    using second_type = U;   // the type of the second element

    T first;        // first element
    U second;       // second element

    // ...
};
```

pair<T,U> (§iso.20.3.2)	
pair p {}	Default constructor: **pair p {T{},U{}};** constexpr
pair p {x,y}	**p.first** is initialized to **x** and **p.second** is initialized to **y**
pair p {p2}	Construct from the **pair p2**: pair p {p2.first,p2.second};
pair p {piecewise_construct,t,t2}	**p.first** is constructed from the elements of **tuple t**, and **p.second** is constructed from the elements of **tuple t2**
p.˜pair()	Destructor: destroy **t.first** and **t.second**
p2=p	Copy assignment: **p2.first=p.first** and **p2.second=p.second**
p2=move{p}	Move assignment: **p2.first=move(p.first)** and **p2.second=move(p.second)**
p.swap(p2)	Exchange the values of **p** and **p2**

An operation on **pair** is **noexcept** if the corresponding operations on its elements are. Similarly, copy or move operations exist for a **pair** if the corresponding operations on its elements do.

The elements **first** and **second** are members that we can directly read and write. For example:

```
void f()
{
    pair<string,int> p {"Cambridge",1209};
    cout << p.first;        // print "Cambridge"
    p.second += 800;     // update year
    // ...
}
```

The **piecewise_construct** is the name of an object of type **piecewise_construct_t** used to distinguish between constructing a **pair** with members of **tuple** types and constructing a **pair** using **tuples** as argument lists for its **first** and **second**. For example:

```
struct Univ {
    Univ(const string& n, int r) : name{n}, rank{r} { }
    string name;
    int rank;
    string city = "unknown";
};
```

```
using Tup = tuple<string,int>;
Tup t1 {"Columbia",11};        // U.S. News 2012
Tup t2 {"Cambridge",2};

pair<Tub,Tub> p1 {t1,t2};                        // pair of tuples
pair<Univ,Univ> p2 {piecewise_construct,t1,t2};  // pair of Univs
```

That is, **p1.second** is **t2**, that is, **{"Cambridge",2}**. To contrast, **p2.second** is **Univ{t2}**, that is, **{"Cambridge",2,"unknown"}**.

pair<T,U> Helpers (§iso.20.3.3, §iso.20.3.4)	
p==p2	p.first==p2.first && p.second==p2.second
p<p2	p.first<p2.first || (!(p2.first<p.first) && p.second<p2.second)
p!=p2	!(p==p2)
p>p2	p2<p
p<=p2	!(p2<p)
p>=p2	!(p<p2)
swap(p,p2)	p.swap(p2)
p=make_pair(x,y)	p is a **pair<decltype(x),decltype(y)>** holding the value **x,y**; if possible, move rather than copy **x** and **y**
tuple_size<T>::value	The size of a **pair** of type **T**
tuple_element<N,T>::type	The type of **first** (if N==0) or **second** (if N==1)
get<N>(p)	A reference to the **Nth** element of the **pair p**; **N** must be **0** or **1**

The **make_pair** function avoids explicit mention of the element types of a **pair**. For example:

```
auto p = make_pair("Harvard",1736);
```

34.2.4.2 tuple

In **<tuple>**, the standard library provides class **tuple** and various supporting facilities. A **tuple** is a sequence of **N** elements of arbitrary types:

```
template<typename... Types>
class tuple {
public:
    // ...
};
```

The number of elements is zero or positive.

For details of **tuple** design, implementation, and use, see §28.5 and §28.6.4.

tuple<Types...> Members (§iso.20.4.2) (continues)	
tuple t {};	Default constructor: the empty **tuple**; constexpr
tuple t {args};	t has one element for each element of **args**; explicit
tuple t {t2};	Construct from **tuple t2**
tuple t {p};	Construct from **pair p**

tuple<Types...> **Members (continued) (§iso.20.4.2)**	
tuple t {allocator_arg_t,a,args};	Construct from **args** using the allocator **a**
tuple t {allocator_arg_t,a,t2};	Construct from **tuple t2**, using the allocator **a**
tuple t {allocator_arg_t,a,p};	Construct from **pair p**, using the allocator **a**
t.~tuple()	Destructor: destroy each element
t=t2	Copy assignment of **tuple**s
t=move(t2)	Move assignment of **tuple**s
t=p	Copy assignment of **pair p**
t=move(p)	Move assignment of **pair p**
t.swap(t2)	Exchange the values of **tuple**s t and t2; noexcept

The types of **tuple** and operands of = and arguments to **swap()**, etc., are *not* required to be the same. An operation is valid if (and only if) the implied operations on elements are valid. For example, we can assign one **tuple** to another if each element of the assigned **tuple** can be assigned to the target element. For example:

```
tuple<string,vector<double>,int> t2 = make_tuple("Hello, tuples!",vector<int>{1,2,3},'x');
```

An operation is **noexcept** if all the element operations are, and an operation throws only if a member operation throws. Similarly, a **tuple** operation is **constexpr** if the element operations are.

The number of elements in each **tuple** of a pair of operands (or arguments) must be the same. Note that the general **tuple** constructor is **explicit**. In particular, this does not work:

```
tuple<int,int,int> rotate(tuple<int,int,int> t)
{
      return {t.get<2>(),t.get<0>(),t.get<1>()};  // error: explicit tuple constructor
}

auto t2 = rotate({3,7,9});  // error: explicit tuple constructor
```

If all you need is two elements, you can use **pair**:

```
pair<int,int> rotate(pair<int,int> p)
{
      return {p.second,p.first};
}

auto p2 = rotate({3,7});
```

For more examples, see §28.6.4.

tuple<Types...> **Helpers (§iso.20.4.2.4, §iso.20.4.2.9) (continues)**	
t=make_tuple(args)	Make **tuple** from **args**
t=forward_as_tuple(args)	t is a **tuple** of rvalue references to the elements in **args** so you can forward the elements of **arg** through t
t=tie(args)	t is a **tuple** of lvalue references to the elements of **args** so you can assign to the elements of **args** through t

tuple<Types...> **Helpers (continued)** (§iso.20.4.2.4, §iso.20.4.2.9)	
t=tuple_cat(args)	Concatenate tuples: args is one or more tuples;
	t has the members of the tuples in args in order
tuple_size<T>::value	The number of elements of the tuple T
tuple_elements<N,T>::type	The type of the Nth element of the tuple T
get<N>(t)	A reference to the Nth element of the tuple t
t==t2	Are all elements of t and t2 equal?
	t and t2 must have the same number of elements
t!=t2	!(t==t2)
t<t2	Does t lexicographically compare less than t2?
t>t2	t2<t
t<=t2	!(t2>t)
t>=t2	!(t2<t)
uses_allocator<T,A>::value	Can a tuple<T> be allocated by an allocator of type A?
swap(t,t2)	t.swap(t2)

For example, tie() can be used to extract elements from a tuple:

```
auto t = make_tuple(2.71828,299792458,"Hannibal");
double c;
string name;
tie(c,ignore,name) = t;          // c=299792458; name="Hannibal"
```

The name ignore refers to an object of a type that ignores assignments. Thus, an ignore in a tie() implies that attempts to assign to its tuple position are ignored. An alternative would be:

```
double c = get<0>(t);          // c=299792458
string name = get<2>(t);       // name="Hannibal"
```

Obviously, this would be more interesting if the tuple came from "elsewhere" so that we didn't trivially know the element values. For example:

```
tuple<int,double,string> compute();
// ...
double c;
string name;
tie(c,ignore,name) = t;          // results in c and name
```

34.3 Resource Management Pointers

A pointer points to an object (or not). However, a pointer does not indicate who (if anyone) owns the objects. That is, looking just at a pointer, we have no idea who is supposed to delete the object pointed to, or how, or if at all. In <memory>, we find "smart pointers" to express ownership:

- unique_ptr (§34.3.1) to represent exclusive ownership
- shared_ptr (§34.3.2) to represent shared ownership
- weak_ptr (§34.3.3) to break loops in circular shared data structures

These resource handles are introduced in §5.2.1.

34.3.1 unique_ptr

The unique_ptr (defined in <memory>) provides a semantics of strict ownership:
- A unique_ptr owns the object to which it holds a pointer. That is, it is the unique_ptr's obligation to destroy the object pointed to (if any) by its contained pointer.
- A unique_ptr cannot be copied (has no copy constructor or copy assignment). However, it can be moved.
- A unique_ptr stores a pointer and deletes the object pointed to (if any) using the associated deleter (if any) when it is itself destroyed (such as when a thread of control leaves the unique_ptr's scope; §17.2.2).

The uses of unique_ptr include:
- Providing exception safety for dynamically allocated memory (§5.2.1, §13.3)
- Passing ownership of dynamically allocated memory to a function
- Returning dynamically allocated memory from a function
- Storing pointers in containers

Think of unique_ptr as being represented by a simple pointer ("the contained pointer") or (if it has a deleter) as a pair of pointers:

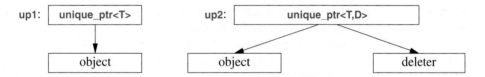

When a unique_ptr is destroyed, its *deleter* is called to destroy the owned object. The deleter represents what it means to destroy an object. For example:
- A deleter for a local variable should do nothing.
- A deleter for a memory pool should return the object to the memory pool and destroy it or not, depending on how that pool is defined.
- The default ("no deleter") version of unique_ptr uses delete. It doesn't even store the default deleter. It can be a specialization or rely on the empty-base optimization (§28.5).

This way unique_ptr supports general resource management (§5.2).

```
template<typename T, typename D = default_delete<T>>
class unique_ptr {
public:
    using pointer = ptr; // type of the contained pointer;
                         // ptr is D::pointer if that is defined, otherwise T*
    using element_type = T;
    using deleter_type = D;

    // ...
};
```

The contained pointer is not directly accessible to users.

unique_ptr<T,D> (§iso.20.7.1.2)	
cp is the contained pointer	
unique_ptr up {}	Default constructor: **cp=nullptr**; constexpr; noexcept
unique_ptr up {p}	**cp=p**; use the default deleter; explicit; noexcept
unique_ptr up {p,del}	**cp=p**; **del** is the deleter; noexcept
unique_ptr up {up2}	Move constructor: **cp.p=up2.p**; **up2.p=nullptr**; noexcept
up.˜unique_ptr()	Destructor: if **cp!=nullptr** invoke **cp**'s deleter
up=up2	Move assigment: **up.reset(up2.cp)**; **up2.cp=nullptr**;
	up gets **up2**'s deleter; **up**'s old object (if any) is deleted; noexcept
up=nullptr	**up.reset(nullptr)**; that is, delete **up**'s old object, if any
bool b {up};	Conversion to **bool**: **up.cp!=nullptr**; explicit
x=*up	**x=up.cp**; for contained non-arrays only
x=up->m	**x=up.cp->m**; for contained non-arrays only
x=up[n]	**x=up.cp[n]**; for contained arrays only
x=up.get()	**x=up.cp**
del=up.get_deleter()	**del** is **up**'s deleter
p=up.release()	**p=up.cp**; **up.cp=nullptr**
up.reset(p)	If **up.cp!=nullptr** call deleter for **up.cp**; **up.cp=p**
up.reset()	**up.cp=pionter{}** (probably **nullptr**);
	call the deleter for the old value of **up.cp**
up.swap(up2)	Exchange **up** and **up2**'s values; noexcept
up==up2	**up.cp==up2.cp**
up<up2	**up.cp<up2.cp**
up!=up2	!(**up==up2**)
up>up2	**up2<up**
up<=up2	!(**up2>up**)
up>=up2	!(**up2<up**)
swap(up,up2)	**up.swap(up2)**

Note: **unique_ptr** does not offer a copy constructor or copy assignment. Had it done so, the meaning of "ownership" would have been very hard to define and/or use. If you feel the need for copies, consider using a **shared_ptr** (§34.3.2).

It is possible to have a **unique_ptr** for a built-in array. For example:

```
unique_ptr<int[]> make_sequence(int n)
{
    unique_ptr p {new int[n]};
    for (int i=0; i<n; ++i)
        p[i]=i;
    return p;
}
```

This is provided as a specialization:

```
template<typename T, typename D>
class unique_ptr<T[],D> {       // specialization for arrays (§iso.20.7.1.3)
                                // the default D=default_delete<T> comes from the general unique_ptr
public:
//      ... like the unique_ptr for individual objects, but with [] instead of * and -> ...
};
```

To avoid slicing (§17.5.1.4), a **Derived[]** is not accepted as an argument to a **unique_ptr<Base[]>** even if **Base** is a public base of **Derived**. For example:

```
class Shape {
    // ...
};

class Circle : public Base {
    // ...
};

unique_ptr<Shape> ps {new Circle{p,20}};                        // OK
unique_ptr<Shape[]> pa {new Circle[] {Circle{p,20}, Circle{p2,40}};    // error
```

How can we best think of a **unique_ptr**? What are the best ways to use a **unique_ptr**? It is called a pointer (_ptr) and I pronounce it "unique pointer," but clearly it is not just an ordinary pointer (or there would be no point in defining it). Consider a simple technical example:

```
unique_ptr<int> f(unique_ptr<int> p)
{
    ++*p;
    return p;
}

void f2(const unique_ptr<int>& p)
{
    ++*p;
}

void use()
{
    unique_ptr<int> p {new int{7}};
    p=f(p);            // error: no copy constructor
    p=f(move(p));      // transfer ownership there and back
    f2(p);             // pass a reference
}
```

The **f2()** body is slightly shorter than **f()** and **f2()** is simpler to call, but I find **f()** easier to think about. The style illustrated by **f()** is explicit about ownership (and the use of **unique_ptr** is typically motivated by ownership issues). See also the discussion of the use of non-**const** references in §7.7.1. On balance, a notation **f(x)** that modifies **x** is more error-prone than a **y=f(x)** notation that does not.

It is a fair estimate that the call of **f2()** is one or two machine instructions faster than a call of **f()** (because of the need to place a **nullptr** in the original **unique_ptr**), but that is unlikely to be significant. On the other hand, access to the contained pointer involves an extra indirection in **f2()** compared to **f()**. This, too, is unlikely to be significant in most programs, so the choice between the styles of **f()** and **f2()** has to be made on reasoning about code quality.

Here is a simple example of a deleter used to provide guaranteed release of data obtained from a C program fragment using **malloc()** (§43.5):

```
extern "C" char* get_data(const char* data); // get data from C program fragment

using PtoCF = void(*)(void*);

void test()
{
    unique_ptr<char,PtoCF> p {get_data("my_data"),free};
    // ... use *p ...
} // implicit free(p)
```

Currently, there is no standard-library **make_unique()** similar to **make_pair()** (§34.2.4.1) and **make_shared()** (§34.3.2). However, it is easily defined:

```
template<typename T, typename... Args>
unique_ptr<T> make_unique(Args&&... args)         // default deleter version
{
        return unique_ptr<T>{new T{args...}};
}
```

34.3.2 shared_ptr

A **shared_ptr** represents shared ownership. It is used where two pieces of code need access to some data but neither has exclusive ownership (in the sense of being responsible for destroying the object). A **shared_ptr** is a kind of counted pointer where the object pointed to is deleted when the use count goes to zero. Think of a shared pointer as a structure with two pointers: one to the object and one to the use count:

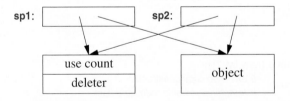

The *deleter* is what is used to delete the shared object when the use count goes to zero. The default deleter is the usual **delete** (invoke the destructor, if any, and deallocate free store).

For example, consider a **Node** in a general graph used by an algorithm that adds and removes both nodes and connections between nodes (edges). Obviously, to avoid resource leaks, a **Node** must be deleted if and only if no other node refers to it. We could try:

```
struct Node {
    vector<Node*> edges;
    // ...
};
```

Given that, answering questions such as "How many nodes points to this node?" is very hard and requires much added "housekeeping" code. We could plug in a garbage collector (§34.5), but that could have negative performance implications if the graph was only a small part of a large application data space. Worse, if the container contained non-memory resources, such as thread handles, file handles, locks, etc., even a garbage collector would leak resources.

Instead, we can use a **shared_ptr**:

```
struct Node {
    vector<shared_ptr<Node>> edges;
    thread worker;
    // ...
};
```

Here, **Node**'s destructor (the implicitly generated destructor will do fine) **delete**s its **edges**. That is, the destructor for each **edges[i]** is invoked, and the **Node** pointed to (if any) is deleted if **edges[i]** was the last pointer to it.

Don't use a **shared_ptr** just to pass a pointer from one owner to another; that's what **unique_ptr** is for, and **unique_ptr** does it better and more cheaply. If you have been using counted pointers as return values from factory functions (§21.2.4) and the like, consider upgrading to **unique_ptr** rather than **shared_ptr**.

Do not thoughtlessly replace pointers with **shared_ptr**s in an attempt to prevent memory leaks; **shared_ptr**s are not a panacea nor are they without costs:

- A circular linked structure of **shared_ptr**s can cause a resource leak. You need some logical complication to break the circle, for example, use a **weak_ptr** (§34.3.3).
- Objects with shared ownership tend to stay "live" for longer than scoped objects (thus causing higher average resource usage).
- Shared pointers in a multi-threaded environment can be expensive (because of the need to prevent data races on the use count).
- A destructor for a shared object does not execute at a predictable time, so the algorithms/logic for the update of any shared object are easier to get wrong than for an object that's not shared. For example, which locks are set at the time of the destructor's execution? Which files are open? In general, which objects are "live" and in appropriate states at the (unpredictable) point of execution?
- If a single (last) node keeps a large data structure alive, the cascade of destructor calls triggered by its deletion can cause a significant "garbage collection delay." That can be detrimental to real-time response.

A **shared_ptr** represents shared ownership and can be very useful, even essential, but shared ownership isn't my ideal, and it always carries a cost (independently of how you represent the sharing). It is better (simpler) if an object has a definite owner and a definite, predictable life span. When there is a choice:

- Prefer unique_ptr to shared_ptr.
- Prefer ordinary scoped objects to objects on the heap owned by a unique_ptr.

The shared_ptr provides a fairly conventional set of operations:

shared_ptr<T> **Operations (§iso.20.7.2.2)**	
cp is the contained pointer; uc is the use count	
shared_ptr sp {}	Default constructor: cp=nullptr; uc=0; noexcept
shared_ptr sp {p}	Constructor: cp=p; uc=1
shared_ptr sp {p,del}	Constructor: cp=p; uc=1; use deleter del
shared_ptr sp {p,del,a}	Constructor: cp=p; uc=1; use deleter del and allocator a
shared_ptr sp {sp2}	Move and copy constructors:
	the move constructor moves and then sets sp2.cp=nullptr;
	the copy constructor copies and sets ++uc for the now-shared uc
sp.˜shared_ptr()	Destructor: --uc; delete the object pointed to by cp if uc became 0,
	using the deleter (the default deleter is delete)
sp=sp2	Copy assignment: ++uc for the now-shared uc; noexcept
sp=move(sp2)	Move assignment: sp2.cp=nullptr for the now-shared uc; noexcept
bool b {sp};	Conversion to bool: sp.uc==nullptr; explicit
sp.reset()	shared_ptr{}.swap(sp); that is, sp contains pointer{},
	and the destruction of the temporary shared_ptr{}
	decreases the use count for the old object; noexcept
sp.reset(p)	shared_ptr{p}.swap(sp); that is, sp.cp=p; uc==1;
	the destruction of the temporary shared_ptr decreases
	the use count for the old object
sp.reset(p,d)	Like sp.reset(p) but with the deleter d
sp.reset(p,d,a)	Like sp.reset(p) but with the deleter d and the allocator a
p=sp.get()	p=sp.cp; noexcept
x=*sp	x=*sp.cp; noexcept
x=sp->m	x=sp.cp->m; noexcept
n=sp.use_count()	n is the value of the use count (0 if sp.cp==nullptr)
sp.unique()	sp.uc==1? (does not check if sp.cp==nullptr)
x=sp.owner_before(pp)	x is an ordering function (strict weak order; §31.2.2.1)
	pp is a shared_ptr or a weak_ptr
sp.swap(sp2)	Exchange sp's and sp2's values; noexcept

In addition, the standard library provides a few helper functions:

shared_ptr<T> **Helpers (§iso.20.7.2.2.6, §iso.20.7.2.2.7) (continues)**	
sp=make_shared(args)	sp is a shared_ptr<T> for an object of type T
	constructed from the arguments args; allocated using new
sp=allocate_shared(a,args)	sp is a shared_ptr<T> for an object of type T
	constructed from the arguments args; allocated using allocator a

shared_ptr<T> **Helpers (continued)** (§iso.20.7.2.2.6, §iso.20.7.2.2.7)	
sp==sp2	sp.cp==sp2.cp; sp or sp2 may be the nullptr
sp<sp2	less<T∗>(sp.cp,sp2.cp); sp or sp2 may be the nullptr
sp!=sp2	!(sp=sp2)
sp>sp2	sp2<sp
sp<=sp2	!(sp>sp2)
sp>=sp2	!(sp<sp2)
swap(sp,sp2)	sp.swap(sp2)
sp2=static_pointer_cast(sp)	static_cast for shared pointers:
	sp2=shared_ptr<T>(static_cast<T∗>(sp.cp)); noexcept
sp2=dynamic_pointer_cast(sp)	dynamic_cast for shared pointers:
	sp2=shared_ptr<T>(dynamic_cast<T∗>(sp.cp)); noexcept
sp2=const_pointer_cast(sp)	const_cast for shared pointers:
	sp2=shared_ptr<T>(const_cast<T∗>(sp.cp)); noexcept
dp=get_deleter<D>(sp)	If sp has a deleter of type D, ∗dp is sp's deleter; otherwise, dp==nullptr; noexcept
os<<sp	Write sp to ostream os

For example:

```
struct S {
    int i;
    string s;
    double d;
    // ...
};

auto p = make_shared<S>(1,"Ankh Morpork",4.65);
```

Now, p is a shared_ptr<S> pointing to an object of type S allocated on the free store, containing {1,string{"Ankh Morpork"},4.65}.

Note that unlike unique_ptr::get_deleter(), shared_ptr's deleter is not a member function.

34.3.3 weak_ptr

A weak_ptr refers to an object managed by a shared_ptr. To access the object, a weak_ptr can be converted to a shared_ptr using the member function lock(). A weak_ptr allows access to an object, owned by someone else, that

- You need access to (only) if it exists
- May get deleted (by someone else) at any time
- Must have its destructor called after its last use (usually to delete a non-memory resource)

In particular, we use weak pointers to break loops in data structures managed using shared_ptrs.

Think of a weak_ptr as a structure with two pointers: one to the (potentially shared) object and one to the use count structure of that object's shared_ptrs:

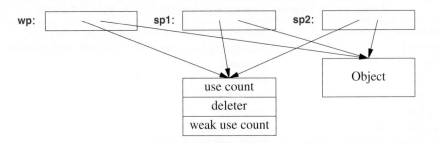

The "weak use count" is needed to keep the use count structure alive because there may be weak_ptrs after the last **shared_ptr** for an object (and the object) is destroyed.

```
template<typename T>
class weak_ptr {
public:
    using element_type = T;
    // ...
};
```

A **weak_ptr** has to be converted to a **shared_ptr** to access "its" object, so it provides relatively few operations:

weak_ptr<T> (§iso.20.7.2.3)	
cp is the contained pointer; **wuc** is the weak use count	
weak_ptr wp {};	Default constructor: **cp=nullptr**; constexpr; noexcept
weak_ptr wp {pp};	Copy constructor: **cp=pp.cp**; **++wuc**;
	pp is a **weak_ptr** or a **shared_ptr**; noexcept
wp.˜weak_ptr()	Destructor: no effect on *cp; **−−wuc**
wp=pp	Copy: decrease **wuc** and set wp to pp: weak_ptr(pp).swap(wp);
	pp is a **weak_ptr** or a **shared_ptr**; noexcept
wp.swap(wp2)	Exchange wp's and wp2's values; noexcept
wp.reset()	Decrease **wuc** and set wp to **nullptr**:
	weak_ptr{}.swap(wp); noexcept
n=wp.use_count()	n is the number of **shared_ptrs** to *cp; noexcept
wp.expired()	Are there any **shared_ptrs** to *cp? noexcept
sp=wp.lock()	Make a new **shared_ptr** for *cp; noexcept
x=wp.owner_before(pp)	x is an ordering function (strict weak order; §31.2.2.1);
	pp is a **shared_ptr** or a **weak_ptr**
swap(wp,wp2)	wp.swap(wp2); noexcept

Consider an implementation of the old "asteroid game." All asteroids are owned by "the game," but each asteroid must keep track of neighboring asteroids and handle collisions. A collision typically leads to the destruction of one or more asteroids. Each asteroid must keep a list of other asteroids in its neighborhood. Note that being on such a neighbor list should not keep an asteroid "alive" (so a **shared_ptr** would be inappropriate). On the other hand, an asteroid must not be destroyed while another asteroid is looking at it (e.g., to calculate the effect of a collision). And obviously, an asteroid destructor must be called to release resources (such as a connection to the graphics system). What we need is a list of asteroids that might still be intact and a way of "grabbing onto one" for a while. A **weak_ptr** does just that:

```
void owner()
{
    // ...
    vector<shared_ptr<Asteroid>> va(100);
    for (int i=0; i<va.size(); ++i) {
        // ... calculate neighbors for new asteroid ...
        va[i].reset(new Asteroid(weak_ptr<Asteroid>(va[neighbor])));
        launch(i);
    }
    // ...
}
```

Obviously, I radically simplified "the owner" and gave each new **Asteroid** just one neighbor. The key is that we give the **Asteroid** a **weak_ptr** to that neighbor. The owner keeps a **shared_ptr** to represent the ownership that's shared whenever an **Asteroid** is looking (but not otherwise). The collision calculation for an **Asteroid** will look something like this:

```
void collision(weak_ptr<Asteroid> p)
{
    if (auto q = p.lock()) {      // p.lock returns a shared_ptr to p's object
        // ... that Asteroid still existed: calculate ...
    }
    else {      // Oops: that Asteroid has already been destroyed
        p.reset();
    }
}
```

Note that even if a user decides to shut down the game and deletes all **Asteroid**s (by destroying the **shared_ptr**s representing ownership), every **Asteroid** that is in the middle of calculating a collision still finishes correctly: after the **p.lock()**, it holds a **shared_ptr** that will not become invalid.

34.4 Allocators

The STL containers (§31.4) and **string** (Chapter 36) are resource handles that acquire and release memory to hold their elements. To do so, they use *allocators*. The basic purpose of an allocator is to provide a source of memory for a given type and a place to return that memory to once it is no longer needed. Thus, the basic allocator functions are:

```
p=a.allocate(n);      // acquire space for n objects of type T
a.deallocate(p,n);    // release space for n objects of type T pointed to by p
```

For example:

```
template<typename T>
struct Simple_alloc {              // use new[] and delete[] to allocate and deallocate bytes
     using value_type = T;

     Simple_alloc() {}

     T* allocate(size_t n)
          { return reinterpret_cast<T*>(new char[n*sizeof(T)]); }
     void deallocate(T* p, size_t n)
          { delete[] reinterpret_cast<char*>(p); }

     // ...
};
```

`Simple_alloc` happens to be the simplest standards-conforming allocator. Note the casts to and from `char*`: `allocate()` does not invoke constructors and `deallocate()` does not invoke destructors; they deal in memory, not typed objects.

I can build my own allocator to allocate from an arbitrary area of memory:

```
class Arena {
     void* p;
     int s;
public:
     Arena(void* pp, int ss); // allocate from p[0..ss-1]
};
```

```
template<typename T>
struct My_alloc {          // use an Arena to allocate and deallocate bytes
     Arena& a;
     My_alloc(Arena& aa) : a(aa) { }
     My_alloc() {}
     // usual allocator stuff
};
```

Once `Arena`s are made, objects can be constructed in the memory allocated:

```
constexpr int sz {100000};
Arena my_arena1{new char[sz],sz};
Arena my_arena2{new char[10*sz],10*sz};

vector<int> v0;// allocate using default allocator

vector<int,My_alloc<int>> v1 {My_alloc<int>{my_arena1}};   // construct in my_arena1

vector<int,My_alloc<int>> v2 {My_alloc<int>{my_arena2}};   // construct in my_arena2

vector<int,Simple_alloc<int>> v3;                          // construct on free store
```

Typically, the verbosity would be alleviated by the use of aliases. For example:

```
template<typename T>
    using Arena_vec = std::vector<T,My_alloc<T>>;
template<typename T>
    using Simple_vec = std::vector<T,Simple_alloc<T>>;

My_alloc<int> Alloc2 {my_arena2};          // named allocator object

Arena_vec<complex<double>> vcd {{{1,2}, {3,4}}, Alloc2};              // explicit allocator
Simple_vec<string> vs {"Sam Vimes", "Fred Colon", "Nobby Nobbs"};    // default allocator
```

An allocator imposes space overhead in a container only if its objects actually have state (like **My_alloc**). This is usually achieved by relying on the empty-base optimization (§28.5).

34.4.1 The Default Allocator

A default allocator that allocates using **new** and deallocates using **delete** is used (by default) by all standard-library containers.

```
template<typename T>
class allocator {
public:
    using size_type = size_t;
    using difference_type = ptrdiff_t;
    using pointer = T*;
    using const_pointer = const T*;
    using reference = T&;
    using const_reference = const T&;
    using value_type = T;

    template<typename U>
        struct rebind { using other = allocator<U>; };

    allocator() noexcept;
    allocator(const allocator&) noexcept;
    template<typename U>
        allocator(const allocator<U>&) noexcept;
    ~allocator();

    pointer address(reference x) const noexcept;
    const_pointer address(const_reference x) const noexcept;

    pointer allocate(size_type n, allocator<void>::const_pointer hint = 0);    // allocate n bytes
    void deallocate(pointer p, size_type n);                                   // deallocate n bytes

    size_type max_size() const noexcept;

    template<typename U, typename... Args>
        void construct(U* p, Args&&... args);       // new(p) U{args}
```

```
template<typename U>
    void destroy(U* p);                          // p->~U()
};
```

The curious **rebind** template is an archaic alias. It should have been:

```
template<typename U>
using other = allocator<U>;
```

However, **allocator** was defined before such aliases were supported by C++. It is provided to allow an allocator to allocate objects of arbitrary type. Consider:

```
using Link_alloc = typename A::template rebind<Link>::other;
```

If **A** is an **allocator**, then **rebind<Link>::other** is an alias for **allocator<Link>**. For example:

```
template<typename T, typename A = allocator<T>>
class list {
private:
    class Link { /* ... */ };

    using Link_alloc = typename A:: template rebind<Link>::other;    // allocator<Link>

    Link_alloc a;    // link allocator
    A alloc;         // list allocator
    // ...
};
```

A more restricted specialization of **allocator<T>** is provided:

```
template<>
class allocator<void> {
public:
    typedef void* pointer;
    typedef const void* const_pointer;
    typedef void value_type;
    template<typename U> struct rebind { typedef allocator<U> other; };
};
```

This allows us to avoid special cases: We can mention **allocator<void>** as long as we don't dereference its pointers.

34.4.2 Allocator Traits

The allocators are "wired together" using **allocator_traits**. A property of an allocator, say, its **pointer** type, is found in its trait: **allocator_traits<X>::pointer**. As usual, the traits technique is used so that I can build an allocator for a type that does not have member types matching the requirements of an allocator, such as **int**, and a type designed without any thought of allocators.

Basically, **allocator_traits** provide defaults for the usual set of type aliases and allocator functions. Compared to the default **allocator** (§34.4.1), **address()** is missing and **select_on_container_copy_construction()** is added:

```
template<typename A>                                    // §iso.20.6.8
struct allocator_traits {
    using allocator_type = A;
    using value_type = A::value_type;
    using pointer = value_type;                                               // trick
    using const_pointer = Pointer_traits<pointer>::rebind<const value_type>;  // trick
    using void_pointer = Pointer_traits<pointer>::rebind<void>;               // trick
    using const_void_pointer = Pointer_traits<pointer>::rebind<const void>;   // trick
    using difference_type = Pointer_traits<pointer>::difference_type;         // trick
    using size_type = Make_unsigned<difference_type>;                         // trick
    using propagate_on_container_copy_assignment = false_type;               // trick
    using propagate_on_container_move_assignment = false_type;               // trick
    using propagate_on_container_swap = false_type;                           // trick

    template<typename T> using rebind_alloc = A<T,Args>;                      // trick
    template<typename T> using rebind_traits = Allocator_traits<rebind_alloc<T>>;

    static pointer allocate(A& a, size_type n) { return a.allocate(n); }      // trick
    static pointer allocate(A& a, size_type n, const_void_pointer hint)       // trick
        { return a.allocate(n,hint); }
    static void deallocate(A& a, pointer p, size_type n) { a.deallocate(p, n); }  // trick

    template<typename T, typename... Args>
        static void construct(A& a, T* p, Args&&... args)                     // trick
        { ::new (static_cast<void*>(p)) T(std::forward<Args>(args)...); }
    template<typename T>
        static void destroy(A& a, T* p) { p->T(); }                          // trick

    static size_type max_size(const A& a)                                     // trick
        { return numeric_limits<size_type>::max() }
    static A select_on_container_copy_construction(const A& rhs) { return a; } // trick
};
```

The "trick" is to use the equivalent member of the allocator **A** if it exists; otherwise, the default specified here. For **allocate(n,hint)**, **A::allocate(n)** will be called if **A** has no **allocate()** taking a hint. The **Args** are any type arguments needed by **A**.

I am no fan of trickery in the definition of the standard library, but liberal use of **enable_if()** (§28.4) allows this to be implemented in C++.

To make the declarations readable, I assume a few type aliases.

34.4.3 Pointer Traits

An allocator uses **pointer_traits** to determine properties of pointers and proxy types for pointers:

```
template<typename P>                                    // §iso.20.6.3
struct pointer_traits {
    using pointer = P;
    using element_type = T;                      // trick
    using difference_type = ptrdiff_t;           // trick
```

```
        template<typename U>
            using rebind = T*;                  // trick

        static pointer pointer_to(a);           // trick
    };

    template<typename T>
    struct pointer_traits<T*> {
        using pointer = T*;
        using element_type = T;
        using difference_type = ptrdiff_t;
        template<typename U>
            using rebind = U*;

        static pointer pointer_to(x) noexcept { return addressof(x); }
    };
```

The "trick" is the same as used by **allocator_traits** (§34.4.2): to use the equivalent member of the pointer **P** if it exists; otherwise, the default specified here. To use the **T**, the template argument **P** must be the first argument of a **Ptr<T,args>** template.

This specification does violence to the C++ language.

34.4.4 Scoped Allocators

A rather sneaky problem can occur when using containers and user-defined allocators: Should an element be in the same allocation area as its container? For example, if you use **Your_allocator** for **Your_string** to allocate its elements and I use **My_allocator** to allocate elements of **My_vector** then which allocator should be used for string elements in **My_vector<Your_allocator>>**?

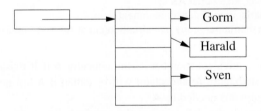

The solution is the ability to tell a container which allocator to pass to elements. The key to that is the class **scoped_allocator**, which provides the mechanism to keep track of an outer allocator (to be used for elements) and an inner allocator (to be passed to elements for their use):

```
    template<typename OuterA, typename... InnerA>          // §iso.20.12.1
    class scoped_allocator_adaptor : public OuterA {
    private:
        using Tr = allocator_traits<OuterA>;
    public:
        using outer_allocator_type = OuterA;
        using inner_allocator_type = see below;
```

```
using value_type = typename Tr::value_type;
using size_type = typename Tr::size_type;
using difference_type = typename Tr::difference_type;
using pointer = typename Tr::pointer;
using const_pointer = typename Tr::const_pointer;
using void_pointer = typename Tr::void_pointer;
using const_void_pointer = typename Tr::const_void_pointer;
using propagate_on_container_copy_assignment = /* see §iso.20.12.2 */;
using propagate_on_container_move_assignment = /* see §iso.20.12.2 */;
using propagate_on_container_swap = /* see §iso.20.12.2 */;

// ...
};
```

We have four alternatives for allocation of **vector**s of **string**s:

```
// vector and string use their own (the default) allocator:
using svec0 = vector<string>;
svec0 v0;

// vector (only) uses My_alloc and string uses its own allocator (the default):
using Svec1 = vector<string,My_alloc<string>>;
Svec1 v1 {My_alloc<string>{my_arena1}};

// vector and string use My_alloc (as above):
using Xstring = basic_string<char,char_traits<char>, My_alloc<char>>;
using Svec2 = vector<Xstring,scoped_allocator_adaptor<My_alloc<Xstring>>>;
Svec2 v2 {scoped_allocator_adaptor<My_alloc<Xstring>>{my_arena1}};

// vector uses its own alloctor (the default) and string uses My_alloc:
using Xstring2 = basic_string<char, char_traits<char>, My_alloc<char>>;
using Svec3 = vector<xstring2,scoped_allocator_adaptor<My_alloc<xstring>,My_alloc<char>>>;
Svec3 v3 {scoped_allocator_adaptor<My_alloc<xstring2>,My_alloc<char>>{my_arena1}};
```

Obviously, the first variant, **Svec0**, will be by far the most common, but for systems with serious memory-related performance constraints, the other versions (especially **Svec2**) can be important. A few more aliases would make that code a bit more readable, but it is good that this is not the kind of code you have to write every day.

The definition of **scoped_allocator_adaptor** is somewhat involved, but basically it is an allocator much like the default **allocator** (§34.4.1) that also keeps track of its "inner" allocator to be passed along for use by contained containers, such as **string**:

scoped_allocator_adaptor<OuterA,InnerA> (Abbreviated, §iso.20.12.1) (continues)	
rebind<T>::other	Alias for a version of this allocator allocating objects of type **T**
x=a.inner_allocator()	**x** is the inner allocator; noexcept
x=a.outer_allocator()	**x** is the outer allocator; noexcept
p=a.allocate(n)	Acquire space for **n** objects of **value_type**

scoped_allocator_adaptor<OuterA,InnerA> (continued) (Abbreviated, §iso.20.12.1)	
p=a.allocate(n,hint)	Acquire space for n objects of value_type hint is an implementation-dependent help for the allocator; often, hint is a pointer to an object to which we would like *p to be near
a.deallocate(p,n)	Free the space for n objects of value_type pointed to by p
n=a.max_size()	n is the largest possible number of elements allocated
t=a.construct(args)	Construct a value_type from args: t=new(p) value_type{args}
a.destroy(p)	Destroy *p: p->˜value_type()

34.5 The Garbage Collection Interface

Garbage collection (automatic recycling of unreferenced regions of memory) is sometimes presented as a panacea. It is not. In particular, resources that are not pure memory can be leaked by a garbage collector. Examples are file handles, thread handles, and locks. I see garbage collection as a convenient last resort after the usual techniques for preventing leaks have been exhausted:

[1]   Use resource handles with the proper semantics for an application whenever possible. The standard library provides string, vector, unordered_map, thread, lock_guard, and more. Move semantics allow such objects to be efficiently returned from a function.

[2]   Use unique_ptrs to hold on to objects that do not implicitly manage their own resources (such as pointers), need to be protected from premature deletion (because they don't have proper destructors), or need to be allocated in ways that require special attention (deleters).

[3]   Use shared_ptrs to hold objects that require shared ownership.

If consistently used, this sequence of techniques ensures the absence of leaks (i.e., no garbage collection is needed because no garbage is generated). However, in a very large number of real-world programs these techniques (all based on RAII; §13.3) are not consistently used and cannot be easily applied because they involve huge amounts of code structured in different ways. These "different ways" often involve complicated pointer uses, naked news and deletes, explicit type conversions that obscure resource ownership, and similar error-prone low-level techniques. In such cases, a garbage collector is an appropriate last resort. It can reclaim/recycle memory, even if it cannot handle non-memory resources. Don't even think of using general "finalizers" called at collection time to try to deal with non-memory resources. A garbage collector can sometimes extend the running time for leaking systems (even systems that leak non-memory resources) significantly. For example, a garbage collector might extend the time between resource exhaustion from hours to days for a system that is taken down every night for maintenance. Also, a garbage collector can be instrumented to find the sources of leaks.

It is worth remembering that a garbage-collected system can have its own variants of leaks. For example, if we put a pointer to an object into a hash table and forget its key, the object is de facto leaked. Similarly, a resource referred to by an infinite thread can live forever, even if the thread wasn't meant to be infinite (e.g., it could be waiting for input that never arrives). Sometimes, resources "living" for an excessive time can be as bad for a system as a permanent leak.

From this basic philosophy it follows that garbage collection is optional in C++. A garbage collector will not be invoked unless explicitly installed and activated. A garbage collector is not even a required part of a standard C++ implementation, but good free and commercial collectors are available. C++ provides a definition of what a garbage collector can do if one is used and an ABI (Application Binary Interface) to help control its actions.

The rules for pointers and lifetimes are expressed in terms of *safely-derived pointers* (§iso.3.7.4.3). A safely-derived pointer is (roughly) "a pointer to something allocated by **new** or to a subobject thereof." Here are some examples of pointers that are *not* safely derived, also known as *disguised pointers*. Make a pointer point "elsewhere" for a while:

```
int* p = new int[100];
p+=10;
// ... collector may run here ...
p -= 10;
*p = 10;   // can we be sure that the int is still there?
```

Hide the pointer in an int:

```
int* p = new int;
int x = reinterpret_cast<int>(p);        // not even portable
p = nullptr;
// ... collector may run here ...
p = reinterpret_cast<int*>(x);
*p = 10;   // can we be sure that the int is still there?
```

Write a pointer to a file and read it back later:

```
int* p = new int;
cout << p;
p = nullptr;
// ... collector may run here ...
cin >> p;
*p = 10;   // can we be sure that the int is still there?
```

Use the "xor trick" to compress doubly-linked lists:

```
using Link = pair<Value,long>;

long xor(Link* pre, Link* suc)
{
    static_assert(sizeof(Link*)<=sizeof(long),"a long is smaller than a pointer");
    return long{pre}^long{suc};
}

void insert_between(Value val, Link* pre, Link* suc)
{
    Link* p = new Link{val,xor(pre,suc)};
    pre->second = xor(xor(pre->second,suc),p);
    suc->second = xor(p,xor(suc->second,pre));
}
```

Using that trick, no undisguised pointers to links are stored.

Don't use such tricks in a program you want to be considered well behaved and comprehensible to ordinary mortals – even if you don't plan to use a garbage collector. There are many more and even nastier tricks, such as scattering the bits of a pointer around in different words.

There are legitimate reasons to disguise pointers (e.g., the xor trick in exceptionally memory-constrained applications), but not as many as some programmers think.

A disguised pointer can still be found by a careful garbage collector if its bitpattern is stored in memory with a wrong type (e.g., **long** or **char[4]**) and is still properly aligned. Such pointers are called *traceable*.

The standard library allows a programmer to specify where there are no pointers to be found (e.g., in an image) and what memory should not be reclaimed even if the collector can't find a pointer into it (§iso.20.6.4):

```
void declare_reachable(void* p);        // the object pointed to by p must not be collected
template<typename T>
        T* undeclare_reachable(T* p);   // undo a declare_reachable()

void declare_no_pointers(char* p, size_t n);     // p[0:n] holds no pointers
void undeclare_no_pointers(char* p, size_t n);   // undo a declare_no_pointers()
```

C++ garbage collectors have traditionally been *conservative collectors*; that is, they do not move objects around in memory and have to assume that every word in memory might contain a pointer. Conservative garbage collection is more efficient than it is reputed to be, especially when a program doesn't generate much garbage, but **declare_no_pointers()** can make it *very* efficient by safely eliminating large parts of memory from consideration. For example, we might use **declare_no_pointers()** to tell the collector where our photographic images are in an application, so as to allow the collector to ignore potentially gigabytes of non-pointer data.

A programmer can inquire which rules for pointer safety and reclamation are in force:

```
enum class pointer_safety {relaxed, preferred, strict };

pointer_safety get_pointer_safety();
```

The standard says (§iso.3.7.4.3): "a pointer value that is not a safely-derived pointer value is an invalid pointer value unless the referenced complete object is of dynamic storage duration and has previously been declared reachable ... the effect of using an invalid pointer value (including passing it to a deallocation function) is undefined."

The enumerators mean:

- **relaxed**: Safely-derived and not safely-derived pointers are treated equivalently (as in C and C++98). Collect every object that does not have a safely derived or traceable pointer to it.
- **preferred**: Like **relaxed**, but a garbage collector may be running as a leak detector and/or a detector of dereferences of "bad pointers."
- **strict**: Safely-derived and not safely-derived pointers may be treated differently; that is, a garbage collector may be running and will ignore pointers that's not safely derived.

There is no standard way of saying which alternative you prefer. Consider that a quality-of-implementation issue or a programming environment issue.

34.6 Uninitialized Memory

Most of the time, it is best to avoid uninitialized memory. Doing so simplifies programming and eliminates many kinds of errors. However, in relatively rare cases, such as when writing memory allocators, implementing containers, and dealing directly with hardware, direct use of uninitialized memory, also known as *raw memory*, is essential.

In addition to the standard **allocator**, the **<memory>** header provides the **fill*** family of functions for dealing with uninitialized memory (§32.5.6). They share the dangerous and occasionally essential property of using a type name **T** to refer to space sufficient to hold an object of type **T** rather than to a properly constructed object of type **T**. These functions are intended primarily for implementers of containers and algorithms. For example, **reserve()** and **resize()** are most easily implemented using these functions (§13.6).

34.6.1 Temporary Buffers

Algorithms often require temporary space to perform acceptably. Often, such temporary space is best allocated in one operation but not initialized until a particular location is actually needed. Consequently, the library provides a pair of functions for allocating and deallocating uninitialized space:

```
template<typename T>
    pair<T*,ptrdiff_t> get_temporary_buffer(ptrdiff_t); // allocate, don't initialize
template<typename T>
    void return_temporary_buffer(T*);                    // deallocate, don't destroy
```

A **get_temporary_buffer<X>(n)** operation tries to allocate space for **n** or more objects of type **X**. If it succeeds in allocating some memory, it returns a pointer to the first uninitialized space and the number of objects of type **X** that will fit into that space; otherwise, the **second** value of the pair is zero. The idea is that a system may keep space ready for fast allocation so that requesting space for **n** objects of a given size may yield space for more than **n**. It may also yield less, however, so one way of using **get_temporary_buffer()** is to optimistically ask for a lot and then use what happens to be available.

A buffer obtained by **get_temporary_buffer()** must be freed for other use by a call of **return_temporary_buffer()**. Just as **get_temporary_buffer()** allocates without constructing, **return_temporary_buffer()** frees without destroying. Because **get_temporary_buffer()** is low-level and likely to be optimized for managing temporary buffers, it should not be used as an alternative to **new** or **allocator::allocate()** for obtaining longer-term storage.

34.6.2 raw_storage_iterator

The standard algorithms that write into a sequence assume that the elements of that sequence have been previously initialized. That is, the algorithms use assignment rather than copy construction for writing. Consequently, we cannot use uninitialized memory as the immediate target of an algorithm. This can be unfortunate because assignment can be significantly more expensive than initialization, and to initialize immediately before overwriting is a waste. The solution is to use a **raw_storage_iterator** from **<memory>** that initializes instead of assigns:

```
template<typename Out, typename T>
class raw_storage_iterator : public iterator<output_iterator_tag,void,void,void,void> {
    Out p;
public:
    explicit raw_storage_iterator(Out pp) : p{pp} { }
    raw_storage_iterator& operator*() { return *this; }

    raw_storage_iterator& operator=(const T& val)
    {
        new(&*p) T{val};      // place val in *p (§11.2.4)
        return *this;
    }

    raw_storage_iterator& operator++() {++p; return *this; }      // pre-increment
    raw_storage_iterator operator++(int)                         // post-increment
    {
        auto t = *this;
        ++p;
        return t;
    }
};
```

A **raw_storage_iterator** should never be used to write to initialized data. This tends to limit its use to the depth of implementations of containers and algorithms. Consider generating a set of permutations (§32.5.5) of **strings** for use in testing:

```
void test1()
{
    auto pp = get_temporary_buffer<string>(1000);    // get uninitialized space
    if (pp.second<1000) {
        // ... handle allocation failure ...
    }
    auto p = raw_storage_iterator<string*,string>(pp.first); // the iterator
    generate_n(p,a.size(),
        [&]{ next_permutation(seed,seed+sizeof(seed)−1); return seed; });
    // ...
    return_temporary_buffer(p);
}
```

This is a somewhat contrived example because I see nothing wrong in allocating default initialized storage for the strings and then assigning the test strings. Also, it fails to use RAII (§5.2, §13.3).

Note that there are no **==** or **!=** operators for **raw_storage_iterator**, so don't try to use it to write to a **[b:e)** range. For example **iota(b,e,0)** (§40.6) will not work if **b** and **e** are **raw_storage_iterators**. Don't mess with uninitialized memory unless you absolutely have to.

34.7 Advice

[1]   Use **array** where you need a sequence with a **constexpr** size; §34.2.1.
[2]   Prefer **array** over built-in arrays; §34.2.1.
[3]   Use **bitset** if you need N bits and N is not necessarily the number of bits in a built-in integer type; §34.2.2.
[4]   Avoid **vector<bool>**; §34.2.3.
[5]   When using **pair**, consider **make_pair()** for type deduction; §34.2.4.1.
[6]   When using **tuple**, consider **make_tuple()** for type deduction; §34.2.4.2.
[7]   Use **unique_ptr** to represent exclusive ownership; §34.3.1.
[8]   Use **shared_ptr** to represent shared ownership; §34.3.2.
[9]   Minimize the use of **weak_ptr**s; §34.3.3.
[10]   Use allocators (only) when the usual **new/delete** semantics is insufficient for logical or performance reasons; §34.4.
[11]   Prefer resource handles with specific semantics to smart pointers; §34.5.
[12]   Prefer **unique_ptr** to **shared_ptr**; §34.5.
[13]   Prefer smart pointers to garbage collection; §34.5.
[14]   Have a coherent and complete strategy for management of general resources; §34.5.
[15]   Garbage collection can be really useful for dealing with leaks in programs with messy pointer use; §34.5.
[16]   Garbage collection is optional; §34.5.
[17]   Don't disguise pointers (even if you don't use garbage collection); §34.5.
[18]   If you use garbage collection, use **declare_no_pointers()** to let the garbage collector ignore data that cannot contain pointers; §34.5.
[19]   Don't mess with uninitialized memory unless you absolutely have to; §34.6.

35

Utilities

The time you enjoy wasting is not wasted time.
– Bertrand Russell

35.1 Introduction

The standard library provides many "utility components" that are so widely useful that they are not easily classified as part of some major standard-library component.

35.2 Time

In **<chrono>**, the standard library provides facilities for dealing with time durations and time points. All **chrono** facilities are in the **std::chrono** (sub)namespace, so we have to either explicitly qualify with **chrono::** or add a **using**-directive:

```
using namespace std::chrono;
```

We often want to time things or to do things that depend on timing. For example, the standard-library mutexes and locks provide the option for a **thread** to wait for a period of time (a **duration**) or to wait until a given point in time (a **time_point**).

If you want to know the current **time_point**, you can call **now()** for one of three clocks: **system_clock, steady_clock, high_resolution_clock**. For example:

```
steady_clock::time_point t = steady_clock::now();
// ... do something ...
steady_clock::duration d = steady_clock::now()–t;      // something took d time units
```

A clock returns a **time_point**, and a **duration** is the difference between two **time_points** from the same clock. As usual, if you are not interested in details, **auto** is your friend:

```
auto t = steady_clock::now();
// ... do something ...
auto d = steady_clock::now()–t;     // something took d time units
cout << "something took " << duration_cast<milliseconds>(d).count() << "ms";  // print as milliseconds
```

The time facilities here are intended to efficiently support uses deep in the system; they do not provide convenience facilities to help you maintain your social calendar. In fact, the time facilities originated with the stringent needs of high-energy physics.

It turns out that "time" is far more complicated to deal with than we usually think. For example, we have leap seconds, clocks that are not accurate and must be adjusted (possibly causing time as reported by a clock to go backward), clocks of differing precision, etc. Furthermore, language facilities for dealing with short time spans (e.g., nanoseconds) must not themselves take significant time. Consequently, the **chrono** facilities are not simple, but many uses of those facilities can be very simple.

The C-style time utilities can be found in §43.6.

35.2.1 duration

In **<chrono>**, the standard library provides type **duration** to represent the time between two points in time (**time_points** §35.2.2):

```
template<typename Rep, typename Period = ratio<1>>
class duration {
public:
     using rep = Rep;
     using period = Period;
     // ...
};
```

duration<Rep,Period> (§iso.20.11.5)	
duration d {};	Default constructor: d becomes {Rep{},Period{}}; constexpr
duration d {r};	Constructor from r;
	r must be convertible to **Rep** without narrowing; constexpr; explicit
duration d {d2};	Copy constructor: d gets the same value as **d2**;
	d2 must be convertible to **Rep** without narrowing; constexpr
d=d2	d gets the same value as **d2**; d2 must be representable as a **Rep**
r=d.count()	r is the number of clock ticks in d; constexpr

We can define a **duration** with a specific **period** value. For example:

```
duration<long long,milli> d1 {7};    // 7 milliseconds
duration<double,pico> d2 {3.33};     // 3.33 picoseconds
duration<int,ratio<1,1>> d3 {};      // 0 seconds
```

A **duration**'s **period** holds the number of *clock ticks* of the **period**.

```
cout << d1.count() << '\n';     // 7
cout << d2.count() << '\n';     // 3.33
cout << d3.count() << '\n';     // 0
```

Naturally, the value of **count()** depends on the **period**:

```
d2=d1;
cout << d1.count() << '\n';     // 7
cout << d2.count() << '\n';     // 7e+009
if (d1!=d2) cerr<<"insane!";
```

Here, **d1** and **d2** are equal but report very different **count()** values.

Care is taken to avoid truncation or loss of precision during initialization (even if the {} notation is not used). For example:

```
duration<int, milli> d {3};       // OK
duration<int, milli> d {3.5};     // error: 3.5 to int is narrowing

duration<int, milli> ms {3};
duration<int, micro> us {ms};     // OK
duration<int, milli> ms2 {us};    // error: we could lose many microseconds
```

The standard library provides meaningful arithmetic operations on **duration**s:

duration<Rep,Period> (continued) (§iso.20.11.5)	
r is a **Rep**; arithmetic is done in the **common_type** of the representations	
++d	++d.r
d++	duration{d.r++}
−−d	−−d.r
d−−	duration{d.r−−}
+d	d
−d	duration{−d.r}
d+=d2	d.r+=d2.r
d−=d2	d.r−=d2.r
d%=d2	d.r%=d2.r.count()
d%=r	d.r+=r
d*=r	d.r+=r
d/=r	d.r+=r

The **period** is a unit system, so there is no = or += taking a plain value. Allowing that would be like allowing the addition of **5** of an unknown SI unit to a length in meters. Consider:

```
duration<long long,milli> d1 {7};      // 7 milliseconds
d1 += 5;           // error

duration<int,ratio<1,1>> d2 {7};           // 7 seconds
d2 = 5;            // error
d2 += 5;           // error
```

What would **5** mean here? **5** seconds? **5** milliseconds? Something else? If you know what you mean, be explicit about it. For example:

```
d1 += duration<long long,milli>{5}; // OK: milliseconds
d3 += decltype(d2){5};              // OK: seconds
```

Arithmetic involving **duration**s with different representations is allowed as long as the combination makes sense (§35.2.4):

duration<Rep,Period> (continued) (§iso.20.11.5)	
r is a **Rep**; arithmetic is done in the **common_type** of the representations	
d3=d+d2	constexpr
d3=d–d2	constexpr
d3=d%d2	constexpr
d2=d%r	d2=d%r.count(); constexpr
d2=d∗x	x is a **duration** or a **Rep**; constexpr
d2=r∗d	constexpr
d2=d/x	x is a **duration** or a **Rep**; constexpr

Comparisons between and explicit conversion between **duration**s with compatible representations are supported:

duration<Rep,Period> (continued) (§iso.20.11.5)	
d=zero()	The **0** for **Rep**: d=duration{duration_values<rep>::zero()}; constexpr
d=min()	The smallest **Rep** value (less than or equal to **zero()**): d=duration{duration_values<rep>::min()}; constexpr
d=max()	The largest **Rep** value (larger than or equal to **zero()**): d=duration{duration_values<rep>::max()}; constexpr
d==d2 d!=d2	Comparison is done in the **common_type** of **d** and **d2**; constexpr !(d==d2)
d<d2 d<=d2	Comparison is done in the **common_type** of **d** and **d2**; constexpr !(d>d2)
d>d2 d>=d2	Comparison is done in the **common_type** of **d** and **d2**; constexpr !(d<d2)
d2=duration_cast<D>(d)	Convert **duration d** to **duration** type **D**; no implicit conversions are used for the representation or period; constexpr

The standard library provides some convenience aliases using the SI units from **<ratio>** (§35.3):

```
using nanoseconds = duration<si64,nano>;
using microseconds = duration<si55,micro>;
using milliseconds = duration<si45,milli>;
using seconds = duration<si35>;
using minutes = duration<si29,ratio<60>>;
using hours = duration<si23,ratio<3600>>;
```

Here, **siN** means "an implementation-defined signed integer type of at least **N** bits."

The **duration_cast** is used to get a **duration** with a known unit of measurement. For example:

```
auto t1 = system_clock::now();
f(x); // do something
auto t2 = system_clock::now();

auto dms = duration_cast<milliseconds>(t2-t1);
cout << "f(x) took " << dms.count() << " milliseconds\n";

auto ds = duration_cast<seconds>(t2-t1);
cout << "f(x) took " << ds.count() << " seconds\n";
```

The reason we need a cast in this example is that we are throwing away information: on the system I used, the **system_clock** counts in **nanoseconds**.

Alternatively, we can simply (try to) construct a suitable **duration**:

```
auto t1 = system_clock::now();
f(x); // do something
auto t2 = system_clock::now();

cout << "f(x) took " << milliseconds(t2-t1).count() << " milliseconds\n";       // error: truncation
cout << "f(x) took " << microseconds(t2-t1).count() << " microseconds\n";
```

The precision of a clock is implementation-dependent.

35.2.2 time_point

In **<chrono>**, the standard library provides type **time_point** to represent a point in time of a given epoch as measured by a given **clock**:

```
template<typename Clock, typename Duration = typename Clock::duration>
class time_point {
public:
    using clock = Clock;
    using duration = Duration;
    using rep = typename duration::rep;
    using period = typename duration::period;
    // ...
};
```

An *epoch* is a range of time determined by a **clock**, measured in terms of a **duration**, starting at the **duration::zero()**:

time_point<Clock,Duration> (§iso.20.11.6)	
time_point tp {};	Default constructor: start of epoch: **duration::zero()**
time_point tp {d};	Constructor: time point d of epoch: **time_point{}+d**; explicit
time_point tp {tp2};	Constructor: **tp** refers to the same point in time as **tp2**;
	tp2's duration type must be implicitly convertible to **tp**'s
d=tp.time_since_epoch()	d is **tp**'s stored duration
tp=tp2	**tp** refers to the same point in time as **tp2**;
	tp2's duration type must be implicitly convertible to **tp**'s

For example:

```
void test()
{
    time_point<steady_clock,milliseconds> tp1(milliseconds(100));
    time_point<steady_clock,microseconds> tp2(microseconds(100*1000));

    tp1=tp2;        // error: would truncate
    tp2=tp1;        // OK

    if (tp1!=tp2) cerr << "Insane!";
}
```

As for **durations**, meaningful arithmetic and comparisons are supported for **time_points**:

time_point<Clock,Duration> (continued) (§iso.20.11.6)	
tp+=d	Move tp forward: **tp.d+=d**
tp-=d	Move tp backward: **tp.d-=d**
tp2=tp+d	tp2=time_point<Clock>{tp.time_since_epoc()+d}
tp2=d+tp	tp2=time_point<Clock>{d+tp.time_since_epoc()}
tp2=tp-d	tp2=time_point<Clock>{tp.time_since_epoc()-d}
d=tp-tp2	d=duration{tp.time_since_epoc()-tp2.time_since_epoc()}
tp2=tp.min()	tp2=time_point(duration::min()); static; constexpr
tp2=tp.max()	tp2=time_point(duration::max()); static; constexpr
tp==tp2	tp.time_since_epoch()==tp2.time_since_epoch()
tp!=tp2	!(tp==tp2)
tp<tp2	tp.time_since_epoch()<tp2.time_since_epoch()
tp<=tp2	!(tp2<tp)
tp>tp2	tp2<tp
tp>=tp2	!(tp<tp2)
tp2=time_point_cast<D>(tp)	Convert the **time_point** tp to **time_point<C,D>**:
	time_point<C,D>(duration_cast<D>(t.time_since_epoch()))

For example:

```
void test2()
{
    auto tp = steady_clock::now();
    auto d1 = time_point_cast<hours>(tp).time_since_epoch().count()/24;   // days since start of epoch

    using days = duration<long,ratio<24*60*60,1>>;                        // a day's duration
    auto d2 = time_point_cast<days>(tp).time_since_epoch().count();       // days since start of epoch

    if (d1!=d2) cout << "Impossible!\n";
}
```

The **time_point** operations that do not access a clock can be **constexpr**, but are not currently guaranteed to be so.

35.2.3 Clocks

The **time_point** and **duration** values are ultimately obtained from hardware clocks. In **<chrono>**, the standard library provides basic interfaces for clocks. Class **system_clock** represents "wall clock time" as obtained from a system's real-time clock:

```
class system_clock {
public:
    using rep = /* implementation-defined signed type */;
    using period = /* implementation-defined ratio<> */;
    using duration = chrono::duration<rep,period>;
    using time_point = chrono::time_point<system_clock>;
    // ...
};
```

All data and function members are **static**. We don't explicitly deal with clock objects. Instead, we use clock types:

Clock Members (§iso.20.11.7)	
is_steady	Is this clock type steady? That is, is **c.now()<=c.now()** for all consecutive calls of **now()** and is the time between clock ticks constant? static
tp=now()	tp is **system_clock**'s **time_point** for the time of call; noexcept
t=to_time_t(tp)	t is the **time_t** (§43.6) for the **time_point** tp; noexcept
tp=from_time_t(t)	tp is the **time_point** for the **time_t** t; noexcept

For example:

```
void test3()
{
    auto t1 = system_clock::now();
    f(x); // do something
    auto t2 = system_clock::now();
    cout << "f(x) took " << duration_cast<milliseconds>(t2–t1).count() << " ms";
}
```

A system provides three named clocks:

Clock Types (§iso.20.11.7)	
system_clock	The system's real-time clock; the system's clock may be reset (jump forward or backward) to match external clocks
steady_clock	A clock where time moves steadily forward; that is, time does not go backward and the time between clock ticks is constant
high_resolution_clock	A clock with the shortest time increment on a system

These three clocks need not be different; a standard-library clock name may be an alias.

We can determine the basic properties of the clocks like this:

```
cout << "min " << system_clock::duration::min().count()
     << ", max " << system_clock::duration::max().count()
     << ", " << (treat_as_floating_point<system_clock::duration>::value ? "FP" : "integral") << '\n';

cout << (system_clock::is_steady?"steady\n": "not steady\n");
```

When I ran it on one of my systems, this produced:

```
min –9223372036854775808, max 9223372036854775807, integral
not steady
```

Different systems and different clocks can give different results.

35.2.4 Time Traits

Implementations of the **chrono** facilities depend on a few standard facilities, collectively known as *time traits*.

The conversion rules for **duration** and **time_point** depend on whether their representation is floating-point (so that rounding is acceptable) or integral:

```
template<typename Rep>
struct treat_as_floating_point : is_floating<Rep> { };
```

A few standard values are provided:

duration_values<Rep> (§iso.20.11.4.2)	
r=zero()	r=Rep(0); static; constexpr
r=min()	r=numeric_limits<Rep>::lowest(); static; constexpr
r=max()	r=numeric_limits<Rep>::max(); static; constexpr

The common type of two **durations** is determined by computing their greatest common denominator (GCD):

```
template<typename Rep1, typename P1, typename Rep2, typename P2>
struct common_type<duration<Rep1,P1>, duration<Rep2, P2>> {
    using type = duration<typename common_type<Rep1,Rep2>::type, GCD<P1,P2>> ;
};
```

This makes **type** an alias for the **duration** with the largest possible tick period so that both **duration** arguments will convert to it without requiring a division operation. This implies that **common_type<R1,P1,R2,P2>::type** can hold any value from **duration<R1,R2>** and **duration<R2,P2>** without truncation error. However, floating-point **duration**s may have round-off errors.

```
template<typename Clock, typename Duration1, typename Duration2>
struct common_type<time_point<Clock, Duration1>, time_point<Clock, Duration2>> {
    using type = time_point<Clock, typename common_type<Duration1, Duration2>::type>;
};
```

In words, to have a **common_type**, two **time_points** must have a common clock type. Their **common_type** is a **time_point** with the **common_type** of their **duration**s.

35.3 Compile-Time Rational Arithmetic

In **<ratio>**, we find class **ratio**, which provides compile-time rational arithmetic. The standard library uses **ratio** to provide a compile-time representation of time duration and time points (§35.2):

```
template<intmax_t N, intmax_t D = 1>
struct ratio {
    static constexpr intmax_t num;
    static constexpr intmax_t den;

    using type = ratio<num,den>;
};
```

The basic idea is to encode the numerator and denominator of a rational number as (value) template arguments. The denominator must always be nonzero.

ratio **Arithmetic Operations (§iso.20.10.4)**	
z=ratio_add<x,y>	z.num=x::num∗y::den+y::num∗x::den; z.den=x::den∗y::den
z=ratio_subtract<x,y>	z.num=x::num∗y::den−y::num∗x::den; z.den=x::den∗y::den
z=ratio_multiply<x,y>	z.num=x::num∗y::num; z.den=x::den∗y::den
z=ratio_divide<x,y>	z.num=x::num∗y::den; z.den=x::den∗y::num
ratio_equal<x,y>	x::num==y::num && x::den==y::den
ratio_not_equal<x,y>	!ratio_equal<x,y>::value
ratio_less<x,y>	x::num∗y::den < y::num∗x::den
ratio_less_equal<x,y>	!ratio_less_equal<y,x>::value
ratio_not_equal<x,y>	!ratio_less<y,x>::value
ratio_greater<x,y>	ratio_less<y,x>::value
ratio_greater_equal<x,y>	!ratio_less<x,y>::value

For example:

```
static_assert(ratio_add<ratio<1,3>, ratio<1,6>>::num == 1, "problem: 1/3+1/6 != 1/2");
static_assert(ratio_add<ratio<1,3>, ratio<1,6>>::den == 2, "problem: 1/3+1/6 != 1/2");
static_assert(ratio_multiply<ratio<1,3>, ratio<3,2>>::num == 1, "problem: 1/3∗3/2 != 1/2");
static_assert(ratio_multiply<ratio<1,3>, ratio<3,2>>::den == 2, "problem: 1/3∗3/2 != 1/2");
```

Obviously, this is not a convenient way of expressing numbers and arithmetic. In **<chrono>**, we find the conventional notation (e.g., **+** and **∗**) for rational arithmetic for time (§35.2). Similarly, to help express unit values, the standard library provides common SI magnitude names:

```
using yocto    = ratio<1,1000000000000000000000000>;    // conditionally supported
using zepto    = ratio<1,1000000000000000000000>;       // conditionally supported
using atto     = ratio<1,1000000000000000000>;
using femto    = ratio<1,1000000000000000>;
using pico     = ratio<1,1000000000000>;
using nano     = ratio<1,1000000000>;
using micro    = ratio<1,1000000>;
using milli    = ratio<1,1000>;
using centi    = ratio<1,100>;
using deci     = ratio<1,10>;
using deca     = ratio<10,1>;
using hecto    = ratio<100,1>;
using kilo     = ratio<1000,1>;
using mega     = ratio<1000000,1>;
using giga     = ratio<1000000000,1>;
using tera     = ratio<1000000000000,1>;
using peta     = ratio<1000000000000000,1>;
using exa      = ratio<1000000000000000000,1>;
using zetta    = ratio<1000000000000000000000,1>;       // conditionally supported
using yotta    = ratio<1000000000000000000000000,1>;    // conditionally supported
```

For an example of use, see §35.2.1.

35.4 Type Functions

In **<type_traits>**, the standard library provides type functions (§28.2) to determine properties of types (type traits; §35.4.1) and to generate new types from existing ones (type generators; §35.4.2). These type functions are primarily used at compile time to support simple, and not so simple, metaprogramming.

35.4.1 Type Traits

In **<type_traits>**, the standard library provides a large set of type functions that allow a programmer to determine properties of a type or a pair of types. Their names are mostly self-explanatory. The *primary type predicates* test fundamental properties of a type:

Primary Type Predicates (§iso.20.9.4.1)	
is_void<X>	Is **X** void?
is_integral<X>	Is **X** an integral type?
is_floating_point<X>	Is **X** a floating-point type?
is_array<X>	Is **X** a built-in array?
is_pointer<X>	Is **X** a pointer (not including pointers to members)?

Primary Type Predicates (continued) (§iso.20.9.4.1)	
is_lvalue_reference<X>	Is X an lvalue reference?
is_rvalue_reference<X>	Is X an rvalue reference?
is_member_object_pointer<X>	Is X a pointer to a non-**static** data member?
is_member_function_pointer<X>	Is X a pointer to a non-**static** member function?
is_enum<X>	Is X an **enum** (either plain of **class enum**)?
is_union<X>	Is X a union?
is_class<X>	Is X a **class** (including **structs**, but not **enums**)?
is_function<X>	Is X a function?

A type trait returns a value that is used as a Boolean. To access that value, use the suffix ::**value**. For example:

```
template<typename T>
void f(T& a)
{
    static_assert(std::is_floating_point<T>::value,"FP type expected");
    // ...
}
```

If you tire of the ::**value** notation, define a **constexpr** function (§28.2.2):

```
template<typename T>
constexpr bool Is_floating_point<T>()
{
    return std::is_floating_point<T>::value;
}

template<typename T>
void f(T& a)
{
    static_assert(Is_floating_point<T>(),"FP type expected");
    // ...
}
```

Ideally, use a library that provides such functions for all standard library type traits.

Some type functions inquire about a combination of fundamental properties:

Composite Type Predicates (§iso.20.9.4.2)	
is_reference<X>	Is x a reference (lvalue or rvalue reference)?
is_arithmetic<X>	Is x an arithmetic type (integral or floating-point; §6.2.1)?
is_fundamental<X>	Is x a fundamental type (§6.2.1)?
is_object<X>	Is x an object type (not a function)?
is_scalar<X>	Is x a scalar type (not a class or a function)?
is_compound<X>	Is x a compound type (!is_fundamental<X>)?
is_member_pointer<X>	Is x a pointer to a non-**static** data or function member?

These *composite type predicates* simply offer notational convenience. For example, is_reference<X> is true if X is either an lvalue reference or an rvalue reference.

Like the primary type predicates, *type property predicates* provide tests for fundamental aspects of a type:

Type property predicates (§iso.20.9.4.3)	
is_const<X>	Is **X** a **const**?
is_volatile<X>	Is **X** a **volatile** (§41.4)?
is_trivial<X>	Is **X** a trivial type (§8.2.6)?
is_trivially_copyable<X>	Can **X** be copied, moved, and destroyed as a simple collection of bits (§8.2.6)?
is_standard_layout<X>	Is **X** a standard-layout type (§8.2.6)?
is_pod<X>	Is **X** a POD (§8.2.6)?
is_literal_type<X>	Does **X** have a **constexpr** constructor (§10.4.3)?
is_empty<X>	Does **X** have a member that requires space in an object?
is_polymorphic<X>	Does **X** have a virtual function?
is_abstract<X>	Does **X** have a pure virtual function?
is_signed<X>	Is **X** an arithmetic type and signed?
is_unsigned<X>	Is **X** an arithmetic type and unsigned?
is_constructible<X,args>	Can an **X** be constructed from **args**?
is_default_constructible<X>	Can an **X** be constructed from {}?
is_copy_constructible<X>	Can an **X** be constructed from an **X&**?
is_move_constructible<X>	Can an **X** be constructed from an **X&&**?
is_assignable<X,Y>	Can a **Y** be assigned to an **X**?
is_copy_assignable<X>	Can a **X&** be assigned to an **X**?
is_move_assignable<X>	Can a **X&&** be assigned to an **X**?
is_destructible<X>	Can an **X** be destroyed (i.e., ˜**X()** has not been deleted)?

For example:

```
template<typename T>
class Cont {
    T∗ elem;    // store elements in an array pointed to by elem
    int sz;     // sz elements
    // ...
    Cont(const Cont& a)      // copy constructor
        :sz(a.sz), elem(new T[a.elem])
    {
        static_assert(Is_copy_constructable<T>(),"Cont::Cont(): no copy");
        if (Is_trivially_copyable<T>())
            memcpy(elem,a.elem,sz∗sizeof(T));        // memcopy optimization
        else
            uninitialized_copy(a.begin(),a.end(),elem);    // use copy constructors
    }
    // ...
}
```

This optimization may be unnecessary, though, because **uninitialized_copy()** is likely to already have been optimized in this way.

For a class to be empty, it can have no virtual functions, no virtual bases, and no base classes for which !is_empty<Base>::value.

The type property predicates don't do access checking depending on where they are used. Instead, they consistently give the result you would expect for a use outside members and friends. For example:

```
class X {
public:
    void inside();
private:
    X& operator=(const X&);
    ~X();
};

void X::inside()
{
    cout << "inside =: " << is_copy_assignable<X>::value << '\n';
    cout << "inside ~: " << is_destructible<X>::value << '\n';
}

void outside()
{
    cout << "outside =: " << is_copy_assignable<X>::value << '\n';
    cout << "outside ~: " << is_destructible<X>::value << '\n';
}
```

Both inside() and outside() will write 00 to report that an X is neither destructible nor copy assignable. Also, if you want to eliminate an operation, use =delete (§17.6.4) rather than relying as private.

Type Property Predicates (continued) (§iso.20.9.4.3)	
is_trivially_constructible<X,args>	Can X be constructed from args using only trivial operations?
is_trivially_default_constructible<X>	
is_trivially_copy_constructible<X>	§8.2.6
is_trivially_move_constructible<X>	
is_trivially_assignable<X,Y>	
is_trivially_copy_assignable<X>	
is_trivially_move_assignable<X>	
is_trivially_destructible<X>	

For example, consider how we might optimize the destructor for a container type:

```
template<class T>
Cont::~Cont()          // destructor for a container Cont
{
    if (!Is_trivially_destructible<T>())
        for (T* p = elem; p!=p+sz; ++p)
            p->~T();
}
```

Type Property Predicates (continued) (§iso.20.9.4.3)	
is_nothrow_constructible<X,args>	Can X be constructed from args using only noexcept operations?
is_nothrow_default_constructible<X>	
is_nothrow_copy_constructible<X>	
is_nothrow_move_constructible<X>	
is_nothrow_assignable<X,Y>	
is_nothrow_copy_assignable<X>	
is_nothrow_move_assignable<X>	
is_nothrow_destructible<X>	
has_virtual_destructor<X>	Does X have a virtual destructor?

Like sizeof(T), a property query returns a numeric value related to a type argument:

Type Property Queries (§iso.20.9.5)	
n=alignment_of<X>	n=alignof(X)
n=rank<X>	If X is an array, n is the number of dimensions; otherwise n==0
n=extent<X,N>	If X is an array, n is the number of elements in the Nth dimension; otherwise n==0
n=extent<X>	n=extent<X,0>

For example:

```
template<typename T>
void f(T a)
{
    static_assert(Is_array<T>(), "f(): not an array");
    constexpr int dn {Extent<a,2>()};    // the number of elements in the 2nd dimension (zero based)
    // ..
}
```

Here, I again used constexpr versions of the type functions returning numeric values (§28.2.2).
    The *type relations* are predicated on two types:

Type Relations (§iso.20.9.6)	
is_same<X,Y>	Is X the same type as Y?
is_base_of<X,Y>	Is X a base of Y?
is_convertible<X,Y>	Can an X be implicitly converted to a Y?

For example:

```
template<typename T>
void draw(T t)
{
    static_assert(Is_same<Shape*,T>() || Is_base_of<Shape,Remove_pointer<T>>(), "");
    t->draw();
}
```

35.4.2 Type Generators

In <type_traits>, the standard library provides type functions for producing a type given other types as arguments.

const **and** volatile **Modification (§iso.20.9.7.1)**	
remove_const<X>	Like X, but with any top-level const removed
remove_volatile<X>	Like X, but with any top-level volatile removed
remove_cv<X>	Like X, but with any top-level const or volatile removed
add_const<X>	If X is a reference, function, or const, then X; otherwise const X
add_volatile<X>	If X is a reference, function, or volatile, then X; otherwise volatile X
struct add_cv<X>	Add const and volatile: add_const<typename add_volatile<T>::type>::type

A type transformer returns a type. To access that type, use the suffix ::type. For example:

```
template<typename K, typename V>
class My_map {
{
    pair<typename add_const<K>::type,V> default_node;
    // ...
};
```

If you tire of the ::type define a type alias (§28.2.1):

```
template<typename T>
using Add_const = typename add_const<T>::type;

template<typename K, typename V>
class My_map {
{
    pair<Add_const<K>,V> default_node;
    // ...
};
```

Ideally, use a support library that provides such aliases systematically for the standard-library type transformers.

Reference Modification (§iso.20.9.7.2, §iso.20.9.7.6)	
remove_reference<X>	If X is a reference type, the referred-to type; otherwise, X
add_lvalue_reference<X>	If X is an rvalue reference Y&&, Y&; otherwise, X&
add_rvalue_reference<X>	If X is a reference, X; otherwise, X&& (§7.7.3)
decay<X>	The type passed by value for a function argument of type X

The decay functions handles array decay as well as reference dereferencing.

The type functions for adding and removing references are important for when writing templates that should work with an argument that may be reference or not. For example:

```
template<typename T>
void f(T v)
{
    Remove_reference<T> x = v;   // copy of v
    T y = v;                     // maybe copy of v; maybe a reference to x
    ++x;                         // increment local variable
    ++y;
    // ...
}
```

Here, x really is a copy of v, but if T is a reference type, y is a reference to v:

```
void user()
{
    int val = 7;
    f(val);    // call f<int&>(): the ++y in f() will increment val
    f(7);      // call f<int>(): the ++y in f will increment a local copy
}
```

In both calls, ++x will increment a local copy.

Sign Modification (§iso.20.9.7.3)	
make_signed<X>	Remove any (explicit or implied) **unsigned** modifier and add **signed**; X must be an integral type (except **bool** or an enumeration)
make_unsigned<X>	Remove any (explicit or implied) **signed** modifier and add **unsigned**; X must be an integral type (except **bool** or an enumeration)

For built-in arrays, we sometimes want to get the element type or to remove a dimension:

Array Modification (§iso.20.9.7.4)	
remove_extent<X>	If X is an array type, the element type; otherwise X
remove_all_extents<X>	If X is an array type, the base type (after removing all array modifiers); otherwise X

For example:

```
int a[10][20];
Remove_extent<decltype(a)> a10;       // an array[10]
Remove_all_extents<decltype(a)> i;    // an int
```

We can make a pointer type pointing to an arbitrary type, or find the pointed-to type:

Pointer Modification (§iso.20.9.7.5)	
remove_pointer<X>	If X is a pointer type, the pointed-to type; otherwise X
add_pointer<X>	remove_reference<X>::type*

For example:

```
template<typename T>
void f(T x)
{
    Add_pointer<T> p = new Remove_reference<T>{};
    T* p = new T{};      // would not work if T is a reference
    // ...
}
```

When dealing with memory at the lowest levels of a system, we must sometimes consider alignment (§6.2.9):

Alignments (§iso.20.9.7.6)	
aligned_storage<n,a>	A POD type with size of at least **n** and whose alignment is a divisor of **a**
aligned_storage<n>	aligned_storage<n,def> where **def** is the largest alignment required for any object type, **T**, with sizeof(T)<=n
aligned_union<n,X...>	A POD type with size of at least **n** that can hold a **union** with members of type **X**

The standard mentions this as a possible implementation of **aligned_storage**:

```
template<std::size_t N, std::size_t A>
struct aligned_storage {
    using type = struct { alignas(A) unsigned char data[N]; };      // N chars aligned to A (§6.2.9)
};
```

The final type functions for type selection, computing common types, etc. are arguably the most useful:

Other Transformations (§iso.20.9.7.6)	
enable_if<b,X>	**X** if b==true; otherwise there is no member ::**type**, leading to substitution failure (§23.5.3.2) for most uses
enable_if<b>	enable_if<b,void>
conditional<b,T,F>	**T** if b==true; otherwise **F**
common_type<X>	The common type of all types of a parameter pack **X**; two types are common if they can be used as true and false types of a ?:-expression
underlying_type<X>	**X**'s underlying type (§8.4); **X** must be an enumeration
result_of<FX>	The type of the result of **F(X)**; **FX** must be a type **F(X)** where **F** is invoked with an argument list **X**

For examples of **enable_if** and **conditional**, see §28.3.1.1 and §28.4.

It is often useful to find a type that can be used for operations on more than one type, such as the result of an addition of two values of related but different types. The type function **common_type** finds such common types. A type is the common type of itself (obviously):

```
template<typename ...T>
struct common_type;

template<typename T>
struct common_type<T> {
    using type = T;
};
```

The common type of two types is what the rules for **?:** (§11.1.3) give us:

```
template<typename T, typename U>
struct common_type<T, U> {
    using type = decltype(true ? declval<T>() : declval<U>());
};
```

The declval<T>() type function returns the type of an unevaluated variable of type **T**.

The common type for N types is found by applying the rules for N==1 and N==2 recursively:

```
template<typename T, typename U, typename... V>
struct common_type<T, U, V...> {
    using type = typename common_type<typename common_type<T, U>::type, V...>::type;
};
```

For example:

```
template<typename T, typename U>
using Common_type = typename common_type<T,U>::type;
```

```
Common_type<int,double> x1;                 // x1 is a double
Common_type<int,string> x2;                 // error: no common type
Common_type<int,short,long,long long> x3;   // x3 is a long long
Common_type<Shape*,Circle*> x4;             // x4 is a Shape*
Common_type<void*,double*,Shape*> x5;       // x5 is a void*
```

Result_of is used to extract the type of the result of a callable type:

```
int ff(int) { return 2; }                   // function
```

```
typedef  bool (*PF)(int);                   // pointer to function
```

```
struct Fct {                                // function object
    double operator()(string);
    string operator()(int,int);
};
```

```
auto fx = [](char ch) { return tolower(ch); };   // lambda
```

```
Result_of<decltype(&ff)()> r1 = 7;          // r1 is a int
Result_of<PF(int)> r2 = true;               // r2 is a bool
Result_of<Fct(string)> r3 = 9.9;            // r3 is a double
Result_of<Fct(int,int)> r4 = "Hero";        // r4 is a string
Result_of<decltype(fx)(char)> r5 = 'a';     // r5 is a char
```

Note that **Result_of** can distinguish between the two versions of **Fct::operator()()**.

Curiously enough, the same does not apply to nonmember functions. For example:

```
int f();                                    // function
string f(int);
Result_of<decltype(&f)()> r1 = 7;           // error: no overload resolution for pointer to function
```

Unfortunately, we don't do overload resolution for pointers to functions, but why did I use **Result_of** in such a roundabout way, instead of:

```
Result_of<ff> r1 = 7;                       // error: no argument specification,
                                            // and ff is a function rather than a type
Result_of<ff()> r1 = 7;                     // error: the argument to Result_of must be a type
Result_of<decltype(f)()> r2 = 7;            // error: decltype(f) is a function type
                                            // rather than a pointer to function type
Result_of<decltype(f)*()> r3 = 7;           // OK: r3 is an int
```

Naturally, **Result_of** is usually found in templates where we can't easily look up the answer in the program text. For example:

```
template<typename F, typename A>
auto temp(F f, A a) -> Result_of<F(A)>
{
    // ...
}

void f4()
{
    temp(ff,1);
    temp(fx,'a');
    temp(Fct(),"Ulysses");
}
```

Note that the function **ff** is converted to a pointer function in the call, so the reliance on pointers to functions in **Result_of** isn't as odd as it may seem at first.

declval() (§iso.20.2.4)	
declval<T>()	Returns an rvalue for **T**: **typename add_rvalue_reference<T>::type**; never use a return value of **declval**

The **declval()** type function is unusual in the standard library because it is actually a function (without users needing to wrap it). It returns a value that must never be used. The intent is to use **declval<X>** as a type where the type of a variable of type **X** is needed. For example:

```
template<typename T, size_t N>
void array<T,N> swap(array& y) noexcept(noexcept(swap(declval<T&>(), declval<T&>())))
{
    for (int i=0; i<a.size(); ++i)
        swap((*this)[i],a[i]);
}
```

See also the definition of **common_type**.

35.5 Minor Utilities

These utilities are minor in size, but not in importance. They don't fit into a larger grouping.

35.5.1 move() and forward()

In <utility>, we find some of the most useful small functions:

Other Transformations (§iso.20.9.7.6)	
x2=forward(x)	x2 is an rvalue; x may not be an lvalue; noexcept
x2=move(x)	x2 is an rvalue; noexcept
x2=move_if_noexcept(x)	If x can be moved, x2=move(x); otherwise x2=x; noexcept

A move() is simply a cast to an rvalue:

```
template<typename T>
Remove_reference<T>&& move(T&& t) noexcept
{
        return static_cast<Remove_reference<T>&&>(t);
}
```

In my opinion, move() should have been called rvalue(), because it doesn't actually move anything. Instead, it produces an rvalue for its argument, so that the object referred to can be moved from.

A move() is used to tell the compiler that an object will not be used anymore in a context, so that its value can be moved and an empty object left behind. The simplest example is the implementation of swap() (§35.5.2).

A forward() produces rvalue from an rvalue only:

```
template<typename T>
T&& forward(Remove_reference<T>& t) noexcept
{
        return static_cast<T&&>(t);
}
```

```
template<typename T>
T&& forward(Remove_reference<T>&& t) noexcept;
{
        static_assert(!Is_lvalue_reference<T>,"forward of lvalue");
        return static_cast<T&&>(t);
}
```

This pair of forward() functions are meant always to be available together, and selection between them should be done by overload resolution. In that case, any lvalue goes to the first version and every rvalue to the second. For example:

```
int i = 7;
forward(i);         // call first version
forward(7);         // call second version
```

The assert is there for programmer who are too clever for their own good and calls the second version with an explicit template argument and an lvalue.

The archetypical use of forward() is for "perfect forwarding" of an argument from one function to another (§23.5.2.1, §28.6.3). The standard-library make_shared<T>(x) (§34.3.2) is a good example.

Use move() when the intent is to "steal the representation" of an object with a move operation, and use forward() for forwarding. Thus, forward(x) is safe, whereas move(x) marks x for destruction so that move(x) should be used with care. The only safe use of an x after a move(x) is destruction or as a target for an assignment. Obviously a particular type could provide further guarantees, and ideally the class's invariant is left intact. However, don't rely on that unless you really know.

35.5.2 swap()

In <utility>, the standard library provides a general swap() and a specialization for built-in arrays:

Other Transformations (§iso.20.2.2)	
swap(x,y)	Exchange the values of x and y; x and y are passed as non-const references; noexcept if x's and y's copy operations are noexcept
swap(a1n,a2n)	a1n and a2n are passed as references to arrays: T(&)[N]; noexcept if *a1n and *a2n's copy operations are noexcept

The relatively obvious implementation swap() is:

```
template<typename T>
void swap(T& a, T& b) noexcept(Is_nothrow_move_constructible<T>()
                               && Is_nothrow_move_assignable<T>())
{
    T tmp {move(a)};
    a = move(b);
    b = move(tmp);
}
```

This implies that swap() cannot be used to exchange rvalues:

```
vector<int> v1 {1,2,3,4};
swap(v,vecor<int>{});        // error: second argument is an rvalue
v.clear();                   // clearer (less obscure)
```

35.5.3 Relational Operators

In <utility>, we find relational operators for arbitrary types in a sub-namespace rel_ops:

Relational Operators in std::rel_ops (§iso.20.2.1)	
x!=y	!(x==y)
x>y	y<x
x<=y	!(y<x)
x>=y	!(x<y)

This requires that the programmer has made sure that x==y and x<y work.

For example:

```
struct Val {
    double d;
    bool operator==(Val v) const { return v.d==d; }
};

void my_algo(vector<Val>& vv)
{
    using namespace std::rel_ops;

    for (int i=0; i<ww.size(); ++i)
        if (0>ww[i]) ww[i]=abs(ww[i]);    // OK: > from rel_ops
}
```

It can be hard to use **rel_ops** without polluting a namespace. In particular:

```
namespace Mine {
    struct Val {
        double d;
        bool operator==(Val v) const { return v.d==d; }
    };

    using namespace std::rel_ops;
}
```

This could expose the perfectly general templates from **rel_ops** to be found by argument-dependent lookup (§14.2.4) and applied to types for which they may be inappropriate. A safer approach is to place **using**-directives in local scopes.

35.5.4 Comparing and Hashing type_info

In **<typeindex>**, the standard library provides support for comparing and hashing **type_index**s. A **type_index** is created from a **type_info** (§22.5), specifically to allow such comparison and hashing.

type_index **Operations (§iso.20.13)**	
tip is a pointer to the **type_info** represented by a **type_index**	
type_index ti {tinf};	ti represents the **type_info** tinf; noexcept
ti==ti2	ti and ti2 represent the same **type_info**: *ti.tip==*ti2.tip); noexcept
ti!=ti2	!(ti==ti2); noexcept
ti<ti2	ti.tip–>before(ti2.tip); noexcept
ti<=ti2	!ti2.tip–>before(ti.tip); noexcept
ti>ti2	ti2.tip–>before(ti.tip); noexcept
ti>=ti2	!ti.tip–>before(ti2.tip); noexcept
n=ti.hash_code()	n=ti.tip–>hash_code()
p=name()	p = ti.tip–>name()
hash<type_index>	A specialization of **hash** (§31.4.3.4)

For example:

```
unordered_map<type_index,type_info*> types;
// ...
types[type_index{something}] = &typeid(something);
```

35.6 Advice

[1]   Use <chrono> facilities, such as **steady_clock, duration,** and **time_point** for timing; §35.2.
[2]   Prefer <clock> facilities over <ctime> facilities; §35.2.
[3]   Use **duration_cast** to get durations in known units of time; §35.2.1.
[4]   Use **system_clock::now()** to get the current time; §35.2.3.
[5]   You can inquire about properties of types at compile time; §35.4.1.
[6]   Use **move(obj)** only when the value of **obj** cannot be used again; §35.5.1.
[7]   Use **forward()** for forwarding; §35.5.1.

36

Strings

Prefer the standard to the offbeat.
– Strunk & White

- Introduction
- Character Classification
    Classification Functions; Character Traits
- Strings
    string vs. C-Style Strings; Constructors; Fundamental Operations; String I/O; Numeric Conversions; STL-like Operations; The **find** Family; Substrings
- Advice

36.1 Introduction

The standard library offers character classification operations in **<cctype>** (§36.2), strings with associated operations in **<string>** (§36.3), regular expression matching in **<regex>** (Chapter 37), and support for C-style strings in **<cstring>** (§43.4). Handling of different character sets, encodings, and conventions (**locale**s) is discussed in Chapter 39.

A simplified **string** implementation is presented in §19.3.

36.2 Character Classification

The standard library provides classification functions to help users to manipulate strings (and other character sequences) and traits specifying properties of a character type to help implementers of operations on strings.

36.2.1 Classification Functions

In **<cctype>**, the standard library provides functions to classify the characters from the basic execution character set:

Character Classification	
isspace(c)	Is c whitespace (space ' ', horizontal tab '\t', newline '\n', vertical tab '\v', form feed '\f', carriage return '\r')?
isalpha(c)	Is c a letter ('a'..'z', 'A'..'Z')? note: not underscore '_'
isdigit(c)	Is c a decimal digit ('0'..'9')?
isxdigit(c)	Is c hexadecimal digit (decimal digit or 'a'..'f' or 'A'..'F')?
isupper(c)	Is c an uppercase letter?
islower(c)	Is c a lowercase letter?
isalnum(c)	isalpha(c) or isdigit(c)
iscntrl(c)	Is c a control character (ASCII 0..31 and 127)?
ispunct(c)	Is c not a letter, digit, whitespace, or invisible control character?
isprint(c)	Is c printable (ASCII ' '..'~')?
isgraph(c)	isalpha(c) or isdigit(c) or ispunct(c)? note: not space

In addition, the standard library provides two useful functions for removing case differences:

Upper- and Lowercase	
toupper(c)	c or c's uppercase equivalent
tolower(c)	c or c's lowercase equivalent

The equivalent functions for wide characters are provided in **<cwctype>**.

The character classification functions are sensitive to the "**C**" locale (§39.5.1, §39.5.2). Equivalent functions for other locales are provided in **<locale>** (§39.5.1).

One reason that these character classification functions are useful is that character classification can be trickier than it might appear. For example, a novice might write:

if ('a'<ch && ch<'z') *// a character*

This is more verbose (and most likely slower) than:

if (islower(ch))   *// a lowercase character*

Also, there is no guarantee that the characters are contiguous in a code space. Furthermore, the use of standard character classifications are far easier to convert to another locale:

if (islower,danish)   *// a lowercase character in Danish*
                          // (assuming "danish" is the name for a Danish locale)

Note that Danish has three more lowercase characters than English, so that the initial explicit test using 'a' and 'z' would be flat wrong.

36.2.2 Character Traits

As shown in §23.2, a string template can, in principle, use any type with proper copy operations as its character type. However, efficiency can be improved and implementations can be simplified for types that don't have user-defined copy operations. Consequently, the standard **string** requires that a type used as its character type be a POD (§8.2.6). This also helps to make I/O of strings simple and efficient.

The properties of a character type are defined by its **char_traits**. A **char_traits** is a specialization of the template:

```
template<typename C> struct char_traits { };
```

All **char_traits** are defined in **std**, and the standard ones are presented in **<string>**. The general **char_traits** itself has no properties; only **char_traits** specializations for a particular character type have. Consider **char_traits<char>**:

```
template<>
struct char_traits<char> {        // char_traits operations should not throw exceptions
    using char_type = char;
    using int_type = int;                 // type of integer value of character
    using off_type = streamoff;           // offset in stream
    using pos_type = streampos;           // position in stream
    using state_type = mbstate_t;         // multibyte stream state (§39.4.6)
    // ...
};
```

The standard provides four specializations of **char_traits** (§iso.21.2.3):

```
template<> struct char_traits<char>;
template<> struct char_traits<char16_t>;
template<> struct char_traits<char32_t>;
template<> struct char_traits<wchar_t>;
```

The members of the standard **char_traits** are all **static** functions:

char_traits<C> static **Members (§iso.21.2)**	
c=to_char_type(i)	int_type to char_type conversion
i=to_int_type(c)	char_type to int_type conversion
eq_int_type(c,c2)	to_int_type(c)==to_int_type(c2)
eq(c,c2)	Is c treated as equal to c2?
lt(c,c2)	Is c treated as less than c2?
i=compare(p,p2,n)	Lexicographical compare of [p:p+n) and [p2:p2+n)
assign(c,c2)	c=c2 for char_type
p2=assign(p,n,c)	Assign n copies of c to [p:p+n); p2=p
p3=move(p,p2,n)	Copy [p:p+n) to [p2:p2+n); [p:p+n) and [p2:p2+n) may overlap; p3=p
p3=copy(p,p2,n)	Copy [p:p+n) to [p2:p2+n); [p:p+n) and [p2:p2+n) may not overlap; p3=p

char_traits<C> static **Members (§iso.21.2)**	
n=length(p)	n is the number of characters in [p:q)
	where *q is the first element so that **eq(q,charT{})**
p2=find(p,n,c)	p points to the first occurrence of **c** in [p:p+n) or **nullptr**
i=eof()	i is the **int_type** value representing end-of-file
i=not_eof(i)	i if !eq_int_type(i,eof()); otherwise i can be any value not equal to **eof()**

Comparing with **eq()** is often not simply an **==**. For example, a case-insensitive **char_traits** would define its **eq()** so that **eq('b','B')** would return **true**.

Because **copy()** does not protect against overlapping ranges, it may be faster than **move()**.

The **compare()** function uses **lt()** and **eq()** to compare characters. It returns an **int**, where **0** represents an exact match, a negative number means that its first argument comes lexicographically before the second, and a positive number means that its first argument comes after its second.

The I/O-related functions are used by the implementation of low-level I/O (§38.6).

36.3 Strings

In **<string>**, the standard library provides a general string template **basic_string**:

```
template<typename C,
          typename Tr = char_traits<C>,
          typename A = allocator<C>>
class basic_string {
public:
      using traits_type = Tr;
      using value_type = typename Tr::char_type;
      using allocator_type = A;
      using size_type = typename allocator_traits<A>::size_type;
      using difference_type = typename allocator_traits<A>::difference_type;
      using reference = value_type&;
      using const_reference = const value_type&;
      using pointer = typename allocator_traits<A>::pointer;
      using const_pointer = typename allocator_traits<A>::const_pointer;
      using iterator = /* implementation-defined */;
      using const_iterator = /* implementation-defined */;
      using reverse_iterator = std::reverse_iterator<iterator>;
      using const_reverse_iterator = std::reverse_iterator<const_iterator>;

      static const size_type npos = −1;    // integer representing end-of-string

      // ...
};
```

The elements (characters) are stored contiguously, so that low-level input operations can safely use a **basic_string**'s sequence of characters as a source or target.

The **basic_string** offers the strong guarantee (§13.2): if a **basic_string** operation throws, the string is left unchanged.

Specializations are offered for a few standard character types:

```
using string = basic_string<char>;
using u16string = basic_string<char16_t>;
using u32string = basic_string<char32_t>;
using wstring = basic_string<wchar_t>;
```

All these strings provide a host of operations.

Like containers (Chapter 31), **basic_string** is not meant to be used as a base class and offers move semantics so that it can be efficiently returned by value.

36.3.1 string vs. C-Style Strings

I assume some familiarity with **string** from the many examples in this book, so I start with a few examples contrasting **string** use with the use of C-style strings (§43.4) which are popular with programmers primarily familiar with C and C-style C++.

Consider making up an email address by concatenating a user identifier and a domain name:

```
string address(const string& identifier, const string& domain)
{
    return identifier + '@' + domain;
}


void test()
{
    string t = address("bs","somewhere");
    cout << t << '\n';
}
```

This is trivial. Now consider a plausible C-style version. A C-style string is a pointer to an array of zero-terminated characters. The user controls allocation and is responsible for deallocation:

```
char* address(const char* identifier, const char* domain)
{
    int iden_len = strlen(identifier);
    int dom_len = strlen(domain);
    char* addr = (char*)malloc(iden_len+dom_len+2);      // remember space for 0 and '@'
    strcpy(identifier,addr);
    addr[iden_len] = '@';
    strcpy(domain,addr+iden_len+1);
    return addr;
}


void test2()
{
    char* t = address("bs","somewhere");
    printf("%s\n",t);
    free(t);
}
```

Did I get that right? I hope so. At least it gave the output I expected. Like most experienced C programmers, I got the C version correct (I hope) the first time, but there are a lot of details to get right. However, experience (i.e., error logs) shows that this is not always the case. Often, such simple programming tasks are given to relative novices who still don't know all the techniques needed to get it right. The implementation of the C-style **address()** contains a lot of tricky pointer manipulation, and its use requires the caller to remember to free the returned memory. Which code would you prefer to maintain?

Sometimes, it is claimed that C-style strings are more efficient than **string**s. However, for most uses, the **string** does fewer allocations and deallocations than a C-style equivalent (because of the small-string optimization and move semantics; §19.3.3, §19.3.1). Also, **strlen()** is a log(N) operation, whereas **string::size()** is a simple read. In the example, this implies that the C-style code traverses each input string twice, whereas the **string** version does only one traversal per input. Efficiency concerns at this level are often misguided, but the **string** version has a fundamental edge.

The fundamental difference between C-style strings and **string** is that **string** is a proper type with conventional semantics, whereas the C-style string is a set of conventions supported by a few useful functions. Consider assignment and comparison:

```
void test3()
{
    string s1 = "Ring";
    if (s1!="Ring") insanity();
    if (s1<"Opera")cout << "check";
    string s2 = address(s1,"Valkyrie");

    char s3[] = "Ring";
    if (strcmp(s3,"Ring")!=0) insanity();
    if (strcmp(s3,"Opera")<0) cout << "check";
    char* s4 = address(s3,"Valkyrie");
    free(s4);
}
```

Finally, consider sorting:

```
void test4()
{
    vector<string> vs = {"Grieg", "Williams", "Bach", "Handel" };
    sort(vs.begin(),vs.end());       // assuming that I haven't defined sort(vs)

    const char* as[] = {"Grieg", "Williams", "Bach", "Handel" };
    qsort(as,sizeof(*as),sizeof(as)/sizeof(*as),(int(*)(const void*,const void*))strcmp);
}
```

The C-style string sort function **qsort()** is presented in §43.7. Again, **sort()** is as fast as (and typically much faster than) **qsort()**, so there is no performance reason to choose the lower-level, more verbose, and less maintainable programming style.

36.3.2 Constructors

A **basic_string** offers a bewildering variety of constructors:

basic_string<C,Tr,A> Constructors (§iso.21.4.2) x can be a basic_string, a C-style string, or an initializer_list<char_type>	
basic_string s {a};	s is an empty string with allocator a; explicit
basic_string s {};	Default constructor: basic_string s {A{}};
basic_string s {x,a};	s gets the characters from x; use allocator a
basic_string s {x};	Move and copy constructor: basic_string s {x,A{}};
basic_string s {s2,pos,n,a};	s gets the characters s2[pos:pos+n}; use allocator a
basic_string s {s2,pos,n};	basic_string s {s2,pos,n,A{};}
basic_string s {s2,pos};	basic_string s {s2,pos,string::npos,A{}};
basic_string s {p,n,a};	Initialize s from [p:p+n); p is a C-style string; use allocator a
basic_string s {p,n};	basic_string s {p,n,A{}};
basic_string s {n,c,a};	s holds n copies of the character c; use allocator a
basic_string s {n,c};	basic_string s {n,c,A{};}
basic_string s {b,e,a};	s gets the characters from [b:e); use allocator a
basic_string s {b,e};	basic_string s {b,e,A{}};
s.˜basic_string()	Destructor: free all resources
s=x	Copy: s gets the characters from x
s2=move(s)	Move: s2 gets the characters from s; noexcept

The most common variants are also the simplest:

```
string s0;                         // the empty string
string s1 {"As simple as that!"};  // construct from C-style string
string s2 {s1};                    // copy constructor
```

Almost always, the destructor is implicitly invoked.

There is no **string** constructor that takes only a number of elements:

```
string s3 {7};      // error: no string(int)
string s4 {'a'};    // error: no string(char)
string s5 {7,'a'};  // OK: 7 'a's
string s6 {0};      // danger: passing nullptr
```

The declaration of **s6** shows a mistake sometimes made by programmers used to C-style strings:

```
const char* p = 0;   // set p to "no string"
```

Unfortunately, the compiler cannot catch the definition of **s6** or the even nastier case of a **const char*** holding the **nullptr**:

```
string s6 {0};      // danger: passing nullptr
string s7 {p};      // may or may not be OK depending on the value of p
string s8 {"OK"};   // OK: pass pointer to C-style string
```

Don't try to initialize a **string** with a **nullptr**. At best, you get a nasty run-time error. At worst, you get mysterious undefined behavior.

If you try to construct a **string** with more characters than your implementation can handle, the constructor throws **std::length_error**. For example:

```
string s9 {string::npos,'x'};    // throw length_error
```

The value **string::npos** represents a position beyond a **string**'s length and is generally used to mean "the end of the string." For example:

```
string ss {"Fleetwood Mac"};
string ss2 {ss,0,9};             // "Fleetwood"
string ss3 {ss,10,string::npos}; // "Mac"
```

Note that the substring notation is (position,length) rather than [start,end).

There are no literals of type **string**. A user-defined literal could be used for that (§19.2.6), for example, **"The Beatles"s** and **"Elgar"s**. Note the s suffix.

36.3.3 Fundamental Operations

A **basic_string** offers comparisons, control of size and capacity, and access operations.

basic_string<C,Tr,A> **Comparisons** (§iso.21.4.8) s or s2 but not both can be a C-style string	
s==s2	Is s equal to s2? compares character values using **traits_type**
s!=s2	!(s==s2)
s<s2	Is s lexicographically before s2?
s<=s2	Is s lexicographically before or equal to s2?
s>s2	Is s lexicographically after s2?
s>=s2	Is s lexicographically after or equal to s2?

For more comparison operations, see §36.3.8.

The size and capacity mechanisms for **basic_string** are the same as those for **vector** (§31.3.3):

basic_string<C,Tr,A> **Size and Capacity** (§iso.21.4.4)	
n=s.size()	n is the number of characters in s
n=s.length()	n=s.size()
n=s.max_size()	n is the largest possible value of s.size()
s.resize(n,c)	Make s.size()==n; added elements get the value c
s.resize(n)	s.resize(n,C{})
s.reserve(n)	Ensure that s can hold n characters without further allocation
s.reserve()	No effect: s.reserve(0)
n=s.capacity()	s can hold n characters without further allocation
s.shrink_to_fit()	Make s.capacity==s.size()
s.clear()	Make s empty
s.empty()	Is s empty?
a=s.get_allocator()	a is s's allocator

A resize() or reserve() that would cause size() to exceed max_size() will throw **std::length_error**.

An example:

```
void fill(istream& in, string& s, int max)
    // use s as target for low-level input (simplified)
{
    s.reserve(max);              // make sure there is enough allocated space
    in.read(&s[0],max);
    const int n = in.gcount();   // number of characters read
    s.resize(n);
    s.shrink_to_fit();           // discard excess capacity
}
```

Here, I "forgot" to make use of the number of characters read. That's sloppy.

basic_string<C,Tr,A> Access (§iso.21.4.5)	
s[i]	Subscripting: s[i] is a reference to the ith element of s; no range check
s.at(i)	Subscripting: s.at(i) is a reference to the ith element of s; throw range_error if s.size()<=i
s.front()	s[0]
s.back()	s[s.size()–1]
s.push_back(c)	Append the character c
s.pop_back()	Remove the last character from s: s.erase(s.size()–1)
s+=x	Append x at the end of s; x can be a character, a string, a C-style string, or an initializer_list<char_type>
s=s1+s2	Concatenation: optimized version of s=s1; s+=s2;
n2=s.copy(s2,n,pos)	s gets the characters from s2[pos:n2] where n2 is min(n,s.size()–pos); throw out_of_range if s.size()<pos
n2=s.copy(s2,n)	s gets all the characters from s2; n=s.copy(s2,n,0)
p=s.c_str()	p is a C-style string version (zero-terminated) of the characters in s; a const C*
p=s.data()	p=s.c_str()
s.swap(s2)	Exchange the values of s and s2; noexcept
swap(s,s2)	s.swap(s2)

An out-of-range access using at() throws std::out_of_range. A +=(), push_back(), or + that would cause size() to exceed max_size() will throw std::length_error.

There is no implicit conversion of a string to a char*. That was tried in many places and found to be error-prone. Instead, the standard library provides the explicit conversion function c_str() to const char*.

A string can contain a zero value character (e.g., '\0'). Using a function, such as strcmp(), that assumes C-style string conventions on the result of s.c_str() or s.data() on a string containing a zero character may cause surprise.

36.3.4 String I/O

A **basic_string** can be written using **<<** (§38.4.2) and read into using **>>** (§38.4.1):

basic_string<C,Tr,A> I/O Operations (§iso.21.4.8.9)	
in>>s	Read a whitespace-separated word into s from in
out<<s	Write s to out
getline(in,s,d)	Read characters from in into s until the character
	d is encountered; d is removed from in but not appended to s
getline(in,s)	getline(in,s,'\n') where '\n' is widened to match the string's character type

An input operation that would cause **size()** to exceed **max_size()** will throw **std::length_error**.

A **getline()** removes its terminator character (by default '\n') from the input stream but does not enter it into the string. This simplifies handling of lines. For example:

```
vector<string> lines;
for (string s; getline(cin,s);)
    lines.push_back(s);
```

The **string** I/O operations all return a reference to their input stream, so that operations can be chained. For example:

```
string first_name;
string second_name;
cin >> first_name >> second_name;
```

The **string** target of an input operation is set to empty before reading and expands to hold the characters read. A read operation can also be terminated by reaching end-of-file (§38.3).

36.3.5 Numeric Conversions

In **<string>**, the standard library provides a set of functions for extracting numeric values from their character representation in a **string** or **wstring** (note: not a **basic_string<C,Tr,A>**). The desired numeric types are encoded in the function names:

Numeric Conversions (§iso.21.5) (continues) s can be a string or a wstring	
x=stoi(s,p,b)	String to int; x is an integer; read starting with s[0]
	if p!=nullptr, *p is set to the number of characters used for x;
	b is the base of the number (between 2 and 36, inclusive)
x=stoi(s,p)	x=stoi(s,p,10); decimal numbers
x=stoi(s)	x=stoi(s,nullptr,10); decimal numbers; don't report the character count
x=stol(s,p,b)	String to long
x=stoul(s,p,b)	String to unsigned long
x=stoll(s,p,b)	String to long long
x=stoull(s,p,b)	String to unsigned long long

Numeric Conversions (continued) (§iso.21.5)	
s can be a **string** or a **wstring**	
x=stof(s,p)	String to **float**
x=stod(s,p)	String to **double**
x=stold(s,p)	String to **long double**
s=to_string(x)	s is a **string** representation of x; x must be an integer or floating-point value
ws=to_wstring(x)	s is a **wstring** representation of x; x must be an integer or floating-point value

Each of these **sto**∗ (String to) functions has three variants, like **stoi**. For example:

```
string s = "123.45";
auto x1 = stoi(s);      // x1 = 123
auto x2 = stod(s);      // x2 = 123.45
```

The second argument of a **sto**∗ function is a pointer used to indicate how far into the string the search for a numeric value progressed. For example:

```
string ss = "123.4567801234";
size_t dist = 0;            // put number of characters read here
auto x = stoi(ss,&dist);   // x = 123 (an int)
++dist;                    // ignore the dot
auto y = stoll(&ss[dist]); // x = 4567801234 (a long long)
```

This is not my favorite interface for parsing several numbers from a string. I prefer to use a **string_stream** (§38.2.2).

Initial whitespace is skipped. For example:

```
string s = "    123.45";
auto x1 = stoi(s);         // x1 = 123
```

The base argument can be in the range [2:36] with the **0123456789abcdefghijklmnopqrstuvwxyz** used as "digits" with their value determined by their position in this sequence. Any further base value will be an error or an extension. For example:

```
string s4 = "149F";
auto x5 = stoi(s4);         // x5 = 149
auto x6 = stoi(s4,nullptr,10);   // x6 = 149
auto x7 = stoi(s4,nullptr,8);    // x7 = 014
auto x8 = stoi(s4,nullptr,16);   // x8 = 0x149F

string s5 = "1100101010100101";  // binary
auto x9 = stoi(s5,nullptr,2);    // x9 = 0xcaa5
```

If a conversion function doesn't find characters in its string argument that it can convert to a number, it throws **invalid_argument**. If it finds a number that it cannot represent in its target type, it throws **out_of_range**; in addition, the conversions to floating-point types set **errno** to **ERANGE** (§40.3). For example:

```
stoi("Hello, World!");            // throws std::invalid_argument
stoi("12345678901234567890");     // throws std::out_of_range; errno=ERANGE
stof("123456789e1000");           // throws std::out_of_range; errno=ERANGE
```

The sto* functions encode their target type in their names. This makes them unsuitable for generic code where the target can be a template parameter. In such cases, consider to<X> (§25.2.5.1).

36.3.6 STL-like Operations

The basic_string provides the usual set of iterators:

basic_string<C,Tr,A> String Iterators (§iso.21.4.3) All operations are noexcept	
p=s.begin()	p is an iterator to the first character of s
p=s.end()	p is an iterator to one beyond the end of s
p=s.cbegin()	p is a const_iterator to the first character
p=s.cend()	p is a const_iterator to one beyond the end of s
p=s.rbegin()	p is the beginning of the reverse sequence for s
p=s.rend()	p is the end of the reverse sequence for s
p=s.crbegin()	p is a const_iterator to the beginning of the reverse sequence for s
p=s.crend()	p is a const_iterator to the end of the reverse sequence for s

Because string has the required member types and the functions for obtaining iterators, strings can be used together with the standard algorithms (Chapter 32). For example:

```
void f(string& s)
{
    auto p = find_if(s.begin(),s.end(),islower);
    // ...
}
```

The most common operations on strings are supplied directly by string. Hopefully, these versions will be optimized for strings beyond what would be easy to do for general algorithms.

The standard algorithms (Chapter 32) are not as useful for strings as one might think. General algorithms tend to assume that the elements of a container are meaningful in isolation. This is typically not the case for a string.

A basic_string offers complex assignment()s:

basic_string<C,Tr,A> Assignment (§iso.21.4.6.3) All operations return the string to which they are applied	
s.assign(x)	s=x; x can be a string, a C-style string, or an initializer_list<char_type>
s.assign(move(s2))	Move: s2 is a string; noexcept
s.assign(s2,pos,n)	s gets the characters s2[pos:pos+n]
s.assign(p,n)	s gets the characters [p:p+n); p is a C-style string
s.assign(n,c)	s gets n copies of the character c
s.assign(b,e)	s gets the characters from [b:e)

We can insert(), append(), and erase() in a basic_string:

basic_string<C,Tr,A> **Insertion and Deletion** (§iso.21.4.6.2, §iso.21.4.6.4, §iso.21.4.6.5) All operations return the string to which they are applied	
s.append(x)	Append x at the end of s; x can be a character, a string, a C-style string, or an initializer_list<char_type>
s.append(b,e)	Append [b:e) at the end of s
s.append(s2,pos,n)	Append s2[pos:pos+n) to the end of s
s.append(p,n)	Append the characters [p:p+n) to the end of s; p is a C-style string
s.append(n,c)	Append n copies of character c to the end of s
s.insert(pos,x)	Insert x before s[pos]; x can be a character, a string, a C-style string, or an initializer_list<char_type>
s.insert(p,c)	Insert c before iterator p
s.insert(p,n,c)	Insert n copies of c before iterator p
insert(p,b,e)	Insert [b:e) before iterator p
s.erase(pos)	Remove trailing characters from s, starting with s[pos]; s.size() becomes pos
s.erase(pos,n)	Remove n characters from s, starting with s[pos]; s.size() becomes max(pos,s.size()−n)

For example:

```
void add_middle(string& s, const string& middle)    // add middle name
{
    auto p = s.find(' ');
    s.insert(p,' '+middle);
}

void test()
{
    string dmr = "Dennis Ritchie";
    add_middle(dmr,"MacAlistair");
    cout << dmr << '\n';
}
```

As for vectors, append()ing (adding characters at the end) is typically more efficient than insert()ing elsewhere.

In the following, I use s[b:e) to denote a sequence of elements [b:e) in s:

basic_string<C,Tr,A> **Replace** (§iso.21.4.6.6) (continues) All operations return the string to which they are applied	
s.replace(pos,n,s2,pos2,n2)	Replace s[pos:pos+n) with s2[pos2:pos2+n2)
s.replace(pos,n,p,n2)	Replace s[pos:pos+n) with [p:p+n2); s2 is a string or a C-style string
s=s.replace(pos,n,s2)	Replace s[pos:pos+n) with s2; s2 is a string or a C-style string
s.replace(pos,n,n2,c)	Replace s[pos:pos+n) with n2 copies of the character c

basic_string<C,Tr,A> **Replace (continued)** (§iso.21.4.6.6)	
All operations return the string to which they are applied	
s.replace(b,e,x)	Replace [b:e] with x; x is a **string**, a C-style string, or an **initializer_list<char_type>**
s.replace(b,e,p,n)	Replace [b:e] with [p:p+n)
s.replace(b,e,n,c)	Replace [b:e] with n copies of the character **c**
s.replace(b,e,b2,e2)	Replace [b:e] with [b2:e2)

The **replace()** replaces one substring with another and adjusts the **string**'s size accordingly. For example:

```
void f()
{
    string s = "but I have heard it works even if you don't believe in it";
    s.replace(0,4,"");                      // erase initial "but "
    s.replace(s.find("even"),4,"only");
    s.replace(s.find(" don't"),6,"");       // erase by replacing with ""
    assert(s=="I have heard it works only if you believe in it");
}
```

Code relying on "magic" constants like the number of characters to be replaced is error-prone.

A **replace()** returns a reference to the object for which it was called. This can be used for chaining operations:

```
void f2()
{
    string s = "but I have heard it works even if you don't believe in it";
    s.replace(0,4,"").replace(s.find("even"),4,"only").replace(s.find(" don't"),6,"");
    assert(s=="I have heard it works only if you believe in it");
}
```

36.3.7 The **find** Family

There is a bewildering variety of functions for finding substrings. As usual, **find()** searches from **s.begin()** onward, whereas **rfind()** searches backward from **s.end()**. The **find** functions use **string::npos** ("not a position") to represent "not found."

basic_string<C,Tr,A> **Find Element** (§iso.21.4.7.2)	
x can be a character, a **string**, or a C-style string. All operations are noexcept	
pos=s.find(x)	Find x in s; pos is the index of the first character found or **string::npos**
pos=s.find(x,pos2)	pos=find(basic_string(s,pos2)
pos=s.find(p,pos2,n)	pos=s.find(basic_string{p,n},pos2)
pos=s.rfind(x,pos2)	Find x in s[0:pos2]; pos is the position of the first character of the x closest to the end of s or **string::npos**
pos=s.rfind(x)	pos=s.rfind(p,string::npos)
pos=s.rfind(p,pos2,n)	pos=s.rfind(basic_string{p,n},pos2)

For example:

```
void f()
{
    string s {"accdcde"};

    auto i1 = s.find("cd");          // i1==2    s[2]=='c' && s[3]=='d'
    auto i2 = s.rfind("cd");         // i2==4    s[4]=='c' && s[5]=='d'
}
```

The **find_*_of()** functions differ from **find()** and **rfind()** by looking for a single character, rather than a whole sequence of characters:

basic_string<C,Tr,A> **Find Elements from a Set (§iso.21.4.7.4)**	
x can be a character, a **string**, or a C-style string; **p** is a C-style string. All operations are noexcept.	
pos2=s.find_first_of(x,pos)	Find a character from **x** in s[pos:s.size()); **pos2** is the position of the first character from **x** in s[pos:s.size()) or string::npos
pos=s.find_first_of(x)	pos=s.find_first_of(s2,0)
pos2=s.find_first_of(p,pos,n)	pos2=s.find_first_of(pos,basic_string{p,n})
pos2=s.find_last_of(x,pos)	Find a character from **x** in s[0:pos); **pos2** is the position of the character from **x** closest to the end of **s** or string::npos
pos=s.find_last_of(x)	pos=s.find_first_of(s2,0)
pos2=s.find_last_of(p,pos,n)	pos2=s.find_last_of(pos2,basic_string{p,n})
pos2=s.find_first_not_of(x,pos)	Find a character not from **x** in s[pos:s.size()); **pos2** is the position of the first character from **x** not in s[pos:s.size()) or string::npos
pos=s.find_first_not_of(x)	pos=s.find_first_not_of(s2,0)
pos2=s.find_first_not_of(p,pos,n)	pos2=s.find_first_not_of(pos,basic_string{p,n})
pos2=s.find_last_not_of(x,pos)	Find a character not from **x** in s[0:pos); **pos** is the position of the character from **x** closest to the end of **s** or string::npos
pos=s.find_last_not_of(x)	pos=s.find_first_not_of(s2,0)
pos2=s.find_last_not_of(p,pos,n)	pos=s.find_last_not_of(pos,basic_string{p,n})

For example:

```
string s {"accdcde"};

auto i1 = s.find("cd");              // i1==2    s[2]=='c' && s[3]=='d'
auto i2 = s.rfind("cd");             // i2==4    s[4]=='c' && s[5]=='d'

auto i3 = s.find_first_of("cd");     // i3==1    s[1]=='c'
auto i4 = s.find_last_of("cd");      // i4==5    s[5]=='d'
auto i5 = s.find_first_not_of("cd"); // i5==0    s[0]!='c' && s[0]!='d'
auto i6 = s.find_last_not_of("cd");  // i6==6    s[6]!='c' && s[6]!='d'
```

36.3.8 Substrings

A basic_string offers a low-level notion of substring:

basic_string<C,Tr,A> Substrings (§iso.21.4.7.8)	
s2=s.substr(pos,n)	s2=basic_string(&s[pos],m) where m=min(s.size()–n,n)
s2=s.substr(pos)	s2=s.substr(pos,string::npos)
s2=s.substr()	s2=s.substr(0,string::npos)

Note that substr() creates a new string:

```
void user()
{
    string s = "Mary had a little lamb";
    string s2 = s.substr(0,4);    // s2 == "Mary"
    s2 = "Rose";                  // does not change s
}
```

We can compare substrings:

basic_string<C,Tr,A> Compare (§iso.21.4.7.9)	
n=s.compare(s2)	A lexicographical comparison of s and s2; using char_traits<C>::compare() for comparison; n=0 if s==s2; n<0 if s<s2; n>0 if s2>s; noexcept;
n2=s.compare(pos,n,s2)	n2=basic_string{s,pos,n}.compare(s2)
n2=s.compare(pos,n,s2,pos2,n2)	n2=basic_string{s,pos,n}.compare(basic_string{s2,pos2,n2})
n=s.compare(p)	n=compare(basic_string{p}); p is a C-style string
n2=s.compare(pos,n,p)	n2=basic_string{s,pos,n}.compare(basic_string{p}); p is a C-style string
n2=s.compare(pos,n,p,n2)	n2=basic_string{s,pos,n}.compare(basic_string{p,n2}); p is a C-style string

For example:

```
void f()
{
    string s = "Mary had a little lamb";
    string s2 = s.substr(0,4);    // s2 == "Mary"
    auto i1 = s.compare(s2);      // i1 is positive
    auto i2 = s.compare(0,4,s2);  // i2==0
}
```

This explicit use of constants to denote positions and lengths is brittle and error-prone.

36.4 Advice

[1]   Use character classifications rather than handcrafted checks on character ranges; §36.2.1.

[2]   If you implement string-like abstractions, use **character_traits** to implement operations on characters; §36.2.2.

[3]   A **basic_string** can be used to make strings of characters on any type; §36.3.

[4]   Use **string**s as variables and members rather than as base classes; §36.3.

[5]   Prefer **string** operations to C-style string functions; §36.3.1.

[6]   Return **string**s by value (rely on move semantics); §36.3.2.

[7]   Use **string::npos** to indicate "the rest of the **string**"; §36.3.2.

[8]   Do not pass a **nullptr** to a **string** function expecting a C-style string; §36.3.2.

[9]   A **string** can grow and shrink, as needed; §36.3.3.

[10]   Use **at()** rather than iterators or **[]** when you want range checking; §36.3.3, §36.3.6.

[11]   Use iterators and **[]** rather than **at()** when you want to optimize speed; §36.3.3, §36.3.6.

[12]   If you use **string**s, catch **length_error** and **out_of_range** somewhere; §36.3.3.

[13]   Use **c_str()** to produce a C-style string representation of a **string** (only) when you have to; §36.3.3.

[14]   **string** input is type sensitive and doesn't overflow; §36.3.4.

[15]   Prefer a **string_stream** or a generic value extraction function (such as **to<X>**) over direct use of **str**∗ numeric conversion functions; §36.3.5.

[16]   Use the **find()** operations to locate values in a **string** (rather than writing an explicit loop); §36.3.7.

[17]   Directly or indirectly, use **substr()** to read substrings and **replace()** to write substrings; §36.3.8.

37

Regular Expressions

If the code and the comments disagree,
then both are probably wrong.
– Norm Schryer

37.1 Regular Expressions

In **<regex>**, the standard library provides regular expressions:

- **regex_match()**: Match a regular expression against a string (of known size).
- **regex_search()**: Search for a string that matches a regular expression in an (arbitrarily long) stream of data.
- **regex_replace()**: Search for strings that match a regular expression in an (arbitrarily long) stream of data and replace them.
- **regex_iterator**: iterate over matches and submatches.
- **regex_token_iterator**: iterate over non-matches.

The result of a **regex_search()** is a collection of matches, typically represented as an **smatch**:

```
void use()
{
    ifstream in("file.txt");      // input file
    if (!in) cerr << "no file\n";

    regex pat {R"(\w{2}\s*\d{5}(-\d{4})?)"};  // U.S. postal code pattern

    int lineno = 0;
    for (string line; getline(in,line);) {
        ++lineno;
        smatch matches;      // matched strings go here
        if (regex_search(line, matches, pat)) {
            cout << lineno << ": " << matches[0] << '\n';   // the complete match
            if (1<matches.size() && matches[1].matched)
                cout << "\t: " << matches[1] << '\n';// submatch
        }
    }
}
```

This function reads a file looking for U.S. postal codes, such as **TX77845** and **DC 20500–0001**. An **smatch** type is a container of regex results. Here, **matches[0]** is the whole pattern and **matches[1]** is the optional four-digit subpattern. I used a raw string (§7.3.2.1) which is particularly suitable for regular expressions because they tend to contain a lot of backslashes. Had I used a conventional string, the pattern definition would have been:

```
regex pat {"\\w{2}\\s*\\d{5}(-\\d{4})?"};   // U.S. postal code pattern
```

The regular expression syntax and semantics are designed so that regular expressions can be compiled into state machines for efficient execution [Cox,2007]. The **regex** type performs this compilation at run time.

37.1.1 Regular Expression Notation

The **regex** library can recognize several variants of the notation for regular expressions (§37.2). Here, I first present the default notation used, a variant of the ECMA standard used for ECMAScript (more commonly known as JavaScript).

The syntax of regular expressions is based on characters with special meaning:

	**Regular Expression Special Characters**		
.	Any single character (a "wildcard")	\	Next character has a special meaning
[	Begin character class	*	Zero or more
]	End character class	+	One or more
{	Begin count	?	Optional (zero or one)
}	End count	|	Alternative (or)
(	Begin grouping	^	Start of line; negation
)	End grouping	$	End of line

For example, we can specify a line starting with zero or more **A**s followed by one or more **B**s followed by an optional **C** like this:

    `^A*B+C?$`

Examples that match:

    AAAAAAAAAAAABBBBBBBBBC
    BC
    B

Examples that do not match:

AAAAA	*// no B*
AAAABC	*// initial space*
AABBCC	*// too many Cs*

A part of a pattern is considered a subpattern (which can be extracted separately from an **smatch**) if it is enclosed in parentheses.

A pattern can be optional or repeated (the default is exactly once) by adding a suffix:

Repetition	
{ n }	Exactly **n** times
{ n, }	**n** or more times
{n,m}	At least **n** and at most **m** times
*	Zero or more, that is, **{0,}**
+	One or more, that is, **{1,}**
?	Optional (zero or one), that is **{0,1}**

For example:

    `A{3}B{2,4}C*`

Examples that match:

    AAABBC
    AAABBB

Example that do not match:

AABBC	*// too few As*
AAABC	*// too few Bs*
AAABBBBBCCC	*// too many Bs*

A suffix **?** after any of the repetition notations makes the pattern matcher "lazy" or "non-greedy." That is, when looking for a pattern, it will look for the shortest match rather than the longest. By default, the pattern matcher always looks for the longest match (similar to C++'s Max Munch rule; §10.3). Consider:

    ababab

The pattern **(ab)*** matches all of **ababab**. However, **(ab)*?** matches only the first **ab**.

The most common character classifications have names:

Character Classes	
alnum	Any alphanumeric character
alpha	Any alphabetic character
blank	Any whitespace character that is not a line separator
cntrl	Any control character
d	Any decimal digit
digit	Any decimal digit
graph	Any graphical character
lower	Any lowercase character
print	Any printable character
punct	Any punctuation character
s	Any whitespace character
space	Any whitespace character
upper	Any uppercase character
w	Any word character (alphanumeric characters plus the underscore)
xdigit	Any hexadecimal digit character

Several character classes are supported by shorthand notation:

Character Class Abbreviations		
\d	A decimal digit	[[:digit:]]
\s	A space (space, tab, etc.)	[[:space:]]
\w	A letter (a-z) or digit (0-9) or underscore (_)	[_[:alnum:]]
\D	Not \d	[^[:digit:]]
\S	Not \s	[^[:space:]]
\W	Not \w	[^_[:alnum:]]

In addition, languages supporting regular expressions often provide:

Nonstandard (but Common) Character Class Abbreviations		
\l	A lowercase character	[[:lower:]]
\u	An uppercase character	[[:upper:]]
\L	Not \l	[^[:lower:]]
\U	Not \u	[^[:upper:]]

For full portability, use the character class names rather than these abbreviations.

As an example, consider writing a pattern that describes C++ identifiers: an underscore or a letter followed by a possibly empty sequence of letters, digits, or underscores. To illustrate the subtleties involved, I include a few false attempts:

```
[:alpha:][:alnum:]*        // wrong: characters from the set ":alph" followed by ...
[[:alpha:]][[:alnum:]]*    // wrong: doesn't accept underscore ('_' is not alpha)
([[:alpha:]]|_)[[:alnum:]]* // wrong: underscore is not part of alnum either
```

```
([[:alpha:]]|_)([[:alnum:]]|_)*      // OK, but clumsy
[[:alpha:]_][[:alnum:]_]*            // OK: include the underscore in the character classes
[_[:alpha:]][_[:alnum:]]*            // also OK
[_[:alpha:]]\w*                      // \w is equivalent to [_[:alnum:]]
```

Finally, here is a function that uses the simplest version of **regex_match()** (§37.3.1) to test whether a string is an identifier:

```
bool is_identifier(const string& s)
{
    regex pat {"[_[:alpha:]]\\w*"};
    return regex_match(s,pat);
}
```

Note the doubling of the backslash to include a backslash in an ordinary string literal. As usual, backslashes can also denote special characters:

Special Characters (§iso.2.14.3, §6.2.3.2)	
\n	Newline
\t	Tab
\\	One backslash
\xhh	Unicode characters expressed using two hexadecimal digits
\uhhhh	Unicode characters expressed using four hexadecimal digits

To add to the opportunities for confusion, two further logically different uses of the backslash are provided:

Special Characters (§iso.28.5.2, §37.2.2)	
\b	The first or last character of a word (a "boundary character")
\B	Not a \b
\i	The ith **sub_match** in this pattern

Using raw string literals alleviates many problems with special characters. For example:

```
bool is_identifier(const string& s)
{
    regex pat {R"([_[:alpha:]]\w*)"};
    return regex_match(s,pat);
}
```

Here are some examples of patterns:

```
Ax*          // A, Ax, Axxxx
Ax+          // Ax, Axxx     Not A
\d-?\d        // 1-2, 12     Not 1--2
\w{2}-\d{4,5} // Ab-1234, XX-54321, 22-5432     Digits are in \w
(\d*:)?(\d+)  // 12:3, 1:23, 123, :123     Not 123:
(bs|BS)      // bs, BS     Not bS
[aeiouy]     // a, o, u     An English vowel, not x
[^aeiouy]    // x, k     Not an English vowel, not e
[a^eiouy]    // a, ^, o, u     An English vowel or ^
```

A **group** (a subpattern) potentially to be represented by a **sub_match** is delimited by parentheses. If you need parentheses that should not define a subpattern, use **(?** rather than plain **(.** For example:

    (\s|:|,)∗(\d∗)   *// spaces, colons, and/or commas followed by a number*

Assuming that we were not interested in the characters before the number (presumably separators), we could write:

    (?\s|:|,)∗(\d∗)   *// spaces, colons, and/or commas followed by a number*

This would save the regular expression engine from having to store the first characters: the **(?** variant has only one subpattern.

Regular Expression Grouping Examples	
\d∗\s\w+	No groups (subpatterns)
(\d∗)\s(\w+)	Two groups
(\d∗)(\s(\w+))+	Two groups (groups do not nest)
(\s∗\w∗)+	One group, but one or more subpatterns; only the last subpattern is saved as a **sub_match**
<(.∗?)>(.∗?)</\1>	Three groups; the \1 means "same as group 1"

That last pattern is useful for parsing XML. It finds tag/end-of-tag markers. Note that I used a non-greedy match (a *lazy match*), .∗?, for the subpattern between the tag and the end tag. Had I used plain .∗, this input would have caused a problem:

    Always look for the <b>bright</b> side of <b>life</b>.

A *greedy match* for the first subpattern would match the first < with the last >. A greedy match on the second subpattern would match the first <b> with the last </b>. Both would be correct behavior, but unlikely what the programmer wanted.

It is possible to vary details of the regular expression notation using options (§37.2). For example, if **regex_constants::grep** is used, **a?x:y** is a sequence of five ordinary characters because **?** does not mean "optional" in grep.

For a more exhaustive presentation of regular expressions, see [Friedl,1997].

37.2 regex

A regular expression is a *matching engine* (usually a state machine) constructed from a sequence of characters, such as a **string**:

```
template<class C, class traits = regex_traits<C>>
class basic_regex {
public:
    using value_type = C;
    using traits_type = traits;
    using string_type = typename traits::string_type;
    using flag_type = regex_constants::syntax_option_type;
    using locale_type = typename traits::locale_type;
```

```
~basic_regex();// not virtual; basic_regex is not meant to be used as a base class
    // ...
};
```

The **regex_traits** are presented in §37.5.

Like **string**, **regex** is an alias for the version that uses **chars**:

```
using regex = basic_regex<char>;
```

The meaning of regular expression patterns is controlled by **syntax_option_type** constants defined identically in **regex_constants** and **regex**:

basic_regex<C,Tr> **Member Constants** (syntax_option_type, §iso.28.5.1)	
icase	No case is used when matching
nosubs	No subexpression matches are stored in the match results
optimize	Prefer fast matching to fast regular expression object construction
collate	Character ranges of the form [a–b] are locale sensitive
ECMAScript	The regular expression grammar is the one used by ECMAScript in ECMA-262 (with minor modifications; §iso.28.13)
basic	The regular expression grammar is the one used by basic regular expressions in POSIX
extended	The regular expression grammar is the one used by extended regular expressions in POSIX
awk	The regular expression grammar is the one used by POSIX awk
grep	The regular expression grammar is the one used by POSIX grep
egrep	The regular expression grammar is the one used by POSIX grep -E

Use the default unless you have a good reason not to. Good reasons include a large body of existing regular expressions in a non-default notation.

A **regex** object can be constructed from a **string** or similar sequence of characters:

basic_regex<C,Tr> **Constructors** (§iso.28.8.2)	
basic_regex r {};	Default constructor: an empty pattern; flags set to regex_constants::ECMAScript
basic_regex r {x,flags};	x can be a basic_regex, a string, a C-style string, or an initializer_list<value_type> with the notation defined by flags; explicit
basic_regex r {x};	basic_regex{x,regex_constants::ECMAScript}; explicit
basic_regex r {p,n,flags};	Construct r from the characters in [p:p+n) with the notation defined by flags
basic_regex r {p,n};	basic_regex{p,n,regex_constants::ECMAScript}
basic_regex r {b,e,flags}	Construct r from the characters in [b:e) with the notation defined by flags
basic_regex r {b,e};	basic_regex{b,e,regex_constants::ECMAScript}

The main use of **regex** is through the search, match, and replace functions (§37.3), but there are also a few operations on **regex** itself:

basic_regex<C,Tr> Operations (§iso.28.8)	
r=x	Copy assignment: **x** can be a **basic_regex**, a C-style string, a **basic_string**, or an **initializer_list<value_type>**
r=move(r2)	Move assignment
r=r.assign(r2)	Copy or move
r=r.assign(x,flags)	Copy or move; set r's flags to **flags x** can be a **basic_string**, a C-style string, or an **initializer_list<value_type>**
r=r.assign(x)	r=r.assign(x,regex_constants::ECMAScript)
r=r.assign(p,n,flags)	Set r's pattern to [p:p+n) and r's flags to **flags**
r=r.assign(b,e,flags)	Set r's pattern to [b:e) and r's flags to **flags**
r=r.assign(b,e)	r=r.assign(b,e,regex_constants::ECMAScript)
n=r.mark_count()	n is the number of marked subexpressions in r
x=r.flags()	x is r's **flags**
loc2=r.imbue(loc)	r gets the locale loc; loc2 is r's previous **locale**
loc=r.getloc()	loc is r's **locale**
r.swap(r2)	Exchange values of r and r2

You can determine the **locale** or a **regex** by a call of **getloc()** and learn what flags are used from **flags()**, but unfortunately there is no (standard) way of reading out its pattern. If you need to output a pattern, keep a copy of the string used to initialize. For example:

```
regex pat1 {R"(\w+\d*)"};        // no way of outputting the pattern in pat1

string s {R"(\w+\d*)"};
regex pat2 {s};
cout << s << '\n';               // the pattern in pat2
```

37.2.1 Match Results

Results from a regular expression match are gathered in a **match_results** object which contains one or more **sub_match** objects:

```
template<class Bi>
class sub_match : public pair<Bi,Bi> {
public:
    using value_type = typename iterator_traits<Bi>::value_type;
    using difference_type = typename iterator_traits<Bi>::difference_type;
    using iterator = Bi;
    using string_type = basic_string<value_type>;

    bool matched; // true if *this contains a match
    // ...
};
```

Bi must be a bidirectional iterator (§33.1.2). A **sub_match** can be seen as a pair of iterators into the string being matched.

sub_match<Bi> **Operations**	
sub_match sm {};	Default constructor: an empty sequence; constexpr
n=sm.length()	**n** is the number of characters matched
s=sm	Implicit conversion of a **sub_match** to a **basic_string**;
	s is a **basic_string** containing the characters matched
s=sm.str()	**s** is a **basic_string** containing the characters matched
x=sm.compare(x)	Lexicographical comparison: **sm.str().compare(x)**;
	x can be a **sub_match**, a **basic_string**, or a C-style string
x==y	Is **x** equal to **y**? **x** and **y** can be a **sub_match** or a **basic_string**
x!=y	!(x==y)
x<y	**x** is lexicographically before **y**
x>y	y<x
x<=y	!(x>y)
x>=y	!(x<y)
sm.matched	**true** if **sm** contains a match; **false** otherwise

For example:

```
regex pat ("<(.*?)>(.*?)</(.*?)>");

string s = "Always look for the <b> bright </b> side of <b> death </b>";

if (regex_search(s1,m,p2))
        if (m[1]==m[3]) cout << "match\n";
```

The output is **match**.

A **match_results** is a container of **sub_match**es:

```
template<class Bi, class A = allocator<sub_match<Bi>>
class match_results {
public:
        using value_type = sub_match<Bi>;
        using const_reference = const value_type&;
        using reference = const_reference;
        using const_iterator = /* implementation-defined */;
        using iterator = const_iterator;
        using difference_type = typename iterator_traits<Bi>::difference_type;
        using size_type = typename allocator_traits<A>::size_type;
        using allocator_type = A;
        using char_type = typename iterator_traits<Bi>::value_type;
        using string_type = basic_string<char_type>;

        ~match_results();     // not virtual

        // ...
};
```

Bi must be a bidirectional iterator (§33.1.2).

As for **basic_string** and **basic_ostream**, a few standard aliases are provided for the most common match_results:

```
using cmatch = match_results<const char*>;              // C-style string
using wcmatch = match_results<const wchar_t*>;          // wide C-style string
using smatch = match_results<string::const_iterator>;   // string
using wsmatch = match_results<wstring::const_iterator>; // wstring
```

A match_results provides access to its match string, its **sub_matches,** and the characters before and after the match:

	m[0]			
m.prefix()	m[1]	...	m[m.size()]	m.suffix()

A match_results provides a conventional set of operations:

regex<C,Tr> **Matches and Submatches (§iso.28.9, §iso.28.10)**	
match_results m {};	Default constructor: use **allocator_type{}**
match_results m {a};	Use allocator a; explicit
match_results m {m2};	Copy and move constructor
m2=m	Copy assignment
m2=move(m)	Move assignment
m.˜match_results()	Destructor: release all resources
m.ready()	Does m hold a complete match?
n=m.size()	n–1 is the number of subexpressions in m; n==0 if there was no match
n=m.max_size()	n is the largest possible number of **sub_matches** for m
m.empty()	m.size()==0?
r=m[i]	r is a **const** reference to the ith **sub_match** of m; m[0] represents the complete match; if i>= size(), m[i] refers to a **sub_match** representing an unmatched subexpression.
n=m.length(i)	n=m[i].length(); the number of characters of m[i]
n=m.length()	n=m.length(0)
pos=m.position(i)	pos=m[i].first; the first character of m[i]
pos=m.position()	pos=position(0)
s=m.str(i)	s=m[i].str(); a string representation of m[i]
s=m.str()	s=m.str(0)
sm=m.prefix()	sm is a **sub_match** representing the characters not matched by m in the input string coming before the match
sm=m.suffix()	sm is a **sub_match** representing the characters not matched by m in the input string coming after the match

regex<C,Tr> **Matches and Submatches (continued)(§iso.28.9, §iso.28.10)**	
p=m.begin()	p points to the first **sub_match** of **m**
p=m.end()	p points to the one-beyond-the-last **sub_match** of **m**
p=m.cbegin()	p points to the first **sub_match** of **m** (**const** iterator)
p=m.cend()	p points to the one-beyond-the-last **sub_match** of **m** (**const** iterator)
a=m.get_allocator()	a is m's allocator
m.swap(m2)	Exchange the states of **m** and **m2**
m==m2	Are the values of **sub_match**es of **m** and **m2** equal?
m!=m2	!(m==m2)

We can subscript a **regex_match** to access a **sub_match**, for example, m[i]. If a subscript, i, refers to a nonexistent **sub_match**, the result of m[i] represents an unmatched **sub_match**. For example:

```
void test()
{
    regex pat ("(AAAA)(BBB)?");
    string s = "AAAA";
    smatch m;
    regex_search(s,m,pat);

    cout << boolalpha;
    cout << m[0].matched << '\n';    // true: we found a match
    cout << m[1].matched << '\n';    // true: there was a first sub_match
    cout << m[2].matched << '\n';    // false: no second sub_match
    cout << m[3].matched << '\n';    // false: there couldn't be a third sub_match for pat
}
```

37.2.2 Formatting

In **regex_replace()**, formatting is done using a **format()** function:

regex<C,Tr> **Formatting (§iso.28.10.5)** Formatting is controlled by **match_flag_type** options	
out=m.format(out,b,e,flags)	Copy [b:e) to **out**; substituting submatches from m for format characters
out=m.format(out,b,e)	out=m.format(out,b,e,regex_constants::format_default)
out=m.format(out,fmt,flags)	out=m.format(out,begin(fmt),end(fmt),flags); fmt can be a **basic_string** or a C-style string
out=m.format(out,fmt)	out=m.format(out,fmt,regex_constants::format_default)
s=m.format(fmt,flags)	Construct **s** as a copy of **fmt**; substituting submatches from m for format characters; fmt can be a **basic_string** or a C-style string
s=m.format(fmt)	s=m.format(fmt,regex_constants::format_default)

Formats can contain formatting characters:

Format Substitution Notation	
$&	The match
$`	The prefix
$'	The suffix
$i	The ith submatch, e.g., $1
$ii	The iith submatch, e.g., $12
$$	Not a match, the $ character

For an example, see §37.3.3.

The details of formatting done by **format()** are controlled by a set of options (flags):

regex<C,Tr> **Formatting Options** (regex_constants::match_flag_type; §iso.28.5.2)	
format_default	Use ECMAScript (ECMA-262) rules (§iso.28.13)
format_sed	Use POSIX sed notation
format_no_copy	Copy only matches
format_first_only	Only the first occurrence of the regular expression is replaced

37.3 Regular Expression Functions

The functions for applying regular expression patterns to data are **regex_search()** for searching in a sequence of characters, **regex_match()** for matching a fixed-length sequence of characters, and **regex_replace()** for doing replacement of patterns.

The details of matching are controlled by a set of options (flags):

regex<C,Tr> **Matching Options** (regex_constants::match_flag_type; §iso.28.5.2)	
match_not_bol	The character ^ is not considered to mean "beginning of line"
match_not_eol	The character $ is not considered to mean "end of line"
match_not_bow	\b does not match the subsequence [first,first)
match_not_eow	\b does not match the subsequence [last,last)
match_any	If more than one match is possible, then any match is acceptable
match_not_null	Do not match an empty sequence
match_continuous	Match only a subsequence that begins at first
match_prev_avail	−−first is a valid iterator position

37.3.1 regex_match()

To look for a pattern matching a whole sequence with a known length, such as a line of text, use **regex_match()**:

Regular Expression Matching (§iso.28.11.2) Matching is controlled by **match_flag_type** options (§37.3)	
regex_match(b,e,m,pat,flags)	Does the input [b:e) match the **regex** pattern **pat**? place the result in **match_results m**; use options **flags**
regex_match(b,e,m,pat)	regex_match(b,e,m,pat,regex_constants::match_default)
regex_match(b,e,pat,flags)	Does the input [b:e) match the **regex** pattern **pat**? use options **flags**
regex_match(b,e,pat)	regex_match(b,e,pat,regex_constants::match_default)
regex_match(x,m,pat,flags)	Does the input **x** match the **regex** pattern **pat**? **x** can be a **basic_string** or a C-style string; place the result in **match_results m**; use options **flags**
regex_match(x,m,pat)	regex_match(x,m,pat,regex_constants::match_default)
regex_match(x,pat,flags)	Does the input **x** match the **regex** pattern **pat**? **x** can be a **basic_string** or a C-style string; use options **flags**
regex_match(x,pat)	regex_match(x,pat,regex_constants::match_default)

As an example, consider a naive program for validating the format of a table. If the table format is as expected, the program writes "all is well" to **cout**; if not, it writes error messages to **cerr**. A table is a series of rows, each with four tab-separated fields, except for the first (title row) which may have only three fields. For example:

```
Class     Boys     Girls     Total
1a        12       15        27
1b        16       14        30
Total     28       29        57
```

The numbers are supposed to add up horizontally and vertically.

The program reads the title line and then does the sums for each line until it reaches the final line labeled "Total":

```
int main()
{
    ifstream in("table.txt");    // input file
    if (!in) cerr << "no file\n";

    string line;      // input buffer
    int lineno = 0;

    regex header {R"(^[\w ]+(\t[\w ]+)*$)"};          // tab-separated words
    regex row {R"(^([\w ]+)(\t\d+)(\t\d+)(\t\d+)$)"};  // label followed by three tab-separated numbers

    if (getline(in,line)) { // check and discard the header line
        smatch matches;
        if (!regex_match(line,matches,header))
            cerr << "no header\n";
    }

    int boys = 0;         // running totals
    int girls = 0;
```

```
while (getline(in,line)) {
    ++lineno;
    smatch matches;                              // submatches go here

    if (!regex_match(line,matches,row))
        cerr << "bad line: " << lineno << '\n';

    int curr_boy = stoi(matches[2]);             // for stoi() see §36.3.5
    int curr_girl = stoi(matches[3]);
    int curr_total = stoi(matches[4]);
    if (curr_boy+curr_girl != curr_total)  cerr << "bad row sum \n";

    if (matches[1]=="Total") {                   // last line
        if (curr_boy != boys) cerr << "boys do not add up\n";
        if (curr_girl != girls) cerr << "girls do not add up\n";
        cout << "all is well\n";
        return 0;
    }
    boys += curr_boy;
    girls += curr_girl;
}

cerr << "didn't find total line\n")
return 1;
}
```

37.3.2 regex_search()

To look for a pattern in a part of a sequence, such as a file, use **regex_search()**:

Regular Expression Searching (§iso.28.11.3)	
Matching is controlled by **match_flag_type** options (§37.3)	
regex_search(b,e,m,pat,flags)	Does the input [b:e) contain a match for the **regex** pattern **pat**? place the result in **match_results m**; use options **flags**
regex_search(b,e,m,pat)	regex_search(b,e,m,regex_constants::match_default)
regex_search(b,e,pat,flags)	Does the input [b:e) contain a match for the the **regex** pattern **pat**? use options **flags**
regex_search(b,e,pat)	regex_search(b,e,pat,regex_constants::match_default)
regex_search(x,m,pat,flags)	Does the input x contain a match for the **regex** pattern **pat**? x can be a **basic_string** or a C-style string; place the result in **match_results m**; use options **flags**
regex_search(x,m,pat)	regex_search(x,m,pat,regex_constants::match_default)
regex_search(x,pat,flags)	Does the input x contain a match for the **regex** pattern **pat**? x can be a **basic_string** or a C-style string; use options **flags**
regex_search(x,pat)	regex_search(x,pat,regex_constants::match_default)

For example, I could look for some of the more popular misspellings of my name like this:

```
regex pat {"[Ss]tro?u?v?p?stra?o?u?p?b?"};

smatch m;
for (string s; cin>>s; )
        if (regex_search(s,m,pat))
              if (m[0]!="stroustrup" && m[0]!="Stroustrup" )
                    cout << "Found: " << m[0] << '\n';
```

Given suitable input, this will output misspellings of **Stroustrup**, such as:

Found: strupstrup
Found: Strovstrup
Found: stroustrub
Found: Stroustrop

Note that **regex_search()** will find its pattern even if it is "hidden" among other characters. For example, it will find **strustrub** in **abstrustrubal**. If you want to match a pattern against every character in an input string, use **regex_match** (§37.3.1).

37.3.3 regex_replace()

To make simple substitutions of a pattern in a part of a sequence, such as a file, use **regex_replace()**:

Regular Expression Replacement (§iso.28.11.4) Matching is controlled by match_flag_type options (§37.3)	
out=regex_replace(out,b,e,pat,fmt,flags)	Copy [b:e) to **out**, searching for the **regex** pattern **pat**; when a match for **pat** is found, copy it to **out** using the format **fmt** controlled by **flags**; fmt can be a **basic_string** or a C-style string
out=regex_replace(out,b,e,pat,fmt)	out=regex_replace(out,b,e,pat,fmt, regex_constants::match_defaults)
s=regex_replace(x,pat,fmt,flags)	Copy **x** to **s**, searching for the **regex** pattern **pat**; when a match for **pat** is found copy it to **s** using the format **fmt** controlled by **flags**; x can be a **basic_string** or a C-style string; fmt can be a **basic_string** or a C-style string
s=regex_replace(x,pat,fmt)	s=regex_replace(x,pat,fmt, regex_constants::match_defaults)

Copying a format is done using the **regex**'s **format()** (§37.2.2) with the **$** prefix notation, for example, **$&** for the match and **$2** for the second submatch. Here is a little test program that takes a string of word and number pairs and outputs them as {word,number}, one per line:

```
void test1()
{
    string input {"x 1 y2 22 zaq 34567"};
    regex pat {"(\w+)\s(\d+)"};        // word space number
    string format {"{$1,$2}\n"};

    cout << regex_replace(input,pat,format);
}
```

The output is:

```
{x,1}
{y2,22}
{zaq,34567}
```

Note the annoying "spurious" spaces at the beginning of the lines. By default, **regex_match()** copies unmatched characters to its output, so the two spaces that were not matched by **pat** are printed.

To eliminate those spaces, we can use the **format_no_copy** option (§37.2.2):

```
cout << regex_replace(input,pat,format,regex_constants::format_no_copy);
```

Now we get:

```
{x,1}
{y2,22}
{zaq,34567}
```

Submatches do not have to be output in order:

```
void test2()
{
    string input {"x 1 y 2 z 3"};
    regex pat {"(\w)\s(\d+)"}; // word space number
    string format {"$2: $1\n"};

    cout << regex_replace(input,pat,format,regex_constants::format_no_copy);
}
```

Now we get:

```
1: x
22: y2
34567: zeq
```

37.4 Regular Expression Iterators

The **regex_search()** function allows us to find a single occurrence of a pattern in a data stream. What if we wanted to find and do something to all such occurrences? If the data is organized as a sequence of easily recognized lines or records, we can iterate over those and use **regex_match()** for each. If what we want to do with each occurrence of a pattern is a simple substitution, we can use

regex_replace(). If we want to iterate over a sequence of characters doing something for each occurrence of a pattern, we use a **regex_iterator**.

37.4.1 regex_iterator

A **regex_iterator** is a bidirectional iterator that searches a sequence for the next match of a pattern when incremented:

```
template<class Bi,
         class C = typename iterator_traits<Bi>::value_type,
         class Tr = typename regex_traits<C>::type>
class regex_iterator {
public:
    using regex_type = basic_regex<C,Tr>;
    using value_type = match_results<Bi>;
    using difference_type = ptrdiff_t;
    using pointer = const value_type*;
    using reference = const value_type&;
    using iterator_category = forward_iterator_tag;
    // ...
}
```

The **regex_traits** are described in §37.5.

The usual set of aliases is provided:

```
using cregex_iterator = regex_iterator<const char*>;
using wcregex_iterator = regex_iterator<const wchar_t*>;
using sregex_iterator = regex_iterator<string::const_iterator>;
using wsregex_iterator = regex_iterator<wstring::const_iterator>;
```

A **regex_iterator** provides a minimal set of iterator operations:

regex_iterator<Bi,C,Tr> (§iso.28.12.1)	
regex_iterator p {};	p is end-of-sequence
regex_iterator p {b,e,pat,flags);	Iterate over [b:e), looking for matches of **pat** using options **flags**
regex_iterator p {b,e,pat);	p is initialized with {b,e,pat,regex_constants::match_default}
regex_iterator p {q};	Copy constructor (no move constructor)
p=q	Copy assignment (no move assignment)
p==q	Does **p** point to the same **sub_match** as **q**?
p!=q	!(p==q)
c=*p	c is the current **sub_match**
x=p–>m	x=(*p).m
++p	Make **p** point to the next occurrence of **p**'s pattern
q=p++	q=p, then ++p

A **regex_iterator** is a bidirectional iterator, so we cannot directly iterate over an **istream**.

As an example, we can output all whitespace-separated words in a **string**:

```
void test()
{
    string input = "aa as; asd ++e^asdf asdfg";
    regex pat {R"(\s+(\w+))"};
    for (sregex_iterator p(input.begin(),input.end(),pat); p!=sregex_iterator{}; ++p)
        cout << (*p)[1] << '\n';
}
```

This outputs:

```
as
asd
asdfg
```

Note that we are missing the first word, **aa**, because it has no preceding whitespace. If we simplify the pattern to R"((\ew+))", we get

```
aa
as
asd
e
asdf
asdfg
```

You cannot write through a **regex_iterator** and **regex_iterator{}** is the only possible end-of-sequence.

37.4.2 regex_token_iterator

A **regex_token_iterator** is an adaptor for **regex_iterator** that iterates over **sub_match**es of the **match_results** found:

```
template<class Bi,
    class C = typename iterator_traits<Bi>::value_type,
    class Tr = typename regex_traits<C>::type>
class regex_token_iterator {
public:
    using regex_type = basic_regex<C,Tr>;
    using value_type = sub_match<Bi>;
    using difference_type = ptrdiff_t;
    using pointer = const value_type*;
    using reference = const value_type&;
    using iterator_category = forward_iterator_tag;
    // ...
```

The **regex_traits** are described in §37.5.

The usual set of aliases is provided:

```
using cregex_token_iterator = regex_token_iterator<const char*>;
using wcregex_token_iterator = regex_token_iterator<const wchar_t*>;
using sregex_token_iterator = regex_token_iterator<string::const_iterator>;
using wsregex_token_iterator = regex_token_iterator<wstring::const_iterator>;
```

A **regex_token_iterator** provides a minimal set of iterator operations:

regex_token_iterator (§iso.28.12.2)	
regex_token_iterator p {};	p is the end-of-sequence
regex_token_iterator p {b,e,pat,x,flags};	x lists the indices of the sub_matches to be included in the iteration or 0, meaning "the whole match," or –1, meaning "represent each character sequence not matched as a sub_match";
	x can be an int, an initializer_list<int>, a const vector<int>&, or a const int (&sub_match)[N]
regex_token_iterator p {b,e,pat,x};	p is initialized with {b,e,pat,x,regex_constants::match_default}
regex_token_iterator p {b,e,pat};	p is initialized with {b,e,pat,0,regex_constants::match_default}
regex_token_iterator p {q};	Copy constructor (no move constructor)
p.˜regex_token_iterator()	Destructor: release all resources
p=q	Copy assignment (no move assignment)
p==q	Does p point to the same sub_match as q?
p!=q	!(p==q)
c=∗p	c is the current sub_match
x=p–>m	x=(∗p).m
++p	Make p point to the next occurrence of p's pattern
q=p++	q=p, then ++p

The **x** argument lists the **sub_match**es to be included in the iteration. For example (iterating over matches **1** and **3**):

```
void test1()
{
    string input {"aa::bb cc::dd ee::ff"};
    regex pat {R"((\w+)([[:punct:]]+)(\w+)\s∗)"};
    sregex_token_iterator end {};
    for (sregex_token_iterator p{input.begin(),input.end(),pat,{1,3}}; p!=end; ++p)
        cout << ∗p << '\n';
}
```

This gives the output:

```
aa
bb
cc
dd
ee
ff
```

The **–1** option basically inverts the strategy for reporting matches by representing each character sequence that does *not* match as a **sub_match**. This is often referred to as *token* **splitting** (that is, splitting a character stream into tokens) because when your pattern matches the token separators, option –1 leaves you with the tokens. For example:

```
void test2()
{
    string s {"1,2 , 3 ,4,5, 6 7"};          // input
    regex pat {R"(\s*,\s*)"};                // use comma as token    separator
    copy(sregex_token_iterator{s.begin(),s.end(),pat,–1}},
        sregex_token_iterator{},
        ostream_iterator<string>{cout,"\n"});
}
```

The output is:

```
1
2
3
4
5
6 7
```

This could equivalently be written using an explicit loop:

```
void test3()
{
    sregex_token_iterator end{};
    for (sregex_token_iterator p {s.begin(),s.end(),pat,–1}; p!=end; ++p)
        cout << *p << '\n';
}
```

37.5 regex_traits

A **regex_traits<T>** represents the correspondence between a character type, a string type, and a locale as needed for a **regex** implementer:

```
template<class C>
struct regex_traits {
public:
    using char_type = C;
    using string_type = basic_string<char_type>;
    using locale_type = locale;
    using char_class_type = /* implementation-defined bitmask type */;
    // ...
};
```

The standard library provides specializations **regex_traits<char>** and **regex_traits<wchar_t>**.

regex_traits<C> **Operations** (§iso.28.7)	
regex_traits tr {};	Make a default **regex_trait<C>**
n=length(p)	n is the number of characters in the C-style string **p**; n=char_traits<C>::length(); static
c2=tr.translate(c)	c2=c, that is, a no-op
c2=tr.translate_nocase(c)	use_facet<ctype<C>>(getloc()).tolower(c); §39.4.5
s=tr.transform(b,e)	s is a string that can be used to compare [b:e) to others strings; §39.4.1
s=tr.transform_primary(b,e)	s is a string that can be used to compare [b:e) to others strings; ignore case; §39.4.1
s=tr.lookup_collatename(b,e)	s is the **string** name of the collating element named [b:e) or the empty string
m=tr.lookup_classname(b,e,ign)	m is the string name of the classification mask for the character classification named [b:e); ignore case if **ign==true**
m=tr.lookup_classname(b,e)	m=tr.lookup_classname(b,e,false)
tr.isctype(c,m)	Is c classified as an m? m is a **class_type**
i=tr.value(c,b)	i is the integer value represented by c in base **b**; b must be **8, 10**, or **16**
loc2=tr.imbue(loc)	Set tr's locale to **loc**; loc2 is tr's previous locale
loc=tr.getloc()	loc is tr's locale

A transform is used to generate strings for fast comparisons in pattern-matching implementations.

A classification name is one of the character classifications listed in §37.1.1, such as **alpha**, **s**, and **xdigit**.

37.6 Advice

[1]   Use **regex** for most conventional uses of regular expressions; §37.1.
[2]   The regular expression notation can be adjusted to match various standards; §37.1.1, §37.2.
[3]   The default regular expression notation is that of ECMAScript; §37.1.1.
[4]   For portability, use the character class notation to avoid nonstandard abbreviations; §37.1.1.
[5]   Be restrained; regular expressions can easily become a write-only language; §37.1.1.
[6]   Prefer raw string literals for expressing all but the simplest patterns; §37.1.1.
[7]   Note that \i allows you to express a subpattern in terms of a previous subpattern; §37.1.1.
[8]   Use **?** to make patterns "lazy"; §37.1.1, §37.2.1.
[9]   **regex** can use ECMAScript, POSIX, awk, grep, and egrep notation; §37.2.
[10] Keep a copy of the pattern string in case you need to output it; §37.2.
[11] Use **regex_search()** for looking at streams of characters and **regex_match()** to look for fixed layouts; §37.3.2, §37.3.1.

38

I/O Streams

What you see is all you get.
– Brian W. Kernighan

38.1 Introduction

The I/O stream library provides formatted and unformatted buffered I/O of text and numeric values. The definitions for I/O stream facilities are found in **<istream>**, **<ostream>**, etc.; see §30.2.

An **ostream** converts typed objects to a stream of characters (bytes):

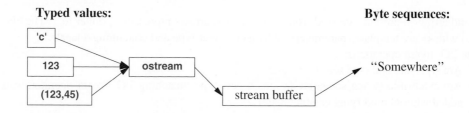

An **istream** converts a stream of characters (bytes) to typed objects:

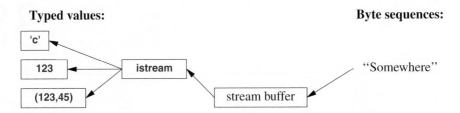

An **iostream** is a stream that can act as both an **istream** and an **ostream**. The buffers in the diagrams are stream buffers (**streambufs**; §38.6). You need them to define a mapping from an **iostream** to a new kind of device, file, or memory. The operations on **istreams** and **ostreams** are described in §38.4.1 and §38.4.2.

Knowledge of the techniques used to implement the stream library is not needed to use the library. So I present only the general ideas needed to understand and use **iostreams**. If you need to implement the standard streams, provide a new kind of stream, or provide a new locale, you need a copy of the standard, a good systems manual, and examples of working code in addition to what is presented here.

The key components of the stream I/O system can be represented graphically like this:

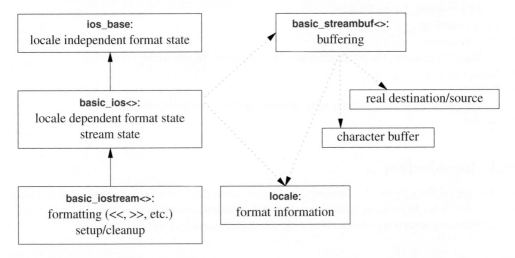

The solid arrows represent "derived from." The dotted arrows represent "pointer to." The classes marked with <> are templates parameterized by a character type and containing a **locale**.

The I/O stream operations:

- Are type-safe and type sensitive
- Are extensible (when someone designs a new type, matching I/O stream operators can be added without modifying existing code)

- Are locale sensitive (Chapter 39)
- Are efficient (though their potential is not always fully realized)
- Are interoperable with C-style stdio (§43.3)
- Include formatted, unformatted, and character-level operations

The **basic_iostream** is defined based on **basic_istream** (§38.6.2) and **basic_ostream** (§38.6.1):

```
template<typename C, typename Tr = char_traits<C>>
class basic_iostream :
    public basic_istream<C,Tr>, public basic_ostream<C,Tr> {
public:
    using char_type = C;
    using int_type = typename Tr::int_type;
    using pos_type = typename Tr::pos_type;
    using off_type = typename Tr::off_type;
    using traits_type = Tr;

    explicit basic_iostream(basic_streambuf<C,Tr>* sb);
    virtual ˜basic_iostream();
protected:
    basic_iostream(const basic_iostream& rhs) = delete;
    basic_iostream(basic_iostream&& rhs);

    basic_iostream& operator=(const basic_iostream& rhs) = delete;
    basic_iostream& operator=(basic_iostream&& rhs);
    void swap(basic_iostream& rhs);
};
```

The template parameters specify the character type and the traits used to manipulate characters (§36.2.2), respectively.

Note that no copy operations are provided: sharing or cloning the fairly complex state of a stream would be difficult to implement and expensive to use. The move operations are intended for use by derived classes and are therefore **protected**. Moving an **iostream** without moving the state of its defining derived class (e.g., an **fstream**) would lead to errors.

There are three standard streams:

Standard I/O Streams	
cout	The standard character output (often by default a screen)
cin	The standard character input (often by default a keyboard)
cerr	The standard character error output (unbuffered)
clog	The standard character error output (buffered)
wcin	**wistream** version of **cin**
wcout	**wostream** version of **cout**
wcerr	**wostream** version of **cerr**
wclog	**wostream** version of **clog**

Forward declarations for stream types and stream objects are provided in **<iosfwd>**.

38.2   The I/O Stream Hierarchy

An **istream** can be connected to an input device (e.g., a keyboard), a file, or a **string**. Similarly, an **ostream** can be connected to an output device (e.g., a text window or an HTML engine), a file, or a **string**. The I/O stream facilities are organized in a class hierarchy:

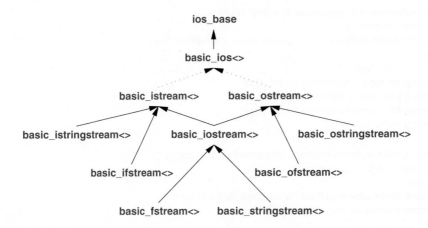

The classes suffixed by <> are templates parameterized on the character type. A dotted line indicates a virtual base class (§21.3.5).

The key class is **basic_ios** in which most of the implementation and many of the operations are defined. However, most casual (and not-so-casual) users never see it: it is mostly an implementation detail of the streams. It is described in §38.4.4. Most of its facilities are described in the context of their function (e.g., formatting; §38.4.5).

38.2.1   File Streams

In <fstream>, the standard library provides streams to and from a file:
- **ifstream**s for reading from a file
- **ofstream**s for writing to a file
- **fstream**s for reading from and writing to a file

The file streams follow a common pattern, so I describe only **fstream**:

```
template<typename C, typename Tr=char_traits<C>>
class basic_fstream
: public basic_iostream<C,Tr> {
public:
     using char_type = C;
     using int_type = typename Tr::int_type;
     using pos_type = typename Tr::pos_type;        // for positions in file
     using off_type = typename Tr::off_type;        // for offsets in file
     using traits_type = Tr;
     // ...
};
```

The set of **fstream** operations is fairly simple:

basic_fstream<C,Tr> (§iso.27.9)	
fstream fs {};	fs is a file stream not attached to a file
fstream fs {s,m};	fs is a file stream opened for a file called s with mode m; s can be a **string** or a C-style string
fstream fs {fs2};	Move constructor: fs2 is moved to fs; fs2 becomes unattached
fs=move(fs2)	Move assignment: fs2 is moved to fs; fs2 becomes unattached
fs.swap(fs2)	Exchange the states of fs and fs2
p=fs.rdbuf()	p is a pointer to fs's file stream buffer (**basic_filebuf<C,Tr>**)
fs.is_open()	Is fs open?
fs.open(s,m)	Open a file called s with mode m and have fs refer to it; sets fs's **failbit** if it couldn't open the file; s can be a **string** or a C-style string
fs.close()	Close the file associated with fs (if any)

In addition, the string streams override the **basic_ios** protected virtual functions **underflow()**, **pback-fail()**, **overflow()**, **setbuf()**, **seekoff()**, and **seekpos()** (§38.6).

A file stream does not have copy operations. If you want two names to refer to the same file stream, use a reference or a pointer, or carefully manipulate file **streambuf**s (§38.6).

If an **fstream** fails to open, the stream is in the **bad()** state (§38.3).

There are six file stream aliases defined in **<fstream>**:

```
using ifstream = basic_ifstream<char>;
using wifstream = basic_ifstream<wchar_t>;
using ofstream = basic_ofstream<char>;
using wofstream = basic_ofstream<wchar_t>;
using fstream = basic_fstream<char>;
using wfstream = basic_fstream<wchar_t>;
```

You can open a file in one of several modes, as specified in **ios_base** (§38.4.4):

Stream Modes (§iso.27.5.3.1.4)	
ios_base::app	Append (i.e., add to the end of the file)
ios_base::ate	"At end" (open and seek to the end)
ios_base::binary	Binary mode; beware of system-specific behavior
ios_base::in	For reading
ios_base::out	For writing
ios_base::trunc	Truncate the file to 0 length

In each case, the exact effect of opening a file may depend on the operating system, and if an operating system cannot honor a request to open a file in a certain way, the result will be a stream that is in the **bad()** state (§38.3). For example:

```
ofstream ofs("target");        // "o" for "output" implying ios::out
if (!ofs)
    error("couldn't open 'target' for writing");
```

```
fstream ifs;                    // "i" for "input" implying ios::in
ifs.open("source",ios_base::in);
if (!ifs)
        error("couldn't open 'source' for reading");
```

For positioning in a file, see §38.6.1.

38.2.2 String Streams

In **<sstream>**, the standard library provides streams to and from a **string**:

- **istringstreams** for reading from a **string**
- **ostringstreams** for writing to a **string**
- **stringstreams** for reading from and writing to a **string**

The string streams follow a common pattern, so I describe only **stringstream**:

```
template<typename C, typename Tr = char_traits<C>, typename A = allocator<C>>
class basic_stringstream
        : public basic_iostream<C,Tr> {
public:
        using char_type = C;
        using int_type = typename Tr::int_type;
        using pos_type = typename Tr::pos_type;        // for positions in string
        using off_type = typename Tr::off_type;  // for offsets in string
        using traits_type = Tr;
        using allocator_type = A;

        // ...
```

The **stringstream** operations are:

basic_stringstream<C,Tr,A> (§iso.27.8)	
stringstream ss {m};	ss is an empty string stream with mode m
stringstream ss {};	Default constructor: stringstream ss {ios_base::out|ios_base::in};
stringstream ss {s,m};	ss is a string stream with its buffer initialized from the string s with mode m
stringstream ss {s};	stringstream ss {s,ios_base::out|ios_base::in};
stringstream ss {ss2};	Move constructor: ss2 is moved to ss; ss2 becomes empty
ss=move(ss2)	Move assignment: ss2 is moved to ss; ss2 becomes empty
p=ss.rdbuf()	p points to ss's string stream buffer (a basic_stringbuf<C,Tr,A>)
s=ss.str()	s is a string copy of the characters in ss: s=ss.rdbuf()–>str()
ss.str(s)	ss's buffer is initialized from the string s: ss.rdbuf()–>str(s);
	if ss's mode is ios::ate ("at end") values written to ss
	are added after the characters from s;
	otherwise values written overwrites the characters from s
ss.swap(ss2)	Exchange the states of ss and ss2

The open modes are described in §38.4.4. For an **istringstream**, the default mode is **ios_base::in**. For an **ostringstream**, the default mode is **ios_base::out**.

In addition, the string streams override the **basic_ios** protected virtual functions **underflow()**, **pbackfail()**, **overflow()**, **setbuf()**, **seekoff()**, and **seekpos()** (§38.6).

A string stream does not have copy operations. If you want two names to refer to the same string stream, use a reference or a pointer.

There are six string stream aliases defined in **<sstream>**:

```
using istringstream = basic_istringstream<char>;
using wistringstream = basic_istringstream<wchar_t>;
using ostringstream = basic_ostringstream<char>;
using wostringstream = basic_ostringstream<wchar_t>;
using stringstream = basic_stringstream<char>;
using wstringstream = basic_stringstream<wchar_t>;
```

For example:

```
void test()
{
    ostringstream oss {"Label: ",ios::ate};        // write at end
    cout << oss.str() << '\n';  // writes "Label: "
    oss<<"val";
    cout << oss.str() << '\n';   // writes "Label: val" ("val" appended after "Label: ")

    ostringstream oss2 {"Label: "};                // write at beginning
    cout << oss2.str() << '\n'; // writes "Label: "
    oss2<<"val";
    cout << oss2.str() << '\n'; // writes "valel: " (val overwrites "Label: ")
}
```

I tend to use **str()** only to read a result from an **istringstream**.

It is not possible to directly output a string stream; **str()** must be used:

```
void test2()
{
    istringstream iss;
    iss.str("Foobar");         // Fill iss

    cout << iss << '\n';       // writes 1
    cout << iss.str() << '\n'; // OK: writes "Foobar"
}
```

The reason for the probably surprising **1** is that an **iostream** converts to its state for testing:

```
if (iss) {   // the last operation of iss succeeded; iss's state is good() or eof()
    // ...
}
else {
    // handle problem
}
```

38.3 Error Handling

An **iostream** can be in one of four states, defined in **basic_ios** from <ios> (§38.4.4):

Stream States (§iso.27.5.5.4)	
good()	The previous **iostream** operations succeeded
eof()	We hit end-of-input ("end-of-file")
fail()	Something unexpected happened (e.g., we looked for a digit and found '**x**')
bad()	Something unexpected and serious happened (e.g., disk read error)

Any operation attempted on a stream that is not in the **good()** state has no effect; it is a no-op. An **iostream** can be used as a condition. In that case, the condition is true (succeeds) if the state of the **iostream** is **good()**. That is the basis for the idiom for reading a stream of values:

```
for (X x; cin>>x;) {   // read into an input buffer of type X
    // ... do something with x ...
}
// we get here when >> couldn't read another X from cin
```

After a read failure, we might be able to clear the stream and proceed:

```
int i;
if (cin>>i) {
    // ... use i ...
} else if (cin.fail()){   // possibly a formatting error
    cin.clear();
    string s;
    if (cin>>s) {     // we might be able to use a string to recover
        // ... use s ...
    }
}
```

Alternatively, errors can be handled using exceptions:

Exception Control: basic_ios<C,Tr> (§38.4.4, §iso.27.5.5)	
st=ios.exceptions()	st is the **iostate** of **ios**
ios.exceptions(st)	Set **ios**'s **iostate** to **st**

For example, we can make **cin** throw a **basic_ios::failure** when its state is set to **bad()** (e.g., by a cin.setstate(ios_base::badbit)):

```
cin.exceptions(cin.exceptions()|ios_base::badbit);
```

For example:

```
struct Io_guard {     // RAII class for iostream exceptions
    iostream& s;
    auto old_e = s.exceptions();
    Io_guard(iostream& ss, ios_base::iostate e) :s{ss} { s.exceptions(s.exceptions()|e); }
    ˜Io_guard() { s.exceptions(old_e); }
};
```

```
    void use(istream& is)
    {
        Io_guard guard(is.ios_base::badbit);
        // ... use is ...
    }
    catch (ios_base::badbit) {
        // ... bail out! ...
    }
```

I tend to use exceptions to handle **iostream** errors that I don't expect to be able to recover from. That usually means all **bad()** exceptions.

38.4 I/O Operations

The complexity of the I/O operations reflects tradition, the need for I/O performance, and the variety of human expectations. The description here is based on the conventional English small character set (ASCII). The ways in which different character sets and different natural languages are handled are described in Chapter 39.

38.4.1 Input Operations

Input operations are provided by **istream** (§38.6.2), found in **<istream>** except for the ones reading into a **string**; those are found in **<string>**. The **basic_istream** is primarily intended as a base class for more specific input classes, such as **istream** and **istringstream**:

```
    template<typename C, typename Tr = char_traits<C>>
    class basic_istream : virtual public basic_ios<C,Tr> {
    public:
        using char_type = C;
        using int_type = typename Tr::int_type;
        using pos_type = typename Tr::pos_type;
        using off_type = typename Tr::off_type;
        using traits_type = Tr;

        explicit basic_istream(basic_streambuf<C,Tr>* sb);
        virtual ˜basic_istream();  // release all resources

        class sentry;
        // ...
    protected:
        // move but no copy:
        basic_istream(const basic_istream& rhs) = delete;
        basic_istream(basic_istream&& rhs);
        basic_istream& operator=(const basic_istream& rhs) = delete;
        basic_istream& operator=(basic_istream&& rhs);
        // ...
    };
```

To users of an **istream**, the **sentry** class is an implementation detail. It provides common code for standard-library and user-defined input operations. Code that needs to be executed first (the "prefix code") – such as flushing a tied stream – is provided as the **sentry**'s constructor. For example:

```
template<typename C, typename Tr = char_traits<C>>
basic_ostream<C,Tr>& basic_ostream<C,Tr>::operator<<(int i)
{
    sentry s {*this};
    if (!s) {                      // check whether all is well for output to start
        setstate(failbit);
        return *this;
    }

    // ... output the int ...
    return *this;
}
```

A **sentry** is used by implementers of input operations rather than by their users.

38.4.1.1 Formatted Input

Formatted input is primarily supplied by the >> ("input," "get," or "extraction") operator:

Formatted Input (§iso.27.7.2.2, §iso.21.4.8.9)	
in>>x	Read from **in** into **x** according to **x**'s type; **x** can be an arithmetic type, a pointer, a **basic_string**, a **valarray**, a **basic_streambuf**, or any type for which the user has supplied a suitable **operator>>()**
getline(in,s)	Read a line from **in** into the **string s**

Built-in types are "known" to **istream** (and **ostream**), so if **x** is a built-in type, **cin>>x** means **cin.operator>>(x)**. If **x** is a user-defined type, **cin>>x**, means **operator>>(cin,x)** (§18.2.5). That is, **iostream** input is type sensitive, inherently type-safe, and extensible. A designer of a new type can provide I/O operations without direct access to the implementation of **iostream**.

If a pointer to a function is the target of >>, that function will be invoked with the **istream** as its argument. For example, **cin>>pf** yields **pf(cin)**. This is the basis for the input manipulators, such as **skipws** (§38.4.5.2). Output stream manipulators are more common than input stream manipulators, so the technique is explained further in §38.4.3.

Unless otherwise stated, an **istream** operation returns a reference to its **istream**, so that we can "chain" operations. For example:

```
template<typename T1, typename T2>
void read_pair(T1& x, T2& y)
{
    cin >> c1 >> x >> c2 >> y >> c3;
    if (c1!='{' || c2!=',' || c3!='}') {          // unrecoverable input format error
        cin.setstate(ios_base::badbit);           // set badbit
        throw runtime_error("bad read of pair");
    }
}
```

By default >> skips whitespace. For example:

```
for (int i; cin>>i && 0<i;)
    cout << i << '\n';
```

This will take a sequence of whitespace-separated positive integers and print them one to a line.

Skipping of whitespace can be suppressed using noskipws (§38.4.5.2).

The input operations are not virtual. That is, a user cannot do an in>>base where base is a class hierarchy and automatically have the >> resolved to an operation on the appropriate derived class. However, a simple technique can deliver that behavior; see §38.4.2.1. Furthermore, it is possible to extend such a scheme to be able to read objects of essentially arbitrary types from an input stream; see §22.2.4.

38.4.1.2 Unformatted Input

Unformatted input can be used for finer control of reading and potentially for improved performance. One use of unformatted input is the implementation of formatted input:

Unformatted Input (§iso.27.7.2.3, §iso.27.7.2.3)	
x=in.get()	Read one character from in and return its integer value; return EOF for end-of-file
in.get(c)	Read a character from in into c
in.get(p,n,t)	Read at most n characters from in into [p:...); consider t a terminator
in.get(p,n)	in.get(p,n,'\n')
in.getline(p,n,t)	Read at most n characters from in into [p:...); consider t a terminator; remove terminator from in
in.getline(p,n)	in.getline(p,n,'\n')
in.read(p,n)	read at most n characters from in into [p:...)
x=in.gcount()	x is the number of characters read by the most recent unformatted input operation on in
in.putback(c)	Put c back into in's stream buffer
in.unget()	Back up in's stream buffer by one, so that the next character read is the same as the previous character
in.ignore(n,d)	Extract characters from in and discard them until either n characters have been discarded or d is found (and discarded)
in.ignore(n)	in.ignore(n,traits::eof())
in.ignore()	in.ignore(1,traits::eof())
in.swap(in2)	Exchange the values of in and in2

If you have a choice, use formatted input (§38.4.1.1) instead these low-level input functions.

The simple get(c) is useful when you need to compose your values out of characters. The other get() function and getline() read sequences of characters into a fixed-size area [p:...). They read until they reach the maximum number of characters or find their terminator character (by default '\n'). They place a 0 at the end of the characters (if any) written to; getline() removes its terminator from the input, if found, whereas get() does not. For example:

```
void f()      // low-level, old-style line read
{
    char word[MAX_WORD][MAX_LINE];          // MAX_WORD arrays of MAX_LINE char each
    int i = 0;
    while(cin.getline(word[i++],MAX_LINE,'\n') && i<MAX_WORD)
        /* do nothing */ ;
    // ...
}
```

For these functions, it is not immediately obvious what terminated the read:

- We found the terminator.
- We read the maximum number of characters.
- We hit end-of-file.
- There was a non-format input error.

The last two alternatives are handled by looking at the file state (§38.3). Typically, the appropriate actions are quite different for these cases.

A **read(p,n)** does not write a **0** to the array after the characters read. Obviously, the formatted input operators are simpler to use and less error-prone than the unformatted ones.

The following functions depend on the detailed interaction between the stream buffer (§38.6) and the real data source and should be used only if necessary and then very carefully:

Unformatted Input (§iso.27.7.2.3)	
x=in.peek()	**x** is the current input character; **x** is not extracted from **in**'s stream buffer and will be the next character read
n=in.readsome(p,n)	If **rdbuf()–>in_avail()==–1**, call **setstate(eofbit)**; otherwise read at **min(n,most rdbuf()–>in_avail())** characters into [p:...); **n** is the number of characters read
x=in.sync()	Synchronize buffers: **in.rdbuf()–>pubsync()**
pos=in.tellg()	**pos** is the position of **in**'s get pointer
in.seekg(pos)	Place **in**'s get pointer at position **pos**
in.seekg(off,dir)	Place **in**'s get pointer at the offset **off** in the direction **dir**

38.4.2 Output Operations

Output operations are provided by **ostream** (§38.6.1), found in **<ostream>** except for the ones writing out a **string**; those are found in **<string>**:

```
template<typename C, typename Tr = char_traits<C>>
class basic_ostream : virtual public basic_ios<C,Tr> {
public:
    using char_type = C;
    using int_type = typename Tr::int_type;
    using pos_type = typename Tr::pos_type;
    using off_type = typename Tr::off_type;
    using traits_type = Tr;
```

```
    explicit basic_ostream(basic_streambuf<char_type,Tr>* sb);
    virtual ~basic_ostream(); // release all resources

    class sentry;   // see §38.4.1
    // ...
protected:
    // move but no copy:
    basic_ostream(const basic_ostream& rhs) = delete;
    basic_ostream(basic_ostream&& rhs);
    basic_ostream& operator=(basic_ostream& rhs) = delete;
    basic_ostream& operator=(const basic_ostream&& rhs);
    // ...
};
```

An **ostream** offers formatted output, unformatted output (output of characters), and simple operations on its **streambuf** (§38.6):

Output Operations (§iso.27.7.3.6, §iso.27.7.3.7, §iso.21.4.8.9)	
out<<x	Write **x** to **out** according to **x**'s type; **x** can be an arithmetic type, a pointer, a **basic_string**, a **bitset**, a **complex**, a **valarray**, or any type for which a user has defined a suitable **operator<<()**
out.put(c)	Write the character **c** to **out**
out.write(p,n)	Write the characters [**p**:**p+n**) to **out**
out.flush()	Empty the character buffer to the destination
pos=out.tellp()	**pos** is the position of **out**'s put pointer
out.seekp(pos)	Place **out**'s put pointer at position **pos**
out.seekp(off,dir)	Place **out**'s put pointer at the offset **off** in the direction **dir**

Unless otherwise stated, an **ostream** operation returns a reference to its **ostream**, so that we can "chain" operations. For example:

```
cout << "The value of x is " << x << '\n';
```

Note that **char** values are output as characters rather than small integers. For example:

```
void print_val(char ch)
{
    cout << "the value of '" << ch << "' is " << int{ch} << '\n';
}

void test()
{
    print_val('a');
    print_val('A');
}
```

This prints:

```
the value of 'a' is 97
the value of 'A' is 65
```

Versions of operator << for user-defined types are usually trivial to write:

```
template<typename T>
struct Named_val {
    string name;
    T value;
};

ostream& operator<<(ostream& os, const Named_val& nv)
{
    return os << '{' << nv.name << ':' << nv.value << '}';
}
```

This will work for every **Named_val<X>** where **X** has a << defined. For full generality, << must be defined for **basic_string<C,Tr>**.

38.4.2.1 Virtual Output Functions

The **ostream** members are not **virtual**. The output operations that a programmer can add are not members, so they cannot be **virtual** either. One reason for this is to achieve close to optimal performance for simple operations such as putting a character into a buffer. This is a place where run-time efficiency is often crucial so that inlining is a must. Virtual functions are used to achieve flexibility for the operations dealing with buffer overflow and underflow only (§38.6).

However, a programmer sometimes wants to output an object for which only a base class is known. Since the exact type isn't known, correct output cannot be achieved simply by defining a << for each new type. Instead, a virtual output function can be provided in an abstract base:

```
class My_base {
public:
    // ...
    virtual ostream& put(ostream& s) const = 0;   // write *this to s
};

ostream& operator<<(ostream& s, const My_base& r)
{
    return r.put(s); // use the right put()
}
```

That is, **put()** is a virtual function that ensures that the right output operation is used in <<.

Given that, we can write:

```
class Sometype : public My_base {
public:
    // ...
    ostream& put(ostream& s) const override;      // the real output function
};

void f(const My_base& r, Sometype& s) // use << which calls the right put()
{
    cout << r << s;
}
```

This integrates the virtual **put()** into the framework provided by **ostream** and **<<**. The technique is generally useful to provide operations that act like virtual functions, but with the run-time selection based on their second argument. This is similar to the technique that under the name *double dispatch* is often used to select an operation based on two dynamic types (§22.3.1). A similar technique can be used to make input operations **virtual** (§22.2.4).

38.4.3 Manipulators

If a pointer to function is given as the second argument to **<<**, the function pointed to is called. For example, **cout<<pf** means **pf(cout)**. Such a function is called a *manipulator*. Manipulators that take arguments can be useful. For example:

```
cout << setprecision(4) << angle;
```

This prints the value of the floating-point variable **angle** with four digits.

To do this, **setprecision** returns an object that is initialized by **4** and calls **cout.precision(4)** when invoked. Such a manipulator is a function object that is invoked by **<<** rather than by **()**. The exact type of that function object is implementation-defined, but it might be defined like this:

```
struct smanip {
    ios_base& (*f)(ios_base&,int);            // function to be called
    int i;                                    // value to be used
    smanip(ios_base&(*ff)(ios_base&,int), int ii) :f{ff}, i{ii} { }
};

template<typename C, typename Tr>
basic_ostream<C,Tr>& operator<<(basic_ostream<C,Tr>& os, const smanip& m)
{
    m.f(os,m.i);     // call m's f with m's stored value
    return os;
}
```

We can now define **setprecision()** like this:

```
inline smanip setprecision(int n)
{
    auto h = [](ios_base& s, int x) -> ios_base& { s.precision(x); return s; };
    return smanip(h,n);          // make the function object
}
```

The explicit specification of the return type for the lambda is needed to return a reference. An **ios_base** cannot be copied by a user.

We can now write:

```
cout << setprecision(4) << angle;
```

A programmer can define new manipulators in the style of **smanip** as needed. Doing this does not require modification of the definitions of standard-library templates and classes.

The standard-library manipulators are described in §38.4.5.2.

38.4.4 Stream State

In `<ios>`, the standard library defines the base class `ios_base` defining most of the interface to a stream class:

```
template<typename C, typename Tr = char_traits<C>>
class basic_ios : public ios_base {
public:
    using char_type = C;
    using int_type = typename Tr::int_type;
    using pos_type = typename Tr::pos_type;
    using off_type = Tr::off_type;
    using traits_type = Tr;
    // ...
};
```

The `basic_ios` class manages the state of a stream:

- The mapping between a stream and its buffers (§38.6)
- The formatting options (§38.4.5.1)
- The use of `locale`s (Chapter 39)
- Error handling (§38.3)
- Connections to other streams and stdio (§38.4.4)

It might be the most complicated class in the standard library.

The `ios_base` holds information that does not depend on template arguments:

```
class ios_base {
public:
    using fmtflags = /* implementation-defined type */;
    using iostate = /* implementation-defined type */;
    using openmode = /* implementation-defined type */;
    using seekdir = /* implementation-defined type */;

    class failure;      // exception class
    class Init;         // initialize standard iostreams
};
```

The implementation-defined types are all *bitmask types*; that is, they support bitwise logical operations, such as `&` and `|`. Examples are `int` (§11.1.2) and `bitset` (§34.2.2).

The `ios_base` controls an `iostream`'s connection (or lack thereof) to `stdio` (§43.3):

Fundamental `ios_base` Operations (§iso.27.5.3.4)	
`ios_base b {};`	Default constructor; protected
`ios.~ios_base()`	Destructor; virtual
`b2=sync_with_stdio(b)`	If `b==true` synchronize `ios` with stdio; otherwise shared buffers might be corrupted; `b` is the previous synchronization state; static
`b=sync_with_stdio()`	`b=sync_with_stdio(true)`

A call of `sync_with_stdio(true)` before the first `iostream` operation in the execution of a program guarantees that the iostream and stdio (§43.3) I/O operations share buffers. A call of sync_with_stdio(false) before the first stream I/O operation prevents buffer sharing and can improve I/O performance significantly on some implementations.

Note that ios_base has no copy or move operations.

ios_base **Stream State** iostate **Member Constants** (§iso.27.5.3.1.3)	
badbit	Something unexpected and serious happened (e.g., a disk read error)
failbit	Something unexpected happened (e.g., we looked for a digit and found 'x')
eofbit	We hit end-of-input (e.g., end-of-file)
goodbit	All is well

Functions for reading these bits (good(), fail(), etc.) in a stream are provided by basic_ios.

ios_base **Mode** openmode **Member Constants** (§iso.27.5.3.1.4)	
app	Append (insert output at end-of-stream)
ate	At end (position to end-of-stream)
binary	Don't apply formatting to characters
in	Input stream
out	Output stream
trunc	Truncate stream before use (set the stream's size to zero)

The exact meaning of ios_base::binary is implementation-dependent. However, the usual meaning is that a character gets mapped to a byte. For example:

```
template<typename T>
char∗ as_bytes(T& i)
{
    return static_cast<char∗>(&i); // treat that memory as bytes
}

void test()
{
    ifstream ifs("source",ios_base::binary);         // stream mode is binary
    ofstream ofs("target",ios_base::binary);         // stream mode is binary

    vector<int> v;

    for (int i; ifs.read(as_bytes(i),sizeof(i));)     // read bytes from binary file
        v.push_back(i);

    // ... do something with v ...

    for (auto i : v)                                  // write bytes to binary file:
        ofs.write(as_bytes(i),sizeof(i));
}
```

Use binary I/O when dealing with objects that are "just bags of bits" and do not have an obvious and reasonable character string representation. Images and sound/video streams are examples.

The **seekg()** (§38.6.2) and **seekp()** (§38.6.2) operations require a direction:

ios_base **Direction** seekdir **Member Constants (§iso.27.5.3.1.5)**	
beg	Seek from beginning of current file
cur	Seek from current position
end	Seek backward from end of current file

Classes derived from **basic_ios** format output and extract objects based on the information stored in their **basic_io**.

The **ios_base** operations can be summarized:

basic_ios<C,Tr> (§iso.27.5.5)	
basic_ios ios {p};	Construct **ios** given the stream buffer pointed to by **p**
ios.˜basic_ios()	Destroy **ios**: release all of **ios**'s resources
bool b {ios};	Conversion to **bool**: **b** is initialized to **!ios.fail()**; explicit
b=!ios	b=ios.fail()
st=ios.rdstate()	**st** is the **iostate** of **ios**
ios.clear(st)	Set the **iostate** of **ios** to **st**
ios.clear()	Set the **iostate** of **ios** to good
ios.setstate(st)	Add **st** to **ios**'s **iostate**
ios.good()	Is the state of **ios** good (is **goodbit** set)?
ios.eof()	Is the state of **ios** end-of-file?
ios.fail()	Is the state of **ios** fail?
ios.bad()	Is the state of **ios** bad?
st=ios.exceptions()	**st** is the exceptions bits of the **iostate** of **ios**
ios.exceptions(st)	Set the exceptions bits of **ios**'s **iostate** to **st**
p=ios.tie()	**p** is a pointer to a tied stream or **nullptr**
p=ios.tie(os)	Tie output stream **os** to **ios**;
	p is a pointer to the previously tied stream or **nullptr**
p=ios.rdbuf()	**p** is a pointer to **ios**'s stream buffer
p=ios.rdbuf(p2)	Set **ios**'s stream buffer to the one pointed to by **p2**;
	p is a pointer to the previous stream buffer
ios3=ios.copyfmt(ios2)	Copy the parts of **io2**'s state related to formatting to **ios**;
	call any **ios2** callback of type **copyfmt_event**;
	copy the values pointed to by **ios2.pword** and **ios2.iword**;
	ios3 is the previous format state
c=ios.fill()	**c** is the fill character of **ios**
c2=ios.fill(c)	Set **c** to be the fill character of **ios**;
	c2 is the previous fill character
loc2=ios.imbue(loc)	Set **ios**'s locale to **loc**; **loc2** is the previous locale
c2=narrow(c,d)	**c2** is a **char** value obtained by converting **c** of **char_type**,
	d is a default value:
	use_facet<ctype<char_type>>(getloc()).narrow(c,d)

basic_ios<C,Tr> (continued) (§iso.27.5.5)	
c2=widen(c)	c2 is a **char_type** value obtained by converting **c** of **char type**: use_facet<ctype<char_type>>(getloc()).widen(c)
ios.init(p)	Set **ios** to the default state and use the stream buffer pointed to by **p**; protected
ios.set_rdbuf(p)	Make **ios** use the stream buffer pointed to by **p**; protected
ios.move(ios2)	Copy and move operation; protected
ios.swap(ios2)	Exchange the states of **ios** and **ios2**; protected; noexcept

The conversion of an **ios** (including **istreams** and **ostreams**) to **bool** is essential to the usual idiom for reading many values:

```
for (X x; cin>>x;) {
    // ...
}
```

Here, the return value of **cin>>x** is a reference to **cin**'s **ios**. This **ios** is implicitly converted to a **bool** representing the state of **cin**. Thus, we could equivalently have written:

```
for (X x; !(cin>>x).fail();) {
    // ...
}
```

The **tie()** is used to ensure that output from a tied stream appears before an input from the stream to which it is tied. For example, **cout** is tied to **cin**:

```
cout << "Please enter a number: ";
int num;
cin >> num;
```

This code does not explicitly call **cout.flush()**, so had **cout** not been tied to **cin**, the user would see the request for input.

ios_base Operations (§iso.27.5.3.5, §iso.27.5.3.6)	
i=xalloc()	**i** is the index of a new (**iword**,**pword**) pair; static
r=iob.iword(i)	**r** is a reference to the **i**th **long**
r=iob.pword(i)	**r** is a reference to the **i**th **void**∗
iob.register_callback(fn,i)	Register callback **fn** to **iword(i)**

Sometimes, people want to add to the state of a stream. For example, one might want a stream to "know" whether a **complex** should be output in polar or Cartesian coordinates. Class **ios_base** provides a function **xalloc()** to allocate space for such simple state information. The value returned by **xalloc()** identifies a pair of locations that can be accessed by **iword()** and **pword()**.

Sometimes, an implementer or a user needs to be notified about a change in a stream's state. The **register_callback()** function "registers" a function to be called when its "event" occurs. Thus, a call of **imbue()**, **copyfmt()**, or ˜**ios_base()** will call a function "registered" for an **imbue_event**, **copyfmt_event**, or **erase_event**, respectively. When the state changes, registered functions are called with the argument **i** supplied by their **register_callback()**.

The **event** and **event_callback** types are defined in **ios_base**:

```
enum event {
    erase_event,
    imbue_event,
    copyfmt_event
};
using event_callback = void (*)(event, ios_base&, int index);
```

38.4.5 Formatting

The format of stream I/O is controlled by a combination of object type, stream state (§38.4.4), format state (§38.4.5.1), locale information (Chapter 39), and explicit operations (e.g., manipulators; §38.4.5.2).

38.4.5.1 Formatting State

In <ios>, the standard library defines a set of formatting constants of an implementation-defined bitmask type fmtflags as members of class ios_base:

ios_base **Formatting** fmtflags **Constants (§iso.27.5.3.1.2)**	
boolalpha	Use symbolic representation of true and false
dec	Integer base is 10
hex	Integer base is 16
oct	Integer base is 8
fixed	Floating-point format dddd.dd
scientific	Scientific format d.ddddEdd
internal	Pad between a prefix (such as +) and the number
left	Pad after the value
right	Pad before the value
showbase	On output, prefix octal numbers by 0 and hexadecimal numbers by 0x
showpoint	Always show the decimal point (e.g., 123.)
showpos	Show + for positive numbers (e.g., +123)
skipws	Skip whitespace on input
unitbuf	Flush after each output operation
uppercase	Use uppercase in numeric output, e.g., 1.2E10 and 0X1A2
adjustfield	Set a value's placement in its field: left, right, or internal
basefield	Set the integer's base: dec, oct, or hex
floatfield	Set the floating-point format: scientific or fixed

Curiously, there are no defaultfloat or hexfloat flags. To get the equivalent, use manipulators defaultfloat and hexfloat (§38.4.5.2), or manipulate the ios_base directly:

```
ios.unsetf(ios_base::floatfield);                              // use the default floating-point format
ios.setf(ios_base::fixed | ios_base::scientific, ios_base::floatfield);        // use hexadecimal floats
```

An iostream's format state can be read and written (set) by operations provided in its ios_base:

ios_base **Formatting** fmtflags **Operations** (§iso.27.5.3.2)	
f=ios.flags()	f is ios's formatting flags
f2=ios.flags(f)	Set ios's formatting flags to f; f2 is the old value of the flags
f2=ios.setf(f)	Set ios's formatting flags to f; f2 is the old value of the flags
f2=ios.setf(f,m)	f2=ios.setf(f&m)
ios.unsetf(f)	Clear the flags f in ios
n=ios.precision()	n is ios's precision
n2=ios.precision(n)	Set ios's precision to n; n2 is the old precision
n=ios.width()	n is ios's width
n2=ios.width(n)	Set ios's width to n; n2 is the old width

Precision is an integer that determines the number of digits used to display a floating-point number:

- The *general* format (defaultfloat) lets the implementation choose a format that presents a value in the style that best preserves the value in the space available. The precision specifies the maximum number of digits.
- The *scientific* format (scientific) presents a value with one digit before a decimal point and an exponent. The precision specifies the maximum number of digits after the decimal point.
- The *fixed* format (fixed) presents a value as an integer part followed by a decimal point and a fractional part. The precision specifies the maximum number of digits after the decimal point. For example, see §38.4.5.2.

Floating-point values are rounded rather than just truncated, and precision() doesn't affect integer output. For example:

```
cout.precision(8);
cout << 1234.56789 << ' ' << 1234.56789 << ' ' << 123456 << '\n';

cout.precision(4);
cout << 1234.56789 << ' ' << 1234.56789 << ' ' << 123456 << '\n';
```

This produces:

```
1234.5679 1234.5679 123456
1235 1235 123456
```

The width() function specifies the minimum number of characters to be used for the next standard-library << output operation of a numeric value, bool, C-style string, character, pointer, string, and bitset (§34.2.2). For example:

```
cout.width(4);
cout << 12;     // print 12 preceded by two spaces
```

The "padding" or "filler" character can be specified by the fill() function. For example:

```
cout.width(4);
cout.fill('#');
cout << "ab";        // print ##ab
```

The default fill character is the space character, and the default field size is 0, meaning "as many characters as needed." The field size can be reset to its default value like this:

```
cout.width(0);  // "as many characters as needed"
```

A call **width(n)** sets the minimum number of characters to **n**. If more characters are provided, they will all be printed. For example:

```
cout.width(4);
cout << "abcdef";   // print abcdef
```

It does not truncate the output to **abcd**. It is usually better to get the right output looking ugly than to get the wrong output looking just fine.

A **width(n)** call affects only the immediately following << output operation. For example:

```
cout.width(4);
cout.fill('#');
cout << 12 << ':' << 13;    // print ##12:13
```

This produces **##12:13**, rather than **##12###:##13**.

If the explicit control of formatting options through many separate operations becomes tedious, we can combine them using a user-defined manipulator (§38.4.5.3).

An **ios_base** also allows the programmer to set an **iostream**'s **locale** (Chapter 39):

ios_base locale **Operations (§iso.27.5.3.3)**	
loc2=ios.imbue(loc)	Set ios's locale to loc; loc2 is the old value of the locale
loc=ios.getloc()	loc is ios's locale

38.4.5.2 Standard Manipulators

The standard library provides manipulators corresponding to the various format states and state changes. The standard manipulators are defined in **<ios>**, **<istream>**, **<ostream>**, and **<iomanip>** (for manipulators that take arguments):

I/O Manipulators from <ios> (§iso.27.5.6, §iso.27.7.4) (continues)	
s<<boolalpha	Use symbolic representation of **true** and **false** (input and output)
s<<noboolalpha	s.unsetf(ios_base::boolalpha)
s<<showbase	On output prefix octal numbers by 0 and hexadecimal numbers by 0x
s<<noshowbase	s.unsetf(ios_base::showbase)
s<<showpoint	Always show decimal point
s<<noshowpoint	s.unsetf(ios_base::showpoint)
s<<showpos	Show + for positive numbers
s<<noshowpos	s.unsetf(ios_base::showpos)
s<<uppercase	Use uppercase in numeric output, e.g., 1.2E10 and 0X1A2
s<<nouppercase	Use lowercase in numeric output, e.g., 1.2e10 and 0x1a2
s<<unitbuf	Flush after each output operation
s<<nounitbuf	Do not flush after each output operation

I/O Manipulators from \<ios\> (continued) (§iso.27.5.6, §iso.27.7.4)	
s\<\<internal	Pad where marked in formatting pattern
s\<\<left	Pad after value
s\<\<right	Pad before value
s\<\<dec	Integer base is 10
s\<\<hex	Integer base is 16
s\<\<oct	Integer base is 8
s\<\<fixed	Floating-point format dddd.dd
s\<\<scientific	Scientific format d.ddddEdd
s\<\<hexfloat	Use base 16 for mantissa and exponent, using **p** to start an exponent, e.g., **A.1BEp−C** and **a.bcdef**
s\<\<defaultfloat	Use the default floating point format
s\>\>skipws	Skip whitespace
s\>\>noskipws	**s.unsetf(ios_base::skipws)**

Each of these operations returns a reference to its first (stream) operand, **s**. For example:

```
cout << 1234 << ',' << hex << 1234 << ',' << oct << 1234 << '\n';        // print 1234,4d2,2322
```

We can explicitly set the output format for floating-point numbers:

```
constexpr double d = 123.456;

cout << d << "; "
     << scientific <<  d << "; "
     << hexfloat <<  d << "; "
     << fixed << d << "; "
     << defaultfloat << d << '\n';
```

This produces:

```
123.456; 1.234560e+002; 0x1.edd2f2p+6; 123.456000; 123.456
```

The floating-point format is "sticky"; that is, it persists for subsequent floating-point operations.

I/O Manipulators from \<ostream\> (§iso.27.5.6, §iso.27.7.4)	
os\<\<endl	Put '\n' and flush
os\<\<ends	Put '\0'
os\<\<flush	Flush stream

An **ostream** is flushed when it is destroyed, when a **tie()**d **istream** needs input (§38.4.4), and when the implementation finds it advantageous. Explicitly flushing a stream is very rarely necessary. Similarly, **\<\<endl** can be considered equivalent to **\<\<'\n'**, but the latter is probably a bit faster. I find

```
cout << "Hello, World!\n";
```

easier to read and write than

```
cout << "Hello, World!" << endl;
```

If you have a genuine need for frequent flushing, consider **cerr** and **unitbuf**.

I/O Manipulators from `<iomanip>` (§iso.27.5.6, §iso.27.7.4)	
`s<<resetiosflags(f)`	Clear flags f
`s<<setiosflags(f)`	Set flags f
`s<<setbase(b)`	Output integers in base b
`s<<setfill(int c)`	Make c the fill character
`s<<setprecision(n)`	Precision is n digits
`s<<setw(n)`	Next field width is n char
`is>>get_money(m,intl)`	Read from is using is's `money_get` facet;
	m is a `long double` or a `basic_string`;
	if intl==true, use standard three-letter currency names
`is>>get_money(m)`	`s>>get_money(m,false)`
`os<<put_money(m,intl)`	Write m to os using os's `money_put` facet;
	that `money_put` determines which types are acceptable for m;
	if intl==true, use standard three-letter currency names
`os<<put_money(m)`	`s<<put_money(m,false)`
`is>>get_time(tmp,fmt)`	Read into ∗tm according to the format fmt,
	using is's `time_get` facet
`os<<put_time(tmp,fmt)`	Write ∗tm to os according to the format fmt,
	using os's `time_put` facet

The time facets are found in §39.4.4 and the time formats in §43.6.

For example:

```
cout << '(' << setw(4) << setfill('#') << 12 << ") (" << 12 << ")\n";        // print (##12) (12)
```

istream Manipulators (§iso.27.5.6, §iso.27.7.4)	
`s>>skipws`	Skip whitespace (in `<ios>`)
`s>>noskipws`	`s.unsetf(ios_base::skipws)` (in `<ios>`)
`is>>ws`	Eat whitespace (in `<istream>`)

By default `>>` skips whitespace (§38.4.1). This default can be modified by `>>skipws` and `>>noskipws`. For example:

```
string input {"0 1 2 3 4"};
istringstream iss {input};
string s;
for (char ch; iss>>ch;)
      s += ch;
cout << s;              // print "01234"

istringstream iss2 {input};
iss>>noskipws;
for (char ch; iss2>>ch;)
      s += ch;
cout << s;              // print "0 1 2 3 4"
}
```

If you want to explicitly deal with whitespace (e.g., to make a newline significant) and still use >>, **noskipws** and **>>ws** become a convenience.

38.4.5.3 User-Defined Manipulators

A programmer can add manipulators in the style of the standard ones. Here, I present an additional style that I have found useful for formatting floating-point numbers.

Formatting is controlled by a confusing multitude of separate functions (§38.4.5.1). For example, a **precision()** persists for all output operations, but a **width()** applies to the next numeric output operation only. What I want is something that makes it simple to output a floating-point number in a predefined format without affecting future output operations on the stream. The basic idea is to define a class that represents formats, another that represents a format plus a value to be formatted, and then an operator << that outputs the value to an **ostream** according to the format. For example:

```
Form gen4 {4};        // general format, precision 4

void f(double d)
{
    Form sci8;
    sci8.scientific().precision(8);        // scientific format, precision 8
    cout << d << ' ' << gen4(d) << ' ' << sci8(d) << ' ' << d << '\n';

    Form sci {10,ios_base::scientific}; // scientific format, precision 10
    cout << d << ' ' << gen4(d) << ' ' << sci(d) << ' ' << d << '\n';
}
```

A call **f(1234.56789)** writes:

```
1234.57 1235 1.23456789e+003 1234.57
1234.57 1235 1.2345678900e+003 1234.57
```

Note how the use of a **Form** doesn't affect the state of the stream, so that the last output of **d** has the same default format as the first.

Here is a simplified implementation:

```
class Form;        // our formatting type

struct Bound_form {        // Form plus value
    const Form& f;
    double val;
};

class Form {
    friend ostream& operator<<(ostream&, const Bound_form&);

    int prc;  // precision
    int wdt;  // width 0 means "as wide as necessary"
    int fmt;  // general, scientific, or fixed (§38.4.5.1)
    // ...
```

```
public:
    explicit Form(int p =6, ios_base::fmtflags f =0, int w =0) : prc{p}, fmt{f}, wdt{w} {}

    Bound_form Form::operator()(double d) const      // make a Bound_form for *this and d
    {
        return Bound_form{*this,d};
    }

    Form& scientific() { fmt = ios_base::scientific; return *this; }
    Form& fixed() { fmt = ios_base::fixed; return *this; }
    Form& general() { fmt = 0; return *this; }

    Form& uppercase();
    Form& lowercase();
    Form& precision(int p) { prc = p; return *this; }

    Form& width(int w) { wdt = w; return *this; }      // applies to all types
    Form& fill(char);

    Form& plus(bool b = true);                         // explicit plus
    Form& trailing_zeros(bool b = true);               // print trailing zeros
    // ...
};
```

The idea is that a `Form` holds all the information needed to format one data item. The default is chosen to be reasonable for many uses, and the various member functions can be used to reset individual aspects of formatting. The () operator is used to bind a value with the format to be used to output it. A `Bound_form` (that is, a `Form` plus a value) can then be output to a given stream by a suitable << function:

```
ostream& operator<<(ostream& os, const Bound_form& bf)
{
    ostringstream s;            // §38.2.2
    s.precision(bf.f.prc);
    s.setf(bf.f.fmt,ios_base::floatfield);
    s << bf.val;                // compose string in s
    return os << s.str();       // output s to os
}
```

Writing a less simplistic implementation of << is left as an exercise.

Note that these declarations make the combination of << and () into a ternary operator; `cout<<sci4{d}` collects the `ostream`, the format, and the value into a single function before doing any real computation.

38.5 Stream Iterators

In `<iterator>`, the standard library provides iterators to allow input and output streams to be viewed as sequences [input-begin:end-of-input) and [output-begin:end-of-output):

```
template<typename T,
         typename C = char,
         typename Tr = char_traits<C>,
         typename Distance = ptrdiff_t>
class istream_iterator
    :public iterator<input_iterator_tag, T, Distance, const T*, const T&> {
    using char_type = C;
    using traits_type = Tr;
    using istream_type = basic_istream<C,Tr>;
    // ...
};

template<typename T, typename C = char, typename Tr = char_traits<C>>
class ostream_iterator: public iterator<output_iterator_tag, void, void, void, void> {
    using char_type = C;
    using traits_type = Tr;
    using ostream_type = basic_ostream<C,Tr>;
    // ...
};
```

For example:

```
copy(istream_iterator<double>{cin}, istream_iterator<double,char>{},
     ostream_iterator<double>{cout,";\n"});
```

When an **ostream_iterator** is constructed with a second (**string**) argument, that string is output as a terminator after every element value. So, if you enter **1 2 3** to that call of **copy()**, the output is:

```
1;
2;
3;
```

The operators provided for a **stream_iterator** are the same as for other iterator adaptors (§33.2.2):

Stream Iterator Operations (§iso.24.6)	
istream_iterator p {st};	Iterator for input stream st
istream_iterator p {p2};	Copy constructor: p is a copy of the istream_iterator p2
ostream_iterator p {st};	Iterator for output stream st
ostream_iterator p {p2};	Copy constructor: p is a copy of the ostream_iterator p2
ostream_iterator p {st,s};	Iterator for output stream st; use the C-style string s as the separator between output elements
p=p2	p is a copy of p2
p2=++p	p and p2 point to the next element
p2=p++	p2=p,++p
*p=x	Insert x before p
*p++=x	Insert x before p, then increment p

Except for the constructors, these operations are typically used by general algorithms, such as **copy()**, rather than directly.

38.6 Buffering

Conceptually, an output stream puts characters into a buffer. Sometime later, the characters are then written to ("flushed to") wherever they are supposed to go. Such a buffer is called a **stream-buf**. Its definition is found in **<streambuf>**. Different types of **streambufs** implement different buffering strategies. Typically, the **streambuf** stores characters in an array until an overflow forces it to write the characters to their real destination. Thus, an **ostream** can be represented graphically like this:

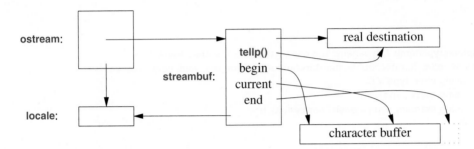

The set of template arguments for an **ostream** and its **streambuf** must be the same, and they determine the type of character used in the character buffer.

An **istream** is similar, except that the characters flow the other way.

Unbuffered I/O is simply I/O where the **streambuf** immediately transfers each character, rather than holding on to characters until enough have been gathered for efficient transfer.

The key class in the buffering mechanisms is **basic_streambuf**:

```
template<typename C, typename Tr = char_traits<C>>
class basic_streambuf {
public:
    using char_type = C;                        // the type of a character
    using int_type = typename Tr::int_type;     // the integer type to which
                                                // a character can be converted
    using pos_type = typename Tr::pos_type;     // type of position in buffer
    using off_type = typename Tr::off_type;     // type of offset from position in buffer
    using traits_type = Tr;
    // ...
    virtual ˜basic_streambuf();
};
```

As usual, a couple of aliases are provided for the (supposedly) most common cases:

```
using streambuf = basic_streambuf<char>;
using wstreambuf = basic_streambuf<wchar_t>;
```

The **basic_streambuf** has a host of operations. Many of the **public** operations simply call a **protected** virtual function that ensures that a function from a derived class implemented the operation appropriately for the particular kind of buffer:

public basic_streambuf<C,Tr> **Operations** (§iso.27.6.3)	
sb.~basic_streambuf()	Destructor: release all resources; virtual
loc=sb.getloc()	loc is sb's locale
loc2=sb.pubimbue(loc)	sb.imbue(loc); loc2 is a pointer to the previous locale
psb=sb.pubsetbuf(s,n)	psb=sb.setbuf(s,n)
pos=sb.pubseekoff(n,w,m)	pos=sb.seekoff(n,w,m)
pos=sb.pubseekoff(n,w)	pos=sb.seekoff(n,w)
pos=sb.pubseekpos(n,m)	pos=sb.seekpos(n,m)
pos=sb.pubseekpos(n)	pos=sb.seekpos(n,ios_base::in|ios_base::out)
sb.pubsync()	sb.sync()

All constructors are **protected** because **basic_streambuf** is designed as a base class.

protected basic_streambuf<C,Tr> **Operations** (§iso.27.6.3)	
basic_streambuf sb {};	Construct **sb** with no character buffer and the global locale
basic_streambuf sb {sb2};	sb is a copy of **sb2** (they share a character buffer)
sb=sb2	sb is a copy of **sb2** (they share a character buffer); sb's old resources are released
sb.swap(sb2)	Exchange the states of **sb** and **sb2**
sb.imbue(loc)	**loc** becomes sb's locale; virtual
psb=sb.setbuf(s,n)	Set sb's buffer; psb=&sb; s is a **const char**∗ and n is a **streamsize**; virtual
pos=sb.seekoff(n,w,m)	Seek with an offset n, a direction w, and a mode m; **pos** is the resulting position or **pos_type(off_type(–1))**, indicating an error; virtual
pos=sb.seekoff(n,w)	pos=sb.seekoff(n,way,ios_base::in|ios_base::out)
pos=sb.seekpos(n,m)	Seek to position n and a mode m; **pos** is the resulting position or **pos_type(off_type(–1))**, indicating an error; virtual
n=sb.sync()	Synchronize the character buffers with the real destination or source; virtual

The exact meaning of the virtual functions are determined by derived classes.

A **streambuf** has a *put area* into which << and other output operations write (§38.4.2), and a *get area* from which >> and other input operations read (§38.4.1). Each area is described by a beginning pointer, current pointer, and one-past-the-end pointer:

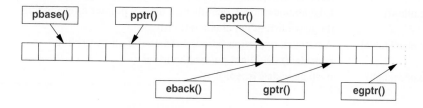

Overflow are handled by the virtual functions **overflow()**, **underflow()**, and **uflow()**.

For a use of positioning, see §38.6.1.

The put-and-get interface is separated into a **public** and a **protected** one:

public **Put and Get** basic_streambuf<C,Tr> **Operations (§iso.27.6.3) (continues)**	
n=sb.in_avail()	If a read position is available, n=sb.egptr()–sb.gptr(); otherwise returns sb.showmanyc()
c=sb.snextc()	Increase sb's get pointer, then c=*sb.gptr()
n=sb.sbumpc()	Increase sb's get pointer
c=sb.sgetc()	If there is no character left to get, c=sb.underflow(); otherwise c=*sb.gptr()
n=sb.sgetn(p,n)	n=sb.xsgetn(p,n); p is a char*
n=sb.sputbackc(c)	Put c back into the get area and decrease the gptr; n=Tr::to_int_type(*sb.gptr()) if the putback succeeded; otherwise n=sb.pbackfail(Tr::to_int_type(c))
n=sb.sungetc()	Decrease the get pointer; n=Tr::to_int_type(*sb.gptr()) if the unget succeeded; otherwise n=sb.pbackfail(Tr::to_int_type())
n=sb.sputc(c)	If there is no character left to put into, n=sb.overflow(Tr::to_int_type(c)); otherwise *sb.sptr()=c; n=Tr::to_int_type(c)
n=sb.sputn(s,n)	n=sb.xsputn(s,n); s is a const char*

The **protected** interface provides simple, efficient, and typically inlined functions manipulating the put and get pointers. In addition, there are virtual functions to be overridden by derived classes.

protected **Put and Get** basic_streambuf<C,Tr> **Operations (continued) (§iso.27.6.3)**	
sb.setg(b,n,end)	The get area is [b,e); the current get pointer is n
pc=sb.eback()	[pc:sb.egptr()) is the get area
pc=sb.gptr()	pc is the get pointer
pc=sb.egptr()	[sb.eback():pc) is the get area
sb.gbump(n)	Increase sb's get pointer
n=sb.showmanyc()	"Show how many characters"; n is an estimate of how many characters can be read without calling sb.underflow() or n=–1 indicating that no characters are ready to be read; virtual
n=sb.underflow()	No more characters in the get area; replenish the get area; n=Tr::to_int_type(c) where c is the new current get character; virtual
n=sb.uflow()	Like sb.underflow(), but advance the get pointer after reading the new current get character; virtual
n=sb.pbackfail(c)	A putback operation failed; n=Tr::eof() if an overriding pbackfail() could not put back; virtual
n=sb.pbackfail()	n=sb.pbackfail(Tr::eof())

protected **Put and Get** basic_streambuf<C,Tr> **Operations (continued)** (§iso.27.6.3)	
sb.setp(b,e)	The put area is [b,e) the current put pointer is **b**
pc=sb.pbase()	[**pc:sb.epptr**()) is the put area
pc=sb.pptr()	**pc** is the put pointer
pc=sb.epptr()	[**sb.pbase**(),**pc**) is the put area
sb.pbump(n)	Add one to the put pointer
n2=sb.xsgetn(s,n)	**s** is a **const char**∗; do **sb.sgetc**(∗p) for each **p** in [**s**:**s**+n);
	n2 is the number of characters read; virtual
n2=sb.xsputn(s,n)	**s** is a [**const char**∗; **sb.sputc**(∗p) for each **p** in [**s**:**s**+n);
	n2 is the number of character written; virtual
n=sb.overflow(c)	Replenish the put area, then n=**sb.sputc(c)**; virtual
n=sb.overflow()	n=sb.overflow(Tr::eof())

The **showmanyc()** ("show how many characters") function is an odd function intended to allow a user to learn something about the state of a machine's input system. It returns an estimate of how many characters can be read "soon," say, by emptying the operating system's buffers rather than waiting for a disk read. A call to **showmanyc()** returns –1 if it cannot promise that any character can be read without encountering end-of-file. This is (necessarily) rather low-level and highly implementation-dependent. Don't use **showmanyc()** without a careful reading of your system documentation and conducting a few experiments.

38.6.1 Output Streams and Buffers

An **ostream** provides operations for converting values of various types into character sequences according to conventions (§38.4.2) and explicit formatting directives (§38.4.5). In addition, an **ostream** provides operations that deal directly with its **streambuf**:

```
template<typename C, typename Tr = char_traits<C>>
class basic_ostream : virtual public basic_ios<C,Tr> {
public:
    // ...
    explicit basic_ostream(basic_streambuf<C,Tr>∗ b);

    pos_type tellp();                               // get current position
    basic_ostream& seekp(pos_type);                 // set current position
    basic_ostream& seekp(off_type, ios_base::seekdir);  // set current position

    basic_ostream& flush();                         // empty buffer (to real destination)

    basic_ostream& operator<<(basic_streambuf<C,Tr>∗ b);    // write from b
};
```

The **basic_ostream** functions override their equivalents in the **basic_ostream**'s **basic_ios** base.

An **ostream** is constructed with a **streambuf** argument, which determines how the characters written are handled and where they eventually go. For example, an **ostringstream** (§38.2.2) or an **ofstream** (§38.2.1) is created by initializing an **ostream** with a suitable **streambuf** (§38.6).

The **seekp()** functions are used to position an **ostream** for writing. The **p** suffix indicates that it is the position used for *putting* characters into the stream. These functions have no effect unless the stream is attached to something for which positioning is meaningful, such as a file. The **pos_type** represents a character position in a file, and the **off_type** represents an offset from a point indicated by an **ios_base::seekdir**.

Stream positions start at **0**, so we can think of a file as an array of **n** characters. For example:

```
int f(ofstream& fout)// fout refers to some file
{
    fout << "0123456789";
    fout.seekp(8);                      // 8 from beginning
    fout << '#';                        // add '#' and move position (+1)
    fout.seekp(–4,ios_base::cur);       // 4 backward
    fout << '*';                        // add '*' and move position (+1)
}
```

If the file was initially empty, we get:

```
01234*67#9
```

There is no similar way to do random access on elements of a plain **istream** or **ostream**. Attempting to seek beyond the beginning or the end of a file typically puts the stream into the **bad()** state (§38.4.4). However, some operating systems have operating modes where the behavior differs (e.g., positioning might resize a file).

The **flush()** operation allows the user to empty the buffer without waiting for an overflow.

It is possible to use **<<** to write a **streambuf** directly into an **ostream**. This is primarily handy for implementers of I/O mechanisms.

38.6.2 Input Streams and Buffers

An **istream** provides operations for reading characters and converting them into values of various types (§38.4.1). In addition, an **istream** provides operations that deal directly with its **streambuf**:

```
template<typename C, typename Tr = char_traits<C>>
class basic_istream : virtual public basic_ios<C,Tr> {
public:
    // ...
    explicit basic_istream(basic_streambuf<C,Tr>* b);
    pos_type tellg();                               // get current position
    basic_istream& seekg(pos_type);                 // set current position
    basic_istream& seekg(off_type, ios_base::seekdir); // set current position

    basic_istream& putback(C c);                    // put c back into the buffer
    basic_istream& unget();                         // put back most recent char read
    int_type peek();                                // look at next character to be read

    int sync();                                     // clear buffer (flush)

    basic_istream& operator>>(basic_streambuf<C,Tr>* b);   // read into b
    basic_istream& get(basic_streambuf<C,Tr>& b, C t = Tr::newline());
```

```
    streamsize readsome(C* p, streamsize n);      // read at most n char
};
```

The **basic_istream** functions override their equivalents in the **basic_istream**'s **basic_ios** base.

The positioning functions work like their **ostream** counterparts (§38.6.1). The **g** suffix indicates that it is the position used for *getting* characters from the stream. The **p** and **g** suffixes are needed because we can create an **iostream** derived from both **istream** and **ostream**, and such a stream needs to keep track of both a get position and a put position.

The **putback()** function allows a program to put a character "back" into an **istream** to be the next character read. The **unget()** function puts the most recently read character back. Unfortunately, backing up an input stream is not always possible. For example, trying to back up past the first character read will set **ios_base::failbit**. What is guaranteed is that you can back up one character after a successful read. The **peek()** function reads the next character and also leaves that character in the **streambuf** so that it can be read again. Thus, **c=peek()** is logically equivalent to **(c=get(),unget(),c)**. Setting **failbit** might trigger an exception (§38.3).

Flushing an **istream** is done using **sync()**. This cannot always be done right. For some kinds of streams, we would have to reread characters from the real source – and that is not always possible or desirable (e.g., for a stream attached to a network). Consequently, **sync()** returns **0** if it succeeded. If it failed, it sets **ios_base::badbit** (§38.4.4) and returns **–1**. Setting **badbit** might trigger an exception (§38.3). A **sync()** on a buffer attached to an **ostream** flushes the buffer to output.

The **>>** and **get()** operations that directly reads from a **streambuf** are primarily useful for implementers of I/O facilities.

The **readsome()** function is a low-level operation that allows a user to peek at a stream to see if there are any characters available to read. This can be most useful when it is undesirable to wait for input, say, from a keyboard. See also **in_avail()** (§38.6).

38.6.3 Buffer Iterators

In **<iterator>**, the standard library provides **istreambuf_iterator** and **ostreambuf_iterator** to allow a user (mostly an implementer of a new kind of **iostream**) to iterate over the contents of a stream buffer. In particular, these iterators are widely used by **locale facets** (Chapter 39).

38.6.3.1 istreambuf_iterator

An **istreambuf_iterator** reads a stream of characters from an **istream_buffer**:

```
template<typename C, typename Tr = char_traits<C>>   // §iso.24.6.3
class istreambuf_iterator
    :public iterator<input_iterator_tag, C, typename Tr::off_type, /*unspecified*/, C> {
public:
    using char_type = C;
    using traits_type = Tr;
    using int_type = typename Tr::int_type;
    using streambuf_type = basic_streambuf<C,Tr>;
    using istream_type = basic_istream<C,Tr>;
    // ...
};
```

The **reference** member of the **iterator** base is not used and is consequently left unspecified.

If you use an **istreambuf_iterator** as an input iterator, its effect is like that of other input iterators: a stream of characters can be read from input using **c=*p++**:

istreambuf_iterator<C,Tr> (§iso.24.6.3)	
istreambuf_iterator p {};	p is an end-of-stream iterator; noexcept; constexpr
istreambuf_iterator p {p2};	Copy constructor; noexcept
istreambuf_iterator p {is};	p is an iterator for **is.rdbuf()**; noexcept
istreambuf_iterator p {psb};	p is an iterator to the **istreambuf** *psb; noexcept
istreambuf_iterator p {nullptr};	p is an end-of-stream iterator
istreambuf_iterator p {prox};	p points to the **istreambuf** designated by **prox**; noexcept
p.˜istreambuf_iterator()	Destructor
c=*p	c is the character returned by the **streambuf**'s **sgetc()**
p–>m	The member m of *p, if that is a class object
p=++p	The **streambuf**'s **sbumpc()**
prox=p++	Let **prox** designate the same position as **p**; then **++p**
p.equal(p2)	Are both **p** and **p2**, or neither, at end-of-stream
p==p2	p.equal(p2)
p!=p2	!p.equal(p2)

Note that any attempt to be clever when comparing **istreambuf_iterators** will fail: you cannot rely on two iterators referring to the same character while input is going on.

38.6.3.2 ostreambuf_iterator

An **ostreambuf_iterator** writes a stream of characters to an **ostream_buffer**:

```
template<typename C, typename Tr = char_traits<C>>   // §iso.24.6.4
class ostreambuf_iterator
      :public iterator<output_iterator_tag, void, void, void, void> {
public:
      using char_type = C;
      using traits_type = Tr;
      using streambuf_type = basic_streambuf<C,Tr>;
      using ostream_type = basic_ostream<C,Tr>;
      // ...
};
```

By most measures, **ostreambuf_iterator**'s operations are odd, but the net effect is that if you use it as an output iterator, its effect is like that of other output iterators: a stream of characters can be written to output using ***p++=c**:

ostreambuf_iterator<C,Tr> (§iso.24.6.4) (continues)	
ostreambuf_iterator p {os};	p is an iterator for **os.rdbuf()**; noexcept
ostreambuf_iterator p {psb};	p is an iterator for the **istreambuf** *psb; noexcept

ostreambuf_iterator<C,Tr> (continued) (§iso.24.6.4)	
p=c	If !p.failed() call the **streambuf**'s **sputc(c)**
*p	Do nothing
++p	Do nothing
p++	Do nothing
p.failed()	Has a **sputc()** on **p**'s streambuf reached **eof**? noexcept

38.7 Advice

[1] Define << and >> for user-defined types with values that have meaningful textual representations; §38.1, §38.4.1, §38.4.2.

[2] Use **cout** for normal output and **cerr** for errors; §38.1.

[3] There are **iostream**s for ordinary characters and wide characters, and you can define an **iostream** for any kind of character; §38.1.

[4] There are standard **iostream**s for standard I/O streams, files, and **strings**; §38.2.

[5] Don't try to copy a file stream; §38.2.1.

[6] Binary I/O is system specific; §38.2.1.

[7] Remember to check that a file stream is attached to a file before using it; §38.2.1.

[8] Prefer **ifstream**s and **ofstream**s over the generic **fstream**; §38.2.1.

[9] Use **stringstream**s for in-memory formatting; §38.2.2.

[10] Use exceptions to catch rare **bad()** I/O errors; §38.3.

[11] Use the stream state **fail** to handle potentially recoverable I/O errors; §38.3.

[12] You don't need to modify **istream** or **ostream** to add new << and >> operators; §38.4.1.

[13] When implementing a **iostream** primitive operation, use **sentry**; §38.4.1.

[14] Prefer formatted input over unformatted, low-level input; §38.4.1.

[15] Input into **string**s does not overflow; §38.4.1.

[16] Be careful with the termination criteria when using **get()**, **getline()**, and **read()**; §38.4.1.

[17] By default >> skips whitespace; §38.4.1.

[18] You can define a << (or a >>) so that it behaves as a virtual function based on its second operand; §38.4.2.1.

[19] Prefer manipulators to state flags for controlling I/O; §38.4.3.

[20] Use **sync_with_stdio(true)** if you want to mix C-style and **iostream** I/O; §38.4.4.

[21] Use **sync_with_stdio(false)** to optimize **iostream**s; §38.4.4.

[22] Tie streams used for interactive I/O; §38.4.4.

[23] Use **imbue()** to make an **iostream** reflect "cultural differences" of a **locale**; §38.4.4.

[24] **width()** specifications apply to the immediately following I/O operation only; §38.4.5.1.

[25] **precision()** specifications apply to all following floating-point output operations; §38.4.5.1.

[26] Floating-point format specifications (e.g., **scientific**) apply to all following floating-point output operations; §38.4.5.2.

[27] **#include <iomanip>** when using standard manipulators taking arguments; §38.4.5.2.

[28] You hardly ever need to **flush()**; §38.4.5.2.

[29] Don't use **endl** except possibly for aesthetic reasons; §38.4.5.2.

[30] If **iostream** formatting gets too tedious, write your own manipulators; §38.4.5.3.

[31] You can achieve the effect (and efficiency) of a ternary operator by defining a simple function object; §38.4.5.3.

39

Locales

When in Rome,
do as the Romans do.
– Proverb

- Handling Cultural Differences
- Class **locale**
    Named **locales**; Comparing **strings**
- Class **facet**
    Accessing **facets** in a **locale**; A Simple User-defined **facet**; Uses of **locales** and **facets**
- Standard **facets**
    string Comparison; Numeric Formatting; Money Formatting; Date and Time Formatting; Character Classification; Character Code Conversion; Messages
- Convenience Interfaces
    Character Classifications; Character Conversions; String Conversions; Buffer Conversions
- Advice

39.1 Handling Cultural Differences

A **locale** is an object that represents a set of cultural preferences, such as how strings are compared, the way numbers appear as human-readable output, and the way characters are represented in external storage. The notion of a *locale* is extensible so that a programmer can add new **facets** to a **locale** representing locale-specific entities not directly supported by the standard library, such as postal codes (zip codes) and phone numbers. The primary use of **locales** in the standard library is to control the appearance of information written to an **ostream** and the format of data read by an **istream**.

This chapter describes how to use a **locale**, how a **locale** is constructed out of **facets**, and how a **locale** affects an I/O stream.

The notion of a locale is not primarily a C++ notion. Most operating systems and application environments have a notion of locale. Such a notion is – in principle – shared among all programs on a system, independently of which programming language they are written in. Thus, the C++ standard-library notion of a locale can be seen as a standard and portable way for C++ programs to access information that has very different representations on different systems. Among other things, a C++ locale is an interface to system information that is represented in incompatible ways on different systems.

Consider writing a program that needs to be used in several countries. Writing a program in a style that allows that is often called *internationalization* (emphasizing the use of a program in many countries) or *localization* (emphasizing the adaptation of a program to local conditions). Many of the entities that a program manipulates will conventionally be displayed differently in those countries. We can handle this by writing our I/O routines to take this into account. For example:

```cpp
void print_date(const Date& d)     // print in the appropriate format
{
     switch(where_am_I) {     // user-defined style indicator
     case DK:           // e.g., 7. marts 1999
         cout << d.day() << ". " << dk_month[d.month()] << " " << d.year();
         break;
     case ISO:          // e.g., 1999-3-7
         cout << d.year() << " - " << d.month() << " / " << d.day();
         break;
     case US:           // e.g., 3/7/1999
         cout << d.month() << "/" << d.day() << "/" << d.year();
         break;
     // ...
     }
}
```

This style of code does the job. However, such code is ugly and hard to maintain. In particular, we have to use this style consistently to ensure that all output is properly adjusted to local conventions. If we want to add a new way of writing a date, we must modify the application code. Worse yet, writing dates is only one of many examples of cultural differences.

Consequently, the standard library provides an extensible way of handling cultural conventions. The iostream library relies on this framework to handle both built-in and user-defined types (§38.1). For example, consider a simple loop copying (Date,double) pairs that might represent a series of measurements or a set of transactions:

```cpp
void cpy(istream& is, ostream& os)// copy (Date,double) stream
{
     Date d;
     double volume;

     while (is >> d >> volume)
         os << d << ' '<< volume << '\n';
}
```

Naturally, a real program would do something with the records and ideally also be a bit careful about error handling.

How would we make this program read a file that conformed to French conventions (where a comma is the character used to represent the decimal point in a floating-point number; for example,

12,5 means twelve and a half) and write it according to American conventions? We can define locales and I/O operations so that cpy() can be used to convert between conventions:

```
void f(istream& fin, ostream& fout, istream& fin2, ostream& fout2)
{
        fin.imbue(locale{"en_US.UTF-8"});         // American English
        fout.imbue(locale{"fr_FR.UTF-8"});        // French
        cpy(fin,fout);                            // read American English, write French
        // ...

        fin2.imbue(locale{"fr_FR.UTF-8"});        // French
        fout2.imbue(locale{"en_US.UTF-8"});       // American English
        cpy(fin2,fout2);                          // read French, write American English
        // ...
}
```

Given these streams:

```
Apr 12, 1999    1000.3
Apr 13, 1999    345.45
Apr 14, 1999    9688.321
...
3 juillet 1950    10,3
3 juillet 1951    134,45
3 juillet 1952    67,9
...
```

this program would produce:

```
12 avril 1999 1000,3
13 avril 1999 345,45
14 avril 1999 9688,321
...
July 3, 1950 10.3
July 3, 1951 134.45
July 3, 1952 67.9
...
```

Much of the rest of this chapter is devoted to describing the mechanisms that make this possible and explaining how to use them. However, most programmers will have little reason to deal with the details of locales and will never explicitly manipulate a locale. At most, they will simply retrieve a standard locale and imbue a stream with it (§38.4.5.1).

The concept of localization (internationalization) is simple. However, practical constraints make the design and implementation of locale quite intricate:

[1]   A locale encapsulates cultural conventions, such as the appearance of a date. Such conventions vary in many subtle and unsystematic ways. These conventions have nothing to do with programming languages, so a programming language cannot standardize them.

[2]   The concept of a locale must be extensible, because it is not possible to enumerate every cultural convention that is important to every C++ user.

[3]   A locale is used in operations (e.g., I/O and sorting) from which people demand run-time efficiency.

[4]   A locale must be invisible to the majority of programmers who want to benefit from facilities "doing the right thing" without having to know exactly what "the right thing" is or how it is achieved.

[5]   A locale must be available to designers of facilities that deal with culture-sensitive information beyond the scope of the standard.

The mechanisms provided to compose those locales and to make them trivial to use constitute a little programming language of their own.

A locale is composed of facets that control individual aspects, such as the character used for punctuation in the output of a floating-point value (decimal_point(); §39.4.2) and the format used to read a monetary value (moneypunct; §39.4.3). A facet is an object of a class derived from class locale::facet (§39.3). We can think of a locale as a container of facets (§39.2, §39.3.1).

39.2 Class locale

The locale class and its associated facilities are presented in <locale>.

locale **Members (§iso.22.3.1)**	
locale loc {};	loc is a copy of the current global locale; noexcept
locale loc {loc2};	Copy constructor: loc holds a copy of loc2; loc.name()==loc2.name(); noexcept
locale loc {s};	Initialize loc to the locale with the name s; s can be a string or a C-style string; loc.name()==s; explicit
locale loc {loc2,s,cat};	loc is a copy of loc2 except for the facet with category cat, which is copied from locale{s}; s can be a string or a C-style string; if loc2 has a name, loc has a name
locale loc {loc2,pf};	loc is a copy of loc2 except for the facet *pf provided pf!=nullptr; loc does not have a name
locale loc {loc2,loc3,cat};	loc is a copy of loc2 except for the facet with category cat, which is copied from loc3; loc has a name if loc2 and loc3 both have names
loc.˜locale()	Destructor; not virtual; noexcept
loc2=loc	Assignment: loc2 is a copy of loc; noexcept
loc3=loc.combine<F>(loc2)	loc3 is a copy of loc except for facet F, which is copied from loc2; loc3 does not have a name
s=loc.name()	s is the name of loc's locale or "*"
loc==loc2	Is loc the same locale as loc2?
loc!=loc2	!(loc==loc2)
loc()(s,s2)	Compare basic_string<C>s and s2, using loc's collate<C> facet
loc2=global(loc)	Set the global locale to loc; loc2 is the previous global locale
loc=classic()	loc is the classic "C" locale

If a **locale** of a given name or a **facet** referred to doesn't exist, the **locale** operation naming it throws a **runtime_error**.

Naming of **locale**s is a bit curious. When you make a new **locale** from another plus a **facet** and the resulting **locale** has a name, that name is implementation-defined. Often, such an implementation-defined name includes the name of the **locale** that supplied most of the **facet**s. For a **locale** without a name, **name()** returns "*".

A **locale** can be thought of as an interface to a **map<id,facet*>**, that is, something that allows us to use a **locale::id** to find a corresponding object of a class derived from **locale::facet**. A real implementation of **locale** is an efficient variant of this idea. The layout will be something like this:

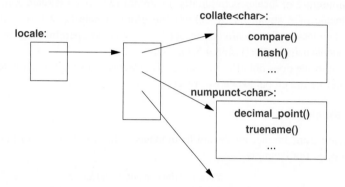

Here, **collate<char>** and **numpunct<char>** are standard-library facets (§39.4). All facets are derived from **locale::facet**.

A **locale** is meant to be copied freely and cheaply. Consequently, a **locale** is almost certainly implemented as a handle to the specialized **map<id,facet*>** that constitutes the main part of its implementation. The **facet**s must be quickly accessible in a **locale**. Consequently, the specialized **map<id,facet*>** will be optimized to provide array-like fast access. The **facet**s of a **locale** are accessed by using the **use_facet<Facet>(loc)** notation; see §39.3.1.

The standard library provides a rich set of **facet**s. To help the programmer manipulate **facet**s in logical groups, the standard **facet**s are grouped into categories, such as **numeric** and **collate** (§39.4):

facet **Categories (§iso.22.3.1)**	
collate	E.g., **collate**; §39.4.1
ctype	E.g., **ctype**; §39.4.5
numeric	E.g., **num_put, num_get, numpunct**; §39.4.2
monetary	**money_put, money_get, moneypunct**; §39.4.3
time	E.g., **time_put, time_get**; §39.4.4
messages	**messages**; §39.4.7
all	**collate	ctype	monetary	numeric	time	messages**
none	

There are no facilities for a programmer to specify a name string for a newly created **locale**. Name strings are either defined in the program's execution environment or created as combinations of such names by **locale** constructors.

A programmer can replace **facets** from existing categories (§39.4, §39.4.2.1). However, there is no way for a programmer to define a new category. The notion of "category" applies to standard-library facets only, and it is not extensible. Thus, a facet need not belong to any category, and many user-defined facets do not.

If a **locale x** does not have a name string, it is undefined whether **locale::global(x)** affects the C global locale. This implies that a C++ program cannot reliably and portably set the C locale to a locale that wasn't retrieved from the execution environment. There is no standard way for a C program to set the C++ global locale (except by calling a C++ function to do so). In a mixed C and C++ program, having the C global locale differ from **global()** is error prone.

By far the dominant use of **locales** is implicitly, in stream I/O. Each **istream** and **ostream** has its own **locale**. The **locale** of a stream is by default the global **locale** (§39.2.1) at the time of the stream's creation. The **locale** of a stream can be set by the **imbue()** operation, and we can extract a copy of a stream's **locale** using **getloc()** (§38.4.5.1).

Setting the global **locale** does not affect existing I/O streams; those still use the **locales** that they were imbued with before the global **locale** was reset.

39.2.1 Named locales

A **locale** is constructed from another **locale** and from **facets**. The simplest way of making a **locale** is to copy an existing one. For example:

```
locale loc1;                              // copy of the current global locale
locale loc2 {""};                         // copy of "the user's preferred locale"

locale loc3 {"C"};                        // copy of the "C" locale
locale loc4 {locale::classic()};          // copy of the "C" locale

locale loc5 {"POSIX"};                    // copy of the locale named "POSIX"
locale loc6 {"Danish_Denmark.1252"};     // copy of the locale named "Danish_Denmark.1252"
locale loc7 {"en_US.UTF-8"};             // copy of the locale named "en_US.UTF-8"
```

The meaning of **locale{"C"}** is defined by the standard to be the "classic" C locale; this is the locale that has been used throughout this book. Other **locale** names are implementation-defined.

The **locale{""}** is deemed to be "the user's preferred locale." This locale is set by extralinguistic means in a program's execution environment. So to see your current "preferred locale," write:

```
locale loc("");
cout << loc.name() << '\n';
```

On my Windows laptop, I got:

```
English_United States.1252
```

On my Linux box, I got:

```
en_US.UTF-8
```

The names of locales are not standardized for C++. Instead, a variety of organizations, such as POSIX and Microsoft, maintain their own (differing) standards across different programming languages. For example:

GNU Locale Name Examples (Based on POSIX)	
ja_JP	Japanese for Japan
da_DK	Danish for Denmark
en_DK	English for Denmark
de_CH	German for Switzerland
de_DE	German for Germany
en_GB	English for Great Britain
en_US	English for the U.S.A.
fr_CA	French for Canada
de_DE	German for Germany
de_DE@euro	German for Germany with the euro symbol €
de_DE.utf8	German for Germany using UTF-8
de_DE.utf8@euro	German for Germany using UTF-8 with the euro symbol €

POSIX recommends a format of a lowercase language name, optionally followed by an uppercase country name, optionally followed by an encoding specifier, for example, **sv_FI@euro** (Swedish for Finland including the euro symbol).

Microsoft Locale Name Examples
Arabic_Qatar.1256
Basque.Spain.1252
Chinese_Singapore.936
English_United Kingdom.1252
English_United States.1252
French_Canada.1252
Greek_Greece.1253
Hebrew_Israel.1255
Hindi_India.1252
Russian_Russia.1251

Microsoft uses a language name followed by a country name optionally followed by a code page number. A *code page* is a named (or numbered) character encoding.

Most operating systems have ways of setting a default locale for a program. Typically, that is done through environment variables with names such as **LC_ALL**, **LC_COLLATE**, and **LANG**. Often, a locale suitable to the person using a system is chosen when that person first encounters a system. For example, I would expect a person who configures a Linux system to use Argentine Spanish as its default setting will find **locale{""}** to mean **locale{"es_AR"}**. However, these names are not standardized across platforms. So, to use named **locale**s on a given system, a programmer must refer to system documentation and experiment.

It is generally a good idea to avoid embedding **locale** name strings in the program text. Mentioning a file name or a system constant in the program text limits the portability of a program and often forces a programmer who wants to adapt a program to a new environment to find and change such values. Mentioning a **locale** name string has similar unpleasant consequences. Instead, **locale**s can be picked up from the program's execution environment (for example, using **locale("")** or reading a file). Alternatively, a program can request a user to specify alternative locales by entering a string. For example:

```
void user_set_locale(const string& question)
{
        cout << question;    // e.g., "If you want to use a different locale, please enter its name"
        string s;
        cin >> s;
        locale::global(locale{s}); // set global locale as specified by user
}
```

It is usually better to let a non-expert user pick from a list of alternatives. A function implementing this would need to know where and how a system keeps its **locale**s. For example, many Linux systems keep their **locale**s in the directory **/usr/share/locale**.

If the string argument doesn't refer to a defined **locale**, the constructor throws the **runtime_error** exception (§30.4.1.1). For example:

```
void set_loc(locale& loc, const char* name)
try
{
        loc = locale{name};
}
catch (runtime_error&) {
        cerr << "locale
        // ...
}
```

If a **locale** has a name string, **name()** will return it. If not, **name()** will return **string("*")**. A name string is primarily a way to refer to a **locale** stored in the execution environment. Secondarily, a name string can be used as a debugging aid. For example:

```
void print_locale_names(const locale& my_loc)
{
        cout << "name of current global locale: " << locale().name() << "\n";
        cout << "name of classic C locale: " << locale::classic().name() << "\n";
        cout << "name of "user's preferred locale": " << locale("").name() << "\n";
        cout << "name of my locale: " << my_loc.name() << "\n";
}
```

39.2.1.1 Constructing New **locales**

A new **locale** is made by taking an existing **locale** and adding or replacing **facet**s. Typically, a new **locale** is a minor variation on an existing one. For example:

```
void f(const locale& loc, const My_money_io* mio)       // My_money_io defined in §39.4.3.1
{
        locale loc1(locale{"POSIX"},loc,locale::monetary); // use monetary facets from loc
        locale loc2 = locale(locale::classic(), mio);               // classic plus mio
        // ...
}
```

Here, **loc1** is a copy of the **POSIX** locale modified to use **loc**'s monetary **facets** (§39.4.3). Similarly, **loc2** is a copy of the **C** locale modified to use a **My_money_io** (§39.4.3.1). The resulting **locales** can be represented like this:

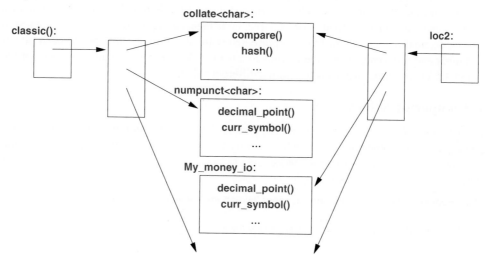

If a **Facet*** argument (here, **My_money_io**) is **nullptr**, the resulting **locale** is simply a copy of the **locale** argument.

In a construction **locale{loc,f}**, the **f** argument must identify a specific **facet** type. A plain **facet*** is not sufficient. For example:

```
void g(const locale::facet* mio1, const money_put<char>* mio2)
{
        locale loc3 = locale(locale::classic(), mio1);      // error: type of facet not known
        locale loc4 = locale(locale::classic(), mio2);      // OK: type of facet known (moneyput<char>)
        // ...
}
```

The **locale** uses the type of the **Facet*** argument to determine the type of the **facet** at compile time. Specifically, the implementation of **locale** uses a **facet**'s identifying type, **facet::id** (§39.3), to find that **facet** in the **locale** (§39.3.1). The constructor

```
template<class Facet> locale(const locale& x, Facet* f);
```

is the only mechanism offered within the language for the programmer to supply a **facet** to be used through a **locale**. Other **locales** are supplied by implementers as named locales (§39.2.1). Named locales can be retrieved from the program's execution environment. A programmer who understands the implementation-specific mechanism used for that might be able to add new **locales**.

The set of constructors for **locale** is designed so that the type of every **facet** is known either from type deduction (of the **Facet** template parameter) or because it came from another **locale** (that knew its type). Specifying a **category** argument specifies the type of **facets** indirectly, because the **locale** knows the type of the **facets** in the categories. This implies that the **locale** class can (and does) keep track of the types of **facets** so that it can manipulate them with minimal overhead.

The **locale::id** member type is used by **locale** to identify **facet** types (§39.3).

There is no way of modifying a **locale**. Instead, the **locale** operations provide ways of making new **locales** from existing ones. The fact that a **locale** is immutable after it has been created is essential for run-time efficiency. This allows someone using a **locale** to call virtual functions of a **facet** and to cache the values returned. For example, an **istream** can know what character is used to represent the decimal point and how **true** is represented without calling **decimal_point()** each time it reads a number and **truename()** each time it reads to a **bool** (§39.4.2). Only a call of **imbue()** for the stream (§38.4.5.1) can cause such calls to return a different value.

39.2.2 Comparing strings

Comparing two **strings** according to a **locale** is possibly the most common use of a **locale** outside I/O. Consequently, this operation is provided directly by **locale** so that users don't have to build their own comparison function from the **collate** facet (§39.4.1). This **string** comparison function is defined as **locale**'s **operator()()**. For example:

```
void user(const string s1, const string s2, const locale& my_locale)
{
    if (my_locale(s,s2)) {      // is s<s2 according to my_locale?
        // ...
    }
}
```

Having the comparison function as the () operator makes it directly useful as a predicate (§4.5.4). For example:

```
void f(vector<string>& v, const locale& my_locale)
{
    sort(v.begin(),v.end());                // sort using < to compare elements
    // ...
    sort(v.begin(),v.end(),my_locale);   // sort according to the rules of my_locale
    // ...
}
```

By default, the standard-library **sort()** uses < for the numerical value of the implementation character set to determine collation order (§32.6, §31.2.2.1).

39.3 Class facet

A **locale** is a collection of **facets**. A **facet** represents one specific cultural aspect, such as how a number is represented on output (**num_put**), how a date is read from input (**time_get**), and how characters are stored in a file (**codecvt**). The standard-library **facets** are listed in §39.4.

A user can define new **facets**, such as a **facet** determining how the names of the seasons are printed (§39.3.2).

A **facet** is represented in a program as an object of a class derived from **std::locale::facet**. Like all other **locale** facilities, **facet** is found in <locale>:

```
class locale::facet {
protected:
      explicit facet(size_t refs = 0);
      virtual ~facet();
      facet(const facet&) = delete;
      void operator=(const facet&) = delete;
};
```

The facet class is designed to be a base class and has no public functions. Its constructor is **protected** to prevent the creation of "plain facet" objects, and its destructor is **virtual** to ensure proper destruction of derived-class objects.

A facet is intended to be managed through pointers stored in locales. A 0 argument to the facet constructor means that locale should delete the facet when the last reference to it goes away. Conversely, a nonzero constructor argument ensures that locale never deletes the facet. A nonzero argument is meant for the rare case in which the lifetime of a facet is controlled directly by the programmer rather than indirectly through a locale.

Each kind of facet interface must have a separate id:

```
class locale::id {
public:
      id();
      void operator=(const id&) = delete;
      id(const id&) = delete;
};
```

The intended use of id is for the user to define a **static** member of type id of each class supplying a new facet interface (for example, see §39.4.1). The locale mechanisms use ids to identify facets (§39.2, §39.3.1). In the obvious implementation of a locale, an id is used as an index into a vector of pointers to facets, thereby implementing an efficient map<id,facet*>.

Data used to define a (derived) facet is defined in the derived class. This implies that the programmer defining a facet has full control over the data and that arbitrary amounts of data can be used to implement the concept represented by a facet.

A facet is intended to be immutable, so all member functions of a user-defined facet should be defined **const**.

39.3.1 Accessing facets in a locale

The facets of a locale are accessed using two template functions:

Non-member locale functions (§iso.22.3.2)	
f=use_facet<F>(loc)	f is a reference to the facet F in loc; throw bad_cast if loc doesn't have F
has_facet<F>(loc)	Does loc have facet F? noexcept

Think of these functions as doing a lookup in their locale argument for their template parameter F. Alternatively, think of use_facet as a kind of explicit type conversion (cast) of a locale to a specific facet. This is feasible because a locale can have only one facet of a given type. For example:

```
void f(const locale& my_locale)
{
    char c = use_facet<numpunct<char>>(my_locale).decimal_point() // use standard facet
    // ...

    if (has_facet<Encrypt>(my_locale)) {      // does my_locale contain an Encrypt facet?
        const Encrypt& f = use_facet<Encrypt>(my_locale);      // retrieve Encrypt facet
        const Crypto c = f.get_crypto();                       // use Encrypt facet
        // ...
    }
    // ...
}
```

The standard facets are guaranteed to be available for all locales (§39.4), so we don't need to use has_facet for standard facets.

One way of looking at the facet::id mechanism is as an optimized implementation of a form of compile-time polymorphism. A dynamic_cast can be used to get very similar results to what use_facet produces. However, the specialized use_facet can be implemented more efficiently than the general dynamic_cast.

An id identifies an interface and a behavior rather than a class. That is, if two facet classes have exactly the same interface and implement the same semantics (as far as a locale is concerned), they should be identified by the same id. For example, collate<char> and collate_byname<char> are interchangeable in a locale, so both are identified by collate<char>::id (§39.4.1).

If we define a facet with a new interface – such as Encrypt in f() – we must define a corresponding id to identify it (see §39.3.2 and §39.4.1).

39.3.2 A Simple User-Defined facet

The standard library provides standard facets for the most critical areas of cultural differences, such as character sets and I/O of numbers. To examine the facet mechanism in isolation from the complexities of widely used types and the efficiency concerns that accompany them, let me first present a facet for a trivial user-defined type:

```
enum Season { spring, summer, fall, winter }; // very simple user-defined type
```

The style of I/O outlined here can be used with little variation for most simple user-defined types.

```
class Season_io : public locale::facet {
public:
    Season_io(int i = 0) : locale::facet{i} { }
    ~Season_io() { }              // to make it possible to destroy Season_io objects (§39.3)

    virtual const string& to_str(Season x) const = 0;              // string representation of x
    virtual bool from_str(const string& s, Season& x) const = 0; // place Season for s in x

    static locale::id id;   // facet identifier object (§39.2, §39.3, §39.3.1)
};

locale::id Season_io::id; // define the identifier object
```

For simplicity, this **facet** is limited to **strings** of **chars**.

The **Season_io** class provides a general and abstract interface for all **Season_io** facets. To define the I/O representation of a **Season** for a particular **locale**, we derive a class from **Season_io**, defining **to_str()** and **from_str()** appropriately.

Output of a **Season** is easy. If the stream has a **Season_io** facet, we can use that to convert the value into a string. If not, we can output the **int** value of the **Season**:

```
ostream& operator<<(ostream& os, Season x)
{
      locale loc {os.getloc()};          // extract the stream's locale (§38.4.4)

      if (has_facet<Season_io>(loc))
             return os << use_facet<Season_io>(loc).to_str(x); // string representation
      return os << static_cast<int>(x);                        // integer representation
}
```

For maximum efficiency and flexibility, standard **facets** tend to operate directly on stream buffers (§39.4.2.2, §39.4.2.3). However, for a simple user-defined type, such as **Season**, there is no need to drop to the **streambuf** level of abstraction.

As is typical, input is a bit more complicated than output:

```
istream& operator>>(istream& is, Season& x)
{
      const locale& loc {is.getloc()};                         // extract the stream's locale (§38.4.4)

      if (has_facet<Season_io>(loc)) {
             const Season_io& f {use_facet<Season_io>(loc)}; // get hold of the locale's Season_io facet

             string buf;
             if (!(is>>buf && f.from_str(buf,x)))              // read alphabetic representation
                    is.setstate(ios_base::failbit);
             return is;
      }

      int i;
      is >> i;                                                 // read numeric representation
      x = static_cast<Season>(i);
      return is;
}
```

The error handling is simple and follows the error-handling style for built-in types. That is, if the input string didn't represent a **Season** in the chosen **locale**, the stream is put into the **fail** state. If exceptions are enabled, this implies that an **ios_base::failure** exception is thrown (§38.3).

Here is a trivial test program:

```
int main()
      // a trivial test
{
      Season x;
```

```
    // use the default locale (no Season_io facet) implies integer I/O:
    cin >> x;
    cout << x << endl;

    locale loc(locale(),new US_season_io{});
    cout.imbue(loc);        // use locale with Season_io facet
    cin.imbue(loc);         // use locale with Season_io facet

    cin >> x;
    cout << x << endl;
}
```

Given the input

```
2
summer
```

this program responds:

```
2
summer
```

To get this, we must derive a class **US_season_io** from **Season_io**, and define an appropriate string representation of the seasons:

```
class US_season_io : public Season_io {
    static const string seasons[];
public:
    const string& to_str(Season) const;
    bool from_str(const string&, Season&) const;

    // note: no US_season_io::id
};

const string US_season_io::seasons[] = {
    "spring",
    "summer",
    "fall",
    "winter"
};
```

Then, we override the **Season_io** functions that convert between the string representation and the enumerators:

```
const string& US_season_io::to_str(Season x) const
{
    if (x<spring || winter<x) {
        static const string ss = "no–such–season";
        return ss;
    }
    return seasons[x];
}
```

```
bool US_season_io::from_str(const string& s, Season& x) const
{
    const string∗ p = find(begin(seasons),end(seasons),s);
    if (p==end)
        return false;

    x = Season(p−begin(seasons));
    return true;
}
```

Note that because **US_season_io** is simply an implementation of the **Season_io** interface, I did not define an **id** for **US_season_io**. In fact, if we want **US_season_io** to be used as a **Season_io**, we must not give **US_season_io** its own **id**. Operations on **locales**, such as **has_facet** (§39.3.1), rely on **facet**s implementing the same concepts being identified by the same **id** (§39.3).

The only interesting implementation question is what to do if asked to output an invalid **Season**. Naturally, that shouldn't happen. However, it is not uncommon to find an invalid value for a simple user-defined type, so it is realistic to take that possibility into account. I could have thrown an exception, but when dealing with simple output intended for humans to read, it is often helpful to produce an "out-of-range" representation for an out-of-range value. Note that for input, the error-handling policy is left to the >> operator, whereas for output, the **facet** function **to_str()** implements an error-handling policy. This was done to illustrate the design alternatives. In a "production design," the **facet** functions would either implement error handling for both input and output or just report errors for >> and << to handle.

This **Season_io** design relies on derived classes to supply the **locale**-specific strings. An alternative design would have **Season_io** itself retrieve those strings from a **locale**-specific repository (see §39.4.7). The possibility of having a single **Season_io** class to which the season strings are passed as constructor arguments is left as an exercise.

39.3.3 Uses of locales and facets

The primary use of **locales** within the standard library is in I/O streams. However, the **locale** mechanism is a general and extensible mechanism for representing culture-sensitive information. The **messages** facet (§39.4.7) is an example of a **facet** that has nothing to do with I/O streams. Extensions to the **iostream** library and even I/O facilities that are not based on streams might take advantage of **locales**. Also, a user may use **locales** as a convenient way of organizing arbitrary culture-sensitive information.

Because of the generality of the **locale/facet** mechanism, the possibilities for user-defined **facets** are unlimited. Plausible candidates for representation as **facets** are dates, time zones, phone numbers, social security numbers (personal identification numbers), product codes, temperatures, general (unit,value) pairs, postal codes (zip codes), clothing sizes, and ISBN numbers.

As with every other powerful mechanism, **facets** should be used with care. That something can be represented as a **facet** doesn't mean that it is best represented that way. The key issues to consider when selecting a representation for cultural dependencies are – as ever – how the various decisions affect the difficulty of writing code, the ease of reading the resulting code, the maintainability of the resulting program, and the efficiency in time and space of the resulting I/O operations.

39.4 Standard facets

In <locale>, the standard library provides these facets:

Standard facets (§iso.22.3.1.1.1)			
collate	String comparison	collate<C>	§39.4.1
numeric	Numeric formatting	numpunct<C> num_get<C,In> num_put<C,Out>	§39.4.2
monetary	Money formatting	moneypunct<C> moneypunct<C,International> money_get<C,In> money_put<C,Out>	§39.4.3
time	Date and time formatting	time_put<C,Out> time_put_byname<C,Out> time_get<C,In>	§39.4.4
ctype	Character classification	ctype<C> codecvt<In,Ex,SS> codecvt_byname<In,Ex,SS>	§39.4.5
messages	Message retrieval	messages<C>	§39.4.7

The details are explained in the referenced subsections.

When instantiating a facet from this table, C must be a character type (§36.1). These facets are guaranteed to be defined for char or wchar_t. In addition, ctype<C> is guaranteed to support char16_t and char32_t. A user who needs standard I/O to deal with another character type X must rely on implementation-specific facet specializations or provide suitable versions of facets for X. For example, codecvt<X,char,mbstate_t> (§39.4.6) might be needed to control conversions between X and char.

International can be true or false; true means that a three-character (plus zero terminator) "international" representation of a currency symbol is used (§39.4.3.1), such as USD and BRL.

A shift-state parameter, SS, is used to represent the shift states of a multibyte character representation (§39.4.6). In <cwchar>, mbstate_t is defined to represent any of the conversion states that can occur in an implementation-defined set of supported multibyte character encoding rules. The equivalent to mbstate_t for an arbitrary character type X is char_traits<X>::state_type (§36.2.2).

In and Out are input iterators and output iterators, respectively (§33.1.2, §33.1.4). Providing the _put and _get facets with these template arguments allows a programmer to provide facets that access nonstandard buffers (§39.4.2.2). Buffers associated with iostreams are stream buffers, so the iterators provided for those are ostreambuf_iterators (§38.6.3, §39.4.2.2). Consequently, the function failed() is available for error handling (§38.6.3).

Each standard facet has a _byname version. An F_byname facet is derived from the facet F. F_byname provides the identical interface to F, except that it adds a constructor taking a string argument naming a locale (e.g., see §39.4.1). The F_byname(name) provides the appropriate semantics for F defined in locale(name). For example:

```
sort(v.begin(),v.end(),collate_byname{"da_DK"});   // sort using character comparison from "da_DK"
```

The idea is to pick a version of a standard facet from a named locale (§39.2.1) in the program's execution environment. This implies that _byname constructors are very slow compared to constructors that do not need to consult the environment. It is almost always faster to construct a locale and then to access its facets than it is to use _byname facets in many places in a program. Thus, reading a facet from the environment once and then using the copy in main memory repeatedly is usually a good idea. For example:

```
locale dk {"da_DK"};     // read the Danish locale (including all of its facets) once
                         // then use the dk locale and its facets as needed

void f(vector<string>& v, const locale& loc)
{
    const collate<char>& col {use_facet<collate<char>>(dk)};
    const ctype<char>& ctyp {use_facet<ctype<char>>(dk)};

    locale dk1 {loc,&col};        // use Danish string comparison
    locale dk2 {dk1,&ctyp};  // use Danish character classification and string comparison

    sort(v.begin(),v.end(),dk2);
    // ...
}
```

This dk2 locale will use Danish-style strings but will retain the default conventions for numbers.

The notion of categories gives a simpler way of manipulating standard facets in locales. For example, given the dk locale, we can construct a locale that reads and compares strings according to the rules of Danish (which has three more vowels than English) but that retains the syntax of numbers used in C++:

```
locale dk_us(locale::classic(),dk,collate|ctype);    // Danish letters, American numbers
```

The presentations of individual standard facets contain more examples of facet use. In particular, the discussion of collate (§39.4.1) brings out many of the common structural aspects of facets.

Standard facets often depend on each other. For example, num_put depends on numpunct. Only if you have a detailed knowledge of individual facets can you successfully mix and match facets or add new versions of the standard facets. In other words, beyond the simple operations (such as imbue() for iostreams and using collate for sort()), the locale mechanisms are not meant to be directly used by novices. For an extensive discussion of locales, see [Langer,2000].

The design of an individual facet is often messy. The reason is partially that facets have to reflect messy cultural conventions outside the control of the library designer, and partially that the C++ standard library-facilities have to remain largely compatible with what is offered by the C standard library and various platform-specific standards.

On the other hand, the framework provided by locales and facets is general and flexible. A facet can be designed to hold any data, and the facet's operations can provide any desired operation based on that data. If the behavior of a new facet isn't overconstrained by convention, its design can be simple and clean (§39.3.2).

39.4.1 string Comparison

The standard **collate** facet provides ways of comparing arrays of characters:

```
template<class C>
class collate : public locale::facet {
public:
    using char_type = C;
    using string_type = basic_string<C>;

    explicit collate(size_t = 0);

    int compare(const C* b, const C* e, const C* b2, const C* e2) const
        { return do_compare(b,e,b2,e2); }

    long hash(const C* b, const C* e) const
        { return do_hash(b,e); }
    string_type transform(const C* b, const C* e) const
        { return do_transform(b,e); }

    static locale::id id;   // facet identifier object (§39.2, §39.3, §39.3.1)

protected:
    ˜collate(); // note: protected destructor

    virtual int do_compare(const C* b, const C* e, const C* b2, const C* e2) const;
    virtual string_type do_transform(const C* b, const C* e) const;
    virtual long do_hash(const C* b, const C* e) const;
};
```

This defines two interfaces:

- The **public** interface for users of the **facet**.
- The **protected** interface for implementers of derived **facet**s.

The constructor argument specifies whether a **locale** or a user is responsible for deleting the **facet**. The default (**0**) means "let the **locale** manage" (§39.3).

All standard-library **facet**s share a common structure, so the salient facts about a **facet** can be summarized by the key functions:

collate<C> facet (§iso.22.4.4.1)
int compare(const C* b, const C* e, const C* b2, const C* e2) const;
long hash(const C* b, const C* e) const;
string_type transform(const C* b, const C* e) const;

To define a **facet** use **collate** as the pattern. To derive from a standard pattern, simply define the **do_*** versions of the key functions providing the **facet**'s functionality. The full declarations of functions are listed (rather than use patterns) to give sufficient information to write an overriding **do_*** function. For an example, see §39.4.1.1.

The **hash()** function calculates a hash value for its imput string. Obviously, this can be useful for building hash tables.

The **transform()** function produces a string that, when compared to another **transform()**ed string, gives the same result as comparing the strings. That is:

> cf.compare(cf.transform(s),cf.transform(s2)) == cf.compare(s,s2)

The purpose of **transform()** is to allow optimization of code in which a string is compared to many others. This is useful when implementing a search among a set of strings.

The **compare()** function does the basic string comparison according to the rules defined for a particular **collate**. It returns:

  1   if the first string is lexicographically greater than the second
  0   if the strings are identical
  –1 if the second string is greater than the first

For example:

```
void f(const string& s1, const string& s2, const collate<char>& cmp)
{
    const char* cs1 {s1.data()};     // because compare() operates on char[]s
    const char* cs2 {s2.data()};

    switch (cmp.compare(cs1,cs1+s1.size(),cs2,cs2+s2.size()) {
    case 0:          // identical strings according to cmp
        // ...
        break;
    case –1:         // s1 < s2
        // ...
        break;
    case 1:          // s1 > s2
        // ...
        break;
    }
}
```

The **collate** member functions compare [b:e) ranges of **C** rather than **basic_string**s or zero-terminated C-style strings. In particular, a **C** with the numeric value **0** is treated as an ordinary character rather than as a terminator.

The standard-library **string** is not **locale** sensitive. That is, it compares strings according to the rules of the implementation's character set (§6.2.3). Furthermore, the standard **string** does not provide a direct way of specifying comparison criteria (Chapter 36). To do a **locale**-sensitive comparison, we can use a **collate**'s **compare()**. For example:

```
void f(const string& s1, const string& s2, const string& name)
{
    bool b {s1==s2};                 // compare using implementation's character set values

    const char* s1b {s1.data()};            // get start of data
    const char* s1e {s1.data()+s1.size()}   // get end of data
    const char* s2b {s2.data()};
    const char* s2e {s2.data()+s2.size()}
```

```
        using Col = collate<char>;

        const Col& global {use_facet<Col>(locale{})};        // from the current global locale
        int i0 {global.compare(s1b,s1e,s2b,s2e)};

        const Col& my_coll {use_facet<Col>(locale{""})};      // from my preferred locale
        int i1 {my_coll.compare(s1b,s1e,s2b,s2e)};

        const Col& n_coll {use_facet<Col>(locale{name})};     // from a named locale
        int i2 {n_coll.compare(s1b,s1e,s2b,s2e)};
    }
```

Notationally, it can be more convenient to use **collate**'s **compare()** indirectly through a **locale**'s **operator()** (§39.2.2). For example:

```
    void f(const string& s1, const string& s2, const string& name)
    {
        int i0 = locale{}(s1,s2);       // compare using the current global locale
        int i1 = locale{""}(s1,s2);     // compare using my preferred locale
        int i2 = locale{name}(s1,s2);   // compare using the named locale
        // ...
    }
```

It is not difficult to imagine cases in which **i0**, **i1**, and **i2** differ. Consider this sequence of words from a German dictionary:

Dialekt, Diät, dich, dichten, Dichtung

According to convention, nouns (only) are capitalized, but the ordering is not case sensitive.

A case-sensitive German sort would place all words starting with **D** before **d**:

Dialekt, Diät, Dichtung, dich, dichten

The **ä** (umlaut a) is treated as "a kind of **a**," so it comes before **c**. However, in most common character sets, the numeric value of **ä** is larger than the numeric value of **c**. Consequently, **int('c')<int('ä')**, and the simple default sort based on numeric values gives:

Dialekt, Dichtung, Diät, dich, dichten

Writing a compare function that orders this sequence correctly according to the dictionary is an interesting exercise.

39.4.1.1 Named collate

A **collate_byname** is a version of **collate** for a **locale** named by a constructor string argument:

```
    template<class C>
    class collate_byname : public collate<C> {    // note: no id and no new functions
    public:
        typedef basic_string<C> string_type;

        explicit collate_byname(const char*, size_t r = 0); // construct from named locale
        explicit collate_byname(const string&, size_t r = 0);
```

```
protected:
    ˜collate_byname();   // note: protected destructor

    int do_compare(const C∗ b, const C∗ e, const C∗ b2, const C∗ e2) const override;
    string_type do_transform(const C∗ b, const C∗ e) const override;
    long do_hash(const C∗ b, const C∗ e) const override;
};
```

Thus, a **collate_byname** can be used to pick out a **collate** from a **locale** named in the program's execution environment (§39.4). One obvious way of storing **facets** in an execution environment would be as data in a file. A less flexible alternative would be to represent a **facet** as program text and data in a _byname facet.

39.4.2 Numeric Formatting

Numeric output is done by a **num_put** facet writing into a stream buffer (§38.6). Conversely, numeric input is done by a **num_get** facet reading from a stream buffer. The format used by **num_put** and **num_get** is defined by a "numerical punctuation" **facet** called **numpunct**.

39.4.2.1 Numeric Punctuation

The **numpunct** facet defines the I/O format of built-in types, such as **bool**, **int**, and **double**:

numpunct<C> facet (§iso.22.4.6.3.1)	
C decimal_point() const;	E.g., '.'
C thousands_sep() const;	E.g., ','
string grouping() const;	E.g., "" meaning "no grouping"
string_type truename() const;	E.g., "true"
string_type falsename() const;	E.g., "false"

The characters of the string returned by **grouping()** are read as a sequence of small integer values. Each number specifies a number of digits for a group. Character **0** specifies the rightmost group (the least significant digits), character **1** the group to the left of that, etc. Thus, "\004\002\003" describes a number such as **123–45–6789** (provided you use '–' as the separation character). If necessary, the last number in a grouping pattern is used repeatedly, so "\003" is equivalent to "\003\003\003". The most common use of grouping is to make large numbers more readable. The **grouping()** and **thousands_sep()** functions define a format for both input and output of integers and the integer part of floating-point values.

We can define a new punctuation style by deriving from **numpunct**. For example, I could define facet **My_punct** to write integer values using spaces to group the digits in sets of three and floating-point values, using a European-style comma as the "decimal point":

```
class My_punct : public numpunct<char> {
public:
    explicit My_punct(size_t r = 0) :numpunct<char>(r) { }
protected:
    char do_decimal_point() const override  { return ','; }        // comma
```

```
        char do_thousands_sep() const override { return '_'; }      // underscore
        string do_grouping() const override { return "\003"; }      // 3-digit groups
};

void f()
{
        cout << "style A: " << 12345678
             << " *** " << 1234567.8
             << " *** " << fixed << 1234567.8 << '\n';
        cout << defaultfloat;                    // reset floating format
        locale loc(locale(),new My_punct);
        cout.imbue(loc);
        cout << "style B: " << 12345678
             << " *** " << 1234567.8
             << " *** " << fixed << 1234567.8 << '\n';
}
```

This produces:

```
style A: 12345678 *** 1.23457e+06 *** 1234567.800000
style B: 12_345_678 *** 1_234_567,800000 *** 1_234_567,800000
```

Note that **imbue()** stores a copy of its argument in its stream. Consequently, a stream can rely on an imbued **locale** even after the original copy of that **locale** has been destroyed. If an **iostream** has its **boolalpha** flag set (§38.4.5.1), the strings returned by **truename()** and **falsename()** are used to represent **true** and **false**, respectively; otherwise, **1** and **0** are used.

A _byname version (§39.4, §39.4.1) of **numpunct** is provided:

```
template<class C>
class numpunct_byname : public numpunct<C> {
        // ...
};
```

39.4.2.2 Numeric Output

When writing to a stream buffer (§38.6), an **ostream** relies on the **num_put** facet:

num_put<C,Out=ostreambuf_iterator<C>> facet (§iso.22.4.2.2)   Put value **v** to buffer position **b** in stream **s**
Out put(Out b, ios_base& s, C fill, bool v) const;
Out put(Out b, ios_base& s, C fill, long v) const;
Out put(Out b, ios_base& s, C fill, long long v) const;
Out put(Out b, ios_base& s, C fill, unsigned long v) const;
Out put(Out b, ios_base& s, C fill, unsigned long long v) const;
Out put(Out b, ios_base& s, C fill, double v) const;
Out put(Out b, ios_base& s, C fill, long double v) const;
Out put(Out b, ios_base& s, C fill, const void* v) const;

The value of **put()** is that iterator positioned one past the last character position written.

The default specialization of num_put (the one where the iterator used to access characters is of type ostreambuf_iterator<C>) is part of the standard locales (§39.4). To write elsewhere using a num_put, we must define an appropriate specialization. For example, here is a very simple num_put for writing into a string:

```
template<class C>
class String_numput : public num_put<C,typename basic_string<C>::iterator> {
public:
    String_numput() :num_put<C,typename basic_string<C>::iterator>{1} { }
};
```

I don't mean for String_numput to go into a locale, so I used the constructor argument to retain ordinary lifetime rules. The intended use is something like this:

```
void f(int i, string& s, int pos)  // format i into s starting at pos
{
    String_numput<char> f;
    f.put(s.begin()+pos,cout,' ',i);  // format i into s; use cout's formatting rules
}
```

The ios_base argument (here, cout) provides information about formatting state and locale. For example:

```
void test(iostream& io)
{
    locale loc = io.getloc();

    wchar_t wc = use_facet<ctype<char>>(loc).widen(c);           // char to C conversion
    string s = use_facet<numpunct<char>>(loc).decimal_point();   // default: '.'
    string false_name = use_facet<numpunct<char>>(loc).falsename();  // default: "false"
}
```

A standard facet, such as num_put<char>, is typically used implicitly through a standard I/O stream function. Consequently, most programmers need not know about it. However, the use of such facets by standard-library functions is interesting because they show how I/O streams work and how facets can be used. As ever, the standard library provides examples of interesting programming techniques.

Using num_put, the implementer of ostream might write:

```
template<class C, class Tr>
basic_ostream<C,Tr>& basic_ostream<C,Tr>::operator<<(double d)
{
    sentry guard(*this);       // see §38.4.1
    if (!guard) return *this;

    try {
        if (use_facet<num_put<C,Tr>>(getloc()).put(*this,*this,this->fill(),d).failed())
            setstate(badbit);
    }
```

```
            catch (...) {
                handle_ioexception(*this);
            }
            return *this;
        }
```

A lot is going on here. The sentry ensures that all prefix and suffix operations are performed (§38.4.1). We get the **ostream**'s **locale** by calling its member function **getloc()** (§38.4.5.1). We extract **num_put** from that **locale** using **use_facet** (§39.3.1). That done, we call the appropriate **put()** function to do the real work. An **ostreambuf_iterator** can be constructed from an **ostream** (§38.6.3), and an **ostream** can be implicitly converted to its base class **ios_base** (§38.4.4), so the first two arguments to **put()** are easily supplied.

A call of **put()** returns its output iterator argument. This output iterator is obtained from a **basic_ostream**, so it is an **ostreambuf_iterator**. Consequently, **failed()** (§38.6.3) is available to test for failure and to allow us to set the stream state appropriately.

I did not use **has_facet**, because the standard **facets** (§39.4) are guaranteed to be present in every **locale**. If that guarantee is violated, **bad_cast** is thrown (§39.3.1).

The **put()** function calls the virtual **do_put()**. Consequently, user-defined code may be executed, and **operator<<()** must be prepared to handle an exception thrown by the overriding **do_put()**. Also, **num_put** may not exist for some character types, so **use_facet()** might throw **bad_cast** (§39.3.1). The behavior of a << for a built-in type, such as **double**, is defined by the C++ standard. Consequently, the question is not what **handle_ioexception()** should do but rather how it should do what the standard prescribes. If **badbit** is set in this **ostream**'s exception state (§38.3), the exception is simply re-thrown. Otherwise, an exception is handled by setting the stream state and continuing. In either case, **badbit** must be set in the stream state (§38.4.5.1):

```
template<class C, class Tr>
void handle_ioexception(basic_ostream<C,Tr>& s)// called from catch-clause
{
    if (s.exceptions()&ios_base::badbit) {
        try {
            s.setstate(ios_base::badbit);   // might throw basic_ios::failure
        }
        catch(...) {
            // ... do nothing ...
        }
        throw;      // re-throw
    }
    s.setstate(ios_base::badbit);
}
```

The **try**-block is needed because **setstate()** might throw **basic_ios::failure** (§38.3, §38.4.5.1). However, if **badbit** is set in the exception state, **operator<<()** must re-throw the exception that caused **handle_ioexception()** to be called (rather than simply throwing **basic_ios::failure**).

The << for a built-in type, such as **double**, must be implemented by writing directly to a stream buffer. When writing a << for a user-defined type, we can often avoid the resulting complexity by expressing the output of the user-defined type in terms of output of existing types (§39.3.2).

39.4.2.3 Numeric Input

When reading from a stream buffer (§38.6), an **istream** relies on the **num_get** facet:

num_get<In = istreambuf_iterator<C>> facet (§iso.22.4.2.1)
Read [b:e) into v, using formatting rules from s, reporting errors by setting **r**
In get(In b, In e, ios_base& s, ios_base::iostate& r, bool& v) const;
In get(In b, In e, ios_base& s, ios_base::iostate& r, long& v) const;
In get(In b, In e, ios_base& s, ios_base::iostate& r, long long& v) const;
In get(In b, In e, ios_base& s, ios_base::iostate& r, unsigned short& v) const;
In get(In b, In e, ios_base& s, ios_base::iostate& r, unsigned int& v) const;
In get(In b, In e, ios_base& s, ios_base::iostate& r, unsigned long& v) const;
In get(In b, In e, ios_base& s, ios_base::iostate& r, unsigned long long& v) const;
In get(In b, In e, ios_base& s, ios_base::iostate& r, float& v) const;
In get(In b, In e, ios_base& s, ios_base::iostate& r, double& v) const;
In get(In b, In e, ios_base& s, ios_base::iostate& r, long double& v) const;
In get(In b, In e, ios_base& s, ios_base::iostate& r, void*& v) const;

Basically, **num_get** is organized like **num_put** (§39.4.2.2). Since it reads rather than writes, **get()** needs a pair of input iterators, and the argument designating the target of the read is a reference.

The **iostate** variable **r** is set to reflect the state of the stream. If a value of the desired type could not be read, **failbit** is set in **r**; if the end-of-input was reached, **eofbit** is set in **r**. An input operator will use **r** to determine how to set the state of its stream. If no error was encountered, the value read is assigned through **v**; otherwise, **v** is left unchanged.

A sentry is used to ensure that the stream's prefix and suffix operations are performed (§38.4.1). In particular, the sentry is used to ensure that we try to read only if the stream is in a good state to start with. For example, an implementer of **istream** might write:

```
template<class C, class Tr>
basic_istream<C,Tr>& basic_istream<C,Tr>::operator>>(double& d)
{
    sentry guard(*this);        // see §38.4.1
    if (!guard) return *this;

    iostate state = 0;          // good
    istreambuf_iterator<C,Tr> eos;
    try {
        double dd;
        use_facet<num_get<C,Tr>>(getloc()).get(*this,eos,*this,state,dd);
        if (state==0 || state==eofbit) d = dd;      // set value only if get() succeeded
        setstate(state);
    }
    catch (...) {
        handle_ioexception(*this);      // see §39.4.2.2
    }
    return *this;
}
```

I took care not to modify the target of the >> unless the read operation succeeded. Unfortunately, that cannot be guaranteed for all input operations.

Exceptions enabled for the **istream** will be thrown by **setstate()** in case of error (§38.3).

By defining a **numpunct**, such as **My_punct** from §39.4.2.1, we can read using nonstandard punctuation. For example:

```
void f()
{
    cout << "style A: "
    int i1;
    double d1;
    cin >> i1 >> d1;          // read using standard "12345678" format

    locale loc(locale::classic(),new My_punct);
    cin.imbue(loc);
    cout << "style B: "
    int i2;
    double d2;
    cin >> i1 >> d2;          // read using the "12_345_678" format
}
```

If we want to read really unusual numeric formats, we have to override **do_get()**. For example, we might define a **num_get** that reads Roman numerals, such as **XXI** and **MM**.

39.4.3 Money Formatting

The formatting of monetary amounts is technically similar to the formatting of "plain" numbers (§39.4.2). However, the presentation of monetary amounts is even more sensitive to cultural differences. For example, a negative amount (a loss, a debit), such as **–1.25**, should in some contexts be presented as a (positive) number in parentheses: **(1.25)**. Similarly, color is in some contexts used to ease the recognition of negative amounts.

There is no standard "money type." Instead, the money **facet**s are meant to be used explicitly for numeric values that the programmer knows to represent monetary amounts. For example:

```
struct Money {               // simple type to hold a monetary amount
    using Value = long long;  // for currencies that have suffered inflation
    Value amount;
};

// ...

void f(long int i)
{
    cout << "value= " << i << " amount= " << Money{i} << '\n';
}
```

The task of the monetary **facet**s is to make it reasonably easy to write an output operator for **Money** so that the amount is printed according to local convention (see §39.4.3.2). The output would vary depending on **cout**'s **locale**. Possible outputs are:

```
value= 1234567 amount= $12345.67
value= 1234567 amount= 12345,67 DKK
value= 1234567 amount= CAD 12345,67
value= –1234567 amount= $–12345.67
value= –1234567 amount= –€12345.67
value= –1234567 amount= (CHF12345,67)
```

For money, accuracy to the smallest currency unit is usually considered essential. Consequently, I adopted the common convention of having the integer value represent the number of cents (pence, øre, fils, cents, etc.) rather than the number of dollars (pounds, kroner, dinar, euro, etc.). This convention is supported by **moneypunct**'s **frac_digits()** function (§39.4.3.1). Similarly, the appearance of the "decimal point" is defined by **decimal_point()**.

The facets **money_get** and **money_put** provide functions that perform I/O based on the format defined by the **money_base** facet.

A simple **Money** type can be used to control I/O formats or to hold monetary values. In the former case, we cast values of (other) types used to hold monetary amounts to **Money** before writing, and we read into **Money** variables before converting them to other types. It is less error-prone to consistently hold monetary amounts in a **Money** type; that way, we cannot forget to cast a value to **Money** before writing it, and we don't get input errors by trying to read monetary values in **locale-**insensitive ways. However, it may be infeasible to introduce a **Money** type into a system that wasn't designed for that. In such cases, applying **Money** conversions (casts) to read and write operations is necessary.

39.4.3.1 Money Punctuation

The **facet** controlling the presentation of monetary amounts, **moneypunct**, naturally resembles the **facet** for controlling plain numbers, **numpunct** (§39.4.2.1):

```cpp
class money_base {
public:
    enum part {                          // parts of value layout
        none, space, symbol, sign, value
    };

    struct pattern {                     // layout specification
        char field[4];
    };
};


template<class C, bool International = false>
class moneypunct : public locale::facet, public money_base {
public:
    using char_type = C;
    using string_type = basic_string<C>;
    // ...
};
```

The **moneypunct** member functions define the layout of money input and output:

moneypunct<C,International>> facet (§iso.22.4.6.3)	
C decimal_point() const;	E.g., '.'
C thousands_sep() const;	E.g., ','
string grouping() const;	E.g., "" meaning "no grouping"
string_type curr_symbol() const;	E.g., "$"
string_type positive_sign() const;	E.g., ""
string_type negative_sign() const;	E.g., "–"
int frac_digits() const;	Number of digits after ".", e.g., **2**
pattern pos_format() const;	**symbol, space, sign, none**, or **value**
pattern neg_format() const;	**symbol, space, sign, none**, or **value**
static const bool intl = International;	Use three-letter international abbreviations

The facilities offered by **moneypunct** are intended primarily for use by implementers of **money_put** and **money_get** facets (§39.4.3.2, §39.4.3.3).

A **_byname** version (§39.4, §39.4.1) of **moneypunct** is provided:

```
template<class C, bool Intl = false>
class moneypunct_byname : public moneypunct<C, Intl> {
    // ...
};
```

The **decimal_point()**, **thousands_sep()**, and **grouping()** members behave as in **numpunct**.

The **curr_symbol()**, **positive_sign()**, and **negative_sign()** members return the string to be used to represent the currency symbol (for example, **$**, **¥**, **INR**, **DKK**), the plus sign, and the minus sign, respectively. If the **International** template argument is **true**, the **intl** member will also be **true**, and "international" representations of the currency symbols will be used. Such an "international" representation is a four-character C-style string. For example:

```
"USD"
"DKK"
"EUR"
```

The last (invisible) character is a terminating zero. The three-letter currency identifier is defined by the ISO-4217 standard. When **International** is **false**, a "local" currency symbol, such as **$**, **£**, and **¥**, can be used.

A **pattern** returned by **pos_format()** or **neg_format()** is four **parts** defining the sequence in which the numeric value, the currency symbol, the sign symbol, and whitespace occur. Most common formats are trivially represented using this simple notion of a pattern. For example:

```
+$ 123.45      // { sign, symbol, space, value } where positive_sign() returns "+"
$+123.45       // { symbol, sign, value, none } where positive_sign() returns "+"
$123.45        // { symbol, sign, value, none } where positive_sign() returns ""
$123.45–       // { symbol, value, sign, none }
–123.45 DKK    // { sign, value, space, symbol }
($123.45)      // { sign, symbol, value, none } where negative_sign() returns "()"
(123.45DKK)    // { sign, value, symbol, none } where negative_sign() returns "()"
```

Representing a negative number using parentheses is achieved by having **negative_sign()** return a string containing the two characters (). The first character of a sign string is placed where **sign** is found in the pattern, and the rest of the sign string is placed after all other parts of the pattern. The most common use of this facility is to represent the financial community's convention of using parentheses for negative amounts, but other uses are possible. For example:

```
–$123.45            // { sign, symbol, value, none } where negative_sign() returns "–"
*$123.45 silly      // { sign, symbol, value, none } where negative_sign() returns "* silly"
```

Each of the values **sign**, **value**, and **symbol** must appear exactly once in a pattern. The remaining value can be either **space** or **none**. Where **space** appears, at least one and possibly more whitespace characters may appear in the representation. Where **none** appears, except at the end of a pattern, zero or more whitespace characters may appear in the representation.

Note that these strict rules ban some apparently reasonable patterns:

```
pattern pat = { sign, value, none, none };        // error: no symbol
```

The **frac_digits()** function indicates where the **decimal_point()** is placed. Often, monetary amounts are represented in the smallest currency unit (§39.4.3). This unit is typically one-hundredth of the major unit (for example, a ¢ is one-hundredth of a $), so **frac_digits()** is often **2**.

Here is a simple format defined as a **facet**:

```
class My_money_io : public moneypunct<char,true> {
public:
    explicit My_money_io(size_t r = 0) :moneypunct<char,true>(r) { }

    char_type do_decimal_point() const { return '.'; }
    char_type do_thousands_sep() const { return ','; }
    string do_grouping() const { return "\003\003\003"; }

    string_type do_curr_symbol() const { return "USD "; }
    string_type do_positive_sign() const { return ""; }
    string_type do_negative_sign() const { return "()"; }

    int do_frac_digits() const { return 2; }     // two digits after decimal point

    pattern do_pos_format() const { return pat; }
    pattern do_neg_format() const { return pat; }
private:
    static const pattern pat;
};

    const pattern My_money_io::pat { sign, symbol, value, none };
```

39.4.3.2 Money Output

The **money_put** facet writes monetary amounts according to the format specified by **moneypunct**. Specifically, **money_put** provides **put()** functions that place a suitably formatted character representation into the stream buffer of a stream:

money_put<C,Out = ostreambuf_iterator<C>> facet (§iso.22.4.6.2)
Put value **v** into buffer position **b**
Out put(Out b, bool intl, ios_base& s, C fill, long double v) const; **Out put(Out b, bool intl, ios_base& s, C fill, const string_type& v) const;**

The **intl** argument indicates whether a standard four-character "international" currency symbol or a "local" symbol is used (§39.4.3.1).

Given **money_put**, we can define an output operator for **Money** (§39.4.3):

```
ostream& operator<<(ostream& s, Money m)
{
     ostream::sentry guard(s);          // see §38.4.1
     if (!guard) return s;

     try {
          const money_put<char>& f = use_facet<money_put<char>>(s.getloc());
          if (m==static_cast<long long>(m)) { // m can be represented as a long long
               if (f.put(s,true,s,s.fill(),m).failed())
                    s.setstate(ios_base::badbit);
          }
          else {
               ostringstream v;
               v << m;          // convert to string representation
               if (f.put(s,true,s,s.fill(),v.str()).failed())
                    s.setstate(ios_base::badbit);
          }
     }
     catch (...) {
          handle_ioexception(s);    // see §39.4.2.2
     }
     return s;
}
```

If a **long long** doesn't have sufficient precision to represent the monetary value exactly, I convert the value to its string representation and output that using the **put()** that takes a **string**.

39.4.3.3 Money Input

The **money_get** facet reads monetary amounts according to the format specified by **moneypunct**. Specifically, **money_get** provides **get()** functions that extract a suitably formatted character representation from the stream buffer of a stream:

money_get<C,In = istreambuf_iterator<C>> facet (§iso.22.4.6.1)
Read [b:e) into **v**, using formatting rules from **s**, reporting errors by setting **r**
In get(In b, In e, bool intl, ios_base& s, ios_base::iostate& r, long double& v) const; **In get(In b, In e, bool intl, ios_base& s, ios_base::iostate& r, string_type& v) const;**

A well-defined pair of **money_get** and **money_put** facets will provide output in a form that can be read back in without errors or loss of information. For example:

```
int main()
{
    Money m;
    while (cin>>m)
        cout << m << "\n";
}
```

The output of this simple program should be acceptable as its input. Furthermore, the output produced by a second run given the output from a first run should be identical to its input.

A plausible input operator for **Money** would be:

```
istream& operator>>(istream& s, Money& m)
{
    istream::sentry guard(s);        // see _io.sentry_
    if (guard) try {
        ios_base::iostate state = 0;    // good
        istreambuf_iterator<char> eos;
        string str;

        use_facet<money_get<char>>(s.getloc()).get(s,eos,true,state,str);

        if (state==0 || state==ios_base::eofbit) { // set value only if get() succeeded
            long long i = stoll(str);        // §36.3.5
            if (errno==ERANGE) {
                state |= ios_base::failbit;
            }
            else {
                m = i;      // set value only if conversion to long long succeeded
            }
            s.setstate(state);
        }
    }
    catch (...) {
        handle_ioexception(s);    // see §39.4.2.2
    }
    return s;
}
```

I use the **get()** that reads into a **string** because reading into a **double** and then converting to a **long long** could lead to loss of precision.

The largest value that can be exactly represented by a **long double** may be smaller than the largest value that can be represented by a **long long**.

39.4.4 Date and Time Formatting

Date and time formats are controlled by **time_get<C,In>** and **time_put<C,Out>**. The representation of dates and times used is **tm** (§43.6).

39.4.4.1 time_put

A **time_put** facet takes a point in time presented as a **tm** and produces a sequence of characters representing it using **strftime()** (§43.6) or an equivalent.

time_put<C,Out = ostreambuf_iterator<C>> facet (§iso.22.4.5.1)
Out put(Out s, ios_base& f, C fill, const tm∗ pt, const C∗ b, const C∗ e) const;
Out put(Out s, ios_base& f, C fill, const tm∗ pt, char format, char mod = 0) const;
Out do_put(Out s, ios_base& ib, const tm∗ pt, char format, char mod) const;

A call s=put(s,ib,fill,pt,b,e) copies [b:e) onto the output stream s. For each **strftime()** format character **x**, with optional modifier **mod**, it calls **do_put(s,ib,pt,x,mod)**. The possible modifier values are **0** (the default meaning "none"), **E**, or **O**. An overriding p=do_put(s,ib,pt,x,mod) is supposed to format the appropriate parts of ∗pt into s and return a value pointing to the position in s after the last character written.

A _byname version (§39.4, §39.4.1) of **messages** is provided:

```
template<class C, class Out = ostreambuf_iterator<C>>
class time_put_byname : public time_put<C,Out>
{
    // ...
};
```

39.4.4.2 time_get

The basic idea is that a **get_time** can read what is produced by a **put_time** using the same **strftime()** format (§43.6):

```
class time_base {
public:
    enum dateorder {
        no_order, // meaning mdy
        dmy,      // meaning "%d%m%y"
        mdy,      // meaning "%m%d%y"
        ymd,      // meaning "%y%m%d"
        ydm       // meaning "%y%d%m"
    };
};

template<class C, class In = istreambuf_iterator<C>>
class time_get : public locale::facet, public time_base {
public:
    using char_type = C;
    using iter_type = In;
    // ...
}
```

In addition to reading according to a format, there are operations for examining the **dateorder** and for reading specific parts of date and time representations, such as **weekday** and **monthname**:

time_get<C,In> facet (§iso.22.4.5.1) Read from [b:e) into *pt
dateorder do_date_order() const;
In get_time(In b, In e, ios_base& ib, ios_base::iostate& err, tm∗ pt) const; In get_date(In b, In e, ios_base& ib, ios_base::iostate& err, tm∗ pt) const; In get_weekday(In b, In e, ios_base& ib, ios_base::iostate& err, tm∗ pt) const; In get_monthname(In b, In e, ios_base& ib, ios_base::iostate& err, tm∗ pt) const; In get_year(In b, In e, ios_base& ib, ios_base::iostate& err, tm∗ pt) const;
In get(In b, In e, ios_base& ib, ios_base::iostate& err, tm∗ pt, char format, char mod) const; In get(In b, In e, ios_base& ib, ios_base::iostate& err, tm∗ pt, char format) const; In get(In b, In e, ios_base& ib, ios_base::iostate& err, tm∗ pt, C∗ fmtb, C∗ fmte) const;

A **get_∗()** function reads from [b:e) into ∗pt, getting its **locale** from b and setting **err** in case of error. It returns an iterator pointing to the first unread character in [b:e).

A call **p=get(b,e,ib,err,pt,format,mod)** reads as indicated by the format character **format** and modifier character **mod**, as specified by **strftime()**. If **mod** is not specified, **mod==0** is used.

A call of **get(b,e,ib,err,pt,fmtb,fmtb)** uses a **strftime()** format presented as a string [fmtb:fmte). This overload, together with the one with the defaulted modifier, does not have **do_get()** interfaces. Instead, they are implemented by calls to the **do_get()** for the first **get()**.

The obvious use of the time and date **facets** is to provide **locale**-sensitive I/O for a **Date** class. Consider a variant of the **Date** from §16.3:

```
class Date {
public:
    explicit Date(int d ={}, Month m ={}, int year ={});
    // ...
    string to_string(const locale& = locale()) const;
};

istream& operator>>(istream& is, Date& d);
ostream& operator<<(ostream& os, Date d);
```

Date::to_string() produces a **locale()**-specific **string** using a **stringstream** (§38.2.2):

```
string Date::to_string(const locale& loc) const
{
    ostringstream os;
    os.imbue(loc);
    return os << *this;
}
```

Given **to_string()**, the output operator is trivial:

```
ostream& operator<<(ostream& os, Date d)
{
    return os<<to_string(d,os.getloc());
}
```

The input operator needs to be careful about state:

```
istream& operator>>(istream& is, Date& d)
{
    if (istream::sentry guard{is}) {
        ios_base::iostate err = goodbit;
        struct tm t;
        use_facet<time_get<char>>(is.getloc()).get_date(is,0,is,err,&t);    // read into t
        if (!err) {
            Month m = static_cast<Month>(t.tm_mon+1);
            d = Date(t.tm_day,m,t.tm_year+1900);
        }
        is.setstate(err);
    }
    return is;
}
```

The +1900 is needed because year 1900 is year zero for **tm** (§43.6).

A _byname version (§39.4, §39.4.1) of **messages** is provided:

```
template<class C, class In = istreambuf_iterator<C>>
class time_get_byname : public time_get<C, In> {
    // ...
};
```

39.4.5 Character Classification

When reading characters from input, it is often necessary to classify them to make sense of what is being read. For example, to read a number, an input routine needs to know which letters are digits. Similarly, §10.2.2 showed a use of standard character classification functions for parsing input.

Naturally, classification of characters depends on the alphabet used. Consequently, a facet **ctype** is provided to represent character classification in a **locale**.

The character classes are described by an enumeration called **mask**:

```
class ctype_base {
public:
    enum mask {            // the actual values are implementation-defined
        space = 1,             // whitespace (in "C" locale: ' ', '\n', '\t', ...)
        print = 1<<1,          // printing characters
        cntrl = 1<<2,          // control characters
        upper = 1<<3,          // uppercase characters
        lower = 1<<4,          // lowercase characters
        alpha = 1<<5,          // alphabetic characters
        digit = 1<<6,          // decimal digits
        punct = 1<<7,          // punctuation characters
        xdigit = 1<<8,         // hexadecimal digits
        blank = 1 << 9;        // space and horizontal tab
        alnum=alpha|digit,     // alphanumeric characters
        graph=alnum|punct
    };
};
```

```
template<class C>
class ctype : public locale::facet, public ctype_base {
public:
    using char_type = C;
    // ...
};
```

This **mask** doesn't depend on a particular character type. Consequently, this enumeration is placed in a (non-template) base class.

Clearly, **mask** reflects the traditional C and C++ classification (§36.2.1). However, for different character sets, different character values fall into different classes. For example, for the ASCII character set, the integer value **125** represents the character }, which is a punctuation character (**punct**). However, in the Danish national character set, **125** represents the vowel å, which in a Danish **locale** must be classified as an **alpha**.

The classification is called a "mask" because the traditional efficient implementation of character classification for small character sets is a table in which each entry holds bits representing the classification. For example:

```
table['P'] == upper|alpha
table['a'] == lower|alpha|xdigit
table['1'] == digit|xdigit
table[' '] == space|blank
```

Given that implementation, **table[c]&m** is nonzero if the character **c** is an **m** and **0** otherwise.

The **ctype** facet is defined like this:

ctype<C> facet (§iso.22.4.1.1)
bool is(mask m, C c) const; const C∗ is(const C∗ b, const C∗ e, mask∗ v) const; const C∗ scan_is(mask m, const C∗ b, const C∗ e) const; const C∗ scan_not(mask m, const C∗ b, const C∗ e) const;
C toupper(C c) const; const C∗ toupper(C∗ b, const C∗ e) const; C tolower(C c) const; const C∗ tolower(C∗ b, const C∗ e) const;
C widen(C c) const; const char∗ widen(const char∗ b, const char∗ e, C∗ b2) const;
char narrow(C c, char def) const; const C∗ narrow(const C∗ b, const C∗ e, char def, char∗ b2) const;

A call **is(m,c)** tests whether the character **c** belongs to the classification **m**. For example:

```
int count_spaces(const string& s, const locale& loc)
{
    const ctype<char>& ct = use_facet<ctype<char>>(loc);
    int i = 0;
```

```
        for(auto p = s.begin(); p!=s.end(); ++p)
            if (ct.is(ctype_base::space,*p))         // whitespace as defined by ct
                ++i;
        return i;
}
```

Note that it is also possible to use **is()** to check whether a character belongs to one of a number of classifications. For example:

```
    ct.is(ctype_base::space|ctype_base::punct,c);     // is c whitespace or punctuation in ct?
```

A call **is(b,e,v)** determines the classification of each character in [**b**:**e**) and places it in the corresponding position in the array **v**.

A call **scan_is(m,b,e)** returns a pointer to the first character in [**b**:**e**) that is an **m**. If no character is classified as an **m**, **e** is returned. As ever for standard **facets**, the public member function is implemented by a call to its **do_** virtual function. A simple implementation might be:

```
    template<class C>
    const C* ctype<C>::do_scan_is(mask m, const C* b, const C* e) const
    {
        while (b!=e && !is(m,*b))
            ++b;
        return b;
    }
```

A call **scan_not(m,b,e)** returns a pointer to the first character in [**b**:**e**) that is not an **m**. If all characters are classified as **m**, **e** is returned.

A call **toupper(c)** returns the uppercase version of **c** if such a version exists in the character set used and **c** itself otherwise.

A call **toupper(b,e)** converts each character in the range [**b**:**e**) to uppercase and returns **e**. A simple implementation might be:

```
    template<class C>
    const C* ctype<C>::to_upper(C* b, const C* e)
    {
        for (; b!=e; ++b)
            *b = toupper(*b);
        return e;
    }
```

The **tolower()** functions are similar to **toupper()** except that they convert to lowercase.

A call **widen(c)** transforms the character **c** into its corresponding **C** value. If **C**'s character set provides several characters corresponding to **c**, the standard specifies that "the simplest reasonable transformation" be used. For example:

```
    wcout << use_facet<ctype<wchar_t>>(wcout.getloc()).widen('e');
```

will output a reasonable equivalent to the character **e** in **wcout**'s **locale**.

Translation between unrelated character representations, such as ASCII and EBCDIC, can also be done by using **widen()**. For example, assume that an **ebcdic** locale exists:

```
char EBCDIC_e = use_facet<ctype<char>>(ebcdic).widen('e');
```

A call **widen(b,e,v)** takes each character in the range [b:e) and places a widened version in the corresponding position in the array **v**.

A call **narrow(ch,def)** produces a **char** value corresponding to the character **ch** from the **C** type. Again, "the simplest reasonable transformation" is to be used. If no such corresponding **char** exists, **def** is returned.

A call **narrow(b,e,def,v)** takes each character in the range [b:e) and places a narrowed version in the corresponding position in the array **v**.

The general idea is that **narrow()** converts from a larger character set to a smaller one and that **widen()** performs the inverse operation. For a character **c** from the smaller character set, we expect:

```
c == narrow(widen(c),0)   // not guaranteed
```

This is true provided that the character represented by **c** has only one representation in "the smaller character set." However, that is not guaranteed. If the characters represented by a **char** are not a subset of those represented by the larger character set (**C**), we should expect anomalies and potential problems with code treating characters generically.

Similarly, for a character **ch** from the larger character set, we might expect:

```
widen(narrow(ch,def)) == ch || widen(narrow(ch,def)) == widen(def)      // not guaranteed
```

However, even though this is often the case, it cannot be guaranteed for a character that is represented by several values in the larger character set but only once in the smaller character set. For example, a digit, such as **7**, often has several separate representations in a large character set. The reason for that is typically that a large character set has several conventional character sets as subsets and that the characters from the smaller sets are replicated for ease of conversion.

For every character in the basic source character set (§6.1.2), it is guaranteed that

```
widen(narrow(ch_lit,0)) == ch_lit
```

For example:

```
widen(narrow('x',0)) == 'x'
```

The **narrow()** and **widen()** functions respect character classifications wherever possible. For example, if **is(alpha,c)**, then **is(alpha,narrow(c,'a'))** and **is(alpha,widen(c))** wherever **alpha** is a valid mask for the **locale** used.

A major reason for using a **ctype** facet in general and for using **narrow()** and **widen()** functions in particular is to be able to write code that does I/O and string manipulation for any character set, that is, to make such code generic with respect to character sets. This implies that **iostream** implementations depend critically on these facilities. By relying on <iostream> and <string>, a user can avoid most direct uses of the **ctype** facet.

A _byname version (§39.4, §39.4.1) of **ctype** is provided:

```
template<class C>
class ctype_byname : public ctype<C> {
    // ...
};
```

39.4.6 Character Code Conversion

Sometimes, the representation of characters stored in a file differs from the desired representation of those same characters in main memory. For example, Japanese characters are often stored in files in which indicators ("shifts") indicate to which of the four common character sets (kanji, katakana, hiragana, and romaji) a given sequence of characters belongs. This is a bit unwieldy because the meaning of each byte depends on its "shift state," but it can save memory because only a kanji requires more than 1 byte for its representation. In main memory, these characters are easier to manipulate when represented in a multibyte character set where every character has the same size. Such characters (for example, Unicode characters) are typically placed in wide characters (**wchar_t**; §6.2.3). Consequently, the **codecvt** facet provides a mechanism for converting characters from one representation to another as they are read or written. For example:

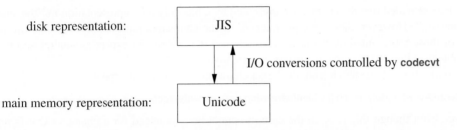

This code conversion mechanism is general enough to provide arbitrary conversions of character representations. It allows us to write a program to use a suitable internal character representation (stored in **char**, **wchar_t**, or whatever) and to then accept a variety of input character stream representations by adjusting the **locale** used by **iostreams**. The alternative would be to modify the program itself or to convert input and output files from/to a variety of formats.

The **codecvt** facet provides conversion between different character sets when a character is moved between a stream buffer and external storage:

```
class codecvt_base {
public:
        enum result {          // result indicators
            ok, partial, error, noconv
        };
};

template<class In, class Ex, class SS>
class codecvt : public locale::facet, public codecvt_base {
public:
        using intern_type = In;
        using extern_type = Ex;
        using state_type = SS;
        // ...
};
```

codecvt<In,Ex,SS> facet (§iso.22.5)
using CI = const In; using CE = const Ex;
result in(SS& st, CE* b, CE* e, CE*& next, In* b2, In* e2, In*& next2) const;
result out(SS& st, CI* b, CI* e, CI*& next, Ex* b2, Ex* e2, Ex*& next2) const;
result unshift(SS& st, Ex* b, Ex* e, Ex*& next) const;
int encoding() const noexcept;
bool always_noconv() const noexcept;
int length(SS& st, CE* b, CE* e, size_t max) const;
int max_length() const noexcept;

A **codecvt** facet is used by **basic_filebuf** (§38.2.1) to read or write characters. A **basic_filebuf** obtains this **facet** from the stream's **locale** (§38.1).

The **State** template argument is the type used to hold the shift state of the stream being converted. **State** can also be used to identify different conversions by specifying a specialization. The latter is useful because characters of a variety of character encodings (character sets) can be stored in objects of the same type. For example:

```
class JISstate { /* .. */ };
```

```
p = new codecvt<wchar_t,char,mbstate_t>;      // standard char to wide char
q = new codecvt<wchar_t,char,JISstate>;       // JIS to wide char
```

Without the different **State** arguments, there would be no way for the **facet** to know which encoding to assume for the stream of **chars**. The **mbstate_t** type from **<cwchar>** or **<wchar.h>** identifies the system's standard conversion between **char** and **wchar_t**.

A new **codecvt** can also be created as a derived class and identified by name. For example:

```
class JIScvt : public codecvt<wchar_t,char,mbstate_t> {
    // ...
};
```

A call **in(st,b,e,next,b2,e2,next2)** reads each character in the range **[b:e)** and tries to convert it. If a character is converted, **in()** writes its converted form to the corresponding position in the **[b2:e2)** range; if not, **in()** stops at that point. Upon return, **in()** stores the position one beyond the last character read in **next** (the next character to be read) and the position one beyond the last character written in **next2** (the next character to be written). The **result** value returned by **in()** indicates how much work was done:

codecvt_base result (§iso.22.4.1.4)	
ok	All characters in [b:e) range were converted
partial	Not all characters in [b:e) were converted
error	A character couldn't be converted
noconv	No conversion was needed

Note that a **partial** conversion is not necessarily an error. Possibly more characters have to be read before a multibyte character is complete and can be written, or maybe the output buffer has to be emptied to make room for more characters.

The **state_type** argument **st** indicates the state of the input character sequence at the start of the call of in(). This is significant when the external character representation uses shift states. Note that **st** is a (non-**const**) reference argument: at the end of the call, **st** holds the shift state of the input sequence. This allows a programmer to deal with **partial** conversions and to convert a long sequence using several calls to in().

A call **out(st,b,e,next,b2,e2,next2)** converts [b:e) from the internal to the external representation in the same way the in() converts from the external to the internal representation.

A character stream must start and end in a "neutral" (unshifted) state. Typically, that state is **state_type{}**.

A call **unshift(ss,b,e,next)** looks at **st** and places characters in [b:e) as needed to bring a sequence of characters back to that unshifted state. The result of **unshift()** and the use of **next** are done just like **out()**.

A call **length(st,b,e,max)** returns the number of characters that in() could convert from [b:e).

Return values from **encoding()** mean:

- −1   The encoding of the external character set uses state (for example, uses shift and unshift character sequences).
- 0   The encoding uses varying number of bytes to represent individual characters (for example, a character representation might use a bit in a byte to indicate whether 1 or 2 bytes are used to represent that character).
- n   Every character of the external character representation is n bytes.

A call **always_noconv()** returns **true** if no conversion is required between the internal and the external character sets and **false** otherwise. Clearly, **always_noconv()==true** opens the possibility for the implementation to provide the maximally efficient implementation that simply doesn't invoke the conversion functions.

A call **cvt.max_length()** returns the maximum value that **cvt.length(ss,p,q,n)** can return for a valid set of arguments.

The simplest code conversion that I can think of is one that converts input to uppercase. Thus, this is about as simple as a **codecvt** can be and still perform a service:

```
class Cvt_to_upper : public codecvt<char,char,mbstate_t> { // convert to uppercase
public:
    explicit Cvt_to_upper(size_t r = 0) : codecvt(r) { }

protected:
    // read external representation, write internal representation:
    result do_in(State& s,
                const char* from, const char* from_end, const char*& from_next,
                char* to, char* to_end, char*& to_next
        ) const override;


    // read internal representation, write external representation:
    result do_out(State& s,
                const char* from, const char* from_end, const char*& from_next,
                char* to, char* to_end, char*& to_next
        ) const override;
```

```
                result do_unshift(State&, E* to, E* to_end, E*& to_next) const override { return ok; }

                int do_encoding() const noexcept override { return 1; }
                bool do_always_noconv() const noexcept override { return false; }

                int do_length(const State&, const E* from, const E* from_end, size_t max) const override;
                int do_max_length() const noexcept override;              // maximum possible length()
        };


        codecvt<char,char,mbstate_t>::result
        Cvt_to_upper::do_out(State& s,
                        const char* from, const char* from_end, const char*& from_next,
                        char* to, char* to_end, char*& to_next) const
        {
                return codecvt<char,char,mbstate_t>::do_out(s,from,from_end,from_next,to,to_end,to_next);
        }


        codecvt<char,char,mbstate_t>::result
        Cvt_to_upper::do_in(State& s,
                        const char* from, const char* from_end, const char*& from_next,
                        char* to, char* to_end, char*& to_next) const
        {
            // ...
        }

        int main()  // trivial test
        {
                locale ulocale(locale(), new Cvt_to_upper);

                cin.imbue(ulocale);

                for (char ch; cin>>ch; )
                        cout << ch;
        }
```

A _byname version (§39.4, §39.4.1) of **codecvt** is provided:

```
        template<class I, class E, class State>
        class codecvt_byname : public codecvt<I,E,State> {
            // ...
        };
```

39.4.7 Messages

Naturally, most end users prefer to use their native language to interact with a program. However, we cannot provide a standard mechanism for expressing **locale**-specific general interactions. Instead, the library provides a simple mechanism for keeping a **locale**-specific set of strings from which a programmer can compose simple messages. In essence, **messages** implements a trivial read-only database:

```
class messages_base {
public:
    using catalog = /* implementation-defined integer type */;  // catalog identifier type
};


template<class C>
class messages : public locale::facet, public messages_base {
public:
    using char_type = C;
    using string_type = basic_string<C>;
    // ...
};
```

The **messages** interface is comparatively simple:

messages<C> facet (§iso.22.4.7.1)

catalog open(const string& s, const locale& loc) const;
string_type get(catalog cat, int set, int id, const basic_string<C>& def) const;
void close(catalog cat) const;

A call **open(s,loc)** opens a "catalog" of messages called **s** for the locale **loc**. A catalog is a set of strings organized in an implementation-specific way and accessed through the **messages::get()** function. A negative value is returned if no catalog named **s** can be opened. A catalog must be opened before the first use of **get()**.

A call **close(cat)** closes the catalog identified by **cat** and frees all resources associated with that catalog.

A call **get(cat,set,id,"foo")** looks for a message identified by **(set,id)** in the catalog **cat**. If a string is found, **get()** returns that string; otherwise, **get()** returns the default string (here, **string("foo")**).

Here is an example of a **messages** facet for an implementation in which a message catalog is a vector of sets of "messages" and a "message" is a string:

```
struct Set {
    vector<string> msgs;
};


struct Cat {
    vector<Set> sets;
};


class My_messages : public messages<char> {
    vector<Cat>& catalogs;
public:
    explicit My_messages(size_t = 0) :catalogs{*new vector<Cat>} { }

    catalog do_open(const string& s, const locale& loc) const;  // open catalog s
    string do_get(catalog cat, int s, int m, const string&) const;  // get message (s,m) in cat
```

```
        void do_close(catalog cat) const
        {
            if (catalogs.size()<=cat)
                catalogs.erase(catalogs.begin()+cat);
        }

    ˜My_messages() { delete &catalogs; }
};
```

All **messages**' member functions are **const**, so the catalog data structure (the **vector<Set>**) is stored outside the **facet**.

A message is selected by specifying a catalog, a set within that catalog, and a message string within that set. A string is supplied as an argument, to be used as a default result in case no message is found in the catalog:

```
string My_messages::do_get(catalog cat, int set, int id, const string& def) const
{
    if (catalogs.size()<=cat)
        return def;
    Cat& c = catalogs[cat];
    if (c.sets.size()<=set)
        return def;
    Set& s = c.sets[set];
    if (s.msgs.size()<=msg)
        return def;
    return s.msgs[id];
}
```

Opening a catalog involves reading a textual representation from disk into a **Cat** structure. Here, I chose a representation that is trivial to read. A set is delimited by <<< and >>>, and each message is a line of text:

```
messages<char>::catalog My_messages::do_open(const string& n, const locale& loc) const
{
    string nn = n + locale().name();
    ifstream f(nn.c_str());
    if (!f) return –1;

    catalogs.push_back(Cat{});          // make in-core catalog
    Cat& c = catalogs.back();

    for(string s; f>>s && s=="<<<"; ) {  // read Set
        c.sets.push_back(Set{});
        Set& ss = c.sets.back();
        while (getline(f,s) && s != ">>>")  // read message
            ss.msgs.push_back(s);
    }
    return catalogs.size()–1;
}
```

Here is a trivial use:

```
int main()
    // a trivial test
{
    if (!has_facet<My_messages>(locale())) {
        cerr << "no messages facet found in" << locale().name() << '\n';
        exit(1);
    }

    const messages<char>& m = use_facet<My_messages>(locale());
    extern string message_directory;       // where I keep my messages

    auto cat = m.open(message_directory,locale());
    if (cat<0) {
        cerr << "no catalog found\n";
        exit(1);
    }

    cout << m.get(cat,0,0,"Missed again!") << endl;
    cout << m.get(cat,1,2,"Missed again!") << endl;
    cout << m.get(cat,1,3,"Missed again!") << endl;
    cout << m.get(cat,3,0,"Missed again!") << endl;
}
```

If the catalog is:

```
<<<
hello
goodbye
>>>
<<<
yes
no
maybe
>>>
```

this program prints

```
hello
maybe
Missed again!
Missed again!
```

39.4.7.1 Using Messages from Other facets

In addition to being a repository for **locale**-dependent strings used to communicate with users, **messages** can be used to hold strings for other **facets**. For example, the **Season_io** facet (§39.3.2) could have been written like this:

```
class Season_io : public locale::facet {
    const messages<char>& m;              // message directory
    messages_base::catalog cat;           // message catalog
public:
    class Missing_messages { };

    Season_io(size_t i = 0)
        : locale::facet(i),
          m(use_facet<Season_messages>(locale())),
          cat(m.open(message_directory,locale()))
    {
        if (cat<0)
            throw Missing_messages();
    }

    ~Season_io() { }       // to make it possible to destroy Season_io objects (§39.3)

    const string& to_str(Season x) const;                 // string representation of x

    bool from_str(const string& s, Season& x) const; // place Season corresponding to s in x

    static locale::id id;   // facet identifier object (§39.2, §39.3, §39.3.1)
};

locale::id Season_io::id; // define the identifier object

string Season_io::to_str(Season x) const
{
    return m->get(cat,0,x,"no–such–season");
}

bool Season_io::from_str(const string& s, Season& x) const
{
    for (int i = Season::spring; i<=Season::winter; i++)
        if (m->get(cat,0,i,"no–such–season") == s) {
            x = Season(i);
            return true;
        }
    return false;
}
```

This **messages**-based solution differs from the original solution (§39.3.2) in that the implementer of a set of **Season** strings for a new **locale** needs to be able to add them to a **messages** directory. This is easy for someone adding a new **locale** to an execution environment. However, since **messages** provides only a read-only interface, adding a new set of season names may be beyond the scope of an application programmer.

A _byname version (§39.4, §39.4.1) of **messages** is provided:

```
template<class C>
class messages_byname : public messages<C> {
    // ...
};
```

39.5   Convenience Interfaces

Beyond simply imbuing an **iostream**, the **locale** facilities can be complicated to use. Consequently, *convenience interfaces* are provided to simplify notation and minimize mistakes.

39.5.1   Character Classification

The most common use of the **ctype** facet is to inquire whether a character belongs to a given classification. Consequently, a set of functions is provided for that:

locale-**Sensitive Character Classification (§iso.22.3.3.1)**	
isspace(c,loc)	Is c a space in **loc**?
isblank(c,loc)	Is c a blank in **loc**?
isprint(c,loc)	Is c printable?
iscntrl(c,loc)	Is c a control character?
isupper(c,loc)	Is c an uppercase letter?
islower(c,loc)	Is c a lowercase letter?
isalpha(c,loc)	Is c a letter?
isdigit(c,loc)	Is c a decimal digit?
ispunct(c,loc)	Is c not a letter, digit, whitespace, or invisible control character?
isxdigit(c,loc)	Is c a hexadecimal digit?
isalnum(c,loc)	isalpha(c) or isdigit(c)
isgraph(c,loc)	isalpha(c) or isdigit(c) or ispunct(c) (note: not space)

These functions are trivially implemented using **use_facet**. For example:

```
template<class C>
inline bool isspace(C c, const locale& loc)
{
    return use_facet<ctype<C>>(loc).is(space,c);
}
```

The one-argument versions of these functions (§36.2.1) use the current C global locale. Except for the rare cases in which the C global locale and the C++ global locale differ (§39.2.1), we can think of a one-argument version as the two-argument version applied to **locale()**. For example:

```
inline int isspace(int i)
{
    return isspace(i,locale());      // almost
}
```

39.5.2 Character Conversions

Case conversions can be **locale** sensitive:

Character Conversion (§iso.22.3.3.2.1)	
c2= **toupper(c,loc)**	**use_facet<ctype<C>>(loc).toupper(c)**
c2= **tolower(c,loc)**	**use_facet<ctype<C>>(loc).tolower(c)**

39.5.3 String Conversions

Character code conversions can be **locale** sensitive. Class template **wstring_convert** performs conversions between a wide string and a byte string. It lets you specify a code conversion **facet** (such as **codecvt**) to perform the conversions, without affecting any streams or **locales**. For example, you might use a code conversion **facet** called **codecvt_utf8** directly to output a UTF-8 multibyte sequence to **cout** without altering **cout**'s **locale**:

```
wstring_convert<codecvt_utf8<wchar_t>> myconv;
string s = myconv.to_bytes(L"Hello\n");
cout << s;
```

The definition of **wstring_convert** is fairly conventional:

```
template<class Codecvt,
         class Wc = wchar_t,
         class Wa = std::allocator<Wc>,     // wide-character allocator
         class Ba = std::allocator<char>    // byte allocator
     >
class wstring_convert {
public:
     using byte_string = basic_string<char, char_traits<char>, Ba>;
     using wide_string = basic_string<Wc, char_traits<Wc>, Wa>;
     using state_type = typename Codecvt::state_type;
     using int_type = typename wide_string::traits_type::int_type;
     // ...
};
```

The **wstring_convert** constructors allow us to specify a character conversion **facet**, an initial conversion state, and values to be used in case of errors:

wstring_convert<Codecvt,Wc,Wa,Ba> (§iso.22.3.3.2.2)	
wstring_convert cvt {};	**wstring_convert cvt {new Codecvt};**
wstring_convert cvt {pcvt,state}	cvt uses the conversion facet ∗**pcvt** and conversion state **state**
wstring_convert cvt {pcvt};	**wstring_convert cvt {pcvt,state_type{}};**
wstring_convert cvt {b_err,w_err};	**wstring_convert cvt{};** use **b_error** and **w_err**
wstring_convert cvt {b_err};	**wstring_convert cvt{};** use **b_error**
cvt.˜wstring_convert();	Destructor

wstring_convert<Codecvt,Wc,Wa,Ba> (§iso.22.3.3.2.2)	
ws=cvt.from_bytes(c)	ws contains the char c converted to Wcs
ws=cvt.from_bytes(s)	ws contains the chars of s converted to Wcs;
	s is a C-style string or a string
ws=cvt.from_bytes(b,e)	ws contains the chars of [b:e) converted to Wcs
s=cvt.to_bytes(wc)	s contains wc converted to chars
s=cvt.to_bytes(ws)	s contains the Wcs of wsconverted to a chars;
	ws is a C-style string or a basic_string<Wc>
s=cvt.to_bytes(b,e)	s contains the Wcs of [b:e) converted to chars
n=cvt.converted()	n is the number of input elements converted by cvt
st=cvt.state()	st is the cvt's state

If a conversion to a **wide_string** fails, functions on a **cvt** constructed with a non-default **w_err** string return that string (as an error message); otherwise, they throw **range_error**.

If a conversion to a **byte_string** fails, functions on a **cvt** constructed with a non-default **b_err** string return that string (as an error message); otherwise, they throw **range_error**.

An example:

```
void test()
{
    wstring_convert<codecvt_utf8_utf16<wchar_t>> converter;

    string s8 = u8"This is a UTF-8 string";
    wstring s16 = converter.from_bytes(s8);
    string s88 = converter.to_bytes(s16);

    if (s8!=s88)
        cerr <"Insane!\n";
}
```

39.5.4 Buffer Conversions

We can use a code conversion **facet** (§39.4.6) to write directly into or to read directly from a stream buffer (§38.6):

```
template<class Codecvt,
        class C = wchar_t,
        class Tr = std::char_traits<C>
    >
class wbuffer_convert
    : public std::basic_streambuf<C,Tr> {
public:
    using state_type = typename Codecvt::state_type;
    // ...
};
```

wbuffer_convert<Codecvt,C,Tr> (§iso.22.3.3.2.3)	
wbuffer_convert wb {psb,pcvt,state};	wb converts from the **streambuf** *psb,
	using converter *pcvt and initial conversion state **state**
wbuffer_convert wb {psb,pcvt};	wbuffer_convert wb {psb,pcvt,state_type{}};
wbuffer_convert wb {psb};	wbuffer_convert wb {psb,new Codecvt{}};
wbuffer_convert wb {};	wbuffer_convert wb {nullptr};
psb=wb.rdbuf()	psb is wb's stream buffer
psb2=wb.rdbuf(psb)	Set wb's stream buffer to *psb;
	*psb2 is wb's previous stream buffer
t=wb.state()	t is wb's conversion state

39.6 Advice

[1] Expect that every nontrivial program or system that interacts directly with people will be used in several different countries; §39.1.

[2] Don't assume that everyone uses the same character set as you do; §39.1, §39.4.1.

[3] Prefer using **locales** to writing ad hoc code for culture-sensitive I/O; §39.1.

[4] Use **locales** to meet external (non-C++) standards; §39.1.

[5] Think of a **locale** as a container of **facets**; §39.2.

[6] Avoid embedding **locale** name strings in program text; §39.2.1.

[7] Keep changes of **locale** to a few places in a program; §39.2.1.

[8] Minimize the use of global format information; §39.2.1.

[9] Prefer **locale**-sensitive string comparisons and sorts; §39.2.2, §39.4.1.

[10] Make **facets** immutable; §39.3.

[11] Let **locale** handle the lifetime of **facets**; §39.3.

[12] You can make your own **facets**; §39.3.2.

[13] When writing **locale**-sensitive I/O functions, remember to handle exceptions from user-supplied (overriding) functions; §39.4.2.2.

[14] Use **numput** if you need separators in numbers; §39.4.2.1.

[15] Use a simple **Money** type to hold monetary values; §39.4.3.

[16] Use simple user-defined types to hold values that require **locale**-sensitive I/O (rather than casting to and from values of built-in types); §39.4.3.

[17] The **time_put** facet can be used for both <chrono>- and <ctime>-style time §39.4.4.

[18] Prefer the character classification functions in which the **locale** is explicit; §39.4.5, §39.5.

40

Numerics

The purpose of computing is insight, not numbers.
– R. W. Hamming

... but for the student,
numbers are often the best road to insight.
– A. Ralston

40.1 Introduction

C++ was not designed primarily with numeric computation in mind. However, numeric computation typically occurs in the context of other work – such as database access, networking, instrument control, graphics, simulation, and financial analysis – so C++ becomes an attractive vehicle for computations that are part of a larger system. Furthermore, numeric methods have come a long way from being simple loops over vectors of floating-point numbers. Where more complex data structures are needed as part of a computation, C++'s strengths become relevant. The net effect is that C++ is widely used for scientific, engineering, financial, and other computation involving sophisticated numerics. Consequently, facilities and techniques supporting such computation have emerged. This chapter describes the parts of the standard library that support numerics. I make no attempt to teach numeric methods. Numeric computation is a fascinating topic in its own right. To understand it, you need a good course in numerical methods or at least a good textbook – not just a language manual and tutorial.

In addition to the standard-library facilities described here, Chapter 29 is an extended example of numerical programming: an N-dimensional matrix.

40.2 Numerical Limits

To do anything interesting with numbers, we typically need to know something about the general properties of built-in numeric types. To allow the programmer to best take advantage of hardware, these properties are implementation-defined rather than fixed by the rules of the language itself (§6.2.8). For example, what is the largest **int**? What is the smallest positive **float**? Is a **double** rounded or truncated when assigned to a **float**? How many bits are there in a **char**?

Answers to such questions are provided by the specializations of the **numeric_limits** template presented in **<limits>**. For example:

```
void f(double d, int i)
{
    char classification[numeric_limits<unsigned char>::max()];

    if (numeric_limits<unsigned char>::digits==numeric_limits<char>::digits ) {
        // chars are unsigned
    }

    if (i<numeric_limits<short>::min() || numeric_limits<short>::max()<i) {
        // i cannot be stored in a short without loss of digits
    }

    if (0<d && d<numeric_limits<double>::epsilon()) d = 0;

    if (numeric_limits<Quad>::is_specialized) {
        // limits information is available for type Quad
    }
}
```

Each specialization provides the relevant information for its argument type. Thus, the general **numeric_limits** template is simply a notational handle for a set of constants and **constexpr** functions:

```
template<typename T>
class numeric_limits {
public:
    static const bool is_specialized = false; // is information available for numeric_limits<T>?
    // ... uninteresting defaults ...
};
```

The real information is in the specializations. Each implementation of the standard library provides a specialization of **numeric_limits** for each fundamental numeric type (the character types, the integer types, the floating-point types, and **bool**) but not for any other plausible candidates such as **void**, enumerations, or library types (such as **complex<double>**).

For an integral type such as **char**, only a few pieces of information are of interest. Here is **numeric_limits<char>** for an implementation in which a **char** has 8 bits and is signed:

```
template<>
class numeric_limits<char> {
public:
        static const bool is_specialized = true;    // yes, we have information

        static const int digits = 7;                        // number of bits ("binary digits") excluding sign

        static const bool is_signed = true;         // this implementation has char signed
        static const bool is_integer = true;         // char is an integral type

        static constexpr char min() noexcept { return –128; }   // smallest value
        static constexpr char max() noexcept { return 127; }    // largest value

        // lots of declarations not relevant to a char
};
```

The functions are **constexpr**, so that they can be used where a constant expression is required and without run-time overhead.

Most members of **numeric_limits** are intended to describe floating-point numbers. For example, this describes one possible implementation of **float**:

```
template<>
class numeric_limits<float> {
public:
        static const bool is_specialized = true;

        static const int radix = 2;                  // base of exponent (in this case, binary)
        static const int digits = 24;                // number of radix digits in mantissa
        static const int digits10 = 9;               // number of base 10 digits in mantissa

        static const bool is_signed = true;
        static const bool is_integer = false;
        static const bool is_exact = false;

        static constexpr float min() noexcept { return 1.17549435E–38F; } // smallest positive
        static constexpr float max() noexcept { return 3.40282347E+38F; } // largest positive
        static constexpr float lowest() noexcept { return –3.40282347E+38F; }   // smallest value

        static constexpr float epsilon() noexcept { return 1.19209290E–07F; }
        static constexpr float round_error() noexcept { return 0.5F; }          // maximum rounding error

        static constexpr float infinity() noexcept { return /* some value */; }
```

```
    static constexpr float quiet_NaN() noexcept { return /* some value */; }
    static constexpr float signaling_NaN() noexcept { return /* some value */; }
    static constexpr float denorm_min() noexcept { return min(); }

    static const int min_exponent = −125;
    static const int min_exponent10 = −37;
    static const int max_exponent = +128;
    static const int max_exponent10 = +38;

    static const bool has_infinity = true;
    static const bool has_quiet_NaN = true;
    static const bool has_signaling_NaN = true;
    static const float_denorm_style has_denorm = denorm_absent;
    static const bool has_denorm_loss = false;

    static const bool is_iec559 = true;   // conforms to IEC-559
    static const bool is_bounded = true;
    static const bool is_modulo = false;
    static const bool traps = true;
    static const bool tinyness_before = true;

    static const float_round_style round_style = round_to_nearest;
};
```

Note that **min()** is the smallest *positive* normalized number and that **epsilon** is the smallest positive floating-point number such that **1+epsilon−1** is larger than **0**.

When defining a scalar type along the lines of the built-in ones, it is a good idea also to provide a suitable specialization of **numeric_limits**. For example, if I write a quadruple-precision type **Quad**, a user could reasonably expect me to provide **numeric_limits<Quad>**. Conversely, if I use a non-numeric type, **Dumb_ptr**, I would expect for **numeric_limits<Dumb_ptr<X>>** to be the primary template that has **is_specialized** set to **false**, indicating that no information is available.

We can imagine specializations of **numeric_limits** describing properties of user-defined types that have little to do with floating-point numbers. In such cases, it is usually better to use the general technique for describing properties of a type than to specialize **numeric_limits** with properties not considered in the standard.

40.2.1 Limit Macros

From C, C++ inherited macros that describe properties of integers. They are found in **<climits>**:

Integer Limit Macros (_iso.diff.library_, abbreviated)	
CHAR_BIT	Number of bits in a **char** (usually 8)
CHAR_MIN	Smallest **char** value (possibly negative)
CHAR_MAX	Largest **char** value (usually 127 if **char** is signed and 255 if **char** is unsigned)
INT_MIN	Smallest **int** value
LONG_MAX	Largest **long** value

Analogously named macros for **signed chars**, **long long**, etc., are also provided.

Similarly, **<cfloat>** and **<float.h>** define macros describing properties of floating-point numbers:

Floating-Point Limit Macros (_iso.diff.library_, abbreviated)	
FLT_MIN	Smallest positive **float** value (e.g., **1.175494351e–38F**)
FLT_MAX	Largest **float** value (e.g., **3.402823466e+38F**)
FLT_DIG	Number of decimal digits of precision of a **float** (e.g., **6**)
FLT_MAX_10_EXP	Largest decimal exponent of a **float** (e.g., **38**)
DBL_MIN	Smallest **double** value
DBL_MAX	Largest **double** value (e.g., **1.7976931348623158e+308**)
DBL_EPSILON	Smallest **double** such that **1.0+DBL_EPSILON!=1.0**

Analogously named macros for **long double** are also provided.

40.3 Standard Mathematical Functions

In **<cmath>** we find what are commonly called the *standard mathematical functions*:

Standard Mathematical Functions	
abs(x)	Absolute value
ceil(x)	Smallest integer >= **x**
floor(x)	Largest integer <= **x**
sqrt(x)	Square root; **x** must be non-negative
cos(x)	Cosine
sin(x)	Sine
tan(x)	Tangent
acos(x)	Arccosine; the result is non-negative
asin(x)	Arcsine; the result nearest to 0 is returned
atan(x)	Arctangent
sinh(x)	Hyperbolic sine
cosh(x)	Hyperbolic cosine
tanh(x)	Hyperbolic tangent
exp(x)	Base e exponential
log(x)	Natural logarithm, base e; **x** must be positive
log10(x)	Base 10 logarithm

There are versions taking **float**, **double**, **long double**, and **complex** (§40.4) arguments. For each function, the return type is the same as the argument type.

Errors are reported by setting **errno** from **<cerrno>** to **EDOM** for a domain error and to **ERANGE** for a range error. For example:

```
void f()
{
    errno = 0; // clear old error state
    sqrt(-1);
    if (errno==EDOM) cerr << "sqrt() not defined for negative argument";
```

```
            pow(numeric_limits<double>::max(),2);
            if (errno == ERANGE) cerr << "result of pow() too large to represent as a double";
    }
```

For historical reasons, a few mathematical functions are found in **<cstdlib>** rather than in **<cmath>**:

More Mathematical Functions (§iso.26.8)	
n2=abs(n)	Absolute value; n is **int**, **long**, or **long long**; n2 has the same type as n
n2=labs(n)	"Long absolute value"; n and n2 are **long**
n2=llabs(n)	"Long long absolute value"; n and n2 are **long long**
p=div(n,d)	p=div(n,d)
p=ldiv(n,d)	Divide n by d; p is {quotient,remainder}; n and d are **long**
p=lldiv(n,d)	Divide n by d; p is {quotient,remainder}; n and d are **long long**

The **l*()** versions are there because C does not support overloading. The results of the **ldiv()** functions are **struct**s **div_t**, **ldiv_t**, and **lldiv_t**, respectively. These **struct**s have members **quot** (for quotient) and **rem** (for remainder) of implementation-defined types.

There is a separate ISO standard for *special mathematical functions* [C++Math,2010]. An implementation may add these functions to **<cmath>**:

Mathematical Special Functions (Optional)			
assoc_laguerre()	assoc_legendre()	beta()	comp_ellint_1()
comp_ellint_2()	comp_ellint_3()	cyl_bessel_i()	cyl_bessel_j()
cyl_bessel_k()	cyl_neumann()	ellint_1()	ellint_2()
ellint_3()	expint()	hermite()	laguerre()
legendre()	riemann_zeta()	sph_bessel()	sph_legendre()
sph_neumann()			

If you don't know these functions, you are unlikely to need them.

40.4 complex Numbers

The standard library provides complex number types **complex<float>**, **complex<double>**, and **complex<long double>**. A **complex<Scalar>** where **Scalar** is some other type supporting the usual arithmetic operations usually works but is not guaranteed to be portable.

```
    template<typename Scalar>
    class complex {
            // a complex is a pair of scalar values, basically a coordinate pair
            Scalar re, im;
    public:
            complex(const Scalar & r = Scalar{}, const Scalar & i = Scalar{}) :re(r), im(i) { }

            Scalar real() const { return re; }          // real part
            void real(Scalar r) { re=r; }
```

```
Scalar imag() const { return im; }          // imaginary part
void imag(Scalar i) { im = i; }

template<typename X>
    complex(const complex<X>&);

complex<T>& operator=(const T&);
complex& operator=(const complex&);
template<typename X>
    complex<T>& operator=(const complex<X>&);

complex<T>& operator+=(const T&);
template<typename X>
    complex<T>& operator+=(const complex<X>&);

// similar for operators -=, *=, /=
};
```

The standard-library **complex** does not protect against narrowing:

```
complex<float> z1 = 1.33333333333333333;    // narrows
complex<double> z2 = 1.33333333333333333;// narrows
z1=z2;                                      // narrows
```

To protect against accidental narrowing, use {} initialization:

```
complex<float> z3 {1.33333333333333333};    // error: narrowing conversion
```

In addition to the members of **complex**, **<complex>** offers a host of useful operations:

complex **Operators**	
z1+z2	Addition
z1−z2	Subtraction
z1*z2	Multiplication
z1/z2	Division
z1==z2	Equality
z1!=z2	Inequality
norm(z)	The square of **abs(z)**
conj(z)	Conjugate: {z.re,−z.im}
polar(x,y)	Make a complex given polar coordinates (rho,theta)
real(z)	Real part
imag(z)	Imaginary part
abs(z)	Distance from (0,0): **sqrt(z.re*z.re+z.im*z.im)**; also known as rho
arg(z)	Angle from positive real axis: **atan2(z.im/z.re)**; also known as theta
out<<z	Complex output
in>>z	Complex input

The standard mathematical functions (§40.3) are also available for complex numbers. Note that **complex** does not provide < or %. For more details, see §18.3.

40.5 A Numerical Array: valarray

Much numeric work relies on relatively simple single-dimensional vectors of floating-point values. In particular, such vectors are well supported by high-performance machine architectures, libraries relying on such vectors are in wide use, and very aggressive optimization of code using such vectors is considered essential in many fields. The **valarray** from **<valarray>** is a single-dimensional numerical array. It provides the usual numeric vector arithmetic operations for an array type plus support for slices and strides:

Numerical Array Classes (§iso.26.6.1)	
valarray<T>	A numerical array of type **T**
slice	A BLAS-like slice (start, length, and stride); §40.5.4
slice_array<T>	A subarray identified by a slice; §40.5.5
gslice	A slice generalized to describe a matrix
gslice_array<T>	A submatrix identified by a generalized slice; §40.5.6
mask_array<T>	A subset of an array identified by a mask; §40.5.2
indirect_array<T>	A subset of an array identified by a list of indices; §40.5.2

The fundamental idea of **valarray** was to provide Fortran-like facilities for dense multidimensional arrays with Fortran-like opportunities for optimization. This can only be achieved with the active support of compiler and optimization suppliers and the addition of more library support on top of the very basic facilities provided by **valarray**. So far, that has not happened for all implementations.

40.5.1 Constructors and Assignments

The **valarray** constructors allow us to initialize **valarray**s from the auxiliary numeric array types and from single values:

valarray<T> Constructors (§iso.26.6.2.2)	
valarray va {};	valarray with no elements
valarray va {n};	valarray of n elements with value **T**{}; explicit
valarray va {t,n};	valarray of n elements with value t
valarray va {p,n};	valarray of n elements with values copied from [p:p+n)
valarray va {v2};	Move and copy constructor
valarray va {a};	Construct **va** with elements from **a**;
	a can be a **slice_array**, **gslice_array**, **mask_array**, or **indirect_array**;
	the number of elements is the number of elements in **a**
valarray va {args};	Construct from the **initializer_list {args}**;
	the number of elements is the number of elements in **{args}**
va.˜valarray()	Destructor

For example:

```
valarray<double> v0;                    // placeholder, we can assign to v0 later
valarray<float> v1(1000);               // 1000 elements with value float()==0.0F
```

```
valarray<int> v2(-1,2000);              // 2000 elements with value -1
valarray<double> v3(100,9.8064);        // bad mistake: floating-point valarray size

valarray<double> v4 = v3;               // v4 has v3.size() elements

valarray<int> v5 {-1,2000};             // two elements
```

In the two-argument constructors, the value comes before the number of elements. This differs from the convention for standard containers (§31.3.2).

The number of elements of an argument **valarray** to a copy constructor determines the size of the resulting **valarray**.

Most programs need data from tables or input. In addition to initializer lists, this is supported by a constructor that copies elements from a built-in array. For example:

```
void f(const int* p, int n)
{
    const double vd[] = {0,1,2,3,4};
    const int vi[] = {0,1,2,3,4};

    valarray<double> v1{vd,4};          // 4 elements: 0,1,2,3
    valarray<double> v2{vi,4};          // type error: vi is not pointer to double
    valarray<double> v3{vd,8};          // undefined: too few elements in initializer
    valarray<int> v4{p,n};              // p had better point to at least n ints
}
```

The **valarray** and its auxiliary facilities were designed for high-speed computing. This is reflected in a few constraints on users and by a few liberties granted to implementers. Basically, an implementer of **valarray** is allowed to use just about every optimization technique you can think of. The **valarray** operations are assumed to be free of side effects (except on their explicit arguments, of course), **valarrays** are assumed to be alias free, and the introduction of auxiliary types and the elimination of temporaries is allowed as long as the basic semantics are maintained. There is no range checking. The elements of a **valarray** must have the default copy semantics (§8.2.6).

Assignment can be with another **valarray**, a scalar, or a subset of a **valarray**:

valarray<T> Assignments (§iso.26.6.2.3)	
va2=va	Copy assignment: **va2**.size() becomes **va**.size()
va2=move(va)	Move assignment: **va** becomes empty
va=t	Scalar assignment: each element of **va** is a copy of t
va={args}	Assignment from the **initializer_list** {args}; the number of elements of **va** becomes {args}.size()
va=a	Assignment from a; a.size() must equal **va**.size(); a can be a **slice_array**, **gslice_array**, **mask_array**, or **indirect_array**
va@=va2	v[i]@=va2[i] for each element of **va**; @ can be /, %, +, -, ^, &, |, <<, or >>
va@=t	v[i]@=t for each element of **va**; @ can be /, %, +, -, ^, &, |, <<, or >>

A **valarray** can be assigned to another of the same size. As one would expect, **v1=v2** copies every element of **v2** into its corresponding position in **v1**. If **valarrays** have different sizes, the result of assignment is undefined.

In addition to this conventional assignment, it is possible to assign a scalar to a **valarray**. For example, **v=7** assigns **7** to every element of the **valarray v**. This may be surprising to some programmers and is best understood as an occasionally useful degenerate case of the operator assignment operations. For example:

```
valarray<int> v {1,2,3,4,5,6,7,8};
v *= 2;     // v=={2,4,6,10,12,14,16}
v = 7;      // v=={7,7,7,7,7,7,7,7}
```

40.5.2 Subscripting

Subscripting can be used to select an element of a **valarray** or a subset of its elements:

valarray<T> **Subscripting** (§iso.26.6.2.4, §iso.26.6.2.5)	
t=va[i]	Subscripting: **t** is a reference to the **i**th element of **va**; no range checking
a2=va[x]	Subset: **x** is a **slice**, a **gslice**, **valarray<bool>**, or a **valarray<size_t>**

Each **operator[]** returns a subset of the elements from a **valarray**. The return type (the type of the object representing the subset) depends on the argument type.

For **const** arguments, the result contains copies of elements. For non-**const** arguments, the result holds references to elements. Since C++ doesn't directly support arrays of references (e.g., we can't say **valarray<int&>**), the implementation will somehow simulate this. This can be done efficiently. An exhaustive list, with examples (based on §iso.26.6.2.5), is in order. In each case, the subscript describes the elements to be returned, and **v1** must be a **vallaray** with an appropriate length and element type:

- A **slice** of a **const valarray**:

  ```
  valarray<T> operator[](slice) const;// copy of elements
  // ...
  const valarray<char> v0 {"abcdefghijklmnop",16};
  valarray<char> v1 {v0[slice(2,5,3)]};       // {"cfilo",5}
  ```

- A **slice** of a non-**const valarray**:

  ```
  slice_array<T> operator[](slice);    // references to elements
  // ...
  valarray<char> v0 {"abcdefghijklmnop",16};
  valarray<char> v1 {"ABCDE",5};
  v0[slice(2,5,3)] = v1;       // v0=={"abAdeBghCjkDmnEp",16}
  ```

- A **gslice** of a **const valarray**:

  ```
  valarray<T> operator[](const gslice&) const; // copies of elements
  // ...
  const valarray<char> v0 {"abcdefghijklmnop",16};
  const valarray<size_t> len {2,3};
  const valarray<size_t> str {7,2};
  valarray<char> v1 {v0[gslice(3,len,str)]};       // v1=={"dfhkmo",6}
  ```

- A **gslice** of a non-**const** valarray:

  ```
  gslice_array<T> operator[](const gslice&);    // references to elements
  // ...
  valarray<char> v0 {"abcdefghijklmnop",16};
  valarray<char> v1 {"ABCDE",5};
  const valarray<size_t> len {2,3};
  const valarray<size_t> str {7,2};
  v0[gslice(3,len,str)] = v1;        // v0=={"abcAeBgCijDlEnFp",16}
  ```

- A **valarray<bool>** (a mask) of a **const** valarray:

  ```
  valarray<T> operator[](const valarray<bool>&) const;   // copies of elements
  // ...
  const valarray<char> v0 {"abcdefghijklmnop",16};
  const bool vb[] {false, false, true, true, false, true};
  valarray<char> v1 {v0[valarray<bool>(vb, 6)]};          // v1=={"cdf",3}
  ```

- A **valarray<bool>** (a mask) of a non-**const** valarray:

  ```
  mask_array<T> operator[](const valarray<bool>&);        // references to elements
  // ...
  valarray<char> v0 {"abcdefghijklmnop", 16};
  valarray<char> v1 {"ABC",3};
  const bool vb[] {false, false, true, true, false, true};
  v0[valarray<bool>(vb,6)] = v1;         // v0=={"abABeCghijklmnop",16}
  ```

- A **valarray<size_t>** (a set of indices) of a **const** valarray:

  ```
  valarray<T> operator[](const valarray<size_t>&) const; // references to elements
  // ...
  const valarray<char> v0 {"abcdefghijklmnop",16};
  const size_t vi[] {7, 5, 2, 3, 8};
  valarray<char> v1 {v0[valarray<size_t>(vi,5)]};         // v1=={"hfcdi",5}
  ```

- A **valarray<size_t>** (a set of indices) of a non-**const** valarray:

  ```
  indirect_array<T> operator[](const valarray<size_t>&); // references to elements
  // ...
  valarray<char> v0 {"abcdefghijklmnop",16};
  valarray<char> v1 {"ABCDE",5};
  const size_t vi[] {7, 5, 2, 3, 8};
  v0[valarray<size_t>(vi,5)] {v1};       // v0=={"abCDeBgAEjklmnop",16}
  ```

Note that subscripting with a mask (a **valarray<bool>**) yields a **mask_array**, and subscripting with a set of indices (a **valarray<size_t>**) yields an **indirect_array**.

40.5.3 Operations

The purpose of **valarray** is to support computation, so a host of basic numerical operations are directly supported:

valarray<T> **Member Operations (§iso.26.6.2.8)**	
va.swap(va2)	Exchange elements of va and va2; noexcept;
n=va.size()	n is the number of elements of va
t=va.sum()	t is the sum of elements of va computed using +=
t=va.min()	t is the smallest element of va found using <
t=va.max()	t is the largest element of va found using <
va2=va.shift(n)	Linear right shift of elements
va2=va.cshift(n)	Circular right shift of elements
va2=va.apply(f)	Apply f: the value of each element va2[i] is va[f(i)]
va.resize(n,t)	Make va a valarray with n elements with the value t
va.resize(n)	va.resize(n,T{})

There is no range checking: the effect of using a function that tries to access an element of an empty **valarray** is undefined.

Note that **resize()** does not retain any old values.

valarray<T> **Operations (§iso.26.6.2.6, §iso.26.6.2.7)**	
v or v2, but not both, can be a scalar; for arithmetic operations, the result is a valarray<T>	
swap(va,va2)	va.swap(va2)
va3=va@va2	Perform @ on elements of va and va2, yielding va3;
	@ can be +, −, *, /, %, &, |, ^, << ,>>, &&, ||
vb=v@v2	Perform @ on elements of v and v2 ,yielding a valarray<bool>;
	@ can be ==, !=, <, <=, >, >=
v2=@(v)	Perform @() on elements of v, yielding v2;
	@ can be abs, acos, asin, atan, cos, cosh, exp, log, log10
v3=atan2(v,v2)	Perform atan2() on elements of v and v2
v3=pow(v,v2)	Perform pow() on v and v2
p=begin(v)	p is a random-access iterator to the first element of v
p=end(v)	p is a random-access iterator to the one-beyond-the-last element of v

The binary operations are defined for **valarray**s and for combinations of a **valarray** and its scalar type. A scalar type is treated as a **valarray** of the right size with every element having the scalar's value. For example:

```
void f(valarray<double>& v, valarray<double>& v2, double d)
{
    valarray<double> v3 = v*v2;    // v3[i] = v[i]*v2[i] for all i
    valarray<double> v4 = v*d;      // v4[i] = v[i]*d for all i
    valarray<double> v5 = d*v2;    // v5[i] = d*v2[i] for all i
    valarray<double> v6 = cos(v);  // v6[i] = cos(v[i]) for all i
}
```

These vector operations all apply their operations to each element of their operand(s) in the way indicated by the * and **cos()** examples. Naturally, an operation can be used only if the corresponding operation is defined for the scalar type. Otherwise, the compiler will issue an error when trying to specialize the operator or function.

Where the result is a **valarray**, its length is the same as its **valarray** operand. If the lengths of the two arrays are not the same, the result of a binary operator on two **valarray**s is undefined.

These **valarray** operations return new **valarray**s rather than modifying their operands. This can be expensive, but it doesn't have to be when aggressive optimization techniques are applied.

For example, if **v** is a **valarray**, it can be scaled like this: **v∗=0.2**, and this: **v/=1.3**. That is, applying a scalar to a vector means applying the scalar to each element of the vector. As usual, ∗= is more concise than a combination of ∗ and = (§18.3.1) and easier to optimize.

Note that the non-assignment operations construct a new **valarray**. For example:

```
double incr(double d) { return d+1; }

void f(valarray<double>& v)
{
    valarray<double> v2 = v.apply(incr);      // produce incremented valarray
    // ...
}
```

This does not change the value of **v**. Unfortunately, **apply()** does not accept a function object (§3.4.3, §11.4) as an argument.

The logical and cyclic shift functions, **shift()** and **cshift()**, return a new **valarray** with the elements suitably shifted and leave the original one unchanged. For example, the cyclic shift **v2=v.cshift(n)** produces a **valarray** so that **v2[i]==v[(i+n)%v.size()]**. The logical shift **v3=v.shift(n)** produces a **valarray** so that **v3[i]** is **v[i+n]** if **i+n** is a valid index for **v**. Otherwise, the result is the default element value. This implies that both **shift()** and **cshift()** shift left when given a positive argument and right when given a negative argument. For example:

```
void f()
{
    int alpha[] = { 1, 2, 3, 4, 5 ,6, 7, 8 };
    valarray<int> v(alpha,8);              // 1, 2, 3, 4, 5, 6, 7, 8
    valarray<int> v2 = v.shift(2);         // 3, 4, 5, 6, 7, 8, 0, 0
    valarray<int> v3 = v<<2;               // 4, 8, 12, 16, 20, 24, 28, 32
    valarray<int> v4 = v.shift(–2);        // 0, 0, 1, 2, 3, 4, 5, 6
    valarray<int> v5 = v>>2;               // 0, 0, 0, 1, 1, 1, 1, 2
    valarray<int> v6 = v.cshift(2);        // 3, 4, 5, 6, 7, 8, 1, 2
    valarray<int> v7 = v.cshift(–2);       // 7, 8, 1, 2, 3, 4, 5, 6
}
```

For **valarray**s, >> and << are bit shift operators, rather than element shift operators or I/O operators. Consequently, <<= and >>= can be used to shift bits within elements of an integral type. For example:

```
void f(valarray<int> vi, valarray<double> vd)
{
    vi <<= 2;          // vi[i]<<=2 for all elements of vi
    vd <<= 2;          // error: shift is not defined for floating-point values
}
```

All of the operators and mathematical functions on **valarray**s can also be applied to **slice_arrays** (§40.5.5), **gslice_arrays** (§40.5.6), **mask_arrays** (§40.5.2), **indirect_arrays** (§40.5.2), and combinations of these types. However, an implementation is allowed to convert an operand that is not a **valarray** to a **valarray** before performing a required operation.

40.5.4 Slices

A **slice** is an abstraction that allows us to manipulate a one-dimensional array (e.g., a built-in array, a **vector,** or a **valarray**) efficiently as a matrix of arbitrary dimension. It is the key notion of Fortran vectors and of the BLAS (Basic Linear Algebra Subprograms) library, which is the basis for much numeric computation. Basically, a **slice** is every **n**th element of some part of an array:

```
class std::slice {
        // starting index, a length, and a stride
public:
        slice();                          // slice{0,0,0}
        slice(size_t start, size_t size, size_t stride);

        size_t start() const;     // index of first element
        size_t size() const;      // number of elements
        size_t stride() const;    // element n is at start()+n*stride()
};
```

A *stride* is the distance (in number of elements) between two elements of the **slice.** Thus, a **slice** describes a mapping of non-negative integers into indices. The number of elements (the **size()**) doesn't affect the mapping (addressing) but allows us to find the end of a sequence. This mapping can be used to simulate two-dimensional arrays within a one-dimensional array (such as **valarray**) in an efficient, general, and reasonably convenient way. Consider a 3-by-4 matrix (three rows, each with four elements):

```
valarray<int> v {
        {00,01,02,03},        // row 0
        {10,11,12,13},        // row 1
        {20,21,22,23}         // row 2
};
```

or graphically:

00	01	02	03
10	11	12	13
20	21	22	23

Following the usual C/C++ conventions, the **valarray** is laid out in memory with row elements first (*row-major* order) and contiguous:

```
for (int x : v) cout << x << ' ';
```

This produces:

```
0 1 2 3 10 11 12 13 20 21 22 23
```

or graphically:

column 0:   0   4   8

00	01	02	03	10	11	12	13	20	21	22	23

row 0:   0   1   2   3

Row x is described by slice(x∗4,4,1). That is, the first element of row x is the x∗4th element of the vector, the next element of the row is the (x∗4+1)th, etc., and there are 4 elements in each row. For example, slice{0,4,1} describes the first row of v (row 0): 00, 01, 02, 03, and slice{1,4,1} describes the second row (row 1).

Column y is described by slice(y,3,4). That is, the first element of column y is the yth element of the vector, the next element of the column is the (y+4)th, etc., and there are 3 elements in each column. For example, slice{0,3,4} describes the first column (column 0): 00, 10, 20, and slice{1,3,4} describes the second column (column 1).

In addition to its use for simulating two-dimensional arrays, a slice can describe many other sequences. It is a fairly general way of specifying very simple sequences. This notion is explored further in §40.5.6.

One way of thinking of a slice is as an odd kind of iterator: a slice allows us to describe a sequence of indices for a valarray. We could build an STL-style iterator based on that:

```cpp
template<typename T>
class Slice_iter {
    valarray<T>* v;
    slice s;
    size_t curr;    // index of current element

    T& ref(size_t i) const { return (*v)[s.start()+i*s.stride()]; }
public:
    Slice_iter(valarray<T>* vv, slice ss, size_t pos =0)
        :v{vv}, s{ss}, curr{0} { }

    Slice_iter end() const { return {this,s,s.size()}; }

    Slice_iter& operator++() { ++curr; return *this; }
    Slice_iter operator++(int) { Slice_iter t = *this; ++curr; return t; }

    T& operator[](size_t i) { return ref(i); }       // C-style subscript
    T& operator()(size_t i) { return ref(i); }       // Fortran-style subscript
    T& operator*() { return ref(curr); }             // current element

    bool operator==(const Slice_iter& q) const
    {
        return curr==q.curr && s.stride()==q.s.stride() && s.start()==q.s.start();
    }
```

```
        bool operator!=(const Slice_iter& q ) const
        {
              return !(*this==q);
        }

        bool operator<(const Slice_iter& q) const
        {
              return curr<q.curr && s.stride()==q.s.stride() && s.start()==q.s.start();
        }
};
```

Since a **slice** has a size, we could even provide range checking. Here, I have taken advantage of **slice::size()** to provide an **end()** operation to provide an iterator for the one-past-the-end element of the **slice**.

Since a **slice** can describe either a row or a column, the **Slice_iter** allows us to traverse a **valarray** by row or by column.

40.5.5 slice_array

From a **valarray** and a **slice**, we can build something that looks and feels like a **valarray** but is really simply a way of referring to the subset of the array described by the slice.

slice_array<T> (§iso.26.6.5)	
slice_array sa {sa2};	Copy constructor: **sa** refers to the same elements as **sa2** does
sa=sa2	Assign the element referred to by **sa[i]** to each corresponding element referred to by **sa2[i]**
sa=va	Assign **va[i]** to each corresponsing element referred to by **sa[i]**
sa=v	Assign **v** to each element referred to by **sa**
sa@=va	**sa[i]@=va[i]** for each element of **sa**; @ can be /, %, +, −, ^, &, |, <<, or >>

A user cannot directly create a **slice_array**. Instead, the user subscripts a **valarray** to create a **slice_array** for a given slice. Once the **slice_array** is initialized, all references to it indirectly go to the **valarray** for which it is created. For example, we can create something that represents every second element of an array like this:

```
        void f(valarray<double>& d)
        {
              slice_array<double>& v_even = d[slice(0,d.size()/2+d.size()%2,2)];
              slice_array<double>& v_odd = d[slice(1,d.size()/2,2)];

              v_even *= v_odd;      // multiply element pairs and store results in even elements
              v_odd = 0;            // assign 0 to every odd element of d
        }
```

A **slice_array** can be copied. For example:

```
slice_array<double> row(valarray<double>& d, int i)
{
    slice_array<double> v = d[slice(0,2,d.size()/2)];
    // ...
    return d[slice(i%2,i,d.size()/2)];
}
```

40.5.6 Generalized Slices

A **slice** (§29.2.2, §40.5.4) can describe a row or a column of an **n**-dimensional array. However, sometimes we need to extract a subarray that is not a row or a column. For example, we might want to extract the 3-by-2 matrix from the top-left corner of a 4-by-3 matrix:

00	01	02
10	11	12
20	21	22
30	31	32

Unfortunately, these elements are not allocated in a way that can be described by a single **slice**:

subarray: 0 1   2 3   4 5

00	01	02	10	11	12	20	21	22	30	31	32

A **gslice** is a "generalized slice" that contains (almost) the information from **n slices**:

```
class std::gslice {
    // instead of 1 stride and one size like slice, gslice holds n strides and n sizes
public:
    gslice();
    gslice(size_t sz, const valarray<size_t>& lengths, const valarray<size_t>& strides);

    size_t start() const;                    // index of first element
    valarray<size_t> size() const;           // number of elements in dimension
    valarray<size_t> stride() const;         // stride for index[0], index[1], ...
};
```

The extra values allow a **gslice** to specify a mapping between **n** integers and an index to be used to address elements of an array. For example, we can describe the layout of the 3-by-2 matrix by a pair of (length,stride) pairs:

```
size_t gslice_index(const gslice& s, size_t i, size_t j)     // max (i,j) to their corresponding index
{
    return s.start()+i*s.stride()[0]+j*s.stride()[1];
}
```

```
valarray<size_t> lengths {2,3};// 2 elements in the first dimension
                              // 3 elements in the second dimension
valarray<size_t> strides {3,1}; // 3 is the stride for the first index
                              // 1 is the stride for the second index


void f()
{
     gslice s(0,lengths,strides);

     for (int i=0; i<3; ++i)       // for each row
          for (int j=0; j<2; ++j) // for each element in row
               cout << "(" << i << "," << j << ")->" << gslice_index(s,i,j) << "; ";    // print mapping
}
```

This prints:

> (0,0)->0; (0,1)->1; (1,0)->3; (1,1)->4; (2,0)->6; (2,1)->7

In this way, a **gslice** with two (length,stride) pairs describes a subarray of a two-dimensional array, a **gslice** with three (length,stride) pairs describes a subarray of a three-dimensional array, etc. Using a **gslice** as the index of a **valarray** yields a **gslice_array** consisting of the elements described by the **gslice**. For example:

```
void f(valarray<float>& v)
{
     gslice m(0,lengths,strides);
     v[m] = 0;                     // assign 0 to v[0],v[1],v[3],v[4],v[6],v[7]
}
```

The **gslice_array** offers the same set of members as **slice_array** (§40.5.5). A **gslice_array** is the result of using a **gslice** as the subscript of a **valarray** (§40.5.2).

40.6 Generalized Numerical Algorithms

In **<numeric>**, the standard library provides a few generalized numeric algorithms in the style of the non-numeric algorithms from **<algorithm>** (Chapter 32). These algorithms provide general versions of common operations on sequences of numerical values:

Numerical Algorithms (§iso.26.7) (continues)	
These algorithms take input iterators	
x=accumulate(b,e,i)	x is the sum of i and the elements of [b:e)
x=accumulate(b,e,i,f)	accumulate using f instead of +
x=inner_product(b,e,b2,i)	x is the inner product of [b:e) and [b2:b2+(e–b)), that is, the sum of i and (*p1)*(*p2) for each p1 in [b:e) and the corresponding p2 in [b2:b2+(e–b))
x=inner_product(b,e,b2,i,f,f2)	inner_product using f and f2 instead of + and *

Numerical Algorithms (continued) (§iso.26.7) These algorithms take input iterators	
p=partial_sum(b,e,out)	Element i of [**out**:**p**) is the sum of elements [**b**:**b**+**i**]
p=partial_sum(b,e,out,f)	**partial_sum** using f instead of +
p=adjacent_difference(b,e,out)	Element i of [**out**:**p**) is (∗**b**+**i**)−∗(**b**+**i**−1) for **i**>0; if **e**−**b**>0, then ∗**out** is ∗**b**
p=adjacent_difference(b,e,out,f)	**adjacent_difference** using f instead of −
iota(b,e,v)	For each element in [**b**:**e**) assign ++**v**; thus the sequence becomes **v**+1, **v**+2, ...

These algorithms generalize common operations such as computing a sum by letting them apply to all kinds of sequences and by making the operation applied to elements of those sequences a parameter. For each algorithm, the general version is supplemented by a version applying the most common operator for that algorithm.

40.6.1 accumulate()

The simple version of **accumulate()** adds elements of a sequence using their + operator:

```
template<typename In, typename T>
T accumulate(In first, In last, T init)
{
        for (; first!=last; ++first)    // for all elements in [first:last)
                init = init + *first;    // plus
        return init;
}
```

It can be used like this:

```
void f(vector<int>& price, list<float>& incr)
{
        int i = accumulate(price.begin(),price.end(),0);        // accumulate in int
        double d = 0;
        d = accumulate(incr.begin(),incr.end(),d);              // accumulate in double

        int prod = accumulate(price.begin,price.end(),1,[](int a, int b) { return a*b; });
        // ...
}
```

The type of the initial value passed determines the return type.

We can provide an initial value and an operation for "combining elements" as arguments to **accumulate()**, so **accumulate()** is not all about addition.

Extracting a value from a data structure is common operation for **accumulate()**. For example:

```
struct Record {
        // ...
        int unit_price;
        int number_of_units;
};
```

```
long price(long val, const Record& r)
{
      return val + r.unit_price * r.number_of_units;
}

void f(const vector<Record>& v)
{
      cout << "Total value: " << accumulate(v.begin(),v.end(),0,price) << '\n';
}
```

Operations similar to **accumulate** are called **reduce**, **reduction**, and **fold** in some communities.

40.6.2 inner_product()

Accumulating from a sequence is very common, and accumulating from a pair of sequences is not uncommon:

```
template<typename In, typename In2, typename T>
T inner_product(In first, In last, In2 first2, T init)
{
      while (first != last)
            init = init + *first++ * *first2++;
      return init;
}

template<typename In, typename In2, typename T, typename BinOp, typename BinOp2>
T inner_product(In first, In last, In2 first2, T init, BinOp op, BinOp2 op2)
{
      while (first != last)
            init = op(init,op2(*first++,*first2++));
      return init;
}
```

As usual, only the beginning of the second input sequence is passed as an argument. The second input sequence is assumed to be at least as long as the first.

The key operation in multiplying a **Matrix** by a **valarray** is an **inner_product**:

```
valarray<double> operator*(const Matrix& m, valarray<double>& v)
{
      valarray<double> res(m.dim2());

      for (size_t i = 0; i<m.dim2(); i++) {
            auto& ri = m.row(i);
            res[i] = inner_product(ri,ri.end(),&v[0],double(0));
      }
      return res;
}
```

```
valarray<double> operator*(valarray<double>& v, const Matrix& m)
{
    valarray<double> res(m.dim1());

    for (size_t i = 0; i<m.dim1(); i++) {
        auto& ci = m.column(i);
        res[i] = inner_product(ci,ci.end(),&v[0],double(0));
    }
    return res;
}
```

Some forms of inner_product are referred to as "dot product."

40.6.3 partial_sum() and adjacent_difference()

The partial_sum() and adjacent_difference() algorithms are inverses of each other and deal with the notion of incremental change.

Given a sequence a, b, c, d, etc., adjacent_difference() produces a, b–a, c–b, d–c, etc.

Consider a vector of temperature readings. We could transform it into a vector of temperature changes like this:

```
vector<double> temps;

void f()
{
    adjacent_difference(temps.begin(),temps.end(),temps.begin());
}
```

For example, 17, 19, 20, 20, 17 turns into 17, 2, 1, 0, –3.

Conversely, partial_sum() allows us to compute the end result of a set of incremental changes:

```
template<typename In, typename Out, typename BinOp>
Out partial_sum(In first, In last, Out res, BinOp op)
{
    if (first==last) return res;
    *res = *first;
    T val = *first;
    while (++first != last) {
        val = op(val,*first);
        *++res = val;
    }
    return ++res;
}

template<typename In, typename Out>
Out partial_sum(In first, In last, Out res)
{
    return partial_sum(first,last,res,plus);   // use std::plus (§33.4)
}
```

Given a sequence **a**, **b**, **c**, **d**, etc., **partial_sum()** produces **a**, **a+b**, **a+b+c**, **a+b+c+d**, etc. For example:

```
void f()
{
    partial_sum(temps.begin(),temps.end(),temps.begin());
}
```

Note the way **partial_sum()** increments **res** before assigning a new value through it. This allows **res** to be the same sequence as the input; **adjacent_difference()** behaves similarly. Thus,

```
partial_sum(v.begin(),v.end(),v.begin());
```

turns the sequence **a**, **b**, **c**, **d** into **a**, **a+b**, **a+b+c**, **a+b+c+d**, and

```
adjacent_difference(v.begin(),v.end(),v.begin());
```

reproduces the original value. Thus, **partial_sum()** turns **17, 2, 1, 0, –3** back into **17, 19, 20, 20, 17**.

For people who think of temperature differences as a boring detail of meteorology or science lab experiments, I note that analyzing changes in stock prices or sea levels involves exactly the same two operations. These operations are useful for analyzing any series of changes.

40.6.4 iota()

A call **iota(b,e,n)** assigns **n+i** to the **i**th element of **[b:e)**. For example:

```
vector<int> v(5);
iota(v.begin(),v.end(),50);
vector<int> v2 {50,51,52,53,54}

if (v!=v2)
    error("complain to your library vendor");
```

The name **iota** is the Latin spelling of the Greek letter ι, which was used for that function in APL.

Do not confuse **iota()** with the non-standard, but not uncommon, **itoa()** (**int**-to-alpha; §12.2.4).

40.7 Random Numbers

Random numbers are essential to many applications, such as simulations, games, sampling-based algorithms, cryptography, and testing. For example, we might want to choose the TCP/IP address for a router simulation, decide whether a monster should attack or scratch its head, or generate a set of values for testing a square root function. In **<random>**, the standard library defines facilities for generating (pseudo-)random numbers. These random numbers are sequences of values produced according to mathematical formulas, rather than unguessable ("truly random") numbers that could be obtained from a physical process, such as radioactive decay or solar radiation. If the implementation has such a truly random device, it will be represented as a **random_device** (§40.7.1).

Four kinds of entities are provided:

- A *uniform random number generator* is a function object returning unsigned integer values such that each value in the range of possible results has (ideally) equal probability of being returned.

- A *random number engine* (an engine) is a uniform random number generator that can be created with a default state **E{}** or with a state determined by a **seed E{s}**.
- A *random number engine adaptor* (an adaptor) is a random number engine that takes values produced by some other random number engine and applies an algorithm to those values in order to deliver a sequence of values with different randomness properties.
- A *random number distribution* (a distribution) is a function object returning values that are distributed according to an associated mathematical probability density function $p(z)$ or according to an associated discrete probability function $P(zi)$.

For details see §iso.26.5.1.

In simpler terms, the users' terms, a random number generator is an engine plus a distribution. The engine produces a uniformly distributed sequence of values, and the distribution bends those into the desired shape (distribution). That is, if you take lots of numbers from a random number generator and draw them, you should get a reasonably smooth graph of their distribution. For example, binding a **normal_distribution** to the **default_random_engine** gives me a random number generator that produces a normal distribution:

```
auto gen = bind(normal_distribution<double>{15,4.0},default_random_engine{});

for (int i=0; i<500; ++i) cout << gen();
```

The standard-library function **bind()** makes a function object that will invoke its first argument given its second argument (§33.5.1).

Using ASCII graphics (§5.6.3), I got:

```
3     **
4     *
5     *****
6     ****
7     ****
8     ******
9     ************
10    ****************************
11    **************************
12    ****************************************
13    **************************************************************
14    ********************************************************
15    **********************************************************
16    ********************************
17    ******************************************************
18    ****************************************
19    **********************************
20    ***************
21    ************
22    ************
23    *******
24    *****
25    ****
26    *
27    *
```

Most of the time, most programmers just need a simple uniform distribution of integers or floating-point numbers in a given range. For example:

```
void test()
{
    Rand_int ri {10,20};      // uniform distribution of ints in [10:20]
    Rand_double rd {0,0.5};   // uniform distribution of doubles in [0:0.5]

    for (int i=0; i<100; ++i)
        cout << ri() << ' ';
    for (int i=0; i<100; ++i)
        cout << rd() << ' ';
}
```

Unfortunately, **Ran_int** and **Rand_double** are not standard classes, but they are easy to build:

```
class Rand_int {
    Rand_int(int lo, int hi) : p{lo,hi} { }    // store the parameters
    int operator()() const { return r(); }
private:
    uniform_int_distribution<>::param_type p;
    auto r = bind(uniform_int_distribution<>{p},default_random_engine{});
};
```

I store the parameters using the distribution's standard **param_type** alias (§40.7.3) so that I can use **auto** to avoid having to name the result of the **bind()**.

Just for variation, I use a different technique for **Rand_double**:

```
class Rand_double {
public:
    Rand_double(double low, double high)
        :r(bind(uniform_real_distribution<>(low,high),default_random_engine())) { }
    double operator()() { return r(); }
private:
    function<double()> r;
};
```

One important use of random numbers is for sampling algorithms. In such algorithms we need to choose a *sample* of some size from a much larger *population*. Here is algorithm R (the simplest algorithm) from a famous old paper [Vitter,1985]:

```
template<typename Iter, typename Size, typename Out, typename Gen>
Out random_sample(Iter first, Iter last, Out result, Size n, Gen&& gen)
{
    using Dist = uniform_int_distribution<Size>;
    using Param = typename Dist::param_type;

    // Fill the reservoir and advance first:
    copy(first,n,result);
    advance(first,n);
```

```
// Sample the remaining values in [first+n:last) by selecting a random
// number r in the range [0:k], and, if r<n, replace it.
// k increases with each iteration, making the probability smaller.
// For random access iterators, k = i-first (assuming we increment i and not first).

Dist dist;
for (Size k = n; first!=last; ++first,++k) {
        Size r = dist(gen,Param{0,k});
        if(r < n)
                *(result + r) = *first;
    }
    return result;
}
```

40.7.1 Engines

A uniform random number generator is a function object that produces an approximately uniformly distributed sequence of values of its **result_type**:

Uniform Random Number Generators: G<T> (§iso.26.5.1.3)	
G::result_type	The type of an element of the sequence
x=g()	Application operator: **x** is the next element of the sequence
x=G::min()	**x** is the smallest element that a **g()** can return
x=G::max()	**x** is the largest element that a **g()** can return

A random number engine is a uniform random number generator with additional properties to make it widely useful:

Random Number Engines: E<T> (§iso.26.5.1.4)	
E e {};	Default constructor
E e {e2};	Copy constructor
E e {s};	**e** will be in a state determined by the seed **s**
E e {g};	**e** will be in a state determined by a call of **generate()** for the seed sequence **g**
e.seed()	**e** will be in the default state
e.seed(s)	**e** will be in a state determined by the seed **s**
e.seed(g)	**e** will be in a state determined by a call of **generate()** for the seed sequence **g**
e.discard(n)	Skip the next **n** elements of the sequence
e==e2	Will **e** and **e2** produce exactly the same sequences?
e!=e2	!(e==e2)
os<<e	Write a representation of **e** to **os**
is>>e	Read a representation of an engine previously written by << from **is** into **e**

A seed is a value in the range $[0:2^{32})$ that can be used to initialize a particular engine. A seed sequence, **g**, is an object that provides a function **g.generate(b,e)** that when called fills [**b**:**e**) with newly generated seeds (§iso.26.5.1.2).

Standard Random Number Engines (§iso.26.5.3)	
default_random_engine	An alias for an engine with wide applicability and low cost
linear_congruential_engine<UI,a,c,m>	$x_{i+1} = (ax_i + c) \bmod m$
mersenne_twister_engine<UI,w,n,m,r,a,u,d,s,t,c,l,f>	§iso.26.5.3.2
subtract_with_carry_engine<UI,w,s,r>	$x_{i+1} = (ax_i) \bmod b$ where $b = m^r - m^s + 1$ and $a = b - (b-1)/m$

The **UI** parameter for a standard random number engine must be an unsigned integer type. For **linear_congruential_engine<UI,a,c,m>**, if the modulus **m** is **0**, the value **numeric_limits<result_type>::max()+1** is used. For example, this writes out the index of the first repetition of a number:

```
map<int,int> m;
linear_congruential_engine<unsigned int,17,5,0> linc_eng;
for (int i=0; i<1000000; ++i)
    if (1<++m[linc_eng()]) cout << i << '\n';
```

I was lucky; the parameters were not too bad and I got no duplicate values. Try **<unsigned int,16,5,0>** instead and see the difference. Use the **default_random_engine** unless you have a real need and know what you are doing.

A *random number engine adaptor* takes a random number engine as an argument and produces a new random number engine with different randomness properties.

Standard Random Number Engine Adaptors (§iso.26.5.4)	
discard_block_engine<E,p,r>	E is the engine; §iso.26.5.4.2
independent_bits_engine<E,w,UI>	Generate w bits in type UI; §iso.26.5.4.3
shuffle_order_engine<E,k>	§iso.26.5.4.4

For example:

```
independent_bits_engine<default_random_engine,4,unsigned int> ibe;
for (int i=0; i<100; ++i)
    cout << '0'+ibe() << ' ';
```

This will produce 100 numbers in the range [48:63] (['0':'0'+2^4-1)).

A few aliases are defined for useful engines:

```
using minstd_rand0 = linear_congruential_engine<uint_fast32_t, 16807, 0, 2147483647>;
using minstd_rand = linear_congruential_engine<uint_fast32_t, 48271, 0, 2147483647>;
using mt19937 = mersenne_twister_engine<uint_fast32_t, 32,624,397,
                    31,0x9908b0df,
                    11,0xffffffff,
                    7,0x9d2c5680,
                    15,0xefc60000,
                    18,1812433253>;
```

```
using mt19937_64 = mersenne_twister_engine<uint_fast64_t, 64,312,156,
                            31,0xb5026f5aa96619e9,
                            29, 0x5555555555555555,
                            17, 0x71d67fffeda60000,
                            37, 0xfff7eee000000000,
                            43, 6364136223846793005>;
using ranlux24_base = subtract_with_carry_engine<uint_fast32_t, 24, 10, 24>;
using ranlux48_base = subtract_with_carry_engine<uint_fast64_t, 48, 5, 12>;
using ranlux24 = discard_block_engine<ranlux24_base, 223, 23>;
using ranlux48 = discard_block_engine<ranlux48_base, 389, 11>;
using knuth_b = shuffle_order_engine<minstd_rand0,256>;
```

40.7.2 Random Device

If an implementation is able to offer a truly random number generator, that source of random numbers is presented as a uniform random number generator called **random_device**:

random_device (§iso.26.5.6)	
random_device rd {s};	The **string s** identifies a source of random numbers; implementation-defined; explicit
d=rd.entropy()	**d** is a **double**; d==0.0 for a pseudo-random number generator

Think of **s** as the name of a random number source, such as a Geiger counter, a Web service, or a file/device containing the record of a truly random source. The **entropy()** is defined as

$$S(P_0, \ldots, P_{n-1}) = - \sum_{i=0}^{i=n-1} P_i \log P_i$$

for a device with n states whose respective probabilities are $P_0, \ldots, P_{n-1}$. The entropy is an estimate of the randomness, the degree of unpredictability, of the generated numbers. In contrast to thermodynamics, high entropy is good for random numbers because that means that it is hard to guess subsequent numbers. The formula reflects the result of repeatedly throwing a perfect n-sided dice.

The **random_device** is intended to be useful for cryptograpic applications, but it would be against all rules of that kind of application to trust an implementation of **random_device** without first studying it closely.

40.7.3 Distributions

A random number distribution is a function object that, when called with a random number generator argument, produces a sequence of values of its **result_type**:

Random Number Distribution D (§iso.26.5.1.6) (continues)	
D::result_type	The type of an element of **D**
D::param_type	The type of the set of arguments needed to construct a **D**
D d {};	Default constructor
D d {p};	Construct from **param_type p**

Random Number Distribution D (continued) (§iso.26.5.1.6)	
d.reset()	Reset to default state
p=d.param()	p is d's parameters of **param_type**
d.param(p)	Reset to the state determined by **param_type** p
x=d(g)	x is a value produced by **d** given the generator **g**
x=d(g,p)	x is a value produced by **d** given the generator **g** and the parameters **p**
x=d.min()	x is the smallest value that **d** can return
x=d.max()	x is the largest value that **d** can return
d==d2	Will **d** and **d2** produce identical sequences of elements?
d!=d2	!(d==d2)
os<<d	Write **d**'s state to **os** so that it can be read back by >>
is>>d	Read a state previously written by << from **is** into **d**

In the following tables, a template argument **R** means a real is required in the mathematical formula and **double** is the default. An **I** means that an integer is required and **int** is the default.

Uniform Distributions (§iso.26.5.8.2)			
Distribution	Precondition	Defaults	Result
uniform_int_distribution<I>(a,b)	$a \leq b$ $P(i\|a, b) = 1/(b - a + 1)$	(0,max)	[a:b]
uniform_real_distribution<R>(a,b)	$a \leq b$ $p(x\|a, b) = 1/(b - a)$	(0.0,1.0)	[a:b)

The *precondition* field specifies requirements on the distribution arguments. For example:

```
uniform_int_distribution<int> uid1 {1,100};    // OK
uniform_int_distribution<int> uid2 {100,1};    // error: a>b
```

The *default* field specifies default arguments. For example:

```
uniform_real_distribution<double> urd1 {};         // use a==0.0 and b==1.0
uniform_real_distribution<double> urd2 {10,20};    // use a==10.0 and b==20.0
uniform_real_distribution<> urd3 {};               // use double and a==0.0 and b==1.0
```

The *result* field specifies the range of the results. For example:

```
uniform_int_distribution<> uid3 {0,5};
default_random_engine e;
for (int i=0; i<20; ++i)
    cout << uid3(e) << ' ';
```

The range for **uniform_int_distribution** is closed, and we see the six possible values:

```
2 0 2 5 4 1 5 5 0 1 1 5 0 0 5 0 3 4 1 4
```

For **uniform_real_distribution**, as for all other distributions with floating-point results, the range is half-open.

Bernoulli distributions reflect sequences of tosses of coins with varying degrees of loading:

Bernoulli Distributions (§iso.26.5.8.3)			
Distribution	Precondition	Defaults	Result
bernoulli_distribution(p)	$0 <= p < 1$	(0.5)	{true,false}
	$P(b\|p) = \begin{cases} p & \text{if } b = true \\ 1 - p & \text{if } b = false \end{cases}$		
binomial_distribution<I>(t,p)	$0 \le p \le 1$ and $0 \le t$	(1,0.5)	[0:∞)
	$P(i\|t, p) = \binom{t}{i} p^i (1 - p)^{t-i}$		
geometric_distribution<I>(p)	$0 < p < 1$	(0.5)	[0:∞)
	$P(i\|p) = p(1 - p)^i$		
negative_binomial_distribution<I>(k,p)	$0 < p < 1$ and $0 < k$	(1,0.5)	[0:∞)
	$P(i\|k, p) = \binom{k + i - 1}{i} p^k (1 - p)^i$		

Poisson distributions express the probability of a given number of events occurring in a fixed interval of time and/or space:

Poisson Distributions (§iso.26.5.8.4)			
Distribution	Precondition	Defaults	Result
poisson_distribution<I>(m)	$0 < m$	(1.0)	[0:∞)
	$P(i\|\mu) = \dfrac{e^{-\mu} \mu^i}{i!}$		
exponential_distribution<R>(lambda)	$1 < lambda$	(1.0)	(0:∞)
	$p(x\|\lambda) = \lambda e^{-\lambda x}$		
gamma_distribution<R,R>(alpha,beta)	$0 < \alpha$ and $0 < \beta$	(1.0,1.0)	(0:∞)
	$p(x\|\alpha, \beta) = \dfrac{e^{-x/\beta}}{\beta^\alpha \Gamma(\alpha)} x^{\alpha-1}$		
weibull_distribution<R>(a,b)	$0 < al$ and $0 < b$	(1.0,1.0)	[0:∞)
	$p(x\|a, b) = \dfrac{a}{b} \left(\dfrac{x}{b}\right)^{a-1} \exp\left(-\left(\dfrac{x}{b}\right)^a\right)$		
extreme_value_distribution<R>(a,b)	$0 < b$	(0.0,1.0)	R
	$p(x\|a, b) = \dfrac{1}{b} \exp\left(\dfrac{a - x}{b} - \exp\left(\dfrac{a - x}{b}\right)\right)$		

Normal distributions map real values into real values. The simplest is the famous "bell curve" that distributes values symmetrically around a peak (mean) with the distance of elements from the mean being controlled by a standard deviation parameter:

Normal Distributions (§iso.26.5.8.5)			
Distribution	Precondition	Defaults	Result
normal_distribution<R>(m,s)	$0 < s$	(0.0,1.0)	R
	$p(x\|\mu,\sigma) = \dfrac{1}{\sigma\sqrt{2\pi}} \exp\left(-\dfrac{(x-\mu)^2}{2\sigma^2}\right)$		
lognormal_distribution<R>(m,s)	$0 < s$	(0.0,1.0)	>0
	$p(x\|m,s) = \dfrac{1}{sx\sqrt{2\pi}} \exp\left(-\dfrac{(\ln x - m)^2}{2s^2}\right)$		
chi_squared_distribution<R>(n)	$0 < n$	(1)	>0
	$p(x\|n) = \dfrac{x^{(n/2)-1}e^{-x/2}}{\Gamma(n/2)2^{n/2}}$		
cauchy_distribution<R>(a,b)	$0 < b$	(0.0,1.0)	R
	$p(x\|a,b) = \left(\pi b\left(1+\left(\dfrac{x-a}{b}\right)^2\right)\right)^{-1}$		
fisher_f_distribution<R>(m,n)	$0 < m$ and $0 < n$	(1,1)	>=0
	$p(x\|m,n) = \dfrac{\Gamma((m+n)/2)}{\Gamma(m/2)\Gamma(n/2)}\left(\dfrac{m}{n}\right)^{m/2} x^{(m/2)-1}\left(1+m\dfrac{x}{n}\right)^{-(m+n)/2}$		
student_t_distribution<R>(n)	$0 < n$	(1)	R
	$p(x\|n) = \dfrac{1}{\sqrt{n\pi}}\dfrac{\Gamma((n+1)/2}{\Gamma}(n/2)\left(1+\dfrac{x^2}{n}\right)^{(n+1)/2}$		

To get a feeling for these distributions, look at graphical representations for a variety of parameters. Such representations are easily generated and even more easily found on the Web.

Sampling distributions map integers into a specific range according to their probability density function **P**:

Sampling Distributions (§iso.26.5.8.6) (continues)			
Distribution	Precondition	Defaults	Result
discrete_distribution<I>{b,e}	$0 <= b[i]$	none	[0:e–b)
	$P(i\|p_0, \cdots p_{n-1}) = p_i$		
	The sequence [b:e) provides weights w_i so		
	$p_i = w_i/S$ and $0 < S = w_0 + \cdots + w_{n?1}$		
	where n = e–b		

Sampling Distributions (continued) (§iso.26.5.8.6)			
Distribution	Precondition	Defaults	Result
discrete_distribution<I>(lst)	discrete_distribution<I>(lst.begin(),lst.end())		
discrete_distribution<I>(n,min,max,f)	discrete_distribution<I>(b,e) where the ith element of [b:e) is obtained by f(min+i*(max?min)/n +(max−min)/(2*n))		
piecewise_constant_distribution<R>{b,e,b2,e2}	$b[i] < b[i+1]$ $P(x\|x_0,\cdots x_n, \rho_0 \cdots \rho_n)$	none	[*b:*(e−1))
piecewise_linear_distribution<R>{b,e,b2,e2}	$b[i] < b[i+1]$ $P(x\|x_0,\cdots x_n, \rho_0 \cdots \rho_n)$ $= p_i \dfrac{b_{i+1} - x}{b_{i+1} - b_i} + \rho_i \dfrac{x - b_i}{b_{i+1} - b_i}$ $b_i < b_{i+1}$ for all b_i in [b:e) $\rho_i = w_i/S$ where $S = \dfrac{1}{2}\sum\limits_{i=0}^{n-1}(w_i + w_{i+1})(b_{i+i} - b_i)$ [b:e] are the interval boundaries [b2:e2] are the weights	none	[*b:*(e−1))

40.7.4 C-Style Random Numbers

In <cstdlib> and <stdlib.h>, the standard library provides a simple basis for the generation of random numbers:

```
#define RAND_MAX implementation_defined /* large positive integer */
```

```
int rand();               // pseudo-random number between 0 and RAND_MAX
void srand(unsigned int i);   // seed random number generator by i
```

Producing a good random number generator isn't easy, and unfortunately not all systems deliver a good **rand()**. In particular, the low-order bits of a random number are often suspect, so **rand()%n** is not a good portable way of generating a random number between **0** and **n−1**. Often, **int((double(rand())/RAND_MAX)*n)** gives acceptable results. However, for serious applications, generators based on **uniform_int_distribution** (§40.7.3) will give more reliable results.

A call **srand(s)** starts a new sequence of random numbers from the *seed*, **s**, given as argument. For debugging, it is often important that a sequence of random numbers from a given seed be repeatable. However, we often want to start each real run with a new seed. In fact, to make games unpredictable, it is often useful to pick a seed from the environment of a program. For such programs, some bits from a real-time clock often make a good seed.

40.8 Advice

[1]   Numerical problems are often subtle. If you are not 100% certain about the mathematical aspects of a numerical problem, either take expert advice, experiment, or do both; §29.1.

[2]   Use variants of numeric types that are appropriate for their use; §40.2.

[3]   Use **numeric_limits** to check that the numeric types are adequate for their use; §40.2.

[4]   Specialize **numeric_limits** for a user-defined numeric type; §40.2.

[5]   Prefer **numeric_limits** over limit macros; §40.2.1.

[6]   Use **std::complex** for complex arithmetic; §40.4.

[7]   Use {} initialization to protect against narrowing; §40.4.

[8]   Use **valarray** for numeric computation when run-time efficiency is more important than flexibility with respect to operations and element types; §40.5.

[9]   Express operations on part of an array in terms of slices rather than loops; §40.5.5.

[10]   Slices is a generally useful abstraction for access of compact data; §40.5.4, §40.5.6.

[11]   Consider **accumulate()**, **inner_product()**, **partial_sum()**, and **adjacent_difference()** before you write a loop to compute a value from a sequence; §40.6.

[12]   Bind an engine to a distribution to get a random number generator; §40.7.

[13]   Be careful that your random numbers are sufficiently random; §40.7.1.

[14]   If you need genuinely random numbers (not just a pseudo-random sequence), use **random_device**; §40.7.2.

[15]   Prefer a random number class for a particular distribution over direct use of **rand()**; §40.7.4.

41

Concurrency

Keep it simple:
as simple as possible,
but no simpler.
– A. Einstein

- Introduction
- Memory Model
    Memory Location; Instruction Reordering; Memory Order; Data Races
- Atomics
    atomic Types; Flags and Fences
- **volatile**
- Advice

41.1 Introduction

Concurrency – the execution of several tasks simultaneously – is widely used to improve through-put (by using several processors for a single computation) or to improve responsiveness (by allow-ing one part of a program to progress while another is waiting for a response).

The C++ standard support for concurrency is introduced in a tutorial manner in §5.3. This chapter and the next provide a more detailed and systematic view.

We call an activity potentially executed concurrently with other activities a *task*. A *thread* is the system-level representation of a computer's facilities for executing a task. A standard-library **thread** (§42.2) can execute a task. A thread may share an address space with other threads. That is, all threads in a single address space can access the same memory locations. One of the central challenges of the programmer of a concurrent system is to make sure that threads access memory in a sensible manner.

The standard library's support for concurrency includes:

- A *memory model*: a set of guarantees for concurrent access to memory (§41.2) that basically ensures that simple and ordinary access works as one would naively expect
- Support for *programming without locks*: fine-grained low-level mechanisms for avoiding data races (§41.3)
- A *thread* library: a set of components supporting traditional threads-and-locks-style system-level concurrent programming, such as **thread, condition_variable**, and **mutex** (§42.2)
- A *task* support library: a few facilities supporting task-level concurrent programming: **future, promise, packaged_task**, and **async()** (§42.4)

These topics are ordered from the most fundamental and low-level to the highest-level. The memory model is common to all programming. For programmer productivity and error minimization, work at the highest feasible level. For example, prefer a **future** over a **mutex** for exchanging information and a **mutex** over an **atomic** for anything but simple counters and the like. Leave the complexities to standard-library implementers whenever feasible.

In the context of the C++ standard library, a *lock* is a **mutex** (a mutual exclusion variable) and any abstraction built upon a **mutex** to provide mutually exclusive access to a resource or to synchronize the progress of several concurrent tasks.

The topic of *processes*, that is, threads of execution in their own address spaces and communicating though inter-process communication mechanisms [Tanenbaum,2007], is not addressed in this book. I suspect that after reading about the problems with and techniques for managing shared data, you may become sympathetic to my view that explicitly shared data is best avoided. Naturally, communication implies some form of sharing, but that sharing most often need not be directly managed by the application programmer.

Please also note that as long as you don't pass pointers to your local data to other threads, your local data is free of the problems mentioned here. This is yet another reason to avoid global data.

This chapter is not a comprehensive guide to concurrent programming or even a complete explanation of the C++ standard-library facilities for concurrent programming. It provides:

- A basic description of the problems facing a programmer who has to deal with concurrency at the system level
- A fairly detailed overview of the concurrency facilities provided by the standard
- An introduction to the basic uses of the standard-library concurrency features at the threads-and-locks level and above

It does not:

- Go into details of the relaxed memory models or lock-free programming
- Teach advanced concurrent programming and design techniques

Concurrent and parallel programming have been popular topics of research and widely used for more than 40 years, so there is an extensive specialized literature (for example, for C++-based concurrency see [Wilson,1996]). In particular, just about any presentation of POSIX threads can be used as a source of examples that can be easily improved by using the standard-library facilities described here.

In contrast to the C-style POSIX facilities and to many older C++ thread-support libraries, the standard-library thread support is type-safe. There is no longer any reason to mess around with macros or **void**∗∗s to pass information among threads. Similarly, we can define tasks as function objects (e.g., lambdas) and pass them to threads without using casts or worrying about type violations. Furthermore, there is no reason to invent elaborate conventions for reporting errors from one thread to another; **futures** (§5.3.5.1, §42.4.4) can transmit exceptions. Given that concurrent software is often complex and that code running in different threads is often separately developed, I consider type safety and a standard (preferably exception-based) error-handling strategy even more important than for single-threaded software. The standard-library thread support also greatly simplifies notation.

41.2 Memory Model

The C++ concurrency mechanisms are mostly supplied as standard-library components. These components rely on a set of language guarantees known as the *memory model*. A memory model is the result of discussions between machine architects and compiler writers about how best to represent computer hardware. The memory model, as specified in the ISO C++ standard, represents a contract between the implementers and the programmers to ensure that most programmers do not have to think about the details of modern computer hardware.

To understand the problems involved, keep one simple fact in mind: operations on an object in memory are never directly performed on the object in memory. Instead, the object is loaded into a processor register, modified there, and then written back. Worse still, an object is typically first loaded from the main memory into a cache memory and from there to a register. For example, consider incrementing a simple integer **x**:

```
// add one to x:
    load x into cache element Cx
    load Cx into register Rx
    Rx=Rx+1;
    store Rx back into Cx
    store Cx back into x
```

Memory can be shared by several threads, and cache memory may (depending on the machine architecture) be shared among threads running on the same or different "processing units" (usually called something like *processors*, *cores*, or *hyper-threads*; this is an area of rapid evolution of both system facilities and terminology). This opens a host of opportunities for a simple operation (such as "add one to **x**") to get corrupted. It will be obvious to machine architecture experts that I am simplifying. For the few who notice that I have not mentioned store buffers, I recommend Appendix C of [McKenney,2012].

41.2.1 Memory Location

Consider two global variables **b** and **c**:

```
// thread 1:                    // thread 2:
    char c = 0;                      char b = 0;
    void f()                         void g()
    {                                {
        c = 1;                           b = 1;
        int x = c;                       int y = b;
    }                                }
```

Now, **x==1** and **y==1** as anyone would expect. Why is this even worth saying? Consider what might happen if a linker allocated **c** and **b** in the same word in memory and (like most modern hardware) the machine could not load or store anything smaller than a word:

word: | c | | b |

Without a well-defined and reasonable memory model, thread 1 might read the word containing **b** and **c**, change **c**, and write the word back into memory. At the same time, thread 2 could do the same with **b**. Then, whichever thread managed to read the word first and whichever thread managed to write its result back into memory last would determine the result. We might get **10**, **01**, or **11** (but not **00**). The memory model saves us from such chaos; we get **11**. The reason that **00** cannot happen is that the initializations of **b** and **c** are done (by the compiler or the linker) before either thread starts.

The C++ memory model guarantees that two threads of execution can update and access separate memory locations without interfering with each other. This is exactly what we would naively expect. It is the compiler's job to protect us from the sometimes very strange and subtle behaviors of modern hardware. How a compiler and hardware combination achieves that is up to the compiler. We program a "machine" that is provided by a combination of hardware and very low-level (compiler-generated) software.

Bit-fields (§8.2.7) give access to parts of a word. If two threads simultaneously access two fields of the same word, all bets are off. If **b** and **c** are two fields of the same word, most hardware has no way of avoiding the problem (the race condition) from the **b**-and-**c** example without using some form of (potentially very expensive) locking. Lock and unlock operations are not a cost we could implicitly impose on bit-fields, which are commonly used in critical device drivers. Consequently, the language defines *memory location* as the unit of memory for which sensible behavior is guaranteed to exclude individual bit-fields.

A *memory location* is either an object of arithmetic type (§6.2.1), a pointer, or a maximal sequence of adjacent bit-fields all having nonzero width. For example:

```
struct S {
        char a;                 // location #1
        int b:5;                // location #2
        unsigned c:11;
        unsigned :0;            // note: :0 is "special" (§8.2.7)
        unsigned d:8;           // location #3
        struct { int ee:8; } e; // location #4
};
```

Here, **S** has exactly four separate memory locations. Don't try to update bit-fields **b** and **c** from separate threads without explicit synchronization.

From the explanation above, you might conclude that if **x** and **y** are of the same type, **x=y** is guaranteed to result in **x** being a copy of **y**. This is true if and only if you don't have a data race (§41.2.4) and if **x** and **y** are memory locations. However, if **x** and **y** are of a multiword **struct** they are not a single memory location, and if you have a data race, all behavior is undefined, so make sure you have proper synchronization in place if you share data (§41.3, §42.3.1).

41.2.2 Instruction Reordering

To gain performance, compilers, optimizers, and hardware reorder instructions. Consider:

```
// thread 1:
    int x;
    bool x_init;

    void init()
    {
        x = initialize();  // no use of x_init in initialize()
        x_init = true;
        // ...
    }
```

For this piece of code there is no stated reason to assign to **x** before assigning to **x_init**. The optimizer (or the hardware instruction scheduler) may decide to speed up the program by executing **x_init=true** first.

We probably meant for **x_init** to indicate whether **x** had been initialized by **initializer()** or not. However, we did not say that, so the hardware, the compiler, and the optimizer do not know that.

Add another thread to the program:

```
// thread 2:
    extern int x;
    extern bool x_init;

    void f2()
    {
        int y;
        while (!x_init)              // if necessary, wait for initialization to complete
            this_thread::sleep_for(milliseconds{10});
        y = x;
        // ...
    }
```

Now we have a problem: thread 2 may never wait and thus will assign an uninitialized **x** to **y**.

Even if thread 1 did not set **x_init** and **x** in "the wrong order," we still may have a problem. In thread 2, there are no assignments to **x_init**, so an optimizer may decide to lift the evaluation of **!x_init** out of the loop, so that thread 2 either never sleeps or sleeps forever.

41.2.3 Memory Order

The time needed to get the value of a word from memory into a cache, then into a register, can be (on a processor's time scale) very long. At best, maybe 500 instructions are executed before the value reaches the register, and another 500 instructions are executed before a new value reaches its intended location. The figure 500 is a guess that depends on machine architecture and varies over time, but for the last decades it has steadily increased. When there is no rush to load and store a particular value because the computation is optimized for throughput, the time taken can be much higher. A value can be "away from its location" for tens of thousands of instruction cycles. This is one of the facts that give modern hardware its amazing performance, but it also opens huge opportunities for confusion as different threads look at a value at different times and in different places in the memory hierarchy. For example, my simplified description mentions only a single cache; many popular architectures use a three-level cache. To illustrate, here is a diagram of a possible two-level cache architecture where each core has its own level-2 cache, a pair of cores share a level-1 cache, and all cores share the memory:

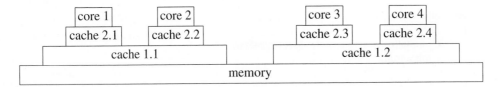

Memory ordering is the term used to describe what a programmer can assume about what a thread sees when it looks at a value from memory. The simplest memory order is called *sequentially consistent*. In a sequentially consistent memory model, every thread sees the effects of every operation done in the same order. The order is as if the instructions were done sequentially in a single thread. A thread can still reorder operations, but at every point where another thread might observe a variable, the set of operations performed before and (therefore) the value of the memory location observed must be well defined and the same for all threads. An operation that "observes" a value and thereby forces a consistent view of a memory location is called an *atomic operation* (see §41.3). A simple read or write does not impose an order.

There are many possible sequentially consistent orders for a given set of threads. Consider:

```
// thread 1:                        // thread 2:
    char c = 0;                         char b = 0;
    extern char b;                      extern char c;
    void f1()                           void f2()
    {                                   {
        c = 1;                              b = 1;
        int x = b;                          int y = c;
    }                                   }
```

Assuming that the initialization of **c** and **b** is done statically (before any thread starts), there are three possible executions:

```
c = 1;        b = 1;        c = 1;
x = b;        y = c;        b = 1;
b = 1;        c = 1;        x = b;
y = c;        x = b;        y = c;
```

The results are **01**, **10**, and **11**, respectively. The only result we cannot get is **00**. Obviously, to get a predictable result, you need some form of synchronization of the access to the shared variables.

The sequential consistent order is just about all a programmer can effectively reason about, but on some machine architectures it imposes significant synchronization costs that can be eliminated by relaxing the rules. For example, two threads running on separate cores might decide to initiate the reads of **x** and **y** before the writes of **a** and **b** or at least before the writes had completed. That could give the nonsequentially consistent result **00**. More relaxed memory models allow that.

41.2.4 Data Races

From these examples, every sensible person will conclude that we have to be very careful when programming threads. But how? First, we must avoid *data races*. Two threads have a data race if both can access a memory location (as defined in §41.2.1) simultaneously and at least one of their accesses is a write. Note that defining "simultaneously" precisely is not trivial. If two threads have a data race, no language guarantees hold: the behavior is undefined. This may sound drastic, but the effects of a data race can (as shown in §41.2.2) be drastic. An optimizer (or a hardware instruction scheduler) may reorder code based on assumptions about values and may execute sections of code (affecting apparently unrelated data) or not based on such assumptions.

There are many ways of avoiding data races:

- Use only a single thread. That eliminates the benefits of concurrency (unless you use processes or co-routines).
- Put a lock on every data item that might conceivably be subject to a data race. That can eliminate the benefits of concurrency almost as effectively as single threading because we easily get into a situation where all but one thread waits. Worse still, heavy use of locks increases the chances of deadlock, where a thread waits for another forever, and other locking problems.
- Try to look carefully at the code and avoid data races by selectively adding locks. This may be the currently most popular approach, but it is error-prone.
- Have a program detect all data races and either report them for the programmer to fix or automatically insert locks. Programs that can do that for programs of commercial size and complexity are not common. Programs that can do that and also guarantee the absence of deadlocks are still research projects.
- Design the code so that threads communicate only through simple put-and-get-style interfaces that do not require two threads to directly manipulate a single memory location (§5.3.5.1, §42.4).
- Use a higher-level library or tool that makes data sharing and/or concurrency implicit or sufficiently stylized to make sharing manageable. Examples include parallel implementations of algorithms in a library, directive-based tools (e.g., OpenMP), and transactional memory (often abbreviated to *TM*).

One way of looking at the rest of this chapter is as a bottom-up approach to arrive at support for one variant of that last style of programming. In the process, we encounter the tools needed to support just about every way of avoiding data races.

Why must programmers suffer all this complexity? An alternative would be to provide only a simple, sequentially consistent model with minimal (or no) opportunities for data races. I can offer two reasons:

- [1] That is not the way the world is. The complexities of machine architectures are real, and a systems programming language, such as C++, must provide the tools for programmers to live with them. Maybe someday machine architects will deliver simpler alternatives, but for now someone must deal with a bewildering variety of low-level facilities provided by machine architects to deliver the performance that their customers demand.
- [2] We (the C++ standards committee) seriously considered that. We would have liked to provide a memory model that was an improved version of what Java and C# provide.

That would have saved a lot of work for the committee and for some programmers. However, this idea was effectively vetoed by the providers of operating systems and virtual machines: they insisted that they needed roughly what was then provided by the various C++ implementations – what is now provided by the C++ standard. The alternative would be for your operating systems and your virtual machines to slow down "by a factor of two or more." I guess that programming language fanatics might have welcomed an opportunity to simplify C++ at the expense of other languages, but doing so would have been neither practical nor professional.

Fortunately, most programmers never have to work directly at the lowest level of the hardware. Most programmers do not need to understand a memory model at all and can think of reordering problems as amusing curiosities:

> *Write data-race-free code and don't mess with memory order (§41.3); then the memory model guarantees that code executes as naively expected. It's even better than sequential consistency.*

I find machine architecture a fascinating topic (e.g., see [Hennesey,2011] [McKenney,2012]), but as sensible and productive programmers, we stay away from the lowest levels of software whenever we can. Leave those for the experts and enjoy the higher levels that those experts provide for you.

41.3 Atomics

Lock-free programming is a set of techniques for writing concurrent programs without using explicit locks. Instead, the programmer relies on primitive operations (directly supported by hardware) to avoid data races (§41.2.4) for small objects (typically a single word or a double word). Primitive operations that do not suffer data races, often called *atomic operations*, can then be used in the implementation of higher-level concurrency mechanisms, such as locks, threads, and lock-free data structures.

With the notable exception of simple atomic counters, lock-free programming is for specialists. In addition to an understanding of language mechanisms, a detailed understanding of specific machine architectures and a knowledge of somewhat specialized implementation techniques are needed. Do not try lock-free programming with only the information provided here. The primary logical advantage of lock-free techniques over lock-based techniques is that classical locking problems, such as deadlock and starvation, cannot happen. For each atomic operation, it is guaranteed that every thread will eventually (and typically soon) make progress even if other threads compete for access to an atomic object. In addition, lock-free techniques can be significantly faster than lock-based alternatives.

The standard atomic types and operations provide a portable alternative to traditional ways of expressing lock-free code. Those typically either rely on assembly code or system-specific primitives. In this sense, the standard support for atomics is another step in C and C++'s long tradition of increasing portable and relatively comprehensible support for systems programming.

A synchronization operation is something that determines when a thread sees the effects of another thread; it determines what is considered to have happened before something else. Between synchronization operations a compiler and a processor are free to reorder code as long as the semantic rules of the language are maintained. In principle, nobody is looking and all that is affected is performance. A synchronization operation on one or more memory locations is a consume operation, an acquire operation, a release operation, or both an acquire and release operation (§iso.1.10).

- For an *acquire operation*, other processors will see its effect before any subsequent operation's effect.
- For a *release operation*, other processors will see every preceding operation's effect before the effect of the operation itself.
- A *consume operation* is a weaker form of an acquire operation. For a consume operation, other processors will see its effect before any subsequent operation's effect, except that effects that do not depend on the consume operation's value may happen before the consume operation.

An atomic operation ensures that the state of the memory is as required by the specified memory order (§41.2.2). By default, the memory order is **memory_order_seq_cst** (sequentially consistent; §41.2.2). The standard memory orders are (§iso.29.3):

```
enum memory_order {
    memory_order_relaxed,
    memory_order_consume,
    memory_order_acquire,
    memory_order_release,
    memory_order_acq_rel,
    memory_order_seq_cst
};
```

The enumerations represent:

- **memory_order_relaxed**: No operation orders memory.
- **memory_order_release, memory_order_acq_rel**, and **memory_order_seq_cst**: A store operation performs a release operation on the affected memory location.
- **memory_order_consume**: A load operation performs a consume operation on the affected memory location
- **memory_order_acquire, memory_order_acq_rel**, and **memory_order_seq_cst**: a load operation performs an acquire operation on the affected memory location.

As an example, consider (§iso.29.3) using **atomic** loads and stores (§41.3.1) to express a relaxed memory order:

```
// thread 1:
    r1 = y.load(memory_order_relaxed);
    x.store(r1,memory_order_relaxed);

// thread 2:
    r2 = x.load(memory_order_relaxed);
    y.store(42,memory_order_relaxed);
```

This is allowed to produce **r2==42**, making it appear that time went backward in thread 2. That is, **memory_order_relaxed** allows this execution order:

```
    y.store(42,memory_order_relaxed);
    r1 = y.load(memory_order_relaxed);
    x.store(r1,memory_order_relaxed);
    r2 = x.load(memory_order_relaxed);
```

For explanations, see the specialist literature, for example, [Boehm,2008] and [Williams,2012].

It is entirely architecture-specific whether a given memory order makes sense. Clearly, a relaxed memory model is not something to be directly used in applications programming. Utilizing a relaxed memory model is an even more specialized task than general lock-free programming. I see it as something done by a small subset of operating system kernel, device driver, and virtual machine implementers. It can also be useful in machine-generated code (as **goto**s can be). If two threads really do not directly share data, some machine architectures deliver significant performance improvements through the use of a relaxed memory model at the cost of complexity in the implementation of message-passing primitives (e.g., **future** and **promise**; §42.4.4).

To allow significant optimizations for architectures with relaxed memory models, the standard provides an attribute [[carries_dependency]] for transmitting memory order dependencies across function calls (§iso.7.6.4). For example:

```
[[carries_dependency]] struct foo* f(int i)
{
    // let the caller use memory_order_consume for the result:
    return foo_head[i].load(memory_order_consume);
}
```

You can also put [[carries__dependency]] on function arguments, and there is a function kill_dependency() for stopping the propagation of such dependencies.

One of the designers of the C++ memory model, Lawrence Crowl, summarizes:

"Dependency ordering is probably the most complex concurrency feature. It's really worth using when
   - you have a machine for which it matters,
   - you have a very high bandwidth read-mostly atomic data structure, and
   - you're willing to spend a couple of weeks in testing and external reviews.

This is real expert territory."

Consider yourself warned.

41.3.1 atomic Types

An *atomic type* is a specialization of the **atomic** template. An operation on an object of an atomic type is *atomic*. That is, it is performed by a single thread without interference from other threads.

The operations on atomics are very simple: loads and stores, swapping, incrementing, etc., on a simple object (usually a single memory location; §41.2.1). They have to be simple or the hardware can't handle them directly.

The following tables aim to give a first impression and an overview (only). Unless explicitly stated, the memory order is **memory_order_seq_cst** (sequentially consistent).

atomic<T> (§iso.29.5)	
x.val represents the value of the atomic x; all operations are **noexcept**	
atomic x;	x is uninitialized
atomic x {};	Default constructor: x.val=T{}; constexpr
atomic x {t};	Constructor: x.val=t; constexpr

atomic<T> **(continued)** (§iso.29.5) x.**val** represents the value of the atomic **x**; all operations are **noexcept**	
x=t	Assignment of **T**: x.**val**=t
t=x	Implicit conversion to **T**: t=x.**val**
x.is_lock_free()	Are operations on **x** lock free?
x.store(t)	x.**val**=t
x.store(t,order)	x.**val**=t; memory order is **order**
t=x.load()	t=x.**val**
t=x.load(order)	t=x.**val**; memory order is **order**
t2=x.exchange(t)	Exchange the values of **x** and t; t2 is **x**'s previous value
t2=x.exchange(t,order)	Exchange the values of **x** and t; memory order is **order**; t2 is **x**'s previous value
b=x.compare_exchange_weak(rt,t)	If b=(x.**val**==rt), x.**val**=t, otherwise rt=x.**val**; rt is a **T&**
b=x.compare_exchange_weak(rt,t,o1,o2)	b=x.compare_exchange_weak(rt,t); use **o1** as the memory order when b==**true**; use **o2** as the memory order when b==**false**
b=x.compare_exchange_weak(rt,t,order)	b=x.compare_exchange_weak(rt,t); use **order** as the memory order (see §iso.29.6.1[21])
b=x.compare_exchange_strong(rt,t,o1,o2)	Like b=x.compare_exchange_weak(rt,t,o1,o2)
b=x.compare_exchange_strong(rt,t,order)	Like b=x.compare_exchange_weak(rt,t,order)
b=x.compare_exchange_strong(rt,t)	Like b=x.compare_exchange_weak(rt,t)

There are no copy or move operations for **atomics**. The assignment operator and constructor take values of the contained type **T** and access the contained value.

A default **atomic** (without an explicit {}) is uninitialized to allow the C standard library to be compatible.

The is_lock_free() operation is there so that you can test if these operations are lock free or if they have been implemented using a lock. On all major implementations, is_lock_free() returns **true** for integral and pointer types.

The **atomic** facilities are designed for types that map to a simple built-in type. Expect atomic<T> to be implemented using locks if **T** objects are large. The template argument type **T** must be trivially copyable (must not have user-defined copy operations).

The initialization of an **atomic** variable is *not* an atomic operation, so an initialization may have a data race with an access from another thread (§iso.29.6.5). However, a data race with an initialization is quite hard to achieve. As ever, keep initialization of nonlocal objects simple and prefer to initialize with constant expressions (you can't have a data race before the program starts).

A simple **atomic** variable is close to ideal for a shared counter, such as a use count for a shared data structure. For example:

```
template<typename T>
class shared_ptr {
public:
    // ...
```

```
        ~shared_ptr()
        {
            if (−−*puc) delete p;
        }
private:
        T* p;                    // pointer to shared object
        atomic<int>* puc;        // pointer to use count
};
```

Here, *puc is an **atomic** (allocated somewhere by a **shared_ptr** constructor), so that the decrement operation (−−) is atomic and the new value is correctly reported in the **thread** destroying a **shared_ptr**.

The first argument of a compare-and-exchange operation (**rt** in the table) is a reference so that the object referred to can be updated if the operation fails to update its target (**x** in the table).

The difference between **compare_exchange_strong()** and **compare_exchange_weak()** is that the weak version can fail for "spurious reasons." That is, some peculiarity of the hardware or the implementation of **x.compare_exchange_weak(rt,t)** may cause a failure even if **x.val==rt**. Allowing such failures makes **compare_exchange_weak()** implementable on architectures where **compare_exchange_strong()** would be difficult or relatively expensive.

The classic compare-and-swap loop can be written like this:

```
atomic<int> val = 0;
// ...
int expected = val.load();        // read current value
do {
        int next = fct(expected); // calculate new value
} while (!val.compare_exchange_weak(expected,next)); // write next to val or to expected
```

The atomic **val.compare_exchange_weak(expected,next)** reads the current value of **val** and compares it to **expected**; if equal, it writes **next** to **val**. If some other thread has written to **val** since we read it in preparation to an update, we have to try again. When we try again, we use the new value of **expected** obtained from **compare_exchange_weak()**. Eventually, the expected value will be written. The value of **expected** is "the current value of **val** as seen by this thread." So, since **expected** is updated to the current value each time the **compare_exchange_weak()** is executed, we should never get an infinite loop.

Operations like **compare_exchange_strong()** are widely known as *compare-and-swap* operations (CAS operations). There is a potentially serious problem with all CAS operations (in any language and on any machine) known as *the ABA problem*. Consider adding a node at the head of a very simple lock-free singly-linked list if the **data** value is less than the head's **data**:

```
extern atomic<Link*> head;         // the shared head of a linked list

Link* nh = new Link(data,nullptr); // make a link ready for insertion
Link* h = head.load();             // read the shared head of the list
do {
        if (h−>data<data) break;   // if so, insert elsewhere
        nh−>next = h;              // next element is the previous head
} while (!head.compare_exchange_weak(h,nh));   // write nh to head or to h
```

This is a simplified version of code that would insert **data** at the right position in an ordered linked list. I read the **head**, use it as the **next** of my new **Link**, and then write the pointer to my new **Link** to **head**. I do that repeatedly until no other thread has managed to change the **head** while I was getting **nh** ready.

Let us examine this code in some detail. Call the value of **head** that I read **A**. If no other thread changed the value of **head** before I executed my **compare_exchange_weak()**, it finds **A** in **head** and succeeds in replacing it with my **nh**. If some other thread changed the value of **head** to **B** after I read **A**, my **compare_exchange_weak()** will fail, and I'll go around my loop to read **head** again.

This looks right. What could possibly go wrong? Well, after I read the value **A**, some other thread changed the value of **head** to **B** and recycled the **Link**. Then, some thread reused the node **A** and reinserted it at the **head** of the list. Now my **compare_exchange_weak()** finds **A** and does the update. However, the list had changed; the value of **head** went from **A** to **B** and then back to **A**. That change may be significant in many different ways, but in this simplified example, **A–>data** may have changed so that the critical **data** comparison may be wrong. ABA problems can be very subtle and hard to detect. There are a variety of ways of dealing with the ABA problem [Dechev,2010]. I mention it here primarily to warn about the subtleties of lock-free programming.

Integral **atomic** types offer atomic arithmetic and bit operations:

atomic<T> **for Integral** T (§iso.29.6.3)	
x.val represents the value of the atomic x; all operations are **noexcept**	
z=x.fetch_add(y)	x.val+=y; z is the previous x.val
z=x.fetch_add(y,order)	z=x.fetch_add(y); use **order**
z=x.fetch_sub(y)	x.val–=y; z is the previous x.val
z=x.fetch_sub(y,order)	z=x.fetch_sub(y); use **order**
z=x.fetch_and(y)	x.val&=y; z is the previous x.val
z=x.fetch_and(y,order)	z=x.fetch_and(y); use **order**
z=x.fetch_or(y)	x.val|=y; z is the previous x.val
z=x.fetch_or(y,order)	z=x.fetch_or(y); use **order**
z=x.fetch_xor(y)	x.val^=y; z is the previous x.val
z=x.fetch_xor(y,order)	z=x.fetch_xor(y); use **order**
++x	++x.val; return x.val
x++	x.val++; return previous x.val
--x	--x.val; return x.val
x--	x.val--; return previous x.val
x+=y	x.val+=y; return x.val
x-=y	x.val-=y; return x.val
x&=y	x.val&=y; return x.val
x|=y	x.val|=y; return x.val
x^=y	x.val^=y; return x.val

Consider the popular *double-checked locking* idiom. The basic idea is that if initializing some **x** must be done under a lock, you may not want to incur the cost of acquiring that lock every time you access **x** to see if the initialization has been done. Instead, you lock and initialize only if a variable **x_init** is **false**:

```
X x;                          // we need a lock to initialize an X
mutex lx;                     // the mutex to be used to lock x during initialization
atomic<bool> x_init {false};  // an atomic used to minimize locking

void some_code()
{
    if (!x_init) {            // proceed if x is uninitialized
        lx.lock();
        if (!x_init) {        // proceed if x is still uninitialized
            // ... initialize x ...
            x_init = true;
        }
        lx.unlock();
    }
    // ... use x ...
}
```

Had **init_x** not been **atomic**, instruction reordering could have moved the initialization of **x** ahead of the apparently unrelated test of **init_x** (see §41.2.2). Making **init_x** atomic prevents that.

The !x_init relies on the implicit conversion from an **atomic<T>** to a **T**.

This code can be simplified further by using RAII (§42.3.1.4).

The double-checked locking idiom is represented in the standard library by **once_flag** and **call_once()** (§42.3.3), so you don't have to write such code directly.

The standard library also supports **atomic** pointers:

atomic<T∗> for Pointers (§iso.29.6.4)	
x.val represents the value of the atomic x; all operations are **noexcept**	
z=x.fetch_add(y)	x.val+=y; z is the previous x.val
z=x.fetch_add(y,order)	z=x.fetch_add(y); use **order**
z=x.fetch_sub(y)	x.val−=y; z is the previous x.val
z=x.fetch_sub(y,order)	z=x.fetch_sub(y); use **order**
++x	++x.val; return x.val
x++	x.val++; return previous x.val
−−x	−−x.val; return x.val
x−−	x.val−−; return previous x.val
x+=y	x.val+=y; return x.val
x−=y	x.val−=y; return x.val

To allow the C standard library to be compatible, the **atomic** member function types have freestanding equivalents:

atomic_∗ operations (§iso.29.6.5) (continues)	
All operations are **noexcept**	
atomic_is_lock_free(p)	Are objects of ∗p's type atomic?
atomic_init(p,v)	Initialize ∗p with v

atomic_* **operations (continued) (§iso.29.6.5)** All operations are **noexcept**	
atomic_store(p,v)	Store **v** in *p
x=atomic_load(p)	Assign *p to **x**
x=atomic_load(p)	Load *p into **x**
b=atomic_compare_exchange_weak(p,q,v) ... about 70 more functions ...	Compare and exchange *p and *q; **b**=(*q==**v**)

41.3.2 Flags and Fences

In addition to the support for atomic types, the standard library offers two lower-level synchronization facilities: atomic flags and fences. The primary use of these is to implement the lowest-level atomic facilities, such as spinlocks and the atomic types. They are the only lock-free mechanisms that are guaranteed to be supported on every implementation (though all major platforms support atomic types).

Essentially no programmers need to use flags or fences. Those who do usually work closely with machine architects.

41.3.2.1 atomic **Flags**

An **atomic_flag** is the simplest atomic type and the only one with operations guaranteed to be atomic for every implementation. An **atomic_flag** represents a single bit of information. If necessary, the other atomic types can be implemented using **atomic_flag**.

The two possible values of an **atomic_flag** are called **set** and **clear**.

atomic_flag **(§iso.29.7)** All operations are **noexcept**	
atomic_flag fl;	The value of **fl** is undefined
atomic_flag fl {};	Default construct: the value of **fl** is **0**
atomic_flag fl {ATOMIC_FLAG_INIT};	Initialize **fl** to **clear**
b=fl.test_and_set()	Set **fl** and **b** is **fl**'s old value
b=fl.test_and_set(order)	Set **fl** and **b** is **fl**'s old value; use memory order **order**
fl.clear()	Clear **fl**
fl.clear(order)	Clear **fl**; use memory order **order**
b=atomic_flag_test_and_set(flp)	Set *flp; **b** is *flp's old value
b=atomic_flag_test_and_set_explicit(flp,order)	Set *flp; **b** is *flp's old value; use memory order **order**
atomic_flag_clear(flp)	Clear *flp
atomic_flag_clear_explicit(flp,order)	Clear *flp; use memory order **order**

The **bool** return values are **true** for set and **false** for clear.

Using {} to initialize **atomic_flag** seems to make sense. However, there is no guarantee that **0** represents clear. A machine where clear is **1** is rumored to exist. Clearing using **ATOMIC_FLAG_INIT** is the only portable and reliable way of initializing an **atomic_flag**. The **ATOMIC_FLAG_INIT** is an implementation-supplied macro.

You can think of an **atomic_flag** as a very simple spin lock:

```
class spin_mutex {
      atomic_flag flag = ATOMIC_FLAG_INIT;
public:
      void lock() { while(flag.test_and_set()); }
      void unlock() { flag.clear(); }
};
```

Note that spin locks can easily become very expensive.

As usual, I leave the memory orders and their proper use to the specialist literature.

41.3.2.2 Fences

A *fence*, also known as a *memory barrier*, is an operation that restricts operation reordering according to some specified memory ordering (§41.2.3). The fence operations do not do anything else. Think of them as simply slowing down a program to a safe speed, allowing the memory hierarchy to reach a reasonably well-defined state.

Fences (§iso.29.8)	
All operations are **noexcept**	
atomic_thread_fence(order)	Enforce memory order **order**
atomic_signal_fence(order)	Enforce memory order **order**
	for a thread and a signal handler executed on that thread

Fences are used in combination with **atomics** (needed to observe the effects of the fences).

41.4   volatile

The **volatile** specifier is used to indicate that an object can be modified by something external to the thread of control. For example:

```
volatile const long clock_register;  // updated by the hardware clock
```

A **volatile** specifier basically tells the compiler not to optimize away apparently redundant reads and writes. For example:

```
auto t1 {clock_register};
// ... no use of clock_register here ...
auto t2 {clock_register};
```

Had **clock_register** not been **volatile**, the compiler would have been perfectly entitled to eliminate one of the reads and assume t1==t2.

Do not use **volatile** except in low-level code that deals directly with hardware.

Do not assume that **volatile** has special meaning in the memory model. It does not. It is not – as in some later languages – a synchronization mechanism. To get synchronization, use an **atomic** (§41.3), a **mutex** (§42.3.1), or a **condition_variable** (§42.3.4).

41.5 Advice

[1]   Use concurrency to improve responsiveness or to improve throughput; §41.1.
[2]   Work at the highest level of abstraction that you can afford; §41.1.
[3]   Prefer **packaged_task** and **futures** over direct use of **thread**s and **mutex**es; §41.1.
[4]   Prefer **mutex**es and **condition_variable**s over direct use of **atomic**s except for simple counters; §41.1.
[5]   Avoid explicitly shared data whenever you can; §41.1.
[6]   Consider processes as an alternative to threads; §41.1.
[7]   The standard-library concurrency facilities are type safe; §41.1.
[8]   The memory model exists to save most programmers from having to think about the machine architecture level of computers; §41.2.
[9]   The memory model makes memory appear roughly as naively expected; §41.2.
[10] Separate threads accessing separate bit-fields of a **struct** may interfere with each other; §41.2.
[11] Avoid data races; §41.2.4.
[12] Atomics allow for lock-free programming; §41.3.
[13] Lock-free programming can be essential for avoiding deadlock and to ensure that every thread makes progress; §41.3.
[14] Leave lock-free programming to experts; §41.3.
[15] Leave relaxed memory models to experts; §41.3.
[16] A **volatile** tells the compiler that the value of an object can be changed by something that is not part of the program; §41.4.
[17] A C++ **volatile** is *not* a synchronization mechanism; §41.4.

42

Threads and Tasks

Keep Calm and Carry On.
– English slogan

- Introduction
- Threads
    Identity; Construction; Destruction; **join()**; **detach()**; Namespace **this_thread**; Killing a **thread**;
    thread_local Data
- Avoiding Data Races
    Mutexes; Multiple Locks; **call_once()**; Condition Variables
- Task-Based Concurrency
    future and **promise**; **promise**; **packaged_task**; **future**; **shared_future**; **async()**; A Parallel **find()**
    Example
- Advice

42.1 Introduction

Concurrency – the execution of several tasks simultaneously – is widely used to improve through-put (by using several processors for a single computation) or to improve responsiveness (by allowing one part of a program to progress while another is waiting for a response).

The C++ standard support for concurrency is introduced in a tutorial manner in §5.3. This chapter and the previous one provide a more detailed and systematic view.

We call an activity potentially executed concurrently with other activities a *task*. A *thread* is the system-level representation of a computer's facilities for executing a task. A **thread** can execute a task. A **thread** may share an address space with other **thread**s. That is, all **thread**s in a single address space can access the same memory locations. One of the central challenges of the programmer of a concurrent system is to make sure that **thread**s access memory in a sensible manner.

42.2 Threads

A **thread** is an abstraction of the computer hardware's notion of a computation. The C++ standard-library **threads** are intended to map one-to-one with the operating system's threads. We use **threads** when several tasks in a program need to progress concurrently. On a system with several processing units ("cores"), **threads** allows us to use those units. All **threads** work in the same address space. If you want hardware protection against data races, use some notion of a process. Stacks are not shared between **threads**, so local variables are not subject to data races, that is, unless you incautiously pass a pointer to a local variable to another **thread**. In particular, beware of by-reference context bindings in lambdas (§11.4.3). Deliberate and careful sharing of stack memory is useful and common, for example, we might pass sections of a local array to a parallel sort.

If a **thread** cannot proceed (e.g., because it has encountered a **mutex** owned by another **thread**), it is said to be *blocked* or *asleep*.

thread (§iso.30.3.1)	
id native_handle_type	The type of a **thread** identifier The type of a system's thread handle; implementation-defined (§iso.30.2.3)
thread t {}; thread t {t2}; thread t {f,args}; t.˜thread(); t=move(t2)	Default constructor: create a **thread** that does not (yet) have a task; noexcept Move constructor; noexcept Constructor: execute f(args) on a new **thread**; explicit Destructor: if t.joinable(), then **terminate()**; otherwise no effect Move assignment: if t.joinable(), then **terminate()**; noexcept
t.swap(t2) t.joinable() t.join() t.detach() x=t.get_id() x=t.native_handle()	Exchange the values of t and t2; noexcept Is there a thread of execution associated with t? t.get_id()!=id{}?; noexcept Join t with the current **thread**; that is, block the current **thread** until t completes; throw **system_error** if a deadlock is detected (e.g., t.get_id()==this_thread::get_id()); throw **system_error** if t.id==id{} Ensure that no system thread is represented by t; throw **system_error** if t.id!=id{} x is the id of t; noexcept x is the native handle for t (of **native_handle_type**)
n=hardware_concurrency() swap(t,t2)	n is the number of hardware processing units (0 means "don't know"); noexcept t.swap(t2); noexcept

A **thread** represents a system resource, a *system thread*, possibly even with dedicated hardware:

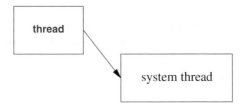

Consequently, a **thread** can be moved but not copied.

After being the source of a move, a **thread** no longer represents a thread of computation. In particular, it cannot be **join()**ed.

The **thread::hardware_concurrency()** operation reports the number of tasks that can simultaneously proceed with hardware support. The exact meaning of that is architecture-dependent, but it is usually less than the number of threads offered by the operating system (e.g., through time multiplexing or time slicing) and sometimes higher than the number of processors or "cores." For example, my little two-core laptop reports four hardware threads (it is using what is sometimes called *hyper-threading*).

42.2.1 Identity

Each thread of execution has a unique identifier represented as a value of type **thread::id**. If a **thread** does not represent a thread of execution, its **id** is the default **id{}**. The **id** of a **thread** t can be obtained by a call of **t.get_id()**.

The **id** of the current **thread** can be obtained by **this_thread::get_id()** (§42.2.6).

A **thread** can have its **id** be **id{}** if

- it has not had a task assigned,
- it has terminated,
- it has been moved from, or
- it has been **detach()**ed.

Every **thread** has an **id**, but a system thread may still be running even though it does not have an **id** (i.e., after a **detach()**).

A **thread::id** can be copied, and **id**s can be compared with the usual comparison operators (==, <, etc.), output using <<, and hashed with a specialization **hash<thread::id>** (§31.4.3.4). For example:

```
void print_id(thread& t)
{
    if (t.get_id()==id{})
        cout << "t not joinable\n";
    else
        cout << "t's id is " << t.get_id() << '\n';
}
```

Note that **cout** is a global shared object so that those output statements are not guaranteed to produce output characters in a recognizable sequence unless you make sure that no two **threads** are writing to **cout** at the same time (§iso.27.4.1).

42.2.2 Construction

A **thread** constructor takes a task to be executed and the arguments required by that task. The number and types of arguments must match what the task requires. For example:

```
void f0();       // no arguments
void f1(int);    // one int argument

thread t1 {f0};
thread t2 {f0,1};                      // error: too many arguments
thread t3 {f1};                        // error: too few arguments
thread t4 {f1,1};
thread t5 {f1,1,2};                    // error: too many arguments
thread t3 {f1,"I'm being silly"};      // error: wrong type of argument
```

After construction, a **thread** starts executing its task as soon as the run-time system can acquire resources for it to run. Think of that as "immediately." There is no separate "start the **thread**" operation.

If you want to build a set of tasks and link them together (e.g., to communicate through message queues), you first build the tasks as function objects and then – when they are all ready to run – start **threads**. For example:

```
template<typename T>
class Sync_queue<T> {   // a queue providing put() and get() without data races (§42.3.4)
    // ...
};

struct Consumer {
    Sync_queue<Message>& head;
    Consumer(Sync_queue<Message>& q) :head(q) {}
    void operator()();     // get messages from head
};

struct Producer {
    Sync_queue<Message>& tail;
    Consumer(Sync_queue<Message>& q) :tail(q) {}
    void operator()();     // put messages on tail
};

Sync_queue<Message> mq;
Consumer c {mq};                // make tasks and "wire them together"
Producer p {mq};

thread pro {p};                 // finally: start threads
thread con {c};

// ...
```

Trying to intersperse **thread** creation with the setup of connections among the tasks to be run by the **thread**s can easily become complicated and error-prone.

The **thread** constructors are variadic templates (§28.6). This implies that to pass a reference to a **thread** constructor, we must use a reference wrapper (§33.5.1). For example:

```
void my_task(vector<double>& arg);

void test(vector<double>& v)
{
    thread my_thread1 {my_task,v};           // oops: pass a copy of v
    thread my_thread2 {my_task,ref(v)};      // OK: pass v by reference
    thread my_thread3 {[&v]{ my_task(v); }}; // OK: dodge the ref() problem
    // ...
}
```

The problem is that the variadic template uses **bind()** or some equivalent mechanism, so that a reference is by default dereferenced and the result copied. So, if **v** was **{1,2,3}** and **my_task** increments elements, **thread1** would never have any effect on **v**. Note that all three **thread**s have a data race on **v**; this is an example of calling conventions, not of good concurrent programming style.

A default-constructed **thread** is primarily useful as the target for a move. For example:

```
vector<thread> worker(1000); // 1000 default threads

for (int i=0; i!=worker.size(); ++i) {
    // ... compute argument for worker[i] and create worker thread tmp ...
    worker[i] = move(tmp);
}
```

Moving a task from one **thread** to another does not affect its execution. A **thread** move simply changes what the **thread**s refer to.

42.2.3 Destruction

Obviously, the **thread** destructor destroys the **thread** object. To prevent a system thread from accidentally outliving its **thread**, the **thread** destructor calls **terminate()** to terminate the program if the **thread** is **joinable()** (that is, if **get_id()!=id{}**). For example:

```
void heartbeat()
{
    while(true) {
        output(steady_clock::now());
        this_thread::sleep_for(second{1}); // §42.2.6
    }
}

void run()
{
    thread t {heartbeat};
}       // terminate because heartbeat() is still running at the end of t's scope
```

If you really need to have a system thread proceed beyond the lifetime of its **thread** see §42.2.5.

42.2.4 join()

A t.join() tells the current **thread** not to proceed until t completes. For example:

```
void tick(int n)
{
    for (int i=0; i!=n; ++i) {
        this_thread::sleep_for(second{1});  // §42.2.6
        output("Alive!");
    }
}

int main()
{
    thread timer {tick,10};
    timer.join();
}
```

This will output **Alive!** ten times at about 1-second intervals. Had the **timer.join()** been missing, the program would have terminated before **tick()** could have printed anything. The **join()** made the main program wait for the **timer** to complete.

As mentioned in §42.2.3, trying to have a **thread** execute past the end of its scope (or more generally, after its destructor is run) without calling **detach()** is considered a fatal (for the program) error. However, we can forget to **join()** a **thread**. When we view a **thread** as a resource, we see that we should consider RAII (§5.2, §13.3). Consider a simple test example:

```
void run(int i, int n)  // warning: really poor code
{
    thread t1 {f};
    thread t2;
    vector<Foo> v;
    // ...
    if (i<n) {
        thread t3 {g};
        // ...
        t2 = move(t3);  // move t3 to outer scope
    }
    v[i] = Foo{};     // might throw
    // ...
    t1.join();
    t2.join();
}
```

Here, I have made several bad mistakes. In particular:

- We may never reach the two **join()**s at the end. In that case, the destructor for **t1** will terminate the program.
- We may reach the two **join()**s at the end without the move **t2=move(t3)** having executed. In that case, **t2.join()** will terminate the program.

For this kind of **thread** use, we need a destructor that implicitly **join()**s. For example:

```
struct guarded_thread : thread {
    using thread::thread;                           // §20.3.5.1
    ˜guarded_thread() { if (t.joinable()) t.join(); }
};
```

Unfortunately, `guarded_thread` is not a standard-library class, but in the best RAII tradition `guarded_thread` makes our code shorter and less error-prone. For example:

```
void run2(int i, int n)      // simple use of a guard
{
    guarded_thread t1 {f};
    guarded_thread t2;
    vector<Foo> v;
    // ...
    if (i<n) {
        thread t3 {g};
        // ...
        t2 = move(t3);  // move t3 to outer scope
    }
    v[i] = Foo{};      // might throw
    // ...
}
```

But why doesn't the `thread`'s destructor just `join()`? There is a long-standing tradition of using system threads that "live forever" or decide for themselves when to terminate. Had it worked, the `timer` executing `tick()` (§42.2.2) would have been an example of such a thread. Threads monitoring data structures provide many more examples. Such threads (and processes) are often called *daemons*. Another use for detached threads is to simply initiate a thread to complete a task and forget about it. Doing so leaves the "housekeeping" to the run-time system.

42.2.5 detach()

Accidentally letting a `thread` try to execute beyond its destructor is considered a very bad error. If you really want a system thread to outlive its `thread` (handle), use `detach()`. For example:

```
void run2()
{
    thread t {heartbeat};
    t.detach();              // let heartbeat run independently
}
```

I have a philosophical problem with detached threads. Given a choice, I would prefer to
- know exactly which threads are running,
- be able to determine if threads are making progress as expected,
- be able to check if threads that are supposed to delete themselves really do so,
- be able to know whether it is safe to use the results of a thread,
- be sure that all resources associated with a thread are properly released, and
- be sure that a thread does not try to access objects from the scope in which it was created after that scope has been destroyed.

Unless I go beyond the standard library (e.g., using **get_native_handle()** and "native" system facilities), I cannot do so for detached threads. Also, how do I debug a system where the behavior of
detached threads cannot be directly observed? What happens if a detached thread holds a pointer to
something in the scope in which it was created? That could lead to corrupted data, a system crash,
or a security violation. Yes, obviously detached threads can be useful and debugged. After all,
people have been doing it for decades. But people have been doing self-destructive things for cen-
turies and deemed them useful. Given a choice, I prefer not to **detach()** threads.

Note that **thread** provides a move assignment and a move constructor. This allows **thread**s to
migrate out of the scope in which they were constructed and often provides an alternative to
detach(). We can migrate **thread**s to a "main module" of a program, access them through
unique_ptrs or **shared_ptr**s, or place them in a container (e.g., **vector<thread>**) to avoid losing track
of them. For example:

```
vector<thread> my_threads;   // keep otherwise detached threads here

void run()
{
    thread t {heartbeat};
    my_threads.push_back(move(t));
    // ...
    my_threads.emplace_back(tick,1000);
}

void monitor()
{
    for (thread& t : my_threads)
        cout << "thread " << t.get_id() << '\n';
}
```

For a more realistic example, I would associate some information with each **thread** in **my_threads**.
Maybe I'd even launch **monitor** as a task.

If you *must* use a **detach()** a **thread**, do make sure that it does not refer to variables in its scope.
For example:

```
void home()     // don't do this
{
    int var;
    thread disaster{[&]{ this_thread::sleep_for(second{7.3});++var; }}
    disaster.detach();
}
```

Apart from the warning comment and the evocative name, this code looks quite innocent. It is not:
the system thread invoked by **disaster()** will "forever" keep writing to the address where **home()**'s
var was allocated, corrupting any data that may later be allocated there. This kind of error is
extremely hard to find because it is only loosely connected to the code in which it manifests itself,
and repeated runs of the program will have different results – many runs may exhibit no symptoms.
Such bugs have been called *Heisenbugs* in honor of the discoverer of the uncertainty principle.

Note that the root problem in that example is a violation of the simple and well known rule
"Don't pass a pointer to a local object out of its scope" (§12.1.4). However, with a lambda, it is

easy (and almost invisible) to create a pointer to a local variable: **[&]**. Fortunately, we have to say **detach()** to allow a **thread** to exit its scope; don't do that without a very good reason, and then only after carefully considering what its task might do.

42.2.6 Namespace this_thread

Operations for the current **thread** are found in namespace **this_thread**:

Namespace this_thread (§iso.30.3.1)	
x=get_id()	x is the **id** of the current **thread**; noexcept
yield()	Give the scheduler the opportunity to run another **thread**; noexcept
sleep_until(tp)	Put the current **thread** to sleep until **time_point** tp
sleep_for(d)	Put the current **thread** to sleep for **duration d**

To get the identity of the current **thread**, call **this_thread::get_id()**. For example:

```
void helper(thread& t)
{
    thread::id me {this_thread::get_id()};
    // ...
    if (t.get_id()!=me) t.join();
    // ...
}
```

Similarly, we can use **this_thread::sleep_until(tp)** and **this_thread::sleep_for(d)** to put the current **thread** to sleep.

The **this_thread::yield()** is used to give another **thread** a chance to proceed. The current **thread** is not blocked, so it will eventually be run again without any other **thread** having to do anything specific to wake it. Thus, **yield()** is primarily useful for waiting for an **atomic** to change state and for cooperative multi-threading. Usually, it is better to use **sleep_for(n)** than to just **yield()**. The argument to **sleep_for()** gives the scheduler a better chance to make rational choices about which **threads** to run when. Consider **yield()** a feature for optimization in very rare and specialized cases.

On all major implementations **thread**s are preemptable; that is, the implementation can switch from one task to another to ensure that all **thread**s progress at a reasonable rate. However, for historical and language technical reasons, preemption is only encouraged rather than required by the standard (§iso.1.10).

Usually, programmers should not mess with system clocks. But if a clock is reset (say, because it has drifted from the true time), a **wait_until()** would be affected, but not a **wait_for()**. The same applies to **wait_until()** and **wait_for()** for a **timed_mutex** (§42.3.1.3).

42.2.7 Killing a thread

I find one important operation missing from **thread**. There is no simple standard way of telling a running **thread** that I have lost interest in its task, so would it please stop running and release all its resources. For example, if I start a parallel **find()** (§42.4.7), I would often like to ask remaining tasks to stop once I have an answer. There are various historical and technical reasons for the lack of this operation (called *kill*, *cancel*, and *interrupt* in various languages and systems).

If needed, application programmers can write their own versions of this idea. For example, many tasks involve a request loop. In that case, a "kindly commit suicide" message would allow the receiving **thread** to release all resources and then terminate. If there is no request loop, a task could periodically examine a "needed" variable to see if results are still wanted.

So, a general cancel operation may be difficult to design and to implement on all systems, but I have never seen an application where a specific cancellation mechanism wasn't relatively easy to implement.

42.2.8 thread_local Data

As indicated by its name, a **thread_local** variable is an object owned by a **thread** and not accessible from other **thread**s unless its owner (incautiously) gives them a pointer to it. In that, a **thread_local** resembles a local variable, but a local variable has its lifetime and access limited by its scope within a function, whereas a **thread_local** is shared among all functions of a **thread** and "lives" for as long as the **thread**. A **thread_local** object can be **extern**.

For most uses, having objects local (on the stack) is preferable to having them shared; **thread_local** storage shares the logical problems of global variables. As usual, namespaces can be used to limit the problems with nonlocal data. However, on many systems, the amount of stack storage for a **thread** is rather limited, so **thread_local** storage becomes important for tasks that require large amounts of nonshared data.

A **thread_local** is said to have *thread storage duration* (§iso.3.7.2). Each **thread** has its own copy of its **thread_local** variables. A **thread_local** is initialized before its first use (§iso.3.2). If constructed, it will be destroyed on **thread** exit.

An important use of **thread_local** storage is for a **thread** to explicitly keep a cache of data for exclusive access. That can complicate the program logic, but on machines with shared caches it can sometimes deliver very significant performance advantages. Also, it can simplify and/or lower the cost of locking by transferring data only in larger batches.

In general, nonlocal memory is a problem for concurrent programming because it is often nontrivial to determine if it is shared and thus a possible source of data races. In particular, **static** class members can be a major problem because they are often hidden from the users of a class, so that potential data races are easily missed. Consider a **Map** design with a per-type default value:

```
template<typename K, typename V>
class Map {
public:
    Map();
    // ...
    static void set_default(const K&,V&);       // set default for all Maps of type Map<K,V>
private:
    static pair<const K,V> default_value;
};
```

Why would a user suspect a data race on two different **Map** objects? Obviously, a user who spotted **set_default()** among the members might suspect, but **set_default()** is an easily overlooked minor feature (§16.2.12).

One-per-class (**static**) values used to be popular. They include default values, use counters, caches, free lists, answers to frequently asked questions, and many obscure uses. When used in a concurrent system, we have a classic problem:

```
// somewhere in thread 1:
    Map<string,int>::set_default("Heraclides",1);

// somewhere in thread 2:
    Map<string,int>::set_default("Zeno",1);
```

This is a potential data race: which **thread** gets to first execute **set_default()**?

Adding **thread_local** helps:

```
template<typename K, typename V>
class Map {
    // ...
private:
    static thread_local pair<const K,V> default_value;
};
```

Now, there is no longer a potential data race. However, there is no longer a single **default_value** shared among all users either. In the example, thread 1 will never see the effect of a **set_default()** in thread 2. As often as not, that was not what was intended in the original code, so by adding **thread_local**, we simply exchanged one error for another. Consider **static** data members suspect (always, because you don't know if your code might someday be executed as part of a concurrent system), and do not consider **thread_local** a panacea.

A namespace variable, a local **static**, and a class **static** member can be declared **thread_local**. As for local **static** variables, the construction of a **thread_local** local variable is protected by a first-time switch (§42.3.3). The order of construction of **thread_locals** is undefined, so keep the construction of different **thread_locals** independent of their order and use compile-time or link-time initialization whenever possible. Like **static** variables, **thread_locals** are by default initialized to zero (§6.3.5.1).

42.3 Avoiding Data Races

The best way to avoid data races is not to share data. Keep interesting data in local variables, in free store not shared with other threads, or in **thread_local** memory (§42.2.8). Do not pass pointers to such data to other **threads**. When such data needs to be processed by another **thread** (e.g., by a parallel sort), pass pointers to a specific section of the data and make sure not to touch that section of the data passed until after the termination of the task.

These simple rules are based on the idea of avoiding attempts to simultaneously access data, so they don't require locking and lead to maximally efficient programs. Where they cannot be used, for example, because lots of data needs to be shared, use some form of locking:

- *Mutexes*: A mutex (a mutual exclusion variable) is an object used to represent the exclusive right to access some resource. To access the resource, acquire the mutex, access, and then release the mutex (§5.3.4, §42.3.1).
- *Condition variables*: A condition variable is a variable used by a **thread** to wait for an event generated by another **thread** or a timer (§5.3.4.1, §42.3.4).

Strictly speaking, condition variables do not prevent data races. Rather, they save us from having to introduce shared data that might become a source of data races.

42.3.1 Mutexes

A **mutex** is an object used to represent exclusive access to some resource. Thus, it can be used to protect against data races and to synchronize access to data shared between multiple **thread**s.

Mutex Classes (§iso.30.4)	
mutex	A nonrecursive mutex; a **thread** will block if it tries to acquire a **mutex** that has already been acquired
recursive_mutex	A mutex that can be repeatedly acquired by a single **thread**
timed_mutex	A nonrecursive mutex with operations to try to acquire the mutex for (only) a specified time
recursive_timed_mutex	A recursive timed mutex
lock_guard<M>	A guard for a **mutex M**
unique_lock<M>	A lock for a **mutex M**

The "plain" **mutex** is the simplest, smallest, and fastest mutex. In exchange for added functionality, recursive and timed mutexes carry a small cost, which may or may not be significant for a given application on a given machine.

Only one **thread** can own a mutex at any one time:

- To *acquire* a mutex means to gain exclusive ownership of it; an acquire operation may block the **thread** executing it.
- To *release* a mutex means relinquishing exclusive ownership; a release operation will allow another **thread** to eventually acquire the mutex. That is, a release operation will unblock waiting **thread**s.

If several **thread**s are blocked on a **mutex** the system scheduler could in principle select the **thread** to be unblocked in such a way that some unfortunate **thread** would never get to run. This is called *starvation*, and a scheduling algorithm that avoids starvation by giving each **thread** an equal chance to make progress is said to be *fair*. For example, a scheduler might always choose the **thread** with the highest **thread::id** to run next, thereby starving a **thread** with a low **id**. The standard does not guarantee fairness, but in reality schedulers are "reasonably fair." That is, they make it extremely unlikely that a **thread** starves forever. For example, a scheduler may pick the next **thread** to run randomly among those blocked.

By itself, a mutex doesn't do anything. Instead, we use a mutex to represent something else. We use ownership of a mutex to represent the right to manipulate a resource, such as an object, some data, or an I/O device. For example, we could define a **cout_mutex** to represent the right to use **cout** from a **thread**:

```
mutex cout_mutex; // represent the right to use cout
```

```
template<typename Arg1, typename Arg2, typename Arg3>
void write(Arg1 a1, Arg2 a2 = {}, Arg3 a3 = {})
{
    thread::id name = this_thread::get_id();
```

```
        cout_mutex.lock();
        cout << "From thread " << name << " : " << a1 << a2 << a3;
        cout_mutex.unlock();
    }
```

If all threads use write() we should get output from different threads properly separated. The snag is that every thread has to use a mutex as intended. The correspondence between a mutex and its resource is implicit. In the cout_mutex example, a thread using cout directly (bypassing cout_mutex) can corrupt output. The standard guarantees that the cout variable is protected against corruption, but there is no protection against output from different threads becoming intermixed.

Note that I locked the mutex only for the one statement that required the lock. To minimize contention and the chances of a thread becoming blocked, we try to minimize the time a lock is held by locking only where it is essential to do so. A section of code protected by a lock is called a *critical section*. To keep code fast and free of problems related to locking, we minimize the size of critical sections.

The standard-library mutexes provide *exclusive ownership semantics*. That is, a single thread (at a time) has exclusive access to the resource. There are other kinds of mutexes. For example, multiple-reader-single-writer mutexes are popular, but the standard library does not (yet) offer one. If you need a different kind of mutex, use one offered by a specific system or write it yourself.

42.3.1.1 mutex and recursive_mutex

Class mutex offers a simple set of operations:

mutex (§iso.30.4.1.2.1)	
mutex m {}; m.˜mutex()	Default constructor: m is not owned by any thread; constexpr; noexcept Destructor: undefined behavior if owned
m.lock() m.try_lock() m.unlock()	Acquire m; block until ownership is acquired Try to acquire m; did acquisition succeed? Release m
native_handle_type nh=m.native_handle()	An implementation-defined system mutex type nh is the system handle for the mutex m

A mutex cannot be copied or moved. Think of a mutex as a resource, rather than a handle of a resource. In fact, a mutex is typically implemented as a handle to a system resource, but since that system resource cannot be shared, leaked, copied, or moved, it is usually a spurious complication to think of them as separate.

The basic uses of a mutex are very simple. For example:

```
mutex cout_mutex;   // initialized to "not owned by any thread"

void hello()
{
    cout_mutex.lock();
    cout << "Hello, ";
    cout_mutex.unlock();
}
```

```
void world()
{
    cout_mutex.lock();
    cout << "World!";
    cout_mutex.unlock();
}

int main()
{
    thread t1 {hello};
    thread t2 {world};

    t1.join();
    t2.join();
}
```

Given that, we will get the output

Hello, World!

or

World! Hello,

We will not get **cout** corrupted or some mixed-up output characters.

The **try_lock()** operation is used when we have some other work we might usefully do if some other **thread** is using a resource. As an example, consider a work generator that composes work requests for other tasks and places them on a work queue:

```
extern mutex wqm;
extern list<Work> wq;

void composer()
{
    list<Work> requests;

    while (true) {
        for (int i=0; i!=10; ++i) {
            Work w;
            // ... compose work request ...
            requests.push_back(w);
        }
        if (wqm.try_lock()) {
            wq.splice(requests);        // splice() requests into the list (§31.4.2)
            wqm.unlock();
        }
    }
}
```

When some server **thread** is examining **wq**, the **composer()** simply makes some more work instead of waiting.

When using locks, we have to beware of deadlock. That is, we must not wait for a lock that can never be released. The simplest form of deadlock requires only one lock and one **thread**. Consider a variant of the thread-safe output operation:

```
template<typename Arg, typename... Args>
void write(Arg a, Args tail...)
{
    cout_mutex.lock();
    cout << a;
    write(tail...);
    cout_mutex.unlock();
}
```

Now, if a **thread** calls **write("Hello,","World!")**, it will deadlock with itself when it tries the recursive call for the **tail**.

Recursive and mutually recursive calls are common enough for the standard to provide a solution. A **recursive_mutex** is just like a plain **mutex**, except that a single **thread** can acquire it repeatedly. For example:

```
recursive_mutex cout_mutex;        // changed to recursive_mutex to avoid deadlock

template<typename Arg, typename... Args>
void write(Arg a, Args tail...)
{
    cout_mutex.lock();
    cout << a;
    write(tail...);
    cout_mutex.unlock();
}
```

Now the recursive call of **write()** is correctly handled by **cout_mutex**.

42.3.1.2 mutex **Errors**

Trying to manipulate a mutex can fail. If so, the mutex operation throws a **system_error**. Some of the possible errors reflect conditions in the underlying system:

Mutex Error Conditions (§iso.30.4.1.2)	
resource_deadlock_would_occur	A deadlock would occur
resource_unavailable_try_again	Some native handle is not available
operation_not_permitted	The **thread** is not allowed to perform the operation
device_or_resource_busy	Some native handle is already locked
invalid_argument	A constructor native handle argument is bad

For example:

```
mutex mtx;
try {
    mtx.lock();
    mtx.lock();        // try to lock a second time
}
catch (system_error& e) {
    mtx.unlock();
    cout << e.what() << '\n';
    cout << e.code() << '\n';
}
```

I got the output

device or resource busy
generic: 16

This looks like a good argument for using a **lock_guard** or a **unique_lock** (§42.3.1.4).

42.3.1.3 timed_mutex and recursive_timed_mutex

A simple **mtx.lock()** is unconditional. If we don't want to block, we can use **mtx.try_lock()**, but when we fail to acquire **mtx**, we often want to wait for a while before trying again. The **timed_mutex** and **recursive_timed_mutex** offer support for that:

timed_mutex (§iso.30.4.1.3.1)	
timed_mutex m {};	Default constructor; **m** is not owned; constexpr; noexcept
m.~timed_mutex()	Destructor: undefined behavior if owned
m.lock()	Acquire **m**; block until ownership is acquired
m.try_lock()	Try to acquire **m**; did the acquisition succeed?
m.try_lock_for(d)	Try to acquire **m** for a maximum **duration** of **d**; did the acquisition succeed?
m.try_lock_until(tp)	Try to acquire **m** until **time_point tp** at the latest; did the acquisition succeed?
m.unlock()	Release **m**
native_handle_type	Implementation-defined system mutex type
nh=m.native_handle()	**nh** is the system handle for the mutex

The **recursive_timed_mutex** interface is identical to the **timed_mutex** interface (just as the **recursive_mutex** interface is identical to the **mutex** interface).

For **this_thread**, we can **sleep_until(tp)** a time_point and **sleep_for(d)** a duration (§42.2.6). More generally, we can **m.try_lock_until(tp)** or **m.try_lock_for(d)** for a **timed_mutex m**. If **tp** is before the current point in time or **d** is less than or equal to zero, the operation is equivalent to a "plain" **try_lock()**.

As an example, consider updating an output buffer with a new image (e.g., in a video game or a visualization):

```
extern timed_mutex imtx;
extern Image buf;
```

```
        void next()
        {
            while (true) {
                Image next_image;
                // ... compute ...

                if (imtx.try_lock(milliseconds{100})) {
                    buf = next_image;
                    imtx.unlock();
                }
            }
        }
```

The assumption here is that if the image cannot be updated reasonably fast (here, in 100 milliseconds), the user would prefer a newer version of the image. Further, it is assumed that missing an image in a sequence of updated images will rarely be noticed, so that a more complicated solution is not needed.

42.3.1.4 lock_guard and unique_lock

A lock is a resource, so we must not forget to release it. That is, each **m.lock()** operation must be matched by an **m.unlock()** operation. The usual opportunities for mistakes exist; for example:

```
    void use(mutex& mtx, Vector<string>& vs, int i)
    {
        mtx.lock();
        if (i<0) return;
        string s = vs[i];
        // ...
        mtx.unlock();
    }
```

The **mtx.unlock()** is there, but if **i<0** or if **i** is out of **vs**'s range and **vs** is range checked, the thread of execution never gets to the **mtx.unlock()** and **mtx** may be locked forever.

The standard library provides two RAII classes, **lock_guard** and **unique_lock**, to handle such problems.

The "plain" **lock_guard** is the simplest, smallest, and fastest guard. In exchange for added functionality, **unique_ptr** carries a small cost, which may or may not be significant for a given application on a given machine.

lock_guard<M> (§iso.30.4.2)	
m is a lockable object	
lock_guard lck {m};	lck acquires m; explicit
lock_guard lck {m,adopt_lock_t};	lck holds m; assume that the current **thread** has already acquired m; noexcept
lck.~lock_guard()	Destructor: calls **unlock()** for the mutex held

For example:

```
void use(mutex& mtx, vector<string>& vs, int i)
{
    lock_guard<mutex> g {mtx};
    if (i<0) return;
    string s = vs[i];
    // ...
}
```

The **lock_guard**'s destructor does the necessary **unlock()** on its argument.

As usual, we should only hold a lock for the minimal amount of time, so a **lock_guard** should not become an excuse for holding a lock until the end of a large scope if we only need the lock for a small section of the scope. Obviously, the checking of i does not require locking, so we could do that before acquiring the lock:

```
void use(mutex& mtx, vector<string>& vs, int i)
{
    if (i<0) return;
    lock_guard<mutex> g {mtx};
    string s = vs[i];
    // ...
}
```

Furthermore, imagine that we only needed the lock for the read of v[i]. Then, we could put the **lock_guard** in a small scope:

```
void use(mutex& mtx, vector<string>& vs, int i)
{
    if (i<0) return;
    string s;
    {
        lock_guard<mutex> g {mtx};
        s = vs[i];
    }
    // ...
}
```

Is such complication of the code worthwhile? Without looking at the code "hidden in the ..." we cannot tell, but we should definitely not use a **lock_guard** just out of unwillingness to consider where locking is needed. Minimizing the size of critical sections is in general a useful thing to do. If nothing else, it forces us to think about exactly where a lock is needed and why.

So, a **lock_guard** (and also a **unique_lock**) is a resource handle ("a guard") for an object that you can lock to acquire ownership and unlock to release.

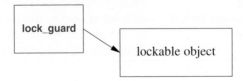

Such an object is called a *lockable object*. The obvious lockable object is of a standard-library mutex type, but users can define their own.

A lock_guard is a very simple class with no interesting operations. All it does is RAII for a mutex. To get an object that provides RAII and operations on a contained mutex, we use a unique_lock:

unique_lock<M> (§iso.30.4.2) m is a lockable object	
unique_lock lck {};	Default constructor: lck does not hold a mutex; noexcept
unique_lock lck {m};	lck acquires m; explicit
unique_lock lck {m,defer_lock_t};	lck holds m but does not acquire it
unique_lock lck {m,try_to_lock_t};	lck holds m and does a m.try_lock(); if the try succeeds lck owns m; otherwise not
unique_lock lck {m,adopt_lock_t};	lck holds m; assume that the current thread has already acquired m
unique_lock lck {m,tp};	lck holds m and calls m.try_lock_until(tp); if the try succeeds, lck owns m; otherwise not
unique_lock lck {m,d};	lck holds m and calls m.try_lock_for(d); if the try succeeds, lck owns m; otherwise not
unique_lock lck {lck2};	Move constructor: lck holds the mutex (if any) held by lck2; lck2 does not hold a mutex
lck.˜unique_lock()	Destructor: calls unlock() for the mutex held (if any)
lck2=move(lck)	Move assignment: lck holds the mutex (if any) held by lck2; lck2 does not hold a mutex
lck.lock()	m.lock()
lck.try_lock()	m.try_lock(); did acquisition succeed?
lck.try_lock_for(d)	m.try_lock_for(d); did acquisition succeed?
lck.try_lock_until(tp)	m.try_lock_until(tp); did acquisition succeed?
lck.unlock()	m.unlock()
lck.swap(lck2)	Exchange the lockable objects of lck and lck2; noexcept
pm=lck.release()	lck no longer owns *pm; noexcept
lck.owns_lock()	Does lck own a lockable object? noexcept
bool b {lck};	Conversion to bool; b==lck.owns_lock(); explicit; noexcept
pm=lck.mutex()	*pm is the owned lockable object, if any; otherwise pm=nullptr; noexcept
swap(lck,lck2)	lck.swap(lck2); noexcept

Obviously, the timed operations are only allowed if the contained mutex is a timed_mutex or a recursive_timed_mutex.

For example:

```
mutex mtx;
timed_mutex mtx2;

void use()
{
    unique_lock<defer_lock_t,mutex> lck {mtx};
    unique_lock<defer_lock_t,timed_mutex> lck2 {mtx2};

    lck.try_lock_for(milliseconds{2});        // error: mutex does not have member try_lock_for()

    lck2.try_lock_for(milliseconds{2});       // OK
    lck2.try_lock_until(steady_clock::now()+milliseconds{2});
    // ...
}
```

If you give a **duration** or a **time_point** as a second argument to a **unique_lock**, the constructor will execute the appropriate try operation. The **owns_lock()** operations allow us to check whether such an acquisition succeeded. For example:

```
timed_mutex mtx2;

void use2()
{
    unique_lock<timed_mutex> lck2 {mtx2,milliseconds{2}};
    if (lck2.owns_lock()) {
        // acquisition succeeded:
        // ... do something ...
    }
    else {
        // timeout:
        // ... do something else ...
    }
}
```

42.3.2 Multiple Locks

It is fairly common to want to acquire multiple resources to do some task. Unfortunately, acquiring two locks implies the opportunity of deadlock. For example:

```
mutex mtx1;    // protects one resource
mutex mtx2;    // protects another resource

void task(mutex& m1, mutex& m2)
{
    unique_lock<mutex> lck1 {m1};
    unique_lock<mutex> lck2 {m2};
    // ... use resources ...
}
```

```
thread t1 {task,ref(mtx1),ref(mtx2)};
thread t2 {task,ref(mtx2),ref(mtx1)};
```

The **ref()** is the **std::ref()** reference wrapper from **<functional>** (§33.5). It is needed to pass a reference through a variadic template (the **thread** constructor; §42.2.2). A mutex cannot be copied or moved, so I must pass them by reference (or use a pointer).

Change the names from **mtx1** and **mtx2** to something that does not indicate order and separate the definitions of **t1** and **t2** from each other in the source text and it will no longer be obvious that there is a good chance that the program will eventually deadlock with **t1** owning **mtx1**, **t2** owning **mtx2**, and each trying to acquire its second mutex forever.

Locks (§iso.30.4.2)	
locks is a sequence of one or more lockable objects **lck1**, **lck2**, **lck3**, ...	
x=try_lock(locks)	Try to acquire all members of **locks**; the locks are acquired in order; **x=–1** if all locks were acquired; otherwise **x=n**, where **n** is the lock that could not be acquired, and no locks are held
lock(locks)	Acquire all members of **locks**; do not deadlock

The actual algorithm for **try_lock()** is unspecified, but one possibility would be:

```
template <typename M1, typename... Mx>
int try_lock(M1& mtx, Mx& tail...)
{
    if (mtx.try_lock()) {
        int n = try_lock(tail...);
        if (n == -1) return -1;      // all locks acquired
        mtx.unlock();                // back out
        return  n+1;
    }
    return 1;                        // couldn't acquire mtx
}

template <typename M1>
int try_lock(M1& mtx)
{
    return (mtx.try_lock()) ? -1 : 0;
}
```

Given **lock()**, the buggy **task()** can be simplified and corrected:

```
void task(mutex& m1, mutex& m2)
{
    unique_lock lck1 {m1,defer_lock_t};
    unique_lock lck2 {m1,defer_lock_t};
    lock(lck1,lck2);
    // ... use resources ...
}
```

Note that applying **lock()** directly to the mutexes, **lock(m1,m2)**, rather than to the **unique_lock**s would have left the programmer with the obligation to explicitly release **m1** and **m2**.

42.3.3 call_once()

We often want to initialize an object without getting into a race condition. The type **once_flag** and the function **call_once()** offer a low-level, efficient, and simple tool for that.

call_once (§iso.30.4.2)	
once_flag fl {};	Default constructor: **fl** has not been used
call_once(fl,f,args)	Call **f(args)** if **fl** hasn't yet been used

For example:

```
class X {
public:
     X();
     // ...
private:
     // ...
     static once_flag static_flag;
     static Y static_data_for_class_X;
     static void init();
};

X::X()
{
     call_once(static_flag,init());
}
```

One way to think about **call_once()** is as a way to simply modify preconcurrency code that relies on initialized **static** data.

Run-time initialization of a local **static** variable is implemented by **call_once()** or by a mechanism very similar to **call_once()**. Consider:

```
Color& default_color()    // user code
{
     static Color def { read_from_environment("background color") };
     return def;
}
```

This may be implemented as

```
Color& default_color()    // generated code
{
     static Color def;
     static_flag __def;
     call_once(__def,read_from_environment,"background color");
     return def;
}
```

I use the double underscore prefix (§6.3.3) to emphasize that this latter version represents compiler-generated code.

42.3.4 Condition Variables

Condition variables are used to manage communication among **threads**. A **thread** can wait (block) on a **condition_variable** until some event, such as reaching a specific time or another **thread** completing, occurs.

condition_variable (§iso.30.5) lck must be a unique_lock<mutex>	
condition_variable cv {}; cv.˜condition_variable()	Default constructor: throw a **system_error** if some system resource cannot be obtained Destructor: no **thread** may be waiting and not notified
cv.notify_one() cv.notify_all()	Unblock one waiting **thread** (if any); noexcept Unblock all waiting **threads**; noexcept
cv.wait(lck) cv.wait(lck,pred) x=cv.wait_until(lck,tp) b=cv.wait_until(lck,tp,pred) x=cv.wait_for(lck,d) b=cv.wait_for(lck,d,pred)	**lck** must be owned by the calling **thread**; atomically calls **lck.unlock()** and blocks; unblocks if notified or "spuriously"; when unblocked calls **lck.lock()** **lck** must be owned by the calling **thread**; while (!pred()) wait(lock); **lck** must be owned by the calling **thread**; atomically calls **lck.unlock()** and blocks; unblocks if notified or timed out at **tp**; when unblocked calls **lck.lock()**; **x** is **timeout** if it timed out; otherwise x=no_timeout while (!pred()) if (wait_until(lck,tp)==cv_status::timeout); b=pred() x=cv.wait_until(lck,steady_clock::now()+d) b=cv.wait_until(lck,steady_clock::now()+d,move(pred))
native_handle_type nh=cv.native_handle()	See §iso.30.2.3 nh is the system handle for **cv**

A **condition_variable** may (or may not) rely on system resources, so a constructor may fail for lack of such a resource. However, like a **mutex**, a **condition_variable** cannot be copied or moved, so it is best to think of a **condition_variable** as a resource in itself, rather than as a handle.

When a **condition_variable** is destroyed, all waiting **threads** (if any) must be notified (i.e., told to wake up) or they may wait forever.

The status returned by **wait_until()** and **wait_for()** is defined as:

enum class cv_status { no_timeout, timeout };

A **condition_variable**'s **unique_lock** is used by the **wait** functions to prevent wake-ups being lost due to contention on the **unique_lock**'s list of waiting **threads**.

The "plain" **wait(lck)** is a low-level operation that should be used with extra care and usually in the implementation of some higher-level abstraction. It can wake up "spuriously." That is, the system may decide to resume **wait()**'s **thread** even though no other **thread** has notified it!

Apparently, allowing spurious wake-up simplifies implementation of condition_variables on some systems. Always use "plain" wait() in a loop. For example:

```
while (queue.empty()) wait(queue_lck);
```

An additional reason for this loop is that some thread may have "snuck up" and invalidated the condition (here, queue.empty()) before the thread calling the unconditional wait() got to run. Such a loop basically is the implementation of a wait with a condition, so prefer those over the unconditional wait().

A thread can wait for an amount of time:

```
void simple_timer(int delay)
{
        condition_variable timer;
        mutex mtx;                          // mutex protecting timer
        auto t0 = steady_clock::now();
        unique_lock<mutex> lck(mtx);        // acquire mtx
        timer.wait_for(lck,milliseconds{delay}); // release and reacquire mtx
        auto t1 = steady_clock::now();
        cout << duration_cast<milliseconds>(t1-t0).count() << "milliseconds passed\n";
} // implicitly release mtx
```

This basically shows the implementation of this_thread::wait_for(). The mutex protects wait_for() against data races. The wait_for() releases its mutex as it goes to sleep and reacquires it as its thread is unblocked. Finally, lck (implicitly) releases the mutex at the end of its scope.

Another simple use of a condition_variable is to control the flow of messages from a producer to a consumer:

```
template<typename T>
class Sync_queue {
public:
        void put(const T& val);
        void put(T&& val);
        void get(T& val);
private:
        mutex mtx;
        condition_variable cond;
        list<T> q;
};
```

The idea is that put() and get() will not get in each other's way. A thread that does a get() will sleep unless there is a value on the queue for it to get.

```
template<typename T>
void Sync_queue::put(const T& val)
{
        lock_guard<mutex> lck(mtx);
        q.push_back(val);
        cond.notify_one();
}
```

That is, a producer put() acquires the queue's mutex, adds a value at the end of the queue, calls notify_one() to wake a possibly blocked consumer, and implicitly releases the mutex. I provided an rvalue version of put() so that we can transmit objects of types that have move, but not copy, operations, such as unique_ptr (§5.2.1, §34.3.1) and packaged_task (§42.4.3).

I used notify_one() rather than notify_all() because I only added one element and wanted to keep put() simple. The possibility of multiple consumers and the possibility of consumers falling behind the producer might make me reconsider.

The get() is a bit more complicated because it should only block its thread if the mutex precludes access or if the queue is empty:

```
template<typename T>
void Sync_queue::get(T& val)
{
    unique_lock<mutex> lck(mtx);
    cond.wait(lck,[this]{ return !q.empty(); });
    val=q.front();
    q.pop_front();
}
```

A caller of get() will remain blocked until the Sync_queue is nonempty.

I used a unique_lock rather than a plain lock_guard because the lock_guard is optimized for simplicity and does not offer the operations needed to unlock and relock the mutex.

I used [this] to enable the lambda to access the Sync_queue object (§11.4.3.3).

I return the value from get() through a reference argument, rather than as a return value, to be sure that an element type with a copy constructor that can throw will not cause trouble. That is the conventional technique (e.g., the STL stack adaptor provides pop() and the containers provide front()). Writing a general get() that directly returns a value is possible, but surprisingly tricky. For an example, see future<T>::get() (§42.4.4).

A simple producer-consumer pair can be very simple:

```
Sync_queue<Message> mq;

void producer()
{
    while (true) {
        Message m;
        // ... fill m ...
        mq.put(m);
    }
}

void consumer()
{
    while (true) {
        Message m;
        mq.get(m);
        // ... use m ...
    }
}
```

```
thread t1 {producer};
thread t2 {consumer};
```

Using a **condition_variable** saves a consumer the bother of explicitly dealing with the case where it runs out of work to do. Had we simply used a **mutex** to control access to the **Sync_queue**, the consumer would have had to repeatedly wake up, look for work on the queue, and decide what to do when it found the queue empty.

I copy values into and out of the **list** I use to hold my queue elements. A copy of an element type may throw an exception, but if it does, the **Sync_queue** will remain unchanged and the **put()** or **get()** simply fails.

A **Sync_queue** is not itself a shared data structure, so we don't use a separate **mutex** for it; only the **put()** and **get()** (updating the head and the tail of the queue, which may be the same element) need to be protected against data races.

For some applications, the simple **Sync_queue** has a fatal flaw: What if a consumer waits forever because a producer stopped adding values? What if a consumer has other things to do so that it cannot wait for a long time? Often there are answers, but one common technique is to add a timeout to **get()**, that is, to specify a maximum time to wait:

```
void consumer()
{
    while (true) {
        Message m;
        mq.get(m,milliseconds{200});
        // ... use m ...
    }
}
```

To make this work, we need to add a second **get()** to **Sync_queue**:

```
template<typename T>
void Sync_queue::get(T& val, steady_clock::duration d)
{
    unique_lock<mutex> lck(mtx);
    bool not_empty = cond.wait_for(lck,d,[this]{ return !q.empty(); });
    if (not_empty) {
        val=q.front();
        q.pop_front();
    }
    else
        throw system_error{"Sync_queue: get() timeout"};
}
```

When using a timeout, we need to consider what to do after the wait: did we get data or did we just time out? Actually, we don't really care about the timeout, but only whether the predicate (expressed in the lambda) is true or not, so that is what **wait_for()** returns. I chose to report the failure of a **get()** with a timeout by throwing an exception. Had I thought that timing out would be a common and "nonexceptional" event, I would have returned a **bool** instead.

The roughly equivalent modification to **put()** would be to wait for the consumer to make inroads into a long queue, but not for too long a time:

```
template<typename T>
void Sync_queue::put(T val, steady_clock::duration d, int n)
{
    unique_lock<mutex> lck(mtx);
    bool not_full = cond.wait_for(lck,d,[this]{ return q.size()<n; });
    if (not_full) {
        q.push_back(val);
        cond.notify_one();
    }
    else {
        cond.notify_all();
        throw system_error{"Sync_queue: put() timeout"};
    }
}
```

For **put()**, the alternative of returning a **bool** to encourage the producer to always explicitly handle both cases seems more attractive than for **get()**. However, to avoid getting into a discussion of how best to handle overflow, I again chose to signal a failure by throwing an exception.

I chose to **notify_all()** if the queue was full. Maybe, some consumer needs a nudge to continue. The choice between **notify_all()** and **notify_one()** depends on the behavior of the application and is not always obvious. Notifying just one **thread** serializes access to the queue and could therefore minimize throughput when there are several potential consumers. On the other hand, notifying all waiting **thread**s may wake up several **thread**s, causing contention on the mutex and possibly having **thread**s repeatedly waking up just to find the queue empty (emptied by other **thread**s). I fall back on the old rule: Don't trust your intuition; measure.

42.3.4.1 condition_variable_any

A **condition_variable** is optimized for **unique_lock<mutex>**. A **condition_variable_any** is functionally equivalent to a **condition_variable** but can use any lockable object for its operations:

condition_variable_any (§iso.30.5.2)
lck can be any lockable object with the operations required
... like **condition_variable** ...

42.4 Task-Based Concurrency

So far, this chapter focused on the mechanisms for running concurrent tasks: the focus was on **thread**s, avoiding race conditions, and synchronizing **thread**s. For many concurrent tasks, I find this focus on mechanisms distracting from the real task (sic!) of specifying concurrent tasks. This section focuses on specifying a simple kind of task: a task that does one thing given arguments and produces one result.

To support this task-based model of concurrency, the standard library offers:

Task Support (§iso.30.6.1)	
packaged_task<F>	Package a callable object of type F to be run as a task
promise<T>	A type of object to which to put one result of type T
future<T>	A type of object from which to move one result of type T
shared_future<T>	A future from which to read a result of type T several times
x=async(policy,f,args)	Launch f(args) to be executed according to policy
x=async(f,args)	Launch with the default policy:
	x=async(launch::async|launch::deferred,f,args)

The presentation of these facilities exposes many details that rarely need to bother an application writer. Please keep in mind the fundamental simplicity of the task model. Most of the more complicated details support rare uses, such as hiding uses of the messier threads-and-locks level.

The standard-library task support is just one example of what can be done to support task-based concurrency. Often, we would like to provide a lot of small tasks and let "the system" worry about how to map their execution onto hardware resources and how to keep them out of problems with data races, spurious wake-ups, excessive waits, etc.

The importance of these facilities is their simplicity to a programmer. In a sequential program, we usually write something like:

```
res = task(args);    // perform a task given arguments and get the result
```

The concurrent version becomes:

```
auto handle = async(task,args);    // perform a task given arguments
// ... do something else ...
res = handle.get()                 // get the result
```

Sometimes, we lose sight of the value of simplicity as we consider alternatives, details, performance, and tradeoffs. By default, use the simplest technique and reserve the more complex solutions for where you know that they are really worthwhile.

42.4.1 future and promise

As mentioned in §5.3.5, communication between tasks is handled by a future/promise pair. A task puts its result into a promise, and a task that needs the result retrieves the result from the corresponding future:

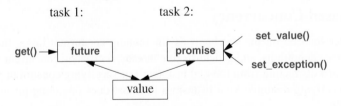

The "value" in this diagram is technically known as the *shared state* (§iso.30.6.4). In addition to the return value or exception, it contains the information needed for two **thread**s to safely exchange the information. At a minimum, a shared state must be able to hold:

- A *value* of the appropriate type or an exception. For a **future** "returning **void**" the value is nothing.
- A *ready bit* to indicate whether a value or exception is ready to be extracted by a **future**.
- The *task* to be executed when a **get()** is called for a **future** for a task launched by **async()** with the launch policy **deferred** (§42.4.6).
- A *use count*, so that the shared state can be destroyed when and only when its last potential user relinquishes access. In particular, if a stored value is of a class with a destructor, its destructor is called when the use count goes to zero.
- Some *mutual exclusion data* to enable unblocking of any **thread** that might be waiting (e.g., a **condition_variable**).

An implementation can take actions on a shared state:

- *Construct*: Possibly using a user-supplied allocator.
- *Make ready*: Set the "ready bit" and unblock any waiting **thread**s.
- *Release*: Decrease the use count and destroy the shared state if this was the last user.
- *Abandon*: If it becomes impossible for a value or exception to be put into the shared state by a **promise** (e.g., because the **promise** is destroyed), a **future_error** exception with the error condition **broken_promise** is stored in the shared state and the shared state is made ready.

42.4.2 promise

A **promise** is the handle to a shared state (§42.4.1). It is where a task can deposit its result to be retrieved through a **future** (§42.4.4).

promise<T> (§iso.30.6.5) (continues)	
promise pr {};	Default constructor: **pr** has a shared state that is not yet ready
promise pr {allocator_arg_t,a};	Construct **pr**; use allocator **a** to construct a shared state that is not yet ready
promise pr {pr2};	Move constructor: **pr** gets **pr2**'s state; **pr2** no longer has a shared state; noexcept
pr.˜promise()	Destructor: abandon the shared state; make the result a **broken_promise** exception.
pr2=move(pr)	Move assignment: **pr2** gets **pr**'s state; **pr** no longer has a shared state; noexcept
pr.swap(pr2)	Exchange the values of **pr** and **pr2**; noexcept
fu=pr.get_future()	**fu** is the **future** corresponding to **pr**
pr.set_value(x)	The result of the task is the value **x**
pr.set_value()	Set the result of the task for a **void future**
pr.set_exception(p)	The result of the task is the exception pointed to by **p**; **p** is an **exception_ptr**

promise<T> (continued) (§iso.30.6.5)	
pr.set_value_at_thread_exit(x)	The result of the task is the value x; don't make the result ready until **thread** exit
pr.set_exception_at_thread_exit(p)	The result of the task is the exception pointed to by **p**; **p** is an **exception_ptr**; don't make the result ready until **thread** exit
swap(pr,pr2)	pr.swap(pr2); noexcept

There are no copy operations for a **promise**.

A **set** function throws **future_error** if a value or exception is already set.

It is only possible to transmit a single result value through a **promise**. That may seem restrictive, but remember that the value is moved into and out of the shared state, rather than copied, so that we can cheaply pass a collection of objects. For example:

```
promise<map<string,int>> pr;
map<string,int> m;
// ... fill m with a million <string,int> pairs ...
pr.set_value(m);
```

A task may then extract that **map** from a corresponding **future** at essentially zero cost.

42.4.3 packaged_task

A **packaged_task** holds a task and a **future/promise** pair.

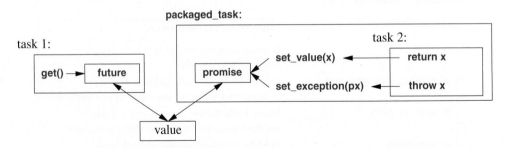

We pass a task (a function or a function object) that we want executed to a **packaged_task**. When our task executes a **return x**, it causes a **set_value(x)** on the **packaged_task**'s **promise**. Similarly, a **throw x** causes a **set_exception(px)** where **px** is an **exception_ptr** for **x**. Basically, the **packaged_task** executes its task, **f(args)**, like this:

```
try {
        pr.set_value(f(args));        // assume that the promise is called pr
}
catch(...) {
        pr.set_exception(current_exception());
}
```

A **packaged_task** offers a fairly conventional set of operations:

packaged_task<R(ArgTypes...)> (§iso.30.6.9)	
packaged_task pt {};	Default constructor: **pt** holds no task; noexcept
packaged_task pt {f};	Construct **pt** holding f; f is moved into **pt**; use the default allocator; explicit
packaged_task pt {allocator_arg_t,a,f};	Construct **pt** holding f; f is moved into **pt**; use allocator **a**; explicit
packaged_task pt {pt2};	Move constructor: **pt** gets **pt2**'s state; after the move **pt2** does not have a task; noexcept
pt=move(pt2)	Move assignment: **pt** gets **pt2**'s state; decrease the use count for **pt**'s former shared state; after the move **pt2** does not have a task; noexcept
pt.~packaged_task();	Destructor: abandon the shared state
pt.swap(pt2)	Exchange the values of **pt** and **pt2**; noexcept
pt.valid()	Does **pt** have a shared state? It does if it has had a task given to it and not been moved from; noexcept
fu=pt.get_future()	**fu** is the **future** for **pt**'s promise; throws **future_error** if called twice
pt()(args)	Execute f(args); a **return x** in f() does a **set_value(x)** to **pt**'s promise, a **throw x** in f() does a **set_exception(px)** to **pt**'s promise; **px** is an **exception_ptr** to **x**
pt.make_ready_at_exit(args)	Call f(args); don't make the result available until **thread** exit
pt.reset()	Reset to initial state; abandon the old state
swap(pt,pt2)	pt.swap(pt2)
uses_allocator<PT,A>	**true_type** if **PT** uses allocator type **A**

A **packaged_task** can be moved but not copied. A **packaged_task** may copy its task, and a copy of a task is assumed to yield the same result as the original. This is important because a task may be moved with its **packaged_task** onto the stack of a new **thread**.

To abandon a shared state (as is done by the destructor and the move) means making it ready. If there is no value or exception stored, a pointer to a **future_error** is stored (§42.4.1).

The advantage of **make_ready_at_exit()** is that the result is not available until destructors for **thread_local** variables have been executed.

There is no **get_promise()** operation to match **get_future()**. The use of the **promise** is completely handled by the **packaged_task**.

For a really simple example we don't even need any **thread**s. First define a simple task:

```
int ff(int i)
{
    if (i) return i;
    throw runtime_error("ff(0)");
}
```

We can now package this function into **packaged_task**s and call them:

```
packaged_task<int(int)> pt1 {ff};        // store ff in pt1
packaged_task<int(int)> pt2 {ff};        // store ff in pt2

pt1(1);                    // let pt1 call ff(1);
pt2(0);                    // let pt2 call ff(0);
```

So far, nothing appears to have happened. In particular, we don't see the exception triggered by ff(0). In fact, pt1(1) did a set_value(1) on the promise attached to pt1, and pt1(0) did a set_exception(px) on the promise attached to pt2; that px is an exception_ptr to a runtime_error("ff(0)").

Later, we can try to retrieve the results. The get_future() operation is used to get hold of the future into which the packaged thread will deposit the result of its task.

```
auto v1 = pt1.get_future();
auto v2 = pt2.get_future();

try {
    cout << v1.get() << '\n';    // will print
    cout << v2.get() << '\n';    // will throw
}
catch (exception& e) {
    cout << "exception: " << e.what() << '\n';
}
```

The output is:

```
1
exception: ff(0)
```

We could have gotten exactly the same effect by simply writing:

```
try {
    cout << ff(1) << '\n'; // will print
    cout << ff(0) << '\n'; // will throw
}
catch (exception& e) {
    cout << "exception: " << e.what() << '\n';
}
```

The point is that the packaged_task version works exactly like the version using ordinary function calls even when the calls of the task (here ff) and the calls of the get()s are in different threads. We can concentrate on specifying the tasks, rather than thinking about threads and locks.

We can move the future, the packaged_task, or both around. Eventually, the packaged_task is invoked and its task deposits its result in the future without having to know either which thread executed it or which thread will receive the result. This is simple and general.

Consider a thread that processes a series of requests. It could be a GUI thread, a thread owning access to a piece of specialized hardware, or indeed any server that serializes access to a resource through a queue. We can implement such a service as a queue of messages (§42.3.4), or we could pass tasks to be executed:

```
using Res = /* result type for server */;
using Args = /* argument types for server */;
```

```
using PTT = Res(Args);

Sync_queue<packaged_task<PTT>> server;

Res f(Args);                              // function: do something
struct G {
    Res operator()(Args);                 // function object: do something
    // ...
};
auto h = [=](Args a) { /* do something */ };   // lambda

packaged_task<PTT> job1(f);
packaged_task<PTT> job2(G{});
packaged_task<PTT> job3(h);

auto f1 = job1.get_future();
auto f2 = job2.get_future();
auto f3 = job3.get_future();

server.put(move(job1));
server.put(move(job2));
server.put(move(job3));

auto r1 = f1.get();
auto r2 = f2.get();
auto r3 = f3.get();
```

The server **thread** would take the **packaged_task**s from the **server** queue and execute them in some suitable order. Typically, the tasks would carry data with them from the calling context.

The tasks are written essentially like ordinary functions, function objects, and lambdas. The server calls the tasks essentially like ordinary (callback) functions. The **packaged_task**s are actually easier for the server to use than ordinary functions because the handling of their exceptions has been taken care of.

42.4.4 future

A **future** is a handle to a shared state (§42.4.1). It is where a task can retrieve a result deposited by a **promise** (§42.4.2).

future<T> (§iso.30.6.6) (continues)	
future fu {};	Default constructor: no shared state; noexcept
future fu {fu2};	Move constructor: **fu** gets **fu2**'s shared state, if any; **fu2** no longer has a shared state; noexcept
fu.˜future()	Destructor: release the shared state, if any
fu=move(fu2)	Move assignment: **fu** gets **fu2**'s shared state, if any; **fu2** no longer has a shared state; release **fu**'s old shared state, if any

future<T> (continued) (§iso.30.6.6)	
sf=fu.share()	Move fu's value into a **shared_future** sf; fu no longer has a shared state
x=fu.get()	fu's value is moved into x; if an exception was stored in fu, throw it; fu no longer has a shared state; don't try to **get()** twice
fu.get()	For **future<void>**: like x=fu.get(), but don't move any value
fu.valid()	Is fu valid? that is, does fu have a shared state? noexcept
fu.wait()	Block until a value arrives
fs=fu.wait_for(d)	Block until a value arrives or for a **duration** d; fs tells if a value is **ready**, a **timeout** occurred, or execution was **deferred**
fs=fu.wait_until(tp)	Block until a value arrives or until a **time_point** tp; fs tells if a value is **ready**, a **timeout** occurred, or execution was **deferred**

A **future** holds a unique value and offers no copy operations.

The value, if any, is *moved* out of a **future**. So **get()** can only be called once. If you potentially need to read a result several times (e.g., by different tasks), use a **shared_future** (§42.4.5).

It is undefined what happens if you try to **get()** twice. In fact, it is undefined what happens if you try to do any operation except a first **get()**, a **valid()**, or a destructor on a **future** that is not **valid()**. The standard "encourages" an implementation to throw a **future_error** with the error condition **future_errc::no_state** in such cases.

If a **future<T>**'s value type, **T**, is **void** or a reference, special rules apply for **get()**:

- **future<void>::get()** doesn't return a value: it just returns or throws an exception.
- **future<T&>::get()** returns a **T&**. A reference isn't an object, so the library must have transmitted something else, such as a **T∗**, and **get()** converts that (back) into a **T&**.

The status of a **future** can be observed by calling **wait_for()** and **wait_until()**:

enum class future_status	
ready	The **future** has a value
timeout	The operation timed out
deferred	The execution of the **future**'s task is deferred until a **get()**

The possible errors from operations on **futures** are:

future **Errors:** future_errc	
broken_promise	A promise abandoned the state before supplying a value
future_already_retrieved	A second **get()** on a **future**
promise_already_satisfied	A second **set_value()** or **set_exception()** on a **promise()**
no_state	An operation tried to access a **promise**'s shared state before that state was created (e.g., **get_future()** or **set_value()**)

In addition, an operation on the **T** value of **shared_future<T>::get()** could possibly throw (e.g., an unusual move operation).

Looking at the **future<T>** table, I find that I miss two useful functions:

- **wait_for_all(args)**: Wait until every **future** in **args** has a value.
- **wait_for_any(args)**: Wait until one **future** in **args** has a value.

I can easily implement a version of **wait_for_all()**:

```
template<typename T>
vector<T> wait_for_all(vector<future<T>>& vf)
{
    vector<T> res;
    for (auto& fu : vf)
        res.push_back(fu.get());
    return res;
}
```

That's easy enough to use, but it has a flaw: if I wait for ten **futures**, I risk my **thread** getting blocked ten times. Ideally, my **thread** would be blocked and unblocked at most once. However, for many uses, this **wait_for_all()** implementation is good enough: if some of the tasks are long-running, the extra waits will not be significant. On the other hand, if all tasks are short, they will most likely have finished after the first wait.

An implementation of **wait_for_any()** is trickier. First we need a way of checking if a **future** is ready. Surprisingly, that is done by using **wait_for()**. For example:

```
future_status s = fu.wait_for(seconds{0});
```

Using **wait_for(seconds{0})** to get the status of a **future** is not obvious, but **wait_for()** will tell us why it resumed, and it tests for ready before suspending. It is common, but unfortunately not guaranteed, that **wait_for(seconds{0})** returns immediately rather than trying to suspend for zero time.

Given **wait_for()**, we can write:

```
template<typename T>
int wait_for_any(vector<future<T>>& vf, steady_clock::duration d)
    // return index of ready future
    // if no future is ready, wait for d before trying again
{
    while(true) {
        for (int i=0; i!=vf.size(); ++i) {
            if (!vf[i].valid()) continue;
            switch (vf[i].wait_for(seconds{0})) {
            case future_status::ready:
                return i;
            case future_status::timeout:
                break;
            case future_status::deferred:
                throw runtime_error("wait_for_all(): deferred future");
            }
        }
        this_thread::sleep_for(d);
    }
}
```

I decided to consider a **deferred** task (§42.4.6) an error for my uses.

Note the check for **valid()**. Trying **wait_for()** on an invalid **future** (e.g., a **future** on which you have already done a **get()**) will cause a hard-to-find error. At best, you can hope for a (probably surprising) exception being thrown.

Like the implementation of **wait_for_all()**, this implementation has a flaw: ideally, the caller of **wait_for_any()** should never have to wake up just to find that no tasks had completed and should be unblocked immediately when one does. This simple implementation only approximates that. With a large **d** a useless wake-up is unlikely but implies the possibility of an unnecessarily long wait.

The **wait_for_all()** and **wait_for_any()** functions are useful building blocks for concurrent algorithms. I use them in §42.4.6.

42.4.5 shared_future

The result value of a **future** can be read only once: it is moved. Thus, if you want to read the value repeatedly or potentially have it read by multiple readers, you must copy it, and then read the copy. That's what a **shared_future** does. Every usable **shared_future** is directly or indirectly initialized by moving the value out of a **future** with the same result type.

shared_future<T> (§iso.30.6.7)	
shared_future sf {};	Default constructor: no shared state; noexcept
shared_future sf {fu};	Constructor: move value from **future fu**;
	fu no longer has a state; noexcept
shared_future sf {sf2};	Copy and move constructor; the move constructor is noexcept
sf.˜future()	Destructor: release the shared state, if any
sf=sf2	Copy assignment
sf=move(sf2)	Move assignment; noexcept
x=sf.get()	sf's value is copied into **x**; if an exception was stored in **fu**, throw it
sf.get()	For **shared_future<void>**: like **x=sf.get()**
	but doesn't copy any value
sf.valid()	Does **sf** have a shared state? noexcept
sf.wait()	Block until a value arrives
fs=sf.wait_for(d)	Block until a value arrives or for a **duration d**;
	fs tells if a value is **ready**, a **timeout** occurred,
	or execution was **deferred**
fs=sf.wait_until(tp)	Block until a value arrives or until a **time_point tp**;
	fs tells if a value is **ready**, a **timeout** occurred,
	or execution was **deferred**

Obviously, **shared_future** is very similar to **future**. The key difference is that a **shared_future** moves its value to a location where it can be repeatedly read and shared. As for **future<T>**, special rules apply for **get()** when a **shared_future<T>**'s value type, **T**, is **void** or a reference:

- **shared_future<void>::get()** doesn't return a value: it just returns or throws an exception.
- **shared_future<T&>::get()** returns a **T&**. A reference isn't an object, so the library must have transmitted something else, such as a **T∗**, and **get()** converts that (back) into a **T&**.
- **shared_future<T>::get()** returns a **const T&** when **T** is not a reference.

Unless the returned object is a reference, it is **const**, so it can safely be accessed from several **thread**s without synchronization. If the returned object is a non-**const** reference, you need some form of mutual exclusion to avoid data races on the referred-to object.

42.4.6 async()

Given **future** and **promise** (§42.4.1) and **packaged_task** (§42.4.3), we can write simple tasks without worrying too much about **thread**s. Given those, a **thread** is just something you give a task to run. However, we still need to consider how many **thread**s to use and whether a task is best run on the current **thread** or on another. Such decisions can be delegated to a *thread launcher*, that is, a function that decides whether to create a new **thread**, to recycle an old **thread**, or simply run the task on the current **thread**.

Asynchronous Task Launcher: async<F,Args>() (§iso.30.6.8)	
fu=async(policy,f,args)	Execute f(args) according to launch policy **policy**
fu=async(f,args)	fu=async(launch::async|launch::deferred,f,args)

The **async()** function is basically a simple interface to a launcher of unknown sophistication. A call of **async()** returns a **future<R>** where **R** is the type of its task's result. For example:

```
double square(int i) { return i*i; }
```

```
future<double> fd = async(square,2);
double d = fd.get();
```

If a **thread** is launched to execute **square(2)**, we may have a record slow way of executing **2*2**. The notation can be simplified by the use of **auto**:

```
double square(int i) { return i*i; }
```

```
auto fd = async(square,2);
auto d = fd.get();
```

In principle, a caller of **async()** could provide a huge variety of information to help the implementation of **async()** decide whether to launch a new **thread**, rather than simply executing the task on the current **thread**. For example, we can easily imagine a programmer wanting to give the launcher a hint about how long a task is likely to run. However, only two policies are currently standard:

Launch Policies: launch	
async	Execute the task as if a new **thread** was created to do so
deferred	Execute the task at the point of a **get()** for the task's **future**

Note the *as if*. The launcher has wide discretionary powers when it comes to launching a new **thread** or not. For example, since the default policy is **async\|deferred** (**async** or **deferred**), it is not too fanciful to imagine an **async()** that decided to use **deferred** for **async(square,2)**, so that the execution reduced to **fd.get()** calling **square(2)**. I could even imagine an optimizer reducing that whole code fragment to

```
double d = 4;
```

However, we should not expect an implementation of **async()** to be optimized for such trivial examples. Implementer efforts are better spent on realistic examples where the task performs a significant amount of computation so that launching on a new or "recycled" **thread** could be reasonably considered.

By a "recycled **thread**" I mean a **thread** from a collection of **threads** (a thread pool) that **async()** may create once and use over and over to execute a variety of tasks. Depending on the implementation of system threads, this can drastically lower the cost of executing a task on a **thread**. If a **thread** is recycled, the launcher must take care that a task does not see leftover state from a previous task executed on the **thread** and that a task does not store pointers to its stack or **thread_local** data (§42.2.8) in nonlocal storage. Such data could conceivably be used for security violations.

A simple and realistic use of **async()** would be to spawn a task to collect input from a user:

```
void user()
{
    auto handle = async([](){ return input_interaction_manager(); });
    // ...
    auto input = handle.get();
    // ...
}
```

Such a task often requires some data from the caller. I used a lambda to make it obvious that I can pass arguments or allow access to local variables. When using a lambda to specify a task, beware of capturing local variables by reference. That could lead to data races or unfortunate cache access patterns by two **threads** accessing the same stack frame. Also, beware that capturing members of an object using **[this]** (§11.4.3.3) implies that the members of the object are accessed indirectly (through **this**), rather than copied, so that the object is subject to data races unless you make certain that it is not. If in doubt, copy (pass or capture by value, **[=]**).

It is often important that we can select a scheduling policy "late" and change it as needed. For example, I might use **launch::deferred** for initial debugging. That would eliminate errors related to concurrency until I had eliminated sequential errors. Also, I can often go back to **launch::deferred** to determine if an error really is related to concurrency.

Over time, more launch policies may become available, and maybe some systems offer better launch policies than others. In such cases, I might be able to improve the performance of my code by a local change of launch policy, rather than by reworking subtle details of the program logic. This, again, is an effect of the fundamental simplicity of the task-based model (§42.4).

Having **launch::async|launch::deferred** as the default launch policy can be a practical problem. Basically, it is not so much a default as a lacking design decision. An implementation might decide that "no concurrency" is a good idea and always use **launch::deferred**. If your experiments with concurrency show results surprisingly similar to single-thread execution, try being explicit about the launch policy.

42.4.7 A Parallel find() Example

A **find()** does a linear search of a sequence. Imagine having millions of items that are not easily sorted so that **find()** is the right algorithm for finding something. This could be slow, so instead of searching once starting at the beginning and going until the end, we might start 100 **find()**s each on a hundredth of the data.

First, we represent the data as a **vector** of **Records**:

```
extern vector<Record> goods;        // data to be searched
```

An individual (sequential) task is simply a use of the standard-library **find_if()**:

```
template<typename Pred>
Record* find_rec(vector<Record>& vr, int first, int last, Pred pr)
{
        vector<Record>::iterator p = std::find_if(vr.begin()+first,vr.begin()+last,pr);
        if (p == vr.begin()+last)
                return nullptr;          // at end: no record found
        return &*p;                      // found: return a pointer to the element
}
```

Unfortunately, we have to decide on a "grain" of parallelism. That is, we need to specify the number of records to be searched sequentially.

```
const int grain = 50000;          // number of records for a linear search
```

Picking a number like that is a very primitive way of choosing a grain size. It is hard to choose well unless a lot is known about the hardware, the library implementation, the data, and the algorithm. Experimentation is essential. Tools and frameworks that save us from having to pick a grain size or help us choose can be most useful. However, for a simple illustration of basic standard-library facilities and the most basic techniques for their use, **grain** is sufficient.

The **pfind()** ("parallel find") function simply does the number of **async()** calls required by the **grain** and the number of **Record**s. Then, it **get()**s the results:

```
template<typename Pred>
Record* pfind(vector<Record>& vr, Pred pr)
{
        assert(vr.size()%grain==0);

        vector<future<Record*>> res;

        for (int i = 0; i!=vr.size(); i+=grain)
                res.push_back(async(find_rec<Pred>,ref(vr),i,i+grain,pr));

        for (int i = 0; i!=res.size(); ++i)     // look for a result in the futures
                if (auto p = res[i].get())      // did the task find a match?
                        return p;

        return nullptr;                          // no match found
}
```

Finally, we can initiate a search:

```
void find_cheap_red()
{
        assert(goods.size()%grain==0);

        Record* p = pfind(goods,
                        [](Record& r) { return r.price<200 && r.color==Color::red; });
        cout << "record "<< *p << '\n';
}
```

This first version of a parallel **find()** first spawns a lot of tasks and then proceeds to wait for them in order. Like **std::find_if()**, it reports the first element that matches the predicate; that is, it finds the element with the lowest index that matches. That may be fine, but:

- We could end up waiting for a lot of tasks that don't find anything (maybe only the last task finds something).
- We may throw away a lot of information that could be useful (maybe a thousand items match our criteria).

The first problem may not be as bad as it sounds. Assume (somewhat recklessly) that launching a **thread** doesn't cost anything and that we have as many processing units as there are tasks; then we would still get the result in roughly the time it took to process one task. That is, we would potentially get our result in the time taken to examine 50,000 records rather than millions. If we have **N** processing units, the results will be delivered in batches of results for **N*50000** records. If no record is found until the last segment of the **vector**, the time will be roughly **vr.size()/(N*grain)** units.

Instead of waiting for each task in order, we could try to look at the results in the order the tasks completed. That is, we could use **wait_for_any()** (§42.4.4). For example:

```
template<typename Pred>
Record* pfind_any(vector<Record>& vr, Pred pr)
{
    vector<future<Record*>> res;

    for (int i = 0; i!=vr.size(); i+=grain)
        res.push_back(async(find_rec<Pred>,ref(vr),i,i+grain,pr));

    for (int count = res.size(); count; --count) {
        int i = wait_for_any(res,microseconds{10});    // find a completed task
        if (auto p = res[i].get())                     // did the task find a match?
            return p;
    }

    return nullptr;                                    // no match found
}
```

A **get()** renders its **future** invalid, so we don't get to look at a partial result twice.

I use **count** to make sure I don't keep looking after all tasks have reported back. Apart from that, **pfind_any()** is as simple as **pfind()**. Whether there is a performance advantage to **pfind_any()** over **pfind()** depends on lots of things, but the key observation is that to (potentially) gain advantages of concurrency, we had to use a slightly different algorithm. Like **find_if()**, **pfind()** returns its first match, whereas **pfind_any()** returns whichever match it first found. Often, the best parallel algorithm for a problem is a variant of the idea for a sequential solution, rather than a simple repetition of the sequential solution.

In this case, the obvious question is "But do you really only need one match?" Given concurrency, it makes more sense to find all matches. Doing so is easy. All we need to do is to let each task return a **vector** of matches, rather than just a simple match:

```
template<typename Pred>
vector<Record*> find_all_rec(vector<Record>& vr, int first, int last, Pred pr)
{
    vector<Record*> res;
    for (int i=first; i!=last; ++i)
        if (pr(vr[i]))
            res.push_back(&vr[i]);
    return res;
}
```

This find_all_rec() is arguably simpler than the original find_rec().

Now we just need to launch find_all_rec() a suitable number of times and wait for the results:

```
template<typename Pred>
vector<Record*> pfind_all(vector<Record>& vr, Pred pr)
{
    vector<future<vector<Record*>>> res;

    for (int i = 0; i!=vr.size(); i+=grain)
        res.push_back(async(find_all_rec<Pred>,ref(vr),i,i+grain,pr));

    vector<vector<Record*>> r2 = wait_for_all(res);

    vector<Record*> r;
    for (auto& x : r2)                    // merge results
        for (auto p : x)
            r.push_back(p);
    return r;
}
```

Had I just returned a vector<vector<Record*>> this pfind_all() would have been the simplest parallelizing function so far. However, by merging the vectors returned into a single one, pfind_all() became an example of a common and popular group of parallel algorithms:

[1]   Create a number of tasks to be run.
[2]   Run the tasks in parallel.
[3]   Merge the results.

This is the basic idea that, when developed into a framework so that the details of concurrent execution have been completely hidden, is commonly referred to as *map-reduce* [Dean,2004].

The example can be run like this:

```
void find_all_cheap_red()
{
    assert(goods.size()%grain==0);

    auto vp = pfind_all(goods,
        [](Record& r) { return r.price<200 && r.color==Color::red; });
    for (auto p : vp)
        cout << "record "<< *p << '\n';
}
```

Finally, we must consider if the effort to parallelize was worthwhile. To do so, I added simple sequential versions to my test:

```
void just_find_cheap_red()
{
    auto p = find_if(goods.begin(),goods.end(),
        [](Record& r) { return r.price<200 && r.color==Color::red; });
    if (p!=goods.end())
            cout << "record "<< *p << '\n';
    else
            cout << "not found\n";
}


void just_find_all_cheap_red()
{
    auto vp = find_all_rec(goods,0,goods.size(),
        [](Record& r) { return r.price<200 && r.color==Color::red; });
    for (auto p : vp)
        cout << "record "<< *p << '\n';
}
```

For my simple test data and my (relatively) simple laptop with only four hardware threads, I did not find any consistent or significant performance differences. In this case, the cost of **thread** creation in the immature implementation of **async()** dominates the effects of concurrency. If I needed significant parallel speedup right now, I would implement my own variant of **async()** based on a pre-created set of **thread**s and a work queue, along the lines of a **Sync_queue** (§42.3.4) of **packaged_task**s (§42.4.3). Note that such a significant optimization can be done without changing my task-based parallel **find()** program. From the application's point of view, replacing the standard-library **async()** with an optimized version is an implementation detail.

42.5 Advice

[1]   A **thread** is a type-safe interface to a system thread; §42.2.
[2]   Do not destroy a running **thread**; §42.2.2.
[3]   Use **join()** to wait for a **thread** to complete; §42.2.4.
[4]   Consider using a **guarded_thread** to provide RAII for **thread**s; §42.2.4.
[5]   Do not **detach()** a **thread** unless you absolutely have to; §42.2.4.
[6]   Use **lock_guard** or **unique_lock** to manage mutexes; §42.3.1.4.
[7]   Use **lock()** to acquire multiple locks; §42.3.2.
[8]   Use **condition_variable**s to manage communication among **thread**s; §42.3.4.
[9]   Think in terms of tasks that can be executed concurrently, rather than directly in terms of **thread**s; §42.4.
[10]   Value simplicity; §42.4.
[11]   Return a result using a **promise** and get a result from a **future**; §42.4.1.
[12]   Don't **set_value()** or **set_exception()** to a **promise** twice; §42.4.2.

[13] Use **packaged_task**s to handle exceptions thrown by tasks and to arrange for value return; §42.4.3.
[14] Use a **packaged_task** and a **future** to express a request to an external service and wait for its response; §42.4.3.
[15] Don't **get()** twice from a **future**; §42.4.4.
[16] Use **async()** to launch simple tasks; §42.4.6.
[17] Picking a good granularity of concurrent tasks is difficult: experiment and measure; §42.4.7.
[18] Whenever possible, hide concurrency behind the interface of a parallel algorithm; §42.4.7.
[19] A parallel algorithm may be semantically different from a sequential solution to the same problem (e.g., **pfind_all()** vs. **find()**); §42.4.7.
[20] Sometimes, a sequential solution is simpler and faster than a concurrent solution; §42.4.7.

43

The C Standard Library

C is a strongly typed,
weakly checked language.
– D. M. Ritchie

- Introduction
- Files
- The **prinf()** Family
- C-Style Strings
- Memory
- Date and Time
- Etc.
- Advice

43.1 Introduction

The standard library for the C language is with very minor modifications incorporated into the C++ standard library. The C standard library provides quite a few functions that have proven useful over the years in a wide variety of contexts – especially for relatively low-level programming.

There are more C standard-library functions than are presented here; see a good C textbook, such as "Kernighan and Ritchie" [Kernighan,1988] or the ISO C standard [C,2011], if you need to know more.

43.2 Files

The **<stdio>** I/O system is based on *files*. A file (a **FILE***) can refer to a file or to one of the standard input and output streams: **stdin**, **stdout**, and **stderr**. The standard streams are available by default; other files need to be opened:

File Open and Close	
f=fopen(s,m)	Open a file stream for a file named **s** with the mode **m**
	f is the **FILE**∗ for the opened file if successful or **nullptr**
x=fclose(f)	Close file stream **f**; return **0** if successful

A file opened with **fopen()** must be closed by **fclose()** or the file will remain open until the operating system closes it. If that is a problem (is considered a leak), use an **fstream** (§38.2.1).

A *mode* is a C-style string containing one or more characters specifying how a file is to be opened (and used after opening):

File Modes	
"r"	Reading
"w"	Writing (discard previous contents)
"a"	Append (add at end)
"r+"	Reading and writing
"w+"	Reading and writing (discard previous contents)
"b"	Binary; use together with one or more other modes

There may be (and usually are) more options on a specific system. For example, **x** is sometimes used to mean "the file must not exist before this open operation." Some options can be combined, for example, **fopen("foo","rb")** tries to open a file called **foo** for binary reading. The I/O modes should be the same for stdio and **iostreams** (§38.2.1).

43.3 The printf() Family

The most popular C standard library functions are the output functions. However, I prefer **iostreams** because that library is type-safe and extensible. The formatted output function, **printf()**, is widely used (also in C++ programs) and widely imitated in other programming languages:

printf()	
n=printf(fmt,args)	Print the format string **fmt** to **stdout**,
	inserting the arguments **args** as appropriate
n=fprintf(f,fmt,args)	Print the format string **fmt** to file **f**,
	inserting the arguments **args** as appropriate
n=sprintf(s,fmt,args)	Print the format string **fmt** to the C-style string **s**,
	inserting the arguments **args** as appropriate

For each version, **n** is the number of characters written or a negative number if the output failed. The return value from **printf()** is essentially always ignored.

The declaration of **printf()** is:

```
int printf(const char∗ format ...);
```

In other words, it takes a C-style string (typically a string literal) followed by an arbitrary number of arguments of arbitrary type. The meaning of those "extra arguments" is controlled by conversion specifications, such as **%c** (print as character) and **%d** (print as decimal integer), in the format string. For example:

```
int x = 5;
const char* p = "Pedersen";
printf("the value of x is '%d' and the value of s is '%s'\n",x,s);
```

A character following a **%** controls the handling of an argument. The first **%** applies to the first "extra argument" (here, **%d** applies to **x**), the second **%** to the second "extra argument" (here, **%s** applies to **s**), and so on. In particular, the output of that call to **printf()** is

> **the value of x is '5' and the value of s is 'Pedersen'**

followed by a newline.

In general, the correspondence between a **%** conversion directive and the type to which it is applied cannot be checked, and when it can, it usually is not. For example:

```
printf("the value of x is '%s' and the value of s is '%x'\n",x,s);        // oops
```

The set of conversion specifications is quite large (and growing over the years) and provides a great degree of flexibility. Various systems support options beyond the ones offered by the C standard. See also the set of options used for **strftime()** formatting (§43.6). Following the **%**, there may be:

- – an optional minus sign that specifies left-adjustment of the converted value in the field;
- + an optional plus sign that specifies that a value of a signed type will always begin with a **+** or – sign;
- 0 an optional zero that specifies that leading zeros are used for padding of a numeric value. If – or a precision is specified this **0** is ignored;
- \# an optional # that specifies that floating-point values will be printed with a decimal point even if no nonzero digits follow, that trailing zeros will be printed, that octal values will be printed with an initial **0**, and that hexadecimal values will be printed with an initial **0x** or **0X**;
- *d* an optional digit string specifying a field width; if the converted value has fewer characters than the field width, it will be blank-padded on the left (or right, if the left-adjustment indicator has been given) to make up the field width; if the field width begins with a zero, zero-padding will be done instead of blank-padding;
- . an optional period that serves to separate the field width from the next digit string;
- *d* an optional digit string specifying a precision that specifies the number of digits to appear after the decimal point, for **e**- and **f**-conversion, or the maximum number of characters to be printed from a string;
- * a field width or precision may be * instead of a digit string. In this case an integer argument supplies the field width or precision;
- h an optional character h, specifying that a following **d, i, o, u, x,** or **X** corresponds to a (signed or unsigned) short integer argument;
- hh an optional pair of characters hh, specifying that a following **d, i, o, u, x,** or **X** argument is treated as a (signed or unsigned) **char** argument;
- l an optional character l (ell), specifying that a following **d, i, o, u, x,** or **X** corresponds to a (signed or unsigned) long integer argument;

ll an optional pair of characters **ll** (ell ell), specifying that a following **d**, **i**, **o**, **u**, **x**, or **X** corresponds to a (signed or unsigned) long long integer argument;

L an optional character **L**, specifying that a following **a**, **A**, **e**, **E**, **f**, **F**, **g**, or **G** corresponds to a long double argument;

j specifying that a following **d**, **i**, **o**, **u**, **x**, or **X** corresponds to a **intmax_t** or **uintmax_t** argument;

z specifying that a following **d**, **i**, **o**, **u**, **x**, or **X** corresponds to a **size_t** argument;

t specifying that a following **d**, **i**, **o**, **u**, **x**, or **X** corresponds to a **ptrdiff_t** argument;

% indicating that the character **%** is to be printed; no argument is used;

c a character that indicates the type of conversion to be applied. The conversion characters and their meanings are:

d The integer argument is converted to decimal notation;

i The integer argument is converted to decimal notation;

o The integer argument is converted to octal notation;

x The integer argument is converted to hexadecimal notation;

X The integer argument is converted to hexadecimal notation;

f The **float** or **double** argument is converted to decimal notation in the style *[−]ddd.ddd*. The number of *d*'s after the decimal point is equal to the precision for the argument. If necessary, the number is rounded. If the precision is missing, six digits are given; if the precision is explicitly **0** and **#** isn't specified, no decimal point is printed;

F Like **%f** but uses capital letters for **INF**, **INFINITY**, and **NAN**.

e The **float** or **double** argument is converted to decimal notation in the scientific style *[−]d.ddd***e**+*dd* or *[−]d.ddd***e**−*dd*, where there is one digit before the decimal point and the number of digits after the decimal point is equal to the precision specification for the argument. If necessary, the number is rounded. If the precision is missing, six digits are given; if the precision is explicitly **0** and **#** isn't specified, no digits and no decimal point are printed;

E As **e**, but with an uppercase **E** used to identify the exponent;

g The **float** or **double** argument is printed in style d, in style f, or in style e, whichever gives the greatest precision in minimum space;

G As **g**, but with an uppercase **E** used to identify the exponent;

a The **double** argument is printed in the hexadecimal format *[−]***0x***h.hhhh***p**+*d* or *[−]***0x***h.hhhh***p**+*d*;

A Like **%a** but using **X** and **P** instead or **x** and **p**;

c The character argument is printed. Null characters are ignored;

s The argument is taken to be a string (character pointer), and characters from the string are printed until a null character or until the number of characters indicated by the precision specification is reached; however, if the precision is 0 or missing, all characters up to a null are printed;

p The argument is taken to be a pointer. The representation printed is implementation-dependent;

u The unsigned integer argument is converted to decimal notation;

n The number of characters written so far by the call of **printf()**, **fprintf()**, or **sprintf()** is *written to* the **int** pointed to by the pointer to **int** argument.

In no case does a nonexistent or small field width cause truncation of a field; padding takes place only if the specified field width exceeds the actual width.

Here is a more elaborate example:

```
char* line_format = "#line %d \"%s\"\n";
int line = 13;
char* file_name = "C++/main.c";

printf("int a;\n");
printf(line_format,line,file_name);
```

which produces:

```
int a;
#line 13 "C++/main.c"
```

Using **printf()** is unsafe in the sense that type checking is not done. For example, here is a well-known way of getting unpredictable output, a segmentation fault, or worse:

```
char x = 'q';
printf("bad input char: %s",x);        // %s should have been %c
```

The **printf()** function does, however, provide great flexibility in a form that is familiar to C programmers.

Because C does not have user-defined types in the sense that C++ has, there are no provisions for defining output formats for user-defined types, such as **complex**, **vector**, or **string**. The format for **strftime()** (§43.6) is an example of the contortions you can get into by trying to design yet another set of format specifiers.

The C standard output, **stdout**, corresponds to **cout**. The C standard input, **stdin**, corresponds to **cin**. The C standard error output, **stderr**, corresponds to **cerr**. This correspondence between C standard I/O and C++ I/O streams is so close that C-style I/O and I/O streams can share a buffer. For example, a mix of **cout** and **stdout** operations can be used to produce a single output stream (that's not uncommon in mixed C and C++ code). This flexibility carries a cost. For better performance, don't mix stdio and **iostream** operations for a single stream. To ensure that, call **ios_base::sync_with_stdio(false)** before the first I/O operation (§38.4.4).

The stdio library provides a function, **scanf()**, that is an input operation with a style that mimics **printf()**. For example:

```
int x;
char s[buf_size];
int i = scanf("the value of x is '%d' and the value of s is '%s'\n",&x,s);
```

Here, **scanf()** tries to read an integer into **x** and a sequence of non-whitespace characters into **s**. A non-format character specifies that the input should contain that character. For example:

```
the value of x is '123' and the value of s is 'string '\n"
```

will read **123** into **x** and string followed by a **0** into **s**. If the call of **scanf()** succeeds, the resulting value (**i** in the call above) will be the number of argument pointers assigned to (hopefully **2** in the example); otherwise, **EOF**. This way of specifying input is error-prone (e.g., what would happen if you forgot the space after string on that input line?). All arguments to **scanf()** must be pointers. I strongly recommend against the use of **scanf()**.

So what can we do for input if we are obliged to use stdio? One popular answer is "use the standard-library function **gets()**":

```
// very dangerous code:
char s[buf_size];
char* p = gets(s);    // read a line into s
```

The call **p=gets(s)** reads characters into **s** until a newline or an end-of-file is encountered and a '\0' is placed after the last character written to **s**. If an end-of-file is encountered or if an error occurred, **p** is set to the **nullptr**; otherwise, it is set to **s**. Never use **gets(s)** or its rough equivalent (**scanf("%s",s)**)! For years, they were the favorites of virus writers: By providing an input that overflows the input buffer (**s** in the example), a program can be corrupted and a computer potentially taken over by an attacker. The **sprintf()** function can suffer similar buffer-overflow problems. The C11 version of the C standard library offers a whole alternate set of stdio input functions that take an extra argument to defend against overflow, such as **gets_s(p,n)**. As for **iostream**'s unformatted input, that leaves the user with the problem of deciding exactly which termination condition was encountered (§38.4.1.2; e.g., too many characters, a terminator character, or an end-of-file).

The stdio library also provides simple and useful character read and write functions:

Stdio Character Functions	
x=getc(st)	Read a character from input stream **st**; **x** is the character's integer value or **EOF** if end-of-file or an error occurred
x=putc(c,st)	Write the character **c** to the output stream **st**; **x** is the integer value of the character written or **EOF** if an error occurred
x=getchar()	x=getc(stdin)
x=putchar(c)	x=putc(c,stdout)
x=ungetc(c,st)	Put **c** back onto the input stream **st**; **x** is the integer value of **c** or **EOF** if an error occurred

The result of these operations is an **int** (not a **char**, or **EOF** could not be returned). For example, this is a typical C-style input loop:

```
int ch;    // note: not "char ch;"
while ((ch=getchar())!=EOF) { /* do something */ }
```

Don't do two consecutive **ungetc()**s on a stream. The result of that is undefined and non-portable.

There are many more stdio functions; see a good C textbook (e.g., "K&R,") if you need to know more.

43.4 C-Style Strings

A C-style string is a zero-terminated array of **char**. This notion of a string is supported by a set of functions defined in **<cstring>** (or **<string.h>**; note: not **<string>**) and **<cstdlib>**. These functions operate on C-style strings through **char*** pointers (**const char*** pointers for memory that is only read, but not **unsigned char*** pointers):

C-Style String Operations	
x=strlen(s)	Count the characters (excluding the terminating **0**)
p=strcpy(s,s2)	Copy **s2** into **s**; [**s**:**s**+n] and [**s2**:**s2**+n] may not overlap; p=**s**; the terminating **0** is copied
p=strcat(s,s2)	Copy **s2** onto the end of **s**; p=**s**; the terminating **0** is copied
x=strcmp(s, s2)	Compare lexicographically: if **s**<**s2**, then **x** is negative; if **s**==**s2**, then **x**==**0**; if **s**>**s2**, then **x** is positive
p=strncpy(s,s2,n)	strcpy of max **n** characters; may fail to copy terminating **0**
p=strncat(s,s2,n)	strcat of max **n** characters; may fail to copy terminating **0**
x=strncmp(s,s2,n)	strcmp of max **n** characters
p=strchr(s,c)	**p** points to the first **c** in **s**
p=strrchr(s,c)	**p** points to the last **c** in **s**
p=strstr(s,s2)	**p** points to the first character of **s** that starts a substring equal to **s2**
p=strpbrk(s,s2)	**p** points to the first character of **s** also found in **s2**

Note that in C++, **strchr()** and **strstr()** are duplicated to make them type-safe (they can't turn a **const char**∗ into a **char**∗ the way the C equivalents can). See also §36.3.2, §36.3.3, and §36.3.7.

C-Style String Numeric Conversions	
p points to the first character of **s** not used for the conversion; **b** is the base of the number [**2**:**36**] or **0**, meaning use C-source-code-style numbers	
x=atof(s)	**x** is a **double** represented by **s**
x=atoi(s)	**x** is an **int** represented by **s**
x=atol(s)	**x** is a **long** represented by **s**
x=atoll(s)	**x** is a **long long** represented by **s**
x=strtod(s,p)	**x** is a **double** represented by **s**
x=strtof(s,p)	**x** is a **float** represented by **s**
x=strtold(s,p)	**x** is a **long double** represented by **s**;
x=strtol(s,p,b)	**x** is a **long** represented by **s**
x=strtoll(s,p,b)	**x** is a **long long** represented by **s**
x=strtoul(s,p,b)	**x** is an **unsigned long** represented by **s**
x=strtoull(s,p,b)	**x** is an **unsigned long long** represented by **s**

The conversions to floating-point values set **errno** to **ERANGE** (§40.3) if their result doesn't fit into the target type. See also §36.3.5.

43.5 Memory

The memory manipulation functions operate on "raw memory" (no type known) through **void**∗ pointers (**const void**∗ pointers for memory that is only read):

C-Style Memory Operations	
q=memcpy(p,p2,n)	Copy **n** bytes from **p2** to **p** (like **strcpy**); [p:p+n] and [p2:p2+n] may not overlap; **q=p**
q=memmove(p,p2,n)	Copy **n** bytes from **p2** to **p**; **q=p**
x=memcmp(p,p2,n)	Compare **n** bytes from **p2** to the equivalent **n** bytes from **p**; **x<0** means <, **x==0** means ==, **0<x** means >
q=memchr(p,c,n)	Find **c** (converted to an **unsigned char**) in [p:p+n]; **q** points to that element; **q=0** if **c** is not found
q=memset(p,c,n)	Copy **c** (converted to an **unsigned char**) into each of [p:p+n]; **q=p**
p=calloc(n,s)	**p** points to **n∗s** bytes initialized to **0** on free store; **p=nullptr** if the bytes could not be allocated
p=malloc(n)	**p** points to **n** uninitialized bytes on free store; **p=nullptr** if the **s** bytes could not be allocated
q=realloc(p,n)	**q** points to **n** bytes on free store; **p** must be a pointer returned by **malloc()** or **calloc()**, or **nullptr**; if possible, reuse the space pointed to by **p**; if not, copy all bytes in the area pointed to by **p** to a new area; **q=nullptr** if **s** bytes could not be allocated
free(p)	Deallocate the memory pointed to by **p**; **p** must be **nullptr** or a pointer returned by **malloc()**, **calloc()**, or **realloc()**

Note that **malloc()**, etc., does not invoke constructors and **free()** doesn't invoke destructors. Do not use these functions for types with constructors or destructors. Also, **memset()** should never be used for any type with a constructor.

Note that **realloc(p,n)** will reallocate (that is, copy) the data stored, from **p** onward, when it needs more memory than is avaliable starting from **p**. For example:

```
int max = 1024;
char* p = static_cast<char*>(malloc(max));
char* current_word = nullptr;
bool in_word = false;
int i=0;
while (cin.get(&p[i]) {
    if (isletter(p[i])) {
        if (!in_word)
            current_word = p;
        in_word = true;
    }
    else
        in_word = false;
    if (++i==max)
        p = static_cast<char*>(realloc(p,max*=2));    // double allocation
    // ...
}
```

I hope you spotted the nasty bug: if **realloc()** was called, **current_word** may (may not) point to a location outside the current allocation pointed to by **p**.

Most uses of **realloc()** are better done using a **vector** (§31.4.1).

The **mem**∗ functions are found in **<cstring>** and the allocation functions in **<cstdlib>**.

43.6 Date and Time

In **<ctime>**, you can find several types and functions related to date and time:

Date and Time Types	
clock_t	An arithmetic type for holding short time intervals (maybe just a few minutes)
time_t	An arithmetic type for holding long time intervals (maybe centuries)
tm	A **struct** for holding the time of a date (since year 1900)

The **struct tm** is defined like this:

```
struct tm {
        int tm_sec;     // second of minute [0:61]; 60 and 61 represent leap seconds
        int tm_min;     // minute of hour [0:59]
        int tm_hour;    // hour of day [0:23]
        int tm_mday;    // day of month [1:31]
        int tm_mon;     // month of year [0:11]; 0 means January (note: not [1:12])
        int tm_year;    // year since 1900; 0 means year 1900, and 115 means 2015
        int tm_wday;    // days since Sunday [0:6]; 0 means Sunday
        int tm_yday;    // days since January 1 [0:365]; 0 means January 1
        int tm_isdst;   // hours of daylight savings time
};
```

A system clock is supported by the function **clock()** supported by a few functions giving meaning to its return type **clock_t**:

Date and Time Functions	
t=clock()	t is the number of clock ticks since the start of the program; t is a **clock_t**
t=time(pt)	t is the current calendar time; pt is a **time_t** or **nullptr**; t is a **clock_t**; if pt!=nullptr ∗pt=t
d=difftime(t2,t1)	d is a **double** representing t2–t1 in seconds
ptm=localtime(pt)	If **pt==nullptr**, ptm=nullptr; otherwise ptm points to the **time_t** local time for ∗pt
ptm=gmtime(pt)	If **pt==nullptr**, ptm=nullptr; otherwise ptm points to the **time_t** for Greenwich Mean Time (GMT) **tm** for ∗pt
t=mktime(ptm)	**time_t** for ∗ptm, or **time_t(–1)**
p=asctime(ptm)	p is a C-style string representation for ∗ptm
p=ctime(t)	**p=asctime(localtime(t))**
n=strftime(p,max,fmt,ptm)	Copy ∗ptm into [p:p+n+1) controlled by the format string **fmt**; characters beyond [p:p+m) are discarded; **n==0** in case of errors; p[n]=0

A example of the result of a call of **asctime()** is

> "Sun Sep 16 01:03:52 1973\n"

Here is an example of how **clock()** can be used to time a function:

```
int main(int argc, char* argv[])
{
    int n = atoi(argv[1]);

    clock_t t1 = clock();
    if (t1 == clock_t(–1)) {          // clock_t(-1) means "clock() didn't work"
        cerr << "sorry, no clock\n";
        exit(1);
    }

    for (int i = 0; i<n; i++)
        do_something();               // timing loop
    clock_t t2 = clock();
    if (t2 == clock_t(–1)) {
        cerr << "sorry, clock overflow\n";
        exit(2);
    }
    cout << "do_something() " << n << " times took "
        << double(t2–t1)/CLOCKS_PER_SEC << " seconds"
        << " (measurement granularity: " << CLOCKS_PER_SEC
        << " of a second)\n";
}
```

The explicit conversion **double(t2–t1)** before dividing is necessary because **clock_t** might be an integer. For values **t1** and **t2** returned by **clock()**, **double(t2–t1)/CLOCKS_PER_SEC** is the system's best approximation of the time in seconds between the two calls.

Compare <ctime> with the facilities provided in <chrono>; see §35.2.

If **clock()** isn't provided for a processor or if a time interval is too long to measure, **clock()** returns **clock_t(–1)**.

The **strftime()** function uses a **printf()** format string to control the output of a **tm**. For example:

```
void almost_C()
{
    const int max = 80;
    char str[max];
    time_t t = time(nullptr);
    tm* pt = localtime(&t);
    strftime(str,max,"%D, %H:%M (%I:%M%p)\n",pt);
    printf(str);
}
```

The output is something like:

> 06/28/12, 15:38 (03:38PM)

The **strftime()** formatting characters almost constitute a small programming language:

Date and Time Formatting	
%a	Abbreviated weekday name
%A	Full weekday name
%b	Abbreviated month name
%B	Full month name
%c	Date and time representation
%C	The year divided by 100 and truncated to a decimal integer [00:99]
%d	The day of the month as a decimal number [01:31]
%D	Equivalent to %m/%d/%y
%e	The day of the month as a decimal number [1:31]; a single digit is preceded by a space
%F	Equivalent to %Y-%m-%d; the ISO 8601 date format
%g	The last two digits of the week-based year as a decimal number [00:99]
%G	The week-based year as a decimal number (e.g., 2012)
%h	Equivalent to %b
%H	The hour (24-hour clock) as a decimal number [00:23]
%I	The hour (12-hour clock) as a decimal number [01:12]
%j	The day of the year as a decimal number [001:366]
%m	The month as a decimal number [01:12]
%M	The minute as a decimal number [00:59]
%n	A newline character
%p	The locale's equivalent of AM/PM for a 12-hour clock
%r	12-hour clock time
%R	Equivalent to %H:%M
%S	The second as a decimal number [00:60]
%t	A horizontal-tab character
%T	Equivalent to %H:%M:%S; the ISO 8601 time format
%u	The ISO 8601 weekday as a decimal number [1:7]; Monday is 1
%U	The week number of the year (the first Sunday is the first day of week 1) as a decimal number [00:53]
%V	The ISO 8601 week number as a decimal number [01:53]
%w	The weekday as a decimal number [0:6]; Sunday is 0
%W	The week number of the year (the first Monday is the first day of week 1) as a decimal number [00:53]
%x	The locale's appropriate date representation
%X	The locale's appropriate time representation
%y	The last 2 digits of the year as a decimal number [00:99]
%Y	The year as a decimal number (e.g., 2012)
%z	The offset from UTC in the ISO 8601 format -0430 (4.5 hours behind UTC, Greenwich); no characters if no time zone is determinable
%Z	The locale's time zone name or abbreviation; nothing if no time zone is known
%%	The character %

The locale referred to is the program's global locale.

Some conversion specifiers can be modified by an **E** or **O** modifier, indicating alternative implementation-specific and locale-specific formatting. For example:

Date and Time Format Modifier Examples	
%Ec	The locale's alternative date and time representation
%EC	The name of the base year (period) in the locale's alternative representation
%OH	The hour (24-hour clock), using the locale's alternative numeric symbols
%Oy	The last two digits of the year, using the locale's alternative numeric symbols

The **strftime()** is used by the **put_time** facet (§39.4.4.1).

For C++-style time facilities, see §35.2.

43.7 Etc.

In **<cstdlib>** we find:

Etc. <stdlib.h> Functions	
abort()	Terminate the program "abnormally"
exit(n)	Terminate the program with value **n**;
	n==0 means successful termination
system(s)	Execute the string as a command (system-dependent)
qsort(b,n,s,cmp)	Sort the array starting at **b** with **n** elements
	of size **s** using the comparison function **cmp**
bsearch(k,b,n,s,cmp)	Search for **k** in the sorted array starting at **b**
	with **n** elements of size **s** using the comparison function **cmp**
d=rand()	**d** is a pseudo-random number in the range [**0**:**RAND_MAX**]
srand(d)	Start a sequence of pseudo-random numbers using **d** as the seed

The comparison function (**cmp**) used by **qsort()** and **bsort()** must have the type

   int (∗cmp)(const void∗ p, const void∗ q);

That is, no type information is known to the sort functions that simply "see" their array arguments as sequences of bytes. The integer returned is

- Negative if ∗**p** is considered less than ∗**q**
- Zero if ∗**p** is considered equal to ∗**q**
- Positive if ∗**p** is considered greater than ∗**q**

This differs from **sort()**, which uses a conventional **<**.

Note that **exit()** and **abort()** do not invoke destructors. If you want destructors called for constructed objects, throw an exception (§13.5.1).

Similarly, **longjmp()** from **<csetjmp>** is a nonlocal **goto** that unravels the stack until it finds the result of a matching **setjmp()**. It does not invoke destructors. Its behavior is undefined if a destructor would be invoked by a **throw** from the same point of a program. Never use **setjmp()** in a C++ program.

For more C standard library functions see [Kernighan,1988] or some other reputable C language reference.

In **<cstdint>**, we find **int_fast16_t** and other standard integer aliases:

Integer Type Aliases	
N can be **8, 16, 32,** or **64**	
int_N_t	Integer type of N bytes, e.g. **int_8_t**
uint_N_t	Unsigned integer type of N bytes, e.g., **uint_16_t**
int_leastN_t	Integer type of at least N bytes, e.g., **int_least16_t**
uint_leastN_t	Unsigned integer type of at least N bytes, e.g., **uint_least32_t**
int_fastN_t	Integer type of at least N bytes, e.g., **int_fast32_t**
uint_leastN_t	Unsigned integer type of at least N bytes, e.g., **uint_fast64_t**

Also in **<cstdint>**, we find type aliases for the largest signed and unsigned integer types for an implementation. For example:

```
typedef long long intmax_t;              // largest signed integer type
typedef unsigned long long uintmax_t;    // largest unsigned integer type
```

43.8 Advice

[1]   Use **fstreams** rather than **fopen()/fclose()** if you worry about resource leaks; §43.2.

[2]   Prefer **<iostream>** to **<stdlib>** for reasons of type safety and extensibility; §43.3.

[3]   Never use **gets()** or **scanf("%s",s)**; §43.3.

[4]   Prefer **<string>** to **<cstring>** for reasons of ease of use and simplicity of resource management; §43.4.

[5]   Use the C memory management routines, such as **memcpy()**, only for raw memory; §43.5.

[6]   Prefer **vector** to uses of **malloc()** and **realloc()**; §43.5.

[7]   Beware that the C standard library does not know about constructors and destructors; §43.5.

[8]   Prefer **<chrono>** to **<ctime>** for timing; §43.6.

[9]   For flexibility, ease of use, and performance, prefer **sort()** over **qsort()**; §43.7.

[10]   Don't use **exit()**; instead, throw an exception; §43.7.

[11]   Don't use **longjmp()**; instead, throw an exception; §43.7.

44

Compatibility

You go ahead and follow your customs,
and I'll follow mine.
– C. Napier

- Introduction
- C++11 Extensions
  Language Features; Standard-Library Components; Deprecated Features; Coping with Older
  C++ Implementations
- C/C++ Compatibility
  C and C++ Are Siblings; "Silent" Differences; C Code That Is Not C++; C++ Code That Is
  Not C
- Advice

44.1 Introduction

This chapter discusses the differences between Standard C++ (as defined by ISO/IEC 14882-2011)
and earlier versions (such as ISO/IEC 14882-1998), Standard C (as defined by ISO/IEC
9899-2011) and earlier versions (such as Classic C). The purposes are

- To concisely list what is new in C++11
- To document differences that can cause problems for a programmer
- To point to ways of dealing with problems

Most compatibility problems surface when people try to upgrade a C program to a C++ program,
try to port a C++ program from an older version of C++ to a newer one (e.g., C++98 to C++11), or
try to compile C++ using modern features with an older compiler. The aim here is not to enumerate every possible compatibility problem but rather to list the most frequently occurring problems
and present their standard solutions.

  When you look at compatibility issues, a key question to consider is the range of implementations under which a program needs to work. For learning C++, it makes sense to use the most

complete and helpful implementation. For delivering a product, a more conservative strategy might be in order to maximize the number of systems on which the product can run. In the past, this has been a reason (and more often just an excuse) to avoid C++ features deemed novel. However, implementations are converging, so the need for portability across platforms is less cause for extreme caution than it once was.

44.2 C++11 Extensions

First, I list the language features and standard-library components that have been added to C++ for the C++11 standard. Next, I discuss ways of coping with older versions (notably C++98).

44.2.1 Language Features

Looking at a list of language features can be quite bewildering. Remember that a language feature is not meant to be used in isolation. In particular, most features that are new in C++11 make no sense in isolation from the framework provided by older features. The order is roughly that of first occurrence in this book:

[1]   Uniform and general initialization using {}-lists (§2.2.2, §6.3.5)
[2]   Type deduction from initializer: **auto** (§2.2.2, §6.3.6.1)
[3]   Prevention of narrowing (§2.2.2, §6.3.5)
[4]   Generalized and guaranteed constant expressions: **constexpr** (§2.2.3, §10.4, §12.1.6)
[5]   Range-**for**-statement (§2.2.5, §9.5.1)
[6]   Null pointer keyword: **nullptr** (§2.2.5, §7.2.2)
[7]   Scoped and strongly typed **enums**: **enum class** (§2.3.3, §8.4.1)
[8]   Compile-time assertions: **static_assert** (§2.4.3.3, §24.4)
[9]   Language mapping of {}-list to **std::initializer_list** (§3.2.1.3, §17.3.4)
[10]   Rvalue references (enabling move semantics; §3.3.2, §7.7.2)
[11]   Nested template arguments ending with >> (no space between the >s; §3.4.1)
[12]   Lambdas (§3.4.3, §11.4)
[13]   Variadic templates (§3.4.4, §28.6)
[14]   Type and template aliases (§3.4.5, §6.5, §23.6)
[15]   Unicode characters (§6.2.3.2, §7.3.2.2)
[16]   **long long** integer type (§6.2.4)
[17]   Alignment controls: **alignas** and **alignof** (§6.2.9)
[18]   The ability to use the type of an expression as a type in a declaration: **decltype** (§6.3.6.1)
[19]   Raw string literals (§7.3.2.1)
[20]   Generalized POD (§8.2.6)
[21]   Generalized **unions** (§8.3.1)
[22]   Local classes as template arguments (§11.4.2, §25.2.1)
[23]   Suffix return type syntax (§12.1.4)
[24]   A syntax for attributes and two standard attributes: **[[carries_dependency]]** (§41.3) and **[[noreturn]]** (§12.1.7)
[25]   Preventing exception propagation: the **noexcept** specifier (§13.5.1.1)

[26] Testing for the possibility of a **throw** in an expression: the **noexcept** operator (§13.5.1.1)
[27] C99 features: extended integral types (i.e., rules for optional longer integer types; §6.2.4); concatenation of narrow/wide strings; **__func__** and **__STDC_HOSTED__** (§12.6.2); **_Pragma(X)** (§12.6.3); vararg macros and empty macro arguments (§12.6)
[28] **inline** namespaces (§14.4.6)
[29] Delegating constructors (§17.4.3)
[30] In-class member initializers (§17.4.4)
[31] Control of defaults: **default** (§17.6) and **delete** (§17.6.4)
[32] Explicit conversion operators (§18.4.2)
[33] User-defined literals (§19.2.6)
[34] More explicit control of **template** instantiation: **extern templates** (§26.2.2)
[35] Default template arguments for function templates (§25.2.5.1)
[36] Inheriting constructors (§20.3.5.1)
[37] Override controls: **override** and **final** (§20.3.4)
[38] Simpler and more general SFINAE rule (§23.5.3.2)
[39] Memory model (§41.2)
[40] Thread-local storage: **thread_local** (§42.2.8)

I have not tried to list every minute change to C++98 in C++11. A historical perspective on these features can be found in §1.4.

44.2.2 Standard_Library Components

The C++11 additions to the standard library come in two forms: new components (such as the regular expression matching library) and improvements to C++98 components (such as move constructors for containers).

[1] **initializer_list** constructors for containers (§3.2.1.3, §17.3.4, §31.3.2)
[2] Move semantics for containers (§3.3.1, §17.5.2, §31.3.2)
[3] A singly-linked list: **forward_list** (§4.4.5, §31.4.2)
[4] Hash containers: **unordered_map**, **unordered_multimap**, **unordered_set**, and **unordered_multiset** (§4.4.5, §31.4.3)
[5] Resource management pointers: **unique_ptr**, **shared_ptr**, and **weak_ptr** (§5.2.1, §34.3)
[6] Concurrency support: **thread** (§5.3.1, §42.2), mutexes (§5.3.4, §42.3.1), locks (§5.3.4, §42.3.2), and condition variables (§5.3.4.1, §42.3.4)
[7] Higher-level concurrency support: **packaged_thread**, **future**, **promise**, and **async()** (§5.3.5, §42.4)
[8] **tuples** (§5.4.3, §28.5, §34.2.4.2)
[9] Regular expressions: **regex** (§5.5, Chapter 37)
[10] Random numbers: **uniform_int_distribution**, **normal_distribution**, **random_engine**, etc. (§5.6.3, §40.7)
[11] Integer type names, such as **int16_t**, **uint32_t**, and **int_fast64_t** (§6.2.8, §43.7)
[12] A fixed-sized contiguous sequence container: **array** (§8.2.4, §34.2.1)
[13] Copying and rethrowing exceptions (§30.4.1.2)
[14] Error reporting using error codes: **system_error** (§30.4.3)

[15] **emplace()** operations for containers (§31.3.6)
[16] Wide use of **constexpr** functions
[17] Systematic use of **noexcept** functions
[18] Improved function adaptors: **function** and **bind()** (§33.5)
[19] **string** to numeric value conversions (§36.3.5)
[20] Scoped allocators (§34.4.4)
[21] Type traits, such as **is_integral** and **is_base_of** (§35.4)
[22] Time utilities: **duration** and **time_point** (§35.2)
[23] Compile-time rational arithmetic: **ratio** (§35.3)
[24] Abandoning a process: **quick_exit** (§15.4.3)
[25] More algorithms, such as **move()**, **copy_if()**, and **is_sorted()** (Chapter 32)
[26] Garbage collection ABI (§34.5)
[27] Low-level concurrency support: **atomics** (§41.3)

More information about the standard library can be found in

- Chapter 4, Chapter 5, and Part IV
- Implementation technique examples: **vector** (§13.6), **string** (§19.3), and **tuple** (§28.5)
- The emerging specialized C++11 standard-library literature, such as [Williams,2012]
- A brief historical perspective can be found in §1.4.

44.2.3 Deprecated Features

By deprecating a feature, the standards committee expresses the wish that the feature will go away (§iso.D). However, the committee does not have a mandate to immediately remove a heavily used feature – however redundant or dangerous it may be. Thus, a deprecation is a strong hint to avoid the feature. It may disappear in the future. Compilers are likely to issue warnings for uses of deprecated features.

- Generation of the copy constructor and the copy assignment is deprecated for a class with a destructor.
- It is no longer allowed to assign a string literal to a **char∗** (§7.3.2).
- C++98 exception specifications are deprecated:

      void f() throw(X,Y);   // *C++98; now deprecated*

  The support facilities for exception specifications, **unexcepted_handler**, **set_unexpected()**, **get_unexpected()**, and **unexpected()**, are similarly deprecated. Instead, use **noexcept** (§13.5.1.1).
- Some C++ standard-library function objects and associated functions are deprecated: **unary_function**, **binary_function**, **pointer_to_unary_function**, **pointer_to_binary_function**, **ptr_fun()**, **mem_fun_t**, **mem_fun1_t**, **mem_fun_ref_t**, **mem_fun_ref1_t**, **mem_fun()**, **const_mem_fun_t**, **const_mem_fun1_t**, **const_mem_fun_ref_t**, **const_mem_fun_ref1_t**, **binder1st**, **bind1st()**, **binder2nd**, **bind2nd()**. Instead, use **function** and **bind()** (§33.5).
- The **auto_ptr** is deprecated. Instead, use **unique_ptr** (§5.2.1, §34.3.1).

In addition, the committee did remove the essentially unused **export** feature, because it was complex and not shipped by the major vendors.

C-style casts should have been deprecated when the named casts (§11.5.2) were introduced. Programmers should seriously consider banning C-style casts from their own programs. Where explicit type conversion is necessary, **static_cast**, **reinterpret_cast**, **const_cast**, or a combination of these can do what a C-style cast can. The named casts should be preferred because they are more explicit and more visible.

44.2.4 Coping with Older C++ Implementations

C++ has been in constant use since 1983 (§1.4). Since then, several versions have been defined, and many separately developed implementations have emerged. The fundamental aim of the standards effort was to ensure that implementers and users would have a single definition of C++ to work from. From 1998, programmers could rely on the ISO C++98 standard, and now we have the ISO C++11 standard.

Unfortunately, it is not uncommon for people to take their first serious look at C++ using a five-year-old implementation. The typical reason is that such implementations are widely available and free. Given a choice, no self-respecting professional would touch such an antique. Also, many modern quality implementations are available for free. For a novice, older implementations come with serious hidden costs. The lack of language features and library support means that the novice must struggle with problems that have been eliminated in newer implementations. Using a feature-poor older implementation, especially if guided by an antique tutorial, warps the novice's programming style and gives a biased view of what C++ is. The best subset of C++ to initially learn is *not* the set of low-level facilities (and not the common C and C++ subset; see §1.3). In particular, to ease learning and to get a good initial impression of what C++ programming can be, I recommend relying on the standard library, and to heavily use classes, templates, and exceptions.

There are still places, where for political reasons or lack of suitable tool chains, C is preferred over C++. If you must use C, write in the common subset of C and C++. That way, you gain some type safety, increase portability, and will be ready when C++ features become available to you. See also §1.3.3.

Use an implementation that conforms to the standard wherever possible, and minimize the reliance on implementation-defined and undefined aspects of the language. Design as if the full language were available, and only use workarounds when necessary. This leads to better organized and more maintainable programs than designing for a lowest-common-denominator subset of C++. Also, use implementation-specific language extensions only when necessary. See also §1.3.2.

44.3 C/C++ Compatibility

With minor exceptions, C++ is a superset of C (meaning C11, defined by ISO/IEC 9899:2011(E)). Most differences stem from C++'s greater emphasis on type checking. Well-written C programs tend to be C++ programs as well. A compiler can diagnose every difference between C++ and C. The C99/C++11 incompatibilities are listed in §iso.C. At the time of writing, C11 is still very new and most C code is Classic C or C99.

44.3.1 C and C++ Are Siblings

Classic C has two main descendants: ISO C and ISO C++. Over the years, these languages have evolved at different paces and in different directions. One result of this is that each language provides support for traditional C-style programming in slightly different ways. The resulting incompatibilities can make life miserable for people who use both C and C++, for people who write in one language using libraries implemented in the other, and for implementers of libraries and tools for C and C++.

How can I call C and C++ siblings? Clearly, C++ is a descendant of C. However, look at a simplified family tree:

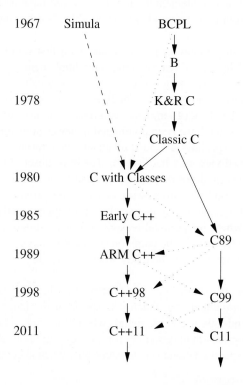

A solid line means a massive inheritance of features, a dashed line a borrowing of major features, and a dotted line a borrowing of minor features. From this, ISO C and ISO C++ emerge as the two major descendants of K&R C, and as siblings. Each carries with it the key aspects of Classic C, and neither is 100% compatible with Classic C. I picked the term "Classic C" from a sticker that used to be affixed to Dennis Ritchie's terminal. It is K&R C plus enumerations and **struct** assignment.

Incompatibilities are nasty for programmers in part because they create a combinatorial explosion of alternatives. Consider a simple Venn diagram:

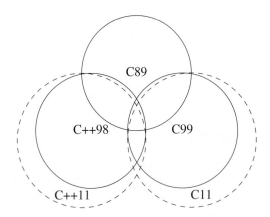

The areas are not to scale. Both C++11 and C11 have most of K&R C as a subset. C++11 has most of C11 as a subset. There are features belonging to most of the distinct areas. For example:

C89 only	Call of undeclared function
C99 only	Variable-length arrays (VLAs)
C++ only	Templates
C89 and C99	Algol-style function definitions
C89 and C++	Use of the C99 keyword **restrict** as an identifier
C++ and C99	// comments
C89, C++, and C99	**struct**s
C++11 only	Move semantics (using rvalue references; **&&**)
C11 only	Type-generic expressions using the **_Generic** keyword
C++11 and C11	Atomics

Note that differences between C and C++ are not necessarily the result of changes to C made in C++. In several cases, the incompatibilities arise from features adopted incompatibly into C long after they were common in C++. Examples are the ability to assign a **T∗** to a **void∗** and the linkage of global **const**s [Stroustrup,2002]. Sometimes, a feature was even incompatibly adopted into C after it was part of the ISO C++ standard, such as details of the meaning of **inline**.

44.3.2 "Silent" Differences

With a few exceptions, programs that are both C++ and C have the same meaning in both languages. Fortunately, these exceptions (often referred to as *silent differences*) are rather obscure:

- In C, the size of a character constant and of an enumeration equals **sizeof(int)**. In C++, **sizeof('a')** equals **sizeof(char)**.
- In C, an enumerator is an **int**, whereas a C++ implementation is allowed to choose whatever size is most appropriate for an enumeration (§8.4.2).
- In C++, the name of a **struct** is entered into the scope in which it is declared; in C, it is not. Thus, the name of a C++ **struct** declared in an inner scope can hide the name in an outer scope. For example:

```
        int x[99];
        void f()
        {
                struct x { int a; };
                sizeof(x);              /* size of the array in C, size of the struct in C++ */
                sizeof(struct x);       /* size of the struct */
        }
```

44.3.3 C Code That Is Not C++

The C/C++ incompatibilities that cause most real problems are not subtle. Most are easily caught
by compilers. This section gives examples of C code that is not C++. Most are deemed poor style
or even obsolete in modern C. A comprehensive list of incompatibilities can be found in §iso.C.

- In C, most functions can be called without a previous declaration. For example:

```
        int main()       // not C++; poor style in C
        {
                double sq2 = sqrt(2);                           /* call undeclared function */
                printf("the square root of 2 is %g\n",sq2);     /* call undeclared function */
        }
```

    Complete and consistent use of function declarations (function prototypes) is generally rec-
    ommended for C. Where that sensible advice is followed, and especially where C compilers
    provide options to enforce it, C code conforms to the C++ rule. Where undeclared functions
    are called, you have to know the functions and the rules for C pretty well to know whether
    you have made a mistake or introduced a portability problem. For example, the previous
    main() contains at least two errors as a C program.

- In C, a function declared without specifying any argument types can take any number of
    arguments of any type at all.

```
        void f();   /* argument types not mentioned */

        void g()
        {
                f(2);       /* poor style in C; not C++ */
        }
```

    Such use is deemed obsolete in ISO C.

- In C, functions can be defined using a syntax that optionally specifies argument types after
    the list of arguments:

```
        void f(a,p,c) char *p; char c; { /* ... */ }            /* C; not C++ */
```

    Such definitions must be rewritten:

```
        void f(int a, char* p, char c) { /* ... */ }
```

- In C, **struct**s can be defined in return type and argument type declarations. For example:

```
struct S { int x,y; } f();          /* C; not C++ */
void g(struct S { int x,y; } y);    /* C; not C++ */
```

The C++ rules for defining types make such declarations useless, and they are not allowed.

- In C, integers can be assigned to variables of enumeration type:

```
enum Direction { up, down };
enum Direction d = 1;               /* error: int assigned to Direction; OK in C */
```

- C++ provides many more keywords than C does. If one of these appears as an identifier in a C program, that program must be modified to make it a C++ program:

<table>
<tr><th colspan="6">C++ Keywords That Are Not C Keywords</th></tr>
<tr><td>alignas</td><td>alignof</td><td>and</td><td>and_eq</td><td>asm</td><td>bitand</td></tr>
<tr><td>bitor</td><td>bool</td><td>catch</td><td>char16_t</td><td>char32_t</td><td>class</td></tr>
<tr><td>compl</td><td>const_cast</td><td>constexpr</td><td>decltype</td><td>delete</td><td>dynamic_cast</td></tr>
<tr><td>explicit</td><td>false</td><td>friend</td><td>inline</td><td>mutable</td><td>namespace</td></tr>
<tr><td>new</td><td>noexcept</td><td>not</td><td>not_eq</td><td>nullptr</td><td>operator</td></tr>
<tr><td>or_eq</td><td>private</td><td>protected</td><td>public</td><td>reinterpret_cast</td><td>static_assert</td></tr>
<tr><td>static_cast</td><td>template</td><td>this</td><td>thread_local</td><td>throw</td><td>true</td></tr>
<tr><td>try</td><td>typeid</td><td>typename</td><td>using</td><td>virtual</td><td>wchar_t</td></tr>
<tr><td>xor</td><td>xor_eq</td><td></td><td></td><td></td><td></td></tr>
</table>

In addition, the word **export** is reserved for future use. C99 adopted **inline**.

- In C, some of the C++ keywords are macros defined in standard headers:

<table>
<tr><th colspan="9">C++ Keywords That Are C Macros</th></tr>
<tr><td>and</td><td>and_eq</td><td>bitand</td><td>bitor</td><td>bool</td><td>compl</td><td>false</td><td>not</td><td>not_eq</td></tr>
<tr><td>or</td><td>or_eq</td><td>true</td><td>wchar_t</td><td>xor</td><td>xor_eq</td><td></td><td></td><td></td></tr>
</table>

This implies that in C they can be tested using **#ifdef**, redefined, etc.

- In C, a global data object may be declared several times in a single translation unit without using the **extern** specifier. As long as at most one such declaration provides an initializer, the object is considered defined only once. For example:

```
int i;
int i; /* just another declaration of a single integer "i"; not C++ */
```

In C++, an entity must be defined exactly once; §15.2.3.

- In C, a **void**∗ may be used as the right-hand operand of an assignment to or initialization of a variable of any pointer type; in C++ it may not (§7.2.1). For example:

```
void f(int n)
{
    int∗ p = malloc(n∗sizeof(int));  /* not C++; in C++, allocate using "new" */
}
```

This is probably the single most difficult incompatibility to deal with. Note that the implicit conversion of a **void**∗ to a different pointer type is *not* in general harmless:

```
char ch;
void* pv = &ch;
int* pi = pv;        // not C++
*pi = 666;           // overwrite ch and other bytes near ch
```

If you use both languages, cast the result of **malloc()** to the right type. If you use only C++, avoid **malloc()**.

- In C, the type of a string literal is "array of **char**," but in C++ it is "array of **const char**," so:

```
char* p = "a string literal is not mutable";     // error in C++; OK in C
p[7] = 'd';
```

- C allows transfer of control to a labeled statement (a **switch** or a **goto**; §9.6) to bypass an initialization; C++ does not. For example:

```
goto foo;            // OK in C; not C++
// ...
{
    int x = 1;
foo:
    if (x!=1) abort();
    /* ... */
}
```

- In C, a global **const** by default has external linkage; in C++ it does not and must be initialized, unless explicitly declared **extern** (§7.5). For example:

```
const int ci;        // OK in C; const not initialized error in C++
```

- In C, names of nested structures are placed in the same scope as the structure in which they are nested. For example:

```
struct S {
    struct T { /* ... */ } t;
    // ...
};
```

```
struct T x;          // OK in C, meaning "S::T x;"; not C++
```

- In C++, the name of a class is entered into the scope in which it is declared; thus it cannot have the same name as another type declared in that scope. For example:

```
struct X { /* ... */ };
typedef int X;       // OK in C; not C++
```

- In C, an array can be initialized by an initializer that has more elements than the array requires. For example:

```
char v[5] = "Oscar"; // OK in C, the terminating 0 is not used; not C++
printf("%s",v);      // likely disaster
```

44.3.3.1 "Classic C" Problems

Should you need to upgrade Classic C programs ("K&R C") or C89 programs, a few more problems will emerge:

- C89 does not have the // comments (though most C89 compilers added them):

      int x;   // not C89

- In C89, the type specifier defaults to **int** (known as "implicit **int**"). For example:

      const a = 7;   /* in C89, type int assumed; not C++ or C99 */

      f()   /* f()'s return type is int by default; not C++ or C99 */
      {
          /* .. */
      }

44.3.3.2 C Features Not Adopted by C++

A few additions to C99 (compared with C89) were deliberately not adopted in C++:

- [1]   Variable-length arrays (VLAs); use **vector** or some form of dynamic array
- [2]   Designated initializers; use constructors

The C11 features are too new to have been considered for C++, except for features such as the memory model and atomics (§41.3) that came from C++.

44.3.4 C++ Code That Is Not C

This section lists facilities offered by C++ but not by C (or adopted by C years after their introduction in C++, as marked, so that they may be missing in old C compilers). The features are sorted by purpose. However, many classifications are possible, and most features serve multiple purposes, so this classification should not be taken too seriously.

- Features primarily for notational convenience:
  - [1]   // comments (§2.2.1, §9.7); added to C99
  - [2]   Support for restricted character sets (§iso.2.4); partially added to C99
  - [3]   Support for extended character sets (§6.2.3); added to C99
  - [4]   Non-constant initializers for objects in **static** storage (§15.4.1)
  - [5]   **const** in constant expressions (§2.2.3, §10.4.2)
  - [6]   Declarations as statements (§9.3); added to C99
  - [7]   Declarations in **for**-statement initializers (§9.5); added to C99
  - [8]   Declarations in conditions (§9.4.3)
  - [9]   Structure names need not be prefixed by **struct** (§8.2.2)
  - [10]   Anonymous **unions** (§8.3.2); added to C11
- Features primarily for strengthening the type system:
  - [1]   Function argument type checking (§12.1); partially added to C (§44.3.3)
  - [2]   Type-safe linkage (§15.2, §15.2.3)
  - [3]   Free-store management using **new** and **delete** (§11.2)

[4]   **const** (§7.5, §7.5); partially added to C
[5]   The Boolean type **bool** (§6.2.2); partially added to C99
[6]   Named casts (§11.5.2)
- Facilities for user-defined types:
    [1]   Classes (Chapter 16)
    [2]   Member functions (§16.2.1) and member classes (§16.2.13)
    [3]   Constructors and destructors (§16.2.5, Chapter 17)
    [4]   Derived classes (Chapter 20, Chapter 21)
    [5]   **virtual** functions and abstract classes (§20.3.2, §20.4)
    [6]   Public/protected/private access control (§16.2.3, §20.5)
    [7]   **friend**s (§19.4)
    [8]   Pointers to members (§20.6)
    [9]   **static** members (§16.2.12)
    [10]   **mutable** members (§16.2.9.3)
    [11]   Operator overloading (Chapter 18)
    [12]   References (§7.7)
- Features primarily for program organization (in addition to classes):
    [1]   Templates (Chapter 23)
    [2]   Inline functions (§12.1.3); added to C99
    [3]   Default arguments (§12.2.5)
    [4]   Function overloading (§12.3)
    [5]   Namespaces (§14.3.1)
    [6]   Explicit scope qualification (operator ::; §6.3.4)
    [7]   Exceptions (§2.4.3.1, Chapter 13)
    [8]   Run-Time Type Identification (Chapter 22)
    [9]   Generalized constant expressions (**constexpr**; §2.2.3, §10.4, §12.1.6)

The C++11 features listed in §44.2 are not in C.

The keywords added by C++ (§44.3.3) can be used to spot most C++-specific facilities. However, some facilities, such as function overloading and **const**s in constant expressions, are not identified by a keyword.

C++'s linking for functions is type-safe, whereas C's rules do not require type safety when linking functions. This implies that on some (most?) implementations, a C++ function must be declared **extern "C"** to be compiled as C++ and also conform to C calling conventions (§15.2.5). For example:

```
double sin(double);              // may not link to C code
extern "C" double cos(double);   // will link to C code
```

The **__cplusplus** macro can be used to determine whether a program is being processed by a C or a C++ compiler (§15.2.5).

In addition to the features listed, the C++ library (§30.1.1, §30.2) is mostly C++-specific. The C standard library offers type-generic macros in **<tgmath.h>** and **_Complex** number support in **<complex.h>**, approximating **<complex>**.

C also offers **<stdbool.h>**, offering **_Bool** and the alias **bool** to approximate C++'s **bool**.

44.4 Advice

[1]   Before using a new feature in production code, try it out by writing small programs to test the standards conformance and performance of the implementations you plan to use; §44.1.

[2]   For learning C++, use the most up-to-date and complete implementation of Standard C++ that you can get access to; §44.2.4.

[3]   The common subset of C and C++ is not the best initial subset of C++ to learn; §1.2.3, §44.2.4.

[4]   Prefer standard facilities to nonstandard ones; §36.1, §44.2.4.

[5]   Avoid deprecated features such as **throw**-specifications; §44.2.3, §13.5.1.3.

[6]   Avoid C-style casts; §44.2.3, §11.5.

[7]   "Implicit **int**" has been banned, so explicitly specify the type of every function, variable, **const**, etc.; §44.3.3.

[8]   When converting a C program to C++, first make sure that function declarations (prototypes) and standard headers are used consistently; §44.3.3.

[9]   When converting a C program to C++, rename variables that are C++ keywords; §44.3.3.

[10]   For portability and type safety, if you must use C, write in the common subset of C and C++; §44.2.4.

[11]   When converting a C program to C++, cast the result of **malloc()** to the proper type or change all uses of **malloc()** to uses of **new**; §44.3.3.

[12]   When converting from **malloc()** and **free()** to **new** and **delete**, consider using **vector**, **push_back()**, and **reserve()** instead of **realloc()**; §3.4.2, §43.5.

[13]   When converting a C program to C++, remember that there are no implicit conversions from **int**s to enumerations; use explicit type conversion where necessary; §44.3.3, §8.4.

[14]   A facility defined in namespace **std** is defined in a header without a suffix (e.g., **std::cout** is declared in **<iostream>**); §30.2.

[15]   Use **<string>** to get **std::string** (**<string.h>** holds the C-style string functions); §15.2.4.

[16]   For each standard C header **<X.h>** that places names in the global namespace, the header **<cX>** places the names in namespace **std**; §15.2.2.

[17]   Use **extern "C"** when declaring C functions; §15.2.5.

I

Index

Knowledge is of two kinds.
We know a subject ourselves,
or we know where
we can find information on it.
— Samuel Johnson

Token

A

E

I

N

Addison
Wesley

Preparation for Programming in the Real World

BJARNE STROUSTRUP

Programming

Principles and Practice Using C++

ISBN-13: 978-0-321-54372-1

From Bjarne Stroustrup, the inventor of C++, comes **Programming: Principles and Practice Using C++**, a general introduction to programming, including object-oriented programming and generic programming, and a solid introduction to the C++ programming language. Stroustrup presents modern C++ programming techniques from the start, introducing the C++ standard library to simplify programming tasks.

The book is primarily designed for people who have never programmed before, and it has been tested with more than ten thousand first-year students and thousands of self-study learners. However, practitioners and advanced students also will gain new insight and guidance by seeing how a recognized master approaches the elements of his art.

For more information and sample content visit
informit.com/title/9780321543721